W9-ANH-749

FILM MUSIC:
From Violins to Video

Compiled and edited
by
JAMES L. LIMBACHER

The Scarecrow Press, Inc.
Metuchen, N. J. 1974

Library of Congress Cataloging in Publication Data

Limbacher, James L comp.
Film music.

Bibliography: p.
1. Moving-picture music--History and criticism.
2. Moving-picture music--Bibliography. I. Title.
ML2075.L54 782.8'5 73-16153
ISBN 0-8108-0651-7

DEDICATED

to the film composers whose talents
have made films even better than
they might have been

ACKNOWLEDGMENTS

The author's appreciation goes to the graciousness of the composers and writers who gave permission to reprint their ideas and articles on film music, and to Mrs. Marie Hamilton, Charles G. Banciu, William H. Rosar and the Composers & Lyricists Guild of America, Inc., all of whom made generous contributions to this book.

The following authors appear in this book and their articles are cited under their names.

LOUIS APPLEBAUM. "The Best Years of Our Lives" (Film Music 6:11, May-June, 1947, and 13:15, January-February, 1954) and "Documentary Film Music" (Film Music 6:13, November-December, 1946) by permission of the author.

ELMER BERNSTEIN. "The Man with the Golden Arm" (Film Music 15:3, Spring, 1956) and "The Ten Commandments" (Film/TV Music 16:3, Winter, 1956) by permission of the author.

SIR ARTHUR BLISS. "Christopher Columbus" (Film Music 9:16, November-December, 1949) by permission of the author.

LOREN G. BUCHANAN. "The Art of Composing Music Scores for Films" (Motion Picture Herald 235:12, October 13, 1965) by permission of Richard Gertner, editor.

MARY ELLEN BUTE. "New Music for New Films" (Film Music 12:15, March-April, 1953) by permission of the author.

PAGE COOK. "What's the Matter with Helen?" (Films in Review 22:501, October, 1971) by permission of the National Board of Review of Motion Pictures.

INGOLF DAHL. "Notes on Cartoon Music" (Film Music 8:3, May-June, 1949) by permission of Dr. Anthony Linick.

GEORGE DUNING. "From Here to Eternity" (Film/TV Music 13:3, March-April, 1954), "Jeanne Eagels" (Film Music 16:7, Late Summer, 1957), "No Sad Songs for Me" (Film/TV Music 9:15, March-April, 1950), "3:10 to Yuma" (Film Music 16:3, Summer, 1957) and "Salome" (Film/TV Music 12:8, March-April, 1953) by permission of the author.

SERGEI M. EISENSTEIN. P R K F V (Soviet Film #167, p. 35) reprinted through Eastern News Distributors.

JEFFREY EMBLER. "The Structure of Film Music" (Films in Review 4:332, August-September, 1953) by permission of the publisher.

GENE FORRELL. "A Time for Bach" (Film Music 9:16, January-February, 1950) by permission of the author.

HERSCHEL BURKE GILBERT. "The Thief" (Film/TV Music 11:4, March-April, 1952) by permission of the author.

JOHN GREEN. "Raintree County" (Film/TV Music 17:3, Fall-Winter, 1957-58) by permission of the author.

OTIS L. GUERNSEY JR. "The Movie Cartoon Is Coming of Age" (Film Music 13:21, November-December, 1953) by permission of the author.

WILLIAM HAMILTON. "The Bad and the Beautiful" (Film/TV Music 12:4, March-April, 1953), "Champion" and "Home of the Brave" (Film Music 8:17, May-June, 1949), "Edge of Doom" (Film Music 10;6, September-October, 1950), "High Noon" (Film/TV Music 12:19, September-October, 1952), "On the Waterfront" (Film/TV Music 14:3, September-October, 1954) and "The Third Man" (Film Music 9:5, January-February, 1950) by permission of the author.

GORDON HENDRICKS. "Film Music Comes of Age" (Films in Review 3:22, January, 1952) by permission of the publisher.

JOHN HUNTLEY. "The African Queen" (Film Music 11:22,

March-April, 1952), "The Music Mixer" (*Film/TV Music* 9:5, January-February, 1950), "The Mudlark" (*Film Music* 10:10, January-February, 1951), "Oliver Twist" (*Film/TV Music* 11:20, September-October, 1951) and "Treasure Island" (*Film Music* 10:6, September-October, 1950) by permission of the author.

PAUL KRESH. "Is There Any Music at the Movies?" (*Stereo Review*, September, 1969, p. 75) by permission of the author and the publisher.

MUIR MATHIESON. "A Note on Hamlet" (*Film Music* 13: 15, January-February, 1954) by permission of the author.

CLIFTON PARKER. "The Sword and the Rose" (*Film Music* 12:14, May-June, 1953) by permission of the author.

DAVID RAKSIN. "Carrie" (*Film Music* 12:13, September-October, 1952) by permission of the author.

FRANCIS RIZZO. "Shadow Opera" (*Opera News*, February 3, 1968, p. 9) by permission of the publisher.

LEONARD ROSENMAN. "East of Eden" (*Film Music* 14:3, May-June, 1955, by permission of the author.

MIKLOS ROZSA. "Julius Caesar" (*Film/TV Music* 13:7, September-October, 1953), "Music from Historical Films" (*Film/TV Music* 11:13, March-April, 1952) and "Quo Vadis" (*Film/TV Music* 11:4, November-December, 1951) by permission of the author.

JIM SHADDUCK. "The Ku-ku Song Man!" (*Pratfall* 1:6, Issue #7, 1972) by permission of the author and Larry M. Byrd, editor.

JACK SHAINDLIN. "Don't Shoot the Piano Player" (*Variety* 241:205, January 5, 1968) and "Cinerama Holiday" (*Film Music* 14:16, January-February, 1955) by permission of the author and the publisher.

LEITH STEVENS. "The Wild One" (*Film Music* 13:3 January-February, 1954) by permission of the executor of the Leith Stevens estate, Abraham Marcus.

DIMITRI TIOMKIN. "Composing for Films" (Films in Review 2:17, November, 1951) by permission of the publisher.

SIR WILLIAM WALTON. "Music for Shakespearean Films" (Film/TV Music 15:20, Spring, 1956) by permission of the author.

MARTIN WILLIAMS. "Jazz at the Movies" (Saturday Review 50:49, July 15, 1967) by permission of the author and the publishers.

MAX WINKLER. "The Origin of Film Music" (Films in Review 2:34, December, 1951) by permission of the publisher.

WILLIAM WOLF. "Facing the Music: Why Movie Scores Are Usually so Awful" (Cue 39:7, December 5, 1970) by permission of the publisher.

In addition to the above permissions, Marie Hamilton has graciously given permission for the inclusion of all articles from Film Music and Film/TV Music magazines, of which she was editor and publisher.

TABLE OF CONTENTS

Part One

Chapter I

THE EARLY DAYS

HOW IT ALL BEGAN

James L. Limbacher

When Thomas A. Edison commercialized the motion picture in the 1890's, he had given little or no thought to actually projecting this new invention on a screen so that more than one person could see it at one time. The "movies" were a penny arcade item, viewed by each individual customer by putting a penny into a Kinetoscope machine and turning the crank to see about 40 seconds' worth of moving images.

It was the arcade owners themselves who first got the idea of projecting them before audiences, thus making much more money per showing. Before 1900, movies were shown in the corner of the arcade, usually in an area blocked off by a wall and containing a white screen and some folding chairs. Despite the fact that the films were silent and very short, audiences grew so large that the arcade owners began renting nearby stores and converting them into little theaters. Since most of these theaters charged five cents admission, they soon got the name of "nickelodeons."

To avoid paying the $500 theater license required by most cities, nickelodeons kept their seating capacity under 199. Those over 200 seats were considered legitimate theaters. Early nickelodeons boasted such coy names as The Idle Hour, Bijou Dream, The Electric, Dreamland, Fairyland, The Rex, etc.

By 1905, the nickelodeon had spread to nearly every city and town in the nation and films gradually grew longer. Larger stores were rented and occasionally an old legitimate theater was converted to movies. Even new theaters strictly for the showing of movies were being constructed.

One of the ways the early theater manager helped to make his film programs more palatable was to hire a versatile pianist to accompany the images on the screen. Larger "first class" houses soon were utilizing the services of a string trio (and once in a while a full orchestra). And so the era of film music began.

A piano accompaniment for a film was said to be first heard in 1895 in France at one of the early presentations by the Lumière Brothers. The vaudeville houses, since they already had a pit orchestra, would sometimes accompany the short 10-minute film program used (at first) to clear the house before the next vaudeville show began. The Edison Company began issuing "Suggestions for Music" sheets as early as 1909.

Music accompanying films began to be standardized and the books of film music were developed into "cue sheets" which categorized the music by its various moods --love, hate, passion, frenzy, comedy, chase, sinister, *furioso*, cartoon, weird, *agitato*, sad, happy, mysterious, etc.

Some of the standard music used in accompanying early movies included "A Bird in a Gilded Cage," "My Buddy," "Hearts and Flowers," "O Solo Mio," "The Curse of an Aching Heart," "You Made Me What I Am Today," "Ragtime Cowboy Joe," "Wait for the Wagon," "Pony Boy" and "Chloe."

The classical repertoire was also raided, resulting in millions of moviegoers being exposed to the classics, although most of them were not sophisticated enough to be aware of the fact. The chase sequences were invariably accompanied by Rossini's "William Tell Overture" and other familiar works included Herold's "Zampa Overture,"

Rubenstein's "Melody in F" and "Kammenoi-Ostrow," Schubert's "Erl König" and "Serenade," Tchaikovsky's "Chant Elégiaque," Wagner's "Evening Star," Chopin's "Nocturne in E," Puccini's "Un Bel Di," Grieg's "To Spring," von Suppe's "Poet and Peasant Overture," Chaminade's "Scarf Dance" and, of course, Elgar's "Pomp and Circumstance."

The development of film music paralleled closely the development of the film as an art. When D. W. Griffith's THE BIRTH OF A NATION appeared in 1915, it was premiered in a legitimate theater on Broadway at $2.00 a ticket. A special score was adapted for the presentation and it was played by a full orchestra. Many times, extra sound effects were added by a crew of "noise makers" stationed behind the screen.

The function of film music in the embryo stages was to underscore the action being presented on the screen. A really versatile pianist or a clever orchestrator could almost synchronize the music with the action, thus combining two arts into one. Much of the early film music became a cliché, but despite certain lapses of taste, the movie pianist was in a sense the predecessor of the film music composer. Although he did little or no actual "composing," he did manage to "arrange" standard music into its effective form to underscore the action on the screen. And most important, he paved the way for the entrance of the arranger who in turn gave way to the film music composer, many of whom became famous in the sound era.

THE ORIGIN OF FILM MUSIC*

Max Winkler

The year 1912 was the beginning of the greatest and most prosperous era in the history of the American amusement industry. Scores of theaters played on Broadway. Victor Herbert was at the peak of his fame. Irving Berlin had begun the ascent to his. Vaudeville prospered throughout the country and the big movie chains, such as Fox and Loew's, had begun to hire vaudeville acts with guarantees that ran to as much as 104 weeks of continuous employment.

All this had tremendous repercussions on the world of music publishing, and soon the exciting waves of prosperity reached the band and orchestra counter in the Carl Fischer store. We began to sell unheard-of amounts of waltzes and songs, of potpourris and marches, of overtures and interludes. Orchestra arrangements of the popular songs of the day arrived from the printers in staggering quantities and were disposed of quickly.

Nothing that happened in the rapidly expanding world of musical comedies, operettas and vaudeville was comparable, however, to the breath-taking development of the silent movies. The men who became the giants of the film industry were beginning to produce films on a large scale in Hollywood. Big movie theatres were being erected, not only in New York but in every town and village. This was of tremendous consequence to the music business. The silent film needed music to bring it to life.

"On the silent screen music must take the place of the spoken word" had become one of the credos of the film industry. Huge theatre orchestras were hired to play in the movie palaces of the big cities, and smaller ensembles, trios, or simply an organist or a pianist, were employed in thousands of towns and villages.

Only in a few isolated theatres in big cities was any effort made to coordinate the goings-on on the screen with the sounds in the musical pit. Thousands of musicians never had a chance to see a picture before they were called upon to play music for it! There they were sitting in the dark, watching the screen, trying to follow the rapidly unfolding events with their music: sad music, funny music, slow music--sinister, agitated, stormy, dramatic, funereal, pursuit, and amorous music. They had to improvise, playing whatever repertoire came to their worried minds, or whatever they made up themselves on the spur of a short moment. It was a terrible predicament--and so, usually, was the music.

One day in the spring of 1912 I went to one of the small movie houses that had so quickly sprung up all over town, to see one of the superb spectacles of the day. It was called WAR BRIDES and featured the exotic Nazimova in the role of a pregnant peasant woman. The king of the mythical country where Nazimova was living passed through her village. Nazimova threw herself in front of him, her hands raised to heaven. She said--no, she didn't say anything but the title on the screen announced: "If you will not give us women the right to vote for or against war I shall not bear a child for such a country."

The king just moved on. Nazimova drew a dagger and killed herself.

The pianist so far had done all right. But I scarcely believed my ears when, just as Nazimova exhaled her last breath, to the heart-breaking sobs of her family, he began to play the old, frivolous favorite, "You Made Me What I Am Today."

The pianist was one of my customers and I just could not resist going backstage afterwards and asking him why he had chosen this particular tune at that particular moment. "Why," he said, "I thought that was perfectly clear. Wasn't it the king's fault that she killed herself?"

More and more musical mishaps began to turn drama and tragedy on the screen into farce and disaster. Exhibitors and theatre managers made frantic efforts to avoid the musical faux pas that made their films appear ridiculous. Carl Fischer's was probably the most famous and certainly the most successful house in the field of orchestra music. I began to understand their problems. We gave advice, we helped some of them, and when they described to us a particular scene in a film, we usually would know of a piece that would fit the mood.

All this had, of course, a very stimulating effect on the volume of business transacted by Carl Fischer's orchestra department, and as the orders came in I had visions of an even more magnificent future.

One day after I had gone home from work I could not fall asleep. The hundreds and thousands of titles, the mountains of music that Fischer's had stored and cataloged, kept going through my mind. There was music, surely to fit any given situation in any picture. If we could only think of a way to let all these orchestra leaders and pianists and organists know what we had! If we could use our knowledge and experience not when it was too late, but much earlier, before they ever had to sit down and play, we would be able to sell them music not by the ton but by the trainload!

The thought suddenly electrified me. It was not a problem of getting the music. We had the music, plenty of it, any conceivable kind, more than anybody could ever want. It was a problem of promoting, timing, and organization. I pulled back the blanket, turned on the light and went over to my little table, took a sheet of paper and began writing feverishly.

Here is what I wrote:

MUSIC CUE SHEET
for
The Magic Valley
Selected and compiled by M. Winkler

Cue

1 Opening - play Minuet No. 2 in G by Beethoven for ninety seconds until title on screen "Follow me dear."

2 Play - "Dramatic Andante" by Vely for two minutes and ten seconds. Note: Play soft during scene where mother cnters. Play Cue No. 2. until scene "hero leaving room."

3 Play - "Love Theme" by Lorenze - for one minute and twenty seconds. Note: Play soft and slow during conversations until title on screen "There they go."

4 Play - "Stampede" by Simon for fifty-five seconds. Note: Play fast and decrease or increase speed of gallop in accordance with action on the screen.

I kept on writing for hours. The Magic Valley was just an imaginary picture with imaginary scenes, situations and moods, but the music was real music. It was music I knew. The years of close contact with it, of carrying it around, of sorting it out, of hearing it, listing it, handling it, living with it, now began to bear unexpected fruit. I went to bed exhausted, and when I woke up the next morning it took me a little time to remember how these densely covered sheets of paper had come into my room.

The next day I copied them cleanly and wrote a letter

to the New York office of the Universal Film Company.

"If you would give me a chance to see your pictures before they are released I could prepare such a cue sheet for each one of them," I wrote. "You could send them out before you release the prints of your films. It would give the local theatre time to prepare adequate musical accompaniment. It will help everybody, the industry, the musicians, and the public." It would also, of course, help the orchestra department of Carl Fischer's, and there was still another party I was hoping the scheme might be able to help, but I didn't mention him in my letter.

Two days later I found myself in the office of Mr. Paul Gulick, publicity director of Universal, in the Mecca Building, 1600 Broadway. It was late in the day. I had not dared to leave my job at the store, not even for so exciting an appointment. Gulick had my letter and the cue sheet for The Magic Valley before him on his desk. He began asking questions. What was I doing? What made me think that I would be the man to fit music to pictures? It wasn't just an occasional picture, he explained, there might be ten, fifteen, twenty every week--I wouldn't have time to go home and think and consult catalogs or listen to a lot of tunes till I found the right one.

"Just give me a chance," I said. "Let me try. I'll show you."

"All right, come up tomorrow night. Be here at seven. We'll see."

Between seven o'clock and a half hour past midnight the next night I was shown sixteen different subjects--slapstick comedies, newsreels, a trip through the Sahara, a Western. I had been provided with a little desk, a stop watch, a stack of paper, a little mountain of pencils. I looked and stopped my watch and wrote. As the pictures flashed by, the bins in the Fischer store appeared before my eyes. I not only heard the music that would fit perfectly to the camels slowly swaying through the sand, I saw the bin that stored Tchaikovsky's "Dance Arabe," and the title I had printed on the card over the bin, and while the camels trotted across the screen I wrote it down on the cue sheet without a moment's hesitation.

Gulick sat there, watched me, and never said a word.

When I had finished at last, everything was going in circles before my exhausted eyes. Gulick took my notes.

"We'll let you know," he said, yawning. "Good night."

The next day--it was 3:30 in the afternoon and I will never forget it--a messenger boy strolled into the Fischer store. He came over to the orchestra counter. He didn't have to ask for me. Before he could say a word I took the letter he held in his hand, signed a receipt with a trembling scrawl. I tore open the envelope. It contained a letter signed by a live vice-president of Universal, engaging me for a four-week period to preview "the films made by this company in advance of actual release date and to prepare music cue sheets for said films, regardless of character or length, such cue sheets to contain only musical compositions published and easily available to our distributors and exhibitors. The films will be shown to you every Tuesday night at Projection Room C in our offices at 1600 Broadway. Your remuneration for said services will be $30 per session. If this meets with your approval please sign the enclosed copy and return same for our files."

During the following weeks I saw more silly comedies, blood-curdling murders and tear-milking melodramas than any other human being has ever been condemned to see. But nobody ever enjoyed them more! Each night Universal rushed my feverishly scribbled notes to the printer and the next day thousands of copies went out to every theatre manager, pianist, organist and orchestra director in every movie theatre in America.

The response was overwhelming. Everybody was delighted. It seemed as simple as Columbus' egg--why had nobody thought of it before? Soon Universal was swamped with requests for cue sheets for films which had been released prior to my appearance on the scene, and Gulick asked me to work an extra night on his old pictures. For the two evening sessions he offered me a salary of forty dollars a week ...

[Mr. Winkler's cue sheets were soon imitated, and he himself worked for other companies than Universal. He left Fischer's and formed a partnership with S. M. Berg, one of his earlier imitators.--Ed.]

Soon we went places. Berg and I had, in the past, been the real stars in the cue sheet world and now that we had become united, we established a virtual monopoly. We supplied the musical cue sheets for Universal, Triangle Films, Douglas Fairbanks, Sr. (then, of course, very much Jr.), William S. Hart, Fox Films, Vitagraph and Goldwyn, and the Great M stars: Mabel Normand, Mary Garden and Mae Marsh.

Every scene, situation, character, action, emotion, every nationality, emergency, wind storm, rain storm and brain storm, every dancer, vamp, cowboy, thief and gigolo, eskimo and zulu, emperor and streetwalker, colibri and elephant--plus every printed title that flickered in the faces of the five-cent to twenty-five-cent audiences--had to be expressed in music, and we soon realized that our catalog of so-called Dramatic and Incidental Music was quite insufficient to furnish the simply colossal amounts of music needed by an ever-expanding industry.

We searched for composers who would supply what we needed and we found them. They were fine musicians, but they were specialists in just one phase of music, film music, and most of them are forgotten today. Who still knows the compositions of Walter Simon, Herman Froml, Gaston Borch, Charles Herbert, Irene Berge, Leo Kempinski, Maurice Baron, Hugo Riesenfeld? Very few, if any, still remember them and yet, in those days, gone only a few decades, their music was heard by more people in this country than was the music of all the great masters combined.

In those days of the silent film these men created the connecting link between the screen and the audience, and the film companies and large theatres which employed orchestras clamored for more and more music. Their instructions to us were: "Once we play a piece of music we don't want it duplicated for at least three months."

This, of course, made our task even more difficult. Our composers were writing film music by the mile, and in order to augment their unceasing efforts we began to import music from Europe, where a whole battery of writers were busy turning their talents to picture music. Among them were: A. W. Ketelbey, world-famous composer of "In a Persian Market"; Ricardo Drigo, whose Serenade from "Les Millions d'Arlequin" is still being played throughout the world; Giuseppe Becce; Patou; and even some of the works of the great Sibelius. Our catalog of Agitatos, Animal Cartoons, Church Music, and such sub-divisions as Sinister, Chase, Sad, Happy, Gypsy, Mysterious, Furious and Majestic, grew and grew.

But no matter how hard we pushed our composers, they had only twenty-four hours a day to put music on paper and that just wasn't enough. We were not only working for the film companies in New York, we had arrangements with some seventy theatres all over the country to view the pictures they booked and to make special musical cue sheets for their orchestras. The cue sheets plus the actual music were to be in their possession a week before the picture went on. The demands upon us grew into staggering dimensions.

In desperation we turned to crime. We began to dismember the great masters. We began to murder the works of Beethoven, Mozart, Grieg, J. S. Bach, Verdi, Bizet, Tchaikovsky and Wagner--everything that wasn't protected by copyright from our pilfering.

The immortal chorales of J. S. Bach became an "Adagio Lamentoso for sad scenes." Extracts from great symphonies and operas were hacked down to emerge again as "Sinister Misterioso" by Beethoven, or "Weird Moderato" by Tchaikovsky. Wagner's and Mendelssohn's wedding marches were used for marriages, fights between husbands and wives, and divorce scenes: we just had them played out of tune, a treatment known in the profession as "souring up the aisle." If they were to be used for happy endings we jazzed them up mercilessly. Finales from famous overtures, with "William Tell" and "Orpheus" the favorites, became galops. Meyerbeer's "Coronation March" was slowed down to a majestic pomposo to give proper background to the inhabitants of Sing Sing's deathhouse. The "Blue Danube" was watered down to a minuet by a cruel change in tempo. Delibes' "Pizzicato Polka" made an excellent accompaniment to a sneaky night scene by counting "one-two" between each pizzicato. Any piece using a trombone prominently would infallibly announce the home-coming of a drunk; no other instrument could hiccup with such virtuosity.

Today I look in shame and awe at the printed copies of these mutilated masterpieces. I hope this belated confession will grant me forgiveness for what I have done. But in those days these pieces saved our lives; no composer could ever catch up with me, blue-pencilling and re-creating with scissors and paste a section of Beethoven's "Pastoral Symphony." Soon we produced these "works" at a breath-taking speed and our list of Dramatic and Incidental music covered almost any situation the most extravagant film writer could think of.

Our firm had grown with the movie industry, for music had become one of the big features of the tremendous movie palaces which had been built all over the country. Hundred-thousand-dollar organs and 60-piece orchestras were advertised in screaming letters everywhere. Also, it was an era of prosperity and a publisher who specialized, as I did, in music for films, and stayed away from other adventures, was bound to prosper. And then, suddenly, it was all over. Completely, with terrifying speed, and with absolute, crushing finality.

There had been rumors about an invention that could make pictures talk. We had shrugged them off. But after attending the grand opening of the first sound film, THE JAZZ SINGER, we couldn't shrug anymore. A few weeks later I had to realize that what had been an industry, what I had made my own and very special business, music for the silent films, would within a short time be a thing of the past. I went home dazed. Again I was faced with the fact that there is no such thing as security. What I had thought was a solid foundation for my life was crumbling.

Within a few months 15,000 film theatres throughout the U.S. were clamoring for sound equipment. If one theatre in a town was able to obtain it, every other house immediately turned into a morgue. Nearly 100,000 musicians found themselves without jobs. It was a grim, sweeping, disastrous collapse.

My tremendous stock of music became worthless overnight. There was nothing to do but to face facts. I sold no less than 70 tons of printed music to a paper mill for 15 cents a hundred pounds. $210 for the entire lot! But two days before it was to pay the $210, the mill went bankrupt, after having been in business for over 90 years. I never received a penny for my entire stock, the fruit of ten years of toil.

For a little while there was just nothing to do but to sit and wait and think. I did not despair. I had seen too many of these changes, and I had acquired enough hope and confidence to take what was coming and to make the best of it.

And then the talkies, which had dealt me so crushing a blow, helped me to catch my breath. The film companies soon realized that nobody could better help them with their new, uncharted task of fitting music to the sound track of pictures, than the men who had done the same type of work for silent pictures. Soon fabulous prices were offered for the services of such men as Hugo Riesenfeld, conductor of the Rivoli Theatre in New York, Erno Rapee of the Roxy, and Nat Finston of the New York Rialto. Within a short time these men found themselves in Hollywood preparing musical scores for sound film. And what was more logical than for them to fall back on the material they had used in the past and knew so well--the mood music, dramatic and incidental, that would fit the situation in sound pictures as it had fitted the situations in silent ones?

The men who were selecting and recording music in Hollywood were all my friends. They knew every piece in my catalog. It was a life-saver for them and for me. I didn't sell sheet music any more. I now sold film companies the right to use my music on sound tracks. This soon became a general practice. I was in business again.

But I knew it couldn't last long. The film companies were paying millions of dollars to publishers and composers for the use of published music. They soon found it more profitable to hire composers to write original music and to organize their own publishing houses. When Warner Brothers spent a million dollars to acquire the old established catalog of M. Witmark and Sons, with thousands of valuable copyrights, the rush was on. Soon most of the major film companies were in the music publishing business and were not interested in outside publications any more. My catalog was again heading for the junk pile, this time for good. I knew that if I wanted to survive I had to draw a final line under the past and find an entirely new field of activity.

DON'T SHOOT THE PIANO PLAYER

Jack Shaindlin

As I recline in a plush semi-mobile seat in my favorite movie house and enjoy the velvety sound of music emanating from the screen and surrounding me, thanks to all the wonders of the latest engineering developments, I can't help thinking back to 1926.

I was 16 years old and played the piano in a barn that had been converted to a movie house in a Chicago suburb. It was a one-story structure with an ominously slanting cement floor. The pianist's chair was frail and the extent of its mobility depended on the weight and sense of balance of the player. The hours were from 6 to 11 p.m., seven nights a week, fitting in perfectly with my conservatory studies during the day. I even had several 15-minute breaks for refreshments. A player piano attachment filled in during my rest periods, hammering out the popular tunes of the day. On one occasion as the villain was dying on the screen, my relief robot was helping him out by playing "Linger Awhile."

The manager sat in the last row watching the film at almost every performance and his chastisement of the "sandwich eaters" was heard above my valiant effort to sustain the proper musical mood of the film. In those days the motion picture, being a relative newcomer to the entertainment media, attracted many "repeaters" who invariably brought their lunch and "made a day of it." Little did the manager know that one day the very "munching" he was trying to discourage would keep many a house from shutting down.

The average film fare in 1926 consisted of a feature picture seldom exceeding 60 minutes in length, a one or two-reel comedy, featuring the popular comedians of the day (Larry Semon, Snub Pollard, Carter DeHaven, Lloyd Hamilton, Our Gang, and others), Aesop's Fables, a five-minute compilation of static reading matter consisting of 15 or 20 jokes, and that inevitable paragon of enlightenment, the sometime topical "International Newsreel," its slogan "The

World at Your Feet" promising a "magic carpet" excursion into the unknown. I still remember some of its fascinating captions: "Federal Agents Smash 600-Gallon Still in New Jersey Hills," "Cuties from 48 States Vie for Beauty Honors," "$10,000 Fire Destroys Warehouse," "A World at Your Feet" indeed!

The style of my playing matched the subtitles of the subject matter on the screen, often resulting in 10 bruised fingers at the evening's end.

My next job at 17 was a cultural, if not a monetary, advancement. I was the leader of a trio consisting of violin, piano and cello in a downtown "grind house." I didn't particularly like the discipline imposed upon me in this job as improvising was out of the question. It is with nostalgia and embarrassment that I recall the girl cellist who straddled her instrument in cowboy fashion, pushing up her dress and revealing her garters.

In those days the musical accompaniment, whether dispersed by a pianist, a trio or an abortive symphony orchestra in the pit, usually duplicated the action on the screen without adding further dimensions. Not that there weren't any "trailblazers" in the orchestra pit at that time. There were many fine mood music makers--Erno Rapee, William Axt, Hugo Riesenfeld and others who pioneered in this field. The patterns they established provided motivations and modus-operandi for the men working in the medium now. Many of these who started in the motion picture business in the 20's have gone on to great things. Eugene Ormandy, who conducts the Philadelphia Orchestra, was the assistant conductor in the Capitol Theatre in New York City and was "allowed" to conduct the newsreel while the "main event" maestro stood in the wings adjusting his white tie.

Since those days, many of the arts involved in film-making--writing, directing, lighting and sometimes acting--have gone through various stages of advancement. However, I feel that the improvements in screen music have been technological rather than intellectual (which is not too surprising since the culture of science and the arts have always been incompatible). Even the widespread use of jazz in film backgrounds seems to be more of an "added attraction" for the paying public than a desire on the part of the composer to set the proper artistic and emotional tone for a film.

Some of the music involved in film (particularly television) scoring today does not differ greatly from the "cueing" done in the mid-1920's when a sizeable pit orchestra in a "deluxe" house gave a good performance of the specially composed music for such films as THE BIG PARADE and WHAT PRICE GLORY?

The other day while watching a Western re-run on television my six-year-old ventured, "I knew he was the robber when I heard the music." Very little has changed from the days when my piano clichês identified the characters. (White hat--good guy; black hat--bad guy.) Sometimes the real "giveaway" on television is the music.

This, of course, is a generalization. There are some fine craftsmen composing for the screen now who often succeed in making a point where the script has failed. They are the ones who are giving film music what validity it has.

Unlike the silent film pianist who tried to "Mickey Mouse" the action on the screen (and usually was either late or early with his cues), the juxtaposition of soundtrack and images on the same piece of film makes exact cueing a relatively simple matter. This is particularly important when music is used to annotate dialog. However, tight schedules in film-making and lack of rapport and collaboration on the part of directors and writers often make it impossible for the composer to set the proper mood for a film.

Today, in my opinion, the arch-enemy of a "perfect movie score" is its illegitimate cousin, the LP soundtrack album. Performing societies pay handsomely for the radio and television performances of film themes. It is not unusual for the composer of a theme that catches on to make more money than the producer of the picture. This has produced a situation in which the tail is wagging the dog. I know a busy and successful composer who turned down an offer to write a score for a film because he did not think it had possibilities as a "hot selling" LP. "I don't think anyone would go for an album of 49 bridges," he declared.

He was right, of course. Most film scores, by their very natures, cannot possibly stand on their own as music that would interest a hi-fi or stereo fan. The story development may require deliberate balance distortions and yards and yards of unobtrusive music which complements or (as is usually the case), mirrors it. This music cannot possibly interest an LP customer who is looking for "sound." Quite often, too, a composer must subvert the music to the requirements of a particular scene so that he can only express himself through the dramatic content of the picture.

In the view of many composers, the requirements of a successful LP are more important than the requirements of the film. They would rather be "on the beat" than "on the beam." I have nothing to lose by saying this because I am well aware that in today's market three nasty letters from Tiomkin can easily be traded for one from Mancini.

My own career, which has involved serving as musical director for hundreds of films, conducting Philharmonic Pop Concerts at Carnegie Hall, and lecturing on film music, has now swung full circle. For a recently televised NBC "Today" show saluting Mack Sennett, the kingmaker of silent screen comedy, I was asked to accompany the shots of slapstick comedy on the piano. The only difference that the passing of 40 years has made is that this time I was heard by millions. So, if you find yourself looking at a movie in a converted barn in a Chicago suburb--don't shoot the piano player. It might be me.

Chapter II

THEORIES AND COMMENTS

THE ART OF COMPOSING MUSIC SCORES FOR FILMS

Loren G. Buchanan

How to write the musical score for a motion picture? Easier said than done, as the old saw goes, but even saying it isn't easy. Veteran screen composer Alex North did his best, however, to explain in simple terms some of the intricacies and approaches to one of man's most complicated accomplishments.

Each picture, as may be imagined, presents a different problem, although several general rules apply to all. The music must complement or point up action, dialogue or other dramatic devices in the picture, North feels, in order even to begin to qualify as a "good" score. He disagrees basically with those who maintain that if the audience is "conscious" of music in the picture, it is a bad score. Examples of this are the bland, innocuous background scores of the thirties, frequently borrowed from the classics, which merely made a "cushion" on which to rest the dialogue, and keep other sequences from being totally silent.

At the other extreme, North said, and perhaps even worse, is what he calls "Mickey Mouse-type" music. Someone goes up a stairs, for example, and the music follows right along, step by step. Each dramatic situation is easily "predicted" by the viewer unfortunate enough to hear this type of soundtrack, and the dramatic impact is thereby dulled, as it might be if a character said, "I'm expecting a phone call" shortly before the phone rang.

Knowing what is bad is part of making something good, though, so let's go on from here. The type of picture and the historical period in which it is set determine, for the most part, the appropriate musical style. Some of the earliest thinking before writing the musical score for 20th-Fox's THE AGONY AND THE ECSTASY consisted, North said, in "soaking up" Gregorian chants and other existing music written during the Renaissance period, as well as its instrumentation, and from this formulating his own style in which to write music specifically for the picture.

A composer is usually called in after a picture is in the can, North said, because music must be written to fit the various scenes, second for second, after final cuts have been made. But the preferable way, one that was used when THE AGONY AND THE ECSTASY, CLEOPATRA, WHO'S AFRAID OF VIRGINIA WOOLF?, and several others were scored, is for the composer to confer with the director even before shooting starts. In this way, dialogue can be eliminated if music would carry the action better, and the drama can be amended as needed, with the music in mind. In the case of CLEOPATRA a temporary score, which was later re-written, was needed to set the tempo for dancers.

Assuming, though, that he is handed a finished picture to score, the first thing he does, North said, is to see the film, stopwatch in hand, as many times as he thinks he needs to, taking copious notes and making a complete breakdown of the film, down to split seconds. He knows before he starts the actual writing of the music, he said, that, for example, a character crosses the room and opens the door at 14-1/2 seconds, and at 21-1/4 seconds the camera cuts to a close-up of a piece of paper in his hand. The music may or may not change during this time, depending on the dramatic context of the situation.

North prefers to be alone the first time he sees a picture he's working on, but likes to sit down with the director shortly thereafter, stopping after each reel and discussing the music desired. The composer said he does not find particular difficulty in writing music to fit odd time periods such as this. A "feel" for it comes with experience.

A six- to 10-week contract is frequently made between composers and film companies, for a score which may run anywhere from 20 minutes to several hours. But the actual writing time may be cut to four or five weeks if previews and advance publicity require its completion before the normal time. To knock out five or six pictures a year as some composers do (North normally scores about two a year) is "physically impossible," at least without help, he contends, "and I like to do every note myself." He composes about half the time at the piano, he said, and half the time away from it, but sitting close by so he can check details as required.

Although he has scored many types of pictures, North observed that he had never done an out-and-out comedy, of the slapstick type, although many films have some comedy in them. There is a certain amount of validity to the idea that composers, like actors, tend to become "type-cast," he conceded. "Different composers have a certain flair for one thing or another," he said, citing a composer who had done a nice job on a particular picture. "Whether he could do THE AGONY AND THE ECSTASY, I don't know."

One of the works of which North is proudest (and one of his most famous), is "Unchained Melody," which enabled the composer to buy a house on the coast for his family. It is now having a resurgence, he said.

After a background of academic study in his chosen field, including studies at Juilliard and a Guggenheim fellowship, and some time spent in writing "serious music" and music for television, he was engaged to compose the music for the Broadway play, "Death of a Salesman," after which he went to Hollywood to do the score for A STREETCAR NAMED DESIRE, his first film. Although most people don't realize it, he was a pioneer in use of original jazz written for a motion picture soundtrack. A STREETCAR NAMED DESIRE was the picture.

Filmgoers over the years may also remember his music from VIVA ZAPATA, THE ROSE TATTOO, THE RAINMAKER, SPARTACUS and CHEYENNE AUTUMN.

Born in Chester, Pa., a suburb of Philadelphia, North spends most of his time in Hollywood, after commuting between coasts for about five years. But he still gets to New York a couple of times a year, he said, finding the seasonal changes refreshing after the monotony of Hollywood weather, and feeling the tempo of the city stimulating.

North is looking for a Broadway play--maybe a musical, "something contemporary, with something to say about our lives today." Broadway star-director Mike Nichols, he said, who directed WHO'S AFRAID OF VIRGINIA WOOLF? is "a very inventive guy, and has a lot to say."

But another North star is ascending, and a father-son team may not be far off. Son Steven, 22, has done "quite well" at theatrical direction in England, the proud father said, and has assisted directors in this country on several films.

And would he enjoy working with his son as director of a picture? The twinkle in his eye made it silly to even ask.

IS THERE ANY MUSIC AT THE MOVIES?

Paul Kresh

"Oh, my!" Emily exclaimed one evening recently, as we were taking our ease after dinner. I was sorting out ball-point pens, trying to separate the ones with ink from the dry ones--a job I had been putting off for weeks. Emily was going through the New York Times; and I could see she was about to indulge that most incorrigible of her habits: reading aloud to me from the newspaper. I waited, attentively but apprehensively. She had cleared her throat. It would probably be something important.

"Waves of magnificent sound," she read, "rolled through the Academy of Music on Fourteenth Street last night as Urbech Associates and the New York Theatre Organ Society presented 'Sounds of the Silents,' a program reviving the musical traditions of the heyday of the movie palace, a period that extended roughly from 1920 to --"

"Tell me in your own words," I interrupted her to plead. The Times' prose is so thorough.

"They fixed the organ," Emily said. "The Wurlitzer."

"That's nice," I muttered. I noticed that there was

ink on my hands from a marking pen, the kind you use on laundry. I wondered how I would ever get it off. "So they fixed the organ," I prompted, trying to show Emily I was on her side.

"Yes. It was built and installed in 1926. It's supposed to be one of the best theater organs in the city. Your fingers are full of ink."

I asked Emily what they had done with the organ after it was fixed, and she was only too glad to tell me. "There's this Lee Erwin," she explained. "He was the organist on the Arthur Godfrey show for twenty-two years. Before that he played the organ on Station WLW in Cincinnati for eleven years in the radio series 'Moon River', and Allen Hughes says he was excellent." She resumed her reading aloud. It seems that Mr. Erwin, at that memorable concert presented by the New York Theatre Organ Society, played the original score he had composed for THE EAGLE, a seventy-minute classic of the silent screen, in addition to which there was a screening of the Charlie Chase comedy CRAZY LIKE A FOX and two Max Fleischer bouncing-ball sing-along cartoons. The affair had been so successful that the New York Theatre Organ Society was planning to restore other organs, including one at the Beacon Theatre on Broadway and 74th Street, and another in Rahway, New Jersey.

I was duly impressed by all this, as I always am when Emily, having combed the Times for its most compelling revelations, presents me with the results of her researches. It set me to thinking about movie music and its evolution from the "sound of the silents" down to THE YELLOW SUBMARINE. As I rummaged clumsily in the kitchen cabinet for some stuff Emily had suggested for taking off indelible ink, I mused on the range of movie music I had been exposed to over the years. It was hard to regard it all as an unmixed blessing.

Now, Emily and I love the movies. We would rather be at the movies than almost anywhere else--even, on Sunday evenings, at home watching the Smothers Brothers (before they were scratched, that is). But I remember Emily reading to me once from an article by Dwight Macdonald, in which he expounded the theory that with each new technological development the motion picture had to give up another aspect of its original flexibility. The advent of the talkies certainly did not please everyone. After seeing his first sound film in 1927, Sir Thomas Beecham is supposed to have exploded: "Now there is no place one can go and hear nothing!" And I vividly remember a song my father used to play on our wind-up Victrola when I was a child. The words went like this:

> Guns go off and whistles blow,
> Music through the whole darned show.
> I can't sleep in the movies any more.

The truth is, movies have never been really silent. Music, Emily tells me, was first brought into the movie house for practical reasons. There was no sound-proof wall between projector and audience in those out-of-the-way halls of London and New York where the cinema first found its public around the turn of the century. Something had to mask the racket made by the projector. And so, before those celebrated pianists in gartered shirtsleeves were hired, hand organs, music boxes, and phonographs were used. Music also helped to solve a peculiar problem of mass psychology: crowds seemed more willing to listen and watch silently than just to watch in silence. Music kept the ears of audiences busy and so kept their mouths from flapping.

In the early years of this century, however, experiments with mechanical reproduction were abandoned in favor of the movie-house pianist and, still later, increasingly elaborate theatre orchestras. The problem of what to play was solved through the compilation of extensive cinema-music libraries. There an enterprising arranger could find every sort of score to meet the movie's requirements. Under "tension-misterioso" he could look up suitable passages for "night: sinister mood" or "night: threatening mood," or "magic: apparition," or "impending doom." In the famous Kinothek in Berlin, for example, under the heading "tension-agitato," the file offered music for "pursuit," "heroic battle," "disturbance," "unrest," "terror," "disturbed masses," "tumult," and three varieties of "natural cataclysm." Climaxes (appassionato) were available in six smashing varieties, from "despair" to "bacchantic." It was all a long way from Dimitri Tiomkin, but it was certainly heading in that direction.

Soon there arose maverick pit conductors who turned up their noses at stock music and preferred to accompany movies with fragments from Debussy and Tchaikovsky, and from there it was a short step to calling upon composers to invent original scores. Edmund Meisel, who wrote the music for Sergei Eisenstein's POTEMKIN, was outstanding among silent-film composers. Richard Strauss came to the Dresden State Opera House to conduct the orchestra for a performance of his opera "Der Rosenkavalier" on film, but he gave up in rehearsal after trying to keep things synchronized and turned his baton over to a professional movie conductor. A few distinguished composers, notably Arthur Honegger, tried their hand at composing for the silents, but no masterpieces came of it, although it might be fun to hear Darius Milhaud's "Actualites," take-off on old newsreel stereotypes.

We all know what happened next. Al Jolson made THE JAZZ SINGER in 1927, and the sound of Vitaphone was heard in the land. Actually, THE JAZZ SINGER and THE SINGING FOOL got their sound from ingenious couplings of the projector with 16-inch phonograph records that, in speed, were precursors of the modern LP--they played at 33-1/3 revolutions per minute. Records wore out fast in those days, though, and synchronization was a tricky business. A few years later this method was replaced by putting the sound on a strip running along the side of the film itself. The impulses on the soundtrack were then translated into music, sound effects, and the clichés of Hollywood dialogue in a way that I could not possibly make clear to you, since I do not understand it too well myself, and neither does Emily.

Concurrent with this development was the growth of the theme song as a device to soften up the audience for the action to come while the credits were gotten out of the way. The use of this device soon reached epidemic proportions, and threatened to hold up the action of movies indefinitely. So the industry, in its wisdom, began to fall back on what has been its Golden Rule ever since: movie music should be *there*, but not *heard*. Movie music, any old Hollywood pro *will* tell you, "*must* not call attention to itself." The "Thou Shalt Not Be Heard" commandment may be one reason why only a handful of major American composers have written for the medium, though England's greatest symphonists --William Walton, Benjamin Britten, Arthur Bliss, Arthur Benjamin, and Ralph Vaughan Williams among them--have produced distinguished motion-picture scores. Honegger, Milhaud, and Georges Auric have all written music you could hear in French films, and Prokofiev and Shostakovich have constructed mighty works, of varying degrees of vulgarity, to enliven the movies of the Soviet Union. Of course, we Americans can point out to foreign detractors that Gershwin wrote his second rhapsody, "Rhapsody in Rivets," for a Hollywood movie, that Aaron Copland contributed lovely scores to OUR TOWN and THE RED PONY, and that Virgil Thomson's music for the documentaries THE PLOW THAT BROKE THE PLAINS, LOUISIANA STORY, and THE RIVER are classic achievements.

But what of the rest? It _is_ there, but are we really not supposed to hear it? Kurt London put it in a nutshell in his book _Film Music._ "Absolute music," he says, "is apprehended _consciously_, film music unconsciously." No wonder, then, that it is all so difficult to remember when you leave the theater. Yet certain exceptions to this dogma are permitted in movieland. A few classical pieces have found their way into the inner sanctum, and may be used as mood-setters. There was a time, not many years ago, when portions of Rachmaninoff's Second Piano Concerto were used as the accompaniment for almost everything. Emily and I wiped our eyes to its strains through Noel Coward's BRIEF ENCOUNTER and perhaps a dozen other pictures of the period. In the newsreel days, I don't think you were allowed to show a horsetrack unless it was accompanied by the breakneck passage from Ponchielli's "Dance of the Hours." Beethoven's "Für Elise" was always heard whenever Spring Byington approached the spinet in the drawing room of her Southern mansion, and you knew that all would not be tranquil for long: Bette Davis or the Civil War was bound to break out any minute. There was a time, too, when you could not start a movie about London without a little scene-setting--the "Knightsbridge March" from Eric Coates' "London Suite," for example.

Other movies have been made in Hollywood for which it has been found necessary not only to draw on the classics, but to make certain alterations in the process. In our long years of moviegoing, Emily and I have come to appreciate the limitless ingenuity with which a Hollywood arranger can improve a masterpiece. Everything Mendelssohn wrote for "A Midsummer Night's Dream" was used in Max Reinhardt's tremendous movie, which touched the heights and sank to the depths as it forged its way through Shakespeare's fantastic comedy, and the producers were even magnanimous enough to call in Erich Wolfgang Korngold to touch up the orchestration a little and provide a couple of transitions which Mendelssohn had thoughtlessly neglected to compose. We'll never forget too that marvelous movie laid in Mexico, with Esther Williams as a lady bullfighter, which used Aaron Copland's "El Salon Mexico" (composed in the movie by an aspiring young Mexican genius, Ricardo Montalban). Almost all of it was played before the movie was over, but in an updated version for piano and orchestra by Johnny Green, the composer of "Body and Soul." Perhaps the most ingenious use of a piece from the standard repertoire was Walt Disney's commandeering of "The Rite of Spring," Stravinsky's ballet about savages in pagan Russia, to illustrate evolution in his movie FANTASIA. (In a state close to shock, the composer is reported to have murmured, "This must have been what I meant in the first place.") To make the piece fit the action, Leopold Stokowski, the conductor for the film, cut and rearranged the score and tactfully eliminated the earthshaking "Dance of Death" at the end.

In the long evolutionary climb from the Tara theme in GONE WITH THE WIND (1939) to Lara's theme in DR. ZHIVAGO (1965), one of the most striking developments has been "original" music by composers schooled in the technique of putting together a patchwork of giant orchestra and chorus, composers who unabashedly thank Tchaikovsky and Rimsky-Korsakov when they walk off with an Academy Award. Perhaps the most wonderful thing about this group of Hollywood composers has been their names: Daniele Amfitheatrof, Dimitri Tiomkin, Bronislau Kaper, Miklos Rozsa, Erich Wolfgang Korngold. And their music is almost as resounding as those grand monikers themselves. What would a screen epic be now without its all-engulfing heaves and swells of sonic overkill? And then there is Max Steiner, who is practically a whole industry in himself. He was at one time virtually the court composer for Bette Davis. Emily and I will never forget the welling up of those great oceanic passages in such movies as OLD ACQUAINTANCE, in which suddenly Miss Davis wasn't listening to Miriam Hopkins any more (or was it the other way around?) and the dialogue was drowned in the subjective turbulence of a Steiner score. He has always favored a kind of leitmotif, haunting in its way, as for example the themes for THE LETTER and SINCE YOU WENT AWAY. He wrote a poignant score of finesse and restraint for THE INFORMER, a harrowing one for KING KONG to climb the Empire State Building by, and 282 episodes, with separate themes for every character from Scarlett to Melanie, and every twist and turn of the plot, for the three-hour production of GONE WITH THE WIND. Despite its longueurs and pretensions, Steiner's score for that recurrent movie classic is much admired, and is still broadcast often, along with such hardy perennials as the score for SPELLBOUND, the suspenseful monotonies of Francis Lai's music for A MAN AND A WOMAN, Richard Addinsell's "Warsaw Concerto" (composed for a forgotten film named DANGEROUS MOONLIGHT), and such other favorites as Ernest Gold's pseudo-Hebraic theme from Otto Preminger's movie EXODUS, John Barry's theme for BORN FREE, and "More" from MONDO CANE.

Much movie music is hard to hear even if you try--the louder it is, perhaps, the harder! In movie musicals, on the other hand, you're supposed to hear the music and, one hopes, be able to recall it afterwards. Only a few days ago, Emily bought one of those 900-page illustrated volumes of the talking picture, and it would be pleasant to pause here and reminisce at length about all those wonderful Saturday afternoons spent watching movie musicals from THE BROADWAY MELODY of 1929 to that cartoon masterpiece, the Beatles' YELLOW SUBMARINE. How could we forget those magic moments when Alice Faye, after a single glance at the score of a brand new song, set the music aside and overwhelmed us with a perfect run-through? How could we ever forget the happy hours we spent listening to those little songbirds MGM used to raise on their back lot in special cages--Judy Garland, Jane Powell, Kathryn Grayson--whose little heartbreaks could be washed away with an ice-cream soda and a few kind words from "Cuddles" Sakall? It would be fun to linger over all the forgotten moments Emily reminded me of--that Ruth Chatterton sang and Nancy Carroll danced in PARAMOUNT ON PARADE; that Bebe Daniels and John Boles were warblers together in RIO RITA, and even Pola Negri sang in A WOMAN COMMANDS (the song was "Paradise"). But the world of Nancy Carroll, Buddy Rogers, Fred Astaire and Ginger Rogers, of Eddie Cantor and Fanny Brice, of Jeanette MacDonald and Nelson Eddy, of Ruby Keeler and Dick Powell, Bing Crosby and Dorothy Lamour, Bob Hope, Frank Sinatra, Judy Garland, Gene Kelly, and Busby Berkeley, however real it seemed at the time, is gone. It was a comforting lotus land, and so were its songs, from Rudolf Friml's to Richard Rodgers'; a new generation is discovering it today on television.

The current crop of Hollywood musicals, especially movie "adaptations" of Broadway shows such as HALF A SIXPENCE and SWEET CHARITY, is getting bigger, louder, and shinier all the time, and losing most of the charm of the originals in the process. The screen musicals Emily and I remember most fondly were written especially for the movies and weren't adaptations at all: SINGIN' IN THE RAIN, for example, with its marvelous score by Nacio Herb Brown and Arthur Freed; SEVEN BRIDES FOR SEVEN BROTHERS, MGM's Western-style version of the Rape of the Sabine Women, with music by Gene de Paul--you didn't exactly go out of the theater whistling it, but it was enormous fun while it lasted. It would be pleasant, too, to linger awhile on the music of those animated cartoons in which the invincible victim arose unscathed from the most vicious sadistic attacks to the sound of a fox-trot. But these are lost worlds too.

In his book What to Listen for in Music, Aaron Copland asserts that most of us movie-goers take the musical accompaniment to dramatic films too much for granted. He reveals that the Hollywood producer, far from considering music unimportant, often secretly hopes that a good score will save a second-rate picture. Copland lists the ways in which music serves the film: the creation of "a more convincing atmosphere" and the evocation of "time and place"; underlining the unspoken thoughts of a character, or the unseen implications of a situation; building continuity, and rounding off the experience--i.e., the music "that blares out at the end of the film."

Emily and I believe that movie music also serves certain other, even more fundamental, purposes. It has to announce to the people waiting in the lobby when the movie is over, so they may begin their rush for seats. It must tell them when the picture starts so they can begin to rattle their candy papers, and also, especially in these times, when the credits are liable to pop up anywhere and go on for any length of time, tell them when the action is really under way. It must also tell them when the end is coming so that they can slip their shoes back on, push their way out to the aisle, and beat everyone else to the door before the rush. And today's movie-goer may wander in at any point; how is he going to catch on fast to earlier developments he has missed? The music will fill him in. Emily boasts that she can close her eyes, listen to the music from any American movie, and recognize at once the nature of the action. As a matter of fact, the movie addict, whether he gets the stuff at movie houses or at home by way of television, could probably provide from memory a suitable score for every occasion in his own life, from trying to start his car on a freezing morning to the big scene when his wife threatens to go home to mother. It is built into us through long years of repetition and "unconscious apprehension."

Recently, movie critics have been demanding that movie music change with the times, that such groups as the Jefferson Airplane and Moby Grape be given their day on the screen as they already have been on television. No doubt the inevitable result of this will be the watering down of originally fresh and rebel styles in order not to offend nervous middle-class ears. Already we have had Simon and Garfunkel singing their songs throughout THE GRADUATE, but this was in some ways more distracting than helpful. And Quicksilver Messenger Service, the Steve Miller Band, and Mother Earth combined forces to whip up a storm of a rock-and-roll score for a movie called REVOLUTION, but that film went--or sank--underground. Meanwhile, what we get are Burt Bacharach (WHAT'S NEW, PUSSYCAT?, CASINO ROYALE); John Barry (THE IPCRESS FILE, THE KNACK, BORN FREE); Elmer Bernstein (THE MAN WITH THE GOLDEN ARM, THE MAGNIFICENT SEVEN, A WALK ON THE WILD SIDE, and THE TEN COMMANDMENTS); Neal Hefti (BAREFOOT IN THE PARK); Quincy Jones (IN THE HEAT OF THE NIGHT and IN COLD BLOOD); Henry Mancini (BREAKFAST AT TIFFANY'S, THE PINK PANTHER, and HATARI); Johnny Mandel (I WANT TO LIVE and THE SANDPIPER); and Leith Stevens (THE WILD ONE and many an eerie score for science-fiction movies). These fellows all show a notable chic in combining a jazz beat with symphonic expansiveness and lush instrumentation. In the contexts for which their pastiches are assembled, they are serviceable, very much in the old tradition, with a little fresh make-up applied to make them sound more "with it." But separated from the film and served up on original soundtrack discs, they are exposed in all their wearying sterility. These "new" composers, like their predecessors, are excellent craftsmen who know exactly what they are about. And that is the trouble. Chaplin could whistle a score into existence (MODERN TIMES, THE GREAT DICTATOR), one that was fresher and apter in its directness and simplicity than all the exertions of these latter-day champions who are always skilled but so very rarely inspired.

What Emily and I remember from movies is music not at its catchiest or most tuneful, but the <u>effect</u> of music in the right place: Bernard Herrmann's score for CITIZEN KANE; Virgil Thomson's idiomatic contributions to those already-named classic documentaries; Aaron Copland's bucolic excellences for THE RED PONY (Westerns nowadays lean heavily on warmed-over imitations of Copland); Georges Auric's music for the films of Jean Cocteau--as well as such brilliant strokes of Cocteau's own as the way he brought in Vivaldi to heighten the dream sequence in LES ENFANTS TERRIBLES; the waltz [by Maurice Jaubert] that expressed all the yearning, frustration, and nostalgia in the ballroom scene of CARNET DU BAL; Honegger's dazzling virtuoso music for the original nonmusical version of PYGMALION; the song that was a plot element in Alfred Hitchcock's THE LADY VANISHES; Arthur Bliss' scare score for the movie of H. G. Wells' prophetic THINGS TO COME; the way a piece was used--it was a rhumba by Xavier Cugat, I believe --in Ben Hecht's CRIME WITHOUT PASSION at the perturbing ironical climax; Leonard Bernstein's galvanically charged musical continuity for ON THE WATERFRONT; Nino Rota's orgies of instrumentation for LA DOLCE VITA and JULIET OF THE SPIRITS; Stanley Myers' inventive, searching score for the Irish movie of Joyce's ULYSSES.

Movie music is at its best when it is written for the purpose for which it is played, knows it place, and does not just drone on monotonously in order <u>not</u> to be heard. It is only when it tries to give itself airs--when Bacharach is exalted over Bach, and Miklos Rozsa over Handel, when the tramp of movie music decks herself out in the ill-fitting raiments of her older sister art--that it truly repels moviegoers like Emily and me. Good movie music need not be self-effacing; it can be as big as William Walton's for the battle scenes in HENRY V, as long as it is real music, celebrating real emotion, whether through full orchestra, Harpo Marx's harp, or the harpsichord of John Addison's tingling score for TOM JONES. We have no objection to raiding the classics, either, when they're deftly matched up to the action, as in Stanley Kubrick's 2001: A SPACE ODYSSEY, in which excerpts from recordings of pieces of Richard and Johann Strauss and others serenaded us during the space trip (are we headed back to the Kinothek?). But it can be overdone. We adored ELVIRA MADIGAN and rushed right out to buy Mozart's Piano Concerto No. 21 so that we could hear again the second-movement theme that had moved us to tears in the movie. To our consternation, we found out that there are twenty-six other concertos by the same composer. We are appalled at the possibility that, somewhere in Hollywood at this very moment, some producer who had made the same discovery may be thinking to himself, "Now, the opening of Number 20 will be just groovy for that rape scene, and for the theme song for LOVES OF CATHERINE THE GREAT there oughta be something in the 'Coronation' . . . "

JAZZ AT THE MOVIES

Martin Williams

What is a good film score? Is it music which is good enough to stand on its own, out of the original context? Or is it, on the other hand, music which is effective in context but which might not stand up in a concert hall?

On film, effective drama is a complex of several things. Movies with sound and dialogue are still primarily visual experiences like their silent forebears. But they begin as written narratives, which portray character, situation, and plot through dialogue. When they are executed, they also include photography, a carefully edited montage of "shots," and some "background" music as a part of their final effect. At the crudest level, one might say that the music is there simply to keep the audience from becoming distracted. And at a somewhat higher level, it is there to underline and perhaps complement mood, situation, and character.

The film composer walks a narrow line; he has to be good enough not to be noticed. If he does not do his job well, he will be noticed, either because he does not contribute to dramatic effect well enough or because, one might say, he contributes too much--he distracts one from the drama and draws too much attention to himself. We would not underline a dramatic film with a Beethoven symphony because, no matter how good the film, the audience might end up listening to Beethoven. In short, good film music is a purely functional aspect of one kind of drama.

One example of ideal movie music would be Max Steiner's score for KING KONG. It sounds perfectly marvelous, is almost totally effective in context, and yet one probably could not bear it for more than five minutes if he were asked to sit attentively during a performance in a concert hall. There are several film scores, however, one thinks particularly of a couple of Aaron Copland's, which manage to sound right in context and yet do stand up on their own.

About ten years ago, the movies began an earnest use of jazz as background music. Naturally, the industry discovered some fairly derivative hacks of its own to grind the stuff out, but it also invited some more-than-capable jazz musicians, and even some first-rate ones, into the fold.

It may seem odd that jazz, a form of music which has been so long determined to free itself from a purely functional role as a background in the barroom and dance hall, should have embraced so enthusiastically still another functional role as background at the movie house. But jazz, as usual, proved to have an unpredictable vitality. John Lewis wrote some very good pieces for the Modern Jazz Quartet to play in the background during a French movie called, in this country, NO SUN IN VENICE (they're on Atlantic 1284). And Lewis wrote a first-rate score for a small orchestra for ODDS AGAINST TOMORROW. That latter score, paradoxically, was even more functionally conceived in terms of the action of the film, but was somewhat better heard on its own. (It was issued on United Artists 4061 but is now out of print.)

Perhaps the most interesting approach was used by Miles Davis for an entirely forgettable French new-wave film called, over here, FRANTIC! Davis and his sidemen watched a screening of the movie and made some notes and sketches. Then they proceeded to improvise their score in direct response to a second screening of the movie in the recording studio. (The results can be heard on Columbia CL 1268.)

One of the two Sonny Rollins records that I am about to discuss is not a film score. It is called "East Broadway Rundown" (Impulse A/As-9121) and presents a Rollins trio on one side and, with the addition of trumpeter Freddy Hubbard, a quartet on the other. Its arrival, however, reminds me that I have neglected to give discussion to Rollins' previous and still recent release, which was a performance of the music he wrote for the British film, ALFIE (Impulse A/AS-9111).

The LP release is not drawn directly from the film's sound track; it features a nine-piece group, with scoring and conducting by Oliver Nelson, and with Rollins as the chief soloist, occasionally spelled by guitarist Kenny Burrell and pianist Roger Kellaway. Rollins' pieces would seem to meet the first, functional requirement of film music very well in sections like "Street Runner with Child" and the waltz, "On Impulse." But, to me, certain portions seem to stand up on their own also. These include the robust main "Alfie's Theme," which Rollins interprets twice, swaggeringly confident before the film's action and introspectively after it. Second a lovely "Child" theme which is played and echoed variously throughout. Rollins is the chief interpreter and improviser, of course, and beside him Burrell and Kellaway seem rather functional, even in the stronger parts of the score. Nelson's orchestrations are appropriately lean and complementary to the saxophonist's writing and playing.

The "East Broadway Rundown" LP features a rather different Rollins. It offers two extended, loosely structured pieces--the "Rundown" title piece and "Blessing in Disguise" --with former John Coltrane associates, Jimmy Garrison on bass and Melvin Jones on drums. On occasion, trumpeter Hubbard, present on the first title only, has also participated in similar "free form" projects with both Coltrane and Ornette Coleman.

Rollins matured in the mid-fifties, at a time when the modern jazz of the period was finding ensemble approaches and forms for itself over and above the take-your-turn, string-of-solos approach with which it had discovered and established its basic language. Rollins, at his best a sort of one-man sextet, functions best (and paradoxically with greater freedom, I think) within the strict tradition of song forms and blues, sometimes fulfilling their "rules" in his highly individual way and sometimes brilliantly extending, or even knowledgeably breaking, those rules. Thus, the best performance here is a relatively brief reading of Richard Rodgers' "We Kiss in a Shadow," which finishes off the LP. When he takes on the currently fashionable loose, "free" forms, as on the other two pieces, Rollins avoids his own best kind of challenge, I think, and we hear one of the most orderly melodists in jazz history courting disorder.

FILM MUSIC COMES OF AGE*

Gordon Hendricks

The tools that a composer of film-music has at his disposal are not unlimited. He has melody, and all too often tries to cram unmelodic situations, characters and ideas into it. He has the leitmotif, the short musical phrase which, by reiteration, can be used to identify a character, a situation, an idea. And there are phrases, commonplace phrases, the clichés of musical expression, which warn an audience that the Indians are coming, or that the feminine lead is going to have a baby.

The leitmotif is not as easy to employ properly as one might suppose. It must be clearly identifiable without possibility of mistake, and it must be inextricably associated with the character, idea or story situation it is to connote. Thus, when we hear a few notes which have been identified with Walter Pidgeon's feeling for Greer Garson, or with Henry V's for the Princess of France, these notes must appear often enough and clearly enough for us to know them. The leitmotif may reappear at any time, by itself, or as part of a musical texture, but it must be clearly identifiable and an integral part of any texture containing it.

A recent example of a less than fortunate use of leitmotif occurred in CYRANO DE BERGERAC, when the composer used and re-used a short musical figure to express the warlike or virile side of Cyrano's nature, but failed to identify it sufficiently with Cyrano. It became lost in the orchestration.

The excellent script and direction of A PLACE IN THE SUN enabled the composer of its score, Franz Waxman, to use a leitmotif effect very judiciously. The impulses to murder that stirred within George Eastman were represented by low-pitched, regularly accented eighth notes that were readily recognizable whenever they occurred. The Elizabeth Taylor motif, a skillful combination containing a jazz reed over varied accompaniments, was the only one of the film techniques assisting her in her characterization of the part that was not over-romanticized.

One of the most moving films I have ever seen, DAY OF WRATH, owed much of its effect to music. The somber mood that permeated the whole film was well adumbrated, during the exhibition of the titles and credits, by employing, as leitmotif material, the Gregorian plainsong "Dies Irae." The deployment, development and supplementation of this simple, unisonous, non-metrical chant, comprised the major part of the film's music, and provided a musical background that colored and strengthened the visual action. It also served the important purpose of tying each episode into an overall unity, which should always be the leitmotif's chief function. There was no patronizing pretentiousness in the way the plainsong was varied and simplified, and no banality. The grave, stark, resistless flow of the music connected the particular story of DAY OF WRATH with the immemorial theme of self-righteousness and intolerance.

The British film ROCKING HORSE WINNER also contained some remarkable uses of leitmotif. I was struck right away by the excellence of the background music for the titles, which forecast in a very satisfying manner the various "motifs" of the story. This was particularly true of the rocking horse music, and the "house" music. Mozart, Rossini, Verdi, Wagner, Puccini and many others put into their overtures indications of material to be used later, and the director of ROCKING HORSE WINNER understood the dramatic reasons for this.

Very early in ROCKING HORSE WINNER there was a sequence of three children singing Christmas carols. I was pleasantly surprised to hear that that is what the sound track had: <u>three children singing Christmas carols</u>. We have all become so conditioned to elaborate choral arrangements under such circumstances, with voice leadings worthy of Fred Waring and orchestrations worthy of Hector Berlioz, that when we hear realism we think we must be in the wrong place.

An extremely skillful and unpatronizing setting was composed for the first appearance of the rocking horse, and contained the fundamental musical materials for which this film was noteworthy. Augmented, extended brass chords promoted the very feeling of "wild and horrid glee" for which the director strove. Later, when the child became identified with this mingled jubilance and terror, it was with a musical texture so fine, and with a directional skill in horizontal cutting so expert, that nothing that the script itself contributed was half so explicit.

The film-making climate of Britain encourages their best composers of serious music to write for films without condescension. In the United States we too often frustrate our serious composer by allowing him too few opportunities, and by compromising his creations by careless unnecessary editing, re-orchestrating, and brazen rewriting. Film music is music. Why not let our best musicians write it?

As for melody, it is greatly misused and abused in films. Movies pretend to represent life. It is pleasant, but idle, to suppose that life or nature, whether it be a kiss or a flowing brook, can be fitted successfully into eight, 16 or 32 measures of "natural" anticipatable melody. Mozart and Haydn would be horrified to know that their developments have been extracted from their position in an overall synthesis and turned into a "tune." When half the instruments of an orchestra are tremolo-ing and vibrato-ing their way through one of these tunes in a rigidly sustained mezzo-forte, over an accompaniment by the other half of the instruments, the result is folly.

A good asymmetrical use of melodic material is contained in Dimitri Tiomkin's score for THE WELL. Large, strong major themes, heard in the strings and reinforced intelligently by brass, were placed skillfully in properly cacophonous textures. They make the musical part of the "shaft" sequence worth listening to. The piano and other percussives are aptly blended with non-musical sounds.

Musical clichés, of course, debilitate otherwise fine musical soundtracks. Too often the "Moonlight Sonata" means moonlight (which it doesn't at all); "William Tell" means a storm; Wagner and Mendelssohn mean wedding bells; Grieg or Sinding mean spring; "Siegfried" means the forest primeval; "Gaudeamus Igitur" means college; drum beats under sixteenth and dotted eighth couplets, mean redskins; and last and perhaps most maddening, a tinkling music-box-glockenspiel combination means a baby.

Although JIM THORPE, ALL-AMERICAN was a moving film in some ways, it was disfigured by three of these clichés. Whenever Burt Lancaster's mind harked back to his native Indian heritage, and whenever an Indian--the picture was full of them--came within a mile of the screen, the drums began to beat and the violins began to sound like "From the Land of the Sky-Blue Water" or "By the Waters of Minnetonka." Again, when Thorpe first put foot on his college campus, "Gaudeamus Igitur" was heard. Years later, when his old college chums came to see him, "Gaudeamus Igitur" was struck up as soon as they rounded the corner. And when Thorpe had his son, our first sight of the two together was chilled by the tinkle of the eternal music-box.

In another recent film, CLOSE TO MY HEART, Ray Milland ascended the stairs to look for his wife, and a music-box tinkled so loud and so long that one expected he would find triplets at least. Even in so inherently brutal a film as M, which contained some of Fritz Lang's starkest realism, a music-box announces the first appearance of a child. In BEDTIME FOR BONZO a music-box connotes a chimpanzee who is raised and treated as a child by two adults (?).

A musical cliché involving directorial cuteness is having an actor turn on the radio or the phonograph, or play the piano. The embarrassing artlessness of this is not relieved by the fact that within a few bars the all too obvious device may be supplemented, and often replaced, by a full symphony orchestra.

The "logical setting" is another cliché used ad nauseum. In JIM THORPE a football team of husky, semi-literate Indians delivered a finely modulated and delicately balanced version of a college song that would have done credit to the Schola Cantorum.

One of the most widespread prejudices among composers of film music is the feeling that movie audiences must be prepared for what will happen on the screen by commonplace musical phrases. Actually very little that happens in a movie is surprising anymore, and musical preparation for it is supererogation.

For example: in MR. IMPERIUM a letter is delivered to Ezio Pinza and six or seven excited little notes in the sound-track tell us the letter brings bad news. A few minutes later, at an airport, the sinister quality of the music foretells us that Sir Cedric Hardwicke is a villain, and that he probably won't deliver the note Pinza had written to Lana Turner.

The value of the absence of "preparation" was shown in THE WELL. The two highest points of interest in the digging sequence, the reaching of the child and the discovery that she was still alive, were unaccompanied by music. The music began after the second point was reached, and the tension had already been largely relieved. Further, in the film's sequence, only camera action indicated that something might happen to the child as she danced through a field to the brink of a well. The music itself was properly "flutey" and conveyed no portent of disaster.

The sudden looming-forth of the convict in GREAT EXPECTATIONS proves that audiences can stand an unprepared surprise. There was no music in this sequence in GREAT EXPECTATIONS, only non-musical sound effects.

Nor did the music in THE THING prepare the audience for seeing the remains of the sled-dog in the greenhouse cupboard. The split-second opening of the cupboard door was simply fortified by an ff in the orchestra.

Of all the malpractices in film music, perhaps the most unfortunate is the use of banal music when it is necessary for the sound track to be unobtrusive, which is often necessary, as during a piece of important dialogue. Non-musical sounds, if carefully used, can be very effective, but rarely are. Unobtrusive music should be intentionally composed. Let there be good unobtrusive music or no music at all.

CYRANO contained especially poor "unobtrusive" music materials. The famous balcony scene was accompanied by an interweaving of exaggerated, meaningless violin melodies. Good, solid music was needed. It does not divert attention; if it did there wouldn't be any successfully dramatic opera.

There is an unfortunate "unobtrusive" spot in A PLACE IN THE SUN, presumably by the hand of a composer other than Waxman. It grew out of the "murder" motif in the lake sequence. Trivial thematic material in an overblown orchestral dress weakened what otherwise would have been effective dialogue.

There was very little music in KIND HEARTS AND CORONETS. In sequence after sequence there was nothing but sound effects. In the last half of the film I can remember only a few measures of triumphant music played when the Houses of Parliament were shown. Nothing whatever was lost by this paucity of music.

I think one important reason why the fine underwater shots of the demolition squad in THE FROGMEN have been so universally praised is because of their economy of sound. There was nothing on the sound-track but the sound of water. In one of the most effective shots the warning "beep" of an electric alarm, added to the water sounds, was overwhelmingly dramatic.

I would like to close this article with a brief discussion of Georges Auric's music for THE LAVENDER HILL MOB. The music for the opening title and credits was a clever little fugue redolent of the humorous incongruities of the whole picture. It was connected skillfully to the Latin orchestra music for the opening shot of the story. It returned during the roll-up of the cast after the picture had ended.

The music for the body of the film was intentionally trivial, designed to heighten the contrast between the pettiness of the thieves and the enormous elements on the screen --the Bank of England, Scotland Yard and the Eiffel Tower itself.

The toy Eiffel Tower music is an excellent example of what can be done by a music box. Whenever it occurred, and it occurred often, it was a part of an intelligently contrived orchestral texture. E.g., when Alec Guinness realized that he had discovered how to get the gold out of the country, the tinkle began <u>after</u> his realization and reenforced the audience's pleasure in the smallness of the means that made possible so large a theft.

The music for the auto truck sequences was very characteristic of Auric. In the waiting sequence, the element of time, always best understood by the ticking of a clock, was represented by the toy Eiffel Tower music in rhythm with the ticking. This was well integrated with the music of the oncoming truck. Auric never condescends, and the second time Guinness rang the bell to stop the truck, we did not hear the bell itself but a dissonant chord in the brass, which created a psychic effect the bell sound could not have instigated.

What I understood as the Guinness leitmotif was a sprightly melody in double-dotted quarter notes and sixteenths that perfectly expressed the specious sycophancy of the grandly scheming bank clerk.

How many other satisfying things were achieved by Mr. Auric in the rich film-music experience that THE LAVENDER HILL MOB is! I cannot refrain from listing more of them: the "night" music in Geegaws, Ltd; the dizzying chase music in the descent of the Eiffel Tower; the scrambled chase music in the police exhibition; and the syncopated pizzicato music for the chase after the last Eiffel Tower child, the coda of which, at the departure of the steamer from Calais, is a gem.

Film music _can_ be wonderful.

The Greeks said that excellence is to be found among scarcely accessible rocks, and that a man may wear his heart out to reach it. I suppose we must not expect film producers and the composers of film music to wear out their hearts, but is it too much to hope that they will try to climb?

FACING THE MUSIC: WHY MOVIE SCORES ARE USUALLY SO AWFUL

William Wolf

The mood is delicate and sensitive. You are engrossed in a drama, and the film has swept you along with its credibility. Suddenly you are jolted by the absurd eruption of a syrupy song on the soundtrack and the impact is ruined for you. That is, it's ruined for _you_. Not for those with a financial interest in the film. That song may become a recording hit and an important added source of revenue for the movie.

What does it have to do with cinematic art? Nothing. Ditto for much of the scoring on today's film scene. In fact, the application of music to movies is one of the most artistically corrupt elements in filmmaking. Not nearly enough public attention has been paid to the low music level. Happily there are directors who make the proper scoring or deliberate non-scoring of a movie an integral part of the production. But often the director is at the mercy of the producing company. Music is tacked on to his film on someone else's say-so.

In the early days of talkies, the use of music was a logical outgrowth of the wonderful new invention, the soundtrack. The mere presence of music was enough of a justification and attraction. The growth of the movie musical as a prime entertainment form lifted singing, dancing, and lush scoring to its own colorful level of fun. The numbers were enjoyed for their own sake, and credibility had nothing to do with it. Musicals had not evolved into a more sophisticated medium with new demands for integration of score and story.

Meanwhile, back at the emotion factory, directors making dramatic films, suspense movies, or just about any variety which seeks an emotional effect, leaned heavily on the score as punctuation. Tender moments called for the sound of violins. Ominous music conjured up thoughts of lurking danger. Explosive scoring accompanied natural disasters. There was no pressure for hit songs, still primarily the province of the musicals. In simplistic terms, music was applied to drama to tell an audience how it should feel at any given crisis.

The subsequent upsurge in realism as a prime movie ingredient, spurred on by post-World War II films from Europe, created new artistic horizons for the more complex and creative use of music. There was also an increasing observation that life had its own music, and it wasn't always necessary to rely fully on a manufactured score. Noises of a city carried a melody stronger than what a composer might write. The chirp of a bird might set a mood impossible to match. The growing stress on cinema verité type of filmmaking has put a further premium on the use of environmental "music." The emergence of the director as _auteur_ also has worked to create a further integration of script, filming, and scoring.

Many developments in the movie industry occurred at a time of enormous upsurge in the recording field, with all of the implications of the lucrative market that developed as the terms LP and Hi-Fi became household words. Movie companies soon discovered that the score of a film drama or catchy music for a comedy, as well as a blockbuster musical, could make an album that would yield substantial revenue. If the film also produced a specific hit song or two, so much the better. This is the basic trend that has developed to its present stage. Now when the financial figures are added up for a movie's potential in the raising and allocating of budgets, the recording picture is automatically a key factor.

The combination of art and record profits is not necessarily incompatible. The music for THE GRADUATE, for example, was a good illustration of an independently successful score ideally suited to its subject. Music from MIDNIGHT COWBOY became an enormous hit, and also worked well in the film. EASY RIDER is another film that provides an example on the constructive side. Exciting scores perfectly matched to subject matter can make good listening at home.

But what has wrecked things is the abuse so often engendered by a pot of gold at the end of a rainbow. In the planning of a film, a basic prerequisite becomes the creation of a "hit" song, and often this means mismatched scores or banal imitations of previous successes in the same way movies themselves are made to imitate a previous bonanza. The rush begins to get a recording artist who's particularly hot, a composer who has proved bankable, and to create a title song in whatever style is popular at the moment. Sometimes the resulting monstrosities are confined to the credits. Sometimes they are tastelessly inserted in the middle, as in I NEVER SANG FOR MY FATHER. It hurts most to see the desecration in quality films.

What control does the director have over this process? Often surprisingly little. Even when a director does get a score he prefers, he may be overruled, and his score replaced by another which seems more commercial or may make a film seem more upbeat to a producer. The old Hollywood idea that incessant music has to pound home a theme to an audience dies hard. When the music bugs me, I try to mentally "tune it out," and am sometimes surprised by the results. I saw gritty scenes in THE MOLLY MAGUIRES, but got romantic vibrations from the score, until I "tuned out" the music and realized the director had done something on film that was being distorted by the soundtrack. Only later did I learn that a gushy Henry Mancini score had been superimposed on the film in place of the first score. Director Martin Ritt apparently had little say in the matter.

Similarly, I understand that director Gilbert Cates did not think the obtrusive song artistically benefitted I NEVER SANG FOR MY FATHER.

Even the outright musicals come in for a share of the pressure. In their case, the issue becomes the use of routinely "commercial" songs versus the more sophisticated approach of integration with a book. I'm curious to see how the SCROOGE album will do. The music is mostly offbeat and subtle, apart from the big production number, and it hardly fits the DOCTOR DOLITTLE syndrome.

The major hope for a more intelligent, less exploitative use of music in films lies with the independent director who is better able to assert taste and will. The tighter directorial control that comes from low budget operations is a factor. But I don't see any panacea on the horizon. Successful, small first films have a tendency to grow into larger second ones, and we are still getting movies like RYAN'S DAUGHTER with their thumping scores. I'm afraid that for some time to come we will have cause to groan at those awful songs and scores that have little to do with the film and less to do with movie art. It is tough to argue with record sales.

Chapter III

TECHNIQUES

COMPOSING FOR FILMS*

Dimitri Tiomkin

In the years that I have been composing and conducting motion picture scores, the importance and value of background music have been increasingly recognized. Only a few years ago music was considered a pleasant, unobtrusive re-enforcement of a sequence's tempo and mood. Today it is far more.

Screen music is still unobtrusive, for being so is the primary characteristic of any movie score that is good. But screen music is now so artfully and effectively integrated with script, direction and the actors themselves, that it has come to be one of the means of story-telling. It is easy to prove this. Just try to transplant any picture's musical score to similar scenes in another picture. You will find that the transplantation doesn't live.

It is of incalculable value to the composer to be able to sit in on story conferences from the beginning. He will not only better comprehend the total trend, mood or purpose of the story, but he will be able to make suggestions that will enable the music to strengthen and fulfill the story.

For example, at random: consider the point in a story at which a man suddenly, without warning, slaps a woman. Let us say the writers conceived the scene to be with two characters standing together talking by a window. Now sudden violence like a slap in the face has more impact if something unobtrusive prepares the audience a second or two in advance. If this split-second preparation is not provided, the mind will resent being taken by surprise. The best "something," it has been found, is music.

When this slapping sequence is discussed in a story conference I might say to the writers, or the director: "I will have to have a few seconds in there just before the slap in order to prepare for it." And we would talk it over and conclude that the man will have to take a few steps in order to slap the woman. This will give me the time I need to presage the violent change of mood.

I have found that a composer will get full cooperation unless his requests alter the story line. Directors and writers know a composer's technical problems. They also know the importance of his contribution.

Not a few writers, and even some directors, have asked me whether a retentive and facile memory of what others have written, or one's own musical inventiveness, is more valuable in scoring a motion picture. I cannot remember ever deliberately cribbing music from others, except when it was intentional, legitimate, and acknowledged, as in my arrangements of Debussy's music for David Selznick's PORTRAIT OF JENNIE.

Possibly even the most conscientious composer now and then inadvertently uses a fragment of melody that has stuck in his subconscious. But deliberately lifting phrases from the compositions of others is not only musical bankruptcy but incompetent craftsmanship.

Maybe I am fortunately equipped. I was born into a family of concert musicians, and have studied music since I was five years old. When you have thought in terms of music as long as I have it is easier to write original music than to bother recalling appropriate bars of music written in the past. After all, scenes and even sequences change so swiftly on the screen that very often there isn't time for more than a couple of measures. It is really simpler and more effective to compose than to rummage around in classical music to find something that expresses the idea.

My first scoring of background music, if it can be

called that, was when I was accompanist for the great European comedian, Max Linder. I sat at the piano and improvised all through his act. He was brilliant and unpredictable, and ad libbed freely and frequently. It was impossible for me to arrange and follow a definite score because he never did his act the same way twice. Consequently I watched him and listened to him and learned to divine intuitively what he would do, and thus to improvise what was actually pure mood music. I would even throw in sound effects, such as laughter, at what I thought were the right times.

Linder was one of the truly great comedians of our time. He worked dumb, in the inelegant show business phrase, but his pantomime and his appeal were eloquent. The only comparable artists today are Chaplin, Jimmy Savo, and possibly Cantinflas, the great Mexican clown.

Some gifted comics are so because of blind and blessed instinct, uninhibited by cerebral processes. Not Linder. He had an inspired comedy sense, of course, but he also had an analytical, ingenious mind. Except for Chaplin, I have never known another comedian who had such an objective view of his own art. Linder was sensitive and responsive to any audience, and could talk audience psychology with the intellectual perspective of a professor. On stage he would introduce a new bit suddenly and without previous thought, but later he could give a profound and apposite reason for having done what he did spontaneously.

My first contact with Linder was typical. A few months before World War I began he was making a triumphant tour that brought him to Petrograd. He arrived in the city by train, but flew from the station to the Astoria Hotel by plane. The effect of such an arrival, especially in 1914, was spectacular. History is beginning to distort Linder as an eccentric given to flashy public appearances and _outré_ living. But it wasn't self indulgence, merely good business. Like Houdini, he was a showman off-stage, too.

Probably because movies were a nearly-perfect vehicle for his pantomime, Linder was enormously enthusiastic over the future of films. Also impatient, because their technological advance seemed to him so slow.

All that now seems to me a far cry from scoring a

motion picture, but it was my first step. After that experience I learned that it was easier, for me, to improvise than to recall and use bits of music from the classics or other sources.

After some years of composing symphony and concert music, I became interested in the ballet. It had always been one of my favorite arts, but at that time in my life I became fascinated by the astonishing correlation of sound and sight, or music and movement, that is the essence of ballet. It was also in this period of my life that I realized, for the first time, how much music contributed to story-telling, or more accurately, to the transmission of mood to the audience. I wrote considerably for the ballet. My numbers met with varying success. I found this my introduction to the composition of "background music."

After composing for several Broadway shows I fell under the spell of the motion picture camera. There is a much closer affinity between ballet and movies than casual thought suggests. The story becomes more involved in ballet, for the screen is a more plastic medium, and its story-telling is therefore simpler. Nevertheless, the eloquence of music is as indispensable to film as to ballet. Sometimes I think a good picture is really just ballet with dialogue.

Dialogue, of course, is of primary importance in determining the genre of background music. It entails problems that must be overcome, and can be overcome only by certain musical techniques. It is difficult for a layman to realize that speaking voices have astonishing variation in pitch and timbre. It may seem incredible, but many actor's voices, however pleasant in themselves, and regardless of pitch, are incompatible with certain instruments. Clarinets, for instance, get in the way of some voices and magnificently complement others. Further, clarinets may be alien to the spirit of a play, or the characterization of a part.

Some actors have voices that are easy to write for. Actors like John Wayne impose almost no burdens on the composer. Wayne's voice happily happens to have a pitch and timbre that fits almost any instrumentation. Jimmie Stewart is another actor for whom it is a delight to write music. Paradoxically, his speaking voice is not "musical." But it has a slightly nasal quality and occasionally "cracks" in a way that is easy to complement. Jean Arthur's voice is somewhat similar.

Just why this type of voice should be easy to write for, I don't know. One might speculate that since these voices have little color in themselves, the complementary musical backdrop doesn't bump into or fall over the dialogue. The mere fact that such voices are unmusical gives them an additional definition.

Imagine an actress whose voice has the right harmonics and overtones of a low register clarinet statement. Assume a voice of incredibly pure, round tones. It might be nice to listen to unaccompanied, but it would be a damned nuisance to write for. You'd have to breach the 13-tone chromatic scale and even abandon Standard Pitch before you got a congenial musical background.

The "crack" in Miss Arthur's and Mr. Stewart's voices is one of those strangely appealing imperfections, like a single strand of rebellious hair on an otherwise impeccable moonlit coiffure. But don't pursue this appeal of imperfect voices too far, or you'll run into Andy Devine.

Jean Arthur and James Stewart also illustrate another point; utilizing music to "soften" a face, or to give it qualities it does not have inherently. This is not necessary with Stewart or Arthur because both have faces that reflect great sincerity. (Frank Capra, with whom I have had the pleasure of working on a number of pictures, once pointed out to me that unless a player has the sort of face that bespeaks sincerity he is not likely ever to become a great star.)

The camera is a merciless, analytical instrument. Even after every artifice of lighting and make-up, the close-up can be cruelly revealing. The composer, by providing pleasant melodic music, can direct attention from what the makeup artist could not hide. And in doing so the composer is surprisingly successful.

To comprehend fully what music does for movies, one should see a picture before the music is added, and again after it has been scored. Not only are all the dramatic effects heightened, but in many instances the faces, voices, and even the personalities of the players are altered by the music.

Because music can add to a personality and even to a player's physical appearance, I paid particular attention to Mala Powers as Roxanne in CYRANO DE BERGERAC, for which I composed and conducted the music. Miss Powers has a lovely, interesting face, but somehow it just didn't look French enough for me. In real life, of course, there are hundreds of thousands of pure-blooded Frenchmen who wouldn't look French. But on the screen a French woman should look like one. Consequently, I used French thematic music for all her appearances in CYRANO DE BERGERAC. By doing so, I like to think, I helped Miss Powers to project the effect of a daughter of France.

While on the subject of typically French music, I would like to point out that much of the music that is accepted as typical of certain races, nationalities and locales, is wholly arbitrary. Audiences have been conditioned to associate certain musical styles with certain backgrounds and peoples, regardless of whether the music is authentic.

For instance, all audiences think a certain type of steady beat of tom-tom or tympani drum, and a high, wailing wind instrument performing in a simple four or five-tone scale, connotes one thing: Indians. I have conducted no exhaustive research into the American Indian's music, but I suspect that this particular stylization of "Indian music" has very little similarity with the genuine article. In the past some composer freely adapted some possibly authentic Indian song, changed and altered it, and came up with the tom-tom effect we all know.

This "conditioned reflex" music, of course, is wholly arbitrary, but it is so effective that sometimes its use is compulsory. I have employed it in any number of Westerns, including Howard Hawks' RED RIVER, which, in my opinion, is a classic movie. I have used the "Indian music" that everyone knows not because I am not resourceful enough to originate other music, but because it is a telegraphic code that audiences recognize. If while the white settlers are resting or enjoying themselves, the background music suddenly takes on that tympani beat, the effect on the audience is electrifying. All know the Redmen are on the warpath even before the camera pans to the smoke signals on a distant hilltop. If I introduced genuine, absolutely authentic Indian tribal music, it probably wouldn't have any effect at all.

This musical conditioning underlies much screen composing. But it must not be hackneyed if it is to be effective. In the Indian music mentioned above I never used standard bars and phrases. I simply employed their mood. The idea is to avoid the usual and the trite, and at the same time to retain the basic ingredients of the musical "codes."

The screen composer, like every artist, must work within limitations. No matter how inventive and resourceful he is, he must also be disciplined. He must, to some extent, compromise. For a motion picture is a collective art, and the composer's contribution must enhance, not dominate.

THE STRUCTURE OF FILM MUSIC*

Jeffrey Embler

Now that film music is being recorded and special programs of it are being broadcast over the radio, now that composers are assigned to write it and awards are given to signalize its excellence, the time has come to establish what film music does, and how. There is practically no film without music, but the music is <u>consciously</u> heard by very few. However, <u>everybody</u> hears it unconsciously, and it is undeniable that music helps to shape the concepts and emotions which a film creates in our minds. This is so importantly true that parts of Alex North's music for A STREETCAR NAMED DESIRE were attacked by the Legion of Decency as "too suggestive."

Why does film need background music? As Ernest Lindgren points out in <u>The Art of the Film</u>, music and film each depend upon the phenomenon of movement, and are thereby allied esthetically. Second, sound movement reinforces visual movement. Third, and most important, music balances the sensual experience of sight with that of sound, and we are more relaxed when we are not straining to comprehend through one sense alone.

What should film music do? It should never dominate a sequence of film nor be the cause that makes characters act or react. It must not repeat what the visual tells, but instead convey what the visual does not show. It should enhance the feelings and emotions of the characters. Film can show fear or loneliness, but because these are feelings and not acts, the shots depicting them are static. Quite often they cannot be sustained long enough to tell the story. But, by the addition of music, moods can be strengthened and protracted. Thus, music can bring movement when film cannot.

The movies' need for musical accompaniment was discovered almost as soon as they were exhibited. Before 1912 the music was whatever occurred spontaneously in the minds of the piano and organ players in the theatres of those days. Naturally, it was often incongruous, irrelevant, or downright inappropriate. The "cue sheet" corrected some of this. Written before the film was publicly shown, distributed to theatre musicians in advance so they could study it, the cue sheet borrowed from all kinds of music, popular, folk and classical.

One result was that when the masses went to the movies they came into contact not only with poor music but also with Beethoven, Brahms and Bach. The "William Tell" overture was long used to help the Lone Ranger on radio and television. Gradually, music was specially arranged for the purpose of supplying more mood meaning to the audience. Tempos and orchestrations were radically changed.

Then some enlightened producers had special scores written for their films. A few of the most notable were Saint-Saëns's Opus 128 for THE ASSASSINATION OF THE DUKE OF GUISE, Joseph Carl Breil's music for THE BIRTH OF A NATION, and Edmund Meisel's score for POTEMKIN. Breil's music was not entirely original, but the parts that were so were mood melodies. Intermingled with the creative film music were themes from "Peer Gynt" and bars from the "Ride of the Valkyries." The arrival of sound did not at once bring forth specially composed music. Arrangers were brought to Hollywood and they again ripped into Beethoven's Ninth, et al.

The first original film music was formed around "the theme," and has continued to be so ever since. This was a logical basis for film music, for ever since the first piano tinkled, melodic variations had been the chief means of enhancing varying moods. There was no unity of style or technique.

Of course the first film composers borrowed; if not actual phrases, certainly the idioms. Hollywood music is still nourished by 19th-century music, from which much of the early borrowed music was taken. This music is the easiest to listen to and does not tax the mind. Most producers still say audiences shouldn't be aware of music anyway. In some cases this kind of film has achieved great success with the mass audience, notably David Raksin's music for LAURA, Miklos Rozsa's for SPELLBOUND, and Alfred Newman's for STREET SCENE. When such music becomes popular, lyrics are written for recordings of it.

Film music today can be broken down into three different styles, all of which employ the same basic elements. The simplest form has only a main theme melody. Of Maurice Jaubert's music for LE CARNET DE BAL, Roger Manvell, in Film, has this to say: "The waltz is the musical theme of the film. It haunts the daydreams of the young widow until it builds into a grand symphony of illusion with lovely waltzing images in a pattern of luxury." Indeed, the waltz is the framework of the film.

In Anton Karas' score for THE THIRD MAN, played by a zither, the background music consists of only one theme. Carol Reed surrounded his characters with sculptural and architectural images for atmosphere, and Karas' music helped in this. It was effective, since atmosphere--i.e., the turmoil of post-war Vienna--plays an important part in THE THIRD MAN.

A more recent example of this is Dimitri Tiomkin's music for HIGH NOON. As Gary Cooper walks the streets of Hadleysville, Tiomkin's one theme effectively emphasizes Cooper's dilemma. Whereas THE THIRD MAN theme was free from other styles of background music, and was enjoyed for that reason, Tiomkin juxtaposed his main theme and other melodies. The Mexican woman has a theme of her own, thunderous pounds on the piano accompany several sequences, and the film's final moments have a typical Tiomkin flourish (booming orchestration) which detracts from the enjoyment of the visual imagery.

The second commonest type of film music is less creative in its own right and comes straight out of the exigencies of the script. Two good examples are the music for THE ASPHALT JUNGLE and THE SNOWS OF KILIMANJARO. In the former, the music comes from a juke box which the audience sees. A pretty girl dances to the sensual jazz rhythms as Sam Jaffe sits watching her movements. The music helps the girl incite Mr. Jaffe's perverted lust.

In Bernard Herrmann's score for THE SNOWS OF KILIMANJARO, a saxophone, seen on the screen, plays an intoxicating blues melody as Gregory Peck lights Ava Gardner's cigarette in a half-lit corner of a Paris cafe. The music was purposefully composed for this scene. The casual moviegoer may think he is affected by the images alone, but the saxophone music is a vital part of the seduction.

The third most prevalent style of film music is the one of which Hollywood is fondest. First, a "leitmotif" representing a character or an idea, is written. Then it is broken down into variations of tempo and orchestrations to express different moods. Nowadays, when the composer works with the finished film before him, and composes the mood melodies for it, he uses a leitmotif to unify the themes.

Some think Miklos Rozsa's music for SPELLBOUND the finest example of this. It consists of eight varying themes. Their moods range from a delightfully mischievous scherzo to the fanatical "Terror on the Ski Run." Most of the themes are variations of each other, adjusted to the mood desired for a particular sequence. The leitmotif is the basis of them all. If SPELLBOUND is not a great score, it is at least an unpretentious one.

A good example of manufactured Hollywood music is Rozsa's score for IVANHOE. It is an overly orchestrated melange of various mood themes. Strong strings, crashing cymbals and blaring horns announce the character of Ivanhoe, and the same theme, watered down to a soft string accompaniment, signifies Rebecca. The music written under the battle of Torquilstone Castle consists of the themes for Ivanhoe and the Norman Knights. Music for such a sequence, one of savage physical movement, requires the best of taste and restraint. Instead, the entire MGM orchestra rips into this theme with chaotic noise.

The score for A PLACE IN THE SUN, by Franz Waxman, also uses a leitmotif. During the credit titles, which are printed over visual action, the entire orchestra plays a theme based on the leitmotif to suggest George's desire for wealth and position. The music for Angela, who represents the life to which George aspires, is a woodwind taking a solo over the muted orchestra and playing the melody of the main orchestrated theme.

Astute directors know how powerful the absence of music can be. In TRADER HORN, YELLOW SKY and DETECTIVE STORY there was no need to sustain mood with music. The rhythmic pace of dialogue and sound effects were sufficient.

There are a few composers in Hollywood who are trying to express in their scores new ideas and new techniques, and to compose music that will be an intrinsic part of one film and one film only. Hitherto a theme expressing love in one film would go quite easily on the sound track of a love scene in another film. But the new composers I have in mind are trying to write music characteristic of one film only.

An illustration of the new technique can be found in a comparison of Victor Young's score for SHANE and Alex North's music for A STREETCAR NAMED DESIRE. Both used a borrowed melody entitled "Put Your Little Foot Right Out." In Young's score it is used as the leitmotif for Jean Arthur and is played on a multitude of violins. But in North's score it is used to recall Blanche's past and is played with music box simulation. North's use is more creative because, by employing one instrument, he produces a sound which, in its direct tone, makes the audience immediately aware of Blanche's immaturity. North has said his music is not a music of action, but of character. It is impossible, when listening to his score divorced from the film, to associate his music with images from other films.

One of the earliest instances of this new technique was David Raksin's music for FOREVER AMBER. His Amber leitmotif changes as her character does. In the music of the opening theme Amber is a young girl searching for idyllic romance. In the final theme horns echo the wantonness of her loves, and the last burst of music suggests a life of complete degeneration. George Antheil's music for THE SNIPER is somewhat similar and tries to describe the inner plight of the psychopathic murderer and to illuminate his rationalizations of his madness.

Romantic music of the 19th-century no longer preoccupies the newer composers in Hollywood--e.g., the sophisticated jazz of Alex North, the semi-modernism of David

Raksin the metallic jazz in ACE IN THE HOLE by Hugo Friedhofer, and Elmer Bernstein's Gershwinesque score for SUDDEN FEAR.

As for future film music, especially for 3-D and wide screen films, I think that, for the full potential of the visual imagery to be realized, the music will have to be music of characterization. If a character's voice and footsteps are to drift across the auditorium as he walks from one side of the screen to the other, the leitmotif will have to be more pronounced. A barrage of strings emerging from a full orchestra for Elizabeth Taylor will be meaningless in 3-D. Imagine, however, the sounds of a lone flute gliding down the aisle and into your ear as Miss Taylor walks out of the screen.

DOCUMENTARY MUSIC

Louis Applebaum

Since the thirties there has existed in the film world a "poor relation" to the rich Hollywood baby. The documentary film, unglamorized and little publicized, has won for itself the wide audience it deserves, and is repaying its many loyal workers and supporters with the satisfaction of recognition. The war years did much to highlight the documentary's job of public education and have in many ways justified to the faithful, the self-centered devotion which this kind of film has managed to win for itself. As is so often the case, the poor relation will demonstrate a pride and self-sufficiency and self-conscious resentment that discourages acceptance and support. Thus, those who make these films are usually the most vociferous in their attacks on what they call Hollywood's lavish but inconsequential product. Their attacks are loud if not altogether true, and biting if not altogether untinged with envy.

This attitude, unfortunately, is reflected in much of the prose writings of the composers who have worked on documentaries. Many, especially those who have not lived through the "Hollywood experience," suggest that supplying music for non-commercial films is a much more gratifying experience than working on the highly technicalized, albeit more lucrative, Hollywood epic. The Hollywood composer, they say, is beset by stifling demands, his imagination is choked by his producer's fear of offending the naive ear of a movie-goer in some small mid-western town, his sensibilities revolted by the suggestions of illiterate and untalented people in the studios' music departments. In short, Hollywood's most important virtue to the composer, they say, is that it pays the composer well for his unappreciated efforts. These arguments are foolish--too foolish to dispute by more than bringing to their attention some fine film works by Waxman, Copland, Herrmann, Deutsch, Antheil and others.

But from such writings it can be inferred that the small, poor, documentary world does offer its composers an acceptance and understanding that draws from them their utmost cooperation and maximum effort. The budgets are small, but the zeal intense. Orchestras are tiny, but audiences are large, specialized and interested. Production facilities are limited, but so are production demands. The composer is a respected and valued participant in an intensely concerted activity. He feels that he is taking part in an exciting, yet worthwhile effort that has something to do with his society's welfare. The fact that he is not very well paid is balanced by the fact that he is more likely to be asked to work on a documentary short than on one of Hollywood's prized and gilded extravaganzas.

The documentary ideal has created many classics in which its supporters take great pride. The U.S. government has been responsible for the creation of several of these: THE RIVER, THE PLOW THAT BROKE THE PLAINS, POWER AND THE LAND, THE CITY, THE MEMPHIS BELLE, titles as significant to documentary's devotees as THE BIRTH OF A NATION, THE INFORMER, THE GOLD RUSH and LOST WEEKEND to Hollywood's.

The composers who worked on these documentaries are equally illustrious: Virgil Thomson, Roy Harris, Douglas Moore, Aaron Copland, Gail Kubick--but note that of all of these, only Aaron Copland can be said to have a continuing association with film. He is one of the very few successful composers of concert music whose work is acceptable in Hollywood. But note too that the others mentioned needed no previous film successes to be asked to work on documentary films. The same is true of other Americans whose names can be found on many films made by OWI, the Army and Navy, and other government film units: William Schuman, Alex North, Paul Creston, Paul Bowles, Lan Adomian, Henry Brant, Jack Shaindlin, Morton Gould, Bob Strassberg and Gene Forrell.

England, where the late John Grierson created the documentary film movement, has asked many of its composers to write for film. The long list of English composers provides two significant names: Benjamin Britten, who worked with Grierson on some of his earliest masterpieces, and has written an orchestral work which forms the basis of Basil Wright's film on the symphony orchestra; and Walter Leigh, whose score to the great SONG OF CEYLON will always remain an object lesson on how film scores can be inspired by and derived from the film idiom.

In Canada, John Grierson was asked by the government in 1939 to form the National Film Board as the Canadian Government's official film voice. Under Grierson's existing leadership, which he forsook on VJ day for activity on an international level, the Film Board grew quickly in size and soon outstripped in enterprise and achievement its equivalent organizations in Britain and the United States. As partners in his effort, Grierson gathered to the Board much of the country's promising talent, people not with established reputations, but youngsters who soon were persuaded to think more of the ideal of possible public education and information than of their private career problems. That his investment was a wise one is reflected in the Board's present stature.

From the first, many Canadian composers, especially the younger ones, were given the opportunity to acquaint themselves with the problems of writing for films, and incidentally, to earn the pittance involved. Since their attitude immediately became one of creation rather than imitation, many interesting and ingenious musical ideas and techniques were evolved. Hollywood's critics might be correct in claiming that similar techniques might not have been possible in Hollywood's commercial environment.

Most important to the Film Board composers' work has probably been the influence that the medium itself has had on their musical thinking. At the Board the composer is encouraged to think as a film-maker as well as a musician. The cutting room paraphernalia is just as familiar to him as his knowledge of key signatures, and consideration of the microphone and the splicing machine is as important as his concern with smooth key modulations. He quickly realized that he was not writing music for concert performance, and therefore adjusted his conception of musical form accordingly. He learned the value of dramatic statement and effective orchestration--he learned too how to get the most out of the small orchestra combinations the limited budgets usually allowed. He was soon on the way to becoming a "film composer"--a musician writing for a specialized, largely mechanized medium, not merely one who can cleverly adapt concert music to functional usages, as so many of our composers do today.

Maurice Blackburn, a very brilliant French Canadian composer, has for many years been on the Board's staff, during which time he has written many very beautiful scores. It is unfortunate that none of his works are at the moment available for quotation. Blackburn studied for two years in Paris under a scholarship given him by the Quebec government. John Weinzweig, Godfrey Ridout, Howard Cable, Robert Fleming, Lucio Agostini, Barbara Pentland, Morris Davis and Phyllis Gummer are some Canadian names which may be known to American readers, if not for their film work, then for their music for radio and the concert. This writer was fortunate enough to have been able to work on about 60 Film Board productions, an experience for which he will forever remain thankful.

One of his first scores was written to a film about the enemy Japan. One sequence in the film concerned itself with the ancient, interesting and sometimes beautiful traditions which in Japan have rejected change. Before writing the music a study was made of traditional Japanese music, the sound of their instruments thought out, and their intonations and scale structure noted. Music was then scored to be played by one flute out of tune, one piano stripped of its action and played by strumming prescribed strings with a screw driver (a disconcerting experience for a dignified pianist with many years of Czerny and Hanon exercises behind him), and by assorted percussion instruments. The microphone was scored in also, because it had to be moved about and waved over the instruments. It disported itself in a very un-electronic fashion. In addition, many incongrous noises were recorded; extra strums of the denuded piano and a few gong crashes, cymbal rolls, and flute twiddles. Once recorded on film, the sound tracks were then assembled in a cutting room, some cut in to sound simultaneously and some cut in backwards so that the normal sound process was reversed. Several sound tracks were thus prepared, re-recorded, and the result, if not truly Japanese, was at least interesting. To some listeners it undoubtedly sounded like a wail from the lips of tortured souls on the River Styx. If so, it was unintended. The musical pirouettes were executed by a composer in search of a Japanese musical sound.

Another involved maneuver was evolved for a film called NEW FACES COME BACK. This film was made to help prepare the people on this side of the battlefields for the ordeal of reaccepting into their normal life, the many badly disfigured casualties that would soon be returning to their homes. The film concerned itself with the affair of one RCAF boy who was severely burned in a plane crash, whose face is later partially rebuilt by plastic surgery, and whose self-consciousness about his appearance and place in society reflected the feelings of the many others in a similar condition. Near the beginning of the film we see the lad's plane crash, his body removed from the burning wreck and taken to an English hospital. For a hospital "motif," to signify the understanding and sympathy which accompanied his long and torturously painful treatments, a theme, built on the 12-tone system, was used. The theme appears often in many guises, sometimes harmonized and sometimes stated by a solo instrument. It acts as a unifying thread for the score.

The boy is prepared for his first visit to the operating room. As he is wheeled out of his room on a hospital cot, the camera very dramatically assumes the position of the patient. It sees as the frightened patient does--looks up into the chin and nostrils of the orderlies wheeling him--sees the ceiling and door tops along the corridors, sees nurses' capped heads pass by, sees with great apprehension the operating lamp loom into view as the cot is wheeled into position under it, sees the Frankenstein monster-like figure of a doctor preparing a hideously savage hypodermic, sees the figure lean over totteringly to apply the anaesthetic--and all goes out of focus as the patient loses consciousness. It is a very effective shot, very dramatically conceived and executed. It needed, of course, a treatment in sound beyond the scope of usual orchestral music, so again recourse was taken to some filmic tricks. The result was not music in the accepted sense, but it must certainly be considered film music. Many separate sounds were recorded on several occasions.

Several sharply attacked chords were recorded together with a heavy rippling strum of piano strings in the low register. Various harp glissandi were recorded. A man's breathing close to a microphone was recorded. Little snatches of the hospital theme and a few hymn-like figures were played by various orchestral groups. In all about 40 separate sounds were recorded. These were prepared in the cutting room for recording into a continuous sound. Some passages were made into sound track loops so that they could sound continuously and be brought into focus whenever desired. Other passages were cut in backwards, some at normal speed, others at increased or lowered speeds, thus altering their pitch and instrumental color. The sharp accents were synchronized to dramatic high points like the first glimpse of the lamp and the plunging of the hypodermic needle. Following the administering of the anaesthetic, the sound of the breathing and the heart beat were made to rise in intensity, then gradually to fade as the film went out of focus.

The point in writing about this is to show that in film, a composer can <u>build</u> his music in a film cutting room. The music that accompanies the above scene could never have been played as a continuous sound by a symphony orchestra. It is music whose creation was possible only through film. Though it is valid music, it is inconceivable to composers not familiar with equipment and techniques. Perhaps all film music will some day be thus built in cutting rooms--or perhaps composers will be able to write their music directly into sound by the twisting of knobs on electronic gadgets. Another essay on that subject might convince skeptics that the suggestion is not entirely a wild and insane one.

Since its founding, the National Film Board of Canada has produced close to one thousand film shorts on many subjects. Some of these are released theatrically under the series titles "WORLD IN ACTION" or "CANADA CARRIES ON." Many more were made for nontheatrical distribution on either the industrial or rural 16mm circuits which the Board organized with such amazing success. It is worth noting that in Canada the Film Board has created an audience for films outside the theatres that is at least as large as its theatrical audience, and that for this nontheatrical audience were produced films specifically attuned to its interests and needs. The workers in plants were shown films concerned with labor-management problems; rural audiences assembled in town halls to see films that helped orient their thinking to vital international as well as national affairs and attitudes. In all of these the composer was a participant. Is it not important to the composer to know that he is thus directly able to cooperate in a vital aspect of his society's welfare and education? Does this present age not suggest that the composer move down from his secluded intellectual garret into the homes of his neighbors, that he may speak with them, work with them and rejoice in their improvement? The composer today must be a contributing member in mundane society. If this is true, the Film Board has done the Canadian musician, writer, painter and poet a great service by making this attitude apparent to him and by enabling him to make out of the attitude a living act.

THE MUSIC MIXER

John Huntley

There are many studio jobs about which little is known even to those working in the film industry. One may well ask, for example, "What is a music mixer?" and indeed even the music mixer himself has difficulty in describing in a few words all that his work entails. Fifty members of the London Symphony Orchestra take their places on the platform of the Music Theatre. The conductor steps on to the mobile rostrom as the oboe sounds an "A" to which the rest of the orchestra tune their instruments. "5M2, gentlemen," says the conductor (meaning section 2 of the music in Reel 5). The players locate 5M2, the baton is raised and the rehearsal begins.

Four Western Electric 639 microphones (Cadioids, so called on account of the heart-shape field of the pick-up) are located on booms of the standard type across the orchestra. Two cover the strings, one the woodwind and horns, and one the noisier brass instruments and the percussion. From each mike, a cable runs back across the wooden floor of the great barn-like stage to the block of equipment rooms at the far end. Here, the Film and Disc Recording room houses two M.S.S. disc cutting machines, two of the latest type Western Electric 200-mil push-pull channels, and the main amplifier and power racks. Above is the Projection Room, with one Super Simplex projector and a single W. E. dummy head for the sound.

On floor level, double sound-proofed doors lead to the Monitor and Control Room which is brightly illuminated by fluorescent strip lighting--a spacious room. The music assistant with two racks of amplifier and equalizer (tone control) units, a monitor speaker, and the control desk are all there. Two double-glass panels let into the wall give a full view of the orchestra and the recording area outside. As the rehearsal proceeds, the composer listens intently to the sounds of the orchestra issuing from the loud-speaker which stands along one wall of the monitor room. The raucous, tinny sounds so often produced by the average projection room monitor have no counterpart here, for the equipment consists of a complete medium-sized theatre unit of the multiple-horn type, with honeycomb high frequency unit mounted above the large baffle of the double-unit middle and low frequency horns. The result is high-fidelity reproduction from which the quality of the sound being recorded can be accurately judged.

Conveniently situated at a diagonal to the monitor speaker is the control or mixing desk. Placed immediately in front of the large window of the monitor room, it consists primarily of a set of potentiometers (or "pots" as they are usually called) with associated switching and metering gear. Each of the four microphone lines leads into a potentiometer on the main panel, thus giving complete control over the volume of sound picked up and transmitted to the recorders from each section of the orchestra. A volume control allows the overall level of sound from the four microphone sources to be controlled, while a volume indicator gives a visual reading on a graduated scale of the amplitude of the sound. Switches allow for the quick cut-in of any microphone line and can be used, for example, to bring into circuit the desk microphone on the sound assistant's panel alongside the conductor's rostrum from which the identification announcements are made before or after each take.

The music mixer for the Recording Theatre has been seated at the control desk throughout the rehearsal, checking the balance and quality of the music as it comes over the monitor speaker. Ted Drake has been the music mixer to the largest music recording theatre in Europe since it opened. Since the days of crystal sets, his main hobbies have been the construction of radio receivers and experimenting with sound reproduction. His knowledge of music and experience in broadcasting led to his present appointment in the Sound Department of Denham Studios, which is supervised by Cyril Crowhurst. The music mixer knows how to place all the microphones before the orchestra arrives. The work of the music mixer is a matter of balance and control. It is one of those jobs you can only learn by doing it yourself. The fundamentals are an outline knowledge of sound recording technique and procedure, with a good background of music and preferably the ability to read a score. It is also very important, of course, to know the characteristic sounds of each instrument of the orchestra, and to be able to pick out and identify these sounds when listening to a full orchestra. This "analytical ear" is, I think, the most important basic requirement of a good music mixer, and can only be developed by continually listening to orchestral music. Closely associated with this is the ability to know what one ought to hear coming from the speaker of the monitor room. For example, the microphone covering the woodwind section of the orchestra picks up the sound of each instrument of that section in the right proportion and perspective, both with regard to the other instruments in the same section and also to those of the rest of the orchestra. This is what is meant by "balance" and it can be achieved by careful planning of the orchestra layout and by correct placing of the microphones.

Should the orchestration require a particular instrument or group of instruments to stand out against the rest, a slight adjustment of the microphone positioning or manipulation of the "pots" on the desk, can produce the desired effect. This is where the ability to read a score is useful. Mr. Drake has a copy of the score (usually in "piano-conductor" form), which indicates the entry of various solo instruments and the groups as well as giving all the musical content of the section being recorded. Thus he can follow the music and adjust the volume of the mixes accordingly, being able to see in advance when certain solo passages which may require predominance are going to occur.

Outside in the main recording area, Muir Mathieson, the music director, steps on to the rostrum and takes over from his assistant. A warning bell comes on outside the stage, and the orchestra becomes silent, ready in their playing positions. As the sound camera and disc recorder turn over, the picture is projected on to the big screen behind the orchestra. The conductor is poised, ready for his cue from the illuminated timing indicator alongside the screen. This final warning is spoken over a loudspeaker system on the stage from a microphone on Ted Drake's mixing desk as he sets the controls, ready for a take. There are a few seconds of absolute silence and then the orchestra springs to life. In the Monitor and Control Room, Ted Drake, music mixer, balances and controls the recording so that cinemagoers may hear the finest possible reproduction of the stirring and noble sounds of the full symphony orchestra now playing in the recording theatre.

Chapter IV

SCORING THE DRAMATIC FILM

THE AFRICAN QUEEN

John Huntley

Allan Gray has had a varied career in all types of music in Europe. At one time a pupil of Schoenberg's, he wrote music for Max Reinhardt's production of "Julius Caesar," a children's opera called 'Wavelength A. B. C.," the German film EMIL AND THE DETECTIVES, and three British Shakespearean productions--"Love's Labours Lost," at Stratford-on-Avon, "Much Ado About Nothing" with Robert Donat, and "Twelfth Night" at the Arts Theatre, London. His British films include THE LIFE AND DEATH OF COLONEL BLIMP, A CANTERBURY TALE, I KNOW WHERE I'M GOING and STAIRWAY TO HEAVEN. Sections of his music for THE AFRICAN QUEEN are published by Peter Maurice.

The sound track of THE AFRICAN QUEEN has been carefully planned in such a way as to give the fullest dramatic values to the elements of sound effects, dialogue and music. After a brief musical introduction, the natural sounds of the jungle take over during a fine crane shot that covers most of the titles and leads into the opening shot. There rises up from the little mission hut a confused, wailing, blurred chant and we discover the missionary leader (played by Robert Morley) attempting to organize some hymn singing with natives who understand little or nothing of European music. Katharine Hepburn is seen playing the organ under difficulties! This is a brilliant exposition of a naturalistic musical effect being used as a dramatic element in the story and immediately reveals the remarkable grasp of film technique possessed by the American director, John Huston.

The little theme for the boat itself makes an early appearance and has some good moments, particularly when it sails forth at the end, in the teeth of a gale, to launch its hand-made torpedoes. Many scenes that might have been over-played with music are expressed through sound only, as in the rain storm. This gives music all the greater point when it is used, notably in the scenes in the thick reeds as the little ship gets stuck completely, only a few yards from open water, although this is not known to the occupants.

The film opens with a song; it ends the same way. Humphrey Bogart and Katharine Hepburn are in the water, swimming towards friendly shores; joyfully, Bogart breaks into a song and the melody is taken up by full orchestra as Allan Gray provides a fitting coda to an unusual and interesting Anglo-American movie.

THE BAD AND THE BEAUTIFUL

William Hamilton

There are two distinct ways to exploit an actor. The more common is to prefabricate a situation where his raw, native quality, virtue, depravity or whatever, will be thrown into the sharpest possible relief. And sometimes it seems even sharper than that. The artistic way is to allow an actor to act: to create with word and deed a unique character among unique characters. Then, the situation becomes as it usually is in life, the product of human activity. The script, direction and performances of THE BAD AND THE BEAUTIFUL combine to make a superb example of this second procedure.

Without troubling to make the usual ethical affirmation, or even to leave a good taste in the mouth, the picture offers a pointed but compassionate account of civilized people casually injuring one another. The struggle is drawn between Jonathan (Kirk Douglas) on the one hand and Fred, Georgia and James Lee (Barry Sullivan, Lana Turner and Dick Powell) on the other. A flashback layout is used, the beginning and end recording the retaliation of the three upon Jonathan, and three interior episodes showing his original provocations. The film gets a lot of sparkle from innumerable tiny touches of fine theatrics, and there is a magnificent sense of the ridiculous at work as well. Watch for the bit where the wardrobe man (uncredited, I'm deeply sorry to say) displays some costumes to Fred and Jonathan for their "Cat-Men" production. These peripheral matters, however, only emphasize my feeling that the propelling force of THE BAD AND THE BEAUTIFUL resides definitely in its personages.

The purpose of all this non-musical discussion is to help explain my one demurrer in the matter of David Raksin's score. His aim is to build scenes, rather than characters. This is so universal a procedure, of course, that there would be no reason to bring it up except for the fact that THE BAD AND THE BEAUTIFUL has such a clear bias in the other direction.

It should not be inferred that the music is a jangling mass of cross-purposes and missed points. On the contrary, it fits like a glove, and I can't recall a single scene that doesn't gain much from it in purely dramatic impetus. The trouble is that the rest of the production is so personal in its nature, that, by contrast, the score often has a detached, above-the-battle quality. Only rarely does it seem to participate, preferring instead to stand off and make objective comment.

Participate or not, Raksin's music abounds in lovely and striking passages, and to say that the loveliness and striking-power arise only from the nicest balance of musical impulse and dramatic requirement is surely no adverse judgment. I suppose that the possibility of refined characterization through music is and must continue to be severely limited as long as movies take their present shape. Action and externals must be attended to before ideas. Otherwise people will complain that the composer ignores the story.

And now some particulars. James Lee and Georgia are identified by themes of their own--his a jagged four-note motive resembling one of Holst's "Planets" and hers a full ABA chorus. The main title music contains the A section and 'preliminary' version of the B. The first sequence is accompanied by a light, scherzando movement, Jonathan Calling, whose opening subject ranks among the main themes of the film, subsequently reappearing a number of times with altered rhythm. The movement which opens the "Fred" episode has a troubled quality: mournful, chromatic melodies, discordant harmonies, throbbing pedal-points. The same movement, varied and extended, recurs at the end of the episode, as Jonathan happily blurts, "and with von Ellstein to direct."

A fascinating recording trick is used for an earlier scene between Fred and Jonathan as they figure out how to make "The Cat-Men" more frightening. Here the microphone was turned on after each chord was struck, so that only the sustained part of the sound, without the impact, was recorded. The effect is totally strange, demonstrating the fact that the quality of an instrument's attack is an essential part of its characteristic "tone." Some will remember the use of this device in Mr. Raksin's LAURA.

The next movement, "hurry," is the background to the preparations for the "Cat-Men" preview. Here the composer develops already stated material with great effectiveness as well as ingenuity. A variant of "Jonathan Calling" begins the movement, and presently the Georgia theme enters at about four times its original speed. These two motifs are worked together for a little over a minute, the cue being succeeded immediately by main and end titles as they might be manufactured for a "Cat-Men" picture.

The second section starts with a variant of the Georgia theme on the alto flute. The scene moves into low-pressure action, and a circumspect allegretto proceeds behind it, fading presently after an especially beautiful cadence. Actually, this cadence has been used, slightly modified, twice before: linking the Georgia and James Lee sequences in the "Jonathan Calling" cue, and shortly after, at the arrival of Georgia, Fred and James Lee in Harry Pebbel's office. I agree heartily with Mr. Raksin's determination to use it again. Most of the music for this section is drawn from the Georgia theme. One of the most distinctive of these cues is heard under the scene where Georgia visits the set alone at night. First the melody is given out softly and intimately by trombone. In a moment the Georgia variant appears accompanied by a dotted figure in somewhat grinding harmony. "The Premiere" is a reworking of the "Hurry" subject.

The doleful theme heard at the beginning of the "Fred" section returns as Georgia arrives at Jonathan's house following the premiere, and a new setting of the agitated Georgia variant follows their scene together. Presently the music fades and is replaced by the sound of the careening automobile.

The third episode, dealing with the adventure of James Lee Bartlow, opens with a longish cue in playful style based on the James Lee motive. This is a most successful movement. (Oddly, I find myself reminded of Elgar by much of the James Lee music when it gets under way. As already mentioned, the theme itself is much like a theme of Holst's.) There are several additional entries of this material similarly reworked. An attractive sample forms the background for the return of James Lee and Jonathan from Arrowhead. This cue finishes with the Georgia cadence.

The present section contains two of Mr. Raksin's quite wonderful takeoffs. The first, entitled "California," is heard as James Lee and wife arrive in Hollywood. I don't believe the composer could have made music more vapid than this, and I like to think that here, at last, is utter refutation of my earlier carping on the subject of characterization. As James Lee gazes around him with obvious distaste, it is only too clear that California is "California" to him. The other spoof is an over-magnificent finish for "The Proud Land," an epic photoplay of which James Lee is the author.

The brief denouement of THE BAD AND THE BEAUTIFUL promptly follows the James Lee section. As Harry Pebbel, in Jonathan's behalf, asks the other three, "What about it--will you do this picture with him?" there is a reprise, slightly extended, of the music for Jonathan's letdown after finishing "Cat-Men." Then follows a complete statement of the Georgia theme in all its glory for the final playoff, end title and screen credits.

In summary, I would acknowledge my great enthusiasm for this score. It is an enthusiasm which has increased with familiarity. Examining the notes has brought to light all sorts of admirable conceptions and manipulations which one fails to notice at a screening. However unobserved they may be in the theatre, there can be no doubt as to the vital role they fill as the elemental ingredients of a gifted composer's style and as the ultimate determinants of his expression.

THE BEST YEARS OF OUR LIVES

Louis Applebaum

The 1946 Academy Award for a dramatic musical score was bestowed on a work about whose merit there can be no question. Not always does this recognition fall on the most deserving of the year's efforts, nor does it always reflect studied judgment and unbiased critical reflection. Film fans, students and critics can find no quarrel with the fact that Sam Goldwyn's and William Wyler's THE BEST YEARS OF OUR LIVES swept off most of the important 1946 Academy prizes, and those interested in film music can be especially happy that Hugo Friedhofer's remarkable score for that film was included in the sweep. Mr. Friedhofer's considerable talents have been known to the handful concerned in the making of film music. In 1945, his score for THE BANDIT OF SHERWOOD FOREST won the Film Music Notes plaque. At last Friedhofer's name and ability are given the widest recognition.

A reading of the score reveals that Mr. Friedhofer, as many composer do, chose to work on the development juxtaposition and superimposition of leitmotifs more or less in the Wagnerian tradition. The material itself is definitely not Wagnerian in character, but the manner of its handling derives from the Wagner of the Niebelungen Ring. As a result, it is possible to list practically all the root material out of which the score as a whole generated.

The most important of the themes is the one on which the Main Title is based. In the score it is called the 'Best Years Theme." Its simplicity, based as it is on the triad, its straightforward, warm harmonization, ably reflects the general theme of the film, principally as it concerns the Harold Russell characterization of "Homer." It has two main sections, each of which is used and developed separately in the course of the score. The first section, A, states the triad motif; the second, B, a chordal, almost hymnal phrase; both are easily recognized and capable of developed treatment.

The second theme is called 'Boone City." It too contains two ideas: A, a five-note motif with the characteristic leap of the major 7th to set it apart, and B, a syncopated, moving, broken-triad motif. The A motif occurs often, and its major 7th interval manages to add interest to the melodic structure of the score. As will be seen later, it was eventually enlarged into a separate theme. A third theme is once more chordal in structure. This one, associated with the neighborly relationship between the families of Homer and that of his girl next door, is most interesting for its harmonization of a tune that is, like the others already mentioned, derived from the simple triad. It seems to suggest strongly the feeling of much of Aaron Copland's recent writing.

Orchestra coloring of a different kind, plus the full utilization of a minimum of musical material, in this case mostly the interval of the 4th, make an exciting moment of Fred's nightmare, his vivid memories of awful war experiences. Here Mr. Friedhofer's clear orchestral thinking, his appreciation and understanding of the orchestra's resources, his sensitive feeling for tone color, and his good taste are apparent.

It is sad that present utilization of film music material does not allow for any kind of distribution of the music itself. True, in rare cases, excerpts from film scores are recorded on commercial discs, and when popular songs are used, they are published; but the full scores, even notable ones such as this are all but ignored. The song, "Among My Souvenirs," which was used often in THE BEST YEARS OF OUR LIVES, can undoubtedly be found in many thousands of homes, but those interested in the score have recourse only to reviews such as this one. The only alternative is to go repeatedly to see the film in order to become more familiar with its music. THE BEST YEARS OF OUR LIVES offers one of those rare cases where this will prove worthwhile.

CARRIE

David Raksin

Some years ago, in the course of a lecture at the

University of Southern California, I was trying to explain that empathy, or identification with the feelings of his characters, is an inner resource indispensable to a film composer. I suggested that talent for a career in film composing might be partially assessed through a "Hecuba Test." The reference was, of course, to the soliloquy ("O, what a rogue and peasant slave am I!") in Act II of Hamlet, wherein the Prince, his own feelings in deep bondage, marvels at the passion with which the First Player invests the contrived emotionality of a playwright. Says Hamlet: "What's Hecuba to him, or he to Hecuba, / That he should weep for her?"

Many are the Hecubas, from LAURA to AMBER, who have been accompanied by noises of my contriving. I have abetted their scheming with clarinets and attenuated their yearnings with cellos--molto vibrato. After 17 years of composing for films, I have learned that empathy is often better tempered with restraint. But there is one character who, more than any other, made restraint difficult. This is George Hurstwood, the tragic lover of Theodore Dreiser's SISTER CARRIE.

In discussing Hurstwood with William Wyler, director of the film (now called CARRIE) I noted that where Dreiser had pitied the man destroyed by his need for love, Wyler had treated him with the sympathy that a man of today might feel for a brother condemned by the rigid morality of an earlier day. It is our compassion toward Carrie and Hurstwood that determines the nature and course of the music in this film.

Thus, the musical material and its development are concerned with expressing the great longing of Hurstwood, as when he plods slowly upstairs, after his son's departure. Again, the music discovers the awakening of Carrie's feelings as Hurstwood leaves, after their scene in the Drouet flat. In the sequence of their first embrace, in the carriage, the music is part of the physical passion, and later reaches out after Carrie as she walks quickly away from Hurstwood.

The soundtrack of the scene in the park is a tour de force of re-recording for which laurels must go to Leon Becker, sound supervisor of the film, and the Paramount dubbing crew. That marvelous actor, Laurence Olivier, had pitched his voice in an almost guttural register to avoid sounding like the cultured Briton he is. Such delivery and expressive music ordinarily do not mix, to the great detriment of the music. But, thanks to the gifted Mr. Becker and his cohorts, the music was able to tell its part of this scene, including a moment of joy when Carrie confesses her love, and a touch of foreboding when Hurstwood cannot find the courage to tell her the truth about himself--that he is married.

Inept dubbing, which afflicts so many pictures, is often responsible for the sad line one sometimes hears from his colleagues in discussion of their film music: "Let me play you the records one day--then you'd really hear the score." But more often it is post-scoring cuts, and their effect upon the continuity and overall sense of the music, that give composers that Kafka look. Such cuts, which are inevitable, and sometimes even necessary, are made on grounds other than musical, and if there is a composer who can equal the dexterity with which a minor executive mutilates the form and context relationship of music to story, I have never met him. Fortunately for CARRIE the hand that did the bidding of the master was that of an artist. In my absence, Mr. Steven Caillag, whose ability as a music cutter approaches genius, made the necessary elisions and extensions. It was he who saw to it that the music of Hurstwood's flight from his wife and employer to Carrie remained intact as to form and meaning.

It was my hope that the music of CARRIE would bear the same relationship to the story that existed between the story and music of some of the wonderful silent movies for which my father conducted the orchestra at the old Metropolitan in Philadelphia. What a warmth there was between the screen and score in those days, when "heart-songs," Kinothek music, and sometimes excerpts of masterpieces followed hard upon one another! The Saturday matinees when I sat in the orchestra pit and responded like a seismograph to the heavings of the Gish sisters had made a deep impression on my young mind, and somehow I now felt that in CARRIE William Wyler had made just such a fable as those I had loved. We agreed that the score should have this "chromo" flavor where feasible.

So the music of Hurstwood's flight does not endeavor to convey torment and urgency through dissonance. It is a kind of distraught aria accompanied by swift, syncopated afterbeats; and the color, which is not a trick of orchestration but a function of the dramatic line, remains the same for many, many bars.

Program notes and sermons upon music are always faintly ridiculous. I console myself that I am, in part, eulogizing a departed friend, for cutting has in places reduced the music to the state of that Priam over whom Hecuba wept: "When she saw Pyrrhus make malicious sport/ In mincing with his sword her husband's limbs." A year and a half ago I may have been one with Hecuba, shedding helpless tears over what Pyrrhus was doing to my poor Priam. Since then, my empathy has receded, through the First Player, through Hamlet, to comparative objectivity. And now, seeing the film, and hearing the score (which I finished in February of 1951), in a projection room in June 1952, I was moved by it. I thought my father and his generation would also have liked it, and I was, after all, glad to have composed the music of CARRIE.

CHAMPION and HOME OF THE BRAVE

William Hamilton

It hardly seems possible that both CHAMPION and HOME OF THE BRAVE were scored by the same man, Dimitri Tiomkin. The virtues of HOME OF THE BRAVE correspond so closely to the flaws of CHAMPION that this discussion could be set down in a tabular form.

In CHAMPION, the music as often as not goes its own sweet way with no regard at all for the purport of the story. (Like HOME OF THE BRAVE, this one is a picture having a very definite moral slant.) As to ingredients, nearly every sequence starts with somebody putting a nickel into a juke box (or more probably a quarter) or walking into a restaurant. So a great deal of what we hear is Muzak-type. Even when the action provides no pretext, such combinations as piano and Hammond organ noodle nondescriptly for what seem like minutes on end, as in the sculpture scene. Another disconcerting mannerism showed itself repeatedly in the way that mis-en-scène became background--and then once or twice, Mickey Mouse. An instance is the scene where Midge (Kirk Douglas) and his brother, having hitched a ride, are making conversation with their host and getting the silent treatment from the host's girl friend. When Midge comments in gesture and grimace on her aloofness, the car radio which, of course, has been on all the while, emits muted trumpets which go, 'wha, wha, wha." Mr. Tiomkin knows better than this, as he demonstrates so easily in the scene where Midge asks his brother to come back. Solo clarinet is heard in long melismatic phrases to form a duet with Midge's wheedling. Here is one of the all-too-few places where the music refers in any way to the character of Midge. The score is not without other successful passages, however. The montage dealing with Midge's basic training is probably the best of them.

A deeply felt point of view is evident throughout HOME OF THE BRAVE. Just the right ingredients are used, and they are consistently handled in such a way as to give greatest support to the script. Mossy's scenes are treated with genuine sympathy which never becomes bathos. The orchestration is varied and fresh-sounding, and the sense of the music shows through, even in tutti passages with 50-calibre machine guns mixed in. The writing for voices is equally apt. The chorus is used to create that old high school gang back home, and more impressionistically, to help develop jungle atmosphere and its effect on the members of the squad. In the landing scene there is a trick, new to me, which should have future possibilities. Here it occurs with a long shot of the beach and one of the jungle, cut back and forth several times. At each cut the level changes; to jungle--up, to beach--down. The effect, of course, is totally different from that of playing alternately louder and softer.

EAST OF EDEN

Leonard Rosenman

Elia Kazan and I, in our preliminary discussions concerning the score to EAST OF EDEN, tried to find a way to score the film so that the music is inextractable from the dramatic framework of the whole project. We agreed that, ideally, the composer should go along entirely with the film, write the necessary music before certain scenes were shot, and, in places where the music plays a great part in determining both the tension and rhythm of the scene, confer with the director as to the problems involved in shooting the scene to the music rather than vice versa. After talks involving the details and spirit of the story, we agreed to work in this somewhat unorthodox manner. Thus I found myself on the first day of shooting on location at Mendicino, California, already brewing musical ideas on the scenes to be shot.

In directing a scene, Kazan seemed to be thinking of every aspect of the project all the time. He would suddenly detach himself from the camera and the actors, walk over to me and whisper, for instance, "Remember, play the kid (James Dean) musically," or words to that effect. Since on location in both Mendicino and Salinas I had access to a piano, I played my daily sketches for Kazan and we discussed the material at hand as it applied to the scenes in question. Thus when the film was rough cut the music was rough cut, too, and when the picture was complete I had only to orchestrate the score, and we recorded it.

Since my concert works are of a highly complex dissonant nature, Kazan and I had something of a friendly disagreement at first. A bargain was made finally to score the children simply, and the adults in a dissonant fashion. There were exceptions dictated by dramatic necessity, of course. Contrary to most thoughts on film music, both Kazan and I agreed that film music should be intrusive, that is to say, music should enter the film medium as a positive part of the plot and not merely for sound effects, or to add redundantly to what the eye and ear perceive to be happening dramatically on the screen. The necessity for music in films is the dramatic necessity for the intrusion of an "unreal" or illusory element for the purpose of creating a new and imaginative reality. Music should illuminate the deepest well of inner life within the character and situation. Too, it should generate that dramatic excitement which the marriage of the arts (ideally the film medium is just that) should bring about, almost in an operatic sense--except that the 'arias' are spoken rather than sung.

With these precepts in mind, certain considerations had to be observed. For example, when scoring under dialogue I took into account that Julie Harris is a high soprano, James Dean a tenor, and Raymond Massey a bass-baritone. The design of the instrumentation and of the thematic material itself was influenced by consideration of these voice ranges and qualities. Often "holes" were left in the scoring for the voice to be utilized as a sort of speaking instrument. Sometimes, in places of high tension or concentrated dialogue, music was not used at all, and entered later for punctuation in quiet reactive moments.

EDGE OF DOOM

William Hamilton

Hugo Friedhofer has again exceeded the requirements by providing not only necessary support to the scenario but also music well worth listening to in its own right. His treatment of Martin Lynn's long-standing grudge against an elderly priest is consistently sure-handed and sensitive, and is typical of the independent musical validity prevailing.

The score features two sharply contrasting motives. One, a linear figure usually stated by solo or unison instruments, seem to express more or less generally the disturbed condition of the central character. A thick, glowering and brazen pronouncement is associated with Martin's ideas of the Church and Father Kirkman. To Martin both are identical, stern and overbearing. Here is an aspect of character told in music with little or no assistance from the script. The latter is far more concerned with Martin's actions than with the emotions which give rise to them. It would be safe to say, therefore, that, without the music, the character of Martin would suffer a serious loss in credibility. There are several occasions where his behavior would seem pretty gratuitous in its absence.

Except for a couple of patches of narration, I don't recall there being any music under dialogue. There seems to be a trend in this direction, and I am all for it. Music heard at low levels while people are talking not only degrades itself, but manages somehow to rob subsequent music of a good part of its effect. The scene involved usually takes on the quality of a laboriously contrived song-cue, and I find myself expecting someone presently to break into "Ah, Sweet Mystery of Life." In EDGE OF DOOM, however, there is a good deal of well-placed silence. Relief from this comes in a wide variety of natural sounds in the scenes which are done with great imagination. There are the usual street noises, a funeral at J. T. Murray's, and particularly striking, the halls and stairways of the house where Martin lives. Immediately the front door is open, we are greeted by a magnificent melange of screaming children, four or five radio programs, and someone practicing arpeggios.

In the scene following the murder of Father Kirkman, Martin hurriedly tries to cover the signs of his visit to the rectory, leaves and passes out through the church into the street. The section beginning with antiphonal alternations between brass and strings is surely the most stunning thing I've heard in pictures. It has a grandeur recalling what they tell us about St. Mark's in Venice in the days of the Gabrielli. Marlin Skiles, who is overlooked in the main credits, is hereby congratulated for having a hand in it.

FROM HERE TO ETERNITY

George Duning

From the viewpoint of a film background composer, the year 1953 was a most interesting one for me. It was my pleasure to score three pictures of highly different subject matter, namely, SALOME, FROM HERE TO ETERNITY and MISS SADIE THOMPSON.

SALOME was a very direct sort of picture of a Biblical nature, and there was very little doubt as to where and what kind of music should be spotted in the background score. MISS SADIE THOMPSON called for a jazz approach, but FROM HERE TO ETERNITY presented a totally different problem--mainly where <u>not</u> to score. Morris Stoloff, music director, Fred Zinnemann, director of the picture, and I spent many hours discussing the approach to the background score. Because of the realism inherent in the picture, we agreed that an over-amount of background music could do more harm than good. The total number of minutes heard amounted to about an hour, divided between source music and actual background scoring. By "source music" I refer to all the bugle calls, the jukebox sequences, the piano playing in the New Congress Club, and the guitar and vocal tracks of Merle Travis.

The tune "From Here to Eternity," by Fred Karger and Bob Wells, was written quite a while before the actual shooting of the picture, and unfortunately when the time came for me to do the background score, it was discovered that there would be very little music back of the scenes between Pruitt and Lorene. I was able to use the tune in two jukebox sequences and once as a scoring cue back of the scene where Lorene brings Pruitt to her apartment. For the Main Title I used a treatment of "Drill Call" which ended in a climax announcing the Main Title and faded out to a snare drum figure as the soldiers get into formation. The music was gradually faded out and the rest of the main title played for sound effects only.

The main part of the original score for the film consisted of a theme for the frustrated love affair between the Captain's wife, Karen, and Sergeant Warden. This theme was heard in various treatments--mainly behind the wonderful scenes on the beach. The first beach scene opens with a sound of crashing waves. Here I had a high violin line playing over the sound, and then the sound was gradually dubbed down so that the main theme, in the celli, is heard.

The music covers the action of Karen and Warden arriving at the beach and deciding to go bathing. The scene then cuts to Pruitt and Lorene at the New Congress Club where a jukebox is heard. From this scene we cut back to the beach and this scene opens on a kiss in the waves. The music at this point remains ecstatic and amorous until the Sergeant starts to doubt Karen as he recalls rumors of her infidelities. At this point I injected a cold minor triad in muted trombones and woodwinds over a bass pedal.

The love theme continues and a gradual change in mood is felt when a dark string chord (non-vibrato) catches her reaction to his distrust. The love theme still continues but this time in a dark flute and bassoon color with gradual ascending thirds in strings over a pedal note for mounting tension. This goes on to the point where the Sergeant accuses her of an affair with a serviceman with the music ending suddenly on a climax.

A little later after Karen has told Warden of her unhappy experience with her husband, the music picks up quietly with a triste treatment of the secondary love theme. When Pruitt starts to run from the guards, the music becomes agitated and mounts to hysterical climax, where it is stopped suddenly by the machine gun sound effect.

For the End Title, I used the obvious but very effective "Aloha" to cover the scene between the two girls, as the boat carried them away from the Islands. At the point where the camera pans to Pruitt's bugle mouthpiece, a distant statement of "Taps" is heard.

HIGH NOON

William Hamilton

Here is one vote for HIGH NOON as the most sophisticated and brilliantly executed western to date. Based upon the leanest of plots, it is a melodrama of almost unrelieved suspense into which is worked a sobering message. The story can be told in a single, somewhat lumpy sentence thus: The retiring Marshal at Hadleyville (Gary Cooper) after learning of the imminent return to town on the noon train of vengeance-bound bad-man, Frank Miller, and after trying fruitlessly to recruit a posse, is obliged finally to receive Miller and company unassisted. In watching this, we are confronted by the uneasy matter of the individual's responsibility to support law and order, rather than count entirely on the efforts of a strong man.

As might be expected, such an argumentative script, developed largely in terms of character and atmosphere, must have a more than commonly high ratio of talk-to-action. And so it is with HIGH NOON. Nevertheless, good old-fashioned dramatic tension is so skillfully maintained that, far from seeming long-winded, the picture gives an impression of unusual brevity. Its running time is 85 minutes (just above average), and it recounts just about 85 minutes worth of story. The camera throughout has a predilection for clocks to help increase our anxiety at the dread approach of twelve. Also, the device of dissolving from one clock to another to follow the action about the town is an effective, if not completely original scene-shifter.

For all these virtues, it still seems to me that much of the film's success must be credited to Dimitri Tiomkin's music score. For the most part, the music is derived from a not very idiomatic song (by Mr. Tiomkin) which is given in full at the beginning, sung in fine, mournful, authentic style by Tex Ritter. Thus stated, the ballad functions as a theme, unifying the score which ranges freely back and forth between the general and the particular.

The sensitiveness and precision with which both speech and movement are accompanied recall the best in operatic practice. Witness the scene where the judge quotes to the marshal the mighty oath of revenge sworn by Miller years ago. Clearly, his words become a text set to the great, towering strokes of the orchestra. Again, in the shoot-it-out sequence near the end, the tactics of battle are practically spelled out in the notes. The tempo hastens and slackens to match the movements of the antagonists so that the eye and ear receive truly concerted stimuli. What might have been a fairly routine spate of gunplay is thereby enhanced sufficiently to top all that went before and provide a properly forceful climax.

As for mood music, the composer has tended to employ simpler and more literal allusions to the theme in a variety of arrangements, vocal and instrumental. Mr. Ritter is heard from time to time, repeating fragments of it with guitar and thumping, and there are passages featuring harmonica and accordian. Never have I heard either of these two instruments so attractively used in orchestral ensemble.

Still under the "general" heading, there are a couple of subsidiary themes relating to the two chief female characters on the scene. The more distinctive of these is a modal, Hispanic melody associated with the queenly Helen Ramirez, and some of the score's most deft changes of pace occur between this and iterations of the ballad theme. The heroine music, on the other hand, is not up to the mark, being just another version of that old andante favori, "The World's Most Beautiful Girl in Distress." However, I do not insist that the heroine, Amy (Grace Kelly) and her controversy with her bridegroom, the marshal, should have been any more powerfully expressed in music. This would have been in full accord with the argument set forth by the ballad:

"No do not forsake me, oh, my darling ... " through ... "till I shoot Frank Miller dead." However, since the story turns mostly on other matters, I can appreciate the wisdom of allowing Will's and Amy's problem to become part of the wallpaper, rather than risk an acute attack of misplaced emphasis. I also liked the rousing reading of the

Battle Hymn of the Republic in the church scene, though I wonder if such a church at such a time and place would be likely to have so fine a choir. And finally, I'm grateful for the harmonium behind Will's and Amy's wedding. Such functions in the movies too often subject us to the Hammond organ.

JEANNE EAGELS

George Duning

In scoring JEANNE EAGELS, the chief problem was to compose a main theme that would meet several requirements. It had to be of such a nature that it could become a pop song, to be used in exploiting the picture. The melody line had to be played in a light, youthful manner for Jeanne Eagels (Kim Novak) in the earlier part of the picture, and it had to get a strong, dark, dramatic treatment in the later reels, as the ambitious girl who wanted both love and stage success continued towards her tragic end. A second theme was used for the character of Elsie Desmond (Virginia Grey), a down and out actress who wants to play Sadie Thompson in "Rain," the role which made Eagels a top Broadway success. The theme is of a pathetic nature, and is usually heard in the woodwinds.

Most of the early part of the picture takes place at a carnival, run by Sal Satori (Jeff Chandler). There is a scene in which Eagels and Satori have a gay time late at night riding on a carousel. I wrote a simple carousel tune called "Love on a Carousel" which we recorded with a calliope, woods, a couple of horns and percussion. Over this I was able to play the main theme in strings, somewhat like the effect I achieved in PICNIC, where I played my main theme against a jazz track. Morris Stoloff, head of the Music Department, and George Sidney, the film's producer-director, liked the combination of the carousel music and the main theme so well that they asked me to use a similar treatment for the Main Title. The Main Title cards were superimposed over a background of the carnival at night, and when Jeanne appears on the scene and her card flashes on, a string treatment of the main theme, recorded separately and reverbed, is superimposed over the carousel music.

THE MAN WITH THE GOLDEN ARM

Elmer Bernstein

First, let me clear up an important point. The score for THE MAN WITH THE GOLDEN ARM is not a jazz score. It is a score in which jazz elements were incorporated toward the end of creating an atmosphere, I should say a highly specialized atmosphere, specific to this particular film. In this respect I was fortunate in that jazz has heretofore been used most sparingly in this manner. Now there are a rash of unpleasant films using jazz more or less skillfully. In the future, therefore, it will be difficult, if not impossible, to create a highly specialized atmosphere merely by using jazz elements. Let us then conclude that my notion was enhanced by fortuitous timing. But enough modesty. Let us get on to more interesting considerations, and the first one that presents itself is: Why Jazz?

I told Otto Preminger, the producer-director, of my intentions after one quick reading of the shooting script. The script had a Chicago slum street, heroin, hysteria, longing, frustration, despair and finally death. Whatever love one could feel in the script was the little, weak emotion left in a soul racked with heroin and guilt, a soul containing its strength in the struggle for the good life and losing pitifully. There is something very American and contemporary about all the characters and their problems. I wanted an element that could speak readily of hysteria and despair, an element that would localize these emotions to our country, to a large city if possible. Ergo, jazz.

This is not a score in which each character has a theme. It is not a score which creates a musical mirror for dialogue. Nor is it a score which psychoanalizes the characters and serves up inner brain on the half shell. It is basically a simple score which deals with a man and his environment. There are only three themes which are exploited in a compositional manner in the development of the score. These can be loosely identified in the following manner: (1) Frank's relationship to his general environment; his job as a dealer in a cheap poker joint, to his fight against the dope habit, to the pusher who sells him the stuff, to the street itself. (2) Frank's relationship to his home environment; his neurotic wife, who feigns a debilitating illness in order to hold him, to the shabby flat with its "lower depth" inhabitants, to his own guilty lack of love for his wife. (3) Frank's relationship with "the other woman," who is a symbol to him of love, and the better life, such small hopes as he has from time to time, and his chance of making it away from the habit and even the neighborhood and its hold on him.

My first move was to avail myself of the counsel and help of two brilliant young jazz musicians, Shorty Rogers and Shelly Manne. Rogers arranged all the band numbers and was of invaluable aid as a guide to the wonders of contemporary jazz. Shelly Manne created his own drum solos where indicated and thus made a unique and exciting contribution to many parts of the score. Since time was of the essence (the score was written in 20 days), an orchestrator of the highest caliber was of great importance. In this my sketches were graced by the great talents of Fred Steiner, a fine composer in his own right, who subsequently went on to score the film, RUN FOR THE SUN.

Upon completion of the score it was apparent that it would take a "super orchestra" of the finest jazz and symphonic musicians available to perform it. This job was entrusted to Bobby Helfer who, with even more than his customary magic, assembled a dream ensemble of 57 musicians from the four corners of the Hollywood symphonic and jazz scene. Perhaps the best way to indicate the cooperation and performance of these artists is to tell you that on one occasion Armand Kaproff was roundly applauded by his colleagues for his performance of a four-bar 'cello solo. There was much applause those days for more spectacular feats by Shelly Manne, Pete Candoli, Milt Bernhart, Mitchell Jurie, Ray Turner, Martin Ruderman, Anatol Kaminsky, but it was the reaction to a short 'cello solo that most eloquently described the degree of concentration and intensity of performance achieved during the recording session.

Once the music was on film its care was entrusted to Leon Birnbaum, who used his vast experience as a music cutter to make life easier on the recording stage, and who was most helpful in preparing the film for transfer to the record album.

Of technical matters there is little to say. The score

was recorded single channel on Westrex equipment. The recording room at RKO is too small to successfully record a full jazz and symphonic ensemble playing at the same time so in one notable case we tried a short cut. Leon Birnbaum built a click track for the main title and we recorded the two ensembles separately and they were reunited in dubbing. Other than that we made no further forays into technical fields.

THE MUDLARK

John Huntley

The score by William Alwyn for this delightful picture, THE MUDLARK, follows a careful plan of musical characterization and delicate point, while avoiding any temptation to over-indulge. Many moments where music could perhaps have been used are left to be played against natural sound or silence. The result is that the occasions when music occurs are all the more significant. The titles contain a wistful theme for the mudlark himself, while at the same time reflecting the pageantry of the Victorian era. A sequence in which the mudlark fights with some other boys in the mud of the river Thames is embellished with a suitable agitato.

The music first comes into its own, however, in the scenes in which the boy Wheeler breaks into Windsor Castle. Although he sees the Castle early in the morning through a Thames-side fog, the undercurrent of the pageantry of the King's Guard within is suggested by the martial music. A skillful example of musical pointing occurs when one of the Guardsmen gives the Cockney classic remark, "Op it!"

The long sequence when Wheeler first explores the interior of the Castle is almost carried by the music, which suddenly becomes subjective and expresses the mood and character of the people rather than the grandeur of the building. Woodwinds delicately pick out the thoughts of the boy; they concentrate the attention on him. When the two lovers are seen plotting an elopement, the music becomes tender and reflects their mood. There is a quick change to a delightful Scottish motif for Mr. Brown's kilted approach, while

Mr. Naseby, head of the kitchen staff, receives a pompous theme in keeping with his character.

There is a return to pageantry in the scenes of the entry of Queen Victoria and her court into the Dining Hall, echoing the initial theme when we first meet the Queen in a lovely tracking shot as the light of some candles falls across her face. Wheeler's nocturnal tour of the Castle gives an opportunity for further neat touches in the score, especially in the great Throne Room when Wheeler mounts the throne and imagines himself King. A carol, sung during the scenes in the Tower, adds pathos to the scene when Wheeler is denied by his friends. In the final sequence when the Queen repents of her seclusion and finally meets the young boy, we have some exquisite moments for the strings, while pageantry re-asserts itself in the triumphant closing shots.

Alwyn's score for this 20th Century-Fox Production, made at Shepperton Studios, London, with Irene Dunne giving a truly remarkable portrayal of Queen Victoria, is discreet, delicately orchestrated and holds back its more powerful effects for the few scenes of majesty that demand it. The musical characterization is consistent and clear-cut.

NO SAD SONGS FOR ME

George Duning

NO SAD SONGS FOR ME is the story of a happily married woman, with a good husband and little daughter, who suddenly discovers that she is dying of cancer and has about eight or ten months to live. Being a woman of unusual fortitude, she does not tell her husband of the imposing tragedy but makes plans which she hopes will lessen the grief of her death. Meanwhile, a young woman, a war widow, goes to work in the husband's office, and the husband suddenly finds himself attracted to the girl. The wife, at first greatly hurt, gradually realizes that this girl, because of her qualities, would make a logical successor. It can be readily seen that the background score called for quite an emotional treatment.

There were several problems encountered in the preparations of the score. First, the story called for a symphonic excerpt which was a favorite work of the wife and later turns out to be a favorite of the other girl. This music was to be heard twice--as a phonograph recording and then as the End Title. The problem involved in the choice of this excerpt was the fact that in both scenes it had to be played under very low dialogue. After much deliberation, the horn solo section of the Brahms First Symphony, Fourth Movement, was chosen because of its great warmth and quiet beauty. It was found that the original orchestration of Brahms dubbed beautifully except for the high flute answer--also the statement of the chorale by the trombones. Being a great worshipper of Brahms it was with extreme reluctance that I reset the high flute solo an octave lower and doubled with an oboe. Arthur Morton, who did a magnificent job on the orchestration of the score, devised an excellent setting of the chorale with a combination of four horns overlaid with woodwinds. Other than these two sections, the Brahms was quoted vertabim on the recordings.

The situation which exists at the end of the picture required that a two-piano version be made of the finale to the Fourth Movement, but again the orchestra was playing from the original score behind the pianos. Regarding the original music in the background score, the main theme had to be a long tune that could be played unaccompanied or with very little underpinning, because of the low husky quality of Margaret Sullavan's voice. In one scene, where Miss Sullavan is writing to her husband regarding her impending death, the violins play this theme muted over a single pedal note with occasional entrances of two flutes in their low register. Considerable use was made of fragments of the main theme, especially the jump of the minor seventh found in the first two notes. The Doctor's theme required a quiet warmth and was generally played as a horn solo or in the violas. The character of Chris, the other girl, required a somewhat cool and out-of-doors flavor and was generally played as a clarinet solo. Only one typically motion picture device was used in this score, namely a reiterated G natural on harp, vibes and celeste which was played over the background scoring whenever reference was made to the wife's impending death. This device was always heard on the same note G regardless of the tonality of the underscoring at the moment. Most of the orchestral settings of the score were typically symphonic with great dependence on the strings, woodwinds in two's and horns; practically no brass.

OLIVER TWIST

John Huntley

With six symphonies, a violin concerto and many other works to his credit, the name of Arnold Bax is well known to all followers of contemporary music. As Sir Arnold Bax, composer of the fanfares for the Royal wedding and anthems for state occasions, he is known to many more in his capacity as Master of the King's Musick, a position he has held since 1942.

In 1943, Sir Arnold wrote his first film music for a documentary picture entitled MALTA G.C., a production of the Army, R.A.F. and Crown Film Units. The recording was made by the R.A.F. Orchestra conducted by Muir Mathieson and the commentary to the film was spoken by Sir Laurence Olivier. The music was afterwards performed as a suite and was recorded by the B.B.C., the score itself was formally presented to the George Cross Island at a ceremony in London at which the composer was present. Of this work, Dr. Hubert Clifford wrote, "Arnold Bax's music for MALTA G.C. is of the highest distinction and ranged from the epic to the naively human in parallel with the exciting subject matter of the film."

Sir Arnold is above all an honest man. Although he had enjoyed the experience and had created a successful film score, his own critical standards were not satisfied. With complete frankness, he wrote of his impressions on music and the film: "I do not think the medium is at present at all satisfactory as far as the composer is concerned, as his music is largely inaudible, toned down to make way for, in many cases, quite unnecessary talk." In fact, after Bax had seen the film, he met Olivier, who said, 'I suppose you are annoyed with me," to which came the reply, "Yes, I jolly well am--chattering away all over my music. Bombs falling in all directions, planes crashing right and left, my music having a wonderful time--and just at the crucial moment, my music is faded down to make way for some fatuous remark like 'an air raid is in progress; it is a time of danger for the population!' "

Now Sir Arnold has written his second film score, this time for the Cineguild production of the famous Charles Dickens novel OLIVER TWIST, which has been directed by David Lean and produced by Ronald Neame. He admits that he enjoyed the experience of writing for a feature film, and feels too that here is a subject in which the music will get its chance, and be able to make a positive contribution to the telling of the story.

Two complete viewings of the finished film, along with typed lists of "music lengths" (i.e., exact timings of all the selections of the film involving music) were sufficient for Sir Arnold to embark on his ten-week task of writing the music itself. Working in his hotel-home in Sussex, the composer had frequent discussions with Muir Mathieson, the music director, before the score was finally completed and sent to the music copyists for the preparation of the orchestral parts. An unusual feature of the music recording was the fact that a complete day was spent on rehearsal alone to ensure that a perfect performance should be obtained for the finished picture and to check on the integration of the music with the film in every possible detail. The composer was present most of the time during the final recording sessions and was particularly fascinated by the way in which the music was fitted to the action, bit by bit.

The highlights of the score have been made into a suite of six items. These include the prelude, an exciting fight scene, two piano pieces (played in the film by Harriet Cohen), the rip-roaring chase scene, with bustling strings, a ripe tune for the brass and plenty of activity for the percussion, a romp, and a finale (which contains one of the most delightful tunes in the picture and is extremely lyrical).

It is interesting to see how the director, David Lean, the music director, Muir Mathieson, and the composer, Sir Arnold Bax, visualized the music, conveyed their ideas, and collaborated in the final result after discussion on all the points involved. For example, here are David Lean's original notes for three sequences, showing how the working out of the music was affected in each case; the result on the screen you must judge for yourself.

"Titles: I haven't the faintest idea what sort of music should accompany the titles, but I should like it gradually to fade away--a fade into an orchestration that suggests that something is about to happen, so that the last two titles on the screen will be in silence, and the first shot of the picture--that of dark clouds--will have a rumble of distant thunder." The title music was eventually worked out with two main musical ideas of the picture. Firstly, there is the "locket theme," the locket being the key of the mystery of Oliver's birth, and secondly, the theme associated with Oliver himself, heard first on divided strings in the upper register. Lean's idea of "something about to happen" and the "last two titles on the screen in silence" eventually became incorporated in the form of a tremulo string sound that quivers through the last of the titles and acts as a bridge into the opening scenes of Oliver's mother in the storm, struggling to the workhouse.

The sequence in which the infant Oliver is carried through the workhouse shows how discussion may sometimes alter the director's original conception of a scene if he hears an idea he likes better. David Lean first wrote: "The mother has died in the lying-in room, and the doctor has said, 'It's all over, Mrs. Thingummy.' As daylight pours in I should like the music to start again. Hopeful: a new day: new life: I should like the music to 'accent' the locket round the girl's neck as it is a very important plot point. The music over the walk through the workhouse changes to a more somber note." The sunlight music and the locket theme were incorporated into the music as Lean indicated, but for the scenes of the workhouse an experiment was tried. It was decided that Oliver himself was the primary factor in the scene introducing the dingy, sordid surroundings of the workhouse. Therefore Bax wrote a part for the piano (played for the film by Harriet Cohen) and as Oliver is carried, crying, through the monstrously ugly and dimly-lit hall, the tentative sounds of a piano are heard to emphasize Oliver and act as a contrast to his miserable surroundings. The piano music has been criticized as "inappropriate," probably because the significance the director and composer were searching for has been missed; it may be therefore that Lean's original conception was the correct one.

A piece of music which came to be known as "Fagin's Romp" started life again as a note on the director's files: "The boys have sat down to supper with Fagin and after the Dodger has brought out his spoils for the day, Fagin raps the table with the toasting fork and says, 'To work.' I should like music to accompany the whole scene of Fagin donning his hat, taking the walking stick and walking round like an old gentleman and finally having his foot trodden on and his pockets picked, causing him to search frantically for his lost wallet and watch, which makes Oliver laugh so much. I think the music should start immediately after 'To work' and end on the dissolve to Oliver lying asleep. This is to me almost the most important piece of music so far, and I should like it to transform the scene into a comic ballet, with only one angry jar in it--the moment when Fagin gives the two boys who have failed to pick his pocket successfully a kick.

Sir Arnold Bax's music does full justice to Lean's requirements. It is highly rhythmic, starting lightly and ending in a rich, vulgar tune. Three chords open out into the main idea which begins on the strings; the development is interrupted with string chords and a rising phrase for trombones. The fun increases with a tune for the horns, with off-the-beat accompaniment by the full orchestra, going on to the trumpets and trombones as the noisy climax is reached and a coda, based on the opening theme, brings the musical sketch to an end. It is interesting to note that, at the recording session at Denham with the Philharmonic Orchestra conducted by Muir Mathieson, the music (known then as "4M1"--that is, the first section of music in reel 4) was first recorded straight through and then an additional sharp roll on the drum (known as "4M1X") was recorded to obtain the effect of the kick mentioned in Lean's notes.

Recalling the writing of the music in retrospect, Bax admitted that it had been hard work and that he had had to struggle considerably with some sections. This however had added to the interest and he had obviously found the whole experience bracing and lively. "OLIVER TWIST is very dramatic in parts and I found I had to adapt my normal musical approach quite a bit, apart from the inevitable restrictions imposed by the stop-watch. Shall I do another film, you ask? No, I can't tell you that at present. But I should like now to try my hand at a particular type of film which would really be in tune with the sort of thing I have tried to do in much of my music. A romantic subject, with beauty and poetry, with color and gaiety, calm and green and pleasing, a subject that would be lyrical and full of the clean, country air."

ON THE WATERFRONT

William Hamilton

In spite of all the fabled terrors of film-score composition, Leonard Bernstein's first try at it has succeeded with the éclat so characteristic of him. As a composer of concert and stage music accustomed to being in control of the proceedings at all times, he planned his WATERFRONT score with a boldness which in the movies could lead to disaster. There are indeed some loose ends--material planted but never dug, passages with intended allusions to others which are never heard, tutti dozens of decibels below the dialog. But these flaws are more disturbing on paper than in screening, where the sweep of the production prevents our lingering over them.

Here are the chief themes in order of their appearance. The first is a sober, somewhat neutral pronouncement given initially in simple two-part canon under the Main Title, and again, (more elaborately) only at the end of the picture where Terry, redeemed, seeks to resume his career as a longshoreman. The impression that this is the theme of the whole story is made stronger by the syntax of its presentations. After the main title it is tagged with a fading, questioning figure which invites the listener to consider the oncoming problem. It is in the nature of things for the final statement to sound final, but ON THE WATERFRONT requires a finality that does not say that everything is going to be just dandy. Hence, instead of the conventional, triumphant cadence over a major-triad-cum-added-6th, the theme is interrupted by discordant snaps (minor 9th to major 7th).

The score's most daring conception is a three-voice fugato for percussion (tympani, tympani, and side drums without snares). It is an overpowering movement of nearly two minutes' length. In the planning, this same movement was to announce each of the three murders in the story in the candid fashion of a Greek chorus. The design was marred, however, in the instance of Kayo Dugan's killing by the fact that the scene in question was shot on location during a genuine unloading, and the sound-track was already too full of dialog and ambient noise to accommodate any music at all. Consequently, the ensuing dead march for Kayo loses much of its point. The "murder movement" does recur for the discovery of the third corpse, and again it fits perfectly the events which it accompanies. However, the sense of repercussion which it was orginally intended to impart is no longer evident.

A very great contrast in treatment appears between the harshness as it is heard in the "murder movement" and the charming setting for flute, harp, oboe, and pigeons which follows it. Again, in the attack on the dissidents in the church basement, the four-note motto from this theme assumes several guises: first, as the soprano 'part' of a series of irregularly spaced staccato clusters, and then in the original snap rhythm with slightly more civilized harmony. Finally, there is a much simpler version in evenly-moving half-notes. A different sort of application using the whole theme occurs in "Blue Goon Blues." It is divided in the middle with the second half placed first. The whole then becomes the subject of a set piece. This "Blues," perhaps a little too sophisticated to be mise-en-scène, is heard toward the end of the saloon sequence.

The "Girl" or "Love" theme is structurally less basic in the score than the other themes. Its frankly melodious character and specific sentiment tend to set it somewhat apart from the main stream. Nevertheless, its appearance is always managed with such ingenuity as to make it sound quite inevitable. It is heard first under the scene where Edie joins the longshoremen's scramble for the last handful of working-tags. It is only after the first phrase of the theme is firmly settled on G that we are aware of the premonitory nature (melodically) of the first of these two figures and the strongly dominant effect of the second. This same scherzo is introduced again under the climatic fight between Terry and Johnny Friendly (wonderful name!).

Another instance of preparation over a much greater distance occurs under the scene in which Terry smashes his way into Edie's apartment. The introduction of the "Edie" theme at this point is identical in shape to the middle section of the "murder" movement. One more entrance of the "Edie" music must be mentioned. It is heard in the sequence "Dead Pigeons," which accompanies the scorn shown by Terry's peers for his apostasy. "Edie" combines with the "Waterfront" theme so perfectly that it is hard to believe that they were composed simultaneously. "Kangaroo Court" has only a very slight developmental function in the score. It is heard a second time, in reverse and much subdued, under the colloquy between Terry and Charlie in the taxi. I found this awesome sound (or, in the words of the composer himself, "terrible noise") one of the most memorable moments of all.

Mr. Bernstein's music for ON THE WATERFRONT merits a much more extended discussion than has been possible here. It cannot be summed up in a few pages. The purposeful unity of the whole work is one of its strongest features, and one which can best be sensed in the screening--or better, a second or third screening.

THE SWORD AND THE ROSE

Clifton Parker

Having worked for ten years on an opera on a medieval subject, just completed and published, I was in close touch with early music and found it very useful for this picture. I did not use any existing music, but composed original music in the style of the various forms I wished to use. In Queen Katherine's audience chamber the players seen on the screen are a consort of viols, represented by a string quartet. They played a fantasia followed by a passepied.

For the practice scene in Mary's drawing room the instrument used was a lute. This has a very sweet but extremely quiet tone, and we had some difficulty in recording because the player's breathing could be heard! The two pieces were an almain [allemand] and la volta, the latter to to be used again in the ballroom scene, and to become, in a slow variant, the romantic theme associated with the lovers. In the ballroom scene the visual orchestra consisted of recorders, serpent, consort of viols and tabor, and lute--represented by harp, flutes, bassoon, string quartet and tenor-drum, and the two dances were a pavane and la volta. The extended version of the latter was in the form of what the Elizabethans called divisions of beat--crotchet [quarter note], quaver [eighth note], semiquaver [16th note], demisemiquaver [32nd note]. This gave us the cumulative effect we wanted. We also cheated a bit by slowly adding a much larger orchestra. The music for the French wedding banquet was based on the rhythmic possibilities of an old Dutch dance called a lesquercade. (Incidentally, there lies the reason for not using actual old music. It would have seemed rather unsophisticated for film purposes, apart from the question of fitting, but many of these old forms, also the instruments on which they were played, suggest all sorts of possibilities which are old enough to be new. For example, the use of trombones--or their old equivalent, the sackbut--to accompany gentle love songs. There was, perhaps fortunately, no opportunity to revive this practice in this film!) In the lesquercade I used little bells (represented by a glockenspiel), which were very popular in early secular music, it seems. The music for the ride in the park was a variation of the lesquercade.

I have confined my remarks to the period music of the score, because the rest of it is normal film music and not, I should think, of any particular interest. I felt this would give more scope for underlining the dramatic side of the story, and as all the period music is actual--that is, belongs to dancing or festive occasions--I don't think there is a conflict of styles. Perhaps one interesting point is the music for Brandon's escape from the Tower. This is a very peculiar score, designed to be used with an echo chamber, and I think it did create some quite strange noises.

THE THIEF

Herschel Burke Gilbert

An important difference in approaching the scoring of THE THIEF from that of a film which contained dialogue, was that all of the music in the film would be audible and thus could truly speak for itself without submergence under dialogue as is usually the case in most films in which even short pieces of music "in the clear" are a rarity. Consequently, I felt this dramatic story which is told completely visually without dialogue and with only the normal, everyday sound effects, must be complemented with music which is broad in scope and which contains as much musical form as I could devise, and yet tell the story which is seen on the screen along with the story which is not seen but which should be heard in the music.

Producer Clarence Greene and director Russell Rouse completely agreed with me that the music must in no way attempt to mimic the characters or imitate sounds or sound effects. Recorded sound effects were to be used for the real everyday sounds we hear around us such as footsteps, traffic noise, clothes rustles, door closes, phone rings, etc. Also, we agreed not to use any musical gimmicks, electrical instruments or popular music score, for I was convinced that only a kind of symphonic sound would be in character with the dignity of the story and the seriousness of the subject matter. Russell Rouse aptly stated that the most important counterpoint to the screen must be the music interpreting the story subjectively rather than objectively.

Before discussing the music in detail, I should like to say something about the philosophy behind the creation of the film. Neither Mr. Greene nor Mr. Rouse had any intention of beginning a series of talkless pictures. Rather, they wanted to create a drama using the art form of motion pictures in its exact sense: a story to be told entirely by the camera with realistic sound effects and music but with no dialogue, printed titles or narration. THE THIEF is not a silent picture; there is no dialogue because it is unnecessary to the telling of the story. In fact, the very nature of the plot precludes any talking, for when the leading characters meet each other, the very nature of their secret mission would make them avoid speaking to each other for fear of detection.

The story is about an eminent nuclear physicist (Ray Milland) who is supplying secret information to an alien power, and the tremendous inner conflict arising in him as a result of his actions. The picture begins with the close-up of a telephone ringing three times, while the camera, now moving through the dark room into a bedroom, pans up the rigid form of a man lying on the bed. The phone begins ringing and again stops after the third ring. A few moments after the final ring the physicist's face relaxes from its tension and the music begins softly on the theme played by unaccompanied solo viola and clarinet in unison.

The bassoon joins with a counterpoint and the bass enters on a G-pedal, sustaining through the downbeat and moves through a semi-cadence in D major back to G minor. Here, the violins, doubled with first oboe, take over the second statement of the first theme in a slightly altered version. The solo viola continues, now playing the counterpoint to the theme it had previously introduced. The celli and additional bass join in and the tympani gives a soft, rhythmic movement to the music. Following the second statement of the main theme which has been extended to nine bars and has now modulated to A minor, comes a five-bar episode and a two-bar extension brings us the second theme. The story is so well devised that it presupposes music with a definite form in accompaniment to it. Our main character has been introduced and we have seen him get up and leave the apartment. Walking through the night he leads us to the story's second subject as the picture cuts directly to Martin Gabel lighting a cigarette while waiting on a dark street corner.

The first statement of the second theme is nine bars long with a full cadence on a D unison. This is followed by the last seven bars of the second theme in a shortened version beginning in the subdominant and returning to D unison. Now begins a fragmentary development of the first theme, introducing along with it a new counterpoint of 16th notes in rhythmic chords of parallel 4ths moving in contrary motion. Here for the first time the music is written in a direct time relationship to the action on the screen. Depicting Dr. Allen Fields' (Ray Milland's) mental conflict, the rhythmic counterpoint nervously continues, even as the first theme broadly and stridently rises to a climax in its own right. The music continues to express Fields' fight with his conscience as he reads and re-reads the message telling him of the mission he must undertake. The music's crescendo emotionally rises as the camera dollies into a large close-up of Fields resigned to the task ahead ... and we fade out with both picture and music.

It is interesting to note that director Rouse did not fall back on the cliché inserts of notes, newspapers and the like to support his picture. In every case where Fields received a message he acted out the intent of the message so that the audience knew what was written in it. I musically punctuated the seriousness of each of these scenes.

Although the entire score is based on two themes and their many variations, there are several motifs used in conjunction with story points. However, I chose several complete sequences to show the method of approach in the music of this film rather than a dissection of the musical motives which may appear in the isolated sections of the score. In most cases these were fragments based on either of the two main themes. The purpose of the music was to subjectively suggest the person or emotion important to that part of the story even though he was not on the screen at the time his music was played. The music was discussed and planned from the beginning to have an overall integrity to the picture and to itself rather than be a series of isolated musical sequences. In some instances music was kept out entirely to let the sound effects supply the realism of the score.

It is interesting to note that instances in which the music needed additional time to rise to important climaxes were helped by film editor Chester Schaeffer who cooperated by adding small portions of film wherever needed. This gave the music the time it required to help give the picture the right feeling. There was no special theme music for the sequences which included Rita Gam. Instead, I wrote "source-music": jazz records from an adjoining apartment, and a mambo and a samba supposedly emanating from Miss Gam's radio or record player.

THE THIRD MAN

William Hamilton

As must be generally realized by this time, THE THIRD MAN represents a most significant and basic development in the "agreeable science" of setting motion picture to music. Mr. Reed has successfully revived accompaniment by a solo instrument without any of the drawback attaching to its early practice. Many of us can recall the old precedure: "Hearts and Flowers" for Deathbed, Foreclosure, Girl-in-Snow; or the 'William Tell" storm for Fire, Trainwreck, Battle, or possibly Storm. By its nature it could hardly be depended on to provide its share of a unified, convincing performance. Also, before electrical recording, image and sound usually emanated from distinctly separate sources which emphasized further the effect of clumsy contrivance.

Without tracing in detail the evolution of the sound

track, let me say that it has made possible a most excellent score of which nearly every note is played by one man, Anton Karas, on the zither. The score appears to consist of selections from Mr. Karas' regular repertory and of free improvisation. Naturally, such pieces as "Unter den Lindenbaum," "Alter Lied," and 'White Chrysanthemums" have no direct bearing on the action. They and Mr. Karas' originals "Cafe Mozart Waltz" and the 'Harry Lime' theme are used mostly to keep us in the mood of time and scene. That the mood which this music calls forth is the right one, can, of course, only be assumed by people unacquainted with postwar Vienna, but authentic or not, it is completely persuasive. In addition, the artful use of the 'Harry Lime" theme, whole and in sections, is highly important to the structure of the story.

The other music pertinent to the action is even more striking in its simplicity and effectivness. It was surely this phase of the work which inspired one critic's allusion to the Homeric bard with his lyre. These are the passages where Mr. Karas abandons 16-bar form and watches the screen with us, punctuating and commenting briefly in a sort of recitative-accompaniment style.

One objection, plausible enough in theory, but in accord with the facts, is that the unrelieved sound of a table model instrument like the zither is bound to start oppressing the ear long before the tale has been told. While it is true that the zither has far fewer notes on it than the piano and lacks the assortment of weird voices available on an organ by Wurlitzer or Hope-Jones, it is an instrument of remarkable variety in expressive resources. In the words of another, somewhat more excitable commentator, the music ranges "from light blue to dark blue to searing, flaming red." Such dazzling extremes depend on the skill of the player, of course, but the instrument itself possesses two basically different sound qualities due to the stringing and to the normal mode of operation.

On the straight side, next to the player, is a set of five metal strings mounted over a fretted fingerboard, as on the guitar. They are sounded by a pick worn on the right thumb and their tone is comparatively big and brilliant. These are color-coded (like harp strings) for ready identification. Plucked with the bare fingers, they have a softer, thinner sound than the five melody strings to which they provide a subservient harmonic background. Since, unlike the guitar, the zither does not have to be held in place, the left hand is free to execute whatever prodigies of fingering practice and natural agility will allow. In this case they allow plenty.

3:10 TO YUMA

George Duning

A good, dramatic Western happens to be one of my favorite types of movies, and so I was delighted to be assigned to do the score for 3:10 TO YUMA. The director of the picture, Delmar Daves, is very sensitive to the value of the background score, and he asked me to compose and record the main theme before he had even started to shoot the picture. In several scenes he had a playback machine on the set and shot the scenes to the mood and timing of the music.

The main theme, sung by Frankie Laine over the main and end titles, is a 48-bar melody, somewhat modal and folksy in character. After writing this theme, I discovered I had written a song using only major and minor chords in the harmonization--no dominant or diminished sevenths! David Heilwell, the producer, and Mr. Daves asked me to use the title song as much as possible throughout the score, even for agitatos, rides, tensions, etc. The guitar became a sort of identification for the bandit. Glenn Ford gives an excellent performance as a bandit leader who is in the custody of an impoverished cattle rancher, played by Van Heflin. The bandit realizes he has missed something in his life as he watched the love and devotion between the rancher, his wife and their boys. A second theme, called "Our Home," was used for scenes involving the rancher and his family.

The balance of the score (which was over 50 minutes in length) was based mainly on tension devices, built out of dissonant chordal structures over nervous tympani patterns. The main theme played over reiterated chords on the guitar became a time device. Because of the length of the main theme, and to accommodate Frankie Laine's tempo, I omitted the usual introductory passages and started the vocal immediately on the opening footage of the Main Title.

TREASURE ISLAND

John Huntley

The music for TREASURE ISLAND, produced by Walt Disney at Denham Studios, England, may be divided into two sections. First came the question of sea shanties to be sung in the film. Under the general supervision of Muir Mathieson (music director to the production), Mrs. Buck, his personal assistant, conducted a research during which over 300 sea shanties and old maritime songs were examined before a final selection was submitted to the production chief, Perce Pearce. It was essential that the songs chosen should not only be correct for the period (1765) but also that they should be suitable in lilt and tempo to the scenes involved. Walt Disney himself heard a number of test recordings before the final selection was madc.

The first of the shanties, "Johnny, Come Down to Hilo," will be heard sung to the accompaniment of a guitar, while "Tom's Gone Down to Hilo" has been recorded by a solo voice, accompanied by a group of pirates humming, and a guitar. The third sea song to be heard in TREASURE ISLAND is not a traditional number as such, but was specially set by Marcus Dods, of Cambridge University; it is the old number, "Yo-Ho-Ho, and a Bottle of Rum."

The second aspect of the music was looked after by the composer of the main musical score, Clifton Parker. This young English writer has been associated with a large number of films and by a strange coincidence, many of them have been about the sea or adventure stories in which the sea played a large part. One of his first successes was the music for WESTERN APPROACHES, the story of a dozen shipwrecked Merchant Seamen adrift in an open boat in mid-Atlantic during the war. There was JOHNNY FRENCHMAN, which dealt with two rival groups of fisherfolk on either side of the English Channel, as well. Many will remember Clifton Parker's music for THE BLUE LAGOON, with Jean Simmons on a tropical island. Of course, not all his scores have been about the sea. For example, there wasn't a drop of water for miles in BLANCHE FURY (except during the fire sequence), CHILDREN ON TRIAL or WHEN THE BOUGH BREAKS.

Clifton Parker is a composer whose views on film music are well-defined. "A composer faces two main problems in films," he will tell you. "Firstly, there are moments when he is allowed to have his say, not as in a symphony, but rather as in opera or ballet, where the eye and the ear must be equally intrigued. Secondly, there are the sections when the sound track must be divided into its three main ingredients--dialogue, sound effects and music. Here the composer must arrange that the music calls for no strong line of its own, but rather the qualities that make it flow smoothly into the general pattern of the sound track. As we are working in the age of sound film, although our eyes are on the screen, our ears are on the sound track. When the composer has it all his own way, he can command half our attention. When he hasn't, then he's lucky if he has one-tenth."

"TREASURE ISLAND has proved to be a most interesting task. First of all, there was the little matter of sea shanties. You have heard how one or two are sung in the film. Then came the great point--should they come into the main musical score? In my younger days, I learned quite a lot of them direct from the first mate of one of the old China Tea Clippers. When it came to the final scoring, it was found impossible to use them because they were too recognisably tuneful. They broke through the action and would have claimed too much of the audience's attention."

However, there is one scene in which the composer was able to include a sea shanty. It comes in the scene where young Jim Hawkins arrives in Bristol for the first time. Everything is new to him: he sees the busy port, the sea, the ships--and then he sees his first sailor walking down the street with a nautical roll, whistling, "Johnny, Come Down to Hilo." Jim promptly imitates the sailor's walk and the music follows him closely as an orchestral echo of the sailor's whistle.

There are many interesting musical moments--for example, a wonderful montage in which the Hispaniola sets to sea on the great voyage of adventure, or a furious scene on the beach when the pirates are grovelling in the sand, hunting for the treasure. But perhaps a description of the music for the opening scenes will in itself sum up the detailed approach that the music writer must adopt on a film of this type. The first shots show a deserted cove, silent and still except for the sound of the sea. The music establishes the mood, carrying the sound of the wind as it appears, and the music makes a transition to a recitative treatment. We see the Smuggler's Inn; Old Captain Bones makes an appearance; there is mystery and drama in the air--but few people will notice the extent to which the mood of the scene has been discreetly launched, not only in the shots themselves, but also in Clifton Parker's music.

WHAT'S THE MATTER WITH HELEN?

Page Cook

David Raksin's score for the latest Henry Farrell "horror" concoction, WHAT'S THE MATTER WITH HELEN?, is rather intriguing music. For one thing, it's the year's most innovative score (timbre sensitivities within its orchestration are brilliantly conceived). So I decided to ask Raksin about the creation of it. To my surprise he at first seemed reluctant to discuss his score for WHAT'S THE MATTER WITH HELEN? Said he: "One works like a demon over some infinitesimal point in the score of a film, with the intention of seeing to it that the music performs its function with some degree of subtlety. Since subtlety is often enhanced by inaudibility, composers get a lot of help in the dubbing room. In any case, moments go by like prairie towns from an Amtrak window: wink, and you've missed them. Not much can be said in words in an instant, and I'm nagged by the suspicion that words about music should be limited in duration to that of the musical event they seek to 'explain'." But I knew that, with a little persistence, I could provoke Raksin into less evasive comments.

HELEN begins with a prologue in the form of a Hearst Movietone newsreel. It informs us of a sensational murder committed by the teenaged sons of Helen Hill and Adele Bruckner. We see the two women leave the trial; pass through a crowd of inquisitive on-lookers, reporters, and "well-wishers." Then, as they get into a car, there's a freeze-frame on their bewildered, grieving faces, and, over this frame, the credits begin to appear. At that moment Raksin jolts our eardrums with a powerful percussive ostinato that rises--duple rhythmic pattern--into desolate fury. As it abates Raksin superimposes a poignant theme which is full of foreboding. Then, and suddenly, this dazzling ostinato, and its ominous but also compassionate thematic overlay, are replaced by a honky-tonk rendition of the song, "Goody, Goody!" This fades out quickly and Raksin returns once again to the paroxysms of the ostinato for the finish of the credits.

The first time I saw HELEN the "Goody, Goody!" interpolation seemed to vitiate the powerfully rhythmic ostinato but the second and third time I saw it, and listened carefully to Raksin's score, the honky-tonkery seemed dramatically effective (knowing the plot, I understood Raksin's reason for interpolating "Goody, Goody!"). Says Raksin: "I really didn't know what to do with such a Main Title, appearing as, and where, it does in the film, and with the primary requirement of the music being that it mustn't let the audience down dramatically--plus my own feeling that this must be accomplished without resort to musical melodrama. I was more than halfway through the score before the idea came to me of how to compose for the titles. The kind of idea I had been looking for isn't something you can hurry. The rhythmic ostinato--it was the first idea for the scoring of the Main Title that came to me (as I was driving down the freeway)--takes care of the basic dramatic requirement of the title music, everything considered. Starting the rhythmic pattern off with percussion was a quick afterthought when, later, I discovered that in order to begin the theme, over the pattern and in sync with the appearance of the first title card, I needed those beats in order to extend the pattern so theme and title would coincide. The pattern, which, with different notes and chords, could show the brighter aspects of its jazz origins, is indeed relentless, partly because of its pace (one quarter note covers 12 frames), but more because of the notes chosen, and because of their relations to the shifting harmony and to the open beats and percussive beats that make the pattern a duple rhythm. Then, over this pattern, with its tragic and propulsive drive, there appears a theme which I described to a local critic as "a loser's tune." Seeing the film and hearing the music the first time around, you are conscious mostly of the energy of the music. The second time, knowing the story, the appropriateness of this "loser's tune" reaches you. Introducing at an early stage ideas and feelings that belong later in the drama is risky, but it's quite legitimate to introduce thematic or other material that will later develop and metamorphose with the story. Not only is this dramatically and musically sound practice, if you can do it, but if properly handled it can help to unify the film. For musical forms per se have integrative power, and music, of course, has the ability to evoke memory.

"As for the interpolation of 'Goody, Goody', it is meant to be a kind of shocker, a seeming irrelevancy, and therefore challenging--a glimpse of a brief and inexplicable tableau in a madhouse you may never know more about. The exploration of the existential nature of this I will leave to whoever has nothing better to do with his time."

The next music of real potency in WHAT'S THE MATTER WITH HELEN?, after this opening credits music, is the soft murmuring of reeds for the vicious telephone calls to Adele. Raksin's scoring of the main theme, when Adele finally tells Linc about her troubled past, is melodious and delicately balanced between sadness and optimism (a typical Raksinism). But Raksin doesn't initially even hint at Helen's nature and I asked Raksin whether or not he thought Helen had a case. His reply: "Helen was a case. After the alleged 'accident' there is a deliberate quiescence, which is not only quite natural but also necessary if 'the matter with Helen' is to remain any kind of mystery beyond reel 3. It was the job of the actress, composer and director to see to it that no note of psychosis crept into that part of the film, which would not only have been phony but would have diminished the surprise introduced by the sudden appearance of Hamilton Starr (by seeming to 'prepare' his entrance)."

The relationship between composer and director is obvious but the one that exists between the composer and actor is not so distant as many think. Actors often resent composers squelching their thespic subtleties and composers are often bored by acting ham. When I asked Raksin about this, he replied: "My purpose is anything but interfering with physical visualization. There's never been a film composer who hasn't incurred the wrath of actors, for the mental processes in which most actors indulge can't be called thinking. One well-known actor even remarked that music was necessary only if the actors did not fulfill their roles. Upon hearing that I told my USC students that if the employment of composers depended on actors not fulfilling their roles all us film hacks would be working 150 per cent of the time."

When Helen first describes the accident in which her husband was killed, Raksin mixes a whirring sound in with his underscoring. During the flashback of the accident itself, and later, when Helen goes berserk backstage during the Kiddystar Revue (with the on-screen orchestra playing "Yankee Doodle Dandy"), the combination of this whirring sound and Raksin's music is audibly very vivid. "The sounds you refer to," Raksin replied when I asked him about this, "were the response of a very good and imaginative sound-effects cutter to the necessity of coming up with a noise to go with the scene in which Helen recounts her story of her husband's death. What she refers to as a plow is actually a disc-harrow, and the cutter had to 'imagine-up' the sound. We all agreed that the sound should ride in the upper register, and that the music should stay out of that part of the spectrum. In some of the scenes--the backstage hallucinations, the death of the intruder--there are quite a few tracks: the effects track (including the disc-harrow); the principal music underscoring tracks; <u>and</u> bits of overlay tracks originally made as improvisations on a good-sized church organ (by me, after the recording of our hymns with 'Sister Alma'). All of which were put through a Buchla synthesizer."

The most gorgeous passage of Raksin's score for WHAT'S THE MATTER WITH HELEN? occurs after Helen has murdered the intruder and she and Adele dispose of the corpse. As the women drag the body in the downpour, the turbulence and pathos of Raksin's lengthy disposition of the thematic material first heard in the titles intensifies the terrifying scene. Not only because Raksin distorts enharmonically, but also because he uses consonant double-reeds, adding a disturbing quietude (which Raksin says is "the characteristic, if anything is, of the score").

One of Raksin's most alluring on-screen tid-bits is his music for the tango Adele does at the riverboat casino. It's an agile intimation of the period's now-obsolete gaiety. He calls it "El Mantenido" and slyly adds: "My purpose here was to interfere with the vissical physualization."

Raksin's lack of compassion for Adele and his sympathy for Helen are necessarily absent from his scoring of the final sequence, in which Helen murders Adele (Helen plays "Goody, Goody" after Adele's corpse is tied up in a mock-dancing position). There's silence during the ensuing roll-up of the cast credits. When I suggested to Raksin that this would have been the perfect place for a postlude of harrowing empathy he answered: "The question of eliciting sympathy for dead Adele is a core issue and refers to the criticism leveled at film music by actors and plenty of others as well. Just as it is pointless to extend sympathy to deaf ears (such as those of the dead), it is pointless to try to evoke sympathy unless that is the purpose of the picture .... It is not the job of the music to give away the story. Therefore, when Helen tells Adele they will be friends again, the music is with Adele, who has to be saying to herself, 'Oh God, no...!' and dying a little. Even when Helen kills Adele, a pretty horrible scene, the music speaks to the tragedy rather than to the horror-film aspect, which would have called for a different kind of dissonance.

"With regard to the use of 'Goody, Goody!' at the very end, played on that rehearsal piano by Helen (actually by Pearl Kaufman, who did the piano recordings for FIVE EASY PIECES), there was no question in our minds about that being the way to end the picture, abrupt cut-off and all, and no music for end cast-titles. As I said, sympathy in such a situation is not only superfluous, it is impossible. To have mourned the dead, or even the bereaved, at that point, would have been to swallow the delusion that sympathy could have made any difference at all. It is, in my mind, questionable enough to 'legitimately' manipulate the multiple arts that comprise the film medium without having the gall to butt in when it is better to leave things unsaid. Adele, with her talent for survival, is dead; Helen, formerly a postulant zombie, is now a pro. This is one of those places in films that music, unless extremely harsh, tends to mitigate, which would not have been the right thing to do.

"Actually, I intended the piano tracks to get far more grotesque at the end. What you hear, at first, is 'Goody, Goody!' played in a very square way, from a dreadful piano arrangement I made (it was played on the beat-up old upright they have on Goldwyn's recording stage). After Helen's brief speech, two more tracks are added. The first is a duplicate of the original track of 'Goody, Goody!' except that it is heard about 4-1/2 frames later at a slightly lower volume, and produces a halting, stammering effect. The second is rather more complex. The piano arrangement was copied backwards and the pianist learned to play it that way, between specific points in the piece, and it was recorded to the same click-track I used for the version recorded in the usual direction. When turned around and played backwards this track sounded out the melody in the correct direction but the impacts were all on the ends of the notes and chords instead of on the beginning, where they usually are. It is an unpleasant sound, a little too much like a concertina with asthma, wheezy. But when played in sync with the original track, into a common reverberation chamber, it produces a remarkable effect. We put together such a track, then added the 4-1/2 frame retarded version, adjusting relative volumes as we experimented. Then I took the resulting tracks out to run through the Buchla synthesizer and we came up with some of the most harrowing (no pun) conceptions of that poor song. The idea was to shift away from the relatively intelligible tracks as we got closer to the end, to edge closer and closer to intolerable levels of volume and distortion. But when the guiding spirits heard what had been wrought on their behalf they liked it not: too extreme, they said. At the time, I thought maybe so. Now, I think not. At the very least we could have won the 5000-meter flesh-crawl, but in order to have understood that we would have had to go all the way. What was achieved was a kind of 'ideal' compromise, in the sense that it defers to the irrelevant rituals of good taste, and therefore neither offends nor satisfies."

One of Raksin's colleagues was recently moved to say: "It's difficult to dislike David, try hard as I may, and implausible as well. His music is like a very fine vintage wine, delicate, subtle--so subtle that the excellence is not often immediately enjoyed by the uninitiated palate. Time is required, familiarity, a return and yet another. More like Racine than Shakespeare. Also, were David not the decent chap he is I'd feel a good deal better, and less odious, in my natural envy of a composer whose tentacular skills equal his unabashed genius. I don't want to be so indelicate as to suggest that the principal fascination of David is his staying power, because he really is an astonishing 'unique'." Raksin's score for WHAT'S THE MATTER WITH HELEN? is genuinely unique and is not going to make the above-quoted colleague feel any better.

THE WILD ONE

Leith Stevens

Stanley Kramer's production of THE WILD ONE, starring Marlon Brando, is a most unusual picture, and one of the outstanding qualities of the film is the high degree of integration of music with story telling and mood progression.

Music could not have been such a definite factor in this film had Mr. Kramer and Lazlo Benedek, the director, followed the usual practice of leaving any consideration of music until after photography is completed. Instead, they brought the composer in for consultation while the shooting script was still in prepartion. Starting at this early point in the development of the film made it possible to plan music as a definite factor in the dramatic impact and progression of the play. For example, scenes were included where the story could be told without dialogue, the dramatic progression being carried forward by action and music alone. Also, there were scenes included where dialogue was not intended to be heard, where an effect important to the story was obtained by a melange of sound--half heard dialogue, music, sound effects, etc. This latter would be impossible unless planned in advance, as most certainly some important plot point would be lost if the dialogue were not written with this effect in mind.

In the beginning there were two possible ways to develop THE WILD ONE with regard to use of music. As the film has a rather strong documentary quality, it could have been done without music, with the exception perhaps of main and end titles. However, the story concerns a few hours in the lives of a group of motorcyclists and the unrelieved sound of these machines could be very tiring for an audience. Further, music could be used in building tensions and assisting in providing certain sudden contrasts necessary to the proper telling of the story, and so it was decided to use a score.

The characters of the play are young people, full of tensions, for the most part inarticulate about their problems, and, though exhibitionistic, still confused and wandering.

These characteristics suggested the use of progressive jazz or bop (call it what you will) as an important segment of the score. This music, with its complicated, nervous searching quality, seemed best suited to complement these characters. This is the first score, to the writer's knowledge, to use contemporary jazz in actual scoring of scenes.

A considerable part of the action takes place in a small town cafe-bar complete with juke-box. The tempo is a slow four (about 60 metronome) and although the style of playing is somewhat reminiscent of the blues idiom, the melodic line and harmonic structure are not typically blues. The searching restless quality of the melody is further emphasized by the introduction of double time rhythm in the seventh, eighth, and ninth bars. After the downbeat of bar 10 the rhythm returns to four and this alternating between slow and fast is continued throughout the piece. The instrumentation is open trumpet solo, with tenor and baritone saxes, trombone and rhythm accompaniment. This theme appears at several points in the score in different forms.

The notable point here is that I used the same theme later in three-four and it still has a very definite jazz quality. This is caused partly by the instrumentation (alto sax solo, with two tenor saxes, baritone sax, trombone and rhythm) and partly by the rhythm section, which although playing basically in the slow three, plays a very light afterbeat for each quarter, thereby giving almost a feeling of six to the bar.

Another treatment of this theme occurs in a quiet scene in a park, where Kathy tries to tell Johnny something of her dreams and hopes. At this point the instrumentation is strings with woodwinds and horns and there is no feeling of jazz as in the other two examples. The theme is used again, as an agitato, in the sequence following the park scene. Here dark colors and tension predominate. English horn, vibraphone and harp play the melodic line and the violas and cellos have the nervous figuration, in octaves punctuated by muted horns and basses.

Many other examples of the converting of contemporary jazz themes to different forms could be mentioned. However, the principle would remain the same. This conversion of themes from one idiom to another serves to give a unity to the score which could not be obtained otherwise. The first exposure, played on a juke-box, calls attention to the material and its significance is strengthened by appearance in other guises in other parts of the score. THE WILD ONE could have been scored in a conventional manner, but no matter how adroitly this might have been done, the impact of the film would have been lessened.

Chapter V

THE FILM SPECTACLE

CHRISTOPHER COLUMBUS

Sir Arthur Bliss

The whole of the first half of the picture, CHRISTOPHER COLUMBUS, is laid in Spain, mostly at the Spanish Court and shows Columbus' frustration at the delay and lack of interest in his first adventure. It is difficult with American and English actors to suggest the atmosphere of Spain--that is what the music has to do--so I have tried using Spanish idioms and tunes akin to those of Spain which convey the feeling and atmosphere of the age in which Columbus set forth from Spain.

The first two climaxes in the film for music are naturally the first sight of the New World and later, the return of Columbus with the triumphant news in Spain. In the voyage across I tried to convey the long suspense as confidence gives way to dejection leading to mutiny aboard. After many trials, land is finally sighted and apprehension gives way to thanks-giving as the new world is reached. The voyage back rises rapidly to a crescendo of excitement as Columbus' ship, the Niña, approaches Spain. A small boy sights it from the cliff tops and rushes into the town spreading the news, "Columbus is back!" The music re-echoes his cries. The townspeople gather at the harbor; the excitement grows intense. The Niña sails into the harbor--and now the scene changes to the Court of Ferdinand and Isabella. The Court trumpeters blow a fanfare and, to a triumphant march, Columbus makes his entry into the grand hall and up to the thrones of the King and Queen of Spain. Musically I found the picture extremely interesting.

CINERAMA HOLIDAY

Jack Shaindlin

When Louis de Rochemont asked me to handle the music for his production of CINERAMA HOLIDAY, I knew that this assignment would turn out to be the most enjoyable one in my 15 years of scoring music for the films. This wasn't "just another job," but an opportunity to explore the possibilities of the finest recording system yet devised. One seldom gets a chance to work with a seven-speaker high-fidelity sound miracle with a range of 15,000 cycles, twice that of the ordinary sound system, and complete control of sound direction.

It was my good fortune to secure the services of Morton Gould to compose the music. Having worked on movie scores with many composers, I was amazed at Gould's technique and facility. Two or three drafts of a single sequence were written in a matter of hours with a minimum of effort and temperament. I was also very fortunate in getting Van Cleave on a loan-out from Paramount Pictures. This brilliant orchestrator was responsible for composing some of the music used in the "Jet Planes" sequence.

CINERAMA HOLIDAY is the story of two couples--their travels and their thrills--as seen through the eyes of the latest cinematic miracle, the Cinerama camera. The Swiss couple visit the United States and discover a new world. At New Orleans, the cradle of jazz, they hear "Down by the Riverside" sung by the congregation of a Baptist church, watch and listen in amazement as the Tuxedo Marching Band plays "When the Saints Come Marching In," and enjoy the improvisations of "Papa" Celestin's Original Tuxedo Dixieland Jazz Band playing "Tiger Rag."

The San Francisco waterfront cafe, the Tin Angel, contributes a duet singing a sea chanty dating from the Gold Rush days--and in another section of the town a group of Chinese musicians play the old love song, "The Luminous Pearl and Magnolia."

Their visit to New Hampshire produces the splendid Dartmouth College Glee Club singing "Men of Dartmouth" and the most glorious autumnal scenes ever filmed are projected to the accompaniment of "Come to the Fair" sung by the University of New Hampshire Glee Club. The Jet Plane Finale culminates in a stirring rendition of "Hail to Our Land" sung by the U.S. Naval Academy Choir. This song was written by me in collaboration with James Peterson, a well known New York choral director.

Meanwhile, the other couple, Americans from Kansas City, embark upon a journey taking them to Paris and Switzerland. The Boy's Choir of the Notre Dame Cathedral in Paris is heard in a Couperin Mass. The famous military band, Garde Republicaine, plays the stirring "Sambre et Meuse" and Jean Phillipe Rameau's 18th-century opera-ballet "Les Indes Galantes" is performed at the plush Opera House. Their adventures in Switzerland end in a visit to Le Ferme in Davos where they join a group of skiers at a cheese fondue party. Here, a couple of yodelers render an old Swiss song, "Hup-sa-sa," with the entire group joining in the chorus.

All the above mentioned musical sequences were filmed with synchronous sound at the place of action. All other sequences were underscored with background music. They included: Plane Ride over the Alps, Swiss Scenic, Simple Skiing, The Ski Waltz, Southland, Vista Dome, Arizona, Paris Valse, The Louvre, Paris Promenade, Joan of Arc, Children's Thursday and Jet Plane Finale. Most of the background music is gay and rhythmic, depicting a holiday not only on the screen but on the sound track as well.

MUSIC FOR HISTORICAL FILMS

Miklos Rozsa

A composer's life in Hollywood often runs in odd cycles. Twelve years ago, before I came to Hollywood, I wrote the music for FOUR FEATHERS, a picture which took place in the Sudan. Immediately other pictures with oriental backgrounds followed, such as THE THIEF OF BAGDAD, JUNGLE BOOK, SUNDOWN, FIVE GRAVES TO CAIRO,

BLOOD ON THE SUN, etc. For years I couldn't write a scale without augmented seconds. Then I wrote SPELLBOUND. An array of psychological subjects followed and my theremin wailed and vibrated subsequently in THE LOST WEEKEND, THE RED HOUSE, SECRET BEYOND THE DOOR and DARK WATERS, to mention only a few. THE KILLERS, a gangster melodrama, was a new departure for a hard-hitting, caustic and somewhat brutal score and BRUTE FORCE, NAKED CITY, CRISS CROSS, DESERT FURY, KISS THE BLOOD OFF MY HANDS came immediately after. Then came QUO VADIS which started a new trend in my life: music to historical films. QUO VADIS, which is set in the 1st century, IVANHOE, which followed, in the 12th century, PLYMOUTH ADVENTURE in the 17th century, JULIUS CAESAR in the 1st century B.C., and KNIGHTS OF THE ROUND TABLE, plays in the 5th century A.D.

In IVANHOE I became my own first disciple (I suppose also the only one!) and followed the example which I set in QUO VADIS. As I tried to recreate the music of the 1st century by using, after thorough research, musical fragments from the period, I have done the same in IVANHOE, by going back to sources of the 12th century. I wanted to create again a score, which sounds and is stylistically authentic. I found a somewhat similar situation in musical matters between 12th-century England and 1st-century Rome. As Roman music was largely influenced by the Greek, so came the music of the Saxons under the influence of the invading Normans. It is a well-known fact that people on a lower level of civilization readily absorb the culture of the invaders or neighboring countries which have a higher civilization, as a subconscious expression of their longing for the higher level of life, which usually goes with higher civilization. The sources of Saxon music are extremely few and far between, but there is a large amount of music from the 12th century available, of the French troubadours and trouveres, who brought their music with the invading Normans to England. The various themes of IVANHOE are partly based on original sources and are partly my own.

Under the opening narration I introduced a theme from a Ballade by Richard the Lionhearted (1157-1199) which recurs later when we come to Sir Cedric's home. The "Norman" theme I developed from a Latin hymn (Reis Glorios) by the troubadour Guiraut de Bornrth (died ca. 1220). This appears the first time with the approaching Normans in Sherwood Forest. Later, during the course of the photoplay, it undergoes various contrapuntal treatments.

The Love Theme of Lady Rowena and Ivanhoe is a free adaptation of an old popular song from the north of France. The manuscript of this melody was found in a collection of songs in the Royal Library of Brussels. The dialect of the text and the orthography are that of the late 12th or early 13th century. It is a lovely melody, breathing the innocently amorous atmosphere of the Middle Ages. I gave it a modal harmonization.

Rebecca, the daughter of Isaac of York, needed a Jewish theme, mirroring not only the tragedy of this lovely character of Sir Walter Scott's, but also that of her persecuted people. Fragments of medieval Jewish motives suggested a theme. At the final scene the main theme returns and the picture ends with the recapitulation of the heroic IVANHOE theme.

PLYMOUTH ADVENTURE is the story of the Mayflower's journey from Plymouth harbor to Plymouth Rock in the year 1620. To be true to my own theories about the scoring of historical pictures, I was looking for a musical theme from the period, which the Pilgrim fathers might have known and which also possessed their indomitable spirit of religious, personal and political freedom. The Pilgrims had one book with music on board: Henry Ainsworth' Psalter, which was printed in Amsterdam in 1612. This book contained the melodies the Pilgrims brought with them to America and sang in their new country. I used as the theme of the Mayflower, the 136th Psalm, a melody which is imbued with vigor and fervent faith. It has a very interesting history. One can trace it back to French Psalters of the early 16th century, and fragments of it (according to Waldo Seldon Pratt's book _Music of the Pilgrims_) can be found in early German chorales. It has been called the "Huguenot Marseillaise," as it has the pulsation of a battle song. It has an unusual rhythm and I found its text most appropriate and, therefore, used it vocally with an orchestral accompaniment for the opening of the picture.

The theme attains its culmination in a sequence of the departure of the Mayflower when the sails of the ship fill with wind to start a voyage into the unknown and the theme appears majestically in the orchestra as a musical confirmation of the faith of the Pilgrims. To give an atmosphere of authenticity I tried to build my other themes in the manner of the 17th-century English lutenist composer whose music the Pilgrim fathers knew and must have brought to our shores. I didn't use any original material, as these themes had to fit closely the situations and personages of our narrative. An innocent and sad theme for little William Button, who dies before the landing of the Mayflower; a theme with a hint of the future, for the first settlers; the picture ends with the departure of the Mayflower and Captain Jones for England. The music swells up and triumphantly reiterates the glorious Psalm tune.

MUSIC FOR SHAKESPEAREAN FILMS

Sir William Walton

HAMLET is my third Shakespearean film. The first was in 1936, for the 20th century-Fox production of AS YOU LIKE IT. Then in 1944, Sir Laurence Olivier approached me to do the score for his Technicolor production of HENRY V. And now, finally, HAMLET. Writing music for the screen is undoubtedly a specialized job. To begin with, the composer is rigidly disciplined in his work by the time factor. For example, in HAMLET (as in all other films) my first contact with the production was the arrival of the script. This meant that I could obtain at least some idea of the treatment envisaged by the producer-director, in translating this monumental work into celluloid. An occasional visit to the film set also gave me some impressions of how the project was coming along.

The real work, however, begins when the picture is complete--complete, that is, in what is called the rough cut. It is only at this stage that the full atmosphere and dramatic impact of the screen play can be seen. However much a composer may examine the scenario, he can never grasp all those little individual touches which a director adds while he is shooting the picture. Then, again, there is this time business. After I have seen the film with the director and music director, the editor passes me a typewritten sheet giving the exact timings of each section of the film to which music will be fitted. For example, a sequence may call for 1 minute 23 seconds of music; 1 minute 24 seconds is too long, and 1 minute 22 seconds is too short. This means that a composer must, right from the start, adjust his approach to the composition. In writing for the concert hall, he can work out his ideas to suit himself. His symphony may run for 20, 30, or 50 minutes. Not so in films. The form and content of the music is governed absolutely by the exacting requirements of the pictures on the screen.

There seems to be an idea among film people that a composer can turn out pages and pages of fully orchestrated manuscript just on the spur of the moment. The sort of things that happen is that the unfortunate writer comes to the studio, is shown the film, finds that there is a total of 50 minutes of music required, and some bright spark in the music office says, "That's lovely. We can book the orchestra in two weeks' time, and get the whole thing in the bag." Frankly, two weeks is no earthly use for 50 minutes' music, as anyone who has attempted full scale composition will know. I think that composers as a whole should decry this bad aspect of film-making and see if some arrangement cannot be made whereby the composer is guaranteed a certain reasonable time in which to deliver his score, and I myself always insist on this.

In the case of HAMLET, I received every consideration from Laurence Olivier, and the film unit, in that the music recording dates were spread over a month, thus giving ample time to consider the results of each of the recording days' work, and allowing time for discussion before proceeding to the next music section. The closest collaboration was maintained between Olivier and myself, and some of my musical ideas were evolved from suggestions from him.

The value to a film of its musical score rests chiefly in the creation of mood, atmosphere, and the sense of period. When the enormous task of re-imagining a Shakespearean drama in terms of the screen has been achieved, these three qualities, which must be common to all film music, appear in high relief. In the case of "mood" I would quote as an example the incidental musical effects in Hamlet's soliloquies which varied their orchestral color according to the shifts of his thought. For "atmosphere" take the music of rejoicing after the victory of Agincourt in HENRY V, which also illustrates the power to evoke a sense of historical period in a special way, for the contemporary Agincourt hymn which has been handed down to us was adapted to my purpose. Indeed the atmosphere of human feeling and the evocation of a past time are often combined, or made to blend from one to the other without any abruptness of transition. At the entry of the players in HAMLET, I took the chance to suggest the musical idiom of the time by using a small sub-section of the orchestra (two violas, cello, oboe, cor anglais, bassoon, harpsichord), then proceeded to make my comment on the action in my own personal idiom.

In a film the visual effect is of course predominant, and the music subserves the visual sequences, providing a subtle form of punctuation--lines can seem to have been given the emphasis of italics, exclamation marks added to details of stage business, phases of the action broken into paragraphs, and the turning of the page at a crossfade or cut can be helped by music's power to summarize the immediate past or heighten expectation of what is to come. The analogy with printer's typography is useful, but beyond this, music offers orchestral "color" to the mind's ear in such a way that at every stage it confirms and reinforces the color on the screen which is engaging the eye.

The composer in the cinema is the servant of the eye. In the opera house he is, of course, the dominating partner. There everyone, beginning with the librettist, must serve him and the needs of the ear. In the film world, however, from the first "rough-cut" where the composer first sees the visual images that his work must reinforce, an opera composer finds his controlling position usurped. He works in the service of a director. Since proportion is as important in music as in any other of the arts, the film composer, no longer his own master, is to a great extent at the mercy of his director. A close and delicate collaboration is essential for the film must be served but music must not be asked to do what it should not or cannot. After a while the composer acquires what has been called "the stop-watch mentality," a quality which I have heard deplored, but I am quite certain the habit, a peculiarly strict form of self-discipline, does a composer far more good than harm when he is working on his own for his own ends. Within or outside the cinema every second counts.

A film composer must have confidence in his director or collaboration will break down. In my three major Shakespearean films I have been particularly blessed in working with a director who knew precisely what he wanted at any given point not only in quantity but in kind. Sir Laurence Olivier understands the composer's problems. He has a genius for thinking up ways of adding to them or increasing those that already exist, but he never demands the impossible, and his challenges have invariably led me to be grateful in the end. In the deployment of his visual resources he is himself a dramatist and though a composer's task is never anything but difficult, the confidence inspired by such a director has certainly made things far easier than they might have been. If the musical aspect of the battle sequences in HENRY V and RICHARD III, for instance, is considered helpful to the general effect, that is due to an unusually complex and close collaboration of sound and screen from one bar or visual movement to the next, the outcome of much patience and exercise of technique certainly, but above all, I think, the fruit of mutual confidence and esteem.

A NOTE ON HAMLET

Muir Mathieson

We recorded Sir Laurence Olivier's HAMLET with the Philharmonia Orchestra on the Music Theatre Stage at Denham with Sir William Walton (as always) present, checking points with the orchestra, discussing improvements with Sir Laurence and taking a most active part in the music making. A single example taken from the famous player's scene will show the method of approach Walton uses in his music. The arrival of the Court is heralded by trumpet calls. Then come the players, introduced and accompanied during their performance by a small group of musicians seated in an alcove overlooking the dais on which the actors present their play. We hear first the music makers; for this, the composer provided a delightful period work for violins, cello, oboe, cor anglais, bassoon and harpsichord. After a section of this "realistic" music, a full symphony orchestra of some 50 players takes up the theme as the camera moves around to show the reactions of the King. The camera, taking in a full orbit in its movements, re-focuses on the actors and the music reverts to the small group of instrumentalists. The actor-king has been poisoned; the King can stand it no longer. The full power of the big orchestra rises up, underlining the dramatic content of the sequence, swamping the small group, and ending in a tremendous "crash chord" as the King roars, "Give me some light." In this example, the music becomes an integral part of the film. The score goes beyond the realism of the small band shown on the screen and extends into the emotional texture of the sequence showing the Court and its badly shaken sovereign; yet it keeps the line of the actor's music in contrast, by the off-setting of the two orchestral groups--one of seven players and one of about 50.

JULIUS CAESAR

Miklos Rozsa

In my previous articles [see page 125] about the music of QUO VADIS, IVANHOE and PLYMOUTH ADVENTURE, I have expanded my theories about music written for historical films. Shakespeare's JULIUS CAESAR presented new problems. If it had been merely a historical film about Julius Caesar I would have undoubtedly tried a reconstruction or approximation of the Roman music of the 1st century B.C. However, it is more than that. It is a Shakespearean tragedy and, with its language, a true mirror of Elizabethan times, and it is principally this language which dictates its style. In Shakespeare's time, as they had few scruples about stylistic correctness, the music was undoubtedly their own--Elizabethan. Should I have composed it in Roman style, it would have been wrong for Shakespeare--should I have tried to treat it as stage music to an Elizabethan drama in Elizabethan style, it would have been anachronistic from the historical point of view. I decided, therefore, to regard it as a universal drama, about the eternal problems of men and the most timely problems about the fate of dictators. I wrote the same music I would have written for a modern state presentation: interpretative incidental music, expressing with my own musical language, for a modern audience, what Shakespeare expressed with his own language for his own audience 350 years ago. The example set by Mendelssohn with his music to A Midsummer Night's Dream was obvious, as he wrote his own highly romantic music which now everybody accepts as authentic, to this romantic play of Shakespeare.

To emphasize the Shakespearean stage drama I wrote an overture, based on the main themes of the music, to precede the play. It was strong and stark, to set the audience in the mood of the following events. It was later replaced by Tchaikovsky's "Capriccio Italien," which oddly enough, some people found more appropriate to precede JULIUS CAESAR.

The four protagonists of the play are Caesar, Marc Antony, Brutus and Cassius. The first two represent the ruthless, ambition-filled, arrogant Roman imperialists; Brutus, the honest, straightforward man who loves Caesar but loves his country better; and finally, Cassius, with a "lean and hungry look" who is filled with envy and jealousy of Caesar. The three main musical themes are these: (1) The theme of Caesar, which also serves later as the theme of Marc Antony, as the two represent the same basic ideas in the play, for "Antony is but a limb of Caesar." It is a martial theme, stern and "constant as the Northern Star," which appears the first time as Caesar's march as he and his entourage come for the "Course" and is interrupted by the soothsayer's voice, "shriller" than all the music.

(2) The theme of "gentle and most noble Brutus" is brooding, musing and sighing, portraying musically the man who is willing to sacrifice his friend (or was he his father?) who knows "no personal cause to spurn at him, but for the general." The theme appears first under the titles as a canon with motives of the Caesar theme interrupting it. (3) We first hear Cassius' theme under his monologue after Brutus' departure, when he first tells about his intriguing. The music portrays the determined character of this envious intriguer who "reads much; is a great observer, looks quite through the deeds of men; loves no plays and hears no music."

This music leads to the street scene of thunder and lightning and disappears with the opening words of Cicero. Calpurnia's dream (this is only mentioned by Shakespeare but in the film we can also see it) about the murder of Caesar, is accompanied by a dissonant muted brass figure in which high violin harmonies eject the Caesar motif. The nervous music follows the scene until Caesar addresses his own statue: "Nor heaven nor earth have been at peace."

Before I set out to compose the music and before I saw the picture, I thought that no dialogue scene should have any music, as on the stage one uses music only for pre- and postludiums, transitions and entr'actes. The filmed stage-play, however, dictates new aesthetics and dramatic rules. Scenes with strongly dramatic content could be emphasized and brought nearer to our consciousness by the use of appropriate music. As Artemidorus waits for Caesar before the Capitol, reads his letter of warning, Caesar and the senators arrive, and until he enters the Senate house, there is a tremendous tension--as we know that he enters the trap laid for him by the conspirators. The music which accompanies this scene is low; dissonant seventh chords are slowly creeping forward on a basso ostinato of tympani and bass pizzicati.

The whole assassination scene in the Senate and the oration of Brutus and Antony at the Forum are without music. These are not only the strongest scenes in the whole tragedy, but undoubtedly the most famous and greatest writing of the entire dramatic literature. Here every line is precise in meaning and does not need any help from any other medium. Music sets in only as final punctuation, as the citizens of Rome rise in mutiny. At Caesar's funeral we hear the lament of women. It is a dirge in the manner of a Greek "Nenia."

After the so-called pricking scene, when Octavius leaves, Antony remains alone, sitting on Caesar's chair and imagining himself as his successor. The brassy music brings back the ominous Caesar-theme. In Brutus' camp, the meeting of Brutus and Cassius, their quarrel over their grievances, etc., are scenes of matter-of-fact realism and did not need any music. After Cassius and his captains leave, Brutus asks his little servant, Lucius, to sing a song. Shakespeare only indicates "music and a song," and I thought that an Elizabethan song, because of its language, would be the most appropriate. I chose John Dowland's, "Now, O now, I needs must part," which was published in 1597 and might have been known to Shakespeare.

The famous scene in the tent when the ghost of Caesar appears before Brutus to tell him that he will see him again at Philippi, is accompanied by a cold, glassy and shimmering sound and we hear the distorted Caesar motif again. It breaks off as the ghostly image of Caesar disappears. The next music we hear is during the battle of Philippi. It starts with the frantic bugles of Brutus' array as it is attacked by Antony's legions. It is rather an impression of the battle instead of a detailed and long debacle and on the victorious close-up of Antony, we hear the victorious Caesar-

Antony theme.

The last music starts after Cassius dies and continues from here to the end of the picture. The themes of Cassius and Brutus appear again in a subdued, low and depressed manner. Brutus appeals to his friends for death and they refuse him. He asks his servant to hold his sword while he runs on it. He dies with the words on his lips: "Caesar, now be still; I kill'd not thee with half so good a will."

Throughout these scenes I wanted to give the impression that the victorious armies of Antony and Octavius are continuously advancing and coming nearer and nearer. This scene, however, is the culmination of the tragedy, when its noblest character, Brutus, like a Greek hero in a Greek drama, faces his inescapable fate. I wrote, therefore, two entirely different scores, contrapuntally worked out, but in content completely independent. The one, which represents Antony's nearing army, is a march based on Caesar's theme and is scored for brass, woodwind and percussion instruments. The other, which plays the scene in the foreground and underlines the tragedy of Brutus, is scored for strings only. Thus there is a complete contrast of color between the two, apart from their emotional, rhythmic and thematic differences. The stereophonic technique, with three loudspeakers behind the screen, came to my help. As the direction of the approaching army is from the right corner of the screen, we put the march track on this loud-speaker and the string track on the two others, screen center and left corner. Thus there is complete separation of the two scores, which were recorded separately, and geographically the listener immediately feels that the army is marching from the right corner of the screen.

As Brutus dies the march becomes louder and louder and the servant runs out from the scene it completely overpowers Brutus' string music and dominates the whole screen. This juxtaposition of two different moods is not entirely my innovation, as Bizet already most effectively used it in the third act of <u>Carmen,</u> when Escamilio enters the arena and Carmen remains alone with Don Jose. In the background we hear the gay, bullfighter music which is interrupted by the orchestra with somber comments about the impending drama in the foreground.

Octavius and Antony arrive in the camp where Brutus'

body lies in a tent and we hear from outside the mournful rhythm of the drums. As Antony finishes his final eulogy on Brutus, "his life was gentle, and the elements, so mixed in him that Nature might stand up, and say to all the world 'This was a man'," the sound of the drums grows with the growing flame of the taper, and breaks off as the taper goes out. There is a moment of silence and then the tragic theme of Brutus concludes the picture.

An MGM record album of the somewhat condensed soundtrack was released. With its beauty of language, rhythm of its words and weight of its thoughts, it can be listened to without seeing the action just as much as one listens to a recording of an orchestra without seeing the performers.

RAINTREE COUNTY

John Green

The composition of the dramatic music score for any "epic" motion picture presents many rough and special problems. Not the least of these is sheer length. A motion picture that is to run in excess of three hours will, the chances are, require a dramatic score of approximately 90 minutes. Some such films will, of course, call for less music; and there will be those, like RAINTREE COUNTY, that demand more. So many notes constitute, to say the least, a large composition chore, even without the stop watch. In the confines of a celluloid strait jacket the task is truly mountainous. Somehow, even with the best advance planning, schedules never seem to come off quite as promised, and inevitably there is that awful pressure on the composer to produce, in a given time unit, what should take, say, twice as much time for a composer blessed with even the greatest facility. RAINTREE COUNTY was no exception; towards the end of the composition period the boom fell and the panic was on. We'll come back to this later.

The novel by Ross Lockridge, Jr., from which the screen play was taken, was by no means a straight-line story. Though effective and moving, it was diffuse and involved. Its emotional complexities, its criss-crossing tensions and surges, its heterogeneous flashbacks demanded of the reader the greatest possible concentration. One found oneself time and again turning back to refresh memory and re-establish contact. These problems had to be faced by Millard Kaufman in constructing the screen play and by Edward Dmytryk in interpreting the development of the story and the characters on the screen. Despite their great skill, vestiges of the diffuseness and involvement of the original came through on the screen to some extent and presented serious problems to the composer.

My first decision had to do with general approach. The time: mid-19th dentury. The place: a fictional and prosperous county in Indiana just preceding, during, and immediately following the Civil War. The atmosphere: the fantasy of the Legend of the Raintree (symbolizing Man's endless quest for the unattainable) superimposed, in not too clear-cut a fashion, on a most realistic and practical set of situations. What should be the style, what should be the content of the music? Because of the overtones of the struggle between the North and the South, would there be the inevitable juxtaposition of "The Battle Hymn of the Republic" against 'Dixie?" Should, indeed, the score be based on indigenous music of the period? Should the music have the "modern sound" and, if so, to what extent? Should block color or should melody be the predominant characteristic? I even considered the possibility of a totally source music score, meaning that all the music would come from a source within the action, either seen on the screen or implied.

Almost immediately I ruled out source music in favor of a completely theatrical approach. Next, I vowed that there would be no "Battle Hymn-Dixie" goings-on and that the thematic material would be original (to the degree that this is possible) with me. I then determined that the score should be romantic in feeling, that it would be melodic and that it should have what we know as "that modern western sound," not "Wagon Wheels" of course, but rather the pentatonic and, to some degree, polytriadic sound that, under the able aegis of certain composers too well-known to require mention, has become the trade mark of the open spaces in recent serious American music.

Next, came a practical and perplexing problem. Should there be a song? The current vogue in so-called title songs has become a bugaboo to all of us who work in films. That it has been overworked to a fare-thee-well there is no doubt. That a small hit title song ranks high among the top exploitation and promotion media that a movie can have is also an established fact. That RAINTREE COUNTY represented a cost of over five and a half million dollars was already common knowledge when I approached the job. Could I, in good composer's conscience, accede to the pressure for a title song? I decided that I could. Hence, "The Song of Raintree County" with lyrics by Paul Francis Webster.

My attempt was to write a melody, with a certain folk feeling, which would serve well as the thematic representation of Raintree County itself, of a locale and its people, have popular appeal as a song and yet dovetail with the color and style of the total score. Webster's problem lyrically was to use the words RAINTREE COUNTY within the title, to create a lyric that would be comprehensible in today's incomprehensible popular song market, to maintain some definite relationship between the words of the song and at least the feeling, if not the story of the picture, to be commercial and yet be literate enough to "belong" in the company of the rest of the elements of the film. Space does not permit a reprint of Webster's entire lyric which fulfills all of the many requirements impressively. However, the essence of it, and indeed the picture, is epitomized in his closing four lines:

For the brave who dare
There's a Raintree everywhere ...
We who dreamed found it so
Long ago.

The developmental treatment of "The Song of Raintree County" is free. Though it occurs often in virtually its basic song form, it frequently appears in other guises. For instance, early in the picture, when Johnny (Montgomery Clift) goes on his futile quest for the Raintree through the big swamp, the melody appears as part of a two-part invention. There is a great deal of linear writing in the score; the fugato treatment of Susanna's (Elizabeth Taylor) Mad Theme occurs somewhat later.

Now, what to do about the diffuseness, the multiple lines, the criss-crossing emotional conflicts? Decision: straightforward leitmotif. A theme or motif for every important character (or combination of characters), locale, emotional element. Result: 13 thematic entities with specific story identifiability (there are additional transitional and independent motifs, of course). Thus I hoped to provide certain clarifying "islands" or "audio-reminders" that would help the audience, if only subconsciously, to orient individual events and character relationships to the whole.

Another "perplexer" to be resolved before actual writing could begin: how would "The Song of Raintree County" be presented? The exploitational and promotional ramifications had to be considered, while still maintaining proper loyalty to the artistic integrities of the film. A hit commercial phonograph record is the sine qua non of important "exposure" for the title of the picture, via a song. Result: vocal presentation in the Main Title by our fine studio chorus or a non-name soloist--OUT. Engage a top name vocalist and make a tie-in deal with his phonograph record company. Result: Nat King Cole and Capitol Records. The original plan was to have Cole sing at both the beginning and the end of the film. When we put it all together, however, we found that the introduction of Cole's solo voice into the final scene of the picture did violate dramatic integrity. Therefore, the reprise of the song at the "finale" is presented by the chorus.

On scene, the "perfesser" refers to the "Golden Raintree," the enormous tree from the Orient, planted by legendary Johnny Appleseed. Its petals of gold, glistening in the sunlight, shower down upon the earth. An orchestral gimmick or shimmer of some kind for the Golden Raintree would be in order. Result: what appears on a percussion line in the orchestral scores as the "Raintree Jimjik." This is the curious sound of descending or cascading and not-quite bells heard throughout the score in one particular bar in "The Song of Raintree County." I hoped that the sound would be intriguing and might evoke questions as to how it was made. Many have asked and here is the answer. A good toy glockenspiel (the kind with the brass tubes rather than the flat rectangular bars), scraped from top to bottom by two pairs of brushes (one pair following the other--two percussionists, of course) produced the effect. On the recording stage, to the naked ear, it was virtually inaudible. It achieves the characteristic heard on the soundtrack via multiple magnification and maximum reverberation (echo chamber). The word, Jimjik, the equivalent of "thing-a-ma-bob," was merely an identifying handle for the effect. The exact method of producing it, known to me when I first conceived and indicated it on paper, was later worked out by trial and error on the recording stage.

The Raintree Jimjik, wherever it occurs, was recorded with earphones against the previously recorded orchestral track. It was, therefore, on a separate film strip (or channel) and could be handled completely independently in re-recording (dubbing). Were this score ever to find its way to the concert stage, it would be necessary to have the Jimjik on a phonograph disc or tape in the manner of the birdcalls in "The Pines of Rome" (with apologies to Respighi).

There was the question of the principal orchestral voice or color of "The Song of Raintree County." My selection of the harmonica was arbitrary and subjective. I did no research in an effort to determine that the harmonica was a popular instrument in Indiana in 1860. It merely felt right to me as the musical voice of Raintree County. The superb playing heard on the Raintree tracks is by George Fields. The harmonica was recorded simultaneously with the rest of the orchestra. However, it was not only on a separate microphone, but also on a separate film strip (channel). Such "separation" from the rest of the orchestra was achieved by the physical placement of the harmonica on the recording stage and by the dynamics within the orchestra itself. The very rhythmic subject allocated to the character of Flash Perkins (Lee Marvin), Raintree County's "rough diamond," speaks principally through the voice of the banjo. Again the choice was the result purely of what I heard in my mind's ear as I studied Flash's character on the screen. At our recording sessions the banjo was placed in the woodwind section (because its line was frequently doubled with two low clarinets in unison) and physical proximity was prerequisite for neat rhythmic ensemble. However, the banjo was <u>closely</u> miked and on a separate film strip. We were lucky with the problem of separation because of the percussive characteristic of the banjo itself and also because of our alert and talented recordist, Fred MacAlpin.

Susanna Drake (Elizabeth Taylor), one of the two leading feminine characters in the story, is a pathetically neurotic figure. She is, so we ultimately learn, actually psychotic, quite paranoid, and is the victim of fear and shame that she is part Negro. She suffers also from the pain of guilt for what she believes to have been her part in the responsibility for the possible murder of her father and the dark-skinned Cuban lady, Henrietta (whom we never meet on the screen, she having died before our story opens). Susanna is neurotically devoted to the memory of Henrietta, by whom she was virtually raised (her own mother having suffered from a progressive mental illness). This emotion gives rise to the Lament for Henrietta (a mutation of the Mad Theme, described presently) which we hear first when Susanna, with her new husband, Johnny, visits her family's burial plot on their once proud plantation.

Susanna's malady advances throughout the course of the action. Among the symptoms of her abnormality is her passion for a large number of boudoir dolls which she takes with her wherever she goes. It was inevitable that there would be a musical identity for Susanna's illness. Again a composer's vow: no vibraphone hazes, no theremin; the onset of dementia to be achieved through some hopefully newer sounds. In discussions of mental aberration there is frequent reference to the victim's constant awareness of some sort of sound which does not actually exist (Robert Schumann's incessant A, for example). Happily having no empirical knowledge of such sounds, I freely devised one for Susanna. "Little bells" are what she hears. The effect was achieved by two pairs of Greek, or finger, cymbals struck simultaneously and very closely miked.

Susanna's Mad Theme is divided into two subjects. The first represents her overall "bad feeling" or dementia. The second is the triplet subject specifically associated with the dolls and particularly with her favorite doll, Jeemie, after whom she names her son. Both subjects are heard for the first time on Susanna and Johnny's wedding night as they travel down the Mississippi on a river boat towards her New Orleans home.

The doll motif, recorded as a separate entity, was composed and orchestrally arranged in such a manner as to be played against the basic Mad Theme during the re-recording or dubbing process. In other words, that which emerges on the soundtrack as a single piece of contrapuntal music, was never played as such on the recording stage. The arithmetical niceties of timing, meter and the like are sufficiently intricate to form the basis for a separate article.

Following an hysterical outburst of self-condemnation in which Susanna begs Johnny to beat her, he suggests that maybe a good start towards lifting the anxieties which plague her would be to get rid of the "damn dolls." Grasping at any straw, Susanna enthusiastically agrees. The two of them sail into an orgy of doll destruction, hurling the "creatures" against the wall. This is accompanied by a variation on the Mad Theme--"in the manner of a sick waltz," according to the direction in the score. The treatment, both rhythmically and harmonically, constitutes something of a departure from the surrounding style. However, it seemed the most effective way in which to speak musically the neurotic delight with which Susanna enters into the futile gesture.

The relationship between Susanna and her husband, Johnny, is most complicated. In fact, it is schizoid. They are either the most ecstatically and idyllically in-love couple imaginable or the most completely frustrated duo in the history of storied romance. I found it impossible to express this relationship musically in terms of one thematic entity treated in two different ways. Therefore, there are two themes for Susanna and Johnny's peculiar alliance; the Happy Love Theme and the Melancholy Love Theme. The first, which is an almost completely diatonic melody, with the simplest of harmony and an orthodox bass line, is in the manner of a love song. Though it was conceived as an instrumental theme and is never sung in the film score, it has been made, apart from the picture, into the published song, "Never Till Now" (lyrics by Paul Francis Webster), of which there are several commercial phonograph recordings. The second or melancholy side of the Susanna-Johnny love is spoken by a more chromatic and harmonically more complicated melody which reaches its climactic statement in a forte full string and horn unison when Susanna's body is found in the Raintree Swamp following her suicide.

There are separate themes for the relationship between Johnny and his school days sweetheart, Nell (Eva Marie Saint), for little Jeemie Shawnessy (son of Susanna and Johnny) and for the Raintree Swamp. There are two additional short motifs which occur and recur with the interplaying anxieties of both Johnny and Susanna, as each realizes that their life together is to be fraught with the inevitable tensions of a union in which one of the partners is mentally unstable and the other is frustrated, fated never to attain fully the goals for which his talents and character had seemingly fitted him. There are two Battle Motifs which underlie the scenes involving Johnny and Flash as soldiers in the Union Army during the Georgia Campaign. All of this thematic material, arranged for piano, is included in a published folio entitled "The Music of Raintree County."

Earlier I referred to the exigencies of schedule and the "lowering of the boom." An orchestrator by profession, I compose my motion picture dramatic music in detailed, seven line orchestral sketches. Why not, then, go the rest of the way and work in full score? Because, regrettably, even before the panic sets in, there just isn't enough time under the scheduling system that still prevails. The small time spread between even the most detailed sketches and full score provides the differential between "making the date" and not making it. There is no orchestration credit on RAINTREE COUNTY because the overwhelmingly major portion of the score was committed to paper in my own fully detailed, seven line sketches. When, however, towards the end of the composition period, my remaining time was suddenly cut in less than half, a group of talented, generous and good friends rallied round to make the impossible recording date possible. After meticulous projection room discussion and sessions at the piano with me, Alexander Courage, Sidney Cutner, Robert Franklyn, Conrad Salinger, and Albert Sendrey each adapted and arranged my detailed thematic material for certain scenes. Sendrey, Franklyn, Albert Woodbury and Arthur Morton all did sections of orchestration.

Any discussion of the music score of RAINTREE COUNTY would be incomplete without enthusiastic thanks to the artist who was at the electronic controls during the rerecording process, William Steinkamp. It is his masterful combining of all the sound elements of the picture that brings the music in its completed state to the soundtrack.

How much producer-director help or supervision (what we musicians are occasionally too inclined to call "interference") is a composer apt to get in creating a score of the proportions of the work we are discussing here? RAINTREE COUNTY, it is pretty generally known, was created in a somewhat hectic atmosphere. As a result, by the time I finally began actual composition of the score, I had had a minimum of contact with the producer and director. During the actual scoring period they were not, shall we say, "on call." However, I did have the distinct benefit of detailed consultation with two of the canniest and most knowledgeable of film minds. I am much indebted for their guidance and advice, for the privilege of sharing their "motion picture sense." One is the distinguished director-producer-executive, Sidney Franklin (THE GOOD EARTH, MRS. MINIVER, RANDOM HARVEST, WATERLOO BRIDGE); the other, the supervising editor of MGM and perhaps the dean of motion picture editors, Miss Margaret Booth. If the score is a helpful adjunct to the emotional and dramatic impact of RAINTREE COUNTY I must share the credit with Mr. Franklin and Miss Booth.

The phonograph LP of the RAINTREE COUNTY score occupies four 12-inch sides and runs 84 minutes and 55 seconds. Lately there has been considerable written criticism of soundtrack LPs on the grounds that while motion picture music may be enormously effective as the accompaniment to dramatic action on the screen, it does not make for good phonograph listening. In an attempt to satisfy the requirements for good listening without benefit of picture, as extensive an editorial job as has ever been attempted went into the preparation of the RAINTREE COUNTY album. Within the limitations of what was on the picture soundtrack, the music was edited with only one frame of reference: does this piece have anything resembling good musical form, and if not are there any editorial procedures by which it can be achieved? Whole sections of bars are transplanted from where they occur in the picture track to a position in which they make for better musical form and sequence. It was not merely a process of cutting out obvious stalls and omitting sections. Within individual sequences, the material was actually "recomposed on track" to produce the optimum in "listening music" consistent with what had been originally recorded for the picture. The extent to which we succeeded is for the listener to decide, but it is germane to this discussion to set down that we did try.

There are over two hours of music in RAINTREE COUNTY. It was a difficult job, but then what motion picture scoring job isn't? Per my discussion of the score in the program notes of the LP, "Raintree" was a challenge--a big one. Meeting it was fascinating, perhaps the most absorbing job I've ever tackled.

SALOME

George Duning

The writing of the background score for the Columbia Pictures SALOME was one of those "once in a blue moon" opportunities for a film composer. The film story by Harry Kleiner presents Salome in a sympathetic light. The main ingredients of the story are the love of Claudius for Salome, the plotting of Queen Herodias against John the Baptist by King Herod. The film was directed by William Dieterle, a director who has a tremendous flair for this type of picture. A great deal of the score, over an hour in length, plays in the open without dialogue or sound effects to cover it. All of the chief characters--Salome, Claudius, King Herod, Queen Herodias, John the Baptist, and Ezra, the king's religious counselor--are more or less of equal importance. The tried but true technique of the leitmotif was suggested.

Unlike QUO VADIS, whose fine score by Miklos Rozsa was stylistically correct and authentic, SALOME was filmed as a dramatic love story, and it was the opinion of Morris Stoloff (head of Columbia Pictures Music Department) and myself that the music should be written in a symphonic manner. I did considerable research in ancient Hebrew music and the music of the Greeks and Romans of that period. I found, in wading through several centuries of music both prior to and following the time of Christ, a remarkable similarity in melodic lines. I noted numerous examples of music settings for Psalms of David in which the same sequence of notes could be found in the Gregorian Chants which came several centuries later. As a matter of fact, when I set up the material for the "Baptist" theme, I instinctively did so in terms of the Gregorian Chants.

The only concessions that were made as to authentic sounds of instruments of the period were the occasional uses of an Irish harp, a viola d'amore, an oboe d'amore, cymbals, camel bells, and flute. My orchestrator, Arthur Morton, and I felt that the occasional use of these colors was sufficient to indicate the geographical flavor of certain scenes. Otherwise, the entire score is written in the grand symphonic manner, using a modern orchestra consisting of full strings, woodwinds in twos, four horns, three trumpets, three trombones, tuba, harp, and a battery of percussion.

The main theme, which is the Salome (Rita Hayworth) and love story theme, was divided into three sections: the first section has a somewhat modal character, while the second section is of a rather light and expressive character. The third section was used for the more moody and dramatic scenes: for instance, the quarrel between Claudius and Salome and the scene where Queen Herodias asked her daughter to dance for the King and Salome storms out of the Queen's quarters.

The Claudius (Stewart Granger) theme is usually heard in horns, or horns and celli. It was written so that it could be played as a counter line to the first section of the Salome theme. The main theme was also used in the light manner. This treatment was used in an amusing scene between Salome and Claudius in which Salome is piqued because she has been supplied with sea water for her bath.

King Herod (Charles Laughton) called for a strong and somewhat pompous theme. This theme usually was played by the low strings in the tutti passages, or as a bass clarinet solo in the quieter dialogue scenes. The Queen Herodias (Judith Anderson) theme is of a fragmentary nature and is usually heard in the cold tones of a pair of muted horns or a clarinet played non-expressive. The character of Pontius Pilate and his Roman followers is set up in a martial piece of music in which I used a unison of horns set above a base line consisting of a succession of paralleled fourths and fifths.

The character of John the Baptist (Alan Badel) was set forth in a melody adapted along the lines of the Gregorian Chants. This melody is usually heard in horns in unison played very softly with a cushion of strings above. In one wonderful scene, near the end of the picture, in which Salome and Claudius visit the Baptist who has been imprisoned in a dungeon in Herod's palace, I was able to use the Baptist theme to greater advantage. The scene is over six minutes in length, and most of it is covered by a long speech by Claudius in which he described the miracles he has seen performed by Christ. Because of the low, soft quality of the dialogue, I had to be extremely careful in the treatment of the background music. I used two groups of strings, one with mutes, and played them against each other. Under one very low line, I even thinned out the orchestra to four violins. At the climax of the scene, where John the Baptist has been overcome with emotion over the realization that the Messiah has come, he gives his blessing to Salome and Claudius and tells them to "go in peace." This dialogue was extremely low and I got over it by resolving the climax achieved with the full string orchestra to a single note which holds over the dialogue line "go in peace."

The caravan scene in which Salome is being transported by the Roman soldiers back to Galilee is beautifully filmed. A great many of the scenes were actually shot in Israel. As a matter of fact, the scene on the river bank in which the Romans attack the Baptist and his followers, was shot on the bank of the river Jordan. Because of the length of the caravan scenes, I set up special material and alternated this material with treatments of the Salome music. When the caravan arrives at the castle of Herod, I was able to alternate the music with the Herod theme.

The picture ends with excerpts from the Sermon on the Mount. Again, I had the problem of a low dialogue level plus the fact that I wished to bring in the Roger Wagner Chorale and work to a climax for the end title. I used four horns in a modal melody which starts on a low "g" played very softly to an organ of high strings. The melody played by the horns gradually climaxes to a high "b" at which point I had all the violins repeat the horn melody in a higher register. The Chorale is singing a supporting structure, the entire scene resolving to "D" major.

The music for the "Dance of the Seven Veils" was written by my eminent colleague, Daniele Amfitheatrof. A 30-minute album of some of the principal scenes in SALOME was recorded for Decca records.

QUO VADIS

Miklos Rozsa

A motion picture with historical background always presents interesting problems to the composer. There have been innumerable other historical pictures produced before QUO VADIS, and they were all alike in their negligent attitude toward the stylistic accuracy of their music. It is interesting to note what painstaking research is usually made to ascertain the year of publication of, let us say, "Yes, We Have No Bananas," if it is used in a picture about the twenties, but no one seems to care much if the early Christians in the 1st century A.D. sing "Onward Christian Soldiers" by Sir Arthur Sullivan, composed a mere 1800 years later! When a period picture is made, the historical background of the script is naturally based on historical facts and the dialogue tries to avoid any anachronistic term or reference. The art director, interior decorator, costume designer, hair-stylist and makeup man start their work only after thorough research, and the greatest care is taken that every building, every piece of furniture, every costume and every hairdo is absolutely authentic according to the period of the picture. During the actual photographing a historical advisor, usually a scholar of reputation, supervises this procedure so that nothing can slip in and spoil the absolute authenticity.

Why is it then when we come to music an exceptionally lofty attitude is felt and no one seems to care much about the genuineness of this most important factor of picture making? The countless dramatizations of antiquity in operas and oratorios naturally have not attempted to recreate the music of the period, as opera is stylized art and, therefore, the music is also a stylized adaptation of a certain historical or nationalistic style. No one expects to hear 16th-century Minnesanger music in _Die Meistersinger_, antique Greek music in _Electra_, or ancient Hebrew music in _Salome_. The orientalism in _Aida_, _Samson and Delilah_ or _Queen of Sheba_ is only used as color and they are full-blooded, romantic operas mirroring the style of the period of their creation with no attempt whatsoever to represent the true style of the period of their action. But the motion picture is different. It is realistic and factual. It not only tries to capture the spirit of bygone eras but also tries to make believe that it projects before the eyes of the spectator the real thing. There are no painted backdrops, fake props, cardboard shields and wooden swords as in an opera, but everything is realistic to the fullest limit and if the public doesn't believe that the Christians were actually eaten by the lions, the photoplay would have completely failed in its objective.

When QUO VADIS was assigned to me I decided to be stylistically, absolutely correct. First, thorough research had to be made. Though my old studies of the music of antiquity came in handy now, I am most indebted to the librarian of Metro-Goldwyn-Mayer studios, Mr. George Schneider, who with unfailing enthusiasm and unceasing effort produced every reference to the period that could be found in the libraries throughout the four corners of the world.

Our first duty was to prepare the blueprints for the antique instruments which had to be made. We reconstructed these from Roman statues (in the Vatican and Naples museums), antique vases and bas-reliefs on columns and tombstones, giving exact measurements for all details. The actual instruments were then produced by Italian instrument makers, so a great array of lyras and cytharas (the chief instruments of the Romans), double pipes (aulos), curved horns (buccina), straight trumpets (salpynx or tuba), tambourines, drums, sistrums, clappers and other percussion instruments were made with amazing likeness to the real ones.

Then the music which was to be performed on-scene had to be prepared. To select music for a historical picture of the middle ages, for instance, would have been an easy task, as there is a wealth of material available. But this is not the case with Roman music from the year A.D. 64. In spite of the fact that a great amount of Roman literature, painting, architecture and sculpture has been preserved, there is absolutely no actual record of any music of the classical times of Roman history. There are a lot of references to music in literary works of the time, so we know what an important part music played in the life of the Romans. Seneca complains that orchestras and choruses grew to gigantic proportions and often there were more singers and players in the theater than spectators. There were numerous schools of music, and daughters of the rich bourgoisie had to learn to play the lyre just as they have to learn the piano today. The slaves of the aristocrats entertained constantly and Seneca complains that "at table no one can talk for the music!" (An early forerunner of the menace of our radios.) All this proves that music was widely practiced and belonged to everyday life.

In QUO VADIS there were three distinguishable styles in which music had to be created. Firstly, the music of the Romans, such as the songs of Nero and the slave girl Eunice, sacrificial hymn of the Vestal, marches and fanfares. Secondly, the hymns of the Christians; and thirdly, the music performed by slaves, which I call the Roman Empire music. As nothing remains of Roman music, this had to be recreated by deduction. We know that the culture of the Romans was entirely borrowed from the Greeks. Greek civilization and religion dominated Roman life and Nero himself preferred to speak Greek rather than Latin. As Greek musicians and instruments were imported and Greek musical theory adopted, the music of the Romans cannot be separated from its Greek models and ideas. It was, therefore, not incorrect to reconstruct this music from Greek examples. About the music of the Greeks we know considerably more. We know their thorough and involved musical systems, we can read their musical notations and we also have about twelve relics of actual music, preserved mostly on tombstones and old papyri. These were of the greatest value in this attempt at reconstruction. The Skolion of Sikilos, which is perhaps the oldest known musical relic with a definite melody in our modern sense, became the basic idea from which I developed Nero's first song, "The Burning of Troy." It is in Phrygian mode and dates from the 1st or 2nd century.

The second song of Nero, "The Burning of Rome," uses a Gregorian anthem, "Omnes sitientos venite ad aquas," as a point of departure. This is a reverse method of reconstruction, but if we accept theory that much Roman music became Christian (as we shall see later), we can select from the early Christian music where the origin cannot be proven, and presume that the original source was Roman. For Eunice's song I used the first Ode of Pindar, music for which was allegedly found in a Sicilian monastery in 1650. Its authenticity is doubtful, but it is constructed entirely on Greek principles and it is a hauntingly beautiful melody. Fragments from an anonymous composer from the 2nd century, which probably were written for a cythara school, were interesting enough to serve as a point of departure for an instrumental piece, used as a bacchanale at Nero's banquet. The 5/8 time is characteristic of Greek music.

The main problem that arose with all these original melodies was how to harmonize them. Whether the Greeks or Romans knew harmonies, or was their music entirely monodic, is still a hotly debated question. Polyphony in our modern sense was, of course, unknown except that of parallel octaves, which hardly can be called polyphony. Only six intervals, the 4th, the 5th, the octaves, and their higher octaves, were known and allowed as consonances.

As the music for QUO VADIS was intended for dramatic use and as entertainment for the lay public, one had to avoid the pitfall of producing only musicalogical oddities instead of music with a universal, emotional appeal. For the modern ear, instrumental music in unison has very little emotional or aesthetic appeal; therefore I had to find a way for an archaic sounding harmonization which gives warmth, color, and emotional values to these melodies. A parallelism with open fifths and fourths came in most handy and also a modal harmonization suggested by the different (Lydian, Phrygian, Dorian, Mixolydian, etc.) modes of the melodies in question. In the second category for which authentic music had to be supplied, were the hymns of the early Christians. These also had to be reconstructed by deduction. Saint Ambrose's collection of liturgical music for the Catholic Church appeared about four hundred years after our period and I wanted to go back to the very source from which the Ambrosian plain chant and later the Gregorian hymnology blossomed. As the early Christians were partly Jews and partly Greeks their liturgical music naturally originates from these two sources. These two influences have been proven and are prevalent in the Gregorian hymns which are the fundamental of the Roman Catholic Church music.

The first time we meet organized Christianity in the picture, we see Saint Paul baptizing new believers and we hear them singing a hymn. A Babylonian Jewish liturgical melody (which found its way into the Gregorian hymnody, becoming a Kyrie) served as basis for this hymn. I used it in the manner of a cantus responsorius, where the priest intones a phrase and the congregation answers it. To achieve the authentic timbre and feeling of its rendition, we engaged a Jewish cantor to sing the part of the priest.

As the second major influence on the early Christian music was Greek, I selected a melody from a Greek hymn which had the beauty and fervor needed for the Christians to sing in the arena. The Hymn to Nemesis which was discovered by Vincenzo Gallilei in the 17th century but dates from the 2nd century, seemed to me perfect for this purpose. The third hymn, which is sung by the Christians burning on the crosses in the arena, had to have a plaintive character which I found in the Ambrosian Aeterna Conditor.

It goes without saying that all these hymns are performed in the picture in unison (or octaves) unharmonized, as they were sung two thousand years ago. The English words were written by Hugh Gray, who also served as historical advisor on the picture and displayed great feeling for the style and character of the time of antiquity.

The third category of the music was the music of the slaves, mostly Babylonians, Syrians, Egyptians, Persians and other conquered nations of oriental origin. There were fragments of the oldest melodies found in Sicily (a Roman province), with Arabian influence, and others found in Cairo, which I could utilize.

The orchestration of the music performed on-scene was another problem. None of the old instruments were available and, therefore, the archaic sound had to be created with our modern instruments. I used a small Scottish harp, the clarsach, and this delicate instrument gave a remarkably true likeness to the sound of the lyre and antique harp. For military music, cornets, mixed with trumpets and trombones, gave the roughness of the early brass instruments. Bass flute and English horn replaced the sound of the aulos. Our modern percussion instruments come close to the antique ones and therefore it was safe to use tambourines, jingles, drums of different shapes and sizes, and cymbals. Bowed stringed instruments, however, could not be used. These came into usage nearly a thousand years after our period so they would have been completely anachronistic. For music that was supposed to be performed by a large group of players I took the liberty of using the string group of the orchestra playing pizzicato to reinforce the main body of the orchestra. Harps and guitars were also added to achieve the percussive quality. Melodic lines, however, were only given to the woodwind and brass instruments to perform.

"Another part of the forest" is the dramatic accompanying music which, for yet undetected reasons, Hollywood semantics calls "the score." The main function of this music is to heighten the drama, create the atmosphere and underline the emotional content of certain scenes. A stylistically, strictly correct music corresponding to our period could not have supplied these aims to the modern spectator and listener. Although I have constructed my themes on classical principles and was able to use a few fragments from historical relics, these had to be harmonized to make them emotionally appealing. A romantic, chromatic harmonization would have been out of place and a simple modal harmonization seemed to me the closest to the character of this music. The modern major and minor triads were unknown factors to the Romans, but our modern ears are so used to these sounds that it would have been impossible to ignore them completely.

The main themes of the score of QUO VADIS are the following: The opening prelude is a choral setting of the words "Quo Vadis Domine?" and its translation, 'Lord, Whither Goest Thou?" The melodic line of this theme was modeled on the Gregorian, "Libera me Domine," and Kyrie. Behind this urging question of Christianity we hear the interrupting fanfares of Romans buccinas. A recurring of faith first appears in the garden where Lygia draws a fish, the symbol of the early Christians. The love theme is first heard in Plautius' gardens in the scene between Lygia and Marcus and is a musical reflection of Lydia's gentle character and deep faith. The Triumph introduces Marcus Vinicius' contrasting theme of pagan heroism and self-confidence. An interesting chromatic motif from the second Delphic hymn was utilized as a motif of menace and tension in the scene where Lygia is taken as hostage. A motif from "The Hymn to the Sun" appears majestically in the brass when Rome is in flames. A motif of four chords introduces the Miracle scene, when the Lord talks to St. Peter and then the voices of angels intone the "Quo Vadis" theme. A theme of doom accompanies the suicide scene of Nero.

The dramatic music of QUO VADIS is much less polyphonic than my previous film scores, for the only reason that extended polyphony would have clashed anachronistically with monodic music performed on-scene throughout the picture. At the end of the picture the voices of humanity take up the 'Quo Vadis" theme and after the answer of Christ they join in a jubilant reprise of the hymn, "By the Light of the Dawn." For those who want to study the music of QUO VADIS more thoroughly, there is a record album from the sound tracks and a piano score, with the most important themes together with pictures and historical notes.

THE TEN COMMANDMENTS

Elmer Bernstein

The composition of the score for THE TEN COMMANDMENTS represents a year and a half of the most exacting work I have ever done. There were so many obstacles to overcome. The first was my own apprehension of scoring what amounts to the birth of civilized ethical concepts, of scoring conversation between man and God, of scoring the birth of freedom and the dignity of man as a free soul under God. I don't think that any true artist should feel equal to that task. I was certainly beset by many fears and doubts. Perhaps it would have been easier if I were being called upon to present a purely personal approach to these great matters. In the composition of motion picture music, however, the composer most often finds himself bypassing his most personal expressions in favor of media and language most certainly communicative. This is one of the primary concerns and responsibilities of the screen composer--the invention and adherence to musical language which communicates easily and spontaneously to the audience. In this case even this problem was not a simple one as I was working under the close supervision of the producer, Cecil B. DeMille.

It seems ridiculous to attempt to examine Mr. DeMille's great involvement with the scoring in one paragraph. First allow me a personal note to say that Cecil B. DeMille is one of the most extraordinary men it has been my pleasure to know. There is no detail of <u>any</u> aspect of picture making which escapes his very sharp scrutiny. From the costuming of the extra players to details of orchestration and sound recording, Mr. DeMille was indeed the master of the fate of his picture. He has very definite concepts about music in his films and is indefatigable in his quest for what he believes to be correct for his films. His concepts are quite Wagnerian both dramatically and musically. He believes firmly in the use of the leitmotif and the interplays of these motifs in scenes which affect the destinies of more than one character. He is a great believer in line and most often would insist upon hearing the lines played on the piano in the belief that weakness of line could be masked by harmonic invention and other orchestral and compositional devices. A piano demonstration of composition played for him in a full, florid piano arrangement would invariably bring a request for a "one finger" demonstration of the line. He is a "spontaneous reactor," becoming warmly enthusiastic about things which please him and equally disturbed about things which irritate him. I found it quite possible to disagree as long as I was completely candid and honest; to attempt to gain an end in devious ways is an extremely dangerous procedure with Mr. DeMille, as he is much too astute a gentleman to be taken in by politicking. To sum up, let's say that Mr. DeMille knew what he wanted and had the energy and drive to keep at it until he got it out of you.

Now some general musical problems. In some cases we were faced with creating Egyptian source music. Since no system of musical notation is extant, we studied the instruments of the period and found a rich assortment of woodwind and percussion instruments. They seemed to indicate a richness of color and a very limited scale. Several compositions in this vein were created, some of which remain in the release print of the picture. A few were cut as it was felt that the sounds, while authentic, might be unpleasant to the modern ear. There are numerous fanfares for which I employed natural horns which impart a wild, barbaric quality to their sound. The only "tricky" effects employed were in the burning bush sequence in which the string choir was reinforced by a novachord, and in the sequence of the pestilence in which several electronic devices were used to help impart a feeling of terror. The orchestra at its greatest strength consisted of 71 musicians. The only unorthodox feature was the presence of eight horns. The music was recorded in a conventional single channel setup on full coat magnetic film and transferred to optical film upon the completion of dubbing.

As I indicated previously, this score was approached on the basis of creating themes for all the major characters and forces. The first is a forthright statement of the theme of Moses as it appears in the Main Title or Prelude. Moses emerges as a complex figure in THE TEN COMMANDMENTS. Found in a basket on the Nile by the daughter of the Pharoah, he is reared in the palace as a prince. He is temporal power, a warrior, a suitor of the throne princess, in all, a glamorous, human figure. Later he is fallen from favor, outcast from Egypt. He is a skeptic concerning his God until, transformed by his experience at the burning bush, he returns to Egypt as God's messenger to lead his people from bondage. The treatment of the theme relates to Moses as a prince of Egypt; its martial stride and "fleshy" orchestration tell of temporal power. The second is a treatment of the Moses theme for his discovery as an infant. Here both rhythmically and in its transparent woodwind setting it is imbued with the feeling of a lullaby.

We now come to the most difficult problem of all. From the very outset all of us concerned with this project had been giving much thought to the projection of the concept of God, which is a vital factor in the unfolding of this picture.

The creative artist who tackles this problem may not find the solution difficult if he is primarily concerned with a subjective expression of his own feeling in relation to God. In a medium like motion pictures, the artist cannot afford the luxury of subjectivity. In a medium which reaches more people in one month than a so-called "serious composer" reaches in an entire lifetime it is necessary that the screen composer have some recognition of the "language barrier" which exists between his own highly sophisticated (we hope) language and the more primitive musical language of his vast and varied audience. The screen composer must also have an honest desire to communicate with his audience. The snob is lost in this medium. His future is an obscure end with a small coterie. The composer who either by choice or necessity invents tortured musical devices to mask a weakness of line or lack of spontaneity of emotion is similarly doomed. Lest there be any misunderstanding let me restate that I am referring to the motion picture as it is constituted today. I am simply saying that when an artist works in a medium in which he has a captive audience, he then has the responsibility to communicate with it in a language it understands. It was an acute awareness of this problem which led me to procrastinate for some time in the creation of music for the scenes which concerned themselves with the presence of God. In music God could be many things; Gregorian chants, Palestrina, Bach, Beethoven, Mozart, or perhaps the Verdi of the Requiem, or perhaps "I Believe." I am not building up to confessing that I took all these elements and fused them in some mechanical way. I mention the foregoing to try to give the reader an understanding of the thoughts that were conditioning my efforts as I approached the problem. After all this introduction I dare not make any comments of my own about these themes. It is, of course, impossible to try to judge whether I have succeeded in what I set out to accomplish with this theme. That is something the millions of people who have seen this film have had to judge for themselves.

Chapter VI

CLASSICAL MUSIC ON THE SCREEN

CLASSICAL COMPOSERS ON THE SCREEN

James L. Limbacher

With the movies only a little over a decade old, foreign film producers began hiring young and talented classical composers to develop special scores for their films. In 1908 alone, Camille Saint-Saëns had composed the background for the French film, THE ASSASSINATION OF THE DUC DE GUISE and Mikhail Ippolitov-Ivanov had done the same for the Russian film, STENKA RAZIN. The latter also was responsible for SONG ABOUT THE MERCHANT KALISHNIKOV in 1909 and VOLGA AND SIBERIA in 1914.

Opera composer Pietro Mascagni contributed scores to two 1915 Italian productions, L'AMICA and RAPSODIA SATANICA, while Darius Milhaud scored the French film, THE BELOVED VAGABOND, and Victor Herbert, THE FALL OF A NATION, that same year. The noted Louis Gottschalk scored D. W. Griffith's BROKEN BLOSSOMS in 1919; Sigmund Romberg, FOOLISH WIVES in 1922, and Charles Wakefield Cadman, THE RUBAIYAT OF OMAR KHAYYAM the same year.

As experiments in sound films were being conducted, more classical composers joined the ranks of film scorers--Erik Satie, Georges Anthiel, Roger Desormiere, Arthur Honegger, Jean Sibelius, Jacques Ibert and Paul Hindemith. All these scores, of course, had to be played by a live orchestra in the deluxe theaters, and few of these scores unfortunately survive today for study.

Other names which are remembered in connection with early film scores include Walter Cleveland Simon, Joseph Carl Briel, Victor Schertzinger, Robert Hood Bowers, Ernst Luz, Hugo Riesenfeld, Oliver Wallace, Carl Edouarde, Louis Silvers, Gottfried Humpertz, Frederick Shepherd Converse, Erno Rapee, Mortimer Wilson, William Axt, David Mendoza, Edmund Meisel, Henry Hadley and Werner Heymann. Many of these composers continued to compose for sound films and in the case of Oliver Wallace, he was still composing for Walt Disney films until his death in the 1960's.

P R K F V

Sergei Eisenstein

"At 12 noon, you'll have the music," he said as we came out of a small preview room. Although it was already midnight, I was quite calm. At exactly 11:55, a small dark-blue car would drive in through the gates of the film studios and out would step Sergei Prokofiev. He would be holding the score for the next passage of ALEXANDER NEVSKY. The next evening we would go through the following part of the film together and on the following morning the next part of the music would be ready.

Prokofiev works like clockwork, like a clock that is never a second slow or fast. Like a sniper, he is always right on the target. Prokofiev's punctuality is not merely business-like pedantry. The well-ordered nature of his timetable is an outward reflection of his well-ordered approach to his art, of the neat precision with which he conveys character via expressive means that he wields with an iron. The precision in his art provides a musical parallel to the precision of Stendhal's laconic style. The crystal purity of Prokofiev's characterization is only equalled by Stendhal.

"Only after a hundred years have passed, will I be understood," wrote Stendhal, who met with so little understanding among his contemporaries, although it is now difficult for us to believe that there was an age when the transparent clarity of Stendhal's style could seem obscure. Prokofiev's fate as an artist was a happier one. His works did not require a hundred years before they found understanding audiences.

Both at home and in the West, Prokofiev's music has been widely acclaimed. Prokofiev's artistic skill lies in his ability to recreate phenomena not as they first appear to him, but transposed like events recast through the lens of a cine-camera.

I was always amazed by the way in which after a mere two (or at the most three) rushes of edited material Prokofiev was able to grasp so astutely and accurately the essence of a passage and the very next day send in music, which in its phrasing and accents would blend perfectly not only with the overall rhythm of action in the given episode but with all the subtle nuances of the editing.

Although we used to watch these rushes in the dark, I could still catch glimpses of Prokofiev's hands on the arms of the chair, those enormous strong hands, which would wield the keys with fingers of steel when in a wild frenzy of inspiration he used to plunge at the keyboard that would shake beneath them.... As the film progressed Prokofiev's long unerring fingers, full of nervous sensitivity, started to move up and down the arms of his chair like a relentless Morse code receiver.

Was Prokofiev "marking out the beat?" No. He was "marking out" a lot more than that. He was measuring out the structural pattern in which the length and rhythm of individual episodes are interwoven with the help of editing techniques, and both these aspects taken together link up with the actions and utterances of the various characters. I reached this conclusion because of Prokofiev's happy exclamation "How great!" at a passage in which a counterpoint of three movements incorporating different rhythms, paces and directions of action were intricately blended together. The next day he would be sending me music in which a counterpoint of sounds would permeate the composition I had achieved through editing.

At the same time it seemed as if he were whispering or muttering something to himself. But woe to anyone who tried to talk to him at such a time! All they would get by way of an answer would be an inaudible grunt (if your question did not disturb his listening) or a horrible snarl, if not curses (if he actually heard what you said!). What was it that Prokofiev heard and was listening out for? It seemed to me that his clear or not-so-clear mumbling contained the melodic equivalent of the scene flitting past across the screen.

I recall another occasion when Prokofiev and I were working with the orchestra, during a rehearsal of one of the most beautiful songs in IVAN THE TERRIBLE--the song: "Oh Ocean-sea, oh Sea of Blue," which was to embody Tsar Ivan's dream of winning an outlet to the sea for his country. Prokofiev's lanky figure hidden to the waist by the sweeping movements of the musicians' bows seemed to be swaying in the midst of rippling corn. He leaned over towards the musicians, listening intently to the interplay of the various instruments' motifs. En passant, he whispered to me, pointing first to one of the musicians and then to another, commenting: "That one is playing the light flickering across the waves ... that one the billowing of the waves ... that one the wide expanses of the ocean ... and that one the mysteries of the deep...."

Each instrument and each group of instruments incorporated into its flow of sound a specific aspect of the watery element, and together they recreated, not copied; they brought to life, rather than imitating life, and in their entirety summoned up a striking image of the ocean, its infinite expanse, its storms churning up the waves so that they break on the shore like thundering horse's hooves, or its blue unruffled calm rocked in the flickering sunlight, as envisaged by the tsar who brought forth a united Russian land from out of scattered chaos. This is no mass-produced print of the "ocean waves," it is not merely an elemental and dynamic image of the real ocean, but an image far more resplendent--lyrical in its childish daydreaming and menacing in its ire--the image of a man and the state he is leading to its indispensable sea frontiers.

Prokofiev is a screen artist in the sense that through the medium of the screen he succeeds in not only revealing the visual impact and essence of phenomena, but also their intrinsic structure, the logic of their essence, the dynamics of their evolution. Prokofiev's music possesses amazing plasticity; it is never merely illustrative but always sparkles with a triumphant wealth of imagery: its revelation of the inner currents of phenomena and their dynamic structure which embody the emotional timbre and significance of events, makes an unforgettable impact.

In the inner nature of phenomena, Prokofiev always succeeds in picking out the structural secret which expresses on an emotional plane precisely their broadest message. After grasping this structural secret, he clothes it in sound patterns of instrumentation making it sparkle with subtle timbre shifts and the stark severity of structural form blossoms forth in the emotional fullness of his orchestration. The resultant dynamic contours of Prokofiev's musical images pierce our consciousness like the blinking rays of a projector tracing moving images onto the white expanse of the screen. This is no mere imprint of phenomena but their piercing light expressed in rays of sound.

I am not referring to Prokofiev's musical technique, I am deciphering the steel roll of his consonants beating out the clear current of ideas in places where many others would merely have a vague sequence of nuances from the sphere of vowels. If Prokofiev were to write articles, he would devote them to the infinitely rational pillars of speech, consonants, just as he writes operas basing his music not on the melody of verse, but on the angular skeleton of unrhythmic prose.... He would have written stanzas in consonants. ... And what have we here? Beneath intricate clauses in contracts, in dedications on phonographs he gives his friends and admirers, in the top right hand corner on the sheets of music for each new work we find one and the same staccato tap-dance of consonants: P-R-K-F-V. This is the composer's normal signature! Even his own name he writes in consonants.

The consonants which stand for the name Prokofiev appear as a symbol of the unswerving consistency of his talent. All that vacillates, all that is transient, accidental and labile has been banished from this composer's music, as from his signature. His signature is reminiscent of the icons of old, on which the words Lord, Tsar, and the Virgin were written in consonants alone. The stern spirit of traditional canons is to be discerned in this removal of all that is chance, transient and terrestrial.

The same spirit pervades the ascetic staccato of the five consonants--P-R-K-F-V--that reverberates through the dazzling gleam of Prokofiev's rays of sound, just as the letters on the frescoes of the Spas-Nereditsa church in Novgorod gleam in their tarnished gold; just as the lyricism of the sepia and cobalt blue rings out in a stern monastic refrain in the murals of Theophan the Greek in the Church of Feodor Stratilat in Novgorod. For side by side with his inexorable severity of style we find the equally magnificent lyricism of Prokofiev's music through which the implacable Aaron's rod of his structural logic comes into its own in the miracle of Prokofiev's inimitable orchestration.

Prokofiev is an essentially Russian artist, but his Russian realism is not the stereotyped pseudo-realism of cabbage soup and kvas. Prokofiev's music is intrinsically Russian in its firm adherence to tradition that can be traced back to the primitive Scythians and the inimitable chiselled beauty of 13th-century stone carving in the Cathedrals of Vladimir and Suzdal. Prokofiev's art turns for inspiration to the emergence of the Russian people's national consciousness which is reflected in medieval frescoes, with their profound folk wisdom, or the icons of the great master Rublev. This explains why the past comes so vividly to life in Prokofiev's music, not by means of archaisms and stylization but via bold, daring patterns of ultra-modern musical style. In his "Hegelian" originality--his primacy--this essentially Russian artist is truly international.

Prokofiev's art finds inspiration not only in patriotic themes taken from his people's past, such as the patriotic wars of the 19th, 16th and 13th centuries (the opera *War and Peace* and the films IVAN THE TERRIBLE and ALEXANDER NEVSKY). Later we find Prokofiev's astringent talent caught up in the passionate world of Shakespeare's Renaissance Italy and giving birth to a ballet based on the most lyrical of all great tragedies, *Romeo and Juliet*.

Amidst the magical phantasmagoria of Gozzi's world, Prokofiev brings to life the fantastic quintessence of Italy in the late 18th century in "Love for Three Oranges." The bestial brutality that raged in the 13th century is epitomized in the pig-headed iron horde of Teutonic Knights galloping like a relentless tank column across the ice in ALEXANDER NEVSKY. In all these works we find the same rigorous methodical approach which links the work of Prokofiev with the masters of the early Renaissance, when painters were philosophers, and sculptors, without fail, mathematicians. All his work is free from impressionistic generalizations, approximating smears and blurred patches of color. In Prokofiev's work it is not an arbitrary paint brush but the unrelenting lens which he holds before us....

The bright lights of the projector were turned off and replaced by mild, even light from the ceiling. Prokofiev was putting on his scarf and I knew I need not fear a sleepless night. Tomorrow morning at 11:55 sharp a small blue car would drive into the film studios and five minutes later the score would be on my desk, complete with the symbolic letters P R K F V.

A TIME FOR BACH

Gene Forrell

Music lovers have very little opportunity to witness a film that they can call their very own, that belongs as much in the category of music as in film itself. And that makes a very special case for the short film--A TIME FOR BACH. It is not only important as music, but film as well. Usually, a film that aims toward the interests of musicians is merely a photographed concert. In most other cases music is relegated to such an incidental role that it might just as well be unheard. This film combines the two arts in an extremely serious and deeply considered manner.

When William H. Scheide, leader of the Bach Aria Group, approached Paul Falkenberg to produce and direct this film about Bach's music as interpreted and experienced by that organization, Mr. Falkenberg felt that "all you had to do was to pick some tuneful Bach aria, prepare your playback breakdown, set your camera, take a few master shots, give the soloists their due with a close-up here, a medium shot there--result: your picture, a music film, nice and conventional--the mixture as before. I was not prepared to do just that." Indeed, he didn't stop or even start at that nice, comfortable formula stage. He goes on to say, "a film with the Bach Aria Group would have to make its point the 'movie way.' From the very outset we agreed that the film would not reproduce the concert rendition of just one or the other aria in full, but would present excerpts from several arias so as to give a glimpse of the immeasurable musical wealth that can be found in Bach's works, a musical wealth that can have a forceful meaning today. Also, no narration was going to bridge any pictorial gaps. The picture sequences alone would have to bear the burden of the statements."

The idea to present the spirit of Bach within the framework of our real, present up-to-the-minute experiences was an inspired one. This is one of the most successful aspects of the picture. Just how this structure took shape in the film maker's mind is best told in a continuation of Mr. Falkenberg's own words. "First, the mood of the Bach period; an organ piece would best provide the broad, noble, sweeping elements so characteristic of the culture Bach lived in. Philip Stapp would create animated variations on a baroque theme, without ever attempting to illustrate the music; a dream-like flight into Baroque space, following the choreographic pattern suggested by the rhythm of the C Major Fugue.

"At a given moment, modern life would clash violently into this Baroque sequence. I felt that a rapid montage could best recreate the nervous tension, the hectic staccato and frantic tempo which pervade our era. In planning the pictorial subject matter of this sequence, we found that some short 'ironical' jingle would provide the right accent, while any narration would have destroyed the stylization this montage attempted." An example of these jingles goes as follows: "Run, run, run (pause) to get your break" and "Run, run, run (pause) to live at all." These and similar phrases were whispered aloud by a small group against a percussion background of a series of regular and occasionally upsetting rhythmic patterns in time with the recitation of the jingles. As this sequence ends, there follows immediately an introduction to the music of the Bach Aria Group through a long, constantly moving and relaxed section of artists and students at work in schools, museums and libraries.

This is at once familiar and comfortable to the music lover as he sits back to enjoy all the beautiful music that is to follow in the rest of the film. As part of each aria is presented, there is one beautiful experience after another to enjoy in the rich and various vocal and instrumental music that Bach contributes to these arias. They are exceedingly well sung and played by the group and we are especially privileged to hear how each is planned according to its own special characterics and meaning it has for the performers. This film is very genuine in its approach and one can be sure of having his appetite for this music ignited to the burning point after seeing it.

SHADOW OPERA

Francis Rizzo

Even before the end of the twenties, when the motion picture found its voice at last, Hollywood had been carrying on a running flirtation with opera and opera singers. Ever since, opera and those who make it have turned up on the movie screen in a surprising variety of guises: we have seen filmed versions of repertory favorites, biographies of great singers (fictitious or purportedly real), and of course standard comedies and dramas enlivened by excerpts from operas.

When, inevitably, screen writers began to introduce opera into films that were not primarily musical, the focus shifted. The onstage excerpt lost much of its importance and became a background element; the real drama was played in the dressing room, the wings or the front of the house. Hollywood has always been a haven for "technical consultants" and other purveyors of authenticity; when opera sequences tailored to the script began to be called for, in the Hollywood tradition they were elaborately faked. The shadow play had bred the shadow opera.

An early example of this hybrid genre dates from the thirties, during the heyday of the famous Charlie Chan series. The Chinese sleuth had been sent practically everywhere in creation in his battle against crime, so in 1936 the public was treated to the adventures of CHARLIE CHAN AT THE OPERA. The plot was properly melodramatic: a famous baritone, long believed dead in a dressing-room fire, but very much alive and in good voice (though hardly in his right mind), runs amok in the San Francisco Opera House. As the deranged singer (whose name, Gravelle, has, one hopes, no bearing on his voice), Boris Karloff was required to sing an aria onstage and, at its climax, stab the soprano with a knife--but not before he has replaced the papier-maché prop with the real thing. As 20th Century-Fox had a Mephistophelean costume worn by Lawrence Tibbett in METROPOLITAN the year before, it was decided that Karloff wear the same costume. And rather than ransack the standard repertory for an appropriate piece, the studio asked Oscar Levant (a charter member of that curious colony of musicians who made Hollywood their home in the late thirties) to provide a made-to-order opera entitled _Carnival._

Recalling the events in his autobiographical _A Smattering of Ignorance,_ Levant says, "I had heard of music being written around a singer, but never for a costume." And as his only previous operatic experience had been a _Pelléas_ parody, _Le Crayon sur la Table_ (text by Berlitz), a pastel wash of whole-tone chords and plaints of "Pourquoi!," he turned to his neighbor Arnold Schoenberg for advice on how to write an opera. The great composer-pedagogue solemnly suggested that he study _Fidelio._

Nothing daunted, Levant addressed himself to the task with enthusiasm. _Carnival_'s plot was a sort of nightmare reminiscence of _Faust,_ with words by songwriter William Kernell. Though the libretto had been put into Italian before he saw the original, Levant came up with a suitably atmospheric score--not only the Karloff scene but a soprano aria and a marche militaire, "a potent mingling of Mussorgsky and pure Levant." Having satisfied the studio's demands, Levant had a requirement of his own: "that at some point I should be allowed to use the word 'Silencio,' which always appealed to me. They compromised by letting me begin one aria with 'Silencio!' " (Compromise indeed, to begin an Italian aria in Spanish.)

It is fitting that one of the most effective "original opera sequences" was written for one of the greatest films ever made, Orson Welles' CITIZEN KANE (1941). Charles Foster Kane, billionaire newspaper magnate, attempts to buy respectability for his second wife, Susan, by forcing her into an opera career, in spite of the lady's obvious lack of talent. (We have an earlier glimpse of her squeaking through "Una voce poco fa" in English.) Kane builds an opera house and inaugurates it with a performance of _Salammbo,_ with his wife in the leading role. The memorable sequence opens on backstage shots of pre-performance pandemonium. Surrounded by vocal coaches, dressers and _régisseurs,_ the reluctant diva is decked out in jeweled robes and a plumed turban and all but thrown onto the stage. To a brilliant orchestra swell, the curtain rises on a scene of oriental splendor. Over a menacing string tremolo, Susan launches into the recitative "Ah, cruel!," and as her pathetic child's voice rises in uncertain spirals toward the top note, the camera moves higher and higher through the flies until it comes to rest on a light-bridge far above the stage, where two bored electricians are manning the follow spots. After listening for a moment in stoic silence, one of them turns toward the other and, with thumb and forefinger, engages his nose in a devastatingly accurate critique of Mme. Kane's performance.

But what about the opera itself? It has all the look and sound of a turn-of-the-century Franco-Oriental sweetmeat, including overripe orchestra effects and a Mary Garden-variety role. Is it by Louis Reyer, who did write a _Salammbo_? Pas du tout. This _Salammbo_ is the work of New York's own Bernard Herrmann, who besides writing all the music for CITIZEN KANE (and Welles' next film) has been a frequent collaborator of Alfred Hitchcock (VERTIGO, NORTH BY NORTHWEST, PSYCHO) and is himself the author of a full-length, bona fide opera based on _Wuthering Heights_.

A later bit of Oriental exotica was featured in 20th Century-Fox's 1949 comedy EVERYBODY DOES IT, written and directed by Nunnally Johnson. What is it that everybody does? Sing, of course. Paul Douglas, the burly boss of a demolition firm, is something of a bathtub baritone. When he discovers that his voice (dubbed by Leonard Warren) is powerful enough to shatter glass, he is persuaded to embark on an opera career. After a trial run on the concert circuit, Douglas makes his stage debut with the America Scala Opera Company in a colorful item called _The Loves of Fatima_ (libretto in Italian and music by Mario Castelnuovo-Tedesco). His leading lady is a sultry diva played by Linda Darnell, and the climactic scene of our hero's first entrance finds her already onstage, looking very much like Amneris in her boudoir, dressed in an Egyptian sheath "stitched together from the 'eyes' of 1783 peacock feathers" (according to studio publicists) and attended by 20 svelte handmaidens (according to on-screen count). She sings out her yearning for her absent lover, unaware that he is still in his dressing room, overcome by stage fright. Backstage, helpful souls are milling about, each with a sure-fire remedy for the jitters--all of them alcoholic. When the great moment comes, Douglas makes his first appearance at the top of a perilously long, steep flight of stairs. Dressed in breastplate, bear pelts and horned helmet, he looks as if he wandered in from a _Götterdämmerung_ rehearsal. He opens his mouth to sing, but the different "cures" have quite undone him. With a crash he finds himself at his beloved's feet--not quite as he had intended.

An entire international repertory could be built around the make-believe operas featured in the several film versions of THE PHANTOM OF THE OPERA. Gaston Leroux's 1908 romantic horror tale has seen screen service no less than three times, and there is little reason to suspect that this source has dried up for good. Lon Chaney's classic 1925 version was of course silent, though the 1930 re-release offered snatches of Faust on a synchronized sound track. But since Chaney first cut free the Paris Opera's chandelier, there have been two "musical" remakes of the venerable chiller--both in color, and both made more colorful still by the inclusion of real and synthetic opera sequences.

The first was Universal's 1943 extravaganza, which offered Nelson Eddy (his "first appearance as a brunet") and Susanna Foster as Anatole and Christine, the story's singing sweethearts, and Claude Rains as Dlaudin, the homicidal Phantom. According to Universal's script, the Phantom starts out as a violinist with the Paris Opera. When advancing age gets the better of his bowing technique, he is cruelly dismissed from the orchestra. He is further mistreated by an unscrupulous publisher, who attempts to steal his life work, a Lisztian piano concerto. Blind with rage, he strangles the man, only to have his face hideously disfigured by printer's acid hurled at him during the fray. He then hies himself to the sewer system beneath the Opera and begins a systematic program of revenge against the musical world. His other objective is to further the career of Christine, a promising chorister.

As leading baritone of the house, Eddy gets to sing Plunkett's drinking song from Martha early in the film. But as the other onstage sequences were meant mainly as background for the Phantom's offstage mayhem, they were pastiche-processed from compositions by Chopin and Tchaikovsky. (Hollywood's cultural commissars seem to agree with Tchaikovsky's opinion of himself as primarily a composer of operas. They never go back to the master's real stage works, however, preferring to raid his symphonic repertory in search of "good tunes." Besides the present instance, they have given opera treatment to several of his symphonies for use by Eddy and MacDonald as well as by Mario Lanza and Kathryn Grayson.)

If the PHANTOM's opera scenes lacked authenticity,

Universal more than made up for this in personnel. For the role of Mme. Biancarolli, the haughty prima donna who tries to block Christine's career, they engaged Jane Farrar, averred to be the niece of the immortal Geraldine. And for the tiny roles of the theatre dressers, they came up with two actresses billed as Rosina Galli and Elvira Curci. As stage director and librettist for the two pastiche operas they hired Wilhelm von Wymetal, veteran of the international opera scene.

The first of the imaginary operas is a French work. (The original title was to have been _Ghislaine d'Armagnac_, but somewhere along the line this was discarded in favor of the snappier _Amour et Gloire_.) In a glittering Empire ballroom, the soprano--Mme. Biancarolli in the role of Ghislaine--sings a melodious descant on themes from a Chopin nocturne as she waits for her baritone lover. He arrives in the person of a dashing officer (Eddy), and together they make a toast to love and glory. It is via the prop goblet that the Phantom administers a Mickey Finn to La Biancarolli, and when she swoons in the wings, Christine, her understudy, steps out of the chorus and into the leading role for a triumphant debut. This does not improve the diva's disposition, and when she recovers from the effects of the drug, the Phantom is obliged to strangle her. (He also gets one of those dressers.)

With Christine successfully launched and the Phantom placated for the moment, all should be well. But the administration, unmindful of critical suggestion, decides to pass up Christine in favor of another soprano (Mme. Lorenzi, played by Nicole Andre) in casting the forthcoming Russian opera, _Le Prince Masque de Caucasie_. Universal asked Wymetal to provide an imaginary opera in which most of the characters could be masked, thus allowing the Phantom--who is always masked anyway--free run of the backstage area. Apparently, no one had heard of _Un Ballo in Maschera_.

The setting of _Le Prince Masque_ is a gypsy encampment in the Caucasus. There is a smoldering soprano-baritone duet, punctuated by cracks of the whip and other features of gypsy romance, sung to a Russian text by Max Rabinowitz, all neatly appliqued over strains of Tchaikovsky's Fourth. Then La Lorenzi has her big solo, but she is spared going for the high note by dreadful doings in the house. As the Phantom saws through the last of its supporting chains, the main chandelier falls in the middle of the parterre, and the soprano's high C becomes a (for once fully justified) shriek. Needless to say, no one ever finds out how *Le Prince Masque* ends.

Nearly 20 years after Universal's version, Hammer Productions, an English company specializing in colorful remakes of horror classics, decided to leave Dracula and Frankenstein to their own devices while they caught up on the Phantom's escapades. As of 1962, our soprano heroine (Heather Sears, dubbed by Patricia Clark) is still called Christine, but instead of the glamorous Anatole her best beau is a stolid, non-singing chap who answers to the name of Harry. The story's locale has been shifted from Paris to London, though the opera house makes no pretense at being Covent Garden, and the chandelier has become a puny affair capable of killing off no more than a handful of somnolent subscribers. Indeed, it eventually falls *onstage*, killing the Phantom instead. The Phantom is now called Professor Petri, and far from being the skull-faced horror played by Chaney or the hoarse, wild-eyed specter offered by Rains, he seems a rather kindly and sentimental sort of music teacher. He has apparently written an opera about Joan of Arc, and it is the theft of the manuscript by another composer that drives him to vengeance.

Hammer, unable to come up with such authentic touches as somebody's niece or a second Galli-Curci team, does provide a sort of Alberich, a malevolent dwarf who performs most of the Phantom's dirty work. This leaves the Phantom plenty of free time, presumably to carry on his composing. Having hit upon some highly sophisticated atonal techniques during the decade when Arnold Schoenberg was just a Viennese teenager enthralled by Wagner, he seems well ahead of the game. His curiously anachronistic opera is the work of Edwin Astley, who composed several scenes from the life of Joan of Arc showing the Maid in battle and court, replete with lines like "You lousy Frenchie, you think this a joke?" *The Observer* observed that the performance sounded "mischievously like a squalling amateur rendition of *Peter Grimes*," and the *New York Herald Tribune* pronounced it the only genuinely horrific part of the proceedings. The *Tribune* went on to wonder if the Phantom might have been driven to homicidal rage by a frustrated desire to hear something sung in French or Italian on the London stage (*pace*, champions of opera in English).

The old question of opera in the vernacular was side-stepped in another British film, THE RED SHOES (1947), with music by Brian Easdale. Though THE RED SHOES is really about ballet, an opera plays a symbolic and decisive role in the story. Early in the film, we learn that Julian Craster, the young composer who writes the ballet score that serves as vehicle for dancer Victoria Page's emergence as prima ballerina, is at work on an opera based on the story of Cupid and Psyche. We twice hear snatches from the opera, most significantly when the BBC broadcasts its opening-night performance from Covent Garden, but we never see the work onstage. And the vocal line, sung offscreen by Margherita Grandi, is a wordless melisma, making Craster's _Cupid and Psyche_ the most shadowy of shadow operas.

Opera without action, opera without words. The next logical step all but leads us back to cinema's first golden age--of silents. Or to bittersweet reflection on those other never-never masterpieces, the real operas that never got written. Who would not trade all Hollywood's paste gems for the briefest scene from Verdi's _King Lear_, Debussy's _House of Usher_ or Wagner's life of _Buddha_? "Heard melodies are sweet, but...."

Chapter VII

ANIMATED FILMS AND COMEDIES

NEW FILM MUSIC FOR NEW FILMS

Mary Ellen Bute

The usual service of music to films is the portrayal of character, to set the mood for the plot and to form a fabric for the knitting together and pointing up of documentary or literary ideas. It is often used as a running commentary developing in parallel or contrary motion with the intellectual mood of the film, and serves as a basic fabric out of which the sound effects and dialogue emerge. It sets the rhythm and pace for the audience's impression of the action. For all this integral relationship with the current cinema, music plays an even more salient part in the absolute film where it is actually intercomposed with the visual material. I have been dedicated to the advancement of absolute film for some time and my interest in it is growing and branching out.

Many contemporary composers have been intrigued with the idea of one kinetic composition to be realized in the two materials (aural and visual) in such a way that they were inter-dependent and neither the musical composition or the picture would be complete alone. I have worked to such an end with the late and deeply lamented Joseph Schillinger and George Gershwin, and with the brilliant and forward-looking composers, Henry Cowell and Edwin Gerschefski. For some years, in order to explore the possibilities of the film medium, I have been working on the visual perception of classical and semi-classical music such as Saint-Saëns' "Dance Macabre" for "Spook Sport," Liszt's "Hungarian Rhapsody No. 2" for "Color Rhapsodie" and Shostakovich's Polka from his "Age of Gold" ballet for "Polka Graph," which used the graph pattern of the music as a springboard for the visual interpretation.

I am doing two films with Leopold Stokowski, who has long been actively interested in this field. The first film which is completed is PASTORAL, a visual interpretation of Bach's "Sheep May Safely Graze." The second, EXUBERANCE, is a visualization of excerpts from "Carmen." The acute reaction of an inspired musician to the visual development of my work is a source of great concern and excitement to me. For instance, in a passage from "Carmen" I have a series of pictures which start in the background of each note and zoom out at the audience. The effect is cumulative and at the end of the phrase I feel that I have approximated the sound effect of Bizet's music. Mr. Stokowski feels that one visual element in a continuous zoom from distant field would be more eloquent of the music. As it was his immediate and spontaneous reaction, I will try it that way and see how it fits in with my overall idea.

EXUBERANCE is like a painting which reveals itself in time continuity. In this way the painter can control the succession of visual impressions delivered to the on-looker and involve his audience aurally at the same time. The picture part of EXUBERANCE is more than a "visual interpretation" of the music. It has the elements of an interrelated composition.

My story is one of metamorphosis, which I am sure no creative worker who may read this will be in the least surprised to hear. As a painter desirous of expressing movement and controlled rhythms in time sequence, I turned to the then existent optical instruments and color organs and went to work with Leon Theremin, the inventor of electronic musical instruments, among which his Theremin Ether Wave instrument is the widest known. There seemed to be no idea that was foreign to Leon Theremin. Among his many incredibly wonderful inventions and devices he had platforms surrounded by magnetic fields. One could dance on these and with the gestures of his arms and legs make his own music. Joseph Schillinger, who was most outstanding himself, said that Leon Theremin's mind was of such a high order that he made everyone else he (Schillinger) knew seem atavistic.

From the first half hour with Theremin I was installing tiny mirrors, about 1/8th inch in diameter, on minute oscillators in tiny tubes of oil to cut down the friction and make them amenable to control. We would reflect light through prisms on these mirrors to get a range of spectral colors, then move the point of colored light about on the screen. We felt that much form is latent in a point, that a travelling point inscribes a line; a point returning on itself a circle, a cube, an angle. From a vibrating point we got a spiral, the figure 8 "line of beauty" and so on.

Needless to say, these visual "goings on" were accompanied by electrical tones and sounds of the most unusual order. The wave lengths of the colors were arithmetically related to the wave length of the sounds and I found the results exhilerating as did the little group in the workshop. But it wasn't enough for wide public demonstration. It was the kernel of something marvelous, but it needed money and concentrated effort to make it grow and flourish. None of us had any money or the ability to interest venture capital in our ideas and Theremin had no bump of self-preservation. So he left the world poorer than it would have been had he been able to sustain himself in it longer.

As this phase of my work shut down, I turned to the film medium and found that with careful budgeting I could buy an adequate amount of 16mm film, use borrowed cameras and carry on my experiments. One day a girl, a friend from Houston, came to see me. Naturally, I exposed her to some of my ideas and showed her my films. She said that she couldn't understand why I skimped and struggled. Why didn't I go to a bank and borrow money to make a proper movie? I put on my hat and went to a bank. With a little research I found I knew two boys with adequate jobs to act as co-makers. So I took a personal loan and made my first absolute film, RHYTHM IN LIGHT, which was then booked by the Radio City Music Hall.

Ted Nemeth, ace cinematographer and film producer, photographed RHYTHM IN LIGHT. He not only filmed my first productions but taught me enough about motion picture photography so that I now expend only about 97.5 per cent of my vital energy on the technical realization of my ideas and have a full 2.5 per cent left over for creative work.

My next film, which is taking shape in my head and is charging my emotions, is entirely new visually and aurally. For it I have turned back to many of my early experiments which I am now technically equipped to develop. A mathematical system serves as a basis for this picture. I take the relationship of two or more numbers, for instance 7:2, 3:4, 9:5:4, fraction them around their axis, raise to powers, permutate, divide, multiply, subtract and invert until I have a complete composition of the desired length in numbers. Then I realize this composition in the materials I have selected to employ. I use this composition of numbers to determine the length, width and depth of the photographic field and everything in it. This numerical composition determines the length, speed, and duration of a zoom, a travel back with the camera, the curve and angle at which the camera approaches a subject. It determines the shape, size, color and luminosity of the subject; how, when and in what relationship to other elements of the composition it develops and moves. The melody, harmony, rhythm, dynamics, etc., of the sound are elaborated from the same numerical composition, thus setting up an exquisite relationship between the structural and rhythmical interferences of the combined materials.

If at some time I compose a visual and aural combination that stands my hair on end, I assure myself that it is my art impulses that are at fault. I am not necessarily to blame, but rather long generations of dull training of visual and aural perceptions have retarded my aesthetic tastes and emotional responses to a point where they are far behind the type of art I am capable of realizing. But I and my indefatigable and far flung confreres feel there are indications that the day is close upon us when we will cast aside our atavistic art attitudes and impulses, leaving ourselves free and unencumbered to be exhilarated by the ever-expanding revelations of this art which is expressive of our culture and refreshing entertainment for modern man.

THE KU-KU SONG MAN!

Jim Shadduck

Marvin Hatley was born April 3, 1905, of illiterate, pioneer, Scotch-Irish parents, in a dug-out on a farm in Reed, Oklahoma (population 100). It is believed that as early as seven months he pestered his grandmother to play the zither. We find his precocious musical inclinations again at about two-and-a-half years old when he got lost in a cotton patch with his little white dog and harmonica, wisely using the time experimenting with the harmonic changes the instrument provided. His parents were natural hillbilly musicians playing hoe-downs, jigs and country music--his mother played the violin, his father, the guitar.

When he was five, Santa Claus brought him a little snare drum which he played with the family orchestra at country dances. At nine years, while living with his grandparents in Mangum, Oklahoma, where he attended grammar school, he became a professional vaudeville drummer. One morning he walked into an old silent movie and vaudeville theater and saw his first big set of drums which he just had to try. The janitor who was cleaning the theater at the time immediately scolded him, but the manager, who was so impressed by how well Marvin kept time, came in and hired him on the spot--there were no unions in those days. He played there accompanying the silent films and vaudeville shows until he was thirteen.

About this time his father gave him a gold ring which he promptly traded for a cornet which he still has. He then taught himself to play both the cornet and piano. In the summer, the minstrels would parade around the town square, four jazzy sliding trombones in front and pounding drums in the rear, with screaming brass trumpets and harmonies echoing from every brick building. It was then that he fell in love with jazz music.

The following year he organized a 25-piece boys' band in which he played cornet and acted as leader, touring Texas for the Elks Club. The next summer was spent in Burkburnet, Texas, a lively oil town, playing in a vaudeville orchestra. A short time later, his father courageously took the family to Inglewood, California, in a Model T Ford. At Inglewood High School he became even more active in music, composing several school songs which are still sung there today, arranging for the band, learning orchestration, and conducting the symphony orchestra in which he played several instruments. It was then also that he began his one-man band, with a set of drums under his feet, cymbals, hot Dixieland cornet with his right hand, swing bass piano with his left hand. He played a lot of local school dances.

After graduation, he attended UCLA as a pre-medical student, taking elective courses in harmony and counterpoint. In mid-term of his fourth year, he was called as a substitute pianist at Warner Brothers Radio Station and was hired to play for a week but ended up staying for two years. Between radio jobs, he toured the West Coast with a vaudeville act in which he played 25 musical instruments. One thing led to another and he never finished UCLA. He was soon hired for another radio station job inside the Hal Roach Motion Picture Studios in Culver City. About this time sound came on film and, being in the right place at the right time with the appropriate talent, Marvin was appointed musical director, founding the music department. He started with a three-piece ensemble which eventually grew to 65 musicians, practically a full symphony orchestra as far as the studio recordings are concerned.

While musical director at the Roach Studios, Mr. Hatley studied conducting with Arthur Kay, a former assistant conductor of the Boston Symphony and musical director of Fox Studios. Mr. Kay taught him the German masters, such as Bach, Brahms, Beethoven, Haydn and Mozart. Marvin also studied with Dr. Albert Coates, conductor of the London Symphony, a most masterful conductor and one of the most genial personalities he ever met. Dr. Coates taught him the Russian school--Stravinsky, Tchaikovsky, Rimsky-Korsakov, Mussorgsky.

Hatley was kept very busy at the Roach Studios scoring most of the films, including all the background music. He wrote over 800 compositions for the films, mostly two-reelers and occasionally features such as PICK A STAR with Jack Haley, SWISS MISS with Laurel and Hardy, ZENOBIA with Hardy and Langdon, TOPPER with Cary Grant and Constance Bennett, CAPTAIN FURY with Brian Aherne and Victor McLaglen, and MERRILY WE LIVE with Patsy Kelly, Billie Burke.

He scored all of the Our Gang, all of the Charlie Chase, and most of the Laurel and Hardy comedies. "I suppose I composed about 200 songs all in all to fit the various actors on the Roach Lot." He had a lot of fun playing with Our Gang kids, their dogs, monkeys and various pets. "And, of course, it was fun writing songs according to the script for them." Hatley feels that his best scores for Laurel and Hardy films can be found in THE MUSIC BOX, in which he played the player piano part, SONS OF THE

DESERT, containing his song "Honolulu Baby," WAY OUT WEST, containing his song "Won't You Be My Lovey Dovey?", A CHUMP AT OXFORD, and SAPS AT SEA.

He originally composed the "coo-coo" theme for an hourly theme for the radio station inside the Roach Studios. "I got the idea from the common coo-coo bellows. I combined a simple silly tune on top and the coo-coo below. The clash of the major second intervals is what makes it funny." He was clowning around in the radio room one day playing the goofy combination. At this time Stan was making silent films there. He came up to the radio station one morning and said that he really liked that little tune and would like to use it in his picture. It was used on the very first Laurel and Hardy sound film and became the popular Laurel and Hardy theme.

"It was Stan's idea, then, to use the coo-coo song; he felt that it just fit his personality, that's the reason he liked it." The top bugle-call-like theme represents Hardy, very domineering and the constant coo-coo part in the base represents little Stan Laurel, just a little off. They are dissonant together, always arguing. "Stan Laurel knows what he wants. It just seemed to fit what he wanted to do his job. He has got the fine sense of picking out things he needs."

"Stan Laurel usually wanted 100 per cent music--he was mainly the boss on his pictures. Because Stan Laurel does a lot of pantomime, he wants some music going on 'cause he feels the scene would be dead without music to push it along." He liked lively music. Stan and his life-long English friend, Charley Rodgers, were the idea men in the Laurel and Hardy comedies. Stan would write most of the ideas and Hardy would do what they told him. Hardy was rather independent compared to Stan--he wasn't so sociable as Stan but he always cooperated with what Stan wanted.

Although Hatley occasionally watched them filming to get some ideas ahead of time, his job usually didn't begin until the filming was completed. After the picture is finished, the director and musical director meet to discuss where the music will be placed. Marvin worked closely with Stan; "Stan was there to tell us what his ideas were." Then Marvin got a print of the film which he cut up and spliced, running it through the movieola and marking it with craryon to fit the cues. He then sat down to the actual task of the composition, writing ideas as they came to him or picking them out on the piano.

"The orchestral colors would come to you about the same time you are making the music. The colors themselves had a lot to do with the mood and the instruments themselves are very important." He would usually take his work home with him. In the back of his home, he had a studio with all kinds of references, phonograph records, and scores. He would do most of his work at home, working all night long when it was quiet and he could think better. "Sometimes I wouldn't go to bed for three weeks."

When the composition was finished, he wrote out the master sheet from which someone copied all the parts. During rehearsal on the set, everyone got his parts down. "We would rehearse and then we'd take it while it was hot." The music was put together in little parts for each section--two, three, five ... at the most ten minutes at a time. The projectionist ran the film on a screen which only the conductor could see. Marvin then began to synchronize the film and music by using crosses previously placed on the film and distributed to fit the scene, or by using headphones to hear clicks punched in the sound part of the film. After sufficient rehearsals, he discarded the full orchestral score and used a thin one-line melody with crosses marked on the score. The conductor really had his hands full just keeping up with the crosses and making the orchestra come out in time to fit the scene.

It usually took about two weeks to compose the music and put it together and about two days to record it. After the music was recorded for the finished picture, the sound department mixed the music under the dialogue with the proper softness so that the dialogue would stand out. Stan then viewed it and never had a complaint--nothing had to be done over. "He was always happy with everything I did."

What was it like working with Laurel and Hardy? "Well, it was a great pleasure. Stan Laurel had a wonderful, sweet personality. He was very humble and he was always ready for a laugh. Hardy was more reticent; that is, he didn't mix in as much as Stan Laurel did." The Hatleys lived in Inglewood while Marvin worked at Roach and they would have Laurel and Hardy over for spaghetti dinner. "You'd be surprised how they ate." Hardy just nibbled at a little plate of spaghetti while Stan ate three or four big plates of it. "Most astounding thing I've ever seen. And then he (Stan) went out and jumped in the swimming pool and almost cracked his head open. I don't know why he did that--really some character."

Mr. Hatley's score for WAY OUT WEST was nominated for an Academy Award. "I thought that was a delightful picture. I enjoyed it because it was such a funny picture and it lent itself to such unusual orchestration." He especially likes the first scene where they are coming down the road with the donkey. "I like the idiotic music that matches Stan Laurel when he walks, that gawky walk he's got--it's in 6/8 time." In this sequence he used a lot of sickly, whiney oboe music to accompany the awkwardness. "I used the coo-coo in thousands of variations in Laurel and Hardy, backwards and forwards, sideways, slow and fast--in all kinds of ways."

Marvin worked for Hal Roach for about 12 years until 1942. When the war started Roach closed down and was making only training films for the army. Then, after the war, Marvin took various jobs as a cocktail pianist and stayed in the business for about 15 years. Since then he has worked on his house, being the "comprehensive designer"--designing all the furniture, sculpture, oil paintings, mosaics, and landscaping. "It's been a full-time job."

Now in his sixties and retired, Marvin is very much alive to his environment--very active mentally and physically. His main hobby is organic gardening--citrus, grapes, figs, peaches, plums, apricots, and vegetables. He walks four miles a day. "I read every book and magazine I can get my hands on." Mr. Hatley has become somewhat of a philosopher. "As you grow older, you automatically become a philosopher whether you want to or not. You get beat up going down the road of life, it makes you think a little bit. It's a great and mysterious world, I'll tell you. Nobody knows it all. Nobody knows it all."

THE MOVIE CARTOON IS COMING OF AGE

Otis L. Guernsey, Jr.

The animated cartoon parade is strutting through theaters all over the world, in a ring-around-the-rosy of cats, mice, dogs, rabbits and birds chasing each other through walls. Most of it is the kind of comedy packaged in a round red cylinder clearly labeled "T. N. T." but the breathless chain of eye-rolling violence is sometimes broken by an unusually rich and imaginative idea. Such a one is Walt Disney's TOOT, WHISTLE, PLUNK AND BOOM which was shown on the program with HOW TO MARRY A MILLIONAIRE. It is an engaging cartoon short about music, remarkable in many respects. It is cleverly drawn and animated, and hilariously funny. Like all good laughs, it is founded in good sense. It is a sort of lesson in musical construction, explaining that all music is based on the four elementary sounds of the title, ripened by modern horn, woodwind, string and percussion instruments.

This short is also the first to be made in the wide-screen CinemaScope process. But most remarkable of all is its style, in which the Disney organization departs from the apple-cheeked, roly-poly drawing of the past. TOOT, WHISTLE, PLUNK AND BOOM is cartooned in the modern manner, with angular line sketches, skeleton backgrounds and flatplanes of delicate color. It resembles closely the work of Stephen Bosustow and his United Productions of America (U. P. A.), the group which created an animated cartoon revolution in 1950 with GERALD McBOING-BOING and has continued with the "Mr. Magoo" series and other specialties. If Disney's name were not printed in large letters on TOOT, WHISTLE, PLUNK AND BOOM, you would swear that it was a U. P. A. cartoon. It is as though, suddenly and unaccountably, a perfect Jaguar were to come off the Cadillac assembly line.

This is actually the second time that the Disney outfit has streamlined its style. The first occasion was in MELODY, a stereoscopic 3-D short. It was the first of a new series called "Adventures in Music," of which TOOT, WHISTLE, PLUNK AND BOOM is the second. In the short his organization shows complete mastery of the impressionistic, childlike movements and fast cutting for laughs. TOOT, WHISTLE, PLUNK AND BOOM starts with a cubistic owl teaching a music class, but its main figures are four crudely drawn cave men making the four basic sounds in primitive fashion. With flashes of Egypt, troubadors and other highlights of a sunny imagination, it goes on to show how the sounds were improved along with the instruments--how, for instance, a horn's pitch is determined by its length, not its shape, so that a long one can be bent to spell "George" and still give out the same note.

It has always been difficult to deal with human beings in the conventional Disney style. The mice stole CINDERELLA from the star, and most of his imitators confine themselves to animals. There is no such difficulty in the new form of caricature, and the Disney group releases its frustration delightfully on everything from a jiving Pharaoh to a stiff-necked modern string quartet.

NOTES ON CARTOON MUSIC

Ingolf Dahl

If film music, as far as critical attention goes, is the poor relation of concert music, then cartoon music must be the destitute nephew of the poor relation. Little has been said, written or thought about the subject and very rarely have the efforts of the makers of short cartoons received much critical interest, least of all those who supply it with music. At the same time be it remembered that it is their joint product which is the only part of the regular cinema fare that unfailingly receives advance applause by the audience, for better or for worse.

Seeing old cartoons again we realize how much the medium has changed. The procedure used to be one of fitting humorous story and action to cheerful, zippy, bouncy music which hovered in style between Gilbert & Sullivan and Zez Confrey. The music was rhythmically defined, symmetrically constructed in eight-bar phrases somewhat on the order of a dance tune, and its changes of mood ("chase," "danger," "villain," "heroism," etc.) were modified by the structural symmetry of popular music and its inherent simplicity. The cartoons presented in essence a kind of humorous "choreography" to catchy music. This analogy can even be carried into details: just as the dancer reserves his more spectacular tricks for the cadences at the end of musical phrases so the cartoonist, probably out of instinct, achieved some of his funniest effects by placing outstanding action (be it the bounce of a ball or the impact of a pie on a face) on the same cadential accents with which in popular music every eighth measure ends. This "cadence plus stylized action" has been changed in most of the newer cartoons to just the opposite approach: the action is determined purely from the story angle and developed independently of musical considerations. I am aware, of course, of the exceptions, such as the cartoons to pre-scored pieces of serious or popular music for which Disney is justly famous. But in the ordinary cartoon nowadays the music is added to a predetermined course of hectic events and is in many cases required to do nothing more than duplicate the action by synchronous illustration, taking the role of sound effect together with the role of musical characterization. It attests to the stubbornness of some few composers that in spite of this more or less mechanical application of their art they still try here and there, to invest their "sound tailoring" with some musical meaning. "Realism of action" (whatever that can be in drawn images) has become more important than rhythmic stylization. This is clearly reflected in the average present-day cartoon score: when we look at the music we see that it makes sense only if considered as "recitative accompaniment" to an action in pantomime.

This is not a new musical form. To quote just two of the most famous historical examples: Beckmesser's pantomime scene in the third act of Die Meistersinger, as well as the opening scene of the third act of Fledermaus. Both are accompanied by such a direct anticipation of cartoon music techniques that once more they give one cause to reflect: have technical advances of our new media called for and developed commensurate musical advances?

The change from the "composed" cartoon to the "realistic" action cartoon has brought with it an attendant confusion of styles which is just as noticeable in some of Disney's Technicolor excesses (one is tempted to quote Frederick Packard from the New Yorker: "Be quiet, Technicoloriot!") as in the cartoon concept of humor. Cartoons are funny, should be funny, but now we are forced to stretch our definition of what is funny in the forties to include continuous sadistic violence in which steam rollers and dynamite sticks constitute the more playful ingredients.

But cartoons, at the same time as they are the buffo intermezzi of modern dramatic entertainment, are also the only completely creative combination of the aural and the plastic arts in movement. As such they have hardly scratched the surface of their possibilities yet. Only comparatively few (such as BOUNDARY LINES, to mention just one) seem to be aware of the possible directions. Considering the opportunities which such a combination offers both to the artists and to general entertainment it is to be hoped that continued critical examinations of the two arts and their common denominators be carried on in discussion and experiment. To be dealt with, among other things, should be the question of repetition (can or should the image repeat as pronouncedly as music must for the sake of its form?), the question of how much rhythmic coincidence is required and where, as well as the relation of variety and order in the pictorial elements to harmonic progression and structure in the music, etc. The experiments of Fischinger and Fischinger-Disney ("Toccato and Fugue"), of the brothers Whitney, Norman McLaren, and others, point to these problems, both through their shortcomings and their achievements.

Much cartoon music is being written in Hollywood as part of the regular schedules of the studios and a considerable amount of talent, thought and hard work goes into the composing and recording of it. To name just a few names of the most prominent composers in the field: Scott Bradley (MGM), Oliver Wallace (Disney), Paul Smith (Disney), Carl Stalling (Warner Brothers).

In order to give an example of the specific techniques of writing cartoon music, let me take you on a visit to Scott Bradley, composer at MGM. After asking him by mail for some information about himself I received a blue slip of paper which I am impelled to quote in toto:

> METRO GOLDWYN MAYER. INTER-OFFICE COMMUNICATION TO: Dahl SUBJECT: Dis-a and dat-a FROM: Bradley. Born ... Russelville, Arkansas (but not an "Arkie" I hasten to add) ... Studied piano, private instruction ... organ and harmony with the English organist Horton Corbet ... Otherwise entirely self-taught in com-

> position and orchestration ... fed large doses of Bach, which I absorbed and asked for more. Conductor at KHJ and KNX in early thirties ... entered the non-sacred realm of pictures in 1932 and started cartoon composing in 1934 with Harmon-Ising Co. Joined MGM in 1937 ... have so far been able to hide from them the fact that I'm not much of a composer. Personal: dislike bridge, slacks and mannish dress on women, all chromatic and diatonic scales, whether written by Beethoven or Bradley. Also, crowds and most people (and especially biographers). Favorite composers: Brahms, Stravinsky, Hindemith, Bartók. This will be boring to most everyone, so cut it as short as you wish. Signed: Scott.

Without comment, one would want to add to this that six Academy Awards have been given to cartoons to which Bradley has written scores (the famous CAT CONCERTO was one of them).

Bradley has his office in the MGM cartoon building which is separated from the main lot by a highway. As we enter his office we see him brooding over a half filled odd-looking sheet of music paper while an old-fashioned pyramidal metronome is clicking away in front of him. The music paper on which he is working is covered, in addition to the few finished measures of music, with all kinds of signs, figures, multi-colored words, directions and descriptions. This is a "detail sheet" for a new Tom and Jerry cartoon which has just been finished by the cartoonist and which is ready for scoring. The music that will have to go on the empty staves of the detail sheet must be composed, orchestrated and recorded within the next two weeks. In order to refresh his memory at any given point and in case the vivid prose on the detail sheet is insufficient to prod his muse into delivering the goods, Bradley has also been given a rough cut of the pencil reel (non-colored) which he can run at any speed, forwards or backwards, through a viewing machine (movieola). Before this he has not seen the cartoon and knows the script only in general outlines. However, if the particular cartoon contains any song-and-dance routines they would have been recorded in pre-scoring before the drawings were made to fit the timing of the music. The detail sheet contains a complete breakdown of all items of action. These are tabulated according to a regular number of frame units on which the animation was based. This unit, whether it be of 10 frames, 16 frames, or whatever number, indicates the smallest rhythmic denominator of the scene. Translated into music, it represents a beat that forms the regular, non-deviating time unit of a scene. The composer determines his metrical structure accordingly. Ten frames equal a metronome (MM) beat of 144, sixteen frames (a beat per foot) equal MM 88, etc. His bar lines will then be set according to the metric scheme in which he wants to group several beats, and only musical requirements plus his ingenuity will determine the meter.

Synchronization in post-scoring will be achieved by means of the "click track," a loop of sound track that is run through a reproducing unit and which is marked, or punched, at regular intervals (ever 10, or 16, etc., frames), thereby producing an audible click in earphones that are worn by the playing musicians. Bradley records most of his music in post-scoring; i.e., like the average dramatic feature film, after the shooting and editing has been completed. The exceptions, as mentioned above, are songs, dances, the cartooning of set concert or popular pieces (right now Bradley is preparing to record the Fledermaus Overture for a future cartoon, without clicks).

The reason for his procedure is that most cartoon directors are not musical and would have difficulty in constructing their action to fit a musical pattern. Therefore the music will have to adjust to the fast shifting image (sometimes one could say "the convulsively shifting image") and the composer will try desperately to find ways of creating a semblance of musical coherence and structure. Expediency is the motto, and a wide variety of styles and techniques a requirement. Musical illustration is another requirement, and the degree to which illustration is lifted above the purely mechanical duplication of action depends again on the inventiveness of the composer. Another problem is the excessively short time in which music must make its points and within which it must accomplish changes of mood, of character, of expression. This calls for constant flexibility in the handling of thematic material and the ability of applying the variation technique to phrases of aphoristic brevity. One sustained melodic note on the violin may consume four feet of film, not to speak of the whole of such a melody. There is little chance for musical extension of any kind.

There are still other restrictions and hazards: the

constant preoccupation with a metronomic beat from which the composer, at least subconsciously, cannot escape, tends to impart a certain rhythmic squareness to his phrases and it takes much conscious effort on his part to overcome this. Tied down, as he is by metronome and timing sheet, it is difficult for him to write music that has flow and overall continuity and that is written across the bar lines rather than shackled by them. But if, on the one hand, he has to fight the constraining influence of the squarely regular time unit he has to try, on the other hand, to create musical symmetry where the cartoon lacks it. The cartoon, being a very extrovert and direct form of entertainment, needs the reassuring directness of symmetrically constructed music. But how to supply this when the direction has crystallized the form of the film entirely outside of musical considerations?

The rigid discipline and regimentation that are imposed by the mechanics of cartoon composition are not the only factors which tie the composer down. The scope of musical expression is equally limited. For how long can a composer continue to restrict himself exclusively to the bright yellows and reds of the musical palette in painting whimsical, cute, hilarious pictures? Even men of genius like Rossini or Offenbach did not have an inexhaustible supply of humorous ideas and there comes a time when piccolo and bassoon in unison will sound rather threadbare. And if it is not whimsy it is violence. With an anguished expression on his usually cheerful face Scott Bradley sighs, "It's fights, fights, fights for me ... and how I am getting tired of them! A beautiful, developed tune--alas, that's never the fate of Scott."

However, there are compensations. Bradley knows how much satisfaction there is in seeing how music can give definition to screen action and how it can invest the drawn characters with personality, from the jocose to the maudlin. At best, music can add charm and profile to the drawings. The good composers realize this and they are straining against the requirements of the "electric buzzer" kind of mickey mousing which is unaware of the richer musical possibilities.

In writing his music the composer will have to consider at all times the scope and the limitations of his orchestra. It is a small group, consisting of anywhere between 16 to 30 musicians. Bradley usually has at his disposal four violins, one viola, one cello, one bass, piano, one percussion player, one each of flute (doubling piccolo), oboe, bassoon, three clarinets (doubling saxophones) three trumpets, two trombones. Microphone placement and recording tricks (such as multi-channel recording of the screened-off sections of the orchestra, parts of which receive artificial reverberation in the dubbing) will have to overcome the inadequacies of balance and instrumental proportion. There is some flexibility in instrumentation and just recently Bradley recorded a whole cartoon (TEXAS TOM) which was scored for only a small woodwind and brass ensemble with very fresh and charming results.

It must be obvious to anyone who has ever seen and heard cartoons that even within the normal orchestral group there are instruments that stand out as cartoon specialists. The marionette quality of the characters and their action finds expression through the comparably "impersonalized" wind instruments, and the above mentioned piccolo and bassoon, as also the dry, jerky xylophone have become cartoon instruments par excellence.

The musically interested person must regret that instances of imaginative instrumentation (I am not talking of the orchestration here) are so rare in a field that actually demands it. It is equally strange that some of the newer devices of tone production have not found their way into a medium that is doubtlessly made for them. I am speaking of sounds like those marvelous chord structures, waves, rolls, strummings, whisperings, crashes, etc. that Henry Cowell gets out of a piano and also of the completely enchanting (as well as radio-genic) sound world of bells, chimes, drums, gongs, underwater xylophones, etc. into which John Cage can transform the piano. Some day a cartoon director is going to wake up to the fact that he is missing a sure-fire bet by not availing himself of the talents of Cage for the cartoon. His sense of sound as well as his remarkably developed rhythmic inventiveness make him (or his techniques) a natural for cartoon music.

Chapter VIII

BIBLIOGRAPHY

ASCAP--30 Years of Motion Picture Music (American Society of Composers, Arrangers and Publishers, 1967), 135p.

Dolan, Robert Emmett. Music in Modern Media (G. Schirmer, 1967), 181p.

Eisler, Hanns. Composing for the Films (Dobson, 1947), 165p.

Faulkner, Robert R. Hollywood Studio Musicians (Aldine-Atherton, 1971), 218p.

Heinsheimer, H. W. Menagerie in F Sharp (Doubleday, 1947), 275p.

Hofmann, Charles. Sounds for Silents (Arno, 1970), n.p.

Lambert, Constant. Music Ho! (Faber, 1934), 341p.

Lang, Edith, and George West. Musical Accompaniment of Moving Pictures (Arno, 1970), 64p.

Levy, Louis. Music for the Movies (Low, 1948), 182p.

London, Kurt. Film Music (Arno, 1970), 280p.

McCarty, Clifford. Film Composers in America (J. Valentine, 1953), 193p.

Mancini, Henry. Sounds and Scores (Northridge Music, 1962), 245p.

Manvell, Roger and John Huntley. Technique of Film Music (Hastings, 1957), 299p.

Meeker, David. _Jazz in the Movies_ (British Film Institute, 1972), 89p.

Rapee, Erno. _Encyclopaedia of Music for Pictures_ (Arno, 1970), 510p.

_______. _Motion Picture Moods for Pianists and Organists_ (Arno, 1970).

Rodriguez, Jose (ed.). _Music and Dance in California_ (Bureau of Musical Research, 1940), 467p.

Sabaneev, Leonid. _Music for the Films_ (Pitman, 1935), 128p.

Saunders, Richard D. (ed.). _Music and Dance in California and the West_ (Bureau of Musical Research, 1948), 311p.

Skinner, Frank. _Underscore_ (Wehman, 1961), 239p.

Smolian, Steve. _A Handbook of Film, Theater and Television Music on Record_ (Record Undertaker, 1970), 2 vols.

Stevens, Leith, and Earle Hagan. _Scoring for Films_ (Criterion, 1972), with recordings.

Tootell, George. _How to Play the Cinema Organ_ (Curwen, 1927), 114p.

Whitworth, Reginald. _The Cinema and Theater Organ_ (London: Musical Opinion, 1932), 112p.

Part Two

INTRODUCTION
(to Chapters IX to XII)

There seem to be many stories about film music composers and there is little doubt that most of them are true. Under studio regimes, several composers worked on a score, although only one may have received official credit. Aaron Copland disowned his score for THE HEIRESS, although he won an Academy Award for it. Much of the score had been scrapped and "Plaisir d'Amour" was substituted. At other studios, several noted composers would help out in bringing together a full score. Important composers such as Andre Previn and David Raksin have had to scrap entire scores when the producer refused to accept them and write new ones or turn them over to another composer altogether. Even Max Steiner is said to have had at least a half-dozen composers working on GONE WITH THE WIND, although only Steiner is credited.

Because of this situation, there will be some challenges on the names listed here, especially those men listed as "musical directors," but some studios in earlier decades did not credit their composers. So these index chapters must be limited to "official" studio credits for the composers listed herein.

Chapter IX, "Film Titles and Dates," is an alphabetical list of all film titles in this volume; it serves as an index to Chapter X, which is arranged chronologically. Each title listed shows the year of the film's release; when more than one year was listed for a particular title in the various sources checked, the earlier date was selected. This is especially important in the case of foreign films which might have been released during a certain year, but did not appear in the United States until perhaps a year or two later.

Chapter X, "Films and Their Composers" has all titles listed by the year of release, together with the name(s) of the composer(s) or musical director of the film. All names were cross-checked for spelling (and there were as many as four different spelling variations for several composers) and the most common spelling was selected in each case.

Chapter XI, "Composers and Their Films," lists the composers and musical directors together with the films credited to them in chronological order by year and alphabetical order within each year.

Chapter XII, "Recorded Musical Scores," lists most known musical scores for films which have been recorded on discs and tapes for commercial release. Musical movies which feature a song score are seldom listed. These are covered in another publication, Theatrical Events on Records and Tapes (Pierian Press).

Chapter IX

FILM TITLES AND DATES

Aaron Slick from Punkin Crick (1952)
Abandon Ship! (1957)
Abandoned (1949)
Abbott and Costello Go to Mars (1953)
Abbott and Costello in Hollywood (1945)
Abbott and Costello in the Foreign Legion (1950)
Abbott and Costello Meet Captain Kidd (1952)
Abbott and Costello Meet Frankenstein (1948)
Abbott and Costello Meet the Invisible Man (1951)
Abbott and Costello Meet the Keystone Kops (1955)
Abbott and Costello Meet the Killer (1949)
Abbott and Costello Meet the Mummy (1955)
The Abductors (1957)
Abdullah's Harem (1956)
Abe Lincoln in Illinois (1940)
Abel, Your Brother (1970)
Abie's Irish Rose (1928)
Abie's Irish Rose (1946)
Abilene Town (1946)
Abilene Trail (1951)
The Abominable Dr. Phibes (1971)
The Abominable Snowman (1957)
About Face (1942)
About Mrs. Leslie (1954)
Above and Beyond (1952)
Above Suspicion (1943)
Above Us the Waves (1956)
Abroad with Two Yanks (1944)
Absent-Minded (1970)
The Absent-Minded Professor (1961)
Absolute Quiet (1936)
Abuse of Authority (1971)
Les Abysses (1963)
Academician Ivan Pavlov (1949)
Accident (1967)
Accomplice (1946)
According to Mrs. Hoyle (1951)
The Accursed (1958)
Accused (1936)
The Accused (1948)
Accused of Murder (1956)
Ace in the Hole (see The Big Carnival)
Aces High (1969)
Across the Bridge (1957)
Across the Pacific (1942)
Across the River (1965)
Across the Wide Missouri (1951)
Act of Love (1953)
An Act of Murder (1948)
Act of the Heart (1970)
Act of Violence (1948)
Act One (1963)
Action in Arabia (1944)
Action in the North Atlantic (1943)
Action of the Tiger (1957)
Actors and Sin (1952)
The Actress (1953)
Actualities (1928)
Ada (1961)
Adam and Eve (1957)
Adam and Evelyn (1949)
Adam Had Four Sons (1941)
Adam 2 (1969)
Adam's Rib (1949)
Adam's Woman (1970)
The Adding Machine (1969)

Address Unknown (1944)
Adios Sabata (1971)
The Admirable Crichton (1957)
Admiral Ushakov (1953)
The Admiral Was a Lady (1950)
Adorable (1933)
Adorable Creatures (1956)
Adrienne Lecouvrer (1938)
Adrift (1971)
Advance to the Rear (1964)
Adventure (1946)
Adventure in Baltimore (1949)
Adventure Island (1947)
The Adventurers (1970)
Adventures in Manhattan (1936)
The Adventures of * (1957)
Adventures of Artyomka (1956)
Adventures of Baron Munchausen (1942)
Adventures of Bullwhip Griffin (1967)
Adventures of Captain Fabian (1951)
Adventures of Casanova (1948)
Adventures of Don Coyote (1947)
Adventures of Don Juan (1948)
Adventures of Gallant Bess (1948)
The Adventures of Hajji Baba (1954)
The Adventures of Huckleberry Finn (1939)
The Adventures of Huckleberry Finn (1960)
The Adventures of Ichabod and Mr. Toad (1949)
Adventures of Marco Polo (1938)
The Adventures of Mark Twain (1944)
The Adventures of Martin Eden (1942)
Adventures of Prince Achmed (1926)
Adventures of Robin Hood (1938)
Adventures of Robinson Crusoe (1954)
The Adventures of Sadie (1955)
The Adventures of Sherlock Holmes (1939)
Adventures of Tom Sawyer (1938)
The Adversary (1971)
Advice to the Lovelorn (1933)
Advise and Consent (1962)
Aerial Gunner (1943)
Aerograd (Frontier) (1936)
The Affair Blum (1948)
Affair in Havana (1957)
Affair in Monte Carlo (1953)
Affair in Reno (1957)
Affair in Trinidad (1952)
An Affair to Remember (1957)
L'Affaire est dans le Sac (1932)
Affairs of Annabel (1938)
The Affairs of Cellini (1934)
Affairs of Dobie Gillis (1953)
Affairs of Geraldine (1946)
The Affairs of Jimmy Valentine (1942)
The Affairs of Martha (1942)
The Affairs of Messalina (1954)
The Affairs of Susan (1945)
Affectionately Yours (1941)
Africa Addio (1966)
Africa Adventure (1954)
Africa Screams (1949)
Africa, Texas Style (1967)
The African Elephant (1971)
The African Lion (1955)
The African Queen (1951)
African Treasure (1952)
After Shadows, Light (1970)
After the Fox (1966)
After the Thin Man (1936)
Again .... Pioneers (1950)
Against All Flags (1952)
Age of Consent (1969)
Age of Infidelity (1958)
Agent 8-3/4 (1965)
The Agony and the Ecstasy (1965)
Ah, Wilderness (1936)
L'Aine Des Ferchaux (1956)
Ain't Misbehavin' (1955)
Air Cadet (1951)
L'air de Paris (1954)
Air Force (1943)
Air Patrol (1962)
Air Raid Wardens (1943)
Airport (1970)
Akran (1969)
Al Capone (1959)
Al Jennings of Oklahoma (1951)
Aladdin and His Lamp (1952)
Alakazam the Great (1961)
The Alamo (1960)

Alaska (1944)
Alaska Highway (1943)
Alaska Passage (1959)
Alaska Patrol (1949)
Alaska Seas (1954)
Albert Schweitzer (1957)
Albuquerque (1948)
Alex in Wonderland (1970)
Alexander Nevsky (1938)
Alexander the Great (1956)
Alfie (1966)
Alfred the Great (1969)
Algiers (1938)
Ali Baba and the Forty Thieves (1944)
Alias a Gentleman (1948)
Alias Billy the Kid (1946)
Alias Bulldog Drummond (1935)
Alias Jesse James (1959)
Alias Nick Beal (1949)
Alias the Champ (1949)
Alice Adams (1935)
Alice in Wonderland (1934)
Alice in Wonderland (1951)
Alice's Restaurant (1969)
The Alienist (1970)
Aliki My Love (1962)
Alimony (1949)
Alisher Navoi (1947)
Alkeste--The Importance of Having Protection (1970)
All About Eve (1950)
The All-American (1953)
All Fall Down (1962)
All Hands on Deck (1961)
All I Desire (1953)
All in a Night's Work (1961)
All Men Are Apes (1965)
All Mine to Give (1957)
All My Sons (1948)
All Neat in Black Stockings (1969)
All Over Town (1949)
All Quiet on the Western Front (1930)
All That Heaven Allows (1955)
All That I Have (1951)
All That Money Can Buy (1941)
All the Brothers Were Valiant (1953)
All the Fine Young Cannibals (1960)
All the Gold in the World (1961)
All the King's Horses (1935)
All the King's Men (1949)
All the Right Noises (1971)
All the Way Home (1963)
All the Way Up (1970)
All the Young Men (1960)
All This and Heaven Too (1940)
All Through the Night (1942)
Allegheny Uprising (1939)
An Alligator Named Daisy (1957)
The Alligator People (1959)
Almost a Man (1966)
Alone (1930)
Alone in the Streets (1956)
Along Came Jones (1945)
Along the Great Divide (1951)
Along the Navajo Trail (1945)
Along the Oregon Trail (1947)
The Alphabet Murders (1966)
Alphaville (1965)
Altar Masterpiece (1952)
The Altarpiece Maker (1970)
Alvarez Kelly (1966)
Always a Bride (1954)
Always Goodbye (1931)
Always in My Heart (1942)
Always Together (1947)
Amateur Daddy (1932)
Amateur Gentleman (1936)
The Amazing Colossal Man (1957)
The Amazing Dr. Clitterhouse (1938)
The Amazing Mrs. Holliday (1943)
The Amazing Mr. Beecham (1949)
Amazon Quest (1949)
The Amazon Trader (1956)
The Ambassador's Daughter (1956)
Ambush (1939)
Ambush (1949)
Ambush at Cimarron Pass (1958)
Ambush at Tomahawk Gap (1953)
Ambush Bay (1966)
Ambush Trail (1946)
The Ambushers (1967)
America, America (1963)
The American Beauty (1916)

An American Dream (1966)
American Empire (1942)
An American Guerrilla in the Philippines (1950)
The American Road (1953)
An American Romance (1944)
American Sexual Revolution (1971)
The American Soldier (1970)
The Americanization of Emily (1964)
The Americano (1955)
L'Amica (1915)
The Amorist (1966)
The Amorous Adventures of Moll Flanders (1965)
Amsterdam Affair (1968)
Anastasia (1956)
Anatomy of the Act of Love (1970)
The Anatomy of Love (1953)
Anatomy of a Murder (1959)
The Ancines Woods (1970)
And Baby Makes Three (1949)
And God Created Woman (1957)
And Now Miguel (1966)
And Now Tomorrow (1944)
And Now Tomorrow (1952)
And Quiet Flows the Don (1957)
And So They Were Married (1936)
And Soon the Darkness (1970)
And Then There Were None (1945)
The Anderson Tapes (1971)
Androcles and the Lion (1952)
The Andromeda Strain (1971)
Andy Hardy Comes Home (1958)
Andy Hardy Gets Spring Fever (1939)
Andy Hardy Meets a Debutante (1940)
Andy Hardy's Blonde Trouble (1944)
Andy Hardy's Double Life (1942)
Andy Hardy's Private Secretary (1941)
Angel and the Badman (1947)
Angel, Angel, Down We Go (1969)
Angel Baby (1961)
An Angel Comes to Brooklyn (1945)
Angel Face (1952)
Angel in Exile (1948)
The Angel Levine (1970)
Angel on My Shoulder (1946)
Angel on the Amazon (1948)
The Angel Wore Red (1960)
Angela (1955)
Angelique (1966)
Angel's Alley (1948)
Angels Die Hard (1970)
Angels from Hell (1968)
Angels in Disguise (1949)
Angels in the Outfield (1951)
Angels One Five (1954)
Angels Wash Their Faces (1939)
Angels with Dirty Faces (1938)
The Angry Hills (1959)
The Angry Silence (1960)
Animal Farm (1955)
The Animal World (1956)
The Animals (1965)
The Animals (1971)
Ann and Eve (1970)
Ann Vickers (1933)
Anna (1970)
Anna and the King of Siam (1946)
The Anna Cross (1954)
Anna Karenina (1935)
Anna Karenina (1968)
Anna Lucasta (1949)
Anna Lucasta (1958)
Annabel Takes a Tour (1938)
An Annapolis Story (1955)
Anne of the Indies (1951)
Anne of the Thousand Days (1969)
Annie Laurie (1927)
Annie Oakley (1936)
The Anniversary (1968)
The Anonymous Venetian (1970)
Another Dawn (1937)
Another Man's Poison (1952)
Another Man's Wife (1967)
Another Part of the Forest (1948)
Another Shore (1948)
Another Thin Man (1939)
Another Time, Another Place (1958)
Antefatto (1971)
Anthony Adverse (1936)
Antigone (1962)

Any Number Can Play (1949)
Any Number Can Win (1963)
Any Wednesday (1966)
Anyone Can Play (1968)
Anything Can Happen (1952)
Anzio (1968)
Aoom (1970)
Apache (1954)
Apache Ambush (1955)
Apache Chief (1949)
Apache Drums (1951)
Apache Gold (1965)
Apache Rifles (1964)
Apache Rose (1947)
Apache Trail (1942)
Apache Uprising (1966)
Apache War Smoke (1952)
Apache Warrior (1957)
Aparajito (1958)
The Apartment (1960)
Apartment for Peggy (1948)
The Ape Man (1943)
The Ape Woman (1964)
Apocalypse (1970)
Apokal (1971)
Apology for Murder (1945)
The Appaloosa (1966)
The Apple (1969)
The Appointment (1969)
Appointment for Love (1941)
Appointment in Berlin (1943)
Appointment in Honduras (1953)
Appointment with Danger (1951)
Appointment with Murder (1948)
The Apprentice (1971)
The April Fools (1969)
Arabesque (1966)
Arabian Nights (1942)
Arch of Triumph (1948)
Arctic Flight (1952)
Arctic Manhunt (1949)
Arde (1971)
Are Husbands Necessary? (1942)
Are You Afraid? (1971)
Are You with It? (1948)
Arabella (1969)
Arena (1953)
Aren't We Wonderful? (1958)
The Argyle Secrets (1948)
Arise, My Love (1940)
The Aristocats (1970)
Arizona (1940)
Arizona Bushwackers (1968)
The Arizona Cowboy (1950)
The Arizona Kid (1939)
Arizona Manhunt (1951)
Arizona Raiders (1965)
The Arizona Ranger (1948)
Arizona Roundup (1942)
Arizona Whirlwind (1944)
Armored Command (1961)
Army Bound (1952)
Army Surgeon (1942)
The Arnelo Affair (1947)
Around is Around (1952)
Around the World (1943)
Around the World in 80 Days (1956)
Around the World Under the Sea (1966)
The Arp Statue (1971)
Arrah-Na-Pough (1911)
The Arrangement (1969)
Arrest Bulldog Drummond (1939)
Arrivederci, Baby (1966)
Arrow in the Dust (1954)
Arrowhead (1953)
Arrowsmith (1931)
Arruza (1971)
Arsene Lupin Returns (1938)
Arsenic and Old Lace (1944)
Arson, Inc. (1949)
Arson Squad (1944)
Arthur Takes Over (1948)
The Art of Love (1965)
Artists and Models (1955)
Arturo's Island (1963)
As Husbands Go (1933)
As Long as They're Happy (1957)
As Long as You Are Healthy (1966)
As the Sea Rages (1960)
As You Like It (1936)
As You Were (1951)
As Young as You Feel (1951)
Ask Any Girl (1959)
The Asphalt Jungle (1950)
The Assassin (1953)
The Assassination Bureau (1969)
The Assassination of the Duc de Guise (1908)
Assault (1957)
Assault (1971)

Assault on a Queen (1966)
Assigned to Danger (1948)
Assignment in Brittany (1943)
Assignment K (1968)
Assignment Paris (1952)
Assignment to Kill (1968)
Asterix and Cleopatra (1969)
Astero (1959)
The Astonished Heart (1950)
The Astro Zombies (1969)
Astrologie (1952)
At Gunpoint (1955)
At Sword's Point (1952)
At the Circus (1939)
L'Atalante (1934)
Athena (1954)
Atilla (1958)
Atlantic City (1944)
Atlantis, the Lost Continent (1961)
The Atomic City (1952)
The Atomic Kid (1954)
The Atomic Submarine (1959)
Atragon (1965)
Attack! (1956)
Attack from the Sea (1953)
Attack of the Crab Monsters (1957)
Attack of the 50-Foot Woman (1958)
Attack on the Iron Coast (1968)
Au Grand Balcon (1949)
Aubervilliers (1947)
Aunt from Chicago (1960)
Auntie Mame (1958)
Autumn Leaves (1956)
Avalanche (1946)
The Avengers (1942)
The Avengers (1950)
The Avenging Rider (1943)
L'Avventura (1961)
The Awakening (1928)
The Awakening (1971)
Away All Boats (1956)

B. F.'s Daughter (1948)
B. S., I Love You (1971)
The Babe Ruth Story (1948)
Babes in Toyland (1961)
Babette Goes to War (1960)
The Baby and the Battleship (1957)
Baby Doll (1956)
Baby Face Morgan (1942)
Baby Face Nelson (1957)
Baby Love (1969)
The Baby Maker (1970)
Baby, the Rain Must Fall (1965)
The Babysitter (1969)
The Bachelor and the Bobby-Soxer (1947)
Bachelor Flat (1961)
Bachelor in Paradise (1961)
The Bachelor Party (1957)
The Bachelor's Daughters (1946)
Back at the Front (1952)
Back Door to Heaven (1939)
Back Door to Hell (1963)
Back from Eternity (1956)
Back from the Dead (1957)
Back Street (1941)
Back Street (1961)
Back Street of Paris (1948)
Back to Bataan (1945)
Back to God's Country (1953)
Back to the Wall (1959)
Backfire (1950)
Backfire (1965)
Background to Danger (1943)
Backlash (1947)
Backlash (1956)
Backtrack (1969)
Backtrail (1948)
The Bad and the Beautiful (1952)
Bad Bascomb (1946)
Bad Boy (1949)
Bad Boys (1960)
Bad Day at Black Rock (1954)
Bad for Each Other (1953)
Bad Lands (1939)
Bad Little Angel (1939)
The Bad Man of Brimstone (1938)
Bad Men of Tombstone (1948)
The Bad Seed (1956)
Bad Sister (1948)
The Bad Sleep Well (1963)
The Badge of Marshal Brennan (1957)
Badlands of Montana (1957)
Badman's Country (1958)
Badman's Territory (1946)
Bagarres (1948)
Bagdad (1949)
The Bailiff (1954)

Bailout at 43,000 (1957)
Bait (1954)
The Baker's Wife (1938)
Bal Tabarin (1952)
The Balcony (1963)
Bali (1971)
The Ball of Count Orgel (1970)
Ballad of a Soldier (1960)
The Ballad of Cable Hogue (1970)
The Ballad of Josie (1967)
Ballerina (1950)
Ballerina (1958)
Ballet Mechanique (1924)
The Ballet of Romeo and Juliet (1955)
Baltic Deputy (1937)
Baltic Express (1959)
A Baltic Tragedy (1970)
Bambole! (1965)
The Bamboo Prison (1954)
The Bamboo Saucer (1968)
Bananas (1971)
Band of Angels (1957)
La Bandera (1935)
Bandido (1956)
The Bandit (O Cangaciero) (1953)
Bandit King of Texas (1949)
The Bandit of Sherwood Forest (1946)
The Bandit of Zhobe (1959)
Bandit Queen (1950)
Bandit Ranger (1942)
Bandits in Milan (1968)
The Bandits of Corsica (1953)
Bandits of the Badlands (1945)
Bandits of the West (1953)
Bandolero (1968)
The Bandwagon (1953)
Bang Bang (1971)
The Bang Bang Gang (1970)
The Bang Bang Kid (1968)
Bang, Bang, You're Dead (1966)
Banjo (1947)
Banjo on My Knee (1936)
The Bank Dick (1940)
Bannerline (1951)
Banquero (1970)
Barabbas (1962)
Barbarella (1968)
The Barbarian and the Geisha (1958)
Barbary Coast (1935)
Barbary Coast Gent (1944)
Barbary Pirate (1949)
The Barefoot Batallion (1954)
The Barefoot Contessa (1954)
The Barefoot Executive (1971)
Barefoot in the Park (1967)
The Barefoot Mailman (1951)
The Baron of Arizona (1950)
The Barretts of Wimpole Street (1934)
The Barretts of Wimpole Street (1957)
Barricade (1939)
Barricade (1950)
The Barrier (The Great Barrier) (1937)
Bartleby (1971)
The Bashful Elephant (1962)
The Basketball Fix (1951)
The Bat (1959)
Bataan (1943)
Batman (1966)
Batouk (1967)
Battle at Bloody Beach (1961)
Battle Beneath the Earth (1968)
Battle Circus (1953)
Battle Cry (1955)
The Battle Cry of Peace (1915)
Battle Flame (1959)
The Battle for Siberia (1940)
Battle Hymn (1956)
Battle in Outer Space (1960)
The Battle of Algiers (1966)
The Battle of Apache Pass (1952)
The Battle of Love's Return (1971)
Battle of Rogue River (1954)
Battle of Russia (1943)
The Battle of Stalingrad (1949)
The Battle of the Bulge (1965)
The Battle of the Bulge--The Brave Rifles (1966)
Battle of the Coral Sea (1959)
The Battle of the Neretva (1969)
Battle of the Rails (1944)
Battle of the Sexes (1928)
The Battle of the Sexes (1960)
The Battle of the Villa Fiorita (1965)
Battle Stations (1956)
Battle Taxi (1955)

Battle Zone (1952)
Battleground (1949)
Bay of Angels (1965)
Bayou (1956)
Be Sick--It's Free (1968)
Beach Ball (1965)
Beach Blanket Bingo (1965)
Beach Party (1963)
The Beach Umbrella (1966)
The Beachcomber (1955)
Beachhead (1954)
The Bear (1970)
Bear Country (1952)
The Bears (1965)
The Beast of Budapest (1958)
The Beast of Hollow Mountain (1956)
The Beast with Five Fingers (1947)
The Beat Generation (1959)
Beat the Devil (1954)
Beau Brummel (1954)
Beau Geste (1926)
Beau Geste (1939)
Beau Geste (1966)
Beau James (1957)
Beauties of the Night (1952)
The Beautiful Blonde from Bashful Bend (1949)
Beautiful but Dangerous (1958)
Beauty and the Bandit (1947)
Beauty and the Beast (1946)
Beauty and the Devil (1949)
Because of Him (1946)
Beaver Valley (1950)
Bebert et le Omnibus (1966)
Bebo's Girl (1963)
Because of You (1952)
Because They're Young (1960)
Becket (1964)
The Beckoning Flame (1916)
Becky Sharp (1935)
Bed of Grass (1957)
Bed of Roses (1933)
The Bed Sitting Room (1969)
Bedazzled (1967)
Bedevilled (1955)
The Bedford Incident (1965)
Bedlam (1946)
Bedside Dentist (1971)
Bedside Manner (1945)
Bedside Mazurka (1970)
Bedtime for Bonzo (1951)
Bedtime Story (1964)
Before Winter Comes (1969)
Beg, Borrow or Steal (1937)
Beggar on Horseback (1925)
Beggars of Life (1928)
Beginning of the End (1957)
The Beginning or the End (1947)
The Beguiled (1971)
Behave Yourself (1951)
Behind City Lights (1945)
Behind Green Lights (1946)
Behind Locked Doors (1948)
Behind the Great Wall (1959)
Behind the High Wall (1956)
Behind the Rising Sun (1943)
Behold a Pale Horse (1964)
Behold Homolka Man (1970)
Bel Ami (1955)
La Bel Indifferent (1957)
Believe in Me (1971)
Bell 'Antonio (1962)
Bell, Book and Candle (1958)
A Bell for Adano (1945)
The Bellboy (1960)
Belle Le Grand (1951)
Belle of Old Mexico (1950)
Belle of the Yukon (1944)
La Belle Que Voila (1949)
Belle Somers (1962)
Belle Starr (1941)
Belle Starr's Daughter (1948)
The Belles of St. Trinian's (1955)
Belles on Their Toes (1952)
The Bells (1931)
Bells of Coronado (1950)
Bells of Rosarita (1945)
The Bells of St. Mary's (1945)
Bells of San Angelo (1947)
Bells of San Fernando (1947)
Beloved (1934)
Beloved Enemy (1937)
Beloved Infidel (1959)
The Beloved Vagabond (1916)
Below the Deadline (1946)
Below the Sahara (1953)
Ben-Hur (1926)
Ben-Hur (1959)
Bend of the River (1952)
Beneath the Planet of the Apes (1970)
Beneath the 12-Mile Reef (1953)
Bengal Brigade (1954)

Bengazi (1955)
The Benny Goodman Story (1955)
La Bergere et le Ramoneur (1952)
Berkeley Square (1933)
Berlin Carnival (1929)
Berlin Correspondent (1942)
Berlin Express (1948)
Berlin--Symphony of a Great City (1927)
The Berliner (1952)
Bermuda Mystery (1944)
Bernardine (1957)
Berserk (1967)
The Bespoke Overcoat (1955)
The Best House in London (1969)
The Best Man (1964)
The Best of Enemies (1962)
The Best of Everything (1959)
Best of the Badmen (1951)
The Best Years of Our Lives (1946)
Betrayal from the East (1945)
Betrayed Women (1955)
Better a Widow (1968)
A Better Tomorrow (1945)
Between Heaven and Hell (1956)
Between Time and Eternity (1960)
Between Two Women (1937)
Between Two Women (1944)
Between Two Worlds (1944)
Between Us (1970)
Beware, My Lovely (1952)
Beware of Children (1961)
Beware of Pity (1949)
Bewitched (1945)
Beyond a Reasonable Doubt (1956)
Beyond Glory (1948)
Beyond Love and Evil (Philosophy of the Boudoir) (1971)
Beyond Mombasa (1957)
Beyond Our Own (1947)
Beyond the Blue Horizon (1942)
Beyond the Forest (1949)
Beyond the Last Frontier (1943)
Beyond the Law (1968)
Beyond the Time Barrier (1960)
Beyond Tomorrow (1940)
Beyond the Valley of the Dolls (1970)
Bhowani Junction (1956)
The Bible (1966)
The Bicycle Thief (1949)
The Bicyclist (1958)
Big Baby Doll (1969)
The Big Beat (1958)
The Big Bluff (1955)
The Big Bonanza (1945)
The Big Boodle (1957)
The Big Bounce (1969)
Big Brown Eyes (1936)
The Big Caper (1957)
The Big Carnival (1951)
The Big Cat (1949)
The Big Chief (1960)
The Big Circus (1959)
Big City (1937)
The Big City (1948)
The Big Clock (1948)
The Big Combo (1955)
The Big Country (1958)
The Big Cube (1969)
Big Deal on Madonna Street (1960)
The Big Fisherman (1959)
The Big Fix (1947)
The Big Gamble (1961)
The Big Gundown (1968)
The Big Gusher (1951)
A Big Hand for the Little Lady (1966)
The Big Hangover (1950)
The Big Heat (1953)
The Big Highway (1971)
Big House, U. S. A. (1955)
Big Jack (1949)
Big Jake (1971)
Big Jim McLain (1952)
The Big Knife (1955)
The Big Land (1957)
The Big Leaguer (1953)
The Big Lift (1950)
The Big Mouth (1967)
The Big Night (1951)
The Big Night (1960)
The Big Noise (1944)
The Big Operator (1959)
The Big Parade (1925)
The Big Punch (1948)
Big Red (1962)
The Big Shot (1942)
The Big Show (1961)
The Big Show-Off (1945)
The Big Sky (1952)

The Big Sky (1970)
The Big Sleep (1946)
The Big Steal (1949)
The Big Store (1941)
The Big Street (1942)
Big Timber (1950)
The Big Tip-Off (1955)
Big Town (1947)
Big Town Scandal (1948)
The Big Trail (1930)
The Big Trees (1952)
The Big Waves (1962)
The Big Wheel (1949)
Bigger Than Life (1956)
The Biggest Bundle of Them All (1968)
Bill and Coo (1947)
A Bill of Divorcement (1932)
A Bill of Divorcement (1940)
Billie (1965)
Billion Dollar Brain (1967)
Billy Budd (1962)
Billy Jack (1971)
Billy Liar (1963)
Billy Rose' Jumbo (see Jumbo)
Billy the Kid (1941)
Bimbo the Great (1961)
Bird Man of Alcatraz (1962)
Bird of Paradise (1932)
Bird of Paradise (1951)
The Bird with the Crystal Plumage (1970)
The Birds and the Bees (1956)
Birds Do It (1966)
Biribi (1971)
The Birth of a Nation (1915)
Birthright (1952)
The Biscuit Eater (1940)
The Bishop Misbehaves (1935)
The Bishop's Wife (1948)
Bitter Creek (1954)
Bitter Fruit (1967)
Bitter Rice (1949)
Bitter Springs (Savage Justice) (1950)
Bitter Victory (1958)
Bizarre, Bizarre (Drôle de Drame) (1937)
Black Angel (1946)
The Black Arrow (1948)
Black Bart (1948)
Black Beauty (1946)
Black Beauty (1971)
The Black Book (see Reign of Terror)
The Black Castle (1952)
The Black Dakotas (1954)
The Black Fox (1963)
Black Gold (1947)
Black Gold (1963)
The Black Hand (1950)
Black Hills (1948)
Black Hills Ambush (1952)
Black Hills Express (1943)
Black Horse Canyon (1954)
The Black Knight (1954)
Black Like Me (1964)
Black Magic (1944)
Black Magic (1949)
Black Market Babies (1945)
Black Midnight (1949)
Black Narcissus (1947)
The Black Orchid (1959)
Black Orpheus (1960)
Black Out (1970)
The Black Parachute (1944)
Black Patch (1957)
The Black Pirate (1926)
The Black Rose (1950)
Black Sabbath (1964)
The Black Scorpion (1957)
The Black Sheep (1968)
The Black Shield of Falworth (1954)
The Black Sleep (1956)
Black Spurs (1965)
Black Sunday (1961)
The Black Swan (1942)
The Black Tent (1957)
Black 13 (1954)
Black Tuesday (1954)
A Black Veil for Lisa (1969)
The Black Whip (1956)
Black Widow (1954)
Black Zoo (1963)
Blackbeard, the Pirate (1952)
Blackbeard's Ghost (1968)
The Blackboard Jungle (1955)
Blackjack Ketchum, Desperado (1956)
Blackmail (1929)
Blackout (1940)
Blackout (1954)
Blanche Fury (1947)
Blast of Silence (1961)

Blaze of Noon (1947)
Blazing Bullets (1951)
The Blazing Forest (1952)
Bleak Morning (1959)
Bless the Beasts and Children (1971)
The Blessing (1970)
Blind Adventure (1933)
Blind Desire (1948)
Blind Goddess (1948)
Blind Spot (1947)
Blindfold (1966)
The Bliss of Mrs. Blossom (1968)
Blithe Spirit (1945)
The Blob (1958)
Blockade (1938)
The Blocked Trail (1943)
Blockheads (1938)
Bloko (The Roundup) (1966)
The Blonde Bandit (1950)
Blonde Dynamite (1950)
Blonde Fever (1944)
Blonde for a Day (1946)
Blonde Ice (1948)
Blonde Ransom (1945)
Blonde Sinner (1956)
Blondie Knows Best (1946)
Blondie's Lucky Day (1946)
Blood Alley (1955)
Blood and Black Lace (1965)
Blood and Roses (1961)
Blood and Sand (1941)
Blood and Steel (1959)
Blood Arrow (1958)
Blood Bath (1966)
Blood Beast from Outer Space (1967)
Blood from the Mummy's Tomb (1971)
The Blood Letting (1971)
Blood of a Poet (1930)
Blood of Dracula (1957)
Blood of the Beasts (1949)
Blood of the Vampire (1958)
Blood on the Arrow (1964)
Blood on the Balcony (1964)
Blood on the Moon (1948)
Blood on the Sun (1945)
Bloodhounds of Broadway (1952)
Bloody Mama (1970)
Bloomfield (1971)
Blossoms in the Dust (1941)
Blow Up (1966)
Blowing Wild (1953)
Blue (1968)
The Blue Angel (1930)
The Blue Angel (1959)
The Blue Bird (1920)
The Blue Bird (1940)
Blue Blood (1951)
The Blue Bonnet (1919)
The Blue Dahlia (1946)
Blue Denim (1959)
The Blue Gardenia (1953)
Blue Hawaii (1961)
Blue Lagoon (1949)
The Blue Max (1966)
Blue Movie (1971)
Blue Murder at St. Trinian's (1958)
The Blue Veil (1951)
Blue Velvet (1970)
Bluebeard (1944)
Bluebeard (Landru) (1963)
Bluebeard's Ten Honeymoons (1960)
A Blueprint for Murder (1953)
Blueprint for Robbery (1961)
Blues Busters (1950)
Blues in the Night (1941)
Blum (1970)
The Boarding School (1970)
The Boatniks (1970)
Bob and Carol and Ted and Alice (1969)
Bob and Sally (1948)
The Bob Mathias Story (1954)
Bobbikins (1960)
Bobby Ware is Missing (1955)
The Bobo (1967)
Boccaccio '70 (1962)
Body and Soul (1947)
The Body Snatcher (1945)
Bodyguard (1948)
Bodyhold (1949)
Boeing Boeing (1965)
The Bofors Gun (1968)
La Boheme (1926)
The Bold and the Brave (1956)
Bolero (1934)
Bomba, the Jungle Boy (1949)
Bomba on Panther Island (1950)
Bombadier (1943)
Bombay Clipper (1942)
Bombay Talkie (1970)

Bombers B-52 (1957)
Bomber's Moon (1943)
Bombs over Burma (1942)
Bon Voyage (1962)
Bondage (1933)
The Bondman (1916)
Bonjour Tristesse (1958)
La Bonne Soupe (1964)
Bonnie and Clyde (1967)
Bonnie Prince Charlie (1948)
Bonzo Goes to College (1952)
Boom (1968)
Boom Town (1940)
Boomerang (1947)
Boot Polish (1958)
Boots Malone (1951)
Bop Girl (1957)
Bora Bora (1968)
The Bordello (1971)
Border Badmen (1945)
Border Bandits (1946)
Border Feud (1947)
Border Incident (1949)
Border Rangers (1950)
Border River (1954)
Border Saddlemates (1952)
Border Street (1948)
Border Treasure (1950)
Borderline (1950)
Bordertown Gun Fighters (1943)
Born Free (1966)
Born Reckless (1959)
Born to Be Bad (1950)
Born to Be Loved (1959)
Born to Kill (1947)
Born to Speed (1947)
Born to Win 1971)
Born Yesterday (1950)
The Borninage (1932)
Borsalino (1970)
The Boss (1956)
Boss of Hangtown Mesa (1943)
Boss of Rawhide (1944)
Botany Bay (1953)
Both Sides of the Law (1954)
The Bottom of the Bottle (1956)
Bottoms Up (1934)
The Bounty Hunter (1954)
The Bounty Killer (1965)
Bowery Battallion (1951)
Bowery Bombshell (1946)
The Bowery Boys Meet the Monsters (1954)
Bowery Buckaroos (1947)
Bowery to Bagdad (1955)
Bowery to Broadway (1944)
Boy (1969)
A Boy ... A Girl (1969)
A Boy, a Girl and a Bike (1949)
The Boy and the Pirates (1960)
Boy, Did I Get a Wrong Number (1966)
Boy from Indiana (1950)
The Boy from Oklahoma (1954)
The Boy Kumasenu (1951)
A Boy Named Charlie Brown (1969)
Boy on a Dolphin (1957)
A Boy Ten Feet Tall (1965)
The Boy Who Caught a Crook (1961)
The Boy Who Stole a Million (1960)
The Boy with Green Hair (1948)
The Boys (1962)
Boys in Brown (1950)
Boy's Night Out (1962)
Boy's Ranch (1946)
Boys' Town (1938)
The Brain Machine (1956)
Brainstorm (1965)
Brainwashed (1961)
The Bramble Bush (1960)
Brand of the Devil (1944)
Brand X (1970)
Branded (1950)
The Brasher Doubloon (1947)
The Brass Bottle (1964)
The Bravados (1958)
The Brave One (1956)
Brave Warrior (1952)
The Brazen Women of Balzac (1971)
Brazil Year 2000 (1970)
Bread, Love and Dreams (1954)
Break in the Circle (1957)
Break to Freedom (1955)
Breakdown (1952)
Breakfast at Tiffany's (1961)
The Breaking Point (1950)
Breaking the Ice (1938)
Breaking the Sound Barrier (1952)
Breakout (1971)
Breakthrough (1950)
A Breath of Scandal (1960)

Brewster McCloud (1970)
Brewster's Millions (1945)
The Bribe (1949)
The Bridal Path (1959)
Bridal Suite (1939)
The Bride and the Beast (1958)
Bride by Mistake (1944)
The Bride Came C.O.D. (1941)
Bride for Sale (1949)
The Bride Goes Wild (1948)
The Bride Is Much Too Beautiful (1958)
Bride of the Gorilla (1951)
Bride of Vengeance (1949)
The Bride Walks Out (1936)
The Bride Wore Boots (1946)
The Brides of Dracula (1960)
The Brides of Fu Manchu (1966)
The Bridge (1960)
The Bridge at Remagen (1969)
The Bridge in the Jungle (1970)
Bridge of San Luis Rey (1929)
The Bridge of San Luis Rey (1944)
The Bridge on the River Kwai (1957)
Bridge to the Sun (1961)
The Bridges at Toko-Ri (1954)
The Brigand (1952)
The Brigand of Kandahar (1965)
Brigham Young (1940)
Bright Leaf (1950)
Bright Road (1953)
Bright Victory (1951)
The Brighton Strangler (1945)
Brimstone (1949)
Bring 'Em Back Alive (1932)
Bring Your Smile Along (1955)
Bringing Up Baby (1938)
Bringing Up Father (1946)
Broadway (1942)
Broadway Bad (1933)
Broadway Musketeers (1938)
Broadway Serenade (1939)
Broadway Thru a Keyhole (1933)
Broadway to Hollywood (1933)
Broken Arrow (1950)
Broken Blossoms (1919)
Broken Journey (1948)
Broken Lance (1954)
The Broken Land (1962)
The Broken Star (1956)
Bronco Bullfrog (1970)
Bronco Buster (1952)
Broth of a Boy (1959)
Brother John (1971)
Brother Orchid (1940)
The Brotherhood (1968)
The Brotherhood of Satan (1971)
Brotherly Love (1970)
The Brothers (1947)
Brothers in the Saddle (1949)
The Brothers Karamazov (1958)
The Brothers Rico (1957)
Brushfire (1962)
The Bubble (1966)
The Buccaneer (1938)
The Buccaneer (1958)
Buccaneer's Girl (1950)
Buckaroo Sheriff of Texas (1950)
A Bucket of Blood (1959)
Brute Force (1947)
Buck Privates Come Home (1947)
Buckskin (1968)
Buckskin Frontier (1943)
The Buckskin Lady (1957)
Buddenbrooks (Part I) (1961)
Buddenbrooks (Part II) (1961)
Buddha (1963)
Buffalo Bill (1944)
Buffalo Bill Rides Again (1947)
The Bug Killer (1971)
Bugles in the Afternoon (1952)
Bulldog Drummond Strikes Back (1934)
Bullet for a Badman (1964)
A Bullet for Joey (1955)
A Bullet for Pretty Boy (1970)
A Bullet Is Waiting (1954)
Bullet Scars (1942)
Bullets and Saddles (1943)
The Bullfighter and the Lady (1951)
The Bullfighters (1945)
Bullitt (1968)
Bullwhip (1958)
Bunco Squad (1950)
Bunker Bean (1936)
Bunny Lake is Missing (1965)
Bunny O'Hare (1971)
Buona Sera, Mrs. Campbell (1968)
The Burglar (1957)

The Burglar (1971)
Burma Victory (1945)
The Burmese Harp (1956)
Burn (1970)
Burn 'Em Up, O'Connor (1939)
Burn Witch Burn (1962)
The Burning Cross (1947)
Bury Me Dead (1947)
The Bus (1965)
The Bus Is Coming (1971)
Bus Riley's Back in Town (1965)
Bus Stop (1956)
The Bushbaby (1970)
The Bushwackers (1951)
The Buster Keaton Story (1957)
The Busy Body (1967)
But Not For Me (1959)
Butch Cassidy and the Sundance Kid (1969)
The Buttercup Chain (1970)
Butterfield 8 (1960)
Bwana Devil (1952)
By Candlelight (1934)
By Love Possessed (1961)
Bye Bye Braverman (1968)

C. C. and Company (1970)
C-Man (1949)
Cabaret (1957)
Cabin in the Sky (1943)
The Cabinet of Caligari (1962)
Cabiria (1914)
Cactus Flower (1969)
The Caddy (1953)
Cafe Metropole (1937)
Cafe Society (1939)
Cage of Evil (1960)
Caged (1950)
Caged Fury (1948)
The Caine Mutiny (1954)
Cairo (1942)
Cairo (1963)
Calamity Jane and Sam Bass (1949)
Calcutta (1947)
Calendar of the Year (1936)
California (1947)
California Firebrand (1948)
California Gold Rush (1946)
California Joe (1943)
California Passage (1950)
The Call (1971)
Call a Messenger (1939)
Call Me Bwana (1963)
Call Me Mathilde (1970)
Call Me Mister (1951)
Call of the Klondike (1950)
Call of the Wild (1935)
Callaway Went Thataway (1951)
Calle Mayor (1956)
Calling All Marines (1939)
Calling Dr. Death (1943)
Calling Dr. Gillespie (1942)
Calling Dr. Kildare (1939)
Calling Bulldog Drummond (1951)
Calling Homicide (1956)
Calling Wild Bill Elliott (1943)
Calliope (1971)
Calypso Heat Wave (1957)
Calypso Joe (1957)
Camille (1927)
Camille (1936)
Camille 2000 (1969)
The Camp on Blood Island (1958)
Campbell's Kingdom (1958)
Campus Rhythm (1943)
Campus Sleuth (1948)
Can Heironymus Merkin Ever Forget Mercy Humppe and Find True Happiness? (1969)
Canadian Pacific (1949)
The Canadians (1961)
Candy (1968)
Cannibal Attack (1954)
The Cannibals (1970)
Cannon for Cordoba (1970)
Canon City (1948)
Can't Help Singing (1944)
The Canterville Ghost (1943)
Canticle (1970)
Canyon City (1943)
Canyon Crossroads (1955)
Canyon Passage (1946)
Canyon River (1955)
Cape Fear (1962)
The Caper of the Golden Bulls (1967)
The Capital City (1945)
Caprice (1967)
The Caprices of Marie (1970)
Captain Apache (1971)
Captain Blood (1935)

Captain Boycott (1947)
Captain Carey, USA (1950)
Captain Caution (1940)
Captain China (1949)
Captain Eddie (1945)
Captain from Castile (1947)
The Captain from Kopenick (1956)
Captain Fury (1939)
Captain Horatio Hornblower (1951)
Captain January (1936)
Capt. John Smith and Pocahontas (1953)
Captain Kidd (1945)
Captain Kidd and the Slave Girl (1954)
Captain Lightfoot (1955)
Captain Newman, M.D. (1963)
Captain of the Guard (1930)
Captain Pirate (1952)
Captain Scarlett (1953)
Captain Sinbad (1963)
Captain Tugboat Annie (1945)
Captains Courageous (1937)
The Captain's Paradise (1953)
The Captain's Table (1960)
The Captive City (1952)
The Captive Heart (1946)
Captive of Billy the Kid (1952)
Captive Wild Woman (1943)
Captive Women (1952)
The Capture (1950)
The Caravan Trail (1946)
Carbine Williams (1952)
Cardboard Cavalier (1949)
The Cardinal (1963)
Cardinal Richelieu (1935)
Career (1939)
Career (1959)
Careful, Soft Shoulder (1942)
Careless Lady (1932)
The Careless Years (1957)
The Caretakers (1963)
Cargo to Capetown (1950)
Caribbean (1952)
The Caribbean Mystery (1945)
The Cariboo Trail (1950)
Carlotta (1971)
Carmen (1915)
Carmen Comes Home (1951)
Un Carnet du Bal (1937)
Carnival (1946)
Carolina Cannonball (1955)
Caroline Cherie (1951)
The Carpenter (1964)
Carrie (1952)
Carry On, Admiral (1958)
Carry On Again Doctor (1969)
Carry On Camping (1969)
Carry On Cleo (1965)
Carry On Cowboy (1966)
Carry On Doctor (1968)
Carry On Nurse (1960)
Carry On Screaming (1966)
Carry On Sergeant (1959)
Carry On Spying (1965)
Carry On Up the Jungle (1970)
Carry On Up the Khyber (1968)
Carson City (1952)
Carson City Cyclone (1943)
Carthage in Flames (1961)
Cartouche (1957)
Cartouche (1964)
Casablan (1963)
Casablanca (1942)
Casanova Brown (1944)
Casanova in Burlesque (1944)
Casanova '70 (1965)
Casanova's Big Night (1954)
The Case Against Brooklyn (1958)
The Case Against Mrs. Ames (1936)
A Case for the Young Hangman (1970)
The Case of Dr. Laurent (1957)
The Case of the Baby Sitter (1947)
The Case of the Red Monkey (1955)
Cash McCall (1959)
Cash on Delivery (1956)
Cash on Demand (1962)
Casino Royale (1967)
Casque D'Or (1952)
Cass Timberlane (1947)
Cast a Giant Shadow (1966)
Cast a Long Shadow (1959)
The Castilian (1963)
Castle Keep (1969)
Castle of Evil (1967)
The Cat (1966)
The Cat and the Canary (1939)
Cat Ballou (1965)

The Cat Burglar (1961)
The Cat Creeps (1946)
Cat o' Nine Tails (1971)
The Cat People (1942)
The Catalina Caper (1967)
Catch as Catch Can (1968)
Catch Me a Spy (1971)
The Catered Affair (1956)
La Cathedrale des Morts (1935)
Catherine the Great (1934)
Catlow (1971)
The Catman of Paris (1946)
The Cat's Paw (1934)
Cattle Drive (1951)
Cattle Empire (1958)
Cattle King (1963)
Cattle Queen of Montana (1954)
Cattle Town (1952)
Caught (1949)
Caught in the Draft (1941)
Cause for Alarm (1951)
Cavalcade (1933)
The Cavalier (1928)
Cavalry Scout (1951)
Cave of Outlaws (1951)
The Cavern (1965)
Cease Fire (1953)
Celeste (1970)
Cell 2455, Death Row (1955)
The Ceremony (1963)
A Certain Smile (1958)
Certain, Very Certain, as a Matter of Fact ... Probable (1970)
Cesar (1936)
Cha-Cha-Cha Boom! (1956)
Chad Hanna (1941)
Chain Lightning (1950)
The Chairman (1969)
The Chalk Garden (1964)
The Challenge (1948)
A Challenge for Robin Hood (1968)
Challenge to Lassie (1949)
The Challenges (1970)
Chamber of Horrors (1966)
Champ for a Day (1953)
Champagne Charlie (1936)
Champagne for Caesar (1950)
Champion (1949)
Chance Meeting (1955)
Chance Meeting (1960)
Chandler (1971)
Change of Habit (1969)
Change of Heart (1934)
Change of Mind (1969)
Chapeyev (1934)
The Chapman Report (1962)
Chappaqua (1966)
Charade (1963)
The Charge at Feather River (1953)
Charge of the Lancers (1954)
The Charge of the Light Brigade (1936)
The Charge of the Light Brigade (1968)
Charley's Aunt (1941)
Charlie, the Lonesome Cougar (1967)
Charlie Bubbles (1968)
Charlie Chan in the Secret Service (1944)
Charlie McCarthy, Detective (1939)
Charly (1968)
Charro (1969)
Chartroose Caboose (1960)
The Chase (1946)
The Chase (1966)
Chase a Crooked Shadow (1958)
The Chasers (1959)
Chastity (1969)
The Chastity Belt (1968)
Chatterbox (1936)
Chatterbox (1943)
Che! (1969)
Che Gioia Vivere (1960)
Cheaper by the Dozen (1950)
The Cheaters (1945)
The Chechahcos (1924)
The Checkered Coat (1948)
Checkers (1919)
Checkpoint (1957)
Cheers for Miss Bishop (1941)
The Cherokee Flash (1945)
Cherry, Harry and Raquel (1969)
Chetniks! (1943)
Cheyenne (1947)
Cheyenne Autumn (1964)
Cheyenne Cowboy (1949)
Cheyenne Roundup (1943)
The Cheyenne Social Club (1970)
Cheyenne Takes Over (1948)
Cheyenne Wildcat (1944)

Chicago Calling (1951)
Chicago Confidential (1957)
Chicago Deadline (1949)
The Chicago Kid (1945)
Chicago Syndicate (1955)
Chicken Every Sunday (1948)
Chief Crazy Horse (1955)
A Child is Waiting (1963)
Child of Divorce (1946)
The Childhood of Maxim Gorky (1938)
Children of Hiroshima (1952)
Children of Paradise (1943)
Children of the Damned (1964)
Children on Trial (1945)
The Children's Hour (1962)
China (1943)
China Clipper (1936)
China Corsair (1951)
China Doll (1958)
China Gate (1957)
China Girl (1942)
China Is Near (1967)
China Seas (1935)
China Sky (1945)
China Venture (1953)
China's Little Devils (1945)
The Chinese Ring (1947)
Chisum (1970)
Les Chouans (1946)
Christa (1971)
The Christian Licorice Store (1971)
Christina (1949)
The Christine Jorgensen Story (1970)
A Christmas Carol (1938)
A Christmas Carol (1951)
A Christmas Carol (1956)
Christmas Eve (1947)
Christmas Holiday (1944)
Christmas in Connecticut (1945)
The Christmas Martian (1971)
The Christmas Tree (1969)
Christopher Columbus (1948)
Chrome and Hot Leather (1971)
Chronicle of a Lady (1971)
Chubasco (1968)
Chuk and Gek (1953)
Chuka (1967)
Cila S'Appelle L'Aurore (1955)
Cimarron (1931)
Cimarron (1960)
The Cincinnati Kid (1965)
Cinderella (1949)
Cinderella Jones (1946)
Cinderella Swings It (1943)
Cinderfella (1960)
Cinerama Holiday (1955)
Cinerama's Russian Adventure (1966)
Les Cinq Gentlemen Maudits (1930)
Circumstantial Evidence (1945)
The Circle (1959)
Circle of Deception (1961)
Circle of Love (1965)
Circus Girl (1956)
Circus of Horrors (1960)
Circus of Love (1958)
Circus World (1964)
Cisco Pike (1971)
The Citadel (1938)
Citizen Kane (1941)
The City (1939)
City Across the River (1949)
City After Midnight (1959)
City Beneath the Sea (1953)
City for Conquest (1940)
City Lights (1931)
City of Bad Men (1953)
City of Fear (1959)
City of Fear (1965)
City of Shadows (1955)
City of Silent Men (1942)
A City Speaks (1948)
City Without Men (1943)
A City's Child (1971)
Civilization (1916)
The Clairvoyant (1936)
Clambake (1967)
Clancy Street Boys (1943)
Clarence, the Cross-Eyed Lion (1965)
Clash by Night (1952)
Claudelle Inglish (1961)
Claudia (1943)
Claudia and David (1946)
Claudine (1939)
The Clay Pigeon (1949)
Cleo from 5 to 7 (1962)
Cleopatra (1934)
Cleopatra (1963)
A Clerk Vanished (1971)
Clickety-Clack (1970)
The Climax (1944)

Clipped Wings (1953)
Cloak and Dagger (1946)
The Clock (1945)
A Clockwork Orange (1971)
A Close Call for Ellery Queen (1946)
Close Quarters (1943)
Close to My Heart (1951)
Close Up (1948)
Cloudburst (1952)
The Clouded Yellow (1951)
The Clown (1953)
The Clowns (1970)
Clue of the Twisted Candle (1968)
Cluny Brown (1946)
C'Mon, Let's Live a Little (1967)
Coalface (1935)
Coast of Skeletons (1965)
Coastal Command (1942)
The Cobra (1968)
The Cobra Strikes (1948)
Cobra Woman (1944)
The Cobweb (1955)
The Cockeyed Cowboys of Calico County (1970)
The Cockeyed Miracle (1946)
The Cockleshell Heroes (1956)
Code of Scotland Yard (1948)
Code of the Outlaw (1942)
Code of the Silver Sage (1950)
Code of the West (1947)
Code Seven, Victim Five (1964)
Code Two (1953)
Cold Turkey (1971)
A Cold Wind in August (1961)
The Colditz Story (1957)
Cole Younger, Gunfighter (1958)
The Collector (1965)
College Confidential (1960)
Colonel Effingham's Raid (1945)
Color Me Dead (1970)
Colorado Ambush (1951)
Colorado Pioneers (1945)
Colorado Ranger (1950)
Colorado Sundown (1952)
Colorado Territory (1949)
The Colossus of New York (1958)
The Colossus of Rhodes (1961)
Colt .45 (1970)
Column South (1953)
Comanche (1956)
Comanche Station (1960)
Comanche Territory (1950)
The Comancheros (1961)
Combat Squad (1953)
Come and Get It (1936)
Come Back, Little Sheba (1952)
Come Blow Your Horn (1963)
Come Dance with Me! (1960)
Come Fill the Cup (1951)
Come Fly with Me (1963)
Come Live with Me (1941)
Come Next Spring (1956)
The Come On (1956)
Come On, Rangers (1938)
Come One, Come All (1970)
Come Out Fighting (1945)
Come September (1961)
Come Spy with Me (1967)
Come, Take My Life (1956)
Come to the Stable (1949)
Come to Your Senses (1971)
Come Together (1971)
The Comedians (1967)
The Comedy of Terrors (1963)
Comet over Broadway (1938)
The Comic (1969)
The Coming Out Party (1934)
A Coming-Out Party (1962)
The Command (1954)
Command Decision (1948)
Commando (1964)
La Commune de Paris (1952)
The Company She Keeps (1950)
Compulsion (1959)
The Computer Wore Tennis Shoes (1969)
Comrade X (1941)
The Concrete Jungle (1962)
The Condemned of Altona (1963)
El Condor (1970)
The Confession of Ina Kahr (1958)
Confession, Theory, Actress (1971)
Confessions of a Nazi Spy (1939)
Confessions of a Police Commissioner to the District Attorney (1971)
Confessions of a Rogue (1948)
Confessions of an Opium Eater (1962)
The Confessions of Felix Krull

(1957)
Confidence Girl (1952)
Confidential Agent (1945)
Confidentially Connie (1953)
Conflict (1936)
Conflict (1945)
The Conformist (1970)
Congo Crossing (1956)
Congress Dances (1931)
The Congress Dances (1957)
The Conjugal Bed (1963)
A Connecticut Yankee (1931)
A Connecticut Yankee in King Arthur's Court (1949)
The Connection (1962)
The Conqueror (1916)
The Conqueror (1956)
The Conqueror Worm (1968)
Conquest of Cheyenne (1946)
Conquest of Cochise (1953)
The Conquest of Everest (1953)
Conquest of Space (1955)
Conquest of the Air (1938)
Conspiracy of Hearts (1960)
The Conspirator (1950)
The Conspirators (1944)
The Constant Nymph (1933)
The Constant Nymph (1943)
Constantine and the Cross (1962)
The Contender (1944)
Convict Stage (1965)
Convicted (1950)
Convicts Four (1962)
Coogan's Bluff (1968)
The Cool and the Crazy (1958)
Cool Hand Luke (1967)
Cool It, Carol (1970)
The Cool Ones (1967)
Cop Hater (1958)
Copacabana (1947)
Copper Canyon (1950)
Copper Sky (1957)
The Copy (1971)
The Corn Is Green (1945)
Cornered (1946)
Coroner Creek (1948
The Corpse Came C.O.D. (1947)
Corregidor (1943)
Corridor of Mirrors (1948)
Corridors of Blood (1963)
The Corrupt Ones (1967)
Corruption (1968)
The Corsican Brothers (1941)
Corvette K-225 (1943)
The Cosmic Man (1959)
Cosmo Jones, Spy Smasher (1943)
The Cossacks (1960)
Cotton Comes to Harlem (1970)
The Couch (1962)
Count Dracula (1971)
Count Five and Die (1958)
The Count of Monte Cristo (1934)
The Count of St. Elmo (1951)
Count Three and Pray (1955)
Count Yorga, Vampire (1970)
Count Your Blessings (1959)
Countdown (1968)
Counter-Attack (1945)
The Counterfeit Killer (1968)
The Counterfeit Plan (1957)
The Counterfeit Traitor (1962)
The Counterfeiters (1948)
The Counterfeiters of Paris (1963)
Counterplan (1932)
Counterplot (1959)
Counterpoint (1967)
The Countess from Hong Kong (1966)
The Countess of Monte Cristo (1948)
Courtin' Trouble (1948)
The Country Girl (1954)
County Fair (1950)
Courage of Black Beauty (1957)
Courage of Lassie (1946)
Court Martial (1962)
The Court Martial of Billy Mitchell (1955)
The Courtship of Andy Hardy (1942)
The Courtship of Eddie's Father (1963)
A Covenant with Death (1966)
Cover-Up (1949)
The Covered Trailer (1939)
The Covered Wagon (1923)
Covered Wagon Days (1943)
Covered Wagon Raid (1950)
The Cow (1971)
The Cow and I (1961)
Cow Country (1953)
Cowards (1970)
Cowboy (1958)

The Cowboy (1954)
The Cowboy and the Lady (1938)
The Cowboy and the Prizefighter (1950)
The Cowboy and the Senorita (1944)
Cowboy Cavalier (1948)
Cowboy Commandos (1943)
Cowboy in Manhattan (1943)
Cowboy Quarterback (1939)
Crack in the Mirror (1959)
Crack in the World (1965)
Crack Up (1946)
Cradle Song (1933)
Craig's Wife (1936)
The Cranes Are Flying (1957)
Crash Dive (1943)
Crash Landing (1958)
Crash of Silence (Mandy) (1953)
Crashing Las Vegas (1956)
Crashout (1955)
Crazy Desire (1964)
Crazy for Love (1957)
Crazy Paradise (1965)
The Crazy World of Laurel and Hardy (1967)
Crazylegs (1953)
The Creature from the Black Lagoon (1954)
The Creature Walks Among Us (1956)
Creature with the Atom Brain (1955)
The Creatures the World Forgot (1971)
The Creeper (1948)
Crest of the Wave (1954)
Crime and Punishment (1935)
Crime and Punishment (1958)
Crime and Punishment, USA (1959)
Crime Against Joe (1956)
The Crime Doctor (1934)
Crime Doctor (1943)
Crime Doctor's Strangest Case (1944)
Crime Doctor's Warning (1946)
Crime Does Not Pay (1962)
Crime in the Streets (1956)
Crime, Inc. (1945)
The Crime of M. Lange (1935)
Crime of Passion (1957)
Crime of the Century (1946)
Crime Wave (1954)
Criminal Court (1946)
Criminal Lawyer (1951)
The Crimson Blade (1964)
The Crimson Canary (1945)
The Crimson Cult (1970)
The Crimson Key (1947)
The Crimson Kimono (1959)
The Crimson Pirate (1952)
Cripple Creek (1952)
Crisis (1939)
Crisis (1950)
Criss Cross (1949)
Critic's Choice (1963)
Cromwell (1970)
The Crooked Circle (1957)
Crooked River (1950)
The Crooked Way (1949)
The Crooked Web (1955)
Crooks and Coronets (1969)
The Cross and the Switchblade (1970)
Cross Channel (1955)
Cross Country Romance (1940)
The Cross-Eyed Saint (1971)
Cross My Heart (1947)
The Cross of Lorraine (1943)
Cross-Up (1958)
Crossed Swords (1954)
Crossed Trails (1948)
Crossfire (1947)
Crossplot (1969)
Crossroads (1942)
Crosswinds (1951)
The Crowd Roars (1938)
Crowded Paradise (1956)
The Crowded Sky (1960)
The Crucible (1957)
The Cruel Sea (1953)
The Cruel Tower (1956)
Cruisin' Down the River (1953)
The Crusades (1935)
The Cry (1970)
The Cry Baby Killer (1958)
Cry Danger (1951)
Cry for Happy (1961)
Cry Freedom (1961)
A Cry from the Streets (1959)
Cry Havoc (1943)
A Cry in the Night (1956)
Cry of Battle (1963)
Cry of the Banshee (1970)

Cry of the City (1948)
Cry of the Hunted (1953)
Cry of the Werewolf (1944)
Cry Terror (1958)
Cry Tough (1959)
Cry Uncle (1971)
Cry Wolf (1947)
The Crystal Ball (1943)
Cuba My Love (1969)
Cuban Fireball (1951)
Cul-de-Sac (1966)
Cult of the Cobra (1955)
The Cumberland Story (1947)
The Cummington Story (1945)
The Cup of Fury (1919)
The Cure for Love (1949)
Curley (1947)
Curly Top (1935)
The Curse of Frankenstein (1957)
Curse of the Cat People (1944)
Curse of the Demon (1958)
The Curse of the Fly (1965)
The Curse of the Living Corpse (1964)
The Curse of the Mummy's Tomb (1965)
Curse of the Undead (1959)
Curse of the Voodoo (1965)
The Curse of the Werewolf (1961)
Curtain Call at Cactus Creek (1950)
Curucu, Beast of the Amazon (1956)
Custer of the West (1967)
Cycle Savages (1970)
The Cyclone Kid (1942)
Cyclops (1957)
Cynthia (1947)
Cyprus is an Island (1945)
Cyrano de Bergerac (1950)
The Czar Wants to Sleep (Lieutenant Kije) (1934)

D-Day, The Sixth of June (1956)
The D.I. (1957)
D.O.A. (1949)
Daddy Long Legs (1931)
Daddy's Gone A-Hunting (1969)
Dad's Diary (1971)
Dagmar's Hot Pants, Inc. (1971)
Daisy Kenyon (1947)
Dakota (1945)
Dakota Incident (1956)
The Dakota Kid (1951)
Dakota Lil (1950)
Daleks Invade Earth 2150 A.D. (1966)
Dallas (1950)
The Dalton Girls (1957)
The Daltons Ride Again (1945)
The Dam Busters (1955)
Les Dames du Bois de Boulogne (1944)
Damn Citizen (1958)
Damn the Defiant! (1962)
The Damned (1969)
The Damned Don't Cry (1950)
Damon and Pythias (1962)
Dance, Girl, Dance (1940)
Dance, Little Lady (1955)
Dance of the Herons (1966)
Dance with Me Henry (1956)
Dancing Co-Ed (1939)
The Dancing Fleece (1950)
Dancing Lady (1933)
The Dancing Masters (1943)
A Dandy in Aspic (1968)
Danger: Diabolik (1968)
Danger in the Pacific (1942)
Danger! Love at Work (1937)
Danger Route (1968)
Danger Signal (1945)
Danger Woman (1946)
Danger Zone (1951)
Dangerous Crossing (1953)
Dangerous Exile (1958)
Dangerous Intruder (1945)
Dangerous Millions (1946)
Dangerous Mission (1954)
Dangerous Money (1946)
Dangerous Number (1937)
Dangerous Partners (1945)
Dangerous Passage (1944)
A Dangerous Profession (1949)
Dangerous Venture (1947)
Dangerous When Wet (1953)
Dangerous Years (1947)
Dangerous Youth (1958)
Dangerously Yours (1933)
Daniel Boone (1936)
Daniel Boone, Trail Blazer (1956)
Danny Boy (1946)

Dante's Inferno (1935)
Daphne (1966)
Daphni (1952)
Darby O'Gill and the Little People (1959)
Darby's Rangers (1958)
Daredevils of the Clouds (1948)
The Daring Caballero (1949)
The Daring Game (1968)
The Daring Young Man (1943)
Dark Angel (1935)
The Dark at the Top of the Stairs (1960)
Dark City (1950)
Dark Command (1940)
Dark Corner (1946)
Dark Delusion (1947)
The Dark House (1946)
Dark Intruder (1965)
The Dark Mirror (1946)
Dark Mountain (1944)
Dark of the Sun (1968)
Dark Passage (1947)
The Dark Past (1948)
Dark Purpose (1964)
Dark River (1953)
Dark Secret (1950)
Dark Victory (1939)
Dark Waters (1944)
Darling (1965)
Darling, How Could You? (1951)
Darling Lili (1970)
D'Artagnan (1916)
Dateline Diamonds (1966)
A Date with Judy (1948)
Daughter of Dr. Jekyll (1957)
The Daughter of Rosie O'Grady (1950)
Daughter of the Gods (1916)
Daughter of the Jungle (1949)
Daughter of the Sands (1952)
Daughter of the West (1949)
Daughters Courageous (1939)
Daughters of Darkness (1971)
David and Bathsheba (1951)
David and Goliath (1961)
David and Lisa (1963)
David Copperfield (1935)
David Copperfield (1970)
David Harum (1934)
Davy Crockett and the River Pirates (1956)
Davy Crockett, Indian Scout (1950)
Davy Crockett, King of the Wild Frontier (1955)
Dawn at Socorro (1954)
Dawn of Iran (1936)
The Dawn of Islam (1971)
The Dawn of Victory (1971)
The Dawn Patrol (1938)
A Day at the Beach (1970)
The Day Mars Invaded Earth (1963)
Day of Anger (1969)
A Day of Fury (1956)
Day of the Bad Man (1958)
Day of the Evil Gun (1968)
Day of the Outlaw (1959)
The Day of the Owl (1968)
Day of the Painter (1960)
The Day of the Triffids (1963)
Day of Triumph (1954)
The Day the Bookies Wept (1939)
The Day the Earth Caught Fire (1962)
The Day the Earth Stood Still (1951)
The Day the Fish Came Out (1967)
The Day They Robbed the Bank of England (1960)
A Day to Remember (1955)
Daybreak (1939)
Daybreak in Udi (1949)
Days and Nights in the Forest (1970)
Days in My Father's House (1968)
Days of Buffalo Bill (1946)
Days of Glory (1944)
Days of Jesse James (1939)
Days of Old Cheyenne (1943)
Days of Thrills and Laughter (1961)
The Days of Water (1971)
Days of Wilfred Owen (1966)
Days of Wine and Roses (1962)
Daytime Wife (1939)
Dayton's Devils (1968)
The Dead Don't Dream (1948)
Dead Man's Eyes (1944)
Dead Man's Gold (1949)
Dead of Night (1945)
Dead of Summer (1970)

The Dead One in the Thames River (1971)
Dead Reckoning (1947)
Dead Ringer (1964)
Dead Run (1969)
Dead to the World (1962)
Deadfall (1968)
Deadlier than the Male (1957)
Deadlier than the Male (1967)
The Deadliest Sin (1956)
Deadline (1948)
Deadline at Dawn (1946)
Deadline for Murder (1946)
Deadline, USA (1952)
Deadlock (1970)
The Deadly Affair (1967)
The Deadly Bees (1967)
The Deadly Companions (1961)
Deadly Decision (1958)
Deadly Duo (1962)
Deadly Is the Female (1949)
The Deadly Mantis (1957)
Deadly Shots on Broadway (1969)
Dear Brat (1951)
Dear Brigitte (1965)
Dear Heart (1964)
Dear Irene (1970)
Dear Mr. Prohack (1948)
Dear Murderer (1948)
Dear Ruth (1947)
Dear Wife (1949)
Death Has No Friends (1970)
Death in Small Doses (1957)
Death in Venice (1971)
Death of a Gunfighter (1969)
Death of a Salesman (1951)
Death of a Scoundrel (1956)
Death Rides a Horse (1969)
Death Takes a Holiday (1934)
Death Took Place Last Night (1970)
Death Valley (1947)
Death Valley Gunfighter (1949)
Death Valley Manhunt (1943)
Death Valley Rangers (1943)
Deathwatch (1966)
The Debut (1971)
The Decameron (1971)
Decameron Nights (1953)
Deception (1946)
Decision Against Time (1957)
Decision at Sundown (1957)
Decision Before Dawn (1951)
The Decision of Christopher Blake (1948)
Decline and Fall (1968)
Deep Adventure (1957)
The Deep Blue Sea (1955)
Deep End (1970)
Deep in the Heart of Texas (1942)
The Deep Six (1958)
Deep Valley (1947)
Deep Waters (1948)
The Deerslayer (1957)
A Defeated People (1945)
The Defector (1966)
The Defiant Ones (1958)
A Degree of Murder (1967)
The Delicate Delinquent (1957)
Delightfully Dangerous (1945)
Delinquent Daughters (1944)
Deliverance (1919)
Delusions of Grandeur (1971)
Dementia (1955)
Demi-Paradise (1949)
Demitrius and the Gladiators (1954)
Demoniaque (1958)
The Demonstrator (1971)
The Denver and the Rio Grande (1952)
The Denver Kid (1948)
Deported (1950)
Deputy Marshal (1949)
Le Dernier Milliadaire (1934)
De Sade (1969)
Desert Attack (1960)
The Desert Fox (1951)
Desert Fury (1947)
Desert Gold (1919)
The Desert Hawk (1950)
Desert Hell (1958)
Desert Legion (1953)
Desert of Lost Men (1951)
Desert Passage (1952)
Desert Patrol (1961)
Desert Pursuit (1952)
The Desert Rats (1953)
Desert Sands (1955)
Desert Victory (1943)
The Deserted Piazza (1971)
The Deserter (1933)
The Deserter (1971)
Design for Death (1948)
Designing Woman (1957)

Desire (1936)
Desire Me (1947)
Desire Under the Elms (1958)
Desiree (1954)
Desk Set (1957)
The Desperado (1954)
The Desperadoes (1943)
The Desperadoes (1969)
The Desperadoes Are in Town (1956)
Desperadoes of Dodge City (1948)
Desperadoes Outpost (1952)
Desperate (1947)
Desperate Characters (1971)
The Desperate Hours (1955)
Desperate Moment (1953)
The Desperate Ones (1968)
Desperate Search (1952)
Destination Big House (1950)
Destination Gobi (1953)
Destination Inner Space (1966)
Destination Moon (1950)
Destination Murder (1950)
Destination 60,000 (1957)
Destination Tokyo (1943)
Destination Unknown (1933)
Destiny (1944)
Destroyer (1943)
The Destructors (1968)
Destry (1954)
Destry Rides Again (1939)
The Detective (1954)
Detective Belli (1970)
Detective Kitty O'Day (1944)
Detour (1945)
Devi (1961)
The Devil and Daniel Webster (see All That Money Can Buy) (1941)
The Devil at Four O'Clock (1961)
Devil Bat's Daughter (1946)
The Devil Dancer (1927)
The Devil Doll (1936)
Devil Goddess (1955)
Devil in the Flesh (1947)
The Devil Is a Sissy (1936)
The Devil on Wheels (1947)
Devil-Ship Pirates (1964)
The Devil Thumbs a Ride (1947)
The Devil with Hitler (1942)
A Devil with Women (1930)
The Devils (1971)
Devil's Angels (1967)
The Devil's Bride (1968)
The Devil's Brigade (1968)
The Devil's Brother (1933)
Devil's Canyon (1953)
Devil's Cargo (1948)
The Devil's Daughter (1956)
The Devil's Disciple (1959)
The Devil's Doorway (1950)
The Devil's 8 (1969)
The Devil's Hairpin (1957)
The Devil's Lottery (1932)
The Devil's Lovers (1971)
Devils of Darkness (1965)
The Devil's Own (1967)
Devil's Playground (1937)
Devotion (1946)
Diabolical Shudder (1971)
Diabolique (1955)
Dial M for Murder (1954)
Dial 1119 (1950)
Dial Red O (1955)
Diamond Head (1962)
Diamond Jim (1935)
The Diamond Queen (1953)
Diamond Safari (1958)
The Diamond Wizard (1954)
Diamonds Are Forever (1971)
Diamonds for Breakfest (1968)
Diane (1955)
A Diary for Timothy (1945)
Diary of a Bachelor (1964)
Diary of a Chambermaid (1946)
The Diary of a Country Priest (1951)
Diary of a High School Bride (1959)
Diary of a Lover (1956)
Diary of a Mad Housewife (1970)
Diary of a Madman (1963)
The Diary of Anne Frank (1959)
Dick Tracy (1945)
Dick Tracy Meets Gruesome (1947)
Dick Tracy vs. Cueball (1946)
Dick Tracy's Dilemma (1947)
Did You Hear the One About the Traveling Saleslady? (1968)
Die! Die! My Darling! (1965)
Die, Monster, Die (1965)
Dig that Uranium (1956)
Dillinger (1945)

Dillinger Is Dead (1969)
Dim Little Island (1948)
Dime with a Halo (1963)
Dimka (1963)
Dimples (1936)
Dinah East (1970)
Dingaka (1965)
Dinner at Eight (1933)
Dino (1957)
Dinosaurus! (1960)
Diplomatic Courier (1952)
Dirty Dingus Magee (1970)
The Dirty Dozen (1967)
Dirty Harry (1971)
The Dirty Heroes (1971)
The Dirty Outlaws (1971)
Dirtymouth (1970)
Disbarred (1939)
The Disembodied (1957)
Dishonored Lady (1947)
Disorder in the Night (1960)
The Disorderly Orderly (1964)
Dispatch from Reuters (1940
Disputed Passage (1939)
Distant Drums (1951)
Distant Journey (1950)
A Distant Trumpet (1964)
Dive Bomber (1941)
Divide and Conquer (1943)
The Divided Heart (1955)
Divorce (1945)
Divorce, American Style (1967)
Divorce, Italian Style (1962)
The Divorce of Lady X (1938)
Dixie Dugan (1943)
Do Not Disturb (1965)
Do Not Throw Cushions Into the Ring (1970)
Doc (1971)
Docks of New Orleans (1948)
The Doctor and the Girl (1949)
Doctor at Large (1957)
Doctor at Sea (1956)
Doctor Beware (1951)
Doctor Blood's Coffin (1961)
Dr. Crippen (1964)
Dr. Cyclops (1940)
Doctor Dolittle (1967)
Dr. Ehrlich's Magic Bullet (1940)
Doctor Fabian--Laughing Is the Best Medicine (1969)
Doctor Faustus (1967)
Dr. Gillespie's Criminal Case (1943)
Dr. Gillespie's New Assistant (1942)
Dr. Goldfoot and the Bikini Machine (1965)
Dr. Goldfoot and the Girl Bombs (1966)
Doctor in Clover (1966)
Doctor in Distress (1964)
Doctor in Love (1962)
Doctor in the House (1955)
Doctor in Trouble (1970)
Dr. Jekyll and Mr. Hyde (1941)
Dr. Jekyll and Sister Hyde (1971)
Dr. Kildare Goes Home (1940)
Dr. No (1963)
Dr. Renault's Secret (1942)
Dr. Strangelove: Or How I Learned to Stop Worrying and Love the Bomb (1963)
The Doctor Takes a Wife (1940)
Dr. Terror's House of Horrors (1965)
Doctor, You've Got to Be Kidding (1967)
Dr. Zhivago (1965)
The Doctor's Dilemma (1958)
Dodge City (1939)
Dodsworth (1936)
A Dog, a Mouse and a Sputnik (1958)
A Dog of Flanders (1959)
A Dog's Best Friend (1960)
La Dolce Vita (1961)
The Doll (1963)
Dollars ($) (1971)
The Domino Kid (1957)
Don Juan (1926)
Don Juan in Sicily (1967)
Don Juan Quilligan (1945)
Don Juan's Night of Love (1955)
Don Q, Son of Zorro (1925)
Don Quixote (1934)
Don Quixote (1957)
Don Quixote de la Mancha (1948)
Dondi (1961)
Donkey Skin (1970)
Donovan's Brain (1953)
Donovan's Reef (1963)
Don't Bother to Knock (1952)
Don't Drink the Water (1969)
Don't Fence Me In (1945)

Don't Fumble, Darling (1970)
Don't Gamble with Strangers (1946)
Don't Give Up the Ship (1959)
Don't Go Near the Water (1957)
Don't Lose Your Head (1967)
Don't Make Waves (1967)
Don't Play with the Martians (1968)
Don't Raise the Bridge, Lower the River (1968)
Don't Trust Your Husband (1948)
Don't Worry (1970)
The Doolins of Oklahoma (1949)
Door-to-Door Maniac (1966)
Dorian Gray (1970)
Double Bunk (1961)
Double Crossbones (1950)
Double Deal (1950)
Double Dynamite (1951)
Double Exposure (1944)
Double Face (1969)
Double Indemnity (1944)
Double Jeopardy (1955)
A Double Life (1947)
The Double Man (1967)
Double Pisces, Scorpio Rising (1970)
Double-Strop (1968)
Double Trouble (1915)
Double Trouble (1967)
Double Wedding (1937)
The Doughgirls (1944)
Douglas (1970)
Dow Dakota Way (1949)
Down Laredo Way (1953)
Down Memory Lane (1949)
Down Missouri Way (1946)
Down the Wyoming Trail (1939)
Down Three Dark Streets (1954)
Down to Earth (1947)
Down to the Sea in Ships (1949)
Downhill Racer (1969)
Downstream from the Sun (1969)
Downtown (1955)
Dracula Has Risen from the Grave (1968)
Dracula, Prince of Darkness (1966)
Les Drageurs (1958)
Dragnet (1947)
Dragnet (1954)
Dragon Seed (1944)
Dragon Sky (1964)
Dragonfly (1955)
Dragonfly Squadron (1954)
Dragon's Gold (1954)
Dragonwyck (1946)
Dragoon Wells Massacre (1957)
Dragstrip Riot (1958)
The Dramatic Life of Abraham Lincoln (1923)
Drango (1957)
The Drawings of Leonardo da Vinci (1954)
Dream Girl (1948)
The Dream Maker (1964)
A Dream of Kings (1969)
Dream Street (1921)
Dream Wife (1953)
Dreamboat (1952)
The Dreamer (1970)
Dreaming Lips (1954)
Dreams that Money Can Buy (1948)
Driftin' River (1946)
Drifting Along (1946)
Driftwood (1947)
Drive a Crooked Road (1954)
Drop Dead, My Love (1968)
Drum Beat (1954)
Drums (1938)
Drums Across the River (1954)
Drums Along the Mohawk (1939)
Drums in the Deep South (1951)
Drums of Africa (1963)
Drums of Love (1929)
Drums of Tahiti (1954)
Drums of the Congo (1942)
Drunken Angel (1948)
Du Barry was a Lady (1943)
The Duck Rings at Half Past Seven (1969)
The Dude Goes West (1948)
Dudes Are Pretty People (1942)
Duel at Apache Wells (1957)
Duel at Diablo (1966)
The Duel at Silver Creek (1952)
Duel in the Jungle (1954)
Duel in the Sun (1947)
Duel of the Titans (1963)
Duel on the Mississippi (1955)
Duffy (1968)
Duffy of San Quentin (1954)
Duke of Chicago (1949)
The Duke of West Point (1938)

Dulcima (1971)
Dulcimer Street (1948)
Dunkirk (1958)
The Dunwich Horror (1970)
Dust Be My Destiny (1939)
Dutchman (1966)
Dynamite (1948)
Dynamite Pass (1950)

Each Dawn I Die (1939)
Eadie Was a Lady (1945)
The Eagle and the Hawk (1950)
Eagle in a Cage (1971)
Eagle Squadron (1942)
The Eagle with Two Heads (1948)
Eagles Attack at Dawn (1970)
Earl Carroll's Vanities (1945)
The Earl of Chicago (1940)
Early Morning (1971)
The Earrings of Madame D... (1953)
The Earth (1970)
The Earth Dies Screaming (1964)
Earth vs. the Flying Saucers (1956)
Earthworm Tractors (1936)
East Meets West (1936)
East of Eden (1954)
East of Java (1935)
East of Sudan (1964)
East of Sumatra (1953)
East of the River (1940)
East Side, West Side (1949)
Easter Island (1934)
Easy Come, Easy Go (1947)
Easy Come, Easy Go (1967)
The Easy Life (1963)
Easy Living (1937)
Easy Living (1949)
Easy to Look At (1945)
Easy to Wed (1946)
L'Eau Vive (1958)
Ebb Tide (1937)
Eclipse (1962)
The Eddy Duchin Story (1956)
Edge of Darkness (1943)
Edge of Doom (1950)
Edge of Eternity (1959)
Edge of Hell (1956)
The Edge of the Abyss (1915)
Edge of the World (1937)
Edison the Man (1940)
Edouard and Caroline (1952)
Edward My Son (1949)
An Eel Worth 300 Million (1971)
The Egg and I (1947)
The Egyptian (1954)
8-1/2 (1963)
Eight Iron Men (1952)
Eight on the Lam (1967)
8 X 8 (1957)
Eighteen and Anxious (1957)
The Eighth (1970)
Eighty Steps to Jonah (1969)
El Alamein (1953)
El Cid (1961)
El Dorado (1951)
El Dorado (1967)
El Paso (1949)
The El Paso Kid (1946)
El Paso Stampede (1953)
Electra (1963)
The Electronic Monster (1960)
Elena and the Men (1955)
Elephant Boy (1936)
An Elephant Called Slowly (1971)
Elephant Gun (1959)
Elephant Walk (1954)
Elevator to the Gallows (1957)
The Eleventh Commandment (1970)
Elmer Gantry (1960)
Elopement (1951)
The Elusive Corporal (1963)
Embraceable You (1948)
Emergency Call (1933)
Emergency Exit (1970)
Emergency Hospital (1956)
Emergency Wedding (1950)
Emil and the Detectives (1931)
Emil and the Detectives (1964)
The Emperor Waltz (1948)
Emperors, Citizens and Comrades (1971)
The Emperor's Nightingale (1951)
Emperor's Waltz (1956)
Empire of the Sun (1957)
The Empty Canvas (1964)
The Enchanted Cottage (1945)
The Enchanted Forest (1945)

Enchanted Island (1958)
The Enchanted Valley (1948)
Enchantment (1948)
Encore (1952)
The End of Belle (1962)
End of Desire (1962)
The End of Pyrenees (1970)
The End of St. Petersburg (1928)
The End of the Affair (1955)
The End of the River (1948)
End of the Road (1970)
Enemies of Women (1923)
The Enemy Below (1957)
Enemy from Space (1957)
The Enemy General (1960)
Enemy of Women (1944)
The Enforcer (1951)
Ensign Pulver (1964)
Enter Arsene Lupin (1944)
Enter Laughing (1967)
The Entertainer (1960)
Entertaining Mr. Sloane (1970)
Entr'acte (1924)
Entree des Artistes (1938)
Equinox (1970)
The Errand Boy (1962)
Escalation (1968)
Escapade (1955)
Escapade in Japan (1957)
Escape (1939)
Escape (1948)
Escape by Night (1964)
Escape from East Berlin (1962)
Escape from Fort Bravo (1953)
Escape from Red Rock (1958)
Escape from San Quentin (1957)
Escape from the Planet of the Apes (1971)
Escape from Yesterday (1939)
Escape from Zahrain (1962)
Escape in the Desert (1945)
Escape Me Never (1935)
Escape Me Never (1947)
Escape to Burma (1955)
Escort West (1959)
Eskimo (1933)
Espionage Agent (1939)
Esther and the King (1960)
Esther Waters (1948)
Eternal Melodies (1948)
The Eternal Return (1944)
The Eternal Sea (1955)
Eternally Yours (1939)
Eugenie--The Story of Her Journey into Perversion (1970)
Eugenie Grandet (1960)
Eureka Stockade (1949)
Eva (1965)
Evangeline (1919)
The Eve of St. Mark (1944)
Evensong (1934)
Events (1970)
Everest Symphony (1971)
Every Day Is a Holiday (1966)
Every Girl Should Be Married (1948)
Every Home Should Have One (1970)
Every Saturday Night (1936)
Everybody Does It (1949)
Everybody Go Home! (1962)
Everybody Sing (1938)
Everybody's Old Man (1936)
Everything But the Truth (1956)
Everything's Ducky (1961)
The Evil of Frankenstein (1964)
The Ex-Mrs. Bradford (1936)
The Executioner (1970)
Exclusive Story (1936)
Excuse Me, My Name is Rocco Papaleo (1971)
Excuse My Dust (1951)
The Exile (1947)
Exile Express (1939)
Exodus (1960)
Experiment Alcatraz (1950)
Experiment in Terror (1962)
Experiment Perilous (1944)
Explosion (1969)
The Explosion (1971)
The Explosive Generation (1961)
Exposed (1947)
Expresso Bongo (1960)
The Exquisite Cadaver (1971)
Extase (1932)
The Extraordinary Seaman (1969)
An Eye for an Eye (1966)
Eye of the Cat (1969)
Eye of the Devil (1967)
Eye Witness (1950)
Eyes in the Night (1942)
The Eyes of Annie Jones (1963)
Eyes of Texas (1948)
Eyes of the Soul (1919)
Eyes without a Face (1959)

Eyewitness (1970)

F.B.I. Code 98 (1963)
F.B.I. Girl (1951)
The F.B.I. Story (1959)
Fabiola (1948)
The Fabulous Dorseys (1947)
The Fabulous Joe (1947)
The Fabulous Senorita (1952)
The Fabulous Suzanne (1946)
The Fabulous Texas (1947)
The Fabulous World of Jules Verne (1961)
A Face in the Crowd (1957)
The Face in the Sky (1933)
Face of a Fugitive (1959)
Face of Fire (1959)
The Face of Fu Manchu (1965)
The Face of Marble (1946)
The Face of Scotland (1938)
The Face of War (1963)
Face to Face (1952)
Face to the Wind (1951)
The Facts of Life (1960)
Fadila (1961)
Fahrenheit 451 (1966)
Fair Wind to Java (1953)
Fait Divers (1924)
Faithful City (1952)
Faithful in My Fashion (1946)
The Fake (1953)
The Falcon in Danger (1943)
The Falcon in San Francisco (1945)
The Falcon Out West (1944)
The Falcon Strikes Back (1943)
The Falcon's Adventure (1946)
The Falcon's Alibi (1946)
Fall Guy (1947)
The Fall of a Nation (1916)
The Fall of Berlin (1945)
The Fall of the Roman Empire (1963)
Fallen Angel (1945)
The Fallen Idol (1948)
Fallen Idols (1919)
Fallen Sparrow (1943)
False Faces (1918)
False Paradise (1948)
Familiarities (1970)
Family Diary (1963)
Family Honeymoon (1948)
The Family Jewels (1965)
Family Portrait (1950)
The Family Secret (1951)
The Family Way (1966)
The Fan (1949)
Fan-Fan La Tulipe (1951)
Fancy Pants (1950)
Fangs of the Arctic (1953)
Fangs of the Wild (1954)
Fanny (1932)
Fanny (1961)
Fanny Hill (1969)
Fantastic Night (1942)
The Fantastic Plastic Machine (1969)
Fantastic Voyage (1966)
Fantomas se Dechaine (1966)
The Far-Away Bride (see Under Sunny Skies)
The Far Country (1955)
Far From the Madding Crowd (1967)
The Far Frontier (1948)
The Far Horizons (1955)
Farewell Doves (1960)
A Farewell to Arms (1957)
Fargo (1952)
The Farmer in the Dell (1936)
The Farmer Takes a Wife (1935)
The Farmer Takes a Wife (1953)
The Farmer's Daughter (1940)
The Farmer's Daughter (1947)
Farrebique (1948)
Fashion Model (1945)
Fast and Furious (1939)
Fast and Sexy (1960)
Fast Company (1938)
Fast Company (1953)
Faster, Pussycat, Kill! Kill! (1966)
The Fastest Guitar Alive (1967)
The Fastest Gun Alive (1956)
The Fat Man (1951)
Fatal Lady (1936)
The Fatal Witness (1945)
Fate Is the Hunter (1963)
Father Goose (1963)
Father Is a Bachelor (1950)
Father Makes Good (1950)
Father of Four in a Sunny Mood (1971)

Father of the Bride (1950)
Father Takes a Wife (1941)
Father Takes the Air (1951)
Father Was a Fullback (1949)
Father's Dilemma (1950)
Father's Doing Fine (1952)
Father's Little Dividend (1951)
Father's Trip (1966)
Father's Wild Game (1950)
Fathom (1967)
Faustina (1968)
Fazil (1928)
Fear in the Night (1947)
The Fear Makers (1958)
Fear Strikes Out (1957)
Fearless Fagan (1952)
The Fearless Vampire Killers (1967)
The Feathered Serpent (1948)
Federal Agent at Large (1950)
Federal Man (1950)
Federal Man Hunt (1939)
The Female Animal (1958)
The Female Animal (1970)
Female on the Beach (1955)
The Female Soldier (1966)
The Feminine Touch (1941)
Fence Riders (1950)
Fernandel, the Dressmaker (1956)
Ferry to Hong Kong (1961)
Feudin' Fools (1952)
Feudin', Fussin' and A-Fightin' (1948)
Fever Heat (1968)
A Fever in the Blood (1961)
The Fickle Finger of Fate (1967)
The Fiend Who Walked the West (1958)
The Fiercest Heart (1961)
Fiesta (1942)
Fiesta (1947)
Fifi La Plume (1965)
Fifth Avenue Girl (1939)
Fifty-Fifty (1971)
50 Roads to Town (1937)
Fifty Years Before Your Eyes (1950)
55 Days at Peking (1963)
Fight for Life (1939)
The Fight for Rome (1969)
The Fighter (1952)
Fighter Attack (1953)
Fighter Squadron (1948)
Fighting Back (1948)
Fighting Bill Carson (1945)
Fighting Bill Fargo (1942)
Fighting Chance (1955)
Fighting Coast Guard (1951)
Fighting Father Dunne (1948)
Fighting Fools (1949)
Fighting Frontier (1943)
The Fighting Gringo (1939)
The Fighting Guardsman (1945)
The Fighting Kentuckian (1949)
The Fighting Lady (1944)
The Fighting Lawman (1953)
Fighting Mad (1948)
Fighting Man of the Plains (1949)
Fighting Mustang (1948)
The Fighting O'Flynn (1949)
The Fighting Prince of Donegal (1966)
The Fighting Ranger (1948)
The Fighting Redhead (1950)
The Fighting Seabees (1944)
The Fighting Stallion (1950)
Fighting Thoroughbreds (1939)
Fighting Trouble (1956)
The Fighting Vigilantes (1948)
The Fighting Wildcats (1957)
Film Record of the Eucharistic Congress (1926)
The Film without a Name (1948)
La Fin du Jour (1939)
The Final Test (1953)
Fincho (1958)
Finders Keepers (1951)
Finders Keepers (1966)
A Fine Madness (1966)
A Fine Pair (1969)
The Finest Hours (1963)
Finger Man (1955)
Finger of Guilt (1956)
Finger on the Trigger (1965)
Fingerprints Don't Lie (1951)
Fingers at the Window (1942)
Fire (1968)
The Fire Brigade (1926)
Fire Down Below (1957)
Fire Over Africa (1954)
Fire Over England (1937)
The Fire Tongue Bowl (1970)
Fire Woman (1971)

The Fireball (1950)
The Firebrand (1962)
Firecreek (1968)
Fired Wife (1943)
Fireman, Save My Child (1954)
Fires of Faith (1919)
Fires on the Plain (1959)
Fires Were Started (1942)
First a Girl (1936)
First Comes Courage (1943)
The First Echelon (1956)
The First Hundred Years (1938)
The First Legion (1951)
First Love (1970)
First Man into Space (1959)
The First Men in the Moon (1963)
The First of the Few (Spitfire) (1942)
The First Texan (1956)
The First Time (1952)
The First Time (1969)
First to Fight (1967)
The First Traveling Saleslady (1956)
The First Yank into Tokyo (1945)
The First Year (1932)
Fitzwilly (1967)
Five (1951)
Five Against the House (1955)
Five Branded Women (1960)
Five Came Back (1939)
Five Card Stud (1968)
Five Finger Exercise (1962)
Five Fingers (1952)
Five Gates to Hell (1959)
Five Golden Hours (1961)
Five Graves to Cairo (1943)
Five Guns to Tombstone (1961)
Five Guns West (1955)
Five Miles to Midnight (1963)
5,000,000 Miles to Earth (1968)
The Five Pennies (1959)
Five Steps to Danger (1957)
Five the Hard Way (1969)
The 5,000 Fingers of Dr. T (1953)
Five Weeks in a Balloon (1962)
Fixed Bayonets (1951)
Fixer Dugan (1939)
The Flame and the Arrow (1950)
The Flame and the Fire (1966)
Flame and the Flesh (1954)
Flame of Araby (1951)
Flame of New Orleans (1941)
Flame of Stamboul (1951)
Flame of the Barbary Coast (1945)
Flame of the Islands (1955)
Flame of the West (1945)
Flame of Youth (1949)
Flame Over India (1960)
Flames of the Volga (1955)
Flaming Feather (1951)
The Flaming Frontier (1926)
Flaming Frontier (1958)
Flaming Frontier (1968)
Flaming Fury (1949)
Flamingo Road (1949)
The Flanders and Alcott Report on Sex Response (1971)
Flap (1970)
Flareup (1969)
Flat Top (1952)
Flaxy Martin (1949)
A Flea in Her Ear (1968)
The Fleet that Came to Stay (1945)
The Flemish Farm (1943)
Flesh and Blood (1951)
Flesh and Desire (1958)
Flesh and Fantasy (1943)
Flesh and Fury (1952)
Flesh and the Woman (1958)
Flick (1970)
The Flight (1971)
Flight at Midnight (1939)
Flight Command (1941)
Flight for Freedom (1943)
Flight from Ashiya (1963)
Flight from Destiny (1941)
Flight Lieutenant (1942)
Flight Nurse (1953)
Flight of the Doves (1971)
Flight of the Lost Balloon (1961)
The Flight of the Phoenix (1965)
Flight of the White Heron (see The Royal Tour of Queen Elizabeth and Philip) (1954)
The Flight that Disappeared (1961)
Flight to Hong Kong (1956)
Flight to Mars (1951)
Flight to Nowhere (1947)

Flight to Tangier (1953)
The Flim Flam Man (1967)
Flipper's New Adventure (1963)
Flirting with Fate (1938)
Flood Tide (1949)
Flood Tide (1958)
Floods of Fear (1959)
Florian (1940)
Flowers of St. Francis (1952)
Flowing Gold (1940)
Fluffy (1965)
The Fly (1958)
The Flying Carpet (1956)
The Flying Classroom (1958)
The Flying Deuces (1939)
The Flying Fontaines (1959)
Flying Hostess (1936)
The Flying Irishman (1939)
Flying Leathernecks (1951)
The Flying Man (1962)
The Flying Missile (1950)
The Flying Saucer (1950)
The Flying Serpent (1946)
Folies Bergere (1958)
Follow Me Boys (1966)
Follow Me Quietly (1949)
Follow that Camel (1967)
Follow that Dream (1962)
Follow that Woman (1945)
Follow the Boys (1944)
Follow the Boys (1963)
Follow the Leader (1944)
Follow the Sun (1951)
Follow Up (1969)
Follow Your Heart (1936)
The Fool (1925)
The Fool Killer (1965)
A Fool There Was (1914)
Foolish Wives (1922)
Fools (1970)
Fool's Gold (1946)
Fool's Parade (1971)
Fools Rush In (1949)
Footsteps in the Dark (1941)
Footsteps in the Fog (1955)
Footsteps in the Night (1957)
For a Few Dollars More (1966)
For a Price (1969)
For Better, For Worse (1961)
For Heaven's Sake (1950)
For Love and Gold (L'Armata Brancaleone) (1966)
For Love of Ivy (1968)
For Love or Money (1963)
For Men Only (The Tall Lie) (1952)
For Singers Only (1968)
For the First Time (1959)
For the Love of Mary (1948)
For the Love of Mike (1960)
For Those Who Dare (1949)
For Those Who Think Young (1964)
For Whom the Bell Tolls (1943)
For You I Die (1947)
Forbidden (1953)
Forbidden Cargo (1956)
Forbidden Fruit (1952)
Forbidden Island (1959)
The Forbidden Street (1949)
Forbidden to Step on the Clouds (1970)
The Forbin Project (1970)
Force of Arms (1951)
Force of Evil (1948)
A Foreign Affair (1948)
Foreign Agent (1942)
Foreign Correspondent (1940)
Foreign Intrigue (1956)
The Foreman (1956)
The Foreman Went to France (1942)
Forever Amber (1947)
Forever and a Day (1943)
Forever Darling (1956)
Forever Female (1953)
Forever My Love (1962)
Forged Passport (1939)
Forgotten Faces (see Till We Meet Again)
The Forgotten Village (1941)
Forgotten Women (1949)
Fort Algiers (1953)
Fort Apache (1948)
Fort Bowie (1958)
Fort Courageous (1965)
Fort Defiance (1951)
Fort Dobbs (1958)
Fort Dodge Stampede (1951)
Fort Massacre (1958)
Fort Osage (1952)
Fort Ti (1953)
Fort Utah (1967)
Fort Vengeance (1953)
Fort Worth (1951)

Fort Yuma (1955)
Fortune and Men's Eyes (1971)
The Fortune Cookie (1966)
Fortunes of Captain Blood (1950)
Forty Guns (1957)
Forty Pounds of Trouble (1962)
The Forty-First (1956)
The Forty-Niners (1954)
The 49th Man (1953)
The Fountain (1934)
The Fountainhead (1949)
Four Bags Full (1956)
Four Boys and a Gun (1957)
Four Chimneys (1953)
Four Clowns (1970)
4-D Man (1959)
Four Daughters (1938)
Four Days in November (1964)
The Four Days of Naples (1963)
4 Devils (1928)
Four Faces West (1948)
Four Fast Guns (1959)
Four Feathers (1929)
Four Feathers (1938)
Four for Texas (1963)
Four Frightened People (1934)
Four Girls in Town (1956)
Four Guns to the Border (1954)
Four Horsemen of the Apocalypse (1921)
The Four Horsemen of the Apocalypse (1962)
The 400 Blows (1959)
The 400 Million (1938)
Four in a Jeep (1951)
Four Men and a Prayer (1938)
The Four Skulls of Jonathan Drake (1959)
Four Sons (1928)
Four Sons (1940)
Four Steps in the Clouds (1942)
Four Wives (1939)
The Fourposter (1952)
Four's a Crowd (1938)
Fourteen Hours (1951)
The Fourth Estate (1939)
The Fox (1967)
The Foxes of Harrow (1947)
Foxfire (1955)
Foxhole in Cairo (1961)
Foxy Lady (1971)
Fragment of Fear (1970)
Framed (1947)
Francis (1949)
Francis Covers the Big Town (1953
Francis Goes to the Races (1951)
Fancis Goes to West Point (1952)
Francis in the Haunted House (1956)
Francis in the Navy (1955)
Francis Joins the Wacs (1954)
Francis of Assisi (1961)
Francois Le Rhinoceros (1952)
Francois Villon (1948)
Frankenstein (1931)
Frankenstein Created Woman (1967)
Frankenstein--1970 (1957)
Frankenstein Meets the Wolf Man (1943)
Frankenstein Must Be Destroyed (1969)
Frankie and Johnny (1966)
Fraulein (1958)
Fraulein Doktor (1969)
Freckles (1960)
Freddie Steps Out (1946)
Free For All (1949)
French Can-Can (1953)
The French Connection (1971)
The French Game (1963)
The French Key (1946)
French Leave (1948)
French Leave (1971)
The French Line (1954)
A French Mistress (1960)
French without Tears (1949)
Frenchie (1950)
Frenchman's Creek (1944)
Freud (1962)
Friend of the Family (1965)
Friendly Enemies (1942)
Friendly Persuasion (1956)
Friends (1971)
Frightened City (1950)
The Frightened City (1962)
Frisco Tornado (1950)
Frisky (1955)
The Frogmen (1951)
From a Roman Balcony (1961)
From Doric to Gothic (1952)
From Ear to Ear (1971)
From Hell It Came (1957)

From Hell to Texas (1958)
From Here to Eternity (1953)
From Russia with Love (1964)
From the Boys (1971)
From the Earth to the Moon (1958)
From the Other Side (1970)
From the Terrace (1960)
From This Day Forward (1946)
Front Page Story (1955)
Frontier Agent (1948)
Frontier Feud (1945)
Frontier Fugitives (1946)
Frontier Gal (1945)
Frontier Gun (1958)
Frontier Investigator (1949)
Frontier Marshal (1939)
Frontier Pony Express (1939)
Frontier Uprising (1961)
The Frozen Dead (1967)
The Frozen Ghost (1945)
The Fugitive (1940)
The Fugitive (1947)
Fugitive Lady (1951)
Fugitive from Sonora (1943)
The Fugitive Kind (1959)
Fugitive of the Plains (1943)
Fugitives for a Night (1938)
Full Confession (1939)
Full of Life (1956)
The Fuller Brush Girl (1950)
The Fuller Brush Man (1948)
Fun and Fancy Free (1947)
Fun in the Streets (1969)
Fun on a Weekend (1947)
Funeral in Berlin (1966)
Funeral Parade of Roses (1970)
The Funniest Man in the World (1967)
Funny Face (1957)
Funnyman (1967)
The Furies (1950)
The Further Perils of Laurel and Hardy (1967)
Fury (1936)
Fury at Furnace Creek (1948)
Fury at Gunsight Pass (1956)
Fury at Smuggler's Bay (1963)
Fury at Sundown (1957)
The Future's in the Air (1936)
Futz (1969)
The Fuzzy Pink Nightgown (1957)

G.I. Blues (1960)
G.I. Honeymoon (1945)
G.I. Jane (1951)
G.I. War Brides (1946)
Gabriel over the White House (1933)
Gaby (1956)
The Gadfly (1955)
Gaily, Gaily (1969)
The Gal Who Took the West (1949)
Galileo (1968)
Gallant Bess (1946)
The Gallant Blade (1948)
The Gallant Hours (1960)
Gallant Journey (1946)
Gallant Lady (1934)
The Gallant Legion (1948)
The Galloping Major (1951)
La Gamberge (1963)
Gambit (1966)
The Gambler from Natchez (1954)
The Gamblers (1969)
Gambler's Choice (1944)
Gambling House (1950)
A Game of Death (1945)
The Game of Love (1954)
Games (1967)
The Games (1970)
Games that Lovers Play (1971)
The Gamma People (1956)
Gang Busters (1955)
The Gang that Couldn't Shoot Straight (1971)
Gang War (1958)
Gangs of the Waterfront (1945)
The Gangster (1947)
Gangsters of the Frontier (1944)
Gangway for Tomorrow (1943)
The Garden of Allah (1917)
The Garden of Allah (1936)
Garden of Eden (1957)
Garden of Evil (1954)
The Garden of the Finzi-Continis (1970)
The Garment Jungle (1957)
Gas House Kids (1946)
Gas House Kids Go West (1947)
Gas House Kids in Hollywood (1947)

Gaslight (1940)
Gaslight (1944)
Gas-s-s-s (1970)
Gates of Paradise (1968)
Gates of Paris (1957)
A Gathering of Eagles (1963)
The Gay Adventure (1953)
The Gay Amigo (1949)
Gay Blades (1946)
The Gay Cavalier (1946)
The Gay Deceivers (1969)
The Gay Deception (1935)
The Gay Desperado (1936)
The Gay Falcon (1941)
The Gay Intruders (1948)
The Gay Lady (Trottie True) (1949)
The Gay Life (1950)
The Gay Ranchero (1948)
The Gay Sisters (1942)
The Gazebo (1959)
The Geisha Boy (1958)
Gelosia (1948)
The Gendarme Gets Married (1968)
The Gene Krupa Story (1959)
The General Died at Dawn (1936)
General Spanky (1936)
General Suvorov (1941)
Generation (1969)
Genevieve (1954)
Genghis Khan (1965)
Gentle Annie (1944)
Gentle Giant (1967)
The Gentle Gunman (1953)
The Gentle Rain (1965)
The Gentle Touch (1957)
A Gentleman After Dark (1942)
Gentleman from Texas (1946)
Gentleman Jim (1942)
Gentleman Joe Palooka (1946)
Gentlemen in White Vests (1970)
Gentlemen Marry Brunettes (1955)
Gentlemen with Guns (1946)
Gentlemen's Agreement (1947)
A Geometry Lesson (1947)
The George Raft Story (1961)
George Washington Slept Here (1942)
Georgy Girl (1966)
Gerald McBoing Boing (1950)
Geraldine (1953)
Germany Year Zero (1947)
Germinal (1963)
Geronimo (1939)
Geronimo (1962)
Gervaise (1957)
Get Carter (1971)
Get Going (1943)
Get Yourself a College Girl (1964)
Getting Gertie's Garter (1945)
Getting Straight (1970)
Ghidrah, The Three-Headed Monster (1965)
The Ghost and Mr. Chicken (1966)
The Ghost and Mrs. Muir (1947)
The Ghost and the Guest (1943)
Ghost Breakers (1940)
Ghost Catchers (1943)
Ghost Diver (1957)
The Ghost Goes Wild (1947)
Ghost Guns (1944)
The Ghost in the Invisible Bikini (1966)
The Ghost of Dragstrip Hollow (1959)
The Ghost of Frankenstein (1942)
Ghost of the China Sea (1958)
The Ghost Ship (1943)
Ghost Ship (1953)
Ghost Town (1955)
Ghost Town Law (1942)
Ghost Town Renegades (1947)
Ghosts Before Breakfast (1929)
Ghosts, Italian Style (1969)
Ghosts on the Loose (1943)
Giacomo Casanova: Childhood and Adolescence (1969)
Giant (1956)
The Giant Behemoth (1959)
The Giant Claw (1957)
The Giant of Marathon (1960)
Gideon of Scotland Yard (1959)
Gidget (1959)
Gidget Goes Hawaiian (1961)
Gidget Goes to Rome (1963)
Gift Horse (1952)
The Gift of Love (1958)
Gigi (1949)
Gigot (1962)

Gilda (1946)
Ginger (1935)
Ginger (1971)
A Girl, a Guy and a Gob (1941)
The Girl and the General (1967)
The Girl Downstairs (1939)
Girl Friends (1936)
The Girl from Alaska (1942)
The Girl from Jones Beach (1949)
The Girl from Manhattan (1948)
The Girl from Mexico (1939)
The Girl from Missouri (1934)
The Girl from San Lorenzo (1950)
Girl Happy (1965)
The Girl He Left Behind (1956)
The Girl Hunters (1963)
The Girl in Black Stockings (1957)
A Girl in Every Port (1952)
The Girl in the Bikini (1955)
The Girl in the Kremlin (1957)
The Girl in the Mist (1955)
The Girl in the Painting (1948)
The Girl in the Red Velvet Swing (1955)
Girl in the Woods (1958)
The Girl in White (1952)
The Girl Next Door (1953)
A Girl Named Tamiko (1962)
Girl No. 217 (1944)
Girl of the Limberlost (1945)
Girl of the Mountains (1958)
Girl of the Night (1960)
The Girl on the Bridge (1951)
Girl Stroke Boy (1971)
Girl Trouble (1942)
The Girl Watchers (1969)
The Girl Who Had Everything (1953)
The Girl Who Knew Too Much (1969)
The Girl with Green Eyes (1964)
The Girl with the Golden Eyes (1962)
Girl without a Room (1933)
Girls and Gynecologists (1971)
Girl's Dormitory (1936)
Girls! Girls! Girls! (1962)
Girls in Chains (1943)
The Girls of Pleasure Island (1953)
Girls of the Night (1959)
Girls of the Big House (1945)
The Girls on the Beach (1965)
Girl's School (1938)
Girl's Town (1942)
Girl's Town (1959)
Give God a Chance on Sunday (1970)
Give the Girl a Break (1953)
The Given Word (1962)
The Gladiator (1938)
Gladiators Seven (1964)
The Glass Alibi (1946)
The Glass Bottom Boat (1966)
The Glass Ceiling (1971)
Glass Houses (1970)
The Glass Key (1942)
The Glass Menagerie (1950)
The Glass Mountain (1948)
The Glass Slipper (1955)
The Glass Wall (1953)
The Glass Web (1953)
The Glenn Miller Story (1954)
A Global Affair (1964)
Glory (1956)
Glory Alley (1952)
The Glory Brigade (1953)
The Glory Guys (1965)
The Gnome-Mobile (1967)
Go for Broke (1951)
Go, Johnny, Go (1959)
Go, Man, Go (1954)
Go Naked Into the World (1961)
Go West (1941)
Goal! (1966)
Gobs and Gals (1952)
God Forgives, I Don't (1969)
God Is My Co-Pilot (1945)
God Is My Partner (1957)
God Needs Men (1951)
God with Us (1970)
The Goddess (1958)
The Goddess of Love (1960)
God's Country (1946)
God's Country and the Woman (1937)
God's Little Acre (1958)
Gods of Pestilence (1970)
Godzilla, King of the Monsters (1956)
Godzilla vs. the Thing (1964)
Gog (1954)

Goin' Down the Road (1970)
Going Home (1971)
Going My Way (1944)
Going Wild (1930)
Gold Fever (1952)
Gold for the Caesars (1964)
Gold for the Tough Guys of the Prairie (1971)
Gold Is Where You Find It (1938)
Gold of the Seven Saints (1961)
Gold Raiders (1951)
The Goldbergs (1950)
Golden Apples of the Sun (1971)
The Golden Arrow (1936)
The Golden Arrow (1964)
The Golden Blade (1953)
Golden Boy (1939)
The Golden Calf (1930)
The Golden Coach (1954)
Golden Earrings (1947)
The Golden Gloves Story (1950)
The Golden Hawk (1952)
Golden Hoofs (1941)
The Golden Horde (1951)
The Golden Idol (1954)
The Golden Mask (1954)
Golden Mountains (1931)
The Golden Salamander (1951)
The Golden Stallion (1949)
The Golden Twenties (1950)
Goldfinger (1964)
Goldtown Ghost Riders (1953)
Golgotha (1937)
Goliath and the Dragon (1960)
Gone with the Wind (1939)
The Good Companions (1933)
The Good Die Young (1955)
The Good Earth (1936)
The Good Fellows (1943)
The Good Guys and the Bad Guys (1969)
The Good Humor Man (1950)
Good Luck, Mr. Yates (1943)
Good Morning ... and Goodbye (1967)
Good Morning, Miss Dove (1955)
Good Neighbor Sam (1964)
The Good Old Soak (1937)
Good Sam (1948)
The Good Soldier Schweik (1963)
The Good, the Bad and the Ugly (1967)
Goodbye Again (1961)
Goodbye Charlie (1964)
Goodbye, Columbus (1969)
Goodbye Gemini (1970)
Goodbye, Mr. Chips (1939)
Goodbye Moscow (1968)
Goodbye My Fancy (1951)
Goodbye, My Lady (1956)
Goodbye, Stork, Goodbye (1971)
The Gorgeous Hussey (1936)
Gorgo (1961)
The Gorgon (1965)
The Gorilla (1939)
Gorilla at Large (1954)
Government Girl (1943)
Goya (1952)
Goya (1971)
Goyokin (1969)
The Gracie Allen Murder Case (1939)
Gradina (1970)
The Graduate (1967)
Un Gran Patron (1951)
Grand Canyon (1949)
Grand Canyon Trail (1948)
Grand Central Murder (1942)
Grand Illusion (1937)
The Grand Olympics (1960)
Grand Prix (1966)
La Grand Rock (1969)
Grand Slam (1967)
Les Grandes Manoeuvres (1955)
Grandma Moses (1951)
The Grapes of Wrath (1940)
Grass (1925)
The Grasshopper (1955)
The Grasshopper (1970)
The Great Adventure (1954)
The Great American Pastime (1956)
The Great Armored Car Swindle (1964)
The Great Bank Robbery (1969)
The Great Battle (1971)
A Great Big Thing (1968)
The Great British Train Robbery (1967)
The Great Caruso (1951)
Great Catherine (1968)
The Great Chase (1963)
A Great Citizen (1938)
The Great Commandment (1939)
The Great Dan Patch (1949)

Great Day in the Morning (1956)
The Great Diamond Robbery (1953)
The Great Dictator (1940)
The Great Escape (1963)
Great Expectations (1934)
Great Expectations (1947)
The Great Flamarion (1945)
The Great Gabbo (1929)
The Great Garrick (1937)
The Great Gatsby (1949)
The Great Glass Blower (1933)
Great Guy (1936)
The Great Impersonation (1935)
The Great Impersonation (1942)
The Great Imposter (1960)
The Great Jewel Robbery (1950)
The Great John L. (1945)
The Great Lie (1941)
The Great Locomotive Chase (1956)
The Great Lover (1949)
The Great Man (1956)
The Great Man Votes (1939)
The Great Man's Lady (1942)
The Great McGinty (1940)
The Great Mike (1944)
The Great Missouri Raid (1950)
The Great Moment (1944)
The Great Plane Robbery (1950)
The Great Race (1965)
The Great Rights (1963)
The Great Rupert (1949)
The Great St. Louis Bank Robbery (1959)
The Great St. Trinian's Train Robbery (1966)
The Great Sinner (1949)
The Great Sioux Massacre (1965)
The Great Sioux Uprising (1953)
The Great Unfenced (1964)
The Great Victor Herbert (1939)
The Great Waltz (1938)
The Great War (1961)
The Greatest Show on Earth (1952)
The Greatest Story Ever Told (1965)
Greece, Land of Dreams (1966)
Greed (1924)
Greed in the Sun (1965)
The Green Berets (1968)
The Green Buddha (1955)
The Green Carnation (1960)
Green Dolphin Street (1947)
The Green-Eyed Blonde (1957)
Green Fire (1954)
The Green Glove (1952)
Green Grass of Wyoming (1948)
The Green Helmet (1961)
The Green Light (1937)
Green Magic (1955)
The Green Man (1957)
Green Mansions (1959)
The Green Pastures (1936)
The Green Promise (1949)
The Green Scarf (1955)
The Green Slime (1969)
The Green Wall (1970)
The Green Years (1946)
Greetings (1968)
The Greenwich Village Story (1963)
Greyfriar's Bobby (1961)
Il Grido (1957)
Grimm's Fairy Tales for Adults (1971)
Grissley's Millions (1945)
The Grissom Gang (1971)
The Groom Wore Spurs (1951)
Grounds for Marriage (1950)
Guadalcanal Diary (1943)
Guendalina (1956)
Guerrilla Girl (1953)
Guess What We Learned in School Today? (1970)
Guess Who's Coming to Dinner (1967)
The Guest (1964)
The Guest (1971)
Guest in the House (1944)
Guest Wife (1945)
The Guide (1965)
A Guide for the Married Man (1967)
The Guilt of Janet Ames (1947)
The Guilty (1947)
Guilty Bystander (1950)
Guilty of Treason (1949)
Guitars of Love (1958)
Gulliver's Travels (1939)
Gumshoe (1971)
Gun Battle at Monterey (1957)
Gun Belt (1953)
Gun Brothers (1956)

Gun Duel in Durango (1957)
Gun Fever (1958)
Gun for a Coward (1957)
Gun Fury (1953)
Gun Glory (1957)
The Gun Hawk (1963)
The Gun Runners (1958)
Gun Smugglers (1948)
Gun Street (1962)
Gun Talk (1947)
The Gun that Won the West (1955)
Gun the Man Down (1956)
A Gunfight (1971)
Gunfight at Comanche Creek (1963)
The Gunfight at Dodge City (1959)
Gunfight at the O.K. Corral (1957)
Gunfight in Abilene (1967)
The Gunfighter (1950)
Gunfighters (1947)
Gunfighters of Abilene (1960)
Gunfighters of Casa Grande (1965)
Gunfire at Indian Gap (1957)
Gung Ho! (1943)
Gunga Din (1939)
Gunman's Walk (1958)
Gunmen of Abilene (1950)
Gunmen of the Rio Grande (1965)
Gunn (1967)
Gunning for Justice (1948)
Gunplay (1951)
Gunpoint (1966)
Guns at Batasi (1964)
Guns for San Sebastian (1968)
Guns, Girls and Gangsters (1958)
The Guns of August (1964)
Guns of Darkness (1962)
The Guns of Fort Petticoat (1957)
Guns of Hate (1948)
The Guns of Navarone (1961)
Guns of the Magnificent Seven (1969)
Guns of the Timberland (1960)
Gunsight Ridge (1957)
Gunsmoke (1953)
Gunsmoke in Tucson (1958)
Gunsmoke Mesa (1944)
The Guru (1969)
A Guy Could Change (1946)
A Guy Named Joe (1943)
The Guy Who Came Back (1951)
Gypsy (1962)
The Gypsy and the Gentleman (1958)
Gypsy Colt (1954)
Gypsy Fury (1951)
The Gypsy Moths (1969)
Gypsy Wildcat (1944)

The H-Man (1959)
Hail the Conquering Hero (1944)
The Hairy Ape (1944)
Half a Hero (1953)
Half Angel (1951)
The Half-Breed (1952)
Half Past Midnight (1948)
Halfway House (1944)
The Hallelujah Trail (1965)
The Halliday Brand (1957)
Halls of Anger (1970)
Halls of Montezuma (1950)
Hallucination Generation (1966)
Hamilton, the Musical Elephant (1963)
Hamlet (1948)
Hamlet (1964)
Hamlet (1969)
Hammer for the Witches (1970)
Hammerhead (1968)
Hand in Hand (1960)
Hand of Death (1962)
Handcuffs (1970)
A Handful of Grain (1959)
Handle with Care (1958)
Hands Across the Border (1943)
Hands Across the Table (1935)
Hands of a Stranger (1962)
Hang 'Em High (1968)
The Hanging Tree (1959)
The Hangman (1959)
Hangman's Knot (1952)
Hangmen Also Die (1942)
Hangover Square (1945)
Hannie Caulder (1971)
Hannibal (1960)
Hannibal Brooks (1969)
Hans Christian Andersen (1952)
Ha'penny Breeze (1950)

The Happening (1967)
The Happiest Days of Your Life (1951)
Happy Anniversary (1959)
Happy Birthday, Davy (1970)
Happy Days (1930)
The Happy Ending (1969)
Happy Go Lucky (1951)
Happy He, Who Like Ulysses (1970)
Happy Is the Bride (1959)
Happy Land (1943)
The Happy Road (1957)
The Happy Thieves (1962)
The Happy Time (1952)
The Happy Years (1950)
Harbor Lights (1963)
Harbor of Missing Men (1950)
Hard Contact (1969)
Hard, Fast and Beautiful (1951)
The Hard Man (1957)
The Hard Ride (1971)
The Hard Road (1970)
The Hard Way (1942)
The Harder They Fall (1956)
Harem (1968)
Harem Girl (1952)
The Harlem Globetrotters (1951)
Harlem Wednesday (1959)
Harlow (1965)
Harlow (1965)
Harold and Maude (1971)
Harold Lloyd's World of Comedy (1962)
Harper (1966)
Harpoon (1948)
Harriet Craig (1950)
Harrigan's Kid (1943)
Harry Black and the Tiger (1958)
Harum Scarum (1965)
Harvest from the Wilderness (1948)
The Harvest Shall Come (1941)
Harvey (1950)
Harvey Middleman, Fireman (1955)
The Hasty Heart (1949)
The Hat Box Mystery (1947)
Hat, Coat and Glove (1934)
Hatari! (1962)
A Hatful of Rain (1957)
Hatikvah (1959)
Haunted Honeymoon (1941)
The Haunted Place (1963)
The Haunted Ranch (1943)
The Haunted Strangler (1958)
The Haunting (1963)
Havana Rose (1951)
Have Rocket, Will Travel (1959)
Having Wonderful Crime (1945)
Hawaii (1966)
The Hawk of Wild River (1952)
Hazard (1948)
He Died After the War (1971)
He Hired the Boss (1943)
He Laughed Last (1956)
He Ran All the Way (1951)
He Rides Tall (1964)
He Stayed for Breakfast (1940)
He Walked by Night (1948)
He Who Must Die (1958)
Head (1968)
The Head (1961)
Head Against the Wall (The Keepers) (1958)
Head of a Tyrant (1960)
Head of the Family (1967)
Head On (1971)
Head Over Heels in Love (1937)
Headin' West (1937)
Heading for Heaven (1947)
Headline Hunters (1955)
Heads or Tails (1971)
The Heart Is a Lonely Hunter (1968)
The Heart of Paula (1916)
Heart of Spain (1937)
The Heart of the Matter (1954)
Heart of the North (1938)
Heart of the Rio Grande (1942)
Heart of the Rockies (1951)
Heart of Virginia (1948)
Heartaches (1947)
Heartbeat (1946)
Heartbreak (1931)
Heartbreak Ridge (1955)
Hearts in Dixie (1929)
Hearts of the World (1918)
Heaven Can Wait (1943)
Heaven Knows, Mr. Alison (1957)
Heaven on Earth (1960)
Heaven Only Knows (1947)
Heaven with a Gun (1969)
The Heavenly Body (1943)
Heavenly Days (1944)

Heidi (1953)
Heidi and Peter (1955)
Heintje--Once the Sun Will Be Shining Again (1970)
The Heiress (1949)
Heldorado (1946)
Helen of Troy (1955)
Hell and High Water (1954)
Hell Below Zero (1954)
Hell Bent for Leather (1960)
Hell Bound (1957)
Hell Canyon Outlaws (1957)
Hell Drivers (1958)
Hell in the Pacific (1968)
Hell Is a City (1960)
Hell Is for Heroes (1962)
Hell on Devil's Island (1957)
Hell on Frisco Bay (1955)
Hell Raiders of the Deep (1953)
Hell Ship Mutiny (1957)
Hell to Eternity (1960)
The Hell with Heroes (1968)
Hellcats of the Navy (1957)
Heller in Pink Tights (1960)
Hellfighters (1968)
Hellfire (1949)
The Hellions (1962)
Hello Down There (1969)
Hello, Elephant! (1953)
Hello, Everybody (1938)
Hello, Goodbye (1970)
Hell's Angels (1930)
Hell's Angels on Wheels (1967)
Hell's Angels '69 (1969)
Hell's Belles (1969)
Hell's Crossroads (1957)
Hell's Five Hours (1958)
Hell's Half Acre (1954)
Hell's Horizon (1955)
Hell's Island (1955)
Hell's Outpost (1955)
The Hellstrom Chronicle (1971)
Help! (1965)
Help Me, My Love (1969)
Helter Skelter (1949)
Hemingway's Adventures of a Young Man (1962)
Henry Aldrich, Boy Scout (1944)
Henry Aldrich Haunts a House (1943)
Henry Aldrich Plays Cupid (1944)
Henry Aldrich's Little Secret (1944)
Henry V (1945)
Henry Moore (1951)
Henry, the Rainmaker (1949)
Her Adventurous Night (1946)
Her Cardboard Lover (1942)
Her First Affair (1941)
Her Highness and the Bellboy (1945)
Her Husband's Affairs (1947)
Her Jungle Love (1938)
Her Kind of Man (1946)
Her Man Gibney (1948)
Her Panelled Door (1951)
Her Primitive Man (1944)
Her Sister's Secret (1946)
Her Twelve Men (1954)
Hercules (1959)
Hercules, Samson and Ulysses (1965)
Hercules Unchained (1960)
Here Come the Girls (1953)
Here Come the Jets (1959)
Here Come the Marines (1952)
Here Come the Nelsons (1952)
Here Comes Kelly (1943)
Here Comes Mr. Jordan (1941)
Here Comes the Band (1935)
Here Comes the Groom (1951)
Here Comes Trouble (1948)
Here We Go Again (1942)
Here's to Romance (1935)
Herod the Great (1960)
Heroes and Sinners (1959)
Heroes of Shipka (1955)
Heroes of Telemark (1965)
Hero's Island (1962)
Hers to Hold (1943)
Hey, Let's Twist (1961)
Hi, Beautiful (1944)
Hi Diddle Diddle (1943)
Hi, Good Lookin' (1944)
Hi, Mom! (1970)
Hi Ya, Chum (1943)
Hi 'Ya, Sailor (1943)
Hiawatha (1952)
The Hidden City (1950)
Hidden Danger (1948)
The Hidden Eye (1945)
Hidden Fear (1957)
Hidden Guns (1956)
Hidden Homicide (1959)
The Hidden Room (1950)

Hidden Valley Outlaws (1944)
Hide and Seek (1964)
Hideout (1949)
Hide-Out (1934)
The Hiding Places (1970)
High and Dry (1954)
The High and the Mighty (1954)
High Barbaree (1947)
High Conquest (1947)
The High Cost of Loving (1958)
High Explosive (1943)
High Flight (1958)
High Fury (1948)
High Hell (1958)
High Lonesome (1950)
High Noon (1952)
High Powered (1945)
High Sierra (1941)
High Society (1955)
High Terrace (1956)
High Tide (1947)
High Time (1960)
High Treason (1952)
High Wall (1947)
High, Wild and Free (1968)
A High Wind in Jamaica (1965)
Highly Dangerous (1951)
Highway Dragnet (1954)
Highway Queen (1971)
Highway 13 (1948)
Highway 301 (1950)
The Highwayman (1951)
Hi-Jacked (1950)
Hilda Crane (1956)
The Hill (1965)
Hill 24 Doesn't Answer (1955)
Hillbilly Blitzkreig (1942)
Hills of Oklahoma (1950)
Hills of Rome (1948)
The Hills Run Red (1967)
L'Hippocampe (1934)
Hippodrome (1961)
The Hired Gun (1957)
The Hired Hand (1971)
The Hired Killer (1967)
Hired Wife (1940)
Hiroshima (1955)
Hiroshima, Mon Amour (1960)
His Brother's Wife (1936)
His Butler's Sister (1943)
His Darker Self (1924)
His Kind of Woman (1951)
His Majesty O'Keefe (1953)
His Night Out (1935)
His Young Wife (1945)
History Is Made at Night (1937)
The History of Mr. Polly (1948)
Hit and Run (1957)
Hit and Run (1966)
Hit Parade of 1943 (1943)
Hit the Deck (1955)
The Hitch Hiker (1953)
Hitchhike to Happiness (1945)
Hitler (1962)
The Hitler Gang (1944)
Hitler's Hangman (1943)
Hiya, Stine (1971)
The Hoaxters (1953)
Hobson's Choice (1954)
Hoffman (1970)
Hold Back the Dawn (1941)
Hold Back the Night (1956)
Hold Back Tomorrow (1955)
Hold On (1966)
Hold that Baby (1949)
Hold that Blonde (1945)
Hold that Ghost (1941)
Hold that Hypnotist (1957)
Hold that Kiss (1938)
Hold that Line (1952)
Holiday (1938)
Holiday Affair (1949)
Holiday Camp (1948)
A Hole in the Ground (1970)
A Hole in the Head (1959)
Holiday for Henrietta (1955)
Holiday for Lovers (1959)
Holiday for Sinners (1952)
Holiday Rhythm (1950)
Hollow Triumph (The Scar) (1948)
Hollywood and Vine (1945)
Hollywood Barn Dance (1947)
Hollywood Cavalcade (1939)
Hollywood or Bust (1956)
The Hollywood Story (1951)
Hollywood Varieties (1949)
Holy Matrimony (1943)
Hombre (1967)
Home Before Dark (1958)
Home from the Hill (1960)
Home in Indiana (1944)
Home in Oklahoma (1946)
Home of the Brave (1949)
Home on the Range (1945)
Home Sweet Homicide (1946)

Home Town Story (1951)
Homecoming (1948)
Homer (1970)
The Homestretch (1947)
Homicidal · (1961)
Homicide (1949)
Homicide for Three (1948)
D'Homme a Homme (1948)
L'Homme et L'Enfant (1957)
Homo Eroticus (1971)
Hondo
The Honest Interview (1971)
The Honey Pot (1967)
Honeychile (1951)
Honeymoon (1947)
Honeymoon Hotel (1964)
The Honeymoon Killers (1969)
The Honeymoon Machine (1961)
Hong Kong (1951)
Hong Kong Affair (1958)
Hong Kong Confidential (1958)
Honky (1971)
Honky Tonk (1941)
The Honorable Catherine (1948)
The Hoodlum (1951)
The Hoodlum (1970)
Hoodlum Empire (1952)
The Hoodlum Priest (1961)
The Hoodlum Saint (1946)
The Hook (1963)
Hook, Line and Sinker (1969)
Hooray for the Blue Hussars (1970)
Hoppy's Holiday (1947)
Horizon (1971)
The Horizontal Lieutenant (1962)
Horizons West (1952)
The Horn Blows at Midnight (1945)
Horror Hotel (1963)
Horror House (1970)
Horror of Dracula (1958)
The Horror of Frankenstein (1970)
The Horror of It All (1964)
Horrors of the Black Museum (1959)
The Horse in the Gray Flannel Suit (1968)
The Horse Soldiers (1959)
The Horsemen (1971)
The Horse's Mouth (1958)
The Hospital (1971)
Hostages (1943)
The Hostess Also Likes to Blow the Horn (1970)
The Hostess Exceeds All Bounds (1970)
Hostile Country (1950)
Hostile Guns (1967)
The Hot Angel (1958)
Hot Blood (1956)
Hot Car Girl (1958)
Hot Cargo (1946)
Hot Cars (1956)
Hot Lead (1951)
Hot Millions (1968)
The Hot Month of August (1966)
Hot News (1953)
Hot Rod (1950)
Hot Rod Rumble (1957)
Hot Rods to Hell (1967)
Hot Shots (1956)
Hot Spell (1958)
Hot Summer Night (1957)
Hot Traces of St. Paul (1971)
Hot Years (1966)
Hotel (1967)
Hotel Berlin (1945)
Hotel Des Invalides (1952)
Hotel Imperial (1939)
Hotel Paradiso (1966)
Hotel Reserve (1944)
Hotel Sahara (1951)
Houdini (1953)
Hound Dog Man (1959)
Hound of the Baskervilles (1939)
The Hound of the Baskervilles (1959)
The Hour Before the Dawn (1944)
Hour of the Gun (1967)
The Hour of Thirteen (1952)
The Hours of Love (1965)
House Across the Bay (1940)
The House Across the Street (1949)
House by the River (1950)
The House I Live In (1957)
The House in the Country (1969)
A House Is Not a Home (1964)
House of a Thousand Candles (1936)
House of Bamboo (1955)

House of Cards (1968)
House of Dracula (1945)
The House of Fear (1945)
House of Frankenstein (1944)
House of Fright (1961)
House of Horrors (1946)
The House of Intrigue (1959)
The House of Light (1970)
House of Numbers (1957)
House of Riccordi (1956)
House of Rothschild (1934)
House of Strangers (1949)
House of the Damned (1963)
House of the Seven Gables (1940)
The House of the Seven Hawks (1959)
The House of Usher (1960)
House of Wax (1953)
House of Women (1962)
The House on Haunted Hill (1958)
The House on 92nd Street (1945)
House on Telegraph Hill (1951)
The House Under the Rocks (1958)
The House Under the Trees (1971)
Houseboat (1958)
The Housekeeper's Daughter (1939)
How Did a Nice Girl Like You Get Into This Business? (1970)
How Do I Love Thee? (1970)
How Do You Do? (1945)
How Green Was My Valley (1941)
How I Won the War (1967)
How Not to Rob a Department Store (1965)
How Short Is the Time for Love (1970)
How Sweet It Is (1968)
How Tasty Was My Little Frenchman (1971)
How the West Was Won (1962)
How to Be Very, Very Popular (1955)
How to Commit Marriage (1969)
How to Frame a Figg (1971)
How to Marry a Millionaire (1955)
How to Murder a Rich Uncle (1957)
How to Murder Your Wife (1965)
How to Save a Marriage and Ruin Your Life (1968)
How to Succeed with Sex (1970)
How to Steal a Million (1966)
How to Stuff a Wild Bikini (1965)
How, When, With Whom (1969)
The Howards of Virginia (1940)
The Hucksters (1947)
Hud (1963)
Hudson's Bay (1941)
Huk (1956)
The Human Beast (1938)
The Human Comedy (1943)
The Human Condition (1959)
Human Desire (1954)
The Human Duplicators (1965)
The Human Jungle (1954)
The Human Monster (1940)
Humoresque (1920)
Humoresque (1947)
The Hunchback of Notre Dame (1940)
The Hunchback of Notre Dame (1957)
Hungarian Rhapsody (1929)
Hungry Hill (1947)
Hunt the Man Down (1950)
The Hunted (1948)
The Hunted Samurai (1971)
The Hunters (1958)
Hunters of the Deep (1955)
The Hunting Party (1971)
Hurrah! Our Parents Aren't There (1970)
Hurrah! The School Is Burning (1970)
Hurray, We Are Bachelors Again (1971)
Hurricane Island (1951)
Hurricane Smith (1952)
Hurry Sundown (1967)
Hush ... Hush, Sweet Charlotte (1965)
The Hustler (1961)
The Hypnotic Eye (1960)
Hysteria (1965)

I Accuse! (1958)
I Accuse My Parents (1944)
I Aim at the Stars (1960)
I Am a Camera (1955)
I Am Suzanne (1934)
I Believe in You (1953)
I Belong to Me (1967)
I Bury the Living (1958)
I Can Get It for You Wholesale (1951)
I Can't ... I Can't (1969)
I Cheated the Law (1949)
I Confess (1953)
I Could Go on Singing (1963)
I Cover the Big Town (1947)
I Cover the Underworld (1955)
I Deal in Danger (1966)
I Died a Thousand Times (1955)
I Dood It (1943)
I Dream Too Much (1935)
I Escaped from the Gestapo (1943)
I Hate Your Guts (1962)
I, Jane Doe (1948)
I Killed Einstein, Gentlemen (1970)
I Killed Geronimo (1950)
I Knew Her Well (1966)
I Like Money (1962)
I Live in Fear (1955)
I Live My Life (1935)
I Love a Bandleader (1945)
I Love a Soldier (1944)
I Love My Wife (1970)
I Love Trouble (1947)
I Love You Again (1940)
I Love You Alice B. Toklas (1968)
I Love You, I Love You (1968)
I Married a Communist (1949)
I Married a Doctor (1936)
I Married a Witch (1942)
I Married a Woman (1958)
I Married Adventure (1940)
I, Mobster (1958)
I Never Sang for My Father (1970)
I Passed for White (1960)
I Remember Mama (1948)
I Ring Doorbells (1946)
I Saw What You Did (1965)
I Shot Billy the Kid (1950)
I Shot Jesse James (1949)
I Stand Accused (1938)
I Start Counting (1970)
I Take This Woman (1940)
I Thank a Fool (1962)
I, the Jury (1953)
I Walk Alone (1947)
I Walk the Line (1970)
I Walked with a Zombie (1943)
I Want a Divorce (1940)
I Want to Live! (1958)
I Want You (1951)
I Wanted Wings (1941)
I Was a Male War Bride (1949)
I Was a Shoplifter (1950)
I Was a Teenage Frankenstein (1957)
I Was a Teenage Werewolf (1957)
I Was an Adventuress (1940)
I Was an American Spy (1951)
I Was Happy Here (1966)
I Was Monty's Double (1959)
I Wouldn't Be in Your Shoes (1948)
I, You, They (1969)
Ice Palace (1960)
Ice Station Zebra (1968)
I'd Climb the Highest Mountain (1951)
I'd Give a Million (1936)
I'd Rather Be Rich (1964)
Idea Girl (1946)
An Ideal Husband (1948)
L'Idee (1934)
Identity Unknown (1945)
The Idiot (1958)
The Idol (1966)
The Idol of Paris (1947)
The Idols (1968)
If ... (1968)
If a Man Answers (1962)
If All the Guys in the World (1957)
If He Hollers, Let Him Go (1968)
If I Were Free (1934)
If I Were King (1938)
If It's Tuesday, This Must Be Belgium (1969)
If Winter Comes (1947)
If You Knew Suzie (1948)
Ikiru (1952)
I'll Be Seeing You (1944)

I'll Be Yours (1947)
I'll Cry Tomorrow (1955)
I'll Never Forget What's 'is Name (1967)
I'll Never Forget You (1951)
I'll Remember April (1945)
I'll Take Happiness (1969)
I'll Take Sweden (1965)
I'll Tell the World (1945)
Illegal (1955)
Illegal Entry (1949)
The Illustrated Man (1969)
I'm All Right, Jack (1960)
I'm from the City (1938)
I'm Going to Get You ... Elliot Boy (1971)
The Image of Love (1965)
Imago (1970)
Imitation of Life (1934)
Imitation of Life (1959)
The Immortal Sergeant (1943)
An Immortal Story (1968)
Impact (1949)
Impasse (1969)
The Impatient Years (1944)
The Imperfect Lady (1947)
The Importance of Being Earnest (1952)
The Important Man (1962)
The Impossible Years (1968)
The Imposter (1944)
In a Lonely Place (1950)
In-Between Age (1958)
In Cold Blood (1967)
In Enemy Country (1968)
In Fast Company (1946)
In Harm's Way (1965)
In His Steps (1936)
In Like Flint (1967)
In Love and War (1958)
In Name Only (1939)
In Old Amarillo (1951)
In Old California (1942)
In Old Chicago (1938)
In Old Kentucky (1935)
In Old Oklahoma (1943)
In Old Sacramento (1946)
In Our Time (1944)
In Person (1935)
In Prison Awaiting Trial (1971)
In Search of Gregory (1970)
In Search of the Castaways (1962)
In Self Defense (1947)
In the Cool of the Day (1963)
In the French Style (1963)
In the Good Old Summertime (1949)
In the Gorge (1971)
In the Green of the Woods (1968)
In the Heat of the Night (1967)
In the Meantime, Darling (1944)
In the Money (1958)
In the Name of the Father (1971)
In the Name of the Italian People (1971)
In the Summertime (1971)
In the Wake of a Stranger (1960)
In the Year of the Lord (1969)
In This Corner (1948)
In This Our Life (1942)
In Which We Serve (1942)
Incident (1948)
The Incident (1967)
Incident at Phantom Hill (1966)
Incident in an Alley (1962)
The Incredible Journey (1963)
The Incredible Mr. Limpet (1964)
The Incredible Shrinking Man (1957)
The Incredible Two-Headed Transplant (1971)
Incubus (1966)
An Indefinite Tenderness (1969)
The Indestructible Man (1956)
The Indian Fighter (1955)
Indian Territory (1950)
Indian Uprising (1952)
Indianapolis Speedway (1939)
Indiscreet (1958)
Indiscretion of an American Wife (1954)
Inferno (1953)
Information Received (1962)
The Informer (1935)
The Ingenue (1969)
Inherit the Wind (1960)
The Inheritors (1970)
L'Inhumaine (1925)
Initiation (1970)
Inn of Evil (1971)
The Inn of the Sixth Happiness (1958)
The Inner Circle (1946)
Inner Sanctum (1948)

An Innocent Affair (1948)
The Innocents (1961)
Innocents of Paris (1955)
Inside Daisy Clover (1965)
Inside Detroit (1955)
Inside Job (1946)
The Inside Story (1948)
Inside Straight (1951)
Inside the Walls of Folsom Prison (1951)
Inspector Clouseau (1968)
The Inspector General (1949)
The Inspector General (Revizor) (1954)
Inspector Maigret (1958)
Insurance Investigator (1951)
Intent to Kill (1958)
Interior Mechanism (1971)
Interlude (1957)
Interlude (1968)
Intermezzo (1939)
International Counterfeiters (1958)
International Crime (1938)
International Lady (1941)
Internes Can't Take Money (1937)
The Interns (1962)
Interrupted Melody (1955)
The Interview (1960)
Intimate Relations (1954)
Intolerance (1916)
Intrigue (1947)
The Intruder (1955)
Intruder in the Dust (1949)
The Invaders (1941)
Invaders from Mars (1953)
Invasion of the Body Snatchers (1956)
Invasion Quartet (1961)
Invasion USA (1952)
Investigation of a Citizen Above Suspicion (1970)
Invisible Avenger (1958)
The Invisible Boy (1957)
The Invisible Informer (1946)
The Invisible Man's Revenge (1944)
The Invisible Wall (1947)
The Invisible Woman (1941)
Invitation (1952)
Invitation to a Gunfighter (1964)
Invitation to Happiness (1939)
Invitation to the Dance (1956)
The Invited One (1969)
The Ipcress File (1965)
Irma La Douce (1963)
The Iron Curtain (1948)
The Iron Glove (1954)
The Iron Horse (1924)
The Iron Major (1943)
The Iron Man (1951)
The Iron Mistress (1952)
Iron Mountain Trail (1953)
The Iron Petticoat (1956)
The Iron Sheriff (1957)
The Iroquois Trail (1950)
Is It Necessary to Be Among the Peoples of the World to Know Them? (1971)
Is Paris Burning? (1966)
Isadora (1968)
The Island (1961)
The Island (1966)
Island in the Sky (1953)
Island in the Sun (1957)
Island of Lost Women (1959)
Island of Love (1963)
Island of Terror (1967)
Island of the Blue Dolphins (1964)
Island of the Doomed (1968)
Island Rescue (1952)
Island Woman (1958)
The Islanders (1938)
Isle of Forgotten Sins (1943)
Isle of Missing Men (1942)
Isle of the Dead (1945)
Isn't It Romantic? (1948)
Isn't Life Wonderful? (1924)
Istanbul (1957)
It (1967)
It Came from Beneath the Sea (1955)
It Came from Outer Space (1953)
It Grows on Trees (1952)
It Had to Be You (1947)
It Had to Happen (1936)
It Happened at the World's Fair (1963)
It Happened in Athens (1962)
It Happened in Broad Daylight (1960)
It Happened in Brooklyn (1947)
It Happened in Rome (1956)
It Happened in the Park (1953)

It Happened on Fifth Avenue (1947)
It Happened to Jane (1959)
It Happened Tomorrow (1944)
It Happens Every Thursday (1953)
It Happens Every Spring (1949)
It Only Happens to Others (1971)
It Should Happen to You (1954)
It Shouldn't Happen to a Dog (1946)
It Started in Naples (1960)
It Started with a Kiss (1959)
It Started with Eve (1941)
It Takes All Kinds (1969)
It! The Terror from Beyond Space (1958)
An Italian in America (1968)
The Italian Job (1969)
The Italian Straw Hat (1927)
Italiano Brava Gente (1965)
It's a Big Country (1951)
It's a Date (1940)
It's a Dog's Life (1955)
It's a Joke, Son! (1947)
It's a Mad, Mad, Mad, Mad World (1963)
It's a Pleasure (1945)
It's a Small World (1950)
It's a Wonderful Life (1946)
It's Great to Be Alive (1933)
It's Hard to Be Good (1948)
It's in the Air (1935)
It's in the Bag (1945)
It's Love Again (1936)
It's Not Cricket (1949)
It's Only Money (1962)
Ivan Pavlov (1950)
Ivan the Terrible (Part I) (1944)
Ivan the Terrible (Part II) (1946)
Ivanhoe (1952)
I've Always Loved You (1946)
I've Lived Before (1956)
Ivory Hunter (Where No Vultures Fly) (1952)
Ivy (1947)

J. W. Coop (1971)
Jack and the Beanstalk (1952)
Jack Johnson (1971)
Jack London (1943)
Jack McCall, Desperado (1953)
Jack of Diamonds (1967)
Jack Slade (1953)
Jack the Giant Killer (1962)
Jack the Ripper (1960)
Jack the Ripper (1971)
The Jackal of Nahueltoro (1970)
Jackass Mail (1942)
The Jackie Robinson Story (1950)
The Jackpot (1950)
Jacqueline (1957)
Jaguar (1956)
Jail Busters (1955)
Jailhouse Rock (1957)
Jalopy (1953)
Jamaica Inn (1939)
Jamaica Run (1953)
Jamboree (1957)
The James Dean Story (1957)
James or Not (1970)
Jane Eyre (1944)
Jane Eyre (1971)
Janice Meredith (1924)
Janie (1944)
Janie Gets Married (1946)
Janosik (1936)
Japanese War Bride (1952)
Jason and the Argonauts (1963)
The Jayhawkers (1959)
Jazz All Around (1969)
Jazz Boat (1960)
The Jazz Singer (1927)
Jealousy (1945)
Jeanne (1957)
Jedda the Uncivilized (1956)
Jeff (1969)
Jennifer (1953)
Jennifer on My Mind (1971)
Jenny (1935)
Jenny (1969)
Jeopardy (1953)
Jesse James vs. the Daltons (1954)
Jesse James' Women (1954)
Jessica (1962)
The Jesus Trip (1971)
Jet Attack (1958)
Jet Generation (1969)
Jet Job (1952)
Jet Pilot (1957)
Jewels of Brandenburg (1947)
Jezebel (1938)

Jiggs and Maggie in Court (1948)
Jiggs and Maggie in Jackpot Jitters (1949)
Jiggs and Maggie in Society (1948)
Jiggs and Maggie Out West (1950)
Jigsaw (1949)
Jigsaw (1968)
Jim Thorpe--All American (1951)
Jinx Money (1948)
Jivaro (1954)
Joan of Arc (1948)
Joan of Arc at the Stake (1954)
Joan of Paris (1942)
Joan of the Angels? (1962)
Joan the Woman (1917)
Joanna (1968)
Joe (1970)
Joe and Ethel Turp Call on the President (1940)
Joe Butterfly (1957)
Joe Dakota (1957)
Joe Hill (1971)
The Joe Louis Story (1953)
Joe Macbeth (1956)
Joe Palooka, Champ (1946)
Joe Palooka in Humphrey Takes a Chance (1950)
Joe Palooka in the Squared Circle (1950)
Joe Palooka in the Big Fight (1949)
Joe Palooka in the Counterpunch (1949)
Joe Palooka in the Knockout (1947)
Joe Palooka in Triple Cross (1951)
Joe Palooka in Winner Take All (1948)
Joe Palooka Meets Humphrey (1950)
Joe Smith, American (1942)
John and Julie (1957)
John and Mary (1969)
John Goldfarb, Please Come Home (1964)
John Loves Mary (1949)
John Meade's Woman (1937)
John Paul Jones (1959)
Johnny Allegro (1949)
Johnny Angel (1945)
Johnny Apollo (1940)
Johnny Belinda (1948)
Johnny Come Lately (1943)
Johnny Comes Flying Home (1946)
Johnny Concho (1956)
Johnny Cool (1963)
Johnny Dark (1954)
Johnny Doesn't Live Here Anymore (1944)
Johnny Frenchman (1945)
Johnny Got His Gun (1971)
Johnny Guitar (1954)
Johnny Holiday (1949)
Johnny O'Clock (1947)
Johnny on the Run (1954)
Johnny Reno (1966)
Johnny Rocco (1958)
Johnny Stool Pigeon (1949)
Johnny Tiger (1966)
Johnny Tremain (1957)
Johnny Trouble (1957)
Johnny Yuma (1967)
The Joker (1961)
The Joker Is Wild (1957)
The Jokers (1967)
Jolson Sings Again (1949)
Jonas (1957)
Josefine Mutzenbacher (1970)
Joseph and His Brethren (1962)
Le Jour se Leve (see Daybreak)
The Journey (1959)
Journey for Margaret (1942)
Journey into Fear (1942)
Journey into History (1952)
Journey into Light (1951)
Journey to Freedom (1957)
Journey to Shiloh (1968)
Journey to South America (1953)
Journey to the Center of the Earth (1959)
Journey to the Far Side of the Sun (1969)
Journey to the Lost City (1960)
Journey Together (1945)
Joy House (1964)
Joy in the Morning (1965)
Joy Ride (1958)
Juarez (1939)
Jubal (1956)

Jubilee Trail (1954)
Jud (1971)
The Judge (1949)
The Judge Steps Out (1949)
Judgment (1970)
Judgment at Nuremberg (1961)
Judith (1966)
The Juggler (1953)
Juke Box Rhythm (1959)
Juke Girl (1942)
Julia Misbehaves (1948)
Julie (1956)
Juliet of the Spirits (1965)
Juliette Ou La Clef Des Songe (1951)
Julius Caesar (1953)
Julius Caesar (1970)
Jumbo (1962)
Jump into Hell (1955)
Jumping over Puddles Again (1971)
June Bride (1948)
The Jungle (1952)
The Jungle Book (1942)
The Jungle Book (1967)
Jungle Cat (1960)
Jungle Gents (1954)
Jungle Goddess (1948)
Jungle Heat (1957)
Jungle Hunters (1951)
Jungle Man Eaters (1954)
Jungle Moon Men (1955)
Jungle of Chang (1951)
Jungle Patrol (1948)
Junior Miss (1945)
Jupiter's Darling (1955)
Just Across the Street (1952)
Just for You (1952)
Just Imagine (1930)
Just Like a Woman (1967)
Just This Once (1952)
Just William's Luck (1948)
Justine (1969)
Jutrzenka: A Winter in Majorca (1971)
Juvenile Jungle (1958)

Kaleidoscope (1966)
Kanchehkungha (1966)
Kangaroo (1952)
The Kangaroo Kid (1950)
Kanku (1970)
The Kansan (1943)
Kansas City Confidential (1952)
Kansas City Kitty (1944)
Kansas Pacific (1953)
Kansas Territory (1952)
Kapo (1959)
Kathleen (1941)
Kathy O' (1958)
Katie Did It (1951)
Kazoku (1971)
Keep 'Em Slugging (1943)
Keep Your Powder Dry (1945)
Keeper of the Bees (1947)
Keeper of the Flame (1942)
The Keepers (see Head Against the Wall) (1958)
Kelly and Me (1957)
Kelly's Heroes (1970)
Kenji Comes Home (1949)
Kenner (1969)
The Kentuckian (1955)
Kentucky (1938)
Kentucky Jubilee (1951)
Kentucky Moonshine (1938)
Kes (1970)
The Kettles in the Ozarks (1956)
The Kettles on Old MacDonald's Farm (1957)
The Key (1958)
Key Largo (1948)
The Key to Paradise (1970)
Key to the City (1950)
Key Witness (1960)
The Keys of the Kingdom (1944)
Khyber Patrol (1954)
The Kid (1921)
A Kid for Two Farthings (Lucky Kid) (1956)
The Kid from Cleveland (1949)
The Kid from Left Field (1953)
The Kid from Texas (1939)
The Kid from Texas (1950)
Kid Galahad (1937)
Kid Galahad (1962)
Kid Glove Killer (1942)
Kid Monk Baroni (1952)
Kid Rodello (1966)
The Kid Sister (1945)
Kidnapped (1938)
Kidnapped (1948)
Kidnapped (1960)
Kidnapped (1971)
Kiki (1931)

Kill! (1968)
Kill a Dragon (1967)
Kill, Baby, Kill (1968)
Kill Her Gently (1958)
Kill Me Tomorrow (1958)
Kill or Be Killed (1950)
Kill or Cure (1962)
Kill the Umpire (1950)
Killer Ape (1953)
Killer at Large (1947)
Killer Dill (1947)
The Killer Is Loose (1956)
Killer Leopard (1954)
Killer McCoy (1947)
Killer Shark (1950)
The Killer that Stalked New York (see Frightened City) (1950)
The Killers (1946)
The Killers (1964)
Killers from Space (1954)
Killer's Kiss (1955)
Killers of Kilimanjaro (1960)
Killers Three (1968)
The Killing (1956)
The Killing of Sister George (1968)
Killing the Devil (1970)
Kilroy Was Here (1947)
Kim (1950)
Kimberley Jim (1965)
Kind Lady (1951)
A Kind of Loving (1962)
King and Country (1965)
The King and Four Queens (1956)
The King and the Chorus Girl (1937)
King Creole (1958)
A King in New York (1957)
King in Shadow (1959)
King Kong (1933)
King Kong vs. Godzilla (1963)
King of Jazz (1930)
King of Kings (1927)
King of Kings (1961)
King of the Bandits (1947)
King of the Bullwhip (1950)
King of the Coral Sea (1956)
King of the Gamblers (1948)
King of the Grizzlies (1970)
King of the Khyber Rifles (1953)
King of the Stallions (1942)
King of the Wild Stallions (1959)
King Rat (1965)
King Richard and the Crusaders (1954)
King Solomon of Broadway (1935)
The King Steps Out (1936)
Kings Go Forth (1958)
Kings of the Sun (1963)
The King's Pirate (1967)
The King's Thief (1955)
Kismet (1920)
Kismet (1931)
Kismet (1944)
Kiss and Tell (1945)
A Kiss Before Dying (1956)
A Kiss for Corliss (1949)
A Kiss in the Dark (1949)
Kiss Me Deadly (1955)
Kiss Me, Stupid (1964)
Kiss of Death (1947)
Kiss of Fire (1955)
Kiss of the Vampire (1963)
Kiss the Blood Off My Hands (1948)
Kiss the Girls and Make Them Die (1966)
Kiss the Other Sheik (1968)
Kiss Them for Me (1957)
Kiss Tomorrow Goodbye (1950)
Kissenga, Man of Africa (1952)
Kisses for My President (1964)
The Kissing Bandit (1948)
Kit Carson (1940)
Kitten with a Whip (1964)
Kitty (1929)
Kitty (1946)
Kitty Foyle (1940)
Klondike Fury (1942)
Klann/Grand Guignol (1970)
The Knack--And How to Get It (1965)
Knife in the Water (1961)
The Knight of the Sword (1970)
Knights of the Round Table (1953)
Knives of the Avenger (1967)
Knock on Any Door (1949)
Knock on Wood (1954)
Kon-Tiki (1951)
Kona Coast (1968)
Konga (1961)
Korea Patrol (1950)
Kotch (1971)

Kotovski (1942)
Krakatit (1951)
Krakatoa, East of Java (1969)
Krazy Kat at the Circus (1927)
The Kremlin Letter (1970)
Kriemhild's Revenge (1923)
Kronos (1957)
Kuhle Wampe (1931)
Kwaidan (1965)

The L-Shaped Room (1963)
Lad: A Dog (1962)
Laddie (1940)
Laddie Loves in All Directions (1969)
Ladies Courageous (1944)
Ladies' Day (1943)
Ladies in Love (1936)
Ladies in Retirement (1941)
Ladies in Washington (1944)
Ladies' Man (1947)
Ladies' Man (1960)
The Ladies' Man (1961)
Ladies Who Do (1963)
The Lady and the Bandit (1951)
The Lady and the Monster (1944)
Lady and the Tramp (1955)
Lady at Midnight (1948)
Lady Caliph (1971)
The Lady Confesses (1945)
The Lady Consents (1936)
The Lady Eve (1941)
Lady for a Night (1942)
The Lady from Cheyenne (1941)
The Lady from Louisiana (1941)
The Lady from Shanghai (1948)
The Lady from Texas (1951)
The Lady Gambles (1949)
Lady Godiva (1955)
Lady Hamilton (1969)
The Lady Has Plans (1942)
Lady in a Jam (1942)
Lady in Cement (1968)
Lady in the Death House (1944)
Lady in the Iron Mask (1952)
Lady in the Lake (1947)
The Lady Is Willing (1942)
Lady L (1965)
Lady Luck (1946)
Lady of Burlesque (1943)
Lady of the Pavements (1929)
Lady of the Tropics (1939)
Lady of Vengeance (1957)
Lady on a Train (1945)
Lady Paname (1951)
The Lady Pays Off (1951)
Lady Possessed (1952)
The Lady Says No (1951)
A Lady Takes a Chance (1943)
The Lady Takes a Flyer (1958)
The Lady Takes a Sailor (1949)
The Lady Wants Mink (1953)
Lady with Red Hair (1940)
The Lady with the Dog (1960)
A Lady Without Passport (1950)
Ladybug, Ladybug (1963)
The Ladykillers (1956)
Lafayette (1963)
Lafayette Escadrille (1958)
The Lair of Love (1966)
Lake Placid Serenade (1944)
The Land (1941)
Land of Fury (1955)
Land of Hunted Men (1943)
Land of the Lawless (1947)
Land of the Outlaws (1944)
Land of the Pharaohs (1955)
Land Raiders (1969)
The Land Unknown (1957)
The Landlord (1970)
Landscape After the Battle (1970)
Larceny (1948)
Larceny in Her Heart (1946)
Larceny, Inc. (1942)
Las Vegas Shakedown (1955)
The Las Vegas Story (1952)
Lassie Come Home (1943)
The Last Act of Martin Weston (1970)
The Last Angry Man (1959)
The Last Bandit (1949)
The Last Blitzkrieg (1958)
The Last Bridge (1953)
The Last Challenge (1967)
The Last Chapter (1966)
The Last Command (1955)
The Last Crooked Mile (1946)
The Last Days of Pompeii (1935)
The Last Days of Pompeii (1960)
The Last Frontier (1955)
Last Frontier Uprising (1947)

The Last Gangster (1937)
The Last Gentleman (1934)
The Last Grenade (1970)
Last Holiday (1950)
The Last Hunt (1956)
The Last Judgment (1961)
The Last Maiden But One (1970)
The Last Man on Earth (1924)
The Last Man to Hang (1956)
The Last Mile (1959)
The Last Movie (1971)
The Last Musketeer (1952)
The Last of Mrs. Cheyney (1937)
Last of the Badmen (1957)
Last of the Buccaneers (1950)
Last of the Comanches (1952)
The Last of the Fast Guns (1958)
The Last of the Mobile Hotshots (1969)
The Last of the Mohicans (1936)
The Last of the Mohicans (1965)
The Last of the Pagans (1935)
Last of the Pony Riders (1953)
Last of the Ski Bums (1969)
Last of the Wild Horses (1948)
The Last Outlaw (1936)
The Last Outpost (1935)
The Last Outpost (1951)
The Last Paradise (1958)
The Last Posse (1953)
The Last Rebel (1971)
The Last Safari (1967)
The Last Shot You Hear (1969)
Last Stagecoach West (1957)
The Last Stop (1948)
Last Summer (1969)
The Last Sunset (1961)
The Last Time I Saw Archie (1961)
The Last Time I Saw Paris (1954)
Last Train from Bombay (1952)
The Last Train from Gun Hill (1959)
The Last Valley (1971)
The Last Voyage (1960)
The Last Wagon (1956)
Last Year at Marienbad (1961)
The Late George Apley (1947)
The Late Liz (1971)
Latin Lovers (1953)
Laughter in the Dark (1969)
Laughing Anne (1954)
Laura (1944)
Laurel and Hardy's Laughing 20's (1965)
The Lavender Hill Mob (1951)
The Law (1960)
Law and Disorder (1958)
Law and Order (1953)
The Law and the Lady (1951)
The Law Is the Law (1959)
Law Men (1944)
Law of the Badlands (1950)
Law of the Golden West (1949)
Law of the Lash (1947)
Law of the Panhandle (1950)
Law of the Valley (1944)
The Law vs. Billy the Kid (1954)
The Law West of Tombstone (1938)
The Lawless (1950)
The Lawless Breed (1952)
The Lawless Eighties (1957)
The Lawless Rider (1954)
A Lawless Street (1955)
Lawman (1971)
Lawrence of Arabia (1962)
The Lawton Story (1949)
The Lawyer (1969)
Lay that Rifle Down (1955)
Leadville Gunslinger (1952)
The Learning Tree (1969)
Lease of Life (1955)
The Leather Burners (1943)
The Leather Saint (1956)
Leave Her to Heaven (1945)
Leave It to Henry (1949)
Leave It to the Marines (1951)
A Lecture on Man (1962)
The Leech Woman (1960)
The Left Hand of God (1955)
The Left Handed Gun (1958)
Left, Right and Center (1961)
The Legend of Lobo (1962)
The Legend of Lylah Clare (1968)
Legend of the Lost (1957)
The Legend of Tom Dooley (1959)
Legions of the Nile (1960)
The Lemon Drop Kid (1951)
Lenin in October (1937)
Lenz (1971)
Leo the Last (1970)
Leonardo da Vinci (1952)
The Leopard (1963)
The Leopard Man (1943)

Lermontov (1943)
Les Girls (1957)
A Lesson in Life (Conflict) (1955)
Let No Man Write My Epitaph (1960)
Let Them Live (1937)
Let's Be Happy (1957)
Let's Dance (1950)
Let's Do It Again (1953)
Let's Go Navy (1951)
Let's Have a Riot (1970)
Let's Kill Uncle (1966)
Let's Live a Little (1948)
Let's Live Again (1948)
Let's Make It Legal (1951)
Let's Make Love (1960)
Let's Make Up (1955)
Let's Play Hide-and-Seek (1970)
Let's Play in the World (1971)
Let's Scare Jessica to Death (1971)
Let's Sing Again (1936)
Let's Talk About Women (1964)
Let's Try Again (1934)
The Letter (1940)
A Letter for Evie (1945)
Letter from an Unknown Woman (1948)
The Letter that Was Never Sent (1959)
A Letter to Three Wives (1948)
Letters from My Windmill (1954)
La Lettre (1938)
Les Liaisons Dangereuses (1959)
Libel (1959)
Libeled Lady (1936)
The Liberation of L. B. Jones (1970)
Liberte I (1963)
The Lickerish Quartet (1970)
Lieutenant Kije (see The Czar Wants to Sleep)
Lt. Robin Crusoe, U. S. N. (1966)
The Lieutenant Wore Skirts (1956)
Life and Death of Colonel Blimp (1943)
Life at the Top (1965)
Life Begins at 8:30 (1942)
Life Begins Tomorrow (1950)
Life Dances On (see Un Carnet du Bal)
Life in Danger (1964)
A Life in the Balance (1955)
Life, Love and Death (1969)
A Life of Her Own (1950)
The Life of Riley (1949)
The Life of Vergie Winters (1934)
Life Upside Down (1965)
Life with Father (1947)
Lifeboat (1943)
The Light Across the Street (1957)
The Light at the Edge of the World (1971)
Light Fantastic (1963)
The Light in the Forest (1958)
Light in the Piazza (1962)
The Light that Failed (1940)
The Light Touch (1951)
The Light Touch (1956)
Lighthouse (1946)
Lightning Bolt (1967)
Lightning Raiders (1946)
Lightning Strikes Twice (1951)
Lights Out in Europe (1940)
A Likely Story (1947)
Li'l Abner (1959)
Lili (1953)
Lili Marlene (1951)
Lilies of the Field (1963)
Liliom (1933)
Lilith (1964)
Lillian Russell (1940)
The Lily and the Rose (1915)
The Limbo Line (1968)
Limelight (1952)
The Limping Man (1953)
Linda Be Good (1947)
Line to the Tschierva Hut (1937)
Lines Horizontal (1960)
The Lion (1962)
The Lion and the Horse (1952)
The Lion Has Wings (1940)
The Lion Hunters (1951)
A Lion in Winter (1968)
A Lion Is in the Streets (1953)
Lion's Love (1969)
The Lion's Share (1971)
The Liquidator (1966)
Lisa (1962)
Lisbon (1956)

The List of Adrian Messenger (1963)
Listen, Darling (1938)
A Little, A Lot, Passionately (1971)
Little Angel (1960)
Little Big Horn (1951)
Little Big Man (1970)
Little Birdie (1971)
Little Boy Lost (1953)
The Little Colonel (1935)
Little Egypt (1951)
Little Fauss and Big Halsy (1970)
The Little Foxes (1941)
The Little Fugitive (1953)
Little Giant (1946)
The Little Hut (1957)
Little Iodine (1946)
Little Joe, the Wrangler (1942)
The Little Kidnappers (1954)
Little Lord Fauntleroy (1936)
Little Miss Big (1946)
Little Mister Jim (1946)
Little Murders (1971)
The Little Nuns (1965)
Little Old New York (1923)
The Little Ones (1965)
Little Savage (1959)
The Little Shepherd of Kingdom Come (1961)
A Little Sun in Cold Water (1971)
Little Women (1934)
Little Women (1949)
The Littlest Hobo (1958)
The Littlest Outlaw (1955)
The Littlest Rebel (1935)
Live a Little, Love a Little (1968)
Live for Life (1967)
Live Today for Tomorrow (see An Act of Murder)
Live Wires (1946)
The Lively Set (1964)
The Living Desert (1953)
The Living Ghost (1942)
The Living Idol (1957)
Living in a Big Way (1947)
Living It Up (1954)
The Living Swamp (1955)
A Lizard in a Woman's Skin (1971)
Lizzie (1957)
Lloyds of London (1937)
The Locket (1947)
The Lodger (1944)
Lola (1961)
Lola Montes (1956)
Lolita (1962)
London Belongs to Me (1949)
London by Night (1937)
The Lone Gun (1954)
Lone Hand (1953)
The Lone Ranger (1956)
The Lone Ranger and the Lost City of Gold (1958)
Lone Star (1952)
Lone Star Trail (1943)
Lone Texan (1959)
The Lone Texas Ranger (1945)
Lone White Sail (1937)
The Loneliness of the Long-Distance Runner (1962)
Lonely Are the Brave (1962)
Lonely Hearts (1958)
Lonely Hearts (1970)
Lonely Hearts Bandits (1950)
The Lonely Man (1957)
The Lonesome Trail (1945)
Long Ago Tomorrow (1971)
The Long Dark Hall (1951)
Long Day's Journey Into Night (1962)
The Long Duel (1967)
The Long Gray Line (1955)
The Long Haul (1957)
The Long, Hot Summer (1958)
Long Is the Road (1948)
Long John Silver (1955)
Long Legs, Long Fingers (1966)
Long Live Life (1969)
Long Live the Bride and Groom (1970)
The Long, Long Trailer (1954)
The Long Memory (1953)
The Long Night (1947)
The Long Ride from Hell (1970)
The Long Rope (1961)
The Long Ships (1964)
The Long Voyage Home (1940)
The Long Wait (1954)
The Longest Day (1962)
The Longest Night (1936)
The Longhorn (1951)
Look Back in Anger (1959)

Look Before You Love (1948)
Look in Any Window (1961)
Look Out, Sister (1949)
Looking for Danger (1957)
Looking for Love (1964)
Looking for Trouble (1934)
The Looking Glass War (1970)
Loophole (1954)
Loose in London (1953)
Loot (1971)
The Looters (1955)
Lord Jeff (1938)
Lord Jim (1965)
Lord Love a Duck (1966)
Lord of the Flies (1963)
Lord of the Jungle (1955)
Lorna Doone (1951)
The Losers (1970)
Loss of Innocence (1961)
Lost (1970)
Lost Angel (1943)
Lost Boundaries (1949)
The Lost Command (1966)
The Lost Continent (1951)
Lost Continent (1957)
The Lost Continent (1968)
Lost Honeymoon (1947)
Lost Horizon (1937)
Lost in a Harem (1944)
Lost in Alaska (1952)
Lost Lagoon (1958)
The Lost Man (1969)
The Lost Missile (1958)
The Lost Moment (1947)
The Lost Patrol (1934)
The Lost Volcano (1950)
The Lost Weekend (1945)
The Lost World (1960)
Louis Lumiere (1954)
Louisa (1950)
Louisiana (1947)
Louisiana Story (1948)
Louisiana Territory (1953)
The Lovable Cheat (1949)
Love (1971)
Love A La Carte (1960)
Love and Anger (1969)
Love and Kisses (1965)
Love and Larceny (1963)
Love and Learn (1947)
Love and Marriage (1966)
Love and the Frenchwoman (1961)
Love Before Breakfast (1936)
The Love Bug (1968)
Love by Rape (1970)
Love Crazy (1941)
Love from a Stranger (1937)
Love from a Stranger (1947)
Love Happy (1949)
Love Has Many Faces (1965)
Love, Honor and Goodbye (1945)
Love in a Goldfish Bowl (1961)
Love in the Afternoon (1957)
Love in the City (1953)
The Love-Ins (1967)
Love Is a Ball (1963)
Love Is a Headache (1938)
Love Is a Many-Splendored Thing (1955)
Love Is Better Than Ever (1952)
Love Is My Profession (1959)
Love Is News (1937)
Love Is Only a Word (1971)
Love Is War (1971)
Love Laughs at Andy Hardy (1946)
Love Letters (1945)
The Love Machine (1971)
Love Me Forever (1935)
Love Me Like I Do (1970)
Love Me or Leave Me (1955)
Love Me Tender (1956)
Love Nest (1951)
Love on a Bet (1936)
Love on a Pillow (1963)
Love on the Dole (1941)
Love on the Run (1936)
Love Slaves of the Amazon (1957)
Love Story (1944)
A Love Story (1958)
Love Story (1970)
Love Story Film (1970)
Love that Brute (1950)
Love with the Proper Stranger (1963)
The Loved One (1965)
A Lovely Monster (1971)
A Lovely Way to Die (1968)
The Lovemaker (1958)
Lover Come Back (1946)
Lover Come Back (1961)
The Lover of Camille (1924)
The Lovers (1959)
The Lovers (1970)

Lovers and Lollipops (1956)
Lovers and Other Strangers (1970)
Lovers and Thieves (1957)
The Lovers of Tereul (1962)
Lovers of Verona (1948)
Loves of a Dictator (1935)
Loves of an Actress (1928)
Loves of Carmen (1927)
The Loves of Carmen (1948)
The Loves of Edgar Allan Poe (1942)
The Loves of Joanna Godden (1947)
Loving (1970)
Loving and Laughing (1971)
The Loving Truth (1970)
Loving You (1957)
The Lower Depths (1936)
The Lower Depths (1957)
Lucie and the Miracles (1971)
The Luck of Ginger Coffey (1964)
The Luck of the Irish (1948)
Lucky Duck (1928)
Lucky Jim (1958)
Lucky Jordan (1942)
Lucky Kid (see A Kid for Two Farthings) (1956)
Lucky Nick Cain (1951)
Lucky Partners (1940)
The Lucky Stiff (1949)
Lucky to Be a Woman (1955)
Lucy Gallant (1955)
Ludwig on the Lookout for a Wife (1970)
Lulu Belle (1948)
Lumberjack (1944)
The Lumiere Years (1971)
Lure of the Wilderness (1952)
Lure of the Swamp (1957)
Lured (Personal Column) (1947)
Lust for Life (1956)
The Lusty Men (1952)
Luv (1967)
Luxury Girls (1953)
Luxury Liner (1948)
Lydia (1941)
Lydia (1970)
Lydia Bailey (1952)

McCabe and Mrs. Miller (1971)
McClintock! (1963)
The McConnell Story (1955)
McHale's Navy (1964)
McHale's Navy Joins the Air Force (1965)
McKenna's Gold (1969)
The McKenzie Break (1970)
The McMasters (1970)

M (1951)
M as in Mathieu (1971)
M*A*S*H (1970)
MGM's Big Parade of Comedy (1964)
Ma and Pa Kettle (1949)
Ma and Pa Kettle at Home (1954)
Ma and Pa Kettle at the Fair (1952)
Ma and Pa Kettle at Waikiki (1955)
Ma and Pa Kettle on Vacation (1953)
Ma Pomme (1951)
Macabre (1958)
Macao (1952)
Macbeth (1948)
Macbeth (1961)
Macbeth (1971)
Machete (1958)
Machine Gun Mama (1944)
The Macomber Affair (1947)
Macumba Love (1960)
Mad Dog Coll (1961)
The Mad Ghoul (1943)
Mad Little Island (1958)
Mad Love (1936)
The Mad Magician (1954)
The Mad Miss Manton (1938)
The Mad Room (1969)
Mad Wednesday (1947)
Madame (1963)
Madame Bovary (1934)
Madame Bovary (1949)
Madame Curie (1943)
Madame Sans-Gene (1925)
Madame X (1937)
Madame X (1966)
Maddalena (1955)
Maddalena (1971)
Made for Each Other (1939)
Made for Each Other (1971)

Made in Paris (1966)
Madeleine (1949)
Madeleine Is (1971)
Mademoiselle de Maupin (1966)
Mademoiselle Docteur (1937)
Mademoiselle Fifi (1944)
Mademoiselle Mosquito (1956)
Madigan (1968)
Madigan's Million (1970)
Madison Avenue (1962)
Madness of the Heart (1949)
Madron (1970)
The Madwoman of Chaillot (1969)
Maedchen in Uniform (1931)
Maedchen in Uniform (1965)
Maeva (1961)
Mafioso (1963)
The Magic Box (1951)
The Magic Canvas (1949)
The Magic Carpet (1951)
The Magic Christian (1969)
The Magic Face (1951)
Magic Fire (1956)
The Magic Garden (1951)
The Magic Garden of Stanley Sweetheart (1970)
The Magic Horse (1941)
The Magic Sword (1962)
Magic Town (1947)
The Magic World of Topo Gigio (1965)
The Magician (1959)
I Magliari (1959)
The Magnet (1951)
The Magnetic Monster (1953)
The Magnificent Ambersons (1942)
The Magnificent Brute (1936)
The Magnificent Dope (1942)
The Magnificent Matador (1955)
Magnificent Obsession (1936)
Magnificent Obsession (1954)
The Magnificent Rogue (1946)
Magnificent Roughnecks (1956)
The Magnificent Seven (1956)
The Magnificent Sinner (1963)
The Magnificent Two (1967)
The Magnificent Yankee (1950)
The Magus (1968)
Maid in Paris (1957)
Maid of Salem (1937)
Mail Order Bride (1964)
Mailbag Robber (1958)
The Main Attraction (1963)
La Main Chaude (1959)
Main Street After Dark (1944)
Main Street to Broadway (1953)
Maintenance Command (1944)
Maisie (1939)
Maisie Gets Her Man (1942)
Maisie Goes to Reno (1944)
Les Maisons de la Misere (1937)
The Major and the Minor (1942)
Major Barbara (1941)
Major Dundee (1965)
A Majority of One (1961)
Make a Face (1971)
Make Haste to Live (1954)
Make Like a Thief (1966)
Make Me an Offer (1956)
Make Way for Lila (1962)
Make Way for Tomorrow (1937)
Make Your Own Bed (1944)
Making It (1971)
Malacarne (1948)
Maladetto Imbroglio (1959)
Malaga (1962)
Malatesta (1970)
Malaya (1949)
The Male Animal (1942)
Malta, G. C. (1942)
The Malta Story (1954)
The Maltese Bippy (1969)
The Maltese Falcon (1941)
Mambo (1955)
Mamma Loves Papa (1945)
Mam'zelle Pigalle (1958)
Man About the House (1949)
Man Afraid (1957)
Man Alive (1945)
A Man Alone (1955)
A Man and a Woman (1966)
The Man Behind the Gun (1952)
The Man Between (1953)
A Man Called Adam (1966)
A Man Called Dagger (1967)
A Man Called Gannon (1969)
A Man Called Peter (1955)
A Man Called Sledge (1971)
A Man Could Get Killed (1966)
Man Crazy (1953)
Man-Eater of Kumaon (1948)
A Man for All Seasons (1966)
The Man from Bitter Ridge (1955)

The Man from Button Willow (1965)
The Man from Colorado (1948)
The Man from Dakota (1940)
Man from Del Rio (1956)
The Man from Down Under (1943)
Man from Frisco (1944)
The Man from Galveston (1964)
The Man from God's Country (1958)
Man from Headquarters (1942)
The Man from Laramie (1955)
The Man from Marrakech (1966)
The Man from Planet X (1951)
The Man from Rainbow Valley (1946)
Man from Sonora (1951)
The Man from Spain (1932)
The Man from Texas (1948)
The Man from the Alamo (1953)
Man from the Black Hills (1952)
The Man from the Diner's Club (1963)
The Man from Thunder River (1943)
Man Hunt (1941)
The Man I Love (1947)
The Man I Married (1940)
The Man in Half Moon Street (1944)
Man in Hiding (1953)
Man in the Attic (1953)
Man in the Dark (1953)
Man in the Dark (1965)
Man in the Dinghy (1951)
The Man in the Gray Flannel Suit (1956)
Man in the Iron Mask (1939)
Man in the Middle (1964)
Man in the Moon (1961)
The Man in the Net (1959)
The Man in the Road (1957)
Man in the Shadow (1957)
The Man in the Trunk (1942)
Man in the Vault (1956)
The Man in the White Suit (1952)
Man in the Wilderness (1971)
The Man Inside (1958)
The Man Is Armed (1956)
Man-Made Monster (1941)
The Man Monster (1942)
Man of a Thousand Faces (1957)
Man of Affairs (1937)
Man of Aran (1934)
Man of Evil (1948)
Man of the People (1937)
Man of the West (1958)
Man of Two Worlds (1934)
Man on a String (1960)
Man on a Tightrope (1953)
Man on Fire (1957)
The Man on the Eiffel Tower (1949)
Man on the Prowl (1957)
Man or Gun (1958)
The Man Outside (1968)
Man-Proof (1938)
A Man to Remember (1938)
Man-Trap (1961)
The Man Who Broke the Bank at Monte Carlo (1935)
The Man Who Came Back (1931)
The Man Who Came for Coffee (1970)
The Man Who Cheated Himself (1950)
The Man Who Could Cheat Death (1959)
The Man Who Died Twice (1958)
The Man Who Had Power Over Women (1970)
The Man Who Knew Too Much (1956)
The Man Who Laughs (1966)
The Man Who Loved Redheads (1955)
The Man Who Never Was (1956)
A Man Who Pleases Me (1969)
The Man Who Shot Liberty Valance (1962)
The Man Who Talked Too Much (1940)
The Man Who Turned to Stone (1957)
The Man Who Understood Women (1959)
The Man Who Walked Alone (1945)
The Man Who Walked Through the Wall (1958)
The Man Who Wouldn't Die (1942)
The Man Who Wouldn't Talk (1960)
The Man with a Gun (1938)

The Man with Balloons (1968)
Man with a Million (1954)
The Man with Connections (1970)
The Man with the Cloak (1951)
The Man with the Golden Arm (1955)
Man with the Gun (1955)
Man without a Star (1955)
The Manchurian Candidate (1962)
The Mandrake (La Mandragola) (1966)
Manfish (1956)
Manhandled (1949)
Manhattan Moon (1935)
Manhunt in the Jungle (1958)
Maniac (1963)
Manila Calling (1942)
Mannequin (1937)
Manon (1949)
Manpower (1941)
Le Mans (1971)
Man's Favorite Sport? (1964)
The Mantrap (1943)
The Many-Colored Paper (1960)
Many Rivers to Cross (1955)
Mara Maru (1952)
Mara of the Wilderness (1965)
Maracaibo (1958)
Marat/Sade (1967)
The Marauders (1947)
Marcel Marceau "In the Park" (1956)
Marcel Marceau's Pantomimes (1955)
Marcellino (1956)
The March Hare (1956)
Marco Polo (1962)
Mardi Gras (1958)
Mare Nostrum (1926)
Margie (1946)
Margin for Error (1943)
Maria Chapdelaine (1934)
Marianne of My Youth (1954)
Marie Antoinette (1938)
Marie du Port (1949)
The Marijuana Story (1952)
Marine Raiders (1944)
Marines, Let's Go (1961)
Marius (1931)
Marjorie Morningstar (1958)
The Mark (1961)
Mark of the Devil (1970)
The Mark of the Hawk (1958)
Mark of the Lash (1948)
Mark of the Renegade (1951)
The Mark of Zorro (1940)
Marked Trails (1944)
Marked Woman (1937)
Marketa Lazarova (1969)
The Marksman (1953)
Marlowe (1969)
Marnie (1964)
Maroc 7 (1967)
The Marriage-Go-Round (1960)
Marriage in the Shadows (1947)
Marriage Is a Private Affair (1944)
Marriage Italian Style (1964)
The Marriage of a Young Stockbroker (1971)
Marriage on the Rocks (1965)
A Married Couple (1969)
The Married Priest (1971)
Marry Me Again (1953)
The Marrying Kind (1952)
La Marseillaise (1938)
Marshal of Amarillo (1948)
Marshal of Cedar Rock (1953)
Marshal of Cripple Creek (1947)
Marshal of Gunsmoke (1944)
Marshal of Laredo (1945)
The Marshal's Daughter (1953)
Marta (1971)
Martin and Gaston (1953)
Martin Luther (1953)
The Martlet's Tale (1970)
Marty (1955)
Martyrs of the Alamo (1915)
Mary Burns, Fugitive (1935)
Mary, Mary (1963)
Mary of Scotland (1936)
Mary, Queen of Scots (1971)
Mary Ryan, Detective (1949)
Maryland (1940)
Mashenka (1942)
The Mask (1961)
Mask of Demitrios (1944)
The Mask of Dijon (1946)
Mask of the Avenger (1951)
Mask of the Dragon (1951)
Masked Raiders (1949)
Masque of the Red Death (1964)
Masquerade (1965)
Masquerade in Mexico (1945)
Massacre (1956)

Massacre Canyon (1954)
Massacre in Grand Canyon (1965)
Massacre River (1949)
Master Minds (1949)
The Master of Ballantrae (1953)
Master of the World (1961)
The Master Race (1944)
Master Spy (1964)
Masters of the Congo Jungle (1959)
Masterson of Kansas (1954)
Mata Hari (1964)
Matchless (1967)
The Matchmaker (1958)
La Maternelle (1932)
The Mating Game (1959)
The Mating of Millie (1948)
The Mating Season (1951)
The Mating Urge (1958)
The Matriarch (1969)
Mattanza (1968)
A Matter of Fat (1970)
A Matter of Honor (1966)
A Matter of Morals (1961)
A Matter of Who (1962)
The Maverick (1952)
The Maverick Queen (1956)
Maya (1966)
Mayerling (1937)
Mayerling (1968)
The Maze (1953)
Me and My Kid Brother and Doggie (1970)
Me and the Colonel (1958)
Me, Me, Me ... and the Others (1966)
Me, Natalie (1969)
The Meanest Man in the World (1943)
Meat Rack (1970)
A Medal for Benny (1945)
The Medium (1951)
Medium Cool (1969)
Meet Danny Wilson (1952)
Meet John Doe (1941)
Meet Me at Dawn (1948)
Meet Me at the Fair (1952)
Meet Me in Las Vegas (1956)
Meet Me in St. Louis (1944)
Meet Nero Wolfe (1936)
Meet the Missus (1937)
Meet the Mob (1942)
Meet the Stewarts (1942)
Meeting on the Elba (1949)
Melba (1953)
Melody (S.W.A.L.K.) (1971)
Melody Cruise (1933)
Melody Parade (1943)
Melody Ranch (1940)
A Member of the Wedding (1952)
Memories of a Gigolo (1970)
Memories of the Future (1970)
The Memphis Belle (1944)
The Men (1950)
The Men (1971)
Men and Ships (1940)
Men Are Not Gods (1937)
Men Are Such Fools (1938)
Men in Danger (1939)
Men in Her Diary (1945)
Men in War (1957)
Men in White (1934)
Men of Boys' Town (1941)
Men of the Fighting Lady (1954)
Men of the Lightship (1940)
Men of Two Worlds (1946)
Men on Call (1930)
Men on Her Mind (1944)
The Men Who Tread on the Tiger's Tail (1945)
Men with Wings (1938)
Menace in the Night (1958)
Menage, Italian Style (1966)
The Mephisto Waltz (1971)
The Mercenary (1970)
Merchant Seaman (1940)
Merrill's Marauders (1962)
Merrily We Live (1938)
Merry Andrew (1958)
The Merry Chase (1948)
Merry-Go-Round (1956)
The Merry Widow (1925)
Merton of the Movies (1947)
The Message (1971)
A Message to Garcia (1936)
Metello (1970)
Metropolis (1926)
Metropolitan (1935)
Mexican Bus Ride (Subida Al Cielo) (1954)
Mexican Hayride (1948)
Mexican Manhunt (1953)
Mexicana (1945)
Miami Exposé (1956)
The Miami Story (1954)
Michael Kohlhaas (1969)

Michael O'Halloran (1948)
Michael Strogoff (1926)
Michael Strogoff (1960)
The Michigan Kid (1947)
Michurin (1947)
Mickey (1918)
Mickey (1948)
Mickey One (1965)
Mictlan (1970)
Midas Run (1969)
Middle of the Night (1959)
Midnight Cowboy (1969)
Midnight Episode (1955)
Midnight Intruder (1938)
Midnight Lace (1960)
The Midnight Story (1957)
The Midnight Sun (1926)
A Midsummer Night's Dream (1936)
A Midsummer Night's Dream (1962) (puppets)
A Midsummer Night's Dream (1969)
Mighty Joe Young (1949)
The Mighty McGurk (1946)
The Mighty Treve (1937)
The Mighty Ursus (1962)
A Milanese Story (1962)
Mildred Pierce (1945)
The Milkman (1950)
Mill on the Floss (1939)
The Miller's Beautiful Wife (1957)
Le Million (1931)
Million Dollar Baby (1941)
$1,000,000 Duck (1971)
Million Dollar Pursuit (1951)
Million Dollar Weekend (1948)
A Millionaire for Christy (1951)
The Millionairess (1961)
Millions in the Air (1935)
The Mind Benders (1963)
Mine Own Executioner (1948)
Minesweeper (1943)
Mingus (1968)
The Mini-Skirt Mob (1968)
Ministry of Fear (1944)
The Miniver Story (1950)
Minne (1951)
Minnesota Clay (1966)
The Minotaur (1961)
Minstrel Man (1944)
A Minute to Pray, A Second to Die (1968)
Miquette (1951)
Mira (1971)
The Miracle (1959)
A Miracle Can Happen (1948)
Miracle in Harlem (1948)
Miracle in Milan (1952)
Miracle in the Rain (1956)
The Miracle of Dr. Petrov (1947)
The Miracle of Fatima (1952)
The Miracle of Morgan's Creek (1944)
The Miracle of the Bells (1948)
The Miracle of the Hills (1959)
The Miracle of the White Stallions (1963)
Miracle of the Wolves (1925)
Miracle on 34th Street (1947)
The Miracle Worker (1962)
Miraculous Journey (1948)
Mirage (1965)
Miranda (1948)
The Mirror Has Two Faces (1959)
Mirrors of Holland (1952)
The Misadventures of Merlin Jones (1964)
Les Miserables (1927)
Les Miserables (1934)
Les Miserables (1935)
Les Miserables (1936)
Les Miserables (1952)
Les Miserables (1952)
The Misfits (1961)
Miss Grant Takes Richmond (1949)
Miss Julie (1952)
Miss Mink of 1949 (1949)
Miss Robin Crusoe (1953)
Miss Sadie Thompson (1953)
Miss Susie Slagle's (1946)
Miss Tatlock's Millions (1948)
Missile Monsters (1958)
The Missing Corpse (1945)
The Missing Lady (1946)
Missing Women (1951)
Mission Over Korea (1953)
Mission to Moscow (1943)
Mississippi Gambler (1929)
Mississippi Gambler (1953)
Mississippi Rhythm (1949)
The Missouri Traveler (1958)
The Missourians (1950)

Mrs. Brown, You've Got a Lovely Daughter (1968)
Mrs. Mike (1949)
Mrs. Miniver (1942)
Mrs. O'Malley and Mr. Malone (1950)
Mrs. Parkington (1944)
Mrs. Wiggs of the Cabbage Patch (1942)
Mr. Ace (1946)
Mr. and Mrs. Juan Lamaglia (1970)
Mr. and Mrs. Smith (1941)
Mr. Arkadin (1962)
Mr. Belvedere Goes to College (1949)
Mr. Belvedere Rings the Bell (1951)
Mr. Blandings Builds His Dream House (1948)
Mister Buddwing (1966)
Mister Cory (1957)
Mr. Deeds Goes to Town (1936)
Mr. District Attorney (1947)
Mr. Drake's Duck (1951)
Mister 880 (1950)
Mr. Hex (1946)
Mr. Hobbs Takes a Vacation (1962)
Mr. Hobo (1935)
Mr. Hulot's Holiday (1954)
Mr. Imperium (1951)
Mr. Lucky (1943)
Mister Moses (1965)
Mr. Muggs Rides Again (1945)
Mr. Orchid (1948)
Mr. Peabody and the Mermaid (1948)
Mr. Peek-A-Boo (1951)
Mr. Perrin and Mr. Traill (1948)
Mr. Potts Goes to Moscow (1954)
Mr. President (1970)
Mr. Reckless (1948)
Mister Roberts (1955)
Mr. Robinson Crusoe (1932)
Mr. Sardonicus (1961)
Mister Scoutmaster (1953)
Mr. Skeffington (1944)
Mr. Smith Goes to Washington (1939)
Mr. Soft Touch (1949)
Mr. Trull Finds Out (1940)
Mr. Universe (1951)
Mr. Winkle Goes to War (1944)
Mr. Wong, Detective (1938)
The Mistress (1953)
Misty (1961)
Mitsou (1958)
M'Liss (1936)
The Mob (1951)
Moby Dick (1956)
The Model and the Marriage Broker (1951)
Model Wife (1941)
Models, Inc. (1952)
Modern Times (1936)
Modesty Blaise (1966)
The Modification (1970)
Mohawk (1956)
The Mojave Firebrand (1944)
The Mole People (1956)
Molly (see The Goldbergs) (1950)
Molly and Me (1945)
The Molly Maguires (1970)
The Moment of Truth (1952)
The Moment of Truth (1965)
Moment to Moment (1966)
Mon Ami Pierre (1951)
Mondo Cane (1963)
Il Mondo Le Condanna (1952)
Mondo Pazzo (1965)
Money from Home (1953)
The Money Jungle (1968)
Money Madness (1948)
The Money Trap (1966)
Monika (1959)
Monique (1970)
The Monitors (1969)
Monkey Business (1952)
Monkey on My Back (1957)
Monkeys Go Home (1967)
The Monkey's Uncle (1965)
The Monolith Monsters (1957)
Monpti (1959)
Monsieur Beaucaire (1946)
Monsieur Ludovic (1946)
Monsieur Verdoux (1947)
Monsieur Vincent (1947)
Monsoon (1953)
The Monster Maker (1944)
The Monster of London City (1967)
The Monster that Challenged the

World (1957)
Montana (1950)
Montana Belle (1952)
Montana Desperado (1951)
Montana Incident (1952)
Montana Territory (1952)
Monte Walsh (1970)
The Moon and Sixpence (1942)
The Moon Is Blue (1953)
The Moon Is Down (1943)
Moon over Burma (1941)
Moon over Montana (1946)
Moon Pilot (1962)
Moon Zero Two (1969)
Moonfleet (1955)
Moonlight in Vermont (1943)
Moonlight Murder (1936)
The Moonlighter (1953)
Moonrise (1948)
The Moon's Our Home (1936)
The Moonshine War (1970)
The Moonspinners (1964)
Moontide (1942)
More Dead Than Alive (1968)
More Than a Miracle (1967)
More Than a Secretary (1936)
The More the Merrier (1943)
Morgan! (1966)
Morgan the Pirate (1961)
Morituri (1965)
Morning Glory (1933)
Morocco (1931)
Moro Witch Doctor (1964)
The Mortal Storm (1940)
Mosquito Squadron (1970)
Moss Rose (1947)
The Most Beautiful Wife (1970)
The Most Dangerous Man Alive (1961)
The Most Dangerous Sin (1956)
The Most Wonderful Moment (1959)
Mother (see 1905) (1955)
Mother Didn't Tell Me (1950)
Mother Is a Freshman (1949)
Mother Knows Best (1928)
Mother Machree (1929)
A Mother's Heart (1969)
Mothra (1962)
The Motive Was Jealousy (1970)
Motor Patrol (1950)
Motorcycle Gang (1957)
Moulin Rouge (1934)
Moulin Rouge (1952)
The Mountain (1956)
Mountain Justice (1937)
The Mountain Road (1960)
Mourning Becomes Electra (1947)
The Mouse that Roared (1959)
Move! (1970)
Move Over, Darling (1963)
The Mudlark (1950)
Mug Town (1943)
The Mugger (1958)
The Mummy (1959)
The Mummy's Curse (1944)
The Mummy's Ghost (1944)
The Mummy's Shroud (1967)
The Mummy's Tomb (1942)
Mumsy, Nanny, Sonny and Girly (1970)
Mumu (1960)
Munna (1957)
Munster, Go Home (1966)
Murder a La Mod (1968)
Murder Ahoy (1964)
Murder at the Gallop (1963)
Murder by Contract (1958)
The Murder Game (1966)
Murder, He Says (1945)
Murder, Inc. (1960)
Murder Is My Beat (1955)
Murder Is My Business (1946)
Murder Man (1935)
Murder Most Foul (1964)
Murder, My Sweet (1945)
Murder on the Blackboard (1934)
Murder Reported (1958)
Murder, She Said (1962)
Murder without Crime (1950)
Murder without Tears (1953)
Murderers Among Us (1946)
Murderer's Row (1966)
Murders in the Rue Morgue (1971)
Muriel (1963)
Murieta (1965)
Murphy's War (1971)
The Music Box Kid (1960)
Music for Millions (1944)
The Music Goes 'Round (1936)
Music in Manhattan (1944)
Music in the Air (1934)
Music Man (1948)

Mustang (1959)
Mutiny (1952)
Mutiny in Outer Space (1965)
Mutiny on the Bounty (1935)
Mutiny on the Bounty (1962)
My Apprenticeship (1939)
My Best Gal (1944)
My Blood Runs Cold (1965)
My Brother Talks to Horses (1947)
My Buddy (1944)
My Cousin Rachel (1952)
My Darling Clementine (1946)
My Dear Secretary (1948)
My Dog Buddy (1960)
My Father's Horses (1956)
My Father's House (1947)
My Favorite Blonde (1942)
My Favorite Brunette (1947)
My Favorite Spy (1942)
My Favorite Spy (1951)
My Favorite Wife (1940)
My Foolish Heart (1949)
My Forbidden Past (1951)
My Friend Flicka (1943)
My Friend Irma (1949)
My Friend Irma Goes West (1950)
My Geisha (1962)
My Girl Friend's Wedding (1969)
My Girl Tisa (1948)
My Gun Is Quick (1957)
My Life with Caroline (1941)
My Lips Betray (1933)
My Little Chickadee (1940)
My Love Came Back (1940)
My Lover, My Son (1970)
My Man and I (1952)
My Man Godfrey (1957)
My Mao (1970)
My Name Is Han (1948)
My Name Is Julia Ross (1945)
My Own True Love (1948)
My Pal Gus (1952)
My Pal Trigger (1946)
My Pal, Wolf (1944)
My Reputation (1946)
My Side of the Mountain (1969)
My Sin (1931)
My Sister's Kids at Their Worst (1971)
My Six Convicts (1952)
My Six Loves (1963)
My Son John (1952)
My Son, My Son (1940)
My Son, the Hero (1943)
My Uncle (1958)
My Uncle Antoine (1971)
My Universities (1940)
My Wife's Best Friend (1952)
Myra Breckinridge (1970)
The Mysterians (1959)
The Mysterious Desperado (1949)
The Mysterious Discovery (1956)
Mysterious Intruder (1946)
Mysterious Island (1961)
The Mysterious Mr. Valentine (1946)
Mystery in Mexico (1948)
The Mystery of Edwin Drood (1935)
The Mystery of Marie Roget (1942)
Mystery of the Black Jungle (1955)
The Mystery of the Golden Eye (1948)
Mystery Ranch (1932)
Mystery Range (1949)
Mystery Street (1950)
Mystery Submarine (1950)
Mystery Submarine (1963)

N. P. (1971)
Nabonga (1945)
Nagin (1956)
Naked Alibi (1954)
The Naked and the Dead (1958)
Naked Autumn (1963)
The Naked Brigade (1965)
Naked City (1948)
The Naked Dawn (1955)
The Naked Edge (1961)
The Naked Eye (1957)
The Naked Heart (1955)
The Naked Hills (1956)
Naked in the Sun (1957)
The Naked Jungle (1954)
The Naked Kiss (1964)
The Naked Maja (1959)
The Naked Night (1956)
The Naked Runner (1967)

Naked Sea (1955)
The Naked Spur (1953)
The Naked Street (1955)
The Name of the Game Is Kill (1968)
Nameless Star (1966)
Namu, the Killer Whale (1966)
Nana (1934)
Nana (1955)
Nana (1971)
Nancy Steele Is Missing (1937)
The Nanny (1965)
Napoleon (1926)
Napoleon (1954)
National Velvet (1944)
Native Land (1942)
Native Son (1951)
Nature's Half Acre (1951)
Naughty Arlette (1949)
Navajo Run (1966)
Navajo Trail Raiders (1949)
Navy Blue and Gold (1937)
The Navy Comes Through (1942)
The Navy Way (1944)
Navy Wife (1956)
Nayak (1966)
Nazi Agent (1942)
The Nazis Strike (1942)
The Neanderthal Man (1953)
Near Orouet (1971)
Nearly a Nasty Accident (1962)
Nearly Eighteen (1943)
The Nebraskan (1953)
Necronomicon--Dreamed Sins (1968)
Necrophagus (1971)
Negatives (1968)
The Negro Soldier (1944)
Neptune's Daughter (1949)
Nettezza Urbana (1948)
Nevada (1944)
Nevada Smith (1966)
The Nevadan (1950)
Never a Dull Moment (1943)
Never a Dull Moment (1950)
Never a Dull Moment (1968)
Never Fear (The Young Lovers) (1950)
Never Let Go (1963)
Never Let Me Go (1953)
Never Love a Stranger (1958)
Never on Sunday (1960)
Never Put It in Writing (1964)
Never Say Goodbye (1946)
Never Say Goodbye (1956)
Never So Few (1959)
Never Steal Anything Small (1959)
Never Too Late (1965)
Never Wave at a Wac (1952)
The New Angels (1961)
New Babylon (1929)
New Earth (1934)
New Faces of 1938 (1937)
The New Gulliver (1935)
The New Interns (1964)
A New Kind of Love (1963)
The New Life Style (1970)
New Mexico (1951)
New Orleans Uncensored (1955)
A New World (1966)
New Worlds for Old (1937)
New York Chiama Superdrago (1966)
New York City--The Most (1968)
New York Confidential (1955)
News Hounds (1947)
Next (see The Secret Vice of Signora Ward) (1971)
Next of Kin (1942)
Next Time We Love (1936)
Next to No Time (1958)
The Next Voice You Hear (1950)
Niagara (1953)
Nice Girl? (1941)
A Nice Girl Like Me (1969)
Nicholas and Alexandra (1971)
Nicholas Nickleby (1946)
Nickel Queen (1971)
Night Affair (1961)
Night Ambush (1957)
Night and Day (1946)
Night and Fog (1955)
Night and the City (1950)
A Night at the Opera (1936)
Night Creatures (1962)
The Night Digger (1971)
Night Encounter (1963)
The Night Fighters (1960)
Night Flight (1933)
Night Freight (1955)
The Night Has a Thousand Eyes (1948)
Night Has Eyes (1946)
The Night Hawk (1938)

The Night Heaven Fell (1958)
The Night Holds Terror (1955)
A Night in Casablanca (1946)
A Night in Paradise (1946)
Night Into Morning (1951)
Night Is My Future (1962)
Night Key (1937)
Night Mail (1936)
Night Monster (1942)
Night Must Fall (1937)
Night Must Fall (1964)
The Night My Number Came Up (1955)
A Night of Adventure (1944)
Night of Dark Shadows (1971)
The Night of San Juan (1971)
Night of the Counting Years (1970)
Night of the Generals (1967)
The Night of the Grizzly (1966)
The Night of the Hunter (1955)
The Night of the Iguana (1964)
Night of the Quarter Moon (1959)
The Night of the Seagull (1970)
Night Passage (1957)
Night People (1954)
Night Raiders (1952)
Night Riders of Montana (1951)
The Night Runner (1957)
Night Shift (1942)
Night Song (1947)
The Night the World Exploded (1957)
The Night They Raided Minsky's (1968)
A Night to Remember (1942)
A Night to Remember (1958)
Night Train (1941)
Night Train to Memphis (1946)
Night Train to Paris (1964)
Night Unto Night (1949)
The Night Visitor (1971)
The Night Walker (1964)
Night Wind (1948)
Night without Sleep (1952)
Night without Stars (1953)
The Nightcomers (1971)
Nightfall (1956)
Nightmare (1956)
Nightmare (1964)
Nightmare Alley (1947)
Nights of Cabiria (1957)
The Nights of Lucretia Borgia (1960)
Nighttime in Nevada (1948)
Nikki, Wild Dog of the North (1961)
Nine Days a Queen (1936)
Nine Days of One Year (1961)
Nine Girls (1944)
Nine Hours to Rama (1963)
Nine Lives (1959)
Nine Men (1943)
1905 (Mother) (1955)
1918 (1958)
1984 (1956)
Ninety-Nine Women (1969)
Nini Tirabuscio (1971)
Ninotchka (1939)
The Ninth Circle (1961)
99 River Street (1953)
No Down Payment (1957)
No Drums, No Bugles (1971)
No Escape (1953)
No Exit (1962)
No Holds Barred (1952)
No Love for Johnnie (1961)
No Man Is an Island (1962)
No Man of Her Own (1950)
No Man's Land (1930)
No Man's Woman (1955)
No Minor Vices (1948)
No More Ladies (1935)
No Name on the Bullet (1959)
No Orchids for Miss Blandish (1948)
No Place for a Lady (1943)
No Place for Jennifer (1951)
No Place Like Homicide (1962)
No Place to Hide (1956)
No Place to Land (1958)
No Questions Asked (1951)
No Resting Place (1952)
No Room for the Groom (1952)
No Sad Songs for Me (1950)
No Shooting Time for Foxes (1966)
No Sun in Venice (1958)
No Time for Comedy (1940)
No Time for Flowers (1952)
No Time for Love (1943)
No Time for Sergeants (1958)
No Time to Be Young (1957)
No Trees in the Street (1959)
No Way Back (1955)

No Way Out (1950)
No Way to Treat a Lady (1968)
Noah's Ark (1928)
Nob Hill (1945)
Nobody Lives Forever (1946)
Nobody Runs Forever (1968)
Nobody Waved Goodbye (1965)
Nobody's Baby (1937)
Nobody's Darling (1943)
Nobody's Perfect (1968)
Nocturne (1946)
None But the Brave (1965)
None But the Lonely Heart (1944)
None Shall Escape (1944)
The Noose Hangs High (1948)
Nora Prentiss (1947)
North by Northwest (1959)
North of the Great Divide (1950)
North Sea (1938)
The North Star (1943)
North to Alaska (1960)
North to the Klondike (1942)
Northern Patrol (1953)
Northern Pursuit (1943)
Northern Safari (1968)
Northwest Mounted Police (1940)
Northwest Outpost (1947)
Northwest Passage (1940)
Northwest Rangers (1942)
Northwest Stampede (1948)
Northwest Trail (1945)
Norwood (1970)
Not as a Stranger (1955)
Not of This Earth (1957)
Not on Your Life! (1965)
Not Wanted (1949)
Not with My Wife, You Don't (1966)
Nothing But the Best (1964)
Nothing But Trouble (1944)
Notorious (1946)
The Notorious Gentleman (1945)
The Notorious Landlady (1962)
The Notorious Mr. Monks (1958)
Notte Bianchi (1957)
Notte Brava (1961)
A Nous la Liberte (1931)
Now I'll Tell (1934)
Now Voyager (1942)
Nowhere to Go (1959)
Nude in a White Car (1959)
Nude Odyssey (1960)
Nudity (1970)
Number One (1969)
The Nun and the Sergeant (1962)
A Nun at the Crossroads (1970)
The Nun's Story (1959)
Nurse Edith Cavell (1939)
Nutty, Naughty Chateau (1964)
The Nutty Professor (1963)

O. Henry's Full House (1952)
O.S.S. (1946)
O.S.S. 117 (1959)
Oasis (1957)
Objective, Burma! (1945)
The Oblong Box (1969)
Obsessed (1951)
Obsessions (1969)
An Occurrence at Owl Creek Bridge (1962)
Ocean's 11 (1960)
October (1928)
October Man (1947)
The Odd Couple (1968)
Odd Man Out (1946)
Odds Against Tomorrow (1959)
Odette (1950)
Odongo (1956)
Oedipus Rex (1957)
Oedipus the King (1968)
Of Human Bondage (1934)
Of Human Bondage (1946)
Of Human Bondage (1964)
Of Human Hearts (1938)
Of Love and Desire (1963)
Of Mice and Men (1940)
Off Limits (1953)
Oh, Amelia (1951)
Oh, Dad, Poor Dad, Mama's Hung You in the Closet and I'm Feeling So Sad (1967)
Oh, Doctor (1937)
Oh, Men! Oh, Women! (1957)
Oh, Sun (1970)
Oh, Susanna (1951)
Oh, What a Lovely War (1969)
Oh, What a Night! (1943)
The Oil Girls (1971)
The Oil Prince (1965)
Okay Bill (1971)
Okinawa (1952)
Oklahoma Annie (1952)
Oklahoma Blues (1948)

Oklahoma Territory (1960)
The Oklahoman (1957)
Old Acquaintance (1943)
The Old Dark House (1963)
Old English (1930)
An Old-Fashioned Girl (1948)
The Old-Fashioned Way (1934)
The Old Frontier (1950)
The Old Homestead (1942)
Old Hutch (1936)
Old Ironsides (1926)
Old Los Angeles (1948)
The Old Maid (1939)
The Old Man and the Sea (1958)
Old Man Rhythm (1935)
The Old Mill (1937)
Old Oklahoma Plains (1952)
Old Surehand (1965)
Old Yeller (1957)
The Oldest Profession in the World (1967)
Ole Rex (1961)
Oliver Twist (1948)
The Olsen Gang in a Fix (1969)
The Olsen Gang in Jutland (1971)
Olympia (1936)
The Olympic Elk (1953)
The Olympics in Mexico (1970)
The Omaha Trail (1942)
Omar Khayyam (1957)
The Omega Man (1971)
Omoo, Omoo, the Shark God (1949)
On Again, Off Again (1937)
On an Island with You (1948)
On Any Sunday (1971)
On Borrowed Time (1939)
On Dangerous Ground (1951)
On Her Majesty's Secret Service (1969)
On Moonlight Bay (1951)
On Our Merry Way (1948)
On the Beach (1959)
On the Bowery (1957)
On the Double (1961)
On the Loose (1951)
On the Point of Death (1971)
On the Sunny Side (1942)
On the Threshold of Space (1956)
On the Waterfront (1954)
On Top of Old Smoky (1953)
Once a Jolly Swagman (1948)
Once a Thief (1950)
Once a Thief (1965)
Once More, My Darling (1949)
Once There Was a Girl (1945)
Once Upon a Dream (1949)
Once Upon a Honeymoon (1942)
Once Upon a Horse (1958)
Once Upon a Time (1944)
Once Upon a Time in the West (1969)
Once You Kiss a Stranger (1969)
One Adventure of Billy the Kid (1971)
One Big Affair (1952)
One Crowded Night (1940)
One Day in the Life of Ivan Denisovich (1971)
One Day Is More Beautiful Than the Other (1970)
One Desire (1955)
One Exciting Night (1945)
One Exciting Week (1946)
One-Eyed Jacks (1961)
One Foot in Heaven (1941)
One Foot in Hell (1960)
One Hundred Rifles (1969)
One Hundred and One Dalmations (1961)
One Last Fling (1949)
One Man's Journey (1933)
One Man's Way (1964)
One Million, B.C. (1940)
The 1,000,000 Eyes of Su-Muru (1967)
One Million Years, B.C. (1966)
One Minute to Zero (1952)
One More River (1934)
One More Time (1970)
One More Tomorrow (1946)
One More Train to Rob (1971)
One Naked Night (1965)
One Night at Dinner (1969)
One Night of Love (1934)
One of Those Things (1971)
One Plus One (1961)
One Potato, Two Potato (1964)
One Rainy Afternoon (1936)
One Romantic Night (1930)
One Spy Too Many (1966)
One Step to Eternity (1955)
One Summer of Happiness (1951)

One Sunday Afternoon (1948)
One-Tenth of a Nation (1940)
The One that Got Away (1958)
1,000 Convicts and a Woman (1971)
1001 Arabian Nights (1959)
One Too Many (1950)
One Touch of Venus (1948)
One Two Three (1961)
One Way Pendulum (1965)
One-Way Street (1950)
One Woman's Story (see The Passionate Friends)
Onibaba (1965)
Onionhead (1958)
The Only Game in Town (1970)
Only One New York (1964)
An Only Son (1969)
Only the French Can (French Can-Can) (1956)
Only the Valiant (1951)
The Only Thing You Know (1971)
Only Two Can Play (1962)
The Only Way (1970)
Only When I Larf (1968)
Open City (1945)
Open Secret (1948)
Open the Door and See All the People (1964)
Operation Amsterdam (1960)
Operation Bikini (1963)
Operation C.I.A. (1965)
Operation Conspiracy (1957)
Operation Crossbow (1965)
Operation Eichmann (1961)
Operation Kid Brother (1967)
Operation Mad Ball (1957)
Operation Manhunt (1954)
Operation Pacific (1951)
Operation Petticoat (1959)
Operation San Gennaro (1966)
Operation Secret (1952)
Operation Snafu (1965)
Operation Snatch (1962)
Operation X (1950)
Operator 13 (1934)
The Opposite Sex (1956)
Opus 3 (1928)
Orchestra Wives (1942)
Orchids to You (1935)
Ordered to Love (1963)
Orders to Kill (1958)
Ordet (1957)
Oregon Passage (1957)
Oregon Trail (1945)
The Oregon Trail (1959)
The Organization (1971)
The Organizer (1964)
The Original Sin (1948)
Orphans of the Storm (1922)
Orpheus (1949)
O'Shaughnessy's Boy (1935)
The Oscar (1966)
Oscar Wilde (1960)
The Ostrich Has Two Eggs (1957)
Othello (1955)
Othello (1960) (ballet)
Othello (1965)
The Other Love (1947)
The Other One (1967)
The Other Woman (1954)
The Other World of Winston Churchill (1967)
Otley (1969)
Our Betters (1933)
Our Country (1944)
Our Daily Bread (1934)
Our Dancing Daughters (1928)
Our Hearts Were Growing Up (1946)
Our Hearts Were Young and Gay (1944)
Our Leading Citizen (1939)
Our Man Flint (1966)
Our Miss Brooks (1956)
Our Mother's House (1967)
Our Town (1940)
Our Very Own (1950)
Our Vines Have Tender Grapes (1945)
Out California Way (1946)
Out of Chaos (1944)
Out of Frame (1969)
Out of the Blue (1947)
Out of the Clouds (1957)
Out of the Past (1947)
Out of the Storm (1948)
Out of This World (1945)
The Out-of-Towners (1970)
Outcast (1937)
The Outcast (1954)
Outcast of the Islands (1952)
Outcasts of Poker Flat (1937)
The Outcasts of Poker Flat (1952)

Outcasts of the City (1958)
Outcasts of the Trail (1949)
The Outlaw (1943)
Outlaw Brand (1948)
Outlaw Gold (1950)
Outlaw Roundup (1945)
The Outlaw Stallion (1954)
Outlaw Trail (1944)
Outlaw Women (1952)
Outlaws (1970)
The Outlaw's Daughter (1954)
The Outlaws Is Coming! (1965)
Outlaws of Pine Ridge (1942)
Outlaw's Son (1957)
Outpost in Malaya (1952)
Outpost in Morocco (1949)
Outrage (1950)
The Outrage (1964)
The Outriders (1950)
Outside the Law (1930)
Outside the Law (1956)
The Outsider (1961)
Over Exposed (1956)
Over My Dead Body (1942)
Over the Hill (1931)
Over There--1914-1918 (1963)
Over 21 (1945)
The Overland Express (1938)
Overland Mail Robbery (1943)
Overland Pacific (1954)
Overland Riders (1946)
Overland Telegraph (1951)
Overland Trails (1948)
The Overlanders (1946)
Overture 1812 (1929)
The Owl and the Pussycat (1970)
The Ox-Bow Incident (1943)

P.J. (1968)
PT 109 (1963)
P.T. Raiders (see The Ship that Died of Shame) (1956)
The Pace that Thrills (1952)
Pacific Blackout (1942)
Pacific Liner (1939)
Pacific 231 (1931)
The Pacifist (1971)
The Pad (And How to Use It) (1966)
Paddy (1970)
The Pagans (1950)
Paid in Full (1949)
Painted Desert (1938)
The Painted Hills (1951)
The Painted Veil (1934)
The Painted Woman (1932)
Paisan (1946)
The Palace of Angels (1970)
The Pale Horseman (1946)
The Paleface (1948)
Palm Beach Story (1942)
Palm Springs (1936)
Palm Springs Weekend (1963)
The Palomino (1950)
Pals of the Golden West (1951)
Panama Sal (1957)
Pandora and the Flying Dutchman (1951)
Panhandle (1948)
Panic (1946)
Panic Button (1964)
Panic in the City (1968)
Panic in the Parlor (1957)
Panic in the Streets (1950)
Panic in Year Zero (1962)
Pantaloons (1957)
Papa, Mama, the Maid and I (1954)
Papa, the Little Boats (1971)
Papanicolis (1971)
Papa's Delicate Condition (1963)
The Paper Lion (1968)
Le Paquebot Tenacity (1934)
The Paradine Case (1947)
Paradise for Three (1938)
Paradise, Hawaiian Style (1966)
Paranoia (1966)
Paranoia (1969)
Paranoiac (1963)
The Paratrooper (1954)
Paratroops (1942)
Pardners (1956)
Pardon My French (1951)
Pardon My Past (1945)
Pardon My Rhythm (1944)
Pardon My Stripes (1942)
The Parent Trap (1961)
Paris After Dark (1943)
Paris Blues (1961)
Paris Calling (1942)
Paris Does Strange Things (1957)

Paris Follies of 1956 (1955)
Paris Holiday (1958)
Paris Hotel (1959)
Paris Model (1953)
Paris 1900 (1948)
Paris Playboys (1954)
Paris Secret (1965)
Paris Underground (1945)
Paris Weekend (1959)
Paris When It Sizzles (1964)
La Parisienne (1958)
Park Row (1952)
Parnell (1937)
Parole (1936)
Parole, Inc. (1948)
Parrish (1961)
The Parson and the Outlaw (1957)
The Parson of Panamint (1941)
Part of the Family (1971)
Un Partie de Campagne (1936)
Partner (1968)
Partners of the Sunset (1948)
Partners of the Trail (1944)
The Party (1968)
Party Girl (1958)
Party Girls for the Candidate (1965)
Passage to Marseille (1944)
Passage West (1951)
Les Passagers de la Grande Ouise (1939)
Passing Days (1970)
Passing of the Third Floor Back (1936)
Passion (1954)
Passion for Life (1952)
The Passion of Joan of Arc (1928)
The Passion of Slow Fire (1961)
Passionate Friends (1949)
Passport to China (1961)
Passport to Destiny (1944)
Passport to Hell (1932)
Passport to Pimlico (1949)
Pastor Hall (1940)
Pat and Mike (1952)
A Patch of Blue (1965)
The Patchwork Girl of Oz (1914)
The Path of Hope (1951)
Pather Panchali (1956)
The Pathfinder (1952)
Paths of Glory (1957)
Patrick the Great (1945)
The Patriot (1928)
The Patsy (1964)
Patton (1970)
Paula (1952)
Le Pave de Paris (1961)
The Pawnbroker (1965)
Pawnee (1957)
Pay or Die (1960)
Payment in Blood (1968)
Payment on Demand (1951)
Payroll (1962)
Pays du Scalp (1929)
The Peace Killers (1971)
Peace over the Fields (1971)
The Peacemaker (1956)
The Peach Thief (1965)
Peak of Fate (1925)
The Pearl (1948)
The Pearl of Death (1944)
Pearl of the South Pacific (1955)
Peasants (1935)
Peck's Bad Boy with the Circus (1938)
A Pedagogical Poem (1955)
Peddlin' In Society (1947)
Peg O' My Heart (1933)
Peggy (1916)
Peggy (1950)
Peking Express (1951)
Peking Remembered (1967)
Pendulum (1969)
Penelope (1966)
Penny Princess (1953)
Penny Serenade (1941)
The Penthouse (1967)
The People Against O'Hara (1951)
People Are Funny (1946)
The People Next Door (1970)
People of the Cumberland (1937)
The People of Warsaw (1970)
People Will Talk (1951)
The People's Land (1942)
Pepe (1960)
Pepe Le Moko (1937)
Pepe Le Moko (1951)
Pepo (1935)
Pepper (1936)
Percy (1971)
Perfect Friday (1970)
The Perfect Furlough (1958)

The Perfect Marriage (1947)
Perfect Strangers (1950)
The Perfect Woman (1949)
Performance (1970)
A Perilous Journey (1953)
Perilous Waters (In Self Defense) (1947)
The Perils of Pauline (1947)
The Perils of Pauline (1967)
Period of Adjustment (1962)
Perrak (1970)
Perri (1957)
A Personal Affair (1954)
Personal Column (see Lured)
Personal Property (1937)
The Persuader (1957)
Peter Ibbetson (1935)
Peter Pan (1953)
Peter the First (Part I) (1937)
Peter the First (Part II) (1938)
Le Petit Soldat (1947)
Pett and Pott (1934)
Petticoat Fever (1936)
The Petty Girl (1950)
Petulia (1968)
Peyton Place (1957)
Phaedra (1962)
The Phantom Chariot (1938)
The Phantom Horse (1956)
Phantom Lady (1944)
Phantom Lovers (1960)
The Phantom of 42nd Street (1945)
The Phantom of Soho (1967)
The Phantom of the Opera (1925)
The Phantom of the Opera (1943)
The Phantom of the Opera (1962)
The Phantom of the Rue Morgue (1954)
The Phantom Plainsman (1942)
The Phantom Stagecoach (1957)
The Phantom Tollbooth (1970)
Pharaoh's Curse (1957)
The Pharaoh's Woman (1961)
Phedre (1968)
The Phenix City Story (1955)
Phffft (1954)
The Philadelphia Story (1940)
Philo Vance Returns (1947)
Philo Vance's Gamble (1947)
Phone Call from a Stranger (1952)
The Phynx (1970)
Picasso (1956)
Piccadilly Incident (1946)
Piccadilly Jim (1936)
Pick a Star (1937)
Pickup (1951)
Pickup Alley (1957)
Pickup on South Street (1953)
The Pickwick Papers (1954)
Picnic (1948)
Picnic (1955)
The Picture of Dorian Gray (1945)
Pieces of Dreams (1970)
The Pied Piper (1942)
Pier 23 (1951)
Pierre of the Plains (1942)
The Pigeon that Took Rome (1962)
Piggies (1970)
The Pilgrim (1922)
The Pilgrim Lady (1947)
The Pillar of Fire (1963)
Pillars of the Sky (1956)
Pillow of Death (1945)
Pillow Talk (1959)
Pillow to Post (1945)
Pilot No. 5 (1943)
Pin-Up Girl (1944)
The Pink Jungle (1968)
The Pink Panther (1964)
Pinky (1949)
Pinocchio (1971)
The Pinto Bandit (1944)
Pioneer Marshal (1950)
The Pirates of Blood River (1962)
Pirates of Monterey (1947)
Pirates of the Prairie (1942)
Pirates of Tortuga (1961)
Pirates of Tripoli (1955)
Pirogov (1947)
Pistol Harvest (1951)
A Pistol Shot (1967)
The Pit and the Pendulum (1961)
Pitfall (1948)
Pittsburgh (1942)
A Place Called Glory (1966)
A Place for Lovers (1969)
A Place in the Sun (1951)

A Place to Live (1941)
The Plague of the Zombies (1966)
Plain People (1945)
The Plainsman (1936)
The Plainsman and the Lady (1946)
Planet of the Apes (1968)
Planet of the Vampires (1965)
The Plank (1967)
The Plastic Dome of Norma Jean (1966)
Platinum High School (1960)
Play Dirty (1969)
Play it Cool (1963)
Play "Misty" for Me (1971)
Playgirl (1954)
Playtime (1967)
Plaza Suite (1971)
Please Believe Me (1950)
Please Don't Eat the Daisies (1960)
Please! Mr. Balzac (1957)
Please Turn Over (1960)
The Pleasure Garden (1953)
The Pleasure of His Company (1961)
The Pleasure Seekers (1964)
The Plough and the Stars (1937)
The Plow that Broke the Plains (1936)
Plunder of the Sun (1953)
Plunder Road (1957)
The Plunderers (1948)
The Plunderers (1960
Plunderers of Painted Flats (1959)
Plymouth Adventure (1952)
The Poacher's Daughter (1960)
Pocketful of Chestnuts (1971)
Pocketful of Miracles (1961)
Poil de Carotte (1932)
Point Blank (1967)
Police Chief Pepe (1969)
Police Nurse (1963)
The Politicians (1970)
Pollyanna (1960)
Pony Express (1925)
Pony Express (1953)
Pony Soldier (1952)
Pool of London (1951)
Poor But Beautiful (1957)
Poor Little Rich Girl (1936)
Popi (1969)
Poppy (1936)
The Poppy Is Also a Flower (1966)
Por Mis Pistolas (1968)
Pork Chop Hill (1959)
Pornography: Copenhagen 1970 (1970)
Port Afrique (1956)
Port of Desire (1957)
Port of Hell (1954)
Port of New York (1949)
Port of Seven Seas (1938)
Port of Shadows (Quai des Brumes) (1938)
Porte de Lilas (1957)
Portes de la Nuit (1946)
Portland Expose (1957)
Portrait in Black (1960)
Portrait of a Mobster (1961)
Portrait of an Unknown Woman (1958)
Portrait of Chicko (1968)
Portrait of Innocence (1948)
Portrait of Jennie (1948)
A Portrait of Marianne (1970)
Portraits of Women (1970)
Posse from Hell (1961)
Possessed (1947)
Post Office Investigator (1949)
The Postman Always Rings Twice (1946)
The Postman Didn't Ring (1942)
Postmark for Danger (1956)
Pot O' Gold (1941)
Potemkin (1925)
Potemkin (re-issued) (1951)
La Poupee (1962)
Powder River (1953)
Powder Town (1942)
Power (1971)
The Power (1968)
Power Among Men (1959)
Power and the Land (1940)
The Power and the Prize (1956)
The Power of the Whistler (1945)
Powered Flight (1953)
Practically Yours (1944)
The Prairie (1948)
Prairie Badmen (1946)
Prairie Chickens (1943)
Prairie Rustlers (1946)
Prehistoric Women (1951)

Prehistoric Women (1951)
Prehistoric Women (1967)
Prejudice (1949)
Prelude to War (1942)
Premature Burial (1962
Presenting Lily Mars (1943)
The President's Analyst (1967)
The President's Lady (1953)
The President's Mystery (1936)
Press for Time (1966)
Pressure Point (1962)
The Pretender (1947)
Pretty Baby (1950)
Pretty Boy Floyd (1960)
Pretty Maids All in a Row (1971)
Pretty Poison (1968)
Pretty Polly (1967)
The Price of Fear (1956)
Pride and Prejudice (1940)
The Pride and the Passion (1957)
Pride of Maryland (1951)
The Pride of St. Louis (1952)
Pride of the Blue Grass (1954)
Pride of the Marines (1945)
Pride of the Plains (1944)
The Pride of the Yankees (1942)
The Priest of St. Paul (1970)
The Priest's Wife (1971)
The Prime of Miss Jean Brodie (1969)
The Primrose Path (1940)
The Prince and the Pauper (1937)
The Prince and the Showgirl (1957)
Prince Bayaya (1954)
A Prince for Cynthia (1954)
Prince of Foxes (1949)
The Prince of Pilsen (1926)
Prince of Pirates (1953)
Prince of Players (1955)
Prince of the Blue Grass (1954)
Prince of the Plains (1949)
Prince Valiant (1954)
The Prince Who Was a Thief (1951)
The Princess and the Pirate (1944)
The Princess and the Plumber (1930)
Princess Cinderella (1955)
Princess of the Nile (1954)
Princess O'Rourke (1943)
Prism (1971)
The Prisoner (1955)
Prisoner of Japan (1942)
The Prisoner of Shark Island (1936)
The Prisoner of the Iron Mask (1962)
Prisoner of the Volga (1960)
Prisoner of War (1954)
The Prisoner of Zenda (1952)
Prisoners in Petticoats (1950)
Prisoners of the Casbah (1953)
The Private Affairs of Bel Ami (1947)
Private Hell 36 (1954)
Private Ivan Brovkin (1955)
The Private Life of Don Juan (1934)
The Private Life of Helen of Troy (1927)
The Private Life of Henry VIII (1933)
The Private Life of Sherlock Holmes (1970)
The Private Lives of Adam and Eve (1960)
Private Lives of Elizabeth and Essex (1939)
Private Number (1936)
The Private Navy of Sgt. O'Farrell (1968)
Private Road (1971)
Private Scandal (1934)
The Private War of Major Benson (1955)
A Private's Affair (1959)
Private's Progress (1956)
Privilege (1967)
The Prize (1963)
A Prize of Gold (1955)
Problem Girls (1953)
The Prodigal (1955)
Professional Soldier (1936)
Professional Sweetheart (1933)
The Professionals (1966)
Professor Hannibal (1957)
El Professor Hippie (1969)
Professor Mamlock (1938)
A Profound Longing for the Gods (1969)
Project M-7 (1953)
Project X (1949)

Project X (1968)
The Projected Man (1967)
The Projectionist (1970)
Prologue (1969)
Promise at Dawn (1970)
Promise Her Anything (1966)
The Promoter (1952)
The Proper Time (1961)
The Prophet of Hunger (1970)
The Protagonists (1968)
The Proud and the Beautiful (1953)
The Proud and the Profane (1956)
Proud, Damned and Dead (1969)
The Proud Heart (1925)
The Proud Ones (1956)
The Proud Rebel (1958)
The Proud Rider (1971)
The Proud Valley (1939)
The Prowler (1951)
Prowlers of the Everglades (1954)
Prudence and the Pill (1968)
Prudence and the Pirate (1916)
Psych-Out (1968)
Psyche '59 (1964)
Psycho (1960)
Psycho-Circus (1967)
Psychomania (1964)
The Psychopath (1966)
Psychout for Murder (1971)
Psychosissimo (1962)
Public Hero No. 1 (1935)
Public Pigeon No. 1 (1957)
Pufnstuf (1970)
The Pumpkin Eater (1964)
Punishment Park (1971)
Punishment to the Traitor (1966)
Puppet on a Chain (1971)
Purgatory Eroica (1971)
Puritan Passions (1923)
The Purple Gang (1960)
The Purple Heart (1944)
The Purple Mask (1955)
Purple Noon (1961)
The Purple Plain (1955)
Pursued (1947)
The Pursuit of Happiness (1971)
Pursuit of the Graf Spee (1957)
The Pusher (1960)
Pushover (1954)
Pussycat, Pussycat, I Love You (1970)
Putney Swope (1969)
Puzzle of a Downfall Child (1970)
Pygmalion (1938)
Pyramid of the Sungods (1965)
Pyro (1964)

Q-bec My Love (1970)
Quackser Fortune Has a Cousin in the Bronx (1970)
Quality Street (1937)
Quantez (1957)
Quantrill's Raiders (1958)
The Quare Fellow (1962)
Quatorze Juillet (1932)
Quebec (1951)
The Queen and the Cardinal (1937)
Queen Bee (1955)
Queen Christina (1934)
Queen Elizabeth (1912)
Queen for a Day (1951)
Queen of Babylon (1956)
Queen of Broadway (1942)
Queen of Burlesque (1946)
Queen of Outer Space (1958)
Queen of Sheba (1953)
The Queen of Spades (1948)
Queen of the Amazons (1947)
The Queens (1968)
The Queen's Necklace (1929)
Quentin Durward (1955)
Quest for Love (1971)
Quest for the Lost City (1954)
A Question of Adultery (1959)
Question Seven (1961)
Quick, Before It Melts (1964)
The Quick Gun (1964)
Quicksand (1950)
The Quiet American (1958)
The Quiet Gun (1957)
The Quiet Man (1952)
A Quiet Place in the Country (1969)
Quiet Please, Murder (1942)
The Quiller Memorandum (1966)
Quincannon, Frontier Scout (1956)
Quo Vadis? (1951)

A Quois Revent Les Jeunes Filles (1924)

R. P. M. (1970)
Rabbit, Run (1970)
The Rabbit Trap (1959)
Race Street (1948)
The Racers (1955)
Rachel and the Stranger (1948)
Rachel Rachel (1968)
Racing Fever (1964)
The Rack (1956)
The Racket (1951)
Radar Secret Service (1950)
Raffles (1940)
Raga (1971)
Rage (1966)
Rage at Dawn (1955)
A Rage to Live (1965)
The Raging Moon (see Long Ago Tomorrow) (1971)
The Raging Tide (1951)
The Raid (Razzia) (1947)
The Raid (1954)
Raid on Rommel (1971)
The Raiders (1952)
The Raiders (1963)
Raiders from Beneath the Sea (1965)
Raiders of San Joaquin (1943)
Raiders of Sunset Pass (1943)
Raiders of the Border (1944)
Raiders of the Range (1942)
Raiders of the Seven Seas (1953)
The Railroad Man (1965)
Railroaded (1947)
Rails into Laramie (1954)
The Railway Children (1970)
Rain (1929)
Rain for a Dusty Summer (1971)
The Rain People (1969)
The Rainbow (1944)
Rainbow Island (1944)
Rainbow Over Texas (1946)
The Rainmaker (1956)
The Rains Came (1939)
The Rains of Ranchipur (1955)
Raintree County (1957)
A Raisin in the Sun (1961)
Raising a Riot (1957)
Rally 'Round the Flag Boys! (1958)
Ramona (1928)
Ramona (1936)
Rampage (1963)
The Ramparts We Watch (1940)
Ramrod (1947)
Rancho Notorious (1952)
Random Harvest (1942)
Range Beyond the Blue (1947)
Range Law (1944)
Range Renegades (1948)
Ranger of Cherokee Strip (1949)
Rangers of Fortune (1940)
The Rangers Ride (1948)
Ransom (1956)
Rape on the Moor (1957)
Rapture (1965)
The Rare Breed (1966)
Rascal (1969)
Rashomon (1952)
Rasputin and the Empress (1933)
Rasputin, the Mad Monk (1966)
Le Rat D'Amerique (1964)
Rat Fink (1966)
The Rat Race (1960)
Rationing (1944)
Raton Pass (1951)
Rattle of a Simple Man (1964)
The Ravagers (1965)
The Raven (1948)
The Raven (1963)
Raw Deal (1948)
The Raw Edge (1956)
Raw Wind in Eden (1958)
Rawhide (1951)
The Rawhide Trail (1958)
The Rawhide Years (1956)
Raymie (1960)
The Razor's Edge (1946)
Razzia (1957)
Reach for Glory (1963)
Reach for the Sky (1957)
Reaching for the Moon (1917)
Reaching for the Moon (1931)
Reaching for the Stars (1958)
Reaching for the Sun (1941)
Reading for the People (1964)
The Real Glory (1939)
Reap the Wild Wind (1942)
Rear Window (1954)
Rebecca (1940)
Rebecca of Sunnybrook Farm (1932)
Rebel City (1953)

Rebel in Town (1956)
The Rebel Set (1959)
Rebel without a Cause (1955)
Recess (1969)
The Reckless Moment (1949)
The Reckoning (1969)
Recruits in Ingolstadt (1971)
The Red and the Black (1954)
The Red Badge of Courage (1951)
The Red Balloon (1956)
Red Canyon (1949)
The Red Circle (1916)
Red Dance (1928)
The Red Danube (1949)
Red Desert (1965)
Red Dragon (1967)
Red Garters (1954)
The Red Horses (1968)
The Red House (1947)
Red Lanterns (1964)
Red Light (1949)
Red Line 7000 (1965)
The Red Menace (1949)
Red Mountain (1951)
Red Planet Mars (1952)
The Red Pony (1949)
Red River (1948)
Red River Renegades (1946)
Red River Shore (1953)
The Red Shoes (1948)
Red Skies of Montana (1952)
Red Sky at Morning (1971)
The Red Stallion (1947)
Red Stallion in the Rockies (1949)
Red Snow (1952)
Red Sun (1971)
Red Sundown (1956)
The Red Tent (1971)
Red Tomahawk (1966)
Red, White and Black (1970)
Red, White and Blue (1971)
Redhead (1970)
The Redhead and the Cowboy (1950)
The Redhead from Wyoming (1952)
Redwood Forest Trail (1950)
Reflections in a Golden Eye (1967)
Reform School Girl (1957)
The Reformer and the Redhead (1950)
Reign of Terror (The Black Book) (1949)
The Reincarnate (1971)
The Reivers (1969)
Relax, Freddie (1966)
Relentless (1948)
The Reluctant Debutante (1958)
The Reluctant Saint (1962)
The Reluctant Widow (1950)
Remains to be Seen (1953)
The Remarkable Andrew (1942)
The Remarkable Mr. Pennypacker (1959)
Remember Pearl Harbor (1942)
Remember the Night (1940)
Rendezvous (1936)
Les Rendezvous Du Diable (1959)
Rendezvous 24 (1946)
Rendezvous with Annie (1946)
Rendezvous with Juliet (1949)
Renegade Girl (1947)
Renegades (1946)
Renegades of Sonora (1948)
Reno (1939)
Repeat Performance (1947)
Repulsion (1965)
Requiem for a Gunfighter (1965)
Requiem for a Heavyweight (1962)
The Rescue (1929)
The Rest Is Silence (1959)
The Restless Breed (1957)
The Restless Years (1958)
The Resurrection of Zachary Wheeler (1971)
Retreat, Hell! (1952)
Return from the Ashes (1965)
Return from the Sea (1954)
The Return of Count Yorga (1971)
The Return of Don Camillo (1956)
The Return of Dracula (1958)
The Return of Frank James (1940)
The Return of Jack Slade (1955)
The Return of Jesse James (1950)
The Return of Maxim Gorky (1936)
The Return of Mr. Moto (1965)

The Return of Monte Cristo (1946)
The Return of October (1948)
The Return of Peter Grimm (1935)
The Return of Rin Tin Tin (1947)
The Return of Ringo (1966)
Return of the Ape Man (1944)
Return of the Bad Man (1948)
The Return of the Fly (1959)
Return of the Frontiersman (1950)
Return of the Lash (1948)
The Return of the Scarlet Pimpernell (1938)
Return of the Seven (1966)
Return of the Texan (1952)
The Return of Ulysses (1915)
The Return of Vasili Bortnikov (1953)
The Return of Wildfire (1948)
Return to Paradise (1953)
Return to Peyton Place (1961)
Return to Treasure Island (1954)
Reunion (1936)
Reunion (1942)
Reunion in Reno (1951)
Reunion in Vienna (1933)
Un Revenant (1946)
Revenge (1928)
The Revenge of Don Mendo (1961)
Revenge of Frankenstein (1958)
Revenge of the Creature (1955)
Revenge of the Gladiators (1965)
Revenue Agent (1950)
Revolt at Fort Laramie (1957)
The Revolt of Gunner Asch (08/15) (1955)
The Revolt of Mamie Stover (1956)
The Revolt of the Slaves (1961)
Revolution, My A- (1970)
The Revolutionaries (1970)
The Revolutionary (1970)
Revolutionists (1936)
The Reward (1965)
Rhapsody (1954)
Rhapsody in Steel (1958)
Rhino! (1964)
Rhodes of Africa (1936)
Rhubarb (1951)
Rhubarb (1970)
Rhythm Inn (1951)
Rhythm Parade (1942)
Rice (1957)
Rich Man, Poor Girl (1938)
Rich, Young and Pretty (1951)
Richard III (1956)
The Richest Girl in the World (1934)
Ricochet Romance (1954)
Ride a Violent Mile (1957)
The Ride Back (1957)
Ride Beyond Vengeance (1966)
Ride Clear of Diablo (1954)
Ride 'Em Cowboy (1942)
Ride in the Whirlwind (1966)
Ride Lonesome (1959)
Ride Out for Revenge (1957)
Ride, Ryder, Ride! (1949)
Ride the High Country (1962)
Ride the High Iron (1956)
Ride the Man Down (1952)
Ride the Pink Horse (1947)
Ride, Vaquero (1953)
Rider from Tucson (1950)
Rider on the Rain (1970)
Riders of the Range (1949)
Riders of the Rio Grande (1943)
Riders to the Stars (1954)
Riding Shotgun (1954)
Rien Que Les Heures (1927)
Riffraff (1936)
Riff Raff (1947)
Rififi (1956)
Rififi in Tokyo (1963)
The Right Approach (1961)
Right Cross (1950)
Right On (1970)
The Right to Be Born (1971)
The Right to Love (1931)
Rimfire (1949)
The Ring (1952)
Ring of Bright Water (1969)
Ring of Fear (1954)
Ring of Fire (1961)
Rings on Her Fingers (1942)
Ringside (1949)
Rio (1939)
Rio Bravo (1959)
Rio Conchos (1964)
Rio Grande Patrol (1950)

Rio Grande Raiders (1946)
Rio Lobo (1970)
Riot (1968)
Riot in Cell Block 11 (1954)
Riot in Juvenile Prison (1959)
Riot on Sunset Strip (1967)
Rip-Off (1971)
Riptide (1934)
The Rise and Fall of Legs Diamond (1960)
The Rise and Fall of Michael Rimmer (1970)
Rise and Shine (1941)
The Rising of the Moon (1957)
The Risk (1961)
The River (1936)
The River (1951)
River Beat (1954)
The River Changes (1956)
The River Gang (1945)
River Lady (1948)
River of No Return (1954)
River of Unrest (1937)
Riverrun (1968)
The River's Edge (1957)
Road Agent (1952)
The Road Back (1937)
Road House (1948)
Road Show (1941)
Road to Alcatraz (1945)
Road to Bali (1952)
The Road to Denver (1955)
Road to Glory (1936)
Road to Happiness (1942)
The Road to Hong Kong (1962)
The Road to Life (1931)
Road to Morocco (1942)
Road to Rio (1947)
Road to Salina (1970)
Road to the Big House (1947)
Road to Utopia (1946)
Roadblock (1951)
Roar of the Crowd (1953)
Roaring City (1951)
Rob Roy, the Highland Rogue (1953)
Robber's Roost (1955)
Robbery (1967)
Robbery Under Arms (1958)
Robby (1968)
The Robe (1953)
Robin and the Seven Hoods (1964)
Robin Hood of El Dorado (1936)
Robinson Crusoe on Mars (1964)
Rock Island Trail (1950)
Rock, Pretty Baby (1956)
Rock-a-Bye Baby (1958)
Rockabilly Baby (1957)
The Rocket Man (1954)
Rocketship X-M (1950)
The Rocking Horse Winner (1949)
Rocky (1948)
Rocky Mountain (1950)
Rodan (1957)
Rodeo (1951)
Rodeo King and the Senorita (1951)
Roger Touhy--Gangster (1944)
Rogue Cop (1954)
Rogue River (1950)
Rogue's Gallery (1945)
Rogue's March (1952)
Rogues of Sherwood Forest (1950)
Rogue's Regiment (1948)
The Role of My Family in the Revolution (1971)
Roll on Texas Moon (1946)
Rolling Home (1947)
Roman Holiday (1953)
The Roman Spring of Mrs. Stone (1961)
Romance of a Horse Theif (1971)
Romance of Rosy Ridge (1947)
Romance of the West (1946)
Romance on the Range (1942)
Romance Sentimentale (1930)
Romanoff and Juliet (1961)
Rome Adventure (1962)
Rome, 11 o'clock (1952)
Romeo (1962)
Romeo and Julie (1968)
Romeo and Juliet (1936)
Romeo and Juliet (1954)
Romeo and Juliet (1968) (ballet)
La Ronde (1950)
The Roof (1956)
Roogie's Bump (1954)
The Rookie (1959)
Rookies on Parade (1941)
Room at the Top (1959)
Room for One More (1952)
Room 43 (1958)

Room Service (1938)
Rooney (1958)
The Roosevelt Story (1947)
The Rooster (1971)
The Roosters of Dawn (1971)
The Roots of Heaven (1958)
Rope (1948)
Rope of Sand (1949)
Rosanna (1956)
The Rose Bowl Story (1952)
A Rose for Everyone (1967)
Rose of Cimarron (1952)
Rose of the Rio Grande (1938)
Rose of the Yukon (1949)
The Rose Tattoo (1955)
Roseanna McCoy (1949)
Rosemary (1958)
Rosemary's Baby (1968)
Roses Are Red (1947)
Rosie (1967)
Rosie the Riveter (1944)
Rotten to the Core (1964)
La Roue (1922)
Rough Night in Jericho (1967)
The Rough Riders (1926)
Rough Riders of Cheyenne (1945)
Rough Riders of Durango (1951)
Roughly Speaking (1945)
Roughshod (1949)
The Rounders (1965)
Roxie Hart (1942)
Royal Affair in Versailles (1954)
The Royal African Rifles (1953)
The Royal Hunt of the Sun (1969)
Royal River (1952)
A Royal Scandal (1945)
The Royal Tour of Queen Elizabeth and Philip (1954)
The Rubaiyat of Omar Khayyam (1922)
Rubens (1948)
Ruby Gentry (1952)
The Rules of the Game (1939)
Rulers of the Sea (1939)
Rumble on the Docks (1956)
Run, Angel, Run (1969)
Run for Cover (1955)
Run for the Sun (1956)
Run Like a Thief (1968)
Run of the Arrow (1957)
Run Silent, Run Deep (1958)
Run Wild, Run Free (1969)
The Runaround (1946)
The Running Man (1963)
Running Target (1956)
Running Wild (1955)
Russian Ballerina (1947)
The Russian Question (1948)
The Russians Are Coming, the Russians Are Coming (1966)
Rustlers (1949)
Rustlers on Horseback (1950)
Ruthless (1948)
Rx Murder (1958)
Ryan's Daughter (1970)

S. O. S. Coast Guard (1942)
S. O. S. Pacific (1960)
Saadia (1953)
Sabaka (1955)
Sabotage (1939)
Saboteur (1942)
Sabre Jet (1953)
Sabrina (1954)
Sabu and the Magic Ring (1957)
Sacco and Vanzetti (1971)
Sacred Fire (1971)
The Sad Horse (1959)
The Sad Sack (1957)
Saddle Legion (1951)
Saddle Pals (1947)
Saddle the Wind (1958)
Saddle Tramp (1950)
Sadismo (1967)
Safari (1940)
Safari (1956)
Safari Drums (1953)
Safe at Home! (1962)
The Safecracker (1958)
The Safety Match (1954)
Saginaw Trail (1953)
Sahara (1943)
Saigon (1948)
Sail a Crooked Ship (1961)
Sailor Beware (1951)
Sailor of the King (1953)
The Sailor Takes a Wife (1945)
St. Benny the Dip (1951)
Saint Denis, in These Times (1970)
Saint Joan (1957)
St. Louis Blues (1958)
Saint Margaret of Cortona (1955)

St. Michael Had a Rooster (1971)
The St. Valentine's Day Massacre (1967)
The Sainted Sisters (1948)
Saintly Sinners (1962)
The Saints from Krajcarek (1970)
The Saint's Girl Friday (1954)
Saladino (1966)
La Salamandre (1971)
Salavat Yulayev (1941)
Sally and Saint Anne (1952)
Salome (1922)
Salome (1953)
Salome Where She Danced (1945)
Salt and Pepper (1968)
Salt Lake Raiders (1950)
Salt to the Devil (1949)
Saltanat (1955)
Salty O'Rourke (1945)
Saludos Amigos (1942)
Salute e Baci (1952)
A Salute to France (1944)
Salute to the Marines (1943)
Sam Whiskey (1969)
Samar (1962)
Samoa (1956)
Samson and Delilah (1949)
Samurai (1955)
Samurai Banners (1969)
San Antone Ambush (1949)
San Antonio (1945)
San Diego, I Love You (1944)
San Francisco (1936)
San Francisco (1945)
The San Francisco Story (1952)
San Quentin (1946)
Sanctuary (1961)
Sand (1949)
The Sand Pebbles (1966)
Sanders of the River (1935)
The Sandpiper (1965)
Sands of Iwo Jima (1949)
Sands of the Kalahari (1965)
The Sandwich Man (1966)
Sangaree (1953)
Sans Famile (1958)
Sans Laisser D'Adresse (1950)
Santa Fe (1951)
Santa Fe Passage (1955)
Santa Fe Saddlemates (1945)
Santa Fe Scouts (1943)
Santa Fe Trail (1941)
Santiago (1956)
Sapho (1970)
Sapphire (1959)
Saraband (1948)
The Saracen Blade (1954)
Saratoga (1937)
Saratoga Trunk (1945)
Sardinia: Ransom (1968)
Sarge Goes to College (1947)
Sarong Girl (1943)
Saskatchewan (1954)
The Satan Bug (1965)
Satan in High Heels (1962)
Satan Never Sleeps (1962)
Satanic Rhapsody (1915)
Satan's Cradle (1949)
Satan's Sadists (1970)
Satan's Satellites (1958)
Saturday's Children (1940)
Saturday's Hero (1951)
The Savage (1952)
Savage Drums (1951)
Savage Frontier (1953)
The Savage Guns (1962)
The Savage Horde (1950)
The Savage Innocents (1960)
Savage Sam (1963)
Savage Splendor (1949)
Savage Triangle (1952)
The Savage Wild (1970)
The Saving of Bill Blewett (1936)
The Savior (1971)
Sawdust and Tinsel (1953)
Sawdust Paradise (1928)
The Saxon Charm (1948)
Say Hello to Yesterday (1971)
Say One for Me (1959)
Sayonara (1957)
The Scalphunters (1968)
Scandal at Scourie (1953)
A Scandal in Paris (1946)
Scandal, Inc. (1956)
Scandal Sheet (1952)
Scandalous John (1971)
The Scapegoat (1959)
The Scar of Dracula (1970)
Scaramouche (1952)
Scared Stiff (1953)
The Scarf (1951)
Scarface (1932)
Scarlet Angel (1952)

The Scarlet Claw (1944)
The Scarlet Clue (1945)
The Scarlet Coat (1955)
The Scarlet Hour (1956)
The Scarlet Letter (1926)
The Scarlet Spear (1954)
Scarlet Street (1945)
Scattergood Baines (1941)
Scattergood Rides High (1942)
Scattergood Survives a Murder (1942)
The Scavengers (1970)
The Scene of the Crash (1971)
Scene of the Crime (1949)
Scent of Mystery (1960)
Schoolgirl Report (1970)
Scorned Flesh (1948)
Scotland Yard Dragnet (1958)
Scotland Yard Investigator (1945)
Scott of the Antarctic (1948)
The Scoundrel (1935)
Scratch Harry (1969)
Scream and Scream Again (1970)
Scream of Fear (1961)
Screaming Eagles (1956)
Scudda Hoo! Scudda Hay! (1948)
The Sea Around Us (1953)
The Sea Chase (1955)
Sea Devils (1937)
Sea Devils (1953)
The Sea Hawk (1940)
The Sea Hornet (1951)
The Sea Horse (1934)
Sea of Grass (1947)
Sea of Lost Ships (1953)
The Sea Pirate (1967)
The Sea Shall Not Have Them (1955)
Sea Spoilers (1936)
Sea Tiger (1952)
Sea Wife (1957)
The Sea Wolf (1941)
Sealed Cargo (1951)
Sealed Verdict (1948)
Seance on a Wet Afternoon (1964)
The Search (1948)
The Search for Bridey Murphy (1956)
Search for Danger (1949)
Search for Paradise (1957)
The Searchers (1956)
The Searching Wind (1946)
Seaside Swingers (1965)
Season of Passion (1961)
Seasons of Our Love (1966)
Second Chance (1947)
Second Chance (1950)
Second Chance (1953)
The Second Face (1951)
Second Fiddle (1939)
The Second Greatest Sex (1955)
Second-Hand Wife (1932)
Second Honeymoon (1937)
The Second Time Around (1961)
The Second Woman (1951)
Seconds (1966)
Secret Agent (1936)
Secret Agent Fireball (1966)
Secret Beyond the Door (1947)
Secret Ceremony (1968)
Secret Command (1944)
The Secret Door (1964)
The Secret Fury (1950)
The Secret Garden (1949)
The Secret Heart (1946)
The Secret Invasion (1964)
The Secret Land (1948)
The Secret Life of an American Wife (1968)
The Secret Life of Walter Mitty (1947)
Secret of Blood Island (1965)
The Secret of Convict Lake (1951)
Secret of Deep Harbor (1961)
The Secret of Magic Island (1965)
The Secret of Monte Cristo (1961)
The Secret of My Success (1965)
The Secret of Santa Vittoria (1969)
Secret of the Incas (1954)
The Secret of the Purple Reef (1960)
Secret of Treasure Mountain (1956)
The Secret Partner (1961)
The Secret Place (1958)
Secret Service Investigator (1948)

Secret Seven (1966)
Secret Venture (1955)
The Secret War of Harry Frigg (1968)
The Secret Ways (1961)
Secrets of a Secretary (1931)
Secrets of a Sorority Girl (1946)
Secrets of Life (1956)
Secrets of Monte Carlo (1951)
Secrets of the Reef (1956)
Secrets of the Underground (1943)
Security Risk (1954)
Seduced and Abandoned (1964)
The Seducers (1962)
See Here, Private Hargrove (1944)
See My Lawyer (1945)
See No Evil (1971)
The Seed of Man (1970)
La Sel de la Terre (1951)
The Sellout (1951)
Seminole (1953)
Seminole Uprising (1955)
The Senator Was Indiscreet (1947)
Send Me No Flowers (1964)
Senechal the Magnificent (1957)
Sensualita (The Barefoot Savage) (1953)
Sentimental Journey (1946)
Separate Tables (1958)
The September Affair (1950)
September Storm (1960)
Serafino (1968)
Serengeti Shall Not Die (1960)
The Sergeant (1968)
Sergeant Deadhead (1965)
Sergeant Rutledge (1960)
Sergeant York (1941)
The Sergeant's Daughter (1955)
Sergeants Three (1962)
Serpent of the Nile (1953)
Servant's Entrance (1934)
The Set-Up (1949)
Seven Angry Men (1955)
Seven Capital Sins (1962)
Seven Cities of Gold (1955)
Seven Days Ashore (1944)
Seven Days in May (1964)
Seven Day's Leave (1942)
Seven Days to Noon (1950)
Seven Doors to Death (1943)
711 Ocean Drive (1950)
Seven Faces (1929)
Seven Faces of Dr. Lao (1964)
Seven Golden Men (1965)
Seven Golden Men Strike Again (1966)
Seven Guns for the MacGregors (1968)
Seven Guns to Mesa (1958)
Seven Guys and a Gal (1967)
The Seven Hills of Rome (1958)
Seven Keys to Baldpate (1936)
Seven Keys to Baldpate (1947)
The Seven Little Foys (1955)
Seven Men from Now (1956)
Seven Miles from Alcatraz (1942)
The Seven Minutes (1971)
Seven Seas to Calais (1963)
Seven Sinners (1936)
Seven Sinners (1940)
Seven Slaves Against the World (1965)
Seven Sweethearts (1942)
Seven Thieves (1960)
Seven Times a Day (1971)
Seven Ways from Sundown (1960)
Seven Women (1965)
Seven Women from Hell (1961)
Seven Wonders of the World (1956)
The Seven Year Itch (1955)
Seventh Cavalry (1956)
The Seventh Cross (1944)
The Seventh Dawn (1964)
The Seventh Floor (1967)
Seventh Heaven (1926)
Seventh Heaven (1937)
The Seventh Juror (1964)
The Seventh Sin (1957)
The Seventh Veil (1945)
The Seventh Victim (1943)
The Seventh Voyage of Sinbad (1958)
A Severed Head (1971)
Sex and the Single Girl (1964)
Sex Kittens Go to College (1960)
The Sex of the Angels (1968)
Sex Perverse (1970)
Sex Power (1970)
Shack Out on 101 (1955)
Shadow in the Sky (1951)

Shadow of a Doubt (1943)
Shadow of a Woman (1946)
Shadow of Fear (1956)
Shadow of Suspicion (1944)
Shadow of Terror (1945)
The Shadow of the Cat (1961)
Shadow of the Eagle (1955)
Shadow of the Thin Man (1941)
Shadow on the Wall (1950)
Shadow on the Window (1957)
The Shadow Returns (1946)
Shadows (1961)
Shadows on the Sage (1942)
Shady Lady (1945)
Shaft (1971)
Shaggy (1948)
The Shaggy Dog (1959)
Shake Hands with Murder (1944)
Shake Hands with the Devil (1959)
Shakedown (1950)
The Shakedown (1960)
Shakespeare: Soul of an Age (1964)
Shakespeare Wallah (1966)
The Shakiest Gun in the West (1968)
Shane (1953)
Shanghai (1935)
The Shanghai Chest (1948)
Shanghai Express (1932)
Shanghai Gesture (1942)
The Shanghai Story (1954)
Shantytown (1943)
Shark River (1953)
The Sharkfighters (1956
She (1935)
She (1965)
She and He (1969)
She Couldn't Say No (1954)
She Devil (1957)
She Knew All the Answers (1941)
She Played with Fire (1958)
She Went to the Races (1945)
The She Wolf (1954)
She-Wolf of London (1946)
She Wore a Yellow Ribbon (1949)
She Wouldn't Say Yes (1945)
Shed No Tears (1948)
The Sheepman (1958)
Shenandoah (1965)
Shep Comes Home (1948)
Shepherd (1971)
Shepherd of the Hills (1941)
Shepherd of the Ozarks (1942)
Sheriff of Cimarron (1945)
The Sheriff of Fractured Jaw (1958)
The Sheriff of Medicine Bow (1948)
Sheriff of Redwood Valley (1946)
Sheriff of Wichita (1949)
Sherlock Holmes (1932)
Sherlock Holmes and the Secret Weapon (1942)
Sherlock Holmes and the Voice of Terror (1942)
Sherlock Holmes Faces Death (1943)
Sherlock Holmes in Washington (1943)
Shield for Murder (1954)
Shinbone Alley (1971)
Shine On, Harvest Moon (1938)
Shine On, Harvest Moon (1944)
The Shining Hour (1938)
Ship of Fools (1965)
The Ship that Died of Shame (P. T. Raiders) (1956)
The Ship Was Loaded (1957)
Ships with Wings (1942)
Shock (1946)
Shock Corridor (1963)
Shock Treatment (1964)
Shockproof (1949)
The Shoes of the Fisherman (1968)
Shoot First (1953)
Shoot Loud, Louder ... I Don't Understand (1966)
Shoot Out (1971)
Shoot-Out at Medicine Bend (1957)
Shoot the Piano Player (1962)
Shoot to Kill (1947)
The Shop Around the Corner (1940)
The Shop on Main Street (1965)
The Shopworn Angel (1938)
Shors (1939)
Short Cut to Hell (1957)
Short Grass (1950)
Short Is the Summer (1969)
The Shot from a Violin Case (1965)

A Shot in the Dark (1964)
Shotgun (1955)
Shoulder Arms (1918)
Show Them No Mercy (1935)
Showdown (1963)
The Showdown (1950)
Showdown at Abilene (1956)
Showdown at Boot Hill (1958)
Showtime (1948)
The Shrike (1955)
Shut My Big Mouth (1942)
The Shuttered Room (1967)
The Sicilians (1969)
The Sickle or the Cross (1949)
Side Street (1949)
The Sidelong Glances of a Pigeon Kicker (Pigeons) (1970)
Sideshow (1950)
Sidewalks of London (1940)
Siege at Red River (1954)
The Siege of Syracuse (1962)
Siege of the Saxons (1963)
Siegfried (1923)
Siegfried (1967)
Sierra (1950)
Sierra Baron (1958)
Sierra Passage (1950)
Sierra Stranger (1957)
Sign of the Cross (1932)
Sign of the Gladiator (1959)
Sign of the Pagan (1954)
The Sign of the Ram (1948)
The Sign of Zorro (1960)
Signore and Signori (1966)
Signpost to Murder (1964)
Signs of Life (1968)
Silence est D'or (1947)
The Silencers (1966)
Silent Barriers (1937)
The Silent Call (1961)
Silent Conflict (1948)
The Silent Enemy (1958)
Silent Friends (1971)
Silent Partner (1944)
The Silent World (1956)
Silk Stockings (1957)
The Silk Noose (1948)
The Silken Affair (1957)
The Silver Bullet (1942)
The Silver Chalice (1954)
Silver City (1951)
Silver City Bonanza (1951)
Silver City Kid (1944)
The Silver Cord (1933)
Silver Lode (1954)
Silver Queen (1942)
Silver Raiders (1950)
Silver Range (1946)
Silver River (1948)
Silver Skates (1943)
Silver Trails (1948)
The Silver Whip (1953)
Simba (1955)
Simon and Laura (1956)
Simon, King of the Witches (1971)
A Simple Case of Money (1952)
Simply Maria (1970)
Sin Town (1942)
Sinbad the Sailor (1947)
Since You Went Away (1944)
Sinful Davey (1969)
Sing and Like It (1934)
Sing, Boy, Sing (1958)
Singapore (1947)
The Singer Not the Song (1961)
Singing Guns (1950)
The Singing Nun (1966)
Sinister Journey (1948)
Sink the Bismark! (1960)
Sinner Take All (1936)
Sins of Casanova (1957)
Sins of Jezebel (1953)
Sins of Man (1936)
The Sins of Rachel Cade (1961)
Sins of Rome (1954)
The Sins of Rose Bernd (1959)
Sins of the Fathers (1928)
Sioux City Sue (1946)
Siren of Atlantis (1948)
Sirocco (1951)
Sister Kenny (1946)
The Sisters (1938)
The Sisters (1957)
Sitting Pretty (1948)
Situation Hopeless, but Not Serious (1965)
Six Black Horses (1962)
Six Bridges to Cross (1955)
Six Gun for Hire (1946)
Six-Gun Gospel (1943)
Six-Gun Serenade (1947)
Six Juin a L'Aube (1947)
633 Squadron (1964)
16 Fathoms Deep (1948)

Sixty Glorious Years (1938)
69 (1970)
Skabenga (1955)
Skaterdater (1965)
Ski Fascination (1966)
Ski Fever (1969)
Ski on the Wild Side (1967)
Ski Party (1965)
Skidoo (1968)
Skin Game (1971)
The Skipper Surprised His Wife (1950)
The Skull (1965)
Skullduggery (1970)
Sky Commando (1953)
Sky Dragons (1949)
Sky Full of Moon (1952)
Sky High (1951)
The Sky Is Blue (1971)
Sky Liner (1949)
The Sky Pirate (1970)
Sky West and Crooked (1966)
Skylark (1941)
Skyline (1931)
The Sky's the Limit (1943)
Slander (1956)
The Slasher (1953)
Slattery's Hurricane (1949)
Slaughter on Tenth Avenue (1957)
Slaughter Trail (1951)
Slave Girl (1947)
Slave Trade in the World Today (1964)
Slaves (1969)
Slaves of Babylon (1953)
Sleep My Love (1948)
Sleeping Beauty (1959)
The Sleeping Car Murder (1966)
Sleeping Car to Trieste (1948)
The Sleeping City (1950)
Sleepy Lagoon (1943)
Sleepytime Gal (1942)
The Slender Thread (1965)
Slide, Kelly, Slide (1927)
A Slight Case of Larceny (1953)
Slightly Dangerous (1943)
Slightly French (1949)
Slightly Honorable (1940)
Slightly Scarlet (1956)
Slim Carter (1957)
The Small Black Room (1952)
The Small Hours (1962)
Small Town Girl (1936)
The Small World of Sammy Lee (1963)
The Smallest Show on Earth (1957)
Smart Alecs (1942)
Smart Girls Don't Talk (1948)
Smart Guy (1944)
Smart Woman (1948)
Smash Up--The Story of a Woman (1947)
The Smashing Bird I Used to Know (1969)
Smashing Time (1967)
Smic, Smac, Smoc (1971)
Smiles of a Summer Night (1957)
Smiley (1957)
Smiley Gets a Gun (1959)
Smilin' Through (1932)
Smith (1969)
Smoke Signals (1955)
Smoky (1946)
Smoky (1966)
Smooth as Silk (1946)
The Smugglers (1948)
Smuggler's Cove (1948)
Smuggler's Gold (1951)
Smuggler's Island (1951)
Snafu (1946)
The Snake Pit (1948)
Snake River Desperadoes (1951)
The Snake Woman (1961)
The Sniper (1952)
Sniper's Ridge (1961)
The Snorkel (1958)
The Snow Creature (1954)
Snow Dog (1950)
The Snow Queen (1959)
Snowbound (1948)
Snowfire (1958)
The Snows of Kilimanjaro (1952)
So Big (1953)
So Dark the Night (1946)
So Dear to My Heart (1948)
So Ends Our Night (1941)
So Evil My Love (1948)
So Goes My Love (1946)
So Long at the Fair (1950)
So Long Gulliver (1971)
So Proudly We Hail (1943)
So Red the Rose (1935)
So This is New York (1948)

So This Is Paris (1954)
So Young, So Bad (1950)
Society of Unrest (1969)
Socrates (1971)
Sodom and Gomorrah (1963)
Sofia (1948)
The Soft Skin (1964)
Sol Madrid (1968)
The Soldier and the Lady (1937)
Soldier Blue (1970)
Soldier in the Rain (1963)
Soldier of Fortune (1955)
Soldiers Three (1951)
The Solid Gold Cadillac (1956)
Solo (1970)
Solomon and Sheba (1959)
Sombrero (1953)
The Sombrero Kid (1942)
Some Came Running (1958)
Some Girls Do (1969)
Some Kind of a Nut (1969)
Some Like It Hot (1959)
Some of My Best Friends Are ... (1971)
Someone to Remember (1943)
Something Big (1971)
Something for Everyone (1970)
Something for the Birds (1952)
Something in the Wind (1947)
Something Money Can't Buy (1953)
Something of Value (1957)
Something to Live For (1952)
Something to Shout About (1943)
Something to Sing About (1937)
Something Wild (1961)
Sometimes a Great Notion (1971)
Somewhere in the Night (1946)
Somewhere I'll Find You (1942)
Son of a Badman (1949)
Son of a Gunfighter (1966)
Son of Ali Baba (1952)
Son of Billy the Kid (1949)
The Son of Captain Blood (1964)
The Son of Dr. Jekyll (1951)
Son of Dracula (1943)
Son of Flubber (1963)
Son of Fury (1942)
Son of God's Country (1948)
Son of Kong (1934)
Son of Lassie (1945)
Son of Paleface (1952)
The Son of Robin Hood (1959)
Son of Sinbad (1955)
A Song About Heroes (1932)
Song About the Merchant Kalashnikov (1909)
A Song for Miss Julie (1945)
Song of Arizona (1946)
The Song of Bernadette (1943)
Song of Ceylon (1934)
Song of India (1949)
Song of Life (1930)
Song of Love (1947)
Song of Mexico (1945)
Song of Russia (1943)
Song of Scheherazade (1947)
Song of Songs (1933)
Song of Surrender (1949)
The Song of the Balalaika (1971)
Song of the Drifter (1948)
Song of the Islands (1942)
Song of the Land (1953)
Song of the North (1917)
Song of the Sarong (1945)
Song of the South (1946)
Song of the Thin Man (1947)
Sons and Lovers (1960)
Sons of Adventure (1948)
The Sons of Katie Elder (1965)
Sons of the Pioneers (1942)
Sophie's Ways (1970)
The Sorcerers (1967)
The Sorceress (1956)
Sorority Girl (1957)
Sorrowful Jones (1949)
The Sorrows of Satan (1926)
Sorry, Wrong Number (1948)
Souls at Sea (1937)
The Sound and the Fury (1959)
The Sound of Fury (1950)
Sound Off! (1952)
South of Caliente (1951)
South of Monterey (1946)
South of Pago Pago (1940)
South of Rio (1949)
South of St. Louis (1949)
South of Santa Fe (1942)
South of the Rio Grande (1945)
South Pacific Trail (1952)
South Riding (1937)
South Sea Adventure (1958)
South Sea Sinner (1950)
South Sea Woman (1953)

A Southern Yankee (1948)
The Southerner (1945)
Southside 1-1000 (1950)
Southwest Passage (1954)
The Space Children (1958)
Space Master X-7 (1958)
Spaceflight IC-1 (1965)
A Spanish Affair (1958)
Spanish Earth (1937)
The Spanish Gardener (1957)
The Spanish Main (1945)
Spanking at School (1969)
Spartacus (1960)
Spawn of the North (1938)
Speaking of Murder (1959)
Special Agent (1949)
Special Delivery (1955)
Special Investigator (1936)
Specter of the Rose (1946)
Speed Crazy (1959)
Speed to Spare (1948)
Speedway (1968)
Spellbound (1945)
Spencer's Mountain (1963)
Spendthrift (1936)
La Spiaggia (1953)
The Spice of Life (1949)
The Spider (1931)
The Spider (1945)
The Spider and the Fly (1949)
Spider Woman (1944)
The Spider's Web (1965)
Spies (1928)
Spin a Dark Web (1956)
Spinout (1966)
The Spiral Road (1962)
The Spiral Staircase (1946)
The Spirit Is Willing (1967)
The Spirit of St. Louis (1957)
The Spiritualist (Amazing Mr. X) (1948)
Spitfire (1934)
Spitfire (see The First of the Few) (1942)
Splendor (1935)
Splendor in the Grass (1961)
The Split (1968)
Split Second (1953)
The Spoilers (1942)
The Spoilers (1955)
Spoilers of the Forest (1957)
Spoilers of the Plains (1951)
Spook Busters (1946)
Spook Chasers (1957)
A Sporting Chance (1945)
The Sporting Club (1971)
Spotlight Scandals (1943)
Spring (1947)
Spring Affair (1960)
Spring and Port Wine (1970)
Spring Madness (1938)
Spring Offensive (1940)
Spring Parade (1940)
Spring Reunion (1957)
Springfield Rifle (1952)
Springtime in Texas (1945)
Springtime in the Rockies (1942)
Springtime in the Sierras (1947)
The Spy (1927)
Spy Chasers (1955)
Spy Hunt (1950)
Spy in the Sky (1958)
Spy in Your Eye (1966)
The Spy Who Came in from the Cold (1965)
The Spy with a Cold Nose (1966)
The Spy with My Face (1966)
Squad Car (1960)
Square Dance Jubilee (1949)
Squadron 992 (1940)
Square Dance Katy (1950)
The Square Jungle (1955)
Square of Violence (1963)
The Square Ring (1955)
The Square Root of Zero (1965)
The Squaw Man (1931)
Squeeze a Flower (1970)
Stablemates (1938)
Stage Fright (1950)
Stage from Blue River (1951)
Stage Struck (1948)
Stage Struck (1958)
Stage to Mesa City (1948)
Stage to Thunder Rock (1964)
Stage to Tucson (1950)
Stagecoach (1939)
Stagecoach (1966)
Stagecoach Buckaroo (1942)
Stagecoach Express (1942)
Stagecoach Kid (1949)
Stagecoach to Dancer's Rock (1962)
Stagecoach to Fury (1956)
Stagedoor Canteen (1943)
Staircase (1969)
Stairway to Heaven (1946)

Stakeout on Dope Street (1958)
Stalag 17 (1953)
Stalingrad (1943)
The Stalking Moon (1968)
Stallion Road (1947)
Stampede (1949)
The Stand at Apache River (1953)
Stand By for Action (1942)
Stand-In (1937)
Stand Up and Cheer (1934)
Stand Up and Fight (1939)
Standing Room Only (1944)
The Star (1953)
Star in the Dust (1956)
A Star Is Born (1937)
Star of India (1956)
The Star of Texas (1953)
The Star of the Season (1971)
Star-Spangled Girl (1971)
Star Spangled Rhythm (1942)
Stardust on the Sage (1942)
Stars (1958)
The Stars are Singing (1953)
Stars in My Crown (1950)
The Stars Look Down (1941)
Stars Over Texas (1946)
Start the Revolution without Me (1970)
State Department File 649 (1949)
State of the Union (1948)
State Penitentiary (1950)
State Secret (The Great Manhunt) (1950)
Station Six--Sahara (1964)
Station West (1948)
The Statue (1971)
Stay Away, Joe (1968)
The Steagle (1971)
Steamboat 'Round the Bend (1935)
The Steel Bayonet (1958)
The Steel Claw (1961)
The Steel Helmet (1950)
The Steel Jungle (1956)
The Steel Lady (1953)
The Steel Trap (1952)
Stella (1950)
Stella (1957)
Stenka Razin (1908)
Step By Step (1946)
Stepchild (1947)
Stephanie (1959)
The Steppe (1963)
Steppin' in Society (1945)
Steps of the Ballet (1948)
The Sterile Cuckoo (1969)
Sticks and Stones (1970)
Stiletto (1969)
Stingaree (1934)
The Stolen Air-Ship (1969)
Stolen Hours (1963)
A Stolen Life (1939)
A Stolen Life (1946)
The Stone (1965)
The Stone Flower (1946)
Stop (1971)
Stop Me Before I Kill (1961)
Stop Press Girl (1949)
Stop that Cab (1951)
Stop Train 349 (1964)
Stop, You're Killing Me (1952)
Stopover Tokyo (1957)
Stork Bites Man (1947)
The Stork Club (1945)
Storm at Daybreak (1933)
Storm Center (1956)
Storm Fear (1956)
Storm Over Lisbon (1944)
Storm Over the Nile (1956)
Storm over Tibet (1951)
Storm over Wyoming (1950)
The Storm Rider (1957)
Storm Warning (1950)
The Storm Within (1949)
Stormbound (1951)
Stormy, the Thoroughbred (1954)
Story of a Girl Alone (1969)
The Story of a Woman (1970)
The Story of Dr. Wassell (1944)
The Story of Esther Costello (1957)
The Story of G.I. Joe (1945)
The Story of Louis Pasteur (1936)
The Story of Mankind (1957)
The Story of Molly X (1949)
The Story of Ruth (1960)
The Story of Seabiscuit (1949)
Story of Shirley Yorke (1950)
The Story of Silver (1955)
The Story of the Count of Monte Cristo (1962)
The Story of Three Loves (1953)
The Story of Time (1949)
The Story of Will Rogers (1952)

The Story of Vickie (1958)
The Story on Page One (1959)
Stowaway (1937)
Stowaway Girl (1957)
Stowaway in the Sky (1960)
La Strada (1954)
Strait-Jacket (1964)
A Strange Adventure (1956)
Strange Affair (1944)
The Strange Affair (1968)
Strange Bargain (1949)
Strange Bedfellows (1964)
Strange Cargo (1940)
The Strange Case of Dr. Manning (1958)
The Strange Case of Dr. RX (1942)
Strange Confession (1945)
Strange Conquest (1946)
The Strange Death of Adolf Hitler (1943)
Strange Deception (Il Cristo Prohibito) (1953)
The Strange Door (1951)
Strange Fascination (1952)
Strange Gamble (1949)
Strange Holiday (1946)
Strange Illusion (1945)
Strange Impersonation (1946)
Strange Intruder (1956)
Strange Journey (1946)
Strange Lady in Town (1955)
The Strange Love of Martha Ivers (1946)
The Strange Mrs. Crane (1948)
The Strange One (1957)
Strange Triangle (1946)
The Strange Vice of Signora Ward (1971)
Strange Victory (1948)
Strange Victory (1964)
Strange Voyage (1945)
The Strange Woman (1946)
Strange World (1952)
The Stranger (1946)
The Stranger (1967)
Stranger at My Door (1956)
The Stranger from Pecos (1943)
Stranger from Santa Fe (1945)
The Stranger In Between (1952)
The Stranger In My Arms (1959)
Stranger In the House (1967)
A Stranger in Town (1943)
A Stranger in Town (1968)
A Stranger Knocks (1963)
The Stranger Left No Card (1954)
Stranger on Horseback (1955)
Stranger on the Prowl (1953)
The Stranger on the Third Floor (1940)
The Stranger Returns (1968)
The Stranger Wore a Gun (1953)
The Stranger's Hand (1955)
Strangers in the City (1962)
Strangers in the Night (1945)
Strangers on a Train (1951)
Strangers When We Meet (1960)
The Strangler (1964)
Strangler of the Swamp (1945)
The Stranglers of Bombay (1960)
Strategic Air Command (1955)
Strategy of Terror (1969)
The Stratton Story (1949)
Straw Dogs (1971)
Strawberry Blonde (1941)
Street Angel (1928)
Street Bandits (1951)
Street Corner (1948)
Street of Chance (1942)
Street of Darkness (1958)
Street of Sinners (1957)
Street Scene (1931)
The Street with No Name (1948)
A Streetcar Named Desire (1951)
Streets of Laredo (1949)
Streets of San Francisco (1949)
Stricken Peninsula (1945)
Strictly Dishonorable (1951)
Strictly Dynamite (1934)
Strike It Rich (1948)
Strike Up the Band (1940
A String of Beads (1947)
The Strip (1951)
The Stripper (1963)
Strogoff (1970)
Stromboli (1950)
The Stud (1970)
The Student Prince (1954)
Studs Lonigan (1960)
Submarine (1928)
Submarine Alert (1943)
Submarine Command (1951)

Submarine D-1 (1937)
Submarine Patrol (1938)
Subterfuge (1969)
The Subterraneans (1960)
The Subversives (1967)
Such Good Friends (1971)
Success at Any Price (1934)
Sudan (1945)
Sudden Danger (1955)
Sudden Fear (1952)
The Sudden Wealth of the Poor People of Kombach (1971)
Suddenly (1954)
Suddenly It's Spring (1947)
Suddenly Last Summer (1959)
Suez (1938)
Sugarfoot (1951)
Suicide Battalion (1958)
Suicide Squadron (1941)
The Suitor (1963)
The Sullivans (1944)
Sullivan's Empire (1967)
Sullivan's Travels (1941)
The Sultans (1966)
The Sultan's Daughter (1943)
Summer and Smoke (1961)
Summer Love (1958)
Summer Magic (1963)
Summer of '42 (1971)
A Summer Place (1959)
Summer Storm (1944)
Summer Trail (1970)
Summertime (1955)
Summit (1968)
The Sun Also Rises (1957)
Sun and Shadow (1961)
The Sun Never Sets (1939)
The Sun Sets at Dawn (1950)
The Sun Shines Bright (1953)
Sun Valley Cyclone (1946)
Sunday Dinner for a Soldier (1944)
Sunday in New York (1963)
Sundays and Cybele (1962)
Sundown (1941)
Sundown at Santa Fe (1948)
The Sundown Kid (1942)
The Sundowners (1950)
Sunflower (1970)
Sunny Beach Revolution (1971)
Sunny Side Up (1929)
Sunrise (1926)
Sunrise at Campobello (1960)
Sunset Boulevard (1950)
Sunset Carson Rides Again (1948)
Sunset in Eldorado (1945)
Sunset in the Desert (1942)
Sunset in the West (1950)
Sunset Pass (1946)
Superman and the Mole Men (1951)
Support Your Local Gunfighter (1971)
Support Your Local Sheriff (1969)
Suppose They Gave a War and Nobody Came (1970)
Surf and Seaweed (1931)
Surprise Package (1960)
Surrender (1950)
Surrender--Hell! (1959)
Survival, 1967 (1968)
Susan and God (1940)
Susan Slade (1961)
Susan Slept Here (1954)
Susanna Pass (1949)
Susannah of the Mounties (1939)
The Suspect (1944)
Suspense (1946)
Suspicion (1941)
Sutter's Gold (1936)
Suzy (1936)
Svengali (1955)
Swamp Fire (1946)
The Swan (1956)
Swanee River (1940)
Sweater Girl (1942)
Sweden--Heaven and Hell (1969)
A Swedish Love Story (1970)
Swedish Wedding Night (1965)
Sweepings (1933)
Sweet Bird of Youth (1962)
The Sweet Body of Deborah (1969)
Sweet Ecstasy (1963)
Sweet Kisses and Languid Caresses (1970)
Sweet Love Bitter (1967)
Sweet November (1968)
The Sweet Ride (1968)
Sweet Savior (1971)
Sweet Smell of Success (1957)
Sweet Sweetback's Baadassss Song (1971)
Sweetheart of Sigma Chi (1946)
Sweetheart of the Navy (1936)

Sweethearts on Parade (1953)
Swell Guy (1946)
The Swimmer (1968)
Swing Fever (1943)
Swing Parade of 1946 (1946)
Swing Shift Maisie (1943)
Swing Your Lady (1938)
The Swinger (1966)
The Swingin' Maiden (1964)
Swingin' on a Rainbow (1945)
Swiss Family Robinson (1940)
Swiss Family Robinson (1960)
Swiss Miss (1938)
Switzerland (1956)
The Sword and the Rose (1953)
Sword in the Desert (1949)
The Sword in the Stone (1963)
The Sword of Ali Baba (1965)
The Sword of Doom (1967)
Sword of Lancelot (1963)
The Sword of Monte Cristo (1951)
Sword of Sherwood Forest (1961)
Sword of the Avenger (1948)
Sword of the Conqueror (1962)
Sword of Venus (1953)
The Swordsman (1947)
Swordsman of Siena (1962)
Sworn Enemy (1936)
Sylvia (1965)
Sylvia Scarlett (1936)
Sylvie and the Phantom (1945)
Symphonie Fantastique (1948)
Symphonie Pastorale (1948)
Symphony for a Massacre (1965)
Symphony for Two Spies (1966)
Symphony of Life (1949)
Synanon (1965)
The System (1953)

T-Men (1947)
THX-1138 (1971)
T. N. P. (1956)
T. R. Baskin (1971)
Tabu (1931)
Taffy and the Jungle Hunter (1965)
Taggart (1964)
A Tailor's Maid (1959)
Take a Giant Step (1959)
Take a Girl Like You (1970)
Take a Letter, Darling (1942)
Take a Little Sunshine (1969)
Take Care of My Little Girl (1951)
Take Her, She's Mine (1963)
Take It Big (1944)
Take Me to Town (1953)
Take Me Out to the Ball Game (1949)
Take My Life (1947)
Take One False Step (1949)
Take the High Ground (1953)
Take the Money and Run (1969)
Tale of the Navajos (1949)
A Tale of Two Cities (1936)
A Tale of Two Cities (1958)
Tales of Beatrix Potter (1971)
Tales of Blood (1970)
Tales of Manhattan (1942)
Tales of Mystery and Imagination (1968)
Tales of Paris (1962)
Tales of Robin Hood (1951)
The Talisman (1968)
Talk About a Stranger (1952)
Talk of the Town (1942)
Tall, Dark and Handsome (1941)
The Tall Headlines (1952)
Tall in the Saddle (1944)
Tall Man Riding (1955)
Tall Story (1960)
The Tall Stranger (1957)
The Tall T (1957)
Tam Lin (1971)
Tamahine (1964)
Tamango (1957)
The Taming (1968)
The Taming of the Shrew (1967)
Taming Sutton's Gal (1957)
Tammy and the Bachelor (1957)
Tammy and the Doctor (1963)
Tammy and the Millionaire (1967)
Tammy Tell Me True (1961)
Tampico (1944)
Tanganyika (1954)
Tangier (1946)
Tangier Incident (1953)
Tank Force (1958)
The Tanks Are Coming (1951)
Tanya (1941)
Tap Roots (1948)
Tarantula (1955)
Taras Bulba (1962)

Taras Shevchenko (1951)
Target (1952)
Target Earth (1954)
Target for Tonight (1941)
Target Hong Kong (1952)
Target Unknown (1951)
Target Zero (1955)
Tarnished (1950)
Tarnished Angel (1938)
Tarnished Angels (1957)
The Tartars (1962)
I Tartassati (1959)
Tartuffe (1926)
Tarzan and the Amazons (1945)
Tarzan and the Great River (1967)
Tarzan and the Huntress (1947)
Tarzan and the Leopard Woman (1946)
Tarzan and the Mermaids (1948)
Tarzan and the Lost Safari (1957)
Tarzan and the She-Devil (1953)
Tarzan and the Slave Girl (1950)
Tarzan Goes to India (1962)
Tarzan, the Ape Man (1959)
Tarzan the Magnificent (1960)
Tarzan Triumphs (1943)
Tarzan's Deadly Silence (1970)
Tarzan's Desert Mystery (1943)
Tarzan's Fight for Life (1958)
Tarzan's Greatest Adventure (1959)
Tarzan's Hidden Jungle (1955)
Tarzan's Magic Fountain (1949)
Tarzan's New York Adventure (1942)
Tarzan's Peril (1951)
Tarzan's Revenge (1938)
Tarzan's Savage Fury (1952)
Task Force (1949)
A Taste of Honey (1962)
The Taste of the Black Earth (1970)
A Taste of Violence (1963)
Taste the Blood of Dracula (1970)
The Tattered Dress (1957)
The Tattooed Police Horse (1964)
The Tattooed Stranger (1950)
Taxi (1953)
Taxi for Tobruk (1965)
Taxi, Mister? (1943)
Taza, Son of Cochise (1954)
Tea and Sympathy (1956)
The Teacher and the Miracle (1961)
Teacher's Pet (1958)
The Teahouse of the August Moon (1956)
Tears for Simon (1957)
Teen-Age Crime Wave (1955)
Teenage Doll (1957)
Teenage Mother (1968)
Teenage Rebel (1956)
Teenage Rebellion (1967)
Tel Aviv Taxi (1956)
The Telephone Book (1971)
Tell It to the Judge (1949)
Tell Me In the Sunlight (1967)
Tell Me Lies (1968)
Tell Me That You Love Me, Junie Moon (1970)
Tell No Tales (1939)
The Tell-Tale Heart (1954)
Tell Them Willie Boy Is Here (1969)
Tembo (1951)
Temperate Zone (1970)
Tempest (1928)
Tempest (1959)
Temptation (1946)
The Ten Commandments (1923)
The Ten Commandments (1956)
Ten Days That Shook the World (1927)
Ten Days to Tulara (1958)
Ten Gentlemen from West Point (1942)
Ten Little Indians (1965)
Ten North Frederick (1958)
10 Rillington Place (1971)
Ten Seconds to Hell (1959)
Ten Tall Men (1951)
10,000 Bedrooms (1957)
10:30 P.M. Summer (1966)
Ten Wanted Men (1955)
Ten Who Dared (1960)
Tender Comrade (1943)
Tender Is the Night (1962)
The Tender Trap (1955)
The Tender Warrior (1971)
The Tender Years (1947)
Tenderly (1969)
Tennessee Champ (1954)

Tennessee Johnson (1942)
Tennessee's Partner (1955)
Tension (1949)
Tension at Table Rock (1956)
Tenth Avenue Angel (1948)
The Tenth Victim (1965)
Tenting Tonight on the Old Camp Ground (1943)
Teorema (1968)
Teresa (1951)
Teresa (1970)
The Terrace (1964)
Terror at Midnight (1956)
Terror in a Texas Town (1958)
Terror in the City (1965)
Terror in the Jungle (1968)
Terror Is a Man (1959)
Terror of the Tongs (1961)
Terror on a Train (1953)
The Terrornauts (1967)
Tess of the Storm Country (1960)
Test Pilot (1938)
The Testament of Dr. Cordelier (1962)
The Testament of Orpheus (1960)
The Texan Meets Calamity Jane (1950)
The Texans (1938)
Texas Across the River (1966)
Texas Bad Man (1953)
Texas, Brooklyn and Heaven (1948)
Texas City (1952)
Texas Lady (1955)
The Texas Rangers (1936)
Thank Heaven for Small Favors (1965)
Thank You, Aunt (1968)
Thank You, Jeeves (1936)
Thank You Very Much (1966)
That Brennan Girl (1946)
That Certain Feeling (1956)
That Cold Day in the Park (1969)
That Dangerous Age (1949)
That Darn Cat (1965)
That Forsyte Woman (1949)
That Funny Feeling (1965)
That Girl from Paris (1936)
That Hagan Girl (1947)
That Hamilton Woman (1941)
That Kind of Woman (1959)
That Lady (1955)
That Little Difference (1970)
That Man from Tangier (1953)
That Night (1957)
That Night with You (1945)
That Other Woman (1942)
That Riviera Touch (1966)
That Splendid November (1971)
That Summer (1971)
That Touch of Mink (1962)
That Uncertain Feeling (1941)
That Way with Women (1947)
That Wonderful Urge (1948)
That's My Baby (1944)
That's My Boy (1951)
That's My Gal (1947)
That's My Man (1947)
That's the Spirit (1945)
Theirs Is the Glory (1946)
Thelma Jordan (1949)
Them! (1954)
Then Came Bronson (1970)
Then Came the Legend (1970)
Theodora Goes Wild (1936)
There Goes Kelly (1945)
There Goes My Heart (1938)
There Grows a Green Pine in the Woods (1971)
There Was a Crooked Man (1970)
There's a Girl in My Soup (1970)
There's Always Tomorrow (1956)
There's Magic in Music (1940)
There's One Born Every Minute (1942)
Therese and Isabelle (1968)
Therese Desqueryoux (1961)
Therese Raquin (1953)
These Are the Damned (1965)
These Thousand Hills (1959)
These Three (1936)
These Wilder Years (1956)
They All Kissed the Bride (1942)
They Are Not Angels (1948)
They Call Me Mister Tibbs (1970)
They Call Me Trinity (1971)
They Came from Beyond Space (1967)
They Came to Blow Up America (1943)
They Came to Cordura (1959)

They Came to Rob Las Vegas (1969)
They Drive by Night (1940)
They Knew What They Wanted (1940)
They Made Me a Killer (1946)
They Met in Moscow (1941)
They Might Be Giants (1971)
They Rode West (1954)
They Shall Have Faith (1944)
They Shall Have Music (1939)
They Shoot Horses, Don't They? (1969)
They Were Expendable (1945)
They Were Not Divided (1950)
They Were So Young (1955)
They Were Ten (1961)
They Won't Believe Me (1947)
They Won't Forget (1937)
They've Changed Faces (1971)
The Thief (1952)
The Thief of Bagdad (1924)
The Thief of Bagdad (1940)
Thief of Bagdad (1961)
The Thief of Venice (1952)
Thieves' Highway (1949)
The Thin Man (1934)
The Thin Man Goes Home (1944)
The Thin Red Line (1964)
The Thing (1951)
Things to Come (1935)
Think of a Number (1969)
The Third Day (1965)
Third Finger, Left Hand (1940)
The Third Key (1957)
The Third Lover (1963)
The Third Man (1950)
Third Man on the Mountain (1959)
Third of a Man (1962)
The Third Part of the Night (1971)
The Third Secret (1964)
The Third Voice (1960)
The Thirst for Love (1967)
Thirteen Days in France (1968)
Thirteen Fighting Men (1960)
Thirteen Frightened Girls (1963)
Thirteen Ghosts (1960)
13 Lead Soldiers (1948)
13 Rue Madeleine (1947)
Thirteen West Street (1962)
The Thirteenth Chair (1937)
The Thirteenth Letter (1951)
-30- (1959)
The 30-Foot Bride of Candy Rock (1959)
Thirty Is a Dangerous Age, Cynthia (1968)
The Thirty Nine Steps (1960)
Thirty Seconds over Tokyo (1944)
Thirty-Six Hours (1964)
36 Hours to Kill (1936)
This Above All (1942)
This Angry Age (1958)
This Could Be the Night (1957)
This Earth is Mine (1959)
This Gun for Hire (1942)
This Happy Feeling (1958)
This Is Cinerama (1952)
This Is My Love (1954)
This Is Russia (1957)
This Island Earth (1955)
This Land Is Mine (1943)
This Love of Ours (1945)
This Man Is Mine (1934)
This Man Is Mine (1946)
This Man's Navy (1945)
This Rebel Breed (1960)
This Side of Heaven (1934)
This Side of the Law (1950)
This Sporting Life (1963)
This Strange Passion (El) (1955)
This Thing Called Love (1941)
This Time for Keeps (1942)
This Transient Life (1970)
This Was Paris (1942)
This Wine of Love (1948)
This Woman Is Dangerous (1952)
Thomas and the Bewitched (1970)
The Thomas Crown Affair (1968)
Thoroughly Modern Millie (1967)
Those Calloways (1964)
Those Crazy Years (1970)
Those Daring Young Men in Their Jaunty Jalopies (1969)
Those Endearing Young Charms (1945)
Those Fantastic Flying Fools (1967)
Those Magnificent Men in Their Flying Machines (1965)
Those Redheads from Seattle (1953)

Those Were the Days (1940)
A Thousand and One Nights (1945)
A Thousand Clowns (1965)
Thousands Cheer (1943)
The Threat (1949)
The Threat (1960)
Three (1969)
Three Bad Sisters (1956)
Three Bites of the Apple (1967)
Three Blind Mice (1938)
Three Brave Men (1957)
Three Came Home (1950)
Three Came to Kill (1960)
Three Cases of Murder (1955)
Three Coins in the Fountain (1954)
Three Comrades (1938)
Three Daring Daughters (1948)
Three Desperate Men (1951)
The Three Faces of Eve (1957)
Three Faces West (1940)
Three for Bedroom C (1952)
Three for Jamie Dawn (1956)
Three for the Show (1955)
Three Forbidden Stores (1952)
Three Godfathers (1948)
Three Guns for Texas (1968)
Three Guys Named Mike (1951)
Three Hearts for Julia (1943)
Three Hours to Kill (1954)
The 300 Spartans (1962)
300-Year Weekend (1971)
Three Husbands (1950)
Three in the Attic (1968)
Three in the Saddle (1945)
Three Into Two Won't Go (1969)
Three Is a Family (1944)
Three Kids and a Queen (1935)
Three Little Sisters (1944)
The Three Lives of Thomasina (1963)
Three Loves has Nancy (1938)
Three Men in a Boat (1959)
Three Men in White (1944)
Three Men on a Horse (1970)
The Three Musketeers (1935)
The Three Musketeers (1948)
Three on a Couch (1966)
Three on a Spree (1961)
Three on a Ticket (1947)
Three Ring Circus (1954)
Three Russian Girls (1943)
Three Secrets (1950)
Three Sisters (1970)
Three Smart Girls (1937)
Three Songs about Lenin (1934)
Three Steps North (1951)
The Three Stooges Go Around the World in a Daze (1963)
The Three Stooges in Orbit (1962)
The Three Stooges Meet Hercules (1962)
Three Strangers (1946)
Three Stripes in the Sun (1955)
3:10 to Yuma (1957)
Three Violent People (1956)
Three Wise Fools (1946)
Three Wise Guys (1936)
Three Women (1951)
The Three Worlds of Gulliver (1960)
Three Young Texans (1954)
Three's a Crowd (1945)
Threesome (1969)
The Threshold of the Void (1971)
Thrill of a Lifetime (1937)
Thrill of a Romance (1945)
The Thrill of it All (1963)
Throne of Blood (1957)
Through Different Eyes (1942)
Thumbs Up (1943)
Thunder Afloat (1939)
Thunder Bay (1953)
Thunder Birds (1942)
Thunder in Carolina (1960)
Thunder in God's Country (1951)
Thunder in the City (1937)
Thunder in the East (1953)
Thunder in the Pines (1949)
Thunder in the Sun (1959)
Thunder in the Valley (1947)
Thunder Island (1963)
Thunder Mountain (1947)
A Thunder of Drums (1961)
Thunder on the Hill (1951)
Thunder over Arizona (1956)
Thunder over Mexico (1933)
Thunder over Tangier (1957)
Thunder over the Plains (1953)
Thunderball (1965)
Thunderbirds (1952)
Thunderbirds (1958)
Thunderbolt (1945)

Thunderhead, Son of Flicka (1945)
Thundering Caravans (1952)
Thundering Jets (1958)
Thunderstorm (1956)
Thursday We Shall Sing Like Sunday (1967)
Tiara Tahiti (1963)
A Ticket to Tomahawk (1950)
Tickle Me (1965)
A Ticklish Affair (1963)
The Tiger and the Flame (1955)
Tiger Fangs (1943)
The Tiger Makes Out (1967)
The Tiger Tamer (1955)
A Tiger Walks (1964)
The Tiger Woman (1945)
Tight Little Island (1949)
Tight Spot (1955)
The Tijuana Story (1957)
Till Death Us Do Part (1968)
Till the End of Time (1946)
Till We Meet Again (1936)
Till We Meet Again (1944)
Timber (1942)
Timber Fury (1950)
Timber Queen (1944)
Timberjack (1955)
Timbuktu (1959)
Time Bomb (1961)
A Time for Dying (1971)
A Time for Killing (1968)
Time Limit (1957)
The Time Machine (1960)
Time of Indifference (1965)
Time of the Wolves (1970)
The Time of Their Lives (1946)
The Time of Your Life (1948)
Time Out for Romance (1937)
Time Out of Mind (1947)
The Time to Die (1970)
The Time, the Place and the Girl (1946)
Time to Kill (1942)
A Time to Love and a Time to Die (1958)
A Time to Sing (1968)
The Time Travelers (1964)
Time Without Pity (1957)
Times Four (1970)
Timetable (1956)
Tin Pan Alley (1940)
The Tin Star (1957)
The Tingler (1959)
Tintin and the Sun Temple (1970)
The Tioga Kid (1948)
Tip on a Dead Jockey (1957)
Tish (1942)
The Titan (1950)
Titanic! (1953)
The Titfield Thunderbolt (1953)
To Be or Not to Be (1942)
To Bed ... Or Not to Bed (1963)
To Catch a Thief (1955)
To Each His Own (1946)
To Hell and Back (1955)
To Hell with School (1969)
To Kill a Mockingbird (1962)
To Love Again (1971)
To Mary, with Love (1936)
To Paris with Love (1955)
To Please a Lady (1950)
To Sir, with Love (1967)
To the Ends of the Earth (1948)
To the Shores of Iwo Jima (1945)
To the Shores of Tripoli (1942)
To the Victor (1948)
To Trap a Spy (1966)
The Toast of New Orleans (1950)
Tobacco Road (1941)
Tobor the Great (1954)
Tobruk (1966)
Toby Tyler (1960)
Toccata for Toy Trains (1958)
The Tocher (1938)
The Todd Killings (1971)
Together Again (1944)
The Toilers (1928)
Toklat (1971)
Tokoloshe (1971)
Tokyo After Dark (1959)
Tokyo File 212 (1951)
Tokyo Joe (1949)
Tokyo Rose (1945)
Tom Brown's Schooldays (1940)
Tom Brown's Schooldays (1951)
Tom, Dick and Harry (1940)
Tom Jones (1963)
Tom Thumb (1958)
Tom Thumb (1967)
Tomahawk (1951)
Tomahawk Trail (1957)
Tomboy and the Champ (1961)

Tombstone--The Town too Tough to Die (1942)
Tomorrow (1970)
Tomorrow Is Another Day (1951)
Tomorrow Is Forever (1946)
Tomorrow Is Too Late (1952)
Tomorrow the World! (1944)
Tomorrow We Live (1942)
Toni (1935)
Tonight at Twelve (1929)
Tonight We Raid Calais (1943)
Tonight's the Night (1954)
Tonka (1958)
Tony Draws a Horse (1950)
Tony Rome (1967)
Too Bad She's Bad (1955)
Too Hot to Handle (1938)
Too Late Blues (1962)
Too Late for Tears (1949)
Too Late the Hero (1970)
Too Little for Such a Big War (1970)
Too Many Girls (1940)
Too Many Husbands (1940)
Too Many Parents (1936)
Too Many Winners (1947)
Too Much, too Soon (1958)
Too Soon to Die (1966)
Too Soon to Love (1960)
Too Young for Love (1955)
Too Young to Kiss (1951)
Too Young to Know (1945)
Top Gun (1955)
Top Man (1943)
Top of the World (1955)
Top Secret Affair (1957)
Top Sergeant (1942)
Topa Topa (1938)
Topaze (1933)
Topeka (1953)
The Topeka Terror (1945)
Topkapi (1964)
Topper (1937)
Topper Returns (1941)
The Torch (1950)
Torch Song (1953)
Torero! (1957)
Tormented (1960)
The Torn Curtain (1966)
Tornado Range (1948)
Torpedo Alley (1953)
Torpedo Boat (1942)
Torrid Zone (1940)
Tortilla Flat (1942)
Torture Garden (1968)
Tostao--The King of Football (1970)
The Touch (1971)
Touch of Evil (1958)
A Touch of Larceny (1960)
A Touch of Love (1969)
The Touchables (1968)
Touchez Ne Pas Au Grisbi (1953)
Tough As They Come (1942)
Tough Assignment (1949)
Tough Guys of the Prairie (1970)
The Tougher They Come (1950)
Toughest Gun in Tombstone (1958)
The Toughest Man Alive (1955)
Toughest Man in Arizona (1952)
Toute Le Memoire Du Monde (1956)
Tovarich (1937)
Toward the Unknown (1956)
Tower of London (1962)
A Town Like Alice (1957)
Town on Trial (1957)
Town Tamer (1965)
The Town Went Wild (1944)
Town without a Face (1963)
Town without Pity (1961)
Toy Tiger (1956)
The Toy Wife (1938)
Toys in the Attic (1963)
Track of the Cat (1954)
Track of Thunder (1968)
Track the Man Down (1956)
Trade Winds (1938)
Trader Horn (1931)
Traffic in Crime (1946)
A Tragedy at Midnight (1942)
Tragic Hunt (1948)
Trail Blazers (1953)
Trail Guide (1952)
Trail of Kit Carson (1945)
The Trail of '98 (1929)
Trail of Robin Hood (1950)
Trail of the Lonesome Pine (1936)
The Trail of the Mounties (1948)
Trail of the Yukon (1949)
Trail Street (1947)
Trail to Mexico (1946)
Trail to San Antone (1947)

The Train (1965)
Train to Alcatraz (1948)
Train of Events (1949)
Train to Tombstone (1950)
The Traitors (1963)
Transatlantic (1931)
Transatlantic Tunnel (1935)
The Trap (1947)
The Trap (1959)
The Trap (1966)
Trapeze (1956)
The Trapp Family (1961)
Trapped (1949)
Trapped in Tangiers (1960)
The Traveling Executioner (1970)
Traveling Saleswoman (1949)
Treasure Island (1934)
Treasure Island (1950)
The Treasure of Lost Canyon (1952)
Treasure of Monte Cristo (1949)
The Treasure of Pancho Villa (1955)
Treasure of the Aztecs (1965)
Treasure of the Golden Condor (1953)
Treasure of the Ruby Hills (1955)
The Treasure of the Sierra Madre (1948)
Treasure of the Silver Lake (1964)
Treat 'Em Rough (1942)
The Tree (1969)
A Tree Grows in Brooklyn (1945)
Trent's Last Case (1953)
The Trespasser (1947)
Trial (1955)
The Trial (1963)
Trial and Error (1962)
The Trial of Vivienne Ware (1932)
Trial without Jury (1950)
Tribute to a Bad Man (1956)
The Tricky Game of Love (1971)
Trigger Fingers (1946)
Trigger, Jr. (1950)
Triggerman (1948)
Trio (1950)
Trip Around My Cranium (1970)
Triple Deception (1957)
Triple Trouble (1950)
Tripoli (1950)
Triumph of the Will (1934)
Trog (1970)
Tropic of Cancer (1970)
Tropic Zone (1953)
Tropical Ecstasy (1970)
Tropical Heat Wave (1952)
Trooper Hook (1957)
Trotta (1971)
Trouble Along the Way (1953)
Trouble for Two (1936)
Trouble in Store (1955)
Trouble in the Glen (1954)
Trouble in the Sky (1961)
Trouble Makers (1948)
Trouble Preferred (1948)
The Trouble with Angels (1966)
The Trouble with Girls (1969)
The Trouble with Harry (1955)
The Trouble with Women (1947)
The Troublemaker (1964)
True Friends (1954)
The True Glory (1945)
True Grit (1969)
The True Story of Jesse James (1957)
The True Story of the Civil War (1957)
True to Life (1943)
True to the Army (1942)
Truman Capote's Trilogy (1969)
The Trunk (1961)
Trunk to Cairo (1966)
The Truth (1961)
The Truth about Murder (1946)
The Truth about Spring (1965)
The Truth about Women (1958)
Try and Get It (1924)
The Trygon Factor (1968)
Tucson (1949)
Tucson Raiders (1944)
Tuesday in November (1945)
Tulsa (1949)
Tumbleweeds (1953)
Tuna Clipper (1949)
Tunes of Glory (1960)
Tunisian Victory (1944)
The Turn of the Tide (1935)
Turn off the Moon (1937)
Turn the Key Softly (1953)
The Turning Point (1952)
The Tuttles of Tahiti (1942)

Twelve Angry Men (1957)
The Twelve Chairs (1970)
Twelve Hours to Kill (1960)
Twelve O'Clock High (1949)
Twelve Plus One (1970)
Twelve to the Moon (1960)
The 25th Hour (1967)
21 Days in Europe (1971)
Twenty Million Miles to Earth (1957)
Twenty Plus Two (1961)
20,000 Eyes (1961)
20,000 Leagues under the Sea (1954)
23-1/2 Hours Leave (1936)
23 Paces to Baker Street (1956)
The 27th Day (1957)
Twice Blessed (1945)
Twice Told Tales (1963)
Twilight for the Gods (1958)
Twilight in the Sierras (1950)
Twilight of Honor (1963)
Twilight on the Rio Grande (1947)
Twilight Women (1953)
Twin Beds (1942)
The Twinkle in God's Eye (1955)
Twinky (1970)
A Twist of Sand (1968)
Twisted Nerve (1968)
The Twisted Road (1948)
Two are Guilty (1964)
Two Dollar Bettor (1951)
Two English Girls and the Continent (1971)
Two-Faced Woman (1941)
Two-Fisted Justice (1943)
Two Flags West (1950)
Two for the Road (1967)
Two for the Seesaw (1962)
Two Gals and a Guy (1951)
Two Gentlemen Sharing (1969)
Two Girls and a Sailor (1944)
Two Grooms for a Bride (1957)
Two Guns and a Badge (1954)
Two Guys from Milwaukee (1946)
The Two-Headed Spy (1959)
200 Motels (1971)
Two in a Crowd (1936)
Two in Revolt (1936)
The Two Little Bears (1961)
Two Lost Worlds (1950)
Two Lovers (1928)
Two Loves (1961)
The Two Mrs. Carrolls (1947)
Two Mules for Sister Sara (1970)
Two O'Clock Courage (1945)
Two of a Kind (1951)
Two on a Guillotine (1965)
Two Rode Together (1961)
Two Smart People (1946)
2001: A Space Odyssey (1968)
Two Thousand Weeks (1969)
Two Thousand Years Later (1969)
Two Tickets to Broadway (1951)
Two Tickets to London (1943)
Two Way Stretch (1961)
Two Weeks in Another Town (1962)
Two Wise Maids (1937)
Two Women (1961)
Two Women Ingold (1971)
Two Yanks in Trinidad (1942)
The Twonky (1953)
Tugboat Annie Sails Again (1940)
Tycoon (1947)
Tyrant of the Sea (1950)

U-Boat 29 (1939)
The Ugly American (1963
Ulysses (1955)
Ulysses (1967)
Umberto D. (1951)
The Umbrellas of Cherbourg (1964)
Uncertain Guy (1944)
Unchained (1955)
Uncle Harry (1945)
Uncle Tom's Cabin (1965)
Uncle Vanya (1958)
Uncle Vanya (1971)
Unconquered (1947)
The Undefeated (1969)
Under Arizona Skies (1946)
Under California Stars (1948)
Under Capricorn (1949)
Under Fire (1957)
Under Mexicali Stars (1950)
Under Milk Wood (1971)
Under My Skin (1950)
Under Nevada Skies (1946)
Under Sunny Skies (The Far-

Away Bride) (1949)
Under Ten Flags (1960)
Under the Cover of Night (1937)
Under the Gun (1950)
Under the Olive Tree (1951)
Under the Red Robe (1923)
Under the Red Robe (1937)
Under the Red Sea (1952)
Under the Roofs of Paris (1930)
Under the Sign of the Scorpion (1969)
Under the Tonto Rim (1947)
Under the Yum Yum Tree (1963)
Under Two Flags (1936)
Under Western Skies (1945)
Under Your Spell (1936)
Undercover Girl (1950)
Undercover Maisie (1947)
The Undercover Man (1949)
The Undercover Woman (1946)
Undercurrent (1946)
The Underdog (1943)
Underground (1941)
Undersea Girl (1957)
Undertow (1949)
Underwater! (1955)
The Underwater City (1962)
Underwater Warrior (1958)
The Underworld Story (see The Whipped) (1950)
Underworld, U.S.A. (1961)
The Undying Monster (1942)
Une Si Jolie Petite Plage (1948)
The Unearthly (1957)
Unexpected Guest (1946)
Unexpected Riches (1942)
The Unfaithful (1947)
Unfaithfully Yours (1948)
Unfinished Business (1941)
The Unfinished Dance (1947)
An Unfinished Story (1955)
The Unforgettable Year--1919 (1952)
The Unforgiven (1960)
The Unguarded Hour (1936)
The Unguarded Moment (1956)
The Unholy Wife (1957)
A Unicorn in the Garden (1954)
Unidentified Flying Objects (1956)
The Uninvited (1944)
United We Stand (1942)
L'Univers d'Utrillo (1954)
The Unknown Guest (1943)
Unknown Island (1948)
The Unknown Man (1951)
The Unknown Soldier (1926)
The Unknown Terror (1957)
The Unknown World (1951)
Union Station (1950)
Unman, Wittering and Zigo (1971)
Unmasked (1950)
The Unseen (1945)
The Unsuspected (1947)
Untamed (1940)
Untamed (1955)
The Untamed Breed (1948)
Untamed Frontier (1952)
Untamed Fury (1947)
Untamed Heiress (1954)
Untamed Women (1952)
Untamed Youth (1957)
Until They Sail (1957)
Unwed Mother (1958)
Uomo de Paglia (1957)
Up from the Beach (1965)
Up Front (1951)
Up Goes Maisie (1946)
Up in Mabel's Room (1944)
Up in Smoke (1957)
Up in the Cellar (1970)
Up Periscope (1959)
Up Pompeii (1971)
Up the Down Staircase (1967)
Up the Junction (1968)
Up the MacGregors (1968)
Upon This Rock (1970)
Upstairs and Downstairs (1961)
Uptight (1968)
The Upturned Glass (1947)
Urubu (1948)
Uranium Boom (1956)
Utah (1945)
Utah Blaine (1957)
Utah Wagon Train (1951)
Utopia (Atoll A) (1955)

The V.I.P.'s (1963)
The Vacation (1971)
Vacation from Love (1938)
Vacation in Reno (1946)
The Vagabond King (1956)
Valdez Is Coming (1971)
Valentino (1951)

Valerie (1957)
The Valiant (1962)
The Valiant Hombre (1948)
Valiant is the Word for Carrie (1936)
The Valley of Decision (1945)
Valley of Fear (1947)
Valley of Headhunters (1953)
Valley of Hunted Men (1942)
Valley of the Dolls (1967)
Valley of the Dragons (1961)
Valley of the Eagles (1952)
The Valley of the Giants (1919)
Valley of the Giants (1938)
Valley of the Kings (1954)
Valley of the Redwoods (1960)
Valley of the Sun (1942)
Valley of the Tennessee (1944)
Valley of the Zombies (1946)
Valley Town (1940)
Valparaiso My Love (1970)
Valparaiso, Valparaiso (1971)
Value for Money (1957)
The Vampire (1957)
The Vampire Lovers (1970)
The Vanishing American (1925)
The Vanishing American (1955)
Vanishing Point (1971)
The Vanishing Prairie (1954)
The Vanishing Westerner (1950)
The Vanquished (1953)
Varieties (1971)
Varieties on Parade (1951)
Variety Girl (1947)
Veils of Bagdad (1953)
Vel'D'Hiv (1957)
The Velvet Touch (1948)
The Velvet Vampire (1971)
Vendetta (1950)
The Venetian Affair (1966)
The Vengeance of Fu Manchu (1968)
The Vengeance of She (1968)
Vengeance Valley (1951)
Venus in Furs (1970)
Vera Cruz (1954)
Verboten! (1959)
The Verdict (1946)
Vertigo (1958)
A Very Handy Man (1966)
A Very Private Affair (1962)
A Very Special Favor (1965)
The Very Thought of You (1944)
Vice Raid (1959)
Vice and Virtue (1965)
Vice Squad (1953)
Vice Versa (1945)
The Vicious Breed (1955)
The Vicious Circle (1948)
The Vicious Years (1950)
Vicki (1953)
Victim (1962)
Victoria and Her Hussar (1957)
Victoria the Great (1937)
The Victors (1963)
Victory (1941)
Victory at Sea (1954)
La Vie Conjugal (1965)
La Vie De Chateau (1965)
The View from Pompey's Head (1955)
A View from the Bridge (1962)
Vigil in the Night (1940)
Vigilante Hideout (1950)
Vigilante Terror (1953)
The Vigilantes Return (1947)
The Viking Queen (1967)
The Viking Who Came from the South (1971)
The Vikings (1958)
Villa! (1958)
Villa Rides (1968)
The Village (1953)
Village Harvest (1938)
Village Harvest (1945)
Village Music (1941)
The Village of the Damned (1960)
Village of the Giants (1965)
Village Teacher (1947)
The Vintage (1957)
Violated (1953)
Violated Paradise (1963)
The Violators (1957)
Violence (1947)
Violent City (1970)
The Violent Men (1955)
The Violent Ones (1967)
Violent Road (1958)
Violent Saturday (1955)
Violin and Roller (1961)
The Violinist (1959)
The Virgin and the Gypsy (1970)
The Virgin Queen (1955)
The Virgin Soldiers (1969)

The Virgin Spring (1960)
Virginia (1940)
Virginia City (1940)
The Virginian (1946)
The Visionaries (1968)
The Visit (1964)
A Visit to a Small Planet (1960)
Les Visiteurs du Soir (1942)
I Vitelloni (1956)
Viva Las Vegas (1964)
Viva Maria (1965)
Viva Max (1969)
Viva Villa! (1934)
Viva Zapata! (1952)
Vivacious Lady (1938)
Vixen (1968)
Voice in the Mirror (1958)
Voice in the Night (1941)
Voice in the Wind (1944)
The Voice of Bugle Ann (1936)
The Voice of Silence (1952)
Voice of the Hurricane (1964)
The Voice of the Turtle (1947)
Volcano (1953)
La Voleur de Paratonnerres (1946)
Volga and Siberia (1914)
The Volga Boatman (1926)
Volga-Volga (1938)
Volochayevsk Days (1938)
Von Richthoven and Brown (1971)
Von Ryan's Express (1965)
Voodoo Island (1957)
Voodoo Man (1944)
Voodoo Tiger (1952)
Vote for Huggett (1949)
Voyage to the Bottom of the Sea (1961)
La Voyageur de la Toussaint (1942)
The Vulture (1967)
The Vyborg Side (1939)

W.I.A. (Wounded in Action) (1966)
"WR"--The Mysteries of the Organism (1971)
W.U.S.A. (1970)
The Wac from Walla Walla (1952)
Waco (1952)
Waco (1966)
The Wackiest Ship in the Army (1960)
The Wages of Fear (1955)
Wagon Team (1952)
Wagon Tracks West (1943)
Wagon Wheels Westward (1945)
Wagonmaster (1950)
Waikiki Wedding (1937)
Wait 'Til the Sun Shines, Nellie (1952)
Wait Until Dark (1967)
Wakamba (1955)
Wake Island (1942)
Wake Me When It's Over (1960)
Wake of the Red Witch (1948)
Wake Up and Dream (1946)
Walk a Crooked Mile (1948)
Walk a Tightrope (1964)
Walk, Don't Run (1966)
Walk East on Beacon (1952)
Walk in the Shadow (1966)
A Walk in the Spring Rain (1970)
A Walk in the Sun (1946)
Walk into Hell (1957)
Walk Like a Dragon (1960)
Walk on the Wild Side (1962)
Walk Softly, Stranger (1950)
Walk Tall (1960)
Walk the Angry Beach (1961)
Walk the Dark Street (1956)
Walk the Proud Land (1956)
A Walk Through the Kurdistan Wilderness (1965)
A Walk with Love and Death (1969)
Walkabout (1971)
The Walking Hills (1949)
Walking My Baby Back Home (1953)
Walking on Air (1936)
The Walking Stick (1970)
Wall of Noise (1963)
Wallflower (1948)
The Walls Came Tumbling Down (1946)
Walls of Fire (1971)
The Walls of Hell (1964)
The Walls of Jericho (1948)
The Walls of Malapaga (1949)
Waltz of the Toreadors (1962)
The Wanderer (1925)
Wanderer of the Wasteland (1945)

Wanted for Murder (1946)
The Wanting Weight (1971)
The War Against Mrs. Hadley (1942)
War and Peace (1956)
War and Peace (1968)
War Arrow (1953)
War Drums (1957)
War Hunt (1962)
War Is Hell (1930)
War Is Hell (1964)
War, Italian Style (1967)
War Kill (1967)
The War Lord (1965)
The War Lover (1962)
The War of the Buttons (1963)
War of the Satellites (1958)
The War of the Worlds (1953)
War Paint (1953)
War Party (1965)
The War Wagon (1967)
Warlock (1959)
Warming Up (1928)
Warning Shot (1966)
Warning to Wantons (1949)
Warpath (1951)
The Warrior and the Slave Girl (1959)
The Warrior Empress (1961)
The Warriors (1955)
Warriors Five (1962)
The Washington Story (1952)
Watch on the Rhine (1943)
Watch the Birdie (1950)
Watch Your Stern (1961)
Waterfront (1944)
Waterfront at Midnight (1948)
Waterhole #3 (1967)
Waterloo (1970)
Waterloo Bridge (1940)
Watermelon Man (1970)
Waters of Time (1951)
The Wave (1935)
A Wave, a Wac and a Marine (1944)
The Way Ahead (1943)
Way Down East (1920)
Way Down East (1935)
Way of a Gaucho (1952)
The Way of All Flesh (1940
The Way Out (1956)
Way Out (1966)
Way Out West (1936)
The Way to the Gold (1957)
The Way to the Stars (1945)
Way ... Way Out (1966)
The Way We Live Now (1970)
The Way West (1967)
Wayward (1931)
The Wayward Bus (1957)
The Wayward Girl (1957)
The Wayward Wife (1955)
We Americans (1928)
We Are All Naked (1970)
We Are from Kronstadt (1936)
We Are Not Alone (1939)
We Are the Marines (1942)
We Chop the Teachers into Mince Meat (1970)
We Live Again (1934)
We Live in Two Worlds (1937)
We Two (1970)
We Two France (1970)
We Went to College (1936)
We Were Dancing (1942)
We Were Strangers (1949)
We Who Are Young (1940)
The Weak and the Wicked (1954)
The Weaker Sex (1948)
The Weapon (1957)
The Web (1947)
Web of Evidence (1959)
The Wedding March (1928)
Wedding Present (1936)
The Wedding Ring (1970)
The Wedding Trip (1969)
Wee Geordie (1956)
Weekend (1963)
Weekend at the Waldorf (1945)
Weekend of Fear (1966)
Weekend with Father (1951)
A Weekend with Lulu (1961)
Weird Woman (1944)
Welcome to Hard Times (1967)
Welcome to the Club (1971)
Welcome Stranger (1947)
Welcome to the Queen (1954)
The Well (1951)
We'll Eat the Fruit of Paradise (1970)
The Well-Groomed Bride (1946)
Wells Fargo (1937)
Wells Fargo Gunmaster (1951)
Weltmelodie (1929)
Went the Day Well? (1942)
We're No Angels (1955)

We're Not Married (1952)
The Werewolf (1956)
Werewolves on Wheels (1971)
West of the Alamo (1946)
West of the Cimarron (1943)
West of the Pecos (1945)
West of the Rio Grande (1944)
West of Wyoming (1950)
West of Zanzibar (1954)
Westbound (1959)
Western Approaches (1944)
Western Heritage (1948)
Western Pacific Agent (1950)
Western Union (1941)
The Westerner (1940)
Westward Bound (1944)
Westward, Ho! (1942)
Westward Ho, the Wagons (1956)
Westward the Women (1951)
The Westward Trail (1948)
What a Blonde (1945)
What a Man! (1943)
What a Way to Go! (1964)
What Did you Do in the War, Daddy? (1966)
What Did You Do in the War, Thanassi? (1971)
What Do You Say to a Naked Lady? (1970)
What Every Woman Knows (1934)
What Next, Corporal Hargrove? (1945)
What Price Glory? (1926)
What Price Glory? (1952)
What Price Hollywood? (1932)
What Price Murder? (1958)
Whatever Happened to Aunt Alice? (1969)
Whatever Happened to Baby Jane? (1962)
What's Good for the Gander (1969)
What's New, Pussycat? (1965)
What's So Bad About Feeling Good? (1968)
What's the Matter with Helen? (1971)
The Wheel Turns in the Shadow (1970)
The Wheeler Dealers (1963)
When a Man Loves (1927)
When Comedy Was King (1960)
When Dinosaurs Ruled the Earth (1970)
When Gangland Strikes (1956)
When Hell Broke Loose (1958)
When I Grow Up (1951)
When in Rome (1952)
When Knighthood Was in Flower (1922)
When Ladies Meet (1941)
When Love Is Young (1937)
When Strangers Marry (1944)
When the Boys Meet the Girls (1965)
When the Clock Strikes (1961)
When the Daltons Rode (1940)
When the Lights Go On Again (1944)
When the Mad Aunts Are Coming (1970)
When the Redskins Rode (1951)
When Willie Comes Marching Home (1950)
When Women Had Tails (1970)
When Worlds Collide (1951)
When You're in Love (1937)
When's Your Birthday? (1937)
Where Angels Go ... Trouble Follows (1968)
Where Danger Lives (1950)
Where Do We Go from Here? (1945)
Where is the Body, Moeller? (1971)
Where It's At (1969)
Where Love Has Gone (1964)
Where Sinners Meet (1934)
Where the Boys Are (1960)
Where the Buffalo Roam (1938)
Where the Bullets Fly (1966)
Where the Hot Wind Blows (see The Law) (1960)
Where the North Begins (1948)
Where the Sidewalk Ends (1950)
Where the Spies Are (1965)
Where the Truth Lies (1962)
Where Were You When the Lights Went Out? (1968)
Where's Jack? (1969)
Where's Poppa? (1970)
Which Way to the Front? (1970)
While I Live (1948)
While the City Sleeps (1956)
While the Sun Shines (1949)

The Whip Hand (1951)
Whiplash (1948)
The Whipped (1950)
Whipsaw (1935)
Whirlpool (1949)
Whirlwind (1951)
The Whisperers (1967)
Whispering City (1947)
Whispering Footsteps (1944)
Whispering Ghosts (1942)
Whispering Smith (1948)
Whispering Smith vs. Scotland Yard (1952)
The Whistle at Eaton Falls (1951)
Whistle Down the Wind (1962)
Whistle Stop (1946)
Whistling in Brooklyn (1943)
Whistling in Dixie (1942)
Whistling in the Dark (1941)
White Banners (1938)
White Cargo (1942)
The White Cliffs of Dover (1944)
White Fang (1936)
White Feather (1955)
White Fire (1954)
White Flood (1940)
White Heat (1949)
White Hell of Pitz Palu (1951)
White Hunter (1937)
White Lightning (1953)
The White Line (1951)
White Mane (1953)
The White Orchid (1954)
The White Reindeer (1956)
The White Room (1970)
The White Rose (1923)
White Savage (1943)
White Shadows of the South Seas (1928)
The White Sheik (1956)
White Sisters (1933)
White Slave Ship (1962)
The White Squaw (1956)
White Tie and Tails (1946)
The White Tower (1950)
White Voices (1965)
The White Warrior (1961)
White Wilderness (1958)
White Witch Doctor (1953)
Whity (1971)
Who Done It? (1942)
Who Is Harry Kellerman and Why Is He Saying Those Terrible Things About Me? (1971)
Who Is Hope Schuyler? (1942)
Who Killed Doc Robbin? (1948)
Who Killed Mary Whats'ername? (1971)
Who Knows? (1967)
Who Says I Can't Ride a Rainbow? (1971)
Who Slew Auntie Roo? (1971)
Who Was That Lady? (1960)
The Whole Truth (1958)
Who's Afraid of Virginia Woolf? (1966)
Who's Been Sleeping in My Bed? (1963)
Who's Got the Action? (1962)
Who's Minding the Mint? (1967)
Who's Minding the Store? (1963)
Why America? (1969)
Why Bother to Knock? (1964)
Why Do They Do It? (1971)
Why Russians are Revolting (1970)
Wichita (1955)
Wicked as They Come (1957)
The Wicked City (1951)
The Wicked Dreams of Paula Schultz (1968)
Wicked Wife (1955)
Wicked Woman (1953)
The Wife of General Ling (1938)
The Wife of Monte Cristo (1946)
The Wife Swappers (1970)
The Wife Takes a Flyer (1942)
Wife Wanted (1946)
Wilbur and the Baby Factory (1970)
The Wild Angels (1966)
The Wild and the Innocent (1959)
Wild and Wonderful (1964)
Wild Beauty (1946)
Wild Bill Hickock Rides (1942)
The Wild Blue Yonder (1951)
The Wild Blue Yonder (1958)
The Wild Bunch (1969)
Wild Cargo (1934)
The Wild Country (1971)
Wild for Kicks (1962)
The Wild Fruit (1958)

Wild Harvest (1947)
The Wild Heart (1952)
Wild Horse Ambush (1952)
Wild Horse Mesa (1947)
Wild Horse Rustlers (1943)
Wild Horse Stampede (1943)
Wild in the Country (1961)
Wild in the Streets (1968)
Wild Is the Wind (1957)
Wild Man of Borneo (1941)
The Wild North (1952)
Wild on the Beach (1965)
The Wild One (1954)
The Wild Party (1956)
The Wild Pussycat (1970)
The Wild Racers (1968)
Wild River (1960)
Wild Rovers (1971)
Wild Seed (1965)
Wild Stallion (1952)
Wild West (1946)
The Wild Westerners (1962)
Wild, Wild Planet (1967)
Wild, Wild Winter (1966)
Wildcat (1942)
Will It Happen Again? (1948)
Will Our Friends Succeed in Finding Their Friend Who Mysteriously Disappeared in Africa? (1969)
Will Penny (1968)
Will Success Spoil Rock Hunter? (1957)
Willard (1971)
Wilson (1944)
Winchester '73 (1950)
The Wind Blows Free (1971)
The Wind Cannot Read (1960)
Windfall in Athens (1953)
Windjammer (1958)
Windom's Way (1958)
The Window (1949)
The Wind's Anger (1971)
The Windsplitter (1971)
A Wing and a Prayer (1944)
Winged Victory (1944)
Wings for the Eagle (1942)
Wings of Chance (1961)
The Wings of Eagles (1957)
Wings of the Hawk (1953)
Wings of the Morning (1937)
Wings over Honolulu (1937)
Wink of an Eye (1958)
The Winner's Circle (1948)
The Winner's Circle (1957)
Winnetou I (see Apache Gold)
Winnetou II (1965)
Winnetou III (1965)
Winnetou and His Friend Old Firehand (1967)
Winning (1969)
Winning of the West (1953)
The Winning Team (1952)
Winter A-Go-Go (1965)
Winter Carnival (1939)
Winter Meeting (1948)
Winter Wonderland (1947)
A Winter's Tale (1968)
Winterset (1936)
Wiretappers (1956)
The Wiser Sex (1931)
Wishing Well Inn (1958)
The Wistful Widow of Wagon Gap (1947)
Witchcraft (1964)
The Witches (1966)
The Witches (1969)
The Witchmaker (1969)
With Love and Kisses (1936)
With Love and Kisses (1971)
Within These Walls (1945)
Without Apparent Motive (1971)
Without Honor (1949)
Without Love (1945)
Without Pity (1948)
Without Prejudice (1949)
Without Reservations (1946)
Without Warning (1952)
Witness for the Prosecution (1957)
Witness to Murder (1954)
The Witnesses (1967)
Wives and Lovers (1963)
The Wizard of Bagdad (1960)
The Wizard of Oz (1939)
Wolf Dog (1958)
The Wolf Hunters (1950)
Wolf Larsen (1958)
Woman Against Woman (1938)
The Woman Alone (Secret Agent) (1937)
Woman Chases Man (1937)
The Woman Disputed (1928)
Woman Eater (1959)
Woman Hater (1948)
Woman Hunt (1962)

The Woman I Abandoned (1969)
The Woman I Love (1937)
Woman in a Dressing Gown (1957)
The Woman in Green (1945)
Woman in Hiding (1949)
The Woman in Question (1950)
The Woman in Room 13 (1932)
Woman in the Dark (1952)
The Woman in the Hall (1947)
The Woman in the Window (1944)
The Woman in White (1948)
A Woman Is a Woman (1964)
Woman Laughs Last (1969)
A Woman Like Satan (1960)
Woman Obsessed (1959)
A Woman of Distinction (1950)
A Woman of Everyone (1970)
Woman of Straw (1964)
Woman of the North Country (1952)
Woman of the River (1957)
The Woman of the Town (1943)
Woman of the Year (1942)
A Woman on Fire (1970)
The Woman on Pier 13 (1949)
The Woman on the Beach (1947)
The Woman on the Moon (1928)
Woman on the Run (1950)
A Woman Rebels (1936)
The Woman They Almost Lynched (1953)
Woman Times Seven (1967)
Woman to Woman (1947)
The Woman Who Came Back (1945)
The Woman Who Wouldn't Die (1965)
The Woman's Angel (1952)
A Woman's Devotion (1956)
A Woman's Face (1941)
A Woman's Secret (1949)
A Woman's Vengeance (1947)
Woman's World (1954)
The Women (1939)
Women from Headquarters (1950)
Women in Bondage (1943)
Women in Love (1969)
Women in Our Time (1949)
Women in the Night (1948)
Women in War (1940)
Women of the Night (1948)
Women of the World (1963)
Women's Prison (1955)
Wonder Man (1945)
The Wonderful Country (1959)
A Wonderful Life (1951)
Wonderful Times (1951)
Wonderful to Be Young (1962)
The Wonderful World of the Brothers Grimm (1962)
The Wonders of Aladdin (1961)
Wonderwall (1969)
The Wooden Horse (1950)
The Woolen Stocking Peddler (1971)
Work Is a Four-Letter Word (1968)
The World at War (1942)
The World by Night (1961)
The World by Night #2 (1962)
World for Ransom (1954)
The World in His Arms (1952)
World in My Corner (1956)
World in My Pocket (1962)
The World Is Just a "B" Movie (1971)
The World Is Ours (1938)
The World Moves On (1934)
The World of Apu (1959)
World of Calder (1950)
The World of Henry Orient (1964)
The World of Paul Delvaux (1947)
World of Plenty (1943)
The World of Suzie Wong (1960)
The World, the Flesh and the Devil (1959)
World without End (1953)
World without End (1956)
World without Sun (1964)
Wow (1971)
The Wreck of the Mary Deare (1959)
Wrecking Crew (1942)
The Wrecking Crew (1968)
The Wrestler and the Clown (1957)
Written on the Wind (1956)
The Wrong Arm of the Law (1963)
The Wrong Box (1966)
The Wrong Man (1957)

Wuthering Heights (1939)
Wuthering Heights (1970)
Wyoming (1947)
The Wyoming Bandit (1949)
Wyoming Mail (1950)
Wyoming Renegades (1955)

X--The Man with the X-Ray Eyes (1963)
X the Unknown (1957)
X-15 (1961)

Y Que Patatin Y Que Patatan (1971)
Yanco (1964)
Yang Kwei Fei (1956)
A Yank at Oxford (1938)
A Yank at Eton (1942)
A Yank in Indo-China (1952)
A Yank in Korea (1951)
A Yank in Viet-Nam (1964)
A Yank on the Burma Road (1942)
Yankee Buccaneer (1952)
Yankee Doodle Dandy (1942)
Yankee Fakir (1947)
Yankee Painter (1964)
The Yanks Are Coming (1942)
Yaqui Drums (1956)
The Yearling (1946)
Yellow Balloon (1953)
The Yellow Cab Man (1950)
The Yellow Canary (1963)
Yellow Cargo (1936)
Yellow Fin (1951)
The Yellow House at Pinnasberg (1970)
Yellow Jack (1938)
The Yellow Mountain (1954)
The Yellow Rolls-Royce (1965)
The Yellow Rose of Texas (1944)
Yellow Sky (1948)
The Yellow Ticket (1931)
The Yellow Tomahawk (1954)
Yellowneck (1955)
Yellowstone (1936)
Yellowstone Kelly (1959)
Yes Sir, Mr. Bones (1951)
Yes, Sir, That's My Baby (1949)
Yesterday and Today (1953)
Yesterday, Today and Tomorrow (1964)
Yojimbo (1961)
Yokel Boy (1942)
Yolande (1924)
You and Me (1938)
You Belong to Me (1941)
You Came Along (1945)
You Can Never Tell (1951)
You Can't Beat the Law (1943)
You Can't Escape Forever (1942)
You Can't Run Away from It (1956)
You Can't See 'Round the Corners (1969)
You Can't Take It with You (1938)
You Can't Win 'em All (1970)
You for Me (1952)
You Gotta Stay Happy (1948)
You Have to Run Fast (1961)
You Know What Sailors Are (1954)
You Must be Joking! (1965)
You Only Live Once (1937)
You Only Live Twice (1967)
You Were Never Lovelier (1942)
You'll Find Out (1940)
Young and Dangerous (1957)
Young and Healthy as a Rose (1971)
The Young and the Brave (1963)
Young and Wild (1958)
Young and Willing (1943)
Young and Willing (1964)
Young Attila (1971)
Young Bess (1953)
Young Billy Young (1969)
The Young Captives (1959)
Young Cassidy (1965)
Young Daniel Boone (1950)
Young Dillinger (1965)
Young Dr. Kildare (1938)
The Young Doctors (1961)
The Young Don't Cry (1957)
Young Fury (1965)
Young Girls of Rochefort (1967)
Young Guard (1947)
The Young Guns (1956)
Young Guns of Texas (1962)
Young Ideas (1943)
The Young in Heart (1938)

Young Jesse James (1960)
The Young Land (1959)
The Young Lions (1958)
The Young Lovers (see Never Fear) (1950)
The Young Lovers (1964)
Young Man with a Horn (1950)
Young Man with Ideas (1952)
Young Mr. Lincoln (1939)
Young People (1940)
The Young Philadelphians (1959)
The Young Racers (1963)
The Young Runaways (1968)
The Young Savages (1961)
The Young Stranger (1957)
The Young, The Evil and the Savage (1968)
The Young Tigers (1968)
The Young Toerless (1966)
Young Tom Edison (1940)
Young Widow (1946)
Youngblood Hawke (1964)
The Younger Brothers (1949)
The Youngest Profession (1943)
Your Child, the Unknown Creature (1970)
Your Husband, the Unknown Creature (1970)
Your Past Is Showing (1958)
Your Uncle Dudley (1935)
You're a Big Boy Now (1966)
You're in the Navy Now (1951)
You're Never Too Young (1955)
You're Only Young Once (1937)
You're Telling Me (1942)
Yours, Mine and Ours (1968)
Youth March (1970)
The Youth of Maxim (1934)
Youth on Parade (1942)
Youth Runs Wild (1944)
Yukon Manhunt (1951)
The Yukon Patrol (1942)
Yukon Vengeance (1954)

Zachariah (1971)
Zamba (1949)
Zamboanga (1937)
Zanzabuku (1956)
Zanzibar (1940)
Zarak (1957)
Zebra in the Kitchen (1965)
Zenobia (1939)
Zeppelin (1971)
Zero for Conduct (1933)
Zero Hour! (1957)
Ziegfeld Girl (1941)
Zigzag (1970)
Zombies of Mora-Tau (1957)
Zombies on Broadway (1945)
Zoo in Budapest (1933)
Zorba the Greek (1964)
Zotz! (1962)
Zoya (1944)
Zulu (1964)

Chapter X

FILMS AND THEIR COMPOSERS/ADAPTORS

Key to Abbreviations

AA	Allied Artists
ABC	American Broadcasting Corp.
AE	Associated Exhibitors
AFR	Africa
AI	American International
ALC	Alco
ALL	Allied
AMB	Ambassador
AP	Associated Producers
API	API Productions
APO	Apollo
ARC	American Releasing Corp.
ARG	Argentina
ARR	Arrow
ART	Artclass or Artcraft
AST	Astor
AUD	Audible Pictures
AUS	Austria
AUT	Australia
BEL	Belgium
BER	Bertad Pictures
BIO	Biograph
BJU	Bob Jones Un.
BOL	Bolex Corp.
BOS	Bosworth
BRA	Brazil
BRI	Great Britain
BRO	Broadway Star
BUL	Bulgaria
CAN	Canada
CAP	Capitol Film Ex.
CBC	Canadian Broadcasting Corp.
CBS	Columbia Broadcasting System
CC	Cinema Center
CEY	Ceylon
CHE	Chesterfield
CHI	Childhood Prod.
CHN	China
CIN	Cinerama
CKY	Clara Kimball Young
CMH	Contemporary/McGraw Hill
COL	Columbia
COM	Colorama or Comicolor
CON	Continental
COR	Coronet Films
COS	Cosmopolitan
CRO	Crown International
CUB	Cuba
CUE	Commonwealth United
CZE	Czechoslovakia
DCA	Distributor's Corp. of America
DEN	Denmark
DER	DeRochemont
DIS	Walt Disney (Buena Vista)
DYN	Dynamic Films
EAS	Eastern
EBE	Encyclopaedia Britannica
ED	Edison
EDU	Educational Pictures
EGY	Egypt
EL	Eagle-Lion
ELE	Electronovision
EMB	Avco-Embassy
EMP	Empire
EPI	Blumenthal-EPI
EQU	Equity
ESS	Essannay
FBO	Film Booking Offices

FC Film Classics
FD First Division
FIN Finland
FN First National
FOR Formosa
FOX Fox Films
FRA France
FRO Frohman
GER Germany
GHA Ghana
GN Grand National
GO Go Pictures
GOL Goldwyn
GOT Gotham
GRE Greece
GRI Griffith
HOD Hodginson
HOF Hoffberg
HOL Holland and Netherlands
HUN Hungary
IN India
INC Ince
IND Independent Release
IRE Ireland
ISR Israel
ITA Italy
JAP Japan
KAL Kalem
KE Klaw & Erlanger
KIN Kinemacolor
KLE Kleine/Edward L. Klein
KOR Korea
LIB Liberty
LIO Lionex
LIP Lippert
LOU Louben Pictures
LUB Lubin
MAG Magna
MAJ Majestic
MAL Malaysia
MAS Mascot
MEX Mexico
MGM Metro-Goldwyn-Mayer
MHF McGraw-Hill Films
MOL Monopol
MON Monogram
MOR Morocco
MUT Mutual
NAT National
NAY Nayfack
NBC National Broadcasting Co.
NET National Educational TV
NG National General
NOR Norway
OCE Ocean Film Corp.
OZ Oz Films
PAL Pallas
PAR Famous Players/Paramount
PAT Pathe/Pathe Freres
PDC Producers Distributing Corp.
PEE Peerless/Brady/World
PEW Peppercorn-Wormser
PHI Philippine Islands
PIO Pioneer
PLA Playboy
PLC Plunkett & Carroll
POL Poland
POR Portugal
POW Powers
PP Peter Pan
PPL Popular Players
PRC Producers Releasing Corp.
PRE Preferred
PRI Principal
PRZ Prizma Pictures
PS Popular Science
PUR Puritan
PWP Public Welfare Pictures
R radio production
RAN Rankin/Bass
RAY Rayart
RC Robertson-Cole
REA Realart
REL Reliable or Reliance
REP Republic
REX Rex/Rex Beach
RKO RKO Radio Pictures
ROS Rosemary Films
ROU Roumania
RUS Russia/Soviet Union
SA South America
SAC Sacred Pictures
SAS Stage & Screen
SEL Selig
SEZ Selznick
SG Screen Guild
SIG Sigma 3
SOL Solax
SPA Spain
SRO Selznick Releasing Org.
STE Sterling
STG Steger
SWE Sweden
SWI Switzerland
SYN Syndicate Pictures
TAI Thailand
TCF 20th Century-Fox

TER	Paul Terry	UA	United Artists
THA	Thanhouser	UN	Universal
TIF	Tiffany	URU	Uruguay
TIM	Time-Life Films	VIT	Vitagraph
TOB	Tobis	WB	Warner Brothers
TPE	Talking Picture Epics	WES	Western
TRI	Triangle	WOL	Wolpar
TUR	Turkey	WOR	World
TV	television production	WW	World Wide/Sono-Art
		YUG	Yugoslavia

1908

The Assassination of the Duc de Guise	FRA	Camille Saint-Saens
Stenka Razin	RUS	Mikhail Ippolitov-Ivanov

1909

Song About the Merchant Kalashnikov	RUS	Mikhail Ippolitov-Ivanov

1911

Arrah-Na-Pough (short)	IND	Walter Cleveland Simon

1912

Queen Elizabeth	PAR	Joseph Carl Briel

1914

Cabiria	ITA	Joseph Carl Briel
A Fool There Was	TCF	B. Gay
The Patchwork Girl of Oz	OZ	Louis Gottschalk
Volga and Siberia	RUS	Mikhail Ippolitov-Ivanov

1915

L'Amica	ITA	Pietro Mascagni
The Battle Cry of Peace	VIT	S. L. Rothapfel
The Birth of a Nation	BRI	Joseph Carl Briel
Carmen	PAR	Hugo Riesenfeld
Double Trouble	TRI	Joseph Carl Briel
The Edge of the Abyss	TRI	Victor Schertzinger
The Lily and the Rose	TRI	Joseph Carl Briel
Martyrs of the Alamo	TRI	Joseph Carl Briel
The Return of Ulysses	FRA	Georges Hue
Satanic Rhapsody	ITA	Pietro Mascagni

1916

The American Beauty	PAR	E.G. Norris

The Beckoning Flame	TRI	Victor Schertzinger
The Beloved Vagabond	FRA	Darius Milhaud
The Bondman	TCF	Max Steiner
Civilization	INC	Victor Schertzinger
The Conqueror	TRI	Victor Schertzinger
D'Artagnan	TRI	Victor Schertzinger
Daughter of the Gods	TCF	Robert Hood Bowers
The Fall of a Nation	NAT	Victor Herbert
The Heart of Paula	PAR	William S. Charles
Intolerance	GRI	Joseph Carl Briel
Peggy	TRI	Victor Schertzinger
Prudence and the Pirate	THA	Ernst Luz
The Red Circle	PAT	Abe Olman

1917

The Garden of Allah	SEL	George A. Little Billy Baskette Leon Flatow
Joan the Woman	PAR	Hugo Riesenfeld
Reaching for the Moon	ART	Oliver Wallace
Song of the North	IND	Frederick Owen Hanks Sol Levy

1918

False Faces	PAR	Pete Wendling
Hearts of the World	GRI	Carl Elinor
Mickey	WES	Neil Moret
Shoulder Arms	FN	Charles Chaplin

1919

The Blue Bonnet	HOD	Fred Fisher
Broken Blossoms	GRI	Louis Gottschalk
Checkers	TCF	Leo Edwards Edgar Allen
The Cup of Fury	GOL	Madelyn Sheppart
Deliverance	IND	George Alfred Lewis
Desert Gold	HOD	Bert Grant
Evangeline	TCF	Fred Fisher
Eyes of the Soul	ART	Fred Fisher
Fallen Idols	TCF	Richard Whiting
Fires of Faith	PAR	M. K. Jerome
The Valley of the Giants	PAR	Bert Grant

1920

The Blue Bird	PAR	Hugo Riesenfeld
Humoresque	PAR	Hugo Riesenfeld
Kismet	RC	Carl Edouarde
Robin Hood	UA	Victor Schertzinger
Way Down East	UA	William Frederick Peters

1921

Dream Street	GRI	Louis Silvers
Four Horsemen of the Apocalypse	MGM	Ernst Luz
The Kid	FN	Charles Chaplin

1922

Foolish Wives	UN	Sigmund Romberg
Orphans of the Storm	UA	Louis Gottschalk William Frederick Peters
The Pilgrim	FN	Charles Chaplin
La Roue	FRA	Arthur Honegger
The Rubaiyat of Omar Khayyam	IND	Charles Wakefield Cadman
Salome	ALL	George M. Rubenstein
When Knighthood Was in Flower	PAR	William Frederick Peters

1923

The Covered Wagon	PAR	Hugo Riesenfeld
The Dramatic Life of Abraham Lincoln	---	Joseph Carl Briel
Enemies of Women	GOL	William Frederick Peters
Kriemhild's Revenge	GER	Gottfried Huppertz
Little Old New York	GOL	William Frederick Peters
Puritan Passions	HOD	Frederick Shepherd Converse
Siegfried	GER	Gottfried Huppertz
The Ten Commandments	PAR	Hugo Riesenfeld
Under the Red Robe	GOL	William Frederick Peters
The White Rose	UA	Joseph Carl Briel

1924

Ballet Mechanique (short)	GER	George Anthiel
The Chechahcos	AE	Edward Kilenyi
Entr'acte (short)	FRA	Erik Satie
Fait Divers	FRA	Arthur Honegger
Greed	MGM	Leo Kempinski
His Darker Self	PDC	Edward Kilenyi
The Iron Horse	TCF	Erno Rapee
Isn't Life Wonderful?	UA	Cesare Sodero Louis Silvers
Janice Meredith	MGM	Deems Taylor
The Last Man on Earth	TCF	Erno Rapee
The Lover of Camille	WB	Mischa Guterson
A Quois Revent Les Jeunes Filles	FRA	Roger Desormiere
The Thief of Bagdad	UA	Mortimer Wilson
Try and Get It	---	Edward Kilenyi
Yolande	MGM	William Frederick Peters

1925

Beggar on Horseback	PAR	Hugo Riesenfeld
The Big Parade	MGM	William Axt David Mendoza
Don Q, Son of Zorro	UA	Mortimer Wilson
The Fool	TCF	Adolph Kornspan
Grass	PAR	Hugo Riesenfeld
L'Inhumaine	FRA	Darius Milhaud
Madame Sans-Gene	PAR	Hugo Riesenfeld
Miracle of the Wolves	FRA	M. Rabaud
The Merry Widow	MGM	William Axt David Mendoza
Peak of Fate	---	James Bradford
The Phantom of the Opera	UN	David Broekman
Pony Express	PAR	Hugo Riesenfeld
Potemkin	RUS	Edmund Meisel
The Proud Heart	---	Edward Kilenyi
The Vanishing American	PAR	Hugo Riesenfeld
The Wanderer	PAR	Hugo Riesenfeld

1926

Adventures of Prince Achmed	GER	Wolfgang Zeller
Beau Geste	PAR	Hugo Riesenfeld
La Boheme	MGM	William Axt David Mendoza
Ben-Hur	MGM	William Axt David Mendoza
The Black Pirate	UA	Mortimer Wilson
Don Juan	WB	William Axt David Mendoza
Film Record of the Eucharistic Congress	TCF	Otto Singenberger Erno Rapee
The Fire Brigade	MGM	William Axt David Mendoza
The Flaming Frontier	UN	Hugo Riesenfeld
Mare Nostrum	MGM	William Axt David Mendoza
Metropolis	GER	Gottfried Huppertz
Michael Strogoff	UN	Edward Kilenyi
The Midnight Sun	UN	Edward Kilenyi
Napoleon	FRA	Arthur Honegger
Old Ironside	PAR	Hugo Riesenfeld J. O. Zamencnik
The Prince of Pilsen	PDC	Hugo Riesenfeld
The Rough Riders	PAR	Hugo Riesenfeld
The Scarlet Letter	MGM	William Axt David Mendoza
Seventh Heaven	TCF	Erno Rapee
The Sorrows of Satan	PAR	Hugo Riesenfeld
Sunrise	TCF	Erno Rapee
Tartuffe	GER	Guiseppe Becce

The Unknown Soldier	IND	Jean Sibelius
The Volga Boatman	PDC	Hugo Riesenfeld
What Price Glory?	TCF	Erno Rapee

1927

Annie Laurie	MGM	William Axt David Mendoza
Berlin--Symphony of a Great City	GER	Edmund Meisel
Camille	FN	William Axt David Mendoza
The Devil Dancer	MGM	Carl Elinor
The Italian Straw Hat	FRA	Jacques Ibert
The Jazz Singer	WB	Louis Silvers
King of Kings	PDC	Hugo Riesenfeld
Krazy Kat at the Circus (short)	RC	Paul Hindemith
Loves of Carmen	TCF	Manuel M. Ponce
Les Miserables	UN	Hugo Riesenfeld
The Private Life of Helen of Troy	FN	Carl Edouarde
Rien Que Les Heures	FRA	Yves de la Casiniere
Slide, Kelly, Slide	MGM	William Axt David Mendoza
The Spy	GER	Werner Heymann
Ten Days that Shook the World	TCF	Edmund Meisel
When a Man Loves	WB	Henry Hadley

1928

Abie's Irish Rose	PAR	J.B. Zamencnik
Actualities (newsreels)	FRA	Darius Milhaud
The Awakening	UA	Hugo Riesenfeld
Battle of the Sexes	UA	Nathaniel Shilkret
Beggars of Life	PAR	Karl Hajos
The Cavalier	TIF	Hugo Riesenfeld
The End of St. Petersburg	RUS	Herbert Stothart
Fazil	TCF	Erno Rapee
4 Devils	TCF	S. L. Rothafel
Four Sons	TCF	Erno Rapee
Loves of an Actress	PAR	Karl Hajos
Lucky Duck (short)	IND	H. Whitney
Mother Knows Best	TCF	S. L. Rothafel
Noah's Ark	WB	Louis Silvers
October	RUS	Edmund Meisel
Opus 3 (short)	GER	Hanns Eisler
Our Dancing Daughters	MGM	William Axt David Mendoza
The Passion of Joan of Arc	FRA	Leo Poufet Victor Allix
The Patriot	PAR	Gerard Carbonara Domenico Savino
Ramona	TCF	L. Wolfe Gilbert Hugo Riesenfeld
Red Dance	TCF	Erno Rapee

Revenge	UA	Hugo Riesenfeld
Sawdust Paradise	PAR	Gerard Carbonara
Sins of the Fathers	PAR	Hugo Riesenfeld
Spies	GER	Werner Heymann
Street Angel	TCF	Erno Rapee
Submarine	COL	Ernest Luz
Tempest	PAR	Hugo Riesenfeld
The Toilers	TIF	Hugo Riesenfeld
Two Lovers	UA	Hugo Riesenfeld
Warming Up	PAR	Gerard Carbonara
We Americans	UN	Josef Cherniavsky
The Wedding March	PAR	J. B. Zamencnik Louis de Francesco
White Shadows of the South Seas	UA	Hugo Riesenfeld
The Woman Disputed	UA	Hugo Riesenfeld
The Woman on the Moon	GER	Willi Schmidt-Gentner

1929

Berlin Carnival (short)	GER	Walter Gronostay
Blackmail	BRI	Hubert Bath
Bridge of San Luis Rey	MGM	Carl Elinor
Drums of Love	UA	Charles Wakefield Cadman
Four Feathers	PAR	William Frederick Peters
Ghosts Before Breakfast (short)	GER	Paul Hindemith
The Great Gabbo	TCF	Howard Jackson
Hearts in Dixie	TCF	Howard Jackson
Hungarian Rhapsody	PAR	William Frederick Peters
Kitty	BRI	Hubert Bath
Lady of the Pavements	UA	Hugo Friedhofer Irving Berlin
Mississippi Gambler	UN	David Broekman
Mother Machree	TCF	Erno Rapee
New Babylon	RUS	Dmitri Shostakovich
Overture 1812 (short)	IND	Hugo Riesenfeld
Pays Du Scalp	FRA	Maurice Jaubert
The Queen's Necklace	FRA	André Roubaud
Rain (short)	HOL	Lon Lichtveld
The Rescue	UA	Hugo Riesenfeld
Seven Faces	TCF	Hugo Riesenfeld
Sunny Side Up	TCF	Howard Jackson
Tonight at Twelve	UN	David Broekman
The Trail of '98	MGM	William Axt David Mendoza
Weltmelodie (short)	GER	Wolfgang Zeller

1930

All Quiet on the Western Front	UN	David Broekman
Alone	RUS	Dmitri Shostakovich
The Big Trail	TCF	Hugo Friedhofer
Blood of a Poet	FRA	Georges Auric
The Blue Angel	PAR	Frederick Hollander

Captain of the Guard	UN	Charles Wakefield Cadman
Les Cinq Gentlemen Maudits	FRA	Jacques Ibert
A Devil with Women	TCF	Hugo Friedhofer
Dynamite	MGM	Herbert Stothart
Going Wild	WB	Erno Rapee
The Golden Calf	TCF	Hugo Friedhofer
Happy Days	TCF	Hugo Friedhofer
Hell's Angels	UA	Hugo Riesenfeld
Just Imagine	TCF	Hugo Friedhofer
King of Jazz	UN	Ferde Grofe
Men on Call	TCF	Hugo Friedhofer
No Man's Land	GER	Hanns Eisler
Old English	WB	Erno Rapee
One Romantic Night	UA	Hugo Riesenfeld
Outside the Law	UN	David Broekman
The Princess and the Plumber	TCF	Hugo Friedhofer
Romance Sentimentale	FRA	A. Alexandrov
Song of Life	GER	Hanns Eisler
Under the Roofs of Paris	FRA	Armand Bernard J. Drejac
War Is Hell	GER	Hanns Eisler

1931

Always Goodbye	TCF	Hugo Friedhofer
Arrowsmith	UA	Alfred Newman
The Bells (short)	BRI	Gustav Holst
Cimarron	RKO	Max Steiner
City Lights	UA	Charles Chaplin
Congress Dances	GER	Werner Heymann
A Connecticut Yankee	TCF	Erno Rapee
Daddy Long Legs	TCF	Hugo Friedhofer
Emil and the Detectives	GER	Allan Gray
Frankenstein	UN	David Broekman
Golden Mountains	RUS	Dmitri Shostakovich
Heartbreak	TCF	Hugo Friedhofer
Kiki	UA	Alfred Newman
Kismet	WB	Edward Ward
Kuhle Wampe	GER	Hanns Eisler
Maedchen in Uniform	GER	Hanson-Milde Meissner
The Man Who Came Back	TCF	Hugo Friedhofer
Marius	FRA	Vincent Scotto
Le Million	FRA	Georges van Parys Armand Bernard Philippe Pares
Morocco	PAR	Karl Hajos
My Sin	PAR	John Green
A Nous La Liberte	FRA	Georges Auric
Over the Hill	TCF	Erno Rapee
Pacific 231 (short)	FRA	Arthur Honegger
Reaching for the Moon	UA	Alfred Newman
The Right to Love	PAR	W. Franke Harling
The Road to Life	RUS	Jacob Stolyar

Secrets of a Secretary	PAR	John Green
Skyline	TCF	Hugo Friedhofer
The Spider	TCF	Hugo Friedhofer
The Squaw Man	PAR	Herbert Stothart
Street Scene	UA	Alfred Newman
Surf and Seaweed (short)	IND	Marc Blitzstein
Tabu	PAR	Hugo Riesenfeld
Trader Horn	MGM	Charles Maxwell
Transatlantic	TCF	Hugo Friedhofer R. H. Bassett
Wayward	PAR	John Green
The Wiser Sex	PAR	John Green
The Yellow Ticket	TCF	Hugo Friedhofer

1932

L'Affaire Est Dans Le Sac	FRA	Maurice Jaubert
Amateur Daddy	TCF	Hugo Friedhofer
A Bill of Divorcement	RKO	Max Steiner
Bird of Paradise	RKO	Max Steiner
The Borinage	BEL	Hans Hauska
Bring 'Em Back Alive	RKO	Gene Rodemich
Careless Lady	TCF	Hugo Friedhofer
Counterplan	RUS	Dmitri Shostakovich
The Devil's Lottery	TCF	Hugo Friedhofer
Extase	CZE	Giuseppe Becce
Fanny	FRA	Vincent Scotto
The First Year	TCF	Hugo Friedhofer
The Man from Spain	FRA	Jean Wiener
La Maternelle	FRA	Edouard Flament
Mr. Robinson Crusoe	UA	Alfred Newman
Mystery Ranch	TCF	Hugo Friedhofer
The Painted Woman	TCF	Hugo Friedhofer
Passport to Hell	TCF	Hugo Friedhofer
Poil de Carotte	FRA	Alexandre Tansman
Quatorze Juillet	FRA	Maurice Jaubert
Rebecca of Sunnybrook Farm	TCF	Hugo Friedhofer
Scarface	UA	Adolph Tandler
Second-Hand Wife	TCF	Hugo Friedhofer
Shanghai Express	PAR	W. Franke Harling
Sherlock Holmes	TCF	Hugo Friedhofer R. H. Bassett
Sign of the Cross	PAR	Rudolph Kopp
Smilin' Through	MGM	William Axt
A Song About Heroes	RUS	Hanns Eisler
The Trial of Vivienne Ware	TCF	Hugo Friedhofer
What Price Hollywood?	RKO	Max Steiner
The Woman in Room 13	TCF	Hugo Friedhofer

1933

Adorable	TCF	Werner Heymann
Advice to the Lovelorn	UA	Alfred Newman

Ann Vickers	RKO	Max Steiner
As Husbands Go	TCF	Hugo Friedhofer
Bed of Roses	RKO	Max Steiner
Berkley Square	TCF	Louis de Francesco
Blind Adventure	RKO	Max Steiner
Bondage	TCF	Hugo Friedhofer
Broadway Bad	TCF	Hugo Friedhofer
Broadway Thru a Keyhole	UA	Alfred Newman
Broadway to Hollywood	MGM	William Axt
Cavalcade	TCF	Louis de Francesco
The Constant Nymph	BRI	Eugene Goossens John Greenwood
Cradle Song	PAR	W. Franke Harling
Dancing Lady	MGM	Louis Silvers
Dangerously Yours	TCF	Hugo Friedhofer
The Deserter	RUS	Y. Shaporin
Destination Unknown	UN	W. Franke Harling
The Devil's Brother	MGM	LeRoy Shield
Dinner at Eight	MGM	William Axt
Emergency Call	RKO	Max Steiner
Eskimo	MGM	William Axt
The Face in the Sky	TCF	Hugo Friedhofer
Gabriel over the White House	MGM	William Axt
Girl without a Room	PAR	Howard Jackson
The Good Companions	TCF	Hugo Friedhofer
The Great Glass Blower (short)	FRA	Jean Wiener
It's Great to Be Alive	TCF	Hugo Friedhofer
King Kong	RKO	Max Steiner
Liliom	GER	Jean Renoir Franz Waxman
Melody Cruise	RKO	Max Steiner
Morning Glory	RKO	Max Steiner
My Lips Betray	TCF	Hugo Friedhofer
Night Flight	MGM	Herbert Stothart
One Man's Journey	RKO	Max Steiner
Our Betters	RKO	Max Steiner
Peg O' My Heart	MGM	Herbert Stothart
Private Life of Henry VIII	BRI	Kurt Schroeder
Professional Sweetheart	RKO	Max Steiner
Rasputin and the Empress	MGM	Herbert Stothart
Reunion in Vienna	MGM	William Axt
The Silver Cord	RKO	Max Steiner
Song of Songs	PAR	Ralph Rainger
Storm at Daybreak	MGM	William Axt
Sweepings	RKO	Max Steiner
This Day and Age	MGM	Howard Jackson
Thunder over Mexico	MEX	Hugo Riesenfeld
Topaze	RKO	Max Steiner
White Sister	MGM	Herbert Stothart
Zero for Conduct	FRA	Maurice Jaubert
Zoo in Budapest	TCF	Hugo Friedhofer

1934

The Affairs of Cellini	UA	Alfred Newman
Alice in Wonderland	PAR	Dimitri Tiomkin
L'Atalante	FRA	Maurice Jaubert
The Barretts of Wimpole Street	MGM	Herbert Stothart
Beloved	UN	Howard Jackson Victor Schertzinger
Bolero	PAR	Ralph Rainger
Bottoms Up	TCF	Constantin Bakaleinikoff
Bulldog Drummond Strikes Back	UA	Alfred Newman
By Candlelight	UA	W. Franke Harling
Catherine the Great	UA	Muir Mathieson
The Cat's Paw	TCF	Alfred Newman
Chapeyev	RUS	Gabriel Popov
Change of Heart	TCF	Hugo Friedhofer
Cleopatra	PAR	Rudolph Kopp
The Coming Out Party	TCF	Hugo Friedhofer
The Count of Monte Cristo	UA	Alfred Newman
The Crime Doctor	RKO	Max Steiner
The Czar Wants to Sleep (Lieutenant Kije)	RUS	Sergei Prokofiev
David Harum	TCF	Louis de Francesco
Death Takes a Holiday	PAR	Sigmund Krumgold
Le Dernier Milliadaire	FRA	Maurice Jaubert
Don Quixote	FRA	Jacques Ibert
Easter Island (short)	FRA	Maurice Jaubert
Evensong	BRI	Louis Levy
The Fountain	RKO	Max Steiner
Four Frightened People	PAR	Karl Hajos
Gallant Lady	UA	Alfred Newman
The Girl from Missouri	MGM	William Axt
Great Expectations	UN	Edward Ward
Hat, Coat and Glove	RKO	Max Steiner
Hide-Out	MGM	William Axt
L'Hippocampe	FRA	Darius Milhaud
House of Rothschild	TCF	Alfred Newman
I Am Suzanne	TCF	Louis de Francesco
L'Idee (short)	FRA	Arthur Honegger
If I Were Free	RKO	Max Steiner
Imitation of Life	UN	Heinz Roemheld
The Last Gentleman	UA	Alfred Newman
Let's Try Again	RKO	Max Steiner
Lieutenant Kije (see The Czar Wants to Sleep)		
The Life of Vergie Winters	RKO	Max Steiner
Little Women	RKO	Max Steiner
Looking for Trouble	UA	Alfred Newman
The Lost Patrol	RKO	Max Steiner
Madame Bovary	FRA	Darius Milhaud
Man of Aran	BRI	John Greenwood
Man of Two Worlds	RKO	Max Steiner
Mari Chapdelaine	FRA	Jean Wiener

Men in White	MGM	William Axt
Les Miserables	FRA	Arthur Honegger
Moulin Rouge	UA	Alfred Newman
Murder on the Blackboard	RKO	Max Steiner
Music in the Air	TCF	Louis de Francesco
Nana	UA	Alfred Newman
New Earth	HOL	Hanns Eisler
Now I'll Tell All	TCF	Hugo Friedhofer
Of Human Bondage	RKO	Max Steiner
The Old-Fashioned Way	PAR	Harry Revel
One More River	UN	W. Franke Harling
One Night of Love	COL	Louis Silvers
Operator 13	MGM	William Axt
Our Daily Bread	UA	Alfred Newman
The Painted Veil	MGM	Herbert Stothart
Le Paquebot Tenacity	FRA	Jean Wiener
Pett and Pott (short)	BRI	Walter Leigh
The Private Life of Don Juan	BRI	Mischa Spoliansky
Private Scandal	PAR	Lee Zahler
Queen Christina	MGM	Herbert Stothart
The Richest Girl in the World	RKO	Max Steiner
Riptide	MGM	Herbert Stothart
The Sea Horse (short)	FRA	Darius Milhaud
Servant's Entrance	TCF	Hugo Friedhofer
Sing and Like It	RKO	Dave Dreyer
Son of Kong	RKO	J. O. Taylor Max Steiner
Song of Ceylon	BRI	Walter Leigh
Spitfire	RKO	Max Steiner
Stand Up and Cheer	TCF	Arthur Lange
Stingaree	RKO	Max Steiner
Strictly Dynamite	RKO	Max Steiner
Success at Any Price	RKO	Max Steiner
The Thin Man	MGM	William Axt
This Man Is Mine	RKO	Max Steiner
This Side of Heaven	MGM	William Axt
Three Sons about Lenin	RUS	Y. Shaporin
Treasure Island	MGM	Herbert Stothart
Triumph of the Will	GER	Herbert Windt
Viva Villa!	MGM	Herbert Stothart
We Live Again	UA	Alfred Newman
What Every Woman Knows	MGM	Herbert Stothart
Where Sinners Meet	RKO	Max Steiner
Wild Cargo	RKO	Winston Sharples
The World Moves On	TCF	Hugo Friedhofer
The Youth of Maxim	RUS	Dmitri Shostakovich

1935

Alias Bulldog Drummond	BRI	Louis Levy
Alice Adams	RKO	Roy Webb
All the King's Horses	PAR	Milan Roder
Anna Karenina	MGM	Herbert Stothart
La Bandera	FRA	Jean Wiener

Barbary Coast	UA	Alfred Newman
Becky Sharp	RKO	Max Steiner
The Bishop Misbehaves	MGM	Edward Ward
Call of the Wild	UA	Alfred Newman
Captain Blood	WB	Erich Wolfgang Korngold
Cardinal Richelieu	UA	Alfred Newman
La Cathedrale Des Morts (short)	FRA	Jean Wiener
China Seas	MGM	Herbert Stothart
Coalface (short)	BRI	Benjamin Britten
Crime and Punishment	FRA	Arthur Honegger
The Crime of M. Lange	FRA	Jean Wiener
The Crusades	PAR	Rudolph Kopp
Curly Top	TCF	Hugo Friedhofer
Dante's Inferno	TCF	Hugo Friedhofer R. H. Bassett Samuel Kaylin
Dark Angel	UA	Alfred Newman
David Copperfield	MGM	William Axt
Diamond Jim	UN	Ferde Grofe Franz Waxman
East of Java	UN	Franz Waxman
Escape Me Never	UA	William Walton
The Farmer Takes a Wife	TCF	Oscar Bradley
The Gay Deception	TCF	Louis de Francesco
Ginger	TCF	Samuel Kaylin
The Great Impersonation	UN	Franz Waxman
Hands Across the Table	PAR	Sam Coslow
Here Comes the Band	MGM	Herbert Stothart
Here's to Romance	TCF	Hugo Friedhofer
His Night Out	UN	Franz Waxman
I Dream Too Much	RKO	Max Steiner
I Live My Life	MGM	Dimitri Tiomkin
In Old Kentucky	TCF	Arthur Lange
In Person	RKO	Roy Webb
The Informer	RKO	Max Steiner
It's in the Air	MGM	William Axt
Jenny	FRA	Joseph Kosma
King Solomon of Broadway	UN	Daniel Mandell
The Last Days of Pompeii	RKO	Roy Webb
The Last of the Pagans	MGM	Hugo Friedhofer Karl Hajos William Axt
The Last Outpost	PAR	Milan Roder
The Little Colonel	TCF	Arthur Lange
The Littlest Rebel	TCF	Cyril J. Mockridge
Love Me Forever	COL	Louis Silvers
Loves of a Dictator	BRI	Karol Rathaus
The Man Who Broke the Bank at Monte Carlo	TCF	Oscar Bradley
Manhattan Moon	UN	Karl Hajos
Mary Burns, Fugitive	PAR	Heinz Roemheld
Metropolitan	TCF	Alfred Newman
Millions in the Air	PAR	Frederick Hollander

Les Miserables	UA	Alfred Newman
Mr. Hobo	BRI	Louis Levy
Murder Man	MGM	William Axt
Mutiny on the Bounty	MGM	Bronislau Kaper
The Mystery of Edwin Drood	UN	Edward Ward
The New Gulliver	RUS	Lev Schwartz
No More Ladies	MGM	Edward Ward
Old Man Rhythm	RKO	Lewis Gensler
Orchids to You	TCF	Hugo Friedhofer
O'Shaughnessy's Boy	MGM	William Axt
Peasants	RUS	V. Pushkov
Pepo	RUS	Aram Khachaturian
Peter Ibbetson	PAR	Ernst Toch
Public Hero No. 1	MGM	Edward Ward
The Return of Peter Grimm	RKO	Alberto Colombo
Sanders of the River	BRI	Mischa Spoliansky
The Scoundrel	PAR	George Anthiel
Shanghai	PAR	Frederick Hollander
She	RKO	Alfred Newman
Show Them No Mercy	TCF	David Buttolph
So Red the Rose	PAR	W. Franke Harling
Splendor	UA	Alfred Newman
Steamboat 'Round the Bend	TCF	Samuel Kaylin
Things to Come	BRI	Sir Arthur Bliss
Three Kids and a Queen	UN	Franz Waxman
The Three Musketeers	RKO	Max Steiner
Toni	FRA	Bozzi
Transatlantic Tunnel	BRI	Louis Levy
The Turn of the Tide (short)	BRI	Sir Arthur Benjamin
The Wave	MEX	Silvestre Revaeltas
Way Down East	TCF	Hugo Friedhofer
The Wedding of Palo	HOF	Emil Reesen
Whipsaw	MGM	William Axt
Your Uncle Dudley	TCF	Samuel Kaylin

1936

Absolute Quiet	MGM	Franz Waxman
Accused	UA	Percival Mackey
Adventures in Manhattan	COL	Morris Stoloff
Aerograd (Frontier)	RUS	Dmitri Kabalevsky
After the Thin Man	MGM	Herbert Stothart
Ah, Wilderness	MGM	Herbert Stothart
Amateur Gentleman	UA	Walter Goehr Richard Addinsell
And So They Were Married	COL	Howard Jackson
Annie Oakley	RKO	Alberto Colombo
Anthony Adverse	WB	Erich Wolfgang Korngold
As You Like It	BRI	William Walton
Banjo on My Knee	TCF	Arthur Lange
Big Brown Eyes	PAR	Gerard Carbonara
The Bride Walks Out	RKO	Roy Webb
Bunker Bean	RKO	Roy Webb

Calendar of the Year (short)	BRI	Sir Benjamin Britten
Camille	MGM	Herbert Stothart
Captain January	TCF	Louis Silvers
The Case Against Mrs. Ames	PAR	Gerard Carbonara
Cesar	FRA	Vincent Scotto
Champagne Charlie	TCF	Samuel Kaylin
The Charge of the Light Brigade	WB	Max Steiner
Chatterbox	RKO	Alberto Colombo
China Clipper	WB	W. Franke Harling
The Clairvoyant	BRI	Sir Arthur Benjamin
Come and Get It	UA	Alfred Newman
Conflict	UN	Herman Heller
Craig's Wife	COL	Morris Stoloff
Daniel Boone	RKO	Arthur Kay
Dawn of Iran (short)	BRI	Walter Leigh
Desire	PAR	Frederick Hollander
The Devil Doll	MGM	Franz Waxman
The Devil Is a Sissy	MGM	Herbert Stothart
Dimples	TCF	Louis Silvers
Dodsworth	UA	Alfred Newman
Earthworm Tractors	WB	Leo F. Forbstein
East Meets West	BRI	Louis Levy
Elephant Boy	BRI	John Greenwood
Every Saturday Night	TCF	Samuel Kaylin
Everybody's Old Man	TCF	David Buttolph
Exclusive Story	MGM	Edward Ward
The Ex-Mrs. Bradford	RKO	Roy Webb
The Farmer in the Dell	RKO	Alberto Colombo
Fatal Lady	PAR	Victor Young
First a Girl	BRI	Louis Levy
Flying Hostess	UN	Herman Heller
Follow Your Heart	REP	Harry Grey
Forgotten Faces (see Till We Meet Again)		
Fury	WB	Franz Waxman
The Future's in the Air (short)	BRI	William Alwyn
The Garden of Allah	UA	Max Steiner
The Gay Desperado	UA	Alfred Newman
The General Died at Dawn	PAR	Werner Janssen Gerard Carbonara
General Spanky	MGM	Marvin Hatley
Girl Friends	RUS	Dmitri Shostakovich
Girl's Dormitory	TCF	Arthur Lange
The Golden Arrow	WB	W. Franke Harling
The Good Earth	MGM	Herbert Stothart
The Gorgeous Hussey	MGM	Herbert Stothart
Great Guy	GN	Marlin Skiles
The Green Pastures	WB	Erich Wolfgang Korngold
His Brother's Wife	MGM	Franz Waxman
House of a Thousand Candles	REP	Arthur Kay
I Married a Doctor	WB	W. Franke Harling
I'd Give a Million	ITA	Gian Luca Tocci
In His Steps	GN	Abe Meyer

It Had to Happen	TCF	Arthur Lange
It's Love Again	BRI	Louis Levy Bretton Byrd
Janosik	CZE	Milos Smatek
The King Steps Out	COL	Howard Jackson
Ladies in Love	TCF	Louis Silvers
The Lady Consents	RKO	Roy Webb
The Last of the Mohicans	UA	Nathaniel Shilkret
The Last Outlaw	RKO	Alberto Colombo
Let's Sing Again	RKO	Hugo Riesenfeld
Libeled Lady	MGM	William Axt
Little Lord Fauntleroy	UA	Max Steiner
The Longest Night	MGM	Edward Ward
Love Before Breakfast	UN	Franz Waxman
Love on a Bet	RKO	Alberto Colombo
Love on the Run	MGM	Franz Waxman
The Lower Depths	FRA	Roger Desormiere Jean Wiener
Mad Love	MGM	Oscar Radin
The Magnificent Brute	UN	Charles Previn
Magnificent Obsession	UN	Franz Waxman
Mary of Scotland	RKO	Carroll Clark
Meet Nero Wolfe	COL	Howard Jackson
A Message to Garcia	TCF	Louis Silvers
A Midsummer Night's Dream	WB	Erich Wolfgang Korngold
Mr. Deeds Goes to Town	COL	Howard Jackson
M'Liss	RKO	Alberto Colombo
Modern Times	UA	Charles Chaplin
The Moon's Our Home	PAR	Gerard Carbonara
Moonlight Murder	MGM	Edward Ward
More than a Secretary	COL	Morris Stoloff
The Music Goes 'Round	COL	Howard Jackson
Next Time We Love	UN	Franz Waxman
A Night at the Opera	MGM	Herbert Stothart
Nine Days a Queen	BRI	Louis Levy
Night Mail (short)	BRI	Benjamin Britten
Old Hutch	MGM	William Axt
Olympia	GER	Herbert Windt
One Rainy Afternoon	UA	Ralph Irwin
Palm Springs	PAR	Boris Morros
Parole	UN	Charles Maxwell
Un Partie de Campagne	FRA	Joseph Kosma
Passing of the Third Floor Back	BRI	Louis Levy
Pepper	TCF	Samuel Kaylin
Petticoat Fever	MGM	William Axt
Piccadilly Jim	MGM	William Axt
The Plainsman	PAR	George Anthiel
The Plow that Broke the Plains (short)	IND	Virgil Thomson
Poor Little Rich Girl	TCF	Louis Silvers
Poppy	PAR	Gerard Carbonara
The President's Mystery	REP	Hugo Riesenfeld

The Prisoner of Shark Island	TCF	Hugo Friedhofer R. H. Bassett
Private Number	TCF	Louis Silvers
Professional Soldier	TCF	Louis Silvers
Ramona	TCF	Alfred Newman
Rendezvous	MGM	William Axt
The Return of Maxim Gorky	RUS	Dmitri Shostakovich
Reunion	MGM	Emil Newman
Revolutionists	RUS	Nikolai Kryukov
Rhodes of Africa	BRI	Hubert Bath
Riffraff	MGM	Edward Ward
The River (short)	IND	Virgil Thomson
Road to Glory	TCF	Louis Silvers
Robin Hood of El Dorado	MGM	Herbert Stothart
Romeo and Juliet	MGM	Herbert Stothart
San Francisco	MGM	Bronislau Kaper
The Saving of Bill Blewett (short)	BRI	Benjamin Britten
Sea Spoilers	UN	Herman Heller
Secret Agent	BRI	Louis Levy
Seven Keys to Baldpate	RKO	Alberto Colombo
Seven Sinners	BRI	Louis Levy
Sinner Take All	MGM	Edward Ward
Sins of Man	TCF	Hugo Friedhofer R. H. Bassett Alexis Archangelsky
Small Town Girl	MGM	Herbert Stothart
Special Investigator	RKO	Roy Webb
Spendthrift	PAR	Gerard Carbonara
The Story of Louis Pasteur	WB	Erich Wolfgang Korngold
Sutter's Gold	UN	Franz Waxman
Suzy	MGM	William Axt
Sweetheart of the Navy	GN	Marlin Skiles
Sworn Enemy	MGM	Edward Ward
Sylvia Scarlett	RKO	Roy Webb
A Tale of Two Cities	MGM	Herbert Stothart
The Texas Rangers	PAR	Gerard Carbonara
Thank You, Jeeves	TCF	Samuel Kaylin
That Girl from Paris	RKO	Nathaniel Shilkret
Theodora Goes Wild	COL	Morris Stoloff
These Three	UA	Alfred Newman
36 Hours to Kill	TCF	Samuel Kaylin
Three Wise Guys	MGM	William Axt
Till We Meet Again	PAR	Frederick Hollander
To Mary, with Love	TCF	Louis Silvers
Too Many Parents	PAR	Milan Roder
Trail of the Lonesome Pine	PAR	Hugo Friedhofer Gerard Carbonara
Trouble for Two	MGM	Franz Waxman
23-1/2 Hours Leave	GN	Marlin Skiles
Two in a Crowd	UN	Charles Previn
Two in Revolt	RKO	Alberto Colombo
Under Two Flags	TCF	Louis Silvers
Under Your Spell	TCF	Arthur Lange

The Unguarded Hour	MGM	William Axt
Valiant Is the Word for Carrie	PAR	Boris Morros
The Voice of Bugle Ann	MGM	Rudolph Kopp
Walking on Air	RKO	Nathaniel Shilkret
Way Out West	MGM	Marvin Hatley
We Are from Kronstadt	RUS	Nikolai Kryukov
We Went to College	MGM	William Axt
Wedding Present	PAR	Gerard Carbonara
White Fang	TCF	Hugo Friedhofer Charles Maxwell
Winterset	RKO	Nathaniel Shilkret
With Love and Kisses	IND	Edward Kay
A Woman Rebels	RKO	Roy Webb
Yellow Cargo	GN	Abe Meyer
Yellowstone	UN	Herman Heller

1937

Another Dawn	WB	Erich Wolfgang Korngold
The Barrier (The Great Barrier)	BRI	Maurice Lawrence
Baltic Deputy	RUS	N. Timofeyev
Beg, Borrow or Steal	MGM	William Axt
Beloved Enemy	UA	Alfred Newman
Between Two Women	MGM	William Axt
Big City	MGM	William Axt
Bizarre, Bizarre (Drole De Drame)	FRA	Maurice Jaubert
Cafe Metropole	TCF	Louis Silvers
Captains Courageous	MGM	Franz Waxman
Un Carnet Du Bal	FRA	Maurice Jaubert
Danger! Love at Work	TCF	David Buttolph
Dangerous Number	MGM	David Snell
Devil's Playground	COL	Morris Stoloff
Double Wedding	MGM	Edward Ward
Easy Living	PAR	Milan Roder
Ebb Tide	PAR	Victor Young
Edge of the World	BRI	Lambert Williamson
50 Roads to Town	TCF	David Buttolph
Fire over England	BRI	Richard Addinsell
God's Country and the Woman	WB	Max Steiner
Golgotha	FRA	Jacques Ibert
The Good Old Soak	MGM	Edward Ward
Grand Illusion	FRA	Joseph Kosma
The Great Garrick	WB	Adolph Deutsch
The Green Light	WB	Max Steiner
Head over Heels in Love	BRI	Louis Levy
Headin' West	COL	Edward Kilenyi
Heart of Spain (short)	IND	Alex North
History Is Made at Night	UA	Alfred Newman
Internes Can't Take Money	PAR	Gregory Stone
John Meade's Woman	PAR	Frederick Hollander
Kid Galahad	WB	Max Steiner
The King and the Chorus Girl	WB	Herman Heller

The Last Gangster	MGM	Edward Ward
The Last of Mrs. Cheyney	MGM	William Axt
Lenin in October	RUS	A. Alexandrov
Let Them Live	UA	Louis Forbes
Line to the Tschierva Hut (short)	BRI	Benjamin Britten
Lloyds of London	TCF	Louis Silvers
London by Night	MGM	William Axt
Lone White Sail	RUS	M. Rauchberger
Lost Horizon	COL	Dimitri Tiomkin
Love from a Stranger	BRI	Benjamin Britten
Love Is News	TCF	David Buttolph
Madame X	MGM	David Snell
Mademoiselle Docteur	FRA	Arthur Honegger
Maid of Salem	PAR	Victor Young
Les Maisons de la Misere	BEL	Maurice Jaubert
Make Way for Tomorrow	PAR	George Anthiel
Man of Affairs	BRI	Louis Levy
Man of the People	MGM	Edward Ward
Mannequin	MGM	Edward Ward
Marked Woman	WB	David. Raksin
Mayerling	FRA	Arthur Honegger
Meet the Missus	RKO	Roy Webb
Men Are Not Gods	BRI	Muir Mathieson
The Mighty Treve	UN	David Raksin
Mountain Justice	WB	W. Franke Harling
Nancy Steele Is Missing	TCF	David Buttolph
Navy Blue and Gold	MGM	Edward Ward
New Faces of 1938	RKO	Roy Webb
New World for Old (short)	BRI	William Alwyn
Night Key	UN	Louis Forbes
Night Must Fall	MGM	Edward Ward
Nobody's Baby	MGM	Marvin Hatley
Oh, Doctor	UN	Louis Forbes
The Old Mill (short)	DIS	Leigh Harline
On Again, Off Again	RKO	Roy Webb
Outcast	PAR	Ernst Toch
Outcasts of Poker Flat	RKO	Roy Webb
Parnell	MGM	William Axt
People of the Cumberland (short)	IND	Alex North Earl Robinson
Pepe Le Moko	FRA	Vincent Scotto Mohammed Ygorbuchen
Personal Property	MGM	Franz Waxman
Peter the First (Part I)	RUS	Vladimir Scherbachev
Pick a Star	MGM	Marvin Hatley
The Plough and the Stars	RKO	Roy Webb
The Prince and the Pauper	WB	Erich Wolfgang Korngold
Quality Street	RKO	Roy Webb
The Queen and the Cardinal	FRA	Maurice Yvain
River of Unrest	BRI	Harry Acres
The Road Back	UN	Dimitri Tiomkin
Saratoga	MGM	Edward Ward
Sea Devils	RKO	Roy Webb

Second Honeymoon	TCF	David Buttolph
Seventh Heaven	TCF	Louis Silvers
Silent Barriers	BRI	Hubert Bath
The Soldier and the Lady	RKO	Nathaniel Shilkret
Something to Sing About	GN	Myrl Alderman
Souls at Sea	PAR	Roland Anderson
South Riding	BRI	Richard Addinsell
Spanish Earth	IND	Marc Blitzstein Virgil Thomson
Stand-In	UA	Heinz Roemheld
A Star Is Born	UA	Max Steiner
Stowaway	TCF	Louis Silvers
Submarine D-1	WB	Adolph Deutsch
They Won't Forget	WB	Adolph Deutsch
The Thirteenth Chair	MGM	David Snell
Three Smart Girls	UN	Charles Previn
Thrill of a Lifetime	PAR	Victor Young
Thunder in the City	COL	Miklos Rozsa
Time Out for Romance	TCF	Samuel Kaylin
Topper	MGM	Marvin Hatley
Tovarich	WB	Adolph Deutsch
Turn Off the Moon	PAR	Sam Coslow
Two Wise Maids	REP	Karl Hajos
Under the Cover of Night	MGM	William Axt
Under the Red Robe	TCF	William Frederick Peters
Victoria the Great	BRI	Anthony Collins
Waikiki Wedding	PAR	Leo Shuken
We Live in Two Worlds	BRI	Maurice Jaubert
Wells Fargo	PAR	Victor Young
When Love Is Young	UN	Charles Previn
When You're in Love	COL	Alfred Newman
When's Your Birthday?	RKO	Sam Wineland
White Hunter	TCF	Arthur Lange
Wings of the Morning	BRI	Sir Arthur Benjamin
Wings Over Honolulu	UN	Charles Previn
The Woman Alone (Secret Agent)	BRI	Louis Levy
Woman Chases Man	UA	Alfred Newman
The Woman I Love	RKO	Arthur Honegger
You Only Live Once	UA	Alfred Newman
You're Only Young Once	MGM	David Snell
Zamboanga	PHI	Edward Kilenyi

1938

Adrienne Lecouvrer	FRA	Maurice Thiriet
Adventures of Marco Polo	UA	Alfred Newman
Adventures of Robin Hood	WB	Erich Wolfgang Korngold
Adventures of Tom Sawyer	UA	Louis Forbes
Affairs of Annabel	RKO	Roy Webb
Alexander Nevsky	RUS	Sergei Prokofiev
Algiers	UA	Vincent Scotto Mohammed Ygorbouchen
Amazing Doctor Clitterhouse	WB	Max Steiner

Angels with Dirty Faces	WB	Max Steiner
Annabel Takes a Tour	RKO	Robert Russell Bennett
Army Girl	REP	Victor Young
Arsene Lupin Returns	MGM	Franz Waxman
The Bad Man of Brimstone	MGM	William Axt
The Baker's Wife	FRA	Vincent Scotto
Blockade	UA	Werner Janssen
Blockheads	MGM	Marvin Hatley
Boys' Town	MGM	Edward Ward
Breaking the Ice	RKO	Victor Young
Bringing Up Baby	RKO	Roy Webb
Broadway Musketeers	WB	Adolph Deutsch
The Buccaneer	PAR	George Anthiel
The Childhood of Maxim Gorky	RUS	Lev Schwartz
A Christmas Carol	MGM	Franz Waxman
The Citadel	MGM	Louis Levy
Come On, Rangers	REP	Cy Feuer
Comet over Broadway	WB	Heinz Roemheld
Conquest of the Air (short)	BRI	Sir Arthur Bliss
The Cowboy and the Lady	UA	Alfred Newman
The Crowd Roars	MGM	Edward Ward
The Dawn Patrol	WB	Max Steiner
The Divorce of Lady X	UA	Miklos Rozsa
Drums	UA	John Greenwood
The Duke of West Point	UA	Frank Tours
Entree Des Artists (short)	FRA	Georges Auric
Everybody Sing	MGM	William Axt
The Face of Scotland (short)	BRI	Walter Leigh
Fast Company	MGM	William Axt
The First Hundred Years	MGM	William Axt
Flirting with Fate	COL	Walter Samuels
Four Daughters	WB	Max Steiner
Four Feathers	BRI	Miklos Rozsa
The 400 Million	IND	Hanns Eisler
Four Men and a Prayer	TCF	Louis Silvers
Four's a Crowd	WB	Adolph Deutsch
Fugitives for a Night	RKO	Robert Russell Bennett
Girl's School	COL	Gregory Stone
The Gladiator	COL	Victor Young
Gold Is Where You Find It	WB	Max Steiner
A Great Citizen	RUS	Dmitri Shostakovich
The Great Waltz	MGM	Dimitri Tiomkin
Heart of the North	WB	Adolph Deutsch
Hello, Everybody	HOL	Darius Milhaud
Her Jungle Love	PAR	Gregory Stone
Hold that Kiss	MGM	Edward Ward
Holiday	COL	Josiah Zuro Sidney Cutner
The Human Beast	FRA	Joseph Kosma
I Stand Accused	RKO	Cy Feuer
If I Were King	PAR	Richard Hageman
I'm from the City	RKO	Roy Webb
In Old Chicago	TCF	Louis Silvers

International Crime	GN	Edward Kilenyi
The Islanders (short)	BRI	Darius Milhaud
Jezebel	WB	Max Steiner
Kentucky	TCF	Louis Silvers
Kentucky Moonshine	TCF	Louis Silvers
Kidnapped	TCF	Arthur Lange
The Law West of Tombstone	RKO	Roy Webb
La Lettre (short)	FRA	Jean Wiener
Life Dances On (see Un Carnet Du Bal)		
Listen, Darling	MGM	William Axt George Stoll
Lord Jeff	MGM	Edward Ward
Love Is a Headache	MGM	Edward Ward
The Mad Miss Manton	RKO	Roy Webb
Man-Proof	MGM	Franz Waxman
A Man to Remember	RKO	Roy Webb
The Man with a Gun	RUS	Dmitri Shostakovich
Marie Antoinette	MGM	Herbert Stothart
La Marseillaise	FRA	Joseph Kosma
Men Are Such Fools	WB	W. Franke Harling
Men with Wings	PAR	W. Franke Harling Gerard Carbonara
Merrily We Live	MGM	Marvin Hatley
Midnight Intruder	UN	Charles Previn
Mr. Wong, Detective	MON	Art Meyer
The Night Hawk	REP	Cy Feuer
North Sea	BRI	Ernst Meyer
Of Human Hearts	MGM	Herbert Stothart
The Overland Express	COL	Edward Kilenyi
Painted Desert	RKO	Roy Webb
Paradise for Three	MGM	Edward Ward
Peck's Bad Boy with the Circus	RKO	Victor Young
Peter the First (Part II)	RUS	Vladimir Scherbachev
The Phantom Chariot	FRA	Jacques Ibert
Port of Seven Seas	MGM	Franz Waxman
Port of Shadows (Quai des Brumes)	FRA	Maurice Jaubert
Professor Mamlock	RUS	N. Timofeyev Y. Kochurov
Pygmalion	MGM	Arthur Honegger
The Return of the Scarlet Pimpernell	UA	Sir Arthur Benjamin
Rich Man, Poor Girl	MGM	William Axt
Room Service	RKO	Roy Webb
Rose of the Rio Grande	MON	Charles Rosoff
Shine On, Harvest Moon	REP	Cy Feuer
The Shining Hour	MGM	Franz Waxman
The Shopworn Angel	MGM	Edward Ward
The Sisters	WB	Max Steiner
Sixty Glorious Years	RKO	Anthony Collins
Spawn of the North	PAR	Dimitri Tiomkin
Spring Madness	MGM	William Axt

Stablemates	MGM	Edward Ward
Submarine Patrol	TCF	Arthur Lange
Suez	TCF	Louis Silvers
Swing Your Lady	WB	Adolph Deutsch
Swiss Miss	MGM	Marvin Hatley
Tarnished Angel	RKO	Frank Tours
Tarzan's Revenge	TCF	Hugo Riesenfeld
Test Pilot	MGM	Franz Waxman
The Texans	PAR	Gerard Carbonara
There Goes My Heart	UA	Marvin Hatley
Three Blind Mice	TCF	Arthur Lange
Three Comrades	MGM	Franz Waxman
Three Loves Has Nancy	MGM	William Axt
The Tocher (short)	BRI	Benjamin Britten
Too Hot to Handle	MGM	Franz Waxman
Topa Topa	IND	Edward Kilenyi
The Toy Wife	MGM	Edward Ward
Valley of the Giants	WB	Hugo Friedhofer Adolph Deutsch
Village Harvest (short)	BRI	Benjamin Britten
Vivacious Lady	RKO	Roy Webb
Volga-Volga	Rus	Isaac Dunayevsky
Volochayevsk Days	RUS	Dmitri Shostakovich
Where the Buffalo Roam	MON	Frank Sanucci
White Banners	WB	Max Steiner
The Wife of General Ling	BRI	Jack Beaver
Woman Against Woman	MGM	William Axt
The World Is Ours	MGM	David Snell
A Yank at Oxford	MGM	Edward Ward
Yellow Jack	MGM	William Axt
You and Me	PAR	Kurt Weill
You Can't Take It with You	COL	Dimitri Tiomkin
Young Dr. Kildare	MGM	David Snell
The Young in Heart	UA	Franz Waxman

1939

The Adventures of Huckleberry Finn	MGM	Franz Waxman
The Adventures of Sherlock Holmes	TCF	Cyril J. Mockridge
Allegheny Uprising	RKO	Anthony Collins
Ambush	PAR	Gerard Carbonara
Andy Hardy Gets Spring Fever	MGM	David Snell Edward Ward
Angels Wash Their Faces	WB	Adolph Deutsch
Another Thin Man	MGM	Edward Ward
The Arizona Kid	REP	Cy Feuer
Arrest Bulldog Drummond	PAR	Gerard Carbonara
At the Circus	MGM	Franz Waxman
Back Door to Heaven	PAR	Erno Rapee
Bad Lands	RKO	Roy Webb
Bad Little Angel	MGM	Edward Ward Herbert Stothart

Barricade	TCF	Alfred Newman
Beau Geste	PAR	Alfred Newman
Bridal Suite	MGM	Arthur Gutmann
Broadway Serenade	MGM	Herbert Stothart
Burn 'Em Up O'Connor	MGM	David Snell
Cafe Society	PAR	Leo Shuken
Calling All Marines	REP	Cy Feuer
Call a Messenger	UN	Hans J. Salter
Calling Dr. Kildare	MGM	David Snell
Captain Fury	UA	Marvin Hatley
Career	RKO	Robert Russell Bennett
The Cat and the Canary	PAR	Ernst Toch
Charlie McCarthy, Detective	UN	Frank Skinner
The City (short)	IND	Aaron Copland
Claudine	FRA	Paul Misraki
Confessions of a Nazi Spy	WB	Max Steiner
The Covered Trailer	REP	Cy Feuer
Cowboy Quarterback	WB	Howard Jackson
Crisis	IND	H. W. Susskind Jaroslav Harvan
Dancing Co-Ed	MGM	Edward Ward
Dark Victory	WB	Max Steiner
Daughters Courageous	WB	Max Steiner
The Day the Bookies Wept	RKO	Arthur Morton
Day-Time Wife	TCF	Cyril J. Mockridge
Daybreak	FRA	Maurice Jaubert
Days of Jesse James	REP	Cy Feuer
Destry Rides Again	UN	Frank Skinner
Disbarred	PAR	Gerard Carbonara
Disputed Passage	PAR	Frederick Hollander John Leipold
Dodge City	WB	Max Steiner
Down the Wyoming Trail	MON	Frank Sanucci
Drums Along the Mohawk	TCF	Alfred Newman
Dust Be My Destiny	WB	Max Steiner
Each Dawn I Die	WB	Max Steiner
Escape	MGM	Franz Waxman
Escape from Yesterday	PAR	Gerard Carbonara
Espionage Agent	WB	Adolph Deutsch
Eternally Yours	UA	Werner Janssen
Exile Express	GN	George Perisch
Fast and Furious	MGM	Daniele Amfitheatrof
Federal Man Hunt	REP	Cy Feuer
Fifth Avenue Girl	RKO	Robert Russell Bennett
Fight for Life (short)	BRI	Louis Gruenberg
The Fighting Gringo	RKO	Roy Webb
Fighting Thoroughbreds	REP	Cy Feuer
La Fin Du Jour	FRA	Maurice Jaubert
Five Came Back	RKO	Roy Webb
Fixer Dugan	RKO	Roy Webb
Flight at Midnight	REP	Cy Feuer
The Flying Deuces	RKO	John Leipold Leo Shuken

The Flying Irishman	RKO	Roy Web
Forged Passport	REP	Cy Feuer
Four Wives	WB	Max Steiner
The Fourth Estate (short)	BRI	Walter Leigh
Frontier Marshal	TCF	David Raksin Charles Maxwell
Frontier Pony Express	REP	Cy Feuer
Full Confession	RKO	Roy Webb
Geronimo	PAR	Gerard Carbonara
The Girl Downstairs	MGM	William Axt
The Girl from Mexico	RKO	Roy Webb
Golden Boy	COL	Victor Young
Goodbye Mr. Chips	MGM	Richard Addinsell
Gone with the Wind	MGM	Max Steiner
The Gorilla	TCF	David Buttolph
The Gracie Allen Murder Case	PAR	Gerard Carbonara
The Great Commandment	TCF	Hans J. Salter
The Great Man Votes	RKO	Roy Webb
The Great Victor Herbert	PAR	Arthur Lange
Gulliver's Travels	PAR	Victor Young
Gunga Din	RKO	Alfred Newman
Hollywood Cavalcade	TCF	Louis Silvers
Hotel Imperial	PAR	Richard Hageman
Hound of the Baskervilles	TCF	Cyril J. Mockridge
The Housekeeper's Daughter	UA	Lud Gluskin
In Name Only	RKO	Roy Webb
Indianapolis Speedway	WB	Adolph Deutsch
Intermezzo	UA	Louis Forbes Heinz Prevost
Invitation to Happiness	PAR	Frederick Hollander
Jamaica Inn	PAR	Eric Fenby
Le Jour Se Leve (see Daybreak)		
Juarez	WB	Erich Wolfgang Korngold
The Kid from Texas	MGM	William Axt
Lady of the Tropics	MGM	Franz Waxman
Made for Each Other	RKO	Hugo Friedhofer David Buttolph
Maisie	MGM	Edward Ward
Man in the Iron Mask	UA	Lucien Moraweck
Men in Danger (short)	BRI	Brian Easdale
Mill on the Floss	BRI	Colin Wark
Mr. Smith Goes to Washington	COL	Dimitri Tiomkin
My Apprenticeship	RUS	Lev Schwartz
Ninotchka	MGM	Werner Heymann
Nurse Edith Cavell	RKO	Anthony Collins
The Old Maid	WB	Max Steiner
On Borrowed Time	MGM	Franz Waxman
Our Leading Citizen	PAR	Gerard Carbonara
Pacific Liner	RKO	Robert Russell Bennett
Les Passagers De La Grande Ouise	FRA	Jean Wiener
Private Lives of Elizabeth and Essex	WB	Erich Wolfgang Korngold

The Proud Valley (short)	BRI	Sir Ernest Irving
The Rains Came	TCF	Alfred Newman
The Real Glory	UA	Alfred Newman
Reno	RKO	Roy Webb
Rio	UN	Charles Previn
The Rules of the Game	FRA	Joseph Kosma
Rulers of the Sea	PAR	Richard Hageman
Sabotage	REP	Cy Feuer
Second Fiddle	TCF	Louis Silvers
Shors	RUS	Dmitri Kabalevsky
Stagecoach	UA	Richard Hageman
Stand Up and Fight	MGM	William Axt
A Stolen Life	PAR	William Walton
The Sun Never Sets	UN	Frank Skinner
Susannah of the Mounties	TCF	Louis Silvers
Tell No Tales	MGM	William Axt
They Shall Have Music	UA	Alfred Newman
Thunder Afloat	MGM	Edward Ward David Snell
U-Boat 29	COL	Miklos Rozsa
Union Pacific	PAR	Sigmund Krumgold John Liepold
The Vyborg Side	RUS	Dmitri Shostakovich
We Are Not Alone	WB	Max Steiner
Winter Carnival	UA	Werner Janssen
The Wizard of Oz	MGM	Herbert Stothart
The Women	MGM	Edward Ward David Snell
Wuthering Heights	UA	Alfred Newman
Young Mr. Lincoln	TCF	Alfred Newman
Zenobia	UA	Marvin Hatley

1940

Abe Lincoln In Illinois	RKO	Roy Webb
All This and Heaven Too	WB	Max Steiner
Andy Hardy Meets a Debutante	MGM	David Snell
Arise My Love	PAR	Victor Young
Arizona	COL	Victor Young
The Bank Dick	UN	Charles Previn
The Battle for Siberia	RUS	Dmitri Shostakovich
Beyond Tomorrow	RKO	Frank Tours
A Bill of Divorcement	RKO	Roy Webb
The Biscuit Eater	PAR	Frederick Hollander
Blackout	UA	Muir Mathieson
The Blue Bird	TCF	Alfred Newman
Boom Town	MGM	Franz Waxman
Brigham Young	TCF	Alfred Newman
Brother Orchid	WB	Heinz Roemheld
Captain Caution	UA	Phil Ohman
City for Conquest	WB	Max Steiner
Cross Country Romance	RKO	Roy Webb
Dance, Girl, Dance	RKO	Edward Ward

Dark Command	REP	Victor Young
Dispatch from Reuters	WB	Max Steiner
Dr. Cyclops	PAR	Ernst Toch Albert Hay Malotte
Dr. Erlich's Magic Bullet	WB	Max Steiner
Dr. Kildare Goes Home	MGM	David Snell
The Doctor Takes a Wife	COL	Morris Stoloff
The Earl of Chicago	MGM	Werner Heymann
East of the River	WB	Adolph Deutsch
Edison the Man	MGM	Herbert Stothart
The Farmer's Daughter	PAR	Leigh Harline
Florian	MGM	Franz Waxman
Flowing Gold	WB	Adolph Deutsch
Foreign Correspondent	UA	Alfred Newman
Four Sons	TCF	David Buttolph
The Fugitive	BRI	Miklos Rozsa
Gaslight	BRI	Richard Addinsell
Ghost Breakers	PAR	Ernst Toch
The Grapes of Wrath	TCF	Alfred Newman
The Great Dictator	UA	Charles Chaplin Meredith Willson
The Great McGinty	PAR	Frederick Hollander
He Stayed for Breakfast	COL	Werner Heymann
Hired Wife	UN	Frank Skinner
House Across the Bay	UA	Werner Janssen
House of the Seven Gables	UN	Frank Skinner
The Howards of Virginia	COL	Richard Hageman
The Human Monster	MON	Guy Jones
The Hunchback of Notre Dame	RKO	Alfred Newman
I Love You Again	MGM	Franz Waxman
I Married Adventure	COL	Morris Stoloff
I Take This Woman	MGM	Bronislau Kaper
I Want a Divorce	PAR	Victor Young
I Was an Adventuress	TCF	David Buttolph
It's a Date	UN	Charles Previn
Joe and Ethel Turp Call on the President	MGM	Edward Ward David Snell
Johnny Apollo	TCF	Cyril J. Mockridge
Kit Carson	UA	Edward Ward
Kitty Foyle	RKO	Roy Webb
Laddie	RKO	Roy Webb
Lady with Red Hair	WB	Heinz Roemheld
The Letter	WB	Max Steiner
The Light that Failed	PAR	Victor Young
Lights Out in Europe	IND	Werner Janssen
Lillian Russell	TCF	Alfred Newman
The Lion Has Wings	UA	Richard Addinsell
The Long Voyage Home	UA	Richard Hageman
Lucky Partners	RKO	Dimitri Tiomkin
The Man from Dakota	MGM	David Snell
The Man I Married	TCF	David Buttolph
The Man who Talked too Much	WB	Heinz Roemheld

The Mark of Zorro	TCF	Alfred Newman Hugo Friedhofer David Buttolph
Maryland	TCF	Alfred Newman
Melody Ranch	REP	Raoul Kraushaar
Men and Ships (short)	BRI	Richard Addinsell
Merchant Seaman (short)	BRI	Constant Lambert
Mr. Trull Finds Out (short)	IND	Gian-Carlo Menotti
The Mortal Storm	MGM	Edward Kane
My Favorite Wife	RKO	Roy Webb
My Little Chickadee	UN	Frank Skinner
My Love Came Back	WB	Heinz Roemheld
My Son, My Son	UA	Edward Ward
My Universities	RUS	Lev Schwartz
No Time for Comedy	WB	Heinz Roemheld
Northwest Mounted Police	PAR	Victor Young
Northwest Passage	MGM	Herbert Stothart
Of Mice and Men	UA	Aaron Copland
One Crowded Night	RKO	Roy Webb
One Million, B.C.	UA	Werner Heymann
One-Tenth of a Nation (short)	IND	Roy Harris
Our Town	UA	Aaron Copland
Pastor Hall	BRI	Charles Brill
The Philadelphia Story	MGM	Franz Waxman
Power and the Land (short)	IND	Douglas Moore
Pride and Prejudice	MGM	Herbert Stothart
The Primrose Path	RKO	Werner Heymann
Raffles	UA	Victor Young
The Ramparts We Watch	RKO	Louis de Francesco Jacques Dallin Pete Brunelli
Rangers of Fortune	PAR	Frederick Hollander
Rebecca	UA	Franz Waxman
Remember the Night	PAR	Frederick Hollander
The Return of Frank James	TCF	David Buttolph
Safari	PAR	Frederick Hollander
Saturday's Children	WB	Adolph Deutsch
The Sea Hawk	WB	Max Steiner
Seven Sinners	UN	Charles Previn
The Shop Around the Corner	MGM	Werner Heymann
Sidewalks of London	BRI	Arthur Johnson
Slightly Honorable	UA	Werner Janssen
South of Pago Pago	UA	Edward Ward
Spring Offensive (short)	BRI	Brian Easdale
Spring Parade	UN	Robert Stolz
Squadron 992 (short)	BRI	Walter Leigh
Strange Cargo	MGM	Franz Waxman
The Stranger on the Third Floor	RKO	Roy Webb
Strike Up the Band	MGM	George Stoll
Susan and God	MGM	Herbert Stothart
Swanee River	TCF	Louis Silvers
Swiss Family Robinson	RKO	Anthony Collins
There's Magic in Music	PAR	Frederick Hollander

They Drive By Night	WB	Adolph Deutsch
They Knew What They Wanted	RKO	Alfred Newman
The Thief of Bagdad	UA	Miklos Rozsa
Third Finger, Left Hand	MGM	David Snell
Those Were the Days	PAR	Victor Young
Three Faces West	REP	Victor Young
Tin Pan Alley	TCF	Alfred Newman
Tom Brown's Schooldays	RKO	Anthony Collins
Tom, Dick and Harry	RKO	Roy Webb
Too Many Girls	RKO	George Bassman
Too Many Husbands	COL	Morris Stoloff
Torrid Zone	WB	Adolph Deutsch
Tugboat Annie Sails Again	WB	Max Steiner
Untamed	PAR	Victor Young
Valley Town (short)	IND	Marc Blitzstein
Vigil in the Night	RKO	Alfred Newman
Virginia	PAR	Victor Young
Virginia City	WB	Max Steiner
Waterloo Bridge	MGM	Herbert Stothart
The Way of All Flesh	PAR	Victor Young
We Who Are Young	MGM	Bronislau Kaper
The Westerner	UA	Dimitri Tiomkin
When the Daltons Rode	UN	Frank Skinner
White Flood (short)	IND	Hanns Eisler
Women in War	REP	Cy Feuer
You'll Find Out	RKO	Roy Webb
Young People	TCF	Alfred Newman
Young Tom Edison	MGM	Edward Ward
Zanzibar	UN	Hans J. Salter

1941

Adam Had Four Sons	COL	W. Franke Harling
Affectionately Yours	WB	Heinz Roemheld
All That Money Can Buy	RKO	Bernard Herrmann
Andy Hardy's Private Secretary	MGM	Herbert Stothart
Appointment for Love	UN	Frank Skinner
Back Street	UN	Frank Skinner
Belle Starr	TCF	Alfred Newman
The Big Store	MGM	George Stoll
Billy the Kid	MGM	David Snell
Blood and Sand	TCF	Vicente Gomez
Blossoms in the Dust	MGM	Herbert Stothart
Blues in the Night	WB	Heinz Roemheld
The Bride Came C.O.D.	WB	Max Steiner
Caught in the Draft	PAR	Victor Young
Chad Hanna	TCF	David Buttolph
Charley's Aunt	TCF	Alfred Newman
Cheers for Miss Bishop	UA	Edward Ward
Citizen Kane	RKO	Bernard Herrmann
Come Live with Me	MGM	Herbert Stothart
Comrade X	MGM	Bronislau Kaper
The Corsican Brothers	UA	Dimitri Tiomkin

The Devil and Daniel Webster (see All That Money Can Buy)		
Dive Bomber	WB	Max Steiner
Dr. Jekyll and Mr. Hyde	MGM	Franz Waxman
Father Takes a Wife	RKO	Roy Webb
The Feminine Touch	MGM	Franz Waxman
Flame of New Orleans	UN	Frank Skinner
Flight Command	MGM	Franz Waxman
Flight from Destiny	WB	Heinz Roemheld
Footsteps in the Dark	WB	Frederick Hollander
The Forgotten Village	MEX	Hanns Eisler
The Gay Falcon	RKO	Paul Sawtell
General Suvorov	RUS	Y. Shaporin
A Girl, A Guy and A Gob	RKO	Roy Webb
Go West	MGM	George Stoll
Golden Hoofs	TCF	Cyril J. Mockridge
The Great Lie	WB	Max Steiner
The Harvest Shall Come (short)	BRI	William Alwyn
Haunted Honeymoon	MGM	Louis Levy
Her First Affair	FRA	Rene Sylvanio
Here Comes Mr. Jordan	COL	Frederick Hollander
High Sierra	WB	Adolph Deutsch
Hold Back the Dawn	PAR	Victor Young
Hold That Ghost	UN	Ted Cain
Honky Tonk	MGM	Franz Waxman
How Green Was My Valley	TCF	Alfred Newman
Hudson's Bay	TCF	Alfred Newman
I Wanted Wings	PAR	Victor Young
International Lady	UA	Lucien Moraweck
The Invaders	BRI	Ralph Vaughan Williams
The Invisible Woman	UN	Charles Previn
It Started with Eve	UN	Hans J. Salter
Kathleen	MGM	Franz Waxman
Ladies in Retirement	COL	Ernst Toch
The Lady Eve	PAR	Leo Shuken
The Lady from Cheyenne	UN	Frank Skinner
The Lady from Louisiana	REP	Cy Feuer
The Land (short)	IND	Richard Arnell
The Little Foxes	UA	Meredith Willson
Love Crazy	MGM	David Snell
Love on the Dole	BRI	Richard Addinsell
Lydia	UA	Miklos Rozsa
The Magic Horse	RUS	V. Oransky
Major Barbara	BRI	William Walton
The Maltese Falcon	WB	Adolph Deutsch
Man Hunt	TCF	Alfred Newman
Manpower	WB	Adolph Deutsch
Man-Made Monster	UN	Charles Previn
Meet John Doe	WB	Dimitri Tiomkin
Men of Boys' Town	MGM	Herbert Stothart
Million Dollar Baby	WB	Frederick Hollander
Mr. and Mrs. Smith	RKO	Edward Ward
Model Wife	UN	Charles Previn

Moon over Burma	PAR	Victor Young
My Life with Caroline	RKO	Werner Heymann
Nice Girl?	UN	Charles Previn
Night Train	BRI	Louis Levy
One Foot in Heaven	WB	Max Steiner
The Parson of Panamint	PAR	John Leipold
Penny Serenade	COL	Morris Stoloff
A Place to Live (short)	IND	David Diamond
Pot O' Gold	UA	Louis Forbes
Reaching for the Sun	PAR	Victor Young
Rise and Shine	TCF	Emil Newman
Road Show	UA	George Stoll
Rookies on Parade	REP	Cy Feuer
Salavat Yulayev	RUS	Aram Khachaturian
Santa Fe Trail	WB	Max Steiner
Scattergood Baines	RKO	Constantin Bakaleinikoff
The Sea Wolf	WB	Erich Wolfgang Korngold
Sergeant York	WB	Max Steiner
Shadow of the Thin Man	MGM	David Snell
She Knew All the Answers	COL	Morris Stoloff
Shepherd of the Hills	PAR	Gerard Carbonara
Skylark	PAR	Victor Young
So Ends Our Night	UA	Louis Gruenberg
The Stars Look Down	BRI	Hans May
Strawberry Blonde	WB	Heinz Roemheld
Suicide Squadron	BRI	Richard Addinsell
Sullivan's Travels	PAR	Leo Shuken
Sundown	UA	Miklos Rozsa
Suspicion	RKO	Franz Waxman
Tall, Dark and Handsome	TCF	Emil Newman
Tanya	RUS	Isaac Dunayevsky
Target for Tonight	BRI	Leighton Lucas
That Hamilton Woman	UA	Miklos Rozsa
That Uncertain Feeling	UA	Werner Heymann
They Met in Moscow	RUS	Tikhon Khrennikov
This Thing Called Love	COL	Morris Stoloff
Tobacco Road	TCF	David Buttolph
Topper Returns	UA	Werner Heymann
Two-Faced Woman	MGM	Bronislau Kaper
Underground	WB	Adolph Deutsch
Unfinished Business	UN	Franz Waxman
Victory	PAR	Frederick Hollander
Village Music (short)	IND	Douglas Moore
Voice in the Night	COL	Nicholas Brodzsky
Western Union	TCF	David Buttolph
When Ladies Meet	MGM	Bronislau Kaper
Whistling in the Dark	MGM	Bronislau Kaper
Wild Man of Borneo	MGM	David Snell
A Woman's Face	MGM	Bronislau Kaper
You Belong to Me	COL	Frederick Hollander
Ziegfeld Girl	MGM	Herbert Stothart

1942

About Face	UA	Edward Ward
Across the Pacific	WB	Adolph Deutsch
Adventures of Baron Munchausen	GER	George Haentzschel
The Adventures of Martin Eden	COL	Morris Stoloff
The Affairs of Jimmy Valentine	REP	Cy Feuer
The Affairs of Martha	MGM	Bronislau Kaper
All Through the Night	WB	Adolph Deutsch
Always in My Heart	WB	Heinz Roemheld
American Empire	UA	Gerard Carbonara
Andy Hardy's Double Life	MGM	Daniele Amfitheatrof
Apache Trail	MGM	Sol Kaplan
Arabian Nights	UN	Frank Skinner
Are Husbands Necessary?	PAR	Robert Emmett Dolan
Arizona Roundup	REP	Cy Feuer
Army Surgeon	RKO	Roy Webb
The Avengers	PAR	Richard Addinsell
Baby Face Morgan	PRC	Leo Erdody
Bandit Ranger	RKO	Paul Sawtell
Berlin Correspondent	TCF	Emil Newman
Beyond the Blue Horizon	PAR	Victor Young
The Big Shot	WB	Adolph Deutsch
The Big Street	RKO	Roy Webb
The Black Swan	TCF	Alfred Newman
Bombay Clipper	UN	Hans J. Salter
Bombs over Burma	PRC	Lee Zahler
Broadway	UN	Frank Skinner
Bullet Scars	WB	Howard Jackson
Cairo	MGM	Herbert Stothart
Calling Dr. Gillespie	MGM	Daniele Amfitheatrof
Captains of the Clouds	WB	Max Steiner
Careful, Soft Shoulder	TCF	Leigh Harline
Casablanca	WB	Max Steiner
The Cat People	RKO	Roy Webb
China Girl	TCF	Hugo Friedhofer
City of Silent Men	PRC	Leo Erdody
Coastal Command	BRI	Ralph Vaughan Williams
Code of the Outlaw	REP	Cy Feuer
The Courtship of Andy Hardy	MGM	David Snell
Crossroads	MGM	Bronislau Kaper
The Cyclone Kid	REP	Cy Feuer
Danger in the Pacific	UN	Hans J. Salter
Deep in the Heart of Texas	UN	Hans J. Salter
The Devil with Hitler	UA	Edward Ward
Dr. Gillespie's New Assistant	MGM	Daniele Amfitheatrof
Dr. Renault's Secret	TCF	David Raksin
Drums of the Congo	UN	Hans J. Salter
Dudes Are Pretty People	UA	Edward Ward
Eagle Squadron	UN	Frank Skinner
Eyes in the Night	MGM	Lennie Hayton
Fantastic Night	FRA	Maurice Thiriet
Fiesta	MGM	Edward Ward Aaron Copland

Fighting Bill Fargo	UN	Hans J. Salter
Fingers at the Window	MGM	Bronislau Kaper
Fires Were Started	BRI	William Alwyn
The First of the Few (Spitfire)	BRI	William Walton
Flight Lieutenant	COL	Werner Heymann
Foreign Agent	MON	Edward J. Kay
The Foreman Went to France	BRI	William Walton
Four Steps in the Clouds	ITA	Alessandro Cicognini
Friendly Enemies	UA	Lucien Moraweck
The Gay Sisters	WB	Max Steiner
A Gentleman After Dark	UA	Dimitri Tiomkin
Gentleman Jim	WB	Heinz Roemheld
George Washington Slept Here	WB	Adolph Deutsch
The Ghost of Frankenstein	UN	Hans J. Salter
Ghost Town Law	MON	Edward J. Kay
The Girl from Alaska	REP	Cy Feuer
Girl Trouble	TCF	Alfred Newman
Girl's Town	PRC	Lee Zahler
The Glass Key	PAR	Victor Young
Grand Central Murder	MGM	David Snell
The Great Impersonation	UN	Hans J. Salter
The Great Man's Lady	PAR	Victor Young
Hangmen Also Die	UA	Hanns Eisler
The Hard Way	WB	Heinz Roemheld
Heart of the Rio Grande	REP	Raoul Kraushaar
Her Cardboard Lover	MGM	Franz Waxman
Here We Go Again	RKO	Roy Webb
Hillbilly Blitzkreig	MON	Paul Sawtell
I Married a Witch	UA	Franz Waxman
In Old California	REP	David Buttolph
In This Our Life	WB	Max Steiner
In Which We Serve	UA	Noel Coward
Isle of Missing Men	MON	Edward J. Kay
Jackass Mail	MGM	David Snell
Joan of Paris	RKO	Roy Webb
Joe Smith, American	MGM	Daniele Amfitheatrof
Journey for Margaret	MGM	Franz Waxman
Journey into Fear	RKO	Roy Webb
Juke Girl	WB	Adolph Deutsch
The Jungle Book	UA	Miklos Rozsa
Keeper of the Flame	MGM	Bronislau Kaper
Kid Glove Killer	MGM	David Snell
King of the Stallions	MON	Frank Sanucci
Klondike Fury	MON	Edward J. Kay
Kotovski	RUS	Sergei Prokofiev
Lady for a Night	REP	David Buttolph
The Lady Has Plans	PAR	Leo Shuken
Lady in a Jam	UN	Frank Skinner
The Lady Is Willing	COL	W. Franke Harling
Larceny, Inc.	WB	Adolph Deutsch
Life Begins at 8:30	TCF	Alfred Newman
Little Joe, the Wrangler	UN	Hans J. Salter
The Living Ghost	MON	Frank Sanucci

The Loves of Edgar Allan Poe	TCF	Emil Newman
Lucky Jordan	PAR	Adolph Deutsch
The Mad Monster	PRC	David Chudnow
The Magnificent Ambersons	RKO	Bernard Herrmann
The Magnificent Dope	TCF	Emil Newman
Maisie Gets Her Man	MGM	Lennie Hayton
The Major and the Minor	PAR	Robert Emmett Dolan
The Male Animal	WB	Heinz Roemheld
Malta, G. C.	BRI	Arnold Bax
Man from Headquarters	MON	Edward J. Kay
The Man in the Trunk	TCF	Cyril Mockridge
The Man Who Wouldn't Die	TCF	Emil Newman
Manila Calling	TCF	Cyril Mockridge David Buttolph David Raksin
Mashenka	RUS	Alexander Glazounóv B. Volsky
Meet the Mob	MON	Edward J. Kay
Meet the Stewarts	COL	Leo Shuken
Mrs. Miniver	MGM	Herbert Stothart
Mrs. Wiggs of the Cabbage Patch	PAR	Victor Young
The Moon and Sixpence	UA	Dimitri Tiomkin
Moontide	TCF	Cyril J. Mockridge David Buttolph
The Mummy's Tomb	UN	Hans J. Salter
My Favorite Blonde	PAR	David Buttolph
My Favorite Spy	RKO	Roy Webb
The Mystery of Marie Roget	UN	Hans J. Salter
Native Land (short)	IND	Marc Blitzstein
The Navy Comes Through	RKO	Roy Webb
Nazi Agent	MGM	Lennie Hayton
The Nazis Strike	IND	Dimitri Tiomkin
Next of Kin	BRI	William Walton
Night Monster	UN	Hans J. Salter
Night Shift (short)	IND	Marc Blitzstein
A Night to Remember	COL	Werner Heymann
North to the Klondike	UN	Hans J. Salter
Northwest Rangers	MGM	Daniele Amfitheatrof David Snell
Now Voyager	WB	Max Steiner
The Old Homestead	REP	Cy Feuer
The Omaha Trail	MGM	David Snell
On the Sunny Side	TCF	David Raksin
Once Upon a Honeymoon	RKO	Robert Emmett Dolan
Orchestra Wives	TCF	Alfred Newman
Outlaws of Pine Ridge	REP	Mort Glickman
Over My Dead Body	TCF	Cyril J. Mockridge
Pacific Blackout	PAR	Gerard Carbonara
Palm Beach Story	PAR	Victor Young
Paratroops (short)	IND	Gail Kubik
Pardon My Stripes	REP	Cy Feuer
Paris Calling	UN	Richard Hageman
The People's Land (short)	BRI	Ralph Vaughan Williams

The Phantom Plainsman	REP	Cy Feuer
The Pied Piper	TCF	Alfred Newman
Pierre of the Plains	MGM	Lennie Hayton
Pirates of the Prairie	RKO	Paul Sawtell
Pittsburgh	UN	Frank Skinner Hans J. Salter
The Postman Didn't Ring	TCF	David Raksin
Powder Town	RKO	David Raksin
Prelude to War	IND	Hugo Friedhofer Leigh Harline Alfred Newman Dimitri Tiomkin
The Pride of the Yankees	RKO	Leigh Harline
Prisoner of Japan	PRC	Leo Erdody
Queen of Broadway	PRC	Leo Erdody
Quiet Please, Murder	TCF	Arthur Lange Charles Maxwell
Raiders of the Range	REP	Cy Feuer
Random Harvest	MGM	Herbert Stothart
Reap the Wild Wind	PAR	Victor Young
The Remarkable Andrew	PAR	Victor Young
Remember Pearl Harbor	REP	Cy Feuer
Reunion	MGM	Franz Waxman
Rhythm Parade	MON	Edward J. Kay
Ride 'Em Cowboy	UN	Frank Skinner
Rings on Her Fingers	TCF	Cyril J. Mockridge
Road to Happiness	MON	Edward J. Kay
Road to Morocco	PAR	Victor Young
Romance on the Range	REP	Cy Feuer
Roxie Hart	TCF	Alfred Newman
S. O. S. Coast Guard	REP	Raoul Kraushaar
Saboteur	UN	Frank Skinner
Saludos Amigos	DIS	Charles Wolcott
Scattergood Rides High	RKO	Paul Sawtell
Scattergood Survives a Murder	RKO	Paul Sawtell
Seven Day's Leave	RKO	Roy Webb
Seven Miles from Alcatraz	RKO	Roy Webb
Seven Sweethearts	MGM	Franz Waxman
Shadows on the Sage	REP	Mort Glickman
Shanghai Gesture	UA	Richard Hageman
Shepherd of the Ozarks	REP	Cy Feuer
Sherlock Holmes and the Secret Weapon	UN	Frank Skinner
Sherlock Holmes and the Voice of Terror	UN	Frank Skinner
Ships with Wings	BRI	Sir Ernest Irving
Shut My Big Mouth	COL	John Leipold
The Silver Bullet	UN	Hans J. Salter
Silver Queen	UA	Victor Young
Sin Town	UN	Hans J. Salter
Sleepytime Gal	REP	Cy Feuer
Smart Alecs	MON	Edward J. Kay
The Sombrero Kid	REP	Cy Feuer

Somewhere I'll Find You	MGM	Bronislau Kaper
Son of Fury	TCF	Alfred Newman
Song of the Islands	TCF	Alfred Newman
Sons of the Pioneers	REP	Cy Feuer
South of Santa Fe	REP	Cy Feuer
Spitfire (see The First of the Few)		
The Spoilers	UN	Hans J. Salter
Springtime in the Rockies	TCF	Alfred Newman
Stand By for Action	MGM	Lennie Hayton
Stagecoach Buckaroo	UN	Hans J. Salter
Stagecoach Express	REP	Cy Feuer
Star-Spangled Rhythm	PAR	Robert Emmett Dolan
Stardust on the Sage	REP	Raoul Kraushaar
The Strange Case of Dr. Rx	UN	Hans J. Salter
Street of Chance	PAR	David Buttolph
The Sundown Kid	REP	Mort Glickman
Sunset on the Desert	REP	Cy Feuer
Sweater Girl	PAR	Victor Young
Take a Letter, Darling	PAR	Victor Young
Tales of Manhattan	TCF	Sol Kaplan
Talk of the Town	COL	Frederick Hollander
Tarzan's New York Adventure	MGM	David Snell
Ten Gentlemen from West Point	TCF	Alfred Newman
Tennessee Johnson	MGM	Herbert Stothart
That Other Woman	TCF	Cyril J. Mockridge
There's One Born Every Minute	UN	Hans J. Salter
They All Kissed the Bride	COL	Werner Heymann
This Above All	TCF	Alfred Newman
This Gun for Hire	PAR	David Buttolph
This Time for Keeps	MGM	Lennie Hayton
This Was Paris	WB	Jack Beaver
Through Different Eyes	TCF	David Raksin
Thunder Birds	TCF	David Buttolph
Timber	UN	Hans J. Salter
Time to Kill	TCF	Emil Newman
Tish	MGM	David Snell
To Be or Not to Be	UA	Werner Heymann
To the Shores of Tripoli	TCF	Alfred Newman
Tombstone--The Town Too Tough to Die	PAR	Gerard Carbonara
Tomorrow We Live	PRC	Leo Erdody
Top Sergeant	UN	Hans J. Salter
Torpedo Boat	PAR	Freddie Rich
Tortilla Flat	MGM	Franz Waxman
Tough as They Come	UN	Hans J. Salter
A Tragedy at Midnight	REP	Cy Feuer
Treat 'Em Rough	UN	Hans J. Slater
True to the Army	PAR	Victor Young
The Tuttles of Tahiti	RKO	Roy Webb
Twin Beds	UA	Dimitri Tiomkin
Two Yanks in Trinidad	COL	John Leipold
The Undying Monster	TCF	David Raksin
Unexpected Riches (short)	MGM	Sol Kaplan

United We Stand	TCF	Louis de Francesco
Valley of Hunted Men	REP	Mort Glickman
Valley of the Sun	RKO	Paul Sawtell
Les Visiteurs Du Soir	FRA	Maurice Thiriet
La Voyageur De La Toussaint	FRA	Jean Wiener
Wake Island	PAR	David Buttolph
The War Against Mrs. Hadley	MGM	David Snell
We Are the Marines	TCF	Jack Shaindlin Frederick Block
We Were Dancing	MGM	Bronislau Kaper
Went the Day Well?	BRI	William Walton
Westward, Ho!	REP	Cy Feuer
Whispering Ghosts	TCF	David Raksin
Whistling in Dixie	MGM	Lennie Hayton
White Cargo	MGM	Bronislau Kaper
Who Done It?	UN	Frank Skinner
Who Is Hope Schuyler?	TCF	David Raksin
The Wife Takes a Flyer	COL	Werner Heymann
Wild Bill Hickock Rides	WB	Howard Jackson
Wildcat	PAR	Freddie Rich
Wings for the Eagle	WB	Frederick Hollander
Woman of the Year	MGM	Franz Waxman
The World at War	IND	Gail Kubik
Wrecking Crew	PAR	Freddie Rich
A Yank at Eton	MGM	Bronislau Kaper
A Yank on the Burma Road	MGM	Lennie Hayton
Yankee Doodle Dandy	WB	Heinz Roemheld
The Yanks Are Coming	PRC	Lee Zahler
Yokel Boy	REP	Cy Feuer
You Can't Escape Forever	WB	Adolph Deutsch
You Were Never Lovelier	COL	Leigh Harline
You're Telling Me	UN	Hans J. Salter
Youth on Parade	REP	Cy Feuer
The Yukon Patrol	REP	Cy Feuer

1943

Above Suspicion	MGM	Bronislau Kaper
Action in the North Atlantic	WB	Adolph Deutsch
Aerial Gunner	PAR	Daniele Amfitheatrof
Air Force	WB	Franz Waxman
Air Raid Wardens	MGM	Nathaniel Shilkret
Alaska Highway	PAR	Freddie Rich
The Amazing Mrs. Holliday	UN	Frank Skinner
The Ape Man	MON	Edward J. Kay
Appointment in Berlin	COL	Anthony Collins
Around the World	RKO	George Duning
Assignment in Brittany	MGM	Lennie Hayton
The Avenging Rider	RKO	Paul Sawtell
Background to Danger	WB	Frederick Hollander
Bataan	MGM	Bronislau Kaper
Battle of Russia	IND	Dimitri Tiomkin
Behind the Rising Sun	RKO	Roy Webb

Beyond the Last Frontier	REP	Mort Glickman
Black Hills Express	REP	Mort Glickman
The Blocked Trail	REP	Mort Glickman
Bombadier	RKO	Roy Webb
Bomber's Moon	TCF	David Buttolph
Bordertown Gun Fighters	REP	Mort Glickman
Boss of Hangtown Mesa	UN	Hans J. Salter
Buckskin Frontier	UA	Victor Young
Bullets and Saddles	MON	Frank Sanucci
Cabin in the Sky	MGM	George Stoll
California Joe	REP	Mort Glickman
Calling Dr. Death	UN	Paul Sawtell
Calling Wild Bill Elliott	REP	Mort Glickman
Campus Rhythm	MON	Edward J. Kay
The Canterville Ghost	MGM	George Bassman
Canyon City	REP	Mort Glickman
Captive Wild Woman	UN	Hans J. Salter
Carson City Cyclone	REP	Mort Glickman
Chatterbox	REP	Walter Scharf
Chetniks!	TCF	Hugo Friedhofer
Cheyenne Roundup	UN	Hans J. Salter
Children of Paradise	FRA	Joseph Kosma Maurice Thiriet
China	PAR	Victor Young
Cinderella Swings It	RKO	Paul Sawtell
City without Men	COL	David Raksin
Clancy Street Boys	MON	Edward J. Kay
Claudia	TCF	Alfred Newman
Close Quarters (short)	BRI	Gordon Jacob
The Constant Nymph	WB	Erich Wolfgang Korngold
Corregidor	PRC	Leo Erdody
Corvette K-225	UN	David Buttolph
Cosmo Jones, Spy Smasher	MON	Edward J. Kay
Covered Wagon Days	REP	Cy Feuer
Cowboy Commandos	MON	Frank Sanucci
Cowboy in Manhattan	UN	Hans J. Salter
Crash Dive	TCF	David Buttolph
Crime Doctor	COL	Lee Zahler
The Cross of Lorraine	MGM	Bronislau Kaper
Cry Havoc	MGM	Daniele Amfitheatrof
The Crystal Ball	UA	Victor Young
The Dancing Masters	TCF	Arthur Lange
The Daring Young Man	COL	John Leipold
Days of Old Cheyenne	REP	Mort Glickman
Death Valley Manhunt	REP	Mort Glickman
Death Valley Rangers	MON	Frank Sanucci
Desert Victory	BRI	William Alwyn
The Desperadoes	COL	John Leipold
Destination Tokyo	WB	Franz Waxman
Destroyer	COL	Anthony Collins
Divide and Conquer	IND	Dimitri Tiomkin
Dixie Dugan	TCF	Emil Newman
Dr. Gillespie's Criminal Case	MGM	Daniele Amfitheatrof

Du Barry Was a Lady	MGM	George Stoll
Edge of Darkness	WB	Franz Waxman
The Falcon in Danger	RKO	Roy Webb
The Falcon Strikes Back	RKO	Roy Webb
The Fallen Sparrow	RKO	Roy Webb
Fighting Frontier	RKO	Paul Sawtell
Fired Wife	UN	Frank Skinner
First Comes Courage	COL	Ernst Toch
Five Graves to Cairo	PAR	Miklos Rozsa
The Flemish Farm (short)	BRI	Ralph Vaughan Williams
Flesh and Fantasy	UN	Alexandre Tansman
Flight for Freedom	RKO	Roy Webb
Forever and a Day	RKO	Anthony Collins
For Whom the Bell Tolls	PAR	Victor Young
Frankenstein Meets the Wolf Man	UN	Hans J. Salter
Fugitive from Sonora	REP	Mort Glickman
Fugitive of the Plains	PRC	Leon N. Todd
Gangway for Tomorrow	RKO	Roy Webb
Get Going	UN	Hans J. Salter
The Ghost and the Guest	PRC	Lee Zahler
Ghost Catchers	UN	Edward Ward
The Ghost Ship	RKO	Roy Webb
Ghosts on the Loose	MON	Edward J. Kay
Girls in Chains	PRC	Leo Erdody
The Good Fellows	PAR	Leo Shuken
Good Luck, Mr. Yates	COL	John Leipold
Government Girl	RKO	Leigh Harline
Guadalcanal Diary	TCF	David Buttolph
Gung Ho!	UN	Frank Skinner
A Guy Named Joe	MGM	Herbert Stothart
Hands Across the Border	REP	Walter Scharf
Happy Land	TCF	Cyril J. Mockridge
Harrigan's Kid	MGM	Daniele Amfitheatrof
The Haunted Ranch	MON	Frank Sanucci
Heaven Can Wait	TCF	Alfred Newman
The Heavenly Body	MGM	Bronislau Kaper
He Hired the Boss	TCF	Cyril J. Mockridge
Henry Aldrich Haunts a House	PAR	Gerard Carbonara
Here Comes Kelly	MON	Edward J. Kay
Hers to Hold	UN	Frank Skinner
Hi Diddle Diddle	UA	Phil Boutelje
High Explosive	PAR	Daniele Amfitheatrof
His Butler's Sister	UN	Hans J. Salter
Hit Parade of 1943	REP	Walter Scharf
Hitler's Hangman	MGM	Karl Hajos
Hi-Ya, Chum	UN	Hans J. Salter
Hi'ya Sailor	UN	Hans J. Salter
Holy Matrimony	TCF	Cyril J. Mockridge
Hostages	PAR	Victor Young
The Human Comedy	MGM	Herbert Stothart
I Dood It	MGM	George Stoll
I Escaped from the Gestapo	MON	W. Franke Harling
The Immortal Sergeant	TCP	David Buttolph

In Old Oklahoma	REP	Walter Scharf
The Iron Major	RKO	Roy Webb
Isle of Forgotten Sins	PRC	Leo Erdody
I Walked with a Zombie	RKO	Roy Webb
Jack London	UA	Freddie Rich
Johnny Come Lately	UA	Leigh Harline
The Kansan	UA	Gerard Carbonara
Keep 'Em Slugging	UN	Hans J. Salter
Ladies' Day	RKO	Roy Webb
Lady of Burlesque	UA	Arthur Lange
A Lady Takes a Chance	RKO	Roy Webb
Land of Hunted Men	MON	Frank Sanucci
Lassie Come Home	MGM	Daniele Amfitheatrof
The Leather Burners	UA	Samuel Kaylin
The Leopard Man	RKO	Roy Webb
Lermontov	RUS	Sergei Prokofiev
Life and Death of Colonel Blimp	BRI	Allan Gray
Lifeboat	TCF	Hugo Friedhofer
Lone Star Trail	UN	Hans J. Salter
Lost Angel	MGM	Daniele Amfitheatrof
Madame Curie	MGM	Herbert Stothart
The Mad Ghoul	UN	Hans J. Salter
Malta, G. C.	BRI	Sir Arnold Bax
The Man from Down Under	MGM	David Snell
The Man from Thunder River	REP	Mort Glickman
The Mantrap	REP	Morton Scott
Margin for Error	TCF	Leigh Harline
The Meanest Man in the World	TCF	Cyril J. Mockridge
Melody Parade	MON	Edward J. Kay
Minesweeper	PAR	Mort Glickman
Mission to Moscow	WB	Max Steiner
The Moon Is Down	TCF	Alfred Newman
Moonlight in Vermont	UN	Edward Ward
The More the Merrier	COL	Leigh Harline
Mr. Lucky	RKO	Roy Webb
Mug Town	UN	Hans J. Salter
My Friend Flicka	TCF	Alfred Newman
My Son, the Hero	PRC	Leo Erdody
Nearly Eighteen	MON	Edward J. Kay
Never a Dull Moment	UN	Hans J. Salter
Nine Men	BRI	John Greenwood
Nobody's Darling	REP	Walter Scharf
No Place for a Lady	COL	Lee Zahler
Northern Pursuit	WB	Adolph Deutsch
The North Star	RKO	Aaron Copland
No Time for Love	PAR	Victor Young
Oh, What a Night!	MON	Edward J. Kay
Old Acquaintance	WB	Franz Waxman
The Outlaw	UA	Victor Young
Overland Mail Robbery	REP	Mort Glickman
The Ox-Bow Incident	TCF	Cyril J. Mockridge
Paris After Dark	TCF	Hugo Friedhofer
The Phantom of the Opera	UN	Edward Ward

Pilot No. 5	MGM	Lennie Hayton
Prairie Chickens	UA	Edward Ward
Presenting Lily Mars	MGM	George Stoll
Princess O'Rourke	WB	Frederick Hollander
Raiders of San Joaquin	UN	Hans J. Salter
Raiders of Sunset Pass	REP	Mort Glickman
Riders of the Rio Grande	REP	Mort Glickman
Sahara	COL	Miklos Rozsa
Salute to the Marines	MGM	Lennie Hayton
Santa Fe Scouts	REP	Mort Glickman
Sarong Girl	MON	Edward J. Kay
Secrets of the Underground	REP	Walter Scharf
Seven Doors to Death	PRC	Lee Zahler
The Seventh Victim	RKO	Roy Webb
Shadow of a Doubt	UN	Dimitri Tiomkin
Shantytown	REP	Walter Scharf
Sherlock Holmes Faces Death	UN	Hans J. Salter
Sherlock Holmes in Washington	UN	Frank Skinner
Silver Skates	MON	Emil Seidel
Six-Gun Gospel	MON	Edward J. Kay
The Sky's the Limit	RKO	Leigh Harline
Sleepy Lagoon	REP	Walter Scharf
Slightly Dangerous	MGM	Bronislau Kaper
So Proudly We Hail	PAR	Miklos Rozsa
Someone to Remember	REP	Walter Scharf
Something to Shout About	COL	David Raksin
Son of Dracula	UN	Hans J. Salter
Song of Bernadette	TCF	Alfred Newman
Song of Russia	MGM	Herbert Stothart
Spotlight Scandals	MON	Edward J. Kay
Stagedoor Canteen	UA	Freddie Rich
Stalingrad	RUS	V. Smirnov
The Strange Death of Adolf Hitler	UN	Hans J. Salter
The Stranger from Pecos	MON	Edward J. Kay
A Stranger in Town	MGM	Daniele Amfitheatrof
Submarine Alert	PAR	Freddie Rich
Submarine Base	PRC	Charles Dant
The Sultan's Daughter	MON	Karl Hajos
Swing Fever	MGM	George Stoll
Swing Shift Maisie	MGM	Lennie Hayton
Tarzan's Desert Mystery	RKO	Paul Sawtell
Tarzan Triumphs	RKO	Paul Sawtell
Taxi, Mister?	UA	Edward Ward
Tender Comrade	RKO	Leigh Harline
Tenting Tonight on the Old Camp Ground	UN	Hans J. Salter
They Came to Blow Up America	TCF	Hugo Friedhofer
Thumbs Up	REP	Walter Scharf
This Land Is Mine	RKO	Lothar Perl
Thousands Cheer	MGM	Herbert Stothart
Three Hearts for Julia	MGM	Herbert Stothart
Three Russian Girls	UA	W. Franke Harling
Tiger Fangs	PRC	Lee Zahler

Tonight We Raid Calais	TCF	Emil Newman
Top Man	UN	Frank Skinner
True to Life	PAR	Victor Young
Two-Fisted Justice	MON	Frank Sanucci
Two Tickets to London	UN	Frank Skinner
The Underdog	PRC	Lee Zahler
The Unknown Guest	MON	Dimitri Tiomkin
Wagon Tracks West	REP	Mort Glickman
Watch on the Rhine	WB	Max Steiner
The Way Ahead	BRI	William Alwyn
West of the Cimarron	REP	Cy Feuer
What a Man!	MON	Edward J. Kay
Whistling in Brooklyn	MGM	George Bassman
White Savage	UN	Frank Skinner
Wild Horse Rustlers	PRC	Leo Erdody
Wild Horse Stampede	MON	Frank Sanucci
The Woman of the Town	UA	Miklos Rozsa
Women in Bondage	MON	Edward J. Kay
World of Plenty	BRI	William Alwyn
You Can't Beat the Law	MON	Edward J. Kay
Young and Willing	UA	Victor Young
The Youngest Profession	MGM	David Snell
Young Ideas	MGM	George Bassman

1944

Abroad with Two Yanks	UA	Lud Gluskin
Action in Arabia	RKO	Roy Webb
Address Unknown	COL	Ernst Toch
The Adventures of Mark Twain	WB	Max Steiner
Alaska	MON	Edward J. Kay
Ali Baba and the Forty Thieves	UN	Edward Ward
An American Romance	MGM	Louis Gruenberg
And Now Tomorrow	PAR	Victor Young
Andy Hardy's Blonde Trouble	MGM	David Snell
Arizona Whirlwind	MON	Frank Sanucci
Arsenic and Old Lace	WB	Max Steiner
Atlantic City	REP	Walter Scharf
Barbary Coast Gent	MGM	David Snell
Battle of the Rails	FRA	Yves Baudrier
Belle of the Yukon	RKO	Arthur Lange
Bermuda Mystery	TCF	Arthur Lange
Between Two Women	MGM	David Snell
Between Two Worlds	WB	Erich Wolfgang Korngold
The Big Noise	TCF	Cyril J. Mockridge
Black Magic	MON	Alexander Laszlo
The Black Parachute	COL	Mario Castelnuevo-Tedesco
Blonde Fever	MGM	Nathaniel Shilkret
Bluebeard	PRC	Leo Erdody
Boss of Rawhide	PRC	Lee Zahler
Bowery to Broadway	UN	Edward Ward
Brand of the Devil	PRC	Lee Zahler
Bride by Mistake	RKO	Roy Webb

The Bridge of San Luis Rey	UA	Dimitri Tiomkin
Buffalo Bill	TCF	David Buttolph
Can't Help Singing	UN	Hans J. Salter
Casanova Brown	RKO	Arthur Lange
Casanova in Burlesque	REP	Walter Scharf
Charlie Chan in the Secret Service	MON	Karl Hajos
Cheyenne Wildcat	REP	Joseph Dubin
Children of Paradise	FRA	Maurice Thiriet Joseph Kosma
Christmas Holiday	UN	Hans J. Salter
The Climax	UN	Edward Ward
Cobra Woman	UN	Edward Ward
The Conspirators	WB	Max Steiner
The Contender	PRC	Albert Glasser
The Cowboy and the Senorita	REP	Walter Scharf
Crime Doctor's Strangest Case	COL	Lee Zahler
Cry of the Werewolf	COL	Mischa Bakaleinikoff
Curse of the Cat People	RKO	Roy Webb
Les Dames Du Bois De Boulogne	FRA	Jean-Jacques Grünenwald
Dangerous Passage	PAR	Alexander Laszlo
Dark Mountain	PAR	Willy Stahl
Dark Waters	UA	Miklos Rozsa
Days of Glory	RKO	Daniele Amfitheatrof
Dead Man's Eyes	UN	Paul Sawtell
Delinquent Daughters	PRC	Lee Zahler
Destiny	UN	Frank Skinner
Detective Kitty O'Day	MON	Edward J. Kay
Double Exposure	PAR	Alexander Laszlo
Double Indemnity	PAR	Miklos Rozsa
The Doughgirls	WB	Adolph Deutsch
Dragon Seed	MGM	Herbert Stothart
Enemy of Women	MON	Arthur Gutmann
Enter Arsene Lupin	UN	Milton Rosen
The Eternal Return	FRA	Georges Auric
The Eve of St. Mark	TCF	Cyril J. Mockridge
Experiment Perilous	RKO	Roy Webb
The Falcon Out West	RKO	Roy Webb
The Fighting Lady	TCF	David Buttolph
The Fighting Seabees	REP	Walter Scharf
Follow the Boys	UN	Leigh Harline
Follow the Leader	MON	Edward J. Kay
Frenchman's Creek	PAR	Victor Young
Gambler's Choice	PAR	Mort Glickman
Gangsters of the Frontier	PRC	Lee Zahler
Gaslight	MGM	Bronislau Kaper
Gentle Annie	MGM	David Snell
Ghost Guns	MON	Edward J. Kay
Girl No. 217	RUS	Aram Khachaturian
Going My Way	PAR	Robert Emmett Dolan
The Great Mike	PRC	Lee Zahler
The Great Moment	PAR	Victor Young
Guest in the House	UA	Werner Janssen
Gunsmoke Mesa	PRC	Lee Zahler

Gypsy Wildcat	UN	Edward Ward
Hail the Conquering Hero	PAR	Werner Heymann
The Hairy Ape	UA	Michel Michelet
Halfway House	BRI	Lord Berners
Heavenly Days	RKO	Leigh Harline
Henry Aldrich, Boy Scout	PAR	Irvin Talbot
Henry Aldrich Plays Cupid	PAR	Irvin Talbot
Henry Aldrich's Little Secret	PAR	Irvin Talbot
Her Primitive Man	UN	Edward Ward
Hi, Beautiful	UN	Frank Skinner
Hi, Good Lookin'	UN	Hans J. Salter
Hidden Valley Outlaws	REP	Mort Glickman
The Hitler Gang	PAR	David Buttolph
Home in Indiana	TCF	Hugo Friedhofer
Hotel Reserve	BRI	Lennox Berkeley
The Hour Before the Dawn	PAR	Miklos Rozsa
House of Frankenstein	UN	Hans J. Salter
I Accuse My Parents	PRC	Lee Zahler
I Love a Soldier	PAR	Robert Emmett Dolan
I'll Be Seeing You	UA	Daniele Amfitheatrof
The Impatient Years	COL	Marlin Skiles
The Imposter	UN	Dimitri Tiomkin
In Our Time	WB	Franz Waxman
In the Meantime, Darling	TCF	David Buttolph
The Invisible Man's Revenge	UN	Hans J. Salter
It Happened Tomorrow	UA	Robert Stolz
Ivan the Terrible (Part I)	RUS	Sergei Prokofiev
Jane Eyre	TCF	Bernard Herrmann
Janie	WB	Heinz Roemheld
Johnny Doesn't Live Here Anymore	MON	Franke W. Harling
Kansas City Kitty	COL	Marlin Skiles
The Keys of the Kingdom	TCF	Alfred Newman
Kismet	MGM	Herbert Stothart
Ladies Courageous	UA	Dimitri Tiomkin
Ladies in Washington	TCF	Cyril J. Mockridge
The Lady and the Monster	REP	Walter Scharf
Lady in the Death House	PRC	Jan Gray
Lake Placid Serenade	REP	Walter Scharf
Land of the Outlaws	MON	Edward J. Kay
Laura	TCF	David Raksin
Law Men	MON	Edward J. Kay
Law of the Valley	MON	Edward J. Kay
The Lodger	TCF	Hugo Friedhofer
Lost in a Harem	MGM	David Snell
Love Story	BRI	Hubert Bath
Lumberjack	UA	Irvin Talbot
Machine Gun Mama	PRC	Mort Glickman
Mademoiselle Fifi	RKO	Werner Heymann
Main Street After Dark	MGM	George Bassman
Maintenance Command (short)	BRI	Gordon Jacob
Maisie Goes to Reno	MGM	David Snell
Make Your Own Bed	WB	Heinz Roemheld

Man from Frisco	REP	Marlin Skiles
The Man in Half Moon Street	PAR	Miklos Rozsa
Marine Raiders	RKO	Roy Webb
Marked Trails	MON	Frank Sanucci
Marriage Is a Private Affair	MGM	Bronislau Kaper
Marshal of Gunsmoke	UN	Hans J. Salter
Marshal of Reno	REP	Joseph Dubin
Mask of Demitrios	WB	Adolph Deutsch
The Master Race	RKO	Roy Webb
Meet Me in St. Louis	MGM	George Stoll
Meet Miss Bobby Socks	COL	Marlin Skiles
The Memphis Belle	PAR	Gail Kubik
Men on Her Mind	PRC	Lee Zahler
Ministry of Fear	PAR	Victor Young
Minstrel Man	PRC	Ferde Grofe
The Miracle of Morgan's Creek	PAR	Leo Shuken Charles Bradshaw
The Mojave Firebrand	REP	Mort Glickman
The Monster Maker	PRC	Albert Glasser
Mr. Skeffington	WB	Franz Waxman
Mrs. Parkington	MGM	Bronislau Kaper
Mr. Winkle Goes to War	COL	Carmen Dragon Paul Sawtell
The Mummy's Curse	UN	Paul Sawtell
The Mummy's Ghost	UN	Hans J. Salter
Music for Millions	MGM	Michel Michelet
Music in Manhattan	RKO	Leigh Harline
My Best Gal	REP	Morton Scott
My Buddy	REP	Morton Scott
My Pal, Wolf	RKO	Werner Heymann
National Velvet	MGM	Herbert Stothart
The Navy Way	PAR	Willy Stahl
The Negro Soldier (short)	IND	Dimitri Tiomkin
Nevada	RKO	Paul Sawtell
A Night of Adventure	RKO	Leigh Harline
Nine Girls	COL	John Leipold
None But the Lonely Heart	RKO	Hanns Eisler
None Shall Escape	COL	Ernst Toch
Nothing But Trouble	MGM	Nathaniel Shilkret
Once Upon a Time	COL	Frederick Hollander
Our Country	BRI	William Alwyn
Our Hearts Were Young and Gay	PAR	Werner Heymann
Out of Chaos (short)	BRI	Lennox Berkeley
Outlaw Trail	MON	Frank Sanucci
Pardon My Rhythm	UN	Hans J. Salter
Partners of the Trail	MON	Edward J. Kay
Passage to Marseille	WB	Max Steiner
Passport to Destiny	RKO	Roy Webb
The Pearl of Death	UN	Paul Sawtell
Phantom Lady	UN	Hans J. Salter
The Pinto Bandit	PRC	Lee Zahler
Pin-Up Girl	TCF	Emil Newman
Practically Yours	PAR	Victor Young

Pride of the Plains	REP	Mort Glickman
The Princess and the Pirate	RKO	David Rose
The Purple Heart	TCF	Alfred Newman
Raiders of the Border	MON	Edward Kay
The Rainbow	RUS	Lev Schwartz
Rainbow Island	PAR	Roy Webb
Range Law	MON	Edward J. Kay
Rationing	MGM	David Snell
Return of the Ape Man	MON	Edward J. Kay
Roger Touhy--Gangster	TCF	Hugo Friedhofer
Rosie the Riveter	REP	Morton Scott
A Salute to France (short)	IND	Kurt Weill
San Diego, I Love You	UN	Hans J. Slater
The Scarlet Claw	UN	Paul Sawtell
Secret Command	COL	Paul Sawtell
See Here, Private Hargrove	MGM	David Snell
Seven Days Ashore	RKO	Constantin Bakaleinikoff
Shadow of Suspicion	MON	Lee Zahler
Shake Hands with Murder	PRC	Lee Zahler
Shine On, Harvest Moon	WB	Heinz Roemheld
Silent Partner	REP	Morton Scott
Silver City Kid	REP	Joseph Dubin
Since You Went Away	UA	Max Steiner
Smart Guy	MON	Edward J. Kay
Spider Woman	UN	Hans J. Salter
Standing Room Only	PAR	Robert Emmett Dolan
Storm over Lisbon	REP	Walter Scharf
The Story of Dr. Wassell	PAR	Victor Young
Strange Affair	COL	Marlin Skiles
The Sullivans	TCF	Cyril J. Mockridge
Summer Storm	UA	Karl Hajos
Sunday Dinner for a Soldier	TCF	Alfred Newman
The Suspect	UN	Frank Skinner
Take It Big	PAR	Rudy Schrager
Tall in the Saddle	RKO	Roy Webb
Tampico	TCF	David Raksin
That's My Baby	REP	Jay Chernis
They Shall Have Faith	MON	Dimitri Tiomkin
The Thin Man Goes Home	MGM	David Snell
Thirty Seconds over Tokyo	MGM	Herbert Stothart
3 Is a Family	UA	Werner Heymann
Three Little Sisters	REP	Morton Scott
Three Men in White	MGM	Nathaniel Shilkret
Till We Meet Again	PAR	David Buttolph
Timber Queen	PAR	Willy Stahl
Together Again	COL	Werner Heymann
Tomorrow the World!	UA	Louis Applebaum
The Town Went Wild	PRC	David Chudnow
Tunisian Victory	MGM	Dimitri Tiomkin William Alwyn
Tucson Raiders	REP	Joseph Dubin
Two Girls and a Sailor	MGM	George Stoll
Uncertain Glory	WB	Adolph Deutsch

The Uninvited	PAR	Victor Young
Up in Mabel's Room	UA	Michel Michelet
Valley of the Tennessee (short)	IND	Henry Brandt
The Very Thought of You	WB	Franz Waxman
Voice in the Wind	UA	Michel Michelet
Voodoo Man	MON	Edward J. Kay
Waterfront	PRC	Lee Zahler
A Wave, a Wac and a Marine	MON	Freddie Rich
Weird Woman	UN	Paul Sawtell
West of the Rio Grande	MON	Edward J. Kay
Western Approaches	BRI	Clifton Parker
Westward Bound	MON	Frank Sanucci
When the Lights Go on Again	PRC	W. Franke Harling
When Strangers Marry	MON	Dimitri Tiomkin
Whispering Footsteps	REP	Morton Scott
The White Cliffs of Dover	MGM	Herbert Stothart
Wilson	TCF	Alfred Newman
A Wing and a Prayer	TCF	Hugo Friedhofer
Winged Victory	TCF	David Rose
The Woman in the Window	RKO	Arthur Lange
The Yellow Rose of Texas	REP	Morton Scott
Youth Runs Wild	RKO	Paul Sawtell
Zoya	RUS	Dmitri Shostakovich

1945

Abbott and Costello in Hollywood	MGM	George Bassman
The Affairs of Susan	PAR	Frederick Hollander
Along Came Jones	RKO	Arthur Lange
Along the Navajo Trail	REP	Morton Scott
And Then There Were None	TCF	Mario Castelnuevo-Tedesco
An Angel Comes to Brooklyn	REP	Morton Scott
Apology for Murder	PRC	Leo Erdody
Arson Squad	PRC	Lee Zahler
Back to Bataan	RKO	Roy Webb
Bandits of the Badlands	REP	Richard Cherwin
Bedside Manner	UA	Emil Newman
Behind City Lights	REP	Richard Cherwin
A Bell for Adano	TCF	Alfred Newman
The Bells of St. Marys	RKO	Robert Emmett Dolan
Bells of Rosarita	REP	Joseph Dubin
Betrayal from the East	RKO	Roy Webb
A Better Tomorrow (short)	IND	Alex North
Bewitched	MGM	Bronislau Kaper
The Big Bonanza	REP	Morton Scott
The Big Show-Off	REP	David Chudnow
Black Market Babies	MON	Edward J. Kay
Blithe Spirit	BRI	Richard Addinsell
Blonde Ransom	UN	Frank Skinner
Blood on the Sun	UA	Miklos Rozsa
The Body Snatcher	RKO	Roy Webb
Border Badmen	PRC	Frank Sanucci
Brewster's Millions	UA	Hugo Friedhofer

The Brighton Strangler	RKO	Leigh Harline
The Bullfighters	TCF	David Buttolph
Burma Victory	BRI	Alan Rawsthorne
The Capital City (short)	IND	Henry Brandt
Captain Eddie	TCF	Cyril J. Mockridge
Captain Kidd	UA	Werner Janssen
Captain Tugboat Annie	REP	Edward J. Kay
The Caribbean Mystery	TCF	David Buttolph
The Cheaters	REP	Walter Scharf
The Cherokee Flash	REP	Richard Cherwin
The Chicago Kid	REP	Morton Scott
Children on Trial	BRI	Clifton Parker
China Sky	RKO	Leigh Harline
China's Little Devils	MON	Dimitri Tiomkin
Christmas in Connecticut	WB	Frederick Hollander
Circumstantial Evidence	TCF	David Buttolph
The Clock	MGM	George Bassman
Colonel Effingham's Raid	TCF	Cyril J. Mockridge
Colorado Pioneers	REP	Richard Cherwin
Come Out Fighting	MON	Edward J. Kay
Confidential Agent	WB	Franz Waxman
Conflict	WB	Frederick Hollander
The Corn Is Green	WB	Hugo Friedhofer
Counter-Attack	COL	Louis Gruenberg
Crime, Inc.	PRC	Walter Greene
The Crimson Canary	UN	Edgar Fairchild
The Cummington Story (short)	IND	Aaron Copland
Cyprus Is an Island (short)	BRI	Petro Petrides
Dakota	REP	Walter Scharf
The Daltons Ride Again	UN	Frank Skinner
Dangerous Intruder	PRC	Karl Hajos
Dangerous Partners	MGM	David Snell
Danger Signal	WB	Adolph Deutsch
Dead of Night	BRI	Georges Auric
A Defeated People (short)	BRI	Guy Warrack
Delightfully Dangerous	UA	Morton Gould
Detour	PRC	Leo Erdody
A Diary for Timothy (short)	BRI	Richard Addinsell
Dick Tracy	RKO	Roy Webb
Dillinger	MON	Dimitri Tiomkin
Divorce	MON	Edward J. Kay
Don Juan Quilligan	TCF	David Raksin
Don't Fence Me In	REP	Morton Scott
Eadie Was a Lady	COL	George Duning
Earl Carroll's Vanities	REP	Walter Scharf
Easy to Look at	UN	Hans J. Salter
The Enchanted Cottage	RKO	Roy Webb
The Enchanted Forest	PRC	Alfred Hay Malotte
Escape in the Desert	WB	Adolph Deutsch
The Falcon in San Francisco	RKO	Paul Sawtell
The Fall of Berlin	RUS	Dmitri Shostakovich
Fallen Angel	TCF	David Raksin
Fashion Model	MON	Edward J. Kay

The Fatal Witness	REP	Richard Cherwin
Fighting Bill Carson	PRC	Frank Sanucci
The Fighting Guardsman	COL	Paul Sawtell
The First Yank into Tokyo	RKO	Leigh Harline
Flame of the Barbary Coast	REP	Morton Scott
Flame of the West	MON	Frank Sanucci
The Fleet that Came to Stay	PAR	Lehman Engel
Follow that Woman	PAR	Alexander Laszlo
Frontier Feud	MON	Frank Sanucci
Frontier Gal	UN	Frank Skinner
The Frozen Ghost	UN	Hans J. Salter
A Game of Death	RKO	Paul Sawtell
Gangs of the Waterfront	REP	Richard Cherwin
Getting Gertie's Garter	UA	Hugo Friedhofer
G.I. Honeymoon	MON	Edward J. Kay
Girl of the Limberlost	COL	Ernest Gold
Girls of the Big House	REP	Joseph Dubin
God Is My Co-Pilot	WB	Franz Waxman
The Great Flamarion	REP	Alexander Laszlo
The Great John L.	UA	Victor Young
Grissley's Millions	REP	Morton Scott
Guest Wife	UA	Daniele Amfitheatrof
Hangover Square	TCF	Bernard Herrmann
Having Wonderful Crime	RKO	Leigh Harline
Henry V	BRI	William Walton
Her Highness and the Bellboy	MGM	George Stoll
The Hidden Eye	MGM	David Snell
High Powered	PAR	Alexander Laszlo
His Young Wife	ITA	Nino Rota
Hitchhike to Happiness	REP	Morton Scott
Hold that Blonde	PAR	Victor Young
Hollywood and Vine	PRC	Lee Zahler
Home on the Range	REP	Dale Butts
The Horn Blows at Midnight	WB	Franz Waxman
Hotel Berlin	WB	Franz Waxman
House of Dracula	UA	Edgar Fairchild
The House of Fear	UN	Paul Sawtell
The House on 92nd Street	TCF	David Buttolph
How Do You Do?	PRC	Howard Jackson
I Love a Bandleader	COL	Paul Sawtell
I'll Remember April	UN	Edgar Fairchild
I'll Tell the World	UN	Hans J. Salter
Identity Unknown	REP	Jay Chernis
Isle of the Dead	RKO	Leigh Harline
It's a Pleasure	RKO	Arthur Lange
It's in the Bag	UA	Werner Heymann
Jealousy	REP	Hanns Eisler
Johnny Angel	RKO	Leigh Harline
Johnny Frenchman	BRI	Clifton Parker
Journey Together	BRI	Gordon Jacob
Junior Miss	TCF	David Buttolph
Keep Your Powder Dry	MGM	David Snell
The Kid Sister	PRC	David Chudnow

Kiss and Tell	COL	Werner Heymann
The Lady Confesses	PRC	Lee Zahler
Lady on a Train	UN	Miklos Rozsa
Leave Her to Heaven	TCF	Alfred Newman
A Letter for Evie	MGM	George Bassman
The Lonesome Trail	MON	Frank Sanucci
The Lone Texas Ranger	REP	Richard Cherwin
Love, Honor and Goodbye	REP	Roy Webb
Love Letters	PAR	Victor Young
The Lost Weekend	PAR	Miklos Rozsa
Mama Loves Papa	RKO	Leigh Harline
Man Alive	RKO	Leigh Harline
The Man Who Walked Alone	PRC	Karl Hajos
Marshal of Laredo	REP	Richard Cherwin
Masquerade in Mexico	PAR	Victor Young
A Medal for Benny	PAR	Victor Young
Men in Her Diary	UN	Milton Rosen
The Men Who Tread on the Tiger's Tail	JAP	Tadashi Hattori
Mexicana	REP	Joseph Dubin
Mildred Pierce	WB	Max Steiner
The Missing Corpse	PRC	Karl Hajos
Molly and Me	TCF	Cyril J. Mockridge
Mr. Muggs Rides Again	MON	Edward J. Kay
Murder, He Says	PAR	Robert Emmett Dolan
Murder, My Sweet	RKO	Roy Webb
My Name Is Julia Ross	COL	Mischa Bakaleinikoff
Nabonga	PRC	David Hudnow
Nob Hill	TCF	Emil Newman
Northwest Trail	SG	Frank Sanucci
The Notorious Gentleman	BRI	William Alwyn
Objective, Burma!	WB	Franz Waxman
Once There Was a Girl	RUS	Benedict Pushkov
One Exciting Night	PAR	Alexander Laszlo
Open City	ITA	Renzo Rossellini
Oregon Trail	REP	Richard Cherwin
Our Vines Have Tender Grapes	MGM	Bronislau Kaper
Out of This World	PAR	Victor Young
Outlaw Roundup	PRC	Lee Zahler
Over 21	COL	Marlin Skiles
Pardon My Past	COL	Dimitri Tiomkin
Paris--Underground	UA	Alexandre Tansman
Patrick the Great	UN	Hans J. Salter
The Phantom of 42nd Street	PRC	Karl Hajos
The Picture of Dorian Gray	MGM	Herbert Stothart
Pillow of Death	UN	Frank Skinner
Pillow to Post	WB	Frederick Hollander
Plain People	RUS	Dmitri Shostakovich
The Power of the Whistler	COL	Wilbur Hatch
Pride of the Marines	WB	Franz Waxman
The River Gang	UN	Hans J. Salter
Road to Alcatraz	REP	Richard Cherwin
Rogues Gallery	PRC	Lee Zahler

Rough Riders of Cheyenne	REP	Richard Cherwin
Roughly Speaking	WB	Max Steiner
A Royal Scandal	TCF	Alfred Newman
The Sailor Takes a Wife	MGM	John Green
Salome, Where She Danced	UN	Edward Ward
Salty O'Rourke	PAR	Robert Emmett Dolan
San Antonio	WB	Max Steiner
San Francisco (short)	IND	Morton Gould
Santa Fe Saddlemates	REP	Richard Cherwin
Saratoga Trunk	WB	Max Steiner
The Scarlet Clue	MON	Edward J. Kay
Scarlet Street	UN	Hans J. Salter
Scotland Yard Investigator	REP	Charles Maxwell
See My Lawyer	UN	Hans J. Salter
The Seventh Veil	BRI	Benjamin Frankel
Shadow of Terror	PRC	Karl Hajos
Shady Lady	UN	Milton Rosen
Sheriff of Cimarron	REP	Richard Cherwin
She Went to the Races	MGM	Nathaniel Shilkret
She Wouldn't Say Yes	COL	Marlin Skiles
Son of Lassie	MGM	Herbert Stothart
A Song for Miss Julie	REP	David Chudnow
Song of the Sarong	UN	Edward Ward
Song of Mexico	REP	Ernesto Lecuona
The Southerner	UA	Werner Janssen
South of the Rio Grande	MON	Edward J. Kay
The Spanish Main	RKO	Hanns Eisler
Spellbound	UA	Miklos Rozsa
The Spider	TCF	David Buttolph
A Sporting Chance	REP	Richard Cherwin
Springtime in Texas	MON	Frank Sanucci
Steppin' in Society	REP	Morton Scott
The Stork Club	PAR	Robert Emmett Dolan
The Story of G.I. Joe	UA	Ann Ronnell Louis Forbes Louis Applebaum
Strange Confession	UN	Frank Skinner
Strange Illusion	PRC	Leo Erdody
Strange Voyage	MON	Lucien Moraweck
Stranger from Santa Fe	MON	Frank Sanucci
Strangers in the Night	REP	Morton Scott
Strangler of the Swamp	PRC	Alexander Steinert
Stricken Peninsula (short)	BRI	Ralph Vaughan Williams
Sudan	UN	Milton Rosen
Sunset in Eldorado	REP	Morton Scott
Swingin' on a Rainbow	REP	Morton Scott
Sylvie and the Phantom	FRA	Rene Cloerc
Tarzan and the Amazons	RKO	Paul Sawtell
That Night with You	UN	Hans J. Salter
That's the Spirit	UN	Hans J. Salter
There Goes Kelly	MON	Edward J. Kay
They Were Expendable	MGM	Herbert Stothart
This Love of Ours	UN	Hans J. Salter

This Man's Navy	MGM	Nathaniel Shilkret
Those Endearing Young Charms	RKO	Roy Webb
A Thousand and One Nights	COL	Marlin Skiles
Three in the Saddle	PRC	Lee Zahler
Three's a Crowd	REP	Richard Cherwin
Thrill of a Romance	MGM	George Stoll
Thunderbolt	IND	Gail Kubik
Thunderhead--Son of Flicka	TCF	Cyril J. Mockridge
The Tiger Woman	REP	Richard Cherwin
Tokyo Rose	PAR	Rudy Schrager
Too Young to Know	WB	Heinz Roemheld
The Topeka Terror	REP	Richard Cherwin
To the Shores of Iwo Jima	IND	William Lava
Trail of Kit Carson	REP	Richard Cherwin
A Tree Grows in Brooklyn	TCF	Alfred Newman
The True Glory	BRI	William Alwyn
Tuesday in November (short)	IND	Virgil Thomson
Twice Blessed	MGM	David Snell
Two O'Clock Courage	RKO	Roy Webb
Uncle Harry	UN	Hans J. Salter
Under Western Skies	UN	Frank Skinner
The Unseen	PAR	Ernst Toch
Utah	REP	Morton Scott
The Valley of Decision	MGM	Herbert Stothart
Vice Versa	BRI	Anthony Hopkins
Village Harvest (short)	BRI	Sir Benjamin Britten
Wagon Wheels Westward	REP	Richard Cherwin
Wanderer of the Wasteland	RKO	Paul Sawtell
The Way to the Stars	BRI	Nicholas Brodzsky
Weekend at the Waldorf	MGM	John Green
West of the Pecos	RKO	Paul Sawtell
What a Blonde	RKO	Leigh Harline
What Next, Corporal Hargrove?	MGM	David Snell
Where Do We Go from Here	TCF	David Raksin
Within These Walls	TCF	David Buttolph
Without Love	MGM	Bronislau Kaper
The Woman in Green	UN	Mark Levant
The Woman Who Came Back	REP	Edward Plumb
Wonder Man	RKO	Ray Heindorf
You Came Along	PAR	Victor Young
Zombies on Broadway	RKO	Roy Web

1946

Abie's Irish Rose	UA	John Scott Trotter
Abilene Town	UA	Nat Finston
Accomplice	PRC	Alexander Laszlo
Adventure	MGM	Herbert Stothart
Affairs of Geraldine	REP	Dale Butts
Alias Billy the Kid	REP	Raoul Kraushaar
Ambush Trail	PRC	Lee Zahler
Angel on My Shoulder	UA	Dimitri Tiomkin
Anna and the King of Siam	TCF	Bernard Herrmann

Avalanche	PRC	Lucien Moraweck
Bachelor's Daughters	UA	Heinz Roemheld
Bad Bascomb	MGM	David Snell
Badman's Territory	RKO	Roy Webb
The Bandit of Sherwood Forest	COL	Hugo Friedhofer
Beauty and the Beast	FRA	Georges Auric
Because of Him	UN	Miklos Rozsa
Bedlam	RKO	Roy Webb
Behind Green Lights	TCF	Emil Newman
Below the Deadline	MON	Edward J. Kay
The Best Years of Our Lives	RKO	Hugo Friedhofer
The Big Sleep	WB	Max Steiner
Black Angel	UN	Frank Skinner
Black Beauty	TCF	Dimitri Tiomkin
Blonde for a Day	PRC	Leo Erdody
Blondie Knows Best	COL	Mischa Bakaleinikoff
Blondie's Lucky Day	COL	Mischa Bakaleinikoff
The Blue Dahlia	PAR	Victor Young
Border Bandits	MON	Frank Sanucci
Bowery Bombshell	MON	Edward J. Kay
Boy's Ranch	MGM	Nathaniel Shilkret
The Bride Wore Boots	PAR	Frederick Hollander
Bringing Up Father	MON	Edward J. Kay
California Gold Rush	REP	Richard Cherwin
Canyon Passage	UN	Frank Skinner
The Captive Heart	BRI	Alan Rawsthorne
The Caravan Trail	PRC	Carl Hoefle
Carnival	BRI	Nicholas Brodzsky
The Cat Creeps	UN	Paul Sawtell
The Catman of Paris	REP	Dale Butts
The Chase	UA	Michel Michelet
Child of Divorce	RKO	Leigh Harline
Les Chouans	FRA	Joseph Kosma
Cinderella Jones	WB	Frederick Hollander
Claudia and David	TCF	Cyril J. Mockridge
Cloak and Dagger	WB	Max Steiner
A Close Call for Ellery Queen	COL	Mischa Bakaleinikoff
Cluny Brown	TCF	Cyril J. Mockridge
The Cockeyed Miracle	MGM	David Snell
Conquest of Cheyenne	REP	Richard Cherwin
Cornered	RKO	Roy Webb
Courage of Lassie	MGM	Bronislau Kaper
Crack-Up	RKO	Leigh Harline
Crime Doctor's Warning	COL	Paul Sawtell
Crime of the Century	REP	Richard Cherwin
Criminal Court	RKO	Paul Sawtell
Danger Woman	UN	Paul Sawtell
Dangerous Millions	TCF	Darrell Calker
Dangerous Money	MON	Edward J. Kay
Danny Boy	PRC	Walter Greene
The Dark Corner	TCF	Cyril J. Mockridge
The Dark House	UN	Hans J. Salter
The Dark Mirror	UN	Dimitri Tiomkin

Days of Buffalo Bill	REP	Richard Cherwin
Deadline at Dawn	RKO	Hanns Eisler
Deadline for Murder	TCF	Rudy Schrager
Deception	WB	Erich Wolfgang Korngold
Devil Bat's Daughter	PRC	Alexander Steinert
Devotion	WB	Erich Wolfgang Korngold
Diary of a Chambermaid	UA	Michel Michelet
Dick Tracy vs. Cueball	RKO	Phil Ohman
Don't Gamble with Strangers	MON	Edward J. Kay
Down Missouri Way	PRC	Karl Hajos
Dragonwyck	TCF	Alfred Newman
Drifting Along	MON	Edward J. Kay
Driftin' River	PRC	Karl Hajos
Easy to Wed	MGM	John Green
The El Paso Kid	REP	Raoul Kraushaar
The Fabulous Suzanne	REP	Arthur Lange
The Face of Marble	MON	Edward J. Kay
Faithful in My Fashion	MGM	Nathaniel Shilkret
The Falcon's Adventure	RKO	Paul Sawtell
The Falcon's Alibi	RKO	Ernest Gold
The Flying Serpent	PRC	Leo Erdody
Fool's Gold	UA	David Chudnow
Freddie Steps Out	MON	Lee Zahler
The French Key	REP	Alexander Laszlo
From This Day Forward	RKO	Leigh Harline
Frontier Fugitives	PRC	Lee Zahler
Gallant Bess	MGM	Rudolph Kopp
Gallant Journey	COL	Marlin Skiles
Gas House Kids	PRC	Leo Erdody
Gay Blades	REP	Morton Scott
The Gay Cavalier	MON	Edward J. Kay
Gentleman Joe Palooka	MON	Edward J. Kay
Gentleman from Texas	MON	Edward J. Kay
Gentlemen with Guns	PRC	Lee Zahler
Gilda	COL	Hugo Friedhofer Marlin Skiles
G.I. War Brides	REP	Ernest Gold
The Glass Alibi	REP	Alexander Laszlo
God's Country	SG	Carl Hoefle
The Green Years	MGM	Herbert Stothart
A Guy Could Change	REP	Richard Cherwin
Heartbeat	RKO	Paul Misraki
Heldorado	REP	Dale Butts
Her Adventurous Night	UN	Hans J. Salter
Her Kind of Man	WB	Franz Waxman
Her Sister's Secret	PRC	Hans Sommer
Home in Oklahoma	REP	Joseph Dubin
Home Sweet Homicide	TCF	David Buttolph
The Hoodlum Saint	MGM	Nathaniel Shilkret
Hot Cargo	PAR	Alexander Laszlo
House of Horrors	UN	Hans J. Salter
Idea Girl	UN	Frank Skinner
In Fast Company	MON	Edward J. Kay

The Inner Circle	REP	Mort Glickman
In Old Sacramento	REP	Morton Scott
Inside Job	UN	Frank Skinner
The Invisible Informer	REP	Richard Cherwin
I Ring Doorbells	PRC	Leo Erdody
It Shouldn't Happen to a Dog	TCF	David Buttolph
It's a Wonderful Life	RKO	Dimitri Tiomkin
Ivan the Terrible (Part II)	RUS	Sergei Prokofiev
I've Always Loved You	REP	Walter Scharf
Janie Gets Married	WB	Frederick Hollander
Joe Palooka, Champ	MON	Alexander Laszlo
Johnny Comes Flying Home	TCF	David Buttolph
The Killers	UN	Miklos Rozsa
Kitty	PAR	Victor Young
Lady Luck	RKO	Leigh Harline
Larceny in Her Heart	PRC	Leo Erdody
The Last Crooked Mile	REP	Richard Cherwin
Lightning Raiders	PRC	Lee Zahler
Lighthouse	PRC	Ernest Gold
Little Giant	UN	Edgar Fairchild
Little Iodine	UA	Alexander Steinert
Little Miss Big	UN	Hans J. Salter
Little Mister Jim	MGM	George Bassman
Live Wires	MON	Edward J. Kay
Love Laughs at Andy Hardy	MGM	David Snell
Lover Come Back	UN	Hans J. Salter
The Magnificent Rogue	REP	Mort Glickman
The Man from Rainbow Valley	REP	Mort Glickman
Margie	TCF	Alfred Newman
The Mask of Dijon	PRC	Karl Hajos
Men of Two Worlds	BRI	Sir Arthur Bliss
The Mighty McGurk	MGM	David Snell
The Missing Lady	MON	Edward J. Kay
Miss Susie Slagle's	PAR	Daniele Amfitheatrof
Monsieur Beaucaire	PAR	Robert Emmett Dolan
Monsieurs Ludovic	FRA	Joseph Kosma
Moon over Montana	MON	Frank Sanucci
Mr. Ace	UA	Heinz Roemheld
Mr. Hex	MON	Edward J. Kay
Murder Is My Business	PRC	Leo Erdody
Murderers Among Us	GER	Ernst Roters
My Darling Clementine	TCF	Cyril J. Mockridge
My Pal Trigger	REP	Morton Scott
My Reputation	WB	Max Steiner
Mysterious Intruder	COL	Wilbur Hatch
The Mysterious Mr. Valentine	REP	Mort Glickman
Never Say Goodbye	WB	Frederick Hollander
Nicholas Nickleby	BRI	Lord Berners
Night and Day	WB	Max Steiner
Night Has Eyes	BRI	Charles Williams
A Night in Casablanca	UA	Werner Janssen
A Night in Paradise	UN	Frank Skinner
Night Train to Memphis	REP	Dale Butts

Nobody Lives Forever	WB	Adolph Deutsch
Nocturne	RKO	Leigh Harline
Notorious	RKO	Roy Webb
O. S. S.	PAR	Daniele Amfitheatrof
Odd Man Out	BRI	William Alwyn
Of Human Bondage	WB	Erich Wolfgang Korngold
One Exciting Week	REP	Dale Butts
One More Tomorrow	WB	Max Steiner
Our Hearts Were Growing Up	PAR	Victor Young
Out California Way	REP	Nathan Scott
Overland Riders	PRC	Lee Zahler
The Overlanders	AUT	John Ireland
Paisan	ITA	Renzo Rossellini
The Pale Horseman (short)	IND	Henry Brandt
Panic	FRA	Jacques Ibert
People Are Funny	PAR	Alexander Laszlo
Piccadilly Incident	BRI	Vivian Ellis
The Plainsman and the Lady	REP	Georges Anthiel
Portes De La Nuit	FRA	Joseph Kosma
The Postman Always Rings Twice	MGM	George Bassman
Prairie Badmen	PRC	Lee Zahler
Prairie Rustlers	PRC	Lee Zahler
Queen of Burlesque	PRC	Karl Hajos
Rainbow over Texas	REP	Morton Scott
The Razor's Edge	TCF	Alfred Newman
Red River Renegades	REP	Mort Glickman
Rendezvous 24	TCF	Emil Newman
Rendezvous with Annie	REP	Joseph Dubin
Renegades	COL	Paul Sawtell
The Return of Monte Cristo	COL	Lucien Moraweck
Un Revenant	FRA	Arthur Honegger
Rio Grande Raiders	REP	Mort Glickman
Road to Utopia	PAR	Leigh Harline
Roll on Texas Moon	REP	Dale Butts
Romance of the West	PRC	Carl Hoefle
The Runaround	UN	Frank Skinner
San Quentin	RKO	Paul Sawtell
A Scandal in Paris	UA	Hanns Eisler
The Searching Wind	PAR	Victor Young
The Secret Heart	MGM	Bronislau Kaper
Secrets of a Sorority Girl	PRC	Karl Hajos
Sentimental Journey	TCF	Cyril Mockridge
Shadow of a Woman	WB	Adolph Deutsch
The Shadow Returns	MON	Edward J. Kay
Sheriff of Redwood Valley	REP	Richard Cherwin
She-Wolf of London	UN	William Lava
Shock	TCF	David Buttolph
The Show-Off	MGM	David Snell
Silver Range	MON	Edward J. Kay
Sioux City Sue	REP	Dale Butts
Sister Kenny	RKO	Alexandre Tansman
Six Gun for Hire	PRC	Lee Zahler
Smoky	TCF	David Raksin

Smooth as Silk	UN	Ernest Gold
Snafu	COL	Paul Sawtell
So Dark the Night	COL	Hugo Friedhofer
So Goes My Love	UN	Hans J. Salter
Somewhere in the Night	TCF	David Buttolph
Song of Arizona	REP	Morton Scott
Song of the South	DIS	Daniele Amfitheatrof
South of Monterey	MON	Edward J. Kay
Specter of the Rose	REP	George Anthiel
The Spiral Staircase	RKO	Roy Webb
Spook Busters	MON	Edward J. Kay
Stairway to Heaven	BRI	Allan Gray
Stars over Texas	PRC	Karl Hajos
Step by Step	RKO	Paul Sawtell
A Stolen Life	WB	Max Steiner
The Stone Flower	RUS	Lev Schwartz
Strange Conquest	UN	Paul Sawtell
Strange Holiday	PRC	Gordon Jenkins
Strange Impersonation	REP	Alexander Laszlo
Strange Journey	TCF	Rudy Schrager
The Strange Love of Martha Ivers	PAR	Miklos Rozsa
Strange Triangle	TCF	David Buttolph
The Strange Woman	UA	Carmen Dragon
The Stranger	RKO	Bronislau Kaper
Sunset Pass	RKO	Paul Sawtell
Sun Valley Cyclone	REP	Richard Cherwin
Suspense	MON	Daniele Amfitheatrof
Swamp Fire	PAR	Rudy Schrager
Sweetheart of Sigma Chi	MON	Edward J. Kay
Swell Guy	UA	David Tamkin
Swing Parade of 1946	MON	Edward J. Kay
Tangier	UN	Milton Rosen
Tarzan and the Leopard Woman	RKO	Paul Sawtell
Temptation	UN	Daniele Amfitheatrof
Theirs Is the Glory (short)	BRI	Guy Warrack
That Brennan Girl	REP	George Anthiel
They Made Me a Killer	PAR	Alexander Laszlo
This Man Is Mine	BRI	Allan Gray
Three Strangers	WB	Adolph Deutsch
Three Wise Fools	MGM	Bronislau Kaper
Till the End of Time	RKO	Leigh Harline
The Time of Their Lives	UN	Milton Rosen
The Time, the Place and the Girl	WB	Frederick Hollander
To Each His Own	PAR	Victor Young
Tomorrow Is Forever	RKO	Max Steiner
Traffic in Crime	REP	Mort Glickman
Trail to Mexico	MON	Frank Sanucci
Trigger Fingers	MON	Edward J. Kay
The Truth About Murder	RKO	Leigh Harline
Two Guys from Milwaukee	WB	Frederick Hollander
Two Smart People	MGM	George Bassman
Two Years Before the Mast	PAR	Victor Young
Under Arizona Skies	MON	Edward J. Kay

The Undercover Woman	REP	Richard Cherwin
Undercurrent	MGM	Herbert Stothart
Under Nevada Skies	REP	Dale Butts
Unexpected Guest	UA	David Chudnow
Up Goes Maisie	MGM	David Snell
Vacation in Reno	RKO	Paul Sawtell
Valley of the Zombies	REP	Richard Cherwin
The Verdict	WB	Frederick Hollander
The Virginian	PAR	Daniele Amfitheatrof
La Voleur De Paratonnerres	FRA	Jean Wiener
Wake up and Dream	TCF	Cyril J. Mockridge
A Walk in the Sun	TCF	Freddie Rich
The Walls Came Tumbling Down	COL	Marlin Skiles
Wanted for Murder	BRI	Mischa Spoliansky
The Well-Groomed Bride	PAR	Roy Webb
West of the Alamo	MON	Frank Sanucci
Whistle Stop	UA	Dimitri Tiomkin
White Tie and Tails	UN	Milton Rosen
The Wife of Monte Cristo	PRC	Paul Desseau
Wife Wanted	MON	Edward J. Kay
Wild Beauty	UN	Paul Sawtell
Wild West	PRC	Karl Hajos
Without Reservations	RKO	Roy Webb
The Yearling	MGM	Herbert Stothart
Young Widow	UA	Carmen Dragon

1947

Adventure Island	PAR	Darrel Calker
Adventures of Don Coyote	UA	David Chudnow
Alisher Navoi	RUS	Rheinhold Gliere T. Sadykov
Along the Oregon Trail	REP	Mort Glickman
Always Together	WB	Werner Heymann
Angel and the Badman	REP	Richard Hageman
Apache Rose	REP	Morton Scott
The Arnelo Affair	MGM	George Bassman
Aubervilliers	FRA	Joseph Kosma Jacques Prevert
The Bachelor and the Bobby-Soxer	RKO	Leigh Harline
Backlash	TCF	Darrel Calker
Banjo	RKO	Alexander Laszlo
The Beast with Five Fingers	WB	Max Steiner
Beauty and the Bandit	MON	Edward J. Kay
The Beginning or the End	MGM	Daniele Amfitheatrof
Bells of San Angelo	REP	Mort Glickman
Bells of San Fernando	SG	Rudy de Saxe
Beyond Our Own	IND	Rudy de Saxe
The Big Fix	PRC	Emil Cadkin
Big Town	PAR	Darrel Calker
Bill and Coo	REP	David Buttolph
Black Gold	AA	Edward J. Kay

Black Narcissus	BRI	Brian Easdale
Blanche Fury	BRI	Clifton Parker
Blaze of Noon	PAR	Adolph Deutsch
Blind Spot	COL	Paul Sawtell
Body and Soul	UA	Hugo Friedhofer
Boomerang	TCF	David Buttolph
Border Feud	PRC	Albert Glasser
Born to Kill	RKO	Paul Sawtell
Born to Speed	PRC	Alvin Levin
Bowery Buckaroos	MON	Edward J. Kay
The Brasher Doubloon	TCF	David Buttolph
The Brothers	BRI	Cedric Thorpe Davie
Brute Force	UN	Miklos Rozsa
Buck Privates Come Home	UN	Walter Schumann
Buffalo Bill Rides Again	SG	Modest Altschuller
The Burning Cross	SG	Ralph Stanley
Bury Me Dead	PRC	Emil Cadkin
Calcutta	PAR	Victor Young
California	PAR	Victor Young
Captain Boycott	BRI	William Alwyn
Captain from Castile	TCF	Alfred Newman
The Case of the Baby Sitter	SG	David Chudnow
Cass Timberlane	MGM	Roy Webb
Cheyenne	WB	Max Steiner
The Chinese Ring	MON	Edward J. Kay
Christmas Eve	UA	Heinz Roemheld
Code of the West	RKO	Paul Sawtell
Copacabana	UA	Edward Ward
The Corpse Came C.O.D.	COL	George Duning
The Crimson Key	REP	Dale Butts
Cross My Heart	PAR	Robert Emmett Dolan
Crossfire	RKO	Roy Webb
Cry Wolf	WB	Franz Waxman
The Cumberland Story (short)	BRI	Sir Arthur Benjamin
Curley	UA	Heinz Roemheld
Cynthia	MGM	Bronislau Kaper
Daisy Kenyon	TCF	David Raksin
Dangerous Venture	UA	David Chudnow
Dangerous Years	TCF	Rudy Schrager
Dark Delusion	MGM	David Snell
Dark Passage	WB	Franz Waxman
Dead Reckoning	COL	Marlin Skiles
Dear Ruth	PAR	Robert Emmett Dolan
Death Valley	SG	Carl Hoefle
Deep Valley	WB	Max Steiner
Desert Fury	PAR	Miklos Rozsa
Desire Me	MGM	Herbert Stothart
Desperate	RKO	Paul Sawtell
Devil in the Flesh	FRA	Rene Cloerec
The Devil on Wheels	PRC	Emil Cadkin
The Devil Thumbs a Ride	RKO	Paul Sawtell
Dick Tracy Meets Gruesome	RKO	Paul Sawtell
Dick Tracy's Dilemma	RKO	Paul Sawtell

Dishonored Lady	UA	Carmen Dragon
A Double Life	UN	Miklos Rozsa
Down to Earth	COL	Heinz Roemheld
Dragnet	SG	Irving Gertz
Driftwood	REP	Nathan Scott
Duel in the Sun	SRO	Dimitri Tiomkin
Easy Come, Easy Go	PAR	Roy Webb
The Egg and I	UN	Frank Skinner
Escape Me Never	WB	Erich Wolfgang Korngold
The Exile	UN	Frank Skinner
Exposed	REP	Ernest Gold
The Fabulous Dorseys	UA	Leo Shuken
The Fabulous Joe	UA	Heinz Roemheld
The Fabulous Texan	REP	Anthony Collins
Fall Guy	MON	Edward J. Kay
The Farmer's Daughter	RKO	Leigh Harline
Fear in the Night	PAR	Rudy Schrager
Fiesta	MGM	John Green Aaron Copland
Flight to Nowhere	SG	Carl Hoefle
Forever Amber	TCF	David Raksin
For You I Die	FC	Paul Sawtell
The Foxes of Harrow	TCF	David Buttolph
Framed	COL	Marlin Skiles
The Fugitive	RKO	Richard Hageman
Fun and Fancy Free	DIS	Eliot Daniel Paul Smith Oliver Wallace
Fun on a Weekend	UA	Lucien Cailliet
The Gangster	AA	Louis Gruenberg
Gas House Kids Go West	PRC	Hans Sommer
Gas House Kids in Hollywood	PRC	Albert Glasser
Gentlemen's Agreement	TCF	Alfred Newman
A Geometry Lesson (short)	ITA	Geofredo Petrassi
Germany Year Zero	ITA	Renzo Rossellini
The Ghost and Mrs. Muir	TCF	Bernard Herrmann
The Ghost Goes Wild	REP	Joseph Dubin
Ghost Town Renegades	PTC	Walter Greene
Golden Earrings	PAR	Victor Young
Great Expectations	BRI	Walter Goehr
Green Dolphin Street	MGM	Bronislau Kaper
The Guilt of Janet Ames	COL	George Duning
The Guilty	MON	Rudy Schrager
Gunfighters	COL	Rudy Schrager
Gun Talk	MON	Edward J. Kay
The Hat Box Mystery	SG	David Chudnow
Heading for Heaven	PRC	Hal Borne
Heartaches	PRC	Emil Cadkin
Heaven Only Knows	UA	Heinz Roemheld
Her Husband's Affairs	COL	George Duning
High Barbaree	MGM	Herbert Stothart
High Conquest	MON	Lud Gluskin
High Tide	MON	Rudy Schrager

High Wall	MGM	Bronislau Kaper
Hollywood Barn Dance	SG	Walter Greene
The Homestretch	TCF	David Raksin
Honeymoon	RKO	Leigh Harline
Hoppy's Holiday	UA	David Chudnow
The Hucksters	MGM	Lennie Hayton
Humoresque	WB	Franz Waxman
Hungry Hill	BRI	John Greenwood
I Cover the Big Town	PAR	Darrel Calker
I Love Trouble	COL	George Duning
I Walk Alone	PAR	Victor Young
If Winter Comes	MGM	Herbert Stothart
I'll Be Yours	UN	Frank Skinner
The Idol of Paris	BRI	Mischa Spoliansky
The Imperfect Lady	PAR	Victor Young
In Self Defense	MON	Rudy Schrager
Intrigue	UA	Louis Forbes
The Invisible Wall	TCF	Dale Butts
It Had to Be You	COL	Morris Stoloff
It Happened in Brooklyn	MGM	John Green
It Happened on Fifth Avenue	AA	Edward Ward
It's a Joke, Son!	EL	Alvin Levin
Ivy	UN	Daniele Amfitheatrof
Jewels of Brandenburg	TCF	Darrell Calker
Joe Palooka in the Knockout	MON	Edward J. Kay
Johnny O'Clock	COL	George Duning
Keeper of the Bees	COL	Paul Sawtell
Killer at Large	PRC	Alvin Levin Albert Glasser
Killer Dill	SG	John Thompson
Killer McCoy	MGM	David Snell
Kilroy Was Here	MON	Edward J. Kay
King of the Bandits	MON	Edward J. Kay
Kiss of Death	TCF	David Buttolph
Ladies' Man	PAR	Irvin Talbot
Lady in the Lake	MGM	David Snell
Land of the Lawless	MON	Edward J. Kay
Last Frontier Uprising	REP	Mort Glickman
The Late George Apley	TCF	Cyril J. Mockridge
Law of the Lash	PRC	Albert Glasser
Life with Father	WB	Max Steiner
A Likely Story	RKO	Leigh Harline
Linda Be Good	PRC	Jack Mason
Living In a Big Way	MGM	Lennie Hayton
The Locket	RKO	Roy Webb
The Long Night	RKO	Dimitri Tiomkin
Lost Honeymoon	EL	Werner Heymann
The Lost Moment	UN	Daniele Amitheatrof
Louisiana	MON	Edward J. Kay
Love and Learn	WB	Max Steiner
Love from a Stranger	EL	Hans J. Salter
The Loves of Joanna Godden	BRI	Ralph Vaughan Williams
Lured (Personal Column)	UA	Michel Michelet

The Macomber Affair	UA	Miklos Rozsa
Mad Wednesday	UA	Werner Heymann
Magic Town	RKO	Roy Webb
The Man I Love	WB	Max Steiner
The Marauders	UA	David Chudnow
Marriage in the Shadows	GER	Wolfgang Zeller
Marshal of Cripple Creek	REP	Mort Glickman
Merton of the Movies	MGM	David Snell
The Michigan Kid	UN	Hans J. Salter
Michurin	RUS	Dmitri Shostakovich
The Miracle of Dr. Petrov	RUS	Benedict Pushkov
Miracle on 34th Street	TCF	Cyril J. Mockridge
Mr. District Attorney	COL	Herschel Burke Gilbert
Monsieur Verdoux	UA	Charles Chaplin
Monsieur Vincent	FRA	Jean-Jacques Grunewald
Moss Rose	TCF	David Buttolph
Mourning Becomes Electra	RKO	Richard Hageman
My Brother Talks to Horses	MGM	Rudolph Kopp
My Father's House	IND	Henry Brandt
My Favorite Brunette	PAR	Robert Emmett Dolan
News Hounds	MON	Edward J. Kay
Nightmare Alley	TCF	Cyril J. Mockridge
Night Song	RKO	Leith Stevens
Nora Prentiss	WB	Franz Waxman
Northwest Outpost	REP	Rudolph Friml
October Man	BRI	William Alwyn
The Other Love	UA	Miklos Rozsa
Out of the Blue	EL	Carmen Dragon
Out of the Past	RKO	Roy Webb
The Paradine Case	SRO	Franz Waxman
Peddlin' in Society	ITA	C. A. Bixio E. Montagnini
The Perfect Marriage	PAR	Frederick Hollander
Perilous Waters (In Self Defense)	MON	Rudy Schrager
The Perils of Pauline	PAR	Robert Emmett Dolan
Personal Column (see Lured)		
Le Petit Soldat	FRA	Joseph Kosma
Philo Vance Returns	PRC	Albert Glasser
Philo Vance's Gamble	PRC	Irving Friedman
The Pilgrim Lady	REP	Richard Cherwin
Pirates of Monterey	UN	Milton Rosen
Pirogov	RUS	Dmitri Shostakovich
Possessed	WB	Franz Waxman
The Pretender	REP	Paul Dessau
The Private Affairs of Bel Ami	UA	Darius Milhaud
Pursued	WB	Max Steiner
Queen of the Amazons	SG	Lee Zahler
The Raid (Razzia)	GER	Werner Eisbrenner
Railroaded	PRC	Alvin Levin
Ramrod	UA	Adolph Deutsch
Range Beyond the Blue	PRC	Walter Greene
The Red House	UA	Miklos Rozsa
The Red Stallion	EL	Frederick Hollander

Renegade Girl	SG	Darrell Calker
Repeat Performance	EL	George Anthiel
The Return of Rin Tin Tin	EL	Leo Erdody
Ride the Pink Horse	UN	Frank Skinner
Riff Raff	RKO	Roy Webb
Road to Rio	PAR	Robert Emmett Dolan
Road to the Big House	SG	Ralph Stanley
Rolling Home	SG	Darrell Calker
Romance of Rosy Ridge	MGM	George Bassman
The Roosevelt Story	IND	Earl Robinson
Roses Are Red	TCF	Rudy Schrager
Russian Ballerina	RUS	Benedict Pushkov
Saddle Pals	REP	Ernest Gold
Sarge Goes to College	MON	Edward J. Kay
Sea of Grass	MGM	Herbert Stothart
Second Chance	TCF	Dale Butts
Secret Beyond the Door	UN	Miklos Rozsa
The Secret Life of Walter Mitty	RKO	David Raksin
The Senator Was Indiscreet	UN	Daniele Amfitheatrof
Seven Keys to Baldpate	RKO	Paul Sawtell
Shoot to Kill	SG	Darrell Calker
Silence Est D'Or	FRA	Georges van Parys
Sinbad the Sailor	RKO	Roy Webb
Singapore	UN	Daniele Amfitheatrof
Six-Gun Serenade	MON	Frank Sanucci
Six Juin A L'Aube	FRA	Jean Gremillon
Slave Girl	UN	Milton Rosen
Smash-Up--The Story of a Woman	UN	Daniele Amfitheatrof
Something in the Wind	UN	John Green
Song of Love	MGM	Bronislau Kaper
Song of Scheherazade	UN	Miklos Rozsa
Song of the Thin Man	MGM	David Snell
Spring	RUS	Isaac Dunayevsky
Springtime in the Sierras	REP	Morton Scott
Stallion Road	WB	Frederick Hollander
Stepchild	PRC	Mario Silva
Stork Bites Man	UA	Raoul Kraushaar
A String of Beads (short)	BRI	Elizabeth Lutyens
Suddenly It's Spring	PAR	Victor Young
The Swordsman	COL	Hugo Friedhofer
T-Men	EL	Paul Sawtell
Take My Life	BRI	William Alwyn
Tarzan and the Huntress	RKO	Paul Sawtell
The Tender Years	TCF	Edward Kilenyi
That Hagan Girl	WB	Franz Waxman
That Way with Women	WB	Frederick Hollander
That's My Girl	REP	Morton Scott
That's My Man	REP	Hans J. Salter
They Won't Believe Me	RKO	Roy Webb
Three on a Ticket	PRC	Emil Cadkin
13 Rue Madeleine	TCF	David Buttolph
Thunder in the Valley	TCF	Cyril J. Mockridge
Thunder Mountain	RKO	Paul Sawtell

Time Out of Mind	UN	Miklos Rozsa
		Mario Castelnovo-Tedesco
Too Many Winners	PRC	Alvin Levin
Trail Street	RKO	Paul Sawtell
Trail to San Antone	REP	Joseph Dubin
The Trap	MON	Edward J. Kay
The Trespasser	REP	Nathan Scott
The Trouble with Women	PAR	Victor Young
Twilight on the Rio Grande	REP	Morton Scott
The Two Mrs. Carrolls	WB	Franz Waxman
Tycoon	RKO	Leigh Harline
Unconquered	PAR	Victor Young
Undercover Maisie	MGM	David Snell
Under the Tonto Rim	RKO	Paul Sawtell
The Unfaithful	WB	Max Steiner
The Unfinished Dance	MGM	Herbert Stothart
The Unsuspected	WB	Franz Waxman
The Untamed Fury	PRC	Alexander Laszlo
The Upturned Glass	BRI	Bernard Stevens
Valley of Fear	MON	Edward J. Kay
Variety Girl	PAR	Joseph J. Lilley
The Vigilantes Return	UN	Paul Sawtell
Village Teacher	RUS	Lev Schwartz
Violence	MON	Edward J. Kay
The Voice of the Turtle	WB	Max Steiner
The Web	UN	Hans J. Salter
Welcome Stranger	PAR	Robert Emmett Dolan
Whispering City	CAN	Andre Mathieu
Wild Harvest	PAR	Hugo Friedhofer
Wild Horse Mesa	RKO	Paul Sawtell
Winter Wonderland	REP	Paul Dessau
The Wistful Widow of Wagon Gap	UN	Walter Schumann
The Woman in the Hall	BRI	Temple Abady
The Woman on the Beach	RKO	Hanns Eisler
Woman to Woman	BRI	George Melachrino
A Woman's Vengeance	UN	Miklos Rozsa
The World of Paul Delvaux	BEL	Andre Souris
Wyoming	REP	Nathan Scott
		Ernest Gold
Yankee Fakir	REP	Alexander Laszlo
Young Guard	RUS	Dmitri Shostakovich

1948

Abbot and Costello Meet Frankenstein	UN	Frank Skinner
The Accused	PAR	Victor Young
An Act of Murder	UN	Daniele Amfitheatrof
Act of Violence	MGM	Bronislau Kaper
Adventures of Casanova	EL	Hugo Friedhofer
Adventures of Don Juan	WB	Max Steiner
Adventures of Gallant Bess	EL	Irving Gertz
The Affair Blum	GER	Herbert Trantow

Albuquerque	PAR	Darrell Calker
Alias a Gentleman	MGM	David Snell
All My Sons	UN	Leith Stevens
Angel in Exile	REP	Nathan Scott
Angel on the Amazon	REP	Nathan Scott
Angel's Alley	MON	Edward J. Kay
Another Part of the Forest	UN	Daniele Amfitheatrof
Another Shore	BRI	Georges Auric
Apartment for Peggy	TCF	David Raksin
Appointment with Murder	FC	Karl Hajos
Arch of Triumph	UA	Louis Gruenberg
Are You with It?	UN	Walter Scharf
The Argyle Secrets	FC	Ralph Stanley
The Arizona Ranger	RKO	Paul Sawtell
Arthur Takes Over	TCF	Darrell Calker
Assigned to Danger	EL	Albert Glasser
B. F.'s Daughter	MGM	Bronislau Kaper
The Babe Ruth Story	AA	Edward Ward
Back Streets of Paris	FRA	Jean Wiener
Back Trail	MON	Edward J. Kay
Bad Men of Tombstone	AA	Roy Webb
Bad Sister	BRI	Bretton Byrd
Bagarres	FRA	Joseph Kosma
Behind Locked Doors	EL	Albert Glasser
Bell Starr's Daughter	TCF	Edward Kilenyi
Berlin Express	RKO	Frederick Hollander
Beyond Glory	PAR	Victor Young
The Big City	MGM	George Stoll
The Big Clock	PAR	Victor Young
The Big Punch	WB	William Lava
Big Town Scandal	PAR	Darrell Calker
The Bishop's Wife	RKO	Hugo Friedhofer
The Black Arrow	COL	Paul Sawtell
Black Bart	UN	Frank Skinner Leith Stevens Hugo Friedhofer
Black Hills	EL	Walter Greene
Blind Desire	FRA	Georges Auric
Blind Goddess	BRI	Bernard Green
Blonde Ice	FC	Irving Gertz
Blood on the Moon	RKO	Roy Webb
Bob and Sally	IND	Milton Rosen
Bodyguard	RKO	Paul Sawtell
Bonnie Prince Charlie	BRI	Ian Whyte
Border Street	POL	Roman Palester
The Boy with Green Hair	RKO	Leigh Harline
The Bride Goes Wild	MGM	Rudolph Kopp
Broken Journey	BRI	John Greenwood
Caged Fury	PAR	Harry Lubin
California Firebrand	REP	Arthur Wilkinson
Campus Sleuth	MON	Edward J. Kay
Canon City	EL	Irving Friedman
The Challenge	TCF	Milton Rosen

The Checkered Coat	TCF	Edward J. Kay
Cheyenne Takes Over	PRC	Walter Greene
Chicken Every Sunday	TCF	Alfred Newman
Christopher Columbus	BRI	Sir Arthur Bliss
A City Speaks (short)	BRI	William Alwyn
Close-Up	EL	Jerome Moross
The Cobra Strikes	EL	Albert Glasser
Code of Scotland Yard	REP	George Melachrino
Command Decision	MGM	Miklos Rozsa
Confessions of a Rogue	FRA	Rene Cloerec
Coroner Creek	COL	Rudy Schrager
Corridor of Mirrors	BRI	George Auric
The Counterfeiters	TCF	Irving Gertz
The Countess of Monte Cristo	UN	Walter Scharf
Courtin' Trouble	MON	Edward J. Kay
Cowboy Cavalier	MON	Edward J. Kay
The Creeper	TCF	Milton Rosen
Crossed Trails	MON	Edward J. Kay
Cry of the City	TCF	Alfred Newman
Daredevils of the Clouds	REP	Morton Scott
The Dark Past	COL	George Duning
A Date with Judy	MGM	George Stoll
The Dead Don't Dream	UA	Ralph Stanley
Deadline	IND	Frank Sanucci
Dear Mr. Prohack	BRI	Temple Abady
Dear Murderer	BRI	Muir Mathieson
The Decision of Christopher Blake	WB	Max Steiner
Deep Waters	TCF	Cyril J. Mockridge
Design for Death	RKO	Paul Sawtell
The Denver Kid	REP	Dale Butts
Desperadoes of Dodge City	REP	Morton Scott
Devil's Cargo	FC	Paul Dessau
Dim Little Island (short)	BRI	Ralph Vaughan Williams
Don Quixote de La Mancha	SPA	Ernesto Halffter
Don't Trust Your Husband	UA	Hans J. Salter
Docks of New Orleans	MON	Edward J. Kay
Dream Girl	PAR	Victor Young
Dreams That Money Can Buy	IND	Louis Applebaum John Cage Paul Bowles David Diamond Darius Milhaud Paul Hindemith Edgar Varese
Drunken Angel	JAP	Fumio Hayasaka
The Dude Goes West	AA	Dimitri Tiomkin
Dulcimer Street	BRI	Benjamin Frankel
Dynamite	PAR	Darrell Calker
The Eagle Has Two Heads	FRA	Georges Auric
Embraceable You	WB	William Lava
The Emperor Waltz	PAR	Victor Young
The Enchanted Valley	EL	Lucien Cailliet

Enchantment	RKO	Hugo Friedhofer
The End of the River	BRI	Lambert Williamson
Escape	TCF	William Alwyn
Esther Waters	BRI	Gordon Jacob
Eternal Melodies	ITA	Alessandro Cicognini
Every Girl Should Be Married	RKO	Leigh Harline
Eyes of Texas	REP	Dale Butts
Fabiola	ITA	Enzo Masetti
The Fallen Idol	BRI	William Alwyn
False Paradise	UA	Ralph Stanley
Family Honeymoon	UN	Frank Skinner
The Far Frontier	REP	Dale Butts
Farrebique	FRA	Henri Sauguet
The Feathered Serpent	MON	Edward J. Kay
Feudin', Fussin' and A-Fightin'	UN	Leith Stevens
Fighter Squadron	WB	Max Steiner
Fighting Back	TCF	Darrell Calker
Fighting Father Dunne	RKO	Roy Webb
Fighting Mad	MON	Edward J. Kay
Fighting Mustang	IND	Frank Sanucci
The Fighting Ranger	MON	Edward J. Kay
The Fighting Vigilantes	EL	Walter Greene
The Film Without a Name	GER	Bernhard Eichhorn
For the Love of Mary	UN	Frank Skinner
Force of Evil	MGM	David Raksin
A Foreign Affair	PAR	Frederick Hollander
Fort Apache	RKO	Richard Hageman
Four Faces West	UA	Paul Sawtell
Francois Villon	FRA	Toni Aubain
French Leave	MON	Edward J. Kay
Frontier Agent	MON	Edward J. Kay
The Fuller Brush Man	COL	Heinz Roemheld
Fury at Furnace Creek	TCF	Alfred Newman
The Gallant Blade	COL	George Duning
The Gallant Legion	REP	Morton Scott
The Gay Intruders	TCF	Ralph Stanley
The Gay Ranchero	REP	Morton Scott
Gelosia	ITA	Enzo Masetti
The Girl from Manhattan	UA	David Chudnow
The Girl in the Painting	BRI	Benjamin Frankel
The Glass Mountain	BRI	Nino Rota
Good Sam	RKO	Robert Emmett Dolan
Grand Canyon Trail	REP	Nathan Scott
Green Grass of Wyoming	TCF	Cyril J. Mockridge
Gun Smuglers	RKO	Paul Sawtell
Gunning for Justice	MON	Edward J. Kay
Guns of Hate	RKO	Paul Sawtell
Half Past Midnight	TCF	Darrell Calker
Hamlet	UN	William Walton
Harpoon	SG	Lucien Cailliet
Harvest from the Wilderness (short)	BRI	Doreen Carwithen
Hazard	PAR	Frank Skinner

He Walked by Night	EL	Irving Friedman
Heart of Virginia	REP	Morton Scott
Her Man Gilbey	BRI	Nicholas Brodzsky
Here Comes Trouble	UA	Heinz Roemheld
Hidden Danger	MON	Edward J. Kay
High Fury	UA	Bernard Grun
Highway 13	SG	David Chudnow
Hills of Home	MGM	Herbert Stothart
The History of Mr. Polly	BRI	William Alwyn
Holiday Camp	BRI	Bob Bushy
Hollow Triumph (The Scar)	EL	Irving Friedman
Homecoming	MGM	Bronislau Kaper
Homicide for Three	REP	Morton Scott
D'Homme a Homme	FRA	Joseph Kosma
The Honorable Catherine	FRA	Henri Sauguet
The Hunted	AA	Edward J. Kay
I, Jane Doe	REP	Heinz Roemheld
I Remember Mama	RKO	Roy Webb
I Wouldn't Be in Your Shoes	MON	Edward J. Kay
An Ideal Husband	BRI	Hubert Clifford
If You Knew Suzie	RKO	Edgar Fairchild
In This Corner	EL	Albert Glasser
Incident	MON	Edward J. Kay
Inner Sanctum	FC	Leon Klatzkin
An Innocent Affair	UA	Hans J. Salter
The Inside Story	REP	Nathan Scott
The Iron Curtain	TCF	Alfred Newman
Isn't It Romantic?	PAR	Joseph J. Lilley
It's Hard to Be Good	BRI	Anthony Hopkins
Jiggs and Maggie in Court	MON	Edward J. Kay
Jiggs and Maggie in Society	MON	Edward J. Kay
Jinx Money	MON	Edward J. Kay
Joan of Arc	RKO	Hugo Friedhofer
Joe Palooka in Winner Take All	MON	Edward J. Kay
Johnny Belinda	WB	Max Steiner
Julia Misbehaves	MGM	Adolph Deutsch
June Bride	WB	David Buttolph
Jungle Goddess	SG	Irving Gertz
Jungle Patrol	TCF	Arthur Lange
Just William's Luck	BRI	Robert Farnon
Key Largo	WB	Max Steiner
Kidnapped	MON	Edward J. Kay
King of the Gamblers	REP	Morton Scott
Kiss the Blood Off My Hands	UN	Miklos Rozsa
The Kissing Bandit	MGM	Nacio Herb Brown
Lady at Midnight	EL	Leo Erdody
The Lady from Shanghai	COL	Heinz Roemheld
Larceny	UN	Leith Stevens
Last of the Wild Horses	SG	Albert Glasser
The Last Stop	POL	Roman Palester
Let's Live Again	TCF	Ralph Stanley
Let's Live a Little	EL	Werner Heymann
Letter from an Unknown Woman	UN	Daniele Amfitheatrof

A Letter to Three Wives	TCF	Alfred Newman
Live Today for Tomorrow (see An Act of Murder)		
Long Is the Road	GER	Lother Bruehne
Look Before You Love	BRI	Bretton Byrd
Louisiana Story	IND	Virgil Thomson
Lovers of Verona	FRA	Joseph Kosma
The Loves of Carmen	COL	Mario Castelnuovo-Tedesco
The Luck of the Irish	TCF	Cyril J. Mockridge
Lulu Belle	COL	Henry Russell
Luxury Liner	MGM	George Stoll
Macbeth	REP	Jacques Ibert
Malacarne	ITA	Oscar Massa
Man-Eater of Kumaon	UN	Hans J. Salter
The Man from Colorado	COL	George Duning
The Man from Texas	EL	Earl Robinson
Man of Evil	BRI	Cedric Mallabey
Mark of the Lash	SG	Walter Greene
Marshal of Amarillo	REP	Morton Scott
The Mating of Millie	COL	Werner Heymann
Meet Me at Dawn	TCF	Mischa Spoliansky
The Merry Chase	ITA	Alessandro Cicognini
Mexican Hayride	UN	Walter Scharf
Michael O'Halloran	MON	Lud Gluskin
Mickey	EL	Marlin Skiles
Million Dollar Weekend	EL	Phil Ohman
Mine Own Executioner	TCF	Benjamin Frankel
A Miracle Can Happen	UA	David Chudnow Skitch Henderson
Miracle in Harlem	SG	Lud Gluskin
The Miracle of the Bells	RKO	Leigh Harline
Miraculous Journey	FC	Leo Erdody
Miranda	BRI	Temple Abady
Miss Tatlock's Millions	PAR	Victor Young
Mr. Blandings Builds His Dream House	RKO	Leigh Harline
Mr. Orchid	FRA	Rene Cloerec
Mr. Peabody and the Mermaid	UN	Robert Emmett Dolan
Mr. Perrin and Mr. Traill	BRI	Alan Gray
Mr. Reckless	PAR	Harry Lubin
Money Madness	FC	Leo Erdody
Moonrise	REP	William Lava
Music Man	MON	Edward J. Kay
My Dear Secretary	UA	Heinz Roemheld
My Girl Tisa	WB	Max Steiner
My Name Is Han	IND	Norman Lloyd
My Own True Love	PAR	Robert Emmett Dolan
Mystery in Mexico	RKO	Paul Sawtell
The Mystery of the Golden Eye	MON	Edward J. Kay
Naked City	UN	Miklos Rozsa Frank Skinner
Nettezza Urbana	ITA	Giovanni Fusco
Night Has a Thousand Eyes	PAR	Victor Young

Nightime in Nevada	REP	Dale Butts
Night Wind	TCF	Ralph Stanley
No Minor Vices	MGM	Franz Waxman
No Orchids for Miss Blandish	BRI	George Melachrino
The Noose Hangs High	EL	Walter Schumann
Northwest Stampede	EL	Paul Sawtell
Oklahoma Blues	MON	Edward J. Kay
An Old-Fashioned Girl	EL	Herschel Burke Gilbert
Old Los Angeles	REP	Ernest Gold Nathan Scott
Oliver Twist	BRI	Arnold Bax
On an Island with You	MGM	George Stoll
On Our Merry Way	UA	Heinz Roemheld
Once a Jolly Swagman	BRI	Bernard Stevens
One Sunday Afternoon	WB	David Buttolph
One Touch of Venus	UN	Leon Arnaud Ann Ronnell
Open Secret	EL	Herschel Burke Gilbert
The Original Sin	GER	Bernhard Eichhorn Adolf Steimel
Out of the Storm	REP	Morton Scott
Outlaw Brand	MON	Edward J. Kay
Overland Trails	MON	Morton Scott
The Paleface	PAR	Victor Young
Panhandle	AA	Rex Dunn
Paris 1900	FRA	Guy Bernard
Parole Inc.	EL	Alexander Laszlo
Partners of the Sunset	MON	Edward J. Kay
The Pearl	RKO	Antonio Diaz Conde
Picnic (short)	IND	Ernest Gold
Pitfall	UA	Louis Forbes
The Plunderers	REP	Dale Butts
Portrait of Innocence	FRA	Marius-Francois Gaillard
Portrait of Jennie	SRO	Dimitri Tiomkin
The Prairie	SG	Alexander Steinert
The Queen of Spades	BRI	Georges Auric
Race Street	RKO	Roy Webb
Rachel and the Stranger	RKO	Roy Webb
Range Renegades	MON	Edward J. Kay
The Rangers Ride	MON	Edward J. Kay
The Raven	FRA	Toni Aubain
Raw Deal	EL	Paul Sawtell
Red River	UA	Dimitri Tiomkin
The Red Shoes	EL	Brian Easdale
Relentless	COL	Marlin Skiles
Renegades of Sonora	REP	Stanley Wilson
The Return of October	COL	George Duning
Return of the Bad Men	RKO	Paul Sawtell
Return of the Lash	EL	Walter Greene
The Return of Wildfire	SG	Albert Glasser
River Lady	UN	Paul Sawtell
Road House	TCF	Cyril J. Mockridge
Rocky	MON	Edward J. Kay

Rogue's Regiment	UN	Daniele Amfitheatrof
Rope	WB	David Buttolph
Rubens	BEL	Raymond Chevreville
The Russian Question	RUS	Aram Khachaturian
Ruthless	EL	Paul Desseau
Saigon	PAR	Robert Emmett Dolan
The Sainted Sisters	PAR	Van Cleave
Saraband	BRI	Alan Rawsthorne
The Saxon Charm	UN	Walter Scharf
Scorned Flesh	ITA	Alessandro Cicognini
Scott of the Antarctic	BRI	Ralph Vaughan Williams
Scudda Hoo! Scudda Hay!	TCF	Cyril J. Mockridge
Sealed Verdict	PAR	Hugo Friedhofer
The Search	MGM	Robert Blum
The Secret Land	MGM	Bronislau Kaper
Secret Service Investigator	REP	Morton Glickman
Shaggy	PAR	Ralph Stanley
The Shanghai Chest	MON	Edward J. Kay
Shed No Tears	EL	Ralph Stanley
Shep Comes Home	SG	Walter Greene
The Sheriff of Medicine Bow	MON	Edward J. Kay
Showtime	BRI	Jack Beaver
The Sign of the Ram	COL	Hans J. Salter
Silent Conflict	UA	Darrell Calker
The Silk Noose	BRI	Charles Williams
Silver River	WB	Max Steiner
Silver Trails	MON	Edward J. Kay
Sinister Journey	UA	Darrell Calker
Siren of Atlantis	UA	Michel Michelet
Sitting Pretty	TCF	Alfred Newman
16 Fathoms Deep	MON	Lucien Moraweck Rene Garriguene
Sleep My Love	UA	Rudy Schrager
Sleeping Car to Trieste	BRI	Benjamin Frankel
Smart Girls Don't Talk	WB	David Buttolph
Smart Woman	AA	Louis Gruenberg
The Smugglers	BRI	Clifton Parker
Smuggler's Cove	MON	Edward J. Kay
The Snake Pit	TCF	Alfred Newman
Snowbound	BRI	Cedric Thorpe Davie
So Dear to My Heart	DIS	Paul Smith
So Evil My Love	PAR	William Alwyn
So This Is New York	UA	Dimitri Tiomkin
Sofia	FC	Raul Lavista
Son of God's Country	REP	Dale Butts
Song of the Drifter	MON	Edward J. Kay
Sons of Adventure	REP	Morton Scott
Sorry, Wrong Number	PAR	Franz Waxman
A Southern Yankee	MGM	David Snell
Speed to Spare	PAR	Darrell Calker
The Spiritualist (Amazing Mr. X)	EL	Alexander Laszlo
Stage Struck	MON	Edward J. Kay
Stage to Mesa City	PRC	Walter Greene

State of the Union	MGM	Victor Young
Station West	RKO	Heinz Roemheld
Steps of the Ballet (short)	BRI	Sir Arthur Benjamin
The Strange Mrs. Crane	EL	Paul Smith
Strange Victory	IND	David Diamond
Street Corner	IND	Bernard Katz
The Street with No Name	TCF	Lionel Newman
Strike It Rich	AA	Rudy Schrager
Sundown at Santa Fe	REP	Stanley Wilson
Sunset Carson Rides Again	IND	Frank Sanucci
Sword of the Avenger	EL	Eddison von Ottenfeld
Symphonie Fantastique	FRA	Maurice-Paul Guillot
Symphonie Pastorale	FRA	George Auric
Tap Roots	UN	Frank Skinner
Tarzan and the Mermaids	RKO	Dimitri Tiomkin
Tenth Avenue Angel	MGM	Rudolph Kopp
Texas, Brooklyn and Heaven	UA	Emil Newman
That Wonderful Urge	TCF	Cyril J. Mockridge
They Are Not Angels	FRA	Maurice Thiriet
13 Lead Soldiers	TCF	Milton Rosen
This Wine of Love	ITA	Giuseppe Morelli
Three Daring Daughters	MGM	George Stoll
Three Godfathers	MGM	Richard Hageman
The Three Musketeers	MGM	Herbert Stothart
The Time of Your Life	UA	Carmen Dragon
The Tioga Kid	EL	Dick Carruth
To the Ends of the Earth	COL	George Duning
To the Victor	WB	David Buttolph
Tornado Range	EL	Walter Greene
Tragic Hunt	ITA	Fernando Previtali
The Trail of the Mounties	SG	Albert Glasser
Train to Alcatraz	REP	Morton Scott
The Treasure of the Sierra Madre	WB	Max Steiner
Triggerman	MON	Edward J. Kay
Trouble Makers	MON	Edward J.. Kay
Trouble Preferred	TCF	David Chudnow
The Twisted Road	RKO	Leigh Harline
Under California Stars	REP	Morton Scott
Une Si Jolie Petite Plage	FRA	Maurice Thiriet
Unfaithfully Yours	TCF	Alfred Newman
Unknown Island	FC	Ralph Stanley
The Untamed Breed	COL	George Duning
Urubu	UA	Albert Glasser
The Valiant Hombre	UA	Albert Glasser
The Velvet Touch	RKO	Leigh Harline
The Vicious Circle	UA	Paul Desseau
Wake of the Red Witch	REP	Nathan Scott
Walk a Crooked Mile	COL	Paul Sawtell
Wallflower	WB	Frederick Hollander
The Walls of Jericho	TCF	Cyril J. Mockridge
Waterfront at Midnight	PAR	Harry Lubin
The Weaker Sex	BRI	Arthur Wilkinson

Western Heritage	RKO	Paul Sawtell
The Westward Trail	EL	Walter Greene
Where the North Begins	SG	Albert Glasser
While I Live	BRI	Charles Williams
Whiplash	WB	Franz Waxman
Whispering City	EL	Jean des Louriers
Who Killed Doc Robbin?	UA	Heinz Roemheld
Will It Happen Again?	FC	Edward Craig
The Winner's Circle	TCF	Lucien Cailliet
Winter Meeting	WB	Max Steiner
Without Pity	ITA	Felice Lattuada
Woman Hater	BRI	Lambert Williamson
The Woman in White	WB	Max Steiner
Women in the Night	FC	Raul Lavista
Women of the Night	JAP	Hisato Nagata
Yellow Sky	TCF	Alfred Newman
You Gotta Stay Happy	UN	Daniele Amfitheatrof

1949

Abandoned	UN	Walter Scharf
Abbott and Costello Meet the Killer	UN	Milton Schwarzwald
Academician Ivan Pavlov	Rus	Dmitri Kabalevsky
Adam and Evelyn	BRI	Mischa Spoliansky
Adam's Rib	MGM	Miklos Rozsa
Adventure in Baltimore	RKO	Frederick Hollander
The Adventures of Ichabod and Mr. Toad	DIS	Oliver Wallace
Africa Screams	UA	Walter Schumann
Alaska Patrol	FC	Mahlon Merrick
Alias Nick Beal	PAR	Franz Waxman
Alias the Champ	REP	Stanley Wilson
Alimony	EL	Alexander Laszlo
All Over Town	BRI	Temple Abady
All the King's Men	COL	Louis Gruenberg
The Amazing Mr. Beecham	BRI	Benjamin Frankel
Amazon Quest	FC	Alexander Laszlo
Ambush	MGM	Rudolph Kopp
And Baby Makes Three	COL	George Duning
Angels in Disguise	MON	Edward J. Kay
Anna Lucasta	COL	David Diamond
Any Number Can Play	MGM	Lennie Hayton
Apache Chief	LIP	Albert Glasser
Arctic Manhunt	UN	Milton Schwarzwald
Arson, Inc.	SG	Raoul Kraushaar
Au Grand Balcon	FRA	Joseph Kosma
Bad Boy	AA	Paul Sawtell
Bagdad	UN	Frank Skinner
Bandit King of Texas	REP	Stanley Wilson
Barbary Pirate	COL	Mischa Bakaleinikoff
The Battle of Stalingrad	RUS	Aram Khachaturian
Battleground	MGM	Lennie Hayton

The Beautiful Blonde from Bashful Bend	TCF	Cyril Mockridge
Beauty and the Devil	FRA	Roman Vlad
La Belle Que Voila	FRA	Joseph Kosma
Beware of Pity	BRI	Nicholas Brodzsky
Beyond the Forest	WB	Max Steiner
The Bicycle Thief	ITA	Alessandro Cicognini
The Big Cat	EL	Paul Sawtell
Big Jack	MGM	Herbert Stothart
The Big Steal	RKO	Leigh Harline
The Big Wheel	UA	Nat Finston
Bitter Rice	ITA	Geoffredo Petrassi
The Black Book (see Reign of Terror)		
Black Magic	UA	Paul Sawtell
Black Midnight	MON	Edward J. Kay
Blood of the Beasts (short)	FRA	Joseph Kosma
Blue Lagoon	BRI	Clifton Parker
Bodyhold	COL	Mischa Bakaleinikoff
Bomba, the Jungle Boy	MON	Edward J. Kay
Border Incident	MGM	Andre Previn
A Boy, a Girl, and a Bike	BRI	Kenneth Pakeman
The Bribe	MGM	Miklos Rozsa
Bride for Sale	RKO	Frederick Hollander
Bride of Vengeance	PAR	Hugo Friedhofer
Brimstone	REP	Nathan Scott
Brothers in the Saddle	RKO	Paul Sawtell
Calamity Jane and Sam Bass	UN	Rudy de Saxe
Canadian Pacific	TCF	Dimitri Tiomkin
Captain China	PAR	Lucien Cailliet
Cardboard Cavalier	BRI	Lambert Williamson
Caught	MGM	Frederick Hollander
Challenge to Lassie	MGM	Andre Previn
Champion	UA	Dimitri Tiomkin
Cheyenne Cowboy	UN	Milton Schwarzwald
Chicago Deadline	PAR	Victor Young
Christina	GER	Herbert Trantow
Cinderella	DIS	Oliver Wallace
City Across the River	UN	Walter Scharf
The Clay Pigeon	RKO	Paul Sawtell
C-Man	FC	Gail Kubik
Colorado Territory	WG	David Buttolph
Come to the Stable	TCF	Cyril J. Mockridge
A Connecticut Yankee in King Arthur's Court	PAR	Victor Young
Cover-Up	UA	Hans J. Salter
Criss Cross	UN	Miklos Rozsa
The Crooked Way	UA	Louis Forbes
The Cure for Love	BRI	William Alwyn
D. O. A.	UA	Dimitri Tiomkin
A Dangerous Profession	RKO	Frederick Hollander
The Daring Caballero	UA	Albert Glasser
Daughter of the Jungle	REP	Stanley Wilson
Daughter of the West	FC	Victor Granadas Juan Duval

Daybreak in Udi	BRI	William Alwyn
Deadly Is the Female	UA	Victor Young
Dead Man's Gold	SG	Walter Greene
Dear Wife	PAR	Joseph J. Lilley
		Van Cleave
Death Valley Gunfighter	REP	Stanley Wilson
Demi-Paradise	BRI	Nicholas Brodszky
Deputy Marshal	LIP	David Chudnow
The Doctor and the Girl	MGM	Rudolph Kopp
The Doolins of Oklahoma	COL	George Duning
		Paul Sawtell
Down Dakota Way	REP	Dale Butts
Down Memory Lane	EL	Sol Kaplan
Down to the Sea in Ships	TCF	Alfred Newman
Duke of Chicago	REP	Stanley Wilson
East Side, West Side	MGM	Miklos Rozsa
Easy Living	RKO	Roy Webb
Edward My Son	MGM	John Woolridge
El Paso	PAR	Darrell Calker
Eureka Stockade	BRI	John Greenwood
Everybody Does It	TCF	Mario Castelnuovo-Tedesco
The Fan	TCP	Daniele Amfitheatrof
The Far-Away Bride (see Under Sunny Skies)		
Father Was a Fullback	TCF	Lionel Newman
Fighting Fools	MON	Edward J. Kay
The Fighting Kentuckian	REP	George Anthiel
Fighting Man of the Plains	TCF	Paul Sawtell
The Fighting O'Flynn	UN	Frank Skinner
Flame of Youth	REP	Stanley Wilson
Flaming Fury	REP	Stanley Wilson
Flamingo Road	WB	Max Steiner
Flaxy Martin	WB	William Lava
Flood Tide	BRI	Robert Irving
Follow Me Quietly	RKO	Leonid Raab
Fools Rush In	BRI	Wilfred Burns
The Forbidden Street	TCF	Malcolm Arnold
Forgotten Women	MON	Edward J. Kay
For Those Who Dare	COL	George Duning
The Fountainhead	WB	Max Steiner
Francis	UN	Frank Skinner
Free for All	UN	Frank Skinner
French without Tears	BRI	Nicholas Brodszky
Frontier Investigator	REP	Stanley Wilson
The Gal Who Took the West	UN	Frank Skinner
The Gay Amigo	UA	Albert Glasser
The Gay Lady	BRI	Benjamin Frankel
Gigi	FRA	Rachel Thoreau
The Girl from Jones Beach	WB	David Buttolph
The Golden Stallion	REP	Nathan Scott
Grand Canyon	SG	Albert Glasser
The Great Dan Patch	UA	Rudy Schrager
The Great Gatsby	PAR	Robert Emmett Dolan
The Great Lover	PAR	Joseph J. Lilley

The Great Rupert	EL	Leith Stevens
The Great Sinner	MGM	Bronislau Kaper
The Green Promise	RKO	Rudy Schrager
Guilty of Treason	EL	Emil Newman
The Hasty Heart	WB	Louis Levy
The Heiress	PAR	Aaron Copland
Hellfire	REP	Dale Butts
Helter Skelter	BRI	Francis Chagrin
Henry, the Rainmaker	MON	Edward J. Kay
Hideout	REP	Stanley Wilson
Hold That Baby	MON	Edward J. Kay
Holiday Affair	RKO	Roy Webb
Hollywood Varieties	LIP	Walter Greene
Home of the Brave	UA	Dimitri Tiomkin
Homicide	WB	William Lava
The House Across the Street	WB	William Lava
House of Strangers	TCF	Daniele Amfitheatrof
I Cheated the Law	TCF	Edward J. Kay
I Married a Communist	RKO	Leigh Harline
I Shot Jesse James	SG	Albert Glasser
I Was a Male War Bride	TCF	Cyril J. Mockridge
Illegal Entry	UN	Milton Schwartzwald
Impact	UA	Michel Michelet
In the Good Old Summertime	MGM	George Stoll
The Inspector General	WB	John Green
Intruder in the Dust	MGM	Adolph Deutsch
It Happens Every Spring	TCF	Leigh Harline
It's Not Cricket	BRI	Arthur Wilkinson
Jiggs and Maggie in Jackpot Jitters	MON	Edward J. Kay
Jigsaw	UA	Robert W. Stringer
Joe Palooka in the Counterpunch	MON	Edward J. Kay
Joe Palooka in the Big Fight	MON	Edward J. Kay
John Loves Mary	WB	David Buttolph
Johnny Allegro	COL	George Duning
Johnny Holiday	UA	Franz Waxman
Johnny Stool Pigeon	UN	Milton Schwarzwald
Jolson Sings Again	COL	George Duning
The Judge	FC	Gene Lanham
The Judge Steps Out	RKO	Leigh Harline
Kenji Comes Home	JAP	Merril Kendrick
The Kid from Cleveland	REP	Nathan Scott
A Kiss for Corliss	UA	Werner Heymann
A Kiss in the Dark	WB	Max Steiner
Knock on Any Door	COL	George Anthiel
The Lady Gambles	UN	Frank Skinner
The Lady Takes a Sailor	WB	Max Steiner
The Last Bandit	REP	Dale Butts
Law of the Golden West	REP	Stanley Wilson
The Lawton Story	IND	Edward J. Kay
Leave It to Henry	MON	Edward J. Kay
The Life of Riley	UN	Frank Skinner
Little Women	MGM	Adolph Deutsch

London Belongs to Me	BRI	Benjamin Frankel
Look Out, Sister	IND	Louis Jordan
Lost Boundaries	FC	Louis Applebaum
The Loveable Cheat	FC	Karl Hajos
Love Happy	UA	Ann Ronnell
The Lucky Stiff	UA	Heinz Roemheld
Ma and Pa Kettle	UN	Milton Schwarzwald
Madame Bovary	MGM	Miklos Rozsa
Madeleine	BRI	William Alwyn
Madness of the Heart	BRI	Allan Gray
The Magic Canvas (short)	BRI	Matyas Seiber
Malaya	MGM	Bronislau Kaper
Man About the House	BRI	Nicholas Brodszky
The Man on the Eiffel Tower	RKO	Michel Michelet
Manhandled	PAR	Darrell Calker
Manon	FRA	Paul Misraki
Marie Du Port	FRA	Joseph Kosma
Mary Ryan, Detective	COL	Mischa Bakaleinikoff
Masked Raiders	RKO	Paul Sawtell
Massacre River	AA	Lud Gluskin
Master Minds	MON	Edward J. Kay
Meeting on the Elba	RUS	Dmitri Shostakovich
Mighty Joe Young	RKO	Roy Webb
Mr. Belvedere Goes to College	TCF	Alfred Newman
Mr. Soft Touch	COL	Heinz Roemheld
Miss Grant Takes Richmond	COL	Heinz Roemheld
Miss Mink of 1949	TCF	Mahlon Merrick
Mrs. Mike	UA	Max Steiner
Mississippi Rhythm	MON	Edward J. Kay
Mother Is a Freshman	TCF	Alfred Newman
My Foolish Heart	RKO	Victor Young
My Friend Irma	PAR	Roy Webb
The Mysterious Desperado	RKO	Paul Sawtell
Mystery Range	SG	Rudy de Saxe
Naughty Arlette	BRI	Charles Williams
Navajo Trail Raiders	REP	Stanley Wilson
Neptune's Daughter	MGM	George Stoll
Night Unto Night	WB	Franz Waxman
Not Wanted	FC	Leith Stevens
Omoo, Omoo, the Shark God	SG	Albert Glasser
Once More, My Darling	UN	Elizabeth Firestone
Once Upon a Dream	BRI	Arthur Wilkinson
One Last Fling	WB	David Buttolph
One Woman's Story (see The Passionate Friends)		
Orpheus	FRA	Georges Auric
Outcasts of the Trail	REP	Stanley Wilson
Outpost in Morocco	UA	Michel Michelet
Paid in Full	PAR	Victor Young
Passionate Friends	BRI	Richard Addinsell
Passport to Pimlico	BRI	Georges Auric
The Perfect Woman	BRI	Arthur Wilkinson
Pinky	TCF	Alfred Newman
Port of New York	EL	Sol Kaplan

Post Office Investigator	REP	Stanley Wilson
Prejudice	IND	Irving Gertz
Prince of Foxes	TCF	Alfred Newman
Prince of the Plains	REP	Stanley Wilson
Project X	FC	Hi Fuchs
Ranger of Cherokee Strip	REP	Stanley Wilson
The Reckless Moment	COL	Hans J. Salter
Red Canyon	UN	Walter Scharf
The Red Danube	MGM	Miklos Rozsa
Red Light	UA	Dimitri Tiomkin
The Red Menace	REP	Nathan Scott
The Red Pony	REP	Aaron Copland
Red Stallion in the Rockies	EL	Lucien Cailliet
Reign of Terror (The Black Book)	EL	Sol Kaplan
Rendezvous with Juliet	FRA	Jean Wiener
Ride, Ryder, Ride!	EL	Darrell Calker
Riders of the Range	RKO	Paul Sawtell
Rimfire	SG	Walter Greene
Ringside	SG	Walter Greene
The Rocking Horse Winner	BRI	William Alwyn
Rope of Sand	PAR	Franz Waxman
Roseanna McCoy	RKO	David Buttolph
Rose of the Yukon	REP	Stanley Wilson
Roughshod	RKO	Roy Webb
Rustlers	RKO	Paul Sawtell
Salt to the Devil	BRI	Benjamin Frankel
Samson and Delilah	PAR	Victor Young
San Antone Ambush	REP	Stanley Wilson
Sand	TCF	Daniele Amfitheatrof
Sands of Iwo Jima	REP	Victor Young
Satan's Cradle	UA	Albert Glasser
Savage Splendor	RKO	Paul Sawtell
Scene of the Crime	MGM	Andre Previn
Search for Danger	FC	Karl Hajos
The Secret Garden	MGM	Bronislau Kaper
The Set-Up	RKO	Constantin Bakaleinikoff
She Wore a Yellow Ribbon	RKO	Richard Hageman
Sheriff of Wichita	REP	Stanley Wilson
Shockproof	COL	George Duning
The Sickle or the Cross	IND	Alberto Colombo
Side Street	MGM	Lennie Hayton
Sky Dragon	MON	Edward J. Kay
Sky Liner	SG	Raoul Kraushaar
Slattery's Hurricane	TCF	Cyril J. Mockridge
Slightly French	COL	Lester Lee
Son of a Badman	SG	Walter Greene
Son of Billy the Kid	SG	Walter Greene
Song of India	COL	Alexander Laszlo
Song of Surrender	PAR	Victor Young
Sorrowful Jones	PAR	Robert Emmett Dolan
South of Rio	REP	Stanley Wilson
South of St. Louis	WB	Max Steiner
Special Agent	PAR	Lucien Cailliet

The Spice of Life	FRA	Rene Cloerec
The Spider and the Fly	BRI	Georges Auric
Square Dance Jubilee	LIP	Walter Greene
Stagecoach Kid	RKO	Paul Sawtell
Stampede	AA	Edward J. Kay
State Department File 649	FC	Lucien Cailliet
Stop Press Girl	BRI	Walter Goehr
The Storm Within	FRA	Georges Auric
The Story of Molly X	UN	Milton Schwartzwald
The Story of Seabiscuit	WB	David Buttolph
The Story of Time (short)	BRI	Guy Warrack
Strange Bargain	RKO	Frederick Hollander
Strange Gamble	UA	Ralph Stanley
The Stratton Story	MGM	Adolph Deutsch
Streets of Laredo	PAR	Victor Young
Streets of San Francisco	REP	Stanley Wilson
Susanna Pass	REP	Morton Scott
Sword in the Desert	UN	Frank Skinner
Symphony of Life	RUS	Nikolai Kriukov
Take Me Out to the Ball Game	MGM	Adolph Deutsch
Take One False Step	UN	Walter Scharf
Tale of the Navajos	MGM	Lan Adomian
Tarzan's Magic Fountain	RKO	Alexander Laszlo
Task Force	WB	Franz Waxman
Tell It to the Judge	COL	Werner Heymann
Tension	MGM	Andre Previn
That Dangerous Age	BRI	Mischa Spoliansky
That Forsyte Woman	MGM	Bronislau Kaper
Thelma Jordan	PAR	Victor Young
Thieves' Highway	TCF	Alfred Newman
The Threat	RKO	Paul Sawtell
Thunder in the Pines	SG	Lucien Cailliet
Tight Little Island	BRI	Georges Auric
Tokyo Joe	COL	George Anthiel
Too Late for Tears	UA	Dale Butts
Tough Assignment	LIP	Albert Glasser
Trail of the Yukon	COL	Edward J. Kay
Train of Events	BRI	Leslie Bridgewater
Trapped	EL	Sol Kaplan
Traveling Saleswoman	COL	Lester Lee Allan Roberts
Treasure of Monte Cristo	LIP	Albert Glasser
Tulsa	EL	Frank Skinner
Tuna Clipper	MON	Edward J. Kay
Tucson	TCF	Darrell Calker
Twelve O'Clock High	TCF	Alfred Newman
Under Capricorn	WB	Richard Addinsell
Under Sunny Skies (The Far-Away Bride)	RUS	K. Korchmaryov
The Undercover Man	COL	George Duning
Undertow	UA	Milton Schwartzwald
Vote for Huggett	BRI	Anthony Hopkins
The Walking Hills	COL	Arthur Morton

The Walls of Malapaga	FRA	Roman Vlad
Warning to Wantons	BRI	Hans May
We Were Strangers	COL	George Anthiel
While the Sun Shines	BRI	Nicholas Brodszky
Whirlpool	TCF	David Raksin
White Heat	WB	Max Steiner
The Window	RKO	Roy Webb
Without Honor	UA	Max Steiner
Without Prejudice	RUS	Nikolai Kriukov
Woman in Hiding	UN	Frank Skinner
A Woman's Secret	RKO	Frederick Hollander
The Woman on Pier 13	RKO	Leigh Harline
Women in Our Time (short)	BRI	Malcolm Arnold
The Wyoming Bandit	REP	Stanley Wilson
Yes, Sir, That's My Baby	UN	Walter Scharf
The Younger Brothers	WB	William Lava
Zamba	EL	Raoul Kraushaar

1950

Abbott and Costello in the Foreign Legion	UN	Joseph Gershenson
The Admiral Was a Lady	UA	Edward J. Kay
Again ... Pioneers	IND	Irving Gertz
All About Eve	TCF	Alfred Newman
An American Guerrilla in the Philippines	TCF	Lionel Newman
The Arizona Cowboy	REP	Stanley Wilson
The Asphalt Jungle	MGM	Miklos Rozsa
The Astonished Heart	BRI	Noel Coward
The Avengers	REP	Nathan Scott
Backfire	WB	Daniele Amfitheatrof
Ballerina	FRA	Robert Lefebvre
Bandit Queen	LIP	Albert Glasser
The Baron of Arizona	LIP	Paul Dunlap
Barricade	WB	William Lava
Beaver Valley (short)	DIS	Paul Smith
Belle of Old Mexico	REP	Stanley Wilson
Bells of Coronado	REP	Dale Butts
The Big Hangover	MGM	Adolph Deutsch
The Big Lift	MGM	Alfred Newman
Big Timber	MON	Edward J. Kay
Bitter Springs (Savage Justice)	BRI	Sir Ernest Irving
Black Hand	MGM	Alberto Colombo
The Black Rose	TCF	Richard Addinsell
The Blonde Bandit	REP	Stanley Wilson
Blonde Dynamite	MON	Edward J. Kay
Blues Busters	MON	Edward J. Kay
Bomba on Panther Island	MON	Edward J. Kay
Borderline	UN	Hans J. Salter
Border Rangers	LIP	Albert Glasser
Border Treasure	RKO	Paul Sawtell
Born to Be Bad	RKO	Frederick Hollander

Born Yesterday	COL	Frederick Hollander
Boy from Indiana	EL	Lud Gluskin
Boys in Brown	BRI	Doreen Carwithen
Branded	PAR	Roy Webb
The Breaking Point	WB	Ray Heindorf
Breakthrough	WB	William Lava
Bright Leaf	WB	Victor Young
Broken Arrow	TCF	Hugo Friedhofer
Buccaneer's Girl	UN	Walter Scharf
Buckaroo Sheriff of Texas	REP	Stanley Wilson
Bunco Squad	RKO	Paul Sawtell
Caged	WB	Max Steiner
California Passage	REP	Nathan Scott
Call of the Klondike	MON	Edward J. Kay
Captain Carey, USA	PAR	Hugo Friedhofer
The Capture	RKO	Daniele Amfitheatrof
Cargo to Capetown	COL	George Duning
The Cariboo Trail	TCF	Paul Sawtell
Chain Lightning	WB	David Buttolph
Champagne for Caesar	UA	Dimitri Tiomkin
Cheaper by the Dozen	TCF	Lionel Newman
Code of the Silver Sage	REP	Stanley Wilson
Colorado Ranger	LIP	Walter Greene
Colt .45	WB	William Lava
Comanche Territory	UN	Frank Skinner
The Company She Keeps	RKO	Leigh Harline
Conspirator	MGM	John Wooldridge
Convicted	COL	George Duning
Copper Canyon	PAR	Daniele Amfitheatrof
County Fair	MON	Ozzie Caswell
Covered Wagon Raid	REP	Stanley Wilson
Cowboy and the Prizefighter	EL	Raoul Kraushaar
Crisis	MGM	Miklos Rozsa
Crooked River	LIP	Walter Greene
Curtain Call at Cactus Creek	UN	Walter Scharf
Cyrano De Bergerac	UA	Dimitri Tiomkin
Dakota Lil	TCF	Dimitri Tiomkin
Dallas	WB	Max Steiner
The Damned Don't Cry	WB	Daniele Amfitheatrof
The Dancing Fleece (short)	BRI	Alan Rawsthorne
Dark City	PAR	Franz Waxman
Dark Secret	BRI	George Melachrino
The Daughter of Rose O'Grady	WB	David Buttolph
Davy Crockett, Indian Scout	UA	Paul Sawtell
Deported	UN	Walter Scharf
The Desert Hawk	UN	Frank Skinner
Destination Big House	REP	Stanley Wilson
Destination Moon	UA	Leith Stevens
Destination Murder	RKO	Irving Gertz
The Devil's Doorway	MGM	Daniele Amfitheatrof
Dial 1119	MGM	Andre Previn
Distant Journey	CZE	Jiri Sternwald
Double Crossbones	UN	Frank Skinner

Double Deal	RKO	Michel Michelet
Dynamite Pass	RKO	Paul Sawtell
The Eagle and the Hawk	PAR	Rudy Schrager
Edge of Doom	RKO	Hugo Friedhofer
Emergency Wedding	COL	Werner Heymann
Experiment Alcatraz	RKO	Irving Gertz
Eye Witness	EL	Malcolm Arnold
Family Portrait (short)	BRI	John Greenwood
Fancy Pants	PAR	Van Cleave
Father Makes Good	MON	Edward J. Kay
Father Is a Bachelor	COL	Arthur Morton
Father of the Bride	MGM	Adolph Deutsch
Father's Dilemma	ITA	Alessandro Cicognini
Father's Wild Game	MON	Edward J. Kay
Federal Agent at Large	REP	Stanley Wilson
Federal Man	EL	Darrell Calker
Fence Riders	MON	Edward J. Kay
50 Years Before Your Eyes	WB	William Lava Howard Jackson
The Fighting Redhead	EL	Darrell Calker
The Fighting Stallion	EL	Darrell Calker
The Fireball	TCF	Victor Young
The Flame and the Arrow	WB	Max Steiner
The Flying Missile	COL	George Duning
The Flying Saucer	FC	Darrell Calker
For Heaven's Sake	TCF	Alfred Newman
Fortunes of Captain Blood	COL	Paul Sawtell
Frenchic	UN	Hans J. Salter
Frightened City	COL	Hans J. Salter
Frisco Tornado	REP	Stanley Wilson
The Fuller Brush Girl	COL	Heinz Roemheld
The Furies	PAR	Franz Waxman
Gambling House	RKO	Roy Webb
Gerald McBoing Boing (short)	COL	Gail Kubik
The Girl from San Lorenzo	UA	Albert Glasser
The Glass Menagerie	WB	Max Steiner
The Good Humor Man	COL	Heinz Roemheld
The Goldbergs	PAR	Van Cleave
The Golden Gloves Story	EL	Arthur Lange Marlin Skiles
The Golden Twenties	RKO	Jack Shaindlin
The Great Jewel Robbery	WB	William Lava
The Great Missouri Raid	PAR	Paul Sawtell
The Great Plane Robbery	UA	Edward J. Kay
Grounds for Marriage	MGM	Bronislau Kaper David Raksin
Guilty Bystander	FC	Dimitri Tiomkin
The Gunfighter	TCF	Alfred Newman
Gunmen of Abilene	REP	Stanley Wilson
Halls of Montezuma	TCF	Sol Kaplan
Ha'Penny Breeze	BRI	Philip Green
The Happy Years	MGM	Leigh Harline

Harbor of Missing Men	REP	Stanley Wilson
Harriet Craig	COL	George Duning
Harvey	UN	Frank Skinner
The Hidden City	MON	Ozzie Caswell
The Hidden Room	BRI	Nino Rota
High Lonesome	EL	Rudy Schrager
Highway 301	WB	William Lava
Hi-Jacked	LIP	Paul Dunlap
Hills of Oklahoma	REP	Stanley Wilson
Holiday Rhythm	LIP	Bert Shefter
Hostile Country	LIP	Walter Greene
Hot Rod	MON	Edward J. Kay
House by the River	REP	George Anthiel
Hunt the Man Down	RKO	Paul Sawtell
I Killed Geronimo	EL	Darrell Calker
I Shot Billy the Kid	LIP	Albert Glasser
I Was a Shoplifter	UN	Milton Schwartzwald
In a Lonely Place	COL	George Anthiel
Indian Territory	COL	Mischa Bakaleinikoff
The Iroquois Trail	UA	Rudy Schrager
It's a Small World	EL	Karl Hajos
The Jackie Robinson Story	EL	Herschel Burke Gilbert
The Jackpot	TCF	Lionel Newman
Jiggs and Maggie Out West	MON	Edward J. Kay
Joe Palooka in Humphrey Takes a Chance	MON	Edward J. Kay
Joe Palooka in the Squared Circle	MON	Edward J. Kay
Joe Palooka Meets Humphrey	MON	Edward J. Kay
The Kangaroo Kid	EL	Wilbur Sampson
Key to the City	MGM	Bronislau Kaper
The Kid from Texas	UN	Milton Schwartzwald
Killer Shark	MON	Edward J. Kay
The Killer that Stalked New York (see Frightened City)		
Kill or Be Killed	EL	Karl Hajos
Kill the Umpire	COL	Heinz Roemheld
Kim	MGM	Andre Previn
King of the Bullwhip	IND	Walter Greene
Kiss Tomorrow Goodbye	WB	Carmen Dragon
Korea Patrol	EL	Alexander Gerens
A Lady without Passport	MGM	David Raksin
Last Holiday	BRI	Francis Chagrin
Last of the Buccaneers	COL	Mischa Bakaleinikoff
The Lawless	PAR	Mahlon Merrick
Law of the Badlands	RKO	Paul Sawtell
Law of the Panhandle	MON	Edward J. Kay
Let's Dance	PAR	Robert Emmett Dolan
Life Begins Tomorrow	FRA	Darius Milhaud
A Life of Her Own	MGM	Bronislau Kaper
Lonely Hearts Bandits	REP	Stanley Wilson
The Lost Volcano	MON	Ozzie Caswell
Louisa	UN	Frank Skinner

Love that Brute	TCF	Cyril J. Mockridge
The Magnificent Yankee	MGM	David Raksin
The Man Who Cheated Himself	TCF	Louis Forbes
The Men	UA	Dimitri Tiomkin
The Milkman	UN	Milton Rosen
The Miniver Story	MGM	Herbert Stothart
The Missourians	REP	Stanley Wilson
Mister 880	TCF	Lionel Newman
Mrs. O'Malley and Mr. Malone	MGM	Adolph Deutsch
Molly (see The Goldbergs)		
Montana	WB	David Buttolph
Mother Didn't Tell Me	TCF	Lionel Newman
Motor Patrol	LIP	Ozzie Caswell
The Mudlark	TCF	William Alwyn
Murder without Crime	BRI	Philip Green
My Friend Irma Goes West	PAR	Leigh Harline
Mystery Street	MGM	Rudolph Kopp
Mystery Submarine	UN	Joseph Gershenson
The Nevadan	COL	Arthur Morton
Never a Dull Moment	RKO	Frederick Hollander
Never Fear (The Young Lovers)	EL	Leith Stevens
The Next Voice You Hear	MGM	David Raksin
Night and the City	TCF	Franz Waxman
No Man of Her Own	PAR	Hugo Friedhofer
No Sad Songs for Me	COL	George Duning
No Way Out	TCF	Alfred Newman
North of the Great Divide	REP	Dale Butts
Odette	BRI	Anthony Collins
The Old Frontier	REP	Stanley Wilson
Once a Thief	UA	Michel Michelet
One Too Many	IND	Bert Shefter Nelly Coletti
One-Way Street	UN	Frank Skinner
Operation X	COL	R. Gallois Montbrun
Our Very Own	RKO	Victor Young
Outlaw Gold	MON	Edward J. Kay
Outrage	RKO	Paul Sawtell
The Outriders	MGM	Andre Previn
The Palomino	COL	Mischa Bakaleinikoff
Panic in the Streets	TCF	Alfred Newman
Peggy	UN	Joseph Gershenson
Perfect Strangers	WB	Leigh Harline
The Petty Girl	COL	Morris Stoloff
Pioneer Marshal	REP	Stanley Wilson
Please Believe Me	MGM	Bonislau Kaper
Pretty Baby	WB	David Buttolph
Prisoners in Petticoats	REP	Stanley Wilson
Quicksand	UA	Louis Gruenberg
Radar Secret Service	LIP	Russell Garcia Richard Hazzard
The Redhead and the Cowboy	PAR	David Buttolph
Redwood Forest Trail	REP	Stanley Wilson
The Reformer and the Redhead	MGM	David Raksin

The Reluctant Widow	BRI	Allan Gray
The Return of Jesse James	LIP	Albert Glasser
Return of the Frontiersman	WB	David Buttolph
Revenue Agent	COL	Mischa Bakaleinikoff
Rider from Tucson	RKO	Paul Sawtell
Right Cross	MGM	David Raksin
Rio Grande Patrol	RKO	Paul Sawtell
Rocketship X-M	LIP	Ferde Grofe
Rock Island Trail	REP	Dale Butts
Rocky Mountain	WB	Max Steiner
Rogue River	EL	Paul Sawtell
Rogues of Sherwood Forest	COL	Heinz Roemheld
La Ronde	FRA	Oscar Straus
Rustlers on Horseback	REP	Stanley Wilson
Saddle Tramp	UN	Joseph Gershenson
Salt Lake Raiders	REP	Stanley Wilson
Sans Laisser D'Adresse	FRA	Joseph Kosma
The Savage Horde	REP	Dale Butts
Second Chance	IND	Louis Forbes
The Secret Fury	RKO	Roy Webb
The September Affair	PAR	Victor Young
Seven Days to Noon	BRI	John Addison
711 Ocean Drive	COL	Sol Kaplan
Shadow on the Wall	MGM	Andre Previn
Shakedown	UN	Joseph Gershenson
Short Grass	MON	Edward J. Kay
The Showdown	REP	Stanley Wilson
Sideshow	MON	Edward J. Kay
Sierra	UN	Walter Scharf
Sierra Passage	MON	Edward J. Kay
Silver Raiders	MON	Edward J. Kay
Singing Guns	REP	Nathan Scott
The Skipper Surprised His Wife	MGM	Bronislau Kaper
The Sleeping City	UN	Frank Skinner
Snow Dog	MON	Edward J. Kay
So Long at the Fair	BRI	Benjamin Frankel
The Sound of Fury	UA	Hugo Friedhofer
South Sea Sinner	UN	Walter Scharf
Southside 1-1000	AA	Paul Sawtell
So Young, So Bad	UA	Robert W. Stringer
Spy Hunt	UN	Walter Scharf
Square Dance Katy	MON	Edward J. Kay
Stage Fright	WB	Leighton Lucas
Stage to Tucson	COL	Paul Sawtell
Stars in My Crown	MGM	Adolph Deutsch
State Penitentiary	COL	Mischa Bakaleinikoff
State Secret (The Great Manhunt)	BRI	William Alwyn
The Steel Helmet	LIP	Paul Dunlap
Stella	TCF	Cyril J. Mockridge
Storm Over Wyoming	RKO	Paul Sawtell
Storm Warning	WB	Daniele Amfitheatrof
Story of Shirley Yorke	BRI	George Melachrino
Stromboli	RKO	Renzo Rossellini

The Sun Sets at Dawn	EL	Leith Stevens
The Sundowners	EL	Alberto Colombo
Sunset Boulevard	PAR	Franz Waxman
Sunset in the West	REP	Dale Butts
Surrender	REP	Nathan Scott
Tarnished	REP	Stanley Wilson
Tarzan and the Slave Girl	RKO	Paul Sawtell
The Tattooed Stranger	RKO	Alan Schulman
The Texan Meets Calamity Jane	COL	Rudy DeSaxe
They Were Not Divided	BRI	Lambert Williamson
The Third Man	SRO	Anton Karas
This Side of the Law	WB	William Lava
Three Came Home	TCF	Hugo Friedhofer
Three Husbands	UA	Herschel Burke Gilbert
Three Secrets	WB	David Buttolph
A Ticket to Tomahawk	TCF	Cyril J. Mockridge
Timber Fury	EL	Ralph Stanley
The Titan	UA	Alois Melichar
To Please a Lady	MGM	Bronislau Kaper
The Toast of New Orleans	MGM	Nicholas Brodszky
Tony Draws a Horse	BRI	Bretton Byrd
The Torch	EL	Antonio Diaz Conde
The Tougher They Come	COL	Ross di Maggio
Trail of Robin Hood	REP	Nathan Scott
Train to Tombstone	LIP	Albert Glasser
Treasure Island	DIS	Clifton Parker
Trial Without Jury	REP	Stanley Wilson
Trigger, Jr.	REP	Dale Butts
Trio	BRI	John Greenwood
Triple Trouble	MON	Edward J. Kay
Tripoli	PAR	Lucien Cailliet
Twilight in the Sierras	REP	Stanley Wilson
Two Flags West	TCF	Hugo Friedhofer
Two Lost Worlds	EL	Michael Terr
Tyrant of the Sea	COL	Mischa Bakaleinikoff
Undercover Girl	UN	Joseph Gershenson
Under Mexicali Stars	REP	Stanley Wilson
Under My Skin	TCF	Daniele Amfitheatrof
Under the Gun	UN	Joseph Gershenson
The Underworld Story (see The Whipped)		
Union Station	PAR	Irvin Talbot
Unmasked	REP	Stanley Wilson
The Vanishing Westerner	REP	Stanley Wilson
Vendetta	RKO	Roy Webb
The Vicious Years	FC	Arthur Lange
Vigilante Hideout	REP	Stanley Wilson
Wagonmaster	RKO	Richard Hageman
Walk Softly, Stranger	RKO	Frederick Hollander
Watch the Birdie	MGM	George Stoll
Western Pacific Agent	LIP	Albert Glasser
West of Wyoming	MON	Edward J. Kay
When Willie Comes Marching Home	TCF	Alfred Newman

Where Danger Lives	RKO	Roy Webb
Where the Sidewalk Ends	TCF	Lionel Newman
The Whipped	UA	David Rose
The White Tower	RKO	Roy Webb
Winchester '73	UN	Joseph Gershenson
The Wolf Hunters	MON	Edward J. Kay
The Woman in Question	BRI	John Wooldridge
A Woman of Distinction	COL	Werner Heymann
Woman on the Run	UN	Arthur Lange
Women from Headquarters	REP	Dale Butts
The Wooden Horse	BRI	Clifton Parker
World of Calder (short)	IND	John Cage
Wyoming Mail	UN	Joseph Gershenson
The Yellow Cab Man	MGM	Paul Bowles Scott Bradley Adolph Deutsch
Young Daniel Boone	MON	Edward J. Kay
The Young Lovers (see Never Fear)		
Young Man with a Horn	WB	Ray Heindorf

1951

Abbott and Costello Meet the Invisible Man	UN	Joseph Gershenson
Abilene Trail	MON	Edward J. Kay
According to Mrs. Hoyle	MON	Edward J. Kay
Ace in the Hole (see The Big Carnival)		
Across the Wide Missouri	MGM	David Raksin
Adventures of Captain Fabian	REP	Rene Cloerec
The African Queen	UA	Del Mar
Air Cadet	UN	Joseph Gershenson
Al Jennings of Oklahoma	COL	Mischa Bakaleinikoff
Alice in Wonderland	DIS	Oliver Wallace
Alice in Wonderland	FRA	Sol Kaplan
All That I Have	IND	Alberto Colombo
Along the Great Divide	WB	David Buttolph
Angels in the Outfield	MGM	Daniele Amfitheatrof
Anne of the Indies	TCF	Franz Waxman
Apache Drums	UN	Hans J. Salter
Appointment with Danger	PAR	Victor Young
Arizona Manhunt	REP	Stanley Wilson
As You Were	LIP	Leon Klatzkin
As Young as You Feel	TCF	Cyril J. Mockridge
Bannerline	MGM	Rudolph G. Kopp
The Barefoot Mailman	COL	George Duning
The Basketball Fix	IND	Raoul Kraushaar
Bedtime for Bonzo	UN	Frank Skinner
Behave Yourself	RKO	Leigh Harline
Belle Le Grand	REP	Victor Young
Best of the Badmen	RKO	Paul Sawtell
The Big Carnival	PAR	Hugo Friedhofer
The Big Gusher	COL	Mischa Bakaleinikoff
The Big Night	UA	Lyn Murray

Bird of Paradise	TCF	Daniele Amfitheatrof
Blazing Bullets	MON	Ozzie Caswell
Blue Blood	MON	Ozzie Caswell
The Blue Veil	RKO	Franz Waxman
Boots Malone	COL	Elmer Bernstein
Bowery Battalion	MON	Edward J. Kay
The Boy Kumasenu (short)	BRI	Elisabeth Lutyens
Bride of the Gorilla	IND	Raoul Krashaar
Bright Victory	UN	Frank Skinner
The Bullfighter and the Lady	REP	Victor Young
The Bushwackers	IND	Albert Glasser
Call Me Mister	TCF	Leigh Harline
Callaway Went Thataway	MGM	Marlin Skiles
Calling Bulldog Drummond	MGM	Rudolph G. Kopp
Captain Horatio Hornblower	WB	Robert Farnon
Carmen Comes Home	JAP	Chuji Kinoshita
		Toshio Uzumi
Caroline Cherie	FRA	Georges Auric
Cattle Drive	UN	Joseph Gershenson
Cause for Alarm	MGM	Andre Previn
Cavalry Scout	MON	Marlin Skiles
Cave of Outlaws	UN	Joseph Gershenson
Chicago Calling	UA	Heinz Roemheld
China Corsair	COL	Mischa Bakaleinikoff
A Christmas Carol	BRI	Richard Addinsell
Close to My Heart	WB	Max Steiner
The Clouded Yellow	COL	Benjamin Frankel
Colorado Ambush	MON	Edward J. Kay
Come Fill the Cup	WB	Ray Heindorf
The Count of St. Elmo	ITA	Jacob Meyerbeer
		Johann Strauss
Criminal Lawyer	COL	Mischa Bakaleinikoff
Crosswinds	PAR	Lucien Cailliet
Cry Danger	RKO	Emil Newman
		Paul Dunlap
Cuban Fireball	REP	Stanley Wilson
The Dakota Kid	REP	Stanley Wilson
Danger Zone	LIP	Bert Shefter
Darling, How Could You?	PAR	Frederick Hollander
David and Bathsheba	TCF	Alfred Newman
The Day the Earth Stood Still	TCF	Bernard Herrmann
Dear Brat	PAR	Van Cleave
Death of a Salesman	COL	Alex North
Decision Before Dawn	TCF	Franz Waxman
The Desert Fox	TCF	Daniele Amfitheatrof
Desert of Lost Men	REP	Stanley Wilson
The Diary of a Country Priest	FRA	Jean-Jacques Grunenwald
Distant Drums	WB	Max Steiner
Doctor Beware	ITA	Renzo Rossellini
Double Dynamite	RKO	Leigh Harline
Drums in the Deep South	RKO	Dimitri Tiomkin
El Dorado (short)	BRI	Elisabeth Lutyens
Elopement	TCF	Cyril J. Mockridge

The Emperor's Nightingale	CZE	Vaclav Trojan
The Enforcer	WB	David Buttolph
Excuse My Dust	MGM	George Stoll
F.B.I. Girl	LIP	Darrell Calker
Face to the Wind	FRA	Jean Wiener
The Family Secret	COL	George Duning
Fan-Fan La Tulipe	FRA	Maurice Thiriet
The Fat Man	UN	Bernard Green
Father Takes the Air	MON	Edward J. Kay
Father's Little Dividend	MGM	Albert Sendrey
Fighting Coast Guard	REP	David Buttolph
Finders Keepers	UN	Hans J. Salter
Fingerprints Don't Lie	LIP	Dudley Chambers
The First Legion	UA	Hans Sommer
Five	COL	Henry Russell
Fixed Bayonets	TCF	Roy Webb
Flame of Araby	UN	Joseph Gershenson
Flame of Stamboul	COL	Ross di Maggio
Flaming Feather	PAR	Paul Sawtell
Flesh and Blood	BRI	Charles Williams
Flight to Mars	MON	Marlin Skiles
Flying Leathernecks	RKO	Roy Webb
Follow the Sun	TCF	Cyril J. Mockridge
Force of Arms	WB	Max Steiner
Fort Defiance	UA	Paul Sawtell
Fort Dodge Stampede	REP	Stanley Wilson
Fort Worth	WB	David Buttolph
Four in a Jeep	UA	Hermann Haller
14 Hours	TCF	Alfred Newman
Francis Goes to the Races	UN	Frank Skinner
The Frogmen	TCF	Cyril J. Mockridge
Fugitive Lady	REP	Alberto Barberis
G.I. Jane	LIP	Walter Greene
The Galloping Major	BRI	Georges Auric
The Girl on the Bridge	TCF	Harold Byrns
Go for Broke	MGM	Alberto Colombo
God Needs Men	FRA	Rene Cloerec
Gold Raiders	UA	Alexandre Starr
The Golden Horde	UN	Hans J. Salter
The Golden Salamander	EL	William Alwyn
Goodbye My Fancy	WB	Ray Heindorf
Un Gran Patron	FRA	Joseph Kosma
Grandma Moses (short)	IND	Hugh Martin
The Great Caruso	MGM	John Green
The Groom Wore Spurs	UN	Arthur Lange
Gunplay	RKO	Paul Sawtell
The Guy Who Came Back	TCF	Leigh Harline
Gypsy Fury	MON	Hugo Alfven Charles Wildman
Half Angel	TCF	Cyril J. Mockridge
The Happiest Days of Your Life	BRI	Mischa Spoliansky
Happy Go Lucky	RKO	Mischa Spoliansky
Hard, Fast and Beautiful	RKO	Roy Webb

The Harlem Globetrotters	COL	Arthur Morton
Havana Rose	REP	Stanley Wilson
He Ran All the Way	UA	Franz Waxman
Heart of the Rockies	REP	Dale R. Butts
Henry Moore (short)	BRI	William Alwyn
Her Panelled Door	BRI	Allan Gray
Here Comes the Groom	PAR	Joseph J. Lilley
Highly Dangerous	LIP	Richard Addinsell
The Highwayman	AA	Herschel Burke Gilbert
His Kind of Woman	RKO	Leigh Harline
The Hollywood Story	UN	Joseph Gershenson
Home Town Story	MGM	Louis Forbes
Honeychile	REP	Victor Young
Hong Kong	PAR	Lucien Cailliet
The Hoodlum	UA	Darrell Calker
Hot Lead	RKO	Paul Sawtell
Hotel Sahara	UA	Benjamin Frankel
House on Telegraph Hill	TCF	Sol Kaplan
Hurricane Island	COL	Mischa Bakaleinikoff
I Can Get It for You Wholesale	TCF	Sol Kaplan
I Want You	RKO	Leigh Harline
I Was an American Spy	AA	Edward J. Kay
I'd Climb the Highest Mountain	TCF	Sol Kaplan
I'll Never Forget You	TCF	William Alwyn
In Old Amarillo	REP	Dale R. Butts
Inside Straight	MGM	Lennie Hayton
Inside the Walls of Folsom Prison	WB	William Lava
Insurance Investigator	REP	Stanley Wilson
The Iron Man	UN	Joseph Gershenson
It's a Big Country	MGM	David Raksin
Jim Thorpe--All American	WB	Max Steiner
Joe Palooka in Triple Cross	MON	Darrell Calker
Journey into Light	TCF	Paul Dunlap
Juliette Ou La Clef Des Songe	FRA	Joseph Kosma
Jungle Hunters	RKO	Paul Sawtell
Jungle of Chang	RKO	Jules Sylvain Gunnar Jonason
Katie Did It	UN	Frank Skinner
Kentucky Jubilee	LIP	Walter Greene
Kind Lady	MGM	David Raksin
Kon-Tiki	RKO	Sune Waldimir
Krakatit	CZE	Jiri Trnka
The Lady and the Bandit	COL	Morris Stoloff
The Lady from Texas	UN	Joseph Kish
Lady Paname	FRA	Georges van Parys
The Lady Pays Off	UN	Frank Skinner
The Lady Says No	UA	Emil Newman
The Last Outpost	PAR	Lucien Cailliet
The Lavender Hill Mob	BRI	Georges Auric
The Law and the Lady	MGM	Carmen Dragon
Leave It to the Marines	LIP	Bert Shefter
The Lemon Drop Kid	PAR	Victor Young
Let's Go Navy	MON	Edward J. Kay

Let's Make It Legal	TCF	Cyril J. Mockridge
The Light Touch	MGM	Miklos Rozsa
Lightning Strikes Twice	WB	Max Steiner
Lili Marlene	RKO	Stanley Black
The Lion Hunters	MON	Marlin Skiles
Little Big Horn	LIP	Paul Dunlap
Little Egypt	UN	Joseph Gershenson
Lone Star	MGM	David Buttolph
The Long Dark Hall	BRI	Benjamin Frankel
The Longhorn	MON	Raoul Kraushaar
Lorna Doone	COL	George Duning
The Lost Continent	LIP	Paul Dunlap
Love Nest	TCF	Cyril J. Mockridge
Lucky Nick Cain	TCF	Walter Goehr
M	COL	Bert Shefter
Ma Pomme	FRA	Jean Marion
The Magic Box	BRI	William Alwyn
The Magic Carpet	COL	Mischa Bakaleinikoff
The Magic Face	COL	Herschel Burke Gilbert
The Magic Garden	BRI	Willard Cele
The Magnet	BRI	William Alwyn
Man in the Dinghy	BRI	Mischa Spoliansky
The Man from Planet X	UA	Charles Koff
Man from Sonora	MON	Edward J. Kay
The Man with the Cloak	MGM	David Raksin
Mark of the Renegade	UN	Frank Skinner
Mask of the Avenger	COL	Mario Castelnuevo-Tedesco
The Mating Season	PAR	Joseph J. Lilley
The Medium	IND	Gian-Carlo Menotti
Million Dollar Pursuit	REP	Stanley Wilson
A Millionaire for Christy	TCF	Victor Young
Minne	FRA	Vincent Scotto
Miquette	FRA	Albert Lasry
Missing Women	REP	Stanley Wilson
Mr. Belvedere Rings the Bell	TCF	Cyril J. Mockridge
Mr. Imperium	MGM	Bronislau Kaper
Mr. Peek-A-Boo	UA	Georges van Parys
Mr. Universe	UA	Dimitri Tiomkin
Mr. Drake's Duck	UA	Bruce Campbell
The Mob	COL	George Duning
The Model and the Marriage Broker	TCF	Cyril J. Mockridge
Mon Ami Pierre	FRA	Joseph Kosma
Montana Desperado	MON	Edward J. Kay
My Favorite Spy	PAR	Victor Young
My Forbidden Past	RKO	Frederick Hollander
Native Son	IND	John Ehlert
Nature's Half Acre (short)	DIS	Paul Smith
New Mexico	UA	Rene Carriguene Lucien Moraweck
Night Into Morning	MGM	Carmen Dragon
Night Riders of Montana	REP	Stanley Wilson
No Place for Jennifer	BRI	Allan Gray

No Questions Asked	MGM	Leith Stevens
Obsessed	BRI	Allan Gray
Oh, Amelia	FRA	Rene Cloerec
Oh, Susanna	REP	Dale R. Butts
On Dangerous Ground	RKO	Bernard Herrmann
On Moonlight Bay	WB	Max Steiner
On the Loose	RKO	Leigh Harline
One Summer of Happiness	SWE	Sven Skjold
Only the Valiant	WB	Franz Waxman
Operation Pacific	WB	Max Steiner
Overland Telegraph	RKO	Paul Sawtell
The Painted Hills	MGM	Daniele Amfitheatrof
Pals of the Golden West	REP	Stanley Wilson
Pandora and the Flying Dutchman	MGM	Hubert Clifford
Pardon My French	UA	Guy Bernard
Passage West	PAR	Mahlon Merrick
The Path of Hope	ITA	Carlo Rustichelli
Payment on Demand	RKO	Victor Young
Peking Express	PAR	Dimitri Tiomkin
The People Against O'Hara	MGM	Carmen Dragon
People Will Talk	TCF	Alfred Newman
Pickup	COL	Harold Byrns
Pier 23	LIP	Bert Shefter
Pistol Harvest	RKO	Paul Sawtell
A Place in the Sun	PAR	Franz Waxman
Pool of London	UN	John Addison
Potemkin (re-issue)	RUS	Nikolai Kruikov
Prehistoric Women	EL	Raoul Kraushaar
Pride of Maryland	REP	Stanley Wilson
The Prince Who Was a Thief	UN	Hans J. Salter
The Prowler	UA	Irving Friedman
Quebec	PAR	Van Cleave
Queen for a Day	UA	Hugo Friedhofer
Quo Vadis?	MGM	Miklos Rozsa
The Racket	RKO	Constantin Bakaleinikoff
The Raging Tide	UN	Frank Skinner
Raton Pass	WB	Max Steiner
Rawhide	TCF	Sol Kaplan
The Red Badge of Courage	MGM	Bronislau Kaper
Red Mountain	PAR	Franz Waxman
Reunion in Reno	UN	Joseph Gershenson
Rhubarb	PAR	Van Cleave
Rhythm Inn	MON	Edward J. Kay
Rich, Young and Pretty	MGM	Nicholas Brodszky
The River	UA	M. A. Partha-Sarathy
Roadblock	RKO	Paul Sawtell
Roaring City	LIP	Bert Shefter
Rodeo	MON	Marlin Skiles
Rodeo King and the Senorita	REP	Stanley Wilson
Rough Riders of Durango	REP	Stanley Wilson
Saddle Legion	RKO	Paul Sawtell
Sailor Beware	PAR	Joseph J. Lilley
St. Benny the Dip	UA	Robert Stringer

Santa Fe	COL	Paul Sawtell
Saturday's Hero	COL	Elmer Bernstein
Savage Drums	LIP	Darrell Calker
The Scarf	UA	Herschel Burke Gilbert
The Sea Hornet	REP	Dale R. Butts
Sealed Cargo	RKO	Roy Webb
The Second Face	UA	Raoul Kraushaar
The Second Woman	UA	Nat Finston
The Secret of Convict Lake	TCF	Sol Kaplan
Secrets of Monte Carlo	REP	Stanley Wilson
La Sel De La Terre	FRA	Guy Bernard
The Sellout	MGM	David Buttolph
Shadow in the Sky	MGM	Bronislau Kaper
Silver City	PAR	Paul Sawtell
Silver City Bonanza	REP	Stanley Wilson
Sirocco	COL	George Anthiel
Sky High	LIP	Bert Shefter
Slaughter Trail	RKO	Darrell Calker
Smuggler's Gold	COL	Mischa Bakaleinikoff
Smuggler's Island	UN	Joseph Gershenson
Snake River Desperadoes	COL	Ross di Maggio
Soldiers Three	MGM	Adolph Deutsch
The Son of Dr. Jekyll	COL	Paul Sawtell
South of Caliente	REP	Dale R. Butts
Spoilers of the Plains	REP	Dale R. Butts
Stage from Blue River	MON	Raoul Kraushaar
Stop That Cab	LIP	John Sentesi
Storm Over Tibet	COL	Arthur Honegger Leith Stevens
Stormbound	REP	Alessandro Cicognini
The Strange Door	UN	Joseph Gershenson
Strangers on a Train	WB	Dimitri Tiomkin
Street Bandits	REP	Stanley Wilson
A Streetcar Named Desire	WB	Alex North
Strictly Dishonorable	MGM	Lennie Hayton
The Strip	MGM	George Stoll
Submarine Command	PAR	David Buttolph
Sugarfoot	WB	Max Steiner
Superman and the Mole Men	LIP	Darrell Calker
The Sword of Monte Cristo	TCF	Raoul Kraushaar
Take Care of My Little Girl	TCF	Alfred Newman
Tales of Robin Hood	LIP	Leon Katzkin
The Tanks Are Coming	WB	William Lava
Taras Shevchenko	RUS	B. Lvatoshinsky
Target Unknown	UN	Joseph Gershenson
Tarzan's Peril	RKO	Michel Michelet
Tembo	RKO	Claude Sweeten
Ten Tall Men	COL	David Buttolph
Teresa	MGM	Louis Applebaum
That's My Boy	PAR	Leigh Harline
The Thing	RKO	Dimitri Tiomkin
The 13th Letter	TCF	Lionel Newman
3 Desperate Men	LIP	Albert Glasser

Three Guys Named Mike	MGM	Bronislau Kaper
Three Steps North	ITA	Roman Vlad
Three Women	FRA	Georges van Parys
Thunder in God's Country	REP	Stanley Wilson
Thunder on the Hill	UN	Hans J. Salter
Tokyo File 212	RKO	Albert Glasser
Tom Brown's Schooldays	UA	Richard Addinsell
Tomahawk	UN	Hans J. Salter
Tomorrow Is Another Day	WB	Daniele Amfitheatrof
Too Young to Kiss	MGM	John Green
Two-Dollar Bettor	IND	Irving Gertz
Two Gals and a Guy	UA	Gail Kubik
Two of a Kind	COL	George Duning
Two Tickets to Broadway	RKO	Walter Scharf
Umberto D.	ITA	Alessandro Cicognini
Under the Olive Tree	ITA	Geofreddo Petrassi
The Unknown Man	MGM	Conrad Salinger
The Unknown World	LIP	Ernest Gold
Up Front	UA	Joseph Gershenson
Utah Wagon Train	REP	Stanley Wilson
Valentino	COL	Heinz Roemheld
Varieties on Parade	LIP	Walter Greene
Vengeance Valley	MGM	Rudolph Kopp
Warpath	PAR	Paul Sawtell
Waters of Time (short)	BRI	Alan Rawsthorne
Weekend with Father	UN	Frank Skinner
The Well	UA	Dimitri Tiomkin
Wells Fargo Gunmaster	REP	Stanley Wilson
Westward the Women	MGM	Jeff Alexander
When I Grow Up	EL	Jerome Moross
When the Redskins Rode	COL	Mischa Bakaleinikoff
When Worlds Collide	PAR	Leith Stevens
The Whip Hand	RKO	Paul Sawtell
Whirlwind	COL	Mischa Bakaleinikoff
The Whistle at Eaton Falls	COL	Louis Applebaum
White Hell of Pitz Palu	SWI	Mark Lothar
The White Line	ITA	Carlo Rustichelli
The Wicked City	UA	Joseph Kosma
The Wild Blue Yonder	REP	Victor Young
A Wonderful Life	IND	Louis Forbes
Wonderful Times	GER	Werner Eisbrenner
A Yank in Korea	COL	Ross di Maggio
Yellow Fin	MON	Edward J. Kay
Yes Sir, Mr. Bones	LIP	Walter Greene
You Can Never Tell	UN	Hans J. Salter
You're in the Navy Now	TCF	Cyril J. Mockridge
Yukon Manhunt	MON	Edward J. Kay

1952

Aaron Slick from Punkin Crick	PAR	Robert Emmett Dolan
Abbott and Costello Meet Captain Kidd	WB	Raoul Kraushaar

Above and Beyond	MGM	Hugo Friedhofer
Actors and Sin	UA	George Anthiel
Affair in Trinidad	COL	George Duning
African Treasure	MON	Raoul Kraushaar
Against All Flags	UN	Hans J. Salter
Aladdin and His Lamp	MON	Marlin Skiles
Altar Masterpiece (short)	POL	Andrzej Panufnik
And Now Tomorrow	IND	Paul Sawtell
Androcles and the Lion	RKO	Frederick Hollander
Angel Face	RKO	Dimitri Tiomkin
Another Man's Poison	UA	Paul Sawtell
Anything Can Happen	PAR	Victor Young
Apache War Smoke	MGM	Alberto Colombo
Arctic Flight	MON	Edward J. Kay
Army Bound	MON	Marlin Skiles
Around Is Around (short)	BRI	Louis Applebaum
Assignment--Paris	COL	George Duning
Astrologie (short)	FRA	Pierre Henry
At Sword's Point	RKO	Constantin Bakaleinikoff
The Atomic City	PAR	Leith Stevens
Back at the Front	UN	Joseph Gershenson
The Bad and the Beautiful	MGM	David Raksin
Bal Tabarin	REP	Dale R. Butts
The Battle of Apache Pass	UN	Hans J. Salter
Battle Zone	AA	Marlin Skiles
Bear Country (short)	DIS	Paul Smith
Beauties of the Night	FRA	Georges van Parys
Because of You	UN	Frank Skinner
Belles on Their Toes	TCF	Lionel Newman
Bend of the River	UN	Hans J. Salter
La Bergere Et Le Ramoneur	FRA	Joseph Kosma
The Berliner	GER	Werner Eisbrenner Gunther Neumann
Beware, My Lovely	RKO	Leith Stevens
Big Jim McLain	WB	Emil Newman
The Big Sky	RKO	Dimitri Tiomkin
The Big Trees	WB	Ray Heindorf
Birthright	IND	Lan Adomian
The Black Castle	UN	Joseph Gershenson
Blackbeard, the Pirate	RKO	Victor Young
Black Hills Ambush	REP	Stanley Wilson
The Blazing Forest	PAR	Lucien Cailliet
Bloodhounds of Broadway	TCF	Lionel Newman
Bonzo Goes to College	UN	Frank Skinner
Border Saddlemates	REP	Stanley Wilson
Brave Warrior	COL	Mischa Bakaleinikoff
Breakdown	IND	Paul Dunlap
Breaking the Sound Barrier	UA	Malcolm Arnold
The Brigand	COL	Morris Stoloff
Bronco Buster	UN	Joseph Gershenson
Bugles in the Afternoon	WB	Ray Heindorf
Bwana Devil	UA	Gordon Jenkins
Captain Pirate	COL	George Duning

The Captive City	UA	Emil Newman
Captive of Billy the Kid	REP	Stanley Wilson
Captive Women	RKO	Charles Koff
Carbine Williams	MGM	Conrad Salinger
Caribbean	PAR	Lucien Cailliet
Carrie	PAR	David Raksin
Carson City	WB	David Buttolph
Casque D'Or	FRA	Georges van Parys
Cattle Town	WB	William Lava
Children of Hiroshima	JAP	Akira Ifukube
Clash by Night	RKO	Constantin Bakaleinikoff
Cloudburst	UA	Frank Spencer
Colorado Sundown	REP	Dale R. Butts
Come Back, Little Sheba	PAR	Franz Waxman
La Commune De Paris	FRA	Joseph Kosma
Confidence Girl	UA	Lucien Cailliet
The Crimson Pirate	WB	William Alwyn
Cripple Creek	COL	Mischa Bakaleinikoff
Daphni	GRE	Howard Brubeck
Daughter of the Sands	AFR	Georges Auric
Deadline, USA	TCF	Lionel Newman
The Denver and the Rio Grande	PAR	Paul Sawtell
Desert Passage	RKO	Constantin Bakaleinikoff
Desert Pursuit	MON	Edward J. Kay
Desperadoes Outpost	REP	Stanley Wilson
Desperate Search	MGM	Rudolph Kopp
Diplomatic Courier	TCF	Lionel Newman
Don't Bother to Knock	TCF	Lionel Newman
Dreamboat	TCF	Cyril J. Mockridge
The Duel at Silver Creek	UN	Hans J. Salter
Edouard and Caroline	FRA	Jean-Jacques Grunenwald
Eight Iron Men	COL	Leith Stevens
Encore	PAR	Richard Addinsell
The Fabulous Senorita	REP	Stanley Wilson
Face to Face	RKO	Hugo Friedhofer
Faithful City	RKO	Eduard Ben Michael
Fargo	MON	Raoul Kraushaar
Father's Doing Fine	BRI	Harold Smart
Fearless Fagan	MGM	Rudolph G. Kopp
Feudin' Fools	MON	Edward J. Kay
The Fighter	UA	Vicente Gomez
The First Time	COL	Morris Stoloff
Five Fingers	TCF	Bernard Herrmann
Flat Top	AA	Marlin Skiles
Flesh and Fury	UN	Hans J. Salter
Flowers of St. Francis	ITA	Renzo Rossellini
For Men Only (The Tall Lie)	LIP	Irving Friedman
Forbidden Fruit	FRA	Paul Durand
Fort Osage	MON	Marlin Skiles
The Fourposter	COL	Dimitri Tiomkin
Francois Le Rhinoceros	FRA	Joseph Kosma
Francis Goes to West Point	UN	Joseph Gershenson
From Doric to Gothic (short)	FRA	Jacques Ibert

Gift Horse	BRI	Clifton Parker
A Girl in Every Port	RKO	Roy Webb
The Girl in White	MGM	David Raksin
Glory Alley	MGM	George Stoll
Gobs and Gals	REP	Stanley Wilson
Gold Fever	MON	Johnny Richards
The Golden Hawk	COL	Mischa Bakaleinikoff
Goya (short)	IND	Vicente Gomez
The Greatest Show on Earth	PAR	Victor Young
The Green Glove	UA	Joseph Kosma
The Half-Breed	RKO	Constantin Bakaleinikoff
Hangman's Knot	COL	Mischa Bakaleinikoff
Hans Christian Andersen	RKO	Walter Scharf
The Happy Time	COL	Dimitri Tiomkin
Harem Girl	COL	Mischa Bakaleinikoff
The Hawk of Wild River	COL	Mischa Bakaleinikoff
Here Come the Marines	MON	Edward J. Kay
Here Come the Nelsons	UN	Joseph Gershenson
Hiawatha	AA	Marlin Skiles
High Noon	UA	Dimitri Tiomkin
High Treason	BRI	John Addison
Hold That Line	MON	Edward J. Kay
Holiday for Sinners	MGM	Alberto Colombo
Hoodlum Empire	REP	Nathan Scott
Horizons West	UN	Joseph Gershenson
Hotel Des Invalides	FRA	Maurice Jarre
The Hour of 13	MGM	John Addison
Hurricane Smith	PAR	Paul Sawtell
Ikiru	JAP	Fumio Yawoguchi
The Importance of Being Earnest	BRI	Benjamin Frankel
Indian Uprising	COL	Ross di Maggio
Invasion USA	COL	Albert Glasser
Invitation	MGM	Bronislau Kaper
The Iron Mistress	WB	Max Steiner
Island Rescue	UN	Benjamin Frankel
It Grows on Trees	UN	Frank Skinner
Ivanhoe	MGM	Miklos Rozsa
Ivory Hunter (Where No Vultures Fly)	BRI	Alan Rawsthorne
Jack and the Beanstalk	WB	Heinz Roemheld
Japanese War Bride	TCF	Emil Newman
Jet Job	MON	Edward J. Kay
Journey into History (short)	BRI	Arnold Bax
The Jungle	LIP	Dakshinamoorthy G. Ramanathan
Just Across the Street	UN	Joseph Gershenson
Just for You	PAR	Emil Newman
Just This Once	MGM	David Rose
Kangaroo	TCF	Alfred Newman
Kansas City Confidential	UA	Paul Sawtell
Kansas Territory	MON	Raoul Kraushaar
Kid Monk Baroni	IND	Herschel Burke Gilbert
Kissenga, Man of Africa	AFR	Muir Mathieson

Lady in the Iron Mask	TCF	Dimitri Tiomkin
Lady Possessed	REP	Nathan Scott
The Las Vegas Story	RKO	Constantin Bakaleinikoff
Last of the Comanches	COL	George Duning
Last Train from Bombay	COL	Mischa Bakaleinikoff
The Last Musketeer	REP	Nathan Scott
The Lawless Breed	UN	Joseph Gershenson
Leadville Gunslinger	REP	Stanley Wilson
Leonardo Da Vinci	ITA	Roman Vlad
Limelight	UA	Charles Chaplin
The Lion and the Horse	WB	William Lava
Lone Star	MGM	David Buttolph
Lost in Alaska	UN	Joseph Gershenson
Love Is Better Than Ever	MGM	Lennie Hayton
Lure of the Wilderness	TCF	Franz Waxman
The Lusty Men	RKO	Roy Webb
Lydia Bailey	TCF	Lionel Newman
Ma and Pa Kettle at the Fair	UN	Joseph Gershenson
Macao	RKO	Constantin Bakaleinikoff
The Man Behind the Gun	WB	David Buttolph
Man from the Black Hills	MON	Raoul Kraushaar
The Man in the White Suit	BRI	Benjamin Frankel
Mara Maru	WB	Max Steiner
The Marijuana Story	ARG	John Ehlert
The Marrying Kind	COL	Morris Stoloff
The Maverick	MON	Raoul Kraushaar
Meet Danny Wilson	UN	Joseph Gershenson
Meet Me at the Fair	UN	Joseph Gershenson
A Member of the Wedding	COL	Alex North
Miracle in Milan	ITA	Alessandro Cicognini
The Miracle of Fatima	WB	Max Steiner
Mirrors of Holland (short)	HOL	Max Vredenburg
Les Miserables	TCF	Alex North
Les Miserables	ITA	Alessandro Cicognini
Miss Julie	SWE	Dag Wiren
Modens, Inc.	IND	Herschel Burke Gilbert
The Moment of Truth	FRA	Paul Misraki
Il Mondo Le Condanna	ITA	Piero Piccioni
Monkey Business	TCF	Lionel Newman
Montana Belle	RKO	Nathan Scott
Montana Incident	MON	Raoul Kraushaar
Montana Territory	COL	Mischa Bakaleinikoff
Moulin Rouge	UA	Georges Auric
Mutiny	UA	Dimitri Tiomkin
My Cousin Rachel	TCF	Franz Waxman
My Man and I	MGM	David Buttolph
My Pal Gus	TCF	Leigh Harline
My Six Convicts	COL	Dimitri Tiomkin
My Son John	PAR	Robert Emmett Dolan
My Wife's Best Friend	TCF	Leigh Harline
Never Wave at a Wac	RKO	Elmer Bernstein
Night Raiders	MON	Raoul Kraushaar
Night Without Sleep	TCF	Cyril J. Mockridge

No Holds Barred	MON	Edward J. Kay
No Resting Place	IRE	William Alwyn
No Room for the Groom	UN	Frank Skinner
No Time for Flowers	RKO	Herschel Burke Gilbert
O. Henry's Full House	TCF	Alfred Newman
Okinawa	COL	Mischa Bakaleinikoff
Oklahoma Annie	REP	Nathan Scott
Old Oklahoma Plains	REP	Stanley Wilson
One Big Affair	UA	L. Hernandez Breton
One Minute to Zero	RKO	Victor Young
Operation Secret	WB	Roy Webb
Outcast of the Islands	UA	Brian Easdale
The Outcasts of Poker Flat	TCF	Lionel Newman
Outlaw Women	LIP	Walter Greene
Outpost in Malaya	UA	Allan Gray
The Pace That Thrills	RKO	Constantin Bakaleinikoff
Park Row	UA	Paul Dunlap
Passion for Life	FRA	Joseph Kosma
Pat and Mike	MGM	David Raksin
The Pathfinder	COL	Mischa Bakaleinikoff
Paula	COL	Morris Stoloff
Phone Call from a Stranger	TCF	Franz Waxman
Plymouth Adventure	MGM	Miklos Rozsa
Pony Soldier	TCF	Alex North
The Pride of St. Louis	TCF	Lionel Newman
The Prisoner of Zenda	MGM	Alfred Newman
The Promoter	BRI	William Alwyn
The Quiet Man	REP	Victor Young
The Raiders	UN	Joseph Gershenson
Rancho Notorious	RKO	Emil Newman
Rashomon	JAP	Takashi Matsuyama
Red Planet Mars	UA	David Chudnow
Red Skies of Montana	TCF	Lionel Newman
Red Snow	COL	Michael Terr
The Redhead from Wyoming	UN	Joseph Gershenson
Retreat, Hell!	WB	William Lava
Return of the Texan	TCF	Lionel Newman
Ride the Man Down	REP	Ned Freeman
The Ring	UA	Herschel Burke Gilbert
Road Agent	RKO	Paul Sawtell
Road to Bali	PAR	Joseph J. Lilley
Rogue's March	MGM	Alberto Colombo
Rome, 11 O'Clock	ITA	Mario Nascimbene
Room for One More	WB	Max Steiner
The Rose Bowl Story	MON	Marlin Skiles
Rose of Cimarron	TCF	Raoul Kraushaar
Royal River (short)	BRI	William Alwyn
Ruby Gentry	TCF	Heinz Roemheld
Sally and Saint Anne	UN	Frank Skinner
Salute E Baci	ITA	S. Barizza
The San Francisco Story	WB	Emil Newman
The Savage	PAR	Paul Sawtell

Savage Triangle	FRA	Paul Misraki
Scandal Sheet	COL	Morris Stoloff
Scaramouche	MGM	Victor Young
Scarlet Angel	UN	Joseph Gershenson
Sea Tiger	MON	Edward J. Kay
A Simple Case of Money	FRA	Jean Marion
Sky Full of Moon	MGM	Paul Sawtell
The Small Back Room	BRI	Brian Easdale
The Sniper	COL	Morris Stoloff
The Snows of Kilimanjaro	TCF	Bernard Herrmann
Something for the Birds	TCF	Sol Kaplan
Something to Live For	PAR	Victor Young
Son of Ali Baba	UN	Joseph Gershenson
Son of Paleface	PAR	Lyn Murray
Sound Off!	COL	Morris Stoloff
South Pacific Trail	REP	Stanley Wilson
Springfield Rifle	WB	Max Steiner
The Steel Trap	TCF	Dimitri Tiomkin
Stop, You're Killing Me	WB	Ray Heindorf
The Story of Will Rogers	WB	Victor Young
Strange Fascination	COL	Vaclav Divina
Strange World	UA	W. Schultz Porto Alegro Emil Velazco
The Stranger in Between	BRI	Hubert Clifford
Sudden Fear	RKO	Elmer Bernstein
Talk About a Stranger	MGM	David Buttolph
The Tall Headlines	BRI	Hans May
Target	RKO	Constantin Bakaleinikoff
Target Hong Kong	COL	Mischa Bakaleinikoff
Tarzan's Savage Fury	RKO	Paul Sawtell
Texas City	MON	Raoul Kraushaar
The Thief	UA	Herschel Burke Gilbert
The Thief of Venice	TCF	Alessandro Cicognini
This Is Cinerama	CIN	Louis Forbes
This Woman Is Dangerous	WB	David Buttolph
Three for Bedroom C	WB	Heinz Roemheld
Three Forbidden Stories	ITA	Antonio Veretti
Thunderbirds	REP	Victor Young
Thundering Caravans	REP	Stanley Wilson
Tomorrow is Too Late	ITA	Alessandro Cicognini
Toughest Man in Arizona	REP	Dale Butts
Trail Guide	RKO	Constantin Bakaleinikoff
The Treasure of Lost Canyon	UN	Joseph Gershenson
Tropical Heat Wave	REP	Stanley Wilson
The Turning Point	PAR	Irvin Talbot
Under the Red Sea	RKO	Bert Grund
The Unforgettable Year--1919	RUS	Dmitri Shostakovich
Untamed Frontier	UN	Hans J. Salter
Untamed Women	UA	Raoul Kraushaar
Valley of the Eagles	LIP	Nino Rota
Viva Zapata!	TCF	Alex North Manuel M. Ponce

The Voice of Silence	ITA	Enzo Masetti
Voodoo Tiger	COL	Mischa Bakaleinikoff
The Wac from Walla Walla	REP	Dale Butts
Waco	MON	Raoul Kraushaar
Wagon Team	COL	Paul Mertz
Wait 'Til the Sun Shines, Nellie	TCF	Alfred Newman
Walk East on Beacon	COL	Jack Shaindlin
Washington Story	MGM	Conrad Salinger
Way of a Gaucho	TCF	Sol Kaplan
We're Not Married	TCF	Lionel Newman
What Price Glory?	TCF	Alfred Newman
When in Rome	MGM	Carmen Dragon
Whispering Smith vs. Scotland Yard	RKO	Frank Spencer
The Wild Heart	RKO	Brian Easdale
Wild Horse Ambush	REP	Stanley Wilson
The Wild North	MGM	Bronislau Kaper
Wild Stallion	MON	Marlin Skiles
The Winning Team	WB	David Buttolph
Without Warning	UA	Herschel Burke Gilbert
Woman in the Dark	REP	Stanley Wilson
Woman of the North Country	REP	Dale Butts
The Woman's Angle	BRI	Kenneth Leslie Smith
The World in His Arms	UN	Frank Skinner
A Yank in Indo-China	COL	Ross di Maggio
Yankee Buccaneer	UN	Joseph Gershenson
You for Me	MGM	Alberto Colombo
Young Man with Ideas	MGM	David Rose

1953

Abbott and Costello Go to Mars	UN	Joseph Gershenson
Act of Love	UA	Michael Emer Joe Hajos
The Actress	MGM	Bronislau Kaper
Admiral Ushakov	RUS	Aram Khachaturian
Affair in Monte Carlo	AA	Robert Gill Philip Green
Affairs of Dobie Gillis	MGM	Jeff Alexander
The All-American	UN	Joseph Gershenson
All I Desire	UN	Joseph Gershenson
All the Brothers Were Valiant	MGM	Miklos Rozsa
Ambush at Tomahawk Gap	COL	Ross di Maggio
The American Road (short)	IND	Alex North
The Anatomy of Love	ITA	Alessandro Cicognini
Appointment in Honduras	RKO	Louis Forbes
Arena	MGM	Rudolph G. Kopp
Arrowhead	PAR	Paul Sawtell
The Assassin	BRI	Nino Rota
Attack from the Sea	RUS	Aram Khachaturian
Back to God's Country	UN	Frank Skinner
Bad for Each Other	COL	Mischa Bakaleinikoff
The Bandwagon	MGM	Adolph Deutsch

The Bandit (O Cangaciero)	BRA	Gabriel Migliori
The Bandits of Corsica	UA	Irving Gertz
Bandits of the West	REP	Stanley Wilson
Battle Circus	MGM	Lennie Hayton
Battles of Chief Pontiac	IND	Elmer Bernstein
Below the Sahara	RKO	Paul Sawtell
Beneath the 12-Mile Reef	TCF	Bernard Herrmann
The Big Heat	COL	Mischa Bakaleinikoff
The Big Leaguer	MGM	Alberto Colombo
Blowing Wild	WB	Dimitri Tiomkin
The Blue Gardenia	WB	Raoul Kraushaar
A Blueprint for Murder	TCF	Lionel Newman
Botany Bay	PAR	Franz Waxman
Bright Road	MGM	David Rose
The Caddy	PAR	Joseph J. Lilley
Capt. John Smith and Pocahontas	UA	Albert Glasser
Captain Scarlett	UA	Elias Breeskin
The Captain's Paradise	BRI	Malcolm Arnold
Cease Fire	PAR	Dimitri Tiomkin
Champ for a Day	REP	Dale R. Butts
The Charge at Feather River	WB	Max Steiner
China Venture	COL	Ross di Maggio
Chuk and Gek	RUS	A. Lepin
City Beneath the Sea	UN	Joseph Gershenson
City of Bad Men	TCF	Lionel Newman
Clipped Wings	AA	Marlin Skiles
The Clown	MGM	David Rose
Code Two	MGM	Alberto Colombo
Column South	UN	Joseph Gershenson
Combat Squad	COL	Paul Dunlap
Confidentially Connie	MGM	David Rose
Conquest of Cochise	UN	Mischa Bakaleinikoff
The Conquest of Everest	UA	Sir Arthur Benjamin
Cow Country	AA	Edward J. Kay
Crash of Silence (Mandy)	BRI	William Alwyn
Crazylegs	REP	Leith Stevens
The Cruel Sea	BRI	Alan Rawsthorne
Cruisin' Down the River	COL	George Duning
Cry of the Hunted	MGM	Joel Freeman
Dangerous Crossing	TCF	Lionel Newman
Dangerous When Wet	MGM	George Stoll
Dark River	ARG	Tito Ribero
Decameron Nights	RKO	Anthony Hopkins
Desert Legion	UN	Frank Skinner
The Desert Rats	TCF	Leigh Harline
Desperate Moment	BRI	Philip Martell
Destination Gobi	TCF	Sol Kaplan
Devil's Canyon	RKO	Daniele Amfitheatrof
The Diamond Queen	WB	Paul Sawtell
Donovan's Brain	UA	Eddie Dunstedter
Down Laredo Way	REP	Stanley Wilson
Dream Wife	MGM	Conrad Salinger
The Earrings of Madame D ...	FRA	Georges van Parys Oscar Straus

East of Sumatra	UN	Joseph Gershenson
El Alamein	COL	Mischa Bakaleinikoff
El Paso Stampede	REP	Stanley Wilson
Escape from Fort Bravo	MGM	Jeff Alexander
Fair Wind to Java	REP	Victor Young
The Fake	UA	Ilona Kabos
Fangs of the Arctic	MON	Edward J. Kay
The Farmer Takes a Wife	TCF	Lionel Newman
Fast Company	MGM	Alberto Colombo
Fighter Attack	AA	Marlin Skiles
The Fighting Lawman	AA	Raoul Kraushaar
The Final Test	BRI	Benjamin Frankel
The 5,000 Fingers of Dr. T	COL	Frederick Hollander
Flight Nurse	REP	Victor Young
Flight to Tangier	PAR	Paul Sawtell
Forbidden	UN	Frank Skinner
Forever Female	PAR	Victor Young
Fort Algiers	UA	Michel Michelet
Fort Ti	WB	Ross di Maggio
Fort Vengeance	AA	Paul Dunlap
The 49th Man	COL	Mischa Bakaleinikoff
Four Chimneys	JAP	Yashushi Akutagawa
Francis Covers the Big Town	UN	Joseph Gershenson
French Can-Can	FRA	Jean Wiener Georges van Parys
From Here to Eternity	COL	George Duning
The Gentle Gunmen	BRI	John Greenwood
Geraldine	REP	Dale R. Butts
Ghost Ship	LIP	Eric Spear
The Girl Next Door	TCF	Joseph Myrow
The Girl Who Had Everything	MGM	Andre Previn
The Girls of Pleasure Island	PAR	Lyn Murray
Give the Girl a Break	MGM	Andre Previn Saul Chaplin
The Glass Wall	COL	Leith Stevens
The Glass Web	UN	Joseph Gershenson
The Glory Brigade	TCF	Lionel Newman
The Golden Blade	UN	Joseph Gershenson
Goldtown Ghost Riders	COL	Mischa Bakaleinikoff
The Great Diamond Robbery	MGM	Rudolph G. Kopp
The Great Sioux Uprising	UN	Joseph Gershenson
Guerilla Girl	UA	Bernard Bossick
Gun Belt	UA	Irving Gertz
Gun Fury	COL	Mischa Bakaleinikoff
Gunsmoke	UN	Joseph Gershenson
Half a Hero	MGM	Paul Sawtell
Heidi	UA	Robert Blum
Hell Raiders of the Deep	ITA	Nina Rota
Hello Elephant!	ITA	Alessandro Cicognini
Here Come the Girls	PAR	Lyn Murray
His Majesty O'Keefe	WB	Dimitri Tiomkin
The Hitch-Hiker	RKO	Leith Stevens
The Hoaxters (short)	MGM	Rudolph G. Kopp

Hondo	WB	Emil Newman Hugo Friedhofer
Hot News	AA	Marlin Skiles
Houdini	PAR	Roy Webb
House of Wax	WB	David Buttolph
How to Marry a Millionaire	TCF	Alfred Newman
I Believe in You	BRI	Sir Ernest Irving
I Confess	WB	Dimitri Tiomkin
I, the Jury	UA	Franz Waxman
Inferno	TCF	Paul Sawtell
Invaders from Mars	TCF	Raoul Kraushaar
Island in the Sky	WN	Emil Newman
It Came from Outer Space	UN	Joseph Gershenson
It Happened in the Park	FRA	Mario Nascimbene
It Happens Every Thursday	UN	Joseph Gershenson
Jack McCall, Desperado	COL	Mischa Bakaleinikoff
Jack Slade	AA	Paul Dunlap
Jalopy	AA	Marlin Skiles
Jamaica Run	PAR	Lucien Cailliet
Jennifer	AA	Ernest Gold
Jeopardy	MGM	Dimitri Tiomkin
The Joe Louis Story	UA	George Bassman
Journey to South America	BRI	Melle Weersma
The Juggler	COL	George Anthiel
Julius Caesar	MGM	Miklos Rozsa
Kansas Pacific	AA	Albert Sendrey
The Kid from Left Field	TCF	Lionel Newman
Killer Apc	COL	Mischa Bakaleinikoff
King of the Khyber Rifles	TCF	Bernard Herrmann
Knights of the Round Table	MGM	Miklos Rozsa
The Lady Wants Mink	REP	Stanley Wilson
The Last Bridge	YUG	Carl de Groof
Last of the Pony Riders	COL	Ross di Maggio
Latin Lovers	MGM	George Stoll
Law and Order	UN	Joseph Gershenson
Let's Do It Again	COL	Morris Stoloff
Lili	MGM	Bronislau Kaper
The Limping Man	LIP	Arthur Wilkinson Eric Spear
A Lion Is in the Streets	WB	Franz Waxman
Little Boy Lost	PAR	Victor Young
The Little Fugitive	IND	Lester Troob Eddy Manson
The Living Desert	DIS	Paul Smith
Lone Hand	UN	Joseph Gershenson
The Long Memory	BRI	William Alwyn
Loose in London	AA	Marlin Skiles
Louisiana Territory	RKO	George Bassman
Love in the City	ITA	Mario Nascimbene
Luxury Girls	ITA	Nino Rota
Ma and Pa Kettle on Vacation	UN	Joseph Gershenson
The Magnetic Monster	UA	Blaine Sanford
Main Street to Broadway	MGM	Ann Ronnell

The Man Between	UA	John Addison
Man Crazy	TCF	Ernest Gold
The Man from the Alamo	UN	Frank Skinner
Man in Hiding	UA	Doreen Carwithen
Man in the Attic	TCF	Lionel Newman
Man in the Dark	COL	Ross di Maggio
Man on a Tightrope	TCF	Franz Waxman
The Marksman	AA	Raoul Kraushaar
Marry Me Again	RKO	Raoul Kraushaar
Marshal of Cedar Rock	REP	Stanley Wilson
The Marshal's Daughter	UA	Darrel Calker
Martin and Gaston (short)	BRI	Temple Abady
Martin Luther	IND	Mark Lothar
The Master of Ballantrae	WB	William Alwyn
Melba	UA	Mischa Spoliansky
Mexican Manhunt	AA	Edward J. Kay
Miss Robin Crusoe	TCF	Elmer Bernstein
Miss Sadie Thompson	COL	Morris Stoloff
Mission over Korea	COL	Mischa Bakaleinikoff
The Mississippi Gambler	UN	Frank Skinner
Mister Scoutmaster	TCF	Cyril J. Mockridge
The Mistress	RUS	Lev Schwartz
Money from Home	PAR	Leigh Harline
Monsoon	UA	Vasant Desai
The Moon Is Blue	UA	Herschel Burke Gilbert
The Moonlighter	WB	Heinz Roemheld
Murder without Tears	AA	Edward J. Kay
The Naked Spur	MGM	Bronislau Kaper
The Neanderthal Man	UA	Albert Glasser
The Nebraskan	COL	Ross di Maggio
Never Let Me Go	MGM	Hans May
Niagara	TCF	Sol Kaplan
Night without Stars	BRI	William Alwyn
99 River Street	UA	Emil Newman
No Escape	UA	Bert Shefter
Northern Patrol	AA	Edward J. Kay
Off Limits	PAR	Van Cleave
The Olympic Elk (short)	DIS	Paul Smith
On Top of Old Smoky	COL	Mischa Bakaleinikoff
Paris Model	COL	Albert Glasser
Penny Princess	BRI	Philip Martell
A Perilous Journey	REP	Victor Young
Peter Pan	DIS	Oliver Wallace
Pickup on South Street	TCF	Leigh Harline
The Pleasure Garden	BRI	Stanley Bates
Plunder of the Sun	WB	Hugo Friedhofer Antonio Diaz Conde
Pony Express	PAR	Paul Sawtell
Powder River	TCF	Lionel Newman
Powered Flight (short)	BRI	William Alwyn
The President's Lady	TCF	Alfred Newman
Prince of Pirates	COL	Mischa Bakaleinikoff
Prisoners of the Casbah	COL	Mischa Bakaleinikoff

Problem Girls	COL	Albert Glasser
Project M-7	BRI	Benjamin Frankel
The Proud and the Beautiful	FRA	Paul Misraki
Queen of Sheba	ITA	Nino Rota
Raiders of the Seven Seas	UA	Paul Sawtell
Rebel City	AA	Raoul Kraushaar
Red River Shore	REP	Dale R. Butts
Remains to Be Seen	MGM	Jeff Alexander
The Return of Vasili Bortnikov	RUS	K. Molchanov
Return to Paradise	UA	Dimitri Tiomkin
Ride, Vaquero	MGM	Bronislau Kaper
Roar of the Crowd	AA	Marlin Skiles
Rob Roy, the Highland Rogue	DIS	Cedric Thorp Davie
The Robe	TCF	Alfred Newman
Roman Holiday	PAR	Georges Auric
The Royal African Rifles	AA	Paul Dunlap
Saadia	MGM	Bronislau Kaper
Sabre Jet	UA	Herschel Burke Gilbert
Safari Drums	AA	Marlin Skiles
Saginaw Trail	COL	Paul Mertz
Sailor of the King	TCF	Muir Mathieson
Salome	COL	Daniele Amfitheatrof George Duning
Sangaree	PAR	Lucien Cailliet
Savage Frontier	REP	Stanley Wilson
Sawdust and Tinsel (Naked Night)	SWE	Karl-Birger Blomdahl
Scandal at Scourie	MGM	Daniele Amfitheatrof
Scared Stiff	PAR	Leith Stevens
The Sea Around Us	RKO	Paul Sawtell
Sea Devils	RKO	Richard Addinsell
Sea of Lost Ships	REP	Dale R. Butts
Second Chance	RKO	Roy Webb
Seminole	UN	Joseph Gershenson
Sensualita (The Barefoot Savage)	ITA	Fernando Previtali
Serpent of the Nile	COL	Mischa Bakaleinikoff
Shane	PAR	Victor Young
Shark River	UA	Irving Gertz
Shoot First	UA	Hans May
The Silver Whip	TCF	Lionel Newman
Sins of Jezebel	LIP	Bert Shefter
Sky Commando	COL	Ross di Maggio
The Slasher	BRI	Lambert Williamson
Slaves of Babylon	COL	Mischa Bakaleinikoff
A Slight Case of Larceny	MGM	Albert Colombo
So Big	WB	Max Steiner
Sombrero	MGM	Leon Arnaud
Something Money Can't Buy	AA	Marlin Skiles
Song of the Land	UA	M. Dupre
South Sea Woman	WB	David Buttolph
La Spiaggia	ITA	Piero Piccioni
Split Second	RKO	Roy Webb
Stalag 17	PAR	Franz Waxman
The Stand at Apache River	UN	Frank Skinner

The Star	TCF	Victor Young
The Star of Texas	AA	Raoul Kraushaar
The Stars Are Singing	PAR	Victor Young
The Steel Lady	UA	Emil Newman
The Story of Three Loves	MGM	Miklos Rozsa
Strange Deception (Il Cristo Prohibito)	ITA	Ugo Giacomazzi
Stranger on the Prowl	UA	G. C. Sonzagno
The Stranger Wore a Gun	COL	Mischa Bakaleinikoff
The Sun Shines Bright	REP	Victor Young
Sweethearts on Parade	REP	Robert Armbruster
The Sword and the Rose	DIS	Clifton Parker
The System	WB	David Buttolph
Take Me to Town	UN	Joseph Gershenson
Take the High Ground	MGM	Dimitri Tiomkin
Tangier Incident	AA	Edward J. Kay
Tarzan and the She-Devil	RKO	Paul Sawtell
Taxi	TCF	Leigh Harline
Terror on a Train	MGM	John Addison
Texas Bad Man	AA	Raoul Kraushaar
That Man from Tangier	UA	Elizabeth Firestone
Therese Raquin	FRA	Maurice Thiriet
Those Redheads from Seattle	PAR	Leo Shuken
Thunder Bay	UN	Frank Skinner
Thunder in the East	PAR	Hugo Friedhofer
Thunder Over the Plains	WB	David Buttolph
Titanic!	TCF	Sol Kaplan
The Titfield Thunderbolt	UN	Georges Auric
Topeka	AA	Raoul Kraushaar
Torch Song	MGM	Adolph Deutsch
Torpedo Alley	AA	Edward J. Kay
Touchez Ne Pas Au Grisbi	FRA	Jean Wiener
Trail Blazers	AA	Edward J. Kay
Treasure of the Golden Condor	TCF	Sol Kaplan
Trent's Last Case	REP	Anthony Collins
Tropic Zone	PAR	Lucien Cailliet
Trouble Along the Way	WB	Max Steiner
Tumbleweeds	UN	Joseph Gershenson
Turn the Key Softly	BRI	Mischa Spoliansky
Twilight Women	LIP	Alan Gray
The Twonky	UA	Jack Meakin
Valley of Headhunters	COL	Mischa Bakaleinikoff
The Vanquished	PAR	Lucien Cailliet
Veils of Bagdad	UN	Joseph Gershenson
Vice Squad	UA	Herschel Burke Gilbert
Vicki	TCF	Leigh Harline
Vigilante Terror	AA	Raoul Kraushaar
The Village	UA	Robert Blum
Violated	IND	Tony Mottola
Volcano	ITA	Enzo Masetti
Walking My Baby Back Home	UN	Joseph Gershenson
War Arrow	UN	Joseph Gershenson
The War of the Worlds	PAR	Leith Stevens

War Paint	UA	Emil Newman
White Lightning	AA	Marlin Skiles
White Mane	FRA	Maurice le Roux
White Witch Doctor	TCF	Bernard Herrmann
Wicked Woman	UA	Buddy Baker
Windfall in Athens	GRE	Andrea Anagnosti
Wings of the Hawk	UN	Frank Skinner
Winning of the West	COL	Ross di Maggio
The Woman They Almost Lynched	REP	Stanley Wilson
World without End	BRI	Elizabeth Lutyens
Yellow Balloon	AA	Philip Green
Yesterday and Today	UA	Eliot Daniel
Young Bess	MGM	Miklos Rozsa

1954

About Mrs. Leslie	PAR	Victor Young
The Adventures of Hajji Baba	TCF	Dimitri Tiomkin
Adventures of Robinson Crusoe	UA	Anthony Collins
The Affairs of Messalina	COL	Renzo Rossellini
Africa Adventure	RKO	Paul Sawtell
L'Air De Paris	FRA	Maurice Thiriet
Alaska Seas	PAR	Irvin Talbot
Always a Bride	BRI	Benjamin Frankel
Angels One Five	BRI	John Wooldridge
The Anna Cross	RUS	Lev Schwartz
Apache	UA	David Raksin
Arrow in the Dust	AA	Marlin Skiles
Athena	MGM	George Stoll
The Atomic Kid	REP	Van Alexander
Bad Day at Black Rock	MGM	Andre Previn
The Bailiff	JAP	Fumio Hayasaka
Bait	COL	Vaclav Divina
The Bamboo Prison	COL	Mischa Bakaleinikoff
The Barefoot Battalion	GRE	Mikis Theodorakis
The Barefoot Contessa	UA	Mario Nascimbene
Battle of Rogue River	COL	Mischa Bakaleinikoff
Beachhead	UA	Emil Newman Arthur Lange
Beat the Devil	UA	Franco Mannino
Beau Brummel	MGM	Richard Addinsell
Bengal Brigade	UN	Joseph Gershenson
Betrayed	MGM	Walter Goehr
Bitter Creek	AA	Raoul Kraushaar
The Black Dakotas	COL	Mischa Bakaleinikoff
Black Horse Canyon	UN	Joseph Gershenson
The Black Knight	COL	John Addison
Blackout	LIP	Ivor Slaney
The Black Shield of Falworth	UN	Joseph Gershenson
Black 13	TCF	Ugo Giacomazzi
Black Tuesday	UA	Paul Dunlap
Black Widow	TCF	Leigh Harline

The Bob Mathias Story	AA	Leith Stevens
Border River	UN	Joseph Gershenson
Both Sides of the Law	UN	Temple Abady
The Bounty Hunter	WB	David Buttolph
The Bowery Boys Meet the Monsters	AA	Marlin Skiles
The Boy from Oklahoma	WB	Max Steiner
Bread, Love and Dreams	ITA	I. Cini
The Bridges at Toko-Ri	PAR	Lyn Murray
Broken Lance	TCF	Leigh Harline
A Bullet Is Waiting	COL	Dimitri Tiomkin
The Caine Mutiny	COL	Max Steiner
Cannibal Attack	COL	Mischa Bakaleinikoff
Captain Kidd and the Slave Girl	UA	Paul Sawtell
Casanova's Big Night	PAR	Lyn Murray
Cattle Queen of Montana	RKO	Louis Forbes
Charge of the Lancers	COL	Ross di Maggio
The Command	WB	Dimitri Tiomkin
The Country Girl	PAR	Victor Young
The Cowboy	LIP	Carl Brandt
The Creature from the Black Lagoon	UN	Joseph Gershenson
Crest of the Wave	MGM	Miklos Rozsa
Crime Wave	WB	David Buttolph
Crossed Swords	UA	Alessandro Cicognini
Dangerous Mission	RKO	Roy Webb
Dawn at Socorro	UN	Joseph Gershenson
Day of Triumph	IND	Daniele Amfitheatrof
Demitrius and the Gladiators	TCF	Franz Waxman Alfred Newman
Desiree	TCF	Alfred Newman Alex North
The Desperado	AA	Raoul Kraushaar
Destry	UN	Joseph Gershenson
Dial M for Murder	WB	Dimitri Tiomkin
The Diamond Wizard	UA	Matyas Seiber
Down Three Dark Streets	UA	Paul Sawtell
Dragnet	WB	Walter Schumann
Dragonfly Squadron	AA	Paul Dunlap
Dragon's Gold	UA	Albert Glasser
The Drawings of Leonardo Da Vinci (short)	BRI	Alan Rawsthorne
Dreaming Lips	GER	Alois Melichar
Drive a Crooked Road	COL	Ross di Maggio
Drum Beat	WB	Victor Young
Drums Across the River	UN	Joseph Gershenson
Drums of Tahiti	COL	Mischa Bakaleinikoff
Duel in the Jungle	WB	Mischa Spoliansky
Duffy of San Quentin	WB	Paul Dunlap
The Egyptian	TCF	Alfred Newman Bernard Herrmann
Elephant Walk	PAR	Franz Waxman
Fangs of the Wild	LIP	Paul Dunlap

Fire over Africa	COL	Benjamin Frankel
Fireman Save My Child	UN	Joseph Gershenson
Flame and the Flesh	MGM	George Stoll
Flight of the White Heron (see The Royal Tour of Queen Elizabeth and Philip)		
The Forty-Niners	AA	Raoul Kraushaar
Four Guns to the Border	UN	Joseph Gershenson
Francis Joins the Wacs	UN	Joseph Gershenson
The French Line	RKO	Walter Scharf
The Gambler from Natchez	TCF	Lionel Newman
The Game of Love	FRA	Rene Cloerec
Garden of Evil	TCF	Bernard Herrmann
Genevieve	UN	Larry Adler
The Glenn Miller Story	UN	Henry Mancini
Go, Man, Go	UA	Alex North
Gog	UA	Harry Sukman
The Golden Coach	ITA	Antonio Vivaldi
The Golden Idol	AA	Marlin Skiles
The Golden Mask	UA	Robert Gill
Gorilla at Large	TCF	Lionel Newman
The Great Adventure	SWE	Lars-Erik Larsson
Green Fire	MGM	Miklos Rozsa
Gypsy Colt	MGM	Rudolph G. Kopp
Hell and High Water	TCF	Alfred Newman
Hell Below Zero	COL	Clifton Parker
Hell's Half Acre	REP	Dale R. Butts
Her 12 Men	MGM	Bronislau Kaper
High and Dry	BRI	John Addison
The High and the Mighty	WB	Dimitri Tiomkin
Highway Dragnet	AA	Edward J. Kay
Hobson's Choice	BRI	Malcolm Arnold
Human Desire	COL	Daniele Amfitheatrof
The Human Jungle	AA	Hans J. Salter
Indiscretion of an American Wife	COL	Alessandro Cicognini
The Inspector General (Revizor)	RUS	N. Timofeyev
Intimate Relations	BRI	Rene Cloerec
The Iron Glove	COL	Mischa Bakaleinikoff
It Should Happen to You	COL	Frederick Hollander
Jesse James vs. the Daltons	COL	Mischa Bakaleinikoff
Jesse James' Women	UA	Walter Greene
Jivaro	PAR	Gregory Stone
Joan of Arc at the Stake	FRA	Arthur Honegger
Johnny Dark	UN	Joseph Gershenson
Johnny Guitar	REP	Victor Young
Johnny on the Run	BRI	Anthony Hopkins
Jubilee Trail	REP	Victor Young
Jungle Gents	AA	Marlin Skiles
Jungle Man-Eaters	COL	Mischa Bakaleinikoff
Khyber Patrol	UA	Irving Gertz
Killer Leopard	AA	Marlin Skiles
Killers from Space	RKO	Manuel Compinsky
King Richard and the Crusaders	WB	Max Steiner

Knock on Wood	PAR	Victor Young
The Last Time I Saw Paris	MGM	Conrad Salinger
Laughing Anne	BRI	Anthony Collins
The Law vs. Billy the Kid	COL	Mischa Bakaleinikoff
The Lawless Rider	UA	Rudy de Saxe
Letters from My Windmill	FRA	Henri Tomasi
The Little Kidnappers	UA	Bruce Montgomery
Living It Up	PAR	Walter Scharf
The Long, Long Trailer	MGM	Adolph Deutsch
The Long Wait	UA	Mario Castelnuevo-Tedesco
Loophole	AA	Paul Dunlap
Louis Lumiere	FRA	Joseph Kosma
Ma and Pa Kettle at Home	UN	Joseph Gershenson
The Mad Magician	COL	Emil Newman Arthur Lange
Magnificent Obsession	UN	Frank Skinner
Make Haste to Live	REP	Elmer Bernstein
The Malta Story	BRI	William Alwyn
Man with a Million	UA	William Alwyn
Marianne of My Youth	FRA	Jacques Ibert
Massacre Canyon	COL	Mischa Bakaleinikoff
Masterson of Kansas	COL	Mischa Bakaleinikoff
Men of the Fighting Lady	MGM	Miklos Rozsa
Mexican Bus Ride (Subida Al Cielo)	MEX	Gustavo Pittaluga
The Miami Story	COL	Mischa Bakaleinikoff
Mr. Hulot's Holiday	FRA	Alain Romans
Mr. Potts Goes to Moscow	BRI	Stanley Black
Naked Alibi	UN	Joseph Gershenson
The Naked Jungle	PAR	Daniele Amfitheatrof
Napoleon	FRA	Jean Francaix
Night People	TCF	Cyril J. Mockridge
On the Waterfront	COL	Leonard Bernstein
Operation Manhunt	UA	Jack Shaindlin
The Other Woman	TCF	Ernest Gold
The Outcast	REP	Dale R. Butts
The Outlaw Stallion	COL	Mischa Bakaleinikoff
The Outlaw's Daughter	TCF	Raoul Kraushaar
Overland Pacific	UA	Irving Gertz
Papa, Mama, the Maid and I	FRA	Georges van Parys
The Paratrooper	COL	John Addison
Paris Playboys	AA	Marlin Skiles
Passion	RKO	Louis Forbes
A Personal Affair	UA	William Alwyn
The Phantom of the Rue Morgue	WB	David Buttolph
Phffft	COL	Frederick Hollander
The Pickwick Papers	BRI	Anthony Hopkins
Playgirl	UN	Joseph Gershenson
Port of Hell	AA	Edward J. Kay
Pride of the Blue Grass	AA	Marlin Skiles
Prince Bayaya	CZE	Vaclav Trojan
A Prince for Cynthia (short)	BRI	Bruce Montgomery
Prince Valiant	TCF	Franz Waxman

Princess of the Nile	TCF	Lionel Newman
Prisoner of War	MGM	Jeff Alexander
Private Hell 36	RKO	Leith Stevens
Prowlers of the Everglades (short)	DIS	Paul Smith
Pushover	COL	Arthur Morton
Quest for the Lost City	RKO	Paul Sawtell
The Raid	TCF	Lionel Newman
Rails into Laramie	UN	Joseph Gershenson
Rear Window	PAR	Franz Waxman
The Red and the Black	FRA	Rene Cloerec
Red Garters	PAR	Joseph J. Lilley
Return from the Sea	AA	Paul Dunlap
Return to Treasure Island	UA	Paul Sawtell
Rhapsody	MGM	John Green
Ricochet Romance	UN	Joseph Gershenson
Ride Clear of Diablo	UN	Joseph Gershenson
Riders to the Stars	UA	Harry Sukman
Riding Shotgun	WB	David Buttolph
Ring of Fear	WB	Emil Newman Arthur Lange
Riot in Cell Block 11	AA	Herschel Burke Gilbert
River Beat	LIP	Hubert Clifford
River of No Return	TCF	Lionel Newman
The Rocket Man	TCF	Lionel Newman
Rogue Cop	MGM	Jeff Alexander
Romeo and Juliet	UA	Roman Vlad
Roogie's Bump	REP	Lehman Engel
Royal Affair in Versailles	FRA	Jean Francaix
The Royal Tour of Queen Elizabeth and Philip	TCF	Stanley Wricken
Sabrina	PAR	Frederick Hollander
The Safety Match	RUS	V. Shirnsky
The Saint's Girl Friday	RKO	Ivor Slaney
The Saracen Blade	COL	Mischa Bakaleinikoff
Saskatchewan	UN	Joseph Gershenson
The Scarlet Spear	UA	Ivor Slaney
Secret of the Incas	PAR	David Buttolph
Security Risk	AA	Edward J. Kay
The Shanghai Story	REP	Dale R. Butts
She Couldn't Say No	RKO	Roy Webb
The She-Wolf	REP	Felice Lattuada
Shield for Murder	UA	Paul Dunlap
Siege at Red River	TCF	Lionel Newman
Sign of the Pagan	UN	Frank Skinner
The Silver Chalice	WB	Franz Waxman
Silver Lode	RKO	Louis Forbes
Sins of Rome	RKO	Renzo Rossellini
The Snow Creature	UA	Manuel Compinsky
So This Is Paris	UN	Joseph Gershenson
Southwest Passage	UA	Emil Newman Arthur Lange
Stormy, the Thoroughbred	DIS	William Lava

La Strada	ITA	Nino Rota
The Stranger Left No Card (short)	BRI	Hugo Alfven
The Student Prince	MGM	Nicholas Brodszky
Suddenly	UA	David Raksin
Susan Slept Here	RKO	Leigh Harline
Tanganyika	UN	Joseph Gershenson
Target Earth	AA	Paul Dunlap
Taza, Son of Cochise	UN	Frank Skinner
The Tell-Tale Heart (short)	COL	Boris Kremenliev
Tennessee Champ	MGM	Conrad Salinger
Them!	WB	Bronislau Kaper
They Rode West	COL	Paul Sawtell
This Is My Love	RKO	Franz Waxman
Three Coins in the Fountain	TCF	Victor Young
Three Hours to Kill	COL	Paul Sawtell
Three Ring Circus	PAR	Walter Scharf
Three Young Texans	TCF	Lionel Newman
Tobor The Great	REP	Howard Jackson
Tonight's the Night	AA	Stanley Black
Track of the Cat	WB	Roy Webb
Trouble in the Glen	REP	Victor Young
True Friends	RUS	Tikhon Khrennikov
20,000 Leagues under the Sea	DIS	Paul Smith
Two Guns and a Badge	AA	Raoul Kraushaar
A Unicorn in the Garden (short)	COL	David Raksin
L'Univers D'Utrillo	FRA	Maurice Jarre
Untamed Heiress	REP	Stanley Wilson
Valley of the Kings	MGM	Miklos Rozsa
The Vanishing Prairie	DIS	Paul Smith
Vera Cruz	UA	Hugo Friedhofer
Victory at Sea	UA	Richard Rodgers
The Weak and the Wicked	AA	Leighton Lucas
Welcome to the Queen (short)	BRI	Sir Arthur Bliss
West of Zanzibar	BRI	Alan Rawsthorne George Sigara
White Fire	LIP	Stanley Black
The White Orchid	UA	Antonio Dias Conde
The Wild One	COL	Leith Stevens
Witness to Murder	UA	Herschel Burke Gilbert
Woman's World	TCF	Cyril J. Mockridge
World for Ransom	AA	Frank de Vol
The Yellow Mountain	UN	Joseph Gershenson
The Yellow Tomahawk	UA	Les Barker
You Know What Sailors Are	BRI	Malcolm Arnold
Yukon Vengeance	AA	Edward J. Kay

1955

Abbott and Costello Meet the Keystone Kops	UN	Joseph Gershenson
Abbott and Costello Meet the Mummy	UN	Joseph Gershenson

The Adventures of Sadie	TCF	Ronald Binge
The African Lion	DIS	Paul Smith
Ain't Misbehavin'	UN	Joseph Gershenson
All That Heaven Allows	UN	Frank Skinner
The Americano	RKO	Roy Webb
Angela	TCF	Mario Nascimbene
Animal Farm	BRI	Matyas Seiber
An Annapolis Story	AA	Marlin Skiles
Apache Ambush	COL	Mischa Bakaleinikoff
Artists and Models	PAR	Walter Scharf
At Gunpoint	AA	Carmen Dragon
The Ballet of Romeo and Juliet	RUS	Serge Prokofiev
Battle Cry	WB	Max Steiner
Battle Taxi	UA	Harry Sukman
The Beachcomber	UA	Francis Chagrin
Bedevilled	MGM	William Alwyn
Bel Ami	FRA	Hanns Eisler
The Belles of St. Trinian's	BRI	Malcolm Arnold
Bengazi	RKO	Roy Webb
The Benny Goodman Story	UN	Henry Mancini
The Bespoke Overcoat (short)	BRI	Georges Auric
Betrayed Women	AA	Edward J. Kay
The Big Bluff	UA	Manuel Compinsky
The Big Combo	AA	David Raksin
Big House, U.S.A.	UA	Paul Dunlap
The Big Knife	UA	Frank de Vol
The Big Tip-Off	AA	Edward J. Kay
The Blackboard Jungle	MGM	Charles Wolcott
Blood Alley	WB	Roy Webb
Bobby Ware Is Missing	AA	Carl Brandt
Bowery to Bagdad	AA	Marlin Skiles
Break to Freedom	UA	Philip Martell
Bring Your Smile Along	COL	George Duning
A Bullet for Joey	UA	Harry Sukman
Canyon Crossroads	UA	George Bassman
Captain Lightfoot	UN	Joseph Gershenson
Carolina Cannonball	REP	Dale R. Butts
The Case of the Red Monkey	AA	Richard Taylor
Cell 2455, Death Row	COL	Mischa Bakaleinikoff
Chance Meeting	BRI	Benjamin Frankel
Chicago Syndicate	COL	Ross di Maggio
Chief Crazy Horse	UN	Frank Skinner
Cila S'Appelle L'Aurore	FRA	Joseph Kosma
Cinerama Holiday	CIN	Morton Gould Van Cleave
City of Shadows	REP	Dale R. Butts
The Cobweb	MGM	Leonard Rosenman
Conquest of Space	PAR	Van Cleave
Count Three and Pray	COL	George Duning
The Court-Martial of Billy Mitchell	WB	Dimitri Tiomkin
Crashout	IND	Leith Stevens
Creature with the Atom Brain	COL	Mischa Bakaleinikoff

The Crooked Web	COL	Mischa Bakaleinikoff
Cross Channel	BRI	Lambert Williamson
Cult of the Cobra	UN	Joseph Gershenson
The Dam Busters	BRI	Leighton Lucas
Dance Little Lady	BRI	Ronald Binge
Davy Crockett, King of the Wild Frontier	DIS	George Bruns
A Day to Remember	REP	Clifton Parker
The Deep Blue Sea	TCF	Malcolm Arnold
Dementia	IND	George Anthiel
Desert Sands	UA	Paul Dunlap
The Desperate Hours	PAR	Gail Kubik
Devil Goddess	COL	Mischa Bakaleinikoff
Diabolique	FRA	Georges van Parys
Dial Red O	AA	Marlin Skiles
Diane	MGM	Miklos Rozsa
The Divided Heart	BRI	Georges Auric
Doctor in the House	BRI	Bruce Montgomery
Don Juan's Night of Love	ITA	Mario Nascimbene
Double Jeopardy	REP	Dale Butts
Downtown	JAP	Akira Ifukube
The Dragonfly	RUS	Sulkhan Tsintsadze
Duel on the Mississippi	COL	Mischa Bakaleinikoff
East of Eden	WB	Leonard Rosenman
Elena and the Men	FRA	Joseph Kosma
The End of the Affair	COL	Benjamin Frankel
Escapade	BRI	Bruce Montgomery
Escape to Burma	RKO	Louis Forbes
The Eternal Sea	REP	Elmer Bernstein
The Far Country	UN	Joseph Gershenson
The Far Horizons	PAR	Hans J. Salter
Female on the Beach	UN	Joseph Gershenson
Fighting Chance	REP	Dale Butts
Finger Man	AA	Paul Dunlap
Five Against the House	COL	George Duning
Five Guns West	IND	Buddy Bregman
Flame of the Islands	REP	Sonny Burke
Flames on the Volga	RUS	Dmitri Kabalevsky
Footsteps in the Fog	COL	Benjamin Frankel
Fort Yuma	UA	Paul Dunlap
Foxfire	UN	Frank Skinner
Francis in the Navy	UN	Joseph Gershenson
Frisky	ITA	Alessandro Cicognini
Front Page Story	BRI	Jackie Brown
The Gadfly	RUS	Dmitri Kabalevsky
Gang-Busters	IND	Richard Aurandt
Gentlemen Marry Brunettes	UA	Robert Farnon
Ghost Town	UA	Paul Dunlap
The Girl in the Bikini	FRA	Jean Yatove
The Girl in the Mist	JAP	Ichito Saito
The Girl in the Red Velvet Swing	TCF	Leigh Harline
The Glass Slipper	MGM	Bronislau Kaper
The Good Die Young	UA	Georges Auric

Good Morning, Miss Dove	TCF	Leigh Harline
Les Grandes Manoeuvres	FRA	Georges van Parys
The Grasshopper	RUS	Nikolai Kryukov
The Green Buddha	REP	Lambert Williamson
Green Magic	ITA	Francesco Lavagnino
The Green Scarf	BRI	Brian Easdale
The Gun that Won the West	COL	Ross di Maggio
Headline Hunters	REP	Dale R. Butts
Heartbreak Ridge	FRA	Claude Arrien
Heidi and Peter	UA	Robert Blum
Helen of Troy	WB	Max Steiner
Hell on Frisco Bay	WB	Max Steiner
Hell's Horizon	COL	Heinz Roemheld
Hell's Island	PAR	Irvin Talbot
Hell's Outpost	REP	Dale R. Butts
Heroes of Shipka	RUS	Nikolai Kryukov F. Kutev
High Society	MON	Marlin Skiles
Hill 24 Doesn't Answer	ISR	Paul Ben Haim
Hiroshima	JAP	Akira Ifukube
Hit the Deck	MGM	George Stoll
Hold Back Tomorrow	UN	Sidney Cutner
Holiday for Henrietta	FRA	Georges Auric
House of Bamboo	TCF	Lionel Newman
How to Be Very, Very Popular	TCF	Lionel Newman
Hunters of the Deep	IND	George Anthiel
I Am a Camera	BRI	Muir Mathieson
I Cover the Underworld	REP	Dale R. Butts
I Died a Thousand Times	WB	David Buttolph
I Live in Fear	JAP	Fumio Hayasaka
I'll Cry Tomorrow	MGM	Alex North
Illegal	WB	Max Steiner
The Indian Fighter	UA	Franz Waxman
Innocents of Paris	BRI	Joseph Kosma
Inside Detroit	Col	Mischa Bakaleinikoff
Interrupted Melody	MGM	Adolph Deutsch
The Intruder	BRI	Muir Mathieson
It Came from Beneath the Sea	COL	Mischa Bakaleinikoff
It's a Dog's Life	MGM	Elmer Bernstein
Jail Busters	AA	Marlin Skiles
Jump into Hell	WB	David Buttolph
Jungle Moon Men	COL	Mischa Bakaleinikoff
Jupiter's Darling	MGM	David Rose
The Kentuckian	UA	Roy Webb
Killer's Kiss	UA	Gerald Fried
The King's Thief	MGM	Miklos Rozsa
Kiss Me Deadly	UA	Frank de Vol
Kiss of Fire	UN	Joseph Gershenson
Lady and the Tramp	DIS	Oliver Wallace
Lady Godiva	UN	Joseph Gershenson
Land of Fury	BRI	William Alwyn
Land of the Pharaohs	WB	Dimitri Tiomkin
Las Vegas Shakedown	AA	Edward J. Kay

The Last Command	REP	Max Steincr
The Last Frontier	COL	Leigh Harline
A Lawless Street	COL	Paul Sawtell
Lay that Rifle Down	REP	Dale R. Butts
Lease of Life	BRI	Alan Rawsthorne
The Left Hand of God	TCF	Victor Young
A Lesson in Life (Conflict)	RUS	A. Filippenko
Let's Make Up	BRI	Robert Farnon
A Life in the Balance	TCF	Raul Lavista
The Littlest Outlaw	DIS	William Lava
The Living Swamp	TCF	Paul Sawtell
The Long Gray Line	COL	George Duning
Long John Silver	TCF	David Buttolph
The Looters	UN	Joseph Gershenson
Lord of the Jungle	AA	Marlin Skiles
Love Is a Many-Splendored Thing	TCF	Alfred Newman
Love Me or Leave Me	MGM	George Stoll
Lucky to Be a Woman	ITA	Alessandro Cicognini
Lucy Gallant	PAR	Van Cleave
Ma and Pa Kettle at Waikiki	UN	Joseph Gershenson
The McConnell Story	WB	Max Steiner
Maddalena	ITA	Antonio Verreti
The Magnificent Matador	TCF	Raoul Kraushaar
Mambo	PAR	Franco Ferrara
A Man Alone	REP	Victor Young
A Man Called Peter	TCF	Alfred Newman
The Man from Bitter Ridge	UN	Joseph Gershenson
The Man from Laramie	COL	George Duning
The Man Who Loved Redheads	UA	Benjamin Frankel
The Man with the Golden Arm	UA	Elmer Bernstein
Man with the Gun	UA	Alex North
Man without a Star	UN	Joseph Gershenson
Many Rivers to Cross	MGM	Cyril J. Mockridge
Marcel Marceau's Pantomimes (short)	FRA	Edgar Bishoff
Marty	UA	Roy Webb
Midnight Episode	BRI	Mischa Spoliansky
Mister Roberts	WB	Franz Waxman
Moonfleet	MGM	Miklos Rozsa
Mother (see 1905)		
Murder Is My Beat	AA	Albert Glasser
Mystery of the Black Jungle	REP	Georges Tzipine Giovanni Fusco
The Naked Dawn	UN	Herschel Burke Gilbert
The Naked Heart	CAN	Guy Bernard
Naked Sea	RKO	Laurindo Almeida
The Naked Street	UA	Emil Newman
Nana	FRA	Georges van Parys
New Orleans Uncensored	COL	Mischa Bakaleinikoff
New York Confidential	WB	Joseph Mullendore
Night and Fog (short)	FRA	Hanns Eisler
Night Freight	AA	Edward J. Kay
The Night Holds Terror	COL	Lucien Cailliet

The Night My Number Came Up	BRI	Malcolm Arnold
The Night of the Hunter	UA	Walter Schumann
1905 (Mother)	RUS	Lev Schwartz
No Man's Woman	REP	Dale R. Butts
No Way Back	GER	Hans-Martin Majewski
Not as a Stranger	UA	George Anthiel
One Desire	UN	Frank Skinner
One Step to Eternity	FRA	Rene Sylviano
Othello	UA	Francesco Lavagnino
Paris Follies of 1956	AA	Frank de Vol
Pearl of the South Pacific	RKO	Louis Forbes
A Pedagogical Poem	RUS	A. Svechnikov
The Phenix City Story	AA	Harry Sukman
Picnic	COL	George Duning
Pirates of Tripoli	COL	Mischa Bakaleinikoff
Prince of Players	TCF	Bernard Herrmann
Princess Cinderella	ITA	Renzo Rossellini
The Prisoner	COL	Benjamin Frankel
Private Ivan Brovkin	RUS	Anatol Lepin
The Private War of Major Benson	UN	Joseph Gershenson
A Prize of Gold	COL	Malcolm Arnold
The Prodigal	MGM	Bronislau Kaper
The Purple Mask	UN	Joseph Gershenson
The Purple Plain	UA	John Veale
Queen Bee	COL	George Duning
Quentin Durward	MGM	Bronislau Kaper
Race at Dawn	RKO	Paul Sawtell
The Racers	TCF	Lionel Newman
The Rains of Ranchipur	TCF	Hugo Friedhofer
Rebel without a Cause	WB	Leonard Rosenman
The Return of Jack Slade	AA	Paul Dunlap
Revenge of the Creature	UN	Joseph Gershenson
The Revolt of Gunner Asch (08/15)	GER	Rolf Wilhelm
The Road to Denver	REP	Dale R. Butts
Robber's Roost	UA	Paul Dunlap
The Rose Tattoo	PAR	Alex North
Run for Cover	PAR	Howard Jackson
Running Wild	UN	Joseph Gershenson
Sabaka	UA	Dakshnimurti
Saint Margaret of Cortona	ITA	Guilio Bonnard
Saltanat	RUS	Aram Khachaturian
Samurai	JAP	Ikuma Dan
Santa Fe Passage	REP	Dale R. Butts
The Scarlet Coat	MGM	Conrad Salinger
The Sea Chase	WB	Roy Webb
The Sea Shall Not Have Them	BRI	Muir Mathieson
The Second Greatest Sex	UN	Joseph Gershenson
Secret Venture	REP	Lambert Williamson
Seminole Uprising	COL	Mischa Bakaleinikoff
The Sergeant's Daughter	GER	Theo Mackeben
Seven Angry Men	AA	Carl Brandt
Seven Cities of Gold	TCF	Hugo Friedhofer
The Seven Little Foys	PAR	Joseph J. Lilley

The Seven Year Itch	TCF	Alfred Newman
Shack Out on 101	AA	Paul Dunlap
Shadow of the Eagle	UA	Hans May
Shotgun	AA	Carl Brandt
The Shrike	UN	Frank Skinner
Simba	BRI	Francis Chagrin
Six Bridges to Cross	UN	Joseph Gershenson
Skabenga	AA	Marlin Skiles
Smoke Signal	UN	Joseph Gershenson
Soldier of Fortune	TCF	Hugo Friedhofer
Son of Sinbad	RKO	Victor Young
Special Delivery	COL	Burhard Kaun
The Spoilers	UN	Joseph Gershenson
Spy Chasers	AA	Marlin Skiles
The Square Jungle	UN	Heinz Roemheld
The Square Ring	BRI	Dock Mathieson
A Story of Silver (short)	DEN	Bent Fabricius-Bjerre
Strange Lady in Town	WB	Dimitri Tiomkin
Stranger on Horseback	UA	Paul Dunlap
The Stranger's Hand	ITA	Nino Rota
Strategic Air Command	PAR	Victor Young
Sudden Danger	AA	Marlin Skiles
Summertime	UA	Alessandro Cicognini
Svengali	MGM	William Alwyn
Tall Man Riding	WB	Paul Sawtell
Tarantula	UN	Joseph Gershenson
Target Zero	WB	David Buttolph
Tarzan's Hidden Jungle	RKO	Paul Sawtell
Teen-Age Crime Wave	COL	Mischa Bakaleinikoff
Ten Wanted Men	COL	Paul Sawtell
The Tender Trap	MGM	Jeff Alexander
Tennessee's Partner	RKO	Louis Forbes
Texas Lady	RKO	Paul Sawtell
That Lady	TCF	John Addison
They Were So Young	LIP	Michael Jary
This Island Earth	UN	Herman Stein
This Strange Passion (El)	MEX	Louis Fernandez Breton
Three Cases of Murder	BRI	Muir Mathieson
Three for the Show	COL	George Duning
Three Stripes in the Sun	COL	George Duning
The Tiger and the Flame	UA	Vasant Desai
The Tiger Tamer	RUS	Moisei Vainberg
Tight Spot	COL	George Duning
Timberjack	REP	Victor Young
To Catch a Thief	PAR	Lyn Murray
To Hell and Back	UN	Joseph Gershenson
To Paris with Love	BRI	Edwin Astley
Too Bad She's Bad	ITA	Alessandro Cicognini
Too Young for Love	ITA	Mario Nascimbene
Top Gun	UA	Irving Gertz
Top of the World	UA	Albert Glasser
The Toughest Man Alive	AA	Edward J. Kay
The Treasure of Pancho Villa	RKO	Leith Stevens

Treasure of the Ruby Hills	AA	Edward J. Kay
Trial	MGM	Daniele Amfitheatrof
Trouble in Store	BRI	Mischa Spoliansky
The Trouble with Harry	PAR	Bernard Herrmann
The Twinkle in God's Eye	REP	Van Alexander
Ulysses	PAR	Alessandro Cicognini
Unchained	WB	Alex North
Underwater!	RKO	Roy Webb
An Unfinished Story	RUS	Gabriel Popov
Untamed	TCF	Franz Waxman
Utopia (Atoll A)	FRA	Paul Misraki
The Vanishing American	REP	Dale R. Butts
The Vicious Breed	BRI	Charles Norman
The View from Pompey's Head	TCF	Elmer Bernstein
The Violent Men	COL	Max Steiner
Violent Saturday	TCF	Lionel Newman
The Virgin Queen	TCF	Franz Waxman
The Wages of Fear	FRA	Georges Auric
Wakamba	RKO	Howard Jackson
The Warriors	AA	Cedric Thorpe Davie
The Wayward Wife	ITA	Franco Mannino
We're No Angels	PAR	Frederick Hollander
White Feather	TCF	Lionel Newman
Wichita	AA	Hans J. Salter
Wicked Wife	AA	John Greenwood
Women's Prison	COL	Mischa Bakaleinikoff
Wyoming Renegades	COL	Mischa Bakaleinikoff
Yellowneck	REP	Laurence Rosenthal
You're Never Too Young	PAR	Walter Scharf

1956

Abdullah's Harem	TCF	Georges Auric
Above Us the Waves	BRI	Sir Arthur Benjamin
Accused of Murder	REP	Dale R. Butts
Adorable Creatures	FRA	Georges van Parys
Adventures of Artyomka	RUS	V. Pushkov
L'Aine des Ferchaux	FRA	Georges Delerue
Alexander the Great	UA	Mario Nascimbene
Alone in the Streets	ITA	Franco Longella
The Amazon Trader	WB	Howard Jackson
The Ambassador's Daughter	UA	Jacques Metehen
Anastasia	TCF	Alfred Newman
The Animal World	WB	Paul Sawtell
Around the World in 80 Days	UA	Victor Young
Attack!	UA	Frank de Vol
Autumn Leaves	COL	Hans J. Salter
Away All Boats	UN	Frank Skinner
Baby Doll	WB	Kenyon Hopkins
Back from Eternity	RKO	Franz Waxman
Backlash	UN	Herman Stein
The Bad Seed	WB	Alex North
Bandido	UA	Max Steiner

Battle Stations	COL	Mischa Bakaleinikoff
Bayou	UA	Fredi Lesse
The Beast of Hollow Mountain	UA	Raul Lavista
Behind the High Wall	UN	Joseph Gershenson
Between Heaven and Hell	TCF	Hugo Friedhofer
Beyond a Reasonable Doubt	RKO	Herschel Burke Gilbert
Bhowani Junction	MGM	Miklos Rozsa
Bigger than Life	TCF	David Raksin
The Birds and the Bees	PAR	Walter Scharf
The Black Sleep	UA	Les Baxter
The Black Whip	TCF	Raoul Kraushaar
Blackjack Ketchum, Desperado	COL	Mischa Bakaleinikoff
Blonde Sinner	AA	Ray Martin
The Bold and the Brave	RKO	Herschel Burke Gilbert
The Boss	UA	Albert Glasser
The Bottom of the Bottle	TCF	Leigh Harline
The Brain Machine	RKO	Richard Taylor
The Brass Legend	UA	Paul Dunlap
The Brave One	RKO	Victor Young
The Broken Star	UA	Paul Dunlap
The Burmese Harp	JAP	Akira Ifukube
The Burning Hills	WB	David Buttolph
Bus Stop	TCF	Alfred Newman
Calle Mayor	SPA	Joseph Kosma
Calling Homicide	AA	Marlin Skiles
Canyon River	AA	Marlin Skiles
The Captain from Kopenick	GER	Bernard Eichhorn
Cash on Delivery	RKO	Lambert Williamson
The Catered Affair	MGM	Andre Previn
Cha-Cha-Cha Boom!	COL	Fred Karger
A Christmas Carol	IND	Bernard Herrmann
Circus Girl	REP	Franz Grothe
The Cockleshell Heroes	COL	John Addison
Comanche	UA	Herschel Burke Gilbert
Come Next Spring	REP	Max Steiner
The Come On	AA	Paul Dunlap
Come, Take My Life	GER	Hans-Otto Borgmann
Congo Crossing	UN	Henry Mancini
The Conqueror	RKO	Victor Young
Crashing Las Vegas	AA	Marlin Skiles
The Creature Walks Among Us	UN	Joseph Gershenson
Crime Against Joe	UA	Paul Dunlap
Crime in the Streets	AA	Franz Waxman
Crowded Paradise	IND	David Broekman
The Cruel Tower	AA	Paul Dunlap
A Cry in the Night	WB	David Buttolph
Curucu, Beast of the Amazon	UN	Raoul Kraushaar
D-Day, the Sixth of June	TCF	Lyn Murray
Dakota Incident	REP	Dale R. Butts
Dance with Me Henry	UA	Paul Dunlap
Daniel Boone, Trail Blazer	REP	Raul Lavista
Davy Crockett and the River Pirates	DIS	George Bruns

A Day of Fury	UN	Joseph Gershenson
The Deadliest Sin	AA	Richard Taylor
Death of a Scoundrel	RKO	Max Steiner
The Desperadoes Are in Town	TCF	Paul Sawtell
		Bert Shefter
The Devil's Daughter	SPA	Guillermo Cases
Diary of a Lover	GER	Alois Melichar
Dig that Uranium	AA	Marlin Skiles
Doctor at Sea	BRI	Bruce Montgomery
Earth vs. The Flying Saucers	COL	Mischa Bakaleinikoff
The Eddy Duchin Story	COL	George Duning
Edge of Hell	UN	Ernest Gold
Emergency Hospital	UA	Paul Dunlap
Emperor's Waltz	GER	Hans Lang
Everything But the Truth	UN	Milton Rosen
The Fastest Gun Alive	MGM	Andre Previn
Fernandel, the Dressmaker	FRA	Paul Misraki
Fighting Trouble	AA	Buddy Bregman
Finger of Guilt	RKO	Trevor Duncan
The First Echelon	RUS	Dmitri Shostakovich
The First Texan	AA	Roy Webb
The First Traveling Saleslady	RKO	Irving Gertz
Flight to Hong Kong	UA	Monty Kelly
The Flying Carpet	RUS	N. Simonyan
Forbidden Cargo	BRI	Lambert Williamson
Foreign Intrigue	UA	Paul Durand
The Foreman	AUS	Carl Zeller
		Hans Lang
Forever Darling	MGM	Bronislau Kaper
The Forty-First	RUS	Nikolai Kruykov
Four Bags Full	FRA	Rene Cloerec
Four Girls in Town	UN	Alex North
Francis in the Haunted House	UN	Joseph Gershenson
Friendly Persuasion	AA	Dimitri Tiomkin
Full of Life	COL	George Duning
Fury at Gunsight Pass	COL	Mischa Bakaleinikoff
Gaby	MGM	Conrad Salinger
The Gamma People	COL	George Melachrino
Giant	WB	Dimitri Tiomkin
The Girl He Left Behind	WB	Roy Webb
Glory	RKO	Frank Perkins
Godzilla, King of the Monsters	JAP	Akira Fukube
Goodbye, My Lady	WB	Laurindo Almeida
The Great American Pastime	MGM	Jeff Alexander
Great Day in the Morning	RKO	Leith Stevens
The Great Locomotive Chase	DIS	Paul Smith
The Great Man	UN	Herman Stein
Guendalina	ITA	Piero Piccioni
Gun Brothers	UA	Irving Gertz
Gun the Man Down	UA	Henry Vars
The Harder They Fall	COL	Hugo Friedhofer
He Laughed Last	COL	Arthur Morton
Hidden Guns	REP	Ramez Idriss

High Terrace	AA	Stanley Black
Hilda Crane	TCF	David Raksin
Hold Back the Night	AA	Hans J. Salter
Hollywood or Bust	PAR	Walter Scharf
Hot Blood	COL	Les Baxter
Hot Cars	UA	Les Baxter
Hot Shots	AA	Marlin Skiles
House of Riccordi	ITA	Renzo Rossellini
Huk	UA	Albert Glasser
The Indestructible Man	AA	Albert Glasser
Invasion of the Body Snatchers	AA	Carmen Dragon
Invitation to the Dance	MGM	Andre Previn Jacques Ibert
The Iron Petticoat	MGM	Benjamin Frankel
It Happened in Rome	ITA	Lelio Luttazzi
I've Lived Before	UN	Herman Stein
Jaguar	REP	Van Alexander
Jedda the Uncivilized	AUT	Isador Goodman
Joe Macbeth	COL	Trevor Duncan
Johnny Concho	UA	Nelson Riddle
Jubal	COL	David Raksin
Julie	MGM	Leith Stevens
The Kettles in the Ozarks	UN	Joseph Gershenson
A Kid for Two Farthings (Lucky Kid)	BRI	Benjamin Frankel
The Killer Is Loose	UA	Lionel Newman
The Killing	UA	Gerald Fried
The King and Four Queens	UA	Alex North
King of the Coral Sea	AA	Wilbur Sampson
A Kiss Before Dying	UA	Lionel Newman
The Ladykillers	BRI	Tristram Cary
The Last Hunt	MGM	Daniele Amfitheatrof
The Last Man to Hang	COL	John Wooldridge
The Last Wagon	TCF	Lionel Newman
The Leather Saint	PAR	Irvin Talbot
The Lieutenant Wore Skirts	TCF	Cyril J. Mockridge
The Light Touch	BRI	John Addison
Lisbon	REP	Nelson Riddle
Lola Montes	FRA	Georges Auric
The Lone Ranger	WB	David Buttolph
Love Me Tender	TCF	Lionel Newman
Lovers and Lollipops	IND	Eddy Manson
Lucky Kid (see A Kid for Two Farthings)		
Lust for Life	MGM	Miklos Rozsa
Mademoiselle Mosquito	GER	Peter Krender
Magic Fire	REP	Erich Wolfgang Korngold
Magnificent Roughnecks	AA	Paul Dunlap
The Magnificent Seven	JAP	Fumio Hayasaka
Make Me an Offer	BRI	John Addison
Man from Del Rio	UA	Fred Steiner
The Man in the Gray Flannel Suit	TCF	Bernard Herrmann
Man in the Vault	RKO	Henry Vars

The Man Is Armed	REP	Dale R. Butts
The Man Who Knew Too Much	PAR	Bernard Herrmann
		Sir Arthur Benjamin
The Man Who Never Was	TCF	Alan Rawsthorne
Manfish	UA	Albert Elms
Marcel Marceau "In the Park" (short)	FRA	Jean Prodromides
Marcellino	SPA	Pablo Sorozabal
The March Hare	BRI	Philip Green
Massacre	TCF	Gonzalo Curiel
The Maverick Queen	REP	Victor Young
Meet Me in Las Vegas	MGM	George Stoll
Merry-Go-Round	HUN	Gyorgy Ranki
Miami Exposé	COL	Mischa Bakaleinikoff
Miracle in the Rain	WB	Franz Waxman
Moby Dick	WB	Philip Sainton
Mohawk	TCF	Raoul Kraushaar
The Mole People	UN	Hans J. Salter
The Most Dangerous Sin	FRA	Maurice Thiriet
The Mountain	PAR	Daniele Amfitheatrof
My Father's Horses	GER	Lothar Bruehne
The Mysterious Discovery	RUS	V. Yurovsky
Nagin	GER	Mermant Kumar
The Naked Hills	AA	Herschel Burke Gilbert
Navy Wife	AA	Hans J. Salter
Never Say Goodbye	UN	Frank Skinner
Nightfall	COL	George Duning
Nightmare	UA	Herschel Burke Gilbert
1984	COL	Malcolm Arnold
No Place to Hide	AA	Herschel Burke Gilbert
Odongo	COL	George Melachrino
On the Threshold of Space	TCF	Lyn Murray
Only the French Can (French Can-Can)	FRA	Georges van Parys
The Opposite Sex	MGM	Nicholas Brodzsky
Othello	RUS	Aram Khachaturian
Our Miss Brooks	WB	Roy Webb
Outside the Law	UN	Milton Rosen
Over-Exposed	COL	Mischa Bakaleinikoff
P.T. Raiders (see The Ship that Died of Shame)		
Pardners	PAR	Frank de Vol
Pather Panchali	IN	Ravi Shankar
The Peacemaker	UA	George Greeley
The Phantom Horse	JAP	Seitaro Omori
Picasso	ITA	Roman Vlad
Pillars of the Sky	UN	Joseph Gershenson
Port Afrique	COL	Malcolm Arnold
Postmark for Danger	RKO	John Veale
The Power and the Prize	MGM	Bronislau Kaper
The Price of Fear	UN	Joseph Gershenson
Private's Progress	BRI	John Addison
The Proud and the Profane	PAR	Victor Young
The Proud Ones	TCF	Lionel Newman

Queen of Babylon	ITA	Renzo Rossellini
Quincannon, Frontier Scout	UA	Les Baxter
The Rack	MGM	Adolph Deutsch
The Rainmaker	PAR	Alex North
Ransom	MGM	Jeff Alexander
Raw Edge	UN	Joseph Gershenson
The Rawhide Years	UN	Frank Skinner
Rebel in Town	UA	Les Baxter
The Red Balloon (short)	FRA	Maurice le Roux
Red Sundown	UN	Hans J. Salter
The Return of Don Camillo	ITA	Alessandro Cicognini
The Revolt of Mamie Stover	TCF	Hugo Friedhofer
Richard III	BRI	William Walton
Ride the High Iron	COL	Melvin Lenard
Rififi	FRA	Georges Auric
The River Changes	WB	Roy Webb
Rock, Pretty Baby	UN	Henry Mancini
The Roof	ITA	Alessandro Cicognini
Rosanna	MEX	Antonio Diaz Conde
Rumble on the Docks	COL	Mischa Bakaleinikoff
Run for the Sun	UA	Fred Steiner
Running Target	UA	Ernest Gold
Safari	AFR	William Alwyn
Samoa (short)	DIS	Oliver Wallace
Santiago	WB	David Buttolph
Scandal, Inc.	REP	Paul Sawtell Bert Shefter
The Scarlet Hour	PAR	Leith Stevens
Screaming Eagles	AA	Harry Sukman
The Search for Bridey Murphy	PAR	Irvin Talbot
The Searchers	WB	Max Steiner
Secret of Treasure Mountain	COL	Mischa Bakaleinikoff
Secrets of Life	DIS	Paul Smith
Secrets of the Reef	CON	Clinton Elliott
Seven Men from Now	WB	Henry Vars
Seven Wonders of the World	CIN	Emil Newman David Raksin Jerome Moross
Seventh Cavalry	COL	Mischa Bakaleinikoff
Shadow of Fear	UA	Leonard Salzedo
The Sharkfighters	UA	Jerome Moross
The Ship that Died of Shame (P. T. Raiders)	BRI	William Alwyn
Showdown at Abilene	UN	Joseph Gershenson
The Silent World	COL	Yves Baudrier
Simon and Laura	BRI	Benjamin Frankel
Slander	MGM	Jeff Alexander
Slightly Scarlet	RKO	Louis Forbes
The Solid Gold Cadillac	COL	Bronislau Kaper
The Sorceress	FRA	Norbert Glanzberg
Spin a Dark Web	COL	Richard Taylor
Stagecoach to Fury	TCF	Paul Dunlap
Star in the Dust	UN	Frank Skinner

Star of India	UA	Nino Rota
The Steel Jungle	WB	David Buttolph
Storm Center	COL	George Duning
Storm Fear	UA	Elmer Bernstein
Storm over the Nile	BRI	Benjamin Frankel
A Strange Adventure	REP	Dale R. Butts
Strange Intruder	AA	Paul Dunlap
Stranger at My Door	REP	Dale R. Butts
The Swan	MGM	Bronislau Kaper
Switzerland (short)	DIS	Paul Smith
T. N. P.	FRA	Maurice Jarre
Tea and Sympathy	MGM	Adolph Deutsch
The Teahouse of the August Moon	MGM	Saul Chaplin
Teenage Rebel	TCF	Leigh Harline
Tel Aviv Taxi	ISR	Edmund Halpern
The Ten Commandments	PAR	Elmer Bernstein
Tension at Table Rock	RKO	Dimitri Tiomkin
Terror at Midnight	REP	Dale R. Butts
That Certain Feeling	PAR	Joseph J. Lilley
There's Always Tomorrow	UN	Heinz Roemheld Ronald Stein
These Wilder Years	MGM	Jeff Alexander
Three Bad Sisters	UA	Paul Dunlap
Three for Jamie Dawn	AA	Walter Scharf
Three Violent People	PAR	Walter Scharf
Thunder over Arizona	REP	Dale R. Butts
Thunderstorm	AA	Paul Misraki
Timetable	UA	Walter Scharf
Toute le Memoire du Monde	FRA	Maurice Jarre
Toward the Unknown	WB	Paul Baron
Toy Tiger	UN	Joseph Gershenson
Track the Man Down	REP	Lambert Williamson
Trapeze	UA	Malcolm Arnold
Tribute to a Bad Man	MGM	Miklos Rozsa
23 Paces to Baker Street	TCF	Leigh Harline
The Unguarded Moment	UN	Herman Stein
Unidentified Flying Objects	UA	Ernest Gold
Uranium Boom	COL	Mischa Bakaleinikoff
The Vagabond King	PAR	Victor Young
I Vitelloni	ITA	Nino Rota
Walk the Dark Street	IND	Paul Dunlap
Walk the Proud Land	UN	Joseph Gershenson
War and Peace	PAR	Nino Rota
The Way Out	RKO	Richard Taylor
Wee Geordie	BRI	William Alwyn
The Werewolf	COL	Mischa Bakaleinikoff
Westward Ho, the Wagons	DIS	George Bruns
When Gangland Strikes	REP	Van Alexander
While the City Sleeps	RKO	Herschel Burke Gilbert
The White Reindeer	FIN	Einar Englund
The White Sheik	ITA	Nino Rota
The White Squaw	COL	Mischa Bakaleinikoff

The Wild Party	UA	Buddy Bregman
Wiretappers	CON	Ralph Carmichael
A Woman's Devotion	REP	Les Baxter
World in My Corner	UN	Joseph Gershenson
World without End	AA	Leith Stevens
Written on the Wind	UN	Frank Skinner
Yang Kwei Fei	JAP	Fumio Hayasaka
Yaqui Drums	AA	Edward J. Kay
You Can't Run Away from It	COL	George Duning
The Young Guns	AA	Imogen Carpenter
Zanzubuku	REP	Ivor Slaney

1957

The Abductors	TCF	Paul Glass
The Abominable Snowman	TCF	John Hollingsworth
Across the Bridge	BRI	James Bernard
Action of the Tiger	MGM	Humphrey Searle
Adam and Eve	IND	Gustavo C. Carreon
The Admirable Crichton	BRI	Douglas Gamley
The Adventures of * (short)	IND	Benny Carter Lionel Hampton
Affair in Havana	AA	Ernest Gold
Affair in Reno	REP	Dale R. Butts
An Affair to Remember	TCF	Hugo Friedhofer
Albert Schweitzer	IND	Alec Wilder
All Mine to Give	UN	Max Steiner
An Alligator Named Daisy	BRI	Stanley Black
The Amazing Colossal Man	AI	Albert Glasser
And God Created Woman	FRA	Paul Misraki
And Quiet Flows the Don	RUS	Yuri Levitin
Apache Warrior	TCF	Paul Dunlap
As Long as They're Happy	BRI	Stanley Black
Assault	FIN	Kalevi Hartti
Attack of the Crab Monsters	AA	Ronald Stein
The Baby and the Battleship	BRI	James Stevens Humphrey Searle
Baby Face Nelson	UA	Van Alexander Frank Spina
The Bachelor Party	UA	Paul Madeira
Back from the Dead	TCF	Raoul Kraushaar
The Badge of Marshal Brennan	AA	Ramez Idriss
Badlands of Montana	TCF	Irving Gertz
Bailout at 43,000	UA	Albert Glasser
Band of Angels	WB	Max Steiner
The Barretts of Wimpole Street	MGM	Bronislau Kaper
Beau James	PAR	Joseph J. Lilley
Bed of Grass	GRE	Manos Hadjidakis
La Bel Indifferent	FRA	Maurice Jarre
Bernardine	TCF	Lionel Newman
Beyond Mombasa	COL	Humphrey Searle
The Big Boodle	UA	Raul Lavista
The Big Caper	UA	Albert Glasser

The Big Land	WB	David Buttolph
Black Patch	WB	Jerry Goldsmith
The Black Scorpion	WB	Paul Sawtell
The Black Tent	BRI	William Alwyn
Blood of Dracula	AI	Paul Dunlap
Bombers B-52	WB	Leonard Rosenman
Bop Girl	UA	Les Baxter
Boy on a Dolphin	TCF	Hugo Friedhofer
Break in the Circle	TCF	Doreen Carwithen
The Bridge on the River Kwai	COL	Malcolm Arnold
The Brothers Rico	COL	George Duning
The Buckskin Lady	UA	Albert Glasser
The Burglar	COL	Sol Kaplan
The Buster Keaton Story	PAR	Victor Young
Cabaret	IND	Willi Schmidt-Centner
Calypso Heat Wave	COL	Paul Mertz Ross di Maggio
Calypso Joe	AA	Richard Hazzard
The Careless Years	UA	Leith Stevens
Cartouche	RKO	Bruce Montgomery
The Case of Dr. Laurent	FRA	Joseph Kosma
Checkpoint	BRI	Bruce Montgomery
Chicago Confidential	UA	Emil Newman
China Gate	TCF	Victor Young
The Colditz Story	COL	Francis Chagrin
The Confessions of Felix Krull	GER	Hans-Martin Majewski
The Congress Dances	REP	Werner Heymann
Copper Sky	TCF	Raoul Kraushaar
The Counterfeit Plan	WB	Richard Taylor
Courage of Black Beauty	TCF	Edward L. Alperson, Jr.
The Cranes Are Flying	RUS	Moisei Vainberg
Crazy for Love	FRA	Paul Misraki
Crime of Passion	UA	Paul Dunlap
The Crooked Circle	REP	Gerald Roberts
The Crucible	FRA	Georges Auric Hanns Eisler
The Curse of Frankenstein	WB	John Hollingsworth
Cyclops	AA	Albert Glasser
The D.I.	WB	David Buttolph
The Dalton Girls	UA	Les Baxter
Daughter of Dr. Jekyll	AA	Melvin Lenard
Deadlier than the Male	FRA	Jean Wiener
The Deadly Mantis	UN	William Lava
Death in Small Doses	AA	Emil Newman
Decision Against Time	MGM	Dock Mathieson
Decision at Sundown	COL	Heinz Roemheld
Deep Adventure	WB	Howard Jackson
The Deerslayer	TCF	Paul Sawtell Bert Shefter
The Delicate Delinquent	PAR	Buddy Bregman
Designing Woman	MGM	Andre Previn
Desk Set	TCF	Cyril J. Mockridge
Destination 60,000	AA	Albert Glasser

The Devil's Hairpin	PAR	Van Cleave
Dino	AA	Franz Waxman
The Disembodied	AA	Marlin Skiles
Doctor at Large	BRI	Bruce Montgomery
The Domino Kid	COL	Mischa Bakaleinikoff
Don Quixote	RUS	Kara Karayev
Don't Go Near the Water	MGM	Bronislau Kaper
Dragoon Wells Massacre	AA	Paul Dunlap
Drango	UA	Elmer Bernstein
Duel at Apache Wells	REP	Gerald Roberts
Edge of the City	MGM	Leonard Rosenman
8 x 8	IND	John Gruen Robert Abramson Hans Richter Douglas Townsend
Eighteen and Anxious	REP	Leith Stevens
Elevator to the Gallows	FRA	Miles Davis
Empire of the Sun	ITA	Francesco Lavagnino
The Enemy Below	TCF	Leigh Harline
Enemy from Space	UA	James Bernard
Escapade in Japan	UN	Max Steiner
Escape from San Quentin	COL	Laurindo Almeida
A Face in the Crowd	WB	Tom Glazer
A Farewell to Arms	TCF	Mario Nascimbene
Fear Strikes Out	PAR	Elmer Bernstein
The Fighting Wildcats	REP	Wilfred Burns
Fire Down Below	COL	Sir Arthur Benjamin
Five Steps to Danger	UA	Paul Sawtell
Footsteps in the Night	AA	Marlin Skiles
Forty Guns	TCF	Harry Sukman
Four Boys and a Gun	UA	Albert Glasser
From Hell It Came	AA	Darrell Calker
Funny Face	PAR	Adolph Deutsch
Fury at Sundown	UA	Harry Sukman
The Fuzzy Pink Nightgown	UA	Billy May
Garden of Eden	IND	Robert McBride
The Garment Jungle	COL	Leith Stevens
Gates of Paris	FRA	Georges Brassens
The Gentle Touch	BRI	Clifton Parker
Gervaise	FRA	Georges Auric
Ghost Diver	TCF	Paul Sawtell Bert Shefter
The Giant Claw	COL	Mischa Bakaleinikoff
The Girl in Black Stockings	UA	Les Baxter
The Girl in the Kremlin	UN	Joseph Gershenson
God Is My Partner	TCF	Paul Dunlap
The Green-Eyed Blonde	WB	Leith Stevens
The Green Man	BRI	Cedric Thorpe Davie
Il Grido	ITA	Giovanni Fusco
Gun Battle at Monterey	AA	Robert Wiley Miller
Gun Duel in Durango	UA	Paul Sawtell Bert Shefter
Gun for a Coward	UN	Joseph Gershenson

Gun Glory	MGM	Jeff Alexander
Gunfight at the O.K. Corral	PAR	Dimitri Tiomkin
Gunfire at Indian Gap	REP	Gerald Roberts
The Guns of Fort Petticoat	COL	Mischa Bakaleinikoff
Gunsight Ridge	UA	David Raksin
The Halliday Brand	UA	Stanley Wilson
The Happy Road	MGM	Georges van Parys
The Hard Man	COL	Mischa Bakaleinikoff
A Hatful of Rain	TCF	Bernard Herrmann
Heaven Knows, Mr. Allison	TCF	Georges Auric
Hell Bound	UA	Les Baxter
Hell Canyon Outlaws	REP	Irving Gertz
Hell on Devil's Island	TCF	Irving Gertz
Hell Ship Mutiny	REP	Paul Sawtell Bert Shefter
Hellcats of the Navy	COL	Mischa Bakaleinikoff
Hell's Crossroads	REP	Gerald Roberts
Hidden Fear	UA	Hans Schreiber
The Hired Gun	MGM	Albert Glasser
Hit and Run	UA	Franz Steininger
Hold that Hypnotist	AA	Marlin Skiles
L'Homme et l'Enfant	FRA	Jeff Davis
Hot Rod Rumble	AA	Alexander Courage
Hot Summer Night	MGM	Andre Previn
The House I Live In	RUS	Yuri Biryukov
House of Numbers	MGM	Andre Previn
How to Murder a Rich Uncle	COL	Kenneth V. Jones
The Hunchback of Notre Dame	AA	Georges Auric
I Was a Teenage Frankenstein	AI	Paul Dunlap
I Was a Teenage Werewolf	AI	Paul Dunlap
If All the Guys in the World	DIS	Georges van Parys
The Incredible Shrinking Man	UN	F. Carling Elliott Lawrence
Interlude	UN	Frank Skinner
The Invisible Boy	MGM	Les Baxter
The Iron Sheriff	UA	Emil Newman
Island in the Sun	TCF	Malcolm Arnold
Istanbul	UN	Joseph Gershenson
Jacqueline	BRI	Cedric Thorpe Davie
Jailhouse Rock	MGM	Jeff Alexander
Jamboree	WB	Otis Blackwell
The James Dean Story	WB	Leith Stevens
Jeanne Eagels	COL	George Duning
Jet Pilot	UN	Bronislau Kaper
Joe Butterfly	UN	Joseph Gershenson
Joe Dakota	UN	Joseph Gershenson
John and Julie	BRI	Philip Green
Johnny Tremain	DIS	George Bruns
Johnny Trouble	WB	Frank de Vol
The Joker Is Wild	PAR	Walter Scharf
Jonas	GER	Duke Ellington
Journey to Freedom	REP	Josef Zimanich
Jungle Heat	UA	Les Baxter

Kelly and Me	UN	Joseph Gershenson
The Kettles on Old MacDonald's Farm	UN	Joseph Gershenson
A King in New York	UA	Charles Chaplin
Kiss Them for Me	TCF	Lionel Newman
Kronos	TCF	Paul Sawtell Bert Shefter
Lady of Vengeance	UA	Phil Cardew
The Land Unknown	UN	Joseph Gershenson
Last of the Badmen	AA	Paul Sawtell
Last Stagecoach West	REP	Gerald Roberts
The Lawless Eighties	REP	Gerald Roberts
Legend of the Lost	UA	Francesco Lavagnino
Les Girls	MGM	Adolph Deutsch
Let's Be Happy	AA	Nicholas Brodzsky
The Light Across the Street	FRA	Norbert Glanzberg
The Little Hut	MGM	Robert Farnon
The Living Idol	MGM	Manuel Esperon Rudolfo Halffter
Lizzie	MGM	Leith Stevens
The Lonely Man	PAR	Van Cleave
The Long Haul	COL	Trevor Duncan
Looking for Danger	AA	Marlin Skiles
Lost Continent	ITA	Francesco Lavagnino
Love in the Afternoon	AA	Franz Waxman
Love Slaves of the Amazon	UN	Joseph Gershenson
Lovers and Thieves	FRA	Jean Francaix
Loving You	PAR	Walter Scharf
The Lower Depths	JAP	Masaru Sato
Lure of the Swamp	TCF	Paul Dunlap
Maid in Paris	FRA	Georges van Parys
Man Afraid	UN	Henry Mancini
The Man in the Road	REP	Philip Martell
Man in the Shadow	UN	Joseph Gershenson
Man of a Thousand Faces	UN	Frank Skinner
Man on Fire	MGM	David Raksin
Man on the Prowl	UA	Ernest Gold
The Man Who Turned to Stone	COL	Ross di Maggio
Men in War	UA	Elmer Bernstein
The Midnight Story	UN	Joseph Gershenson
The Miller's Beautiful Wife	ITA	Francesco Lavagnino
Mister Cory	UN	Joseph Gershenson
Monkey on My Back	UA	Paul Sawtell Bert Shefter
The Monolith Monsters	UN	Joseph Gershenson
The Monster that Challenged the World	UA	Heinz Roemheld
Motorcycle Gang	AI	Albert Glasser
Munna	IN	Anil Biswas
My Gun Is Quick	UA	Marlin Skiles
My Man Godfrey	UN	Frank Skinner
The Naked Eye	IND	Elmer Bernstein
Naked in the Sun	AA	Laurence Rosenthal

Night Passage	UN	Dimitri Tiomkin
The Night Runner	UN	Joseph Gershenson
The Night the World Exploded	COL	Ross di Maggio
Nights of Cabiria	ITA	Nino Rota
No Down Payment	TCF	Leigh Harline
No Time to Be Young	COL	Mischa Bakeleinikoff
Not of This Earth	AA	Ronald Stein
Notte Bianchi	ITA	Nino Rota
Oasis	FRA	Paul Misraki
Oedipus Rex	CAN	Cedric Thorpe Davie
Oh, Men! Oh, Women!	TCF	Cyril J. Mockridge
		Hugo Friedhofer
The Oklahoman	AA	Hans J. Salter
Old Yeller	DIS	Oliver Wallace
Omar Khayyam	PAR	Victor Young
On the Bowery	IND	Charles Mills
Operation Conspiracy	REP	Wilfred Burns
Operation Mad Ball	COL	George Duning
Ordet	DEN	Paul Shierbeck
Oregon Passage	AA	Paul Dunlap
The Ostrich Has Two Eggs	FRA	Henri Sauguet
Out of the Clouds	BRI	Richard Addinsell
Outlaw's Son	UA	Les Baxter
Panama Sal	REP	Gerald Roberts
Panic in the Parlor	BRI	Peter Akister
Pantaloons	FRA	Henri Sauguet
Paris Does Strange Things	FRA	Joseph Kosma
The Parson and the Outlaw	COL	Joe Sodja
Paths of Glory	UA	Gerald Fried
Pawnee	REP	Paul Sawtell
Perri	DIS	Paul Smith
The Persuader	AA	Ralph Carmichael
Peyton Place	TCF	Franz Waxman
The Phantom Stagecoach	COL	Mischa Bakaleinikoff
Pharaoh's Curse	UA	Les Baxter
Pickup Alley	COL	Richard Rodney Bennett
Please! Mr. Balzac	FRA	Paul Misraki
Plunder Road	TCF	Irving Gertz
Poor But Beautiful	ITA	Piero Morgan
Port of Desire	FRA	Jean Ledrut
Porte de Lilas	FRA	Georges Brassens
Portland Exposé	AA	Paul Dunlap
The Pride and the Passion	UA	George Anthiel
The Prince and the Showgirl	WB	Richard Addinsell
Professor Hannibal	HUN	Zdenko Tamassy
Public Pigeon No. 1	RKO	David Rose
Pursuit of the Graf Spee	BRI	Brian Easdale
Quantez	UN	Herman Stein
The Quiet Gun	TCF	Paul Dunlap
Raintree County	MGM	John Green
Raising a Riot	BRI	Bruce Montgomery
Rape on the Moor	GER	Werner Bochmann
Razzia	FRA	Marc Lanjean

Reach for the Sky	BRI	John Addison
Reform School Girl	AI	Ronald Stein
The Restless Breed	TCF	Raoul Kraushaar
Revolt at Fort Laramie	UA	Les Baxter
Rice	JAP	Yashushi Akutagawa
Ride a Violent Mile	TCF	Raoul Kraushaar
The Ride Back	UA	Frank de Vol
Ride Out for Revenge	UA	Leith Stevens
The Rising of the Moon	WB	Eammon O. Gallagher
The River's Edge	TCF	Louis Forbes
Rockabilly Baby	TCF	Paul Dunlap
Rodan	JAP	Akira Ifukube
Run of the Arrow	UN	Victor Young
Sabu and the Magic Ring	AA	Harry Sukman
The Sad Sack	PAR	Walter Scharf
Saint Joan	UA	Mischa Spoliansky
Sayonara	WB	Franz Waxman
Sea Wife	TCF	William Alwyn
Search for Paradise	CIN	Dimitri Tiomkin
Senechal the Magnificent	FRA	Paul Misraki
The Seventh Sin	MGM	Miklos Rozsa
Shadow on the Window	COL	George Duning
She Devil	TCF	Paul Sawtell Bert Shefter
The Ship Was Loaded	BRI	Philip Green
Shoot-Out at Medicine Bend	WB	Roy Webb
Short Cut to Hell	PAR	Irvin Talbot
Sierra Stranger	COL	Alexander Courage
Silk Stockings	MGM	Andre Previn
The Silken Affair	BRI	Peggy Stuart
Sins of Casanova	ITA	Francesco Lavagnino
The Sisters	RUS	Dmitri Kabalevsky
Slaughter on Tenth Avenue	UN	Richard Rodgers Herschel Burke Gilbert
Slim Carter	UN	Herman Stein
The Smallest Show on Earth	BRI	William Alwyn
Smiles of a Summer Night	SWE	Erik Nordgren
Smiley	AUT	William Alwyn
Something of Value	MGM	Miklos Rozsa
Sorority Girl	AI	Ronald Stein
The Spanish Gardener	BRI	John Veale
The Spirit of St. Louis	WB	Franz Waxman
Spoilers of the Forest	REP	Gerald Roberts
Spook Chasers	AA	Marlin Skiles
Spring Reunion	UA	Herbert Spencer Earle Hagen
Stella	GRE	Manos Hadjidakis
Stopover Tokyo	TCF	Paul Sawtell
The Storm Rider	TCF	Les Baxter
The Story of Esther Costello	COL	Georges Auric
The Story of Mankind	WB	Paul Sawtell
Stowaway Girl	PAR	William Alwyn
The Strange One	COL	Kenyon Hopkins

Street of Sinners	UA	Albert Glasser
The Sun Also Rises	TCF	Hugo Friedhofer
Sweet Smell of Success	UA	Elmer Bernstein
The Tall Stranger	AA	Hans J. Salter
The Tall T	COL	Heinz Roemheld
Tamango	FRA	Joseph Kosma
Taming Sutton's Gal	REP	Gerald Roberts
Tammy and the Bachelor	UN	Frank Skinner
Tarnished Angels	UN	Frank Skinner
Tarzan and the Lost Safari	MGM	Clifton Parker
The Tattered Dress	UN	Frank Skinner
Tears for Simon	REP	Benjamin Frankel
Teenage Doll	AA	Walter Greene
10,000 Bedrooms	MGM	George Stoll
That Night	UN	Mario Nascimbene
The Third Key	BRI	Gerard Schurmann
This Could Be the Night	MGM	George Stoll
This Is Russia	UN	Joseph Gershenson
Three Brave Men	TCF	Hans J. Salter
The Three Faces of Eve	TCF	Robert Emmett Dolan
3:10 to Yuma	COL	George Duning
Throne of Blood	JAP	Masaru Sato
Thunder over Tangier	REP	Wilfred Burns
The Tijuana Story	COL	Mischa Bakaleinikoff
Time Limit	UA	Fred Steiner
Time without Pity	BRI	Tristram Cary
The Tin Star	PAR	Elmer Bernstein
Tip on a Dead Jockey	MGM	Miklos Rozsa
Tomahawk Trail	UA	Les Baxter
Top Secret Affair	WB	Roy Webb
Torero!	COL	Rodolfo Halffter
A Town Like Alice	BRI	Matyas Seiber
Town on Trial	COL	Tristram Cary
Triple Deception	BRI	Hubert Clifford
Trooper Hook	UA	Gerald Fried
The True Story of Jesse James	TCF	Leigh Harline
The True Story of the Civil War (short)	IND	Ernest Gold
12 Angry Men	UA	Kenyon Hopkins
20 Million Miles to Earth	COL	Mischa Bakaleinikoff
The 27th Day	COL	Mischa Bakaleinikoff
Two Grooms for a Bride	TCF	Stanley Black
Under Fire	TCF	Paul Dunlap
Undersea Girl	AA	Alexander Courage
The Unearthly	REP	Henry Vars
The Unholy Wife	UN	Daniele Amfitheatrof
The Unknown Terror	TCF	Raoul Kraushaar
Untamed Youth	WB	Les Baxter
Until They Sail	MGM	David Raksin
Uomo de Paglia	ITA	Carlo Rustichelli
Up in Smoke	AA	Marlin Skiles
Utah Blaine	COL	Ross di Maggio
Valerie	UA	Albert Glasser

Value for Money	BRI	Malcolm Arnold
The Vampire	UA	Gerald Fried
Vel'D'Hiv	FRA	Maurice Jarre
Victoria and Her Hussar	GER	Mischa Spoliansky
The Vintage	MGM	David Raksin
The Violators	UN	Elliot Lawrence
Voodoo Island	UA	Les Baxter
Walk into Hell	AUT	Georges Auric
War Drums	UA	Les Baxter
The Way to the Gold	TCF	Lionel Newman
The Wayward Bus	TCF	Leigh Harline
The Wayward Girl	REP	Gerald Roberts
The Weapon	REP	James Stevens
Wicked as They Come	COL	Malcolm Arnold
Wild Is the Wind	PAR	Dimitri Tiomkin
Will Success Spoil Rock Hunter?	TCF	Cyril J. Mockridge
The Wings of Eagles	MGM	Jeff Alexander
The Winner's Circle	FRA	Rene Cloerec
Witness for the Prosecution	UA	Ernest Gold
Woman in a Dressing Gown	WB	Louis Levy
Woman of the River	COL	Francesco Lavagnino
The Wrestler and the Clown	RUS	Yuri Biryukov
The Wrong Man	WB	Bernard Herrmann
X the Unknown	WB	James Bernard
Young and Dangerous	TCF	Paul Dunlap
The Young Don't Cry	COL	George Anthiel
The Young Stranger	RKO	Leonard Rosenman
Zarak	COL	William Alwyn
Zero Hour!	PAR	Ted Dale
Zombies of Mora-Tau	COL	Mischa Bakaleinikoff

1958

The Accursed	AA	Jackie Brown
Age of Infidelity	SPA	Izidor Maiztegui
Ambush at Cimarron Pass	TCF	Paul Sawtell
		Bert Shefter
Andy Hardy Comes Home	MGM	Van Alexander
Anna Lucasta	UA	Elmer Bernstein
Another Time, Another Place	PAR	Douglas Gamley
Aparajito	IN	Ravi Shankar
Aren't We Wonderful?	GER	Franz Grothe
Atilla	ITA	Enzo Masetti
Attack of the 50-Foot Woman	AA	Ronald Stein
Auntie Mame	WB	Bronislau Kaper
Badman's Country	WB	Irving Gertz
Ballerina	GER	Herbert Windt
The Barbarian and the Geisha	TCF	Hugo Friedhofer
The Beast of Budapest	AA	Marlin Skiles
Beautiful But Dangerous	TCF	Renzo Rosellini
Bell, Book and Candle	COL	George Duning
The Bicyclist (short)	DEN	Bent Fabricius-Bjerre
The Big Beat	UN	Henry Mancini

The Big Country	UA	Jerome Moross
Bitter Victory	COL	Maurice la Roux
The Blob	PAR	Jean Yeaworth
Blood Arrow	TCF	Raoul Kraushaar
Blood of the Vampire	UN	Stanley Black
Blue Murder at St. Trinian's	BRI	Malcolm Arnold
Bonjour Tristesse	COL	Georges Auric
Boot Polish	IN	Shankar Jaikishan
The Bravados	TCF	Hugo Friedhofer Alfred Newman
The Bride and the Beast	AA	Les Baxter
The Bride Is Much Too Beautiful	FRA	Norbert Glanzberg
The Brothers Karamazov	MGM	Bronislau Kaper
The Buccaneer	PAR	Elmer Bernstein
Bullwhip	AA	Leith Stevens
The Camp on Blood Island	COL	Gerard Schurmann
Campbell's Kingdom	BRI	Clifton Parker
Carry On, Admiral	BRI	Philip Green
The Case Against Brooklyn	COL	Mischa Bakaleinikoff
Cattle Empire	TCF	Paul Sawtell Bert Shefter
A Certain Smile	TCF	Alfred Newman
Chase a Crooked Shadow	WB	Matyas Seiber
China Doll	UA	Henry Vars
Circus of Love	GER	Willi Schmidt-Gentner
Cole Younger, Gunfighter	AA	Marlin Skiles
The Colossus of New York	PAR	Van Cleave
The Confession of Ina Kahr	GER	Erwin Halletz
The Cool and the Crazy	AI	Raoul Kraushaar
Cop Hater	UA	Leith Stevens
Count Five and Die	TCF	John Wooldridge
Cowboy	COL	George Duning
Crash Landing	COL	Mischa Bakaleinikoff
Crime and Punishment	FRA	Maurice Thiriet
Cross-Up	UA	Stanley Black
The Cry-Baby Killer	AA	Gerald Fried
Cry Terror	MGM	Howard Jackson
Curse of the Demon	COL	Clifton Parker
Damn Citizen	UN	Henry Mancini
Dangerous Exile	BRI	Georges Auric
Dangerous Youth	WB	Stanley Black
Darby's Rangers	WB	Max Steiner
Day of the Bad Man	UN	Hans J. Salter
Deadly Decision	GER	Siegfried Franz
The Deep Six	WB	David Buttolph
The Defiant Ones	UA	Ernest Gold
Demoniaque	FRA	Joseph Kosma
Desert Hell	TCF	Raoul Kraushaar
Desire Under the Elms	PAR	Elmer Bernstein
Diamond Safari	TCF	Woolf Phillips
The Doctor's Dilemma	MGM	Joseph Kosma
A Dog, a Mouse and a Sputnik	FRA	Paul Misraki
Les Drageurs	FRA	Maurice Jarre

Dragstrip Riot	AI	Nicholas Carras
Dunkirk	MGM	Malcolm Arnold
L'Eau Vive	FRA	Guy Bearts
Enchanted Island	WB	Raul Lavista
Escape from Red Rock	TCF	Les Baxter
The Fearmakers	UA	Irving Gertz
The Female Animal	UN	Hans J. Salter
The Fiend Who Walked the West	TCF	Leon Klatzkin
Fincho	AFR	Alexander Laszlo
Flaming Frontier	TCF	John Bath
Flesh and Desire	FRA	Georges Auric
Flesh and the Woman	FRA	Georges van Parys
Flood Tide	UN	Henry Mancini William Lava
The Fly	TCF	Paul Sawtell
The Flying Classroom	GER	Hans-Martin Majewski
Folies Bergere	FRA	Philippe Gerard
Fort Bowie	UA	Les Baxter
Fort Dobbs	WB	Max Steiner
Fort Massacre	UA	Marlin Skiles
Frankenstein--1970	AA	Paul Dunlap
Fraulein	TCF	Daniele Amfitheatrof
From Hell to Texas	TCF	Daniele Amfitheatrof
From the Earth to the Moon	WB	Louis Forbes
Frontier Gun	TCF	Paul Dunlap
Gang War	TCF	Paul Dunlap
The Geisha Boy	PAR	Walter Scharf
Ghost of the China Sea	COL	Alexander Laszlo
The Gift of Love	TCF	Cyril J. Mockridge
Girl in the Woods	REP	Albert Glasser
Girl of the Mountains	GRE	Takis Morekis
The Goddess	COL	Virgil Thomson
God's Little Acre	UA	Elmer Bernstein
Guitars of Love	GER	Willy Mattes
Gun Fever	UA	Paul Dunlap
The Gun Runners	UA	Leith Stevens
Gunman's Walk	COL	George Duning
Guns, Girls and Gangsters	UA	Buddy Bregman
Gunsmoke in Tucson	AA	Sidney Cutner
The Gypsy and the Gentleman	BRI	Hans May
Handle with Care	MGM	Alexander Courage
Harry Black and the Tiger	TCF	Clifton Parker
The Haunted Strangler	MGM	Buxton Orr
He Who Must Die	FRA	Georges Auric
Head Against the Wall (The Keepers)	FRA	Maurice Jarre
Hell Drivers	BRI	Hubert Clifford
Hell's Five Hours	AA	Nicholas Carras
The High Cost of Loving	MGM	Jeff Alexander
High Flight	COL	Kenneth V. Jones
High Hell	PAR	Phil Cardew
Home Before Dark	WB	Franz Waxman
Hong Kong Affair	COL	Louis Forbes

Hong Kong Confidential	UA	Paul Sawtell Bert Shefter
Horror of Dracula	UN	John Hollingsworth
The Horse's Mouth	UA	Kenneth V. Jones
The Hot Angel	PAR	Richard Markowitz
Hot Car Girl	AA	Cal Tjader
Hot Spell	PAR	Alex North
The House on Haunted Hill	AA	Von Dexter
The House Under the Rocks	HUN	Istvan Sarkozi
Houseboat	PAR	George Duning
The Hunters	TCF	Paul Sawtell
I Accuse!	MGM	William Alwyn
I Bury the Living	UA	Gerald Fried
I Married a Woman	UN	Cyril J. Mockridge
I, Mobster	TCF	Gerald Fried
I Want to Live!	UA	Johnny Mandel
The Idiot	RUS	Nikolai Kryukov
In-Between Age	AA	Philip Green
In Love and War	TCF	Hugo Friedhofer
In the Money	AA	Marlin Skiles
Indiscreet	WB	Richard Rodney Bennett Kenneth V. Jones
The Inn of the Sixth Happiness	TCF	Malcolm Arnold
Inspector Maigret	FRA	Paul Misraki
Intent to Kill	TCF	Kenneth V. Jones
International Counterfeiters	REP	Herbert Trantow
Invisible Avenger	REP	Edward Dutrell
Island Women	UA	Boyd Raeburn
It! The Terror from Beyond Space	UA	Paul Sawtell Bert Shefter
Jet Attack	AI	Ronald Stein
Johnny Rocco	AA	Edward J. Kay
Joy Ride	AA	Marlin Skiles
Juvenile Jungle	REP	Gerald Roberts
Kathy O'	UN	Frank Skinner
The Keepers (see Head Against the Walls)		
The Key	COL	Malcolm Arnold
Kill Her Gently	COL	Edwin Astley
Kill Me Tomorrow	BRI	Temple Abady
King Creole	PAR	Walter Scharf
Kings Go Forth	UA	Elmer Bernstein
La Parisienne	UA	Hubert Rostaing
The Lady Takes a Flyer	UN	Herman Stein
Lafayette Escadrille	WB	Leonard Rosenman
The Last Blitzkrieg	COL	Hugo de Groot
The Last of the Fast Guns	UN	Joseph Gershenson
The Last Paradise	UA	Francesco Lavagnino
Law and Disorder	BRI	Humphrey Searle
The Left Handed Gun	WB	Alexander Courage
The Light in the Forest	DIS	Paul Smith
The Littlest Hobo	AA	Ronald Stein
The Lone Ranger and the Lost City of Gold	UA	Les Baxter

Lonely Hearts	UA	Conrad Salinger
The Long, Hot Summer	TCF	Alex North
Lost Lagoon	UA	Hubert Smith
The Lost Missile	UA	Gerald Fried
A Love Story	GER	Werner Eisbrenner
The Lovemaker	SPA	Joseph Kosma
Lucky Jim	BRI	John Addison
Macabre	AA	Les Baxter
Machete	UA	Paul Sawtell Bert Shefter
Mad Little Island	BRI	Cedric Thorpe Davie
Mailbag Robbery	BRI	Stanley Black
Mam'zelle Pigalle	FRA	Henri Crolla
The Man from God's Country	AA	Marlin Skiles
The Man Inside	COL	Richard Rodney Bennett
Man of the West	UA	Leigh Harline
Man or Gun	REP	Ramez Idriss
The Man Who Died Twice	REP	Gerald Roberts
The Man Who Walked Through the Wall	GER	Franz Grothe
Manhunt in the Jungle	WB	Howard Jackson
Maracaibo	PAR	Laurindo Almeida
Mardi Gras	TCF	Lionel Newman
Marjorie Morningstar	WB	Max Steiner
The Mark of the Hawk	UN	Matyas Seiber
The Matchmaker	PAR	Adolph Deutsch
The Mating Urge	IND	Stanley Wilson
Me and the Colonel	COL	George Duning
Menace in the Night	UA	Richard Rodney Bennett
Merry Andrew	MGM	Nelson Riddle
Missile Monsters	REP	Stanley Wilson
The Missouri Traveler	DIS	Jack Marshall
Mitsou	FRA	Georges van Parys
The Mugger	UA	Albert Glasser
Murder by Contract	COL	Perry Botkin
Murder Reported	COL	Reg Owen
My Uncle	FRA	Alain Romans Franck Barcellini
The Naked and the Dead	WB	Bernard Herrmann
Never Love a Stranger	AA	Raymond Scott
Next to No Time	BRI	Georges Auric
Night Ambush	BRI	Mikis Theodorakis
The Night Heaven Fell	FRA	Georges Auric
A Night to Remember	BRI	William Alwyn
1918	RUS	Dmitri Kabalevsky
No Place to Land	REP	Alec Compinsky
No Sun in Venice	ITA	John Lewis
No Time for Sergeants	WB	Ray Heindorf
The Notorious Mr. Monks	REP	Gerald Roberts
The Old Man and the Sea	WB	Dimitri Tiomkin
Once Upon a Horse	UN	Frank Skinner
The One that Got Away	BRI	Hubert Clifford
Onionhead	WB	David Buttolph

Orders to Kill	BRI	Benjamin Frankel
Outcasts of the City	REP	Harry Sukman
The Pagans	AA	Franco Ferrara
Paris Holiday	UA	Joseph J. Lilley
Party Girl	MGM	Jeff Alexander
The Perfect Furlough	UN	Frank Skinner
Portrait of an Unknown Woman	UN	Franz Grothe
The Proud Rebel	DIS	Jerome Moross
Quantrill's Raiders	AA	Marlin Skiles
Queen of Outer Space	AA	Marlin Skiles
The Quiet American	UA	Mario Nascimbene
Rally 'Round the Flag, Boys!	TCF	Cyril J. Mockridge
Raw Wind in Eden	UN	Hans J. Salter
The Rawhide Trail	AA	Andre S. Brummer
Reaching for the Stars	GER	Werner Eisbrenner
The Reluctant Debutante	MGM	Eddie Warner
The Restless Years	UN	Frank Skinner
The Return of Dracula	UA	Gerald Fried
Revenge of Frankenstein	COL	Leonard Salzedo
Rhapsody in Steel (short)	IND	Dimitri Tiomkin
Robbery Under Arms	BRI	Matyas Seiber
Rock-A-Bye Baby	PAR	Walter Scharf
Room 43	BRI	Kenneth V. Jones
Rooney	BRI	Philip Green
The Roots of Heaven	TCF	Malcolm Arnold
Rosemary	GER	Norbert Schultz
Run Silent, Run Deep	UA	Franz Waxman
Rx Murder	TCF	John Wooldridge
Saddle the Wind	MGM	Jeff Alexander
The Safecracker	MGM	Richard Rodney Bennett
St. Louis Blues	PAR	Nelson Riddle
Sans Famile	FRA	Paul Misraki
Satan's Satellites	REP	Stanley Wilson
Scotland Yard Dragnet	REP	Trevor Duncan
The Secret Place	BRI	Clifton Parker
Separate Tables	UA	David Raksin
Seven Guns to Mesa	AA	Leith Stevens
The Seven Hills of Rome	MGM	George Stoll
The 7th Voyage of Sinbad	COL	Bernard Herrmann
She Played with Fire	COL	William Alwyn
The Sheepman	MGM	Jeff Alexander
The Sheriff of Fractured Jaw	TCF	Robert Farnon
Showdown at Boot Hill	TCF	Albert Harris
Sierra Baron	TCF	Paul Sawtell Bert Shefter
The Silent Enemy	UN	William Alwyn
Sing, Boy, Sing	TCF	Lionel Newman
The Snorkel	COL	Francis Chagrin
Snowfire	AA	Albert Glasser
Some Came Running	MGM	Elmer Bernstein
South Seas Adventure	CIN	Alex North
The Space Children	PAR	Van Cleave
Space Master X-7	TCF	Josef Zimanich

A Spanish Affair	PAR	Daniele Amfitheatrof
Spy in the Sky	AA	Hugo de Groot
Stage Struck	DIS	Alex North
Stakeout on Dope Street	WB	Richard Markowitz
Stars	BUL	Simeon Pironkov
The Steel Bayonet	UA	Leonard Salzedo
The Story of Vickie	DIS	Anton Profes
The Strange Case of Dr. Manning	REP	John Bath
Street of Darkness	REP	Frank Worth
Suicide Battalion	AI	Ronald Stein
Summer Love	UN	Henry Mancini
A Tale of Two Cities	BRI	Richard Addinsell
Tank Force	COL	Kenneth V. Jones
Tarzan's Fight for Life	MGM	Ernest Gold
Teacher's Pet	PAR	Roy Webb
Tempestuous Love	GER	Herbert Trantow
Ten Days to Tulara	UA	Lan Adomian
Ten North Frederick	TCF	Leigh Harline
Terror in a Texas Town	UA	Gerald Fried
This Angry Age	COL	Nino Rota
This Happy Feeling	UN	Frank Skinner
Thunderbirds	REP	Victor Young
Thundering Jets	TCF	Irving Gertz
A Time to Love and a Time to Die	UN	Miklos Rozsa
Toccata for Toy Trains (short)	IND	Elmer Bernstein
Tom Thumb	MGM	Douglas Gamley Kenneth V. Jones
Tonka	DIS	Oliver Wallace
Too Much, Too Soon	WB	Ernest Gold
Touch of Evil	UN	Henry Mancini
Toughest Gun in Tombstone	UN	Paul Dunlap
The Truth About Women	BRI	Bruce Montgomery
Twilight for the Gods	UN	David Raksin
Uncle Vanya	CON	Werner Janssen
Underwater Warrior	MGM	Harry Sukman
Unwed Mother	AA	Emil Newman
Vertigo	PAR	Bernard Herrmann
The Vikings	UA	Mario Nascimbene
Villa!	TCF	Paul Sawtell Bert Shefter
Violent Road	WB	Leith Stevens
Voice in the Mirror	UN	Henry Mancini
War of the Satellites	AA	Walter Greene
What Price Murder	FRA	Paul Durand
When Hell Broke Loose	PAR	Albert Glasser
White Wilderness	DIS	Oliver Wallace
The Whole Truth	BRI	Mischa Spoliansky
The Wild Blue Yonder	REP	Victor Young
The Wild Fruit	FRA	Joseph Kosma
Windjammer	IND	Morton Gould
Windom's Way	BRI	James Bernard
Wink of an Eye	UA	Ernest Gold
Wishing Well Inn	BRI	Edwin Astley

Wolf Dog	TCF	John Bath
Wolf Larsen	AA	Paul Dunlap
Young and Wild	REP	Gerald Roberts
The Young Lions	TCF	Hugo Friedhofer
Your Past Is Showing	BRI	Stanley Black

1959

Al Capone	AA	David Raksin
Alaska Passage	TCF	Alex Alexander
Alias Jesse James	UA	Joseph J. Lilley
The Alligator People	TCF	Irving Gertz
Anatomy of a Murder	COL	Duke Ellington
The Angry Hills	MGM	Richard Rodney Bennett
Ask Any Girl	MGM	Jeff Alexander
Astero	GRE	Takis Morekis
The Atomic Submarine	AA	Alexander Laszlo
Aunt from Chicago	GRE	Takis Morekis
Back to the Wall	FRA	Richard Cornu
Baltic Express	POL	Andrej Trzaskowski
The Bandit of Zhobe	COL	Kenneth V. Jones
The Bat	AA	Louis Forbes
Battle Flame	AA	Marlin Skiles
Battle of the Coral Sea	COL	Ernest Gold
The Beat Generation	MGM	Albert Glasser
Behind the Great Wall	CON	Francesco Lavagnino
Beloved Infidel	TCF	Franz Waxman
Ben-Hur	MGM	Miklos Rozsa
The Best of Everything	TCF	Alfred Newman
The Big Circus	AA	Paul Sawtell Bert Shefter
The Big Fisherman	DIS	Albert Hay Malotte
The Big Operator	MGM	Van Alexander
The Black Orchid	PAR	Alessandro Cicognini
Bleak Morning	RUS	Dmitri Kabalevsky
Blood and Steel	TCF	Calvin Jackson
The Blue Angel	TCF	Hugo Friedhofer
Blue Denim	TCF	Bernard Herrmann
Born Reckless	WB	Buddy Bregman
Born to Be Loved	UA	Franz Steininger
The Bridal Path	BRI	Cedric Thorpe Davie
Broth of a Boy	IRE	Stanley Black
A Bucket of Blood	AI	Fred Katz
But Not for Me	PAR	Leith Stevens
Career	PAR	Franz Waxman
Carry on Sergeant	BRI	Bruce Montgomery
Cash McCall	WB	Max Steiner
Cast a Long Shadow	UA	Gerald Fried
The Chasers	FRA	Maurice Jarre
The Circle	BRI	Stanley Black
City After Midnight	RKO	Stanley Black
City of Fear	COL	Jerry Goldsmith
Compulsion	TCF	Lionel Newman

The Cosmic Man	AA	Paul Sawtell Bert Shefter
Count Your Blessings	MGM	Franz Waxman
Counterplot	UA	Paul Sawtell Bert Shefter
Crack in the Mirror	TCF	Maurice Jarre
Crime and Punishment, USA	AA	Herschel Burke Gilbert
The Crimson Kimono	COL	Harry Sukman
A Cry from the Streets	BRI	Larry Adler
Cry Tough	UA	Laurindo Almeida
Curse of the Undead	UN	Irving Gertz
Darby O'Gill and the Little People	DIS	Oliver Wallace
Day of the Outlaw	UA	Alexander Courage
The Devil's Disciple	UA	Richard Rodney Bennett
Diary of a High School Bride	AI	Ronald Stein
The Diary of Anne Frank	TCF	Alfred Newman
The Dog of Flanders	TCF	Paul Sawtell Bert Shefter
Don't Give Up the Ship	PAR	Walter Scharf
Edge of Eternity	COL	Daniele Amfitheatrof
Elephant Gun	BRI	James Bernard
Escort West	UA	Henry Vars
Eyes without a Face	FRA	Maurice Jarre
The F.B.I. Story	WB	Max Steiner
Face of a Fugitive	COL	Jerry Goldsmith
Face of Fire	AA	Erik Nordgren
Fires on the Plain	JAP	Yashushi Akutagawa
First Man into Space	MGM	Buxton Orr
Five Gates to Hell	TCF	Harry Gerstad
The Five Pennies	PAR	Leith Stevens
Floods of Fear	BRI	Alan Rawsthorne
The Flying Fontaines	COL	Mischa Bakaleinikoff
For the First Time	MGM	George Stoll
Forbidden Island	COL	Alexander Laszlo
4-D Man	UN	Ralph Carmichael
Four Fast Guns	UN	Alec Compinsky
The 400 Blows	FRA	Jean Constantin
The Four Skulls of Jonathan Drake	UA	Paul Dunlap
The Fugitive Kind	UA	Kenyon Hopkins
The Gazebo	MGM	Jeff Alexander
The Gene Krupa Story	COL	Leith Stevens
The Ghost of Dragstrip Hollow	AI	Ronald Stein
The Giant Behemoth	AA	Edwin Astley
Gideon of Scotland Yard	COL	Douglas Gamley
Gidget	COL	Morris Stoloff
Girls of the Night	FRA	Guy Magenta
Girl's Town	MGM	Val Alexander
Go, Johnny, Go	IND	Leon Klatzkin
The Great St. Louis Bank Robbery	UA	Bernardo Segall
Green Mansions	MGM	Heitor Villa-Lobos
The Gunfight at Dodge City	UA	Hans J. Salter
The H-Man	COL	Masaru Sato

A Handful of Grain	IN	Naushad
The Hanging Tree	WB	Max Steiner
The Hangman	PAR	Harry Sukman
Happy Anniversary	UA	Sol Kaplan
Happy Is the Bride	BRI	Benjamin Frankel
Harlem Wednesday (short)	IND	Benny Carter
Hatikvah	ISR	Moshe Wilinsky
Have Rocket, Will Travel	COL	Mischa Bakaleinikoff
Hercules	WB	Enzo Masetti
Here Come the Jets	TCF	Paul Dunlap
Heroes and Sinners	FRA	Louiguy
Hidden Homicide	REP	Otto Ferrari
A Hole in the Head	UA	Nelson Riddle
Holiday for Lovers	TCF	Leigh Harline
Horrors of the Black Museum	AI	Gerard Schurmann
The Horse Soldiers	UA	David Buttolph
Hound-Dog Man	TCF	Cyril J. Mockridge
The Hound of the Baskervilles	UA	James Bernard
The House of Intrigue	AA	Nino Rota
The House of the Seven Hawks	MGM	Clifton Parker
The Human Condition	JAP	Chuji Kinoshita
I Was Monty's Double	BRI	John Addison
Imitation of Life	UN	Frank Skinner
Island of Lost Women	WB	Raoul Kraushaar
It Happened to Jane	COL	George Duning
It Started with a Kiss	MGM	Jeff Alexander
The Jayhawkers	PAR	Jerome Moross
John Paul Jones	WB	Max Steiner
The Journey	MGM	Georges Auric
Journey to the Center of the Earth	TCF	Bernard Herrmann
Juke Box Rhythm	COL	Hal Belfer
Kapo	ITA	Carlo Rustichelli
King in Shadow	GER	Werner Eisbrenner
King of the Wild Stallions	AA	Marlin Skiles
The Last Angry Man	COL	George Duning
The Last Mile	UA	Van Alexander
The Last Train from Gun Hill	PAR	Dimitri Tiomkin
The Law Is the Law	CON	Nino Rota
The Legend of Tom Dooley	COL	Ronald Stein
The Letter that Was Never Sent	RUS	Nikolai Kryukov
Les Liaisons Dangereuses	FRA	Thelonius Monk Jack Murray
Libel	MGM	Benjamin Frankel
Li'l Abner	PAR	Nelson Riddle Joseph J. Lilley
Little Savage	TCF	Raul Lavista
Lone Texan	TCF	Paul Dunlap
Look Back in Anger	WB	John Addison
Love Is My Profession	FRA	Rene Cloerec
The Lovers	FRA	Alain de Rosnay
The Magician	SWE	Erik Nordgren
I Magliari	ITA	Piero Piccioni
La Main Chaude	FRA	Maurice Jarre

Maladetto Imbroglio	ITA	Carlo Rustichelli
The Man in the Net	UA	Hans J. Salter
The Man Who Could Cheat Death	PAR	Richard Rodney Bennett
The Man Who Understood Women	TCF	Robert Emmett Dolan
Masters of the Congo Jungle	TCF	Richard Cornu
The Mating Game	MGM	Jeff Alexander
Middle of the Night	COL	George Bassman
The Miracle	WB	Elmer Bernstein
The Miracle of the Hills	TCF	Paul Sawtell Bert Shefter
The Mirror Has Two Faces	FRA	Louiguy
Monika	SWE	Les Baxter
Monpti	GER	Bernard Eichhorn
The Most Wonderful Moment	ITA	Nino Rota
The Mouse that Roared	COL	Edwin Astley
The Mummy	UN	Franz Reisenstein
The Mustang	UA	Raoul Kraushaar
The Mysterians	JAP	Akira Ifukube
The Naked Maja	UA	Francesco Lavagnino
Never So Few	MGM	Hugo Friedhofer
Never Steal Anything Small	UA	Allie Wrubel
Night of the Quarter Moon	MGM	Albert Glasser
Nine Lives	NOR	Gunnar Sonstevold
No Name on the Bullet	UN	Herman Stein
No Trees in the Street	BRI	Laurie Johnson
North by Northwest	MGM	Bernard Herrmann
Nowhere to Go	MGM	Dizzy Reece
Nude in a White Car	FRA	Andre Gosselain
The Nun's Story	WB	Franz Waxman
O. S. S. 117	REP	Jean Marion
Odds Against Tomorrow	UA	John Lewis
On the Beach	UA	Ernest Gold
1001 Arabian Nights	COL	George Duning
Operation Petticoat	UN	David Rose
The Oregon Trail	TCF	Paul Dunlap
Paris Hotel	PAR	Paul Durand
Paris Weekend (short)	FRA	Edgar Bishoff
Pillow Talk	UN	Frank de Vol
Plunderers of Painted Flats	REP	Alec Compinsky
Pork Chop Hill	UA	Leonard Rosenman
Power Among Men	IND	Virgil Thomson
A Private's Affair	TCF	Cyril J. Mockridge
A Question of Adultry	BRI	Philip Green
The Rabbit Trap	UA	Jack Marshall
The Rebel Set	AA	Paul Dunlap
The Remarkable Mr. Pennypacker	TCF	Leigh Harline
Les Rendezvous du Diable	FRA	Marius-Francois Gaillard
The Rest Is Silence	GER	Bernhard Eichhorn
The Return of the Fly	TCF	Paul Sawtell
Ride Lonesome	COL	Heinz Roemheld
Rio Bravo	WB	Dimitri Tiomkin
Riot in Juvenile Prison	UA	Emil Newman
The Rookie	TCF	Paul Dunlap

Room at the Top	BRI	Mario Nascimbene
The Sad Horse	TCF	Paul Sawtell Bert Shefter
Sapphire	UN	Philip Green
Say One for Me	TCF	Lionel Newman
The Scapegoat	MGM	Bronislau Kaper
The Shaggy Dog	DIS	Paul Smith
Shake Hands with the Devil	UA	William Alwyn
Sign of the Gladiator	AI	Francesco Lavagnino
The Sins of Rose Bernd	GER	Herbert Windt
Sleeping Beauty	DIS	George Bruns
Smiley Gets a Gun	AUT	Wilbur Sampson
The Snow Queen	UN	Frank Skinner
Solomon and Sheba	UA	Mario Nascimbene
Some Like It Hot	UA	Adolph Deutsch
The Son of Robin Hood	TCF	Leighton Lucas
The Sound and the Fury	TCF	Alex North
Speaking of Murder	FRA	Denis Kieffer
Speed Crazy	AA	Richard LaSalle
Stephanie	GER	Georg Haentzschel
The Story on Page One	TCF	Elmer Bernstein
Stranger in My Arms	UN	Joseph Gershenson
Suddenly Last Summer	COL	Malcolm Arnold Buxton Orr
A Summer Place	WB	Max Steiner
Surrender--Hell!	AA	Francisco Buencamino
A Tailor's Maid	ITA	Alessandro Cicognini
Take a Giant Step	UA	Jack Marshall
I Tartassati	ITA	Pierro Piccioni
Tarzan, the Ape Man	MGM	Shorty Rogers
Tarzan's Greatest Adventure	PAR	Douglas Gamley
Tempest	PAR	Piero Piccioni
Ten Seconds to Hell	UA	Kenneth V. Jones
Terror Is a Man	IND	Ariston Auelino
That Kind of Woman	PAR	Van Cleave
These Thousand Hills	TCF	Leigh Harline
They Came to Cordura	COL	Elie Siegmeister
Third Man on the Mountain	DIS	William Alwyn
-30-	WB	Ray Heindorf
The 30-Foot Bride of Candy Rock	COL	Raoul Kraushaar
This Earth Is Mine	UN	Hugo Friedhofer
3 Men in a Boat	BRI	John Addison
Thunder in the Sun	PAR	Cyril J. Mockridge
Timbuktu	UA	Gerald Fried
The Tingler	COL	Von Dexter
Tokyo After Dark	PAR	Alexander Courage
The Trap	PAR	Irvin Talbot
The Two-Headed Spy	COL	Gerard Schurmann
Up Periscope	WB	Ray Heindorf
Verboten!	COL	Harry Sukman
Vice Raid	UA	Paul Sawtell Bert Shefter

The Violinist (short)	IND	Ernest Pintoff
Warlock	TCF	Leigh Harline
The Warrior and the Slave Girl	COL	Roberto Nicolosi
Web of Evidence	AA	Douglas Gamley
Westbound	WB	David Buttolph
The Wild and the Innocent	UN	Hans J. Salter
Woman Eater	COL	Edwin Astley
Woman Obsessed	TCF	Hugo Friedhofer
The Wonderful Country	UA	Alex North
The World of Apu	IN	Ravi Shankar
The World, the Flesh and the Devil	MGM	Miklos Rozsa
The Wreck of the Mary Deare	MGM	George Duning
Yellowstone Kelly	WB	Howard Jackson
The Young Captives	PAR	Richard Markowitz
The Young Land	COL	Dimitri Tiomkin
The Young Philadelphians	WB	Ernest Gold

1960

The Adventures of Huckleberry Finn	MGM	Jerome Moross
The Alamo	UA	Dimitri Tiomkin
All the Fine Young Cannibals	MGM	Jeff Alexander
All the Young Men	COL	George Duning
The Angel Wore Red	MGM	Bronislau Kaper
The Angry Silence	BRI	Malcolm Arnold
The Apartment	UA	Adolph Deutsch
As the Sea Rages	COL	Friedrich Meyer
Babette Goes to War	COL	Gilbert Becaud
Bad Boys	JAP	Toru Takemitsu
Ballad of a Soldier	RUS	Mikhail Siv
Battle in Outer Space	COL	Akira Ifukube
The Battle of the Sexes	BRI	Stanley Black
Because They're Young	COL	Johnny Williams
The Bellboy	PAR	Walter Scharf
Between Time and Eternity	UN	Bert Grund
Beyond the Time Barrier	AI	Darrel Calker
The Big Chief	FRA	Gerard Calvi
Big Deal on Madonna Street	ITA	Piero Umiliani
The Big Night	PAR	Richard LaSalle
Black Orpheus	BRA	Antonio Carlos Jobim Luiz Bonfa
Bluebeard's Ten Honeymoons	AA	Albert Elms
Bobbikins	TCF	Philip Green
The Boy and the Pirates	UA	Albert Glasser
The Boy Who Stole a Million	PAR	Tristram Cary
The Bramble Bush	WB	Leonard Rosenman
A Breath of Scandal	PAR	Alessandro Cicognini
The Brides of Dracula	BRI	Malcolm Williamson
The Bridge	AA	Hans-Martin Majewski
Butterfield 8	MGM	Bronislau Kaper
Cage of Evil	UA	Paul Sawtell
The Captain's Table	TCF	Frank Cordell

Carry on Nurse	BRI	Bruce Montgomery
Chance Meeting	PAR	Richard Rodney Bennett
Chartroose Caboose	UN	Darrell Calker
Che Gioia Vivere	ITA	Francesco Lavagnino
Cimarron	MGM	Franz Waxman
Cinderfella	PAR	Walter Scharf
Circus of Horrors	AI	Franz Reisenstein Muir Mathieson
College Confidential	UN	Dean Elliott
Comanche Station	COL	Mischa Bakaleinikoff
Come Dance with Me!	FRA	Henri Crolla
Conspiracy of Hearts	PAR	Francesco Lavagnino
The Cossacks	UN	Giovanni Fusco
The Crowded Sky	WB	Leonard Rosenman
The Dark at the Top of the Stairs	WB	Max Steiner
Day of the Painter (short)	IND	Eddy Manson
The Day They Robbed the Bank of England	MGM	Edwin Astley
Desert Attack	TCF	Leighton Lucas
Dinosaurus!	UN	Ronald Stein
Disorder in the Night	FRA	Jean Yatove
A Dog's Best Friend	UA	Paul Sawtell Bert Shefter
The Electronic Monster	COL	Richard Taylor
Elmer Gantry	UA	Andre Previn
The Enemy General	COL	Mischa Bakaleinikoff
The Entertainer	BRI	John Addison
Esther and the King	TCF	Francesco Lavagnino
Eugenie Grandet	RUS	V. Yurovsky
Exodus	UA	Ernest Gold
Expresso Bongo	BRI	Robert Farnon Norrie Paramor
The Facts of Life	UA	Leigh Harline
Farewell Doves	RUS	M. Fradkin
Fast and Sexy	COL	Alessandro Cicognini
Five Branded Women	PAR	Francesco Lavagnino
Flame over India	TCF	Mischa Spoliansky
For the Love of Mike	TCF	Raul Lavista
Freckles	TCF	Henry Vars
A French Mistress	BRI	John Addison
From the Terrace	TCF	Elmer Bernstein
G.I. Blues	PAR	Joseph J. Lilley
The Gallant Hours	UA	Roger Wagner
The Giant of Marathon	MGM	Roberto Nicolosi
Girl of the Night	WB	Sol Kaplan
The Goddess of Love	TCF	Michel Michelet
Goliath and the Dragon	AI	Les Baxter
The Grand Olympics	ITA	Francesco Lavagnino
The Great Imposter	UN	Henry Mancini
The Green Carnation	BRI	Ron Goodwin
Gunfighters of Abilene	UA	Paul Dunlap
Guns of the Timberland	WB	David Buttolph

Hand in Hand	COL	Stanley Black
Hannibal	WB	Carlo Rustichelli
Head of a Tyrant	UN	Carlo Savina
Heaven on Earth	ITA	Alberico Vitalini
Hell Bent for Leather	UN	William Lava
Hell Is a City	COL	Stanley Black
Hell to Eternity	AA	Leith Stevens
Heller in Pink Tights	PAR	Daniele Amfitheatrof
Hercules Unchained	WB	Enzo Masetti
Herod the Great	AA	Carlo Savina
High Time	TCF	Henry Mancini
Hiroshima, Mon Amour	FRA	Giovanni Fusco Georges Delerue
Home from the Hill	MGM	Bronislau Kaper
The House of Usher	AI	Les Baxter
The Hypnotic Eye	AA	Marlin Skiles
I Aim at the Stars	COL	Laurie Johnson
I Passed for White	AA	Johnny Williams
Ice Palace	WB	Max Steiner
I'm All Right, Jack	COL	Ron Goodwin
In the Wake of a Stranger	PAR	Edwin Astley
Inherit the Wind	UA	Ernest Gold
The Interview (short)	IND	Stan Getz
It Happened in Broad Daylight	CON	Bruno Canfora
It Started in Naples	PAR	Alessandro Cicognini
Jack the Ripper	PAR	Jimmy McHugh Pete Rugolo
Jazz Boat	COL	Kenneth V. Jones
Journey to the Lost City	AI	Michel Michelet
Jungle Cat	DIS	Oliver Wallace
Kapo	ITA	Carlo Rustichelli
Key Witness	MGM	Charles Wolcott
Kidnapped	DIS	Cedric Thorpe Davie
Killers of Kilimanjaro	COL	Muir Mathieson
Ladies' Man	FRA	Claude Bolling
The Lady with the Dog	RUS	N. Simonyan
The Last Days of Pompeii	UA	Francesco Lavagnino
The Last Voyage	MGM	Rudy Schrager
The Law	ITA	Roman Vlad
The Leech Woman	UN	Irving Gertz
Legions of the Nile	TCF	Renzo Rossellini
Let No Man Write My Epitaph	COL	George Duning
Let's Make Love	TCF	Lionel Newman
Lines Horizontal (short)	CAN	Pete Seeger
Little Angel	MEX	Raul Lavista
The Lost World	TCF	Paul Sawtell Bert Shefter
Love a la Carte	ITA	Piero Piccioni
Macumba Love	UA	Enrico Simonetti
Man on a String	COL	George Duning
The Man Who Wouldn't Talk	BRI	Stanley Black
The Many-Colored Paper (short)	IND	Pete Seeger
The Marriage-Go-Round	TCF	Dominic Frontiere

Michael Strogoff	CON	Serge Baudo
Midnight Lace	UN	Frank Skinner
The Mountain Road	COL	Jerome Moross
Murder, Inc.	TCF	Frank de Vol
Mumu	RUS	Alexei Muravlyov
The Music Box Kid	UA	Paul Sawtell Bert Shefter
My Dog Buddy	COL	Jack Marshall
Never on Sunday	GRE	Manos Hadjidakis
The Night Fighters	UA	Cedric Thorpe Davie
The Nights of Lucretia Borgia	COL	Alexander Derevitsky
North to Alaska	TCF	Lionel Newman
Nude Odyssey	ITA	Francesco Lavagnino
Ocean's 11	WB	Nelson Riddle
Oklahoma Territory	UA	Albert Glasser
One Foot in Hell	TCF	Dominic Frontiere
Operation Amsterdam	TCF	Philip Green
Oscar Wilde	BRI	Kenneth V. Jones
Othello	RUS	Aram Khachaturian
Pay or Die	AA	David Raksin
Pepe	COL	John Green
Phantom Lovers	ITA	Nino Rota
Platinum High School	MGM	Van Alexander
Please Don't Eat the Daisies	MGM	David Rose
Please Turn Over	COL	Bruce Montgomery
The Plunderers	AA	Leonard Rosenman
The Poacher's Daughter	IRE	Ivor Slaney
Pollyanna	DIS	Paul Smith
Portrait in Black	UN	Frank Skinner
Pretty Boy Floyd	CON	Del Serino William Sanford
Prisoner of the Volga	PAR	Norbert Glanzberg
The Private Lives of Adam and Eve	UN	Van Alexander
Psycho	PAR	Bernard Herrmann
The Purple Gang	AA	Paul Dunlap
The Pusher	UA	Raymond Scott
The Rat Race	PAR	Elmer Bernstein
Raymie	AA	Ronald Stein
The Rise and Fall of Legs Diamond	WB	Leonard Rosenman
S.O.S. Pacific	UN	Georges Auric
The Savage Innocents	PAR	Francesco Lavagnino
Scent of Mystery	IND	Mario Nascimbene
The Secret of the Purple Reef	TCF	Buddy Bregman
September Storm	TCF	Raoul Kraushaar
Serengeti Shall Not Die	AA	Wolfgang Zeller
Sergeant Rutledge	WB	Howard Jackson
Seven Thieves	TCF	Dominic Frontiere
Seven Ways from Sundown	UN	William Lava Irving Gertz
Sex Kittens Go to College	AA	Dean Elliott
The Shakedown	UN	Philip Green

The Sign of Zorro	DIS	William Lava
Sink the Bismark!	TCF	Clifton Parker
Sons and Lovers	TCF	Mario Nascimbene
Spartacus	UN	Alex North
Spring Affair	IND	Manuel Francisco
Squad Car	TCF	Hall Daniels
The Story of Ruth	TCF	Franz Waxman
Stowaway in the Sky	FRA	Jean Prodromides
Strangers When We Meet	COL	George Duning
The Stranglers of Bombay	COL	James Bernard
Studs Lonigan	UA	Jerry Goldsmith
The Subterraneans	MGM	Andre Previn
Sunrise at Campobello	WB	Franz Waxman
Surprise Package	COL	Benjamin Frankel
Swiss Family Robinson	DIS	William Alwyn
Tall Story	WB	Cyril J. Mockridge
Tarzan the Magnificent	PAR	Kenneth V. Jones
Ten Who Dared	DIS	Oliver Wallace
Tess of the Storm Country	TCF	Paul Sawtell Bert Shefter
The Testament of Orpheus	FRA	Georges Auric
The 3rd Voice	TCF	Johnny Mandel
13 Fighting Men	TCF	Irving Gertz
13 Ghosts	COL	Von Dexter
The 39 Steps	TCF	Clifton Parker
This Rebel Breed	WB	David Rose
The Threat	WB	Ronald Stein
Three Came to Kill	UA	Bert Shefter
The 3 Worlds of Gulliver	COL	George Duning
Thunder in Carolina	IND	Walter Greene
The Time Machine	MGM	Russell Garcia
Toby Tyler	DIS	Buddy Baker
Too Soon to Love	UN	Ronald Stein
Tormented	AA	Albert Glasser
A Touch of Larceny	PAR	Philip Green
Trapped in Tangiers	TCF	Lelio Luttazzi
Tunes of Glory	BRI	Malcolm Arnold
Twelve Hours to Kill	TCF	Paul Dunlap
12 to the Moon	COL	Michael Anderson
Under Ten Flags	PAR	Nino Rota
The Unforgiven	UA	Dimitri Tiomkin
Valley of the Redwoods	TCF	Buddy Bregman
The Village of the Damned	MGM	Ron Goodwin
The Virgin Spring	SWE	Erik Nordgren
A Visit to a Small Planet	PAR	Leigh Harline
The Wackiest Ship in the Army	COL	George Duning
Wake Me When It's Over	TCF	Cyril J. Mockridge
Walk Like a Dragon	PAR	Paul Dunlap
Walk Tall	TCF	Richard D. Aurandt
When Comedy Was King	TCF	Ted Royal
Where the Boys Are	MGM	George Stoll
Where the Hot Wind Blows (see The Law)		
Who Was that Lady?	COL	Andre Previn

Wild River	TCF	Kenyon Hopkins
The Wind Cannot Read	TCF	Francesco Lavagnino
The Wizard of Bagdad	TCF	Irving Gertz
A Woman Like Satan	UA	Jean Wiener
The World of Suzie Wong	PAR	George Duning
Young Jesse James	TCF	Irving Gertz

1961

The Absent-Minded Professor	DIS	George Bruns
Ada	MGM	Bronislau Kaper
Alakazam the Great	AI	Les Baxter
All Hands on Deck	TCF	Cyril J. Mockridge
All in a Night's Work	PAR	Andre Previn
All the Gold in the World	FRA	Georges van Parys
Angel Baby	AA	Wayne Shankin
Armored Command	AA	Bert Grund
Atlantis, the Lost Continent	MGM	Russell Garcia
L'Avventura	ITA	Giovanni Fusco
Babes in Toyland	DIS	George Bruns
Bachelor Flat	TCF	Johnny Williams
Bachelor in Paradise	MGM	Henry Mancini
Back Street	UN	Frank Skinner
Battle at Bloody Beach	TCF	Henry Vars
Beware of Children	AI	Bruce Montgomery
The Big Gamble	TCF	Maurice Jarre
The Big Show	TCF	Paul Sawtell
Bimbo the Great	WB	Theo Mackeben Klaus Orgermann
Black Sunday	AI	Les Baxter
Blast of Silence	UN	Meyer Kupferman
Blood and Roses	PAR	Jean Prodromides
Blue Hawaii	PAR	Joseph J. Lilley
Blueprint for Robbery	PAR	Van Cleave
The Boy Who Caught a Crook	UA	Richard La Salle
Brainwashed	AA	Hans-Martin Majewski
Breakfast at Tiffany's	PAR	Henry Mancini
Bridge to the Sun	MGM	Georges Auric
Buddenbrooks (Part I)	GER	Werner Eisbrenner
Buddenbrooks (Part II)	GER	Werner Eisbrenner
By Love Possessed	UA	Elmer Bernstein
The Canadians	TCF	Ken Darby
Carthage in Flames	COL	Mario Nascimbene
The Cat Burglar	UA	Buddy Bregman
Circle of Deception	TCF	Clifton Parker
Claudelle Inglish	WB	Howard Jackson
A Cold Wind in August	IND	Gerald Fried
The Colossus of Rhodes	MGM	Francesco Lavagnino
The Comancheros	TCF	Elmer Bernstein
Come September	UN	Hans J. Salter
The Cow and I	FRA	Paul Durand
Cry for Happy	COL	George Duning
Cry Freedom	PHI	Restie Umali

The Curse of the Werewolf	UN	Benjamin Frankel
David and Goliath	AA	Carlo Innocenzi
Days of Thrills and Laughter	TCF	Jack Shaindlin
The Deadly Companions	IND	Marlin Skiles
Desert Patrol	BRI	Clifton Parker
Devi	IN	Alik Akbar Khan
The Devil at 4 O'Clock	COL	George Duning
Doctor Blood's Coffin	UA	Buxton Orr
La Dolce Vita	ITA	Nino Rota
Dondi	AA	Earl Schuman
Double Bunk	BRI	Stanley Black
El Cid	AA	Miklos Rozsa
Everything's Ducky	COL	Bernard Green
The Explosive Generation	UA	Francesco Lavagnino
The Fabulous World of Jules Verne	WB	Sydney Fox
Fadila (short)	AFR	Alain Romans
Fanny	WB	Harold Rome
Ferry to Hong Kong	TCF	Kenneth V. Jones
A Fever in the Blood	WB	Ernest Gold
The Fiercest Heart	TCF	Irving Gertz
Five Golden Hours	COL	Stanley Black
Five Guns to Tombstone	UA	Paul Sawtell Bert Shefter
Flight of the Lost Balloon	IND	Hal Borne
The Flight that Disappeared	UA	Richard La Salle
For Better, for Worse (short)	BRI	Matyas Seiber
Foxhole in Cairo	PAR	Wolfram Roehrig
Francis of Assisi	TCF	Mario Nascimbene
From a Roman Balcony	ITA	Piero Piccioni
Frontier Uprising	UA	Paul Sawtell Bert Shefter
The George Raft Story	AA	Jeff Alexander
Gidget Goes Hawaiian	COL	George Duning
Go Naked into the World	MGM	Adolph Deutsch
Gold of the Seven Saints	WB	Howard Jackson
Goodbye Again	UA	Georges Auric
Gorgo	MGM	Francesco Lavagnino
The Great War	ITA	Nino Rota
The Green Helmet	MGM	Kenneth V. Jones
Greyfriar's Bobby	DIS	Francis Chagrin
The Guns of Navarone	COL	Dimitri Tiomkin
The Head	GER	Willy Mattes Jacques Lasry
Hey, Let's Twist	PAR	Henry Glover
Hippodrome	GER	Bert Grund
Homicidal	COL	Hugo Friedhofer
The Honeymoon Machine	MGM	Leigh Harline
The Hoodlum Priest	UA	Richard Markowitz
House of Fright	AI	Monty Norman David Henneker
The Hustler	TCF	Dan Terry
The Innocents	TCF	Georges Auric

Invasion Quartet	MGM	Ron Goodwin
The Island	JAP	Hikaru Hayashi
The Joker	FRA	Georges Delerue
Judgment at Nuremberg	UA	Ernest Gold
King of Kings	MGM	Miklos Rozsa
Knife in the Water	POL	Kryzstof Komeda
Konga	AI	Gerard Schurmann
The Ladies' Man	PAR	Walter Scharf
The Last Judgment	ITA	Alessandro Cicognini
The Last Sunset	UN	Ernest Gold
The Last Time I Saw Archie	UA	Frank Comstock
Last Year at Marienbad	FRA	Francis Seyrig
Left, Right and Center	BRI	Humphrey Searle
The Little Shepherd of Kingdom Come	TCF	Henry Vars
Lola	FRA	Michel Legrand
The Long Rope	TCF	Paul Sawtell Bert Shefter
Look in Any Window	AA	Richard Shores
Loss of Innocence	COL	Richard Addinsell
Love and the Frenchwoman	FRA	Jean Constantin Henri Crolla Georges Delerue Norbert Glanzberg Joseph Kosma Jacques Metehen Paul Misraki
Love in a Goldfish Bowl	PAR	Jimmie Haskell
Lover Come Back	UN	Frank de Vol
Macbeth	BRI	Richard Addinsell
Mad Dog Coll	COL	Stu Philips
Maeva	FRA	Teiji Ito
A Majority of One	WB	Max Steiner
Man in the Moon	BRI	Philip Green
Man-Trap	PAR	Leith Stevens
Marines, Let's Go	TCF	Irving Gertz
The Mark	CON	Richard Rodney Bennett
The Mask	WB	Louis Applebaum
Master of the World	AI	Les Baxter
A Matter of Morals	UA	Dag Wiren
The Millionairess	TCF	Georges van Parys
The Minotaur	UA	Carlo Rustichelli
The Misfits	UA	Alex North
Mr. Sardonicus	COL	Von Dexter
Misty	TCF	Paul Sawtell
Morgan the Pirate	MGM	Franco Mannino
The Most Dangerous Man Alive	COL	Louis Forbes
Mysterious Island	COL	Bernard Herrmann
The Naked Edge	UA	William Alwyn
The New Angels	ITA	Piero Umiliani
Night Affair	FRA	Jean Yatove
Nikki, Wild Dog of the North	DIS	Oliver Wallace
Nine Days of One Year	RUS	D. Ter-Tatevosian

The Ninth Circle	RUS	Branimin Sakac
No Love for Johnnie	BRI	Malcolm Arnold
Notte Brava	ITA	Piero Piccione
Ole Rex	UN	Donald Bagley William Hinshaw
On the Double	PAR	Leith Stevens
One-Eyed Jacks	PAR	Hugo Friedhofer
One Hundred and One Dalmations	DIS	George Bruns
1 Plus 1	CAN	John Bath
One, Two, Three	UA	Andre Previn
Operation Eichmann	AA	Alex Alexander
The Outsider	UN	Leonard Rosenman
The Parent Trap	DIS	Paul Smith
Paris Blues	UA	Duke Ellington
Parrish	WB	Max Steiner
The Passion of Slow Fire	FRA	Georges Delerue
Passport to China	COL	Edwin Astley
Le Pave De Paris	FRA	Joseph Kosma
The Pharaoh's Woman	UN	Giovanni Fusco
Pirates of Tortuga	TCF	Paul Sawtell Bert Shefter
The Pit and the Pendulum	AI	Les Baxter
The Pleasure of His Company	PAR	Alfred Newman
Pocketful of Miracles	UA	Walter Scharf
Portrait of a Mobster	WB	Max Steiner
Posse from Hell	UN	Joseph Gershenson
The Proper Time	IND	Shelly Manne
Purple Noon	FRA	Nino Rota
Question 7	GER	Hans-Martin Majewski
A Raisin in the Sun	COL	Lawrence Rosenthal
Return to Peyton Place	TCF	Franz Waxman
The Revenge of Don Mendo	SPA	Rafael de Andres
The Revolt of the Slaves	UA	Francesco Lavagnino
The Right Approach	TCF	Dominic Frontiere
Ring of Fire	MGM	Duane Eddy
The Risk	BRI	John Wilkes
The Roman Spring of Mrs. Stone	WB	Richard Addinsell
Romanoff and Juliet	UA	Mario Nascimbene
Sail a Crooked Ship	COL	George Duning
Sanctuary	TCF	Alex North
Scream of Fear	COL	Clifton Parker
Season of Passion	UA	Benjamin Frankel
The Second Time Around	TCF	Gerald Fried
Secret of Deep Harbor	UA	Richard La Salle
The Secret of Monte Cristo	MGM	Clifton Parker
The Secret Partner	MGM	Philip Green
The Secret Ways	UN	Johnny Williams
7 Women from Hell	TCF	Paul Dunlap
The Shadow of the Cat	UN	Mikis Theodorakis
Shadows	IND	Charles Mingus
The Silent Call	TCF	Richard D. Aurandt
The Singer Not the Song	WB	Philip Green
The Sins of Rachel Cade	WB	Max Steiner

The Snake Woman	UA	Buxton Orr
Sniper's Ridge	TCF	Richard La Salle
Something Wild	UA	Aaron Copland
Splendor in the Grass	WB	David Amram
The Steel Claw	WB	Harry Zimmerman
Stop Me Before I Kill	COL	Stanley Black
Summer and Smoke	PAR	Elmer Bernstein
Sun and Shadow	BUL	Simeon Pironkov
Susan Slade	WB	Max Steiner
Sword of Sherwood Forest	COL	Stanley Black
Tammy Tell Me True	UN	Percy Faith
The Teacher and the Miracle	ITA	Carlo Innocenzi
Terror of the Tongs	COL	James Bernard
Therese Desqueryoux	FRA	Maurice Jarre
They Were 10	ISR	Gari Bertini
Thief of Bagdad	MGM	Carlo Rustichelli
Three on a Spree	UA	Philip Martell
A Thunder of Drums	MGM	Harry Sukman
Time Bomb	AA	Henri Crolla
Tomboy and the Champ	UN	Richard Shores
Town without Pity	UA	Dimitri Tiomkin
The Trapp Family	TCF	Franz Grothe
Trouble in the Sky	UN	Gerald Schurmann
The Trunk	COL	John Fox
The Truth	FRA	J. Tremble
Twenty Plus Two	AA	Gerald Fried
20,000 Eyes	TCF	Albert Glasser
The Two Little Bears	TCF	Henry Vars
Two Loves	MGM	Bronislau Kaper
Two Rode Together	COL	George Duning
Two Way Stretch	BRI	Kenneth V. Jones
Two Women	ITA	Armando Trovajoli
Underworld, U.S.A.	COL	Harry Sukman
Upstairs and Downstairs	TCF	Philip Green
Valley of the Dragons	COL	Ruby Raskin
Violin and Roller	RUS	Byechesav Ovchinnikov
Voyage to the Bottom of the Sea	TCF	Paul Sawtell
Walk the Angry Beach	IND	Bill Marx
The Warrior Empress	COL	Francesco Lavagnino
Watch Your Stern	BRI	Bruce Montgomery
A Weekend with Lulu	COL	Tony Osborne
When the Clock Strikes	UA	Richard La Salle
The White Warrior	WB	Robert Nicolosi
Wild in the Country	TCF	Kenyon Hopkins
Wings of Chance	UN	Michael Andersen
The Wonders of Aladdin	MGM	Francesco Lavagnino
The World by Night	WB	Piero Piccioni
X-15	UA	Nathan Scott
Yojimbo	JAP	Masaru Sato
You Have to Run Fast	UA	Richard La Salle
The Young Doctors	UA	Elmer Bernstein
The Young Savages	UA	David Amram

1962

Advise and Consent	COL	Jerry Fielding
Air Patrol	TCF	Albert Glasser
Aliki My Love	GRE	Manos Hadjidakis
All Fall Down	MGM	Alex North
Antigone	GRE	Arghyris Kounadis
Barabbas	COL	Mario Nascimbene
The Bashful Elephant	AA	Ronald Stein
Bell'Antonio	ITA	Piero Piccioni
Belle Somers	COL	Harry Sukman
The Best of Enemies	COL	Nino Rota
Big Red	DIS	Oliver Wallace
The Big Wave	AA	Toshiro Mayazumi
Billy Budd	AA	Anthony Hopkins
Billy Rose's Jumbo (see Jumbo)		
Bird Man of Alcatraz	UA	Elmer Bernstein
Boccaccio '70	ITA	Nino Rota
Bon Voyage	DIS	Paul Smith
The Boys	BRI	The Shadows
Boy's Night Out	MGM	Frank de Vol
The Broken Land	TCF	Richard La Salle
Brushfire	PAR	Irving Gertz
Burn Witch Burn	AI	William Alwyn
The Cabinet of Caligari	TCF	Gerald Fried
Cape Fear	UN	Bernard Herrmann
Cash on Demand	COL	Wilfred Josephs
The Chapman Report	WB	Leonard Rosenman
The Children's Hour	UA	Alex North
Cleo from 5 to 7	FRA	Michel Legrand
A Coming-Out Party	BRI	Reg Owen
The Concrete Jungle	BRI	John Dankworth
Confessions of an Opium Eater	AA	Albert Glasser
The Connection	IND	Freddie Redd
Constantine and the Cross	ITA	Mario Nascimbene
Convicts 4	AA	Leonard Rosenman
The Couch	WB	Frank Perkins
The Counterfeit Traitor	PAR	Alfred Newman
Court Martial	UA	Werner Eisbrenner
Crime Does Not Pay	FRA	Georges Delerue
Damn the Defiant!	COL	Clifton Parker
Damon and Pythias	MGM	Francesco Lavagnino
The Day the Earth Caught Fire	UN	Stanley Black
Days of Wine and Roses	WB	Henry Mancini
Dead to the World	UA	Charlie Byrd
Deadly Duo	UA	Richard La Salle
Diamond Head	COL	Johnny Williams
Divorce--Italian Style	ITA	Carlo Rustichelli
Doctor in Love	BRI	Bruce Montgomery
Eclipse	ITA	Giovanni Fusco
The End of Belle	FRA	Georges Delerue
End of Desire	FRA	Roman Vlad
The Errand Boy	PAR	Walter Scharf

Escape from East Berlin	MGM	Hans-Martin Majewski
Escape from Zahrain	PAR	Lyn Murray
Everybody Go Home!	ITA	Francesco Lavagnino
Experiment in Terror	COL	Henry Mancini
The Firebrand	TCF	Richard La Salle
Five Finger Exercise	COL	Jerome Moross
Five Weeks in a Balloon	TCF	Paul Sawtell
The Flying Man (short)	BRI	Ron Goodwin
Follow that Dream	UA	Hans J. Salter
Forever My Love	PAR	Anton Profes
40 Pounds of Trouble	UN	Mort Lindsay
The Four Horsemen of the Apocalypse	MGM	Andre Previn
Freud	UN	Jerry Goldsmith
The Frightened City	AA	Norrie Paramor
Geronimo	UA	Hugo Friedhofer
Gigot	TCF	Jackie Gleason
A Girl Named Tamiko	PAR	Elmer Bernstein
The Girl with the Golden Eyes	FRA	Narciso Yepes
Girls! Girls! Girls!	PAR	Joseph J. Lilley
The Given Word	BRA	Gabriel Migliori
Gun Street	UA	Richard La Salle
Guns of Darkness	WB	Benjamin Frankel
Gypsy	WB	Frank Perkins
Hand of Death	TCF	Sonny Burke
Hands of a Stranger	AA	Richard La Salle
The Happy Thieves	UA	Mario Nascimbene
Harold Lloyd's World of Comedy	CON	Walter Scharf
Hatari!	PAR	Henry Mancini
Hell Is for Heroes	PAR	Leonard Rosenman
The Hellions	COL	Larry Adler
Hemmingway's Adventures of a Young Man	TCF	Franz Waxman
Hero's Island	UA	Dominic Frontiere
Hitler	AA	Hans J. Salter
The Horizontal Lieutenant	MGM	George Stoll
House of Women	WB	Howard Jackson
How the West Was Won	MGM	Alfred Newman
I Hate Your Guts	IND	Herman Stein
I Like Money	TCF	Georges van Parys
I Thank a Fool	MGM	Gail Kubik
If a Man Answers	UN	Hans J. Salter
The Important Man	MEX	Raul Lavista
In Search of the Castaways	DIS	William Alwyn
Incident in an Alley	UA	Richard La Salle
Information Received	UN	Martin Slavin
The Interns	COL	Leith Stevens
It Happened in Athens	TCF	Manos Hadjidakis
It's Only Money	PAR	Walter Scharf
Jack the Giant Killer	UA	Paul Sawtell Bert Shefter
Jessica	UA	Mario Nascimbene
Joan of the Angels?	POL	Adam Walacinski

Film	Studio	Composer
Joseph and His Brethren	ITA	Mario Nascimbene
Jumbo	MGM	George Stoll
Kid Galahad	UA	Jeff Alexander
Kill or Cure	MGM	Ron Goodwin
A Kind of Loving	BRI	Ron Grainer
Lad: A Dog	WB	Heinz Roemheld
Lawrence of Arabia	COL	Maurice Jarre
A Lecture on Man (short)	BRI	Tristram Cary
The Legend of Lobo	DIS	Oliver Wallace
Light in the Piazza	MGM	Mario Nascimbene
The Lion	TCF	Malcolm Arnold
Lisa	TCF	Malcolm Arnold
Lolita	MGM	Nelson Riddle
The Loneliness of the Long-Distance Runner	BRI	John Addison
Lonely Are the Brave	UN	Jerry Goldsmith
Long Day's Journey into Night	EMB	Andre Previn
The Longest Day	TCF	Maurice Jarre
The Lovers of Tereul	FRA	Mikis Theodorakis
Madison Avenue	TCF	Harry Sukman
The Magic Sword	UA	Richard Markowitz
Make Way for Lila	SWE	Lars-Erik Larsson
Malaga	WB	Matyas Seiber
The Man Who Shot Liberty Valance	PAR	Cyril J. Mockridge
The Manchurian Candidate	UA	David Amram
Marco Polo	AI	Les Baxter Francesco Lavagnino
A Matter of Who	BRI	Edwin Astley
Merrill's Marauders	WB	Howard Jackson
A Midsummer Night's Dream	CZE	Vaclav Trojan
The Mighty Ursus	UA	Roman Vlad
A Milanese Story	ITA	John Lewis
The Miracle Worker	UA	Laurence Rosenthal
Mr. Arkadin	IND	Paul Misraki
Mr. Hobbs Takes a Vacation	TCF	Henry Mancini
Moon Pilot	DIS	Paul Smith
Mothra	COL	Yuji Koseki
Murder She Said	MGM	Ron Goodwin
Mutiny on the Bounty	MGM	Bronislau Kaper
My Geisha	PAR	Franz Waxman
Nearly a Nasty Accident	BRI	Kenneth V. Jones
Night Creatures	UN	Don Banks
Night Is My Future	SWE	Erland von Koch
No Exit	ARG	Vladimir Ussachevsky
No Man Is an Island	UN	Restie Umali
No Place Like Homicide	BRI	Muir Mathieson
The Notorious Landlady	COL	George Duning
The Nun and the Sergeant	UA	Jerry Fielding
An Occurrence at Owl Creek Bridge (short)	FRA	Henri Lanoe
Only Two Can Play	COL	Richard Rodney Bennett
Operation Snatch	CON	Kenneth V. Jones

Panic in Year Zero	AI	Les Baxter
Payroll	AA	Reg Owen
Period of Adjustment	MGM	Lyn Murray
Phaedra	GRE	Mikis Theodorakis
The Phantom of the Opera	UN	Edwin Astley
The Pigeon that Took Rome	PAR	Alessandro Cicognini
The Pirates of Blood River	COL	Gary Hughes
La Poupee	FRA	Joseph Kosma
Premature Burial	AI	Ronald Stein
Pressure Point	UA	Ernest Gold
The Prisoner of the Iron Mask	AI	Carlo Innocenzi
Psycosissimo	ITA	Carlo Rustichelli
The Quare Fellow	IRE	Alexander Faris
The Reluctant Saint	ITA	Nino Rota
Requiem for a Heavyweight	COL	Laurence Rosenthal
Ride the High Country	MGM	George Bassman
The Road to Hong Kong	UA	Robert Farnon
Rome Adventure	WB	Max Steiner
Romeo (short)	RUS	Sergei Prokofiev
Safe at Home!	COL	Van Alexander
Saintly Sinners	UA	Richard La Salle
Samar	WB	Harry Zimmerman
Satan in High Heels	IND	Mundell Lowe
Satan Never Sleeps	TCF	Richard Rodney Bennett
The Savage Guns	MGM	Anton Garcia Abril
The Seducers	IND	Mort Lindsay
Sergeants 3	UA	Billy May
7 Capital Sins	FRA	Michel Legrand
Shoot the Piano Player	FRA	Georges Delerue
The Siege of Syracuse	PAR	Francesco Lavagnino
Six Black Horses	UN	Joseph Gershenson
The Small Hours	IND	Danny Hart
The Spiral Road	UN	Jerry Goldsmith
Stagecoach to Dancer's Rock	UN	Franz Steininger
The Story of the Count of Monte Cristo	WB	Rene Cloerec
Strangers in the City	ITA	Robert Prince
Sundays and Cybele	FRA	Maurice Jarre
Sweet Bird of Youth	MGM	Harold Gelman
Sword of the Conqueror	UA	Carlo Rustichelli
Swordsman of Siena	MGM	Mario Nascimbene
Tales of Paris	FRA	Georges Garvarentz
Taras Bulba	UA	Franz Waxman
The Tartars	MGM	Renzo Rossellini
Tarzan Goes to India	MGM	Kenneth V. Jones
A Taste of Honey	BRI	John Addison
Tender Is the Night	TCF	Bernard Herrmann
The Testament of Dr. Cordelier	FRA	Joseph Kosma
That Touch of Mink	UN	George Duning
Third of a Man	UN	Samuel Matlovsky
13 West Street	COL	George Duning
The 300 Spartans	TCF	Manos Hadjidakis
The Three Stooges in Orbit	COL	Paul Dunlap

The Three Stooges Meet Hercules	COL	Paul Dunlap
To Kill a Mockingbird	UN	Elmer Bernstein
Too Late Blues	PAR	David Raksin
Tower of London	UA	Michael Andersen
Trial and Error	MGM	Kenny Ball
Two for the Seesaw	UA	Andre Previn
Two Weeks in Another Town	MGM	David Raksin
The Underwater City	COL	Ronald Stein
The Valiant	UA	Christopher Whelen
A Very Private Affair	FRA	Fiorenzo Carpi
Victim	BRI	Philip Green
A View from the Bridge	CON	Maurice le Roux
Walk on the Wild Side	COL	Elmer Bernstein
Waltz of the Toreadors	BRI	Richard Addinsell
War Hunt	UA	Bud Shank
The War Lover	COL	Richard Addinsell
Warriors Five	AI	Armando Trovajoli
Whatever Happened to Baby Jane?	WB	Frank de Vol
Where the Truth Lies	PAR	Pierre Henry
Whistle Down the Wind	BRI	Malcolm Arnold
White Slave Ship	AI	Les Baxter
Who's Got the Action?	PAR	George Duning
Wild for Kicks	BRI	John Barry
The Wild Westerners	COL	Ross di Maggio
Woman Hunt	TCF	Henry Vars
Wonderful to Be Young	PAR	Stanley Black
The Wonderful World of the Brothers Grimm	MGM	Leigh Harline
The World by Night #2	WB	Piero Piccioni
World in My Pocket	MGM	Claude Bolling
Young Guns of Texas	TCF	Paul Sawtell
Zotz!	COL	Bernard Green

1963

Les Abysses	FRA	Pierre Barbaud
Act One	WB	Skitch Henderson
All the Way Home	PAR	Bernard Green
America, America	WB	Manos Hadjidakis
Any Number Can Win	FRA	Michel Magne
Arturo's Island	ITA	Carlo Rustichelli
The Bad Sleep Well	JAP	Masaru Sato
The Balcony	CON	Igor Stravinsky
Beach Party	AI	Les Baxter
Billy Liar	CON	Richard Rodney Bennett
The Black Fox	IND	Ezra Laderman
Black Gold	WB	Howard Jackson
Black Zoo	AA	Paul Dunlap
Bluebeard (Landru)	FRA	Pierre Jansen
Buddha	JAP	Akira Ifukube
Cairo	MGM	Kenneth V. Jones
Call Me Bwana	UA	Muir Mathieson

Captain Newman, M.D.	UN	Frank Skinner
Captain Sinbad	GER	Michel Michelet
The Cardinal	COL	Jerome Moross
The Caretakers	UA	Elmer Bernstein
The Castilian	WB	Jose Buenagu
Cattle King	MGM	Paul Sawtell
The Ceremony	UA	Gerard Schurmann
Charade	UN	Henry Mancini
A Child Is Waiting	UA	Ernest Gold
Cleopatra	TCF	Alex North
Come Blow Your Horn	PAR	Nelson Riddle
Come Fly with Me	MGM	Lyn Murray
The Comedy of Terrors	AI	Les Baxter
The Condemned of Altona	TCF	Dmitri Shostakovich
The Conjugal Bed	ITA	Teo Usuelli
Corridors of Blood	MGM	Buxton Orr
The Counterfeiters of Paris	FRA	Frances Remarque Michel Legrand
The Courtship of Eddie's Father	MGM	George Stoll
Critic's Choice	WB	George Duning
Cry of Battle	AA	Richard Markowitz
David and Lisa	CON	Mark Lawrence
The Day Mars Invaded Earth	TCF	Richard La Salle
The Day of the Triffids	AA	Ron Goodwin
Diary of a Madman	UA	Richard La Salle
Dime with a Halo	MGM	Ronald Stein
Dimka	RUS	Nikolai Yakovlev
Dr. No	UA	Monty Norman
Donovan's Reef	PAR	Cyril J. Mockridge
Drums of Africa	MGM	Johnny Mandel
The Duel of the Titans	ITA	Piero Piccioni
The Easy Life	ITA	Riz Ortolani
8-1/2	ITA	Nino Rota
Electra	GRE	Mikis Theodorakis
The Elusive Corporal	FRA	Joseph Kosma
The Face of War	JAP/SWE	George Riedel
Family Diary	ITA	Geoffredo Petrassi
55 Days at Peking	AA	Dimitri Tiomkin
Five Miles to Midnight	UA	Mikis Theodorakis
Follow the Boys	MGM	Ron Goodwin
For Love or Money	UN	Frank de Vol
The Four Days of Naples	ITA	Carlo Rustichelli
4 for Texas	WB	Nelson Riddle
The French Game	FRA	Michel Legrand
Fury at Smuggler's Bay	BRI	Harold Geller
La Gamberge	FRA	Guy Bearts
A Gathering of Eagles	UA	Jerry Goldsmith
Germinal	FRA	Michel Magne
Gidget Goes to Rome	COL	Johnny Williams
The Girl Hunters	IND	Philip Green
The Good Soldier Schweik	GER	Bernhard Eichhorn
The Great Chase	CON	Larry Adler
The Great Escape	UA	Elmer Bernstein

The Great Rights (short)	IND	Gerald Fried
The Greenwich Village Story	IND	Hy Gubernick
The Gun Hawk	AA	Jimmie Haskell
Gunfight at Comanche Creek	AA	Marlin Skiles
Hamilton, the Musical Elephant (short)	BRI	John Dankworth
Harbor Lights	TCF	Paul Sawtell
The Haunted Palace	AI	Ronald Stein
The Haunting	MGM	Humphrey Searle
The Hook	MGM	Larry Adler
Horror Hotel	BRI	Kenneth V. Jones
House of the Damned	TCF	Henry Vars
Hud	PAR	Elmer Bernstein
I Could Go on Singing	UA	Mort Lindsay
In the Cool of the Day	MGM	Francis Chagrin
In the French Style	COL	Joseph Kosma
The Incredible Journey	DIS	Oliver Wallace
Irma La Douce	UA	Andre Previn
Island of Love	WB	George Duning
It Happened at the World's Fair	MGM	Leith Stevens
It's a Mad, Mad, Mad, Mad World	UA	Ernest Gold
Jason and the Argonauts	COL	Bernard Herrmann
Johnny Cool	UA	Billy May
King Kong vs. Godzilla	UN	Peter Zinner
Kings of the Sun	UA	Elmer Bernstein
Kiss of the Vampire	UN	James Bernard
The L-Shaped Room	COL	John Barry
Ladies Who Do	BRI	Ron Goodwin
Ladybug, Ladybug	UA	Robert Cobert
Lafayette	FRA	Steve Laurent Pierre Duclos
The Leopard	TCF	Nino Rota
Liberte I	FRA	J. Drejac
Light Fantastic	IND	Joseph Liebman
Lilies of the Field	UA	Jerry Goldsmith
The List of Adrian Messenger	UN	Jerry Goldsmith
Lord of the Flies	CON	Raymond Leppard
Love and Larceny	ITA	Pippo Barzizza
Love Is a Ball	UA	Michel Legrand
Love on a Pillow	FRA	Michel Magne
Love with the Proper Stranger	PAR	Elmer Bernstein
McClintock!	UA	Frank de Vol
Madame	FRA/ITA	Francesco Lavagnino
Mafioso	ITA	Piero Piccioni
The Magnificent Sinner	FRA	Joseph Kosma
The Main Attraction	MGM	Andrew Dorian
The Man from the Diner's Club	COL	Stu Philips
Maniac	COL	Stanley Black
Mary, Mary	WB	Frank Perkins
The Mind Benders	AI	Georges Auric
The Miracle of the White Stallions	DIS	Paul Smith
Mondo Cane	ITA	Riz Ortolani

Move Over, Darling	TCF	Lionel Newman
Murder at the Gallop	MGM	Ron Goodwin
Muriel	FRA	Hans Werner Henze
My Six Loves	PAR	Walter Scharf
Mystery Submarine	UN	John Hollingsworth
Naked Autumn	FRA	Maurice le Roux
Never Let Go	CON	John Barry
A New Kind of Love	PAR	Leith Stevens
Night Encounter	FRA	Andre Gosselain
Nine Hours to Rama	TCF	Malcolm Arnold
The Nutty Professor	PAR	Walter Scharf
Of Love and Desire	TCF	Ronald Stein
The Old Dark House	COL	Benjamin Frankel
Operation Bikini	AI	Les Baxter
Ordered to Love	GER	Gerhard Becker
Over There--1914-1918	FRA	Serge Kaufmann
PT 109	WB	William Lava David Buttolph
Palm Springs Weekend	WB	Frank Perkins
Papa's Delicate Condition	PAR	Joseph J. Lilley
Paranoiac	UN	Elizabeth Lutyens
The Pillar of Fire	ISR	Moshe Wilensky
Play It Cool	AA	Norrie Paramor
Police Nurse	TCF	Richard La Salle
The Prize	MGM	Jerry Goldsmith
The Raiders	UN	Morton Stevens
Rampage	WB	Elmer Bernstein
The Raven	AI	Les Baxter
Reach for Glory	BRI	Bob Russell
Rififi in Tokyo	FRA/JAP	Georges Delerue
The Running Man	COL	William Alwyn
Savage Sam	DIS	Oliver Wallace
Seven Seas to Calais	MGM	Franco Mannino
Shock Corridor	AA	Paul Dunlap
Showdown	UN	Hans J. Salter
Siege of the Saxons	COL	Laurie Johnson
The Small World of Sammy Lee	BRI	Kenny Graham
Sodom and Gomorrah	TCF	Miklos Rozsa
Soldier in the Rain	AA	Henry Mancini
Son of Flubber	DIS	George Bruns
Spencer's Mountain	WB	Max Steiner
Square of Violence	YUG	Franco Ferrara
The Steppe	ITA	Guido Turchi
Stolen Hours	UA	Mort Lindsay
A Stranger Knocks	DEN	Erik Fiehn
The Stripper	TCF	Jerry Goldsmith
The Suitor	FRA	Jean Paillaud
Summer Magic	DIS	Buddy Baker
Sunday in New York	MGM	Peter Nero
Sweet Ecstasy	FRA	George Garvarentz
The Sword in the Stone	DIS	George Bruns
Sword of Lancelot	UN	Ron Goodwin
Take Her, She's Mine	TCF	Jerry Goldsmith

Tammy and the Doctor	UN	Frank Skinner
A Taste of Violence	WB	Jean-Michel Demase
The Third Lover	FRA	Pierre Jansen
13 Frightened Girls	COL	Van Alexander
This Sporting Life	CON	Roberto Gerhard
The Three Lives of Thomasina	DIS	Paul Smith
The Three Stooges Go Around the World in a Daze	COL	Paul Dunlap
The Thrill of It All	UN	Frank de Vol
Thunder Island	TCF	Paul Sawtell Bert Shefter
Tiara Tahiti	BRI	Philip Green
A Ticklish Affair	MGM	George Stoll Robert van Eps
To Bed ... Or Not to Bed	ITA	Piero Piccioni
Tom Jones	UA	John Addison
Town without a Face	CZE	Janos Guylai-Gaal
Toys in the Attic	UA	George Duning
The Traitors	BRI	Johnny Douglas
The Trial	FRA	Jean Ledrut
Twice Told Tales	UA	Richard La Salle
Twilight of Honor	MGM	John Green
The Ugly American	UN	Frank Skinner
Under the Yum Yum Tree	COL	Frank de Vol
The V.I.P.'s	MGM	Miklos Rozsa
The Victors	COL	Sol Kaplan
Violated Paradise	JAP	Marcello Abbado
Wall of Noise	WB	William Lava
The War of the Buttons	FRA	Jose Bergkmans
Weekend	DEN	Erik Moseholm
The Wheeler Dealers	MGM	Frank de Vol
Who's Been Sleeping in My Bed?	PAR	George Duning
Who's Minding the Store?	PAR	Joseph J. Lilley
Wives and Lovers	PAR	Lyn Murray
Women of the World	ITA	Riz Ortolani Nino Oliviero
The Wrong Arm of the Law	BRI	John Hollingsworth
X--The Man with the X-Ray Eyes	AI	Les Baxter
The Yellow Canary	TCF	Kenyon Hopkins
The Young and the Brave	MGM	Ronald Stein
The Young Racers	AI	Les Baxter

1964

Advance to the Rear	MGM	Randy Sparks
The Americanization of Emily	MGM	Johnny Mandel
Apache Rifles	TCF	Richard La Salle
The Ape Woman	ITA	Teo Usuelli
Back Door to Hell	TCF	Mike Velerde
Bebo's Girl	ITA	Carlo Rustichelli
Becket	PAR	Laurence Rosenthal
Bedtime Story	UN	Hans J. Salter

Behold a Pale Horse	COL	Maurice Jarre
The Best Man	UA	Mort Lindsay
Black Like Me	CON	Meyer Kupferman
Black Sabbath	AI	Les Baxter
Blood on the Arrow	AA	Richard La Salle
Blood on the Balcony	ITA	Roberto Nicolosi
The Brass Bottle	UN	Bernard Green
Bullet for a Badman	UN	Frank Skinner
The Carpenter	PAR	Elmer Bernstein
Cartouche	FRA	George Delerue
Casablan	GRE	Costa Capnissis
The Chalk Garden	UN	Malcolm Arnold
Cheyenne Autumn	WB	Alex North
Children of the Damned	MGM	Ron Goodwin
Circus World	PAR	Dimitri Tiomkin
Code 7 Victim 5	COL	Johnny Douglas
Commando	AI	Francesco Lavagnino
Crazy Desire	ITA	Ennio Morricone
The Crimson Blade	COL	Gary Hughes
The Curse of the Living Corpse	TCF	Bill Holmes
Dark Purpose	UN	Francesco Lavagnino
Dead Ringer	WB	Andre Previn
Dear Heart	WB	Henry Mancini
Devil-Ship Pirates	COL	Gary Hughes
Diary of a Bachelor	AI	Jack Pleis
The Disorderly Orderly	PAR	Joseph J. Lilley
A Distant Trumpet	WB	Max Steiner
Dr. Crippen	WB	Kenneth V. Jones
Doctor in Distress	BRI	Norrie Paramor
Dr. Strangelove: or How I Learned to Stop Worrying and Love the Bomb	COL	Laurie Johnson
The Doll	SWE	Ulrik Neumann
Dragon Sky	FRA	Maurice Jarre
The Dream Maker	UN	Philip Green
The Earth Dies Screaming	TCF	Elizabeth Lutyens
East of Sudan	COL	Laurie Johnson
Emil and the Detectives	DIS	Heinz Schreiter
The Empty Canvas	EMB	Luis Enrique Bacalov
Ensign Pulver	WB	George Duning
Escape by Night	AA	Philip Martell
The Evil of Frankenstein	UN	Don Banks
The Eyes of Annie Jones	TCF	Buxton Orr
F.B.I. Code 98	WB	Max Steiner
The Fall of the Roman Empire	PAR	Dimitri Tiomkin
Fate Is the Hunter	TCF	Jerry Goldsmith
Father Goose	UN	Cy Coleman
The Finest Hours	COL	Ron Grainer
The First Men in the Moon	COL	Laurie Johnson
Flight from Ashiya	UA	Frank Cordell
Flipper's New Adventure	MGM	Henry Vars
For Those Who Think Young	UA	Jerry Fielding
Four Days in November	UA	Elmer Bernstein

From Russia with Love	UA	John Barry
Get Yourself a College Girl	MGM	George Stoll
The Girl with Green Eyes	BRI	John Addison
Gladiators 7	MGM	Marcello Giombini
A Global Affair	MGM	Dominic Frontiere
Godzilla vs. the Thing	AI	Akira Ifukube
Gold for the Caesars	MGM	Franco Mannino
The Golden Arrow	MGM	Mario Nascimbene
Goldfinger	UA	John Barry
Good Neighbor Sam	COL	Frank de Vol
Goodbye Charlie	TCF	Andre Previn
The Great Armored Car Swindle	BRI	Albert Elms
The Great Unfenced (short)	IND	Robert Muczynski
The Guest	BRI	Ron Grainer
Guns at Batasi	TCF	John Addison
The Guns of August	UN	Sol Kaplan
Hamlet	RUS	Dmitri Shostakovich
He Rides Tall	UN	Irving Gertz
Hide and Seek	UN	Muir Mathieson
Honeymoon Hotel	MGM	Walter Scharf
The Horror of It All	TCF	Douglas Gamley
A House Is Not a Home	EMB	Joseph Weiss
I'd Rather Be Rich	UN	Percy Faith
The Incredible Mr. Limpet	WB	Frank Perkins
Invitation to a Gunfighter	UA	David Raksin
Island of the Blue Dolphins	UN	Paul Sawtell
John Goldfarb, Please Come Home	TCF	Johnny Williams
Joy House	MGM	Lalo Schifrin
The Killers	UN	Johnny Williams
Kiss Me Stupid	UA	Andre Previn
Kisses for My President	WB	Bronislau Kaper
Kitten with a Whip	UN	Joseph Gershenson
La Bonne Soupe	FRA	Raymond le Senechal
Let's Talk About Women	ITA	Armando Trovajoli
Life in Danger	AA	William Davies
Lilith	COL	Kenyon Hopkins
The Lively Set	UN	Bobby Darin
The Long Ships	COL	Dusan Radic
Looking for Love	MGM	George Stoll
The Luck of Ginger Coffey	CAN	Bernardo Segall
MGM's Big Parade of Comedy	MGM	Bernie Green
McHale's Navy	UN	Jerry Fielding
Mail Order Bride	MGM	George Bassman
The Man from Galveston	WB	David Buttolph
Man in the Middle	TCF	John Barry
Man's Favorite Sport?	UN	Henry Mancini
Marnie	UN	Bernard Herrmann
Marriage Italian Style	ITA	Armando Trovajoli
Masque of the Red Death	AI	David Lee
Master Spy	AA	Ken Thorne
Mata Hari	FRA	Georges Delerue
Misadventures of Merlin Jones	DIS	Buddy Baker

The Moonspinners	DIS	Ron Grainer
Moro Witch Doctor	TCF	Ariston Auelino
Murder Ahoy	MGM	Ron Goodwin
Murder Most Foul	MGM	Ron Goodwin
The Naked Kiss	AA	Paul Dunlap
Never Put It in Writing	AA	Frank Cordell
The New Interns	COL	Earle Hagen
Night Must Fall	MGM	Ron Grainer
The Night of the Iguana	MGM	Benjamin Frankel
Night Train to Paris	TCF	Kenny Graham
The Night Walker	UN	Vic Mizzy
Nightmare	UN	Don Banks
Nothing But the Best	BRI	Ron Grainer
Nutty, Naughty Chateau	FRA	Raymond le Senchal
Of Human Bondage	MGM	Ron Goodwin
One Man's Way	UA	Richard Markowitz
One Potato, Two Potato	IND	Gerald Fried
Only One New York	FRA	Milton DeLugg
Open the Door and See All the People	IND	Alec Wilder
The Organizer	ITA	Carlo Rustichelli
The Outrage	MGM	Alex North
Panic Button	IND	George Garvarentz
Paris When It Sizzles	PAR	Nelson Riddle
The Patsy	PAR	David Raksin
The Pink Panther	UA	Henry Mancini
The Pleasure Seekers	TCF	Lionel Newman
Psyche '59	COL	Kenneth V. Jones
Psychomania	IND	W. L. Holcombe
The Pumpkin Eater	BRI	Georges Delerue
Pyro	AI	Jose Sola
Quick, Before It Melts	MGM	David Rose
The Quick Gun	COL	Richard La Salle
Racing Fever	AA	Al Jacobs
Le Rat D'Amerique	FRA	Georges Garvarentz
Rattle of a Simple Man	CON	Stanley Black
Ready for the People	WB	Frank Perkins
Red Lanterns	GRE	Stavros Xarchakos
Rhino!	MGM	Lalo Schifrin
Rio Conchos	TCF	Jerry Goldsmith
Robin and the 7 Hoods	WB	Nelson Riddle
Robinson Crusoe on Mars	PAR	Van Cleave
Rotten to the Core	BRI	Michael Dress Robin Miller
Seance on a Wet Afternoon	BRI	John Barry
The Secret Door	AA	Tony Osborne
The Secret Invasion	UA	Hugo Friedhofer
Seduced and Abandoned	ITA	Carlo Rustichelli
Send Me No Flowers	UN	Frank de Vol
Seven Days in May	PAR	Jerry Goldsmith
Seven Faces of Dr. Lao	MGM	Leigh Harline
The 7th Dawn	UA	Riz Ortolani

The Seventh Juror	FRA	Jean Yatove
Sex and the Single Girl	WB	Neal Hefti
Shakespeare: Soul of an Age	IND	George Kleinsinger
Shock Treatment	TCF	Jerry Goldsmith
A Shot in the Dark	UA	Henry Mancini
Signpost to Murder	MGM	Lyn Murray
633 Squadron	UA	Ron Goodwin
Slave Trade in the World Today	CON	Teo Usuelli
The Soft Skin	IND	Georges Delerue
The Son of Captain Blood	PAR	Gregory Segura
Stage to Thunder Rock	PAR	Paul Dunlap
Station Six--Sahara	AA	Ron Grainer
Stop Train 349	AA	Peter Thomas
Strait-Jacket	COL	Van Alexander
Strange Bedfellows	UN	Leigh Harline
Strange Victory	IND	David Diamond
The Strangler	AA	Marlin Skiles
The Swingin' Maiden	COL	Eric Rogers
Taggart	UN	Herman Stein
Tamahine	MGM	Malcolm Arnold
The Tattooed Police Horse	DIS	William Lava
The Terrace	ARG	Jorge Lopez Ruiz
The Thin Red Line	AA	Malcolm Arnold
The Third Secret	TCF	Richard Arnell
36 Hours	MGM	Dimitri Tiomkin
Those Calloways	DIS	Max Steiner
A Tiger Walks	DIS	Buddy Baker
The Time Travelers	AI	Richard La Salle
Topkapi	UA	Manos Hadjidakis
Treasure of the Silver Lake	GER	Martin Boetticher
The Troublemaker	IND	Cy Coleman
Two Are Guilty	MGM	Louiguy
The Umbrellas of Cherbourg	FRA	Michel Legrand
The Visit	TCF	Hans-Martin Majewski
Viva Las Vegas	MGM	George Stoll
Voice of the Hurricane	IND	Paul Dunlap
Walk a Tightrope	PAR	Buxton Orr
The Walls of Hell	IND	Tito Arevalo
War Is Hell	AA	Ronald Stein
What a Way to Go!	TCF	Nelson Riddle
Where Love Has Gone	PAR	Walter Scharf
Why Bother to Knock?	BRI	Elizabeth Lutyens
Wild and Wonderful	UN	Morton Stevens
Witchcraft	TCF	Philip Martell
A Woman Is a Woman	FRA	Michel Legrand
Woman of Straw	UA	Muir Mathieson
The World of Henry Orient	UA	Elmer Bernstein
World without Sun	COL	Andre Hodier Henri Crolla
Yanco	MEX	Gustavo C. Carreon
A Yank in Viet-Nam	AA	Richard La Salle
Yankee Painter (short)	IND	Robert Muczynski
Yesterday, Today and Tomorrow	ITA	Armando Trovajoli

Young and Willing	UN	Norrie Paramor
The Young Lovers	MGM	Sol Kaplan
Youngblood Hawke	WB	Max Steiner
Zorba the Greek	TCF	Mikis Theodorakis
Zulu	EMB	John Barry

1965

Across the River	IND	Charles Gross
Agent 8-3/4	BRI	Francesco Lavagnino
The Agony and the Ecstasy	TCF	Alex North
All Men Are Apes	IND	Irv Dwier
Alphaville	FRA	Paul Misraki
The Amorous Adventures of Moll Flanders	PAR	John Addison
The Animals	FRA	Maurice Jarre
Apache Gold	COL	Martin Boetticher
Arizona Raiders	COL	Richard La Salle
The Art of Love	UN	Cy Coleman
Atragon	JAP	Akira Ifukube
Baby, the Rain Must Fall	COL	Elmer Bernstein
Backfire	FRA	Martial Solal
Bambole!	ITA	Armando Trovajoli
The Battle of the Bulge	WB	Benjamin Frankel
The Battle of the Villa Fiorita	WB	Mischa Spoliansky
Day of Angels	FRA	Michel Legrand
Beach Ball	PAR	Frank Wilson
Beach Blanket Bingo	AI	Les Baxter
The Bears	FRA	Jean Prodromides
The Bedford Incident	COL	Gerard Schurmann
Billie	UA	Dominic Frontiere
Black Spurs	PAR	Jimmie Haskell
Blood and Black Lace	ITA	Carlo Rustichelli
Boeing Boeing	PAR	Neal Hefti
The Bounty Killer	EMB	Ronald Stein
A Boy Ten Feet Tall	PAR	Tristram Cary
Brainstorm	WB	George Duning
The Brigand of Kandahar	COL	Don Banks
Bunny Lake Is Missing	COL	Paul Glass
The Bus	IND	Richard Markowitz
Bus Riley's Back in Town	UN	Richard Markowitz
Cary on Cleo	BRI	Eric Rogers
Carry on Spying	BRI	Eric Rogers
Casanova '70	EMB	Armando Trovajoli
Cat Ballou	COL	Frank de Vol
The Cavern	ITA	Carlo Rustichelli
The Cincinnati Kid	MGM	Lalo Schifrin
Circle of Love	FRA	Michel Magne
City of Fear	AA	Jerry Goldsmith
Clarence, the Cross-Eyed Lion	MGM	Shelly Manne
Coast of Skeletons	AFR	Christopher Whelen
The Collector	COL	Maurice Jarre
Convict Stage	TCF	Richard La Salle

Crack in the World	PAR	Johnny Douglas
Crazy Paradise	DEN	I. B. Glindemann
The Curse of the Fly	TCF	Bert Shefter
The Curse of the Mummy's Tomb	COL	Carlo Martelli
Curse of the Voodoo	AA	Brian Fahey
Dark Intruder	UN	Stanley Wilson
Darling	EMB	John Dankworth
Dear Brigitte	TCF	George Duning
Devils of Darkness	TCF	Bernie Felton
Die! Die! My Darling!	COL	Wilfred Josephs
Die, Monster, Die	AI	Don Banks
Dingaka	EMB	Bertha Egnos
		Eddie Domingo
		Basil Gray
Do Not Disturb	TCF	Lionel Newman
Dr. Goldfoot and the Bikini Machine	AI	Les Baxter
Dr. Terror's House of Horrors	PAR	Kenny Lynch
Doctor Zhivago	MGM	Maurice Jarre
Eva	FRA	Michel Legrand
The Face of Fu Manchu	BRI	Christopher Whelen
The Family Jewels	PAR	Pete King
Fifi La Plume	FRA	Jean Michel Defave
Finger on the Trigger	AA	Jose Sola
The Flight of the Phoenix	TCF	Frank de Vol
Fluffy	UN	Irving Gertz
The Fool Killer	IND	Gustavo C. Carreon
Fort Courageous	TCF	Richard La Salle
Friend of the Family	FRA	Raymond le Senechal
Genghis Khan	COL	Dusan Radic
The Gentle Rain	BRA	Luiz Bonfa
Ghidran, the Three-Headed Monster	JAP	Akira Ifukube
Girl Happy	MGM	George Stoll
The Girls on the Beach	PAR	Gary Usher
The Glory Guys	UA	Riz Ortolani
The Gorgon	COL	James Bernard
The Great Race	WB	Henry Mancini
The Great Sioux Massacre	COL	Emil Newman
The Greatest Story Ever Told	UA	Alfred Newman
Greed in the Sun	FRA	Georges Delerue
The Guide	IN	S. D. Burman
Gunfighters of Casa Grande	MGM	Johnny Douglas
Gunmen of the Rio Grande	AA	Francesco Lavagnino
The Hallelujah Trail	UA	Elmer Bernstein
Harlow	IND	Nelson Riddle
		Al Ham
Harlow	PAR	Neal Hefti
Harum Scarum	MGM	Fred Karger
Harvey Middleman, Fireman	COL	Bernard Green
Help!	UA	The Beatles
Hercules, Samson and Ulysses	MGM	Francesco Lavagnino
Heroes of Telemark	COL	Malcolm Arnold

Title	Studio	Composer
A High Wind in Jamaica	TCF	Larry Adler
The Hill	MGM	Art Noel Don Pelosi
The Hours of Love	ITA	Luiz Bonfa
How Not to Rob a Department Store	FRA	Georges Garvarentz
How to Murder Your Wife	UA	Neal Hefti
How to Stuff a Wild Bikini	AI	Les Baxter
The Human Duplicators	AA	Gordon Zahler
Hush ... Hush, Sweet Charlotte	TCF	Frank de Vol
Hysteria	MGM	Don Banks
I Saw What You Did	UN	Van Alexander
I'll Take Sweden	UA	Jimmie Haskell
The Image of Love	IND	Ezra Laderman
In Harm's Way	PAR	Jerry Goldsmith
Inside Daisy Clover	WB	Andre Previn
The Ipcress File	UN	John Barry
Italiano Brava Gente	ITA	Armando Trovajoli
Joy in the Morning	MGM	Bernard Herrmann
Juliet of the Spirits	ITA	Nino Rota
Kimberley Jim	EMB	Bill Walker
King and Country	BRI	Larry Adler
King Rat	COL	John Barry
The Knack--And How to Get It	UA	John Barry
Kwaidan	JAP	Toru Takemitsu
Lady L	MGM	Jean Wiener
The Last of the Mohicans	GER	Peter Thomas
Laurel and Hardy's Laughing 20's	MGM	Skeets Alquist
Life at the Top	BRI	Richard Addinsell
Life Upside Down	FRA	Jacques Loussier
The Little Nuns	ITA	Ennio Morricone
The Little Ones	COL	Malcolm Lockyer
Lord Jim	COL	Bronislau Kaper
Love and Kisses	UN	Jimmie Haskell William Loose
Love Has Many Faces	COL	David Raksin
The Loved One	MGM	John Addison
McHale's Navy Joins the Air Force	UN	Jerry Fielding
Maedchen in Uniform	GER	Peter Sandloff
The Magic World of Topo Gigio	COL	Armando Trovajoli
Major Dundee	COL	Daniele Amfitheatrof
The Man from Button Willow	IND	George Stoll Robert van Eps
Man in the Dark	UN	Brian Fahey
Mara of the Wilderness	AA	Harry Bluestone
Marriage on the Rocks	WB	Nelson Riddle
Masquerade	UA	Philip Green
Massacre in Grand Canyon	ITA	Gianni Ferrio
Mickey One	COL	Eddie Sauter
Mirage	UN	Quincy Jones
Mister Moses	UA	John Barry
The Moment of Truth	ITA	Piero Piccioni

Mondo Pazzo	ITA	Nino Oliviero
The Monkey's Uncle	DIS	Buddy Baker
Morituri	TCF	Jerry Goldsmith
Murieta	WB	Antonio Perez Olea
Mutiny in Outer Space	AA	Gordon Zahler
My Blood Runs Cold	WB	George Duning
The Naked Brigade	UN	Theo Fanidi
The Nanny	TCF	Richard Rodney Bennett
Never Too Late	WB	David Rose
Nobody Waved Goodbye	CAN	Eldon Rathburn
None But the Brave	WB	Johnny Williams
Not on Your Life!	SPA	Miguel Asins Arbo
The Oil Prince	GER	Martin Boetticher
Old Surehand	GER	Martin Boetticher
Once a Thief	MGM	Lalo Schifrin
One Naked Night	IND	Chet McIntyre
One Way Pendulum	BRI	Richard Rodney Bennett
Onibaba	JAP	Hikaru Hayashi
Operation C.I.A.	AA	Leonard Blair
Operation Crossbow	MGM	Ron Goodwin
Operation Snafu	AI	Malcolm Arnold
Othello	BRI	Richard Hampton
The Outlaws Is Coming!	COL	Paul Dunlap
Paris Secret	FRA	Alain Goraguer
Party Girls for the Candidate	IND	Steve Karman
A Patch of Blue	MGM	Jerry Goldsmith
The Pawnbroker	IND	Quincy Jones
The Peach Thief	BUL	Simeon Pironkov
Planet of the Vampires	AI	Gino Marinuzzi
Pyramid of the Sungods	GER	Erwin Halletz
A Rage to Live	UA	Nelson Riddle
Raiders from Beneath the Sea	TCF	Hank Levine
The Railroad Man	ITA	Carlo Rustichelli
Rapture	FRA	Georges Delerue
The Ravagers	IND	Tito Arevalo
Red Desert	ITA	Giovanni Fusco
Red Line 7000	PAR	Nelson Riddle
Repulsion	BRI	Chico Hamilton
Requiem for a Gunfighter	EMB	Ronald Stein
Return from the Ashes	BRI	John Dankworth
The Return of Mr. Moto	TCF	Douglas Gamley
Revenge of the Gladiators	ITA	Francesco de Masi
The Reward	TCF	Elmer Bernstein
The Rounders	MGM	Jeff Alexander
The Sandpiper	MGM	Johnny Mandel
Sands of the Kalahari	PAR	John Dankworth
The Satan Bug	UA	Jerry Goldsmith
Seaside Swingers	BRI	Tony Osborne
Secret of Blood Island	UN	James Bernard
The Secret of Magic Island	FRA	Richard Cornu
The Secret of My Success	MGM	Roland Shaw
Sergeant Deadhead	AI	Les Baxter
Seven Golden Men	ITA	Armando Trovajoli

Seven Slaves Against the World	ITA	Francesco de Masi
7 Women	MGM	Elmer Bernstein
She	MGM	James Bernard
Shenandoah	UN	Frank Skinner
Ship of Fools	COL	Ernest Gold
The Shop on Main Street	CZE	Zdenek Liska
The Shot from a Violin Case	GER	Peter Thomas
Situation Hopeless, But Not Serious	PAR	Harold Byrne
Skaterdater (short)	IND	Mike Curb
Ski Party	AI	Gary Usher
The Skull	PAR	Elizabeth Lutyens
The Slender Thread	COL	Quincy Jones
The Sons of Katie Elder	PAR	Elmer Bernstein
Spaceflight IC-1	BRI	Elizabeth Lutyens
The Spider's Web	BRI	Tony Crombie
The Spy Who Came in from the Cold	PAR	Sol Kaplan
The Square Root of Zero	IND	Elliot Kaplan
The Stone	GRE	Stavros Xarchakos
Swedish Wedding Night	SWE	Georg Riedel
The Sword of Ali Baba	UN	Frank Skinner
Sylvia	PAR	David Raksin
Symphony for a Massacre	FRA	Michel Magne
Synanon	COL	Neal Hefti
Taffy and the Jungle Hunter	AA	Shorty Rogers
Taxi for Tobruk	FRA	Georges Garvarentz
Ten Little Indians	BRI	Malcolm Lockyer
The 10th Victim	ITA	Piero Piccioni
Terror in the City	AA	Robert Mersey
Thank Heaven for Small Favors	FRA	Joseph Kosma
That Darn Cat	DIS	Robert F. Brunner
That Funny Feeling	UN	Bobby Darin
These Are the Damned	COL	James Bernard
The Third Day	WB	Percy Faith
Those Magnificent Men in Their Flying Machines	TCF	Ron Goodwin
A Thousand Clowns	UA	Jerry Mulligan
Thunderball	UA	John Barry
Tickle Me	AA	Walter Scharf
Time of Indifference	ITA	Giovanni Fusco
Town Tamer	PAR	Jimmie Haskell
The Train	UA	Maurice Jarre
Treasure of the Aztecs	GER	Erwin Halletz
The Truth About Spring	UN	Robert Farnon
Two on a Guillotine	WB	Max Steiner
Uncle Tom's Cabin	GER	Peter Thomas
Up from the Beach	TCF	Edgar Cosma
A Very Special Favor	UN	Vic Mizzy
Vice and Virtue	FRA	Michel Magne
La Vie Conjugal	FRA	Guy Bearts
La Vie De Chateau	FRA	Michel Legrand
Village of the Giants	EMB	Jack Nitzsche

Viva Maria	FRA	Georges Delerue
Von Ryan's Express	TCF	Jerry Goldsmith
A Walk Through the Kurdistan Wilderness	GER	Raimund Rosenberger
The War Lord	UN	Jerome Moross
War Party	TCF	Richard La Salle
What's New, Pussycat?	UA	Burt Bacharach
When the Boys Meet the Girls	MGM	Fred Karger
Where the Spies Are	MGM	Brian Fahey
White Voices	ITA	Gino Marinuzzi
Wild on the Beach	TCF	Jimmie Haskell
Wild Seed	UN	Richard Markowitz
Winnetou I (see Apache Gold)		
Winnetou II	GER	Martin Boetticher
Winnetou III	GER	Martin Boetticher
Winter A-Go-Go	COL	Harry Betts
The Woman Who Wouldn't Die	WB	Carlo Martelli
The Yellow Rolls-Royce	MGM	Riz Ortolani
You Must Be Joking!	COL	Laurie Johnson
Young Cassidy	MGM	Sean O'Riada
Young Dillinger	AA	Shorty Rogers
Young Fury	PAR	Paul Dunlap
Zebra in the Kitchen	MGM	Warren Barker

1966

Africa Addio	ITA	Riz Ortolani
After the Fox	UA	Burt Bacharach
Alfie	PAR	Sonny Rollins
Almost a Man	ITA	Ennio Morricone
The Alphabet Murders	MGM	Ron Goodwin
Alvarez Kelly	COL	John Green
Ambush Bay	UA	Richard La Salle
An American Dream	WB	Johnny Mandell
The Amorist	JAP	Toshiro Mayazumi
And Now Miguel	UN	Philip Lambro
Angelique	FRA	Michel Magne
Any Wednesday	WB	George Duning
Apache Uprising	PAR	Jimmie Haskell
The Appaloosa	UN	Frank Skinner
Arabesque	UN	Henry Mancini
Arrivederci, Baby	PAR	Dennis Farnon
Around the World under the Sea	MGM	Harry Sukman
As Long as You Are Healthy	FRA	Jean Paillauo
Assault on a Queen	PAR	Duke Ellington
Bang, Bang, You're Dead	AI	Malcolm Lockyer
Batman	TCF	Nelson Riddle
The Battle of Algiers	ALG/ITA	Ennio Morricone Gillo Pontecorvo
The Battle of the Bulge--The Brave Rifles	IND	Ruby Raskin
The Beach Umbrella	FRA/ITA	Lelio Luttazzi
Beau Geste	UN	Hans J. Salter

Bebert Et Le Omnibus	FRA	M. Phillippe-Gerard
The Bible	TCF	Toshiro Mayazumi
A Big Hand for the Little Lady	WB	David Raksin
Birds Do It	COL	Samuel Matlovsky
Blindfold	UA	Lalo Schifrin
Bloko (The Roundup)	GRE	Mikis Theodorakis
Blood Bath	AI	Mark Lowry
Blow-Up	BRI	Herbert Hancock
The Blue Max	TCF	Jerry Goldsmith
Born Free	COL	John Barry
Boy, Did I Get a Wrong Number	UA	Richard La Salle By Durham
The Brides of Fu Manchu	BRI	Bruce Montgomery
The Bubble	IND	Paul Sawtell Bert Shefter
Carry on Cowboy	BRI	Eric Rogers
Carry on Screaming	BRI	Eric Rogers
Cast a Giant Shadow	UA	Elmer Bernstein
The Cat	EMB	Stan Worth
Chamber of Horrors	WB	William Lava
Chappaqua	IND	Ravi Shankar
The Chase	COL	John Barry
Cinerama's Russian Adventure	CIN	Aleksandr Lohskin Ilya Schweitzer Yuri Effimov
The Countess from Hong Kong	UN	Charles Chaplin
A Covenant with Death	WB	Leonard Rosenman
Cul-De-Sac	BRI	Kryzstof Komeda
Daleks Invade Earth 2150 A.D.	BRI	Bill McGuffie
Dance of the Herons	GER/HOL	Jurrihan Andriessen
Daphne	JAP	Toshiro Mayazumi
Dateline Diamonds	BRI	Johnny Douglas
Days of Wilfred Owen (short)	IND	Richard Lewis
Deathwatch	IND	Gerald Fried
The Defector	SA	Serge Gainsbourg
Destination Inner Space	MAG	Paul Dunlap
Dr. Goldfoot and the Girl Bombs	AI	Les Baxter
Doctor in Clover	BRI	John (Patrick) Scott
Door-to-Door Maniac	AI	Gene Kauer
Dracula--Prince of Darkness	BRI	James Bernard
Duel at Diablo	UA	Neal Hefti
Dutchman	IND	John Barry
Every Day Is a Holiday	SPA	Augusto Alguero
An Eye for an Eye	EMB	Raoul Kraushaar
Fahrenheit 451	UN	Bernard Herrmann
The Family Way	BRI	Paul McCartney
Fantastic Voyage	TCF	Leonard Rosenman
Fantomas Se Dechaine	FRA	Michel Magne
Faster, Pussycat, Kill! Kill!	IND	Paul Sawtell
Father's Trip	FRA	Georges Garvarentz
The Female Soldier	MEX	Raul Lavista
The Fighting Prince of Donegal	DIS	George Bruns
Finders Keepers	BRI	The Shadows

A Fine Madness	WB	John Addison
The Flame and the Fire	FRA	Michael Colicchio
Follow Me Boys	DIS	George Bruns
For a Few Dollars More	ITA	Ennio Morricone
For Love and Gold (L'Armata Brancaleone)	ITA	Carlo Rustichelli
The Fortune Cookie	UA	Andre Previn
Frankie and Johnny	UA	Fred Karger
Funeral in Berlin	PAR	Conrad Elfers
Gambit	UN	Maurice Jarre
Georgy Girl	COL	Alexander Paris
The Ghost and Mr. Chicken	UN	Vic Mizzy
The Ghost in the Invisible Bikini	AI	Les Baxter
The Glass Bottom Boat	MGM	Frank de Vol
Goal!	BRI	John Hawkesworth
Grand Prix	MGM	Maurice Jarre
The Great St. Trinian's Train Robbery	BRI	Malcolm Arnold
Greece, Land of Dreams	GER	Manos Hadjidakis
Gunpoint	UN	Hans J. Salter
Hallucination Generation	IND	Bernardo Segall
Harper	WB	Johnny Mandell
Hawaii	UA	Elmer Bernstein
Hit and Run	JAP	Masaru Sato
Hold On	MGM	Fred Karger
The Hot Month of August	GRE	Stavros Xarchacos
Hot Years	YUG	Dusan Radic
Hotel Paradiso	MGM	Laurence Rosenthal
How to Steal a Million	TCF	Johnny Williams
I Deal in Danger	TCF	Lalo Schifrin
I Knew Her Well	UN	Hans J. Salter
I Was Happy Here	BRI	John Addison
The Idol	BRI	John Dankworth
Incident at Phantom Hill	UN	Hans J. Salter
Incubus	IND	Dominic Frontiere
Is Paris Burning?	PAR	Maurice Jarre
The Island	SWE	Erik Nordgren
Johnny Reno	PAR	Jimmie Haskell
Johnny Tiger	UN	John Green
Judith	PAR	Sol Kaplan
Kaleidoscope	BRI	Stanley Myers
Kanchehkungha	IN	Satyajit Ray
Kid Rodello	PAR	Johnny Douglas
Kiss the Girls and Make Them Die	COL	Mario Nascimbene
The Lair of Love	FRA	Georges Delerue
The Last Chapter	IND	Vladimir Heifetz
Let's Kill Uncle	UN	Herman Stein
Lt. Robin Crusoe, U.S.N.	DIS	Robert F. Brunner
The Liquidator	MGM	Lalo Schifrin
Long Legs--Long Fingers	GER	Martin Boetticher
Lord Love a Duck	UA	Neal Hefti
The Lost Command	COL	Franz Waxman

Love and Marriage	ITA	Marcello Giombini
Madame X	UN	Frank Skinner
Made in Paris	MGM	George Stoll
Mademoiselle de Maupin	ITA	Franco Mannino
Make Like a Thief	FIN	Erkki Meloski
A Man and a Woman	FRA	Francis Lai
A Man Called Adam	EMB	Benny Carter
A Man Could Get Killed	UN	Bert Kaempfert
A Man for All Seasons	COL	Georges Delerue
The Man from Marrakech	FRA	Alain Goraguer
The Man Who Laughs	ITA	Piero Piccioni
The Mandrake (La Mandragola)	FRA/ITA	Gino Marinuzzi
A Matter of Honor	FRA/ITA	Luis Enrique Bacalov
Maya	MGM	Riz Ortolani
Menage, Italian Style	ITA	Ennio Morricone
Me, Me, Me ... and the Others	ITA	Carlo Rustichelli
Minnesota Clay	ITA	Piero Piccioni
Mister Buddwing	MGM	Kenyon Hopkins
Modesty Blaise	TCF	John Dankworth
Moment to Moment	UN	Henry Mancini
The Money Trap	MGM	Hal Schaefer
Morgan!	BRI	John Dankworth
Munster, Go Home	UN	Jack Marshall
The Murder Game	BRI	Carlo Martelli
Murderer's Row	COL	Lalo Schifrin
Nameless Star	FRA/RUM	Georges Delerue
Namu, the Killer Whale	UA	Samuel Matlovsky
Navajo Run	AI	Emil Cadkin
		William Loose
Nayak	IN	Satyajit Ray
Nevada Smith	PAR	Alfred Newman
A New World	FRA	Michel Colombier
New York Chiama Superdrago	ITA	Benedetto Ghiglia
The Night of the Grizzly	PAR	Leith Stevens
No Shooting Time for Foxes	GER	Hans Posegga
Not with My Wife, You Don't	WB	Johnny Williams
One Million Years, B.C.	BRI	Mario Nascimbene
One Spy Too Many	MGM	Gerald Fried
Operation San Gennaro	FRA/GER/ITA	Armando Trovajoli
The Oscar	EMB	Percy Faith
Our Man Flint	TCF	Jerry Goldsmith
The Pad (And How to Use It)	UN	Russell Garcia
Paradise, Hawaiian Style	PAR	Joseph J. Lilley
Paranoia	FRA/ITA	Nino Rota
		Teo Usuelli
		Luiz Enrique Bacalov
Penelope	MGM	Johnny Williams
A Place Called Glory	GER/SPA	Angel Arteaga
The Plague of the Zombies	BRI	James Bernard
The Plastic Dome of Norma Jean	IND	Michel Legrand
The Poppy Is also a Flower	IND	Georges Auric
Press for Time	BRI	Mike Vickers
The Professionals	COL	Maurice Jarre

Promise Her Anything	PAR	Lyn Murray
The Psychopath	BRI	Philip Martell
Punishment to the Traitor	ARG	Adolfo Morpurgo
The Quiller Memorandum	BRI	John Barry
Rage	COL	Gustavo C. Carreon
The Rare Breed	UN	Johnny Williams
Rasputin--The Mad Monk	TCF	Don Banks
Rat Fink	IND	Ronald Stein
Red Tomahawk	PAR	Jimmie Haskell
Relax, Freddie	DEN	Bent Fabricius-Bjerre
The Return of Ringo	ITA	Ennio Morricone
Return of the Seven	UA	Elmer Bernstein
Ride Beyond Vengeance	COL	Richard Markowitz
Ride in the Whirlwind	IND	Robert Drasnin
The Russians Are Coming, The Russians Are Coming	UA	Johnny Mandel
Saladino	ITA	Francesco Lavagnino
The Sand Pebbles	TCF	Jerry Goldsmith
The Sandwich Man	BRI	Mike Vickers
Seasons of Our Love	ITA	Carlo Rustichelli
Seconds	PAR	Jerry Goldsmith
Secret Agent Fireball	AI	Carlo Savina
Secret Seven	ITA/SPA	Carlo Franci
Seven Golden Men Strike Again	ITA	Armando Trovajoli
Shakespeare Wallah	IN	Satyajit Ray
Shoot Loud, Louder ... I Don't Understand	ITA	Nino Rota
Signore and Signori	FRA/ITA	Carlo Rustichelli
The Silencers	COL	Elmer Bernstein
The Singing Nun	MGM	Harry Sukman
Ski Fascination	GER	Benny Golson
Sky West and Crooked	BRI	Malcolm Arnold
The Sleeping Car Murder	FRA	Michel Magne
Smoky	TCF	Leith Stevens
Son of a Gunfighter	MGM	Frank Barber
Spinout	MGM	George Stoll
Spy in Your Eye	AI	Riz Ortolani
The Spy with a Cold Nose	BRI	Riz Ortolani
The Spy with My Face	MGM	Morton Stevens
Stagecoach	TCF	Jerry Goldsmith
The Sultans	FRA	Georges Garvarentz
The Swinger	PAR	Marty Paich
Symphony for Two Spies	ITA	Francesco de Masi
10:30 P.M. Summer	LOP	Cristobal Halffter
Texas Across the River	UN	Frank de Vol
Thank You Very Much	ITA	Piero Piccioni
That Riviera Touch	BRI	Ron Goodwin
Three on a Couch	COL	Louis Brown
To Trap a Spy	MGM	Jerry Goldsmith
Tobruk	UN	Bronislau Kaper
Too Soon to Die	FRA/ITA	Ennio Morricone
The Torn Curtain	UN	John Addison
The Trap	BRI	Ron Grainer

The Trouble with Angels	COL	Jerry Goldsmith
Trunk to Cairo	AI	Dov Seltzer
The Venetian Affair	MGM	Lalo Schifrin
A Very Handy Man	ITA	Carlo Savina
W.I.A. (Wounded in Action)	PHI	Leopold Silos
Waco	PAR	Jimmie Haskell
Walk, Don't Run	COL	Quincy Jones
Walk in the Shadow	BRI	William Alwyn
Warning Shot	PAR	Jerry Goldsmith
Way Out	IND	Kurt Kaiser
Way ... Way Out	TCF	Lalo Schifrin
Weekend of Fear	IND	William H. Lockwood
What Did You Do in the War, Daddy?	UA	Henry Mancini
Where the Bullets Fly	BRI	Ron Briges
Who's Afraid of Virginia Woolf?	WB	Alex North
The Wild Angels	AI	Mike Curb
Wild, Wild Winter	UN	Jerry Long
The Witches	BRI	Richard Rodney Bennett
The Wrong Box	BRI	John Barry
You're a Big Boy Now	SA	John Sebastian
The Young Toerless	FRA/GER	Hans Werner Henze

1967

Accident	BRI	John Dankworth
Adventures of Bullwhip Griffin	DIS	George Bruns
Africa--Texas Style	PAR	Malcolm Arnold
The Ambushers	COL	Hugo Montenegro
Another Man's Wife	SPA	Ernesto Halffter
The Ballad of Josie	UN	Frank de Vol
Barefoot in the Park	PAR	Neal Hefti
Batouk	FRA	Michel Magne
Bedazzled	TCF	Dudley Moore
Berserk	COL	John (Patrick) Scott
The Big Mouth	COL	Harry Betts
Billion Dollar Brain	UA	Richard Rodney Bennett
Bitter Fruit	FRA/ITA/YUG	Joseph Kosma
Blood Beast from Outer Space	BRI	John Gregory
The Bobo	WB	Francis Lai
Bonnie and Clyde	WB	Charles Strouse
The Busy Body	PAR	Vic Mizzy
The Caper of the Golden Bulls	EMB	Vic Mizzy
Caprice	TCF	Frank de Vol
Casino Royale	COL	Burt Bacharach
Castle of Evil	IND	Paul Dunlap
The Catalina Caper	IND	Jerry Long
Charlie, the Lonesome Cougar	DIS	Franklyn Marks
China Is Near	ITA	Ennio Morricone
Chuka	PAR	Leith Stevens
Clambake	UA	Jeff Alexander
C'mon, Let's Live a Little	PAR	Don Ralke
Come Spy with Me	TCF	Bob Bowers

The Comedians	MGM	Lawrence Rosenthal
Cool Hand Luke	WB	Lalo Schifrin
The Cool Ones	WB	Ernie Freeman
The Corrupt Ones	GER	Georges Garvarentz
Counterpoint	UN	Bronislau Kaper
The Crazy World of Laurel and Hardy	IND	Jerry Fielding
Custer of the West	CIN	Bernardo Segall
The Day the Fish Came Out	GRE	Mikis Theodorakis
Deadlier than the Male	BRI	Malcolm Lockyer
The Deadly Affair	BRI	Quincy Jones
The Deadly Bees	BRI	Wilfred Josephs
A Degree of Murder	GER	Brian Jones
Devil's Angels	AI	Mike Curb
The Devil's Own	BRI	Richard Rodney Bennett
The Dirty Dozen	MGM	Frank de Vol
Divorce American Style	COL	Dave Grusin
Doctor Dolittle	TCF	Leslie Bricusse
Doctor Faustus	COL	Mario Nascimbene
Doctor, You've Got to Be Kidding	MGM	Kenyon Hopkins
Don Juan in Sicily	ITA	Armando Trovajoli
Don't Lose Your Head	BRI	Eric Rogers
Don't Make Waves	MGM	Vic Mizzy
The Double Man	BRI	Ernie Freeman
Double Trouble	MGM	Jeff Alexander
Easy Come, Easy Go	PAR	Joseph J. Lilley
Eight on the Lam	UA	George Romanis
El Dorado	PAR	Nelson Riddle
Enter Laughing	COL	Quincy Jones
Eye of the Devil	BRI	Gary McFarland
Far from the Madding Crowd	MGM	Richard Rodney Bennett
The Fastest Guitar Alive	MGM	Fred Karger
Fathom	TCF	John Dankworth
The Fearless Vampire Killers	MGM	Kryzstof Komeda
The Fickle Finger of Fate	SPA/USA	Gregory Segura
First to Fight	WB	Fred Steiner
Fitzwilly	UA	Johnny Williams
The Flim Flam Man	TCF	Jerry Goldsmith
Follow That Camel	BRI	Eric Rogers
Fort Utah	PAR	Jimmie Haskell
The Fox	CAN	Lalo Schifrin
Frankenstein Created Woman	TCF	James Bernard
The Frozen Dead	BRI	Don Banks
The Funniest Man in the World	IND	Johnny Douglas
Funnyman	IND	Peter Schickele
The Further Perils of Laurel and Hardy	TCF	John Parker
Games	UN	Samuel Matlovsky
Gentle Giant	PAR	Samuel Matlovsky
The Girl and the General	ITA	Ennio Morricone
The Gnome-Mobile	DIS	Buddy Baker
The Good, the Bad and the Ugly	ITA	Ennio Morricone
Good Morning ... And Goodbye	IND	Igo Kantor

The Graduate	EMB	Dave Grusin
Grand Slam	PAR	Ennio Morricone
The Great British Train Robbery	GER	Heinz Funk
Guess Who's Coming to Dinner	COL	Frank de Vol
A Guide for the Married Man	TCF	Johnny Williams
Gunfight in Abilene	UN	Bobby Darin
Gunn	PAR	Henry Mancini
The Happening	COL	Frank de Vol
Head of the Family	FRA/ITA	Carlo Rustichelli
Hell's Angels on Wheels	IND	Stu Philips
The Hills Run Red	UA	Leo Nichols
The Hired Killer	PAR	Robby Poitevin
Hombre	TCF	David Rose
The Honey Pot	UA	John Addison
Hostile Guns	PAR	Jimmie Haskell
Hot Rods to Hell	MGM	Fred Karger
Hotel	WB	Johnny Keating
Hour of the Gun	UA	Jerry Goldsmith
How I Won the War	BRI	Ken Thorne
Hurry Sundown	PAR	Hugo Montenegro
I Belong to Me	DEN	Bent Fabricius-Bjerre
I'll Never Forget What's 'Is Name	BRI	Francis Lai
In Cold Blood	COL	Quincy Jones
In Like Flint	TCF	Jerry Goldsmith
In the Heat of the Night	UA	Quincy Jones
The Incident	TCF	Terry Knight
Island of Terror	BRI	Malcolm Lockyer
It	BRI	Carlo Martelli
Jack of Diamonds	MGM	Peter Thomas
Johnny Yuma	ITA	Nora Orlandi
The Jokers	UN	Johnny Pearson
The Jungle Book	DIS	George Bruns
Just Like a Woman	BRI	Ken Napper
Kill a Dragon	UA	Philip Springer
The King's Pirate	UN	Ralph Ferraro
Knives of the Avenger	ITA	Marcello Giombini
The Last Challenge	MGM	Richard Shores
The Last Safari	PAR	John Dankworth
Lightning Bolt	ITA	Riz Ortolani
Live for Life	FRA	Francis Lai
The Long Duel	BRI	John (Patrick) Scott
The Love-Ins	COL	Fred Karger
Luv	COL	Gerry Mulligan
The Magnificent Two	BRI	Ron Goodwin
A Man Called Dagger	MGM	Steve Allen
Marat/Sade	BRI	Richard Peaslee
Maroc 7	BRI	Kenneth V. Jones
Matchless	ITA	Ennio Morricone Gino Marinuzzi
Monkeys Go Home	DIS	Robert F. Brunner
The Monster of London City	GER	Martin Boetticher
More Than a Miracle	MGM	Piero Piccioni

The Mummy's Shroud	TCF	Don Banks
The Naked Runner	WB	Harry Sukman
Night of the Generals	COL	Maurice Jarre
Oh, Dad, Poor Dad, Mama's Hung You in the Closet and I'm Feelin' So Sad	PAR	Neal Hefti
The Oldest Profession in the World	FRA	Michel Legrand
The 1,000,000 Eyes of Su-Muru	AI	John (Patrick) Scott
Operation Kid Brother	UA	Ennio Morricone
The Other One	FRA	Serge Gainsbourg
The Other World of Winston Churchill	BRI	Carl Davis
Our Mother's House	MGM	Georges Delerue
Peking Remembered	IND	Andrew Belling
The Penthouse	PAR	John Hawkesworth
The Perils of Pauline	UN	Vic Mizzy
The Phantom of Soho	GER	Martin Boetticher
A Pistol Shot	RUS	Karen Kachaturian
The Plank	BRI	Brian Fahey
Playtime	FRA	Francis Lamarque
Point Blank	MGM	Johnny Mandel
Prehistoric Women	BRI	Carlo Mantelli
The President's Analyst	PAR	Lalo Schifrin
Pretty Polly	UN	Michel Legrand
Privilege	BRI	Mike Leander
The Projected Man	BRI	Kenneth V. Jones
Psycho-Circus	BRI	Johnny Douglas
Red Dragon	GER/ITA	Riz Ortolani
Reflections in a Golden Eye	WB	Toshiro Mayazumi
Riot on Sunset Strip	AI	Fred Karger
Robbery	BRI	Johnny Keating
A Rose for Everyone	ITA	Luis Enriquez
Rosie	UN	Lyn Murray
Rough Night in Jericho	UN	Don Costa
Sadismo	IND	Les Baxter
The St. Valentine's Day Massacre	TCF	Fred Steiner
The Sea Pirate	FRA/ITA/SPA	Georges Garvarentz
Seven Guys and a Gal	FRA	Paul Misraki
The Seventh Floor	ITA	Teo Usuelli
The Shuttered Room	BRI	Basil Kirchin
Siegfried	GER/YUG	Rolf Wilhelm
Ski on the Wild Side	IND	Billy Allen
Smashing Time	BRI	John Addison
The Sorcerers	BRI	Paul Ferris
The Spirit Is Willing	PAR	Vic Mizzy
The Stranger	FRA/ITA	Piero Piccioni
Stranger in the House	BRI	John (Patrick) Scott
The Subversives	ITA	Giovanni Fusco
Sullivan's Empire	UN	Lalo Schifrin
Sweet Love Bitter	IND	Mal Waldron
The Sword of Doom	JAP	Masaru Sato
The Taming of the Shrew	COL	Nino Rota

Tammy and the Millionaire	UN	Jack Marshall
Tarzan and the Great River	PAR	William Loose
Teenage Rebellion	IND	Mike Curb
Tell Me in the Sunlight	IND	Michael Anderson
The Terrornauts	BRI	Elizabeth Lutyens
They Came from Beyond Space	BRI	James Stevens
The Thirst for Love	JAP	Toshiro Mayazumi
Thoroughly Modern Millie	UN	Elmer Bernstein
Those Fantastic Flying Fools	AI	John (Patrick) Scott
Three Bites of the Apple	MGM	Eddy Manson
Thursday We Shall Sing Like Sunday	FRA/BEL	Georges Delerue
The Tiger Makes Out	COL	Ron Grainer
To Sir, with Love	COL	Ron Grainer
Tom Thumb	MEX	Raul Lavista
Tony Rome	TCF	Billy May
The 25th Hour	MGM	Georges Delerue
Two for the Road	TCF	Henry Mancini
Ulysses	CON	Stanley Myers
Up the Down Staircase	WB	Fred Karlin
Valley of the Dolls	TCF	Johnny Williams
The Viking Queen	TCF	Philip Martell
The Violent Ones	IND	Marlin Skiles
The Vulture	PAR	Eric Spear
Wait Until Dark	WB	Henry Mancini
War--Italian Style	ITA	Piero Umiliani
War Kill	IND	Gene Kaurer Douglas Lackey
The War Wagon	UN	Dimitri Tiomkin
Waterhole #3	PAR	Dave Grusin
The Way West	UA	Bronislau Kaper
Welcome to Hard Times	MGM	Harry Sukman
The Whisperers	BRI	John Barry
Who Knows?	ITA	Luis Enrique Bacalov
Who's Minding the Mint?	COL	Lalo Schifrin
Wild, Wild Planet	ITA	Francesco Lavagnino
Winnetou and His Friend Old Firehand	GER	Peter Thomas
The Witnesses	FRA	Maurice Jarre
Woman Times Seven	EMB	Riz Ortolani
You Only Live Twice	UA	John Barry
Young Girls of Rochefort	FRA	Michel Legrand

1968

Amsterdam Affair	BRI	John (Patrick) Scott
Angels from Hell	AI	Stu Philips
Anna Karenina	RUS	Rodion Chtchedrine
The Anniversary	BRI	Philip Martell
Anyone Can Play	ITA	Armando Trovajoli
Anzio	COL	Riz Ortolani
Arizona Bushwackers	PAR	Jimmie Haskell
Assignment K	COL	Basil Kirchin

Assignment to Kill	WB	William Lava
Attack on the Iron Coast	UA	Gerard Schurmann
The Bamboo Saucer	NTA	Edward Paul
Bandits in Milan	ITA	Riz Ortolani
Bandolero	TCF	Jerry Goldsmith
The Bang Bang Kid	ITA/SPA	Nico Tedenco
Barbarella	PAR	Bob Crewe
		Charles Fox
Battle Beneath the Earth	BRI	Kenneth V. Jones
Be Sick--It's Free	ITA	Piero Piccioni
Better a Widow	ITA	Carlo Rustichelli
Beyond the Law	IND	Frank Conroy
The Big Gundown	FRA/ITA	Ennio Morricone
The Biggest Bundle of Them All	MGM	Riz Ortolani
The Black Sheep	ITA	Luis Enriquez
Blackbeard's Ghost	DIS	Robert F. Brunner
The Bliss of Mrs. Blossom	BRI	Riz Ortolani
Blue	PAR	Manos Hadjidakis
The Bofors Gun	BRI	Carl Davis
Boom	UN	John Barry
Bora Bora	FRA/ITA	Piero Piccioni
The Brotherhood	PAR	Lalo Schifrin
The Brute and the Beast	ITA	Lallo Gori
Buckskin	PAR	Jimmie Haskell
Bullitt	WB	Lalo Schifrin
Buona Sera, Mrs. Campbell	WB	Riz Ortolani
Bye Bye Braverman	WB	Peter Matz
Candy	CIN	Dave Grusin
Carry on Doctor	BRI	Eric Rogers
Carry on Up the Khyber	BRI	Eric Rogers
Catch as Catch Can	ITA	Luis Enrique Bacalov
A Challenge for Robin Hood	BRI	Gary Hughes
The Charge of the Light Brigade	UA	John Addison
Charlie Bubbles	BRI	Mischa Donat
Charly	CIN	Ravi Shankar
The Chastity Belt	WB	Riz Ortolani
Chubasco	WB	William Lava
Clue of the Twisted Candle	BRI	Francis Chagrin
The Cobra	ITA/SPA	Jose Antonio Abril
The Conqueror Worm	AI	Paul Ferris
Coogan's Bluff	UN	Lalo Schifrin
Corruption	BRI	Bill McGuffie
Countdown	WB	Leonard Rosenman
The Counterfeit Killer	UN	Quincy Jones
A Dandy in Aspic	COL	Quincy Jones
Danger: Diabolik	FRA/ITA	Ennio Morricone
Danger Route	BRI	John Mayer
The Daring Game	PAR	George Bruns
Dark of the Sun	BRI	Jacques Loussier
Day of the Evil Gun	MGM	Jeff Alexander
The Day of the Owl	FRA/ITA	Giovanni Fusco
Days in My Father's House	DEN/USA	Gil Evans
Dayton's Devils	IND	Marlin Skiles

Deadfall	BRI	John Barry
Decline and Fall	BRI	Ron Goodwin
The Desperate Ones	SPA/USA	Cristobal Halffter
The Destructors	IND	Paul Dunlap
The Devil's Bride	WB	James Bernard
The Devil's Brigade	UA	Alex North
Diamonds for Breakfast	BRI	Norman Kaye
Did You Hear the One About the Traveling Saleslady?	UN	Vic Mizzy
Don't Play with the Martians	FRA	Henri Lanoe
Don't Raise the Bridge, Lower the River	COL	David Whitaker
Double-Strop	IND	David Davis
Dracula Has Risen from the Grave	BRI	James Bernard
Drop Dead, My Love	ITA	Armando Trovajoli
Duffy	BRI	Ernie Freeman
Escalation	ITA	Ennio Morricone
Faustina	ITA	Armando Trovajoli
Fever Heat	PAR	Jaime Mendoza-Nava
Fire	ITA	Franco Potenza
Firecreek	WB	Alfred Newman
Five Card Stud	PAR	Maurice Jarre
5,000,000 Miles to Earth	BRI	Tristram Cary
Flaming Frontier	GER/YUG	Martin Boetticher
A Flea in Her Ear	TCF	Bronislau Kaper
For Love of Ivy	CIN	Quincy Jones
For Singles Only	UN	Fred Karger
Galileo	ITA/BUL	Ennio Morricone
Gates to Paradise	BRI	Ward Swingle
The Gendarme Gets Married	FRA	Raymond Lefevre
Goodbye Moscow	JAP	Toshiro Mayazumi
A Great Big Thing	CAN	Robert Prince
Great Catherine	WB	Dimitri Tiomkin
The Green Berets	WB	Miklos Rozsa
Greetings	SIG	Children of Paradise
Guns for San Sebastian	MGM	Ennio Morricone
Hammerhead	COL	David Whitaker
Hang 'Em High	UA	Dominic Frontiere
Harem	FRA/GER/ITA	Ennio Morricone
Head	COL	Ken Thorne
The Heart Is a Lonely Hunter	WB	Dave Grusin
Hell in the Pacific	CIN	Lalo Schifrin
The Hell with Heroes	UN	Quincy Jones
Hellfighters	UN	Leonard Rosenman
High, Wild and Free	AI	Jaime Mendoza-Nava
The Horse in the Gray Flannel Suit	DIS	George Bruns
Hot Millions	BRI	Laurie Johnson
House of Cards	BRI	Francis Lai
How Sweet It Is	NGP	Pat Williams
How to Save a Marriage and Ruin Your Life	COL	Michel Legrand

I Love You, Alice B. Toklas	WB	Elmer Bernstein
I Love You, I Love You	FRA	Krzystov Penderecki
Ice Station Zebra	MGM	Michel Legrand
The Idols	FRA	Stephane Willar
If ...	BRI	Marc Wilkinson
If He Hollers, Let Him Go	CIN	Harry Sukman
An Immortal Story	FRA	Erik Satie
The Impossible Years	MGM	Don Costa
In Enemy Country	UN	William Lava
In the Green of the Woods	DEN	Bent Fabricius-Bjerre
Inspector Clouseau	UA	Ken Thorne
Interlude	COL	Georges Delerue
Isadora	UN	Maurice Jarre
Island of the Doomed	GER/SPA	Anton Garcia Abril
An Italian in America	ITA	Piero Piccioni
Joanna	TCF	Rod McKuen
Jigsaw	UN	Quincy Jones
Journey to Shiloh	UN	David Gates
Kill!	JAP	Masaru Sato
Kill, Baby, Kill	ITA	Carlo Rustichelli
Killers Three	AI	Mike Curb Harley Hatcher
The Killing of Sister George	CIN	Gerald Fried
Kiss the Other Sheik	FRA/ITA	Luis Enrique Bacalov
Kona Coast	WB	Jack Marshall
Lady in Cement	TCF	Hugo Montenegro
The Legend of Lylah Clare	MGM	Frank de Vol
The Limbo Line	BRI	Johnnie Spence
A Lion in Winter	BRI	John Barry
Live a Little, Love a Little	BRI	Billy Strange
The Lost Continent	BRI	Gerard Schurmann
The Love Bug	DIS	George Bruns
A Lovely Way to Die	BRI	Kenyon Hopkins
Madigan	UN	Don Costa
The Magus	TCF	John Dankworth
The Man Outside	BRI	Johnnie Spence
The Man with Balloons	FRA/ITA	Teo Usuelli
Mattanza	ITA	Benedetto Ghiglia
Mayerling	BRA/FRA	Francis Lai
Mingus	IND	Charles Mingus
The Mini-Skirt Mob	AI	Les Baxter
A Minute to Pray, a Second to Die	ITA	Carlo Rustichelli
Mrs. Brown, You've Got a Lovely Daughter	MGM	Ron Goodwin
The Money Jungle	IND	Paul Dunlap
More Dead Than Alive	UA	Philip Springer
Murder a la Mod	IND	John Herbert McDowell
The Name of the Game Is Kill	IND	Stu Philips
Necronomicon--Dreamed Sins	GER	Friedrich Gulda
Negatives	BRI	Basil Kirchin
Never a Dull Moment	DIS	Robert F. Brunner
New York City--The Most	IND	Sol Kaplan

The Night They Raided Minsky's	UA	Charles Strouse
No Way to Treat a Lady	PAR	Stanley Myers
Nobody Runs Forever	BRI	George Delerue
Nobody's Perfect	UN	Irving Gertz
Northern Safari	AUD	Frank Smith
The Odd Couple	PAR	Neal Hefti
Oedipus the King	BRI	Janni Cristou
Only When I Larf	BRI	Ron Grainer
P. J.	UN	Neal Hefti
Panic in the City	IND	Paul Dunlap
The Paper Lion	UA	Roger Kellaway
Partner	ITA	Ennio Morricone
The Party	UA	Henry Mancini
Payment in Blood	ITA	Francesco de Masi
Petulia	WB	John Barry
The Pink Jungle	UN	Ernie Freeman
Planet of the Apes	TCF	Jerry Goldsmith
Por Mis Pistolas	MEX	Sergio Guerrero
Portrait of Chicko	JAP	Masaru Sato
The Power	MGM	Miklos Rozsa
Pretty Poison	TCF	Johnny Mandel
The Private Navy of Sgt. O'Farrell	UA	Harry Sukman
Project X	PAR	Van Cleave
The Protagonists	ITA	Luis Enrique Bacalov
Prudence and the Pill	TCF	Bernard Ebbinghouse
Psych-Out	ITA	Armando Trovajoli
The Queens	ITA	Armando Trovajoli
Rachel, Rachel	WB	Jerome Moross
The Red Horses	DEN	Bent Fabricius-Bjerre
Riot	PAR	Kryzstof Komeda
Riverrun	IND	Richard Greene Peter Berg
Robby	IND	John Randolph Eaton
Romeo and Juliet	BRI	Nino Rota
Romeo and Juliet	ITA	Peter Tchaikovsky Serge Rachmaninoff
Rosemary's Baby	PAR	Kryzstof Komeda
Run Like a Thief	IND	Johnny Douglas
Salt and Pepper	UA	John Dankworth
Sardinia: Ransom	ITA	Riz Ortolani
The Scalphunters	UA	Elmer Bernstein
Secret Ceremony	BRI	Richard Rodney Bennett
The Secret Life of an American Wife	TCF	Billy May
The Secret War of Harry Frigg	UN	Carlo Rustichelli
Serafino	FRA/ITA	Carlo Rustichelli
The Sergeant	WB	Michel Magne
7 Guns for the MacGregors	ITA/SPA	Ennio Morricone
The Sex of the Angels	GER/ITA	Giovanni Fusco
The Shakiest Gun in the West	UN	Vic Mizzy
The Shoes of the Fisherman	MGM	Alex North
Signs of Life	GER	Stavros Xarchakos

Skidoo	PAR	(Harry) Nilsson
Sol Madrid	MGM	Lalo Schifrin
Speedway	MGM	Jeff Alexander
The Split	MGM	Quincy Jones
The Stalking Moon	NGP	Fred Karlin
Stay Away, Joe	MGM	Jack Marshall
The Strange Affair	BRI	Basil Kirchin
A Stranger in Town	ITA	Benedetto Ghiglia
The Stranger Returns	ITA	Stelvio Cipriani
Summit	FRA/ITA	Mario Nascimbene
Survival, 1967	ISR	Irwin Bazelon
Sweet November	WB	Michel Legrand
The Sweet Ride	TCF	Pete Rugolo
The Swimmer	COL	Marvin Hamlisch
Tales of Mystery and Imagination	FRA/ITA	Nino Rota
The Talisman	IND	Jaime Mendoza-Nava
The Taming	IND	Marcel Aimee
Teenage Mother	IND	Steve Karmen
Tell Me Lies	BRI	Richard Peaslee
Teorema	ITA	Ennio Morricone
Terror in the Jungle	IND	Les Baxter Stan Hofman
Thank You, Aunt	ITA	Ennio Morricone
Therese and Isabelle	FRA	Georges Auric
13 Days in France	FRA	Francis Lai
30 Is a Dangerous Age, Cynthia	BRI	Dudley Moore
The Thomas Crown Affair	UA	Michel Legrand
Three Guns for Texas	UN	Russell Garcia
Three in the Attic	AI	Chad Stuart
Till Death Us Do Part	BRI	Wilfred Burns
A Time for Killing	COL	Van Alexander
A Time to Sing	MGM	Fred Karger
Torture Garden	COL	Don Banks James Bernard
The Touchables	BRI	Ken Thorne
Track of Thunder	UA	John Caper, Jr.
The Trygon Factor	BRI	Peter Thomas
A Twist of Sand	BRI	Tristram Cary
Twisted Nerve	BRI	Bernard Herrmann
2001: A Space Odyssey	MGM	Richard Strauss Johann Strauss, Jr. Gyorgy Ligeti Aram Khachaturian
Up the Junction	BRI	Mike Hugg
Up the MacGregors	ITA/SPA	Ennio Morricone
Uptight	PAR	Booker T. Jones
The Vengeance of Fu Manchu	BRI	Malcolm Lockyer
The Vengeance of She	BRI	Mario Nascimbene
Villa Rides	PAR	Maurice Jarre
The Visionaries	ITA	Gustav Mahler
Vixen	IND	Igo Kantor
War and Peace	RUS	Vyecheslav Ovchinnikov

What's So Bad About Feeling Good?	UN	Frank de Vol
Where Angels Go ... Trouble Follows	COL	Lalo Schifrin
Where Were You When the Lights Went Out?	MGM	Dave Grusin
The Wicked Dreams of Paula Schultz	UA	Jimmie Haskell
Wild in the Streets	AI	Les Baxter
The Wild Racers	AI	Mike Curb
Will Penny	PAR	David Raksin
A Winter's Tale	WB	Jim Dale
Work Is a Four-Letter Word	BRI	Guy Woolfenden
The Wrecking Crew	COL	Hugo Montenegro
The Young Runaways	MGM	Fred Karger
The Young, the Evil and the Savage	ITA	Carlo Savina
The Young Tigers	ITA	Piero Piccioni
Yours, Mine and Ours	UA	Fred Karlin

1969

Aces High	ITA	Carlo Rustichelli
Adam 2	GER	Joseph Anton Reidl
The Adding Machine	BRI	Mike Leander
Age of Consent	AUT	Peter Sculthorpe
Akran	IND	Fred Coulter
Alfred the Great	MGM	Raymond Leppard
Alice's Restaurant	UA	Arlo Guthrie Garry Sherman
All Neat in Black Stockings	BRI	Robert Comford
Angel, Angel, Down We Go	AI	Fred Karger
Anne of the Thousand Days	UN	Georges Delerue
The Apple	SWI	Jacques Oliver
The Appointment	MGM	John Barry
The April Fools	NGP	Marvin Hamlisch
Arabella	ITA	Ennio Morricone
The Arrangement	WB	David Amram
The Assassination Bureau	BRI	Ron Grainer
Asterix and Cleopatra	FRA	Gerard Calvi
The Astro Zombies	IND	Nico Karaski
Baby Love	BRI	Max Harris
The Babysitter	IND	Robert O. Ragland
Backtrack	UN	Jack Marshall
The Battle of the Neretva	CUE	Vladimir Rajteric-Kraus
The Bed Sitting Room	BRI	Ken Thorne
Before Winter Comes	COL	Ron Grainer
The Best House in London	BRI	Mischa Spoliansky
Big Baby Doll	ITA	Luis Enrique Bacalov
The Big Bounce	WB	Mike Curb
The Big Cure	MEX/USA	Val Johns
A Black Veil for Lisa	GER/ITA	Richard Markowitz
Bob and Carol and Ted and Alice	COL	Quincy Jones

Boy	JAP	Hikaru Hayashi
A Boy ... A Girl	IND	Joe Green
A Boy Named Charlie Brown	NGP	Vince Guaraldi
The Bridge at Remagen	UA	Elmer Bernstein
Butch Cassidy and the Sundance Kid	TCF	Burt Bacharach
Cactus Flower	COL	Quincy Jones
Camille 2000	FRA/ITA	Piero Piccioni
Can Heironymus Merkin Ever Forget Mercy Humppe and Find True Happiness?	BRI	Anthony Newley
Carry on Again, Doctor	BRI	Eric Rogers
Carry on Camping	BRI	Eric Rogers
Castle Keep	COL	Michel Legrand
The Chairman	TCF	Jerry Goldsmith
Change of Habit	UN	Ben Weisman
Change of Mind	CIN	Duke Ellington
Charro	NGP	Hugo Montenegro
Chastity	AI	Sonny Bono
Che!	TCF	Lalo Schifrin
Cherry, Harry and Raquel	IND	Igo Kantor
The Christmas Tree	FRA	Georges Auric
The Comic	COL	Jack Elliott
The Computer Wore Tennis Shoes	DIS	Robert F. Brunner
Crooks and Coronets	BRI	John (Patrick) Scott)
Crossplot	BRI	Stanley Black
Cuba My Love	JAP	Teizo Matsumara
Daddy's Gone A-Hunting	NGP	Johnny Williams
The Damned	WB	Maurice Jarre
Day of Anger	GER/ITA	Riz Ortolani
Dead Run	IND	Gerard Calvi
Deadly Shots on Broadway	GER	Peter Thomas
Death of a Gunfighter	UN	Oliver Nelson
Death Rides a Horse	ITA	Ennio Morricone
De Sade	AI	Billy Strange
The Desperados	COL	David Whitaker
The Devil's 8	AI	Mike Curb
Dillinger Is Dead	ITA	Teo Usuelli
Doctor Fabian--Laughing Is the Best Medicine	GER	Martin Boetticher
Don't Drink the Water	EMB	Pat Williams
Double Face	GER/ITA	Carlo Rustichelli
Downhill Racer	PAR	Kenyon Hopkins
Downstream from the Sun	YUG	Dusan Radic
A Dream of Kings	NGP	Alex North
The Duck Rings at Half Past Seven	GER/ITA	Martin Boetticher
80 Steps to Jonah	WB	George Shearing
Explosion	CAN	Sol Kaplan
The Extraordinary Seaman	MGM	Maurice Jarre
Eye of the Cat	UN	Lalo Schifrin
Fanny Hill	SWE	George Riedel

The Fantastic Plastic Machine	IND	Harry Betts
The Fight for Rome	GER/RUM	Riz Ortolani
A Fine Pair	NGP	Ennio Morricone
The First Time	UA	Kenyon Hopkins
Five the Hard Way	IND	Mike Curb
Flareup	MGM	Les Baxter
Follow Me	CIN	Stu Phillips
For a Price	ITA	Ennio Morricone
Fun in the Streets	DEN	Sven Gyldmark
Frankenstein Must Be Destroyed	BRI	James Bernard
Fraulein Doktor	ITA/YUG	Ennio Baragli
Futz	CUE	Tom O'Horgan
Gaily, Gaily	UA	Henry Mancini
The Gamblers	IND	John Morris
The Gay Deceivers	IND	Stu Philips
Generation	EMB	Ben Chapman
Ghosts--Italian Style	FRA/ITA	Luis Enrique Bacalov
Giacomo Casanova: Childhood and Adolescence	ITA	Fiorenzo Carpi
The Girl Watchers	BRA	Roberto Carlos
The Girl Who Knew Too Much	CUE	Joe Green
God Forgives--I Don't	ITA/SPA	Angel Oliver Pina
The Good Guys and the Bad Guys	WB	William Lava
Goodbye Columbus	PAR	Charles Fox
Goyokin	JAP	Masaru Sato
La Grand Rock	CAN	Eldon Rathburn
The Great Bank Robbery	WB	Nelson Riddle
The Green Slime	MGM	Toskiaki Tumasawa
Guns of the Magnificent Seven	UA	Elmer Bernstein
The Guru	TCF	Ustad Vilaya
The Gypsy Moths	MGM	Elmer Bernstein
Hamlet	COL	Patrick Gowers
Hannibal Brooks	BRI	Francis Lai
The Happy Ending	UA	Michel Legrand
Hard Contract	TCF	Alex North
Heaven with a Gun	MGM	Johnny Mandel
Hello Down There	PAR	Jeff Barry
Hell's Angels '69	AI	Tony Bruno
Hell's Belles	AI	Les Baxter
Help Me, My Love	ITA	Piero Piccioni
The Honeymoon Killers	AI	Gustav Mahler
Hook, Line and Sinker	COL	Dick Stabile
The House in the Country	FRA	Raymond Lefevre
How to Commit Marriage	CIN	Joseph J. Lilley
How, When, with Whom	ITA	Armando Trovajoli
I Can't ... I Can't	IRE	Cyril Ornadel
I, You, They	FRA	Bernard Parmegiani
If It's Tuesday, This Must Be Belgium	UA	Donovan
I'll Take Happiness	DEN	Bent Fabricius-Bjerre
The Illustrated Man	WB	Jerry Goldsmith
Impasse	UA	Philip Springer
In the Year of the Lord	ITA	Armando Trovajoli

Film	Origin	Composer
An Indefinite Tenderness	FRA	Francois de Roubaix
The Ingenue	GER	Hans-Martin Majewsky
The Invited One	FRA	Georges Garvarentz
It Takes All Kinds	AUS/USA	Bob Young
The Italian Job	PAR	Quincy Jones
Jazz All Around	DEN	Bent Fabricius-Bjerre
Jeff	FRA	Francois de Roubaix
Jenny	CIN	Michael Small
Jet Generation	GER	David Llewellyn
John and Mary	TCF	Quincy Jones
Journey to the Far Side of the Sun	UN	Barry Gray
Justine	TCF	Jerry Goldsmith
Kenner	MGM	Piero Piccioni
Krakatoa--East of Java	CIN	Frank de Vol
Laddie Loves in All Directions	GER	Martin Boetticher
Lady Hamilton	FRA/GER/ITA	Riz Ortolani
Land Raiders	COL	Bruno Nicolai
The Last of the Mobile Hotshots	WB	Quincy Jones
Last of the Ski Bums	IND	The Sandals
The Last Shot You Hear	BRI	Bert Shefter
Last Summer	AA	John Simon
Laughter in the Dark	BRI	Raymond Leppard
The Lawyer	PAR	Malcolm Dodds
The Learning Tree	WB	Gordon Parks
Life, Love and Death	FRA	Francis Lai
Lion's Love	IND	Joseph Byrd
Long Live Life	ARG	Sergio Ortega
The Lost Man	UN	Quincy Jones
Love and Anger	FRA/ITA	Giovanni Fusco
McKenna's Gold	COL	Quincy Jones
The Mad Room	COL	Dave Grusin
The Madwoman of Chaillot	WB	Michael J. Lewis
The Magic Christian	CUE	Ken Thorne
The Maltese Bippy	MGM	Nelson Riddle
A Man Called Gannon	UN	Dave Grusin
A Man Who Pleases Me	FRA	Francis Lai
Marketa Lazarova	CZE	Zdenek Liska
Marlowe	MGM	Peter Matz
A Married Couple	CAN	Zal Yanovsky Doug Bush
The Matriarch	ITA	Armando Trovajoli
Me, Natalie	NGP	Henry Mancini
Medium Cool	PAR	Mike Bloomfield
Michael Kohlhaas	GER	Stanley Myers
Midas Run	CIN	Elmer Bernstein
Midnight Cowboy	UN	John Barry
A Midsummer Night's Dream	BRI	Guy Woolfenden
The Monitors	CUE	Fred Katz
Moon Zero Two	BRI	Don Ellis
A Mother's Heart	ITA	Ennio Morricone
My Girl Friends' Wedding	IND	Al Kooper
My Side of the Mountain	PAR	Wilfred Josephs

A Nice Girl Like Me	EMB	Pat Williams
99 Women	BRI/SPA	Bruno Nicolai
Number One	UA	Dominic Frontiere
The Oblong Box	AI	Harry Robinson
Obsessions	BRI/SPA	Bernard Herrmann
Oh, What a Lovely War	BRI	Alfred Ralston
The Olsen Gang in a Fix	BEN	Bent Fabricius-Bjerre
On Her Majesty's Secret Service	UA	John Barry
Once Upon a Time in the West	PAR	Ennio Morricone
Once You Kiss a Stranger	WB	Jimmie Fagas
100 Rifles	TCF	Jerry Goldsmith
One Night at Dinner	ITA	Ennio Morricone
An Only Son	FRA	J. P. Drouet
Otley	BRI	Stanley Myers
Out of Frame	ITA	Fiorenzo Carpi
Paranoia	FRA/ITA	Piero Umiliani
Pendulum	COL	Walter Scharf
A Place for Lovers	MGM	Maurice de Sica
Play Dirty	BRI	Michel Legrand
Police Chief Pepe	ITA	Armando Trovajoli
Popi	UA	Dominic Frontiere
The Prime of Miss Jean Brodie	TCF	Rod McKuen
El Professor Hippie	ARG	Jorge Lopez Ruiz
A Profound and Longing for the Gods	JAP	Toshiro Mayazumi
Prologue	CAN	William Brooks
Proud, Damned and Dead	IND	Gene Kauer Douglas Lackey
Putney Swope	IND	Charley Cuva
A Quiet Place in the Country	FRA/ITA	Ennio Morricone
The Rain People	WB	Ronald Stein
Rascal	DIS	Buddy Baker
Recess	IND	Luther Henderson
The Reckoning	BRI	Malcolm Arnold
The Reivers	NGP	Johnny Williams
Ring of Bright Water	BRI	Frank Cordell
The Royal Hunt of the Sun	BRI	Marc Wilkinson
Run, Angel, Run	IND	Stu Philips
Run Wild, Run Free	COL	David Whitaker
Sam Whiskey	UN	Herschel Burke Gilbert
Samurai Banners	JAP	Mararu Sato
Scratch Harry	IND	Ken Lauber
The Secret of Santa Vittoria	UA	Ernest Gold
She and He	ITA	Ennio Morricone
Short Is the Summer	SWE	Hilding Rosenberg
The Sicilians	FRA	Ennio Morricone
Sinful Davey	BRI	Ken Thorne
Ski Fever	AA	Guy Hemric Jerry Styner
Slaves	CON	Bobby Scott
The Smashing Bird I Used to Know	BRI	Bobby Richards
Smith	DIS	Robert F. Brunner

Society of Unrest	ITA	Don Backy
Some Girls Do	BRI	Charles Blackwell
Some Kind of a Nut	UA	Johnny Mandel
Spanking at School	GER	Martin Boetticher
Staircase	TCF	Dudley Moore
The Sterile Cuckoo	PAR	Fred Karlin
Stiletto	EMB	Sid Ramin
The Stolen Air-Ship	CZE/ITA	Jan Novak
Story of a Girl Alone	ITA/SPA	Francesco Lavagnino
Strategy of Terror	UN	Lynn Murray
Subterfuge	BRI/USA	Cyril Ornadel
Support Your Local Sheriff	UA	Jeff Alexander
Sweden--Heaven and Hell	ITA	Piero Umiliani
The Sweet Body of Deborah	WB	Nora Orlandi
Take a Little Sunshine	DEN	Sven Gyldmark
Take the Money and Run	GIN	Marvin Hamlisch
Tell Them Willie Boy Is Here	UN	Dave Grusin
Tenderly	ITA	Riz Ortolani
That Cold Day in the Park	CAN	Johnny Mandel
They Came to Rob Las Vegas	WB	Georges Garvarentz
They Shoot Horses, Don't They?	ABC	John Green
Think of a Number	DEN	Bent Fabricius-Bjerre
Those Daring Young Men in Their Jaunty Jalopies	PAR	Ron Goodwin
Three	BRI	Laurence Rosenthal
3 Into 2 Won't Go	BRI	Francis Lai
Threesome	IND	David Whittaker
To Hell with School	GER	Peter Thomas
A Touch of Love	BRI	Michael Dress
The Tree	IND	Kenyon Hopkins
The Trouble with Girls	MGM	Billy Strange
True Grit	PAR	Elmer Bernstein
Truman Capote's Trilogy	AA	Meyer Kupferman
Two Gentlemen Sharing	BRI	Stanley Myers
2,000 Weeks	AUT	Don Burrows
2,000 Years Later	WB	Stu Phillips
The Undefeated	TCF	Hugo Montenegro
Under the Sign of the Scorpion	ITA	Vittorio Gelmatti
The Virgin Soldiers	COL	Peter Greenwell
Viva Max	Cue	Hugo Montenegro
A Walk with Love and Death	TCF	Georges Delerue
The Wedding Trip	GER/ITA	Carlo Savina
What Ever Happened to Aunt Alice?	CIN	Gerald Fried
What's Good for the Gander	BRI	Reg Tilsley
Where It's At	UA	Benny Golson
Where's Jack?	BRI	Elmer Bernstein
Why America?	FRA	Eddie Harris
The Wild Bunch	WB	Jerry Fielding
Will Our Friends Succeed in Finding Their Friend Who Mysteriously Disappeared in Africa?	ITA	Armando Trovajoli
Winning	UN	Dave Grusin

The Witches	FRA/ITA	Piero Piccioni
The Witchmaker	IND	Jaime Mendoza-Nava
The Woman I Abandoned	JAP	Toshiro Mayazumi
Woman Laughs Last	ITA	Stelvio Cipriani
Women in Love	BRI	Georges Delerue
Wonderwall	BRI	George Harrison
You Can't See 'Round the Corners	AUT	Thomas Tycho
Young Billy Young	UA	Shelly Manne

1970

Abel, Your Brother	POL	Waldemar Kazanecki
Absent-Minded	FRA	Vladimir Cosma
Act of the Heart	CAN	Harry Freedman
Adam's Woman	AUT	Bob Young
The Adventurers	PAR	Antonio Carlos Jobim
After Shadows, Light	EGY	Andre Ryder
Airport	UN	Alfred Newman
Alex in Wonderland	MGM	Tom O'Horgan
The Alienist	BRA	Guilherme Megalhaes Vaz
Alkeste--The Importance of Having Protection	AUS	Erich Kleinschuster
All the Way Up	BRI	Howard Blake
The Altarpiece Maker	BUL	Milcho Leviev
The American Soldier	GER	Peer Raben
Anatomy of the Act of Love	GER	Maurice Ravel
The Ancines Woods	SPA	Antonio Perez Olea
And Soon the Darkness	BRI	Laurie Johnson
The Angel Levine	UA	William Eaton
Angels Die Hard	IND	Richard Hieronymous Waldorf
Anne and Eve	SWE	Bengt-Arne Wallin
Anna	FIN	Claes Afgeyerstam
The Anonymous Venetian	ITA	Stelvio Cipriani
Aoom	SPA	Alfonso Sainz
Apocalypse	FRA	Alain Kremski Laurett Petitgirard
The Aristocats	DIS	George Bruns
The Baby Maker	NGP	Fred Karlin
The Ball of Count Orgel	FRA	Raymond le Senchal
The Ballad of Cable Hogue	WB	Jerry Goldsmith
A Baltic Tragedy	SWE	Bengt Emryd
The Bang Bang Gang	IND	Allen Alper
Barquero	UA	Dominic Frontiere
The Bear	POL	Wojcieck Kilar
Bedside Mazurka	DEN	Ole Hoeyer
Behold Homolka Man	CZE	Karel Mares
Beneath the Planet of the Apes	TCF	Leonard Rosenman
Between Us	SWE	Joe Hill Rage Siven
Beyond the Valley of the Dolls	TCF	Stu Philips
The Big Sky	IN	Salil Chowdhury

Film		Composer
The Bird with the Crystal Plumage	IND	Ennio Morricone
Black-Out	SWI	Alphonse Roy
The Blessing	IN	Vasant Desai
Bloody Mama	AI	Don Randl
Blue Velvet	GER	The Soft Machine
Blum	ARG	Jorge Lopez Ruiz
The Boarding School	SPA	Waldo de los Rios
The Boatniks	DIS	Robert F. Brunner
Bombay Talkie	IN	Shankar Jaikishan
Borsalino	FRA	Claude Bolling
Brand X	IND	Ken Lauber
Brazil Year 2000	BRA	Rogerio Duprat
Brewster McCloud	MGM	Gene Page
The Bridge in the Jungle	UA	Leroy Holmes
Bronco Bullfrog	BRI	Howard Werth Tony Connor Keith Gemmell Trevor Williams
Brotherly Love	BRI	John Addison
A Bullet for Pretty Boy	AI	Harley Hatcher
Burn	UA	Ennio Morricone
The Bushbaby	MGM	Les Reed
The Buttercup Chain	BRI	Richard Rodney Bennett
C.C. and Company	EMB	Lenny Stack
Call Me Mathilde	FRA	Michel Legrand
The Cannibals	ITA	Ennio Morricone
Cannon for Cordoba	UA	Elmer Bernstein
Canticle	SPA	Antonio Perez Olea
The Caprices of Marie	FRA	Georges Delerue
Carry on up the Jungle	BRI	Eric Rogers
A Case for the Young Hangman	CZE	Zdenek Liska
Celeste	FRA	Guy Pederssen
Certain, Very Certain, as a Matter of Fact ... Probable	ITA	Carlo Rustichelli
The Challenges	SPA	Luis de Pablo
The Cheyenne Social Club	NGP	Walter Scharf
Chisum	WB	Dominic Frontiere
The Christine Jorgensen Story	UA	Paul Sawtell Bert Shefter
The Cockeyed Cowboys of Calico County	UN	Lyn Murray
Clickety-Clack	JAP	Toru Takemitsu
The Clowns	FRA/GER/ITA	Nino Rota
Color Me Dead	AUT	Bob Young
Come One, Come All	IND	David Kenzie
El Condor	NGP	Maurice Jarre
The Conformist	FRA/ITA	Georges Delerue
Cool It, Carol	BRI	Cyril Ornandel
Cotton Comes to Harlem	UA	Galt MacDermot
Count Yorga, Vampire	AI	Bill Marx
Cowards	IND	The Merry-Go-Round
The Crimson Cult	BRI	Peter Knight

Cromwell	BRI	Frank Cordell
The Cross and the Switchblade	IND	Ralph Carmichael
The Cry	ITA	Fiorenzo Carpi
Cry of the Banshee	AI	Les Baxter
Cycle Savages	AI	Jerry Styner
Darling Lili	PAR	Henry Mancini
David Copperfield	TCF	Malcolm Arnold
A Day at the Beach	IND	Mort Schuman
Days and Nights in the Forest	IN	Satyajit Ray
Dead of Summer	FRA/ITA	Peppino de Luca Carlo Pas
Deadlock	CIN	The Can
Dear Irene	YUG	Dubravko Defonj
Death Has No Friends	ISR	Herb Newman
Death Took Place Last Night	GER/ITA	Gianni Ferrio
Deep End	GER/USA	Cat Ten
Detective Belli		Fred Bongusto
Dinah East	IND	Ernie Freeman
Dirty Dingus Magee	MGM	Jeff Alexander
Dirtymouth	IND	Emanuel Vardi Leonid Hambro
Do Not Throw Cushions into the Ring	IND	Nicholas Carras
Doctor in Trouble	BRI	Eric Rogers
Donkey Skin	FRA	Michel Legrand
Don't Fumble, Darling	GER	Christian Schultze
Don't Worry	RUS	J. Kancheli
Dorian Gray	AI	Peppino de Luca Carlo Pas
Double Pisces, Scorpio Rising	BRI	Peter Townshend Speedy Kean
Douglas	NOR	Egil-Monn Iversen
The Dreamer	ISR	Gershon Kingsley
The Dunwich Horror	AI	Les Baxter
Eagles Attack at Dawn	ISR	Dov Seltzer
The Earth	EGY	Aly Ismail
The Eighth	BUL	Milcho Leviev
The Eleventh Commandment	YUG	Bosco Petrovic
Emergency Exit	FRA	Philippe Sarde
The End of Pyrenees	FRA	Andre Ellart Philippe Langlet
End of the Road	AA	Teo Macero
Entertaining Mr. Sloane	BRI	Georgie Fame
Equinox	IND	John Cape
Eugenie--The Story of Her Journey into Perversion	BRI	Bruno Nicolai
Events	GRO	Eric Gale
Every Home Should Have One	BRI	John Cameron
The Executioner	BRI	Ron Goodwin
Eyewitness	BRI	Fairfield Parlor Van der Graff Generator
Familiarities	MEX	Joaquin Gutierrez Heras

The Female Animal	ITA/SPA	Clay Pitts
The Fire Tongue Bowl	GER	Bernhard Eichhorn
First Love	GER/SWI	Mark London
Flap	WB	Marvin Hamlisch
Flick	CAN	Paul Hoffert
Fools	CIN	The First Edition
Forbidden to Step on the Clouds	SA	Luis (Chino) Urquidi
The Forbin Project	UN	Michel Colombier
Four Clowns	TCF	Manny Albam
Fragment of Fear	BRI	Johnny Harris
From the Other Side	YUG	Urban Koder
Funeral Parade of Roses	JAP	Joii Yuassa
The Games	TCF	Francis Lai
The Garden of the Finzi-Continis	ITA	Manuel de Sica
Gas-s-s-s	AI	Harry Melton
Gentlemen in White Vests	GER	Peter Thomas
Getting Straight	COL	Ronald Stein
Give God a Chance on Sunday	DEN	Patrick Gowers
Glass Houses	IND	David Raksin
God with Us	ITA	Ennio Morricone
Gods of Pestilence	GER	Peer Raben
Goin' Down the Road	CAN	Bruce Cockburn
Goodbye Gemini	BRI	Christopher Gunning
Gradina	ITA	Mario Nascimbene
The Grasshopper	NGP	Billy Goldenberg
The Green Wall	SA	John Fiddy Alan Hawkshaw
Guess What We Learned in School Today?	IND	Moose Charlap
Halls of Anger	UA	Dave Grusin
Hammer for the Witches	CZE	Jiri Srnka
Handcuffs	YUG	Miljanko Prohaska
Happy Birthday, Davy	IND	Lou Nanager
Happy He, Who Like Ulysses	FRA	Georges Delerue
The Hard Road	IND	Jaime Mendoza-Nava
Heintje--Once the Sun Will Be Shining Again	GER	Raimund Rosenberger
Hello--Goodbye	TCF	Francis Lai
Hi, Mom!	IND	Eric Katz
The Hiding Places	SPA	Juan Prado
Hoffman	BRI	Ron Grainer
A Hole in the Grounds	POL	Tomasz Stanko
Homer	NGP	Don Scardino
The Hoodlum	FRA	Francis Lai
Hooray for the Blue Hussars	DEN	Sven Gyldmark
Horror House	AI	Reg Tilsley
The Horror of Frankenstein	BRI	Malcolm Williamson
The Hostess Also Likes to Blow the Horn	GER/ITA	Gianni Ferrio
The Hostess Exceeds All Bounds	AUS/GER	Gerhard Heinz
The House of Light	CAN	Walter Boudreau

Title	Country/Studio	Composer
How Did a Nice Girl Like You Get into This Business?	GER	Klaus Dildinger
How Do I Love Thee?	CIN	Randy Sparks
How Short Is the Time for Love	GER	Jerry van Royen
How to Succeed with Sex	IND	Forest Hamilton Sean Bonniwell
Hurrah! Our Parents Aren't There	GER	Pepe Ederer
Hurrah! The School Is Burning	GER	Rolf Wilhelm
I Killed Einstein, Gentlemen	CZE	Vlastimil Hala
I Love My Wife	UN	Lalo Schifrin
I Never Sang for My Father	COL	Al Gorgoni Barry Mann
I Start Counting	BRI	Basil Kirchin
I Walk the Line	COL	Johnny Cash
Imago	IND	Lalo Schifrin
In Search of Gregory	UN	Ron Grainer
The Inheritors	ARG	Jorge Lopez Ruiz
Initiation	CAN	Francois Cousineau
Investigation of a Citizen above Suspicion	ITA	Ennio Morricone
The Jackal of Nahueltoro	SA	Sergio Ortega
James or Not	SWI	Guy Bovet
Joe	IND	Bobby Scott
Josefine Mutzenbacher	AUS/GER	Gerhard Heinz
Judgment	HUN/RUM	Cornel Taranu
Julius Caesar	BRI	Michael Lewis
Kanku	IN	Dilip Kholakia
Kelly's Heroes	MGM	Lalo Schifrin
Kes	BRI	John Cameron
The Key to Paradise	DEN	Bent Fabricius-Bjerre
Killing the Devil	CZE	Angelo Michajilov
King of the Grizzlies	DIS	Buddy Baker
Klann/Grand Guignol	BEL/FRA	Patrick Ledoux
The Knight of the Sword	ARG	Ariel Ramirez
The Kremlin Letter	TCF	Robert Drasnin
The Landlord	UA	Al Kooper
Landscape after the Battle	POL	Zygmunt Konieczny
The Last Act of Martin Weston	CAN/CZE	Milan Kymlicka
The Last Grenade	CIN	John Dankworth
The Last Maiden But One	BRA	Egberto Giamonte
Leo the Last	BRI	Fred Myrow
Let's Have a Riot	ITA	Piero Piccioni
Let's Play Hide-and-Seek	DEN/NOR	Eigil Monn-Iversen
The Liberation of L. B. Jones	COL	Elmer Bernstein
The Lickerish Quartet	GER/ITA/USA	Stelvio Cipriani
Little Big Man	NGP	John Hammond
Little Fauss and Big Halsy	PAR	Johnny Cash Bob Dylan Carl Perkins
Lonely Hearts	ITA	Luiz Enriquez
Long Live the Bride and Groom	SPA	Antonio Perez Olea
The Long Ride from Hell	ITA	Carlo Savina

The Looking Glass War	CAL	Wally Stott
The Losers	IND	Stu Philips
Lost	CHI	Domingo Lam
Love By Rape	GER	Irwin Schmidt
Love Me Like I Do	IND	Esla Singman
Love Story	PAR	Francis Lai
Love Story Film	HUN	Janos Gonda
The Lovers	RUS	B. Trotsuk
Lovers and Other Strangers	CIN	Fred Karlin
Loving	COL	Bernardo Segall
The Loving Truth	IND	Gary Le Mel Norman Green Jim Helms
Ludwig on the Lookout for a Wife	GER	Rolf Wilhelm
Lydia	GER	Peter Kiesewetter
The McKenzie Break	UA	Riz Ortolani
The McMasters	IND	Coleridge-Taylor Perkinson
Madigan's Million	AI	Gregory Segura
Madron	IND	Riz Ortolani
The Magic Garden of Stanley Sweetheart	MGM	Jerry Styner
Malatesta	GER	Georges Gruntz
The Man Who Came for Coffee	ITA	Fred Bongusto
The Man Who Had Power over Women	EMB	Johnny Mandel
The Man with Connections	FRA	Georges Moustaki
Mark of the Devil	BRI/GER	Michael Holm
The Martlet's Tale	ITA	Manos Hadjidakis
M*A*S*H	TCF	Johnny Mandel
A Matter of Fat	CAN	Robert Fleming
Me and My Kid Brother and Doggie	DEN	Sven Gyldmark
Meat Rack	IND	Donald Skinner
Memories of a Gigolo	BRA	Antonio Adolfo Tiberio Gaspar
Memories of the Future	GER	Peter Thomas
The Mercenary	ITA/SPA	Ennio Morricone
Metello	ITA	Ennio Morricone
Mictlan	MEX	Guillermo Noriega
Mr. and Mrs. Juan Lamaglia	ARG	Roberto Lar
Mr. President	ARG	Virtu Margano
The Modification	FRA	Francis Lai
The Molly Maguires	PAR	Henry Mancini
Monique	FRA	Jacques Loussier
Monte Walsh	NGP	John Barry
The Moonshine War	MGM	Fred Karger
Mosquito Squadron	UA	Frank Cordell
The Most Beautiful Wife	ITA	Ennio Morricone
The Motive Was Jealousy	ITA	Armando Trovajoli
Move!	TCF	Marvin Hamlisch
Mumsy, Nanny, Sonny and Girly	CIN	Bernard Ebbinghouse
My Lover, My Son	BRI	Norrie Paramor
My Mao	ITA	Teo Usuelli

Myra Breckinridge	TCF	John Philips
The New Life Style	GER/USA	Danny Domino Horace Diaz Athena Hosey
Night of the Counting Years	EGY	Mario Nascimbene
The Night of the Seagull	JAP	Chumei Watanabe
Norwood	PAR	Al de Lory
Nudity	CZE	Lubos Fiser
A Nun at the Croosroads	ITA/SPA	Giovanni Fusco
Oh, Sun	FRA	Georges Anderson
The Olympics in Mexico	COL	Joaquin Guiterrez Heras
One Day Is More Beautiful Than the Other	GER	Franz Grothe
One More Time	UA	Les Reed
The Only Game in Town	TCF	Maurice Jarre
The Only Way	DEN/USA	Carl Davis
The Out-of-Towners	PAR	Quincy Jones
Outlaws	JAP	Masaru Sato
The Owl and the Pussycat	COL	Richard Halligan
Paddy	AA	John Rubenstein
The Palace of Angels	FRA	Rogerio Duprat
Passing Days	YUG	Vojislav Kostic
Patton	TCF	Jerry Goldsmith
The People Next Door	EMG	Don Sebesky
The People of Warsaw	POL	Zygmunt Konieczny
Perfect Friday	BRI	John Dankworth
Performance	BRI	Jack Nitzsche
Perrak	GER	Rolf Kuehn
The Phantom Tollbooth	MGM	Dean Elliott
The Phynx	WB	Mike Stoller
Pieces of Dreams	UA	Michel Legrand
Piggies	GER	Serge Gainsbourg
The Politicians	IND	John Bath
Pornography: Copenhagen 1970	DEN	Frederick Magius
A Portrait of Marianne	FRA	Philippe Carson
Portraits of Women	FIN	Claes Af Guerstam
The Priest of St. Pauli	GER	Erwin Halletz
The Private Life of Sherlock Holmes	UA	Miklos Rozsa
The Projectionist	IND	Igo Kantor Erma E. Levin
Promise at Dawn	EMB	Georges Delerue
The Prophet of Hunger	BRA	Rinaldo Rossi
Pufnstuf	UN	Charles Fox
Pussycat, Pussycat, I Love You	UA	Lalo Schifrin
Puzzle of a Downfall Child	UN	Michael Small
Q-Bec My Love	CAN	Andree Paul
Quackser Fortune Has a Cousin in the Bronx	IND	Michael Dress
R. P. M.	COL	Barry de Vorzon
Rabbit, Run	WB	Ray Burton Brian King
The Railway Children	BRI	Johnny Douglas

Red, White and Black	IND	Stu Philips
Redhead	FIN	Otto Donner
Revolution, My A--	DEN	Bent Fabricius-Bjerre
The Revolutionaries	SA	Claudio Rebagliatti Armando Guevara Ochoa
The Revolutionary	BRI	Michael Small
Rhubarb	BRI	Brian Fahey
Rider on the Rain	FRA	Francis Lai
Right On	LEA	Abdul Hakien Jim Pollard Harold Sorel
Rio Lobo	NGP	Jerry Goldsmith
The Rise and Rise of Michael Rimmer	BRI	John Cameron
Road to Salina	FRA/ITA	Michel Magne
Ryan's Daughter	MGM	Maurice Jarre
Saint Denis, in These Times	CAN	Francois Dompierre
The Saints from Krejcarek	CZE	Zdenek Liska
Sapho	FRA	Georges Garvarentz
Satan's Sadists	IND	Harley Hatcher
The Savage Wild	AI	Jaime Mendoza-Nava
The Scar of Dracula	BRI	James Bernard
The Scavengers	ITA	Gianni Ferrio
Schoolgirl Report	GER	Gert Wilden
Scream and Scream Again	AI	David Whittaker
The Seed of Man	ITA	Teo Usuelli
Sex Perverse	GER	Christian Schultze
Sex Power	FRA	Vangelis Papathanassiou
The Sidelong Glances of a Pigeon Kicker (Pigeons)	MGM	Pat Williams Lee Holdridge Chris Dedrick Warren Marley
Simply Maria	SA	Tito Ribero
69	FIN/SWE	Claes Af Geigerstam
Skullduggery	UN	Oliver Nelson
The Sky Pirate	IND	Brian Trentham
Soldier Blue	EMB	Roy Budd
Solo	FRA	Georges Moustaki
Something for Everyone	NGP	John Kander
Sophie's Ways	FRA	Art Ensemble Chicago
Spring and Port Wine	BRI	Douglas Gamley
Squeeze a Flower	AUT	Tommy Leonetti
Start the Revolution without Me	WB	John Addison
Sticks and Stones	IND	Mary Jo Frontiera
The Story of a Woman	ITA/SWE	Johnny Williams
Strogoff	GER/ITA	Teo Usuelli
The Stud	FRA	Francois de Roubaix
Summer Trail	FIN	Rauno Lehtinen
Sunflower	ITA	Henry Mancini
Suppose They Gave a War and Nobody Came	CIN	Jerry Fielding
A Swedish Love Story	SWE	Bjorn Isfalt

Sweet Kisses and Languid Caresses	ITA	Peppino de Luca Carlo Pes
Take a Girl Like You	BRI	Stanley Myers
Tales of Blood	YUG	Vojislav Kostic
Tarzan's Deadly Silence	NGP	Walter Greene
The Taste of the Black Earth	POL	Wojciech Kilar
Taste the Blood of Dracula	BRI	James Bernard
Tell Me That You Love Me, Junie Moon	PAR	Philip Springer
Temperate Zone	HUN	Janos Gonda
Teresa	FRA	Wladimir Kosma
That Little Difference	FRA/ITA	Maestro Ghiglia
Then Came Bronson	MGM	George Duning
Then Came the Legend	RUM	Radu Serban
There Was a Crooked Man	WB	Charles Strouse
There's a Girl in My Soup	COL	Mike d'Abo
They Call Me Mister Tibbs	UA	Quincy Jones
This Transient Life	JAP	Toru Fuyuki
Thomas and the Bewitched	ITA	Amadeo Tommasi
Those Crazy Years	ARG	Tito Ribero
Three Men on a Horse	FRA	Gerard Calvi
Three Sisters	BRI	William Walton
Time of the Wolves	FRA	Georges Garvarentz
The Time to Die	FRA	Karel Trow
Times Four	BRI	Gavin Bryars
Tintin and the Sun Temple	BEL/FRA	Francois Rauber
Tomorrow	BRI	Hugo Montenegro
Too Late the Hero	CIN	Gerald Fried
Too Little for Such a Big War	RUM	Cornel Cezar
Tostao--The King of Football	BRA	Milton Nascimento
Tough Guys of the Prairie	DEN	Sven Gyldmark
The Traveling Executioner	MGM	Jerry Goldsmith
Trip Around My Cranium	HUN	Gyorgy Ranki
Trog	WB	John (Patrick) Scott
Tropic of Cancer	PAR	Stanley Myers
Tropical Ecstasy	ARG	Luis Alberto del Parana
The 12 Chairs	UMC	John Morris
12 Plus 1	FRA/ITA	Piero Poletto
Twinky	BRI/ITA	John (Patrick) Scott
Two Mules for Sister Sara	UN	Ennio Morricone
Up in the Cellar	AI	Don Randi
Upon This Rock	IND	Michael J. Lewis
Valparaiso My Love	SA	Gustavo Becerra
The Vampire Lovers	BRI	Harry Robinson
A Vampire's Dream	BRA	Joao Silverio Trevisan
Venus in Furs	AI	Manfred Mann Mike Hugg
Violent City	ITA	Ennio Morricone
The Virgin and the Gypsy	BRI	Patrick Gowers
W. U. S. A.	PAR	Lalo Schifrin
A Walk in the Spring Rain	COL	Elmer Bernstein
The Walking Stick	MGM	Stanley Myers
Waterloo	COL	Nino Rota

Watermelon Man	COL	Melvin van Peebles
The Way We Live Now	UA	Nate Sassover
We Are All Naked	FRA	Jean-Paul Mengeon
We Chop the Teachers into Mince Meat	GER	Rolf Wilhelm
We--Two	GER	Xhol Caravan
We Two France	FRA	Memphis Slim
The Wedding Ring	FRA	Gilbert Amy
We'll Eat the Fruit of Paradise	BEL/CZE	Zdenek Liska
What Do You Say to a Naked Lady?	UA	Steve Karman
The Wheel Turns in the Shadow	JAP	Takashi Akutagawa
When Dinosaurs Ruled the Earth	BRI	Mario Nascimbene
When the Mad Aunts Are Coming	GER	Gerhard Heinrich
When Women Had Tails	ITA	Ennio Morricone
Where's Poppa?	UA	Jack Elliott
Which Way to the Front?	WB	Louis Brown
The White Room	BUL	Dimiter Vulchev
Why Russians Are Revolting	IND	Robert Hennessy
The Wife Swappers	BRI	Michael Eaton John Fiddy
Wilbur and the Baby Factory	IND	Michael Teresco
The Wild Pussycat	GRE	Nikolai Ignatoff
The Woman of Everyone	BRA	Ana Rosalina
A Woman on File	ITA	Gino Peguri
Wuthering Heights	AI	Michel Legrand
The Yellow House at Pinnasberg	GER	Rolf Kuehn
You Can't Win 'Em All	COL	Bert Kaempfert
Your Child, the Unknown Creature	GER	Heinz Kissling Peter Schirmann
Your Husband, the Unknown Creature	GER	Heinz Kissling
Youth March	ITA	Piero Piccioni
Zigzag	UN	Oliver Nelson

1971

The Abominable Dr. Phibes	AI	Basil Kirchin Jack Nathan
Abuse of Authority	GRE	Mimas Plessas
Adios Sabata	UA	Bruno Nicolai
Adrift	CZE/USA	Zdenek Liska
The Adversary	IN	Satyajit Ray
The African Elephant	NGP	Laurence Rosenthal
All the Right Noises	BRI	Melanie
American Sexual Revolution	IND	Carlos Rodrigues
The Anderson Tapes	COL	Quincy Jones
The Andromeda Strain	UN	Gil Melle
The Animals	IND	Rupert Holmes
Antefatto	ITA	Stelvio Cipriani
Apokal	GER	Peter Janssens
The Apprentice	CAN	Roger Gravel
Arde	MEX	Luciano Michelini

Are You Afraid?	DEN	Burnin' Red Ivanhoe
The Arp Statue	BRI	James L. Fox
Arruza	IND	Raul Lavista
Assault	BRI	Eric Rogers
The Awakening	CAN	Francois Cousineau
B.S., I Love You	TCF	Jim Dale Mark Shekter
Bali	GER/ITA	Giorgio Gaslini
Bananas	UA	Marvin Hamlisch
Bang Bang	BRA	Mario Fongaro Murano
The Barefoot Executive	DIS	Robert F. Brunner
Bartleby	BRI	Roger Webb
The Battle of Love's Return	IND	Lloyd Kaufman Andre Golino
Bedside Dentist	DEN	Ole Hoeyer
The Beguiled	UN	Lalo Schifrin
Believe in Me	MGM	Fred Karlin
Beyond Love and Evil (Philosophy of the Boudoir)	FRA	Jean Claude Pelletier
The Big Highway	ARG	Jorge Lopez Ruiz
Big Jake	NGP	Elmer Bernstein
Billy Jack	WB	Mundell Lowe
Biribi	FRA	Mikis Theodorakis
Black Beauty	BRI	Lionel Bart
Bless the Beasts and Children	COL	Barry de Vorzon Perry Botkin, Jr.
Blood from the Mummy's Tomb	BRI	Tristram Cary
The Blood Letting	UA	Eddy Vartan
Bloomfield	BRI/ISR	Johnny Harris
Blue Movie	GER/HOL	Jurgen Drews Les Humphreys
The Bordello	GER	Otto Schuett
Born to Win	UA	William S. Fisher
The Brazen Women of Balzac	GER	Claudius Alzner
Breakout	HUN	Gyorgy Vukan
Brother John	COL	Quincy Jones
The Brotherhood of Satan	COL	Jaime Mendoza-Nava
The Bug Killer	YUG	Miodrac Ilic-Bell
Bunny O'Hare	AI	Billy Strange
The Burglar	FRA	Ennio Morricone
The Bus Is Coming	IND	Tom McIntosh
The Call	POL	Andrej Trzaskowski
Calliope	IND	Tommy Oliver
Captain Apache	SPA	Dolores Claman
Carlotta	HUN	Zdenko Tamassy Gabor Presser
Cat O' Nine Tails	NGP	Ennio Morricone
Catch Me a Spy	BRI/FRA	Claude Bolling
Catlow	SPA	Roy Budd
Chandler	MGM	George Romanis
Christa	DEN/USA	Manfred Mann
The Christian Licorice Store	NGP	Lalo Schifrin
The Christmas Martian	CAN	Jacques Perron

Film	Country/Studio	Composer
Chrome and Hot Leather	AI	Porter Jordan
Chronicle of a Lady	ARG	Roberto Lar
Cisco Pike	COL	Kris Kristoffersen
A City's Child	AUT	Peter Pinne
A Clerk Vanished	DEN	Henning Christiansen
A Clockwork Orange	WB	Walter Carlos
Cold Turkey	UA	Randy Newman
Come to Your Senses	NGP	Rod McKuen, et al
Come Together	ITA	Stelvio Cipriani
Confession, Theory, Actress	JAP	Ichiyangi Toshi
Confessions of a Police Commissioner to the District Attorney	ITA	Riz Ortolani
The Cop	ISR	Nurit Hirsch
Count Dracula	GER/ITA/SPA	Bruno Nicolai
The Cow	ITA	Mormoz Ferhat
The Creatures the World Forgot	BRI	Mario Nascimbene
The Cross-Eyed Saint	ITA	Maurizio de Angelis Guido de Angelis
Cry Uncle	IND	Harper MacKay
Dad's Diary	BRI	Wilfred Burns
Dagmar's Hot Pants, Inc.	DEN	Jimmie Haskell
Daughters of Darkness	FRA/USA	Francois de Roubaix
The Dawn of Islam	EGY	Fouad El-Zahrey
The Dawn of Victory	GRE	Costas Kapnissis
The Days of Water	CUB	Leo Brouwer
The Dead One in the Thames River	GER	Peter Thomas
Death in Venice	ITA	Gustav Mahler
The Debut	RUS	B. Bigerba
The Decameron	ITA	Pier Paolo Passolini Ennio Morricone
Delusions of Grandeur	FRA	Michel Polnareff
The Demonstrator	AUT	Bob Young
The Deserted Piazza	ITA	Jacqueline Perrotin
The Deserter	PAR	Piero Piccioni
Desertoren	DEN	Pelle Gudmundsen Holmgren
Desperate Characters	BRI	Lee Konitz Jim Hall Ron Carter
The Devils	WB	Peter Maxwell Davis
The Devil's Lovers	ITA/SPA	Carlo Savina Mariano Girolani
Diabolical Shudder	SPA	Jose Espeitia
Diamonds Are Forever	UA	John Barry
Dirty Harry	WB	Lalo Schifrin
The Dirty Heroes	FRA/GER/ITA	Ennio Morricone
The Dirty Outlaws	ITA	Gianni Ferrio
Doc	UA	Jimmy Webb
Dr. Jekyll and Sister Hyde	BRI	David Whittaker
Dollars ($)	COL	Quincy Jones
Dulcima	BRI	Johnny Douglas
Eagle in a Cage	NGP	Marc Wilkinson
Early Morning	FRA	Francis Lai

An Eel Worth 300 Million	ITA	Fiorenzo Carpi
An Elephant Called Slowly	BRI	Bert Kaempfert
Emperors, Citizens and Comrades	GER	Wolfgang de Gelmini
Escape from the Planet of the Apes	TCF	Jerry Goldsmith
Everest Symphony	JAP	Ikuma Dan
Excuse Me, My Name Is Rocco Papaleo	ITA	Armando Trovajoli
The Explosion	BEL/CAN/FRA	Henri Salvador
The Exquisite Cadaver	SPA	Marco Rossi
Father of Four in a Sunny Mood	DEN	Sven Gyldmark
Fifty-Fifty	ISR	David Krivoskey
Fire Woman	KOR	Han Sang-Ky
The Flanders and Alcott Report on Sex Response	IND	Randy Scott
The Flight	RUS	Nikolai Karetnikov
Flight of the Doves	COL	Roy Budd
Fool's Parade	COL	Henry Vars
Fortune and Men's Eyes	MGM	Galt MacDermot
Foxy Lady	CAN	Doug Riley
The French Connection	TCF	Don Ellis
French Leave	FRA	Michel Legrand
Friends	PAR	Elton John
From Ear to Ear	FRA	Clay Pitts
From the Boys	FRA/ITA	Michel Magne
Games That Lovers Play	BRI	David Lindup
The Gang That Couldn't Shoot Straight	MGM	Dave Grusin
Get Carter	MGM	Roy Budd
Ginger	IND	Harry D. Glass
Girl Stroke Boy	BRI	John (Patrick) Scott
Girls and Gynecologists	GER	Erwin Halletz
The Glass Ceiling	SPA	Angel Arteaga
Going Home	MGM	Bill Walker
Gold for the Tough Guys of the Prairie	DEN	Sven Gyldmark
Golden Apples of the Sun	CAN	Galt MacDermot
Goodbye, Stork, Goodbye	SPA	Antonio Perez Olea
Goya	SPA	Luis de Pablo
The Great Battle	RUS	A. Levitin
Grimm's Fairy Tales for Adults	GER	Joe Beck Regis Mull
The Grissom Gang	CIN	Gerald Fried
The Guest	ITA	Giocchino Rossini
Gumshoe	BRI	Andrew Lloyd Webber
A Gunfight	PAR	Laurence Rosenthal
Hannie Caulder	PAR	Ken Thorne
The Hard Ride	AI	Harley Hatcher
Harold and Maude	PAR	Cat Stevens
He Died After the War	JAP	Toru Takemitsu
Head On	IND	William G. St. Pierre
Heads or Tails	CAN	Stephane Venne

The Hellstrom Chronicle	WOL	Lalo Schifrin
Highway Queen	ISR	Dov Seltzer
The Hired Hand	UN	Bruce Langhorne
Hiya, Stine	DEN	Bengt-Arne Wallin
Homo Eroticus	ITA	Armando Trovajoli
The Honest Interview	GER	The Cats
Honky	IND	Quincy Jones
Horizon	HUN	Janos Gonda
The Horsemen	COL	Georges Delerue
The Hospital	UA	Morris Surdin
Hot Traces of St. Pauli	GER	Peter Schirmann
The House under the Trees	FRA	Gilbert Becaud
How Tasty Was My Little Frenchman	BRA	Guilherme Mangalhaes Vaz
How to Frame a Figg	UN	Vic Mizzy
The Hunted Samurai	JAP	Hajime Kaburagi
The Hunting Party	UA	Riz Ortolani
Hurray, We Are Bachelors Again	GER	Peter Schirmann
I'm Going to Get You ... Elliot Boy	CAN	Allen Aller
In Prison Awaiting Trial	ITA	Carlo Rustichelli
In the Gorge	YUG	Joze Drivsek
In the Name of the Father	ITA	Nicola Provani
In the Name of the Italian People	ITA	Carlo Rustichelli
In the Summertime	ITA	Bruno Lanzi
The Incredible Two-Headed Transplant	AI	John Barber
Inn of Evil	JAP	Toru Takemitsu
Interior Mechanism	SPA	G. Gil-San
Is It Necessary to Be Among the Peoples of the World to Know Them?	CAN	Michael Garneau
It Only Happens to Others	FRA/ITA	Michel Poinareff
J. W. Coop	COL	Louie Shelton Don Randi
Jack Johnson	IND	Miles Davis
Jack the Ripper	ITA/SPA	Piero Piccioni
Jane Eyre	BRI	Johnny Williams
Jennifer on My Mind	UA	Stephen J. Lawrence
The Jesus Trip	IND	Bernardo Segall
Joe Hill	SWE/USA	Stefan Crossman
Johnny Got His Gun	IND	Jerry Fielding
Jud	IND	Stu Phillips
Jumping over Puddles Again	CZE	Zdenek Liska
Jutrzenka: A Winter in Majorca	SPA	Frederic Chopin
Kazoku	JAP	Masaru Sato
Kidnapped	BRI	Roy Budd
Kotch	CIN	Marvin Hamlisch
Lady Caliph	FRA/ITA	Ennio Morricone
The Last Movie	UN	Kris Kristoffersen
The Last Rebel	COL	Jon Lord Tony Ashton

Title	Country/Studio	Composer
The Last Valley	CIN	John Barry
The Late Liz	IND	Ralph Carmichael
Lawman	UA	Jerry Fielding
Le Mans	NGP	Michel Legrand
Lenz	GER	David Llewellyn
Let's Play in the World	ARG	Marito Cosentino
Let's Scare Jessica to Death	PAR	Orville Steober
The Light at the Edge of the World	NGP	Piero Piccioni
The Lion's Share	FRA	Georges Garvarentz
A Little, A Lot, Passionately	FRA	Francois de Roubaix
Little Birdie	HUN	Gabor Presser
Little Murders	TCF	Fred Katz
A Little Sun in Cold Water	FRA	Michel Legrand
A Lizard in a Woman's Skin	FRA/ITA/SPA	Ennio Morricone
Long Ago Tomorrow	BRI	Stanley Myers
Loot	BRI	Keith Mansfield Richard Willington-Denton
Love	HUN	Andras Mihaly
Love Is Only a Word	GER	Erich Ferstl
Love Is War	NOR	Ragnar Lasse
The Love Machine	COL	Artie Butler
A Lovely Monster	FRA	Georges Garvarentz
Loving and Laughing	CAN	Dean Morgan
Lucie and the Miracles	CZE	Lubos Fiser
The Lumiere Years	FRA	Pierre Dutour
M as in Mathieu	FRA	Antoine Duhamel
Macbeth	COL	The Third Ear Band
McCabe and Mrs. Miller	WB	Leonard Cohen
Maddalena	ITA	Ennio Morricone
Made for Each Other	TCF	Trade Martin
Madeleine Is	CAN	Ross Barrett
Make a Face	IND	Tony Cohan
Making It	TCF	Norman Gimpel Charles Fox
A Man Called Sledge	COL	Gianni Ferrio
Man in the Wilderness	WB	Johnny Harris
The Marriage of a Young Stockbroker	TCF	Fred Karlin
The Married Priest	ITA	Armando Trovajoli
Marta	ITA/SPA	Piero Piccione
Mary, Queen of Scots	UN	John Barry
Melody (S.W.A.L.K.)	BRI	The Bee Gees
The Men	CAN	Stephane Venne
The Mephisto Waltz	TCF	Jerry Goldsmith
The Message	POR	Rui Cardoso
Mira	BEL/HOL	Georges Delerue
Murders in the Rue Morgue	AI	Waldo de los Rios
Murphy's War	BRI	John Barry
My Sister's Kids at Their Worst	DEN	Sven Gyldmark
My Uncle Antoine	CAN	Jean Cousineau
N. P.	ITA	Nicola Piovani
Nana	SWE	George Riedel

Near Orouet	FRA	Daevid Allen Gilli Smythe
Necrophagus	SPA	Alfonso Santisteben
Next (see The Secret Vice of Signora Ward)		
Nicholas and Alexandra	COL	Richard Rodney Bennett
Nickel Queen	AUT	Sven Libaek
The Night Digger	MGM	Bernard Herrmann
Night of Dark Shadows	MGM	Robert Cobert
The Night of San Juan	ITA	Roberto Lar
The Night Visitor	UMC	Henry Mancini
The Nightcomers	BRI	Jerry Fielding
Nini Tirabuscio	ITA	Carlo Rustichelli
No Drums, No Bugles	CIN	Lyle Ritz
The Oil Girls	FRA	Francis Lai
Okay Bill	IND	Charles G. Morrow
The Olsen Gang in Jutland	DEN	Bent Fabricius-Bjerre
The Omega Man	WB	Ron Grainer
On Any Sunday	CIV	Dominic Frontiere
On the Point of Death	ITA	Dimitri Nicolau Golovnyi
One Adventure of Billy the Kid	FRA	Patriee Moullet
One Day in the Life of Ivan Denisovich	CIN	Arne Nordheim
$1,000,000 Duck	DIS	Buddy Baker
One More Train to Rob	UN	David Shire
One of Those Things	DEN	Bent Fabricius-Bjerre
1,000 Convicts and a Woman	BRI	Peter J. Elliott
The Only Thing You Know	CAN	Paul Craven Ian Ewing
The Organization	UA	Gil Melle
The Pacifist	FRA/GER/ITA	Giorgio Gaslini
Papa, the Little Boats	FRA	Andre Popp
Papanicolis	GRE	Costas Kapnissis
Part of the Family	IND	Marc Ling Clarke Meyer
The Peace Killers	IND	Kenneth Wannberg Ruthann Friedman
Peace over the Fields	BEL	Paul Uy
Percy	MGM	Roy Davies
Pinocchio	IND	John Barber
Plaza Suite	PAR	Maurice Jarre
Play "Misty" for Me	UN	Dee Barton
Pocketful of Chestnuts	ITA	Carlo Rustichelli
Power	ITA	Eugenia Tretti Manzoni
Pretty Maids All in a Row	MGM	Lalo Schifrin
The Priest's Wife	ITA	Armando Trovajoli
Prism	IND	Tom Manhoff
Private Road	BRI	George Fenton Michael Feast David Dundas
The Proud Rider	CAN	Sol Sherman
Psychout for Murder	ITA	Benedetto Ghiglia
Punishment Park	IND	Paul Motian
Puppet on a Chain	CIN	Piero Piccioni

Purgatory Eroica	JAP	Ichiyangi Toshi
The Pursuit of Happiness	COL	Dave Grusin
Quest for Love	BRI	Eric Rogers
Raga	BRI	Colin Walcott
The Raging Moon (see Long Ago Tomorrow)		
Raid on Rommel	UN	Hal Mooney
Rain for a Dusty Summer	SPA/USA	Wade Denning
Recruits in Ingolstadt	GER	Peer Raben
Red Sky at Morning	UN	Billy Goldenberg
Red Sun	FRA	Maurice Jarre
The Red Tent	PAR	Ennio Morricone
Red, White and Blue	IND	New Hope
The Reincarnate	CAN	Milan Kymlicka
The Resurrection of Zachary Wheeler	IND	Marlin Skiles
The Return of Count Yorga	AI	Bill Marx
The Right to Be Born	MEX	Gustavo C. Carreon
Rip-Off	CAN	Murray McLaughlan
The Role of My Family in the Revolution	YUG	Jornelije Kovac
Romance of a Horse Thief	AA	Mort Schuman
The Rooster	ISR	Rahum Heiman
The Roosters of Dawn	SPA	Ernesto Halffter
Sacco and Vanzetti	ITA	Ennio Morricone
Sacred Fire	FRA	Alain Kremski
St. Michael Had a Rooster	ITA	Benedetto Ghiglia
La Salamandre	SWI	Patrick Moraz
The Savior	FRA	Pierre Jansen
Say Hello to Yesterday	CIN	Riz Ortolani
Scandalous John	DIS	Rod McKuen
The Scene of the Crash	YUG	Zivan Czitkovic
See No Evil	COL	Elmer Bernstein
The Seven Minutes	TCF	Stu Phillips
Seven Times a Day	CAN	Francois Cousineau
A Severed Head	COL	Stanley Myers
Shaft	MGM	Isaac Hayes
Shepherd	YUG	Bojan Adamic
Shinbone Alley	AA	George Kleinsinger
Shoot Out	UN	Dave Grusin
Silent Friends	CAN/RUM	Gheorges Gregorium
Simon, King of the Witches	IND	Stu Phillips
Skin Game	WB	David Shire
The Sky Is Blue	FRA	Francois de Roubaix
Smic, Smac, Smoc	FRA	Francis Lai
So Long Gulliver	ITA	Piero Piccioni
Socrates	ITA	Mario Nascimbene
Some of My Best Friends Are...	AI	Gordon Rose
Something Big	NGP	Marvin Hamlisch
Sometimes a Great Notion	UN	Henry Mancini
The Song of the Balalaika	FRA/GER	Caravelli
The Sporting Club	EMB	Michael Small
The Star of the Season	POL	Wojciech Kilar
Star-Spangled Girl	PAR	Charles Fox

The Statue	CIN	Riz Ortolani
The Steagle	EMB	Fred Myrow
Stop	CAN	Pierre F. Brault
The Strange Vice of Signora Ward	ITA/SPA	Nora Orlandi
Straw Dogs	CIN	Jerry Fielding
Such Good Friends	PAR	Thomas Z. Shepard
The Sudden Wealth of the Poor People of Kombach	GER	Klaus Doldinger
Summer of '42	WB	Michel Legrand
Sunny Beach Revolution	DEN	Kaspar Winding Bo Stief
Support Your Local Gunfighter	UA	Jack Elliott Allyn Ferguson
Sweet Savior	IND	Jeff Barry Gilbert Slavin
Sweet Sweetback's Baadassss Song	IND	Melvin van Peebles
T. R. Baskin	PAR	Jack Elliott
THX-1138	WB	Lalo Schifrin
Tales of Beatrix Potter	BRI	John Lanchbery
Tam Lin	AI	Stanley Myers
The Telephone Book	IND	Nate Sassover
10 Rillington Place	BRI	John Dankworth
The Tender Warrior	IND	Kenneth Wannberg
That Splendid November	FRA/ITA	Ennio Morricone
That Summer	GRE	Yannis Spanos
There Grows a Green Pine in the Woods	YUG	Andelko Klobucar
They Call Me Trinity	ITA	Franco Micalizzi
They Might Be Giants	UN	John Barry
They've Changed Faces	ITA	Amadeo Tommasi
The Third Part of the Night	POL	Andrej Korzynski
300-Year Weekend	CIN	Gilbert Fuller
The Threshold of the Void	FRA	Jack Arel
A Time for Dying	IND	Harry Betts
To Love Again	JAP	Shinichi Magaino
The Todd Killings	NGP	Leonard Rosenman
Toklat	IND	Larry Bastian A. Gean Snow
Tokoloshe	SA	Sam Sklair
The Touch	SWE/USA	Jan Johansson
The Tricky Game of Love	CZE	Zdenek Liska
Trotta	GER	Eberhard Schoener
21 Days in Europe	IND	Helmut Schmidt
Two English Girls and the Continent	FRA	Georges Delerue
200 Motels	UA	Frank Zappa
Two Women In Gold	CAN	Robert Charlebois
Uncle Vanya	RUS	A. Shnitke
Under Milk Wood	BRI	Brian Gascoigne
Unman, Wittering and Zigo	BRI	Michael J. Lewis
Up Pompeii	BRI	Ken Howard Alan Blaikey

The Vacation	ITA	Fiorenzo Carpi
Valdez Is Coming	UA	Charles Gross
Valparaiso, Valparaiso	FRA	Ivrey Gitlis
Vanishing Point	TCF	Jimmy Bowen
Varieties	SPA	Gregory Segura
The Velvet Vampire	IND	Clancy B. Gross, III Roger Dollarhide
The Viking Who Came from the South	ITA	Armando Trovajoli
Von Richthoven and Brown	UA	Hugo Friedhofer
"WR"--The Mysteries of the Organism	YUG	Bojana Makavejev
Walkabout	BRI	John Barry
Walls of Fire	MEX/USA	Jimmie Haskell
The Wanting Weight	GER	Georges Gruntz
Welcome to the Club	COL	Ken Thorne
Werewolves on Wheels	IND	Don Gere
What Did You Do in the War, Thanassi?	GRE	Mimas Plessas
What's the Matter with Helen?	UA	David Raksin
Where Is the Body, Moeller?	DEN	Poul Godske
Whity	GER	Peer Rabin
Who Is Harry Kellerman and Why Is He Saying Those Terrible Things about Me?	NGP	Shel Silverstein
Who Killed Mary What'sername?	IND	Gary McFarland
Who Says I Can't Ride a Rainbow?	IND	Bobby Scott
Who Slew Auntie Roo?	AI	Kenneth V. Jones
Why Do They Do It?	DEN	Ole Hoeyer
The Wild Country	DIS	Robert F. Brunner
Wild Rovers	MGM	Jerry Goldsmith
Willard	CIN	Alex North
The Wind Blows Free	ITA	Ennio Morricone
The Wind's Anger	ITA/SPA	Augusto Martelli
The Windsplitter	IND	Jackie Mills Al Capps
With Love and Kisses	DEN	Bent Fabricius-Bjerre
Without Apparent Motive	FRA	Ennio Morricone
The Woolen Stocking Peddler	DEN	Thorkild Knudsen
The World Is Just a "B" Movie	IND	Bob Ling
Wow	CAN	Joe Solkin
Y Que Patatin y Que Patatan	ARG	Juan Cedron
Young and Healthy as a Rose	YUG	Baronijan Vartkes
Young Attila	ITA	Francesco de Masi
Zachariah	CIN	Jimmie Haskell
Zeppelin	WB	Roy Budd

1972

A.W.O.L.	SWE/USA	Rupert Holmes
The Abductors	IND	Robert G. Orpin
Adult Fun	BRI	Simon Standage

Adventure Is Adventure	FRA	Francis Lai
Adventures of Barry McKenzie	AUT	Peter Best
		David McKay
The Algerian War	FRA	Francois de Charby
		Jean Brassat
		Francis Moraine
Alice's Adventures in Wonderland	BRI	John Barry
And Baby Makes Three	IND	Harry D. Glass
And Hope to Die	TCF	Francis Lai
Angry Youth	GRE	Yannis Spanos
Another Smith for Paradise	CAN	Don Druik
The Annuity	FRA	Gerard Calvi
Antony and Cleopatra	BRI	John (Patrick) Scott
The Apple War	SWE	Sven-Bertil Taube
Arid Land	CEY	S. Elvitigalor
The Artless One	FRA	Georges Delerue
The Assassination	FRA	Ennio Morricone
Assassination of Trotsky	FRA/ITA	Egisto Macchi
The Audience	ITA	Teo Usuelli
Bad Company	PAR	Harvey Schmidt
Banked Fires	RUS	Andrei Petrov
The Bar at the Crossing	FRA	Jacques Brel
Baron Blood	ITA	Les Baxter
Bedside Head	DEN	Ole Hoeyer
Bedside Highway	DEN	Ole Hoeyer
Ben	CIN	Walter Scharf
The Bengal Tiger	IND	Gordon Zahler
La Betia	ITA/YUG	Carlo Rustichelli
Beware the Blob	IND	Mort Garson
The Big Bird Cage	IND	William Castleman
		William Loose
The Birds	HUN	Gabor Presser
The Biscuit Eater	DIS	Robert F. Brunner
The Black Belly of the Tarantula	MGM	Ennio Morricone
Black Fantasy	IND	Morris Goldberg
Black Girl	CIN	Ed Boggs
		Ray Shanklin
		Jesse Osborne
		Mort Saunders
Blacula	AI	Gene Page
Blindman	TCF	Stelvio Cipriani
Blow for Blow	FRA	Jacky Moreau
Bluebeard	CIN	Ennio Morricone
Bob & Daryl & Ted & Alex	IND	The Electric Banana
Bone	IND	Gil Melle
Boom	GRE	Costas Kapnissis
Boxcar Bertha	AI	Gib Guilbean
		Thad Maxwell
Buck and the Preacher	COL	Benny Carter
Butterflies Are Free	COL	Bob Alcivar
Cactus in the Show	IND	Joe Parnello
Cancel My Reservation	WB	Dominic Frontiere

The Candidate	WB	John Rubenstein
The Captain	GER	James Last
The Carey Treatment	MGM	Roy Budd
The Cat Ate the Parakeet	IND	Ted Roberts
Chaplinesque, My Life and Hard Times	IND	Stuart Oderman
Chato's Land	UA	Jerry Fielding
Child's Play	PAR	Michael Small
Chut	FRA	Francois de Roubaix
Closed Ward	NOR	Freddy Lindquist
Come Back Charleston Blue	WB	Donny Hathaway Quincy Jones
Conquest of the Planet of the Apes	TCF	Tom Scott
Cool Breeze	MGM	Solomon Burke
A Cop	FRA	Michel Colombier
Corky	MGM	Jerry Styner
Count Your Bullets	IND	Richard Markowitz
The Cowboys	WB	John Williams
Crescendo	WB	Malcolm Williamson
Crimes of Petiot	SPA	Angel Arteaga
Cruel Sea	AFR	Bo Tarik
The Cry of the Black Wolves	GER	Gerhart Heinz
Cuban Fight Against Demons	CUB	Leo Brouwer
The Culpepper Cattle Co.	TCF	Tom Scott Jerry Goldsmith
Dagmar Is Where It's At	DEN	Palle Mikhelborg
The Darwin Adventure	BRI	Marc Wilkinson
The Daughter-In-Law	RUS	Redjep Redjepov
Daughters of Satan	UA	Richard La Salle
The Dead Are Alive	ITA	Riz Ortolani
Dead Landscape	HUN	Andras Szollossy
Dealing: Or the Berkeley-to-Boston Forty-Brick Lost-Bag Blues	WB	Michael Small
Dear Louise	FRA	Georges Delerue
Dear Summer Sister	JAP	Toru Takemitsu
The Death of Ipu	RUM	Tiberiu Olah
Deliverance	WB	Eric Weissberg
Diamonds on Your Naked Body	GRE	Andreas Prezas
Diary of an Italian	ITA	Guiliano Illiani
A Diverse World: The Test and the Care Conscience	BUL	Konstantin Kotsev
Dr. Phibes Rises Again	AI	John Gale
Doctor Popoul	FRA	Pierre Jansen
Double by Half	ITA	Daniele Patucchi
The Doves	CAN	Michel Conte
Downpour	IRAN	Sheyda Gharache-Daghi
Dracula A.D. 1972	WB	Mike Vickers
The Dreamed Life	FRA	Emmanuel Charpentier
Duck, You Sucker (Fistful of Dynamite)	UA	Ennio Morricone
Dyn Ako	BRI	Gavin Byars

Dynamite	IND	Firth DeMule
Ecny Meeny Miney Moe	FRA	Ghorghe Zamfir
The Effect of Gamma Rays on Man-in-the-Moon Marigolds	TCF	Maurice Jarre
Eglantine	FRA	Jean-Jacques Debout
Embassy	BRI	Jonathan Hodge
The Enrico Mattei Affair	ITA	Piero Piccioni
The Epidemic	POL	Alina Kielanowski
The Erotic Adventures of Zorro	FRA/GER	Betty Allen William Loose
Escape to the Sun	FRA/GER/ISR	Dov Seltzer
Every Little Crook and Nanny	MGM	Fred Karlin
Every Sunday Morning	ITA	Teo Usuelli
Everything You Always Wanted to Know about Sex But Were Afraid to Ask	UA	Mundell Lowe
F. T. A.	AI	Aminadev Aloni
The Fall	SWI	Walter Baumgartner
The Family with 100 Children	DEN	Benny E. Andersen
A Fan's Notes	CAN	Ron Collier
Far from the Trees	SPA	Marco Rossi Johnny Galvao Carlos Maleras
Fat City	COL	Kris Kristoffersen Marvin Hamlisch
Faustine and the Beautiful Summer	FRA	Bruno Rigutto
Felix and Otilia	RUM	Anatol Vieru
Field Lilies	CZE	Ilja Zeijenka
The Final Comedown	IND	Wade Marcus
The Five-Leaf Clover	FRA	Georges Moustaki
Flock	ISR	Alex Cagan
Four Flies on Gray Velvet	FRA/ITA	Ennio Morricone
Franz	BEL/FRA	Jacques Brel
Frenzy	UN	Ron Goodwin
Friends: Let's Go to the Party	ITA	Ettore Ballotta
Fritz the Cat	IND	Ed Boggs Ray Shanklin
Frogs	AI	Les Baxter
From the Police, with Thanks	GER/ITA	Stelvio Cipriani
Funeral Rites	IN	Reijiev Taranath
Fuzz	UA	Dave Grusin
Ganga Zumba	BRA	Moacyr Santos
Gas Lamps	CZE	Labos Fiser
The Gates of Fire	FRA	Alain Goaguer
The Genesis Children	IND	Jerry Styner
Georgia, Georgia	DEN	Sven-Olaf Waldorf
Get to Know Your Rabbit	WB	Jack Elliott Allyn Ferguson
The Getaway	NGP	Quincy Jones
The Girl from Australia	ITA	Piero Piccioni
Girl from the Mountains	YUG	Darko Kraljic
The Girl Passing Through	ITA	Gianni Casciello

The Goalie's Anxiety at the Penalty Kick	AUS/GER	Jurgen Knieper
The Goat Horn	BUL	Simeon Pironkov
The Godfather	PAR	Nino Rota
The Golden Thing	GER	Nikos Mamangates
Greaser's Palace	IND	Jack Nitzsche
The Great Northfield, Minnesota, Raid	UN	Dave Grusin
The Great Scuttling	CAN/FRA	Derry Hall
The Groundstar Conspiracy	CAN	Paul Hoffert
Guernica	ITA	Stelvio Cipriani
Hail	IND	Trade Martin
Hammer	UA	Solomon Burke
Hammersmith Is Out	BRI	Dominic Frontiere
The Happiness Cage	CIN	Phil Ramone Chris Dedrick
Havoc	GER	The X-Holes
The Heartbreak Kid	TCF	Garry Sherman
Hearth Fires	FRA	Michel Legrand
Heat	IND	John Cale
Hello Jerusalem	FRA	Vangelis Papathanassiou
Henry VIII and His Six Wives	BRI	David Munrow
Here Comes Every Body	BRI	Tony Rawlins
Heroine	ARG	Roberto Lar
Hickey and Boggs	UA	Ted Ashford
Hippocrates	GRE	Costas Kapnissis
The Hitchhikers	IND	Danny Cohen
The Hoax	IND	Ray Martin
Home Sweet Home	FRA	Roland Vincent
The Honkers	UA	Jimmie Haskell
Hot Circuit	IND	Michael Sahl
The Hot Rock	TCF	Quincy Jones
House of the Doves	ITA/SPA	Francesco de Masi
The House without Boundaries	SPA	Carmelo Bernaola
How to Behave in a Fourposter Bed	DEN	Sigurd Jansen
Howzer	IND	Stephen Scull
I Love You, Rosa	ISR	Dov Seltzer
I Want What I Want	BRI	Johnny Harris
Images	BRI	John Williams
The Interview	IN	Vijay Raghava Rao
The Intruders	FRA	Georges Garvarentz
It Ain't Easy	IND	Blue Batch
The Italian of the Roses	FRA	Jose Bertel
Jamilya	RUS	N. Sidelnikov
Jeremiah Johnson	WB	John Rubenstein Tim McIntire
Joe Kidd	UN	Lalo Schifrin
The Jerusalem File	MGM	John (Patrick) Scott
Joao	HOL	Heitor Villa-Lobos
Journey	CAN	Luke Gibson
Journey through Rosebud	CIN	Jerry Fielding
Just Peter	POR	Manuel Jorge Veloso

Justine de Sade	FRA	Francoise and Roger Cotts
Kansas City Bomber	MGM	Don Ellis
Katz and Karasso	ISR	Nurit Hirsch
Kill the Black Sheep	POL	Jerzy Matuszkiewicz
The Killer	FRA	Ennio Morricone
King, Queen, Knave	GER/USA	Stanley Myers
Klara Lust	SWE	Gustav Mahler
Lady Caroline Lamb	UA	Richard Rodney Bennett
Lady Sings the Blues	PAR	Michel Legrand
Laia	SPA	Angel Arteaga
Last Tango in Paris	UA	Gato Barbieri
Lautare	RUS	E. Doga
Left-Handed	IND	Stan Finkelstein
The Legend about the Death and Resurrection of Two Young Men	HUN	Emil Petrovics
The Legend of Boggy Creek	IND	Jaime Mendoza-Nava
The Legend of Nigger Charley	PAR	John Bennings
Lenin, You Rascal You	DEN	Erik Moseholm
The Leopard	SYR	Suheil Arafe
Liberty	ITA/YUG	Egisto Macchi
The Life and Times of Judge Roy Bean	NGP	Maurice Jarre
Life Is Tough, Eh Providence?	FRA/GER/ITA	Ennio Morricone
Life of a Shock-Force Worker	YUG	Bojan Adamic
Limbo	UN	Anita Kerr
The Little Ark	NGP	Fred Karlin
Little Mother	IND	George Craig
Living Free	COL	Sol Kaplan
Liza	FRA/ITA	Philippe Sarde
Love, Swedish Style	IND	Jirh Christopher
The Lover	BEL	Arsene Souffriau
Luminous Procuress	IND	Warner Jepson
Lycistrata	GRE	Stavros Xarhacos
Made	BRI	John Cameron
The Mafia	ARG	Gustavo Beytelman
The Magnificent Seven Ride	UA	Elmer Bernstein
Main Thing Holiday	GER	Heinz Keissling
Malpertius	BEL/FRA	Georges Delerue
The Man	PAR	Jerry Goldsmith
Man and Boy	IND	J. J. Johnson
A Man from the East	FRA/ITA	Guido and Maurizio de Angelis
Manson	IND	B. Poston
Marco's Theme	ITA	Marco Migliori
The Master and Margherita	ITA	Ennio Morricone
The Mechanic	UA	Jerry Fielding
Melinda	MGM	Jerry Butler
The Merry Wives of Windsor	CAN	Terry Bush
Mimi, the Metalworker	ITA	Piero Piccioni
Mio	FRA/ITA/JAP	Jean Guillou
Mirage	SA	Enrique Pinilla

Mr. Forbush and the Penguins	BRI	John Addison
Money Talks	UA	Mark Barkan
Moonwalk One	IND	Charles G. Morrow
Morbidness	SPA	Jacques Daugean
The Morals of Ruth Halbfass	GER	Friedrich Meyer
A Murder Is a Murder	FRA	Paul Misraki
My Dearest Lady	SPA	Rafael Luis
Napoleon and Samantha	DIS	Buddy Baker
Nathalie Granger	FRA	Marguerite Duras
Necromancy	CIN	Fred Karger
Neither By Day Nor By Night	ISR	Vladimir Cosma
The New Centurions	COL	Quincy Jones
The Newcomers	IND	Main Squeez
The Night Evelyn Came out of the Grave	ITA	Bruno Nicolai
Night of the Lepus	MGM	Jimmie Haskell
Nightshade	GER	E. G. Bearbitung
Nocturne	GER	Tugen Thomass
Now You See Him, Now You Don't	DIS	Robert F. Brunner
Oasis	CZE	Jiri Sternwald
Oh, to Be on the Bandwagon	DEN	Bent Fabricius-Bjerre
The Old Maid	FRA	Michel Legrand
The Olsen Gang's Big Score	DEN	Bent Fabricius-Bjerre
Olympia-Olympia	GER	Wolfgang de Gelmini
One Is a Lonely Number	MGM	Michel Legrand
One on Top of the Other	ITA	Riz Ortolani
The Only Way Home	IND	Dan Foliart Ukie Hart Tom Shapiro
The Other	TCF	Jerry Goldsmith
The Other Side of the Underneath	BRI	Sally Minford
Our Willi Is the Best	GER	Peter Thomas
Outside In	IND	Randy Edelman
Parades	IND	Garry Sherman
Paulina 1800	FRA	Nicolas Nabokov
Pearl in the Crown	POL	Wojcieck Kilar
Pete 'n Tillie	UN	John Williams
Pictures from a Strange Land	GER	Wolfgang de Gelmini
The Pied Piper	PAR	Donovan
A Place Called Today	EMB	Robert G. Orpin
Play It Again, Sam	PAR	Billy Goldenberg
Pocket Money	NGP	Alex North
Poor Little Maria	FIN	Elsa Helasvuo
Pope Joan	BRI	Maurice Jarre
Portnoy's Complaint	WB	Michel Legrand
The Poseidon Adventure	TCF	John Williams
The Possession of Joel Delaney	PAR	Joe Raposo
The Power and the Truth	RUM	Tiberiu Olah
Praised Be What Hardens You	GER	Bernd Kampka
Preludio A Espaja	SPA	Isaac Albeniz
Present Times	HUN	Gyorgy Vukan
Prime Cut	NGP	Lalo Schifrin
Private Collection	AUT	Mike Perjanik

Film	Country/Studio	Composer
The Public Eye	UN	John Barry
Pulp	BRI	George Martin
The Puzzle of the Silver Half-Moon	GER/ITA	Riz Ortolani
Quadroon	IND	Jack Brokensha
Quite Good Chaps	CZE	Zdenek Liska
The Ra Expeditions	SWE	Ed Norton
Rage	WB	Lalo Schifrin
The Ragman's Daughter	BRI	Kenny Clayton
Rampart of Desire	FRA	Michel Delpech Roland Vincent
The Rendezvous	JAP	Yasushi Miyagawa
Repeated Absences	FRA	Jean-Pierre Stora
The Revengers	EMB	Peter Matz
The Right to Love	FRA	Philippe Sarde
Roma	FRA/ITA	Nino Rota
The Rowdyman	CAN	Ben McPeak
The Ruling Class	BRI	John Cameron
St. Pauli Report	GER	Siegfried Franz
The Salzburg Connection	TCF	Lionel Newman
Sapporo Winter Olympics	JAP	Masaru Sato
Savages	IND	Joe Raposo
Scarecrow in a Garden of Cucumbers	IND	Jerry Blatt
Schoolgirls Report III	GER	Siegfried Franz
The Scientific Cardplayer	ITA	Piero Piccioni
The Secret of the Green Pins	GER/ITA	Ennio Morricone
A Separate Peace	PAR	Charles Fox
Shaft's Big Score	MGM	Gordon Parks Isaac Hayes
She No Longer Talks ... She Shoots	FRA	Eddy Vartan
Shirley Thompson vs. the Aliens	AUT	Ralph Tyrell
A Silence	JAP	Toru Takemitsu
Silence! The Court Is in Session	IN	Jitendra Abhishkel
Silent Running	UN	Peter Schickele
Sitting Target	BRI	Stanley Myers
Skyjacked	MGM	Perry Botkin, Jr.
Slap the Monster on Page One	FRA/ITA	Ennio Morricone
Slaughter	AI	Luchi de Jesus
Slaughterhouse-Five	UN	Glenn Gould
Sleuth	TCF	John Addison
A Slip-Up	POL	Jerzy Matuszkiewicz
Smugglers	TUR	Arif Erkin
Snow Job	WB	Jacques Loussier
Snowball Express	DIS	Robert F. Brunner
Soho Gorilla	GER	Peter Thomas
Something to Hide	BRI	Roy Budd
Somewhere, Someone	FRA	Georges Delerue
Sounder	TCF	Taj Mahal
Squares	IND	Donald Vincent
Stadium Nuts	FRA	Charlot
Stand Up and Be Counted	COL	Ernie Wilkins

Title	Country/Studio	Composer
Stella Da Falla	SWI	Jode Purpora
Strange City	GER	John Andrews
Strangers	IND	Jack Ackerman
The Stuff that Dreams Are Made Of	GER	Peter Thomas
Suburban Wives	BRI	Terry Warr
Summer Lightning	GER	Stanley Myers
Summer Soldiers	JAP	Toru Takemitsu
Summertime Killer	FRA/ITA/SPA	De Mellis
Suns of Easter Island	BRA/SA/FRA	Bernard Parmegiani
Superbeast	UA	Richard La Salle
Superfly	WB	Curtis Mayfield
The Swinger	FRA	Pierre Fanen
Swords of Death	JAP	Taichiro Rosugi
Szindbad	HUN	Zoltan Jeney
Take 2	IND	Noam Sreriff
Thanassi Get Your Gun	GRE	Mimis Plessas
That Dawn Should Be Peaceful	RUS	Kirill Molchianov
There's Always Vanilla	IND	Barefoot in Athens Steve Gorn
They Only Kill Their Masters	MGM	Perry Botkin, Jr.
The Thing with Two Heads	AI	Robert O. Ragland
Those Quiet Japanese	JAP	Tayama Masamitsu
Thumb Tripping	EMB	Bob Thompson
The Time of the Hunt	CAN	Pierre F. Brault
'Tis a Pity She's a Whore (Addio, Fratello Crudele)	ITA	Ennio Morricone
To Be Free	IND	Lalo Schifrin
To Find a Man	COL	David Shire
To Kill in Silence	ITA	Stelvio Cipriani
Together	IND	Emmanuel Vardi
Together for Days	IND	Coleridge-Taylor Perkinson
Too Pretty to Be Honest	FRA	Serge Gainsbourg
Top of the Heap	IND	J. J. Johnson
Toys Are Not for Children	IND	Cathy Lynn Jacques Urbont Emmanuel Vardi Leonid Hambro
Traces	MOR	Kama Dominique Helleboid
Trastevere	ITA	Guido and Maurizio de Angelis
Travels with My Aunt	MGM	Tony Hatch
The Treasure	CEY	Premasiri Khemadasa
Treasure Island	NGP	Natal Massara
Trial of the Catonsville Nine	IND	Shelly Manne
Trinity Is Still My Name	ITA	Guido and Maurizio de Angelis
Trotta	GER	Richard Schoner
Trouble Man	TCF	Marvin Gaye
The True Story of Bernadette	CAN	Pierre F. Brault
Two Heartbeats	ISR	Misha Segal
Two Seasons of Life	BEL	Ennio Morricone
Ulzana's Raid	UN	Frank de Vol

Under the Flag of the Rising Sun	JAP	Hikaru Hayashi
The Unholy Rollers	AI	Bobby Hart
The United Family Awaits the Visit of Hallewyn	ARG	Jorge Lopez Ruiz
Unto a Good Land	SWE	Bengt Emryd
Up the Sandbox	NGP	Billy Goldenberg
The Valachi Papers	COL	Riz Ortolani
The Valley	FRA	Pink Floyd
Venus Planet	ITA	Norman and Stelvio Cipriani
The Vicar of Vejlby	DEN	Henning Christiansen
Vietnam	JAP	Masao Oki
The War Between Men and Women	NGP	Marvin Hamlisch
War Is War	FRA	Gerard Calvi
The Warmth of Your Hands	RUS	Revez Laguidze
Wedding in White	CAN	Milan Kymlicka
Wedding without Rings	CZE	Stepan Lucky
The Weekend Murders	MGM	Francesco de Masi
Welcome Home, Soldier Boys	TCF	Ken Wanniberg
We'll Call Him Andreas	ITA	Manuel de Sica
What a Flash	FRA	Les Axis
What Is to Be Done?	SA	Country Joe McDonald
What's Up, Doc?	WB	Artie Butler
When the Heavens Fell	FIN	Kaj Chydenius
When the Legends Die	TCF	Glenn Paxton
Where Does It Hurt?	CIN	Keith Allison
The White Rat	IND	Tony Esposito
The White Rose	MEX	Raul Lavista
Who Fears the Devil?	IND	Roger Kellaway
The Wild Pack	AI	Louis Oliveira
Willi Manages the Whole Thing	GER	Martin Boetticher
Without Family	ITA	Fiorenzo Carpi
The Wolves	JAP	Masaru Sato
Women of Doom	SPA	James Perez
The Working Class Goes to Heaven	ITA	Ennio Morricone
The Wrath of God	MGM	Lalo Schifrin
X, Y and Zee	COL	Stanley Myers
Yes, But ...	GRE	Demetrios Melios
You and Me	RUS	Alfred Snitche
You'll Like My Mother	UN	Gil Melle
Young Winston	COL	Alfred Ralston

Chapter XI

COMPOSERS AND THEIR FILMS

ABADY, TEMPLE
The Woman in the Hall (1947)
Dear Mr. Prohack (1948)
Miranda (1948)
All over Town (1949)
Martin and Gaston (1953)
Both Sides of the Law (1954)
Kill Me Tomorrow (1958)

ABBADO, MARCELLO
Violated Paradise (1963)

ABHISHKEI, JITENDRA
Silence! The Court Is in Session (1972)

ABRAMSON, ROBERT
8 X 8 (1957)

ABRIL, ANTON GARCIA
The Savage Guns (1962)
Island of the Doomed (1968)

ABRIL, JOSE ANTONIO
The Cobra (1968)

ACKERMAN, JACK
Strangers (1972)

ACRES, HARRY
River of Unrest (1937)

ADAMIC, BOJAN
Shepherd (1971)
Life of a Shock-Force Worker (1972)

ADDINSELL, RICHARD
Amateur Gentleman (1936)
Fire over England (1937)
South Riding (1937)
Goodbye, Mr. Chips (1939)
Gaslight (1940)
The Lion Has Wings (1940)
Men of the Lightship (1940)
Love on the Dole (1941)
Suicide Squadron (1941)
The Avengers (1942)
Blithe Spirit (1945)
A Diary for Timothy (1945)
Passionate Friends (1949)
Under Capricorn (1949)
The Black Rose (1950)
A Christmas Carol (1951)
Highly Dangerous (1951)
Tom Brown's Schooldays (1951)
Encore (1952)
Sea Devils (1953)
Beau Brummel (1954)
Out of the Clouds (1957)
The Prince and the Showgirl (1957)
A Tale of Two Cities (1958)
Loss of Innocence (1961)
Macbeth (1961)
The Roman Spring of Mrs. Stone (1961)
Waltz of the Toreadors (1962)
The War Lover (1962)
Life at the Top (1965)

ADDISON, JOHN
Seven Days to Noon (1950)
Pool of London (1951)
High Treason (1952)
The Hour of 13 (1952)
The Man Between (1953)
Terror on a Train (1953)
The Black Knight (1954)
High and Dry (1954)

The Paratrooper (1954)
That Lady (1955)
The Cockleshell Heroes (1956)
The Light Touch (1956)
Make Me an Offer (1956)
Private's Progress (1956)
Three Men in a Boat (1956
Reach for the Sky (1957)
Lucky Jim (1958)
I Was Monty's Double (1959)
Look Back in Anger (1959)
The Entertainer (1960)
A French Mistress (1960)
The Loneliness of the Long-Distance Runner (1962)
A Taste of Honey (1962)
Tom Jones (1963)
The Girl with the Green Eyes (1964)
Guns at Batasi (1964)
The Amorous Adventures of Moll Flanders (1965)
The Loved One (1965)
A Fine Madness (1966)
I Was Happy Here (1966)
The Torn Curtain (1966)
The Honey Pot (1967)
Smashing Time (1967)
The Charge of the Light Brigade (1968)
Brotherly Love (1970)
Start the Revolution without Me (1970)
Mr. Forbush and the Penguins (1972)
Sleuth (1972)

ADLER, LARRY
Genevieve (1954)
A Cry from the Streets (1959)
The Hellions (1962)
The Great Chase (1963)
The Hook (1963)
A High Wind in Jamaica (1965)
King and Country (1965)

ADOLFO, ANTONIO
Memories of a Gigolo (1970)

ADOMIAN, LAN
Tale of the Navajos (1949)
Birthright (1952)
Ten Days to Tulara (1958)

AFGEYERSTAM, CLAES
Anna (1970)

AIMEE, MARCEL
The Taming (1968)

AKISTER, PETER
Panic in the Parlor (1957)

AKUTAGAWA, TAKASHI
The Wheel Turns in the Shadow (1970)

AKUTAGAWA, YASHUSHI
Four Chimneys (1953)
Rice (1957)
Fires on the Plain (1959)

ALBAM, MANNY
Four Clowns (1970)

ALBENIZ, ISAAC
Preludio a Espaja (1972)

ALCIVAR, BOB
Butterflies Are Free (1972)

ALDERMAN, MYRL
Something to Sing About (1937)

ALEGRO, PORTO
Strange World (1952)

ALEXANDER, ALEX
Alaska Passage (1959)
Operation Eichmann (1961)

ALEXANDER, JEFF
Westward the Women (1951)
Affairs of Dobie Gillis (1953)
Escape from Fort Bravo (1953)
Remains to Be Seen (1953)
Prisoner of War (1954)
Rogue Cop (1954)
The Tender Trap (1955)
The Great American Pastime (1956)
Ransom (1956)
Slander (1956)
These Wilder Years (1956)
Gun Glory (1957)
Jailhouse Rock (1957)
The Wings of Angels (1957)

The High Cost of Loving (1958)
Party Girl (1958)
Saddle the Wind (1958)
The Sheepman (1958)
Ask Any Girl (1959)
The Gazebo (1959)
It Started with a Kiss (1959)
The Mating Game (1959)
All the Fine Young Cannibals (1960)
The George Raft Story (1961)
Kid Galahad (1962)
The Rounders (1965)
Clambake (1967)
Double Trouble (1967)
Day of the Evil Gun (1968)
Speedway (1968)
Dirty Dingus Magee (1970)

ALEXANDER, VAN
The Atomic Kid (1954)
The Twinkle in God's Eye (1955)
Jaguar (1956)
When Gangland Strikes (1956)
Baby Face Nelson (1957)
Andy Hardy Comes Home (1958)
The Big Operator (1959)
Girls Town (1959)
Platinum High School (1960)
The Private Lives of Adam and Eve (1960)
Safe at Home! (1962)
13 Frightened Girls (1963)
Strait-Jacket (1964)
I Saw What You Did (1965)
A Time for Killing (1968)

ALEXANDROV, A.
Romance Sentimentale (1930)
Lenin in October (1937)

ALFVEN, HUGO
Gypsy Fury (1951)
The Stranger Left No Card (1954)

ALGUERO, AUGUSTO
Every Day Is a Holiday (1966)

ALLEN, BETTY
The Erotic Adventures of Zorro (1972)

ALLEN, BILLY
Ski on the Wild Side (1967)

ALLEN, DAEVID
Near Orouet (1971)

ALLEN, EDGAR
Checkers (1919)

ALLEN, STEVE
A Man Called Dagger (1967)

ALLER, ALLEN
I'm Going to Get You ... Elliot Boy (1971)

ALLISON, KEITH
Where Does It Hurt? (1972)

ALLIX, VICTOR
The Passion of Joan of Arc (1928)

ALMEIDA, LAURINDO
Naked Sea (1955)
Goodbye, My Lady (1956)
Escape from San Quentin (1957)
Maracaibo (1958)
Cry Tough (1959)

ALONI, ALMINADEV
F.T.A. (1972)

ALPER, ALLEN
The Bang Bang Gang (1970)

ALPERSON, EDWARD L., JR.
Courage of Black Beauty (1957)

ALQUIST, SKEETS
Laurel and Hardy's Laughing 20's (1965)

ALTSCHULLER, MODEST
Buffalo Bill Rides Again (1947)

ALWYN, WILLIAM
The Future's in the Air (1936)
New Worlds for Old (1937)
The Harvest Shall Come (1941)
Fires Were Started (1942)
Desert Victory (1943)
The Way Ahead (1943)

World of Plenty (1943)
Our Country (1944)
Tunisian Victory (1944)
The Notorious Gentleman (1945)
The True Glory (1945)
Odd Man Out (1946)
Captain Boycott (1947)
October Man (1947)
Take My Life (1947)
A City Speaks (1948)
Escape (1948)
Fallen Idol (1948)
The History of Mr. Polly (1948)
So Evil My Love (1948)
The Cure for Love (1949)
Daybreak in Udi (1949)
Madeleine (1949)
The Rocking Horse Winner (1949)
The Mudlark (1950)
State Secret (1950)
The Golden Salamander (1951)
Henry Moore (1951)
I'll Never Forget You (1951)
The Magic Box (1951)
The Magnet (1951)
The Crimson Pirate (1952)
No Resting Place (1952)
The Promoter (1952)
Royal River (1952)
Crash of Silence (Mandy) (1953)
The Long Memory (1953)
Master of Ballantrae (1953)
Night without Stars (1953)
Powered Flight (1953)
The Malta Story (1954)
Man with a Million (1954)
A Personal Affair (1954)
Bedevilled (1955)
Land of Fury (1955)
Svengali (1955)
Safari (1956)
The Ship That Died of Shame (P. T. Raiders) (1956)
Wee Geordie (1956)
The Black Tent (1957)
Sea Wife (1957)
The Smallest Show on Earth (1957)
Smiley (1957)
Stowaway Girl (1957)
Zarak (1957)
I Accuse! (1958)
A Night to Remember (1958)
She Played with Fire (1958)
The Silent Enemy (1958)
Shake Hands with the Devil (1959)
Third Man on the Mountain (1959)
Swiss Family Robinson (1960)
The Naked Edge (1961)
Burn Witch Burn (1962)
In Search of the Castaways (1962)
Walk in the Shadow (1966)

ALZNER, CLAUDIUS
The Brazen Women of Balzac (1971)

AMFITHEATROF, DANIELE
Fast and Furious (1939)
Andy Hardy's Double Life (1942)
Calling Dr. Gillespie (1942)
Dr. Gillespie's New Assistant (1942)
Joe Smith, American (1942)
Northwest Rangers (1942)
Aerial Gunner (1943)
Cry Havoc (1943)
Dr. Gillespie's Criminal Case (1943)
Harrigan's Kid (1943)
High Explosive (1943)
Lassie Come Home (1943)
Lost Angel (1943)
A Stranger in Town (1943)
Days of Glory (1944)
I'll Be Seeing You (1944)
Guest Wife (1945)
Miss Susie Slagle's (1946)
O.S.S. (1946)
Song of the South (1946)
Suspense (1946)
Temptation (1946)
The Virginian (1946)
The Beginning or the End (1947)
Ivy (1947)
The Lost Moment (1947)
The Senator was Indiscreet (1947)

Singapore (1947)
Smash-Up, the Story of a Woman (1947)
Act of Murder (1948)
Another Part of the Forest (1948)
Letter from an Unknown Woman (1948)
Rogue's Regiment (1948)
You Gotta Stay Happy (1948)
The Fan (1949)
House of Strangers (1949)
Sand (1949)
Backfire (1950)
The Capture (1950)
Copper Canyon (1950)
The Damned Don't Cry (1950)
The Devil's Doorway (1950)
I Killed Geronimo (1950)
Storm Warning (1950)
Under My Skin (1950)
Angels in the Outfield (1951)
Bird of Paradise (1951)
The Desert Fox (1951)
The Painted Hills (1951)
Tomorrow Is Another Day (1951)
Devil's Canyon (1953)
Salome (1953)
Scandal at Scourie (1953)
Day of Triumph (1954)
Human Desire (1954)
The Naked Jungle (1954)
Trial (1955)
Edge of Eternity (1956)
The Last Hunt (1956)
The Mountain (1956)
The Unholy Wife (1957)
Fraulein (1958)
From Hell to Texas (1958)
A Spanish Affair (1958)
Heller in Pink Tights (1960)
Major Dundee (1965)

AMRAM, DAVID
Splendor in the Grass (1961)
The Young Savages (1961)
The Manchurian Candidate (1962)
The Arrangement (1969)

AMY, GILBERT
The Wedding Ring (1970)

ANAGNOSTI, ANDREA
Windfall in Athens (1953)

ANDERSEN, BENNY E.
The Family with 100 Children (1972)

ANDERSON, GEORGES
Oh, Sun (1970)

ANDERSON, MICHAEL
Twelve to the Moon (1960)
Wings of Chance (1961)
Tower of London (1962)
Tell Me in the Sunlight (1967)

ANDERSON, ROLAND
Souls at Sea (1937)

ANDREWS, JOHN
Strange City (1972)

ANDRIESSEN, JURRIHAN
Dance of the Herons (1966)

ANGELIS, GUIDO and MAURIZIO
A Man from the East (1972)
Trastevere (1972)
Trinity is Still My Name (1972)

ANTHIEL, GEORGE
Ballet Mechanique (1924)
Millions in the Air (1935)
The Scoundrel (1935)
The Plainsman (1936)
Make Way for Tomorrow (1937)
The Buccaneer (1938)
The Plainsman and the Lady (1946)
That Brennan Girl (1946)
Specter of the Rose (1946)
Repeat Performance (1947)
The Fighting Kentuckian (1949)
Knock on Any Door (1949)
Tokyo Joe (1949)
We Were Strangers (1949)
House by the River (1950)
In a Lonely Place (1950)
Sirocco (1951)
Actors and Sin (1952)

The Juggler (1953)
Dementia (1955)
Hunters of the Deep (1955)
Not as a Stranger (1955)
The Pride and the Passion (1957)
The Young Don't Cry (1957)

APPLEBAUM, LOUIS
Tomorrow the World! (1944)
The Story of G. I. Joe (1945)
Dreams That Money Can Buy (1948)
Lost Boundaries (1949)
Teresa (1951)
The Whistle at Eaton Falls (1951)
Around Is Around (1952)
The Mask (1961)

ARAFE, SUHEIL
The Leopard (1972)

ARBO, MIGUEL ASINS
Not on Your Life! (1965)

ARCHANGELSKY, ALEXIS
Sins of Man (1936)

AREL, JACK
The Threshold of the Void (1971)

AREVALO, TITO
The Walls of Hell (1964)
The Ravagers (1965)

ARMBRUSTER, ROBERT
Sweethearts on Parade (1953)

ARNAUD, LEON
One Touch of Venus (1948)
Sombrero (1953)

ARNELL, RICHARD
The Land (1941)
The Third Secret (1964)

ARNOLD, MALCOLM
The Forbidden Street (1949)
Women in Our Time (1949)
Eye Witness (1950)
Breaking the Sound Barrier (1952)
The Captain's Paradise (1953)
Hobson's Choice (1954)
You Know What Sailors Are (1954)
The Belles of St. Trinian's (1955)
The Deep Blue Sea (1955)
The Night My Number Came Up (1955)
A Prize of Gold (1955)
1984 (1956)
Port Afrique (1956)
Trapeze (1956)
The Bridge on the River Kwai (1957)
Island in the Sun (1957)
Value for Money (1957)
Wicked as They Come (1957)
Blue Murder at St. Trinian's (1958)
Dunkirk (1958)
The Inn of the Sixth Happiness (1958)
The Key (1958)
The Roots of Heaven (1958)
Suddenly Last Summer (1959)
The Angry Silence (1960)
Tunes of Glory (1960)
No Love for Johnnie (1961)
The Lion (1962)
Lisa (1962)
Whistle Down the Wind (1962)
Nine Hours to Rama (1963)
The Chalk Garden (1964)
Tamahine (1964)
The Thin Red Line (1964)
Heroes of Telemark (1965)
Operation Snafu (1965)
The Great St. Trinian's Train Robbery (1966)
Sky West and Crooked (1966)
Africa--Texas Style (1967)
The Reckoning (1969)
David Copperfield (1970)

ARRIEU, CLAUDE
Heartbreak Ridge (1955)

ART ENSEMBLE CHICAGO
Sophie's Way (1970)

ARTEAGA, ANGEL
A Place Called Glory (1966)
The Glass Ceiling (1971)
Crimes of Petiot (1972)
Laia (1972)

ASHFORD, TED
Hickey and Boggs (1972)

ASHTON, TONY
The Last Rebel (1971)

ASTLEY, EDWIN
To Paris with Love (1955)
Kill Her Gently (1958)
Wishing Well Inn (1958)
The Giant Behemoth (1959)
The Mouse that Roared (1959)
Woman Eater (1959)
The Day They Robbed the Bank of England (1960)
In the Wake of a Stranger (1960)
Passport to China (1961)
A Matter of Who (1962)
The Phantom of the Opera (1962)

AUBAIN, TONI
Francois Villon (1948)
The Raven (1948)

AUELINO, ARISTON
Terror Is a Man (1959)
Moro Witch Doctor (1964)

AURANDT, RICHARD D.
Gang Busters (1955)
Walk Tall (1960)
The Silent Call (1961)

AURIC, GEORGES
Blood of a Poet (1930)
A Nous La Liberte (1931)
Entree Des Artists (1938)
The Eternal Return (1944)
Dead of Night (1945)
Beauty and the Beast (1946)
Another Shore (1948)
Blind Desire (1948)
Corridor of Mirrors (1948)
The Eagle with Two Heads (1948)
The Queen of Spades (1948)
Symphonie Pastorale (1948)
Orpheus (1949)
Passport to Pimlico (1949)
The Spider and the Fly (1949)
The Storm Within (1949)
Tight Little Island (1949)
Caroline Cherie (1951)
The Lavender Hill Mob (1951)
The Galloping Major (1951)
Daughter of the Sands (1952)
Moulin Rouge (1952)
Roman Holiday (1953)
The Titfield Thunderbolt (1953)
The Bespoke Overcoat (1955)
The Divided Heart (1955)
The Good Die Young (1955)
Holiday for Henrietta (1955)
The Wages of Fear (1955)
Abdullah's Harem (1956)
Lola Montes (1956)
Rififi (1956)
The Crucible (1957)
Heaven Knows, Mr. Allison (1957)
The Hunchback of Notre Dame (1957)
The Story of Esther Costello (1957)
Walk into Hell (1957)
Bonjour Tristesse (1958)
Dangerous Exile (1958)
Flesh and Desire (1958)
He Who Must Die (1958)
Next to No Time! (1958)
The Night Heaven Fell (1958)
The Journey (1959)
S.O.S. Pacific (1960)
The Testament of Orpheus (1960)
Bridge to the Sun (1961)
Goodbye Again (1961)
The Mind Benders (1963)
The Poppy Is Also a Flower (1966)
Therese and Isabelle (1968)
The Christmas Tree (1969)

AXIS, LES
What a Flash (1972)

AXT, WILLIAM
The Big Parade (1925)
The Merry Widow (1925)
La Boheme (1926)
Ben-Hur (1926)
Don Juan (1926)
The Fire Brigade (1926)
Mare Nostrum (1926)
The Scarlet Letter (1926)
Annie Laurie (1927)
Camille (1927)
Slide, Kelly Slide (1927)
Our Dancing Daughters (1928)
White Shadows of the South Seas (1928)
The Trail of '98 (1929)
Smilin' Through (1932)
Broadway to Hollywood (1933)
Dinner at Eight (1933)
Eskimo (1933)
Gabriel over the White House (1933)
Reunion in Vienna (1933)
Storm at Daybreak (1933)
The Girl from Missouri (1934)
Hide-Out (1934)
Men in White (1934)
Operator 13 (1934)
The Thin Man (1934)
This Side of Heaven (1934)
David Copperfield (1935)
It's in the Air (1935)
The Last of the Pagans (1935)
Murder Man (1935)
O'Shaughnessy's Boy (1935)
Whipsaw (1935)
Libeled Lady (1936)
Old Hutch (1936)
Petticoat Fever (1936)
Piccadilly Jim (1936)
Rendezvous (1936)
Suzy (1936)
Three Wise Guys (1936)
The Unguarded Hour (1936)
We Went to College (1936)
Beg, Borrow or Steal (1937)
Between Two Women (1937)
Big City (1937)
The Last of Mrs. Cheyney (1937)
London by Night (1937)
Parnell (1937)
Under the Cover of Night (1937)
Bad Man of Brimstone (1938)
Everybody Sing (1938)
Fast Company (1938)
The First Hundred Years (1938)
Listen, Darling (1938)
Rich Man, Poor Girl (1938)
Spring Madness (1938)
Three Loves Has Nancy (1938)
Woman Against Woman (1938)
Yellow Jack (1938)
The Girl Downstairs (1939)
The Kid from Texas (1939)
Stand Up and Fight (1939)
Tell No Tales (1939)

BACALOV, LUIS ENRIQUE
The Empty Canvas (1964)
Paranoia (1966)
A Matter of Honor (1966)
Who Knows? (1967)
Catch as Catch Can (1968)
Kiss the Other Sheik (1968)
The Protagonists (1968)
Big Baby Doll (1969)
Ghosts--Italian Style (1969)

BACHARACH, BURT
What's New, Pussycat? (1965)
After the Fox (1966)
Casino Royale (1967)
Butch Cassidy and the Sundance Kid (1969)

BACKY, DON
Society of Unrest (1969)

BAGLEY, DONALD
Ole Rex (1961)

BAKALEINIKOFF, CONSTANTIN
Bottoms Up (1934)
Scattergood Baines (1941)
Seven Days Ashore (1944)
The Set-Up (1949)
The Racket (1951)
At Sword's Point (1952)
Clash by Night (1952)
Desert Passage (1952)
The Half-Breed (1952)
The Las Vegas Story (1952)
Macao (1952)

The Pace That Thrills (1952)
Target (1952)
Trail Guide (1952)

BAKALEINIKOFF, MISCHA
Cry of the Werewolf (1944)
My Name is Julia Ross (1945)
Blondie Knows Best (1946)
Blondie's Lucky Day (1946)
Close Call for Ellery Queen (1946)
Barbary Pirate (1949)
Bodyhold (1949)
Mary Ryan, Detective (1949)
Indian Territory (1950)
Last of the Buccaneers (1950)
The Palomino (1950)
Revenue Agent (1950)
State Penitentiary (1950)
Tyrant of the Sea (1950)
Al Jennings of Oklahoma (1951)
The Big Gusher (1951)
China Corsair (1951)
Criminal Lawyer (1951)
Hurricane Island (1951)
The Magic Carpet (1951)
Smuggler's Gold (1951)
When the Redskins Rode (1951)
Whirlwind (1951)
Brave Warrior (1952)
Cripple Creek (1952)
The Golden Hawk (1952)
Hangman's Knot (1952)
Harem Girl (1952)
The Hawk of Wild River (1952)
Last Train from Bombay (1952)
Montana Territory (1952)
Okinawa (1952)
The Pathfinder (1952)
Target Hong Kong (1952)
Voodoo Tiger (1952)
Bad for Each Other (1953)
The Big Heat (1953)
Conquest of Cochise (1953)
El Alamein (1953)
The 49th Man (1953)
Goldtown Ghost Riders (1953)
Gun Fury (1953)
Jack McCall, Desperado (1953)
Killer Ape (1953)
Mission Over Korea (1953)
On Top of Old Smoky (1953)
Prince of Pirates (1953)
Prisoners of the Casbah (1953)
Serpent of the Nile (1953)
Slaves of Babylon (1953)
The Stranger Wore a Gun (1953)
Valley of Headhunters (1953)
The Bamboo Prison (1954)
Battle of Rogue River (1954)
The Black Dakotas (1954)
Cannibal Attack (1954)
Drums of Tahiti (1954)
The Iron Glove (1954)
Jesse James vs. the Daltons (1954)
Jungle Man-Eaters (1954)
The Law vs. Billy the Kid (1954)
Massacre Canyon (1954)
Masterson of Kansas (1954)
The Miami Story (1954)
The Outlaw Stallion (1954)
The Saracen Blade (1954)
Apache Ambush (1955)
Cell 2455, Death Row (1955)
Creature with the Atom Brain (1955)
The Crooked Web (1955)
Devil Goddess (1955)
Duel on the Mississippi (1955)
Inside Detroit (1955)
It Came from Beneath the Sea (1955)
Jungle Moon Men (1955)
New Orleans Uncensored (1955)
Pirates of Tripoli (1955)
Seminole Uprising (1955)
Teen-Age Crime Wave (1955)
Women's Prison (1955)
Wyoming Renegades (1955)
Battle Stations (1956)
Blackjack Ketchum, Desperado (1956)
Earth vs. the Flying Saucers (1956)
The Flying Fontaines (1956)
Fury at Gunsight Pass (1956)
Have Rocket, Will Travel (1956)
Miami Expose (1956)
Over-Exposed (1956)
Rumble on the Docks (1956)
Secret of Treasure Mountain

(1956)
Seventh Cavalry (1956)
Uranium Boom (1956)
The Werewolf (1956)
The White Squaw (1956)
The Domino Kid (1957)
The Giant Claw (1957)
The Guns of Fort Petticoat (1957)
The Hard Man (1957)
Hellcats of the Navy (1957)
No Time to Be Young (1957)
The Phantom Stagecoach (1957)
The Tijuana Story (1957)
20 Million Miles to Earth (1957)
The 27th Day (1957)
Zombies of Mora-Tau (1957)
The Case Against Brooklyn (1958)
Crash Landing (1958)
Comanche Station (1960)
The Enemy General (1960

BAKER, BUDDY
Wicked Woman (1953)
Toby Tyler (1960)
Summer Magic (1963)
The Misadventures of Merlin Jones (1964)
The Monkey's Uncle (1965)
The Gnome-Mobile (1967)
Rascal (1969)
King of the Grizzlies (1970)
$1,000,000 Duck (1971)
Napoleon and Samantha (1972)

BALL, KENNY
Trial and Error (1962)

BALLOTTA, ETTORE
Friends: Let's Go to the Party (1972)

BANKS, DON
Night Creatures (1962)
The Evil of Frankenstein (1964)
Nightmare (1964)
The Brigand of Kandahar (1965)
Die, Monster, Die (1965)
Hysteria (1965)
Rasputin--The Mad Monk (1966)
The Frozen Dead (1967)
The Mummy's Shroud (1967)
Torture Garden (1968)

BARAGLI, ENNIO
Fraulein Doktor (1969)

BARBAUD, PIERRE
Les Abysses (1963)

BARBER, FRANK
Son of a Gunfighter (1966)

BARBER, JOHN
The Incredible Two-Headed Transplant (1971)
Pinocchio (1971)

BARBERIS, ALBERTO
Fugitive Lady (1951)

BARBIERI, CATO
Last Tango in Paris (1972)

BARCELLINI, FRANCK
My Uncle (1958)

BAREFOOT IN ATHENS
There's Always Vanilla (1972)

BARIZZA, S.
Salue e Baci (1952)

BARKAN, MARK
Money Talks (1972)

BARKER, WARREN
Zebra in the Kitchen (1965)

BARON, PAUL
Toward the Unknown (1956)

BARRETT, ROSS
Madeleine Is (1971)

BARRY, JEFF
Hello Down There (1969)
Sweet Savior (1971)

BARRY, JOHN
Wild for Kicks (1962)
The L-Shaped Room (1963)
Never Let Go (1963)
From Russia with Love (1964)
Goldfinger (1964)
Man in the Middle (1964)
Seance on a Wet Afternoon (1964)
Zulu (1964)
The Ipcress File (1965)
King Rat (1965)
The Knack--And How to Get It (1965)
Mister Moses (1965)
Thunderball (1965)
Born Free (1966)
The Chase (1966)
Dutchman (1966)
The Quiller Memorandum (1966)
The Wrong Box (1966)
The Whisperers (1967)
You Only Live Twice (1967)
Boom (1968)
Deadfall (1968)
Lion in Winter (1968)
Petulia (1968)
The Appointment (1969)
Midnight Cowboy (1969)
On Her Majesty's Secret Service (1969)
Monte Walsh (1970)
Diamonds Are Forever (1971)
The Last Valley (1971),
Mary, Queen of Scots (1971)
Murphy's War (1971)
They Might be Giants (1971)
Walkabout (1971)
Alice's Adventures in Wonderland (1972)
The Public Eye (1972)

BART, LIONEL
Black Beauty (1971)

BARTON, DEE
Play Misty for Me (1971)

BARZIZZA, PIPPO
Love and Larceny (1963)

BASKETTE, BILLY
The Garden of Allah (1917)

BASSETT, R. H.
Transatlantic (1931)
Sherlock Holmes (1932)
Dante's Inferno (1935)
The Prisoner of Shark Island (1936)
Sins of Man (1936)

BASSMAN, GEORGE
Too Many Girls (1940)
The Canterville Ghost (1943)
Whistling in Brooklyn (1943)
Young Ideas (1943)
Main Street After Dark (1944)
Abbot and Costello in Hollywood (1945)
The Clock (1945)
A Letter for Evie (1945)
Little Mister Jim (1946)
The Postman Always Rings Twice (1946)
Two Smart People (1946)
The Arnelo Affair (1947)
Romance of Rosy Ridge (1947)
The Joe Louis Story (1953)
Louisiana Territory (1953)
Canyon Crossroads (1955)
Middle of the Night (1959)
Ride the High Country (1962)
Mail Order Bride (1964)

BASTIAN, LARRY
Toklat (1971)

BATES, STANLEY
The Pleasure Garden (1953)

BATH, HUBERT
Blackmail (1929)
Kitty (1929)
Rhodes of Africa (1936)
Silent Barriers (1937)
Love Story (1944)

BATH, JOHN
Flaming Frontier (1958)
The Strange Case of Dr. Manning (1958)
Wolf Dog (1958)
1 Plus 1 (1961)
The Politicians (1970)

BAUDO, SERGE
Michael Strogoff (1960)

BAUDRIER, YVES
Battle of the Rails (1944)
The Silent World (1956)

BAUMGARTNER, WALTER
The Fall (1972)

BAX, ARNOLD
Malta, G. C. (1942)
Oliver Twist (1948)
Journey into History (1952)

BAXTER, LES
The Yellow Tomahawk (1954)
The Black Sleep (1956)
Hot Blood (1956)
Hot Cars (1956)
Quincannon, Frontier Scout (1956)
Rebel in Town (1956)
A Woman's Devotion (1956)
Bop Girl (1957)
The Dalton Girls (1957)
The Girl in Black Stockings (1957)
Hell Bound (1957)
The Invisible Boy (1957)
Jungle Heat (1957)
Outlaw's Son (1957)
Pharoah's Curse (1957)
Revolt at Fort Laramie (1957)
The Storm Rider (1957)
Tomahawk Trail (1957)
Untamed Youth (1957)
Voodoo Island (1957)
War Drums (1957)
The Bride and the Beast (1958)
Escape from Red Rock (1958)
Fort Bowie (1958)
The Lone Ranger and the Lost City of Gold (1958)
Macabre (1958)
Monika (1959)
Goliath and the Dragon (1960)
The House of Usher (1960)
Alakazam the Great (1961)
Black Sunday (1961)
Master of the World (1961)
The Pit and the Pendulum (1961)
Marco Polo (1962)
Panic in Year Zero (1962)
White Slave Ship (1962)
Beach Party (1963)
The Comedy of Terrors (1963)
Operation Bikini (1963)
The Raven (1963)
X--The Man with the X-Ray Eyes (1963)
The Young Racers (1963)
Black Sabbath (1964)
Beach Blanket Bingo (1965)
Dr. Goldfoot and the Bikini Machine (1965)
How to Stuff a Wild Bikini (1965)
Sergeant Deadhead (1965)
Dr. Goldfoot and the Girl Bombs (1966)
The Ghost in the Invisible Bikini (1966)
Sadismo (1967)
The Mini-Skirt Mob (1968)
Terror in the Jungle (1968)
Wild in the Streets (1968)
Flareup (1969)
Hell's Belles (1969)
Cry of the Banshee (1970)
The Dunwich Horror (1970)
Baron Blood (1972)
Frogs (1972)

BAZELON, IRWIN
Survival, 1967 (1968)

BEARBITUNG, E. G.
Nightshade (1972)

BEARTS, GUY
L'eau Vive (1958)
La Gamberge (1963)
La Vie Conjugal (1965)

THE BEATLES
Help! (1965)

BEAVER, JACK
The Wife of General Ling (1938)
This Was Paris (1942)
Showtime (1948)

BECAUD, GILBERT
Babette Goes to War (1960)
The House under the Trees (1971)

BECCE, GUISEPPE
Tartuffe (1926)
Extase (1932)

BECERRA, GUSTAVO
Valparaiso My Love (1970)

BECK, JOE
Grimm's Fairy Tales for Adults (1971)

BECKER, GERHARD
Ordered to Love (1963)

THE BEE GEES
Melody (S. W. A. L. K.) (1971)

BELFER, HAL
Juke Box Rhythm (1959)

BELLING, ANDREW
Peking Remembered (1967)

BENJAMIN, SIR ARTHUR
The Turn of the Tide (1935)
The Clairvoyant (1936)
Wings of the Morning (1937)
The Return of the Scarlet Pimpernell (1938)
The Cumberland Story (1947)
Steps of the Ballet (1948)
The Conquest of Everest (1953)
Above Us the Waves (1956)
The Man Who Knew Too Much (1956)
Fire Down Below (1957)

BENNETT, RICHARD RODNEY
The Angry Hills (1956)
The Devil's Disciple (1956)
The Man Who Could Cheat Death (1956)
Pickup Alley (1957)
Indiscreet (1958)
The Man Inside (1958)
Menace in the Night (1958)
The Safecracker (1958)
Chance Meeting (1960)
The Mark (1961)
Only Two Can Play (1962)
Satan Never Sleeps (1962)
Billy Liar (1963)
The Nanny (1965)
One Way Pendulum (1965)
The Witches (1966)
Billion Dollar Brain (1967)
The Devil's Own (1967)
Far from the Madding Crowd (1967)
Secret Ceremony (1968)
The Buttercup Chain (1970)
Nicholas and Alexandra (1971)
Lady Caroline Lamb (1972)

BENNETT, ROBERT RUSSELL
Annabel Takes a Tour (1938)
Fugitives for a Night (1938)
Career (1939)
Fifth Avenue Girl (1939)
Pacific Liner (1939)

BENNINGS, JOHN
The Legend of Nigger Charley (1972)

BERG, PETER
Riverrun (1968)

BERGKMANS, JOSE
The War of the Buttons (1963)

BERKELEY, LENNOX
Hotel Reserve (1944)
Out of Chaos (1944)

BERLIN, IRVING
Lady of the Pavements (1929)

BERNAOLA, CARMELO
The House without Boundaries (1972)

BERNARD, ARMAN
Under the Roofs of Paris (1930)
Le Million (1931)

BERNARD, GUY
Paris 1900 (1948)
Pardon My French (1951)
La Sel de la Terre (1951)

The Naked Heart (1955)

BERNARD, JAMES
Across the Bridge (1957)
Enemy from Space (1957)
X The Unknown (1957)
Windom's Way (1958)
Elephant Gun (1959)
The Hound of the Baskervilles (1959)
The Stranglers of Bombay (1960)
Terror of the Tongs (1961)
Kiss of the Vampire (1963)
The Gorgon (1965)
Secret of Blood Island (1965)
She (1965)
These Are the Damned (1965)
Dracula--Prince of Darkness (1966)
The Plague of the Zombies (1966)
Frankenstein Created Woman (1967)
The Devil's Bride (1968)
Dracula Has Risen from the Grave (1968)
Torture Garden (1968)
Frankenstein Must be Destroyed (1969)
The Scar of Dracula (1970)
Taste the Blood of Dracula (1970)

BERNERS, LORD
Halfway House (1944)
Nicholas Nickleby (1946)

BERNSTEIN, ELMER
Boots Malone (1951)
Saturday's Hero (1951)
Never Wave at a Wac (1952)
Sudden Fear (1952)
Battles of Chief Pontiac (1953)
Miss Robin Crusoe (1953)
Make Haste to Live (1954)
The Eternal Sea (1955)
It's a Dog's Life (1955)
The Man with the Golden Arm (1955)
The View from Pompey's Head (1955)
Storm Fear (1956)
The Ten Commandments (1956)
Drango (1957)
Fear Strikes Out (1957)
Men in War (1957)
The Naked Eye (1957)
Sweet Smell of Success (1957)
The Tin Star (1957)
Anna Lucasta (1958)
The Buccaneer (1958)
Desire Under the Elms (1958)
God's Little Acre (1958)
Kings Go Forth (1958)
Some Came Running (1958)
Toccata for Toy Trains (1958)
The Miracle (1959)
The Story on Page One (1959)
From the Terrace (1960)
The Rat Race (1960)
By Love Possessed (1961)
The Comancheros (1961)
Summer and Smoke (1961)
The Young Doctors (1961)
Bird Man of Alcatraz (1962)
A Girl Named Tamiko (1962)
To Kill a Mockingbird (1962)
Walk on the Wild Side (1962)
The Caretakers (1963)
The Great Escape (1963)
Hud (1963)
Kings of the Sun (1963)
Love with the Proper Stranger (1963)
Rampage (1963)
The Carpenter (1964)
Four Days in November (1964)
The World of Henry Orient (1964)
Baby the Rain Must Fall (1965)
The Hallelujah Trail (1965)
The Reward (1965)
Seven Women (1965)
The Sons of Katie Elder (1965)
Cast a Giant Shadow (1966)
Hawaii (1966)
Return of the Seven (1966)
The Silencers (1966)
Thoroughly Modern Millie (1967)
I Love You, Alice B. Toklas (1968)
The Scalphunters (1968)
The Bridge at Remagen (1969)

Guns of the Magnificent Seven (1969)
The Gypsy Moths (1969)
Midas Run (1969)
True Grit (1969)
Where's Jack! (1969)
Cannon for Cordoba (1970)
The Liberation of L.B. Jones (1970)
A Walk in the Spring Rain (1970)
Big Jake (1971)
See No Evil (1971)
The Magnificent Seven Ride (1972)

BERNSTEIN, LEONARD
On the Waterfront (1954)

BERTEL, JOSE
The Italian of the Roses (1972)

BERTINI, GARI
They Were Ten (1961)

BEST, PETER
Adventures of Barry McKenzie (1972)

BETTS, HARRY
Winter A-Go-Go (1965)
The Big Mouth (1967)
The Fantastic Plastic Machine (1969)
A Time for Dying (1971)

BEYTELMAN, GUSTAVO
The Mafia (1972)

BIGERBA, B.
The Debut (1971)

BINGE, RONALD
The Adventures of Sadie (1955)
Dance Little Lady (1955)

BIRYUKOV, YURI
The House I Love In (1957)
The Wrestler and the Clown (1957)

BISHOFF, EDGAR
Marcel Marceau's Pantomimes (1955)
Paris Weekend (1959)

BISWAS, ANIL
Munna (1957)

BIXIO, C. A.
Peddlin' in Society (1947)

BLACK, STANLEY
Lili Marlene (1951)
Mr. Potts Goes to Moscow (1954)
White Fire (1954)
Tonight's the Night (1954)
High Terrace (1956)
An Alligator Named Daisy (1957)
As Long as They're Happy (1957)
Two Grooms for the Bride (1957)
Blood of the Vampire (1958)
Cross-Up (1958)
Dangerous Youth (1958)
Mailbag Robbery (1958)
Your Past Is Showing (1958)
Broth of a Boy (1959)
The Circle (1959)
City After Midnight (1959)
The Battle of the Sexes (1960)
Hand in Hand (1960)
Hell Is a City (1960)
The Man Who Wouldn't Talk (1960)
Double Bunk (1961)
Five Golden Hours (1961)
Stop Me Before I Kill (1961)
Sword of Sherwood Forest (1961)
The Day the Earth Caught Fire (1962)
Wonderful to be Young (1962)
Maniac (1963)
Rattle of a Simple Man (1964)
Crossplot (1969)

BLACKWELL, CHARLES
Some Girls Do (1969)

BLACKWELL, OTIS
Jamboree (1957)

BLAIKEY, ALAN
Up Pompeii (1971)

BLAIR, LEONARD
Operation C. I. A. (1965)

BLAKE, HOWARD
All the Way Up (1970)

BLATT, JERRY
Scarecrow in a Garden of Cucumbers (1972)

BLISS, SIR ARTHUR
Things to Come (1935)
Conquest of the Air (1938)
Men of Two Worlds (1946)
Christopher Columbus (1948)
Welcome to the Queen (1954)

BLITZSTEIN, MARC
Surf and Seaweed (1931)
Spanish Earth (1937)
Valley Town (1940)
Native Land (1942)
Night Shift (1942)

BLOCK, FREDERICK
We Are the Marines (1942)

BLOMDAHL, KARL-BIRGER
Sawdust and Tinsel (Naked Night) (1953)

BLOOMFIELD, MIKE
Medium Cool (1969)

BLUE BATCH
It Ain't Easy (1972)

BLUESTONE, HARRY
Mara of the Wilderness (1965)

BLUM, ROBERT
The Search (1948)
Heidi (1953)
The Village (1953)
Heidi and Peter (1955)

BOCHMANN, WERNER
Rape on the Moor (1957)

BOETTICHER, MARTIN
Treasure of the Silver Lake (1964)
Apache Gold (1965)
The Oil Prince (1965)
Old Surehand (1965)
Winnetou II (1965)
Winnetou III (1965)
Long Legs--Long Fingers (1966)
The Monster of London City (1967)
The Phantom of Soho (1967)
Flaming Frontier (1968)
Doctor Fabian--Laughing is the Best Medicine (1969)
The Duck Rings at Half Past Seven (1969)
Laddie Loves in All Directions (1969)
Spanking at School (1969)
Willi Manages the Whole Thing (1972)

BOGGS, ED
Black Girl (1972)
Fritz the Cat (1972)

BOLLING, CLAUDE
Ladies' Man (1960)
World in My Pocket (1962)
Borsalino (1970)
Catch Me a Spy (1971)

BONFA, LUIZ
Black Orpheus (1960)
The Gentle Rain (1965)
The Hours of Love (1965)

BONGUSTO, FRED
Detective Belli (1970)
The Man Who Came for Coffee (1970)

BONNARD, GUILIO
Saint Margaret of Cortona (1955)

BONNIWELL, SEAN
How to Succeed with Sex (1970)

BONO, SONNY
Chastity (1969)

BORGMANN, HANS-OTTO
Come, Take My Life (1956)

BORNE, HAL
Flight of the Lost Balloon (1961)
Heading for Heaven (1947)

BOSSICK, BERNARD
Guerrilla Girl (1953)

BOTKIN, PERRY
Murder by Contract (1958)

BOTKIN, PERRY, JR.
Bless the Beasts and Children (1971)
Skyjacked (1972)
They Only Kill Their Masters (1972)

BOUDREAU, WALTER
The House of Light (1970)

BOUTELJE, PHIL
Hi Diddle Diddle (1943)

BOWEN, JIMMY
Vanishing Point (1971)

BOWERS, BOB
Come Spy with Me (1967)

BOWERS, ROBERT HOOD
Daughter of the Gods (1916)

BOWLES, PAUL
Dreams That Money Can Buy (1948)
The Yellow Cab Man (1950)

BOZZI
Toni (1935)

BRADFORD, JAMES
Peak of Fate (1925)

BRADLEY, OSCAR
The Farmer Takes a Wife (1935)
The Man Who Broke the Bank at Monte Carlo (1935)

BRADLEY, SCOTT
The Yellow Cab Man (1950)

BRADSHAW, CHARLES
The Miracle of Morgan's Creek (1944)

BRANDT, CARL
The Cowboy (1954)
Bobby Ware Is Missing (1955)
Seven Angry Men (1955)
Shotgun (1955)

BRANDT, HENRY
Valley of the Tennessee (1944)
The Capital City (1945)
The Pale Horseman (1946)
My Father's House (1947)

BRASSAT, JEAN
The Algerian War (1972)

BRASSENS, GEORGES
Gates of Paris (1957)
Porte de Lilas (1957)

BRAULT, PIERRE F.
Stop (1971)
The Time of the Hunt (1972)
The True Story of Bernadette (1972)

BREESKIN, ELIAS
Captain Scarlett (1953)

BREGMAN, BUDDY
Five Guns West (1955)
Fighting Trouble (1956)
The Wild Party (1956)
The Delicate Delinquent (1957)
Guns, Girls and Gangsters (1958)
Born Reckless (1959)
The Secret of the Purple Reef (1960)
Valley of the Redwoods (1960)
The Cat Burglar (1961)

BREL, JACQUES
The Bar at the Crossing (1972)
Franz (1972)

BRETON, LUIS FERNANDEZ
This Strange Passion (El) (1955)

BRETON, L. HERNANDEZ
One Big Affair (1952)

BRICUSSE, LESLIE
Doctor Dolittle (1967)

BRIDGEWATER, LESLIE
Train of Events (1949)

BRIEL, JOSEPH CARL
Queen Elizabeth (1912)
Cabiria (1914)
The Birth of a Nation (1915)
Double Trouble (1915)
The Lily and the Rose (1915)
Martyrs of the Alamo (1915)
Intolerance (1916)
The Dramatic Life of Abraham Lincoln (1923)
The White Roses (1923)

BRIGES, RON
Where the Bullets Fly (1966)

BRILL, CHARLES
Pastor Hall (1940)

BRITTEN, BENJAMIN
Coalface (1935)
Calendar of the Year (1936)
Night Mail (1936)
The Saving of Bill Blewett (1936)
Line to the Tschierva Hut (1937)
Love from a Stranger (1937)
The Tocher (1938)
Village Harvest (1938)
Village Harvest (1945)

BRODZSKY, NICHOLAS
Voice in the Night (1941)
The Way to the Stars (1945)
Carnival (1946)
Her Man Gilbey (1948)
Beware of Pity (1949)
Demi-Paradise (1949)
French without Tears (1949)
Man About the House (1949)
While the Sun Shines (1949)
The Toast of New Orleans (1950)
Rich, Young and Pretty (1951)
The Student Prince (1954)
The Opposite Sex (1956)
Let's Be Happy (1957)

BROEKMAN, DAVID
The Phantom of the Opera (1925)
Mississippi Gambler (1929)
Tonight at Twelve (1929)
All Quiet on the Western Front (1930)
Outside the Law (1930)
Frankenstein (1931)
Crowded Paradise (1956)

BROKENSHA, JACK
Quadroon (1972)

BROOKS, WILLIAM
Prologue (1969)

BROUWER, LEO
The Days of Water (1971)
Cuban Fight Against Demons (1972)

BROWN, JACKIE
Front Page Story (1955)
The Accursed (1958)

BROWN, LOUIS
Three on a Couch (1966)
Which Way to the Front? (1970)

BROWN, NACIO HERB
The Kissing Bandit (1948)

BRUBECK, HOWARD
Daphni (1952)

BRUEHNE, LOTHAR
Long Is the Road (1948)
My Father's Horse (1956)

BRUMMER, ANDRE S.
The Rawhide Trail (1958)

BRUNELLI, PETE
The Ramparts We Watch (1940)

BRUNNER, ROBERT F.
That Darn Cat (1965)
Lt. Robin Crusoe, U.S.N. (1966)
Monkeys Go Home (1967)
Blackbeard's Ghost (1968)
Never a Dull Moment (1968)
The Computer Wore Tennis Shoes (1969)
Smith (1969)
The Boatniks (1970)
The Barefoot Executive (1971)
The Wild Country (1971)
The Biscuit Eater (1972)
Now You See Him, Now You Don't (1972)
Snowball Express (1972)

BRUNO, TONY
Hell's Angels '69 (1969)

BRUNS, GEORGE
Davy Crockett, King of the Wild Frontier (1955)
Davy Crockett and the River Pirates (1956)
Westward Ho, the Wagons (1956)
Johnny Tremain (1957)
Sleeping Beauty (1959)
The Absent-Minded Professor (1961)
Babes in Toyland (1961)
One Hundred and One Dalmations (1961)
Son of Flubber (1963)
The Sword in the Stone (1963)
The Fighting Prince of Donegal (1966)
Follow Me Boys (1966)
Adventures of Bullwhip Griffin (1967)
The Jungle Book (1967)
The Daring Game (1968)
The Horse in the Gray Flannel Suit (1968)
The Love Bug (1968)
The Aristocats (1970)

BRYARS, GAVIN
Times Four (1970)

BUDD, ROY
Soldier Blue (1970)
Catlow (1971)
Flight of the Doves (1971)
Get Carter (1971)
Kidnapped (1971)
Zeppelin (1971)
The Carey Treatment (1972)
Something to Hide (1972)

BUENAGU, JOSE
The Castilian (1963)

BUENCAMINO, FRANCISCO
Surrender--Hell! (1959)

BURKE, SOLOMON
Cool Breeze (1972)
Hammer (1972)

BURKE, SONNY
Flame of the Islands (1955)
Hand of Death (1962)

BURNIN' RED IVANHOE
Are You Afraid? (1971)

BURNS, WILFRED
Fools Rush In (1949)
The Fighting Wildcats (1957)
Operation Conspiracy (1957)
Thunder over Tangier (1957)
Till Death Us Do Part (1968)
Dad's Diary (1971)

BURROWS, DON
2,000 Weeks (1969)

BURTON, RAY
Rabbit, Run (1970)

BUSH, DOUG
A Married Couple (1969)

BUSH, TERRY
The Merry Wives of Windsor (1972)

BUSHY, BOB
Holiday Camp (1948)

BUTLER, ARTIE
The Love Machine (1971)
What's Up, Doc? (1972)

BUTLER, JERRY
Melinda (1972)

BUTTOLPH, DAVID
Show Them No Mercy (1935)
Everybody's Old Man (1936)
Danger! Love at Work (1937)
Fifty Roads to Town (1937)
Love Is News (1937)
Nancy Steels Is Missing (1937)
Second Honeymoon (1937)
The Gorilla (1939)
Made for Each Other (1939)
Four Sons (1940)
I Was an Adventuress (1940)
The Man I Married (1940)
The Mark of Zorro (1940)
The Return of Frank James (1940)
Chad Hanna (1941)
Tobacco Road (1941)
Western Union (1941)
In Old California (1942)
Lady for a Night (1942)
Manila Calling (1942)
Moontide (1942)
My Favorite Blonde (1942)
Street of Chance (1942)
This Gun for Hire (1942)
Thunder Birds (1942)
Wake Island (1942)
Bomber's Moon (1943)
Corvette K-225 (1943)
Crash Dive (1943)
Guadalcanal Diary (1943)
The Immortal Sergeant (1943)
Buffalo Bill (1944)
The Fighting Lady (1944)
The Hitler Gang (1944)
In the Meantime, Darling (1944)
Till We Meet Again (1944)
The Bullfighters (1945)
The Caribbean Mystery (1945)
Circumstantial Evidence (1945)
The House on 92nd Street (1945)
Junior Miss (1945)
The Spider (1945)
Within These Walls (1945)
Home Sweet Homicide (1946)
It Shouldn't Happen to a Dog (1946)
Johnny Comes Flying Home (1946)
Shock (1946)
Somewhere in the Night (1946)
Strange Triangle (1946)
Bill and Coo (1947)
Boomerang (1947)
The Brasher Doubloon (1947)
The Foxes of Harrow (1947)
Kiss of Death (1947)
Moss Rose (1947)
13 Rue Madeleine (1947)
June Bride (1948)
One Sunday Afternoon (1948)
Rope (1948)
Smart Girls Don't Talk (1948)
To the Victor (1948)
Colorado Territory (1949)
The Girl from Jones Beach (1949)
John Loves Mary (1949)
One Last Fling (1949)
Roseanna McCoy (1949)
The Story of Sea Biscuit (1949)
Chain Lightning (1950)
The Daughter of Rosie O'Grady (1950)
Montana (1950)
Pretty Baby (1950)
The Redhead and the Cowboy (1950)
Return of the Frontiersman (1950)
Three Secrets (1950)
Along the Great Divide (1951)
The Enforcer (1951)
Fighting Coast Guard (1951)
Fort Worth (1951)
Lone Star (1951)
The Sellout (1951)
Submarine Command (1951)
Ten Tall Men (1951)
Carson City (1952)

Lone Star (1952)
The Man Bandit the Gun (1952)
My Man and I (1952)
Talk About a Stranger (1952)
This Woman Is Dangerous (1952)
The Winning Team (1952)
House of Wax (1953)
South Sea Woman (1953)
The System (1953)
Thunder Over the Plains (1953)
The Bounty Hunter (1954)
Crime Wave (1954)
Phantom of the Rue Morgue (1954)
Riding Shotgun (1954)
Secret of the Incas (1954)
I Die a Thousand Times (1955)
Jump Into Hell (1955)
Long John Silver (1955)
Target Zero (1955)
The Burning Hills (1956)
A Cry in the Night (1956)
The Lone Ranger (1956)
Santiago (1956)
The Steel Jungle (1956)
The Big Land (1957)
The D. I. (1957)
The Deep Six (1958)
Onionhead (1958)
The Horse Soldiers (1959)
Westbound (1959)
Guns of the Timberland (1960)
PT-109 (1963)
The Man from Galveston (1964)

BUTTS, DALE

Home on the Range (1945)
Affairs of Geraldine (1946)
The Catman of Paris (1946)
Heldorado (1946)
Night Train to Memphis (1946)
One Exciting Week (1946)
Roll On Texas Moon (1946)
Sioux City Sue (1946)
Under Nevada Skies (1946)
The Crimson Key (1947)
The Invisible Wall (1947)
Second Chance (1947)
The Denver Kid (1948)
Eyes of Texas (1948)
The Far Frontier (1948)
Nightime in Nevada (1948)
The Plunderers (1948)
Son of God's Country (1948)
Down Dakota Way (1949)
Hellfire (1949)
The Last Bandit (1949)
Too Late for Tears (1949)
Bells of Coronado (1950)
North of the Great Divide (1950)
Rock Island Trail (1950)
The Savage Horde (1950)
Sunset in the West (1950)
Trigger, Jr. (1950)
Heart of the Rockies (1951)
In Old Amarillo (1951)
Oh, Susanna (1951)
The Sea Hornet (1951)
South of Caliente (1951)
Spoilers of the Plains (1951)
Bal Tabarin (1952)
Colorado Sundown (1952)
Toughest Man in Arizona (1952)
The Wac from Walla Walla (1952)
Woman of the North Country (1952)
Champ for a Day (1953)
Geraldine (1953)
Red River Shore (1953)
Sea of Lost Ships (1953)
Hell's Half Acre (1954)
The Outcast (1954)
The Shanghai Story (1954)
Carolina Cannonball (1955)
City of Shadows (1955)
Double Jeopardy (1955)
Fighting Chance (1955)
Headline Hunters (1955)
Hell's Outpost (1955)
I Cover the Underworld (1955)
Lay that Rifle Down (1955)
No Man's Woman (1955)
The Road to Denver (1955)
Santa Fe Passage (1955)
The Vanishing American (1955)
Accused of Murder (1956)
Dakota Incident (1956)
The Man Is Armed (1956)
A Strange Adventure (1956)
Stranger at My Door (1956)
Terror at Midnight (1956)
Thunder over Arizona (1956)
Affair in Reno (1957)

BYARS, GAVIN
Dyn Ako (1972)

BYRD, BRETTON
It's Love Again (1936)
Bad Sister (1948)
Look Before You Love (1948)
Tony Draws a Horse (1948)

BYRD, CHARLIE
Dead to the World (1962)

BYRD, JOSEPH
Lion's Love (1969)

BYRNE, HAROLD
Situation Hopeless, But Not Serious (1965)

BYRNS, HAROLD
The Girl on the Bridge (1951)
Pickup (1951)

CADKIN, EMIL
The Big Fix (1947)
Bury Me Dead (1947)
The Devil on Wheels (1947)
Heartaches (1947)
Three on a Ticket (1947)
Navajo Run (1966)

CADMAN, CHARLES WAKEFIELD
The Rubaiyat of Omar Khayyam (1922)
Drums of Love (1929)
Captain of the Guard (1930)

CAGAN, ALEX
Flock (1972)

CAGE, JOHN
Dreams That Money Can Buy (1948)
World of Calder (1950)

CAILLIET, LUCIEN
Fun on a Weekend (1947)
The Enchanted Valley (1948)
Harpoon (1948)
The Winner's Circle (1948)
Captain China (1949)
Red Stallion in the Rockies (1949)
Special Agent (1949)
State Department File 649 (1949)
Thunder in the Pines (1949)
Crosswinds (1951)
Hong Kong (1951)
The Last Outpost (1951)
The Blazing Forest (1952)
Caribbean (1952)
Confidence Girl (1952)
Jamaica Run (1953)
Tropic Zone (1953)
The Vanquished (1953)
The Night Holds Terror (1955)

CAIN, TED
Hold That Ghost (1941)

CALE, JOHN
Heat (1972)

CALKER, DARRELL
Dangerous Millions (1946)
Adventure Island (1947)
Backlash (1947)
Big Town (1947)
I Cover the Big Town (1947)
Jewels of Brandenburg (1947)
Renegade Girl (1947)
Rolling Home (1947)
Shoot to Kill (1947)
Albuquerque (1948)
Arthur Takes Over (1948)
Big Town Scandal (1948)
Dynamite (1948)
Fighting Back (1948)
Half Past Midnight (1948)
Silent Conflict (1948)
Sinister Journey (1948)
Speed to Spare (1948)
El Paso (1949)
Manhandled (1949)
Ride, Ryder, Ride! (1949)
Tucson (1949)
Federal Man (1950)
The Fighting Redhead (1950)
The Fighting Stallion (1950)
The Flying Saucer (1950)
F.B.I. Girl (1951)
The Hoodlum (1951)
Joe Palooka in Triple Cross (1951)
Savage Drums (1951)

Slaughter Trail (1951)
Superman and the Mole Men (1951)
The Marshal's Daughter (1953)
From Hell It Came (1957)
Beyond the Time Barrier (1960)
Chartroose Caboose (1960)

CALVI, GERARD
The Big Chief (1960)
Asterix and Cleopatra (1969)
Dead Run (1969)
Three Men on a Horse (1970)
The Annuity (1972)
War is War (1972)

CAMERON, JOHN
Every Home Should Have One (1970)
Kes (1970)
The Rise and Rise of Michael Rimmer (1970)
Made (1972)
The Ruling Class (1972)

CAMPBELL, BRUCE
Mr. Drake's Duck (1951)

THE CAN
Deadlock (1970)

CANFORA, BRUNO
It Happened in Broad Daylight (1960)

CAPE, JOHN
Equinox (1970)

CAPER, JOHN, JR.
Track of Thunder (1968)

CAPNISSIS, COSTA
Casablan (1964)

CAPPS, AL
The Windsplitter (1971)

CARAVAN, XHOL
We-Two (1970)

CARAVELLI
The Song of the Balalaika (1971)

CARBONARA, GERARD
The Patriot (1928)
Sawdust Paradise (1928)
Warming Up (1928)
Big Brown Eyes (1936)
The Case Against Mrs. Ames (1936)
The General Died at Dawn (1936)
The Moon's Our Home (1936)
Poppy (1936)
Spendthrift (1936)
The Texas Rangers (1936)
Trail of the Lonesome Pine (1936)
Wedding Present (1936)
Men with Wings (1938)
The Texans (1938)
Ambush (1939)
Arrest Bulldog Drummond (1939)
Disbarred (1939)
Escape from Yesterday (1939)
Geronimo (1939)
The Gracie Allen Murder Case (1939)
Our Leading Citizen (1939)
Shepherd of the Hills (1941)
American Empire (1942)
Pacific Blackout (1942)
Tombstone--The Town Too Tough to Die (1942)
Henry Aldrich Haunts a House (1943)
The Kansan (1943)

CARDEW, PHIL
Lady of Vengeance (1957)
High Hell (1958)

CARDOSO, RUI
The Message (1971)

CARLING, F.
The Incredible Shrinking Man (1957)

CARLOS, ROBERTO
The Girl Watchers (1969)

CARLOS, WALTER
A Clockwork Orange (1971)

CARMICHAEL, RALPH
Wiretappers (1956)
The Persuader (1957)
4-D Man (1959)
The Cross and the Switchblade (1970)
The Late Liz (1971)

CARPENTER, IMOGEN
The Young Guns (1956)

CARPI, FIORENZO
A Very Private Affair (1962)
Giacomo Casanova: Childhood and Adolescence (1969)
Out of Frame (1969)
The Cry (1970)
An Eel Worth 300 Million (1971)
The Vacation (1971)
Without Family (1972)

CARRAS, NICHOLAS
Dragstrip Riot (1958)
Hell's Five Hours (1958)
Do Not Throw Cushions Into the Ring (1970)

CARREON, GUSTAVO C.
Adam and Eve (1957)
Yanco (1964)
The Fool Killer (1965)
Rage (1966)
The Right to Be Born (1971)

CARRIGUENE, RENE
New Mexico (1951)

CARRUTH, DICK
The Tioga Kid (1948)

CARSON, PHILIPPE
A Portrait of Marianne (1970)

CARTER, BENNY
The Adventures of * (1957)
Harlem Wednesday (1959)
A Man Called Adam (1966)
Buck and the Preacher (1972)

CARTER, RON
Desperate Characters (1971)

CARWITHEN, DOREEN
Harvest from the Wilderness (1948)
Boys in Brown (1950)
Man in Hiding (1953)
Break in the Circle (1957)

CARY, TRISTRAM
The Ladykillers (1956)
Time without Pity (1957)
Town on Trial (1957)
The Boy Who Stole a Million (1960)
A Lecture on Man (1962)
A Boy Ten Feet Tall (1965)
5,000,000 Miles to Earth (1968)
A Twist of Sand (1968)
Blood from the Mummy's Tomb (1971)

CASCIELLO, GIANNI
The Girl Passing Through (1972)

CASES, GUILLERMO
The Devil's Daughter (1956)

CASH, JOHNNY
I Walk the Line (1970)
Little Fauss and Big Halsy (1970)

CASTLEMAN, WILLIAM
The Big Bird Cage (1972)

CASTELNUEVO-TEDESCO, MARIO
The Black Parachute (1944)
And Then There Were None (1945)
Time Out of Mind (1947)
The Loves of Carmen (1948)
Everybody Does It (1949)
Mask of the Avenger (1951)
The Long Wait (1954)

CASWELL, OZZIE
County Fair (1950)
The Hidden City (1950)

The Lost Volcano (1950)
Motor Patrol (1950)
Blazing Bullets (1951)
Blue Blood (1951)

CAT TEN
Deep End (1970)

THE CATS
The Honest Interview (1971)

CEDRON, JUAN
Y Que Patatin Y Que Patatan (1971)

CELE, WILLIAM
The Magic Garden (1951)

CEZAR, CORNEL
Too Little Such a Big War (1970)

CHAGRIN, FRANCIS
Helter Skelter (1949)
Last Holiday (1950)
The Beachcomber (1955)
Simba (1955)
The Colditz Story (1957)
The Snorkel (1958)
Greyfriar's Bobby (1961)
In the Cool of the Day (1963)
Clue of the Twisted Candle (1968)

CHAMBERS, DUDLEY
Fingerprints Don't Lie (1951)
Mask of the Dragon (1951)

CHAPLIN, CHARLES
Shoulder Arms (1918)
The Kid (1921)
The Pilgrim (1922)
City Lights (1931)
Modern Times (1936)
The Great Dictator (1940)
Monsieur Verdoux (1947)
Limelight (1952)
A King in New York (1957)
The Countess from Hong Kong (1966)

CHAPLIN, SAUL
Give the Girl a Break (1953)
The Teahouse of the August Moon (1956)

CHAPMAN, BEN
Generation (1969)

CHARLAP, MOOSE
Guess What We Learned in School Today? (1970)

CHARLEBOIS, ROBERT
Two Women in Gold (1971)

CHARLES, WILLIAM S.
The Heart of Paula (1916)

CHARLOT
Stadium Nuts (1972)

CHARPENTIER, EMMANUEL
The Dreamed Life (1972)

CHERNIAVSKY, JOSEF
We Americans (1928)

CHERNIS, JAY
That's My Baby (1944)
Identity Unknown (1945)

CHERWIN, RICHARD
Bandits of the Bandlands (1945)
Behind City Lights (1945)
The Cherokee Flash (1945)
Colorado Pioneers (1945)
The Fatal Witness (1945)
Gangs of the Waterfront (1945)
The Lone Texas Ranger (1945)
Marshal of Laredo (1945)
Oregon Trail (1945)
Road to Alcatraz (1945)
Rough Riders of Cheyenne (1945)
Santa Fe Saddlemates (1945)
Sheriff of Cimarron (1945)
A Sporting Chance (1945)
Three's a Crowd (1945)
The Tiger Woman (1945)
The Topeka Terror (1945)
Trail of Kit Carson (1945)
Wagon Wheels Westward (1945)

California Gold Rush (1946)
Conquest of Cheyenne (1946)
Crime of the Century (1946)
Days of Buffalo Bill (1946)
A Guy Could Change (1946)
The Invisible Informer (1946)
The Last Crooked Mile (1946)
Sheriff of Redwood Valley (1946)
Sun Valley Cyclone (1946)
The Undercover Man (1946)
Valley of the Zombies (1946)
The Pilgrim Lady (1947)

CHEVREVILLE, RAYMOND
Rubens (1948)

CHILDREN OF PARADISE
Greetings (1968)

CHOPIN, FREDERIC
Jutrzenka: A Winter in Majorca (1971)

CHOWDHURY, SALIL
The Big Sky (1970)

CHRISTIANSEN, HENNING
A Clerk Vanished (1971)
The Vicar of Vejlby (1972)

CHRISTOPHER, JIRH
Love, Swedish Style (1972)

CHTCHEDRINE, RODION
Anna Karenina (1968)

CHUDNOW, DAVID
The Mad Monster (1942)
The Town Went Wild (1944)
The Big Show-Off (1945)
The Kid Sister (1945)
Nabonga (1945)
A Song for Miss Julie (1945)
Fool's Gold (1946)
Unexpected Guest (1946)
Adventures of Don Coyote (1947)
The Case of the Baby Sitter (1947)
Dangerous Venture (1947)
The Hat Box Mystery (1947)
Hoppy's Holiday (1947)
The Marauders (1947)
The Girl from Manhattan (1948)
Highway 13 (1948)
A Miracle Can Happen (1948)
Trouble Preferred (1948)
Deputy Marshal (1949)
Red Planet Mars (1952)

CHYDENIUS, KAJ
When the Heavens Fell (1972)

CICOGNINI, ALESSANDRO
Four Steps in the Clouds (1942)
Eternal Melodies (1948)
The Merry Chase (1948)
Scorned Flesh (1948)
The Bicycle Thief (1949)
Father's Dilemma (1950)
Stormbound (1951)
Umberto D. (1951)
Miracle in Milan (1952)
Les Miserables (1952)
The Thief of Venice (1952)
Tomorrow Is Too Late (1952)
The Anatomy of Love (1953)
Hello Elephant (1953)
Crossed Swords (1954)
Indiscretion of an American Wife (1954)
Frisky (1955)
Lucky to be a Woman (1955)
Summertime (1955)
Too Bad She's Bad (1955)
Ulysses (1955)
The Return of Don Camillo (1956)
The Roof (1956)
The Black Orchid (1959)
A Tailor's Maid (1959)
A Breath of Scandal (1960)
Fast and Sexy (1960)
It Started in Naples (1960)
The Last Judgment (1961)
The Pigeon that Took Rome (1962)

CINI, I.
Bread, Love and Dreams (1954)

CIPRIANI, NORMAN
Venus Planet (1972)

CIPRIANI, STELVIO
The Stranger Returns (1968)
Woman Laughs Last (1969)
The Anonymous Venetian (1970)
The Lickerish Quartet (1970)
Antefatto (1971)
Come Together (1971)
Blindman (1972)
From the Police, with Thanks (1972)
Guernica (1972)
To Kill in Silence (1972)
Venus Planet (1972)

CLAMAN, DOLORES
Captain Apache (1971)

CLARK, CARROLL
Mary of Scotland (1936)

CLAYTON, KENNY
The Ragman's Daughter (1972)

CLEAVE, VAN
The Sainted Sisters (1948)
Dear Wife (1949)
Fancy Pants (1950)
The Goldbergs (1950)
Dear Brat (1951)
Quebec (1951)
Rhubarb (1951)
Off Limits (1953)
Cinerama Holiday (1955)
Conquest of Space (1955)
Lucy Gallant (1955)
The Devil's Hairpin (1957)
The Lonely Man (1957)
The Colossus of New York (1958)
The Space Children (1958)
That Kind of Woman (1959)
Blueprint for Robbery (1961)
Robinson Crusoe on Mars (1964)
Project X (1968)

CLIFFORD, SIR HUBERT
An Ideal Husband (1948)
Pandora and the Flying Dutchman (1951)
The Stranger in Between (1952)
River Beat (1954)
Triple Deception (1957)
Hell Drivers (1958)
The One That Got Away (1958)

CLOEREC, RENE
Sylvie and the Phantom (1945)
Devil in the Flesh (1947)
Confessions of a Rogue (1948)
Mr. Orchid (1948)
The Spice of Life (1949)
Adventures of Captain Fabian (1951)
God Needs Men (1951)
Oh, Amelia (1951)
The Game of Love (1954)
Intimate Relations (1954)
The Red and the Black (1954)
Four Bags Full (1956)
The Winner's Circle (1957)
Love Is My Profession (1959)
The Story of the Count of Monte Cristo (1962)

COBERT, ROBERT
Ladybug, Ladybug (1963)
Night of Dark Shadows (1971)

COCKBURN, BRUCE
Goin' Down the Road (1970)

COHAN, TONY
Make a Face (1971)

COHEN, DANNY
The Hitchhikers (1972)

COHEN, LEONARD
McCabe and Mrs. Miller (1971)

COLEMAN, CY
Father Goose (1964)
The Troublemaker (1964)
The Art of Love (1965)

COLICCHIO, MICHAEL
The Flame and the Fire (1966)

COLLIER, RON
A Fan's Notes (1972)

COLLINS, ANTHONY
Sixty Glorious Years (1938)
Allegheny Uprising (1939)
Nurse Edith Cavell (1939)
Swiss Family Robinson (1940)
Tom Brown's Schooldays (1940)
Destroyer (1943)
Forever and a Day (1943)
The Fabulous Texan (1947)
Odette (1950)
Trent's Last Case (1953)
Adventures of Robinson Crusoe (1954)
Laughing Anne (1954)

COLOMBIER, MICHEL
A New World (1966)
The Forbin Project (1970)
A Cop (1972)

COLOMBO, ALBERTO
The Return of Peter Grimm (1935)
Annie Oakley (1936)
Chatterbox (1936)
The Farmer in the Dell (1936)
The Last Outlaw (1936)
Love on a Bet (1936)
M'Liss (1936)
Seven Keys to Baldpate (1936)
Two in Revolt (1936)
The Sickle or the Cross (1949)
The Black Hand (1950)
The Sundowners (1950)
All That I Have (1951)
Go for Broke (1951)
Apache War Smoke (1952)
Holiday for Sinners (1952)
Rogue's March (1952)
You for Me (1952)
The Big Leaguer (1953)
Code Two (1953)
Fast Company (1953)
A Slight Case of Larceny (1953)

COMFORD, ROBERT
All Neat in Black Stockings (1969)

COMPINSKY, ALEC
No Place to Land (1958)
Four Fast Guns (1959)
Plunderers of Painted Flats (1959)

COMPINSKY, MANUEL
Killers from Space (1954)
The Snow Creature (1954)
The Big Bluff (1955)

COMSTOCK, FRANK
The Last Time I Saw Archie (1961)

CONDE, ANTONIO DIAZ
The Pearl (1948)
The Torch (1950)
Plunder of the Sun (1953)
The White Orchid (1954)
Rosanna (1956)

CONNOR, TONY
Bronco Bullfrog (1970)

CONSTANTIN, JEAN
The 400 Blows (1959)
Love and the Frenchwoman (1961)

CONTE, MICHEL
The Doves (1972)

CONVERSE, FREDERICK SHEPHERD
Puritan Passions (1923)

COPLAND, AARON
The City (1939)
Of Mice and Men (1940)
Our Town (1940)
Fiesta (1942)
The North Star (1943)
The Cummington Story (1945)
Fiesta (1947)
The Heiress (1949)
The Red Pony (1949)
Something Wild (1961)

CORDELL, FRANK
The Captain's Table (1960)

Flight from Ashiya (1964)
Never Put It in Writing (1964)
Ring of Bright Water (1969)
Cromwell (1970)
Mosquito Squadron (1970)

CORNU, RICHARD
Back to the Wall (1959)
Masters of the Congo Jungle (1959)
The Secret of Magic Island (1965)

COSENTINO, MARITO
Let's Play in the World (1971)

COSLOW, SAM
Hands Across the Table (1935)
Turn Off the Moon (1937)

COSMA, EDGAR
Up from the Beach (1965)

COSMA, VLADIMIR
Absent Minded (1970)
Neither By Day Nor By Night (1972)

COSTA, DON
Rough Night in Jericho (1967)
The Impossible Years (1968)
Madigan (1968)

COTTS, FRANCOISE and ROGER
Justine de Sade (1972)

COULTER, FRED
Akran (1969)

COURAGE, ALEXANDER
Hot Rod Rumble (1957)
Sierra Stranger (1957)
Undersea Girl (1957)
Handle with Care (1958)
The Left-Handed Gun (1958)
Day of the Outlaw (1959)
Tokyo After Dark (1959)

COUSINEAU, FRANCOIS
Initiation (1970)
The Awakening (1971)
Seven Times a Day (1971)

COUSINEAU, JEAN
My Uncle Antoine (1971)

COWARD, NOEL
In Which We Serve (1942)
The Astonished Heart (1950)

CRAIG, EDWARD
Will It Happen Again? (1948)

CRAIG, GEORGE
Little Mother (1972)

CRAVEN, PAUL
The Only Thing You Know (1971)

CREWE, BOB
Barbarella (1968)

CRISTOU, JANNI
Oedipus the King (1968)

CROLLA, HENRI
Mamzelle Pigalle (1958)
Come Dance with Me! (1960)
Love and the Frenchwoman (1961)
Time Bomb (1961)
World without Sun (1964)

CROMBIE, TONY
The Spider's Web (1965)

CROSSMAN, STEFAN
Joe Hill (1971)

CURB, MIKE
Skaterdater (1965)
The Wild Angels (1966)
Devil's Angels (1967)
Teenage Rebellion (1967)
Killers Three (1968)
The Wild Racers (1968)
The Big Bounce (1969)
The Devil's 8 (1969)
Five the Hard Way (1969)

CURIEL, GONZALO
Massacre (1956)

CUTNER, SIDNEY
Holiday (1938)

Hold Back Tomorrow (1955)
Gunsmoke in Tucson (1958)

CUVA, CHARLEY
Putney Swope (1969)

CZITKOVIC, ZIVAN
The Scene of the Crash (1971)

D'ABO, MIKE
There's a Girl in My Soup (1970)

DAKSHNIMURTI
Sabaka (1955)

DALE, JIM
A Winter's Tale (1968)
B. S., I Love You (1971)

DALE, TED
Zero Hour! (1957)

DALLIN, JACQUES
The Ramparts We Watch (1940)

DAN, IKUMA
Samurai (1955)
Everest Symphony (1971)

DANIEL, ELIOT
Fun and Fancy Free (1947)
Yesterday and Today (1953)

DANIELS, HALL
Squad Car (1960)

DANKWORTH, JOHN
The Concrete Jungle (1962)
Hamilton, the Musical Elephant (1963)
Darling (1965)
Return from the Ashes (1965)
Sands of the Kalahari (1965)
The Idol (1966)
Modesty Blaise (1966)
Morgan! (1966)
Accident (1967)
Fathom (1967)
The Last Safari (1967)
The Magus (1968)
Salt and Pepper (1968)
The Last Grenade (1970)
Perfect Friday (1970)
10 Rillington Place (1971)

DANT, CHARLES
Submarine Base (1943)

DARBY, KEN
The Canadians (1961)

DARIN, BOBBY
The Lively Set (1964)
That Funny Feeling (1965)
Gunfight in Abilene (1967)

DAUGEAN, JACQUES
Morbidness (1972)

DAVIE, CEDRIC THORPE
The Brothers (1947)
Snowbound (1948)
Rob Roy, the Highland Rogue (1953)
The Warriors (1955)
The Green Man (1957)
Jacqueline (1957)
Oedipus Rex (1957)
Mad Little Island (1948)
The Bridal Path (1959)
Kidnapped (1960)
The Night Fighters (1960)

DAVIES, ROY
Percy (1971)

DAVIES, WILLIAM
Life in Danger (1964)

DAVIS, CARL
The Other World of Winston Churchill (1967)
The Bofors Gun (1968)
The Only Way (1970)

DAVIS, DAVID
Double-Strop (1968)

DAVIS, JEFF
L'Homme et L'Enfant (1957)

DAVIS, MILES
Elevator to the Gallows (1957)
Jack Johnson (1971)

DAVIS, PETER MAXWELL
The Devils (1971)

DE ANDRES, RAFAEL
The Revenge of Don Mendo (1961)

DE ANGELIS, GUIDO
The Cross-Eyed Saint (1971)

DE ANGELIS, MAURIZIO
The Cross-Eyed Saint (1971)

DE CHARBY, FRANCOIS
The Algerian War (1972)

DE FRANCESCO, LOUIS
The Wedding March (1928)
Berkeley Square (1933)
Cavalcade (1933)
David Harum (1934)
I Am Suzanne (1934)
Music in the Air (1934)
The Gay Deception (1935)
The Ramparts We Watch (1940)
United We Stand (1942)

DE GELMINI, WOLFGANG
Emperors, Citizens and Comrades (1971)
Olympia-Olympia (1972)
Pictures from a Strange Land (1972)

DE GROOF, CARL
The Last Bridge (1953)

DE GROOT, HUGO
The Last Blitzkrieg (1958)
Spy in the Sky (1958)

DE JESUS, LUCHI
Slaughter (1972)

DE LA CASINIERE, YVES
Rien Que Les Heures (1927)

DE LORY, AL
Norwood (1970)

DE LOS RIOS, WALDO
The Boarding School (1970)
Murders in the Rue Morgue (1971)

DE LUCA, PEPPINO
Dead of Summer (1970)
Dorian Gray (1970)
Sweet Kisses and Languid Caresses (1970)

DE MASI, FRANCESCO
Revenge of the Gladiators (1965)
Seven Slaves Against the World (1965)
Symphony for Two Spies (1966)
Payment in Blood (1968)
Young Attila (1971)
House of the Doves (1972)
The Weekend Murders (1972)

DE MELLIS
The Summertime Killer (1972)

DE MULE, FIRTH
Dynamite (1972)

DE PABLO, LUIS
The Challenges (1970)
Goya (1971)

DE ROSNAY, ALAIN
The Lovers (1959)

DE ROUBAIX, FRANCOIS
An Indefinite Tenderness (1969)
Jeff (1969)
The Stud (1970)
Daughters of Darkness (1971)
A Little, a Lot, Passionately (1971)
The Sky Is Blue (1971)
Chut (1972)

DE SAXE, RUDY
Bells of San Fernando (1947)
Beyond Our Own (1947)
Calamity Jane and Sam Bass (1949)
Mystery Range (1949)
The Texan Meets Calamity Jane (1950)

The Lawless Rider (1954)

DE SICA, MANUEL
The Garden of the Finzi-Continis (1970)
We'll Call Him Andreas (1972)

DE SICA, MAURICE
A Place for Lovers (1969)

DE VOL, FRANK
World for Ransom (1954)
The Big Knife (1955)
Kiss Me Deadly (1955)
Paris Follies of 1956 (1955)
Attack! (1956)
Pardners (1956)
Johnny Trouble (1957)
The Ride Back (1957)
Pillow Talk (1959)
Murder, Inc. (1960)
Lover Come Back (1961)
Boys' Night Out (1962)
Whatever Happened to Baby Jane? (1962)
For Love or Money (1963)
McClintock! (1963)
The Thrill of It All (1963)
Under the Yum-Yum Tree (1963)
The Wheeler Dealers (1963)
Good Neighbor Sam (1964)
Send Me No Flowers (1964)
Cat Ballou (1965)
The Flight of the Phoenix (1965)
Hush ... Hush, Sweet Charlotte (1965)
The Glass Bottom Boat (1966)
Texas Across the River (1966)
The Ballad of Josie (1967)
Caprice (1967)
The Dirty Dozen (1967)
Guess Who's Coming to Dinner? (1967)
The Happening (1967)
The Legend of Lylah Clare (1968)
What's So Bad About Feeling Good? (1968)
Krakatoa--East of Java (1969)
Ulzana's Raid (1972)

DE VORZON, BARRY
R. P. M. (1970)
Bless the Beasts and Children (1971)

DEBOUT, JEAN-JACQUES
Eglantine (1972)

DEDRICK, CHRIS
The Sidelong Glances of a Pigeon Kicker (Pigeons) (1970)
The Happiness Cage (1972)

DEFAVE, JEAN MICHEL
Fifi La Plume (1965)

DEFONJ, DUBRAVKO
Dear Irene (1970)

DEL PARANA, LUIS ALBERTO
Tropical Ecstasy (1970)

DELERUE, GEORGES
L'aine des Ferchaux (1956)
Hiroshima, Mon Amour (1960)
The Joker (1961)
Love and the Frenchwoman (1961)
The Passion of Slow Fire (1961)
Crime Does Not Pay (1962)
The End of Belle (1962)
Shoot the Piano Player (1962)
Rififi in Tokyo (1963)
Cartouche (1964)
Mata Hari (1964)
The Pumpkin Eater (1964)
The Soft Skin (1964)
Greed in the Sun (1965)
Rapture (1965)
Viva Maria (1965)
The Lair of Love (1966)
A Man for All Seasons (1966)
Nameless Star (1966)
Our Mother's House (1967)
Thursday We Shall Sing Like Sunday (1967)
The 25th Hour (1967)
Interlude (1968)
Nobody Runs Forever (1968)
Anne of the 1000 Days (1969)

A Walk with Love and Death (1969)
Women in Love (1969)
The Caprices of Marie (1970)
The Conformist (1970)
Happy He, Who Like Ulysses (1970)
Promise at Dawn (1970)
The Horsemen (1971)
Mira (1971)
Two English Girls (1971)
The Artless One (1972)
Dear Louise (1972)
Malpertius (1972)
Somewhere, Someone (1972)

DELPECH, MICHEL
Rampart of Desire (1972)

DELUGG, MILTON
Only One New York (1964)

DEMASE, JEAN-MICHEL
A Taste of Violence (1963)

DENNING, WADE
Rain for a Dusty Summer (1971)

DER GRAFF, GENERATOR VAN
Eyewitness (1970)

DEREVITZKY, ALEXANDER
The Nights of Lucretia Borgia (1960)

DESAI, VASANT
Monsoon (1953)
The Tiger and the Flame (1955)
The Blessing (1970)

DES LOURIERS, JEAN
Whispering City (1948)

DESORMIERE, ROGER
A Quois Revent Les Jeunes Filles (1924)
The Lower Depths (1936)

DESSEAU, PAUL
The Wife of Monte Cristo (1946)
The Pretender (1947)
Winter Wonderland (1947)
Devil's Cargo (1948)
Ruthless (1948)
The Vicious Circle (1948)

DEUTSCH, ADOLPH
The Great Garrick (1937)
Submarine D-1 (1937)
They Won't Forget (1937)
Tovarich (1937)
Broadway Musketeers (1938)
Four's a Crowd (1938)
Heart of the North (1938)
Swing Your Lady (1938)
Valley of the Giants (1938)
Angels Wash Their Faces (1939)
Espionage Agent (1939)
Indianapolis Speedway (1939)
East of the River (1940)
Flowing Gold (1940)
Saturday's Children (1940)
They Drive By Night (1940)
Torrid Zone (1940)
High Sierra (1941)
The Maltese Falcon (1941)
Manpower (1941)
Underground (1941)
Across the Pacific (1942)
All Through the Night (1942)
The Big Shot (1942)
George Washington Slept Here (1942)
Juke Girl (1942)
Larceny, Inc. (1942)
Lucky Jordan (1942)
You Can't Escape Forever (1942)
Action in the North Atlantic (1943)
Northern Pursuit (1943)
The Doughgirls (1944)
The Mask of Demitrios (1944)
Uncertain Glory (1944)
Danger Signal (1945)
Escape in the Desert (1945)
Nobody Lives Forever (1946)
Shadow of a Woman (1946)
Three Strangers (1946)
Blaze of Noon (1947)
Ramrod (1947)
Julia Misbehaves (1948)

Intruder in the Dust (1949)
Little Women (1949)
The Stratton Story (1949)
Take Me out to the Ball Game (1949)
The Big Hangover (1950)
Father of the Bride (1950)
Mrs. O'Malley and Mr. Malone (1950)
Stars in My Crown (1950)
The Yellow Cab Man (1950)
Soldiers Three (1951)
The Bandwagon (1953)
Torch Song (1953)
The Long, Long Trailer (1954)
Interrupted Melody (1955)
The Rack (1956)
Tea and Sympathy (1956)
Funny Face (1957)
Les Girl (1957)
The Matchmaker (1958)
Some Like It Hot (1959)
The Apartment (1960)
Go Naked into the World (1961)

DEXTER, VON
The House on Haunted Hill (1958)
The Tingler (1959)
Thirteen Ghosts (1960)
Mr. Sardonicus (1961)

DI MAGGIO, ROSS
The Tougher They Come (1950)
Flame of Stamboul (1951)
Snake River Desperadoes (1951)
A Yank in Korea (1951)
Indian Uprising (1952)
A Yank in Indo-China (1952)
Ambush at Tomahawk Gap (1953)
China Venture (1953)
Last of the Pony Riders (1953)
Man in the Dark (1953)
The Nebraskan (1953)
Sky Commando (1953)
The Winning of the West (1953)
Charge of the Lancers (1954)
Drive a Crooked Road (1954)
Chicago Syndicate (1955)
The Gun That Won the West (1955)
Calypso Heat Wave (1957)
The Man Who Turned to Stone (1957)
The Night the World Exploded (1957)
Utah Blaine (1957)
The Wild Westerners (1962)

DIAMOND, DAVID
A Place to Live (1941)
Dreams That Money Can Buy (1948)
Strange Victory (1948)
Anna Lucasta (1949)
Strange Victory (1964)

DIAZ, HORACE
The New Life Style (1970)

DILDINGER, KLAUS
How Did a Nice Girl Like You Get into This Business? (1970)
The Sudden Wealth of the Poor People of Kombach (1971)

DIVINA, VACLAV
Strange Fascination (1952)
Bait (1954)

DODDS, MALCOLM
The Lawyer (1969)

DOGA, E.
Lautare (1972)

DOLAN, ROBERT EMMETT
Are Husbands Necessary? (1942)
The Major and the Minor (1942)
Once Upon a Honeymoon (1942)
Star Spangled Rhythm (1942)
Going My Way (1944)
I Love a Soldier (1944)
Standing Room Only (1944)
The Bells of St. Mary's (1945)
Murder, He Says (1945)
Salty O'Rourke (1945)
The Stork Club (1945)
Monsieur Beaucaire (1946)
Cross My Heart (1947)

Dear Ruth (1947)
My Favorite Brunette (1947)
The Perils of Pauline (1947)
The Road to Rio (1947)
Welcome Stranger (1947)
Good Sam (1948)
Mr. Peabody and the Mermaid (1948)
My Own True Love (1948)
Saigon (1948)
The Great Gatsby (1949)
Sorrowful Jones (1949)
Let's Dance (1950)
Aaron Slick from Punkin Creek (1952)
My Son John (1952)
The Three Faces of Eve (1957)
The Man Who Understood Women (1959)

DOLLARHIDE, ROGER
The Velvet Vampire (1971)

DOMINGO, EDDIE
Dingaka (1965)

DOMINO, DANNY
The New Life Style (1970)

DOMPIERRE, FRANCOIS
Saint Denis, in These Times (1970)

DONAT, MISCHA
Charlie Bubbles (1968)

DONNER, OTTO
Redhead (1970)

DONOVAN
If It's Tuesday, This Must be Belgium (1969)
The Pied Piper (1972)

DORIAN, ANDREW
The Main Attraction (1963)

DOUGLAS, JOHNNY
The Traitors (1963)
Code 7 Victim 5 (1964)
Crack in the World (1965)
Gunfighters of Casa Grande (1965)
Dateline Diamonds (1966)
Kid Rodello (1966)
The Funniest Man in the World (1967)
Psycho-Circus (1967)
Run Like a Thief (1968)
The Railway Children (1970)
Dulcima (1971)

DRAGON, CARMEN
Mr. Winkle Goes to War (1944)
The Strange Woman (1946)
Young Widow (1946)
Dishonored Lady (1947)
Out of the Blue (1947)
The Time of Your Life (1948)
Kiss Tomorrow Goodbye (1950)
The Law and the Lady (1951)
Night into Morning (1951)
The People Against O'Hara (1951)
When in Rome (1952)
At Gunpoint (1955)
Invasion of the Body Snatchers (1956)

DRASNIN, ROBERT
Ride in the Whirlwind (1966)
The Kremlin Letter (1970)

DREJAC, J.
Under the Roofs of Paris (1930)
Liberte I (1963)

DRESS, MICHAEL
Rotten to the Core (1964)
A Touch of Love (1969)
Quackser Fortune has a Cousin in the Bronx (1970)

DREWS, JURGEN
Blue Movie (1971)

DREYER, DAVE
Sing and Like It (1934)

DRIVSEK, JOZE
In the Gorge (1971)

DROUET, J. P.
An Only Son (1969)

DRUICK, DON
Another Smith for Paradise (1972)

DUBIN, JOSEPH
Cheyenne Wildcat (1944)
Marshal of Reno (1944)
Silver City Kid (1944)
Tucson Raiders (1944)
Bells of Rosarita (1945)
Girls of the Big House (1945)
Mexicana (1945)
Home in Oklahoma (1946)
Rendezvous with Annie (1946)
The Ghost Goes Wild (1947)
Trail to San Antone (1947)

DUCLOS, PIERRE
Lafayette (1963)

DUHAMEL, ANTOINE
M as in Mathieu (1971)

DUNAYEVSKY, ISAAC
Volga-Volga (1938)
Tanya (1941)
Spring (1947)

DUNCAN, TREVOR
Finger of Guilt (1956)
Joe Macbeth (1956)
The Long Haul (1957)
Scotland Yard Dragnet (1958)

DUNDAS, DAVID
Private Road (1971)

DUNING, GEORGE
Around the World (1943)
Eadie Was a Lady (1945)
The Corpse Came C.O.D. (1947)
The Guilt of Janet Ames (1947)
Her Husband's Affairs (1947)
I Love Trouble (1947)
Johnny O'Clock (1947)
The Dark Past (1948)
Gallant Blade (1948)
The Man from Colorado (1948)
The Return of October (1948)
To the Ends of the Earth (1948)
The Untamed Breed (1948)
And Baby Makes Three (1949)
The Doolins of Oklahoma (1949)
For Those Who Dare (1949)
Johnny Allegro (1949)
Jolson Sings Again (1949)
Shockproof (1949)
Undercover Man (1949)
Cargo to Capetown (1950)
Convicted (1950)
The Flying Missile (1950)
Harriet Craig (1950)
No Sad Songs for Me (1950)
The Barefoot Mailman (1951)
The Family Secret (1951)
Lorna Doone (1951)
The Mob (1951)
Two of a Kind (1951)
Affair in Trinidad (1952)
Assignment Paris (1952)
Captain Pirate (1952)
Last of the Comanches (1952)
Cruisin' Down the River (1953)
From Here to Eternity (1953)
Salome (1953)
The Eddy Duchin Story (1956)
Full of Life (1956)
Nightfall (1956)
Storm Center (1956)
You Can't Run Away from It (1956)
The Brothers Rico (1957)
Jeanne Eagels (1957)
Operation Mad Ball (1957)
Shadow on the Window (1957)
3:10 to Yuma (1957)
Bell, Book and Candle (1958)
Cowboy (1958)
Gunman's Walk (1958)
Houseboat (1958)
It Happened to Jane (1959)
The Last Angry Man (1959)
1001 Arabian Nights (1959)
The Wreck of the Mary Deare (1959)
All the Young Men (1960)
Let No Man Write My Epitaph (1960)

Man on a String (1960)
Strangers When We Meet (1960)
The Three Worlds of Gulliver (1960)
The Wackiest Ship in the Army (1960)
The World of Suzie Wong (1960)
Cry for Happy (1961)
The Devil at Four O'Clock (1961)
Gidget Goes Hawaiian (1961)
Sail a Crooked Ship (1961)
Two Rode Together (1961)
The Notorious Landlady (1962)
That Touch of Mink (1962)
Thirteen West Street (1962)
Who's Got the Action? (1962)
Critic's Choice (1963)
Island of Love (1963)
Toys in the Attic (1963)
Who's Been Sleeping in My Bed? (1963)
Ensign Pulver (1964)
Brainstorm (1965)
Dear Brigitte (1965)
My Blood Runs Cold (1965)
Any Wednesday (1966)
Then Came Bronson (1970)

DUNLAP, PAUL
The Baron of Arizona (1950)
Hi-Jacked (1950)
The Steel Helmet (1950)
Cry Danger (1951)
Journey into Light (1951)
Little Big Horn (1951)
The Lost Continent (1951)
Breakdown (1952)
Park Row (1952)
Combat Squad (1953)
Fort Vengeance (1953)
Jack Slade (1953)
The Royal African Rifles (1953)
Black Tuesday (1954)
Dragonfly Squadron (1954)
Duffy of San Quentin (1954)
Fangs of the Wild (1954)
Loophole (1954)
Return from the Sea (1954)
Shield for Murder (1954)
Target Earth (1954)
Big House, U.S.A. (1955)
Desert Sands (1955)
Finger Man (1955)
Fort Yuma (1955)
Ghost Town (1955)
The Return of Jack Slade (1955)
Robber's Roost (1955)
Shack Out on 101 (1955)
Stranger on Horseback (1955)
The Brass Legend (1956)
The Broken Star (1956)
The Come On (1956)
Crime Against Joe (1956)
The Cruel Tower (1956)
Dance with Me Henry (1956)
Emergency Hospital (1956)
Magnificent Roughnecks (1956)
Stagecoach to Fury (1956)
Strange Intruder (1956)
Three Bad Sisters (1956)
Walk the Dark Street (1956)
Apache Warrior (1957)
Blood of Dracula (1957)
Crime of Passion (1957)
Dragoon Wells Massacre (1957)
God Is My Partner (1957)
I Was a Teenage Frankenstein (1957)
I Was a Teenage Werewolf (1957)
Lure of the Swamp (1957)
Oregon Passage (1957)
Portland Expose (1957)
The Quiet Gun (1957)
Rockabilly Baby (1957)
Under Fire (1957)
Young and Dangerous (1957)
Frankenstein 1970 (1958)
Frontier Gun (1958)
Gang War (1958)
Gun Fever (1958)
Toughest Gun in Tombstone (1958)
Wolf Larsen (1958)
The Four Skulls of Jonathan Drake (1959)
Here Come the Jets (1959)
Lone Texan (1959)
The Oregon Trail (1959)
The Rebel Set (1959)
The Rookie (1959)
Gunfighters of Abilene (1960)
The Purple Gang (1960)

Twelve Hours to Kill (1960)
Walk Like a Dragon (1960)
Seven Women from Hell (1961)
The Three Stooges in Orbit (1962)
The Three Stooges Meet Hercules (1962)
Black Zoo (1963)
Shock Corridor (1963)
The Three Stooges Go around the World in a Daze (1963)
The Naked Kiss (1964)
Stage to Thunder Rock (1964)
Voice of the Hurricane (1964)
The Outlaws Is Coming! (1965)
Young Fury (1965)
Destination Inner Space (1966)
Castle of Evil (1967)
The Destructors (1968)
The Money Jungle (1968)
Panic in the City (1968)

DUNN, REX
Panhandle (1948)

DUNSTEDTER, EDDIE
Donovan's Brain (1953)

DUPRAT, ROGERIO
Brazil Year 2000 (1970)
The Palace of Angels (1970)

DUPRE, M.
Song of the Land (1953)

DURAND, PAUL
Forbidden Fruit (1952)
Foreign Intrigue (1956)
What Price Murder (1958)
Paris Hotel (1959)
The Cow and I (1961)

DURAS, MARGUERITE
Nathalie Granger (1972)

DURHAM, BY
Boy, Did I Get a Wrong Number (1966)

DURMAN, S. D.
The Guide (1965)

DUTOUR, PIERRE
The Lumicre Years (1971)

DUTRELL, EDWARD
Invisible Avenger (1958)

DUVAL, JUAN
Daughter of the West (1949)

DWIER, IRV
All Men Are Apes (1965)

DYLAN, BOB
Little Fauss and Big Halsy (1970)

EASDALE, BRIAN
Men in Danger (1939)
Spring Offensive (1940)
Black Narcissus (1947)
The Red Shoes (1948)
Outcast of the Islands (1952)
The Small Back Room (1952)
The Wild Heart (1952)
The Green Scarf (1955)
Pursuit of the Graf Spee (1957)

EATON, JOHN RANDOLPH
Robby (1968)

EATON, MICHAEL
The Wife Swappers (1970)

EATON, WILLIAM
The Angel Levine (1970)

EBBINGHOUSE, BERNARD
Prudence and the Pill (1968)
Mumsy, Nanny, Sonny and Girly (1970)

EDDY, DUANE
Ring of Fire (1961)

EDELMAN, RANDY
Outside In (1972)

EDERER, PEPE
Hurrah! Our Parent's Aren't There (1970)

EDOUARDE, CARL
Kismet (1920)

The Private Life of Helen of Troy (1927)

EDWARDS, LEO
Checkers (1919)

EFFIMOV, YURI
Cinerama's Russian Adventure (1966)

EGNOS, BERTHA
Dingaka (1965)

EHLERT, JOHN
Native Son (1951)
The Marijuana Story (1952)

EICHHORN, BERNHARD
The Film Without a Name (1948)
The Original Sin (1948)
The Captain from Kopenick (1956)
Monpti (1959)
The Rest Is Silence (1959)
The Good Soldier Schweik (1963)
The Fire Tongue Bowl (1970)

EISBRENNER, WERNER
The Raid (Razzia) (1947)
Wonderful Times (1951)
The Berliner (1952)
A Love Story (1958)
Reaching for the Stars (1958)
King in Shadow (1959)
Buddenbrooks (Part I) (1961)
Buddenbrooks (Part II) (1961)
Court Martial (1962)

EISLER, HANNS
Opus 3 (1928)
No Man's Land (1930
Song of Life (1930)
War Is Hell (1930)
Kuhle Wampe (1931)
A Song About Heroes (1932)
New Earth (1934)
The 400 Million (1938)
White Flood (1940)
The Forgotten Village (1941)
Hangmen Also Die (1942)
None But the Lonely Heart (1944)
Jealousy (1945)
The Spanish Main (1945)
Deadline at Dawn (1946)
A Scandal in Paris (1946)
The Woman on the Beach (1947)
Bel Ami (1955)
Night and Fog (1955)
The Crucible (1957)

ELECTRIC BANANA, THE
Bob & Daryl & Ted & Alex

ELFERS, CONRAD
Funeral in Berlin (1966)

ELINOR, CARL
Hearts of the World (1918)
The Devil Dancer (1927)
Bridge of San Luis Rey (1929)

ELLART, ANDRE
The End of Pyrenees (1970)

ELLINGTON, DUKE
Jonas (1957)
Anatomy of a Murder (1959)
Paris Blues (1961)
Assault on a Queen (1966)
Change of Mind (1969)

ELLIOTT, CLINTON
Secrets of the Reef (1956)

ELLIOTT, DEAN
College Confidential (1960)
Sex Kittens Go to College (1960)
The Phantom Tollbooth (1970)

ELLIOTT, JACK
The Comic (1969)
Where's Poppa? (1970)
Support Your Local Gunfighter (1971)
T. R. Baskin (1971)
Get to Know Your Rabbit (1972)

ELLIOTT, PETER J.
1,000 Convicts and a Woman (1971)

ELLIS, DON
Moon Zero Two (1969)
The French Connection (1971)
Kansas City Bomber (1972)

ELLIS, VIVIAN
Piccadilly Incident (1946)

ELMS, ALBERT
Manfish (1956)
Bluebeard's Ten Honeymoons (1960)
The Great Armored Car Swindle (1964)

ELVITOGALOR, S.
Arid Land (1972)

EL-ZAHREY, FOUAD
The Dawn of Islam (1971)

EMER, MICHAEL
Act of Love (1953)

EMRYD, BENGT
A Baltic Tragedy (1970)
Unto a Good Land (1972)

ENGEL, LEHMAN
The Fleet That Came to Stay (1945)
Roogie's Rump (1954)

ENGLUND, EINAR
The White Reindeer (1956)

ENRIQUEZ, LUIS
A Rose for Everyone (1967)
The Black Sheep (1968)
Lonely Hearts (1970)

ERDODY, LEO
Baby Face Morgan (1942)
City of Silent Men (1942)
Prisoner of Japan (1942)
Queen of Broadway (1942)
Tomorrow We Live (1942)
Corregidor (1943)
Girls in Chains (1943)
Isle of Forgotten Sins (1943)
My Son, the Hero (1943)
Wild Horse Rustlers (1943)
Bluebeard (1944)
Apology for Murder (1945)
Detour (1945)
Strange Illusion (1945)
Blonde for a Day (1946)
The Flying Serpent (1946)
Gas House Kids (1946)
I Ring Doorbells (1946)
Larceny in Her Heart (1946)
Murder Is My Business (1946)
The Return of Rin Tin Tin (1947)
Lady at Midnight (1948)
Miraculous Journey (1948)
Money Madness (1948)

ERKIN, ALF
Smugglers (1972)

ESPEITIA, JOSE
Diabolical Shudder (1971)

ESPERON, MANUEL
The Living Idol (1957)

ESPOSITO, TONY
The White Rat (1972)

EVANS, GIL
Days in My Father's House (1968)

EWING, LAN
The Only Thing You Know (1971)

FABRICIUS-BJERRE, BENT
A Story of Silver (1955)
The Bicyclist (1958)
Relax, Freddie (1966)
I Belong to Me (1967)
In the Green of the Woods (1968)
The Red Horses (1968)
I'll Take Happiness (1969)
Jazz All Around (1969)
The Olsen Gang in a Fix (1969)
Think of a Number (1969)
The Key to Paradise (1970)

Revolution, My A-- (1970)
The Olsen Gang in Jutland (1971)
One of Those Things (1971)
With Love and Kisses (1971)
Oh, to Be on the Bandwagon (1972)
The Olsen Gang's Big Score (1972)

FAGAS, JIMMIE
Once You Kiss a Stranger (1969)

FAHEY, BRIAN
Curse of the Voodoo (1965)
Man in the Dark (1965)
Where the Spies Are (1965)
The Plank (1967)
Rhubarb (1970)

FAIRCHILD, EDGAR
The Crimson Canary (1945)
House of Dracula (1945)
I'll Remember April (1945)
Little Giant (1946)
If You Knew Suzie (1948)

FAITH, PERCY
Tammy Tell Me True (1961)
I'd Rather Be Rich (1964)
The Third Day (1965)
The Oscar (1966)

FAME, GEORGIE
Entertaining Mr. Sloane (1970)

FANEN, PIERRE
The Swinger (1972)

FANIDI, THEO
The Naked Brigade (1965)

FARIS, ALEXANDER
The Quare Fellow (1962)

FARNON, DENNIS
Arrivederci, Baby (1966)

FARNON, ROBERT
Just William's Luck (1948)
Captain Horatio Hornblower (1951)
Gentlemen Marry Brunettes (1955)
Let's Make Up (1955)
The Little Hut (1957)
The Sheriff of Fractured Jaw (1958)
Expresso Bongo (1960)
The Road to Hong Kong (1962)
The Truth About Spring (1965)

FEAST, MICHAEL
Private Road (1971)

FELTON, BERNIE
Devils of Darkness (1965)

FENBY, ERIC
Jamaica Inn (1939)

FENTON, GEORGE
Private Road (1971)

FERGUSON, ALLYN
Support Your Local Gunfighter (1971)
Get to Know Your Rabbit (1972)

FERHAT, MORMOZ
The Cow (1971)

FERRARA, FRANCO
Mambo (1955)
The Pagans (1958)
Square of Violence (1963)

FERRARI, OTTO
Hidden Homicide (1959)

FERRARO, RALPH
The King's Pirate (1967)

FERRIO, GIANNI
Massacre in Grand Canyon (1965)
Death Took Place Last Night (1970)
The Hostess also Likes to Blow the Horn (1970)
The Scavengers (1970)
The Dirty Outlaws (1971)
A Man Called Sledge (1971)

FERRIS, PAUL
The Sorcerers (1967)
The Conqueror Worm (1968)

FERSTL, ERICH
Love Is Only a Word (1971)

FEUER, CY
Come On, Rangers (1938)
I Stand Accused (1938)
The Night Hawk (1938)
Shine On, Harvest Moon (1938)
The Arizona Kid (1939)
Calling All Marines (1939)
The Covered Trailer (1939)
Days of Jesse James (1939)
Federal Man Hunt (1939)
Fighting Thoroughbreds (1939)
Flight at Midnight (1939)
Forged Passport (1939)
Frontier Pony Express (1939)
Sabotage (1939)
Women in War (1940)
The Lady from Louisiana (1941)
Rookies on Parade (1941)
The Affairs of Jimmy Valentine (1942)
Arizona Roundup (1942)
Code of the Outlaw (1942)
The Cyclone Kid (1942)
The Girl from Alaska (1942)
The Old Homestead (1942)
Pardon My Stripes (1942)
The Phantom Plainsman (1942)
Raiders of the Range (1942)
Remember Pearl Harbor (1942)
Romance on the Range (1942)
Shepherd of the Ozarks (1942)
Sleepytime Gal (1942)
The Sombrero Kid (1942)
Sons of the Pioneers (1942)
South of Santa Fe (1942)
Stagecoach Express (1942)
Sunset on the Desert (1942)
A Tragedy at Midnight (1942)
Westward, Ho! (1942)
Yokel Boy (1942)
Youth on Parade (1942)
The Yukon Patrol (1942)
Covered Wagon Days (1943)
West of the Cimarron (1943)

FIDDY, JOHN
The Green Wall (1970)
The Wife Swappers (1970)

FIEHN, ERIK
A Stranger Knocks (1963)

FIELDING, JERRY
Advise and Consent (1962)
The Nun and the Sergeant (1962)
For Those Who Think Young (1964)
McHale's Navy (1964)
McHale's Navy Joins the Air Force (1965)
The Crazy World of Laurel and Hardy (1967)
The Wild Bunch (1969)
Suppose They Gave a War and Nobody Came (1970)
Johnny Got His Gun (1971)
Lawman (1971)
The Nightcomers (1971)
Straw Dogs (1971)
Chato's Land (1972)
Journey Through Rosebud (1972)
The Mechanic (1972)

FILIPPENKO, A.
A Lesson in Life (Conflict) (1955)

FINKELSTEIN, STAN
Left-Handed (1972)

FINSTON, NAT
Abilene Town (1946)
The Big Wheel (1949)
The Second Woman (1951)

FIRESTONE, ELIZABETH
Once More, My Darling (1949)
That Man from Tangier (1953)

THE FIRST EDITION
Fools (1970)

FISER, LUBOS
Nudity (1970)
Lucie and the Miracles (1971)
Gas Lamps (1972)

FISHER, FRED
The Blue Bonnet (1919)
Evangeline (1919)
Eyes of the Soul (1919)

FISHER, WILLIAM S.
Born to Win (1971)

FLAMENT, EDOUARD
La Maternelle (1932)

FLATOW, LEON
The Garden of Allah (1917)

FLEMING, ROBERT
A Matter of Fact (1970)

FOLIART, DAN
The Only Way Home (1972)

FORBES, LOUIS
Let Them Live (1937)
Oh, Doctor (1937)
Adventures of Tom Sawyer (1938)
Intermezzo (1939)
Pot O' Gold (1941)
The Story of G. I. Joe (1945)
Intrigue (1947)
Pitfall (1948)
The Crooked Way (1949)
The Man Who Cheated Himself (1950)
Second Chance (1950)
Home Town Story (1951)
A Wonderful Life (1951)
This Is Cinerama (1952)
Appointment in Honduras (1953)
Cattle Queen of Montana (1954)
Passion (1954)
Silver Lode (1954)
Escape to Burma (1955)
Pearl of the South Pacific (1955)
Tennessee's Partner (1955)
Slightly Scarlet (1956)
The River's Edge (1957)
From the Earth to the Moon (1958)
Hong Kong Affair (1958)
The Bat (1959)
The Most Dangerous Man Alive (1961)

FORBSTEIN, LEO F.
Earthworm Tractors (1936)

FOX, CHARLES
Barbarella (1968)
Goodbye Columbus (1969)
Pufnstuf (1970)
Making It (1971)
Star Spangled Girl (1971)
A Separate Peace (1972)

FOX, JAMES
The Arp Statue (1971)

FOX, JOHN
The Trunk (1961)

FOX, SYDNEY
The Fabulous World of Jules Verne (1961)

FRADKIN, M.
Farewell Doves (1960)

FRANCAIX, JEAN
Napoleon (1954)
Royal Affair in Versailles (1954)
Lovers and Thieves (1957)

FRANCI, CARLO
Secret Seven (1966)

FRANCISCO, MANUEL
Spring Affair (1960)

FRANKEL, BENJAMIN
The Seventh Veil (1945)
Dulcimer Street (1948)
The Girl in the Painting (1948)
Mine Own Executioner (1948)
Sleeping Car to Trieste (1948)
The Amazing Mr. Beecham (1949)
The Gay Lady (1949)
London Belongs to Me (1949)
Salt to the Devil (1949)
So Long at the Fair (1950)
The Clouded Yellow (1951)
Hotel Sahara (1951)
The Long Dark Hall (1951)

The Importance of Being Earnest (1952)
Island Rescue (1952)
The Man in the White Suit (1952)
The Final Test (1953)
Project M-7 (1953)
Always a Bride (1954)
Fire over Africa (1954)
Chance Meeting (1955)
The End of the Affair (1955)
Footsteps in the Fog (1955)
The Man Who Loved Redheads (1955)
The Prisoner (1955)
The Iron Petticoat (1956)
A Kid for Two Farthings (Lucky Kid) (1956)
Simon and Laura (1956)
Storm over the Nile (1956)
Tears for Simon (1957)
Orders to Kill (1958)
Happy Is the Bride (1959)
Libel (1959)
Surprise Package (1960)
The Curse of the Werewolf (1961)
Season of Passion (1961)
Guns of Darkness (1962)
The Old Dark House (1963)
The Night of the Iguana (1964)
The Battle of the Bulge (1965)

FRANZ, SIEGFRIED
Deadly Decision (1958)
St. Pauli Report (1972)
Schoolgirls Report III (1972)

FREEDMAN, HARRY
Act of the Heart (1970)

FREEMAN, ERNIE
The Cool Ones (1967)
The Double Man (1967)
Duffy (1968)
The Pink Jungle (1968)
Dinah East (1970)

FREEMAN, JOEL
Cry of the Hunted (1953)

FREEMAN, NED
Ride the Man Down (1952)

FRIED, GERALD
Killer's Kiss (1955)
The Killing (1956)
Paths of Glory (1957)
Trooper Hook (1957)
The Vampire (1957)
The Cry Baby Killer (1958)
I Bury the Living (1958)
I, Monster (1958)
The Last Missile (1958)
The Return of Dracula (1958)
Terror in a Texas Town (1958)
Cast a Long Shadow (1959)
Timbuktu (1959)
A Cold Wind in August (1961)
The Second Time Around (1961)
Twenty Plus Two (1961)
The Cabinet of Caligari (1962)
The Great Rights (1963)
One Potato, Two Potato (1964)
Deathwatch (1966)
One Spy Too Many (1966)
The Killing of Sister George (1968)
Whatever Happened to Aunt Alice? (1969)
Too Late the Hero (1970)
The Grissom Gang (1971)

FRIEDHOFER, HUGO
Lady of the Pavements (1929)
The Big Trail (1930)
A Devil with Women (1930)
The Golden Calf (1930)
Happy Days (1930)
Just Imagine (1930)
Men on Call (1930)
The Princess and the Plumber (1930)
Always Goodbye (1931)
Daddy Long Legs (1931)
Heartbreak (1931)
The Man Who Came Back (1931)
Skyline (1931)
The Spider (1931)
Transatlantic (1931)
The Yellow Ticket (1931)
Amateur Daddy (1932)
Careless Lady (1932)
The Devil's Lottery (1932)
The First Year (1932)

Mystery Ranch (1932)
The Painted Woman (1932)
Passport to Hell (1932)
Rebecca of Sunnybrook Farm (1932)
Second-Hand Wife (1932)
Sherlock Holmes (1932)
The Trial of Vivienne Ware (1932)
The Woman in Room 13 (1932)
As Husbands Go (1933)
Bondage (1933)
Broadway Bad (1933)
Dangerously Yours (1933)
The Face in the Sky (1933)
The Good Companions (1933)
It's Great to Be Alive (1933)
My Lips Betray (1933)
Zoo in Budapest (1933)
Change of Heart (1934)
The Coming Out Party (1934)
Now I'll Tell All (1934)
Servant's Entrance (1934)
The World Moves On (1934)
Curly Top (1935)
Dante's Inferno (1935)
Here's to Romance (1935)
The Last of the Pagans (1935)
Orchids to You (1935)
Way Down East (1935)
The Prisoner of Shark Island (1936)
Sins of Man (1936)
Trail of the Lonesome Pine (1936)
White Fang (1936)
Valley of the Giants (1938)
Made for Each Other (1939)
The Mark of Zorro (1940)
China Girl (1942)
Prelude to War (1942)
Chetniks! (1943)
Lifeboat (1943)
Paris After Dark (1943)
They Came to Blow Up America (1943)
Home in Indiana (1944)
The Lodger (1944)
Roger Touhy--Gangster (1944)
A Wing and a Prayer (1944)
Brewster's Millions (1945)
The Corn Is Green (1945)
Getting Gertie's Garter (1945)
The Bandit of Sherwood Forest (1946)
The Best Years of Our Lives (1946)
Gilda (1946)
So Dark the Night (1946)
Body and Soul (1947)
The Swordsman (1947)
Wild Harvest (1947)
Adventures of Casanova (1948)
The Bishop's Wife (1948)
Black Bart (1948)
Enchantment (1948)
Joan of Arc (1948)
Sealed Verdict (1948)
Bride of Vengeance (1949)
Broken Arrow (1950)
Captain Carey, USA (1950)
Edge of Doom (1950)
No Man of Her Own (1950)
The Sound of Fury (1950)
Three Came Home (1950)
Two Flags West (1950)
The Big Carnival (1951)
Queen for a Day (1951)
Above and Beyond (1952)
Face to Face (1952)
Hondo (1953)
Plunder of the Sun (1953)
Thunder in the East (1953)
Vera Cruz (1954)
The Rains of Ranchipur (1955)
Seven Cities of Gold (1955)
Soldier of Fortune (1955)
Between Heaven and Hell (1956)
The Harder They Fall (1956)
The Revolt of Mamie Stover (1956)
An Affair to Remember (1957)
Boy on a Dolphin (1957)
Oh, Men! Oh, Women! (1957)
The Sun Also Rises (1957)
The Barbarian and the Geisha (1958)
The Bravados (1958)
In Love and War (1958)
The Young Lions (1958)
The Blue Angel (1959)
Never So Few (1959)
This Earth Is Mine (1959)
Woman Obsessed (1959)
Homicidal (1961)
One-Eyed Jacks (1961)

Geronimo (1962)
The Secret Invasion (1964)
Von Richthoven and Brown (1971)

FRIEDMAN, IRVING
Philo Vance's Gamble (1947)
Canon City (1948)
He Walked By Night (1948)
Hollow Triumph (The Scar) (1948)
The Prowler (1951)
For Men Only (The Tall Lie) (1952)

FRIEDMAN, RUTHANN
The Peace Killers (1971)

FRIML, RUDOLPH
Northwest Outpost (1947)

FRONTIERA, MARY JO
Sticks and Stones (1970)

FRONTIERE, DOMINIC
The Marriage-Go-Round (1960)
One Foot in Hell (1960)
Seven Thieves (1960)
The Right Approach (1961)
Hero's Island (1962)
A Global Affair (1964)
Billie (1965)
Incubus (1966)
Hang 'Em High (1968)
Number One (1969)
Popi (1969)
Barquero (1970)
Chisum (1970)
On Any Sunday (1971)
Cancel My Reservation (1972)
Hammersmith Is Out (1972)

FUCHS, HI
Project X (1949)

FUKUBE, AKIRA
Godzilla, King of the Monsters (1956)

FULLER, GILBERT
300-Year Weekend (1971)

FUNK, HEINZ
The Great British Train Robbery (1967)

FUSCO, GIOVANNI
Nettezza Urbana (1948)
Mystery of the Black Jungle (1955)
Il Grido (1957)
The Cossacks (1960)
Hiroshima, Mon Amour (1960)
L'Avventura (1961)
The Pharoah's Woman (1961)
Eclipse (1962)
Red Desert (1965)
Time of Indifference (1965)
The Subversives (1967)
The Day of the Owl (1968)
The Sex of the Angels (1968)
Love and Anger (1969)
A Nun at the Crossroads (1970)

FUYUKI, TORU
This Transient Life (1970)

GAILLARD, MARIUS-FRANCOIS
Portrait of Innocence (1948)
Les Rendezvous du Diable (1959)

GAINSBOURG, SERGE
The Defector (1966)
The Other One (1967)
Piggies (1970)
Too Pretty to Be Honest (1972)

GALE, ERIC
Events (1970)

GALE, JOHN
Dr. Phibes Rises Again (1972)

GALLAGHER, EAMMON O.
The Rising of the Moon (1957)

GALVAO, JOHNNY
Far from the Trees (1972)

GAMLEY, DOUGLAS
The Admirable Crichton (1957)
Another Time, Another Place (1958)

Tom Thumb (1958)
Gideon of Scotland Yard (1959)
Tarzan's Greatest Adventure (1959)
Web of Evidence (1959)
The Horror of It All (1964)
The Return of Mr. Moto (1965)
Spring and Port Wine (1970)

GARCIA, RUSSELL
Radar Secret Service (1950)
The Time Machine (1960)
Atlantis, The Lost Continent (1961)
The Pad (and How to Use It) (1966)
Three Guns for Texas (1968)

GARNEAU, MICHAEL
Is It Necessary to Be Among the Peoples of the World to Know Them? (1971)

GARRIGUENE, RENE
16 Fathoms Deep (1948)

GARSON, MORT
Beware the Blob (1972)

GARVARENTZ, GEORGES
Tales of Paris (1962)
Sweet Ecstasy (1963)
Panic Button (1964)
Le Rat D'Amerique (1964)
How Not to Rob a Department Store (1965)
Taxi for Tobruk (1965)
Father's Trip (1966)
The Sultans (1966)
The Corrupt Ones (1967)
The Sea Pirate (1967)
The Invited One (1969)
They Came to Rob Las Vegas (1969)
Sapho (1970)
Time of the Wolves (1970)
The Lion's Share (1971)
A Lovely Monster (1971)
The Intruders (1972)

GASCOIGNE, BRIAN
Under Milk Wood (1971)

GASLINI, GIORGIO
Bali (1971)
The Pacifist (1971)

GASPAR, TIBERIO
Memories of a Gigolo (1970)

GATES, DAVID
Journey to Shiloh (1968)

GAY, B.
A Fool There Was (1914)

GAYE, MARVIN
Trouble Man (1972)

GEIGERSTAM, CLAES AF
69 (1970)

GELLER, HAROLD
Fury at Smuggler's Bay (1963)

GELMAN, HAROLD
Sweet Bird of Youth (1962)

GELMATTI, VITTORIO
Under the Sign of the Scorpion (1969)

GEMMELL, KEITH
Bronco Bullfrog (1970)

GENSLER, LEWIS
Old Man Rhythm (1935)

GERARD, PHILIPPE
Folies Bergere (1958)

GERE, DON
Werewolves on Wheels (1971)

GERENS, ALEXANDER
Korea Patrol (1950)

GERHARD, ROBERTO
This Sporting Life (1963)

GERSHENSON, JOSEPH
Abbott and Costello in the Foreign Legion (1950)
Mystery Submarine (1950)
Peggy (1950)
Saddle Tramp (1950)

Shakedown (1950)
Under the Gun (1950)
Undercover Girl (1959)
Winchester '73 (1950)
Wyoming Mail (1950)
Abbott and Costello Meet the Invisible Man (1951)
Air Cadet (1951)
Cattle Drive (1951)
Cave of Outlaws (1951)
Flame of Araby (1951)
The Hollywood Story (1951)
The Iron Man (1951)
Little Egypt (1951)
Reunion in Reno (1951)
Smuggler's Island (1951)
The Strange Door (1951)
Target Unknown (1951)
Up Front (1951)
Back at the Front (1952)
The Black Castle (1952)
Bronco Buster (1952)
Francis Goes to West Point (1952)
Here Come the Nelsons (1952)
Horizons West (1952)
Just Across the Street (1952)
The Lawless Breed (1952)
Lost in Alaska (1952)
Ma and Pa Kettle at the Fair (1952)
Meet Danny Wilson (1952)
Meet Me at the Fair (1952)
The Raiders (1952)
The Redhead from Wyoming (1952)
Scarlet Angel (1952)
Son of Ali Baba (1952)
The Treasure of Lost Canyon (1952)
Yankee Buccaneer (1952)
Abbott and Costello Go to Mars (1953)
The All-American (1953)
All I Desire (1953)
City Beneath the Sea (1953)
Column South (1953)
East of Sumatra (1953)
Francis Covers the Big Town (1953)
The Glass Web (1953)
The Golden Blade (1953)
The Great Sioux Uprising (1953)
Gunsmoke (1953)
It Came from Outer Space (1953)
Law and Order (1953)
The Lone Hand (1953)
Ma and Pa Kettle on Vacation (1953)
Seminole (1953)
Take Me to Town (1953)
Tumbleweeds (1953)
Veils of Bagdad (1953)
Walking My Baby Back Home (1953)
War Arrow (1953)
Bengal Brigade (1954)
Black Horse Canyon (1954)
The Black Shield of Falworth (1954)
Border River (1954)
Dawn at Socorro (1954)
Destry (1954)
Drums Across the River (1954)
Fireman, Save My Child (1954)
Four Guns to the Border (1954)
Francis Joins the Wacs (1954)
Johnny Dark (1954)
Ma and Pa Kettle at Home (1954)
Naked Alibi (1954)
Playgirl (1954)
Rails into Laramie (1954)
Ricochet Romance (1954)
Ride Clear of Diablo (1954)
Saskatchewan (1954)
So This Is Paris (1954)
Tanganyika (1954)
The Yellow Mountain (1954)
Abbott and Costello Meet the Keystone Kops (1955)
Abbott and Costello Meet the Mummy (1955)
Ain't Misbehavin' (1955)
Captain Lightfoot (1955)
Cult of the Cobra (1955)
The Far Country (1955)
Female on the Beach (1955)
Francis in the Navy (1955)
Kiss of Fire (1955)
Lady Godiva (1955)
The Looters (1955)
Ma and Pa Kettle at Waikiki (1955)
The Man from Bitter Ridge (1955)

Man without a Star (1955)
The Private War of Major Benson (1955)
The Purple Mask (1955)
Revenge of the Creature (1955)
Running Wild (1955)
The Second Greatest Sex (1955)
Six Bridges to Cross (1955)
Smoke Signal (1955)
The Spoilers (1955)
Tarantula (1955)
To Hell and Back (1955)
Behind the High Wall (1956)
The Creature Walks Among Us (1956)
A Day of Fury (1956)
Francis in the Haunted House (1956)
The Kettles in the Ozarks (1956)
Pillars of the Sky (1956)
The Price of Fear (1956)
Raw Edge (1956)
Showdown at Abilene (1956)
Toy Tiger (1956)
Walk the Proud Land (1956)
World in My Corner (1956)
The Girl in the Kremlin (1957)
Gun for a Coward (1957)
Istanbul (1957)
Joe Butterfly (1957)
Joe Dakota (1957)
Kelly and Me (1957)
The Kettles on Old MacDonald's Farm (1957)
The Land Unknown (1957)
Love Slaves of the Amazon (1957)
Man in the Shadow (1957)
The Midnight Story (1957)
Mister Cory (1957)
The Monolith Monsters (1957)
The Night Runner (1957)
This Is Russia (1957)
The Last of the Fast Guns (1958)
Stranger in My Arms (1959)
Posse from Hell (1961)
Six Black Horses (1962)
Kitten with a Whip (1964)

GERSTAD, HARRY
Five Gates to Hell (1959)

GERTZ, IRVING
Dragnet (1947)
Adventures of Gallant Bess (1948)
Blonde Ice (1948)
The Counterfeiters (1948)
Jungle Goddess (1948)
Prejudice (1949)
Again ... Pioneers (1950)
Destination Murder (1950)
Experiment Alcatraz (1950)
Two-Dollar Bettor (1951)
The Bandits of Corsica (1953)
Gun Belt (1953)
Shark River (1953)
Khyber Patrol (1954)
Overland Pacific (1954)
Top Gun (1955)
The First Traveling Saleslady (1956)
Gun Brothers (1956)
Badlands of Montana (1957)
Hell Canyon Outlaws (1957)
Hell on Devil's Island (1957)
Plunder Road (1957)
Badman's Country (1958)
The Fearmakers (1958)
Thundering Jets (1958)
The Alligator People (1959)
Curse of the Undead (1959)
The Leech Woman (1960)
Seven Ways from Sundown (1960)
Thirteen Fighting Men (1960)
The Wizard of Bagdad (1960)
Young Jesse James (1960)
The Fiercest Heart (1961)
Marines, Let's Go (1961)
Brushfire (1962)
He Rides Tall (1964)
Fluffy (1965)
Nobody's Perfect (1968)

GETZ, STAN
The Interview (1960)

GHARACHE-DAGHI, SHEYDA
Downpour (1972)

GHIGLIA, BENEDETTO
New York Chiama Superdrago (1966)
Mattanza (1968)

A Stranger in Town (1968)
Psychout for Murder (1971)
St. Michael Had a Rooster (1971)

GHIGLIA, MAESTRO
That Little Difference (1970)

GIACOMAZZI, UGO
Strange Deception (Il Cristo Prohibito) (1953)
Black 13 (1954)

GIAMONTE, EGBERTO
The Last Maiden But One (1970)

GIBSON, LUKE
Journey (1972)

GILBERT, HERSCHEL BURKE
Mr. District Attorney (1947)
An Old-Fashioned Girl (1948)
Open Secret (1948)
The Jackie Robinson Story (1950)
Three Husbands (1950)
The Highwayman (1951)
The Magic Face (1951)
The Scarf (1951)
Kid Monk Baroni (1952)
Models, Inc. (1952)
No Time for Flowers (1952)
The Ring (1952)
The Thief (1952)
Without Warning (1952)
The Moon Is Blue (1953)
Sabre Jet (1953)
Vice Squad (1953)
Riot in Cell Block 11 (1954)
Witness to Murder (1954)
The Naked Dawn (1955)
Beyond a Resonable Doubt (1956)
The Bold and the Brave (1956)
Comanche (1956)
The Naked Hills (1956)
Nightmare (1956)
No Place to Hide (1956)
While the City Sleeps (1956)
Slaughter on Tenth Avenue (1957)

Crime and Punishment (1959)
Sam Whiskey (1969)

GILBERT, L. WOLFE
Ramona (1928)

GILL, ROBERT
Affair in Monte Carlo (1953)
The Golden Mask (1954)

GIL-SAN, G.
Interior Mechanism (1971)

GIMPEL, NORMAN
Making It (1971)

GIOMBINI, MARCELLO
Gladiators 7 (1964)
Love and Marriage (1966)
Knives of the Avenger (1967)

GIROLANI, MARIANO
The Devil's Lovers (1971)

GITLIS, IVREY
Valparaiso, Valparaiso (1971)

GLANZBERG, NORBERT
The Sorceress (1956)
The Light Across the Street (1957)
The Bride Is Much Too Beautiful (1958)
Prisoner of the Volga (1960)
Love and the Frenchwoman (1961)

GLASS, HARRY D.
Ginger (1971)
And Baby Makes Three (1972)

GLASS, PAUL
The Abductors (1957)
Bunny Lake Is Missing (1965)

GLASSER, ALBERT
The Contender (1944)
The Monster Maker (1944)
Border Feud (1947)
Gas House Kids in Hollywood (1947)
Killer at Large (1947)

Law of the Lash (1947)
Philo Vance Returns (1947)
Assigned to Danger (1948)
Behind Locked Doors (1948)
The Cobra Strikes (1948)
In This Corner (1948)
Last of the Wild Horses (1948)
The Return of Wildfire (1948)
The Trail of the Mounties (1948)
Urubu (1948)
The Valiant Hombre (1948)
Where the North Begins (1948)
Apache Chief (1949)
The Daring Caballero (1949)
The Gay Amigo (1949)
Grand Canyon (1949)
I Shot Jesse James (1949)
Omoo, Omoo, the Shark God (1949)
Satan's Cradle (1949)
Tough Assignment (1949)
Treasure of Monte Cristo (1949)
Bandit Queen (1950)
Border Rangers (1950)
The Girl from San Lorenzo (1950)
I Shot Billy the Kid (1950)
The Return of Jesse James (1950)
Train to Tombstone (1950)
Western Pacific Agent (1950)
The Bushwackers (1951)
Three Desperate Men (1951)
Tokyo File 212 (1951)
Invasion USA (1952)
Capt. John Smith and Pocahontas (1953)
The Neanderthal Man (1953)
Paris Model (1953)
Problem Girls (1953)
Dragon's Gold (1954)
Murder Is My Beat (1955)
Top of the World (1955)
The Boss (1956)
Huk (1956)
The Indestructible Man (1956)
The Amazing Colossal Man (1957)
Bailout at 43,000 (1957)
The Big Caper (1957)
The Buckskin Lady (1957)
Cyclops (1957)
Destination 60,000 (1957)
Four Boys and a Gun (1957)
The Hired Gun (1957)
Motorcycle Gang (1957)
Street of Sinners (1957)
Valerie (1957)
Girl in the Woods (1958)
The Mugger (1958)
Snowfire (1958)
When Hell Broke Loose (1958)
The Beat Generation (1959)
Night of the Quarter Moon (1959)
The Boy and the Pirates (1960)
Oklahoma Territory (1960)
Tormented (1960)
20,000 Eyes (1961)
Air Patrol (1962)
Confessions of an Opium Eater (1962)

GLAZOUNOV, ALEXANDER
Mashenka (1942)

GLEASON, JACKIE
Gigot (1962)

GLICKMAN, MORT
Outlaws of Pine Ridge (1942)
Shadows on the Sage (1942)
The Sundown Kid (1942)
Valley of Hunted Men (1942)
Beyond the Last Frontier (1943)
Black Hills Express (1943)
The Blocked Trail (1943)
Bordertown Gunfighters (1943)
California Joe (1943)
Calling Wild Bill Elliott (1943)
Canyon City (1943)
Carson City Cyclone (1943)
Days of Old Cheyenne (1943)
Death Valley Manhunt (1943)
Fugitive from Sonora (1943)
The Man from Thunder River (1943)
Minesweeper (1943)
Overland Mail Robbery (1943)
Raiders of Sunset Pass (1943)
Riders of the Rio Grande (1943)
Santa Fe Scouts (1943)
Wagon Tracks West (1943)
Gambler's Choice (1944
Hidden Valley Outlaws (1944)

Machine Gun Mama (1944)
The Mojave Firebrand (1944)
Pride of the Plains (1944)
The Inner Circle (1946)
The Magnificent Rogue (1946)
The Man from Rainbow Valley (1946)
The Mysterious Mr. Valentine (1946)
Red River Renegades (1946)
Rio Grande Raiders (1946)
Traffic in Crime (1946)
Along the Oregon Trail (1947)
Bells of San Angelo (1947)
Last Frontier Uprising (1947)
Marshal of Cripple Creek (1947)
Secret Service Investigator (1948)

GLIERE, RHEINHOLD
Alisher Navoi (1947)

GLINDEMANN, I. B.
Crazy Paradise (1965)

GLOVER, HENRY
Hey, Let's Twist (1961)

GLUSKIN, LUD
The Housekeeper's Daughter (1939)
Abroad with Two Yanks (1944)
High Conquest (1947)
Michael O'Halloran (1948)
Miracle in Harlem (1948)
Massacre River (1949)
Boy from Indiana (1950)

GODSKE, POUL
Where Is the Body, Moeller? (1971)

GOEHR, WALTER
Amateur Gentleman (1936)
Great Expectations (1947)
Stop Press Girl (1949)
Lucky Nick Cain (1951)
Betrayed (1954)

GOLD, ERNEST
Girl of the Limberlost (1945)
The Falcon's Alibi (1946)
G.I. War Brides (1946)
Lighthouse (1946)
Smooth as Silk (1946)
Exposed (1947)
Saddle Pals (1947)
Old Los Angeles (1948)
Picnic (1948)
The Unknown World (1951)
Jennifer (1953)
Man Crazy (1953)
The Other Woman (1954)
Edge of Hell (1956)
Running Target (1956)
Unidentified Flying Objects (1956)
Affair in Havana (1957)
Man on the Prowl (1957)
The True Story of the Civil War (1957)
Witness for the Prosecution (1957)
The Defiant Ones (1958)
Tarzan's Fight for Life (1958)
Too Much, Too Soon (1958)
Wink of an Eye (1958)
Battle of the Coral Sea (1959)
On the Beach (1959)
The Young Philadelphians (1959)
Exodus (1960)
Inherit the Wind (1960)
A Fever in the Blood (1961)
Judgment at Nurenburg (1961)
The Last Sunset (1961)
Pressure Point (1962)
A Child Is Waiting (1963)
It's a Mad Mad Mad Mad World (1963)
Ship of Fools (1965)
The Secret of Santa Vittoria (1969)

GOLDBERG, MORRIS
Black Fantasy (1972)

GOLDENBERG, BILLY
The Grasshopper (1970)
Red Sky at Morning (1971)
Play It Again, Sam (1972)
Up the Sandbox (1972)

GOLDSMITH, JERRY
Black Patch (1957)
City of Fear (1959)
Face of a Fugitive (1959)
Studs Lonigan (1960)
Freud (1962)
Lonely Are the Brave (1962)
The Spiral Road (1962)
A Gathering of Eagles (1963)
Lilies of the Field (1963)
The List of Adrian Messenger (1963)
The Prize (1963)
The Stripper (1963)
Take Her, She's Mine (1963)
Fate is the Hunter (1964)
Rio Conchos (1964)
Seven Days in May (1964)
Shock Treatment (1964)
City of Fear (1965)
In Harm's Way (1965)
Morituri (1965)
A Patch of Blue (1965)
The Satan Bug (1965)
Von Ryan's Express (1965)
The Blue Max (1966)
Our Man Flint (1966)
The Sand Pebbles (1966)
Seconds (1966)
Stagecoach (1966)
To Trap a Spy (1966)
The Trouble with Angels (1966)
Warning Shot (1966)
The Flim Flam Man (1967)
Hour of the Gun (1967)
In Like Flint (1967)
Bandolero (1968)
Planet of the Apes (1968)
The Chairman (1969)
The Illustrated Man (1969)
Justine (1969)
100 Rifles (1969)
The Ballad of Cable Hogue (1970)
Patton (1970)
Rio Lobo (1970)
The Traveling Executioner (1970)
Escape from the Planet of the Apes (1971)
The Mephisto Waltz (1971)
Wild Rovers (1971)
The Culpepper Cattle Co. (1972)
The Man (1972)
The Other (1972)

GOLETTI, NELLY
One Too Many (1950)

GOLINO, ANDRE
The Battle of Love's Return (1971)

GOLOVNYI, DIMITRI NICOLAU
On the Point of Death (1971)

GOLSON, BENNY
Ski Fascination (1966)
Where It's At (1969)

GOMEZ, VICENTE
Blood and Sand (1941)
The Fighter (1952)
Goya (1952)

GONDA, JANOS
Love Story Film (1970)
Temperate Zone (1970)
Horizon (1971)

GOODMAN, ISADOR
Jedda the Uncivilized (1956)

GOODWIN, RON
The Green Carnation (1960)
I'm All Right, Jack (1960)
The Village of the Damned (1960)
Invasion Quartet (1961)
The Flying Man (1962)
Kill or Cure (1962)
Murder She Said (1962)
The Day of the Triffids (1963)
Follow the Boys (1963)
Ladies Who Do (1963)
Murder at the Gallop (1963)
Sword of Lancelot (1963)
Children of the Damned (1964)
Murder Ahoy (1964)
Murder Most Foul (1964)
Of Human Bondage (1964)
633 Squadron (1964)
Operation Crossbow (1965)
Those Magnificent Men in Their Flying Machines (1965)

The Alphabet Murders (1966)
That Riviera Touch (1966)
The Magnificent Two (1967)
Decline and Fall (1968)
Mrs. Brown, You've Got a Lovely Daughter (1968)
Those Daring Young Men in Their Jaunty Jalopies (1969)
The Executioner (1970)
Frenzy (1972)

GOOSSENS, EUGENE
The Constant Nymph (1933)

GORAGUER, ALAIN
Paris Secret (1965)
The Man from Marrakech (1966)
The Gates of Fire (1972)

GORGONI, AL
I Never Sang for My Father (1970)

GORI, LALLO
The Brute and the Beast (1968)

GORN, STEVE
There's Always Vanilla (1972)

GOSSELAIN, ANDRE
Nude in a White Car (1959)
Night Encounter (1963)

GOTTSCHALK, LOUIS
The Patchwork Girl of Oz (1914)
Broken Blossoms (1919)
Orphans of the Storm (1922)

GOULD, GLENN
Slaughterhouse-Five (1972)

GOULD, MORTON
Delightfully Dangerous (1945)
San Francisco (1945)
Cinerama Holiday (1955)
Windjammer (1958)

GOWERS, PATRICK
Hamlet (1969)
Give God a Chance on Sunday (1970)
The Virgin and the Gypsy (1970)

GRAHAM, KENNY
The Small World of Sammy Lee (1963)
Night Train to Paris (1964)

GRAINER, RON
A Kind of Loving (1962)
The Finest Hours (1964)
The Guest (1964)
The Moonspinners (1964)
Night Must Fall (1964)
Nothing but the Best (1964)
Station Six--Sahara (1964)
The Trap (1966)
The Tiger Makes Out (1967)
To Sir with Love (1967)
Only When I Larf (1968)
The Assassination Bureau (1969)
Before Winter Comes (1969)
Hoffman (1970)
In Search of Gregory (1970)
The Omega Man (1971)

GRANADAS, VICTOR
Daughter of the West (1949)

GRANT, BERT
Desert Gold (1919)
The Valley of the Giants (1919)

GRAVEL, ROGER
The Apprentice (1971)

GRAY, ALLAN
Emil and the Detectives (1931)
Life and Death of Colonel Blimp (1943)
Stairway to Heaven (1946)
This Man Is Mine (1946)
Mr. Perrin and Mr. Traill (1948)
Madness of the Heart (1949)
The Reluctant Widow (1950)
No Place for Jennifer (1951)
Obsessed (1951)
Outpost in Malaya (1952)
Twilight Women (1953)

GRAY, BARRY
Journey to the Far Side of the Sun (1969)

GRAY, BASIL
Dingaka (1965)

GRAY, JAN
Lady in the Death House (1944)

GREELEY, GEORGE
The Peacemaker (1956)

GREEN, B.
The Brass Bottle (1964)

GREEN, BERNARD
Blind Goddess (1948)
The Fat Man (1951)
Everything's Ducky (1961)
Zotz! (1962)
All the Way Home (1963)
MGM's Big Parade of Comedy (1964)
Harvey Middleman, Fireman (1965)

GREEN, JOE
A Boy ... A Girl (1969)
The Girl Who Knew Too Much (1969)

GREEN, JOHN
My Sin (1931)
Secrets of a Secretary (1931)
Wayward (1931)
The Wiser Sex (1931)
The Sailor Takes a Wife (1945)
Weekend at the Waldorf (1945)
Easy to Wed (1946)
Fiesta (1947)
It Happened in Brooklyn (1947)
Something in the Wind (1947)
The Inspector General (1949)
The Great Caruso (1951)
Too Young to Kiss (1951)
Rhapsody (1954)
Raintree County (1957)
Pepe (1960)
Twilight of Honor (1963)
Alvarez Kelly (1966)
Johnny Tiger (1966)
They Shoot Horses, Don't They? (1969)

GREEN, NORMAN
The Loving Truth (1970)

GREEN, PHILIP
Ha'Penny Breeze (1950)
Murder without Crime (1950)
Affair in Monte Carlo (1953)
Yellow Balloon (1953)
The March Hare (1956)
John and Julie (1957)
The Ship Was Loaded (1957)
Carry on Admiral (1958)
In-Between Age (1958)
Rooney (1958)
A Question of Adultry (1959)
Sapphire (1959)
Bobbykins (1960)
Operation Amsterdam (1960)
The Shakedown (1960)
A Touch of Larceny (1960)
Man in the Moon (1961)
The Secret Partner (1961)
The Singer Not the Song (1961)
Upstairs and Downstairs (1961)
Victim (1962)
The Girl Hunters (1963)
Tiara Tahiti (1963)
The Dream Maker (1964)
Masquerade (1965)

GREENE, RICHARD
Riverrun (1968)

GREENE, WALTER
Crime, Inc. (1945)
Danny Boy (1946)
Ghost Town Renegades (1947)
Hollywood Barn Dance (1947)
Range Beyond the Blue (1947)
The Black Hills (1948)
Cheyenne Takes Over (1948)
The Fighting Vigilantes (1948)
Mark of the Lash (1948)
Return of the Lash (1948)
Shep Comes Home (1948)
Stage to Mesa City (1948)
Tornado Range (1948)
The Westward Trail (1948)
Dead Man's Gold (1949)
Hollywood Varieties (1949)
Rimfire (1949)
Ringside (1949)
Son of a Badman (1949)

Son of Billy the Kid (1949)
Square Dance Jubilee (1949)
Colorado Ranger (1950)
Crooked River (1950)
Hostile Country (1950)
King of the Bullwhip (1950)
G. I. Jane (1951)
Kentucky Jubilee (1951)
Varieties on Parade (1951)
Yes Sir, Mr. Bones (1951)
Outlaw Women (1952)
Jesse James' Women (1954)
Teenage Doll (1957)
War of the Satellites (1958)
Thunder in Carolina (1960)
Tarzan's Deadly Silence (1970)

GREENWELL, PETER
The Virgin Soldiers (1969)

GREENWOOD, JOHN
The Constant Nymph (1933)
Man of Aran (1934)
Elephant Boy (1936)
Drums (1938)
Nine Men (1943)
Hungry Hill (1947)
Broken Journey (1948)
Eureka Stockade (1949)
Family Portrait (1950)
Trio (1950)
The Gentle Gunman (1953)
Wicked Wife (1955)

GREGORIUM, GHEORGES
Silent Friends (1971)

GREMILLION, JEAN
Six Juin a l'aube (1947)

GREY, HARRY
Follow Your Heart (1936)

GROFE, FERDE
King of Jazz (1930)
Diamond Jim (1935)
Minstrel Man (1944)
Rocketship X-M (1950)

GRONOSTAY, WALTER
Berlin Carnival (1929)

GROSS, CHARLES
Across the River (1965)
Valdez Is Coming (1971)

GROSS, CLANCY B., III
The Velvet Vampire (1971)

GROTHE, FRANZ
Circus Girl (1956)
Aren't We Wonderful? (1958)
The Man Who Walked through the Wall (1958)
Portrait of an Unknown Woman (1958)
The Trapp Family (1961)
One Day Is More Beautiful than the Other (1970)

GRUEN, JOHN
8 X 8 (1957)

GRUENBERG, LOUIS
Fight for Life (1939)
So Ends Our Night (1941)
An American Romance (1944)
Counter Attack (1945)
The Gangster (1947)
Arch of Triumph (1948)
Smart Woman (1948)
All the King's Men (1949)
Quicksand (1950)

GRUN, BERNARD
High Fury (1948)

GRUND, BERT
Under the Red Sea (1952)
Between Time and Eternity (1960)
Armored Command (1961)
Hippodrome (1961)

GRUNENWALD, JEAN-JACQUES
Les Dames Du Bois De Boulogne (1944)
Monsieur Vincent (1947)
The Diary of a Country Priest (1951)
Edouard and Caroline (1952)

GRUNTZ, GEORGES
Malatesta (1970)
The Wanting Weight (1971)

GRUSIN, DAVE
Divorce American Style (1967)
The Graduate (1967)
Waterhole #3 (1967)
Candy (1968)
The Heart Is a Lonely Hunter (1968)
Where Were You When the Lights Went Out? (1968)
The Mad Room (1969)
A Man Called Gannon (1969)
Tell Them Willie Boy Is Here (1969)
Winning (1969)
Halls of Anger (1970)
The Gang that Couldn't Shoot Straight (1971)
The Pursuit of Happiness (1971)
Shoot Out (1971)
Fuzz (1972)
The Great Northfield, Minnesota, Raid (1972)

GUARALDI, VINCE
A Boy Named Charlie Brown (1969)

GUBERNICK, HY
The Greenwich Village Story (1963)

GUERRERO, SERGIO
Por Mis Pistolas (1968)

GUERSTAM, CLAES AF
Portraits of Women (1970)

GUILBEAN, GIB
Boxcar Bertha (1972)

GUILLOT, MAURICE-PAUL
Symphonie Fantastique (1948)

GUILLOU, PIERO
Mio (1972)

GULDA, FRIEDRICH
Necronomicon--Dreamed Sins (1968)

GUNNING, CHRISTOPHER
Goodbye Gemini (1970)

GUTERSON, MISCHA
The Lover of Camille (1924)

GUTHRIE, ARLO
Alice's Restaurant (1969)

GUTMANN, ARTHUR
Bridal Suite (1939)
Enemy of Women (1944)

GYLDMARK, SVEN
Fun in the Streets (1969)
Take a Little Sunshine (1969)
Hurray for the Blue Hussars (1970)
Me and My Kid Brother and Doggie (1970)
The Saints from Krejcarek (1970)
Tough Guys of the Prairie (1970)
Father of Four in a Sunny Mood (1971)
Gold for the Tough Guys of the Prairie (1971)
My Sister's Kids at Their Worst (1971)

GYULAI-GAAL, JANOS
Town without a Face (1963)

HADJIDAKIS, MANOS
Bed of Grass (1957)
Stella (1957)
Never on Sunday (1960)
Aliki My Love (1962)
It Happened in Athens (1962)
The 300 Spartans (1962)
America, America (1963)
Topkapi (1964)
Greece, Land of Dreams (1966)
Blue (1968)
The Martlet's Tale (1970)

HADLEY, HENRY
When a Man Loves (1927)

HAENTZSCHEL, GEORG
The Adventures of Baron Munchausen (1942)
Stephanie (1959)

HAGEMAN, RICHARD
If I Were King (1938)
Hotel Imperial (1939)
Rulers of the Sea (1939)
Stagecoach (1939)
The Howards of Virginia (1940)
The Long Voyage Home (1940)
Paris Calling (1942)
Shanghai Gesture (1942)
Angel and the Badman (1947)
The Fugitive (1947)
Mourning Becomes Electra (1947)
Fort Apache (1948)
Three Godfathers (1948)
She Wore a Yellow Ribbon (1949)
Wagonmaster (1950)

HAGEN, EARLE
Spring Reunion (1957)
The New Interns (1964)

HAIM, PAUL BEN
Hill 24 Doesn't Answer (1955)

HAJOS, JOE
Act of Love (1953)

HAJOS, KARL
Beggars of Life (1928)
Loves of an Actress (1928)
Morocco (1931)
Four Frightened People (1934)
The Last of the Pagans (1935)
Manhattan Moon (1935)
Two Wise Maids (1937)
Hitler's Hangman (1943)
The Sultan's Daughter (1943)
Charlie Chan in the Secret Service (1944)
Summer Storm (1944)
Dangerous Intruder (1945)
The Man Who Walked Alone (1945)
The Missing Corpse (1945)
The Phantom of 42nd Street (1945)
Shadow of Terror (1945)
Down Missouri Way (1946)
Driftin' River (1946)
The Mask of Dijon (1946)
Queen of Burlesque (1946)
Secrets of a Sorority Girl (1946)
Stars over Texas (1946)
Wild West (1946)
Appointment with Murder (1948)
The Lovable Cheat (1949)
Search for Danger (1949)
It's a Small World (1950)
Kill or Be Killed (1950)

HAKIEN, ABDUL
Right On (1970)

HALA, VLASTIMIL
I Killed Einstein, Gentlemen (1970)

HALFFTER, CRISTOBAL
10:30 P.M. Summer (1966)
The Desperate Ones (1968)

HALFFTER, ERNESTO
Don Quixote de la Mancha (1948)
Another Man's Wife (1967)
The Roosters of Dawn (1971)

HALFFTER, RUDOLFO
The Living Idol (1957)
Torero! (1957)

HALL, DERRY
The Great Scuttling (1972)

HALL, JIM
Desperate Characters (1971)

HALLER, HERMANN
Four in a Jeep (1951)

HALLETZ, ERWIN
The Confession of Ina Kahr (1958)
Pyramid of the Sungods (1965)
Treasure of the Aztecs (1965)
The Priest of St. Pauli (1970)

Girls and Gynecologists (1971)

HALLIGAN, RICHARD
The Owl and the Pussycat (1970)

HALPERN, EDMUND
Tel Aviv Taxi (1956)

HAM, AL
Harlow (1965)

HAMBRO, LEONID
Dirtymouth (1970)
Toys Are Not for Children (1972)

HAMILTON, CHICO
Repulsion (1965)

HAMILTON, FOREST
How to Succeed with Sex (1970)

HAMLISCH, MARVIN
The Swimmer (1968)
The April Fools (1969)
Take the Money and Run (1969)
Flap (1970)
Move! (1970)
Bananas (1971)
Kotch (1971)
Something Big (1971)
Fat City (1972)
The War Between Men and Women (1972)

HAMMOND, JOHN
Little Big Man (1970)

HAMPTON, LIONEL
The Adventures of * (1957)

HAMPTON, RICHARD
Othello (1965)

HANCOCK, HERBERT
Blow Up (1966)

HANKS, FREDERICK OWEN
Song of the North (1917)

HARLINE, LEIGH
The Old Mill (1937)
The Farmer's Daughter (1940)
Careful, Soft Shoulder (1942)
Prelude to War (1942)
Pride of the Yankees (1942)
You Were Never Lovelier (1942)
Government Girl (1943)
Johnny Come Lately (1943)
Margin for Error (1943)
The More the Merrier (1943)
The Sky's the Limit (1943)
Tender Comrade (1943)
Follow the Boys (1944)
Heavenly Days (1944)
Music in Manhattan (1944)
A Night of Adventure (1944)
The Brighton Strangler (1945)
China Sky (1945)
First Yank into Tokyo (1945)
Having Wonderful Crime (1945)
Isle of the Dead (1945)
Johnny Angel (1945)
Man Alive (1945)
Mama Loves Papa (1945)
What a Blonde (1945)
Child of Divorce (1946)
Crack-Up (1946)
From This Day Forward (1946)
Lady Luck (1946)
Nocturne (1946)
Road to Utopia (1946)
Till the End of Time (1946)
The Truth about Murder (1946)
The Bachelor and the Bobby-Soxer (1947)
The Farmer's Daughter (1947)
Honeymoon (1947)
A Likely Story (1947)
Tycoon (1947)
The Boy with Green Hair (1948)
Every Girl Should Be Married (1948)
The Miracle of the Bells (1948)
Mr. Blandings Builds His Dream House (1948)
The Twisted Road (1948)
The Velvet Touch (1948)
The Big Steal (1949)
I Married a Communist (1949)
It Happens Every Spring (1949)
The Judge Steps Out (1949)

The Woman on Pier 13 (1949)
The Company She Keeps (1950)
The Happy Years (1950)
My Friend Irma Goes West (1950)
Perfect Strangers (1950)
Behave Yourself (1951)
Call Me Mister (1951)
Double Dynamite (1951)
The Guy Who Came Back (1951)
His Kind of Woman (1951)
I Want You (1951)
On the Loose (1951)
That's My Boy (1951)
My Pal Gus (1952)
My Wife's Best Friend (1952)
The Desert Rats (1953)
Money from Home (1953)
Vicki (1953)
Black Widow (1954)
Broken Lance (1954)
Susan Slept Here (1954)
The Girl in the Red Velvet Swing (1955)
Good Morning, Miss Dove (1955)
The Last Frontier (1955)
The Bottom of the Bottle (1956)
Great Day in the Morning (1956)
Teenage Rebel (1956)
23 Paces to Baker Street (1956)
The Enemy Below (1957)
No Down Payment (1957)
The True Story of Jesse James (1957)
The Wayward Bus (1957)
Man of the West (1958)
Ten North Frederick (1958)
Holiday for Lovers (1959)
The Remarkable Mr. Pennypacker (1959)
These Thousand Hills (1959)
Warlock (1959)
The Facts of Life (1960)
A Visit to a Small Planet (1960)
The Honeymoon Machine (1961)
The Wonderful World of the Brothers Grimm (1962)
Seven Faces of Dr. Lao (1964)
Strange Bedfellows (1964)

HARLING, W. FRANKE
The Right to Love (1931)
Shanghai Express (1932)
Cradle Song (1933)
Destination Unknown (1933)
By Candlelight (1934)
One More River (1934)
So Red the Rose (1935)
China Clipper (1936)
The Golden Arrow (1936)
I Married a Doctor (1936)
Mountain Justice (1937)
Men Are Such Fools (1938)
Men with Wings (1938)
Adam Had Four Sons (1941)
The Lady Is Willing (1942)
I Escaped from the Gestapo (1943)
Three Russian Girls (1943)
Johnny Doesn't Live Here Anymore (1944)
When the Lights Go On Again (1944)

HARRIS, ALBERT
Showdown at Boot Hill (1958)

HARRIS, EDDIE
Why America? (1969)

HARRIS, JOHNNY
Fragment of Fear (1970)
Bloomfield (1971)
Man in the Wilderness (1971)
I Want What I Want (1972)

HARRIS, MAX
Baby Love (1969)

HARRIS, ROY
One-Tenth of a Nation (1940)

HARRISON, GEORGE
Wonderwall (1969)

HART, BOBBY
The Unholy Rollers (1972)

HART, DANNY
The Small Hours (1962)

HART, UKIE
The Only Way Home (1972)

HARTTI, KALEVI
Assault (1957)

HARVAN, JAROSLAV
Crisis (1939)

HASKELL, JIMMIE
Love in a Goldfish Bowl (1961)
The Gun Hawk (1963)
Black Spurs (1965)
I'll Take Sweden (1965)
Love and Kisses (1965)
Town Tamer (1965)
Wild on the Beach (1965)
Apache Uprising (1966)
Johnny Reno (1966)
Red Tomahawk (1966)
Waco (1966)
Fort Utah (1967)
Hostile Guns (1967)
Arizona Bushwackers (1968)
Buckskin (1968)
The Wicked Dreams of Paula Schultz (1968)
Dagmar's Hot Pants, Inc. (1971)
Walls of Fire (1971)
Zachariah (1971)
The Honkers (1972)
Night of the Lepus (1972)

HATCH, TONY
Travels with My Aunt (1972)

HATCH, WILBUR
The Power of the Whistler (1945)
Mysterious Intruder (1946)

HATCHER, HARLEY
Killers Three (1968)
A Bullet for Pretty Boy (1970)
Satan's Sadists (1970)
The Hard Ride (1971)

HATHAWAY, DONNY
Come Back Charleston Blue (1972)

HATLEY, MARVIN
General Spanky (1936)
Way Out West (1936)
Nobody's Baby (1937)
Pick a Star (1937)
Topper (1937)
Blockheads (1938)
Merrily We Live (1938)
Swiss Miss (1938)
There Goes My Heart (1938)
Captain Fury (1939)
Zenobia (1939)

HATTORI, TADASHI
The Men Who Tread on the Tiger's Tail (1945)

HAUSKA, HANS
The Borinage (1932)

HAWKESWORTH, JOHN
Goal! (1966)
The Penthouse (1967)

HAWKSHAW, ALAN
The Green Wall (1970)

HAYASAKA, FUMIO
Drunken Angel (1948)
The Bailiff (1954)
I Live in Fear (1955)
The Magnificent Seven (1956)
Yang Kwei Fei (1956)

HAYASHI, HIKARU
The Island (1961)
Onibaba (1965)
Boy (1969)
Under the Flag of the Rising Sun (1972)

HAYES, ISAAC
Shaft (1971)
Shaft's Big Score (1972)

HAYTON, LENNIE
Eyes in the Night (1942)
Maisie Gets Her Man (1942)
Nazi Agent (1942)
Pierre of the Plains (1942)
Stand By for Action (1942)
This Time for Keeps (1942)
Whistling in Dixie (1942)

A Yank on the Burma Road (1942)
Assignment in Brittany (1943)
Pilot No. 5 (1943)
Salute to the Marines (1943)
Swing Swift Maisie (1943)
The Hucksters (1947)
Living in a Big Way (1947)
Any Number Can Play (1949)
Battleground (1949)
Side Street (1949)
Inside Straight (1951)
Strictly Dishonorable (1951)
Love Is Better Than Ever (1952)
Battle Circus (1953)

HAZZARD, RICHARD
Radar Secret Service (1950)
Calypso Joe (1957)

HEFTI, NEAL
Sex and the Single Girl (1964)
Boeing Boeing (1965)
Harlow (1965)
How to Murder Your Wife (1965)
Synanon (1965)
Duel at Diablo (1966)
Lord Love a Duck (1966)
Barefoot in the Park (1967)
Oh, Dad, Poor Dad, Mama's Hung You in the Closet and I'm Feeling So Sad (1967)
The Odd Couple (1968)
P. J. (1968)

HEIFETZ, VLADIMIR
The Last Chapter (1966)

HEIMAN, NAHUM
The Rooster (1971)

HEINDORF, RAY
Wonder Man (1945)
The Breaking Point (1950)
Young Man with a Horn (1950)
Come Fill the Cup (1951)
Goodbye My Fancy (1951)
The Big Trees (1952)
Bugles in the Afternoon (1952)
Stop, You're Killing Me (1952)
No Time for Sergeants (1958)
-30- (1959)
Up Periscope (1959)

HEINRICH, GERHARD
When the Mad Aunts Are Coming (1970)

HEINZ, GERHARD
The Hostess Exceeds All Bounds (1970)
Josefine Mulzenbacher (1970)
The Cry of the Black Wolves (1972)

HELASVUO, ELSA
Poor Little Maria (1972)

HELLEBOID, KAMA DOMINIQUE
Traces (1972)

HELLER, HERMAN
Conflict (1936)
Flying Hostess (1936)
Sea Spoilers (1936)
Yellowstone (1936)
The King and the Chorus Girl (1937)

HELMS, JIM
The Loving Truth (1970)

HEMRIC, GUY
Ski Fever (1969)

HENDERSON, LUTHER
Recess (1969)

HENDERSON, SKITCH
A Miracle Can Happen (1948)
Act One (1963)

HENNEKER, DAVID
House of Fright (1961)

HENNESSY, ROBERT
Why Russians Are Revolting (1970)

HENRY, PIERRE
Astrologie (1952)
Where the Truth Lies (1962)

HENZE, HANS WERNER
Muriel (1963)
The Young Toerless (1966)

HERAS, JOAQUIN GUTIERREZ
Familiarities (1970)
The Olympics in Mexico (1970)

HERBERT, VICTOR
The Fall of a Nation (1916)

HERRMANN, BERNARD
All That Money Can Buy (1941)
Citizen Kane (1941)
The Magnificent Ambersons (1942)
Jane Eyre (1944)
Hangover Square (1945)
Anna and the King of Siam (1946)
The Ghost and Mrs. Muir (1947)
The Day the Earth Stood Still (1951)
On Dangerous Ground (1951)
Five Fingers (1952)
The Snows of Kilimanjaro (1952)
Beneath the Twelve Mile Reef (1953)
King of the Khyber Rifles (1953)
White Witch Doctor (1953)
The Egyptian (1954)
Garden of Evil (1954)
Prince of Players (1955)
The Trouble with Harry (1955)
A Christmas Carol (1956)
The Man in the Grey Flannel Suit (1956)
The Man Who Knew Too Much (1956)
A Hatful of Rain (1957)
The Wrong Man (1957)
The Naked and the Dead (1958)
The Seventh Voyage of Sinbad (1958)
Vertigo (1958)
Blue Denim (1959)
Journey to the Center of the Earth (1959)
North by Northwest (1959)
Psycho (1960)
Mysterious Island (1961)
Cape Fear (1962)
Tender Is the Night (1962)
Jason and the Argonauts (1963)
Marnie (1964)
Joy in the Morning (1965)
Fahrenheit 451 (1966)
Twisted Nerve (1968)
Obsessions (1969)
The Night Digger (1971)

HEYMANN, WERNER
The Spy (1927)
Spies (1928)
Congress Dances (1931)
Adorable (1933)
Ninotchka (1939)
The Earl of Chicago (1940)
He Stayed for Breakfast (1940)
One Million B.C. (1940)
The Primrose Path (1940)
The Shop around the Corner (1940)
My Life with Caroline (1941)
That Uncertain Feeling (1941)
Topper Returns (1941)
Flight Lieutenant (1942)
A Night to Remember (1942)
They All Kissed the Bride (1942)
To Be or Not to Be (1942)
The Wife Takes a Flyer (1942)
Hail the Conquering Hero (1944)
Mademoiselle Fifi (1944)
My Pal, Wolf (1944)
Our Hearts Were Young and Gay (1944)
Three Is a Family (1944)
Together Again (1944)
It's in the Bag (1945)
Kiss and Tell (1945)
Always Together (1947)
Lost Honeymoon (1947)
Mad Wednesday (1947)
Let's Live a Little (1948)
The Mating of Millie (1948)
A Kiss for Corliss (1949)
Tell It to the Judge (1949)
Emergency Wedding (1950)
A Woman of Distinction (1950)
The Congress Dances (1957)

HILL, JOE
Between Us (1970)

HINDEMITH, PAUL
Krazy Kat at the Circus (1927)
Ghosts Before Breakfast (1929)
Dreams That Money Can Buy (1948)

HINSHAW, WILLIAM
Ole Rex (1961)

HIRSCH, NURIT
The Cop (1971)
Katz and Karasso (1972)

HODGE, JONATHAN
Embassy (1972)

HODIER, ANDRE
World without Sun (1964)

HOEFLE, CARL
The Caravan Trail (1946)
God's Country (1946)
Romance of the West (1946)
Death Valley (1947)

HOEYER, OLE
Beside Mazurka (1970)
Bedside Dentist (1971)
Why Do They Do It? (1971)
Bedside Head (1972)
Bedside Highway (1972)

HOFFERT, PAUL
Flick (1970)
The Groundstar Conspiracy (1972)

HOFMAN, STAN
Terror in the Jungle (1968)

HOLCOMBE, W. L.
Psychomania (1964)

HOLDRIDGE, LEE
The Sidelong Glances of a Pigeon Kicker (Pigeons) (1970)

HOLLANDER, FREDERICK
The Blue Angel (1930)
Shanghai (1935)
Desire (1936)
Till We Meet Again (1936)
John Meade's Woman (1937)
Disputed Passage (1939)
Invitation to Happiness (1939)
The Biscuit Eater (1940)
The Great McGinty (1940)
Rangers of Fortune (1940)
Remember the Night (1940)
Safari (1940)
There's Magic in Music (1940)
Footsteps in the Dark (1941)
Here Comes Mr. Jordan (1941)
Million Dollar Baby (1941)
Victory (1941)
You Belong to Me (1941)
Talk of the Town (1942)
Wings for the Eagle (1942)
Background to Danger (1943)
Princess O'Rourke (1943)
Once Upon a Time (1944)
The Affairs of Susan (1945)
Christmas in Connecticut (1945)
Conflict (1945)
Pillow to Post (1945)
The Bride Wore Boots (1946)
Cinderella Jones (1946)
Janie Gets Married (1946)
Never Say Goodbye (1946)
The Time, the Place and the Girl (1946)
Two Guys from Milwaukee (1946)
The Verdict (1946)
The Perfect Marriage (1947)
The Red Stallion (1947)
Stallion Road (1947)
That Way with Women (1947)
Berlin Express (1948)
A Foreign Affair (1948)
Wallflower (1948)
Adventure in Baltimore (1949)
Bride for Sale (1949)
Caught (1949)
A Dangerous Profession (1949)
Strange Bargain (1949)
A Woman's Secret (1949)
Born to Be Bad (1950)

Born Yesterday (1950)
Never a Dull Moment (1950)
Walk Softly, Stranger (1950)
Darling, How Could You? (1951)
My Forbidden Past (1951)
Androcles and the Lion (1952)
The 5,000 Fingers of Dr. T (1953)
It Should Happen to You (1954)
Phffft (1954)
Sabrina (1954)
We're No Angels (1955)

HOLLINGSWORTH, JOHN
The Abominable Snowman (1957)
The Curse of Frankenstein (1957)
Horror of Dracula (1958)
Mystery Submarine (1963)
The Wrong Arm of the Law (1963)

HOLM, MICHAEL
Mark of the Devil (1970)

HOLMES, BILL
The Curse of the Living Corpse (1964)

HOLMES, LEROY
The Bridge in the Jungle (1970)

HOLMES, RUPERT
The Animals (1971)
A.W.O.L. (1972)

HOLMGREN, PELLE GUDMUNDSEN
Desertoren (1971)

HOLST, GUSTAV
The Bells (1931)

HONEGGER, ARTHUR
La Roue (1922)
Fait Divers (1924)
Napoleon (1926)
Pacific 231 (1931)
L'Idee (1934)
Les Miserables (1934)
Crime and Punishment (1935)
Mademoiselle Docteur (1937)
Mayerling (1937)
The Woman I Love (1937)
Pygmalion (1938)
Un Revenant (1946)
Storm over Tibet (1951)
Joan of Arc at the Stake (1954)

HOPKINS, ANTHONY
Vice Versa (1945)
It's Hard to Be Good (1948)
Vote for Huggett (1949)
Decameron Nights (1953)
Johnny on the Run (1954)
The Pickwick Papers (1954)
Billy Budd (1962)

HOPKINS, KENYON
Baby Doll (1956)
The Strange One (1957)
Twelve Angry Men (1957)
The Fugitive Kind (1959)
Wild River (1960)
Wild in the Country (1961)
The Yellow Canary (1963)
Lilith (1964)
Mister Buddwing (1966)
Doctor, You've Got to be Kidding (1967)
A Lovely Way to Die (1968)
Downhill Racer (1969)
The First Time (1969)
The Tree (1969)

HOSEY, ATHENA
The New Life Style (1970)

HOWARD, KEN
Up Pompeii (1971)

HUE, GEORGES
The Return of Ulysses (1915)

HUGG, MIKE
Up the Junction (1968)
Venus in Furs (1970)

HUGHES, GARY
The Pirates of Blood River (1962)
The Crimson Blade (1964)

Devil-Ship Pirates (1964)
A Challenge for Robin Hood (1968)

HUMPHREYS, LES
Blue Movie (1971)

HUPPERTZ, GOTTFRIED
Kriemhild's Revenge (1923)
Siegfried (1923)
Metropolis (1926)

IBERT, JACQUES
The Italian Straw Hat (1927)
Les Cinq Gentlemen Maudits (1930)
Don Quixote (1934)
Golgotha (1937)
The Phantom Chariot (1938)
Panic (1946)
Macbeth (1948)
From Doric to Gothic (1952)
Marianne of My Youth (1954)
Invitation to the Dance (1946)

IDRISS, RAMEZ
Hidden Guns (1956)
The Badge of Marshal Brennan (1957)
Man or Gun (1958)

IFUKUBE, AKIRA
Children of Hiroshima (1952)
Downtown (1955)
Hiroshima (1955)
The Burmese Harp (1956)
Rodan (1957)
The Mysterians (1959)
Battle in Outer Space (1960)
Buddha (1963)
Godzilla vs. the Thing (1964)
Atragon (1965)
Ghidrah, the Three-Headed Monster (1965)

IGNATOFF, NIKOLAI
The Wild Pussycat (1970)

ILIC-BELL, MIODRAC
The Bug Killer (1971)

ILLIANI, GUILIANO
Diary of an Italian (1972)

INNOCENZI, CARLO
David and Goliath (1961)
The Teacher and the Miracle (1961)
The Prisoner of the Iron Mask (1962)

IPPOLITOV-IVANOV, MIKHAIL
Stenka Razin (1908)
Song about the Merchant Kalashnikov (1909)
Volga and Siberia (1914)

IRELAND, JOHN
The Overlanders (1946)

IRVING, SIR ERNEST
The Proud Valley (1939)
Ships with Wings (1942)
Bitter Springs (Savage Justice) (1950)
I Believe in You (1953)

IRVING, ROBERT
Flood Tide (1949)

IRWIN, RALPH
One Rainy Afternoon (1936)

ISFALT, BJORN
A Swedish Love Story (1970)

ISMAIL, ALY
The Earth (1970)

ITO, TEIJI
Maeva (1961)

IVERSEN, EGIL-MONN
Douglas (1970)

JACKSON, CALVIN
Blood and Steel (1959)

JACKSON, HOWARD
The Great Gabbo (1929)
Hearts in Dixie (1929)
Sunny Side Up (1929)
Girl without a Room (1933)
This Day and Age (1933)

Beloved (1934)
And So They Were Married (1936)
The King Steps Out (1936)
Meet Nero Wolfe (1936)
Mr. Deeds Goes to Town (1936)
The Music Goes 'Round (1936)
Cowboy Quarterback (1939)
Bullet Scars (1942)
Wild Bill Hickock Rides (1942)
How Do You Do? (1945)
Fifty Years Before Your Eyes (1950)
Tobor the Great (1954)
Run for Cover (1955)
Wakamba (1955)
The Amazon Trader (1956)
Deep Adventure (1957)
Cry Terror (1958)
Manhunt in the Jungle (1958)
Yellowstone Kelly (1959)
Sergeant Rutledge (1960)
Claudelle Inglish (1961)
Gold of the Seven Saints (1961)
House of Women (1962)
Merrill's Marauders (1962)
Black Gold (1963)

JACOB, GORDON
Close Quarters (1943)
Maintenance Command (1944)
Journey Together (1945)
Esther Waters (1948)

JACOBS, AL
Racing Fever (1964)

JAIKISHAN, SHANKAR
Boot Polish (1958)
Bombay Talkie (1970)

JANSEN, PIERRE
Bluebeard (Landru) (1963)
The Third Lover (1963)
The Savior (1971)
Doctor Popoul (1972)

JANSEN, SIGURD
How to Behave in a Fourposter Bed (1972)

JANSSEN, WERNER
The General Died at Dawn (1936)
Blockade (1938)
Eternally Yours (1939)
Winter Carnival (1939)
House Across the Bay (1940)
Lights out in Europe (1940)
Slightly Honorable (1940)
Guest in the House (1944)
Captain Kidd (1945)
The Southerner (1945)
A Night in Casablanca (1946)
Uncle Vanya (1958)

JANSSENS, PETER
Apokal (1971)

JARRE, MAURICE
Hotel Des Invalides (1952)
L'univers d'Utrillo (1954)
T. N. P. (1956)
Toute Le Memoire du Monde (1956)
La Bel Indifferent (1957)
Vel'd'Hiv (1957)
Les Drageurs (1958)
Head Against the Wall (The Keepers) (1958)
The Chasers (1959)
Crack in the Mirror (1959)
Eyes without a Face (1959)
La Main Chaude (1959)
The Big Gamble (1961)
Therese Desqueryoux (1961)
Lawrence of Arabia (1962)
The Longest Day (1962)
Sundays and Cybele (1962)
Behold a Pale Horse (1964)
Dragon Sky (1964)
The Animals (1965)
The Collector (1965)
Doctor Zhivago (1965)
The Train (1965)
Gambit (1966)
Grand Prix (1966)
Is Paris Burning? (1966)
The Professionals (1966)
The Night of the Generals (1967)
The Witnesses (1967)
Five Card Stud (1968)
Isadora (1968)
Villa Rides (1968)

The Damned (1969)
The Extraordinary Seaman (1969)
El Condor (1970)
The Only Game in Town (1970)
Ryan's Daughter (1970)
Plaza Suite (1971)
Red Sun (1971)
The Effect of Gamma Rays on Man-in-the-Moon Marigolds (1972)
The Life and Times of Judge Roy Bean (1972)
Pope Joan (1972)

JARY, MICHAEL
They Were So Young (1955)

JAUBERT, MAURICE
Pays Du Scalp (1929)
L'Affair Est Dans Le Sac (1932)
Quatorze Juillet (1932)
Zero for Conduct (1933)
L'Atalante (1934)
Le Dernier Milliadaire (1934)
Easter Island (1934)
Bizarre, Bizarre (Drole De Drame) (1937)
Un Carnet Du Bal (1937)
Les Maisons de la Misere (1937)
We Live in Two Worlds (1937)
Port of Shadows (Quai Des Brumes) (1938)
Daybreak (1939)
La Fin Du Jour (1939)

JENEY, ZOLTAN
Szindbad (1972)

JENKINS, GORDON
Strange Holiday (1946)
Bwana Devil (1952)

JEPSON, WARNER
Luminous Procuress (1972)

JEROME, M. K.
Fires of Faith (1919)

JOBIM, ANTONIO CARLOS
Black Orpheus (1960)
The Adventurors (1970)

JOHANSSON, JAN
The Touch (1971)

JOHN, ELTON
Friends (1971)

JOHNS, VAL
The Big Cube (1969)

JOHNSON, ARTHUR
Sidewalks of London (1940)

JOHNSON, J. J.
Man and Boy (1972)
Top of the Heap (1972)

JOHNSON, LAURIE
No Trees in the Street (1959)
I Aim at the Stars (1960)
Siege of the Saxons (1963)
Dr. Strangelove: Or How I Stopped Worrying and Began to Love the Bomb (1964)
East of Sudan (1964)
The First Man in the Moon (1964)
You Must Be Joking! (1965)
Hot Millions (1968)
And Soon the Darkness (1970)

JONASON, GUNNAR
Jungle of Chang (1951)

JONES, BOOKER T.
Uptight (1968)

JONES, BRIAN
A Degree of Murder (1967)

JONES, GUY
The Human Monster (1940)

JONES, KENNETH V.
How to Murder a Rich Uncle (1957)
High Flight (1958)
The Horse's Mouth (1958)
Indiscreet (1958)
Intent to Kill (1958)
Room 43 (1958)
Tank Force (1958)

Tom Thumb (1958)
The Bandit of Zhobe (1959)
Ten Seconds to Hell (1959)
Jazz Boat (1960)
Oscar Wilde (1960)
Tarzan the Magnificent (1960)
Ferry to Hong Kong (1961)
The Green Helmet (1961)
Two Way Stretch (1961)
Nearly a Nasty Accident (1962)
Operation Snatch (1962)
Tarzan Goes to India (1962)
Cairo (1963)
Horror Hotel (1963)
Dr. Crippen (1964)
Psyche '59 (1964)
Maroc 7 (1967)
The Projected Man (1967)
Battle Beneath the Earth (1968)
Who Slew Auntie Roo? (1971)

JONES, QUINCY
Mirage (1965)
The Pawnbroker (1965)
The Slender Thread (1965)
Walk, Don't Run (1966)
The Deadly Affair (1967)
Enter Laughing (1967)
In Cold Blood (1967)
In the Heat of the Night (1967)
The Counterfeit Killer (1968)
A Dandy in Aspic (1968)
For Love of Ivy (1968)
The Hell with Heroes (1968)
Jigsaw (1968)
The Split (1968)
Bob and Carol and Ted and Alice (1969)
Cactus Flower (1969)
The Italian Job (1969)
John and Mary (1969)
The Last of the Mobile Hot-shots (1969)
The Lost Man (1969)
McKenna's Gold (1969)
The Out-of-Towners (1970)
They Call Me Mister Tibbs (1970)
The Anderson Tapes (1971)
Brother John (1971)
Dollars ($) (1971)
Honky (1971)
Come Back Charleston Blue (1972)
The Getaway (1972)
The Hot Rock (1972)
The New Centurions (1972)

JORDAN, LOUIS
Look Out, Sister (1949)

JORDAN, PORTER
Chrome and Hot Leather (1971)

JOSEPHS, WILFRED
Cash on Demand (1962)
Die! Die! My Darling! (1965)
The Deadly Bees (1967)
My Side of the Mountain (1969)

KABALEVSKY, DMITRI
Aerograd (Frontier) (1936)
Shors (1939)
Academician Ivan Pavlov (1949)
Ivan Pavlov (1950)
Flames on the Volga (1955)
The Gadfly (1955)
The Sisters (1957)
1918 (1958)
Bleak Morning (1959)

KABOS, ILONA
The Fake (1953)

KABURAGI, HAJIME
The Hunted Samurai (1971)

KACHATURIAN, KAREN
A Pistol Shot (1967)

KAEMPFERT, BERT
A Man Could Get Killed (1966)
You Can't Win 'Em All (1970)
An Elephant Called Slowly (1971)

KAISER, KURT
Way Out (1966)

KAMPKA, BERND
Praised Be What Hardens You (1972)

KANCHELI, J.
Don't Worry (1970)

KANDER, JOHN
Something for Everyone (1970)

KANE, EDWARD
The Mortal Storm (1940)

KANTOR, IGO
Good Morning ... and Goodbye (1967)
Vixen (1968)
Cherry, Harry and Raquel (1969)
le Projectionist (1970)

KAPER, BRONISLAU
Mutiny on the Bounty (1935)
San Francisco (1936)
I Take This Woman (1940)
We Who Are Young (1940)
Comrade X (1941)
Two-Faced Woman (1941)
When Ladies Meet (1941)
Whistling in the Dark (1941)
A Woman's Face (1941)
Fingers at the Window (1942)
Keeper of the Flame (1942)
Somewhere I'll Find You (1942)
We Were Dancing (1942)
White Cargo (1942)
A Yank at Eton (1942)
Crossroads (1942)
Above Suspicion (1943)
Bataan (1943)
The Cross of Lorraine (1943)
The Heavenly Body (1943)
Slightly Dangerous (1943)
Gaslight (1944)
Marriage Is a Private Affair (1944)
Mrs. Parkington (1944)
Bewitched (1945)
Our Vines Have Tender Grapes (1945)
Without Love (1945)
Courage of Lassie (1946)
The Secret Heart (1946)
The Stranger (1946)
Three Wise Fools (1946)
Cynthia (1947)
Green Dolphin Street (1947)
High Wall (1947)
Song of Love (1947)
Act of Violence (1948)
B.F.'s Daughter (1948)
Homecoming (1948)
The Secret Land (1948)
The Great Sinner (1949)
Malaya (1949)
The Secret Garden (1949)
That Forsyte Woman (1949)
Grounds for Marriage (1950)
Key to the City (1950)
A Life of Her Own (1950)
Please Believe Me (1950)
The Skipper Surprised His Wife (1950)
To Please a Lady (1950)
Mr. Imperium (1951)
The Red Badge of Courage (1951)
Shadow in the Sky (1951)
Three Guys Named Mike (1951)
Invitation (1952)
The Wild North (1952)
The Actress (1953)
Lili (1953)
The Naked Spur (1953)
Ride, Vaquero (1953)
Saadia (1953)
Her Twelve Men (1954)
Them! (1954)
The Glass Slipper (1955)
The Prodigal (1955)
Quentin Durward (1955)
Forever Darling (1956)
The Power and the Prize (1956)
The Solid Gold Cadillac (1956)
The Swan (1956)
The Barretts of Wimpole Street (1957)
Don't Go Near the Water (1957)
Jet Pilot (1957)
Auntie Mame (1958)
The Brothers Karamazov (1958)
The Scapegoat (1959)
The Angel Wore Red (1960)
Butterfield 8 (1960)
Home from the Hill (1960)
Ada (1961)
Two Loves (1961)
Mutiny on the Bounty (1962)
Kisses for My President (1964)

Lord Jim (1965)
Tobruk (1966)
Counterpoint (1967)
The Way West (1967)
A Flea in Her Ear (1968)

KAPLAN, ELLIOT
The Square Root of Zero (1965)

KAPLAN, SOL
Apache Trail (1942)
Tales of Manhattan (1942)
Unexpected Riches (1942)
Down Memory Lane (1949)
Port of New York (1949)
Reign of Terror (The Black Book) (1949)
Trapped (1949)
Halls of Montezuma (1950)
711 Ocean Drive (1950)
Alice in Wonderland (1951)
House on Telegraph Hill (1951)
I Can Get It for You Wholesale (1951)
I'd Climb the Highest Mountain (1951)
Rawhide (1951)
The Secret of Convict Lake (1951)
Something for the Birds (1952)
Way of a Gaucho (1952)
Destination Gobi (1953)
Niagara (1953)
Titanic! (1953)
Treasure of the Golden Condor (1953)
The Burglar (1957)
Happy Anniversary (1959)
Girl of the Night (1960)
The Victors (1963)
The Guns of August (1964)
The Young Lovers (1964)
The Spy Who Came in from the Cold (1965)
Judith (1966)
New York City--The Most (1968)
Explosion (1969)
Living Free (1972)

KAPNISSIS, COSTAS
The Dawn of Victory (1971)
Papanicolis (1971)
Boom (1972)
Hippocrates (1972)

KARAS, ANTON
The Third Man (1950)

KARASKI, NICO
The Astro Zombies (1969)

KARAYEV, KARA
Don Quixote (1957)

KARETNIKOV, NIKOLAI
The Flight (1971)

KARGER, FRED
Cha-Cha-Cha Boom! (1956)
Harum Scarum (1965)
When the Boys Meet the Girls (1965)
Frankie and Johnny (1966)
Hold On (1966)
The Fastest Guitar Alive (1967)
Hot Rods to Hell (1967)
The Love-Ins (1967)
Riot on Sunset Strip (1967)
For Singles Only (1968)
A Time to Sing (1968)
The Young Runaways (1968)
Angel, Angel, Down We Go (1969)
The Moonshine War (1970)
Necromancy (1972)

KARLIN, FRED
Up the Down Staircase (1967)
The Stalking Moon (1968)
Yours, Mine and Ours (1968)
The Sterile Cuckoo (1969)
The Baby Maker (1970)
Lovers and Other Strangers (1970)
Believe in Me (1971)
The Marriage of a Young Stockbroker (1971)
Every Little Crook and Nanny (1972)
The Little Ark (1972)

KARMAN, STEVE
Party Girls for the Candidate (1965)
Teenage Mother (1968)
What Do You Say to a Naked Lady? (1970)

KATZ, BERNARD
Street Corner (1948)

KATZ, ERIC
Hi, Mom! (1970)

KATZ, FRED
A Bucket of Blood (1959)
The Monitors (1969)
Little Murders (1971)

KAUER, GENE
Door-to-Door Maniac (1966)
Proud, Damned and Dead (1969)

KAUFMAN, LLOYD
The Battle of Love's Return (1971)

KAUFMANN, SERGE
Over There--1914-1918 (1963)

KAUN, BURHARD
Special Delivery (1955)

KAURER, GENE
War Kill (1967)

KAY, ARTHUR
Daniel Boone (1936)
House of a Thousand Candles (1936)

KAY, EDWARD J.
With Love and Kisses (1936)
Foreign Agent (1942)
Ghost Town Law (1942)
Isle of Missing Men (1942)
Klondike Fury (1942)
Man from Headquarters (1942)
Meet the Mob (1942)
Rhythm Parade (1942)
Road to Happiness (1942)
Smart Alecs (1942)
The Ape Man (1943)
Campus Rhythm (1943)
Clancy Street Boys (1943)
Cosmo Jones, Spy Smasher (1943)
Ghosts on the Loose (1943)
Here Comes Kelly (1943)
Melody Parade (1943)
Nearly Eighteen (1943)
Oh, What a Night! (1943)
Sarong Girl (1943)
Six-Gun Gospel (1943)
Spotlight Scandals (1943)
The Stranger from Pecos (1943)
What a Man! (1943)
Women in Bondage (1943)
You Can't Beat the Law (1943)
Alaska (1944)
Detective Kitty O'Day (1944)
Ghost Guns (1944)
Land of the Outlaws (1944)
Law Men (1944)
Law of the Valley (1944)
Partners of the Trail (1944)
Raiders of the Border (1944)
Range Law (1944)
Return of the Ape Man (1944)
Smart Guy (1944)
Voodoo Man (1944)
West of the Rio Grande (1944)
Black Market Babies (1945)
Captain Tugboat Annie (1945)
Come Out Fighting (1945)
Divorce (1945)
Fashion Model (1945)
G.I. Honeymooon (1945)
Mr. Muggs Rides Again (1945)
The Scarlet Clue (1945)
South of the Rio Grande (1945)
There Goes Kelly (1945)
Below the Deadline (1946)
Bowery Bombshell (1946)
Bringing Up Father (1946)
Dangerous Money (1946)
Don't Gamble with Strangers (1946)
Drifting Along (1946)
The Face of Marble (1946)
The Gay Cavalier (1946)

Gentleman Joe Palooka (1946)
Gentleman from Texas (1946)
In Fast Company (1946)
Live Wires (1946)
The Missing Lady (1946)
Mr. Hex (1946)
The Shadow Returns (1946)
Silver Range (1946)
South of Monterey (1946)
Spook Busters (1946)
Sweetheart of Sigma Chi (1946)
Swing Parade of 1946 (1946)
Trigger Fingers (1946)
Under Arizona Skies (1946)
Wife Wanted (1946)
Black Gold (1947)
Beauty and the Bandit (1947)
Bowery Buckaroos (1947)
The Chinese Ring (1947)
Fall Guy (1947)
Gun Talk (1947)
Joe Palooka in the Knockout (1947)
Kilroy Was Here (1947)
King of the Bandits (1947)
Land of the Lawless (1947)
Louisiana (1947)
News Hounds (1947)
Sarge Goes to College (1947)
The Trap (1947)
Valley of Fear (1947)
Violence (1947)
Angel's Alley (1948)
Backtrail (1948)
Campus Sleuth (1948)
The Checkered Coat (1948)
Courtin' Trouble (1948)
Cowboy Cavalier (1948)
Crossed Trails (1948)
Docks of New Orleans (1948)
The Feathered Serpent (1948)
Fighting Man (1948)
The Fighting Ranger (1948)
French Leave (1948)
Frontier Agent (1948)
Gunning for Justice (1948)
Hidden Danger (1948)
The Hunted (1948)
I Wouldn't Be in Your Shoes (1948)
Incident (1948)
Jiggs and Maggie in Court (1948)
Jinx Money (1948)
Joe Palooka in Winner Take All (1948)
Kidnapped (1948)
Music Man (1948)
The Mystery of the Golden Eye (1948)
Oklahoma Blues (1948)
Outlaw Brand (1948)
Partners of the Sunset (1948)
Range Renegades (1948)
The Rangers Ride (1948)
Rocky (1948)
The Shanghai Chest (1948)
The Sheriff of Medicine Bow (1948)
Silver Trails (1948)
Smuggler's Cove (1948)
Song of the Drifter (1948)
Stage Struck (1948)
Triggerman (1948)
Trouble Makers (1948)
Angels in Disguise (1949)
Black Midnight (1949)
Bomba, the Jungle Boy (1949)
Fighting Fools (1949)
Forgotten Women (1949)
Henry, the Rainmaker (1949)
Hold That Baby (1949)
I Cheated the Law (1949)
Jiggs and Maggie in Jackpot Jitters (1949)
Joe Palooka in the Big Fight (1949)
Joe Palooka in the Counter-punch (1949)
The Lawton Story (1949)
Leave It to Henry (1949)
Masterminds (1949)
Mississippi Rhythm (1949)
Sky Dragons (1949)
Stampede (1949)
Trail of the Yukon (1949)
Tuna Clipper (1949)
The Admiral Was a Lady (1950)
Big Timber (1950)
Blonde Dynamite (1950)
Blues Busters (1950)
Bomba on Panther Island (1950)
Call of the Klondike (1950)
Father Makes Good (1950)
Father's Wild Game (1950)
Fence Rider (1950)

The Great Plane Robbery (1950)
Hot Rod (1950)
Jiggs and Maggie Out West (1950)
Joe Palooka in Humphrey Takes a Chance (1950)
Joe Palooka in the Squared Circle (1950)
Joe Palooka Meets Humphrey (1950)
Killer Shark (1950)
Law of the Panhandle (1950)
Outlaw Gold (1950)
Short Grass (1950)
Sideshow (1950)
Sierra Passage (1950)
Silver Raiders (1950)
Snow Dog (1950)
Square Dance Katy (1950)
Triple Trouble (1950)
West of Wyoming (1950)
The Wolf Hunters (1950)
Young Daniel Boone (1950)
Abilene Trail (1951)
According to Mrs. Hoyle (1951)
Bowery Battalion (1951)
Colorado Ambush (1951)
Father Takes the Air (1951)
I Was an American Spy (1951)
Let's Go Navy (1951)
Man from Sonora (1951)
Montana Desperado (1951)
Rhythm Inn (1951)
Yellow Fin (1951)
Yukon Manhunt (1951)
Arctic Flight (1952)
Desert Pursuit (1952)
Feudin' Fools (1952)
Here Come the Marines (1952)
Hold That Line (1952)
Jet Job (1952)
No Holds Barred (1952)
Sea Tiger (1952)
Cow Country (1953)
Fangs of the Arctic (1953)
Mexican Manhunt (1953)
Murder without Tears (1953)
Northern Patrol (1953)
Tangier Incident (1953)
Torpedo Alley (1953)
Trail Blazers (1953)
Highway Dragnet (1954)
Port of Hell (1954)
Security Risk (1954)
Yukon Vengeance (1954)
Betrayed Women (1955)
The Big Tip-Off (1955)
Las Vegas Shakedown (1955)
Night Freight (1955)
The Toughest Man Alive (1955)
Treasure of the Ruby Hills (1955)
Yaqui Drums (1956)
Johnny Rocco (1958)

KAYE, NORMAN
Diamonds for Breakfast (1968)

KAYLIN, SAMUEL
Dante's Inferno (1935)
Ginger (1935)
Steamboat 'Round the Bend (1935)
Your Uncle Dudley (1935)
Champagne Charlie (1936)
Every Saturday Night (1936)
Pepper (1936)
Thank You, Jeeves (1936)
36 Hours to Kill (1936)
Time Out for Romance (1937)
The Leather Burners (1943)

KAZANECKI, WALDEMAR
Abel, Your Brother (1970)

KEAN, SPEEDY
Double Pisces, Scorpio Rising (1970)

KEATING, JOHNNY
Hotel (1967)
Robbery (1967)

KEISSLING, HEINZ
Main Thing Holiday (1972)

KELLAWAY, ROGER
The Paper Lion (1968)
Who Fears the Devil? (1972)

KELLY, MONTY
Flight to Hong Kong (1956)

KEMPINSKI, LEO
Greed (1924)

KENDRICK, MERRIL
Kenji Comes Home (1949)

KENZIE, DAVID
Come One, Come All (1970)

KERR, ANITA
Limbo (1972)

KHACHATURIAN, ARAM
Pepo (1935)
Salavat Yulayev (1941)
Girl No. 217 (1944)
The Russian Question (1948)
The Battle of Stalingrad (1949)
Admiral Ushakov (1953)
Attack from the Sea (1953)
Saltanat (1955)
Othello (1960)
2001: A Space Odyssey (1968)

KHAN, ALIK AKBAR
Devi (1961)

KHEMADASA, PREMASIRI
The Treasure (1972)

KHOLAKIA, DILIP
Kanku (1970)

KHRENNIKOV, TIKHON
They Met in Moscow (1941)
True Friends (1954)

KIEFFER, DENIS
Speaking of Murder (1959)

KIELANOWSKI, ALINA
The Epidemic (1972)

KIESEWETTER, PETER
Lydia (1970)

KILAR, WOJCIECK
The Bear (1970)
The Taste of the Black Earth (1970)
The Star of the Season (1971)
Pearl in the Crown (1972)

KILENYI, EDWARD
The Chechahcos (1924)
His Darker Self (1924)
Try and Get It (1924)
The Proud Heart (1925)
Michael Strogoff (1926)
The Midnight Sun (1926)
Headin' West (1937)
Zambonga (1937)
International Crime (1938)
The Overland Express (1938)
Topa Topa (1938)
The Tender Years (1947)
Belle Starr's Daughter (1948)

KING, BRIAN
Rabbit, Run (1970)

KING, PETE
The Family Jewels (1965)

KINOSHITA, CHUJI
Carmen Comes Home (1951)
The Human Condition (1959)

KIRCHIN, BASIL
The Shuttered Room (1967)
Assignment K (1968)
Negatives (1968)
The Strange Affair (1968)
I Start Counting (1970)
The Abominable Dr. Phibes (1971)

KISH, JOSEPH
The Lady from Texas (1951)

KISSLING, HEINZ
Your Child, the Unknown Creature (1970)
Your Husband, the Unknown Creature (1970)

KLATZKIN, LEON
Inner Sanctum (1948)
As You Were (1951)
Tales of Robin Hood (1951)
The Fiend Who Walked the West (1958)
Go, Johnny, Go (1959)

KLEINSCHUSTER, ERICH
Alkeste--The Importance of

Having Protection (1970)

KLEINSINGER, GEORGE
Shakespeare: Soul of an Age (1964)
Shinbone Alley (1971)

KLOBUCAR, ANDELKO
There Grows a Green Pine in the Woods (1971)

KNIEPER, JURGEN
The Goalie's Anxiety at the Penalty Kick (1972)

KNIGHT, PETER
The Crimson Cult (1970)

KNIGHT, TERRY
The Incident (1967)

KNUDSEN, THORKILD
The Woolen Stocking Peddler (1971)

KOCHUROV, Y.
Professor Mamlock (1938)

KODER, URBAN
From the Other Side (1970)

KOFF, CHARLES
The Man from Planet X (1951)
Captive Women (1952)

KOMEDA, KRYZSTOF
Knife in the Water (1961)
Cul de Sac (1966)
The Fearless Vampire Killers (1967)
Riot (1968)
Rosemary's Baby (1968)

KONIECZNY, ZYGMUNT
Landscape After the Battle (1970)
The People of Warsaw (1970)

KONITZ, LEE
Desperate Characters (1971)

KOOPER, AL
My Girl Friend's Wedding (1969)
The Landlord (1970)

KOPP, RUDOLPH
Sign of the Cross (1932)
Cleopatra (1934)
The Crusades (1935)
The Voice of Bugle Ann (1936)
Gallant Bess (1946)
My Brother Talks to Horses (1947)
The Bride Goes Wild (1948)
Tenth Avenue Angel (1948)
Ambush (1949)
The Doctor and the Girl (1949)
Mystery Street (1950)
Bannerline (1951)
Calling Bulldog Drummond (1951)
Vengeance Valley (1951)
Desperate Search (1952)
Fearless Fagan (1952)
Arena (1953)
The Great Diamond Robbery (1953)
The Hoaxters (1953)
Gypsy Colt (1954)

KORCHMARYOV, K.
Under Sunny Skies (The Far-Away Bride) (1949)

KORNGOLD, ERICH WOLFGANG
Captain Blood (1935)
Anthony Adverse (1936)
The Green Pastures (1936)
A Midsummer Night's Dream (1936)
The Story of Louis Pasteur (1936)
Another Dawn (1937)
The Prince and the Pauper (1937)
The Adventures of Robin Hood (1938)
Juarez (1939)
The Private Lives of Elizabeth and Essex (1939)
The Sea Wolf (1941)
The Constant Nymph (1943)
Between Two Worlds (1944)

Deception (1946)
Devotion (1946)
Of Human Bondage (1946)
Escape Me Never (1947)
Magic Fire (1956)

KORNSPAN, ADOLPH
The Fool (1925)

KORZYNSKI, ANDREJ
The Third Part of the Night (1971)

KOSEKI, YUJI
Mothra (1962)

KOSMA, JOSEPH
Jenny (1935)
Un Partie de Campagne (1936)
Grand Illusion (1937)
The Human Beast (1938)
La Marseillaise (1938)
The Rules of the Game (1939)
Children of Paradise (1943)
Les Chouans (1946)
Monsieur Ludovic (1946)
Portes de la Nuit (1946)
Aubervilliers (1947)
Le Petit Soldat (1947)
Bagarres (1948)
Au Grand Balcon (1949)
La Belle Que Voila (1949)
Blood of the Beasts (1949)
Marie du Port (1949)
San Laisser D'Adresse (1950)
Un Gran Patron (1951)
Juliette ou la Clef Des Songe (1951)
La Bergere et le Ramoneur (1952)
La Commune de Paris (1952)
Francois le Rhinoceros (1952)
The Green Glove (1952)
Louis Lumiere (1954)
Cila S'Appelle L'aurore (1955)
Elena and the Men (1955)
Innocents of Paris (1955)
Calle Mayor (1956)
The Case of Dr. Laurent (1957)
Paris Does Strange Things (1957)
Tamango (1957)
Demoniaque (1958)
The Doctor's Dilemma (1958)
The Lovemaker (1958)
The Wild Fruit (1958)
Love and the Frenchwoman (1961)
Le Pave de Paris (1961)
La Poupee (1962)
The Testament of Dr. Cordelier (1962)
The Elusive Corporal (1963)
In the French Style (1963)
The Magnificent Sinner (1963)
Thank Heaven for Small Favors (1965)
Bitter Fruit (1967)

KOSMA, WLADIMIR
Teresa (1970)

KOSTIC, VOJISLAV
Passing Days (1970)
Tales of Blood (1970)

KOTSEV, KONSTANTIN
A Diverse World: The Test and the Care Conscience (1972)

KOUNADIS, ARGHYRIS
Antigone (1962)

KOVAC, JORNELIJE
The Role of My Family in the Revolution (1971)

KRALJIC, DARKO
Girl from the Mountains (1972)

KRAUSHAAR, RAOUL
Melody Ranch (1940)
Heart of the Rio Grande (1942)
S.O.S. Coast Guard (1942)
Stardust on the Sage (1942)
Alias Billy the Kid (1946)
The El Paso Kid (1946)
Stork Bites Man (1947)
Arson, Inc. (1949)
Sky Liner (1949)
Zamba (1949)
Cowboy and the Prizefighter (1950)
The Basketball Fix (1951)
Bride of the Gorilla (1951)

The Longhorn (1951)
Prehistoric Women (1951)
The Second Face (1951)
Stage from Blue River (1951)
The Sword of Monte Cristo (1951)
Abbott and Costello Meet Captain Kidd (1952)
African Treasure (1952)
Fargo (1952)
Kansas Territory (1952)
Man from Black Hills (1952)
The Maverick (1952)
Montana Incident (1952)
Night Raiders (1952)
Rose of Cimarron (1952)
Texas City (1952)
Untamed Women (1952)
Waco (1952)
The Blue Gardenia (1953)
The Fighting Lawman (1953)
The Marksman (1953)
Marry Me Again (1953)
Rebel City (1953)
The Star of Texas (1953)
Texas Bad Man (1953)
Topeka (1953)
Vigilante Terror (1953)
Bitter Creek (1954)
The Desperado (1954)
The Forty-Niners (1954)
The Outlaw's Daughter (1954)
Two Guns and a Badge (1954)
The Magnificent Matador (1955)
The Black Whip (1956)
Curucu, Beast of the Amazon (1956)
Mohawk (1956)
Back from the Dead (1957)
Copper Sky (1957)
The Restless Breed (1957)
Ride a Violent Mile (1957)
The Unknown Terror (1957)
Blood Arrow (1958)
The Cool and the Crazy (1958)
Desert Hell (1958)
Island of Lost Women (1959)
Mustang (1959)
The 30-Foot Bride of Candy Rock (1959)
September Storm (1960)
An Eye for an Eye (1966)

KREMENLIEV, BORIS
The Tell-Tale Heart (1954)

KREMSKI, ALAIN
Apocalypse (1970)
Sacred Fire (1971)

KRENDER, PETER
Mademoiselle Mosquito (1956)

KRISTOFFERSON, KRIS
Cisco Pike (1971)
The Last Movie (1971)
Fat City (1972)

KRIVOSKEY, DAVID
Fifty-Fifty (1971)

KRUMGOLD, SIGMUND
Death Takes a Holiday (1934)
Union Pacific (1939)

KRYUKOV, NIKOLAI
We Are from Kronstadt (1936)
Revolutionists (1936)
Symphony of Life (1949)
Without Prejudice (1949)
Potemkin (re-issue) (1951)
The Grasshopper (1955)
Heroes of Shipka (1955)
The Forty-First (1956)
The Idiot (1958)
The Letter That Was Never Sent (1959)

KUBIK, GAIL
Men and Ships (1940)
Paratroops (1942)
The World at War (1942)
The Memphis Belle (1944)
Thunderbolt (1945)
C-Man (1949)
Gerald McBoing Boing (1950)
Two Gals and a Guy (1951)
The Desperate Hours (1955)
I Thank a Fool (1962)

KUEHN, ROLF
Perrak (1970)
The Yellow House at Pinnasberg (1970)

KUMAR, MERMANT
Nagin (1956)

KUPFERMAN, MEYER
Blast of Silence (1961)
Black Like Me (1964)
Truman Capote's Trilogy (1969)

KUTEV, F.
Heroes of Shipka (1955)

KYMLICKA, MILAN
The Last Act of Martin Weston (1970)
The Reincarnate (1971)
Wedding in White (1972)

LA SALLE, RICHARD
Speed Crazy (1959)
The Big Night (1960)
The Boy Who Caught a Crook (1961)
The Flight that Disappeared (1961)
Secret of Deep Harbor (1961)
Sniper's Ridge (1961)
When the Clock Strikes (1961)
You Have to Run Fast (1961)
The Broken Land (1962)
Deadly Duo (1962)
The Firebrand (1962)
Gun Street (1962)
Hands of a Stranger (1962)
Incident in an Alley (1962)
Saintly Sinners (1962)
The Day Mars Invaded Earth (1963)
Diary of a Madman (1963)
Police Nurse (1963)
Twice Told Tales (1963)
Apache Rifles (1964)
Blood on the Arrow (1964)
The Quick Gun (1964)
The Time Travelers (1964)
A Yank in Viet Nam (1964)
Arizona Raiders (1965)
Convict Stage (1965)
Fort Courageous (1965)
War Party (1965)
Ambush Bay (1966)
Boy, Did I Get a Wrong Number (1966)
Daughters of Satan (1972)
Superbeast (1972)

LACKEY, DOUGLAS
War Kill (1967)
Proud, Damned and Dead (1969)

LADERMAN, EZRA
The Black Fox (1963)
The Image of Love (1965)

LAGUIDZE, REVEZ
The Warmth of Your Hands (1972)

LAI, FRANCIS
A Man and a Woman (1966)
The Bobo (1967)
I'll Never Forget What's 'is Name (1967)
Live for Life (1967)
House of Cards (1968)
Mayerling (1968)
13 Days in France (1968)
Hannibal Brooks (1969)
Life, Love and Death (1969)
A Man Who Pleases Me (1969)
Three into Two Won't Go (1969)
The Games (1970)
Hello--Goodbye (1970)
The Hoodlum (1970)
Love Story (1970)
The Modification (1970)
Rider on the Rain (1970)
Early Morning (1971)
The Oil Girls (1971)
Smic, Smac, Smoc (1971)
Adventure Is Adventure (1972)
And Hope to Die (1972)

LAM, DOMINGO
Lost (1970)

LAMARQUE, FRANCIS
Playtime (1967)

LAMBERT, CONSTANT
Merchant Seaman (1940)

LAMBRO, PHILIP
And Now Miguel (1966)

LANCHBERY, JOHN
Tales of Beatrix Potter (1971)

LANG, HANS
Emperor's Waltz (1956)
The Foreman (1956)

LANGE, ARTHUR
Stand Up and Cheer (1934)
In Old Kentucky (1935)
The Little Colonel (1935)
Banjo on My Knee (1936)
Girl's Dormitory (1936)
It Had to Happen (1936)
Under Your Spell (1936)
White Hunter (1937)
Kidnapped (1938)
Submarine Patrol (1938)
Three Blind Mice (1938)
The Great Victor Herbert (1939)
Quiet Please, Murder (1942)
The Dancing Masters (1943)
Lady of Burlesque (1943)
Belle of the Yukon (1944)
Bermuda Mystery (1944)
Casanova Brown (1944)
The Woman in the Window (1944)
Along Came Jones (1945)
It's a Pleasure (1945)
The Fabulous Suzanne (1946)
Jungle Patrol (1948)
The Golden Gloves Story (1950)
The Vicious Years (1950)
Woman on the Run (1950)
The Groom Wore Spurs (1951)
Beachhead (1954)
The Mad Magician (1954)
Ring of Fear (1954)
Southwest Passage (1954)

LANGHORNE, BRUCE
The Hired Hand (1971)

LANGLET, PHILIPPE
The End of Pyrenees (1970)

LANHAM, GENE
The Judge (1949)

LANJEAN, MARC
Razzia (1957)

LANOE, HENRI
An Occurrence at Owl Creek Bridge (1962)
Don't Play with the Martians (1968)

LANZI, BRUNO
In the Summertime (1971)

LAR, ROBERTO
Mr. and Mrs. Juan Lamaglia (1970)
Chronicle of a Lady (1971)
The Night of San Juan (1971)
Heroine (1972)

LARSSON, LARS-ERIK
The Great Adventure (1954)
Make Way for Lila (1962)

LASRY, ALBERT
Miquette (1951)

LASRY, JACQUES
The Head (1961)

LASSE, RAGNAR
Love Is War (1971)

LAST, JAMES
The Captain (1972)

LASZLO, ALEXANDER
Black Magic (1944)
Dangerous Passage (1944)
Double Exposure (1944)
Follow That Woman (1945)
The Great Flamarion (1945)
High Powered (1945)
One Exciting Night (1945)
Accomplice (1946)
The French Key (1946)
The Glass Alibi (1946)
Hot Cargo (1946)
Joe Palooka, Champ (1946)
People Are Funny (1946)
Strange Impersonation (1946)
They Made Me a Killer (1946)
Banjo (1947)
Untamed Fury (1947)

Yankee Fakir (1947)
Parole, Inc. (1948)
Alimony (1948)
Amazon Quest (1949)
Song of India (1949)
Tarzan's Magic Foundation (1949)
The Spiritualist (Amazing Mr. X) (1948)
Forbidden Island (1956)
Fincho (1958)
Ghost of the China Sea (1958)
The Atomic Submarine (1959)

LATTUADA, FELICE
Without Pity (1948)
The She-Wolf (1954)

LAUBER, KEN
Scratch Harry (1969)
Brand X (1970)

LAURENT, STEVE
Lafayette (1963)

LAVA, WILLIAM
To the Shores of Iwo Jima (1945)
She-Wolf of London (1946)
The Big Punch (1948)
Embraceable You (1948)
Moonrise (1948)
Flaxy Martin (1949)
Homicide (1949)
The House Across the Street (1949)
The Younger Brothers (1949)
Barricade (1950)
Breakthrough (1950)
Colt .45 (1950)
Fifty Years Before Your Eyes (1950)
The Great Jewel Robbery (1950)
Highway 301 (1950)
This Side of the Law (1950)
Inside the Walls of Folsom Prison (1951)
The Tanks Are Coming (1951)
Cattle Town (1952)
The Lion and the Horse (1952)
Retreat, Hell! (1952)
Stormy, the Thoroughbred (1954)
The Littlest Outlaw (1955)
The Deadly Mantis (1957)
Flood Tide (1958)
Hell Bent for Leather (1960)
Seven Ways from Sundown (1960)
The Sign of Zorro (1960)
PT-109 (1963)
Wall of Noise (1963)
The Tattooed Police Horse (1964)
Chamber of Horrors (1966)
Assignment to Kill (1968)
Chubasco (1968)
In Enemy Country (1968)
The Good Guys and the Bad Guys (1969)

LAVAGNINO, FRANCESCO
Green Magic (1955)
Othello (1955)
Empire of the Sun (1957)
Legend of the Lost (1957)
Lost Continent (1957)
The Miller's Beautiful Wife (1957)
Sins of Casanova (1957)
Woman of the River (1957)
The Last Paradise (1958)
Behind the Great Wall (1959)
The Naked Maja (1959)
Sign of the Gladiator (1959)
Che Gioia Vivere (1960)
Conspiracy of Hearts (1960)
Esther and the King (1960)
Five Branded Women (1960)
The Grand Olympics (1960)
The Last Days of Pompeii (1960)
Nude Odyssey (1960)
The Savage Innocents (1960)
The Wind Cannot Read (1960)
The Colossus of Rhodes (1961)
The Explosive Generation (1961)
Gorgo (1961)
The Revolt of the Slaves (1961)
The Warrior Empress (1961)
The Wonders of Aladdin (1961)
Damon and Pythias (1962)
Everybody Go Home! (1962)
Marco Polo (1962)
The Siege of Syracuse (1962)

Madame (1963)
Commando (1964)
Dark Purpose (1964)
Agent 8-3/4 (1965)
Gunmen of the Rio Grande (1965)
Hercules, Samson and Ulysses (1965)
Saladino (1966)
Wild, Wild Planet (1967)
Story of a Girl Alone (1969)

LAVISTA, RAUL
Sofia (1948)
Women in the Night (1948)
A Life in the Balance (1955)
The Beast of Hollow Mountain (1956)
Daniel Boone, Trail Blazer (1956)
The Big Boodle (1957)
Enchanted Island (1958)
Little Savage (1959)
For the Love of Mike (1960)
Little Angel (1960)
The Important Man (1962)
The Female Soldier (1966)
Tom Thumb (1967)
Arruza (1971)
The White Rose (1972)

LAWRENCE, ELLIOTT
The Incredible Shrinking Man (1957)
The Violators (1957)

LAWRENCE, MARK
David and Lisa (1963)

LAWRENCE, MAURICE
The Barrier (The Great Barrier) (1937)

LAWRENCE, STEPHEN J.
Jennifer on My Mind (1971)

LE FEBVRE, ROBERT
Ballerina (1950)

LE MEL, GARY
The Loving Truth (1970)

LE ROUX, MAURICE
White Mane (1953)
The Red Balloon (1956)
Bitter Victory (1958)
A View from the Bridge (1962)
Naked Autumn (1963)

LE SENECHAL, RAYMOND
La Bonne Soupe (1964)
Nutty, Naughty Chateau (1964)
Friend of the Family (1965)
The Ball of Count Orgel (1970)

LEANDER, MIKE
Privilege (1967)
The Adding Machine (1969)

LECUONA, ERNESTO
Song of Mexico (1945)

LEDOUX, PATRICK
Klann/Grand Guignol (1970)

LEDRUT, JEAN
Port of Desire (1957)
The Trial (1963)

LEE, DAVID
Masque of the Red Death (1964)

LEE, LESTER
Slightly French (1949)
Traveling Saleswoman (1949)

LEFEVRE, RAYMOND
The Gendarme Gets Married (1968)
The House in the Country (1969)

LEGRAND, MICHEL
Lola (1961)
Cleo from 5 to 7 (1962)
Seven Capital Sins (1962)
The Counterfeiters of Paris (1963)
The French Game (1963)
Love Is a Ball (1963)
The Umbrellas of Cherbourg (1964)
A Woman Is a Woman (1964)
Bay of Angels (1965)
Eva (1965)
La Vie de Chateau (1965)

The Plastic Dome of Norma Jean (1966)
The Oldest Profession in the World (1967)
Pretty Polly (1967)
Young Girls of Rochefort (1967)
How to Save a Marriage and Ruin Your Life (1968)
Ice Station Zebra (1968)
Sweet November (1968)
The Thomas Crown Affair (1968)
Castle Keep (1969)
The Happy Ending (1969)
Play Dirty (1969)
Call Me Mathilde (1970)
Donkey Skin (1970)
Pieces of Dreams (1970)
Wuthering Heights (1970)
French Leave (1971)
Le Mans (1971)
A Little Sun in Cold Water (1971)
Summer of '42 (1971)
Hearth Fires (1972)
Lady Sings the Blues (1972)
The Old Maid (1972)
One Is a Lonely Number (1972)
Portnoy's Complaint (1972)

LEHTINEN, RAUNO
Summer Trail (1970)

LEIGH, WALTER
Pett and Pott (1934)
Song of Ceylon (1934)
Dawn of Iran (1936)
The Face of Scotland (1938)
The Fourth Estate (1939)
Squadron 992 (1940)

LEIPOLD, JOHN
Disputed Passage (1939)
Flying Deuces (1939)
Union Pacific (1939
The Parson of Panamint (1941)
Shut My Big Mouth (1942)
Two Yanks in Trinidad (1942)
The Daring Young Man (1943)
The Desperadoes (1943)
Good Luck, Mr. Yates (1943)
Nine Girls (1944)

LENARD, MELVIN
Ride the High Iron (1956)
Daughter of Dr. Jekyll (1957)

LEONETTI, TOMMY
Squeeze a Flower (1970)

LEPIN, A.
Chuk and Gek (1953)
Private Ivan Brovkin (1955)

LEPPARD, RAYMOND
Lord of the Flies (1963)
Alfred the Great (1969)
Laughter in the Dark (1969)

LESSE, FREDI
Bayou (1956)

LEVANT, MARK
The Woman in Green (1945)

LEVIEV, MILCHO
The Altarpiece Maker (1970)
The Eighth (1970)

LEVIN, ALVIN
Born to Speed (1947)
It's a Joke, Son! (1947)
Killer at Large (1947)
Railroaded (1947)
Too Many Winners (1947)

LEVIN, ERMA E.
The Projectionist (1970)

LEVINE, HANK
Raiders from Beneath the Sea (1965)

LEVITIN, A.
The Great Battle (1971)

LEVITIN, YURI
And Quiet Flows the Don (1957)

LEVY, LOUIS
Evensong (1934)
Alias Bulldog Drummond (1935)

Mr. Hobo (1935)
Transatlantic Tunnel (1935)
East Meets West (1936)
First a Girl (1936)
It's Love Again (1936)
Nine Days a Queen (1936)
Passing of the Third Floor Back (1936)
Secret Agent (1936)
Seven Sinners (1936)
Head Over Heels in Love (1937)
Man of Affairs (1937)
The Woman Alone (Secret Agent) (1937)
The Citadel (1938)
Haunted Honeymoon (1941)
Night Train (1941)
The Hasty Heart (1949)
Woman in a Dressing Gown (1957)

LEVY, SOL
Song of the North (1917)

LEWIS, GEORGE ALFRED
Deliverance (1919)

LEWIS, JOHN
No Sun in Venice (1958)
Odds Against Tomorrow (1959)
A Milanese Story (1962)

LEWIS, MICHAEL J.
The Madwoman of Chaillot (1969)
Julius Caesar (1970)
Upon This Rock (1970)
Unman, Wittering and Zigo (1971)

LEWIS, RICHARD
Days of Wilfred Owen (1966)

LIBAEK, SVEN
Nickel Queen (1971)

LICHTVELD, LON
Rain (1929)

LIEBMAN, JOSEPH
Light Fantastic (1963)

LIGETI, GYORGY
2001: A Space Odyssey (1968)

LILLEY, JOSEPH J.
Variety Girl (1947)
Isn't It Romantic? (1948)
Dear Wife (1949)
The Great Lover (1949)
Here Comes the Groom (1951)
The Mating Season (1951)
Sailor Beware (1951)
Road to Bali (1952)
The Caddy (1953)
Red Garters (1954)
The Seven Little Foys (1955)
Alias Jesse James (1956)
Li'l Abner (1956)
That Certain Feeling (1956)
Beau James (1957)
Paris Holiday (1958)
G.I. Blues (1960)
Blue Hawaii (1961)
Girls! Girls! Girls! (1962)
Papa's Delicate Condition (1963)
Who's Minding the Store? (1963)
The Disorderly Orderly (1964)
Paradise, Hawaiian Style (1966)
Easy Come, Easy Go (1967)
How to Commit Marriage (1969)

LINDQUIST, FREDDY
Closed Ward (1972)

LINDSAY, MORT
40 Pounds of Trouble (1962)
The Seducers (1962)
I Could Go On Singing (1963)
Stolen Hours (1963)
The Best Man (1964)

LINDUP, DAVID
Games That Lovers Play (1971)

LING, BOB
The World Is Just a "B" Movie (1971)

LING, MARC
Part of the Family (1971)

LISKA, ZDENEK
The Shop on Main Street (1965)
Marketa Lazarova (1969)
A Case for the Young Hangman (1970)
We'll Eat the Fruit of Paradise (1970)
Adrift (1971)
Jumping over Puddles Again (1971)
The Tricky Game of Love (1971)
Quite Good Chaps (1972)

LITTLE, GEORGE A.
The Garden of Allah (1917)

LLEWELLYN, DAVID
Jet Generation (1969)
Lenz (1971)

LLOYD, NORMAN
My Name Is Han (1948)

LOCKWOOD, WILLIAM H.
Weekend of Fear (1966)

LOCKYER, MALCOLM
The Little Ones (1965)
Ten Little Indians (1965)
Bang, Bang, You're Dead (1966)
Deadlier than the Male (1967)
Island of Terror (1967)
The Vengeance of Fu Manchu (1968)

LOHSKIN, ALEKSANDR
Cinerama's Russian Adventure (1966)

LONDON, MARK
First Love (1970)

LONG, JERRY
Wild, Wild Winter (1966)
The Catalina Caper (1967)

LONGELLA, FRANCO
Alone in the Streets (1956)

LOOSE, WILLIAM
Love and Kisses (1965)
Navajo Run (1966)
Tarzan and the Great River (1967)
The Big Bird Cage (1972)
The Erotic Adventures of Zorro (1972)

LORD, JON
The Last Rebel (1971)

LOTHAR, MARK
White Hell of Pitz Palu (1951)
Martin Luther (1953)

LOUIGUY
Heroes and Sinners (1959)
The Mirror Has Two Faces (1959)
Two Are Guilty (1964)

LOUSSIER, JACQUES
Life Upside Down (1965)
Dark of the Sun (1968)
Monique (1970)
Snow Job (1972)

LOWE, MUNDELL
Satan in High Heels (1962)
Billy Jack (1971)
Everything You Always Wanted to Know About Sex But Were Afraid to Ask (1972)

LOWRY, MARK
Blood Bath (1966)

LUBIN, HARRY
Caged Fury (1948)
Mr. Reckless (1948)
Waterfront at Midnight (1948)

LUCAS, LEIGHTON
Target for Tonight (1941)
Stage Fright (1950)
The Weak and the Wicked (1954)
The Dam Busters (1955)
The Son of Robin Hood (1959)
Desert Attack (1960)

LUCKY, STEPAN
Wedding without Rings (1972)

LUIS, RAFAEL
My Dearest Lady (1972)

LUTTAZZI, LELIO
It Happened in Rome (1956)
Trapped in Tangiers (1960)
The Beach Umbrella (1966)

LUTYENS, ELIZABETH
A String of Beads (1947)
The Boy Kumasenu (1951)
El Dorado (1951)
World without End (1953)
Paranoiac (1963)
The Earth Dies Screaming (1964)
Why Bother to Knock? (1964)
The Skull (1965)
Spaceflight IC-1 (1965)
The Terrornauts (1967)

LUZ, ERNST
Prudence and the Pirate (1916)
Four Horsemen of the Apocalypse (1921)
Submarine (1928)
Two Lovers (1929)

LVATOSHINSKY, B.
Taras Shevchenko (1951)

LYNCH, KENNY
Dr. Terror's House of Horrors (1965)

LYNN, CATHY
Toys Are Not for Children (1972)

McBRIDE, ROBERT
Garden of Eden (1957)

McCARTNEY, PAUL
The Family Way (1966)

MACCHI, EGISTO
The Assassination of Trotsky (1972)
Liberty (1972)

MacDERMOT, GALT
Cotton Comes to Harlem (1970)
Fortune and Men's Eyes (1971)
Golden Apples of the Sun (1971)

McDONALD, COUNTRY JOE
What Is to Be Done? (1972)

McDOWELL, JOHN HERBERT
Murder a la Mod (1968)

MACERO, TEO
End of the Road (1970)

McFARLAND, GARY
Eye of the Devil (1967)
Who Killed Mary Whats'ername? (1971)

McGUFFIE, BILL
Daleks Invade Earth 2150 A.D. (1966)
Corruption (1968)

McHUGH, JIMMY
Jack the Ripper (1960)

McINTIRE, TIM
Jeremiah Johnson (1972)

McINTOSH, TOM
The Bus Is Coming (1971)

McINTYRE, CHET
One Naked Night (1965)

McKAY, DAVID
Adventures of Barry McKenzie (1972)

MacKAY, HARPER
Cry Uncle (1971)

MACKEBEN, THEO
The Sergeant's Daughter (1955)
Bimbo the Great (1961)

MACKEY, PERCIVAL
Accused (1936)

McKUEN, ROD
Joanna (1968)
The Prime of Miss Jean Brodie (1969)

Come to Your Senses (1971)
Scandalous John (1971)

McLAUGHLAN, MURRAY
Rip Off (1971)

McPEAK, BEN
The Rowdyman (1972)

MADEIRA, PAUL
The Bachelor Party (1957)

MAGAINO, SHINICHI
To Love Again (1971)

MAGENTA, GUY
Girls of the Night (1959)

MAGIUS, FREDERICK
Pornography: Copenhagen 1970 (1970)

MAGNE, MICHEL
Any Number Can Win (1963)
Germinal (1963)
Love on a Pillow (1963)
Circle of Love (1965)
Symphony for a Massacre (1965)
Vice and Virtue (1965)
Angelique (1966)
Fantomas se Dechaine (1966)
The Sleeping Car Murder (1966)
Batouk (1967)
The Sergeant (1968)
Road to Salina (1970)
From the Boys (1971)

MAHAL, TAJ
Sounder (1972)

MAHLER, GUSTAV
The Visionaries (1968)
The Honeymoon Killers (1969)
Death in Venice (1971)
Klara Lust (1972)

MAIN SQUEEZ
The Newcomers (1972)

MAIZTEGUI, IZIDOR
Age of Infidelity (1958)

MAJEWSKI, HANS-MARTIN
No Way Back (1955)
The Confessions of Felix Krull (1957)
The Flying Classroom (1958)
The Bridge (1960)
Brainwashed (1961)
Question 7 (1961)
Escape from East Berlin (1962)
The Visit (1964)
The Ingenue (1969)

MAKAVEJEV, BOJANA
"WR"--The Mysteries of the Organism (1971)

MALERAS, CARLOS
Far from the Trees (1972)

MALLABEY, CEDRIC
Man of Evil (1948)

MALOTTE, ALBERT HAY
Dr. Cyclops (1940)
The Enchanted Forest (1945)
The Big Fisherman (1959)

MAMANGATES, NIKOS
The Golden Thing (1972)

MANCINI, HENRY
The Glenn Miller Story (1954)
The Benny Goodman Story (1955)
Congo Crossing (1956)
Rock, Pretty Baby (1956)
Man Afraid (1957)
The Big Beat (1958)
Damn Citizen (1958)
Flood Tide (1958)
Summer Love (1958)
Touch of Evil (1958)
Voice in the Mirror (1958)
The Great Imposter (1960)
High Time (1960)
Bachelor in Paradise (1961)
Breakfast at Tiffany's (1961)
Days of Wine and Roses (1962)
Experiment in Terror (1962)

Hatari! (1962)
Mr. Hobbs Takes a Vacation (1962)
Charade (1963)
Soldier in the Rain (1963)
Dear Heart (1964)
Man's Favorite Sport? (1964)
The Pink Panther (1964)
A Shot in the Dark (1964)
The Great Race (1965)
Arabesque (1966)
Moment to Moment (1966)
What Did You Do in the War, Daddy? (1966)
Gunn (1967)
Two for the Road (1967)
Wait Until Dark (1967)
The Party (1968)
Gaily, Gaily (1969)
Me, Natalie (1969)
Darling Lili (1970)
The Molly Maguires (1970)
Sunflower (1970)
The Night Visitor (1971)
Sometimes a Great Notion (1971)

MANDEL, JOHNNY
I Want to Live! (1958)
The Third Voice (1960)
Drums of Africa (1963)
The Americanization of Emily (1964)
The Sandpiper (1965)
An American Dream (1966)
Harper (1966)
The Russians Are Coming, the Russians Are Coming (1966)
Point Blank (1967)
Pretty Poison (1968)
Heaven with a Gun (1969)
Some Kind of a Nut (1969)
That Cold Day in the Park (1970)
M*A*S*H (1970)
The Man Who Had Power over Women (1970)

MANDELL, DANIEL
King Solomon of Broadway (1935)

MANHOFF, TOM
Prism (1971)

MANN, BARRY
I Never Sang for My Father (1970)

MANN, MANFRED
Venus in Furs (1970)
Christa (1971)

MANNE, SHELLY
The Proper Time (1961)
Clarence, the Cross-Eyed Lion (1965)
Young Billy Young (1969)
Trial of the Catonsville Nine (1972)

MANNINO, FRANCO
Beat the Devil (1954)
The Wayward Wife (1955)
Morgan the Pirate (1961)
Seven Seas to Calais (1963)
Gold for the Caesars (1964)
Mademoiselle de Maupin (1966)

MANSFIELD, KEITH
Loot (1971)

MANSON, EDDY
The Little Fugitive (1953)
Lovers and Lollipops (1956)
Day of the Painter (1960)
Three Bites of the Apple (1967)

MANZONI, EUGENIA TRETTI
Power (1971)

MAR, DEL
The African Queen (1951)

MARCUS, WADE
The Final Comedown (1972)

MARES, KAREL
Behold Homolka Man (1970)

MARGANO, VIRTU
Mr. President (1970)

MARINUZZI, GINO
Planet of the Vampires (1965)
White Voices (1965)
The Mandrake (La Mandragola) (1966)
Matchless (1967)

MARION, JEAN
Ma Pomme (1951)
O.S.S. 117 (1959)
A Simple Case of Money (1952)

MARKOWITZ, RICHARD
The Hot Angel (1958)
Stakeout on Dope Street (1958)
The Young Captives (1959)
The Hoodlum Priest (1961)
The Magic Sword (1962)
Cry of Battle (1963)
One Man's Way (1964)
The Bus (1965)
Bus Riley's Back in Town (1965)
Wild Seed (1965)
Ride Beyond Vengeance (1966)
A Black Veil for Lisa (1969)
Count Your Bullets (1972)

MARKS, FRANKLYN
Charlie, the Lonesome Cougar (1967)

MARLEY, WARREN
The Sidelong Glances of a Pigeon Kicker (Pigeons) (1970)

MARSHALL, JACK
The Missouri Traveler (1958)
The Rabbit Trap (1959)
Take a Giant Step (1959)
My Dog Buddy (1960)
Munster, Go Home (1966)
Tammy and the Millionaire (1967)
Kona Coast (1968)
Stay Away, Joe (1968)
Backtrack (1969)

MARTELL, PHILIP
Desperate Moment (1953)
Penny Princess (1953)
Break to Freedom (1955)
The Man in the Road (1957)
Three on a Spree (1961)
Escape by Night (1964)
Witchcraft (1964)
The Psychopath (1966)
The Viking Queen (1967)
The Anniversary (1968)

MARTELLI, AUGUSTO
The Wind's Anger (1971)

MARTELLI, CARLO
The Curse of the Mummy's Tomb (1965)
The Woman Who Wouldn't Die (1965)
The Murder Game (1966)
It (1967)
Prehistoric Women (1967)

MARTIN, GEORGE
Pulp (1972)

MARTIN, HUGH
Grandma Moses (1951)

MARTIN, RAY
Blonde Sinner (1956)
The Hoax (1972)

MARTIN, TRADE
Made for Each Other (1971)
Hail (1972)

MARX, BILL
Walk the Angry Beach (1961)
Count Yorga, Vampire (1970)
The Return of Count Yorga (1971)

MASAMITSU, TAYAMA
Those Quiet Japanese (1972)

MASCAGNI, PIETRO
L'Amica (1915)
Satanic Rhapsody (1915)

MASETTI, ENZO
Fabiola (1948)
Gelosia (1948)
Volcano (1953)

Atilla (1958)
Hercules (1959)
Hercules Unchained (1960)

MASON, JACK
Linda Be Good (1947)

MASSA, OSCAR
Malacarne (1948)

MASSARA, NATAL
Treasure Island (1972)

MATHIESON, DOCK
The Square Ring (1955)
Decision Against Time (1957)

MATHIESON, MUIR
Catherine the Great (1934)
Men Are Not Gods (1937)
Blackout (1940)
Dear Murderer (1948)
Kissenga, Man of Africa (1952)
Sailor of the King (1953)
I Am a Camera (1955)
The Intruder (1955)
The Sea Shall Not Have Them (1955)
Three Cases of Murder (1955)
Circus of Horrors (1960)
Killers of Kilimanjaro (1960)
No Place Like Homicide (1962)
Call Me Bwana (1963)
Hide and Seek (1964)
Woman of Straw (1964)

MATHIEU, ANDRE
Whispering City (1947)

MATLOVSKY, SAMUEL
Third of a Man (1962)
Birds Do It (1966)
Namu, the Killer Whale (1966)
Games (1967)
Gentle Giant (1967)

MATSUMARA, TEIZO
Cuba My Love (1969)

MATSUYAMA, TAKASHI
Rashomon (1952)

MATTES, WILLY
Guitars of Love (1958)
The Head (1961)

MATUSZKIEWICZ, JERZY
Kill the Black Sheep (1972)
A Slip-Up (1972)

MATZ, PETER
Bye Bye Braverman (1968)
Marlowe (1969)
The Revengers (1972)

MAXWELL, CHARLES
Trader Horn (1931)
Parole (1936)
White Fang (1936)
Frontier Marshal (1939)
Quiet Please, Murder (1942)
Scotland Yard Investigator (1945)

MAXWELL, THAD
Boxcar Bertha (1972)

MAY, BILLY
The Fuzzy Pink Nightgown (1957)
Sergeants 3 (1962)
Johnny Cool (1963)
Tony Rome (1967)
The Secret Life of an American Wife (1968)

MAY, HANS
The Stars Look Down (1941)
Warning to Wantons (1949)
The Tall Headlines (1952)
Never Let Me Go (1953)
Shoot First (1953)
Shadow of the Eagle (1955)
The Gypsy and the Gentleman (1958)

MAYAZUMI, TOSHIRO
The Big Wave (1962)
The Amorist (1966)
The Bible (1966)
Daphne (1966)
Reflections in a Golden Eye (1967)
The Thirst for Love (1967)
Goodbye Moscow (1968)
A Profound Longing for the Gods (1969)
The Woman I Abandoned (1969)

MAYER, JOHN
Danger Route (1968)

MAYFIELD, CURTIS
Superfly (1972)

MEAKIN, JACK
The Twonky (1953)

MEISEL, EDMUND
Potemkin (1925)
Berlin--Symphony of a Great City (1927)
Ten Days That Shook the World (1927)
October (1928)

MEISSNER, HANSON-MILDE
Maedchen in Uniform (1931)

MELACHRINO, GEORGE
Woman to Woman (1947)
Code of Scotland Yard (1948)
No Orchids for Miss Blandish (1948)
Dark Secret (1950)
Story of Shirley Yorke (1950)
The Gamma People (1956)
Odongo (1956)

MELANIE
All the Right Noises (1971)

MELICHAR, ALOIS
The Titan (1950)
Dreaming Lips (1954)
Diary of a Lover (1956)

MELIOS, DEMETRIOS
Yes, But ... (1972)

MELLE, GIL
The Andromeda Strain (1971)
The Organization (1971)
Bone (1972)
You'll Like My Mother (1972)

MELOSKI, ERKKI
Make Like a Thief (1966)

MELTON, HARRY
Gas-s-s-s (1970)

MEMPHIS SLIM
We Two France (1970)

MENDOZA, DAVID
The Big Parade (1925)
The Merry Widow (1925)
La Boheme (1926)
Ben-Hur (1926)
Don Juan (1926)
The Fire Brigade (1926)
Mare Nostrum (1926)
The Scarlet Letter (1926)
Annie Laurie (1927)
Camille (1927)
Slide, Kelly, Slide (1927)
Our Dancing Daughters (1928)
White Shadows of the South Seas (1928)
The Trail of '98 (1929)

MENDOZA-NAVA, JAIME
Fever Heat (1968)
High, Wild and Free (1968)
The Talisman (1968)
The Witchmaker (1969)
The Hard Road (1970)
The Savage Wind (1970)
The Brotherhood of Satan (1971)
The Legend of Boggy Creek (1972)

MENGEON, JEAN-PAUL
We Are All Naked (1970)

MENOTTI, GIAN-CARLO
Mr. Trull Finds Out (1940)
The Medium (1951)

MERRICK, MAHLON
Alaska Patrol (1949)
Miss Mink of 1949 (1949)
The Lawless (1950)
Passage West (1951)

THE MERRY-GO-ROUND
Cowards (1970)

MERSEY, ROBERT
Terror in the City (1965)

MERTZ, PAUL
Wagon Team (1952)

Calypso Heat Wave (1957)

METEHEN, JACQUES
The Ambassador's Daughter (1956)
Love and the Frenchwoman (1961)

MEYER, ABE
In His Steps (1936)
Yellow Cargo (1936)

MEYER, ART
Mr. Wong, Detective (1938)

MEYER, CLARKE
Part of the Family (1971)

MEYER, ERNST
North Sea (1938)

MEYER, FRIEDRICH
As the Sea Rages (1960)
The Morals of Ruth Halbfass (1972)

MEYERBEER, JACOB
The Count of St. Elmo (1951)

MICALIZZI, FRANCO
They Call Me Trinity (1971)

MICHAEL, EDUARD BEN
Faithful City (1952)

MICHAJILOV, ANGELO
Killing the Devil (1970)

MICHELET, MICHEL
The Hairy Ape (1944)
Music for Millions (1944)
Up in Mabel's Room (1944)
Voice in the Wind (1944)
The Chase (1946)
Diary of a Chambermaid (1946)
Lured (Personal Column) (1947)
Siren of Atlantis (1948)
Impact (1949)
The Man on the Eiffel Tower (1949)
Outpost in Morocco (1949)
Double Deal (1950)
Once a Thief (1950)
Tarzan's Peril (1951)
Fort Algiers (1953)
The Goddess of Love (1960)
Journey to the Lost City (1960)
Captain Sinbad (1963)

MICHELINI, LUCIANO
Arde (1971)

MIGLIORI, GABRIEL
The Bandit (O Cangaciero) (1953)
The Given Word (1962)

MIGLIORI, MARCO
Marco's Theme (1972)

MIHALY, ANDRAS
Love (1971)

MIKHELBORG, PALLE
Dagmar Is Where It's At (1972)

MILHAUD, DARIUS
The Beloved Vagabond (1916)
L'Inhumaine (1925)
Actualities (1928) (newsreels)
L'Hippocampe (1934)
Madame Bovary (1934)
The Sea Horse (1934)
Hello Everybody (1938)
The Islanders (1938)
The Private Affairs of Bel Ami (1947)
Dreams That Money Can Buy (1948)
Life Begins Tomorrow (1950)

MILLER, ROBERT WILEY
Gun Battle at Monterey (1957)

MILLER, ROBIN
Rotten to the Core (1964)

MILLS, CHARLES
On the Bowery (1957)

MILLS, JACKIE
The Windsplitter (1971)

MINFORD, SALLY
The Other Side of the Underneath (1972)

MINGUS, CHARLES
Shadows (1961)
Mingus (1968)

MISRAKI, PAUL
Claudine (1939)
Heartbeat (1946)
Manon (1949)
The Moment of Truth (1952)
Savage Triangle (1952)
The Proud and the Beautiful (1953)
Utopia (Atoll A) (1955)
Fernandel, the Dressmaker (1956)
Thunderstorm (1956)
And God Created Woman (1957)
Crazy for Love (1957)
Oasis (1957)
Please! Mr. Balzac (1957)
Senechal the Magnificent (1957)
A Dog, a Mouse and a Sputnik (1958)
Inspector Maigret (1958)
Sans Famile (1958)
Love and the Frenchwoman (1961)
Mr. Arkadin (1962)
Alphaville (1965)
Seven Guys and a Gal (1967)
A Murder Is a Murder (1972)

MIYAGAWA, YASUSHI
The Rendezvous (1972)

MIZZY, VIC
The Night Walker (1964)
A Very Special Favor (1965)
The Ghost and Mr. Chicken (1966)
The Busy Body (1967)
The Caper of the Golden Bulls (1967)
Don't Make Waves (1967)
The Perils of Pauline (1967)
The Spirit Is Willing (1967)
Did You Hear the One about the Traveling Saleslady? (1968)
The Shakiest Gun in the West (1968)
How to Frame a Figg (1971)

MOCKRIDGE, CYRIL J.
The Littlest Rebel (1935)
The Adventures of Sherlock Holmes (1939)
Day-Time Wife (1939)
Hound of the Baskervilles (1939)
Johnny Apollo (1940)
Golden Hoofs (1941)
The Man in the Trunk (1942)
Manila Calling (1942)
Moontide (1942)
Over My Dead Body (1942)
Rings on Her Fingers (1942)
That Other Woman (1942)
Happy Land (1943)
He Hired the Boss (1943)
Holy Matrimony (1943)
The Meanest Man in the World (1943)
The Ox-Bow Incident (1943)
The Big Noise (1944)
The Eve of St. Mark (1944)
Ladies in Washington (1944)
The Sullivans (1944)
Captain Eddie (1945)
Colonel Effingham's Raid (1945)
Molly and Me (1945)
Thunderhead, Son of Flicka (1945)
Claudia and David (1946)
Cluny Brown (1946)
The Dark Corner (1946)
My Darling Clementine (1946)
Sentimental Journey (1946)
Wake Up and Dream (1946)
The Late George Apley (1947)
Miracle on 34th Street (1947)
Nightmare Alley (1947)
Thunder in the Valley (1947)
Deep Waters (1948)
Green Grass of Wyoming (1948)
The Luck of the Irish (1948)
Road House (1948)
Scudda Hoo! Scudda Hay! (1948)
That Wonderful Urge (1948)
The Walls of Jericho (1948)

The Beautiful Blonde from Bashful Bend (1949)
Come to the Stable (1949)
I Was a Male War Bride (1949)
Slattery's Hurricane (1949)
Love that Brute (1950)
Stella (1950)
A Ticket to Tomahawk (1950)
As Young as You Feel (1951)
Elopement (1951)
Follow the Sun (1951)
The Frogmen (1951)
Half Angel (1951)
Let's Make It Legal (1951)
Love Nest (1951)
Mr. Belvedere Rings the Bell (1951)
The Model and the Marriage Broker (1951)
You're In the Navy Now (1951)
Dreamboat (1952)
Night without Sleep (1952)
Mister Scoutmaster (1953)
Night People (1954)
Woman's World (1954)
The Lieutenant Wore Skirts (1956)
Desk Set (1957)
Oh, Men! Oh, Women! (1957)
Will Success Spoil Rock Hunter (1957)
The Gift of Love (1958)
I Married a Woman (1958)
Rally Round the Flag, Boys! (1958)
Hound Dog Man (1959)
A Private's Affair (1959)
Thunder in the Sun (1959)
Tall Story (1960)
Wake Me When It's Over (1960)
All Hands on Deck (1961)
The Man Who Shot Liberty Valance (1962)
Donovan's Reef (1963)

MOLCHANOV, KIRILL
The Return of Vasili Bortnikov (1953)
That Dawn Should Be Peaceful (1972)

MONK, THELONIUS
Les Liaisons Dangereuses (1959)

MONN-IVERSEN, EIGIL
Let's Play Hide-and-Seek (1970)

MONTAGNINI, E.
Peddlin' in Society (1947)

MONTENEGRO, HUGO
The Ambushers (1967)
Hurry Sundown (1967)
Lady in Cement (1968)
The Wrecking Crew (1968)
Charro (1969)
The Undefeated (1969)
Viva Max (1969)
Tomorrow (1970)

MONTBRUN, R. GALLOIS
Operation X (1950)

MONTGOMERY, BRUCE
The Little Kidnappers (1954)
A Prince for Cynthia (1954)
Doctor in the House (1955)
Escapade (1955)
Doctor at Sea (1956)
Cartouche (1957)
Checkpoint (1957)
Doctor at Large (1957)
Raising a Riot (1957)
The Truth about Women (1958)
Carry on Sergeant (1959)
Carry on Nurse (1960)
Please Turn over (1960)
Beware of Children (1961)
Watch Your Stern (1961)
Doctor in Love (1962)
The Brides of Fu Manchu (1966)

MOONEY, HAL
Raid on Rommel (1971)

MOORE, DOUGLAS
Power and the Land (1940)
Village Music (1941)

MOORE, DUDLEY
Bedazzled (1967)
30 Is a Dangerous Age, Cynthia (1968)

Staircase (1969)

MORAINE, FRANCIS
The Algerian War (1972)

MORAWECK, LUCIEN
Man in the Iron Mask (1939)
International Lady (1941)
Friendly Enemies (1942)
Strange Voyage (1945)
Avalanche (1946)
The Return of Monte Cristo (1946)
16 Fathoms Deep (1948)
New Mexico (1951)

MORAZ, PATRICK
La Salamandre (1971)

MOREAU, JACKY
Blow for Blow (1972)

MOREKIS, TAKIS
Girl of the Mountains (1958)
Astero (1959)
Aunt from Chicago (1959)

MORELLI, GIUSEPPE
This Wine of Love (1948)

MORET, NEIL
Mickey (1918)

MORGAN, DEAN
Loving and Laughing (1971)

MORGAN, PIERO
Poor but Beautiful (1957)

MOROSS, JEROME
Close-Up (1948)
When I Grow Up (1951)
Seven Wonders of the World (1956)
The Sharkfighters (1956)
The Big Country (1958)
The Proud Rebel (1958)
The Jayhawkers (1959)
The Adventures of Huckleberry Finn (1960)
The Mountain Road (1960)
Five Finger Exercise (1962)
The Cardinal (1963)
The War Lord (1965)
Rachel Rachel (1968)

MORPURGO, ADOLFO
Punishment to the Traitor (1966)

MORRICONE, ENNIO
Crazy Desire (1964)
The Little Nuns (1965)
Almost a Man (1966)
The Battle of Algiers (1966)
For a Few Dollars More (1966)
Menage, Italian Style (1966)
The Return of Ringo (1966)
Too Soon to Die (1966)
China Is Near (1967)
The Girl and the General (1967)
The Good, the Bad and the Ugly (1967)
Grand Slam (1967)
Matchless (1967)
Operation Kid Brother (1967)
The Big Gundown (1968)
Danger: Diabolik (1968)
Escalation (1968)
Galileo (1968)
Guns for San Sebastian (1968)
Harem (1968)
Partner (1968)
Seven Guns for the MacGregors (1968)
Teorema (1968)
Thank You, Aunt (1968)
Up the MacGregors (1968)
Arabella (1969)
Death Rides a Horse (1969)
A Fine Pair (1969)
For a Price (1969)
A Mother's Heart (1969)
Once Upon a Time in the West (1969)
One Night at Dinner (1969)
A Quiet Place in the Country (1969)
She and He (1969)
The Sicilians (1969)
The Bird with the Crystal Plumage (1970)
Burn (1970)

The Cannibals (1970)
God with Us (1970)
Investigation of a Citizen above Suspicion (1970)
Metello (1970)
The Mercenary (1970)
The Most Beautiful Wife (1970)
Two Mules for Sister Sara (1970)
Violent City (1970)
When Women Had Tails (1970)
The Burglar (1971)
Cat O'Nine Tails (1971)
The Decameron (1971)
The Dirty Heroes (1971)
Lady Caliph (1971)
A Lizard in a Woman's Skin (1971)
Maddelena (1971)
The Red Tent (1971)
Sacco and Vanzetti (1971)
The Wind Blows Free (1971)
Without Apparent Motive (1971)
The Assassination (1972)
The Black Belly of the Tarantula (1972)
Bluebeard (1972)
Duck, You Sucker (1972)
Four Flies on Gray Velvet (1972)
The Killer (1972)
Life Is Tough, Eh Providence? (1972)
The Master and Margherita (1972)
The Secret of the Green Pins (1972)
Slap the Monster on Page One (1972)
'Tis a Pity She's a Whore (1972)
Two Seasons of Life (1972)
The Working Class Goes to Heaven (1972)

MORRIS, JOHN
The Gamblers (1969)
The 12 Chairs (1970)

MORROS, BORIS
Palm Springs (1936)
Valiant Is the Word for Carrie (1936)

MORROW, CHARLES G.
Okay Bill (1971)
Moonwalk One (1972)

MORTON, ARTHUR
The Day the Bookies Wept (1939)
The Walking Hills (1949)
Father Is a Bachelor (1950)
The Nevadan (1950)
The Harlem Globetrotters (1951)
Pushover (1954)
He Laughed Last (1956)

MOSEHOLM, ERIK
Weekend (1963)
Lenin, You Rascal You (1972)

MOTIAN, PAUL
Punishment Park (1971)

MOTTOLA, TONY
Violated (1953)

MOULLET, PATRICE
One Adventure of Billy the Kid (1971)

MOUSTAKI, GEORGES
The Man with Connections (1970)
Solo (1970)
The Five-Leaf Clover (1972)

MUCZYNSKI, ROBERT
The Great Unfenced (1964)
Yankee Painter (1964)

MULL, REGIS
Grimm's Fairy Tales for Adults (1971)

MULLENDORE, JOSEPH
New York Confidential (1955)

MULLIGAN, GERRY
A Thousand Clowns (1965)
Luv (1967)

MUNROW, DAVID
Henry VIII and His Six Wives (1972)

MURANO, MARIO FONGARO
Bang Bang (1971)

MURAVLYOV, ALEXEI
Mumu (1960)

MURRAY, JACK
Les Liaisons Dangereuses (1959)

MURRAY, LYN
The Big Night (1951)
Son of Paleface (1952)
The Girls of Pleasure Island (1953)
Here Come the Girls (1953)
The Bridges at Toko-Ri (1954)
Casanova's Big Night (1954)
To Catch a Thief (1955)
D-Day, the Sixth of June (1956)
On the Threshold of Space (1956)
Escape from Zahrain (1962)
Period of Adjustment (1962)
Come Fly with Me (1963)
Wives and Lovers (1963)
Signpost to Murder (1964)
Promise Her Anything (1966)
Rosie (1967)
Strategy of Terror (1969)
The Cockeyed Cowboys of Calico County (1970)

MYERS, STANLEY
Kaleidoscope (1966)
Ulysses (1967)
No Way to Treat a Lady (1968)
Michael Kohlhaas (1969)
Otley (1969)
Two Gentlemen Sharing (1969)
Take a Girl Like You (1970)
Tropic of Cancer (1970)
The Walking Stick (1970)
Long Ago Tomorrow (1971)
A Severed Head (1971)
Tam Lin (1971)
King, Queen, Knave (1972)
Sitting Target (1972)
Summer Lightning (1972)
X, Y and Zee (1972)

MYROW, FRED
Leo the Last (1970)
The Steagle (1971)

MYROW, JOSEPH
The Girl Next Door (1953)

NABAKOV, NICOLAS
Paulina 1800 (1972)

NAGATA, HISATO
Women of the Night (1948)

NANAGER, LOU
Happy Birthday, Davy (1970)

NAPPER, KEN
Just Like a Woman (1967)

NASCIMBENE, MARIO
Rome, 11 O'clock (1952)
It Happened in the Park (1953)
Love in the City (1953)
The Barefoot Contessa (1954)
Angela (1955)
Don Juan's Night of Love (1955)
Too Young for Love (1955)
Alexander the Great (1956)
A Farewell to Arms (1957)
That Night (1957)
The Quiet American (1958)
The Vikings (1958)
Room at the Top (1959)
Solomon and Sheba (1959)
Scent of Mystery (1960)
Sons and Lovers (1960)
Carthage in Flames (1961)
Francis of Assisi (1961)
Romanoff and Juliet (1961)
Barabbas (1962)
Constantine and the Cross (1962)
The Happy Thieves (1962)
Jessica (1962)
Joseph and His Brethren (1962)
Light in the Piazza (1962)
Swordsman of Siena (1962)
The Golden Arrow (1964)

Kiss the Girls and Make Them Die (1966)
One Million Years, B.C. (1966)
Doctor Faustus (1967)
Summit (1968)
The Vengeance of She (1968)
Gradina (1970)
Night of the Counting Years (1970)
When Dinosaurs Ruled the Earth (1970)
The Creatures the World Forgot (1971)
Socrates (1971)

NASCIMENTO, MILTON
Tostao--The King of Football (1970)

NATHAN, JACK
The Abominable Dr. Phibes (1971)

NAUSHAD
A Handful of Grain (1959)

NELSON, OLIVER
Death of a Gunfighter (1969)
Skullduggery (1970)
Zigzag (1970)

NERO, PETER
Sunday in New York (1963)

NEUMANN, ELRIK
The Doll (1964)

NEUMANN, GUNTHER
The Berliner (1952)

NEW HOPE
Red, White and Blue (1971)

NEWLEY, ANTHONY
Can Heironymus Merkin Ever Forget Mercy Humppe and Find True Happiness? (1969)

NEWMAN, ALFRED
Arrowsmith (1931)
Kiki (1931)
Reaching for the Moon (1931)
Street Scene (1931)
Mr. Robinson Crusoe (1932)
Advice to the Lovelorn (1933)
Broadway Thru a Keyhole (1933)
The Affairs of Cellini (1934)
Bulldog Drummond Strikes Back (1934)
The Cat's Paw (1934)
The Count of Monte Cristo (1934)
Gallant Lady (1934)
House of Rothschild (1934)
The Last Gentleman (1934)
Looking for Trouble (1934)
Moulin Rouge (1934)
Nana (1934)
Our Daily Bread (1934)
We Live Again (1934)
Barbary Coast (1935)
Call of the Wild (1935)
Cardinal Richelieu (1935)
Dark Angel (1935)
Metropolitan (1935)
Les Miserables (1935)
She (1935)
Splendor (1935)
Come and Get It (1936)
Dodsworth (1936)
The Gay Desperado (1936)
Ramona (1936)
These Three (1936)
Beloved Enemy (1937)
History Is Made at Night (1937)
When You're in Love (1937)
Woman Chases Man (1937)
You Only Live Once (1937)
Adventures of Marco Polo (1938)
The Cowboy and the Lady (1938)
Trade Winds (1938)
Barricade (1939)
Beau Geste (1939)
Drums Along the Mohawk (1939)
Gunga Din (1939)
The Rains Came (1939)
The Real Glory (1939)
They Shall Have Music (1939)
Wuthering Heights (1939)

Young Mr. Lincoln (1939)
The Blue Bird (1940)
Brigham Young (1940)
Foreign Correspondent (1940)
The Grapes of Wrath (1940)
The Hunchback of Notre Dame (1940)
Lillian Russell (1940)
The Mark of Zorro (1940)
Maryland (1940)
They Knew What They Wanted (1940)
Tin Pan Alley (1940)
Vigil in the Night (1940)
Young People (1940)
Belle Starr (1941)
Charley's Aunt (1941)
How Green Was My Valley (1941)
Hudson's Bay (1941)
Man Hunt (1941)
The Black Swan (1942)
Girl Trouble (1942)
Life Begins at 8:30 (1942)
Orchestra Wives (1942)
The Pied Piper (1942)
Prelude to War (1942)
Roxie Hart (1942)
Son of Fury (1942)
Song of the Islands (1942)
Springtime in the Rockies (1942)
Ten Gentlemen from West Point (1942)
This Above All (1942)
To the Shores of Tripoli (1942)
Claudia (1943)
Heaven Can Wait (1943)
The Moon Is Down (1943)
My Friend Flicka (1943)
Song of Bernadette (1943)
The Keys of the Kingdom (1944)
The Purple Heart (1944)
Sunday Dinner for a Soldier (1944)
Wilson (1944)
A Bell for Adano (1945)
Leave Her to Heaven (1945)
A Royal Scandal (1945)
A Tree Grows in Brooklyn (1945)
Dragonwyck (1946)
Margie (1946)
The Razor's Edge (1946)
Captain from Castile (1947)
Gentleman's Agreement (1947)
Chicken Every Sunday (1948)
Cry of the City (1948)
Fury at Furnace Creek (1948)
The Iron Curtain (1948)
A Letter to Three Wives (1948)
Sitting Pretty (1948)
The Snake Pit (1948)
Unfaithfully Yours (1948)
Yellow Sky (1948)
Down to the Sea in Ships (1949)
Mr. Belvedere Goes to College (1949)
Mother Is a Freshman (1949)
Pinky (1949)
Prince of Foxes (1949)
Thieves' Highway (1949)
Twelve O'Clock High (1949)
All About Eve (1950)
The Big Lift (1950)
For Heaven's Sake (1950)
The Gunfighter (1950)
No Way Out (1950)
Panic in the Streets (1950)
When Willie Comes Marching Home (1950)
David and Bathsheba (1951)
Fourteen Hours (1951)
People Will Talk (1951)
Take Care of My Little Girl (1951)
Kangaroo (1952)
O. Henry's Full House (1952)
The Prisoner of Zenda (1952)
Wait Till the Sun Shines, Nellie (1952)
What Price Glory? (1952)
How to Marry a Millionaire (1953)
The President's Lady (1953)
The Robe (1953)
Demitrius and the Gladiators (1954)
Desiree (1954)
The Egyptian (1954)
Hell and High Water (1954)
Love Is a Many-Splendored

Thing (1955)
A Man Called Peter (1955)
The Seven Year Itch (1955)
Anastasia (1956)
Bus Stop (1956)
The Bravados (1958)
A Certain Smile (1958)
The Best of Everything (1959)
The Diary of Anne Frank (1959)
The Pleasure of His Company (1961)
The Counterfeit Traitor (1962)
How the West Was Won (1962)
The Greatest Story Ever Told (1965)
Nevada Smith (1966)
Firecreek (1968)
Airport (1970)

NEWMAN, EMIL
Reunion (1936)
Rise and Shine (1941)
Tall, Dark and Handsome (1941)
Berlin Correspondent (1942)
The Loves of Edgar Allan Poe (1942)
The Magnificent Dope (1942)
The Man Who Wouldn't Die (1942)
Time to Kill (1942)
Dixie Dugan (1943)
Tonight We Raid Calais (1943)
Pin-Up Girl (1944)
Bedside Manner (1945)
Nob Hill (1945)
Behind Green Lights (1946)
Rendezvous 24 (1946)
Texas, Brooklyn and Heaven (1948)
Guilty of Treason (1949)
Cry Danger (1951)
The Lady Says No (1951)
The 13th Letter (1951)
Big Jim McLain (1952)
The Captive City (1952)
Japanese War Bride (1952)
Just for You (1952)
Rancho Notorious (1952)
The San Francisco Story (1952)
Hondo (1953)
Island in the Sky (1953)
99 River Street (1953)
The Steel Lady (1953)
War Paint (1953)
Beachhead (1954)
The Mad Magician (1954)
Ring of Fear (1954)
Southwest Passage (1954)
The Naked Street (1955)
Chicago Confidential (1957)
Death in Small Doses (1957)
The Iron Sheriff (1957)
Unwed Mother (1958)
Riot in Juvenile Prison (1959)
The Great Sioux Massacre (1965)

NEWMAN, HERB
Death Has No Friends (1970)

NEWMAN, LIONEL
The Street with No Name (1948)
Father Was a Fullback (1949)
An American Guerrilla in the Philippines (1950)
Cheaper by the Dozen (1950)
The Jackpot (1950)
Mister 880 (1950)
Mother Didn't Tell Me (1950)
Where the Sidewalk Ends (1950)
Belles on Their Toes (1952)
Bloodhounds of Broadway (1952)
Deadline, USA (1952)
Diplomatic Courier (1952)
Don't Bother to Knock (1952)
Lydia Bailey (1952)
Monkey Business (1952)
The Outcasts of Poker Flat (1952)
The Pride of St. Louis (1952)
Red Skies of Montana (1952)
Return of the Texan (1952)
We're Not Married (1952)
A Blueprint for Murder (1953)
City of Bad Men (1953)
Dangerous Crossing (1953)
The Farmer Takes a Wife (1953)
The Kid from Left Field (1953)

Man in the Attic (1953)
Powder River (1953)
The Gambler from Natchez (1954)
Gorilla at Large (1954)
Princess of the Nile (1954)
The Raid (1954)
River of No Return (1954)
The Rocket Man (1954)
Siege at Red River (1954)
Three Young Texans (1954)
House of Bamboo (1955)
How to Be Very, Very Popular (1955)
The Racers (1955)
Violent Saturday (1955)
White Feather (1955)
The Killer Is Loose (1956)
A Kiss Before Dying (1956)
The Last Wagon (1956)
Love Me Tender (1956)
The Proud Ones (1956)
Bernardine (1957)
Kiss Them for Me (1957)
Mardi Gras (1958)
Sing, Boy, Sing (1958)
Compulsion (1959)
Say One for Me (1959)
Let's Make Love (1960)
North to Alaska (1960)
Move Over, Darling (1963)
The Pleasure Seekers (1964)
Do Not Disturb (1965)
The Salzburg Connection (1972)

NEWMAN, RANDY
Cold Turkey (1971)

NICHOLS, LEO
The Hills Run Red (1967)

NICOLAI, BRUNO
Land Raiders (1969)
99 Women (1969)
Eugenie--The Story of Her Journey into Perversion (1970)
Adios Sabata (1971)
Count Dracula (1971)
The Night Evelyn Came Out of the Grave (1972)

NICOLOSI, ROBERTO
The Warrior and the Slave Girl (1959)
The Giant of Marathon (1960)
The White Warrior (1961)
Blood on the Balcony (1964)

NILSSON (HARRY)
Skidoo (1968)

NITZSCHE, JACK
Village of the Giants (1965)
Performance (1970)
Greaser's Palace (1972)

NOEL, ART
The Hill (1965)

NORDGREN, ERIK
Smiles of a Summer Night (1957)
Face of Fire (1959)
The Magician (1959)
The Virgin Spring (1960)
The Island (1966)

NORDHEIM, ARNE
One Day in the Life of Ivan Denisovich (1971)

NORIEGA, GUILLERMO
Mictlan (1970)

NORMAN, MONTY
House of Fright (1961)
Dr. No (1963)

NORRIS, E. G.
The American Beauty (1916)

NORTH, ALEX
Heart of Spain (1937)
People of the Cumberland (1937)
A Better Tomorrow (1945)
Death of a Salesman (1951)
A Streetcar Named Desire (1951)
A Member of the Wedding (1952)
Les Miserables (1952)
Pony Soldier (1952)
Viva Zapata! (1952)
The American Road (1953)

Desiree (1954)
Go, Man, Go (1954)
I'll Cry Tomorrow (1955)
Man with a Gun (1955)
The Rose Tattoo (1955)
Unchained (1955)
The Bad Seed (1956)
Four Girls in Town (1956)
The King and Four Queens (1956)
The Rainmaker (1956)
Hot Spell (1958)
The Long Hot Summer (1958)
South Seas Adventure (1958)
Stage Struck (1958)
The Sound and the Fury (1959)
The Wonderful Country (1959)
Spartacus (1960)
The Misfits (1961)
Sanctuary (1961)
All Fall Down (1962)
The Children's Hour (1962)
Cleopatra (1963)
Cheyenne Autumn (1964)
The Outrage (1964)
The Agony and the Ecstasy (1965)
Who's Afraid of Virginia Woolf? (1966)
The Devil's Brigade (1968)
The Shoes of the Fisherman (1968)
A Dream of Kings (1969)
Hard Contract (1969)
Willard (1971)
Pocket Money (1972)

NORTON, ED
The Ra Expeditions (1972)

NOVAK, JAN
The Stolen Air-Ship (1969)

OCHOA, ARMANDO GUEVARA
The Revolutionaries (1970)

ODERMAN, STUART
Chaplinesque, My Life and Hard Times (1972)

OHMAN, PHIL
Captain Caution (1940)
Dick Tracy vs. Cueball (1946)
Million Dollar Weekend (1948)

O'HORGAN, TOM
Futz (1969)
Alex in Wonderland (1970)

OKI, MASAO
Vietnam (1972)

OLAH, TIBERIU
The Death of Ipu (1972)
The Power and the Truth (1972)

OLEA, ANTONIO PEREZ
Murieta (1965)
The Ancines Woods (1970)
Canticle (1970)
Long Live the Bride and Groom (1970)
Goodbye, Stork, Goodbye (1971)

OLIVEIRA, LOUIS
The Wild Pack (1972)

OLIVER, JACQUES
The Apple (1969)

OLIVER, TOMMY
Calliope (1971)

OLIVIERO, NINO
Women of the World (1963)
Mondo Pazzo (1965)

OLMAN, ABE
The Red Circle (1916)

OMORI, SEITARO
The Phantom Horse (1956)

ORANSKY, V.
The Magic Horse (1941)

ORGERMANN, KLAUS
Bimbo the Great (1961)

O'RIADA, SEAN
Young Cassidy (1965)

ORLANDI, NORA
Johnny Yuma (1967)
The Sweet Body of Deborah (1969)
The Strange Vice of Signora Ward (1971)

ORNADEL, CYRIL
I Can't ... I Can't (1969)
Subterfuge (1969)
Cool It, Carol (1970)

ORPIN, ROBERT G.
The Abductors (1972)
A Place Called Today (1972)

ORR, BUXTON
The Haunted Strangler (1958)
First Man into Space (1959)
Suddenly Last Summer (1959)
Doctor Blood's Coffin (1961)
The Snake Woman (1961)
Corridors of Blood (1963)
The Eyes of Annie Jones (1964)
Walk a Tightrope (1964)

ORTEGA, SERGIO
Long Live Life (1969)
The Jackal of Nahueltoro (1970)

ORTOLANI, RIZ
The Easy Life (1963)
Mondo Cane (1963)
Women of the World (1963)
The Seventh Dawn (1964)
The Glory Guys (1965)
The Yellow Rolls Royce (1965)
Africa Addio (1966)
Maya (1966)
Spy in Your Eye (1966)
The Spy with a Cold Nose (1966)
Lightning Bolt (1967)
Red Dragon (1967)
Woman Times Seven (1967)
Anzio (1968)
Bandits in Milan (1968)
The Biggest Bundle of Them All (1968)
The Bliss of Mrs. Blossom (1968)
Buona Sera, Mrs. Campbell (1968)
The Chastity Belt (1968)
Sardinia: Ransom (1968)
Day of Anger (1969)
The Fight for Rome (1969)
Lady Hamilton (1969)
Tenderly (1969)
The McKenzie Break (1970)
Madron (1970)
Confessions of a Police Commissioner to the District Attorney (1971)
The Hunting Party (1971)
Say Hello to Yesterday (1971)
The Statue (1971)
The Dead Are Alive (1972)
One on Top of the Other (1972)
The Puzzle of the Silver Half-Moon (1972)
The Valachi Papers (1972)

OSBORNE, JESSE
Black Girl (1972)

OSBORNE, TONY
A Weekend with Lulu (1961)
The Secret Door (1964)
Seaside Swingers (1965)

OVCHINNIKOV, VYECHESLAV
Violin and Roller (1961)
War and Peace (1968)

OWEN, REG
Murder Reported (1958)
A Coming-Out Party (1962)
Payroll (1962)

PAGE, GENE
Brewster McCloud (1970)
Blacula (1972)

PAICH, MARTY
The Swinger (1966)

PAILLAUD, JEAN
The Suitor (1963)
As Long As You Are Healthy (1966)

PAKEMAN, KENNETH
A Boy, a Girl and a Bike (1949)

PALESTER, ROMAN
Border Street (1948)

PANUFNIK, ANDRZEJ
Altar Masterpiece (1952)

PAPATHANASSIOU, VANGELIS
Sex Power (1970)
Hello Jerusalem (1972)

PARAMOR, NORRIE
Expresso Bongo (1960)
The Frightened City (1962)
Play It Cool (1963)
Doctor in Distress (1964)
Young and Willing (1964)
My Lover, My Son (1970)

PARES, PHILIPPE
Le Million (1931)

PARIS, ALEXANDER
Georgy Girl (1966)

PARKER, CLIFTON
Western Approaches (1944)
Children on Trial (1945)
Johnny Frenchman (1945)
Blanche Fury (1947)
The Smugglers (1948)
Blue Lagoon (1949)
Treasure Island (1950)
The Wooden Horse (1950)
Gift Horse (1952)
The Sword and the Rose (1953)
Hell Below Zero (1954)
A Day to Remember (1955)
The Gentle Touch (1957)
Tarzan and the Lost Safari (1957)
Campbell's Kingdom (1958)
Curse of the Damned (1958)
Harry Black and the Tiger (1958)
The Secret Place (1958)
The House of the Seven Hawks (1959)
Sink the Bismark! (1960)
The 39 Steps (1960)
Circle of Deception (1961)
Desert Patrol (1961)
Scream of Fear (1961)
The Secret of Monte Carlo (1961)
Damn the Defiant! (1962)

PARKER, JOHN
The Further Perils of Laurel and Hardy (1967)

PARKS, GORDON
The Learning Tree (1969)
Shaft's Big Score (1972)

PARLOR, FAIRFIELD
Eyewitness (1970)

PARMEGIANI, BERNARD
I, You, They (1969)
The Suns of Easter Island (1972)

PARNELLO, JOE
Cactus in the Snow (1972)

PARTHA-SARATHY, M. A.
The River (1951)

PAS, CARLO
Dead of Summer (1970)
Dorian Gray (1970)

PASSOLINI, PIER PAOLO
The Decameron (1971)

PATUCCHI, DANIELE
Double by Half (1972)

PAUL, ANDREE
Q-Bec My Love (1970)

PAUL, EDWARD
The Bamboo Saucer (1968)

PAXTON, GLENN
When the Legends Die (1972)

PEARSON, JOHNNY
The Jokers (1967)

PEASLEE, RICHARD
Marat/Sade (1967)
Tell Me Lies (1968)

PEDERSSEN, GUY
Celeste (1970)

PEGURI, GINO
A Woman on Fire (1970)

PELLETIER, JEAN CLAUDE
Beyond Love and Evil (Philosophy of the Boudoir) (1971)

PELOSI, DON
The Hill (1965)

PENDERECKI, KRZYSTOV
I Love You, I Love You (1968)

PEREZ, JAMES
Women of Doom (1972)

PERISCH, GEORGE
Exile Express (1939)

PERJANIK, MIKE
Private Collection (1972)

PERKINS, CARL
Little Fauss and Big Halsy (1970)

PERKINS, FRANK
Glory (1956)
The Couch (1962)
Gypsy (1962)
Mary, Mary (1963)
Palm Springs Weekend (1963)
The Incredible Mr. Limpet (1964)
Ready for the People (1964)

PERKINSON, COLERIDGE-TAYLOR
The McMasters (1970)
Together for Days (1972)

PERL, LOTHAR
This Land Is Mine (1943)

PERRON, JACQUES
The Christmas Martian (1971)

PERROTIN, JACQUELINE
The Deserted Piazza (1971)

PES, CARLO
Sweet Kisses and Languid Caresses (1970)

PETERS, WILLIAM FREDERICK
Way Down East (1920)
Orphans of the Storm (1922)
When Knighthood Was in Flower (1922)
Enemies of Women (1923)
Little Old New York (1923)
Under the Red Robe (1923)
Yolande (1924)
Four Feathers (1929)
Hungarian Rhapsody (1929)
Under the Red Robe (1937)

PETITGIRARD, LAURETT
Apocalypse (1970)

PETRASSI, GEOFREDO
A Geometry Lesson (1947)
Bitter Rice (1949)
Under the Olive Tree (1951)
Family Diary (1963)

PETRIDES, PETRO
Cyprus Is an Island (1945)

PETROV, ANDREI
Banked Fires (1972)

PETROVIC, BOSCO
The Eleventh Commandment (1970)

PETROVICS, EMIL
The Legend About the Death and Resurrection of Two Young Men (1972)

PHILIPS, STU
Mad Dog Coll (1961)
The Man from the Diner's Club (1963)
Hell's Angels on Wheels (1967)
Angels from Hell (1968)
The Name of the Game Is Kill (1968)
Follow Me (1969)
The Gay Deceivers (1969)
Run, Angel, Run (1969)
2,000 Years Later (1969)
Beyond the Valley of the Dolls (1970)

The Losers (1970)
Red, White and Black (1970)
Jud (1971)
The Seven Minutes (1971)
Simon, King of the Witches (1971)

PHILIPS, JOHN
Myra Breckinridge (1970)

PHILLIPPE-GERARD, M.
Bebert et le Omnibus (1966)

PHILLIPS, WOOLF
Diamond Safari (1958)

PICCIONI, PIERO
Il Mondo le Condanna (1952)
La Spiaggia (1953)
Guendalina (1956)
I Magliari (1959)
I Tartassati (1959)
Tempest (1959)
Love a la Carte (1960)
From a Roman Balcony (1961)
Notte Brava (1961)
The World by Night (1961)
Bell 'Antonio (1962)
The World by Night #2 (1962)
The Duel of the Titans (1963)
Mafioso (1963)
To Bed ... or Not to Bed (1963)
The Moment of Truth (1965)
The Tenth Victim (1965)
The Man Who Laughs (1966)
Minnesota Clay (1966)
Thank You Very Much (1966)
More Than a Miracle (1967)
The Stranger (1967)
Be Sick ... It's Free (1968)
Bora Bora (1968)
An Italian in America (1968)
The Young Tigers (1968)
Camille 2000 (1969)
Help Me, My Love (1969)
Kenner (1969)
The Witches (1969)
Let's Have a Riot (1970)
Youth March (1970)
The Deserter (1971)
Jack the Ripper (1971)
The Light at the Edge of the World (1971)
Marta (1971)
Puppet on a Chain (1971)
So Long Gulliver (1971)
The Enrico Mattei Affair (1972)
The Girl from Australia (1972)
Mimi, the Metalworker (1972)
The Scientific Cardplayer (1972)

PINA, ANGEL OLIVER
God Forgives--I Don't (1969)

PINILLA, ENRIQUE
Mirage (1972)

PINK FLOYD
The Valley (1972)

PINNE, PETER
A City's Child (1971)

PINTOFF, ERNEST
The Violinist (1959)

PIRONKOV, SIMEON
Stars (1958)
Sun and Shadow (1961)
The Peach Thief (1965)
The Goat Horn (1972)

PITTALUGA, GUSTAVO
Mexican Bus Ride (Subida Al Cielo) (1954)

PITTS, CLAY
The Female Animal (1970)
From Ear to Ear (1971)

PLEIS, JACK
Diary of a Bachelor (1964)

PLESSAS, MIMAS
Abuse of Authority (1971)
What Did You Do in the War, Thanassi? (1971)
Thanassi Get Your Gun (1972)

PLUMB, EDWARD
The Woman Who Came Back (1945)

POINAREFF, MICHEL
It Only Happens to Others (1971)

POITEVIN, ROBBY
The Hired Killer (1967)

POLLARD, JIM
Right On (1970)

POLNAREFF, MICHEL
Delusions of Grandeur (1971)

PONCE, MANUEL M.
Loves of Carmen (1927)
Viva Zapata! (1952)

PONTECORVO, GILLO
The Battle of Algiers (1966)

POPOV, GABRIEL
Chapeyev (1934)
An Unfinished Story (1955)

POPP, ANDRE
Papa, the Little Boats (1971)

POSEGGA, HANS
No Shooting Time for Foxes (1966)

POSTON, B.
Manson (1972)

POTENZA, FRANCO
Fire (1968)

POUFET, LEO
The Passion of Joan of Arc (1928)

PRADO, JUAN
The Hiding Places (1970)

PRESSER, GABOR
Carlotta (1971)
Little Birdie (1971)
The Birds (1972)

PREVERT, JACQUES
Aubervillers (1947)

PREVIN, ANDRE
Border Incident (1949)
Challenge to Lassie (1949)
Scene of the Crime (1949)
Tension (1949)
Dial 1119 (1950)
Kim (1950)
The Outriders (1950)
Shadow on the Wall (1950)
Cause for Alarm (1951)
The Girl Who Had Everything (1953)
Give the Girl a Break (1953)
Bad Day at Black Rock (1954)
The Catered Affair (1956)
The Fastest Gun Alive (1956)
Invitation to the Dance (1956)
Designing Woman (1957)
Hot Summer Night (1957)
House of Numbers (1957)
Silk Stockings (1957)
Elmer Gantry (1960)
The Subterraneans (1960)
Who Was That Lady? (1960)
All in a Night's Work (1961)
One Two Three (1961)
The Four Horsemen of the Apocalypse (1962)
Long Day's Journey into Night (1962)
Two for the Seesaw (1962)
Irma La Douce (1963)
Dead Ringer (1964)
Goodbye Charlie (1964)
Kiss Me Stupid (1964)
Inside Daisy Clover (1965)
The Fortune Cookie (1966)

PREVIN, CHARLES
The Magnificent Brute (1936)
Two in a Crowd (1936)
Three Smart Girls (1937)
When Love Is Young (1937)
Wings over Honolulu (1937)
Midnight Intruder (1938)
Rio (1939)
The Bank Dick (1940)
It's a Date (1940)
Seven Sinners (1940)
The Invisible Woman (1941)

Man-Made Monster (1941)
Model Wife (1941)
Nice Girl? (1941)

PREVITALI, FERNANDO
Tragic Hunt (1948)
Sensualita (The Barefoot Savage) (1953)

PREVOST, HEINZ
Intermezzo (1939)

PREZAS, ANDREAS
Diamonds on Your Naked Body (1972)

PRINCE, ROBERT
Strangers in the City (1962)
A Great Big Thing (1968)

PRODROMIDES, JEAN
Marcel Marceau "In the Park" (1956)
Stowaway in the Sky (1960)
Blood and Roses (1961)
The Bears (1965)

PROFES, ANTON
The Story of Vickie (1958)
Forever My Love (1962)

PROHASKA, MILJANKO
Handcuffs (1970)

PROKOFIEV, SERGEI
The Czar Wants to Sleep (1934)
Alexander Nevsky (1938)
Kotovski (1942)
Lermontov (1943)
Ivan the Terrible (Part I) (1944)
Ivan the Terrible (Part II) (1946)
The Ballet of Romeo and Juliet (1955)
Romeo (1962)

PROVANI, NICHOLA
In the Name of the Father (1971)
N. P. (1971)

PURPORA, JODE
Stella da Falla (1972)

PUSHKOV, BENEDICT
Once There Was a Girl (1945)
The Miracle of Dr. Petrov (1947)
Russian Ballerina (1947)

PUSHKOV, V.
Peasants (1935)
Adventures of Artyomka (1956)

RAAB, LEONID
Follow Me Quietly (1949)

RABAUD, M.
Miracle of the Wolves (1925)

RABEN, PEER
The American Soldier (1970)
Gods of Pestilence (1970)
Recruits in Ingolstadt (1971)
Whity (1971)

RACHMANINOFF, SERGE
Romeo and Juliet (1968)

RADIC, DUSAN
The Long Ships (1964)
Genghis Khan (1965)
Hot Years (1966)
Downstream from the Sun (1969)

RADIN, OSCAR
Mad Love (1936)

RAEBURN, BOYD
Island Woman (1958)

RAGLAND, ROBERT O.
The Thing with Two Heads (1972)

RAINGER, RALPH
Song of Songs (1933)
Bolero (1934)

RAJTERIC-KRAUS, VLADIMIR
The Battle of the Neretva (1969)

RAKSIN, DAVID
Marked Woman (1937)
The Mighty Treve (1937)
Frontier Marshal (1939)
Dr. Renault's Secret (1942)
Manila Calling (1942)
On the Sunny Side (1942)
The Postman Didn't Ring (1942)
Powder Town (1942)
Through Different Eyes (1942)
The Undying Monster (1942)
Whispering Ghosts (1942)
Who Is Hope Schuyler? (1942)
City without Men (1943)
Something to Shout About (1943)
Laura (1944)
Tampico (1944)
Don Juan Quilligan (1945)
Fallen Angel (1945)
Where Do We Go from Here? (1945)
Smoky (1946)
Daisy Kenyon (1947)
Forever Amber (1947)
The Homestretch (1947)
The Secret Life of Walter Mitty (1947)
Apartment for Peggy (1948)
Force of Evil (1948)
Whirlpool (1949)
Grounds for Marriage (1950)
A Lady without Passport (1950)
The Magnificent Yankee (1950)
The Next Voice You Hear (1950)
The Reformer and the Redhead (1950)
Right Cross (1950)
Across the Wide Missouri (1951)
It's a Big Country (1952)
Kind Lady (1951)
The Man with the Cloak (1951)
The Bad and the Beautiful (1952)
Carrie (1952)
The Girl in White (1952)
Pat and Mike (1952)
Apache (1954)
Suddenly (1954)
A Unicorn in the Garden (1954)
The Big Combo (1955)
Al Capone (1956)
Bigger Than Life (1956)
Hilda Crane (1956)
Jubal (1956)
Seven Wonders of the World (1956)
Gunsight Ridge (1957)
Man on Fire (1957)
Until They Sail (1957)
The Vintage (1957)
Separate Tables (1958)
Twilight for the Gods (1958)
Pay or Die (1960)
Too Late Blues (1962)
Two Weeks in Another Town (1962)
Invitation to a Gunfighter (1964)
The Patsy (1964)
Love Has Many Faces (1965)
Sylvia (1965)
A Big Hand for the Little Lady (1966)
Will Penny (1968)
Glass Houses (1970)
What's the Matter with Helen? (1971)

RALKE, DON
C'Mon, Let's Live a Little (1967)

RALSTON, ALFRED
Oh, What a Lovely War (1969)
Young Winston (1972)

RAMANATHAN, DAKSHINAMOORTHY G.
The Jungle (1952)

RAMIN, SID
Stiletto (1969)

RAMIREZ, ARIEL
The Knight of the Sword (1970)

RAMONE, PHIL
The Happiness Cage (1972)

RANDI, DON
Bloody Mama (1970)

Up in the Cellar (1970)
J. W. Coop (1971)

RANKI, GYORGY
Merry-Go-Round (1956)
Trip Around My Cranium (1970)

RAO, VIJAY RAGHAVA
The Interview (1972)

RAPEE, ERNO
The Iron Horse (1924)
The Last Man on Earth (1924)
Film Record of the Eucharistic Congress (1926)
Seventh Heaven (1926)
Sunrise (1926)
What Price Glory? (1926)
Fazil (1928)
Four Sons (1928)
Red Dance (1928)
Street Angel (1928)
Mother Machree (1929)
Going Wild (1930)
Old English (1930)
A Connecticut Yankee (1931)
Over the Hill (1931)
Back Door to Heaven (1939)

RAPOSO, JOE
The Possession of Joel Delaney (1972)
Savages (1972)

RASKIN, RUBY
Valley of the Dragons (1961)
The Battle of the Bulge--The Brave Rifles (1966)

RATHAUS, KAROL
Loves of a Dictator (1935)

RATHBURN, ELDON
Nobody Waved Goodbye (1965)
La Grand Rock (1969)

RAUBER, FRANCOIS
Tintin and the Sun Temple (1970)

RAUCHBERGER, M.
Lone White Sail (1937)

RAVEL, MAURICE
Anatomy of the Act of Love (1970)

RAWLINS, TONY
Here Comes Every Body (1972)

RAWSTHORNE, ALAN
Burma Victory (1945)
The Captive Heart (1946)
Saraband (1948)
The Dancing Fleece (1950)
Waters of Time (1951)
Ivory Hunter (Where No Vultures Fly) (1952)
The Cruel Sea (1953)
The Drawings of Leonardo Da Vinci (1954)
West of Zanzibar (1954)
Lease of Life (1955)
The Man Who Never Was (1956)
Floods of Fear (1959)

RAY, SATYAJIT
Kanchehkungha (1966)
Nayak (1966)
Shakespeare Wallah (1966)
Days and Nights in the Forest (1970)
The Adversary (1971)

REBAGLIATTI, CLAUDIO
The Revolutionaries (1970)

REDD, FREDDIE
The Connection (1962)

REDJEPOV, REDJEP
The Daughter-in-Law (1972)

REECE, DIZZY
Nowhere to Go (1959)

REED, LES
The Bushbaby (1970)
One More Time (1970)

REIDL, JOSEPH ANTON
Adam 2 (1969)

REISENSTEIN, FRANZ
The Mummy (1959)
Circus of Horrors (1960)

REMARQUE, FRANCES
The Counterfeiters of Paris (1963)

RENOIR, JEAN
Liliom (1933)

REVAELTAS, SILVESTRE
The Wave (1935)

REVEL, HARRY
The Old-Fashioned Way (1934)

RIBERO, TITO
Dark River (1953)
Simply Maria (1970)
Those Crazy Years (1970)

RICH, FREDDIE
Torpedo Boat (1942)
Wildcat (1942)
Wrecking Crew (1942)
Alaska Highway (1943)
Jack London (1943)
Stagedoor Canteen (1943)
Submarine Alert (1943)
A Wave, a Wac and a Marine (1944)
A Walk in the Sun (1946)

RICHARDS, BOBBY
The Smashing Bird I Used to Know (1969)

RICHARDS, JOHNNY
Gold Fever (1952)

RICHTER, HANS
8 X 8 (1957)

RIDDLE, NELSON
Johnny Concho (1956)
Lisbon (1956)
Merry Andrew (1958)
St. Louis Blues (1958)
A Hole in the Head (1959)
Li'l Abner (1959)
Ocean's 11 (1960)
Lolita (1962)
Come Blow Your Horn (1963)
Four for Texas (1963)
Paris When It Sizzles (1964)
Robin and the 7 Hoods (1964)
What a Way to Go! (1964)
Harlow (1965)
Marriage on the Rocks (1965)
A Rage to Live (1965)
Red Line 7000 (1965)
Batman (1966)
El Dorado (1967)
The Great Bank Robbery (1969)
The Maltese Bippy (1969)

RIEDEL, GEORGE
The Face of War (1963)
Swedish Wedding Night (1965)
Nana (1971)

RIESENFELD, HUGO
Carmen (1915)
Joan the Woman (1917)
The Blue Bird (1920)
Humoresque (1920)
The Covered Wagon (1923)
The Ten Commandments (1923)
Beggar on Horseback (1925)
Grass (1925)
Madame Sans-Gene (1925)
Pony Express (1925)
The Vanishing American (1925)
The Wanderer (1925)
Beau Geste (1926)
The Flaming Frontier (1926)
Old Ironsides (1926)
The Prince of Pilsen (1926)
The Rough Riders (1926)
The Sorrows of Satan (1926)
The Volga Boatman (1926)
King of Kings (1927)
Les Miserables (1927)
The Awakening (1928)
The Cavalier (1928)
Ramona (1928)
Revenge (1928)
Sins of the Fathers (1928)
Tempest (1928)
The Toilers (1928)
Two Lovers (1928)
The Woman Disputed (1928)
Overture 1812 (1929)
The Rescue (1929)
Seven Faces (1929)

Hell's Angels (1930)
One Romantic Night (1930)
Tabu (1931)
Thunder over Mexico (1933)
Let's Sing Again (1936)
The President's Mystery (1936)
Tarzan's Revenge (1938)

RIGUTTO, BRUNO
Faustine and the Beautiful Summer (1972)

RILEY, DOUG
Foxy Lady (1971)

RITZ, LYLE
No Drums, No Bugles (1971)

ROBERTS, ALLAN
Traveling Saleswoman (1949)

ROBERTS, GERALD
The Crooked Circle (1957)
Duel at Apache Wells (1957)
Gunfire at Indian Gap (1957)
Hell's Crossroads (1957)
Last Stagecoach West (1957)
The Lawless Eighties (1957)
Panama Sal (1957)
Spoilers of the Forest (1957)
Taming Sutton's Gal (1957)
The Wayward Girl (1957)
Juvenile Jungle (1958)
The Man Who Died Twice (1958)
The Notorious Mr. Monks (1958)
Young and Wild (1958)

ROBERTS, TED
The Cat Ate the Parakeet (1972)

ROBINSON, EARL
People of the Cumberland (1937)
The Roosevelt Story (1947)
The Man from Texas (1948)

ROBINSON, HARRY
The Oblong Box (1969)
The Vampire Lovers (1970)

RODEMICH, GENE
Bring 'Em Back Alive (1932)

RODER, MILAN
All the King's Horses (1935)
The Last Outpost (1935)
Too Many Parents (1936)
Easy Living (1937)

RODGERS, RICHARD
Victory at Sea (1954)
Slaughter on Tenth Avenue (1957)

RODRIGUES, CARLOS
American Sexual Revolution (1971)

ROEHRIG, WOLFRAM
Foxhole in Cairo (1961)

ROEMHELD, HEINZ
Imitation of Life (1934)
Mary Burns, Fugitive (1935)
Stand-In (1937)
Comet over Broadway (1938)
Brother Orchid (1940)
Lady with Red Hair (1940)
The Man Who Talked Too Much (1940)
My Love Came Back (1940)
No Time for Comedy (1940)
Affectionately Yours (1941)
Blues in the Night (1941)
Flight from Destiny (1941)
Strawberry Blonde (1941)
Always in My Heart (1942)
Gentleman Jim (1942)
The Hard Way (1942)
The Male Animal (1942)
Yankee Doodle Dandy (1942)
Janie (1944)
Make Your Own Bed (1944)
Shine On Harvest Moon (1944)
Too Young to Know (1945)
The Bachelor's Daughters (1946)
Mr. Ace (1946)
Christmas Eve (1947)
Curley (1947)
Down to Earth (1947)
The Fabulous Joe (1947)
Heaven Only Knows (1947)

The Fuller Brush Man (1948)
Here Comes Trouble (1948)
I, Jane Doe (1948)
Lady from Shanghai (1948)
My Dear Secretary (1948)
On Our Merry Way (1948)
Station West (1948)
Who Killed Doc Robbin? (1948)
The Lucky Stiff (1949)
Mr. Soft Touch (1949)
Miss Grant Takes Richmond (1949)
The Fuller Brush Girl (1950)
The Good Humor Man (1950)
Kill the Umpire (1950)
Rogues of Sherwood Forest (1950)
Chicago Calling (1951)
Valentino (1951)
Jack and the Beanstalk (1952)
Ruby Gentry (1952)
Three for Bedroom C (1952)
The Moonlighter (1953)
Hell's Horizon (1955)
The Square Jungle (1955)
There's Always Tomorrow (1956)
Decision at Sundown (1957)
The Monster that Challenged the World (1957)
The Tall "T" (1957)
Ride Lonesome (1959)
Lad: A Dog (1962)

ROGERS, ERIC
The Swingin' Maiden (1964)
Carry on Cleo (1965)
Carry on Spying (1965)
Carry on Cowboy (1966)
Don't Lose Your Head (1967)
Follow That Camel (1967)
Carry on Doctor (1968)
Carry on Up the Khyber (1968)
Carry on Again, Doctor (1969)
Carry on Camping (1969)
Carry on Up the Jungle (1970)
Doctor in Trouble (1970)
Assault (1971)
Quest for Love (1971)

ROGERS, SHORTY
Tarzan, the Ape Man (1959)
Taffy and the Jungle Hunter (1965)
Young Dillinger (1965)

ROLLINS, SONNY
Alfie (1966)

ROMANIS, GEORGE
Eight on the Lam (1967)
Chandler (1971)

ROMANS, ALAIN
Mr. Hulot's Holiday (1954)
My Uncle (1958)
Fadila (1961)

ROMBERG, SIGMUND
Foolish Wives (1922)

ROME, HAROLD
Fanny (1961)

RONNELL, ANN
The Story of G.I. Joe (1945)
One Touch of Venus (1948)
Love Happy (1949)
Main Street to Broadway (1953)

ROSALINA, ANA
The Woman of Everyone (1970)

ROSE, DAVID
The Princess and the Pirate (1944)
Winged Victory (1944)
The Whipped (1950)
Just This Once (1952)
Young Man with Ideas (1952)
Bright Road (1953)
The Clown (1953)
Confidentially Yours (1953)
Jupiter's Darling (1955)
Public Pigeon No. 1 (1957)
Operation Petticoat (1959)
Please Don't Eat the Daisies (1960)
This Rebel Breed (1960)
Quick, Before It Melts (1964)
Never Too Late (1965)
Hombre (1967)

ROSE, GORDON
Some of My Best Friends Are . . . (1971)

ROSEN, MILTON
Enter Arsene Lupin (1944)
Men in Her Diary (1945)
Shady Lady (1945)
Sudan (1945)
Tangier (1946)
The Time of Their Lives (1946)
White Tie and Tails (1946)
Pirates of Monterey (1947)
Slave Girl (1947)
Bob and Sally (1948)
The Challenge (1948)
The Creeper (1948)
Thirteen Lead Soldiers (1948)
The Milkman (1950)
Everything but the Truth (1956)
Outside the Law (1956)

ROSENBERG, HILDING
Short Is the Summer (1969)

ROSENBERGER, RAIMUND
A Walk Through the Kurdistan Wilderness (1965)
Heintje--Once the Sun Will Be Shining Again (1970)

ROSENMAN, LEONARD
The Cobweb (1955)
East of Eden (1955)
Rebel without a Cause (1955)
Bombers B-52 (1957)
Edge of the City (1957)
The Young Stranger (1957)
Lafayette Escadrille (1958)
Pork Chop Hill (1959)
The Bramble Bush (1960)
The Crowded Sky (1960)
The Plunderers (1960)
The Rise and Fall of Legs Diamond (1960)
The Outsider (1961)
The Chapman Report (1962)
Convicts Four (1962)
Hell Is for Heroes (1962)
A Covenant with Death (1966)
Fantastic Voyage (1966)
Countdown (1968)
Hellfighters (1968)
Beneath the Planet of the Apes (1970)
The Todd Killings (1971)

ROSENTHAL, LAURENCE
Yellowneck (1955)
Naked in the Sun (1957)
A Raisin in the Sun (1961)
The Miracle Worker (1962)
Requiem for a Heavyweight (1962)
Becket (1964)
Hotel Paradiso (1966)
The Comedians (1967)
Three (1969)
The African Elephant (1971)
A Gunfight (1971)

ROSOFF, CHARLES
Rose of the Rio Grande (1938)

ROSSELLINI, RENZO
Open City (1945)
Paisan (1946)
Germany Year Zero (1947)
Stromboli (1950)
Doctor Beware (1951)
Flowers of St. Francis (1952)
The Affairs of Messalina (1954)
Sins of Rome (1954)
Princess Cinderella (1955)
House of Riccordi (1956)
Queen of Babylon (1956)
Beautiful but Dangerous (1958)
Legions of the Nile (1960)
The Tartars (1962)

ROSSI, MARCO
The Exquisite Cadaver (1971)
Far from the Trees (1972)

ROSSI, RINALDO
The Prophet of Hunger (1970)

ROSSINI, GIOCCHINO
The Guest (1971)

ROSTAING, HUBERT
La Parisienne (1958)

ROSUGI, TAICHIRO
Swords of Death (1972)

ROTA, NINO
His Young Wife (1945)
The Glass Mountain (1948)
The Hidden Room (1950)
Valley of the Eagles (1952)
The Assassin (1953)
Hell Raiders of the Deep (1953)
Luxury Girls (1953)
Queen of Sheba (1953)
La Strada (1954)
The Stranger's Hand (1955)
Star of India (1956)
I Vitelloni (1956)
War and Peace (1956)
The White Shiek (1956)
Nights of Cabiria (1957)
Notte Bianchi (1957)
This Angry Age (1958)
The House of Intrigue (1959)
The Law is the Law (1959)
The Most Wonderful Moment (1959)
Phantom Lovers (1960)
Under Ten Flags (1960)
La Dolce Vita (1961)
The Great War (1961)
The Innocents (1961)
Purple Noon (1961)
The Best of Enemies (1962)
Boccaccio '70 (1962)
The Reluctant Saint (1962)
8-1/2 (1963)
The Leopard (1963)
Juliet of the Spirits (1965)
Paranoia (1966)
Shoot Loud, Louder ... I Don't Understand (1966)
The Taming of the Shrew (1967)
Romeo and Juliet (1968)
Tales of Mystery and Imagination (1968)
The Clowns (1970)
Waterloo (1970)
The Godfather (1972)
Roma (1972)

ROTERS, ERNST
Murderers Among Us (1946)

ROTHAFEL, S. L.
The Battle Cry of Peace (1915)
4 Devils (1928)
Mother Knows Best (1928)

ROUBAUD, ANDRE
The Queen's Necklace (1929)

ROY, ALPHONSE
Black-Out (1970)

ROYAL, TED
When Comedy Was King (1960)

ROZSA, MIKLOS
Thunder in the City (1937)
The Divorce of Lady X (1938)
Four Feathers (1938)
U-Boat 29 (1939)
The Fugitive (1940)
The Thief of Bagdad (1940)
Lydia (1941)
Sundown (1941)
That Hamilton Woman (1941)
The Jungle Book (1942)
Five Graves to Cairo (1943)
Sahara (1943)
So Proudly We Hail (1943)
The Woman of the Town (1943)
Dark Waters (1944)
Double Indemnity (1944)
The Hour Before the Dawn (1944)
The Man in Half Moon Street (1944)
Blood on the Sun (1945)
Lady on a Train (1945)
The Lost Weekend (1945)
Spellbound (1945)
Because of Him (1946)
The Killers (1946)
The Strange Love of Martha Ivers (1946)
Brute Force (1947)
Desert Fury (1947)
A Double Life (1947)
The Macomber Affair (1947)
The Other Love (1947)
The Red House (1947)
Secret Beyond the Door (1947)
Song of Scheherazade (1947)
Time out of Mind (1947)
A Woman's Vengeance (1947)
Command Decision (1948)
Kiss the Blood Off My Hands (1948)
Naked City (1948)
Adam's Rib (1949)
The Bribe (1949)

Criss Cross (1949)
East Side, West Side (1949)
Madame Bovary (1949)
The Red Danube (1949)
The Asphalt Jungle (1950)
Crisis (1950)
The Light Touch (1951)
Quo Vadis? (1951)
Ivanhoe (1952)
Plymouth Adventure (1952)
All the Brothers Were Valiant (1953)
Julius Caesar (1953)
Knights of the Round Table (1953)
The Story of Three Loves (1953)
Young Bess (1953)
Crest of the Wave (1954)
Green Fire (1954)
Men of the Fighting Lady (1954)
Valley of the Kings (1954)
Diane (1955)
The King's Thief (1955)
Moonfleet (1955)
Bhowani Junction (1956)
Lust for Life (1956)
Tribute to a Bad Man (1956)
The Seventh Sin (1957)
Something of Value (1957)
Tip on a Dead Jockey (1957)
A Time to Love and a Time to Die (1958)
Ben-Hur (1959)
The World, the Flesh and the Devil (1959)
El Cid (1961)
King of Kings (1961)
Sodom and Gomorrah (1963)
The VIP's (1963)
The Green Berets (1968)
The Power (1968)
The Private Life of Sherlock Holmes (1970)

RUBENSTEIN, GEORGE M.
Salome (1922)

RUBENSTEIN, JOHN
Paddy (1970)
The Candidate (1972)
Jeremiah Johnson (1972)

RUGOLO, PETE
Jack the Ripper (1960)
The Sweet Ride (1968)

RUIZ, JORGE LOPEZ
The Terrace (1964)
El Professor Hippie (1969)
Blum (1970)
The Inheritors (1970)
The Big Highway (1971)
The United Family Awaits the Visit of Hallewyn (1972)

RUSSELL, BOB
Reach for Glory (1963)

RUSSELL, HENRY
Lulu Belle (1948)
Five (1951)

RUSTICHELLI, CARLO
The Path of Hope (1951)
The White Line (1951)
Uomo de Paglia (1957)
Kapo (1959)
Maladetto Imbroglio (1959)
Hannibal (1960)
The Minotaur (1961)
Thief of Bagdad (1961)
Divorce Italian Style (1962)
Psycosissimo (1962)
Sword of the Conqueror (1962)
Arturo's Island (1963)
The Four Days of Naples (1963)
Bebo's Girl (1964)
The Organizer (1964)
Seduced and Abandoned (1964)
Blood and Black Lace (1965)
The Cavern (1965)
The Railroad Man (1965)
For Love and Gold (L'Armata Brancaleone) (1966)
Me, Me, Me ... and the Others (1966)
Seasons of Our Love (1966)
Signore and Signori (1966)
Head of the Family (1967)
Better a Widow (1968)
Kill, Baby, Kill (1968)
A Minute to Pray, a Second to Die (1968)
The Sècret War of Harry Frigg (1968)
Serafino (1968)

Aces High (1969)
Double Face (1969)
Certain, Very Certain, as a Matter of Fact ... Probable (1970)
In Prison Awaiting Trial (1971)
In the Name of the Italian People (1971)
Nini Tirabuscio (1971)
Pocketful of Chestnuts (1971)
La Betia (1972)

RYDER, ANDRE
After Shadows, Light (1970)

SADYKOV, T.
Alisher Navoi (1947)

SAHL, MICHAEL
Hot Circuit (1972)

ST. PIERRE, WILLIAM G.
Head On (1971)

SAINT-SAENS, CAMILLE
The Assassination of the Duc De Guise (1908)

SAINTON, PHILIP
Moby Dick (1956)

SAINZ, ALFONSO
Aoom (1970)

SAITO, ICHITO
The Girl in the Mist (1955)

SAKAC, BRANIMIN
The Ninth Circle (1961)

SALINGER, CONRAD
The Unknown Man (1951)
Carbine Williams (1952)
Washington Story (1952)
Dream Wife (1953)
The Last Time I saw Paris (1954)
Tennessee Champ (1954)
The Scarlet Coat (1955)
Gaby (1956)
Lonelyhearts (1958)

SALTER, HANS J.
Call a Messenger (1939)
The Great Commandment (1939)
Zanzibar (1940)
It Started with Eve (1941)
Bombay Clipper (1942)
Danger in the Pacific (1942)
Deep in the Heart of Texas (1942)
Drums of the Congo (1942)
Fighting Bill Fargo (1942)
The Ghost of Frankenstein (1942)
The Great Impersonation (1942)
Little Joe, the Wrangler (1942)
The Mummy's Tomb (1942)
The Mystery of Marie Roget (1942)
Night Monster (1942)
North to the Klondike (1942)
Pittsburgh (1942)
The Silver Bullet (1942)
Sin Town (1942)
The Spoilers (1942)
Stagecoach Buckaroo (1942)
The Strange Case of Dr. RX (1942)
There's One Born Every Minute (1942)
Timber (1942)
Top Sergeant (1942)
Tough as They Come (1942)
Treat 'Em Rough (1942)
You're Telling Me (1942)
Boss of Hangtown Mesa (1943)
Captive Wild Woman (1943)
Cheyenne Roundup (1943)
Cowboy in Manhattan (1943)
Frankenstein Meets the Wolf Man (1943)
Get Going (1943)
His Butler's Sister (1943)
Hi Ya, Chum (1943)
Hi'Ya, Sailor (1943)
Keep 'Em Slugging (1943)
Lone Star Trail (1943)
The Mad Ghoul (1943)
Mug Town (1943)
Never a Dull Moment (1943)
Raiders of San Joaquin (1943)
Sherlock Holmes Faces Death (1943)

Son of Dracula (1943)
The Strange Death of Adolph Hitler (1943)
Tenting Tonight on the Old Camp Ground (1943)
Can't Help Singing (1944)
Christmas Holiday (1944)
Hi, Good Lookin' (1944)
House of Frankenstein (1944)
The Invisible Man's Revenge (1944)
Marshal of Gunsmoke (1944)
The Mummy's Ghost (1944)
Pardon My Rhythm (1944)
Phantom Lady (1944)
San Diego, I Love You (1944)
Spider Woman (1944)
Easy to Look At (1945)
The Frozen Ghost (1945)
I'll Tell the World (1945)
Patrick the Great (1945)
The River Gang (1945)
Scarlet Street (1945)
See My Lawyer (1945)
That Night with You (1945)
That's the Spirit (1945)
This Love of Ours (1945)
Uncle Harry (1945)
The Dark House (1946)
Her Adventurous Night (1946)
House of Horror (1946)
Little Miss Big (1946)
Lover Come Back (1946)
So Goes My Love (1946)
Love from a Stranger (1947)
The Michigan Kid (1947)
That's My Man (1947)
The Web (1947)
Don't Trust Your Husband (1948)
An Innocent Affair (1948)
Man-Eater of Kumaon (1948)
The Sign of the Ram (1948)
Cover-Up (1949)
The Reckless Moment (1949)
Borderline (1950)
Frenchie (1950)
Frightened City (1950)
Woman from Headquarters (1950)
Apache Drums (1951)
Finders Keepers (1951)
The Golden Horde (1951)
The Prince Who Was a Thief (1951)
Thunder on the Hill (1951)
Tomahawk (1951)
You Can Never Tell (1951)
Against All Flags (1952)
The Battle of Apache Pass (1952)
Bend of the River (1952)
The Duel at Silver Creek (1952)
Flesh and Fury (1952)
Untamed Frontier (1952)
The Human Jungle (1954)
The Far Horizons (1955)
Wichita (1955)
Autumn Leaves (1956)
Hold Back the Night (1956)
The Mole People (1956)
Navy Wife (1956)
Red Sundown (1956)
The Oklahoman (1957)
The Tall Stranger (1957)
Three Brave Men (1957)
Day of the Bad Man (1958)
The Female Animal (1958)
Raw Wind in Eden (1958)
The Gunfight at Dodge City (1959)
Man in the Net (1959)
The Wild and the Innocent (1959)
Come September (1961)
Follow that Dream (1962)
Hitler (1962)
If a Man Answers (1962)
Showdown (1963)
Bedtime Story (1964)
Beau Geste (1966)
Gunpoint (1966)
I Knew Her Well (1966)
Incident at Phantom Hill (1966)

SALVADOR, HENRI
The Explosion (1971)

SALZEDO, LEONARD
Shadow of Fear (1956)
Revenge of Frankenstein (1958)
The Steel Bayonet (1958)

SAMPSON, WILBUR
The Kangaroo Kid (1950)

King of the Coral Sea (1956)
Smiley Gets a Gun (1959)

SAMUELS, WALTER
Flirting with Fate (1938)

THE SANDALS
Last of the Ski Bums (1969)

SANDLOFF, PETER
Maedchen in Uniform (1965)

SANFORD, BLAINE
The Magnetic Monster (1953)

SANFORD, WILLIAM
Pretty Boy Floyd (1960)

SANG-KY, HAN
Fire Woman (1971)

SANTISTEBEN, ALFONSO
Necrophagus (1971)

SANTOS, MOACYR
Ganga Zumba (1972)

SANUCCI, FRANK
Where the Buffalo Roam (1938)
Down the Wyoming Trail (1939)
King of the Stallions (1942)
The Living Ghost (1942)
Land of Hunted Men (1943)
Bullets and Saddles (1943)
Cowboy Commandos (1943)
Death Valley Rangers (1943)
The Haunted Ranch (1943)
Two-Fisted Justice (1943)
Wild Horse Stampede (1943)
Arizona Whirlwind (1944)
Marked Trails (1944)
Outlaw Trail (1944)
Westward Bound (1944)
Border Badmen (1945)
Fighting Bill Carson (1945)
Flame of the West (1945)
Frontier Feud (1945)
The Lonesome Trail (1945)
Northwest Trail (1945)
Springtime in Texas (1945)
Stranger from Santa Fe (1945)
Border Bandits (1946)
Moon over Montana (1946)
Trail to Mexico (1946)
West of the Alamo (1946)
Six-Gun Serenade (1947)
Deadline (1948)
Fighting Mustang (1948)
Sunset Carson Rides Again (1948)

SARDE, PHILIPPE
Emergency Exit (1970)
Liza (1972)
The Right to Love (1972)

SARKOZI, ISTVAN
The House under the Rocks (1958)

SASSOVER, NATE
The Way We Live Now (1970)
The Telephone Book (1971)

SATIE, ERIK
Entr'acte (1924)
An Immortal Story (1968)

SATO, MASARU
The Lower Depths (1957)
Throne of Blood (1957)
The H-Man (1959)
Yojimbo (1961)
The Bad Sleep Well (1963)
Hit and Run (1966)
The Sword of Doom (1967)
Kill! (1968)
Portrait of Chicko (1968)
Goyokin (1969)
Samurai Banners (1969)
Outlaws (1970)
Kazoku (1971)
Sapporo Winter Olympics (1972)
The Wolves (1972)

SAUGUET, HENRI
Farrebique (1948)
The Honorable Catherine (1948)
The Ostrich Has Two Eggs (1957)
Pantaloons (1957)

SAUNDERS, MORT
Black Girl (1972)

SAUTER, EDDIE
Mickey One (1965)

SAVINA, CARLO
Head of a Tyrant (1960)
Herod the Great (1960)
Secret Agent Fireball (1966)
A Very Handy Man (1966)
The Young, the Evil and the Savage (1968)
The Wedding Trip (1969)
The Long Ride from Hell (1970)
The Devil's Lovers (1971)

SAVINO, DOMENICO
The Patriot (1928)

SAWTELL, PAUL
The Gay Falcon (1941)
Bandit Ranger (1942)
Hillbilly Blitzkreig (1942)
Pirates of the Prairie (1942)
Scattergood Rides High (1942)
Scattergood Survives a Murder (1942)
Valley of the Sun (1942)
The Avenging Rider (1943)
Calling Dr. Death (1943)
Cinderella Swings It (1943)
Fighting Frontier (1943)
Tarzan's Desert Mystery (1943)
Tarzan Triumphs (1943)
Dead Man's Eyes (1944)
Mr. Winkle Goes to War (1944)
The Mummy's Curse (1944)
Nevada (1944)
The Pearl of Death (1944)
The Scarlet Claw (1944)
Secret Command (1944)
Weird Woman (1944)
Youth Runs Wild (1944)
The Falcon in San Francisco (1945)
The Fighting Guardsman (1945)
A Game of Death (1945)
The House of Fear (1945)
I Love a Bandleader (1945)
Tarzan and the Amazons (1945)
Wanderer of the Wasteland (1945)
West of the Pecos (1945)
The Cat Creeps (1946)
Crime Doctor's Warning (1946)
Criminal Court (1946)
Danger Woman (1946)
The Falcon's Adventure (1946)
Renegades (1946)
San Quentin (1946)
Snafu (1946)
Step by Step (1946)
Strange Conquest (1946)
Sunset Pass (1946)
Tarzan and the Leopard Woman (1946)
Vacation in Reno (1946)
Wild Beauty (1946)
Blind Spot (1947)
Born to Kill (1947)
Code of the West (1947)
Desperate (1947)
The Devil Thumbs a Ride (1947)
Dick Tracy Meets Gruesome (1947)
Dick Tracy's Dilemma (1947)
For You I Die (1947)
Keeper of the Bees (1947)
Seven Keys to Baldpate (1947)
T-Men (1947)
Tarzan and the Huntress (1947)
Thunder Mountain (1947)
Trail Street (1947)
Under the Tonto Rim (1947)
The Vigilantes Return (1947)
Wild Horse Mesa (1947)
The Arizona Ranger (1948)
The Black Arrow (1948)
Bodyguard (1948)
Design for Death (1948)
Four Faces West (1948)
Gun Smugglers (1948)
Guns of Hate (1948)
Mystery in Mexico (1948)
Northwest Stampede (1948)
Raw Deal (1948)
Return of the Bad Men (1948)
River Lady (1948)
Walk a Crooked Mile (1948)
Western Heritage (1948)
Bad Boy (1949)

The Big Cat (1949)
Black Magic (1949)
Brothers in the Saddle (1949)
The Clay Pigeon (1949)
The Doolins of Oklahoma (1949)
Fighting Man of the Plains (1949)
Masked Raiders (1949)
The Mysterious Desperado (1949)
Riders of the Range (1949)
Rustlers (1949)
Savage Splendor (1949)
Stagecoach Kid (1949)
The Threat (1949)
Border Treasure (1950)
Bunco Squad (1950)
The Cariboo Trail (1950)
Davy Crockett, Indian Scout (1950)
Dynamite Pass (1950)
Fortunes of Captain Blood (1950)
The Great Missouri Raid (1950)
Hunt the Man Down (1950)
Law of the Badlands (1950)
Outrage (1950)
Rider from Tucson (1950)
Rio Grande Patrol (1950)
Rogue River (1950)
Southside 1-1000 (1950)
Stage to Tucson (1950)
Storm over Wyoming (1950)
Tarzan and the Slave Girl (1950)
Best of the Badmen (1951)
Flaming Feather (1951)
Fort Defiance (1951)
Gunplay (1951)
Hot Lead (1951)
Jungle Hunters (1951)
Overland Telegraph (1951)
Pistol Harvest (1951)
Roadblock (1951)
Saddle Legion (1951)
Santa Fe (1951)
Silver City (1951)
The Son of Dr. Jekyll (1951)
Warpath (1951)
The Whip Hand (1951)
And Now Tomorrow (1952)
Another Man's Poison (1952)
The Denver and the Rio Grande (1952)
Hurricane Smith (1952)
Kansas City Confidential (1952)
Road Agent (1952)
The Savage (1952)
Sky Full of Moon (1952)
Tarzan's Savage Fury (1952)
Arrowhead (1953)
Below the Sahara (1953)
The Diamond Queen (1953)
Flight to Tangier (1953)
Forever Female (1953)
Half a Hero (1953)
Inferno (1953)
Pony Express (1953)
Raiders of the Seven Seas (1953)
The Sea Around Us (1953)
Tarzan and the She-Devil (1953)
Africa Adventure (1954)
Captain Kidd and the Slave Girl (1954)
Down Three Dark Streets (1954)
Quest for the Lost City (1954)
Return to Treasure Island (1954)
They Rode West (1954)
Three Hours to Kill (1954)
A Lawless Street (1955)
The Living Swamp (1955)
Rage at Dawn (1955)
Tall Man Riding (1955)
Tarzan's Hidden Jungle (1955)
Ten Wanted Men (1955)
Texas Lady (1955)
The Animal World (1956)
The Desperadoes Are in Town (1956)
Scandal, Inc. (1956)
The Black Scorpion (1957)
The Deerslayer (1957)
Five Steps to Danger (1957)
Ghost Diver (1957)
Gun Duel in Durango (1957)
Hell Ship Mutiny (1957)
Kronos (1957)
Last of the Badmen (1957)
Monkey on My Back (1957)
Pawnee (1957)
She Devil (1957)
Stopover Tokyo (1957)
The Story of Mankind (1957)

Ambush at Cimarron Pass (1958)
Cattle Empire (1958)
The Fly (1958)
Hong Kong Confidential (1958)
The Hunters (1958)
It! The Terror from Beyond Space (1958)
Machete (1958)
Sierra Baron (1958)
Villa! (1958)
The Big Circus (1959)
The Cosmic Man (1959)
Counterplot (1959)
A Dog of Flanders (1959)
The Miracle of the Hills (1959)
The Return of the Fly (1959)
The Sad Horse (1959)
Vice Raid (1959)
Cage of Evil (1960)
A Dog's Best Friend (1960)
The Lost World (1960)
The Music Box Kid (1960)
Tess of the Storm Country (1960)
The Big Show (1961)
Five Guns to Tombstone (1961)
Frontier Uprising (1961)
The Long Rope (1961)
Misty (1961)
Pirates of Tortuga (1961)
Voyage to the Bottom of the Sea (1961)
Five Weeks in a Balloon (1962)
Jack the Giant Killer (1962)
Young Guns of Texas (1962)
Cattle King (1963)
Harbor Lights (1963)
Thunder Island (1963)
Island of the Blue Dolphins (1964)
The Bubble (1966)
Faster, Pussycat, Kill! Kill! (1966)
The Christine Jorgensen Story (1970)

SCARDINO, DON
Homer (1970)

SCHAEFER, HAL
The Money Trap (1966)

SCHARF, WALTER
Chatterbox (1943)
Hands Across the Border (1943)
Hit Parade of 1943 (1943)
In Old Oklahoma (1943)
Nobody's Darling (1943)
Secrets of the Underground (1943)
Shantytown (1943)
Sleepy Lagoon (1943)
Someone to Remember (1943)
Thumbs Up (1943)
Atlantic City (1944)
Casanova in Burlesque (1944)
The Cowboy and the Senorita (1944)
The Fighting Seebees (1944)
The Lady and the Monster (1944)
Lake Placid Serenade (1944)
Storm over Lisbon (1944)
The Cheaters (1945)
Dakota (1945)
Earl Carroll's Vanities (1945)
I've Always Loved You (1946)
Are You with It? (1948)
The Countess of Monte Cristo (1948)
Mexican Hayride (1948)
The Saxon Charm (1948)
Abandoned (1949)
City Across the River (1949)
Red Canyon (1949)
Take One False Step (1949)
Buccaneer's Girl (1950)
Curtain Call at Cactus Creek (1950)
Deported (1950)
Sierra (1950)
South Sea Sinner (1950)
Spy Hunt (1950)
Two Tickets to Broadway (1951)
Hans Christian Andersen (1952)
Living It Up (1954)
Three Ring Circus (1954)
The French Line (1954)
Artists and Models (1955)
You're Never Too Young (1955)
The Birds and the Bees (1956)
Hollywood or Bust (1956)
Three for Jamie Dawn (1956)
Three Violent People (1956)

Timetable (1956)
The Joker Is Wild (1957)
Loving You (1957)
The Sad Sack (1957)
The Geisha Boy (1958)
King Creole (1958)
Rock-a-bye Baby (1958)
Don't Give Up the Ship (1959)
The Bellboy (1960)
Cinderfella (1960)
The Ladies' Man (1961)
Pocketful of Miracles (1961)
The Errand Boy (1962)
Harold Lloyd's World of Comedy (1962)
It's Only Money (1962)
My Six Loves (1963)
The Nutty Professor (1963)
Honeymoon Hotel (1964)
Where Love Has Gone (1964)
Tickle Me (1965)
Pendulum (1969)
The Cheyenne Social Club (1970)
Ben (1972)

SCHERBACHEV, VLADIMIR
Peter the First (Part I) (1937)
Peter the First (Part II) (1938)

SCHERTZINGER, VICTOR
The Edge of the Abyss (1915)
The Beckoning Flame (1916)
Civilization (1916)
The Conqueror (1916)
D'Artagnan (1916)
Peggy (1916)
Robin Hood (1920)
Beloved (1934)

SCHICKELE, PETER
Funnyman (1967)
Silent Running (1972)

SCHIFRIN, LALO
Joy House (1964)
Rhino! (1964)
The Cincinnati Kid (1965)
Once a Thief (1965)
Blindfold (1966)
I Deal in Danger (1966)
The Liquidator (1966)
Murderer's Row (1966)
The Venetian Affair (1966)
Way ... Way Out (1966)
Cool Hand Luke (1967)
The Fox (1967)
The President's Analyst (1967)
Sullivan's Empire (1967)
Who's Minding the Mint? (1967)
The Brotherhood (1968)
Bullitt (1968)
Coogan's Bluff (1968)
Hell in the Pacific (1968)
Sol Madrid (1968)
Where Angels Go ... Trouble Follows (1968)
Che! (1969)
Eye of the Cat (1969)
I Love My Wife (1970)
Imago (1970)
Kelly's Heroes (1970)
Pussycat, Pussycat, I Love You (1970)
W.U.S.A. (1970)
The Beguiled (1971)
The Christian Licorice Store (1971)
Dirty Harry (1971)
The Hellstrom Chronicle (1971)
Pretty Maids All in a Row (1971)
THX-1138 (1971)
Joe Kidd (1972)
Prime Cut (1972)
Rage (1972)
To Be Free (1972)
The Wrath of God (1972)

SCHIRMANN, PETER
Your Child, the Unknown Creature (1970)
Hot Traces of St. Pauli (1971)
Hurray, We Are Bachelors Again (1971)

SCHMIDT, HARVEY
Bad Company (1972)

SCHMIDT, HELMUT
21 Days in Europe (1971)

SCHMIDT, IRWIN
Love by Rape (1970)

SCHMIDT GENTNER, WILLI
The Woman on the Moon (1928)
Cabaret (1957)
Circus of Love (1958)

SCHOENER, EBERHARD
Trotta (1971)

SCHRAGER, RUDY
Take It Big (1944)
Tokyo Rose (1945)
Deadline for Murder (1946)
Strange Journey (1946)
Swamp Fire (1946)
Dangerous Years (1947)
Fear in the Night (1947)
The Guilty (1947)
Gunfighters (1947)
High Tide (1947)
In Self Defense (1947)
Perilous Waters (1947)
Roses Are Red (1947)
Coroner Creek (1948)
Sleep My Love (1948)
Strike It Rich (1948)
The Great Dan Patch (1949)
The Green Promise (1949)
The Eagle and the Hawk (1950)
High Lonesome (1950)
The Iroquois Trail (1950)
The Last Voyage (1960)

SCHREIBER, HANS
Hidden Fear (1957)

SCHREITER, HEINZ
Emil and the Detectives (1964)

SCHROEDER, KURT
Private Life of Henry VIII (1933)

SCHUETT, OTTO
The Bordello (1971)

SCHULMAN, ALAN
The Tattooed Stranger (1950)

SCHULTHORPE, PETER
Age of Consent (1969)

SCHULTZ, NORBERT
Rosemary (1958)

SCHULTZ, W.
Strange World (1952)

SCHULTZE, CHRISTIAN
Don't Fumble, Darling (1970)
Sex Perverse (1970)

SCHUMAN, EARL
Dondi (1961)

SCHUMAN, MORT
A Day at the Beach (1970)
Romance of a Horse Thief (1971)

SCHUMANN, WALTER
Buck Privates Come Home (1947)
The Wistful Widow of Wagon Gap (1947)
The Noose Hangs High (1948)
Africa Screams (1949)
Dragnet (1954)
The Night of the Hunter (1955)

SCHURMANN, GERARD
The Third Key (1957)
The Camp on Blood Island (1958)
Horrors of the Black Museum (1959)
The Two-Headed Spy (1959)
Konga (1961)
Trouble in the Sky (1961)
The Ceremony (1963)
The Bedford Incident (1965)
Attack on the Iron Coast (1968)
The Lost Continent (1968)

SCHWARTZ, LEV
The New Gulliver (1935)
The Childhood of Maxim Gorky (1938)
My Apprenticeship (1939)
My Universities (1940)
The Rainbow (1944)
The Stone Flower (1946)
Village Teacher (1947)
The Mistress (1953)
The Anna Cross (1954)
1905 (Mother) (1955)

SCHWARZWALD, MILTON
Abbott and Costello Meet the Killer (1949)
Arctic Manhunt (1949)
Cheyenne Cowboy (1949)
Illegal Entry (1949)
Johnny Stool Pigeon (1949)
Ma and Pa Kettle (1949)
The Story of Molly X (1949)
Undertow (1949)
I Was a Shoplifter (1950)
The Kid from Texas (1950)

SCHWEITZER, ILYA
Cinerama's Russian Adventure (1966)

SCOTT, BOBBY
Slaves (1969)
Joe (1970)
Who Says I Can't Ride a Rainbow? (1971)

SCOTT, (PATRICK) JOHN
Doctor in Clover (1966)
Berserk (1967)
The Long Duel (1967)
The 1,000,000 Eyes of Su-Muru (1967)
Stranger in the House (1967)
Those Fantastic Flying Fools (1967)
Amsterdam Affair (1968)
Crooks and Coronets (1969)
Trog (1970)
Twinky (1970)
Girl Stroke Boy (1971)
Antony and Cleopatra (1972)
The Jerusalem File (1972)

SCOTT, MORTON
The Mantrap (1943)
My Best Gal (1944)
My Buddy (1944)
Rosie the Riveter (1944)
Silent Partner (1944)
Three Little Sisters (1944)
Whispering Footsteps (1944)
The Yellow Rose of Texas (1944)
Along the Navajo Trail (1945)
An Angel Comes to Brooklyn (1945)
The Big Bonanza (1945)
The Chicago Kid (1945)
Don't Fence Me In (1945)
Flame of the Barbary Coast (1945)
Grissley's Millions (1945)
Hitchhike to Happiness (1945)
Steppin' in Society (1945)
Strangers in the Night (1945)
Sunset in Eldorado (1945)
Swingin' on a Rainbow (1945)
Utah (1945)
Gay Blades (1946)
In Old Sacramento (1946)
My Pal Trigger (1946)
Out California Way (1946)
Rainbow over Texas (1946)
Song of Arizona (1946)
Apache Rose (1947)
Springtime in the Sierras (1947)
That's My Gal (1947)
Twilight on the Rio Grande (1947)
Daredevils of the Clouds (1948)
Desperadoes of Dodge City (1948)
The Gallant Legion (1948)
Gay Ranchero (1948)
Heart of Virginia (1948)
Homicide for Three (1948)
King of the Gamblers (1948)
Marshal of Amarillo (1948)
Out of the Storm (1948)
Overland Trails (1948)
Sons of Adventure (1948)
Train to Alcatraz (1948)
Under California Stars (1948)
Susanna Pass (1949)

SCOTT, NATHAN
Driftwood (1947)
The Trespasser (1947)
Wyoming (1947)
Angel in Exile (1948)
Angel on the Amazon (1948)
Grand Canyon Trail (1948)
The Inside Story (1948)
Old Los Angeles (1948)
Wake of the Red Witch (1948)
Brimstone (1949)
The Golden Stallion (1949)
The Kid from Cleveland (1949)

The Red Menace (1949)
The Avengers (1950)
California Passage (1950)
Singing Guns (1950)
Surrender (1950)
Trail of Robin Hood (1950)
Hoodlum Empire (1952)
Lady Possessed (1952)
The Last Musketeer (1952)
Montana Belle (1952)
Oklahoma Annie (1952)
X-15 (1961)

SCOTT, RANDY
The Flanders and Alcott Report on Sex Response (1971)

SCOTT, RAYMOND
Never Love a Stranger (1958)
The Pusher (1960)

SCOTT, TOM
Conquest of the Planet of the Apes (1972)
The Culpepper Cattle Co. (1972)

SCOTTO, VINCENT
Marius (1931)
Fanny (1932)
Cesar (1936)
Pepe Le Moko (1937)
Algiers (1938)
The Baker's Wife (1938)
Minne (1951)

SCULL, STEPHEN
Howzer (1972)

SEARLE, HUMPHREY
Action of the Tiger (1957)
Beyond Mombasa (1957)
Law and Disorder (1958)
Left, Right and Center (1961)
The Haunting (1963)

SEBASTIAN, JOHN
You're a Big Boy Now (1966)

SEBESKY, DON
The People Next Door (1970)

SEEGER, PETE
Lines Horizontal (1960)
The Many-Colored Paper (1960)

SEGAL, MISHA
Two Heartbeats (1972)

SEGALL, BERNARDO
The Great St. Louis Bank Robbery (1959)
The Luck of Ginger Coffey (1964)
Hallucination Generation (1966)
Custer of the West (1967)
Loving (1970)
The Jesus Trip (1971)

SEGURA, GREGORY
The Son of Captain Blood (1964)
The Fickle Finger of Fate (1967)
Madigan's Million (1970)
Varieties (1971)

SEIBER, MATYAS
The Magic Canvas (1949)
The Diamond Wizard (1954)
Animal Farm (1955)
Chase a Crooked Shadow (1958)
The Mark of the Hawk (1958)
Robbery Under Arms (1958)
For Better, for Worse (1961)
Malaga (1962)

SEIDEL, EMIL
Silver Skates (1943)

SELTZER, DOV
Trunk to Cairo (1966)
Eagles Attack at Dawn (1970)
Highway Queen (1971)
Escape to the Sun (1972)
I Love You, Rosa (1972)

SENDREY, ALBERT
Father's Little Dividend (1951)
Kansas Pacific (1953)

SENTESI, JOHN
Stop That Cab (1951)

SERBAN, RADU
Then Came the Legend (1970)

SERINO, DEL
Pretty Boy Floyd (1960)

SEYRIG, FRANCIS
Last Year at Marienbad (1961)

THE SHADOWS
The Boys (1962)
Finders Keepers (1966)

SHAINDLIN, JACK
We Are the Marines (1942)
The Golden Twenties (1950)
Walk East on Beacon (1952)
Operation Manhunt (1954)
Days of Thrills and Laughter (1961)

SHANK, BUD
War Hunt (1962)

SHANKAR, RAVI
Pather Panchali (1956)
Aparajito (1958)
The World of Apu (1959)
Chappaqua (1966)
Charly (1968)

SHANKIN, WAYNE
Angel Baby (1961)

SHANKLIN, RAY
Black Girl (1972)
Fritz the Cat (1972)

SHAPIRO, TOM
The Only Way Home (1972)

SHAPORIN, Y.
The Deserter (1933)
Three Songs About Lenin (1934)
General Suvorov (1941)

SHARPLES, WINSTON
Wild Cargo (1934)

SHAW, ROLAND
The Secret of My Success (1965)

SHEARING, GEORGE
80 Steps to Jonah (1969)

SHEFTER, BERT
Holiday Rhythm (1950)
One Too Many (1950)
Danger Zone (1951)
Leave It to the Marines (1951)
"M" (1951)
Pier 23 (1951)
Roaring City (1951)
Sky High (1951)
No Escape (1953)
The Desperadoes Are in Town (1956)
Scandal, Inc. (1956)
The Deerslayer (1957)
Ghost Diver (1957)
Gun Duel in Durango (1957)
Hell Ship Mutiny (1957)
Kronos (1957)
Monkey on My Back (1957)
She Devil (1957)
Ambush at Cimarron Pass (1958)
Cattle Empire (1958)
Hong Kong Confidential (1958)
It! The Terror from Beyond Space (1958)
Machete (1958)
Sierra Baron (1958)
Villa! (1958)
The Big Circus (1959)
The Cosmic Man (1959)
Counterplot (1959)
A Dog of Flanders (1959)
The Miracle of the Hills (1959)
The Sad Horse (1959)
Vice Raid (1959)
A Dog's Best Friend (1960)
The Lost World (1960)
Tess of the Storm Country (1960)
Three Came to Kill (1960)
Five Guns to Tombstone (1961)
Frontier Uprising (1961)
The Long Rope (1961)
Pirates of Tortuga (1961)
Jack the Giant Killer (1962)
Thunder Island (1963)

The Curse of the Fly (1965)
The Bubble (1966)
The Last Shot You Hear (1969)
The Christine Jorgensen Story (1970)

SHEKTER, MARK
B. S., I Love You (1971)

SHELTON, LOUIE
J. W. Coop (1971)

SHEPARD, THOMAS Z.
Such Good Friends (1971)

SHEPPART, MADELYN
The Cup of Fury (1919)

SHERMAN, GARRY
Alice's Restaurant (1969)
The Heartbreak Kid (1972)
Parades (1972)

SHERMAN, SOL
The Proud Rider (1971)

SHIELD, LEROY
The Devil's Brother (1933)

SHIERBECK, POUL
Ordet (1957)

SHILKRET, NATHANIEL
Battle of the Sexes (1928)
The Last of the Mohicans (1936)
That Girl from Paris (1936)
Walking on Air (1936)
Winterset (1936)
The Soldier and the Lady (1937)
Air Raid Wardens (1943)
Blonde Fever (1944)
Nothing But Trouble (1944)
Three Men in White (1944)
She Went to the Races (1945)
This Man's Navy (1945)
Boy's Ranch (1946)
Faithful in My Fashion (1946)
The Hoodlum Saint (1946)

SHIRE, DAVID
One More Train to Rob (1971)
Skin Game (1971)
To Find a Man (1972)

SHIRNSKY, V.
The Safety Match (1954)

SHNITKE, A.
Uncle Vanya (1971)

SHORES, RICHARD
Look in Any Window (1961)
Tomboy and the Champ (1961)
The Last Challenge (1967)

SHOSTAKOVICH, DMITRI
New Babylon (1929)
Alone (1930)
Golden Mountains (1931)
Counterplan (1932)
The Youth of Maxim (1934)
Girl Friends (1936)
The Return of Maxim Gorky (1936)
A Great Citizen (1938)
The Man with a Gun (1938)
Volochayevsk Days (1938)
The Vyborg Side (1939)
The Battle for Siberia (1940)
Zoya (1944)
The Fall of Berlin (1945)
Plain People (1945)
Michurin (1947)
Pirogov (1947)
Young Guard (1947)
Meeting on the Elba (1949)
The Unforgettable Year--1919 (1952)
The First Echelon (1956)
The Condemned of Altona (1963)
Hamlet (1964)

SHUKEN, LEO
Waikiki Wedding (1937)
Cafe Society (1939)
The Flying Deuces (1939)
The Lady Eve (1941)
Sullivan's Travels (1941)
The Lady Has Plans (1942)
Meet the Stewarts (1942)
The Good Fellows (1943)
The Miracle of Morgan's Creek (1944)
The Fabulous Dorseys (1947)
Those Redheads from Seattle (1953)

SIBELIUS, JEAN
The Unknown Soldier (1926)

SIDELNIKOV, N.
Jamilya (1972)

SIEGMEISTER, ELIE
They Came to Cordura (1959)

SIGARA, GEORGE
West of Zanzibar (1954)

SILOS, LEOPOLD
W.I.A. (Wounded in Action) (1966)

SILVA, MARIO
Stepchild (1947)

SILVERS, LOUIS
Way Down East (1920)
Dream Street (1921)
Isn't Life Wonderful? (1924)
The Jazz Singer (1927)
Noah's Ark (1928)
Dancing Lady (1933)
One Night of Love (1934)
Love Me Forever (1935)
Captain January (1936)
Dimples (1936)
Ladies in Love (1936)
A Message to Garcia (1936)
Poor Little Rich Girl (1936)
Private Number (1936)
Professional Soldier (1936)
Road to Glory (1936)
To Mary, with Love (1936)
Under Two Flags (1936)
Cafe Metropole (1937)
Lloyds of London (1937)
Seventh Heaven (1937)
Stowaway (1937)
Four Men and a Prayer (1938)
In Old Chicago (1938)
Kentucky (1938)
Kentucky Moonshine (1938)
Suez (1938)
Hollywood Cavalcade (1939)
Second Fiddle (1939)
Susannah of the Mounties (1939)
Swanee River (1940)

SILVERSTEIN, SHEL
Who Is Harry Kellerman and Why Is He Saying Those Terrible Things About Me? (1971)

SIMON, JOHN
Last Summer (1969)

SIMON, WALTER CLEVELAND
Arrah-Na-Pough (1911)

SIMONETTI, ENRICO
Macumba Love (1960)

SIMONYAN, N.
The Flying Carpet (1956)
The Lady with the Dog (1960)

SINGENBERGER, OTTO
Film Record of the Eucharistic Congress (1926)

SINGMAN, ESLA
Love Me Like I Do (1970)

SIV, MIKHAIL
Ballad of a Soldier (1960)

SIVEN, RAGE
Between Us (1970)

SKILES, MARLIN
Great Guy (1936)
Sweetheart of the Navy (1936)
Twenty-three and One-half Hours Leave (1936)
The Impatient Years (1944)
Kansas City Kitty (1944)
Man from Frisco (1944)
Meet Miss Bobby Socks (1944)
Strange Affair (1944)
Over 21 (1945)
She Wouldn't Say Yes (1945)
A Thousand and One Nights (1945)
Gallant Journey (1946)
Gilda (1946)
The Walls Came Tumbling Down (1946)
Dead Reckoning (1947)
Framed (1947)
Mickey (1948)

Relentless (1948)
The Golden Gloves Story (1950)
Callaway Went Thataway (1951)
Cavalry Scout (1951)
Flight to Mars (1951)
The Lion Hunters (1951)
Rodeo (1951)
Aladdin and His Lamp (1952)
Army Bound (1952)
Battle Zone (1952)
Flat Top (1952)
Fort Osage (1952)
Hiawatha (1952)
The Rose Bowl Story (1952)
Wild Stallion (1952)
Clipped Wings (1953)
Fighter Attack (1953)
Hot News (1953)
Jalopy (1953)
Loose in London (1953)
Roar of the Crowd (1953)
Safari Drums (1953)
Something Money Can't Buy (1953)
White Lightning (1953)
Arrow in the Dust (1954)
The Bowery Boys Meet the Monsters (1954)
The Golden Idol (1954)
Jungle Gents (1954)
Killer Leopard (1954)
Paris Playboys (1954)
Pride of the Blue Grass (1954)
An Annapolis Story (1955)
Bowery to Bagdad (1955)
Dial Red 0 (1955)
High Society (1955)
Jail Busters (1955)
Lord of the Jungle (1955)
Skabenga (1955)
Spy Chasers (1955)
Sudden Danger (1955)
Calling Homicide (1956)
Canyon River (1956)
Crashing Las Vegas (1956)
Dig That Uranium (1956)
Hot Shots (1956)
The Disembodied (1957)
Footsteps in the Night (1957)
Hold That Hypnotist (1957)
Looking for Danger (1957)
My Gun Is Quick (1957)
Spook Chasers (1957)
Up in Smoke (1957)
The Beast of Budapest (1958)
Cole Younger, Gunfighter (1958)
Fort Massacre (1958)
In the Money (1958)
Joy Ride (1958)
The Man from God's Country (1958)
Quantrill's Raiders (1958)
Queen of Outer Space (1958)
Battle Flame (1959)
King of the Wild Stallions (1959)
The Hypnotic Eye (1960)
The Deadly Companions (1961)
Gunfight at Comanche Creek (1963)
The Strangler (1964)
The Violent Ones (1967)
Dayton's Devils (1968)
The Resurrection of Zachary Wheeler (1971)

SKINNER, DONALD
Meat Rack (1970)

SKINNER, FRANK
Charlie McCarthy, Detective (1939)
Destry Rides Again (1939)
The Sun Never Sets (1939)
Hired Wife (1940)
House of the Seven Gables (1940)
My Little Chickadee (1940)
When the Daltons Rode (1940)
Appointment for Love (1941)
Back Street (1941)
Flame of New Orleans (1941)
The Lady from Cheyenne (1941)
Arabian Nights (1942)
Broadway (1942)
Eagle Squadron (1942)
Lady in a Jam (1942)
Pittsburgh (1942)
Ride 'Em Cowboy (1942)
Saboteur (1942)
Sherlock Holmes and the Secret Weapon (1942)
Sherlock Holmes and the Voice of Terror (1942)

Who Done It? (1942)
The Amazing Mrs. Holliday (1943)
Fired Wife (1943)
Gung Ho! (1943)
Hers to Hold (1943)
Sherlock Holmes in Washington (1943)
Top Man (1943)
Two Tickets to London (1943)
White Savage (1943)
Destiny (1944)
Hi, Beautiful (1944)
The Suspect (1944)
Blonde Ransom (1945)
The Daltons Ride Again (1945)
Frontier Gal (1945)
Pillow of Death (1945)
Strange Confession (1945)
Under Western Skies (1945)
Black Angel (1946)
Canyon Passage (1946)
Idea Girl (1946)
Inside Job (1946)
Night in Paradise (1946)
The Runaround (1946)
The Egg and I (1947)
The Exile (1947)
I'll Be Yours (1947)
Ride the Pink Horse (1947)
Abbott and Costello Meet Frankenstein (1948)
Black Bart (1948)
Family Honeymoon (1948)
For the Love of Mary (1948)
Hazard (1948)
Naked City (1948)
Tap Roots (1948)
Bagdad (1949)
The Fighting O'Flynn (1949)
Francis (1949)
Free for All (1949)
The Gal Who Took the West (1949)
The Lady Gambles (1949)
The Life of Riley (1949)
Sword in the Desert (1949)
Tulsa (1949)
Woman in Hiding (1949)
Comanche Territory (1950)
The Desert Hawk (1950)
Double Crossbones (1950)
Harvey (1950)
Louisa (1950)
One-Way Street (1950)
The Sleeping City (1950)
Bedtime for Bonzo (1951)
Bright Victory (1951)
Francis Goes to the Races (1951)
Katie Did It (1951)
The Lady Pays Off (1951)
Mark of the Renegade (1951)
The Raging Tide (1951)
Weekend with Father (1951)
Because of You (1952)
Bonzo Goes to College (1952)
It Grows on Trees (1952)
No Room for the Groom (1952)
Sally and Saint Anne (1952)
The World in His Arms (1952)
Back to God's Country (1953)
Desert Legion (1953)
Forbidden (1953)
The Man from the Alamo (1953)
Mississippi Gambler (1953)
The Stand at Apache River (1953)
Thunder Bay (1953)
Wings of the Hawk (1953)
Magnificent Obsession (1954)
Sign of the Pagan (1954)
Taza, Son of Cochise (1954)
All That Heaven Allows (1955)
Chief Crazy Horse (1955)
Foxfire (1955)
One Desire (1955)
The Shrike (1955)
Away All Boats (1956)
Battle Hymn (1956)
Never Say Goodbye (1956)
The Rawhide Years (1956)
Star in the Dust (1956)
Written on the Wind (1956)
Interlude (1957)
Man of a Thousand Faces (1957)
My Man Godfrey (1957)
Tammy and the Bachelor (1957)
Tarnished Angels (1957)
The Tattered Dress (1957)
Kathy O' (1958)
Once Upon a Horse (1958)
The Perfect Furlough (1958)

The Restless Years (1958)
This Happy Feeling (1958)
Imitation of Life (1959)
The Snow Queen (1959)
Midnight Lace (1960)
Portrait in Black (1960)
Back Street (1961)
Captain Newman, M.D. (1963)
Tammy and the Doctor (1963)
The Ugly American (1963)
Bullet for a Badman (1964)
Shenandoah (1965)
The Sword of Ali Baba (1965)
The Appoloosa (1966)
Madame X (1966)

SKJOLD, SVEN
One Summer of Happiness (1951)

SKLAIR, SAM
Tokoloshe (1971)

SLANEY, IVOR
Blackout (1954)
The Saint's Girl Friday (1954)
The Scarlet Spear (1954)
Zanzabuku (1956)
The Poacher's Daughter (1960)

SLAVIN, GILBERT
Sweet Savior (1971)

SLAVIN, MARTIN
Information Received (1962)

SMALL, MICHAEL
Jenny (1969)
Puzzle of a Downfall Child (1970)
The Revolutionary (1970)
The Sporting Club (1971)
Child's Play (1972)
Dealing: or the Berkeley-to-Boston Forty-Brick Lost-Bag Blues (1972)

SMART, HAROLD
Father's Doing Fine (1952)

SMATEK, MILOS
Janosik (1936)

SMIRNOV, V.
Stalingrad (1943)

SMITH, FRANK
Northern Safari (1968)

SMITH, HUBERT
Lost Lagoon (1958)

SMITH, KENNETH LESLIE
The Woman's Angle (1952)

SMITH, PAUL
Fun and Fancy Free (1947)
So Dear to My Heart (1948)
The Strange Mrs. Crane (1948)
Beaver Valley (1950)
Nature's Half Acre (1951)
Bear Country (1952)
The Living Desert (1953)
The Olympic Elk (1953)
Prowlers of the Everglades (1954)
20,000 Leagues Under the Sea (1954)
The Vanishing Prairie (1954)
The African Lion (1955)
The Great Locomotive Chase (1956)
Secrets of Life (1956)
Switzerland (1956)
Perri (1957
The Light in the Forest (1958)
The Shaggy Dog (1959)
Pollyanna (1960)
The Parent Trap (1961)
Bon Voyage (1962)
Moon Pilot (1962)
The Miracle of the White Stallions (1963)
The Three Loves of Thomasina (1963)

SMYTHE, GILLI
Near Orouet (1971)

SNELL, DAVID
Dangerous Number (1937)
Madame X (1937)
The Thirteenth Chair (1937)
You're Only Young Once (1937)
The World Is Ours (1938)
Young Dr. Kildare (1938)

Andy Hardy Gets Spring Fever (1939)
Burn 'Em Up, O'Connor (1939)
Calling Dr. Kildare (1939)
Thunder Afloat (1939)
The Women (1939)
Andy Hardy Meets a Debutante (1940)
Dr. Kildare Goes Home (1940)
Joe and Ethel Turp Call on the President (1940)
The Man from Dakota (1940)
Third Finger, Left Hand (1940)
Billy the Kid (1941)
Love Crazy (1941)
Shadow of the Thin Man (1941)
Wild Man of Borneo (1941)
The Courtship of Andy Hardy (1942)
Grand Central Murder (1942)
Jackass Mail (1942)
Kid Glove Killer (1942)
Northwest Rangers (1942)
The Omaha Trail (1942)
Tarzan's New York Adventure (1942)
Tish (1942)
The War Against Mrs. Hadley (1942)
Northwest Rangers (1942)
The Man from Down Under (1943)
The Youngest Profession (1943)
Andy Hardy's Blonde Trouble (1944)
Barbary Coast Gent (1944)
Between Two Women (1944)
Gentle Annie (1944)
Lost in a Harem (1944)
Maisie Goes to Reno (1944)
Rationing (1944)
See Here, Private Hargrove (1944)
The Thin Man Goes Home (1944)
Dangerous Partners (1945)
The Hidden Eye (1945)
Keep Your Powder Dry (1945)
Twice Blessed (1945)
What Next, Corporal Hargrove? (1945)
Bad Bascomb (1946)
The Cockeyed Miracle (1946)
Love Laughs at Andy Hardy (1946)
The Mighty McGurk (1946)
The Show-Off (1946)
Up Goes Maisie (1946)
Dark Delusion (1947)
Killer McCoy (1947)
Lady in the Lake (1947)
Merton of the Movies (1947)
Song of the Thin Man (1947)
Undercover Maisie (1947)
Alias a Gentleman (1948)
A Southern Yankee (1948)

SNITCHE, ALFRED
You and Me (1972)

SNOW, A. GEAN
Toklat (1971)

SODERO, CESARE
Isn't Life Wonderful? (1924)

SODJA, JOE
The Parson and the Outlaw (1957)

THE SOFT MACHINE
Blue Velvet (1970)

SOLA, JOSE
Pyro (1964)
Finger on the Trigger (1965)

SOLAL, MARTIAL
Backfire (1965)

SOLKIN, JOE
Wow (1971)

SOMMER, HANS
Her Sister's Secret (1946)
Gas House Kids Go West (1947)
The First Legion (1951)

SONSTEVOLD, GUNNAR
Nine Lives (1959)

SONZAGNO, G. C.
Stranger on the Prowl (1953)

SOREL, HAROLD
Right On (1970)

SOROZABAL, PABLO
Marcellino (1956)

SOUFFRIAU, ARSENE
The Lover (1972)

SOURIS, ANDRE
The World of Paul Delvaux (1947)

SPANOS, YANNIS
That Summer (1971)
Angry Youth (1972)

SPARKS, RANDY
Advance to the Rear (1964)
How Do I Love Thee? (1970)

SPEAR, ERIC
Ghost Ship (1953)
The Limping Man (1953)
The Vulture (1967)

SPENCE, JOHNNIE
The Limbo Line (1968)
The Man Outside (1968)

SPENCER, FRANK
Cloudburst (1952)
Whispering Smith vs. Scotland Yard (1952)

SPENCER, HERBERT
Spring Reunion (1957)

SPINA, FRANK
Baby Face Nelson (1957)

SPOLIANSKY, MISCHA
The Private Life of Don Juan (1934)
Sanders of the River (1935)
Wanted for Murder (1946)
The Idol of Paris (1947)
Meet Me at Dawn (1948)
Adam and Evelyn (1949)
That Dangerous Age (1949)
The Happiest Days of Your Life (1951)
Happy Go Lucky (1951)
Man in the Dinghy (1951)
Melba (1953)
Turn the Key Softly (1953)
Duel in the Jungle (1954)
Midnight Episode (1955)
Trouble in Store (1955)
Saint Joan (1957)
Victoria and Her Hussar (1957)
The Whole Truth (1958)
Flame over India (1960)
The Battle of the Villa Fiorita (1965)
The Best House in London (1969)

SPRINGER, PHILIP
Kill a Dragon (1967)
More Dead Than Alive (1968)
Impasse (1969)
Tell Me That You Love Me, Junie Moon (1970)

SRERIFF, NOAM
Take 2 (1972)

SRNKA, JIRI
Krakatit (1951)
Hammer for the Witches (1970)

STABILE, DICK
Hook, Line and Sinker (1969)

STACK, LENNY
C. C. and Company (1970)

STAHL, WILLY
Dark Mountain (1944)
The Navy Way (1944)
Timber Queen (1944)

STANDAGE, SIMON
Adult Fun (1972)

STANKO, TOMASZ
A Hole in the Ground (1970)

STANLEY, RALPH
The Burning Cross (1947)
Road to the Big House (1947)
The Argyle Secrets (1948)
The Dead Don't Dream (1948)
False Paradise (1948)
The Gay Intruders (1948)
Let's Live Again (1948)
Night Wind (1948)
Shaggy (1948)

Shed No Tears (1948)
Unknown Island (1948)
Strange Gamble (1949)
Timber Fury (1950)

STARR, ALEXANDRE
Gold Raiders (1951)

STEIMEL, ADOLF
The Original Sin (1948)

STEIN, HERMAN
This Island Earth (1955)
Backlash (1956)
The Great Man (1956)
I've Lived Before (1956)
The Unguarded Moment (1956)
Quantez (1957)
Slim Carter (1957)
The Lady Takes a Flyer (1958)
No Name on the Bullet (1959)
I Hate Your Guts (1962)
Taggart (1964)
Let's Kill Uncle (1966)

STEIN, RONALD
There'a Always Tomorrow (1956)
Attack of the Crab Monsters (1957)
Not of This Earth (1957)
Reform School Girl (1957)
Sorority Girl (1957)
Attack of the 50-Foot Woman (1958)
Jet Attack (1958)
The Littlest Hobo (1958)
Suicide Battalion (1958)
Diary of a High School Bride (1959)
The Ghost of Dragstrip Hollow (1959)
The Legend of Tom Dooley (1959)
Dinosaurus! (1960)
Raymie (1960)
The Threat (1960)
Too Soon to Love (1960)
The Bashful Elephant (1962)
Premature Burial (1962)
The Underwater City (1962)
Dime with a Halo (1963)
The Haunted Place (1963)
Of Love and Desire (1963)
The Young and the Brave (1963)
War Is Hell (1964)
The Bounty Killer (1965)
Requiem for a Gunfighter (1965)
Rat Fink (1966)
The Rain People (1969)
Getting Straight (1970)

STEINER, FRED
Man from Del Rio (1956)
Run for the Sun (1956)
Time Limit (1957)
First to Fight (1967)
The St. Valentine's Day Massacre (1967)

STEINER, MAX
The Bondman (1916)
Cimarron (1931)
A Bill of Divorcement (1932)
Bird of Paradise (1932)
What Price Hollywood? (1932)
Ann Vickers (1933)
Bed of Roses (1933)
Blind Adventure (1933)
Emergency Call (1933)
King Kong (1933)
Melody Cruise (1933)
Morning Glory (1933)
One Man's Journey (1933)
Our Betters (1933)
Professional Sweetheart (1933)
The Silver Cord (1933)
Sweepings (1933)
Topaze (1933)
The Crime Doctor (1934)
The Fountain (1934)
Hat, Coat and Glove (1934)
If I Were Free (1934)
Let's Try Again (1934)
The Life of Vergie Winters (1934)
Little Women (1934)
The Lost Patrol (1934)
Man of Two Worlds (1934)
Murder on the Blackboard (1934)
Of Human Bondage (1934)
The Richest Girl in the World (1934)

Son of Kong (1934)
Spitfire (1934)
Stingaree (1934)
Strictly Dynamite (1934)
Success at Any Price (1934)
This Man Is Mine (1934)
Where Sinners Meet (1934)
Becky Sharp (1935)
I Dream Too Much (1935)
The Informer (1935)
The Three Musketeers (1935)
The Charge of the Light Brigade (1936)
The Garden of Allah (1936)
Little Lord Fauntleroy (1936)
God's Country and the Woman (1937)
The Green Light (1937)
Kid Galahad (1937)
A Star Is Born (1937)
The Amazing Doctor Clitterhouse (1938)
Angels with Dirty Faces (1938)
The Dawn Patrol (1938)
Four Daughters (1938)
Gold Is Where You Find It (1938)
Jezebel (1938)
The Sisters (1938)
White Banners (1938)
Confessions of a Nazi Spy (1939)
Dark Victory (1939)
Daughters Courageous (1939)
Dodge City (1939)
Dust Be My Destiny (1939)
Each Dawn I Die (1939)
Four Wives (1939)
Gone with the Wind (1939)
The Old Maid (1939)
We Are Not Alone (1939)
All This and Heaven Too (1940)
City for Conquest (1940)
Dispatch from Reuters (1940)
Dr. Ehrlich's Magic Bullet (1940)
The Letter (1940)
The Sea Hawk (1940)
Tugboat Annie Sails Again (1940)
Virginia City (1940)
The Bride Came C.O.D. (1941)
Dive Bomber (1941)
The Great Lie (1941)
One Foot in Heaven (1941)
Santa Fe Trail (1941)
Sergeant York (1941)
Captains of the Clouds (1942)
Casablanca (1942)
The Gay Sisters (1942)
In This Our Life (1942)
Now Voyager (1942)
Mission to Moscow (1943)
Watch on the Rhine (1943)
The Adventures of Mark Twain (1944)
Arsenic and Old Lace (1944)
The Conspirators (1944)
Passage to Marseille (1944)
Since You Went Away (1944)
Mildred Pierce (1945)
Saratoga Trunk (1945)
The Big Sleep (1946)
Cloak and Dagger (1946)
My Reputation (1946)
Night and Day (1946)
One More Tomorrow (1946)
A Stolen Life (1946)
Tomorrow Is Forever (1946)
Beast with Five Fingers (1947)
Cheyenne (1947)
Deep Valley (1947)
Life with Father (1947)
Love and Learn (1947)
The Man I Love (1947)
Pursued (1947)
The Unfaithful (1947)
Voice of the Turtle (1947)
Adventures of Don Juan (1948)
The Decision of Christopher Blake (1948)
Fighter Squadron (1948)
Johnny Belinda (1948)
Key Largo (1948)
My Girl Tisa (1948)
Silver River (1948)
The Treasure of the Sierra Madre (1948)
Winter Meeting (1948)
The Woman in White (1948)
Flamingo Road (1949)
The Fountainhead (1949)
A Kiss in the Dark (1949)

The Lady Takes a Sailor (1949)
Mrs. Mike (1949)
South of St. Louis (1949)
White Heat (1949)
Without Honor (1949)
Caged (1950)
Dallas (1950)
The Flame and the Arrow (1950)
The Glass Menagerie (1950)
Rocky Mountain (1950)
Close to My Heart (1951)
Distant Drums (1951)
Force of Arms (1951)
Jim Thorpe, All-American (1951)
Lightning Strikes Twice (1951)
On Moonlight Bay (1951)
Operation Pacific (1951)
Raton Pass (1951)
Sugarfoot (1951)
The Iron Mistress (1952)
Mara Maru (1952)
The Miracle of Fatima (1952)
Room for One More (1952)
Springfield Rifle (1952)
The Charge at Feather River (1953)
So Big (1953)
Trouble Along the Way (1953)
The Boy from Oklahoma (1954)
The Caine Mutiny (1954)
King Richard and the Crusaders (1954)
Battle Cry (1955)
Helen of Troy (1955)
Hell on Frisco Bay (1955)
Illegal (1955)
The Last Command (1955)
The McConnell Story (1955)
The Violent Men (1955)
Bandido (1956)
Come Next Spring (1956)
Death of a Scoundrel (1956)
The Searchers (1956)
All Mine to Give (1957)
Band of Angels (1957)
Escapade in Japan (1957)
Darby's Raiders (1958)
Fort Dobbs (1958)
Marjorie Morningstar (1958)
Cash McCall (1959)
The FBI Story (1959)
The Hanging Tree (1959)
John Paul Jones (1959)
A Summer Place (1959)
The Dark at the Top of the Stairs (1959)
Ice Palace (1959)
A Majority of One (1961)
Parrish (1961)
Portrait of a Mobster (1961)
The Sins of Rachel Cade (1961)
Susan Slade (1961)
Rome Adventure (1962)
Spencer's Mountain (1963)
A Distant Trumpet (1964)
F.B.I. Code 98 (1964)
Those Calloways (1964)
Youngblood Hawke (1964)
Two on a Guillotine (1965)

STEINERT, ALEXANDER
Strangler of the Swamp (1945)
Devil Bat's Daughter (1946)
Little Iodine (1946)
The Prairie (1948)

STEININGER, FRANZ
Hit and Run (1957)
Born to Be Loved (1959)
Stagecoach to Dancer's Rock (1962)

STEOBER, ORVILLE
Let's Scare Jessica to Death (1971)

STERNWALD, JIRI
Distant Journey (1950)
Oasis (1972)

STEVENS, BERNARD
The Upturned Glass (1947)
Once a Jolly Swagman (1948)

STEVENS, CAT
Harold and Maude (1971)

STEVENS, JAMES
The Weapon (1957)
They Came from Beyond Space (1967)

STEVENS, LEITH
Night Song (1947)
All My Sons (1948)
Black Bart (1948)
Feudin', Fussin' and A-Fightin' (1948)
Larceny (1948)
The Great Rupert (1949)
Not Wanted (1949)
Destination Moon (1950)
Never Fear (1950)
The Sun Sets at Dawn (1950)
No Questions Asked (1951)
Storm over Tibet (1951)
When Worlds Collide (1951)
The Atomic City (1952)
Beware, My Lovely (1952)
Eight Iron Men (1952)
Crazylegs (1953)
The Glass Wall (1953)
The Hitchhiker (1953)
Scared Stiff (1953)
The War of the Worlds (1953)
The Bob Mathias Story (1954)
Private Hell 36 (1954)
The Wild One (1954)
Crashout (1955)
The Treasure of Pancho Villa (1955)
Julie (1956)
The Scarlet Hour (1956)
World without End (1956)
The Careless Years (1957)
Eighteen and Anxious (1957)
The Garment Jungle (1957)
The Green-Eyed Blonde (1957)
The James Dean Story (1957)
Lizzie (1957)
Ride Out for Revenge (1957)
Bullwhip (1958)
Cop Hater (1958)
The Gun Runners (1958)
Seven Guns to Mesa (1958)
Violent Road (1958)
But Not for Me (1959)
The Five Pennies (1959)
The Gene Krupa Story (1959)
Hell to Eternity (1960)
Man Trap (1961)
On the Double (1961)
The Interns (1962)
It Happened at the World's Fair (1963
A New Kind of Love (1963)
The Night of the Grizzly (1966)
Smoky (1966)
Chuka (1967)

STEVENS, MORTON
The Raiders (1963)
Wild and Wonderful (1964)
The Spy with My Face (1966)

STIEF, BO
Sunny Beach Revolution (1971)

STOLL, GEORGE
Listen, Darling (1938)
Strike Up the Band (1940)
The Big Store (1941)
Go West (1941)
Road Show (1941)
Cabin in the Sky (1943)
DuBarry Was a Lady (1943)
I Dood It (1943)
Presenting Lily Mars (1943)
Swing Fever (1943)
Meet Me in St. Louis (1944)
Two Girls and a Sailor (1944)
Her Highness and the Bellboy (1945)
Thrill of a Romance (1945)
The Big City (1948)
A Date with Judy (1948)
Luxury Liner (1948)
On an Island with You (1948)
Three Daring Daughters (1948)
In the Good Old Summertime (1949)
Neptune's Daughter (1949)
Watch the Birdie (1950)
Excuse My Dust (1951)
The Strip (1951)
Glory Alley (1952)
Dangerous When Wet (1953)
Latin Lovers (1953)
Athena (1954)
Flame and the Flesh (1954)
Hit the Deck (1955)
Love Me or Leave Me (1955)
Meet Me in Las Vegas (1956)
10,000 Bedrooms (1957)
This Could Be the Night (1957)
The Seven Hills of Rome (1958)

For the First Time (1959)
Where the Boys Are (1960)
The Horizontal Lieutenant (1962)
Jumbo (1962)
The Courtship of Eddie's Father (1963)
A Ticklish Affair (1963)
Get Yourself a College Girl (1964)
Looking for Love (1964)
Viva Las Vegas (1964)
Girl Happy (1965)
The Man from Button Willow (1965)
Made in Paris (1966)
Spinout (1966)

STOLLER, MIKE
The Phynx (1970)

STOLOFF, MORRIS
Adventures in Manhattan (1936)
Craig's Wife (1936)
More Than a Secretary (1936)
Theodora Goes Wild (1936)
Devil's Playground (1937)
The Doctor Takes a Wife (1940)
I Married Adventure (1940)
Too Many Husbands (1940)
Penny Serenade (1941)
She Knew All the Answers (1941)
This Thing Called Love, (1941)
The Adventures of Martin Eden (1942)
It Had to Be You (1947)
The Petty Girl (1950)
The Lady and the Bandit (1951)
The Brigand (1952)
The First Time (1952)
The Marrying Kind (1952)
Paula (1952)
Scandal Sheet (1952)
The Sniper (1952)
Sound Off! (1952)
Let's Do It Again (1953)
Miss Sadie Thompson (1953)
Gidget (1959)

STOLYAR, JACOB
The Road to Life (1931)

STOLZ, ROBERT
Spring Parade (1940)
It Happened Tomorrow (1944)

STONE, GREGORY
Internes Can't Take Money (1937)
Girl's School (1938)
Her Jungle Love (1938)
Jivaro (1954)

STORA, JEAN-PIERRE
Repeated Absences (1972)

STOTHART, HERBERT
The End of St. Petersburg (1928)
Dynamite (1929)
The Squaw Man (1931)
Night Flight (1933)
Peg O' My Heart (1933)
Rasputin and the Empress (1933)
White Sister (1933)
The Barretts of Wimpole Street (1934)
The Painted Veil (1934)
Queen Christina (1934)
Riptide (1934)
Treasure Island (1934)
Viva Villa! (1934)
What Every Woman Knows (1934)
Anna Karenina (1935)
China Seas (1935)
Here Comes the Band (1935)
After the Thin Man (1936)
Ah, Wilderness (1936)
Camille (1936)
The Devil Is a Sissy (1936)
The Good Earth (1936)
The Gorgeous Hussey (1936)
A Night at the Opera (1936)
Robin Hood of El Dorado (1936)
Romeo and Juliet (1936)
Small Town Girl (1936)
A Tale of Two Cities (1936)
Marie Antoinette (1938)
Of Human Hearts (1938)
Bad Little Angel (1939)
Broadway Serenade (1939)
The Wizard of Oz (1939)
Edison the Man (1940)

Northwest Passage (1940)
Pride and Prejudice (1940)
Susan and God (1940)
Waterloo Bridge (1940)
Andy Hardy's Private Secretary (1941)
Blossoms in the Dust (1941)
Come Live with Me (1941)
Men of Boys' Town (1941)
Ziegfeld Girl (1941)
Cairo (1942)
Mrs. Miniver (1942)
Random Harvest (1942)
Tennessee Johnson (1942)
A Guy Named Joe (1943)
The Human Comedy (1943)
Madame Curie (1943)
Song of Russia (1943)
Thousands Cheer (1943)
Three Hearts for Julia (1943)
Dragon Seed (1944)
Kismet (1944)
National Velvet (1944)
Thirty Seconds over Tokyo (1944)
The White Cliffs of Dover (1944)
The Picture of Dorian Gray (1945)
Son of Lassie (1945)
They Were Expendable (1945)
The Valley of Decision (1945)
Adventure (1946)
The Green Years (1946)
Undercurrent (1946)
The Yearling (1946)
Desire Me (1947)
High Barbaree (1947)
If Winter Comes (1947)
Sea of Grass (1947)
The Unfinished Dance (1947)
Hills of Home (1948)
The Three Musketeers (1948)
Big Jack (1949)
The Miniver Story (1950)

STOTT, WALLY
The Looking Glass War (1970)

STRANGE, BILLY
Live a Little, Love a Little (1968)
De Sade (1969)
The Trouble with Girls (1969)
Bunny O'Hare (1971)

STRAUS, OSCAR
La Ronde (1950)
The Earrings of Madame D ... (1953)

STRAUSS, JOHANN
The Count of St. Elmo (1951)

STRAUSS, JOHANN, JR.
2001: A Space Odyssey (1968)

STRAUSS, RICHARD
2001: A Space Odyssey (1968)

STRAVINSKY, IGOR
The Balcony (1963)

STRINGER, ROBERT W.
Jigsaw (1949)
So Young, So Bad (1950)
St. Benny the Dip (1951)

STROUSE, CHARLES
Bonnie and Clyde (1967)
The Night They Raided Minsky's (1968)
There Was a Crooked Man (1970)

STUART, CHAD
Three in the Attic (1968)

STUART, PEGGY
The Silken Affair (1957)

STYNER, JERRY
Ski Fever (1969)
Cycle Savages (1970)
The Magic Garden of Stanley Sweetheart (1970)
Corky (1972)
The Genesis Children (1972)

SUKMAN, HARRY
Gog (1954)
Riders to the Stars (1954)
Battle Taxi (1955)
A Bullet for Joey (1955)
The Phenix City Story (1955)
Screaming Eagles (1956)

Forty Guns (1957)
Fury at Sundown (1957)
Sabu and the Magic Ring (1957)
Outcasts of the City (1958)
Underwater Warrior (1958)
The Crimson Kimono (1959)
The Hangman (1959)
Verboten! (1959)
A Thunder of Drums (1961)
Underworld, U.S.A. (1961)
Belle Somers (1962)
Madison Avenue (1962)
Around the World under the Sea (1966)
The Singing Nun (1966)
The Naked Runner (1967)
Welcome to Hard Times (1967)
If He Hollers, Let Him Go (1968)
The Private Navy of Sgt. O'-Farrell (1968)

SURDIN, MORRIS
The Hospital (1971)

SUSSKIND, H. W.
Crisis (1939)

SVECHNIKOV, A.
A Pedagogical Poem (1955)

SWEETEN, CLAUDE
Tembo (1951)

SWINGLE, WARD
Gates to Paradise (1968)

SYLVAIN, JULES
Jungle of Chang (1951)

SYLVIANO, RENE
Her First Affair (1941)
One Step to Eternity (1955)

SZOLLOSSY, ANDRAS
Dead Landscape (1972)

TAKEMITSU, TORU
Bad Boys (1960)
Kwaidan (1965)
Clickety-Clack (1970)
He Died After the War (1971)
Inn of Evil (1971)
Dear Summer Sister (1972)
A Silence (1972)
Summer Soldiers (1972)

TALBOT, IRVIN
Henry Aldrich, Boy Scout (1944)
Henry Aldrich Plays Cupid (1944)
Henry Aldrich's Little Secret (1944)
Lumberjack (1944)
Ladies' Man (1947)
Union Station (1950)
The Turning Point (1952)
Alaska Seas (1954)
Hell's Island (1955)
The Leather Saint (1956)
The Search for Bridey Murphy (1956)
Short Cut to Hell (1957)
The Trap (1959)

TAMASSY, ZDENKO
Professor Hannibal (1957)
Carlotta (1971)

TAMKIN, DAVID
Swell Guy (1946)

TANDLER, ADOLPH
Scarface (1932)

TANSMAN, ALEXANDRE
Poil De Carotte (1932)
Flesh and Fantasy (1943)
Paris Underground (1945)
Sister Kenny (1946)

TARANATH, REJIEV
Funeral Rites (1972)

TARANU, CORNEL
Judgment (1970)

TARIK, BO
Cruel Sea (1972)

TAUBE, SVEN-BERTIL
The Apple War (1960)

TAYLOR, DEEMS
Janice Meredith (1924)

TAYLOR, J. O.
Son of Kong (1934)

TAYLOR, RICHARD
The Case of the Red Monkey (1955)
The Brain Machine (1956)
The Deadliest Sin (1956)
Spin a Dark Web (1956)
The Way Out (1956)
The Counterfeit Plan (1957)
The Electronic Monster (1960)

TCHAIKOVSKY, PETER
Romeo and Juliet (1968)

TEDENCO, NICO
The Bang Bang Kid (1968)

TERESCO, MICHAEL
Wilbur and the Baby Factory (1970)

TERR, MICHAEL
Two Lost Worlds (1950)
Red Snow (1952)

TERRY, DAN
The Hustler (1961)

TER-TATEVOSIAN, D.
Nine Days of One Year (1961)

THEODORAKIS, MIKIS
The Barefoot Battalion (1954)
Night Ambush (1958)
The Shadow of the Cat (1961)
The Lovers of Tereul (1962)
Phaedra (1962)
Electra (1963)
Five Miles to Midnight (1963)
Zorba the Greek (1964)
Bloko (The Roundup) (1966)
The Day the Fish Came Out (1967)
Biribi (1971)

THE THIRD EAR BAND
Macbeth (1971)

THIRIET, MAURICE
Adrienne Lecouvrer (1938)
Fantastic Night (1942)
Les Visiteurs du Soir (1942)
Children of Paradise (1943)
They Are Not Angels (1948)
Une si Jolie Petite Plage (1948)
Fan Fan, La Tulipe (1951)
Therese Raquin (1953)
L'air de Paris (1954)
The Most Dangerous Sin (1956)
Crime and Punishment (1958)

THOMAS, PETER
Stop Train 349 (1964)
The Last of the Mohicans (1965)
The Shot from a Violin Case (1965)
Uncle Tom's Cabin (1965)
Jack of Diamonds (1967)
Winnetou and His Friend, Old Firehand (1967)
The Trygon Factor (1968)
Deadly Shots on Broadway (1969)
To Hell with School (1969)
Gentlemen in White Vests (1970)
Memories of the Future (1970)
The Dead One in the Thames River (1971)
Our Willi Is the Best (1972)
Soho Gorilla (1972)
The Stuff That Dreams Are Made Of (1972)

THOMAS, TUGEN
Nocturne (1972)

THOMPSON, BOB
Thumb Tripping (1972)

THOMPSON, JOHN
Killer Dill (1947)

THOMSON, VIRGIL
The Plow That Broke the Plains (1936)
The River (1936)
Spanish Earth (1937)
Tuesday in November (1945)

Louisiana Story (1948)
The Goddess (1958)
Power Among Men (1959)

THOREAU, RACHEL
Gigi (1949)

THORNE, KEN
Master Spy (1964)
How I Won the War (1967)
Head (1968)
Inspector Clouseau (1968)
The Touchables (1968)
Hannie Caulder (1971)
Welcome to the Club (1971)

TILSLEY, REG
What's Good for the Gander (1969)
Horror House (1970)

TIMOFEYEV, N.
Baltic Deputy (1937)
Professor Mamlock (1938)
The Inspector General (Revizor) (1954)

TIOMKIN, DIMITRI
Alice in Wonderland (1934)
I Live My Life (1935)
Lost Horizon (1937)
The Road Back (1937)
The Great Waltz (1938)
Spawn of the North (1938)
You Can't Take It with You (1938)
Mr. Smith Goes to Washington (1939)
Lucky Partners (1940)
The Westerner (1940)
The Corsican Brothers (1941)
Meet John Doe (1941)
A Gentleman After Dark (1942)
The Moon and Sixpence (1942)
The Nazis Strike (1942)
Prelude to War (1942)
Twin Beds (1942)
Battle of Russia (1943)
Divide and Conquer (1943)
Shadow of a Doubt (1943)
The Unknown Guest (1943)
The Bridge of San Luis Rey (1944)
The Imposter (1944)
Ladies Courageous (1944)
The Negro Soldier (1944)
They Shall Have Faith (1944)
Tunisian Victory (1944)
When Strangers Marry (1944)
China's Little Devils (1945)
Dillinger (1945)
Pardon My Past (1945)
Angel on My Shoulder (1946)
Black Beauty (1946)
The Dark Mirror (1946)
It's a Wonderful Life (1946)
Whistle Stop (1946)
Duel in the Sun (1947)
The Long Night (1947)
The Dude Goes West (1948)
Portrait of Jennie (1948)
Red River (1948)
So This Is New York (1948)
Tarzan and the Mermaids (1948)
Canadian Pacific (1949)
Champion (1949)
D. O. A. (1949)
Home of the Brave (1949)
Red Light (1949)
Champagne for Caesar (1950)
Cyrano de Bergerac (1950)
Dakota Lil (1950)
Guilty Bystander (1950)
The Men (1950)
Drums in the Deep South (1951)
Mr. Universe (1951)
Peking Express (1951)
Strangers on a Train (1951)
The Thing (1951)
The Well (1951)
Angel Face (1952)
The Big Sky (1952)
The Fourposter (1952)
The Happy Time (1952)
High Noon (1952)
Lady in the Iron Mask (1952)
Mutiny (1952)
My Six Convicts (1952)
The Steel Trap (1952)
Blowing Wild (1953)
Cease Fire (1953)
His Majesty O'Keefe (1953)
I Confess (1953)
Jeopardy (1953)

Return to Paradise (1953)
Take the High Ground (1953)
The Adventures of Hajja Baba (1954)
A Bullet Is Waiting (1954)
The Command (1954)
Dial "M" for Murder (1954)
The High and the Mighty (1954)
Land of the Pharoahs (1955)
Strange Lady in Town (1955)
Friendly Persuasion (1956)
Giant (1956)
Tension at Table Rock (1956)
Gunfight at the O.K. Corral (1957)
Night Passage (1957)
Search for Paradise (1957)
Wild Is the Wind (1957)
The Old Man and the Sea (1958)
Rhapsody in Steel (1958)
The Last Train from Gun Hill (1959)
Rio Bravo (1959)
The Young Land (1959)
The Alamo (1960)
The Unforgiven (1960)
The Guns of Navarone (1961)
Town without Pity (1961)
55 Days at Peking (1963)
Circus World (1964)
The Fall of the Roman Empire (1964)
36 Hours (1964)
The War Wagon (1967)
Great Catherine (1968)

TJADER, CAL
Hot Car Girl (1958)

TOCCI, GIAN LUCA
I'd Give a Million (1936)

TOCH, ERNST
Peter Ibbetson (1935)
Outcast (1937)
The Cat and the Canary (1939)
Dr. Cyclops (1940)
Ghost Breakers (1940)
Ladies in Retirement (1941)
First Comes Courage (1943)
Address Unknown (1944)
None Shall Escape (1944)
The Unseen (1945)

TODD, LEON N.
Fugitive of the Plains (1943)

TOMASI, HENRY
Letters from My Windmill (1954)

TOMMASI, AMADEO
Thomas and the Bewitched (1970)
They've Changed Faces (1971)

TOSHI, ICHIYANGI
Confession, Theory, Actress (1971)
Purgatory Eroica (1971)

TOURS, FRANK
The Duke of West Point (1938)
Tarnished Angel (1938)
Beyond Tomorrow (1940)

TOWNSEND, DOUGLAS
8 X 8 (1957)

TOWNSHEND, PETER
Double Pisces, Scorpio Rising (1970)

TRANTOW, HERBERT
The Affair Blum (1948)
Christina (1949)
International Counterfeiters (1958)
Tempestuous Love (1958)

TREMBLE, J.
The Truth (1961)

TRENTHAM, BRIAN
The Sky Pirate (1970)

TREVISAN, JOAO SILVERIO
A Vampire's Dream (1970)

TROJAN, VACLAV
The Emperor's Nightingale (1951)
Prince Bayaya (1954)
A Midsummer Night's Dream (1962)

TROOB, LESTER
The Little Fugitive (1953)

TROTSUK, B.
The Lovers (1970)

TROTTER, JOHN SCOTT
Abie's Irish Rose (1946)

TROVAJOLI, ARMANDO
Two Women (1961)
Warriors Five (1962)
Let's Talk About Women (1964)
Marriage Italian Style (1964)
Yesterday, Today and Tomorrow (1964)
Bambole! (1965)
Casanova '70 (1965)
Italiano Brava Gente (1965)
The Magic World of Topo Gigio (1965)
Seven Golden Men (1965)
Operation San Gennero (1966)
Seven Golden Men Strike Again (1966)
Don Juan in Sicily (1967)
Anyone Can Play (1968)
Drop Dead, My Love (1968)
Faustina (1968)
Psych-Out (1968)
The Queens (1968)
How, When, with Whom (1969)
In the Year of the Lord (1969)
The Matriarch (1969)
Police Chief Pepe (1969)
Will Our Friends Succeed in Finding Their Friend Who Mysteriously Disappeared in Africa? (1969)
The Motive Was Jealousy (1970)
Excuse Me, My Name is Rocco Papalev (1971)
Homo Eroticus (1971)
The Married Priest (1971)
The Priest's Wife (1971)
The Viking Who Came from the South (1971)

TROW, KAREL
The Time to Die (1970)

TRZASKOWSKI, ANDREJ
Baltic Express (1959)
The Call (1971)

TSINTSADZE, SULKHAN
The Dragonfly (1955)

TUMASAWA, TOSKIAKI
The Green Slime (1969)

TURCHI, GUIDO
The Steppe (1963)

TYCHO, THOMAS
You Can't See 'Round the Corners (1969)

TYRELL, RALPH
Shirley Thompson vs. the Aliens (1972)

TZIPINE, GEORGES
Mystery of the Black Jungle (1955)

UMALI, RESTIE
Cry Freedom (1961)
No Man Is an Island (1962)

UMILIANI, PIERO
Big Deal on Madonna Street (1960)
The New Angels (1961)
War--Italian Style (1967)
Paranoia (1969)
Sweden--Heaven and Hell (1969)

URBONT, JACQUES
Toys Are Not for Children (1972)

URQUIDI, LUIX (CHINO)
Forbidden to Step on the Clouds (1970)

USHER, GARY
The Girls on the Beach (1965)
Ski Party (1965)

USSACHEVSKY, VLADIMIR
No Exit (1962)

USUELLI, TEO
The Conjugal Bed (1963)

The Ape Woman (1964)
Slave Trade in the World Today (1964)
Paranoia (1966)
The Seventh Floor (1967)
The Man with Balloons (1968)
Dillinger Is Dead (1969)
My Mao (1970)
The Seed of Man (1970)
Strogoff (1970)
The Audience (1972)
Every Sunday Morning (1972)

UY, PAUL
Peace over the Fields (1971)

UZUMI, TOSHIO
Carmen Comes Home (1951)

VAINBERG, MOISEI
The Tiger Tamer (1955)
The Cranes are Flying (1957)

VAN EPS, ROBERT
A Ticklish Affair (1963)
The Man from Button Willow (1965)

VAN PARYS, GEORGES
Le Million (1931)
Silence est D'or (1947)
Lady Paname (1951)
Mr. Peek-a-Boo (1951)
Three Women (1951)
Beauties of the Night (1952)
Casque D'or (1952)
The Earrings of Madame D ... (1953)
French Can-Can (1953)
Papa, Mama, the Maid and I (1954)
Diabolique (1955)
Les Grandes Manoeuvres (1955)
Nana (1955)
Adorable Creatures (1956)
Only the French Can (French Can-Can) (1956)
The Happy Road (1957)
If All the Guys in the World (1957)
Maid in Paris (1957)
Flesh and the Woman (1958)
Mitsou (1958)
All the Gold in the World (1961)
The Millionairess (1961)
I Like Money (1962)

VAN PEEBLES, MELVIN
Watermelon Man (1970)
Sweet Sweetback's Baadassss Song (1971)

VAN ROYEN, JERRY
How Short Is the Time for Love (1970)

VARDI, EMANUEL
Dirtymouth (1970)
Together (1972)
Toys Are Not for Children (1972)

VARESE, EDGAR
Dreams That Money Can Buy (1948)

VARS, HENRY
Gun the Man Down (1956)
Man in the Vault (1956)
Seven Men from Now (1956)
The Unearthly (1957)
China Doll (1958)
Escort West (1959)
Freckles (1960)
Battle at Bloody Beach (1961)
The Little Shepherd of Kingdom Come (1961)
The Two Little Bears (1961)
Woman Hunt (1962)
House of the Damned (1963)
Flipper's New Adventure (1964)
Fool's Parade (1971)

VARTAN, EDDY
The Blood Letting (1971)
She No Longer Talks ... She Shoots (1972)

VARTKES, BARONIJAN
Young and Healthy as a Rose (1971)

VAZ, GUILHERME MEGALHAES
The Alienist (1970)
How Tasty Was My Little Frenchman (1971)

VEALE, JOHN
The Purple Plain (1955)
Postmark for Danger (1956)
The Spanish Gardener (1957)

VELAZCO, EMIL
Strange World (1952)

VELERDE, MIKE
Back Door to Hell (1964)

VELOSO, MANUEL JORGE
Just Peter (1972)

VENNE, STEPHANE
Heads or Tails (1971)
The Men (1971)

VERRETI, ANTONIO
Maddalena (1955)

VICKERS, MIKE (MICHAEL)
Press for Time (1966)
Dracula A.D. 1972 (1972)

VIERU, ANATOL
Felix and Otilia (1972)

VILAYA, USTAD
The Guru (1969)

VILLA-LOBOS, HEITOR
Green Mansions (1959)
Joao (1972)

VINCENT, DONALD
Squares (1972)

VINCENT, ROLAND
Home Sweet Home (1972)
Rampart of Desire (1972)

VITALINI, ALBERICO
Heaven on Earth (1960)

VIVALDI, ANTONIO
The Golden Coach (1954)

VLAD, ROMAN
Beauty and the Devil (1949)
The Walls of Malapaga (1949)
Three Steps North (1951)
Leonardo Da Vinci (1952)
Romeo and Juliet (1954)
Picasso (1956)
The Law (1960)
End of Desire (1962)
The Mighty Ursus (1962)

VOLSKY, B.
Mashenka (1942)

VON KOCH, ERLAND
Night Is My Future (1962)

VON OTTENFELD, EDDISON
Sword of the Avenger (1948)

VREDENBURG, MAX
Mirrors of Holland (1952)

VUKAN, GYORGY
Breakout (1971)
Present Times (1972)

VULCHEV, DIMITER
The White Room (1970)

WAGNER, ROGER
The Gallant Hours (1960)

WALACINSKI, ADAM
Joan of the Angels? (1962)

WALCOTT, COLIN
Raga (1971)

WALDIMIR, SUNE
Kon-Tiki (1951)

WALDORF, RICHARD HIERONYMOUS
Angels Die Hard (1970)

WALDORF, SVEN-OLAF
Georgia, Georgia (1972)

WALDRON, MAL
Sweet Love Bitter (1967)

WALKER, BILL
Kimberley Jim (1965)
Going Home (1971)

WALLACE, OLIVER
Reaching for the Moon (1917)
Fun and Fancy Free (1947)
The Adventures of Ichabod and Mr. Toad (1949)
Cinderella (1949)
Alice in Wonderland (1951)
Peter Pan (1953)
Lady and the Tramp (1955)
Samoa (1956)
Old Yeller (1957)
Tonka (1958)
White Wilderness (1958)
Darby O'Gill and the Little People (1959)
Jungle Cat (1960)
Ten Who Dared (1960)
Nikki, Wild Dog of the North (1961)
Big Red (1962)
The Legend of Lobo (1962)
The Incredible Journey (1963)
Savage Sam (1963)

WALLIN, BENGT-ARNE
Ann and Eve (1970)
Hiya, Stine (1971)

WALTON, WILLIAM
Escape Me Never (1935)
As You Like It (1936)
A Stolen Life (1939)
Major Barbara (1941)
The First of the Few (Spitfire) (1942)
The Foreman Went to France (1942)
Next of Kin (1942)
Went the Day Well? (1942)
Henry V (1945)
Hamlet (1948)
Richard III (1956)
Three Sisters (1970)

WANNBERG, KENNETH
The Peace Killers (1971)
The Tender Warrior (1971)
Welcome Home, Soldier Boys (1972)

WARD, EDWARD
Kismet (1931)
Great Expectations (1934)
The Bishop Misbehaves (1935)
The Mystery of Edwin Drood (1935)
No More Ladies (1935)
Public Hero No. 1 (1935)
Exclusive Story (1936)
The Longest Night (1936)
Moonlight Murder (1936)
Riffraff (1936)
Sinner Take All (1936)
Sworn Enemy (1936)
Double Wedding (1937)
The Good Old Soak (1937)
The Last Gangster (1937)
Man of the People (1937)
Mannequin (1937)
Navy Blue and Gold (1937)
Night Must Fall (1937)
Saratoga (1937)
Boys' Town (1938)
The Crowd Roars (1938)
Hold That Kiss (1938)
Lord Jeff (1938)
Love Is a Headache (1938)
Paradise for Three (1938)
The Shopworn Angel (1938)
Stablemates (1938)
The Toy Wife (1938)
Vacation from Love (1938)
A Yank at Oxford (1938)
Andy Hardy Gets Spring Fever (1939)
Another Thin Man (1939)
Bad Little Angel (1939)
Dancing Co-Ed (1939)
Maisie (1939)
Thunder Afloat (1939)
The Women (1939)
Dance, Girl Dance (1940)
Joe and Ethel Turp Call on the President (1940)
Kit Carson (1940)
My Son, My Son (1940)
South of Pago Pago (1940)
Young Tom Edison (1940)
Cheers for Miss Bishop (1941)
Mr. and Mrs. Smith (1941)

About Face (1942)
The Devil with Hitler (1942)
Dudes Are Pretty People (1942)
Fiesta (1942)
Ghost Catchers (1943)
Moonlight in Vermont (1943)
The Phantom of the Opera (1943)
Prairie Chickens (1943)
Taxi, Mister? (1943)
Ali Baba and the Forty Thieves (1944)
Bowery to Broadway (1944)
The Climax (1944)
Cobra Woman (1944)
Gypsy Wildcat (1944)
Her Primitive Man (1944)
Salome, Where She Danced (1945)
Song of the Sarong (1945)
Copacabana (1947)
It Happened on Fifth Avenue (1947)
The Babe Ruth Story (1948)

WARK, COLIN
Mill on the Floss (1939)

WARNER, EDDIE
The Reluctant Debutante (1958)

WARR, TERRY
Suburban Wives (1972)

WARRACK, GUY
A Defeated People (1945)
Theirs Is the Glory (1946)
The Story of Time (1949)

WATANABE, CHUMEI
The Night of the Seagull (1970)

WAXMAN, FRANZ
Liliom (1933)
Diamond Jim (1935)
East of Java (1935)
The Great Impersonation (1935)
His Night Out (1935)
Three Kids and a Queen (1935)
Absolute Quiet (1936)
The Devil Doll (1936)
Fury (1936)
His Brother's Wife (1936)
Love Before Breakfast (1936)
Love on the Run (1936)
Magnificent Obsession (1936)
Next Time We Love (1936)
Sutter's Gold (1936)
Trouble for Two (1936)
Captains Courageous (1937)
Personal Property (1937)
Arsene Lupin Returns (1938)
A Christmas Carol (1938)
Man-Proof (1938)
Port of Seven Seas (1938)
The Shining Hour (1938)
Test Pilot (1938)
Three Comrades (1938)
Too Hot to Handle (1938)
The Young in Heart (1938)
The Adventures of Huckleberry Finn (1939)
At the Circus (1939)
Escape (1939)
Lady of the Tropics (1939)
On Borrowed Time (1939)
Boom Town (1940)
Florian (1940)
I Love You Again (1940)
The Philadelphia Story (1940)
Rebecca (1940)
Strange Cargo (1940)
Dr. Jekyll and Mr. Hyde (1941)
The Feminine Touch (1941)
Flight Command (1941)
Honky Tonk (1941)
Kathleen (1941)
Suspicion (1941)
Unfinished Business (1941)
Her Cardboard Lover (1942)
I Married a Witch (1942)
Journey for Margaret (1942)
Reunion (1942)
Seven Sweethearts (1942)
Tortilla Flat (1942)
Woman of the Year (1942)
Air Force (1943)
Destination Tokyo (1943)
Edge of Darkness (1943)
Old Acquaintance (1943)
In Our Time (1944)
Mr. Skeffington (1944)
The Very Thought of You (1944)
Confidential Agent (1945)

God Is My Co-Pilot (1945)
The Horn Blows at Midnight (1945)
Hotel Berlin (1945)
Objective, Burma! (1945)
Pride of the Marines (1945)
Roughly Speaking (1945)
San Antonio (1945)
Her Kind of Man (1946)
Cry Wolf (1947)
Dark Passage (1947)
Humoresque (1947)
Nora Prentiss (1947)
The Paradine Case (1947)
Possessed (1947)
That Hagan Girl (1947)
The Two Mrs. Carrolls (1947)
The Unsuspected (1947)
No Minor Vices (1948)
Sorry, Wrong Number (1948)
Whiplash (1948)
Alias Nick Beal (1949)
Johnny Holiday (1949)
Night Unto Night (1949)
Rope of Sand (1949)
Task Force (1949)
Dark City (1950)
The Furies (1950)
Night and the City (1950)
Sunset Boulevard (1950)
Anne of the Indies (1951)
The Blue Veil (1951)
Decision Before Dawn (1951)
He Ran All the Way (1951)
Only the Valiant (1951)
A Place in the Sun (1951)
Red Mountain (1951)
Come Back, Little Sheba (1952)
Lure of the Wilderness (1952)
My Cousin Rachel (1952)
Phone Call from a Stranger (1952)
Botany Bay (1953)
I, the Jury (1953)
A Lion Is in the Streets (1953)
Man on a Tightrope (1953)
Stalag 17 (1953)
Demitrius and the Gladiators (1954)
Elephant Walk (1954)
Prince Valiant (1954)
Rear Window (1954)
The Silver Chalice (1954)
This Is My Love (1954)
The Indian Fighter (1955)
Mister Roberts (1955)
Untamed (1955)
The Virgin Queen (1955)
Back from Eternity (1956)
Crime in the Streets (1956)
Miracle in the Rain (1956)
Dino (1957)
Love in the Afternoon (1957)
Peyton Place (1957)
Sayonara (1957)
The Spirit of St. Louis (1957)
Home Before Dark (1958)
Run Silent, Run Deep (1958)
Beloved Infidel (1959)
Career (1959)
Count Your Blessings (1959)
The Nun's Story (1959)
Cimarron (1960)
The Story of Ruth (1960)
Sunrise at Campobello (1960)
Return to Peyton Place (1961)
Hemingway's Adventures of a Young Man (1962)
My Geisha (1962)
Taras Bulba (1962)
The Lost Command (1966)

WEBB, JIMMY
Doc (1971)

WEBB, ROGER
Bartleby (1971)

WEBB, ROY
Alice Adams (1935)
In Person (1935)
The Last Days of Pompeii (1935)
The Bride Walks Out (1936)
Bunker Bean (1936)
The Ex-Mrs. Bradford (1936)
The Lady Consents (1936)
Special Investigator (1936)
Sylvia Scarlett (1936)
A Woman Rebels (1936)
Meet the Missus (1937)
New Faces of 1938 (1937)
On Again, Off Again (1937)
Outcasts of Poker Flat (1937)
The Plough and the Stars (1937)
Quality Street (1937)

Sea Devils (1937)
Affairs of Annabel (1938)
Bringing Up Baby (1938)
I'm from the City (1938)
The Law West of Tombstone (1938)
The Mad Miss Manton (1938)
A Man to Remember (1938)
Painted Desert (1938)
Room Service (1938)
Vivacious Lady (1938)
Bad Lands (1939)
The Fighting Gringo (1939)
Five Came Back (1939)
Fixer Dugan (1939)
The Flying Irishman (1939)
Full Confession (1939)
The Girl from Mexico (1939)
The Great Man Votes (1939)
In Name Only (1939)
Reno (1939)
Abe Lincoln in Illinois (1940)
A Bill of Divorcement (1940)
Cross Country Romance (1940)
Kitty Foyle (1940)
Laddie (1940)
My Favorite Wife (1940)
One Crowded Night (1940)
The Stranger on the Third Floor (1940)
Tom, Dick and Harry (1940)
You'll Find Out (1940)
Father Takes a Wife (1941)
A Girl, a Guy and a Gob (1941)
Army Surgeon (1942)
The Big Street (1942)
The Cat People (1942)
Here We Go Again (1942)
Joan of Paris (1942)
Journey into Fear (1942)
My Favorite Spy (1942)
The Navy Comes Through (1942)
Seven Day's Leave (1942)
Seven Miles from Alcatraz (1942)
The Tuttles of Tahiti (1942)
Behind the Rising Sun (1943)
Bombadier (1943)
The Falcon in Danger (1943
The Falcon Strikes Back (1943)
Fallen Sparrow (1943)
Flight for Freedom (1943)
Gangway for Tomorrow (1943)
The Ghost Ship (1943)
The Iron Major (1943)
I Walked with a Zombie (1943)
Ladies' Day (1943)
The Lady Takes a Chance (1943)
The Leopard Man (1943)
Mr. Lucky (1943)
The Seventh Victim (1943)
Action in Arabia (1944)
Bride by Mistake (1944)
Curse of the Cat People (1944)
Experiment Perilous (1944)
The Falcon Out West (1944)
Marine Raiders (1944)
The Master Race (1944)
Passport to Destiny (1944)
Rainbow Island (1944)
Tall in the Saddle (1944)
Back to Bataan (1945)
Betrayal from the East (1945)
The Body Snatcher (1945)
Dick Tracy (1945)
The Enchanted Cottage (1945)
Love, Honor and Obey (1945)
Murder, My Sweet (1945)
Those Endearing Young Charms (1945)
Two O'Clock Courage (1945)
Zombies on Broadway (1945)
Badman's Territory (1946)
Bedlam (1946)
Cornered (1946)
Notorious (1946)
The Spiral Staircase (1946)
The Well-Groomed Bride (1946)
Without Reservations (1946)
Crossfire (1947)
The Locket (1947)
Magic Town (1947)
Out of the Past (1947)
Riff Raff (1947)
Sinbad the Sailor (1947)
They Won't Believe Me (1947)
Bad Men of Tombstone (1948)
Blood on the Moon (1948)
Fighting Father Dunne (1948)
I Remember Mama (1948)
Race Street (1948)
Rachel and the Stranger (1948)
Easy Living (1949)
Holiday Affair (1949)

Mighty Joe Young (1949)
My Friend Irma (1949)
Roughshod (1949)
The Window (1949)
Branded (1950)
Gambling House (1950)
The Secret Fury (1950)
Vendetta (1950)
Where Danger Lives (1950)
The White Tower (1950)
Fixed Bayonets (1951)
Flying Leathernecks (1951)
Hard, Fast and Beautiful (1951)
Sealed Cargo (1951)
A Girl in Every Port (1952)
The Lusty Men (1952)
Operation Secret (1952)
Houdini (1953)
Second Chance (1953)
Dangerous Mission (1954)
She Couldn't Say No (1954)
Track of the Cat (1954)
The Americano (1955)
Bengazi (1955)
Blood Alley (1955)
The Kentuckian (1955)
Marty (1955)
The Sea Chase (1955)
Underwater! (1955)
The First Texan (1956)
The Girl He Left Behind (1956)
Our Miss Brooks (1956)
The River Changes (1956)
Shoot-Out at Medicine Bend (1957)
Top Secret Affair (1957)
Teacher's Pet (1958)

WEBBER, ANDREW LLOYD
Gumshoe (1971)

WEERSMA, MELLE
Journey to South America (1953)

WEILL, KURT
You and Me (1938)
A Salute to France (1944)

WEISMAN, BEN
Change of Habit (1969)

WEISS, JOSEPH
A House Is Not a Home (1964)

WEISSBERG, ERIC
Deliverance (1972)

WENDLING, PETE
False Faces (1918)

WERTH, HOWARD
Bronco Bullfrog (1970)

WHELEN, CHRISTOPHER
The Valiant (1962)
Coast of Skeletons (1965)
The Face of Fu Manchu (1965)

WHITAKER, DAVID
Don't Raise the Bridge, Lower the River (1968)
Hammerhead (1968)
Scream and Scream Again (1970)
Dr. Jekyll and Sister Hyde (1971)

WHITING, RICHARD
Fallen Idols (1919)

WHITNEY, H.
Lucky Duck (1928)

WHYTE, IAN
Bonnie Prince Charlie (1948)

WIENER, JEAN
The Man from Spain (1932)
The Great Glass Blower (1933)
Maria Chapdelaine (1934)
Le Paquebot Tenacity (1934)
La Bandera (1935)
La Cathedrale Des Morts (1935)
The Crime of M. Lange (1935)
The Lower Depths (1936)
La Lettre (1938)
Les Passagers De La Grande Ouise (1939)
La Voyageur de la Toussaint (1942)
La Voleur de Paratonnerres (1946)
Back Streets of Paris (1948)
Rendezvous with Juliet (1949)
Face to the Wind (1951)
French Can-Can (1953)
Touchez ne pas au Grisbi (1953)

Deadlier Than the Male (1957)
A Woman Like Satan (1960)
Lady L (1965)

WILDEN, GERT
Schoolgirl Report (1970)

WILDER, ALEC
Albert Schweitzer (1957)
Open the Door and See All the People (1964)

WILDMAN, CHARLES
Gypsy Fury (1951)

WILHELM, ROLF
The Revolt of Gunner Asch (08/15) (1955)
Siegfried (1967)
Hurrah! The School Is Burning (1970)
Ludwig on the Lookout for a Wife (1970)
We Chop the Teachers into Mince Meat (1970)

WILINSKY, MOSHE
Hatikvah (1959)
The Pilar of Fire (1963)

WILKES, JOHN
The Risk (1961)

WILKINS, ERNIE
Stand Up and Be Counted (1972)

WILKINSON, ARTHUR
California Firebrand (1948)
The Weaker Sex (1948)
It's Not Cricket (1949)
Once Upon a Dream (1949)
The Perfect Woman (1949)
The Limping Man (1953)

WILKINSON, MARC
If ... (1968)
The Royal Hunt of the Sun (1969)
Eagle in a Cage (1971)
The Darwin Adventure (1972)

WILLAR, STEPHANE
The Idols (1968)

WILLIAMS, CHARLES
Night Has Eyes (1946)
The Silk Noose (1948)
While I Live (1948)
Naughty Arlette (1949)
Flesh and Blood (1951)

WILLIAMS, JOHNNY (JOHN)
Because They're Young (1960)
I Passed for White (1960)
Bachelor Flat (1961)
The Secret Ways (1961)
Diamond Head (1962)
Gidget Goes to Rome (1963)
John Goldfarb, Please Come Home (1964)
The Killers (1964)
None But the Brave (1965)
How to Steal a Million (1966)
Not with My Wife, You Don't (1966)
Penelope (1966)
The Rare Breed (1966)
Fitzwilly (1967)
A Guide for the Married Man (1967)
Valley of the Dolls (1967)
Daddy's Gone A-Hunting (1969)
The Reivers (1969)
The Story of a Woman (1970)
Jane Eyre (1971)
The Cowboys (1972)
Images (1972)
Pete 'n Tillie (1972)
The Poseidon Adventure (1972)

WILLIAMS, PAT
How Sweet It Is (1968)
Don't Drink the Water (1969)
A Nice Girl Like Me (1969)
The Sidelong Glances of a Pigeon Kicker (Pigeons) (1970)

WILLIAMS, RALPH VAUGHAN
The Invaders (1941)
Coastal Command (1942)
The Invaders (1942)
The People's Land (1942)
The Flemish Farm (1943)

Stricken Peninsula (1945)
The Loves of Joanna Godden (1947)
Dim Little Island (1948)
Scott of the Antarctic (1948)

WILLIAMS, TREVOR
Bronco Bullfrog (1970)

WILLIAMSON, LAMBERT
Edge of the World (1937)
The End of the River (1948)
Woman Hater (1948)
Cardboard Cavalier (1949)
They Were Not Divided (1950)
The Slasher (1953)
Cross Channel (1955)
The Green Buddha (1955)
Secret Venture (1955)
Cash on Delivery (1956)
Forbidden Cargo (1956)
Track the Man Down (1956)

WILLIAMSON, MALCOLM
The Brides of Dracula (1960)
The Horror of Frankenstein (1970)
Crescendo (1972)

WILLINGTON-DENTON, RICHARD
Loot (1971)

WILLSON, MEREDITH
The Great Dictator (1940)
The Little Foxes (1941)

WILSON, FRANK
Beach Ball (1965)

WILSON, MORTIMER
The Thief of Bagdad (1924)
Don Q, Son of Zorro (1925)
The Black Pirate (1926)

WILSON, STANLEY
Renegades of Sonora (1948)
Sundown at Santa Fe (1948)
Alias the Champ (1949)
Bandit King of Texas (1949)
Daughter of the Jungle (1949)
Death Valley Gunfighter (1949)
Duke of Chicago (1949)
Flame of Youth (1949)
Flaming Fury (1949)
Frontier Investigator (1949)
Hideout (1949)
Law of the Golden West (1949)
Navajo Trail Raiders (1949)
Outcasts of the Trail (1949)
Post Office Investigator (1949)
Prince of the Plains (1949)
Ranger of Cherokee Strip (1949)
Rose of the Yukon (1949)
San Antone Ambush (1949)
Sheriff of Wichita (1949)
South of Rio (1949)
Streets of San Francisco (1949)
The Wyoming Bandit (1949)
The Arizona Cowboy (1950
Belle of Old Mexico (1950)
The Blonde Bandit (1950)
Buckaroo Sheriff of Texas (1950)
Code of the Silver Sage (1950)
Covered Wagon Raid (1950)
Destination Big House (1950)
Federal Agent at Large (1950)
Frisco Tornado (1950)
Gunmen of Abilene (1950)
Harbor of Missing Men (1950)
Lonely Hearts Bandits (1950)
The Missourians (1950)
The Old Frontier (1950)
Pioneer Marshal (1950)
Prisoners in Petticoats (1950)
Redwood Forest Trail (1950)
Rustlers on Horseback (1950)
The Showdown (1950)
Tarnished (1950)
Trial without Jury (1950)
Twilight in the Sierras (1950)
Under Mexicali Skies (1950)
Unmasked (1950)
The Vanishing Westerner (1950)
Vigilante Hideout (1950)
Arizona Manhunt (1951)
Cuban Fireball (1951)
The Dakota Kid (1951)
Desert of Lost Men (1951)
Fort Dodge Stampede (1951)
Havana Rose (1951)
Insurance Investigator (1951)
Million Dollar Pursuit (1951)
Missing Women (1951)

Night Riders of Montana (1951)
Pals of the Golden West (1951)
Pride of Maryland (1951)
Rodeo King and the Senorita (1951)
Rough Riders of Durango (1951)
Secrets of Monte Carlo (1951)
Silver City Bonanza (1951)
Street Bandits (1951)
Thunder in God's Country (1951)
Utah Wagon Train (1951)
Wells Fargo Gunmaster (1951)
Black Hills Ambush (1952)
Border Saddlemates (1952)
Captive of Billy the Kid (1952)
Desperadoes Outpost (1952)
The Fabulous Senorita (1952)
Gobs and Gals (1952)
Leadville Gunslinger (1952)
Old Oklahoma Plains (1952)
South Pacific Trail (1952)
Thundering Caravans (1952)
Tropic Heat Wave (1952)
Wild Horse Ambush (1952)
Woman in the Dark (1952)
Bandits of the West (1953)
Down Laredo Way (1953)
El Paso Stampede (1953)
Marshal of Cedar Rock (1953)
Savage Frontier (1953)
The Woman They Almost Lynched (1953)
Untamed Heiress (1954)
The Halliday Brand (1957)
The Mating Urge (1958)
Missile Monsters (1958)
Satan's Satellites (1958)
Dark Intruder (1965)

WINDING, KASPAR
Sunny Beach Revolution (1971)

WINDT, HERBERT
Triumph of the Will (1934)
Olympia (1936)
Ballerina (1958)
The Sins of Rose Bernd (1959)

WINELAND, SAM
When's Your Birthday?

WIREN, DAG
Miss Julie (1952)

A Matter of Morals (1961)

WOLCOTT, CHARLES
Saludos, Amigos (1942)
The Blackboard Jungle (1955)
Key Witness (1960)

WOOLFENDEN, GUY
Work Is a Four-Letter Word (1968)
A Midsummer Night's Dream (1969)

WOOLRIDGE, JOHN
Edward My Son (1949)
Conspirator (1950)
The Woman in Question (1950)
Angels One Five (1954)
The Last Man to Hang (1956)
Count Five and Die (1958)
RX Murder (1958)

WORTH, FRANK
Street of Darkness (1958)

WORTH, STAN
The Cat (1966)

WRICKEN, STANLEY
The Royal Tour of Queen Elisabeth and Philip (1954)

WRUBEL, ALLIE
Never Steal Anything Small (1959)

X-HOLES, THE
Havoc (1972)

XARCHAKOS, STAVROS
Red Lanterns (1964)
The Stone (1965)
The Hot Month of August (1966)
Signs of Life (1968)
Lycistrata (1972)

YAKOVLEV, NIKOLAI
Dimka (1963)

YANOVSKY, ZAL
A Married Couple (1969)

YATOVE, JEAN
The Girl in the Bikini (1955)
Disorder in the Night (1960)
Night Affair (1961)
The Seventh Juror (1964)

YAWOGUCHI, FUMIO
Ikiru (1952)

YEAWORTH, JEAN
The Blob (1958)

YEPES, NARCISCO
The Girl with the Golden Eyes (1962)

YGORBOUCHEN, MOHAMMED
Pepe le Moko (1937)
Algiers (1938)

YOUNG, BOB
It Takes All Kinds (1969)
Color Me Dead (1970)
Adam's Woman (1970)
The Demonstrator (1971)

YOUNG, VICTOR
Fatal Lady (1936)
Ebb Tide (1937)
Maid of Salem (1937)
Thrill of a Lifetime (1937)
Wells Fargo (1937)
Army Girl (1938)
Breaking the Ice (1938)
The Gladiator (1938)
Peck's Bad Boy with the Circus (1938)
Golden Boy (1939)
Gulliver's Travels (1939)
Arise My Love (1940)
Arizona (1940)
Dark Command (1940)
I Want a Divorce (1940)
The Light That Failed (1940)
Northwest Mounted Police (1940)
Raffles (1940)
Those Were the Days (1940)
Three Faces West (1940)
Untamed (1940)
Virginia (1940)
The Way of All Flesh (1940)
Caught in the Draft (1941)
Hold Back the Dawn (1941)
I Wanted Wings (1941)
Moon over Burma (1941)
Reaching for the Sun (1941)
Skylark (1941)
Beyond the Blue Horizon (1942)
The Glass Key (1942)
The Great Man's Lady (1942)
Mrs. Wiggs of the Cabbage Patch (1942)
The Palm Beach Story (1942)
Reap the Wild Wind (1942)
The Remarkable Andrew (1942)
Road to Morocco (1942)
Silver Queen (1942)
Sweater Girl (1942)
Take a Letter, Darling (1942)
True to the Army (1942)
Buckskin Frontier (1943)
China (1943)
The Crystal Ball (1943)
For Whom the Bell Tolls (1943)
Hostages (1943)
No Time for Love (1943)
The Outlaw (1943)
True to Life (1943)
Young and Willing (1943)
And Now Tomorrow (1944)
Frenchman's Creek (1944)
The Great Moment (1944)
Ministry of Fear (1944)
Practically Yours (1944)
The Story of Dr. Wassell (1944)
The Uninvited (1944)
The Great John L. (1945)
Hold That Blonde (1945)
Love Letters (1945)
Masquerade in Mexico (1945)
A Medal for Benny (1945)
Out of This World (1945)
You Came Along (1945)
The Blue Dahlia (1946)
Kitty (1946)
Our Hearts Were Growing Up (1946)
The Searching Wind (1946)
To Each His Own (1946)
Two Years Before the Mast (1946)
Calcutta (1947)

California (1947)
Golden Earrings (1947)
I Walk Alone (1947)
Imperfect Lady (1947)
Suddenly It's Spring (1947)
The Trouble with Women (1947)
Unconquered (1947)
The Accused (1948)
Beyond Glory (1948)
The Big Clock (1948)
Dream Girl (1948)
The Emperor Waltz (1948)
Miss Tatlock's Millions (1948)
The Night Has a 1,000 Eyes (1948)
The Paleface (1948)
State of the Union (1948)
Chicago Deadline (1949)
A Connecticut Yankee in King Arthur's Court (1949)
Deadly is the Female (1949)
My Foolish Heart (1949)
Paid in Full (1949)
Samson and Delilah (1949)
Sands of Iwo Jima (1949)
Song of Surrender (1949)
Streets of Laredo (1949)
Thelma Jordan (1949)
Bright Leaf (1950)
The Fireball (1950)
Our Very Own (1950)
September Affair (1950)
Appointment with Danger (1951)
Belle Le Grand (1951)
The Bullfighter and the Lady (1951)
Honeychile (1951)
The Lemon Drop Kid (1951)
A Millionaire for Christy (1951)
My Favorite Spy (1951)
Payment on Demand (1951)
The Wild Blue Yonder (1951)
Anything Can Happen (1952)
Blackbeard, the Pirate (1952)
The Greatest Show on Earth (1952)
One Minute to Zero (1952)
The Quiet Man (1952)
Scaramouche (1952)
Something to Live For (1952)
The Story of Will Rogers (1952)
Thunderbirds (1952)
Fair Wind to Java (1953)
Flight Nurse (1953)
Little Boy Lost (1953)
A Perilous Journey (1953)
Shane (1953)
The Star (1953)
The Stars Are Singing (1953)
The Sun Shines Bright (1953)
About Mrs. Leslie (1954)
The Country Girl (1954)
Drum Beat (1954)
Johnny Guitar (1954)
Jubilee Trail (1954)
Knock on Wood (1954)
Three Coins in the Fountain (1954)
Trouble in the Glen (1954)
The Left Hand of God (1955)
A Man Alone (1955)
Son of Sinbad (1955)
Strategic Air Command (1955)
Timberjack (1955)
Around the World in Eighty Days (1956)
The Brave One (1956)
The Conqueror (1956)
The Maverick Queen (1956)
The Proud and the Profane (1956)
The Vagabond King (1956)
The Buster Keaton Story (1957)
China Gate (1957)
Omar Khayyam (1957)
Run of the Arrow (1957)
Thunderbirds (1958)
The Wild Blue Yonder (1958)

YUASSA, JOJI
Funeral Parade of Roses (1970)

YUROVSKY, V.
The Mysterious Discovery (1956)
Eugenie Grandet (1960)

YVAIN, MAURICE
The Queen and the Cardinal (1937)

ZAHLER, GORDON
The Human Duplicators (1965)
Mutiny in Outer Space (1965)

The Bengal Tiger (1972)

ZAHLER, LEE
The Yanks Are Coming (1942)
Crime Doctor (1943)
The Ghost and the Guest (1943)
No Place for a Lady (1943)
Seven Doors to Death (1943)
Tiger Fangs (1943)
The Underdog (1943)
Boss of Rawhide (1944)
Brand of the Devil (1944)
Crime Doctor's Strangest Case (1944)
Delinquent Daughters (1944)
Gangsters of the Frontier (1944)
The Great Mike (1944)
Gunsmoke Mesa (1944)
I Accuse My Parents (1944)
Men on Her Mind (1944)
The Pinto Bandit (1944)
Shadow of Suspicion (1944)
Shake Hands with Murder (1944)
Waterfront (1944)
Arson Squad (1945)
Hollywood and Vine (1945)
The Lady Confesses (1945)
Outlaw Roundup (1945)
Rogues Gallery (1945)
Three in the Saddle (1945)
Ambush Trail (1946)
Freddie Steps Out (1946)
Frontier Fugitives (1946)
Gentlemen with Guns (1946)
Lightning Raiders (1946)
Overland Riders (1946)
Prairie Badmen (1946)
Prairie Rustler (1946)
Six-Gun for Hire (1946)
Queen of the Amazons (1947)

ZAMENCNIK, J. B.
Old Ironsides (1926)
Abie's Irish Rose (1928)
The Wedding March (1928)

ZAMFIR, GHORGHE
Eeeny Meeny Miney Moe (1972)

ZAPPA, FRANK
200 Motels (1971)

ZEIJENKA, ILJA
Field Lilies (1972)

ZELLER, CARL
The Foreman (1956)

ZELLER, WOLFGANG
Adventures of Prince Achmed (1926)
Weltmelodie (1929)
Marriage in the Shadows (1947)
Serengeti Shall Not Die (1960)

ZIMANICH, JOSEF
Journey to Freedom (1957)
Space Master X-7 (1958)

ZIMMERMAN, HARRY
The Steel Claw (1961)
Samar (1962)

ZINNER, PETER
King Kong vs. Godzilla (1963)

ZURO, JOSIAH
Holiday (1938)

Chapter XII

RECORDED MUSICAL SCORES
(A Discography)

This discography consists of a majority of film music on discs in 78, 45, and 33-1/3 r.p.m. Because soundtrack albums are usually commercially withdrawn a year or two after a film completes its first and second runs, most of the albums listed will no longer be generally available for sale, but may be purchased through record collectors or checked out from some public library record collections.

Complete scores and suites (or albums containing at least three themes from a film) are underlined. Other versions are usually single themes only. Where two record numbers are given, the first is monaural and the second, a stereo version. Numbers or letters in parenthesis before a record number indicate a stereo version.

Availability of tape, cartridge and cassette versions of these scores may be checked in the latest edition of the Schwann Record and Tape Guide and the Harrison Tape Catalog.

THE ABOMINABLE DR. PHIBES (American International, 1971)
Basil Kirchin/Jack Nathan
AIR 1040

ABOUT MRS. LESLIE (Paramount, 1954) Victor Young
Jubilee 1034
Mercury 25192

ABOVE THE STARS (n.d.) composer unlisted
Columbia 1880/8680
Mercury 20810/60810

THE ABSENT-MINDED PROFESSOR (Disney, 1961) George Bruns
Buena Vista 373

THE ACCUSED (Paramount, 1948) Victor Young
Decca 5265

ADA (MGM, 1961) William Fowler, Warren Roberts
MGM (S) 3988 and (S) 4064

ADAM'S RIB (MGM, 1949) Miklos Rozsa
RCA LSP-1401

ADDIO GROVINEZZA see FAREWELL TO YOUTH

ADDIO, ZIO TOM see GOODBYE, UNCLE TOM

THE ADVENTURERS (Paramount, 1970) Antonio Carlos Jobim
Paramount 6001
RCA 4350

ADVENTURES OF A YOUNG MAN see HEMINGWAY'S ADVENTURES OF A YOUNG MAN

ADVENTURES OF DON JUAN (Warner Bros., 1948) Max Steiner
RCA 1170

ADVENTURES OF HAJJI BABA (Fox, 1954) Dimitri Tiomkin
Coral 57006

THE ADVENTURES OF ROBIN HOOD (Warner Bros., 1938) Erich Wolfgang Korngold
RCA LSC-3330
Warner Bros. (S) 1438

ADVISE AND CONSENT (Columbia, 1962) Jerry Fielding
Columbia 1880/8680
Epic 20414/26014
RCA LSO-1068

AFFAIR IN MONTE CARLO (TWENTY-FOUR HOURS OF A WOMAN'S LIFE) (British, 1952) Philip Green
English Columbia 3138

AN AFFAIR TO REMEMBER (Fox, 1957) Hugo Friedhofer
Columbia 1371/8172 and 1013
Harmony 7108
Liberty 3135/7135 and 3306/7306
Mercury 20483/60162
RCA (S) 2895
Warner Bros. (S) 1319 and (S) 1368
Wing 12504

AFRICA ADDIO (Italy, 1966) Riz Ortolani
Italian Ariete 2001
United Artists 69 and 4141/5141

AFTER THE FOX (United Artists, 1966) Burt Bacharach
United Artists 4148/5148 and 3570/6570

THE AGONY AND THE ECSTASY (Fox, 1965) Alex North
Capitol (S) WAO 2427

AIMEZ-VOUS LES FEMMES? see DO YOU LIKE GIRLS?

L'AINE DES FERCHAUX (France, 1966) Georges Delerue
French Philips 77.233 and 432.973

AIRPORT (Universal, 1970) Alfred Newman
Decca 79173
Decca 75212
RCA 4350

ALAKAZAM THE GREAT (American-International, 1961) Les Baxter
Vee Jay 6000

THE ALAMO (United Artists, 1960) Dimitri Tiomkin
Columbia 1558/8358
Dot 3349/25349
Kapp 1297/3297
Liberty 13011/14011
London 3231/224 and 3257/246, SP-44173
MGM (S) 3894
Mercury 20640/60640
Polydor 184023
Richmond 20095/30095
Time (S) 304
United Artists 3122/6122

ALEXANDER NEVSKY (Russia, 1938) Serge Prokofiev
Artia (7)202
Columbia 5706/6306
Colosseum 228
Melodiya/Angel (S) 40010
Monitor (S) 2062
RCA (S) 2395
Vanguard (S) 451
Westminster 18144

ALEXANDER THE GREAT (United Artists, 1956) Mario Nascimbene
Mercury 20148 and 20037
United Artists 3001

ALFIE (Paramount, 1966) Sonny Rollins
Camden (S) 2133
Columbia GP-10
Command (S) 5005
Fox (S) 3192
Harmony 11315
Impulse (S) 9111
London 44112
United Artists 69

ALFRED THE GREAT (MGM, 1970) Ray Leppard
English MGM 8112

ALICE'S RESTAURANT (United Artists, 1969) Arlo Guthrie
United Artists 5195 and 6731

ALIKI--MY LOVE (Greece, 1963) Manos Hadjidakis
Capitol (S) 2527
Fontana 26523/67523

ALL ABOUT EVE (Fox, 1950) Alfred Newman
Mercury 20037

ALL FALL DOWN (MGM, 1962) Alex North
Columbia 1880/8680

ALL I DESIRE (Universal, 1953) David Lieber
MGM 3134

ALL NIGHT LONG (Britain, 1962) Dave Brubeck, Johnny Dankworth, Philip Green, Johnny Scott
Epic 16032/17032

ALL THE LOVING COUPLES (Cottage, 1969) Casanova
Crescendo 2051
United Artists 6742

ALL THE WAY HOME (Paramount, 1963) Bernard Green
Command (S) 871
United Artists 3376/6376

THE ALPHABET MURDERS (France, 1966) Ron Goodwin
Command (S) 5005

AMERICA, AMERICA (Warner Bros., 1963) Manos Hadjidakis
Time (S) 2131
Warner Bros. (S) 1527 and (S) 1535

AN AMERICAN DREAM (Warner Bros., 1966) Johnny Mandel
MGM (S) 4491
Project 3 5016

AN AMERICAN DREAMER (EYR, 1971) Various folk artists
Mediarts 41-12

THE AMERICANIZATION OF EMILY (MGM, 1964) Johnny Mandel
MGM (S) 4271
RCA (S) 3342 and (S) 3491
Reprise (S) 6151
Time (S) 2169 and (S) 304

THE AMERICANO (RKO, 1955) Roy Webb
Mercury 20115

AMOROUS ADVENTURES OF MOLL FLANDERS (Paramount, 1965)
John Addison

Command (S) 887
RCA LSO 1113

L'AMOUR DESCEND DU CIEL (France, n.d.) composer unlisted
Dot 3120

ANASTASIA (Fox, 1956) Alfred Newman
Capitol (S) 1652
Coral 57125
Decca 8460 and (7) 4362
Forum Circle (S) 9080
Roulette 25023

ANATOMY OF A MURDER (Columbia, 1959) Duke Ellington
Columbia 1360/8166 and 1421/8218

AND GOD CREATED WOMAN (France, 1957) Paul Misraki
Capitol (S) 8603
Decca 8685
Dot 3120

AND NOW TOMORROW (Paramount, 1944) Victor Young
Decca 8140

AND SUDDENLY IT'S MURDER (Italy, 1960) composer unlisted
Capitol (S) 8608

AND THE ANGELS SING (Paramount, 1944) Victor Young
Capitol 10068 (45)

THE ANDROMEDA STRAIN (Universal, 1971) Gil Melle
Kapp 5513

ANGEL, ANGEL, DOWN WE GO (American-International) Fred Karger
Tower 5161

ANGEL UNCHAINED (American-International, 1970) Randy Sparks
AIR 1037

THE ANGEL WORE RED (MGM, 1960) Bronislau Kaper
Carlton (S) 126

ANGELIQUE MARQUISE DES ANGES (France, 1966) Michel Magne
Dance Along 1318
Ducretet Thomson 300-V-145 and 460-V-660 (45)

ANGELS FROM HELL (American-International, 1968) Stu Phillips
Tower 5128

THE ANIMALS (France, 1965) Maurice Jarre
French Philips 77.233 and 434.822 (45)

ANNA (Italy, 1950) Roman Vatro
Atco (S) 170
Capitol (S) 1986 and (S) 8608
Columbia 593 and 659
Decca 8051 and 8312
Dunhill (S) 50012
Epic 3593
Liberty 3491/7491
London 44020
MGM 3485
Mercury 20123, 20483/60162 and 20648/60648
Reprise (9) 6009
Riviera 6580
United Artists 3360/6360
Vox 25180

ANNA FROM BROOKLYN see FAST AND SEXY

ANNA LUCASTA (United Artists, 1958) Elmer Bernstein
Ava (S) 11

ANNE OF THE THOUSAND DAYS (Universal, 1969) Georges Delerue
Decca 79174 and 75212

THE ANONYMOUS VENETIAN (Italy, 1971) Stelvio Cipriani
Ampex 10129
United Artists UAS 5218

ANOTHER DAWN (Warners, 1937) Erich Wolfgang Korngold
RCA 1782

ANOTHER TIME, ANOTHER PLACE (Paramount, 1958) Douglas Gamley
Columbia 1180
Wing 12136/12501

ANTHONY ADVERSE (Warner Bros., 1936) Erich Wolfgang Korngold
RCA LSC-3330
Warner Bros. (S) 1438

ANY WEDNESDAY (Warner Bros., 1966) George Duning
Warner Bros. (S) 1669

APACHE GOLD see WINNETOU I

THE APARTMENT (United Artists, 1960) Adolph Deutsch
Ascot 13500/16500
Cameo (S) 4003
Carlton (S) 126
Columbia 1627/8427
Decca (7) 4083
Epic 24014/26014
Kapp 1297/3297

Liberty 3306/7306
London 3261/249 and 44092
Mercury 20649/60649
Richmond 20095/30095
United Artists 3105, 3003/6303, 3122/6122 and 3475/6475
Warner Bros. (S) 1476

THE APRIL FOOLS (National General, 1969) Percy Faith
Columbia 3340, 9906

ARABESQUE (Universal, 1966) Henry Mancini
RCA LSC 3623

AROUND THE WORLD IN 80 DAYS (United Artists, 1956) Victor Young
Alshire (S) 5085
Capitol (S) 1986
Columbia 1371/8172
Crown (S) 101
Decca (7) 4362 and (7) 9046
Dot 3091/25097 and 3364/25364
Forum Circle (S) 9080
Fontana 67584
Grand Award 214
Hamilton 108/12108
Harmony 7351/11151
Jubilee 1034
Liberty 13011/14011
London 3117/164 and 3313/44025
MGM (S) 3894, (S) 4077, and (S) 4132 and (S) 4432
Mayfair 9591
Mercury 25023 and 20483/60162
Richmond 20061/30061
RCA (S) 2380 and (S) 2381
Roulette 25023
Specialty 2101
Time (5) 2046
Unart 20025/21025
United Artists 30001 and 3633/6633
Waldorf 1249
Warner Bros. (S) 1291 and (S) 1368
Wing 12504

AROUND THE WORLD UNDER THE SEA (MGM, 1966) Harry Sukman
Monument 8050/18050

THE ARRANGEMENT (Warners, 1969) David Amram
United Artists 6742
Warner Bros. 1824

THE ART OF LOVE (Universal, 1965) Cy Coleman
Capitol (S) 2355

L'ASCENSEUR POUR L'ECHAFAUD (France, 1957) Miles Davis
Columbia 1268
English Fontana 135
French Fontana 600213

L'ASSOLUTO NATURALE (Italy, 1972) Ennio Morricone
Italian Cinevox MDF-3323

THE ASTONISHED HEART (Britain, 1950) Noel Coward
His Master's Voice 3953 (78)

L'ATALANTE (France, 1934) Maurice Jaubert
Vega 30A98

ATHENA (MGM, 1954) George Stoll
Coral 61226
Decca 8102
Mercury 70465

ATLANTIS see FORBIDDEN ISLAND

AUNTIE MAME (Warner Bros., 1958) Bronislau Kaper
Mercury 20483/60162
Warner Bros. (S) 1242

L'AVVENTURA (Italy, 1961) Giovanni Fusco
RCA (S) 4

THE AWAKENING (United Artists, 1928) Irving Berlin
RCA (S) 2560

AWAY ALL BOATS (Universal, 1956) Frank Skinner
Coral 57065
Decca 8629

B. S., I LOVE YOU (Fox, 1971) Jim Dale/Mark Shekter
Mercury 1-610

BABY DOLL (Warner Bros., 1956) Kenyon Hopkins
Columbia CL-958
Epic 9194
MGM 3480

BABY FACE NELSON (United Artists, 1957) Van Alexander and Frank Spina
Jubilee 2021

THE BABY MAKER (National General, 1970) Fred Karlin
Ode 77002

BABY THE RAIN MUST FALL (Parmount, 1965) Elmer Bernstein
Dunhill (S) 50015
Mainstream 56056/6056

BACHELOR FLAT (Fox, 1961) Johnny Williams
RCA (S) 3491

BACHELOR IN PARADISE (MGM, 1961) Henry Mancini
MGM (S) 3988
RCA (S) 2604

BACHELOR PARTY (United Artists, 1957) Alex North
RCA 47-6896 (45)

BACK STREET (Universal, 1961) Frank Skinner
Capital (S) 1652
Decca (7) 9097
Mercury 20640/60640

THE BAD AND THE BEAUTIFUL (MGM, 1952) David Raksin
Capitol (S) 1599 and (S) 1652
Columbia 6255
Decca 8051
MGM 3134 and (S) 4261
RCA 1205
Warner Bros. (S) 1319

THE BAD SEED (Warner Bros., 1956) Alex North
RCA LPM-1395

BALLAD OF A SOLDIER (Russia, 1960) Mikhail Siv
Kapp (S) 1289
Warner Bros. (S) 1548

BAND OF ANGELS (Warner Bros., 1957) Max Steiner
RCA LPM-1557

BAND OF THIEVES (Britain, 1964) Composer unlisted
English Columbia 8178 (45)

BANDOLERO! (Fox, 1968) Jerry Goldsmith
Project 3 5026
United Artists 6710

BANNING (Universal, 1967) Quincy Jones
Project 3 5016

BARABBAS (Columbia, 1962) Mario Nascimbene
Colpix (S) 510, (S) 456 and (S) 464
London 3261/249

BARBARELLA (France, 1968) Bob Crewe, Charles Fox
Dynavoice 31908
United Artists 6701

THE BARBARIAN AND THE GEISHA (Fox, 1958) Hugo Friedhofer
Fox 3004

BAREFOOT ADVENTURE (SLIPPERY WHEN WET) (Independent, n.d.) Bud Shank
Pacific Jazz (S) 350
World 1265

THE BAREFOOT CONTESSA (United Artists, 1954) Mario Nascimbene
Capitol (S) 1986
RCA 2381

BAREFOOT IN THE PARK (Paramount, 1967) Neal Hefti
Dot 3803/25803

BARNABE (France, 1938) R. Dumas
French Decca 164.077

THE BARRETTS OF WIMPOLE STREET (MGM, 1956) Herbert Stothart
Coral 57125
MGM 3694

THE BASILISKS (Italy, n.d.) composer unlisted
Capitol (S) 8608

THE BAT (Allied Artists, 1959) Louis Forbes
Capitol 4239 (45)

BATTLE CRY (Warner Bros., 1955) Max Steiner
MGM 1156 (45)

THE BATTLE FOR STALINGRAD (Russia, 1944) Aram Khatchaturian
Classic Editions 3009

THE BATTLE OF ALGIERS (France, 1967) Gillo Pontecorvo, Ennio Morricone
United Artists 4171/5171

BATTLE OF BRITAIN (Britain, 1969) Ron Goodwin; "Battle of the Air" by Sir William Walton
United Artists 5201

THE BATTLE OF THE BULGE (Warner Bros., 1965) Benjamin Frankel
Warner Bros. (S) 1617

BATTLE STRIPE see THE MEN

BAY OF ANGELS (France, 1965) Michel Legrand
French Philips 77.233 and 432.885 (45)

BEAR SKIN (France, n.d.) composer unlisted
Dot 3120
French Philips 432.526 (45)

THE BEARS (France, 1965) Jean Prodromides
French Philips 432.526 (45)

BEBERT ET L'OMNIBUS (France, 1966) M. Philippe-Gerard
French Philips 77.233 and 434.814 (45)

BEBO'S GIRL (Italy, 1965) Carlo Rustichelli
Capitol (S) 2316
Polydor 184023

BECAUSE THEY'RE YOUNG (Columbia, 1960) Johnny Williams
Carlton (S) 126

BECKET (Paramount, 1964) Laurence Rosenthal
Decca (7) 9117

BEDAZZLED (Fox, 1968) Dudley Moore
London (S) 82009

BEHIND THE GREAT WALL (Italy, 1959) Francesco Lavagnino
Capitol 10401
Monitor 525

BEHOLD A PALE HORSE (Columbia, 1964) Maurice Jarre
Colpix (S) 519
Time (5) 2169

BELL, BOOK AND CANDLE (Columbia, 1959) George Duning
Colpix 502

BELLE LE GRAND (Republic, 1951) Victor Young
Decca 8060

BENEATH THE PLANET OF THE APES (Fox, 1970) Leonard Rosenman
Amos 8001

BEN-HUR (MGM, 1959) Miklos Rozsa
Capitol (S) 2837
Columbia 1783/8583
Liberty 6011/7711
Lion (S) 70123
London 3257/246, 3516/516, SP-44173
MGM (S) 1, (S) 242, S 3823, (S) 3894, (S) 3988, (S) 4112, (S) 4132, (S) 3900 and (S) 4417
Mercury 20640/60640
Metro (S) 503 and (S) 600
Somerset 16400
Stereo Fidelity 16400

THE BEST OF EVERYTHING (Fox, 1959) Alfred Newman
Decca (7) 4083

THE BEST YEARS OF OUR LIVES (RKO, 1946) Hugo Friedhofer
Columbia 2034/8834
Decca 5413 and 8364

BETWEEN TWO WORLDS (Warners, 1944) Erich Wolfgang Korngold
RCA LSC-3330

BEYOND MOMBASA (Britain, 1947) Humphrey Searle
Capitol 41460 (45)
English Columbia 3827

BEYOND THE GREAT WALL see BEHIND THE GREAT WALL

BEYOND THE VALLEY OF THE DOLLS (Fox, 1970) Stu Phillips
Fox 4211

THE BIBLE (Fox, 1966) Toshiro Mayuzumi
Camden (S) 2133
Capitol (S) 2627
Fox (S) 4184 and (S) 3192
Kapp 1501/3501
Liberty 6011/7711
London 516
MGM (S) 4417
Metro (s) 593 and (S) 600
Somerset 26800
Stereo Fidelity 26800

LES BICYCLETTES DE BELSIZE (Britain, 1969) Les Reed
English Polydor 584728

THE BIG BOUNCE (Warner Bros., 1968) Mike Curb
Warner Bros. (S) 1781

THE BIG CIRCUS (Allied Artists, 1959) Paul Sawtell and Bert Shefter
Todd 5001

THE BIG COUNTRY (United Artists, 1958) Jerome Moross
Ascot 13504/16504
London 3261/249 and 3313/44025
United Artists 40004/5004 and 3122/6122

THE BIG DAY see JOUR DE FETE

THE BIG GUNDOWN (United Artists, 1968) Ennio Morricone
United Artists 69, 5190 and 6710

A BIG HAND FOR THE LITTLE LADY (Warner Bros., 1966) David Raksin
Command (S) 5005

BIG RED (Disney, 1962) Oliver Wallace
Buena Vista (S) 3119

THE BIGGEST BUNDLE OF THEM ALL (MGM, 1968) Riz Ortolani
MGM (S) 4446

A BILL OF DIVORCEMENT (TV Title: The Right to Love) (RKO, 1932) Max Steiner
RCA LPM-1170

BILLIE (United Artists, 1965) Dominic Frontiere
United Artists 3131/5131

BILLION DOLLAR BRAIN (United Artists, 1968) Richard Rodney Bennett
United Artists 4174/5174

BILLY JACK (Warner Bros., 1971) Mundell Lowe
Sunset 1926
Warner Bros. 1926

BILLY LIAR (Britain, 1963) Richard Rodney Bennett
Atco (S) 170

BIRD OF PARADISE (RKO, 1932) Max Steiner
RCA LPM-1170

THE BIRD WITH THE CRYSTAL PLUMAGE (UMC, 1971) Ennio Morricone
Capitol 642

THE BIRDS, THE BEES, AND THE ITALIANS (SIGNORE AND SIGNORI) (Italy, 1966) Carlo Rustichelli
Italian CAM 100-013
United Artists 4157/5147 and 3625/6625

THE BIRTH OF A NATION (Griffith, 1915) Joseph Carl Briel
Golden Crest 4019
RCA (S) 2560

BITTER RICE (Italy, 1950) Goffredo Petrassi
MGM 3485

THE BLACK ORCHID (Paramount, 1959) Alessandro Cicognini
Dot 3178/25178

BLACK ORPHEUS (ORFEO NEGRO) (Brazil, 1959) Luis Bonfa
Antonio Carlos Jobim
Capitol (S) 8603
Deram 12706
Dunhill (S) 50012 and (S) 50015
Fontana 27520/67520
Kapp 1512/3512

London (S) 44020 and (S) 44078
MGM (S) 4185 and (S) 4491
Medallion (S) 7513
Musicor 2049/3049
RCA (S) 3887
Reprise (9) 6009
United Artists 69
Warner Bros. (S) 1548

BLACK SABBATH (Italy, 1964) Les Baxter
RCA Italian 10394

BLACK TIGHTS (Magna, 1962) various composers
RCA (S) 3

THE BLACKBOARD JUNGLE (MGM, 1953) Charles Wolcott
MGM 3220

BLACULA (American International, 1972) Gene Page
RCA LSP-4806

BLESS THE BEASTS AND CHILDREN (Columbia, 1971) Barry de Vorzon/Perry Botkin, Jr.
A&M SP-4322

LES BLEUS DE LA MARINE (France, n.d.) R. Dumas
French Decca 164.007

BLIND DATE see CHANCE MEETING

THE BLISS OF MRS. BLOSSOM (Paramount, 1968) Riz Ortolani
RCA (S) 4080

BLITHE SPIRIT (Britain, 1945) Richard Addinsell
Camden 130 and 233
Decca 8112
Mercury 16399

BLOOD AND SAND (Fox, 1941) Vicente Gomez
Decca 5380 and 8279

BLOOMFIELD (Britain/Israel, 1971) Johnny Harris
English Pye NSPL-18376

BLOW-UP (MGM, 1966) Herbie Hancock
MGM (S) 242, (S) 4447

BLUE (Paramount, 1968) Manos Hadjidakis
Dot 25855

THE BLUE ANGEL (Paramount, 1930) Frederick Hollander
Columbia 1178

THE BLUE MAX (Fox, 1966) Jerry Goldsmith
Command (S) 5005
Mainstream 56081/6081

THE BLUEBIRD (Fox, 1940) Alfred Newman
Decca 8123

BOB & CAROL & TED & ALICE (Columbia, 1969) Quincy Jones
Bell 1200
United Artists 6742

THE BOBO (Warner Bros., 1967) Francis Lai
Warner Bros. (S) 1711

BOCCACCIO '70 (Italy, 1962) Nino Rota, Armando Trovajoli
RCA (S) 5 and (S) 2604

THE BODY (MGM, 1971) Ron Geesin/Roger Waters
EMI Harvest 4008

BOEING, BOEING (Paramount, 1965) Neal Hefti
RCA LSO-1121

BONJOUR TRISTESSE (United Artists, 1958) Georges Auric
Mercury 20188
RCA LOC-1040
Wing 12136/12501

LA BONNE OCCASE (France, n.d.) composer unlisted
Ducretet Thomson 460-V-670 (45)

LES BONNES CAUSES (France, 1963) composer unlisted
French Barclay 70536 (45)

BONNIE AND CLYDE (Warner Bros., 1967) Charles Strouse
Alshire (S) 5097
Camden (S) 2210, (S) 2253
United Artists 69 and 3666/6633
Warner Bros. (S) 1742

BOOM! (Universal, 1968) John Barry
English MCA (S) 360

BORA BORA (American International, n.d.) composer unlisted
AIR 1029

BORN FREE (Britain, 1966) John Barry
Columbia 2493/9293 and 2708/9508
Command (S) 5005
Dunhill (S) 5002
Kapp 1501/3501
London 3516/516
MGM (S) 4368, (S) 242

Mercury (S) 16348
Metro (S) 600
Philip 200231/600231
RCA (S) 3887
Solid 17013/18013

BORSALINO (France, 1970) Claude Bolling
Paramount 5019

BOY ON A DOLPHIN (Fox, 1957) Hugo Friedhofer
Coral 57125
Decca 8580

THE BOYS (Britain, 1962) "The Shadows"
Capitol (S) 2075

THE BRAVADOS (Fox, 1958) Hugo Friedhofer and Alfred Newman
Fox 106 (45)

THE BRAVE ONE (RKO, 1957) Victor Young
Decca 8344

BREAD, LOVE AND DREAMS (Italy, 1954) I. Cini
Columbia 880
MGM 3485
United Artists 3360/6360

BREAKFAST AT TIFFANY'S (Paramount, 1961) Henry Mancini
Camden (S) 373 and (S) 736, (S) 2161
Cameo (S) 4003
Columbia GP-10
Decca (7) 4647
Dunhill (S) 50008
Epic 24014/26014
Harmony 7351/11151
Kapp 1297/3297
London 3261/249 and 3313/44025
MGM (S) 13
Mercury 20810/60810 and 21125/61125
Metro (S) 551
Philips 200213/ 600213
Polydor 184023
RCA (S) 2362 (S) 2693 and (S) 3887
Reprise (9) 6105
Somerset 20700
Stereo Fidelity 20700
United Artists 3197/6197

BREWSTER McCLOUD (MGM, 1971) John Phillips
MGM 28

BRIAN'S SONG (Screen Gems, 1971)
Bell 6071

THE BRIDE WORE BLACK (France, 1968) Bernard Herrmann
French United Artists 36.122 (45)

THE BRIDGE AT REMAGEN (United Artists, 1969) Elmer Bernstein
United Artists 6731

THE BRIDGE ON THE RIVER KWAI (Columbia, 1957) Malcolm Arnold
Capitol (S) 1986
Colpx (S) 458 and (S) 464
Columbia 1100
Dunhill (S) 50015
Epic 3809/1147
Kapp 3005
London 3106/159
MGM (S) 3894, (S) 3988 and (S) 4132
RCA 2381
Warner Bros. 1247 and (S) 1319
Wing 12504

BRIDGE TO THE SUN (MGM, 1962) Georges Auric
Epic 3809/1147
MGM (S) 3988 and (S) 4064

THE BRIDGES AT TOKO-RI (Paramount, 1954) Lyn Murray
MGM 3172
Mercury 20156

BROKEN ARROW (Fox, 1950) Alfred Newman
Dot 3097/25097

THE BROTHERS KARAMAZOV (MGM, 1958) Bronislau Kaper
MGM 12624 (45)

BRUTE FORCE (Universal, 1947) Miklos Rozsa
Decca (7) 10015

THE BUCCANEER (Paramount, 1958) Elmer Bernstein
Columbia 1278

A BULLET FOR PRETTY BOY (American International, 1970) Harley Hatcher
AIR 1034

A BULLET IS WAITING (Columbia, 1954) Dimitri Tiomkin
Coral 57006
MGM 3172

THE BULLFIGHTER AND THE LADY (Republic, 1951) Victor Young
Columbia 39851 (45)

BUNNY LAKE IS MISSING (Columbia, 1965) Paul Glass
RCA (S) 1115

BUNNY O'HARE (American International, 1971) Billy Strange
AIR 1041

BUONA SERA, MRS. CAMPBELL (United Artists, 1969) Riz Ortolani
United Artists 69, 5192, and 6701

BURN! (United Artists, 1970) Ennio Morricone
Italian United Artists SR-620

BUTCH CASSIDY AND THE SUNDANCE KID (Fox, 1969) Burt Bacharach
A&M 4227
Mercury 61279
RCA 4350

BUTTERFIELD 8 (MGM, 1960) Bronislau Kaper
Kapp (S) 1289
MGM (S) 3894, (S) 3988, (S) 4132, (S) 4144 and (S) 4261

THE BUTTON WAR see WAR OF THE BUTTONS

BY LOVE POSSESSED (United Artists, 1961) Elmer Bernstein
Mercury 20640/60640

BYE BYE BRAVERMAN (Warner Bros., 1968) Peter Matz
Camden (S) 2210
Mercury 21149/ 61149

THE CABINET OF CALIGARI (Fox, 1962) Gerald Fried
London 3347/347

CACTUS FLOWER (Columbia, 1969) Quincy Jones
Bell 1201

THE CAINE MUTINY (Columbia, 1954) Max Steiner
Decca 8085
RCA 1013

THE CANDIDATE (n. d.) Steve Karmen
Jubilee 5029

CANDY (Cinerama, 1968) Dave Grusin
ABC (S) 9

THE CAPER OF THE GOLDEN BULLS (Embassy, 1967) Vic Mizzy
Tower (S) 5086

CAPTAIN BLOOD (Warners, 1935) Erich Wolfgang Korngold
RCA LSC-3330

CAPTAIN CAREY, USA (Paramount, 1950) Jay Livingston
Columbia 2025/8826
Kapp 1297/3297

London 3106/159 and 3201
Mercury 20061
RCA 1110

THE CAPTAIN FROM CASTILE (Fox, 1947) Alfred Newman
Capitol (S) 1652
Liberty 55001
Mercury 20005 and 16399
Philips 200098/600098
RCA (S) 3887

CAPTAIN HORATIO HORNBLOWER (Warner Bros., 1951) Robert Farnon
Philips 200098/600098

CAPTAIN NEWMAN, M.D. (Universal, 1963) Frank Skinner
Time (S) 2131

THE CAPTAIN'S PARADISE (Britain, 1953) Malcolm Arnold
MGM (S) 4271

THE CARDINAL (Columbia, 1963) Jerome Moross
Capitol (S) 2063
Diplomat (S) 2305
Liberty 6011/7711
London 3347/347
Mercury 20887/60887
RCA LSO 1084
Time (5) 2112 and (S) 2131
Warner Bros. (S) 1535

THE CARETAKERS (United Artists, 1963) Elmer Bernstein
Ava (S) 31
MGM (S) 4192

UN CARNET DU BAL (France, 1937) Maurice Jaubert
Capitol (S) 8603
French Victor 440.138

CARNIVAL (Britain, 1946) Nicholas Brodszky
English Columbia 2180 (78)

CARNIVAL NIGHT (Russia, n.d.) A. Lepin
Russian Melodiya 11797-98

THE CARPETBAGGERS (Paramount, 1964) Elmer Bernstein
Ava (S) 45 and (S) 49
Command (S) 871
Decca (7) 4669
MGM (S) 4271

CARRY IT ON! (Independent, 1971) Joan Baez
Vanguard VSD-79313

CARTHACALLA (France, n.d.) M. Yvain
French Victor 440.138

CASABLANCA (Warner Bros., 1943) Max Steiner
RCA 4350

CASANOVA '70 (Italy, 1965) Armando Trovajoli
Epic 24195/26195

CASINO ROYALE (Columbia, 1967) Burt Bacharach
A&M (S) 844
Colgems (S) 5005
London 3514/514
Musicor 2133/3133
Philips 200260/600260
Sunset 1184/5184

CASSE, LE (n.d.)
Bell C-062-92889

CAST A GIANT SHADOW (United Artists, (1966) Elmer Bernstein
United Artists 4138/5138 and 3570/6570

CAT ON A HOT TIN ROOF (MGM, 1958) composer unlisted
MGM (S) 4144 and (S) 4261

THE CATERED AFFAIR (MGM, 1956) Andre Previn
Coral 57065
English Vogue 72187
MGM 3397

CAVALCADE (Fox, 1933) Noel Coward
London 1062

C'ERA UNA VOLTA IL WEST see ONCE UPON A TIME IN THE WEST

A CERTAIN SMILE (Fox, 1958) Alfred Newman
Columbia 1194/8068
London 3117/164
Mercury 20483/60162
Richmond 20060/30060 and 20101/30101

THE CHAIRMAN (Fox, 1969) Jerry Goldsmith
Tetragrammaton 5007
United Artists 6731

CHAMPION (United Artists, 1949) Dimitri Tiomkin
Coral 57006

CHANCE MEETING (BLIND DATE) (Britain, 1959) Richard Rodney Bennett
Top Rank 5005

THE CHAPLIN REVUE (United Artists, 1959) Charles Chaplin
Decca 4040
Paramount PAS-6026

CHAPLIN'S ART OF COMEDY (n.d.) Elias Breeskin
Mainstream 56089/6089

THE CHAPMAN REPORT (Warner Bros., 1962) Leonard Rosenman
Warner Bros. (S) 1478

CHAPPAQUA (Independent, 1968) Ravi Shankar
Columbia (S) 3230

CHARADE (Universal, 1963) Henry Mancini
Camden (S) 799
Decca (7) 4647 and (7) 4669
Diplomat (S) 2305
Liberty 3353/7353
London (3) 419, 104, and 3347/347
Mercury 20887/60887
Philips 200098/600098
Polydor 184023
RCA (S) 2755, (S) 2693 and (S) 3887
Time (5) 2112 and (S) 2131
United Artists 3376/6376
Warner Bros. (S) 1535

THE CHARGE OF THE LIGHT BRIGADE (Warner Bros., 1936) Max Steiner
RCA LPM-1287

THE CHARGE OF THE LIGHT BRIGADE (Britain, 1968) John Addison
United Artists 69 and 5177

CHARLY (Cinerama, 1968) Ravi Shankar
World Pacific (S) 21454

THE CHASE (Columbia, 1966) John Barry
Columbia 6560/2960 and 2493, 9293
Command (S) 894

CHASTITY (American-International, 1969) Sonny Bono
Atco 302

CHATEAU EN SUEDE (France, 1963) Raymond le Senechal
Polydor 184023

CHE! (Fox, 1969) Lalo Schifrin
Mercury 61279
Tetragrammaton 5006

CHE GIOIA VIVERE (Italy, 1960) Francesco Lavagnino
RCA (S) 4

CHEINS PERDUS SANS COLLIER (France, n.d.) Paul Misraki
French Victor 440.138

A CHILD IS WAITING (United Artists, 1963) Ernest Gold
London 3320/320

CHITTY CHITTY BANG BANG (United Artists, 1968) Richard and Robert Sherman
Columbia (S) 9823 and (S) 9835
Command (S) 941
United Artists (S) 6669 and (S) 6701

EL CID (Allied Artists, 1961) Miklos Rozsa
Columbia 1783/8583
Capitol (S) 2837
Command (S) 835
Kapp (S) 1289
Liberty 3306/7306
MGM (S) 3977, (S) 4078, (S) 4112, 2 (S) 13
United Artists 3197/6197
Warner Bros. (S) 1476

CIMARRON (MGM, 1960) Franz Waxman
MGM (S) 3894 and (S) 3988

THE CINCINNATI KID (MGM, 1966) Lalo Schifrin
Command (S) 894
MGM (S) 4313

CINDERFELLA (Paramount, 1960) Walter Scharf
Dot (3) 8001

CINERAMA HOLIDAY (Cinerama, 1955) Morton Gould
Forum Circle (S) 9080
Mercury 20059

CINERAMA SOUTH SEAS ADVENTURE see SOUTH SEAS ADVENTURE

CIRCLE OF LOVE (France, 1965) Michel Magne
Monitor (S) 602

CIRCUS OF HORRORS (Britain, 1960) Franz Reizenstein and Muir Mathieson; "Look for a Star" by Mark Anthony
Carlton (S) 126
Dunhill (S) 50015
Imperial 9129
London 3247/237

CIRCUS WORLD (Paramount, 1964) Dimitri Tiomkin
MGM (S) 4252

CITIZEN KANE (RKO, 141) Bernard Herrmann
London ST-44144
Virtuoso 13010

CITTA VIOLENTA (Italy, 1970) Ennio Morricone
RCA Italiana KOLS-1010

CITY LIGHTS (United Artists, 1931) Charles Chaplin
French Vogue SLD-837
London 3431/44066 and 3474/474
Paramount PAS-6026

CITY OF WOMEN (CITY WITHOUT MEN) (Columbia, 1943) Victor Young
Jubilee 1034

CLEO FROM 5 TO 7 (France, 1962) Michel Legrand
French Philips 432.596 (45)
Philips 200071/600071

CLEOPATRA (Fox, 1963) Alex North
Capitol (S) 2075
Command (S) 854
Fox (S) 4105 and (S) 5008
London 3327/44031
MGM (S) 4144
Mercury 20887/60887
RCA (S) 2766
Somerset 20200
Stereo Fidelity 20200
Time (S) 304
United Artists 3290/6290 and 3303/6303

A CLOCKWORK ORANGE (Warners, 1971) Walter Carlos
Angel 36855
Warner Brothers 2573

THE CLOWNS (Italy, 1971) Nino Rota
Columbia 30772

LE CLUB DE SOUPERANTS (France, n.d.) George Van Parys
French Decca 164.077

THE COBWEB (MGM, 1956) Leonard Rosenman
MGM 3501

COCKLESHELL HEROES (Columbia, 1956) John Addison
London 1443

THE COLLECTOR (Columbia, 1965) Maurice Jarre
Mainstream (5) 6053 and 56063/6063

COLLEGE CONFIDENTIAL (Universal, 1960) Dean Elliott
Chancellor (S) 5016

COLONEL BLIMP see THE LIFE AND DEATH OF COLONEL BLIMP

COMANCHE (United Artists, 1957) Herschel Burke Gilbert
Coral 57040

THE COMANCHEROS (Fox, 1961) Elmer Bernstein
Capitol 4664 (45)

COME BACK, CHARLESTON BLUE (Warner Bros., 1972) Donny Hathaway
Atco 7010

COME BLOW YOUR HORN (Paramount, 1963) Nelson Riddle
Reprise (9) 6071

COME SEPTEMBER (Universal, 1961) Hans J. Salter
Columbia 1753/8553
Dot 3396/25396 and 16262 (45)

COME TO THE STABLE (Fox, 1949) Alfred Newman
Decca 8123

COME TOGETHER (Italy, 1971) Stelvio Cipriani
Apple SW-3377

THE COMEDIANS (MGM, 1967) Laurence Rosenthal
MGM (S) 4494

COMMANDO (Germany/Italy/Spain, 1963) Armando Trovajoli
French Victor 430.667 (45)
Italian RCA 10382
London 104

COMMENT TROUVEZ-VOUS MA SOEUR? (France, n.d.) Serge Gainsbourg
French Philips 77.233 and 434.850 (45)

THE CONDEMNED OF ALTONA (Fox, 1963) Dimitri Shostakovich, based on his "Symphony 11"
Angel (S) 3586
Artia 201
Capitol (S) 8448

CONFESSIONE DI UN COMMISARIO DI POLIZIA AL PROCURATORE DELLA REPUBLICA (Italy, 1971) Riz Ortolani
Italian RCA OLS-6

CONGO CROSSING (Universal, 1956) Henry Mancini
Coral 57065

THE CONQUEROR (RKO, 1956) Victor Young
Decca 29855 (45)

THE CONSTANT NYMPH (Warner Bros., 1943) Erich Wolfgang Korngold
RCA LSC-3330
Warner Bros. (S) 1438

CONTEMPT (LE MEPRIS) (France, 1964) Georges Delerue
French Philips 434. 809 (45) and 77. 233 (45)

COOL HAND LUKE (Warner Bros., 1967) Lalo Schifrin
Dot 3833/25833
United Artists 3633/6633

THE COOL WORLD (Independent, 1964) Mal Waldron
English Philips 7636

THE CORRUPT ONES (Warner Bros., 1967) George Garvarentz
English Philips 7782
Sunset 1184/5184
United Artists 4158/5158 and 3625/6625

COTTON COMES TO HARLEM (United Artists, 1970) Galt McDermott
United Artists UAS-5211

COUNT YOUR BLESSINGS (MGM, 1959) Franz Waxman
MGM 12784 (45)

A COUNTESS FROM HONG KONG (Universal, 1967) Charles Chaplin
Camden (S) 2161
Columbia GP-10
Decca (7) 1501
French Vogue SLD-837
London 3516, 516, 44112
Musicor 2133/3133

THE COUNTRY GIRL (Paramount, 1954) Victor Young
Mercury 20156

A COUNTRY SINGS (Czechoslovakia, c1935) Frantisek Skvor
Supraphon 480

THE COVERED WAGON (Paramount, 1923) Hugo Reisenfeld
Golden Crest 4019
RCA (S) 2560

COWBOY (Columbia, 1958) George Duning
Decca 8684
Wing 12136/12501

THE CREATURE FROM THE BLACK LAGOON (Universal, 1956)
Hans J. Salter
Coral (7) 57240

THE CREATURE FROM UNDER THE SEA (n.d.) composer unlisted
Epic 24125/26125

THE CREATURE WALKS AMONG US (Universal, 1956) Henry Mancini
Coral (7) 57240

CRIME IN THE STREETS (Allied Artists, 1956) Franz Waxman
Decca 8376

THE CRIMSON KIMONO (Columbia, 1959) Harry Sukman
Liberty 3135/7135 and 55210 (45)

CROMWELL (Columbia, 1970) Frank Cordell
Capitol 640

CRUELLE MEPRISE (France, n.d.) composer unlisted
Ducretet Thomson 460-V-657 (45)

LA CUCURACHA (Mexico, n.d.) composer unlisted
Columbia WL-161

THE CURE FOR LOVE (Britain, 1949) William Alwyn
His Master's Voice 9879 (78)

CUSTER OF THE WEST (Cinerama, 1968) Bernardo Segall
ABC (S) 5

THE CYCLIST RAIDERS see THE WILD ONE

CYNTHIA (MGM, 1947) Edward Powell
Decca 8060

THE CZAR WANTS TO SLEEP (LIEUTENANT KIJE) (Russia, 1934)
Serge Prokofiev
Artia (S) 191
Capitol (S) 8508
Columbia 4683, 5101 and 5945/6545
Everest 6054/3054
London (S) 9142
RCA (S) 2150 and (S) 2621
Vanguard 1028/2010 and (S) 174
Vox 9180
Westminster 18266

THE DAM BUSTERS (Britain, 1955) Leighton Lucas
His Master's Voice 8265 (78)

DAMN THE DEFIANT! (Britain, 1962) Clifton Parker
Colpix (S) 511, (S) 458 and (S) 464

THE DAMNED (Warners, 1969) Maurice Jarre
Decca 75212
Warner Bros. 1829

DANGEROUS MOONLIGHT see SUICIDE SQUADRON

THE DARK AT THE TOP OF THE STAIRS (Warners, 1960) Max Steiner
Columbia 1627/8427
Dot 3349/25349
Mercury 20688/60688

DARK OF THE SUN (MGM, 1968) Jacques Loussier
London 44112
MGM (S) 4544

DARK SECRET (Britain, 1950) George Melachrino
His Master's Voice 9805 (78)

DARK VICTORY (Warners, 1939) Max Steiner
Columbia 794
RCA LPM-1170

DARLING (Britain, 1965) John Dankworth
Epic 24195/26195

DAVID AND BATHSHEBA (Fox, 1951) Alfred Newman
Decca 8123
RCA 1007

DAVID AND LISA (Continental, 1963) Mark Lawrence
Ava (S) 21
London 3298/298
MGM (S) 4192
RCA (S) 2895

THE DAY AND THE HOUR (France, n.d.) composer unlisted
French Barclay 70528 (45)

A DAY AT THE RACES (MGM, 1937) Bronislau Kaper
London 1588

A DAY IS WORTH A LIFETIME (Russia, n.d.) Dmitri Shostakovich
Angel SR-40181

DAY OF ANGER (National General, 1967) Riz Ortolanti
RCA LSO-1165
United Artists UAS-6710

THE DAY THE FISH CAME OUT (Fox, 1967) Mikis Theodorakis
Decca (7) 4956
Fox (S) 4194

DAYS OF WINE AND ROSES (Warners, 1962) Henry Mancini
Ava (S) 23
Camden (S) 736
Capitol (S) 1877 and (S) 2063
Columbia GP-10 and 2026/8826
Command (S) 954
Decca (7) 4647 and (7) 4669
Kapp 3610
Liberty 3287/7287
Mercury 21125/61125
Philips 200213/600213
Reprise (9) 6105
RCA (S) 2604, (S) 2693, (S) 2895 and (S) 3887
Somerset 19300 and 20700
Stereo Fidelity 19300 and 20070
Time (5) 2078
United Artists 3315/6315

DE SADE (American International, 1969) Billy Strange
United Artists 6742

DEAD RINGER (Warners, 1964) Andre Previn
Warner Bros. (S) 1536

DEADFALL (Fox, 1968) John Barry
Fox (S) 4203

THE DEADLY AFFAIR (MGM, 1967) Quincy Jones
Verve (6) 8679

THE DEADLY MANTIS (Universal, 1957) William Lava
Coral 57240

DEAR HEART (Warners, 1964) Henry Mancini
Camden (S) 2162
Command (S) 887
DCP 3806/6806
Decca (7) 4647 and (7) 4669
Dot 3616/25616
London (3) 419
Musicor 2049/3049
RCA (S) 3342
United Artists 3392/6392

DEAR JOHN (Sweden, 1965) Bengt Arne Wallin
Dunhill (S) 55001 and (S) 50012

DEATH IN VENICE (Italy, 1971) Gustav Mahler
Ampex 10129

DGG 2538-124
English Classics for Pleasure CFP-186

DECEPTION (Warners, 1946) Erich Wolfgang Korngold
RCA LSC-3330

DELICIOUS (Fox, 1931) George Gershwin's "Second Rhapsody"
Capitol (S) 8581
Decca 8024

DESERT VICTORY (Britain, 1943) William Alwyn
English Columbia 2140 (78)

DESIRE UNDER THE ELMS (Paramount, 1958) Elmer Bernstein
Dot 3095
Wing 12136/12501

DESIREE (Fox, 1954) Alfred Newman, Alex North
Columbia 569
Decca 8123
Dot 3107

DESTINATION MOON (Eagle-Lion, 1950) Leith Stevens
Columbia 6151
Omega 3

THE DEVIL AND DANIEL WEBSTER (RKO, 1941) Bernard Herrmann
London ST-44144
Virtuoso 13010

THE DEVIL AT 4 O'CLOCK (Columbia, 1961) George Duning
Colpix (S) 509

DEVIL IN THE FLESH (France, 1947) Rene Cloerec
Capitol (S) 8603

THE DEVIL'S BRIGADE (United Artists, 1968) Alex North
Project 3 (S) 5027
United Artists 3654/6654 and 69

THE DEVIL'S COMMANDMENT (Italy, 1957) Martini Brighetti
RCA (S) 4

DEVOTION (Warners, 1946) Erich Wolfgang Korngold
RCA LSC-3330

DIAL "M" FOR MURDER (Warner Bros., 1954) Dimitri Tiomkin
Coral 57006 and 61211
Mercury 20156

DIAMOND HEAD (Columbia, 1963) Johnny Williams; theme by Hugo Winterhalter

Colpix (S) 440, (S) 458 and (S) 464
London 3298/298
Mercury 20810/60810

DIAMONDS ARE FOREVER (United Artists, 1971) John Barry
United Artists PAS-5220

DIANE (MGM, 1955) Miklos Rozsa
Columbia 794
MGM (S) 4033 and (S) 4112

DIARY OF A BACHELOR (American-International, 1964) Jack Pleis
United Artists 3392/6392

THE DIARY OF ANNE FRANK (Fox, 1959) Alfred Newman
Fox (S) 3012

DIME WITH A HALO (MGM, 1963) Ronald Stein
Capitol (S) 2075
Reprise (9) 6105

DINGAKA (Embassy, 1965) Bertha Egnos-Eddie Domingo
Mercury 21013/61013

DINO (Allied Artists, 1957) Gerald Fried
Epic 3404

DIRTY DINGUS MAGEE (MGM, 1971) Jeff Alexander
MGM 24

THE DIRTY DOZEN (MGM, 1967) Frank de Vol
MGM (S) 4445

THE DIRTY GAME (American International, 1966) Gian Piero Reverheri
Laurie (S) 2034

THE DISCOVERY OF BRAZIL (Brazil, 1937) Heitor Villa-Lobos
Pathé 602/603

DIVORCE AMERICAN STYLE (Columbia, 1967) Dave Grusin
United Artists 4163/5163

DIVORCE--ITALIAN STYLE (Italy, 1962) Carlo Rustichelli
Ascot 13505/16505
Atco (S) 170
Capitol (S) 8608
London 3347/347
United Artists 4106/5106, 3303/6303 and 3360/6360

DO YOU LIKE GIRLS? (France, 1966) Ward Swingle
French Philips 77.233 and 434.902 (45)

DR. DOLITTLE (Fox, 1967) Leslie Bricusse
Alshire (S) 5097
MGM (S) 4491
Unart 20015/21015
United Artists 3633/6633

DR. GOLDFOOT AND THE GIRL BOMBS (American International, 1966) Les Baxter
Tower 5053

DR. NO (United Artists, 1963) Monty Norman
Ascot 13504/16504
Capitol (S) 2455
Columbia 2708/9508
London (3) 412
United Artists 4108/5108 and 3303/6303

DR. STRANGELOVE (Columbia, 1964) Laurie Johnson
Colpix (S) 464

DOCTOR ZHIVAGO (MGM, 1965) Maurice Jarre
Camden (S) 2133
Capitol (S) 302
Columbia GP-10
Command (S) 894
Decca (7) 4754
Dunhill (S) 50008
Fox (S) 3192
Kapp 1470/3470
London 44092, 3516/516, 44112, 44173
MGM (S) 6, (S) 242
Mercury (S) 16348 and 21125/61125
Metro (S) 570 and (S) 600
Philips 200213/600213
RCA (S) 3887, (S) 3041
Solid 17013/18013
Somerset 24800
Stereo Fidelity 24800
United Artists 3526/6525 and 3570/6570
Viva (S) 6001

A DOG OF FLANDERS (Fox, 1960) Paul Sawtell and Bert Shefter
Fox (S) 3026

A DOG'S LIFE (First National, 1918) Charles Chaplin
Decca 4040
French Vogue SLD-837

LA DOLCE VITA (Italy, 1961) Nino Rota
Camden (S) 373
Capitol (S) 1877 and (S) 8608
Command (S) 835
Deram 12706

Epic 24014/26014
Kapp (S) 1289
Liberty 3491/7491
London 44020
MGM (S) 4033
RCA (S) 1 and (S) 4
Reprise (S) 6009
Time (S) 304
United Artists 3360/6360 and 3376/6376
Warner Bros. (S) 1548

THE DOLL see LA POUPEE

DON'T MAKE WAVES (MGM, 1967) Vic Mizzy
MGM (S) 4483

D'OU VIENS-TU JOHNNY? (France, n.d.) J. J. Debout
French Philips 77.233

DRACULA (Universal, 1931) composer unlisted
Epic 24125/26125

THE DRAGONFLY (Russia, 1955) Sulkhan Tsintsadze
Monitor 530

DRANGO (United Artists, 1957) Elmer Bernstein
Liberty 3036

A DREAM OF KINGS (National General, 1970) Alex North
National General 1000

DREAM OF OLWEN see WHILE I LIVE

DROP DEAD ... DARLING (BRI, 1967) Dennis Farnon
English Victor 7846

DUEL AT DIABLO (United Artists, 1966) Neal Hefti
United Artists 4139/5139, 3570/6570, and 3573/6573

DUEL IN THE SUN (Selznick, 1946) Dimitri Tiomkin
Columbia 612
Coral 57006
MGM 3480
RCA 1008 and 1083 (78)

DUSTY AND SWEETS McGEE (Warners, 1971) various composers
Warner Brothers S-1936

DUTCHMAN (Britain, 1967) John Barry
Columbia 2708/9508

THE EAGLE (United Artists, 1925) Lee Erwin
Concert Recording 0045

THE EARRINGS OF MADAME D .... (France, 1954) composer unlisted
Riviera 6580

EAST OF EDEN (Warner Bros., 1955) Leonard Rosenman
Columbia 941
Coral 57065 and 57099
Decca 8364
Polydor 184023
RKO 109
Warner Bros. (S) 1478

THE EASY LIFE (Italy, 1963) Riz Ortolani
United Artists 3360/6360

EASY RIDER (Columbia, 1969) various composers
Dunhill 50063

L'EAU VIVE (France, 1956) Guy Béarts
Capitol (S) 8603

ECCO! (Italy, 1965) Riz Ortolani
Warner Bros. (S) 1600

THE EDDY DUCHIN STORY (Columbia, 1956) George Duning
Decca (7) 4362

EDGE OF THE CITY (MGM, 1956) Leonard Rosenman
MGM 3501

EDGE OF THE WORLD (Britain, 1937) Lambert Williamson
English Decca 1579 (78)

THE EGYPTIAN (Fox, 1954) Alfred Newman and Bernard Herrmann
Decca 9014

8-1/2 (Italy, 1963) Nino Rota
Capitol (S) 8608
Liberty 3491/7491
London 3347/347
Mercury 20887/60887
RCA (S) 6
United Artists 3360/6360
Warner Bros. (S) 1548

8 ON THE LAM (United Artists, 1967) George Romanis
United Artists 4156/5156

EL DORADO (Paramount, 1967) Nelson Riddle
Epic 13114/15114

ELEKTRA (Greece, 1963) Mikis Theodorakis
Greek Philips 600508

AN ELEPHANT CALLED SLOWLY (Britain, 1970) Bert Kaempfert
Bell 1202

ELIZABETH AND ESSEX see THE PRIVATE LIVES OF ELIZABETH AND ESSEX

ELMER GANTRY (United Artists, 1960) Andre Previn
United Artists 4069/5069

ELVIRA MADIGAN (Sweden, 1967) Wolfgang Amadeus Mozart: Piano Concerto 21
Ampex 10129
Angel COLH-67 and 3593
Artia 159
Columbia 6095/6695 and (S) 9835
DGG 138783
Epic 6062/162
Kapp 3610
London 44112
RCA (S) 2634, (S) 3041 and LSC-3245
Turnabout (S) 34080

EMILY see THE AMERICANIZATION OF EMILY

THE EMPEROR'S NIGHTINGALE (Czechoslovakia, 1951) Vaclav Trojan
Supraphon 199

EMPIRE OF THE SUN (Latin America, 1957) Francesco Lavagnino
Columbia 107

THE ENDLESS SUMMER (Independent, 1966) The Sandals
World Pacific (S) 1832

ENTER LAUGHING (Columbia, 1967) Quincy Jones
Liberty 16004/17004

ERIC SOYA'S 17 see 17

ERNEST THE REBEL (France, 1937) C. Oberfeld
French Decca 164.077

ESCAPADE (MGM, 1935) Bronislau Kaper
MGM 3511

ESCAPE ME NEVER (Warners, 1947) Erich Wolfgang Korngold
RCA LSC-3330

ESERCITO DI 5 UOMINI (Italy, 1971) composer unlisted
Ariete 2009

EVA (France, n.d.) composer unlisted
French Philips 432.821 (45)

EXODUS (United Artists, 1960) Ernest Gold
Ascot 13500/16500
Camden (S) 799
Cameo (S) 4003
Capitol (S) 1661 and (S) 2627
Columbia 1627/8427
Command (S) 935
DCP 3802/6802
Epic 3809/1147
Harmony 7351/11151
Kapp 1297/3297 and 3610
Liberty 3306/7306
London 3231/224, 3257/246, 3320/320 and 3322/322
MGM (S) 3892, (S) 4077 and (S) 4132
Mercury 20688/60688, 20702/60702 and 20810/60810
Metro (S) 585
RCA (S) 1058 and (S) 3887
Time (5) 2046
United Artists 3122/6122, 3123/6123 and 3303/6303
Warner Bros. (S) 1476

EXPERIMENT IN TERROR (Columbia, 1962) Henry Mancini
Camden (S) 736
RCA (S) 2442 and (S) 2693

THE FBI STORY (Warners, 1959) Max Steiner
Columbia 1421/8218

A FACE IN THE CROWD (Warners, 1957) Tom Glazer
Capitol 872

FACES (Continental, 1968) Jack Ackerman
Columbia (S) 3290

FALL OF A NATION (National, 1916) Victor Herbert
Decca 8145

THE FALL OF BERLIN (Russia, 1949) Dmitri Shostakovich
Classic Editions 9

FALL OF THE ROMAN EMPIRE (Paramount, 1964) Dimitri Tiomkin
Columbia 6060/2460
Time (S) 304 and (S) 2131

THE FAMILY WAY (BRI, 1967) Paul McCartney
London 76007/82007

FANNY (Warners, 1961) Harold Rome, arr. by Harry Sukman
Camden (S) 373
Epic 3809/1147
London 3261/249
United Artists 2197/6197
Warner Bros. (S) 1416

FANNY HILL (Independent, 1965) composer unlisted
Command (S) 887

FANNY HILL (Sweden, 1969) The Oven
Canyon 7700
United Artists 6742

FANTASMI A ROMA see THE PHANTOM LOVERS

THE FANTASTIC PLASTIC MACHINE (Crown-International, 1969)
Harry Betts
Epic 26469

FANTOMAS SE DECHAINE (France, 1966) Michel Magne
French Barclay 70.916 (45)

FAR FROM THE MADDING CROWD (MGM, 1967) Richard Rodney Bennett
Decca (7) 4956
MGM (S) 11, (S) 242
Philips 200260/600260

A FAREWELL TO ARMS (Fox, 1958) Mario Nascimbene
Camden (S) 830
Capitol 918
MGM (S) 4033
Mercury 20371/60017
Wing 12136/12501

FAREWELL TO YOUTH (ADDIO GROVINEZZA) (Italy, 1940) S. Blanc
Epic 3593

FAREWELL, UNCLE TOM see GOODBYE, UNCLE TOM

FARREBIQUE (France, 1948) Henri Sauget
Vega 30A98

FAST AND SEXY (ANNA OF BROOKLYN) (Italy, 1958) Alessandro Cicognini
Epic 3593

FATE IS THE HUNTER (Fox, 1964) Jerry Goldsmith
Command (S) 871

FATHER OF THE BRIDE (MGM, 1950) Adolph Deutsch
MGM (S) 4144

FATHER'S DOING FINE (Britain, 1952) Harold Smart
Parlophone 3596 (78)

FATHOM! (Fox, 1967) John Dankworth
Fox 4195

LA FAUSSE MAITRESSE (France, n.d.) M. Yvain
French Victor 440.138

FELLINI SATYRICON (Italy, 1970) Nino Rota
United Artists 5208

FEMALE ON THE BEACH (Universal, 1955) Joseph Gershenson
Decca 2956 (45)
RCA 20-6194 (45)

THE FEMALE PRISONER see LA PRISONIERE

UNE FEMME EST UNE FEMME see A WOMAN IS A WOMAN

DES FEMMES DISPARAISSENT see GIRLS DISAPPEAR

FEMMINIE INSAZIABILI (Italy, 1970) composer unlisted
Ariete 2006

FERRY TO HONG KONG (Britain, 1961) Kenneth V. Jones
Top Rank 151

FESTIVAL (TRESPASS) (Britain, 1947) Richard Addinsell
London 127

LE FETE A HENRIETTE see HOLIDAY FOR HENRIETTA

FIESTA (MGM, 1947) Aaron Copland, based on his "El Salon Mexico"
Columbia 920, 5755/6355 and 5841/6441
Mercury 50172/90172
RCA 1008 and 1928
Vanguard 439
Westminster 18284, 18840 and (S) 14063

FIEVRE (France, 1921) R. Lucchesi
French Victor 440.138

FIFI LA PLUME (France, 1965) Jean Michel Defave
Ducretet Thomson 460-V-680 (45)

55 DAYS AT PEKING (Allied Artists, 1963) Dimitri Tiomkin
Columbia 2028/8828
Command (S) 954
MGM (S) 4185

THE FIGHTER (United Artists, 1952) Vicente Gomez
Decca 5415

THE FINAL COMEDOWN (Independent, 1972) Wade Marcus
Blue Note BST-84415

FINNEGANS WAKE (Expanding Cinema, 1967) Elliot Kaplan
RCA (S) 118

FIRE DOWN BELOW (Columbia, 1957) Kenneth V. Jones and Vivian Coma; themes by Jack Lemmon, Ned Washington and Lester Lee
Decca 8597
RCA (S) 3491

THE FIRST OF THE FEW (SPITFIRE) (Britain, 1943) William Walton
English Columbia TWO-272
English HMV 3359 (78)

A FISTFUL OF DOLLARS (Italy, 1966) Ennio Morricone
RCA (S) 1135, (S) 4049
RCA International PML-10414
Unart 20032/21032

FITZWILLY (MGM, 1968) Johnny Williams
MGM (S) 4491
United Artists 4173/5173

FIVE DAYS AND FIVE NIGHTS (Russia, n.d.) Dimitri Shostakovich
Russian Melodiya 11327-28

FIVE EASY PIECES (Columbia, 1970) various composers
Epic 30456
RCA LSC-3245

FIVE GATES TO HELL (Fox, 1959) Paul Dunlap
Capitol 4293 (45)

5 SONS OF DOGS (Italy, 1970) composer unlisted
Ariete 2004

FLAME AND THE FLESH (MGM, 1954) Nicholas Brodszky
MGM 1080 (45) and 30851 (45)

A FLEA IN HER EAR (Fox, 1968) Bronislau Kaper
Fox 4200

FLESH AND BLOOD (Britain, 1951) Charles Williams
English Columbia 2836 (78)

FLESH AND FANTASY (Universal, 1943) Alexandre Tansman
Camden 205 and 233

FLIGHT OF THE DOVES (Columbia, 1971) Roy Budd
London XPS-591

FLIGHT OF THE PHOENIX (Fox, 1964) Frank de Vol
Command (S) 894 and (S) 899

Dunhill (S) 50008
Kapp 1467/3467

FLIPPER (MGM, 1963) Henry Vars
Capitol (S) 2075

FOLLOW ME (Universal, 1969) Stu Phillips
Uni 73056

A FOOL THERE WAS (Fox, 1941) B. Gay
Golden Crest 4019

FOOLS (Cinerama, 1971) Shorty Rogers
Reprise 6429

FOOTSTEPS IN THE FOG (Columbia, 1955) Benjamin Frankel
Epic 9117 and 9064 (45)

FOR A FEW DOLLARS MORE (United Artists, 1967) Ennio Morricone
RCA International PML-10414
Unart 20015/21015 and 20032/21032
United Artists 3608/6608 and 3625/6625

FOR LOVE OF IVY (Palomar, 1968) Quincy Jones
ABC 7
Columbia (S) 9835
Command (S) 941
RCA (S) 4022
United Artists 69

FOR WHOM THE BELL TOLLS (Paramount, 1943) Victor Young
Capitol (S) 1599
Columbia 612
Decca 8008, 8461 and (7) 4362
Dot 3097/25097 and 3364/25364
Hamilton 108/12108
Jubilee 1034
London SP-44173
Mercury 20369
Warner Bros. (S) 1201

FORBIDDEN GAMES (France, 1952) Narcisso Yepes
Capitol (S) 8603
Deram 12706/13706
French Decca 75505 (45)
London 44020

FORBIDDEN ISLAND (Columbia, 1959) Alexander Laszlo
Carlton 106

FORBIDDEN PLANET (MGM, 1956) theme by David Rose; electronic music by Louis and Bebe Barron

MGM 3397 and (S) 4271

FOREIGN INTRIGUE (United Artists, 1956) Paul Durand
Capitol 3478 (45)
MGM 12281 (45)

FOREVER AMBER (Fox, 1947) David Raksin
RCA 197 (78)

FOREVER DARLING (MGM, 1956) Bronislau Kaper
MGM 12478 (45)

FOREVER FEMALE (Paramount, 1954) Victor Young
Decca 8051

40 POUNDS OF TROUBLE (Universal, 1963) Mort Lindsay
Mercury 20784/60784 and 20810/60810

49TH PARALLEL see THE INVADERS

THE FORTUNE COOKIE (United Artists, 1966) Andre Previn
United Artists 4145/5145 and 3570/6570

FOUR DAYS OF NAPLES (MGM, 1963) Carlo Rustichelli
Capitol (S) 8608
United Artists 3360/6360

FOUR GIRLS IN TOWN (Universal, 1957) Alex North
Decca 8424

THE FOUR HORSEMEN OF THE APOCALYPSE (MGM, 1921) E. Luz
Golden Crest 4019

FOUR HORSEMEN OF THE APOCALYPSE (MGM, 1962) Andre Previn
Columbia 1782/8583
Command (S) 835
London 3261/249
MGM (S) 3993 and (S) 4078

THE 400 BLOWS (France, 1959) Jean Constantin
French Vogue 7631 (45)
Reprise (9) 6009

FOUR IN THE MORNING (Britain, 1967) John Barry
Ember NR-5029
Roulette (S) 805

FOUR SONS (Fox, 1928) Erno Rapee
RCA (S) 2560

FOUR WIVES (Warners, 1939) Max Steiner
Decca 8629
MGM 3354

Roulette 25023
RCA LPM-1287

THE FOURPOSTER (Columbia, 1952) Dimitri Tiomkin
RCA LPM-1007

THE FOX (Warners, 1968) Lalo Schifrin
Camden (S) 2253
Columbia (S) 9835
Mercury 21149/61149
Warner Bros. (S) 1738

FRANCIS OF ASSISI (Fox, 1961) Franco Ferrara
Capitol (S) 2627
Fox (S) 3053
London 3257/246

FRANKENSTEIN (Universal, 1931) David Broekman
Epic 24125/26125

FRANTIC see ASCENSUR A L'ECHAFAUD

FRENCH CAN-CAN see ONLY THE FRENCH CAN

A FRENCH MISTRESS (Britain, 1960) John Addison
London 3238/231

FRIENDLY PERSUASION (Allied Artists, 1956) Dimitri Tiomkin
Columbia 107
Coral 57125
London 3106/159, 3117/164 and 3322/322
MGM 3480 and (S) 4064
Metro (S) 585
Mercury 20371/60017
Philips 200098/600098 and 200260/600260
RKO-Unique 110
Wing 12504

FRIENDS (Paramount, 1971) Elton John
Paramount 6004

FRITZ THE CAT (Cinemation, 1972) various composers
Fantasy 9406

FROM HERE TO ETERNITY (Columbia, 1953) George Duning
Colpix (S) 458 and (S) 464
Coral 56105
Decca 8396 and (7) 4362
London 3322/322

FROM RUSSIA WITH LOVE (United Artists, 1964) John Barry; theme by Lionel Bart
Atco (S) 170

Camden (S) 913
Capitol (S) 2075, (S) 2455, (S) 2527
Columbia 2493/9293, 2708/9508
Command (S) 871
Liberty 3353/7353
London (3) 412, 3474/474 and 44078
Metro (S) 520
Polydor 184023
Time (S) 2131
United Artists 4114/5114, 3376/6376 and 3424/6424

FROM THE TERRACE (Fox, 1960) Elmer Bernstein
Carlton (S) 126

FRONTIER HELLCAT (OLD SUREHAND) (Columbia, 1964) Martin Boetticher
German Polydor 237422

THE FUGITIVE KIND (United Artists, 1960) Kenyon Hopkins
United Artists (S) 4065

FULL OF LIFE (Columbia, 1956) George Duning
Decca 30167 (45)
English Brunswick 05666 (45)

FUNERAL IN BERLIN (Paramount, 1967) Konrad Elfers
RCA (S) 1136

THE FUZZY PINK NIGHTGOWN (United Artists, 1957) Billy May
Imperial 9042

THE GADFLY (Russia, 1955) Dmitri Shostakovich
Russian MK 0123/4

GAILY, GAILY (United Artists, 1969) Henry Mancini
United Artists 5202 and 6731

GALIA (France, 1967) Ward Swingle--Bach's "Largo"
Philips 200225/600225

LA GAMBERGE (France, 1963) Guy Beart
French Philips 432.748 (45)
Philips 200071/600071

THE GAME IS OVER (France, 1967) Jean-Pierre Bourtayre, Jean Bouchety
Atco (S) 205

GAMES (Universal, 1967) Samuel Matlovsky
Mercury 21149/61149

THE GARDEN OF THE FINZI-CONTINIS (Italy, 1971) Manuel de Sica
RCA Italiano KOLS-1013
RCA LSP-4712

GAS-S-S-S (American International, 1970) Harry Melton
AIR 1038

GATES OF PARIS see PORTE DE LILAS

GEISHA BOY (Paramount, 1958) Walter Scharf
Jubilee (S) 1096

GENEVIEVE (Britain, 1953) Larry Adler
Angel 64014
Columbia CL-577
English Columbia 3327 (78)

THE GENTLE RAIN (Brazil, 1965) Luiz Bonfa
Mercury 21016/61016

GEORGY GIRL (Britain, 1966) Tom Springfield
Kapp 1512/3512 and 3610
Mercury (S) 16348
RCA (S) 3041

GERALDINE (Republic, 1953) Victor Young
Decca 8060

GERMINAL (France, 1963) Michel Mange
French Barclay 70.570 (45)

GERVAISE (France, 1957) Georges Auric
Columbia 107
Mercury 20188

GETTING STRAIGHT (Columbia, 1970) Ronald Stein
Colgems 5010

GHENGIS KHAN (Columbia, 1965) Dusan Radic
Liberty 3412/7412

GHOSTS IN ROME see THE PHANTOM LOVERS

GIANT (Warners, 1956) Dimitri Tiomkin
Capitol (S) 773
Columbia 940
Coral 57099 and 57125
Imperial 9021
MGM 3397 and (S) 4144
RKO-Unique 109

THE GIFT OF LOVE (Fox, 1958) Cyril Mockridge
Columbia 1113

GIGI (France, 1950) Rachel Thoreau
Columbia 593
Mercury 20371/60017

GIGOT (Fox, 1962) Jackie Gleason
Capitol (S) 1754

THE GIRL FROM SAN FREDIANO (Italy, n.d.) S. Masheroni
Epic 3593

THE GIRL IN THE BIKINI (France, 1955) Jean Yatove
Poplar 1002

A GIRL NAMED TAMIKO (Paramount, 1963) Elmer Bernstein
Time (5) 2078

GIRL ON A MOTORCYCLE (France, 1968) Les Reed
English Polydor 583714
Tetragrammaton (S) 5000

THE GIRL WITH THE GOLDEN EYES (France, 1963) Narcisso Yepes
Philips 200071/600071

GIRLS AT PLAY see IT HAPPENED IN ROME

GIRLS DISAPPEAR (France, 1958) Art Blakey
English Fontana 135

IL GIUDIZIO UNIVERSALE see THE LAST JUDGMENT

THE GLASS MOUNTAIN (Britain, 1950) Nino Rota
London 1513
Saga 5018

THE GLASS SLIPPER (MGM, 1955) Bronislau Kaper
Capitol 843
MGM 3397, 3511 and 3694
Warner Bros. 1212

THE GLENN MILLER STORY (Universal, 1954) Henry Mancini
Camden (S) 799
Decca 8060 and 8226
RCA (S) 2604

GLI UOMINI CHE MASCALZONI see WHAT RASCALS MEN ARE

THE GLORY GUYS (United Artists, 1965) Riz Ortolani
United Artists 4126/5126 and 3476/6476

THE GLORY STOMPERS (American-International, 1968) various composers
Sidewalk (S) 5910

THE GO-BETWEEN (Britain, 1971) Michel Legrand
Bell 6071

GO, GO, GO WORLD (Italy, 1965) Nino Oliviero, Bruno Nicolai
Musicor 2059/3059

GOD'S LITTLE ACRE (United Artists, 1958) Elmer Bernstein
United Artists 40002, 3122/6122 and 3158/6158

GOG (United Artists, 1954) Harry Sukman
Decca 8060

THE GOLD OF NAPLES (Italy, 1957) composer unlisted
MGM 3599

THE GOLD RUSH (United Artists, 1925) Charles Chaplin
French Vogue SLD-837

THE GOLDEN BREED (Independent, 1968) Mike Curb/Jerry Styner
Capitol (S) 2886

THE GOLDEN COACH (Italy, 1954) Gino Marinuzzi, based on themes by Antonio Vivaldi
MGM 3111

GOLDEN EARRINGS (Paramount, 1947) Victor Young
Capitol (S) 302
Columbia 1371/8172
Decca 8008
Jubilee 1034
Liberty 13011/14011
MGM (S) 4432
Mercury 20369

THE GOLDEN MOUNTAINS see LE MONTS D'OR

GOLDFINGER (United Artists, 1954) John Barry
Camden (S) 913
Capitol (S) 2455
Columbia 2493/9293 and 2708/9508
Command (S) 887
DCP 3806/6806
Decca (7) 4647
London (S) 412 and 44078 and 3516/516
Metro (S) 520 and (S) 551
Musicor 2049/3049
RCA (S) 3342
Sunset 1184/5184
Time (5) 2189
United Artists 4117/5117, 3392/6392 and 3424/6424

GOLIATH AND THE BARBARIANS (American International, 1960) Les Baxter
AIR 1001

GONE WITH THE WAVE (Independent, 1965) Lalo Schifrin
Colpix (S) 492

GONE WITH THE WIND (MGM, 1939) Max Steiner
Alshire (S) 5080
Camden 625 and (S) 2161
Capitol (S) 1599
Columbia GP-10, 1627/8427 and 612
Decca 5413, 8102 and 8364
Dot 3097/25097 and 3364/25364
Kapp 3005
London 3298/298, 3327/44031 and 3156/516
MGM (S) 10, (S) 242, (S) 3954, 3172, (S) 3894, (S) 3988, (S) 4104, (S) 4132 and (S) 4491
Mercury 21149/61149 and 16399
Metro (S) 613, (S) 585 and (S) 600
Mercury 20648/60648
Philips 200213/600213
RCA 1287, 2381 and (S) 3859
Somerset 29100
Stereo Fidelity 29100
Unart 20015/21015
United Artists 3158/6158, 3625/6625 and 3633/6633
Warner Bros. (S) 1242, (S) 1219 and (S) 1268

THE GOOD LIFE (France, 1964) composer unlisted
Capitol (S) 8603

GOOD NEIGHBOR SAM (Columbia, 1964) Frank de Vol
United Artists 3376/6376

THE GOOD, THE BAD AND THE UGLY (Italy, 1967) Ennio Morricone
Camden (S) 2253
Harmony 11315
London 44112
Project 3 (S) 5027
RCA (S) 4049
Unart 20032/21032
United Artists 4172/5172, 3633/6633

GOODBYE AGAIN (United Artists, 1961) Georges Auric
Camden (S) 373
London 3261/249
Ultra 7514/8514
United Artists (S) 4091 and 3158/6158

GOODBYE CHARLIE (Fox, 1964) Andre Previn
Fox 3165/4165
United Artists 3392/6392

GOODBYE, COLUMBUS (Paramount, 1969) The Association
Warner Bros. 1786

GOODBYE, MR. CHIPS (MGM, 1969) Leslie Bricusse
United Artists 6731

GOODBYE, UNCLE TOM (Italy, 1971) Riz Ortolani
RCA International OLS-8

THE GOSPEL ACCORDING TO ST. MATTHEW (Continental, 1966)
Bach, Prokofiev, Mozart, Webern and folk music
Mainstream 54000/4000

THE GRADUATE (Embassy, 1967) Paul Simon, David Grusin
Camden (S) 2253
Columbia (S) 3180
Harmony 11315
Project 3 (S) 5027

LE GRAND BLUFF (France, 1957) composer unlisted
Dot 3120

THE GRAND OLYMPICS (Italy, 1960) Francesco Lavagnino
RCA (S) 4

GRAND PRIX (MGM, 1966) Maurice Jarre
MGM (S) 8, (S) 242
Philips 200231/600231
Somerset 27600
Stereo Fidelity 27600

THE GRASS IS GREENER (Universal, 1960) Noel Coward
Medallion 603

THE GRASSHOPPER (National General, 1970) Billy Goldenberg
National General 1001

THE GREAT DICTATOR (United Artists, 1940) Charles Chaplin
French Vogue SLD-837
Paramount PAS-6026

THE GREAT ESCAPE (United Artists, 1963) Elmer Bernstein
Capitol (S) 2075
United Artists 4107/5107 and 3303/6303

GREAT EXPECTATIONS (Britain, 1947) Walter Goehr
English Decca 1596 (78)

THE GREAT IMPOSTER (Universal, 1960) Henry Mancini
Camden (S) 928
Capitol (S) 1626
Choreo 62250 (45)
RCA 47-7830 (45)

THE GREAT RACE (Warners, 1965) Henry Mancini
Camden (S) 926

Decca (7) 4617
RCA (S) 3402

THE GREATEST SHOW ON EARTH (Paramount, 1952) Victor Young
RCA LPM-3018

THE GREATEST STORY EVER TOLD (United Artists, 1965) Alfred Newman
Capitol (S) 2627
DCP 3806/6806
Liberty 6011/7711
MGM (S) 4417
Metro (S) 600
United Artists 4120/5120 and 3476/6476

GREECE, LAND OF DREAMS (Germany, 1966) Manos Hadjidakis
Fontana 680-241

THE GREEN CARNATION see THE TRIALS OF OSCAR WILDE

GREEN DOLPHIN STREET (MGM, 1947) Bronislau Kaper
MGM (S) 4033
Mercury 20648/60648
RCA (S) 2895
Warner Bros. 1242

GREEN FIRE (MGM, 1954) Miklos Rozsa
Mercury 20156 and 20301

GREEN MANSIONS (MGM, 1959) Bronislau Kaper; special themes by Heitor Villa-Lobos
MGM 12784 (45)

GREENGAGE SUMMER see LOSS OF INNOCENCE

LE GRISBI see TOUCHEZ PAS AU GRISBI

GROUNDS FOR MARRIAGE (MGM, 1950) David Raksin
MGM 30315 (78)

GROUPIE GIRL (Britain, 1970) various artists
Polydor 2384.021

LA GUERRE EST FINIE (France, 1967) Giovanni Fusco
Bell 6012

GUESS WHO'S COMING TO DINNER (Columbia, 1967) Frank de Vol
Camden (S) 2110
Colgems (S) 108

THE GUIDE (India, 1967) various composers
Odeon MOCE-1038

THE GUN HAWK (Allied Artists, 1964) Jimmy Haskell
Capitol (S) 2075

GUNN (Paramount, 1967) Henry Mancini
RCA (S) 3840

THE GUNS OF NAVARONE (Columbia, 1961) Dimitri Tiomkin
Camden (S) 373
Columbia 1655/8455
Kapp 1297/3297
London 3247/237
Mercury 20810/60810
United Artists 3197/6197

THE GURU (Fox, 1969) Ustad Vilayat Khan
RCA (S) 1158

GYPSY GIRL (Britain, 1967) Milton de Lugg
Mainstream 56090/6090

HAGBARD AND SIGNE see THE RED MANTLE

HALLELUJAH THE HILLS! (Independent, 1963) Meyer Kupferman
Fontana 27524/67524

HALLELUJAH TRAIL, THE (United Artists, 1965) Elmer Bernstein
Mainstream 56063/6063
United Artists 4127/5127 and 3476/6476

HAMLET (Universal, 1948) Sir William Walton
Angel (S) 36198
RCA 1273 (78) and 1924

HAMMERHEAD (Columbia, 1968) David Whittaker
Colgems (S) 110

HAND IN HAND (Britain, 1961) Stanley Black
Mercury 20688/60688

HANG 'EM HIGH (United Artists, 1968) Dominic Frontiere
Project 3 (S) 5027
RCA 4002, 4049
United Artists 69, 5179 and 6710

HANGOVER SQUARE (Fox, 1945) Bernard Herrmann
Camden 205

HANNIBAL BROOKS (United Artists, 1969) Francis Lai
United Artists 5196 and 69

HA'PENNY BREEZE (Britain, 1950) Philip Green
English Columbia 1724 (78)

THE HAPPENING (Columbia, 1967) Frank de Vol
Colgems (S) 5006

THE HAPPY ENDING (United Artists, 1970) Michel Legrand
Bell 6071
Mercury 61279
United Artists 5203

THE HAPPY THIEVES (United Artists, 1962) Mario Nascimbene
United Artists 3197/6197

THE HAPPY TIME (Columbia, 1952) Dimitri Tiomkin
RCA 1007

A HARD DAY'S NIGHT (United Artists, 1964) Paul McCartney, John Lennon
Command (S) 871
United Artists 3392/6392

THE HARD RIDE (Paramount, 1971) Harley Hatcher
Paramount 6005

HARLOW (Paramount, 1965) Neal Hefti
Columbia 6390/2790
RCA (S) 3496

HARLOW (Magna, 1965) Nelson Riddle, Al Ham
Warner Bros. (S) 1599

HARPER (THE MOVING TARGET) (Warners, 1966) Johnny Mandel
Mainstream 56078/6078
RCA (S) 3491

HARRY, CHERRY AND RAQUEL (Independent, 1969) Igo Kantor, William Loose
Beverly Hills 23

HATARI! (Paramount, 1962) Henry Mancini
Camden (S) 736, (S) 2162
Columbia CL-1880/CS-8680
RCA (S) 2559 and (S) 2693
United Artists 3249/6249

THE HAUNTING (MGM, 1963) Humphrey Searle
MGM (S) 4185 and (S) 4192

HAWAII (United Artists, 1966) Elmer Bernstein
Command (S) 5005
Fox (S) 3192
Somerset 26900
Stereo Fidelity 26900
Unart 20015/21015
United Artists 4143/5143 and 3570/6570

THE HEART IS A LONELY HUNTER (Warners, 1968) David Grusin
Columbia (S) 9835
RCA LSC-3245
Warner Bros. (S) 1759

HEAVEN WITH A GUN (MGM, 1969) Johnny Mandel
United Artists 6710

THE HEIRESS (Paramount, 1949) Aaron Copland
Everest 19403 (45)

HELEN OF TROY (Warners, 1954) Max Steiner
Capitol 3336 (45)
MGM 3294 and 3480
RCA 1170

HELL CATS (Four Star, 1964) various composers
Tower S-5124

HELL TO ETERNITY (Allied Artists, 1960) Leith Stevens
Warwick 2030

HELLRAIDERS OF THE DEEP (Italy, 1954) P. G. Redi
MGM 3485

HELL'S ANGELS '69 (American International, 1969) Tony Bruno
Capitol 303

HELL'S BELLES (American International, 1969) Les Baxter
Sidewalk 5919

HELP! (United Artists, 1965) Paul McCartney, John Lennon
Metro (S) 551
United Artists 3476/6476

HEMINGWAY'S ADVENTURES OF A YOUNG MAN (Fox, 1962) Frank Waxman
RCA (S) 1074

HENRY V (United Artists, 1946) Sir William Walton
Angel (S) 36198
English Odeon 1444
Epic 3809/1147
London 3313/44025
RCA 1924

HERE WE GO 'ROUND THE MULBERRY BUSH (Britain, 1968) various composers
United Artists 4175/5175

THE HERO (Britain, 1972) Johnny Harris
Capitol SW-11098

THE HEROES OF TELEMARK (Columbia, 1965) Malcolm Arnold
Mainstream 56064/6064

THE HIDDEN ROOM (OBSESSION) (Britain, 1950) Nino Rota
English Parlophone 3264 (78)

THE HIGH AND THE MIGHTY (Warners, 1954) Dimitri Tiomkin
Cameo (S) 4001
Capitol 594 and (S) 1599
Coral 57006
Decca 8085, 8102 and 8312
Harmony 7351/11151
London 3106/159, 3117/164 and 3257/246
MGM 3172, (S) 4132 and (S) 13
Mercury 20123 and 20483/60162
RCA 2381 and 1042
Richmond 20101/30101
Warner Bros. (S) 1319

HIGH NOON (United Artists, 1952) Dimitri Tiomkin
Cameo (S) 4003
Columbia 2826/8826 and 1178
Coral 57006
Harmony 7108 and 7351/11151
London 1700/124
Mercury 20156, 20648/60648 and 20702/60702
RCA 1007 and (S) 2897
Time (5) 2046
United Artists 30001

HIGH TIME (Fox, 1960) Henry Mancini
Camden (S) 928

HIS WIFE'S HABIT (Independent, 1970) Jim Helms, Gary LeMel, Norma Green
Capitol 641

HOLIDAY FOR HENRIETTA (France, 1955) Georges Auric
Columbia 2599 and 107

HOLIDAY IN SPAIN see SCENT OF MYSTERY

HOMBRE (Fox, 1967) David Rose
MGM (S) 4491

HOMER (National General, 1970) Various artists
Cotillion 9037

L'HOMME A FEMMES (LADIES' MAN) (France, 1960) Claude Bolling
French Philips 432.512 (45)

L'HOMME ET L'ENFANT (THE MAN AND THE CHILD) (France, 1957) Jeff Davis
Dot 3120

THE HONEY POT (United Artists, 1967) John Addison
Unart 20015/21015
United Artists 4149/5149

THE HONEYMOON MACHINE (MGM, 1961) Leigh Harline
MGM (S) 3988

HONG KONG AFFAIR (Allied Artists, 1958) Louis Forbes
Lion (S) 70136

HONOR AMONG THIEVES see TOUCHEZ PAS AU GRISBI

HORROR OF DRACULA (Universal, 1958) James Bernard
Coral (7) 57240

THE HORSE SOLDIERS (United Artists, 1960) David Buttolph
Ascot 13502/16502
United Artists 4035/5035 and 3122/6122

HOT ROD RUMBLE (Allied Artists, 1957) Alexander Courage
Liberty 3048

HOT SPELL (Paramount, 1958) Alex North
RCA (S) 1445

HOTEL (Warners, 1967) Johnny Keating
Warner Bros. (S) 1682

HOTEL PARADISO (MGM, 1966) Laurence Rosenthal
MGM (S) 4419

HOUDINI (Paramount, 1953) Roy Webb
Columbia 39975 (45)
Decca 28590 (45)

HOUR OF THE GUN (United Artists, 1967) Jerry Goldsmith
United Artists 4165/5165

A HOUSE IS NOT A HOME (Embassy, 1964) Joseph Weiss
Ava (S) 50
Musicor 2049/3049

THE HOUSE OF BAMBOO (Fox, 1955) Leigh Harline
Capitol 662 (45) and 3202 (45)

HOUSE OF FRANKENSTEIN (Universal, 1945) F. Dessau and Hans J. Salter
Coral (7) 57240

HOUSEBOAT (Paramount, 1958) George Duning
Columbia 1222
Lion (S) 70136

HOW GREEN WAS MY VALLEY (Fox, 1941) Alfred Newman
Capitol (S) 1599
Mercury 20000 and 1150

HOW SWEET IT IS (National General, 1968) Pat Williams
RCA (S) 4037

HOW THE WEST WAS WON (MGM, 1962) Alfred Newman
Command (S) 854
MGM (S) 5, (S) 242
Mercury 20887, 60887
Metro (S) 600
Polydor 184023
Time (S) 304, (5) 2078 and (5) 2112
United Artists 3003/6303

HOW TO MURDER YOUR WIFE (United Artists, 1965) Neal Hefti
DCP 3806/6806
United Artists 4119/5119 and 3476/647 and 3573/6573

HOW TO SAVE A MARRIAGE AND RUIN YOUR LIFE (Columbia, 1968) Michel Legrand
Columbia (S) 3140

HOW TO STEAL A MILLION (Fox, 1966) Johnny Williams
Fox (S) 4183

HUD (Paramount, 1963) Elmer Bernstein
Command (S) 854
Dunhill (S) 50015
MGM (S) 4185

HUNGARIAN FREEDOM FIGHTERS see WHILE I LIVE

HUNGRY HILL (Britain, 1947) John Greenwood
English Decca 1579 (78)

THE HUNTERS (Fox, 1958) Paul Sawtell
Fox 106 (45)

THE HURRICANE (United Artists, 1937) Alfred Newman
Capitol (S) 1652
Decca 8123 and 8312

HURRY SUNDOWN (Paramount, 1967) Hugo Montenegro
Musicor 2133/3133
RCA (S) 1133

HUSH, HUSH ... SWEET CHARLOTTE (Fox, 1965) Frank de Vol
ABC-Paramount (S) 513
Camden (S) 926
United Artists 3434/6434

THE HUSTLER (Fox, 1961) Kenyon Hopkins
Command (S) 835
Kapp 1264/3264 and 430 (45)

I, A WOMAN--PART II (Sweden, 1969) Sven Gyldmark
MGM 18

I AM A CAMERA (Britain, 1955) Malcolm Arnold
Columbia 1525/8325

I CONFESS (Warners, 1953) Dimitri Tiomkin
Coral 57006

I KILLED RASPUTIN (France, 1966) Andre Hossein
French Philips 70.426

I NEVER SANG FOR MY FATHER (Columbia, 1970) Al Gorgoni, Barry Mann
Bell 1204

I TRE VOLTI see BLACK SABBATH

I WALK THE LINE (Columbia, 1970) Johnny Cash
Columbia 30397

I WANT TO LIVE! (United Artists, 1958) Johnny Mandel
Ascot 13501/16501
United Artists 4005/5005 and 3122/6122

ICE STATION ZEBRA (MGM, 1968) Michel Legrand
Command (S) 941
MGM (S) 14

THE IDOL (Embassy, 1966) John Dankworth
Fontana 27559/67559

IDOL OF PARIS (Britain, 1947) Mischa Spoliansky
Entre 3029

IF HE HOLLERS, LET HIM GO (Cinerama, 1968) Harry Sukman; songs by Sammy Fain
Tower (S) 5152

IF IT'S TUESDAY, THIS MUST BE BELGIUM (United Artists, 1969) Walter Scharf
United Artists 5197

IF VERSAILLES WERE TOLD TO ME see ROYAL AFFAIRS IN VERSAILLES

IGNACE (France, n.d.) R. Dumas
French Decca 164.077

I'LL CRY TOMORROW (MGM, 1955) Alex North
Mercury 20123

ILL MET BY MOONLIGHT see NIGHT AMBUSH

I'LL NEVER FORGET WHAT'S 'ISNAME (Britain, 1968) Francis Lai
Decca 79163

I'LL TAKE SWEDEN (United Artists, 1965) Jimmie Haskell, by Durham
United Artists 4121/5121 and 3476/6476

IMITATION OF LIFE (Universal, 1959) Frank Skinner
Decca (7) 8879 and (7) 4362

IMMORTAL GARRISON, THE (Russia, 1956) A. Petrov
Russian MK 022043/4

IMPOSSIBLE FAMILY, THE (Italy, n.d.) S. Astore
Epic 3593

IN COLD BLOOD (Columbia, 1967) Quincy Jones
Colgems (S) 107

IN HARM'S WAY (Paramount, 1965) Jerry Goldsmith
RCA (S) 1100

IN LIKE FLINT (Fox, 1967) Jerry Goldsmith
Fox (S) 4193

IN THE FRENCH STYLE (Columbia, 1963) Joseph Kosma
Colpix (S) 464

IN THE HEAT OF THE NIGHT (United Artists, 1967) Quincy Jones
Camden (S) 2253
RCA (S) 4022
Unart 20015/21015
United Artists 4160/5160

THE INCREDIBLE MAN (Universal, 1957) F. Carling and Elliott Lawrence
Coral (7) 57240

THE INDIAN FIGHTER (United Artists, 1955) Franz Waxman
Capitol 3355 (45)

INDISCREET (Warners, 1958) Richard Rodney Bennett, Kenneth V. Jones
Lion (S) 70136
Roulette 4084 (45)

INDISCRETION OF AN AMERICAN HOUSEWIFE (Columbia, 1954)
Alessandro Cicognini
Atco (S) 170
Columbia 593, 612 and 6277
MGM 3485
Mercury 16399

THE INFORMER (RKO, 1935) Max Steiner
Capitol 387
Columbia 794
Decca (7) 9079

INHERIT THE WIND (United Artists, 1960) Ernest Gold
London 3320/320

THE INN OF THE SIXTH HAPPINESS (Fox, 1958) Malcolm Arnold
Fox (S) 3011
London 3298/298
RCA 2381

INSENSIBLEMENT (France, n.d.) composer unlisted
Dot 3120

INSIDE DAISY CLOVER (Warners, 1965) Andre Previn
Command (S) 894
RCA (S) 3491
Warner Bros. (S) 1616

INSPECTOR CLOUSEAU (United Artists, 1968) Ken Thorne
United Artists 69 and 5186

INTERLUDE (Universal, 1957) Frank Skinner
Coral 57159
Decca 8364

INTERLUDE (Columbia, 1968) Georges Delerue
Colgems (S) 5007
Project 3 (S) 5027

INTERMEZZO (United Artists, 1939) Heinz Provost
Capitol (S) 1599
Columbia 218, 1322/8124 and 1681/8481
Decca (7) 9079
Liberty 3135/7135
London 1700/124
MGM 3215 and (S) 4033
Mercury 25063 and 20648/60648
RCA 1245 and (S) 2380
Richmond 20095/30095 and 20101/30101
Vista (S) 3309
Warner Bros. (S) 1249

THE INTERNS (Columbia, 1962) Leith Stevens
Colpix (S) 427 and (S) 464

THE INVADERS (49TH PARALLEL) (Britain, 1942) Ralph Vaughan Williams
London 5053 (78)
His Master's Voice 9879 (78)

THE INVISIBLE BOY (MGM, 1957) Les Baxter
Capitol 3842 (45)

INVITATION (MGM, 1952) Bronislau Kaper
Capitol 594 and (S) 1652
Columbia 577 and 1681/8481
Decca 5413, 8341, 8364 and 8629
Liberty 3135/7135
MGM 3303, 3694 and (S) 4003
Mercury 20648/60648
Philips 200213/600213
RCA 2381
Warner Bros. 1242

INVITATION TO THE DANCE (MGM, 1956) Jacques Ibert, Andre Previn
MGM 3207

IO, IO, IO ... E GLI ALTRI (Italy, 1966) Carlo Rustichelli
Italian CAM 100-011

THE IPCRESS FILE (Universal, 1964) John Barry
Columbia 2493/9293
Decca (7) 9124

IRMA LA DOUCE (United Artists, 1963) Andre Previn, based on themes by Marguerite Monnot
Ava (S) 30
Columbia 2034/8834
Fox (S) 4105
United Artists 4109/5109, 3134/5134 and 3303/6306

IS PARIS BURNING? (Paramount, 1966) Maurice Jarre
Columbia 6630/3030
Command (S) 5005

ISADORA see THE LOVES OF ISADORA

THE ISLAND (Japan, 1961) Hikaru Hayashi
French Barclay 70.420 (45)

ISLAND IN THE SKY (Warners, 1953) Hugo Friedhofer, Emil Newman
Decca 7029

ISLAND OF APHRODITE (Greece, 1964) Mikis Theodorakis
Greek Odeon 45
English HMV 9

ISLAND WOMEN (ISLAND OF LOST WOMEN) (Warners, 1959) Raoul Kraushaar
Art 22

IT CAME FROM OUTER SPACE (Universal, 1953) Herman Stein
Coral (7) 57240

IT COMES UP MURDER see THE HONEY POT

IT HAPPENED IN ROME (Italy, 1956) Lelio Luttazzi
Epic 3593

IT STARTED IN NAPLES (Paramount, 1960) Alessandro Cicognini, Carlo Savina
Dot 3324/25324

IT WON'T RUB OFF, BABY see SWEET LOVE, BITTER

IT'S A MAD, MAD, MAD, MAD WORLD (United Artists, 1963) Ernest Gold
Fox (S) 4105
London 3320/320
Mercury 20887/60887
Time (5) 2112
United Artists 4110/5110 and 3376/6376
Warner Bros. (S) 1535

THE ITALIAN JOB (Paramount, 1969) Quincy Jones
Paramount (S) 5007

ITALIANI BRAVA GENTE see COMMANDO

IVAN THE TERRIBLE, PART I (Russia, 1944) Serge Prokofiev
Melodiya/Angel (S) 4103
Russian MK 1323/4

IVAN THE TERRIBLE, PART II (Russia, 1946) Serge Prokofiev
Melodiya/Angel (S) 4103
Russian MK 1323/4

IVANHOE (MGM, 1952) Miklos Rozsa
MGM 3507
RCA 1007

JACK JOHNSON (Independent, 1970) Miles Davis
Columbia 30455

JACK THE RIPPER (Paramount, 1960) Jimmy McHugh, Pete Rugolo
Camden 590

RCA (S) 2199

J'AI TUE RASPUTINE see I KILLED RASPUTIN

THE JAMES DEAN STORY (Warners, 1957) Leith Stevens
Capitol 881
World Pacific 2005

JANE EYRE (Fox, 1944) Bernard Herrmann
London ST-44144

JANE EYRE (Britain, 1971) John Williams
Capitol SW-749

JE M'BALADE DANS MOSCOU (France, n.d.) composer unlisted
Ducretet Thomson 460-V-658 (45)

JEANNE EAGLES (Columbia, 1957) George Duning
Decca 8574

JESSICA (United Artists, 1962) Mario Nascimbene, Marguerite Monnot
Capitol (S) 1986
London 104
United Artists 4096/5096

JOANNA (Fox, 1968) Rod McKuen
Command (S) 941
Fox (S) 4202
United Artists 69 and 6701

JOE (Cannon, 1970) Jerry Butler, Exuma
Mercury 605

THE JOE LOUIS STORY (United Artists, 1953) George Bassman
MGM 221

JOHN AND MARY (Fox, 1969) Quincy Jones
A&M 4230
Mercury 61279
United Artists 6742

JOHN F. KENNEDY: YEARS OF LIGHTNING, DAYS OF DRUMS (Independent, 1965) Bruce Herschenson
Capitol (S) 2486

JOHN PAUL JONES (Warners, 1959) Max Steiner
Warner Bros. (S) 1293

JOHNNY BELINDA (Warners, 1948) Max Steiner
RCA LPM-1170

JOHNNY CONCHO (United Artists, 1956) Nelson Riddle
Capitol 1-754 (45) and 2-754 (45)

JOHNNY COOL (United Artists, 1963) Billy May
Ascot 13504/15404
United Artists 4111/5111 and 3376/6376

JOHNNY GUITAR (Republic, 1954) Victor Young
English Columbia 3492
Jubilee 1034
Polydor 184023

THE JOKER IS WILD (Paramount, 1957) Walter Scharf
London 320
Mercury 20483/60162
Richmond 20101/30101
Wing 12504

JOUR DE FETE (France, 1952) Jacques Tati
English Philips (S) 7858

LE JOUR ET L'HEURE see THE DAY AND THE HOUR

JOY HOUSE (MGM, 1964) Lalo Schifrin
Verve (6) 8624

JUAREZ (Warners, 1939) Erich Wolfgang Korngold
RCA LSC-3330

JUBILEE TRAIL (Republic, 1954) Victor Young
Decca 8060

JUDGMENT AT NUREMBURG (United Artists, 1961) Ernest Gold
Ascot 13502/16502
London 3261/249 and 3320/320
Medallion (S) 7535
United Artists 4095/5095 and 3197/6197

JUDITH (Paramount, 1966) Sol Kaplan
Command (S) 894
Kapp 1467/3467
RCA (S) 1119

JULES ET JIM (France, 1962) Georges Delerue
French Victor 440.138 and 432.728 (45)
Philips 200071/600071
Warner Bros. (S) 1548

JULIA MISBEHAVES (MGM, 1948) Adolph Deutsch
MGM (S) 4144

JULIE (MGM, 1956) Leith Stevens
Capitol 843
MGM 3397

JULIET OF THE SPIRITS (Italy, 1965) Nino Rota
Kapp 1467/3467
Mainstream 56062/6062 and 56063/6063

JULIUS CAESAR (MGM, 1953) Miklos Rozsa
Dot 3107
MGM 3033

THE JUNGLE BOOK (United Artists, 1942) Miklos Rozsa
RCA 2118

JUSTINE (Fox, 1969) Jerry Goldsmith
Mercury 61279
Monument 18123
United Artists 6731

KALEIDOSCOPE (Warners, 1966) Stanley Myers
Warner Bros. (S) 1663

KAPO (Italy, 1960) Carlo Rustichelli
RCA (S) 4

KATIA (France, n.d.) Wal Berg
French Victor 440.138 (45)

THE KENTUCKIAN (United Artists, 1955) Roy Webb
MGM 3220
United Artists 30001

THE KEY (Columbia, 1958) Malcolm Arnold
Columbia 1185
Warner Bros. (S) 1247

KEY WITNESS (MGM, 1961) Sonny Skylar
London 3238/231

KIIARTOUM (United Artists, 1966) Frank Cordell
Camden 2106
Command (S) 5005
United Artists 3140/5140, 3526/6526 and 3570/6570

THE KID (Firsl National, 1921) Charles Chaplin
Decca 4040

A KID FOR TWO FARTHINGS (LUCKY KID) (Britain, 1956) Benjamin Frankel
London 1443

KIDNAPPED (American International, 1971) Roy Budd
AIR 1042

THE KILLERS (Universal, 1946) Miklos Rozsa
Decca (7) 10015

THE KILLING OF SISTER GEORGE (Cinerama, 1969) Gerald Fried
Command (S) 941

KINFOLKS (Independent, 1958) folk music and speech
Folkways 3852

A KING IN NEW YORK (Britain, 1957) Charles Chaplin
English Decca 10918 (45)
French Vogue SLD-837
Paramount PAS-6026

KING KONG (RKO, 1933) Max Steiner
Decca (7) 9079
Epic 24125/26125

KING OF HEARTS (United Artists, 1967) Georges Delerue
United Artists 4150/5150

KING OF KINGS (MGM, 1961) Miklos Rozsa
Capitol (S) 2627 and (S) 2837
Command (S) 835
Kapp (S) 1289
Liberty 3306/7306 and 6011/7711
MGM (S) 2, (S) 4078, (S) 4112 and (S) 4417
Mercury 20640/60640
Somerset 16400
Stereo Fidelity 16400
United Artists 3197/6197

KING RAT (Columbia, 1965) John Barry
Columbia 2493/9293
Mainstream 56061/6061 and 56063/6063

KINGS GO FORTH (United Artists, 1958) Elmer Bernstein
Capitol 1063

KINGS ROW (Warners, 1941) Erich Wolfgang Korngold
Columbia 794
RCA LSC-3330
Warner Bros. (S) 1438

KISENGA, MAN OF AFRICA see MEN OF TWO WORLDS

A KISS BEFORE DYING (United Artists, 1956) Lionel Newman
MGM 3380

KISS ME, STUPID (United Artists, 1965) Andre Previn
United Artists 3392/6392

KISS THEM FOR ME (Fox, 1957) Lionel Newman
Coral 57160

THE KNACK--AND HOW TO GET IT (United Artists, 1964) John Barry
Columbia 2493/9293
United Artists 4129/5129 and 3476/6476

KRAKATOA--EAST OF JAVA (Cinerama, 1969) Frank de Vol
ABC (S) 8

LADIES' MAN see L'HOMME A FEMMES

LADY IN CEMENT (Fox, 1968) Hugo Montenegro
Fox (S) 4204
RCA (S) 4104

LADY IN THE DARK (Paramount, 1944) Robert Emmet Dolan, based on the score by Kurt Weill
Decca 8085

LADY L (MGM, 1966) Jean Francaix
Command (S) 5005

A LADY SURRENDERS (LOVE STORY) (Britain, 1947) "Cornish Rhapsody" by Hubert Bath
Camden 233
Capitol (S) 8326, (S) 8386 and (S) 8598
Columbia 744
Decca 8285
Harmony 7237 and 7258/11035
London 1700/124 and 1513/112
Liberty 9003
MGM 3199 and (S) 3868
RCA (S) 2380
Ron-lette 47 and 528
English Saga 5018
Somerset 6700
Stereo Fidelity 6700
Urania (5) 8011
Vox 25180
Warner Bros. (S) 1249

LAFAYETTE (France, 1963) Steve Laurent, Pierre Duclos
Philips 200071/600071

LAND OF THE PHAROAHS (Warners, 1955) Dimitri Tiomkin
Coral 57006
MGM 3172 and 3220
RCA LPM-1170

THE LANDLORD (United Artists, 1970) Al Kooper
United Artists 5209

THE LAST COMMAND (Republic, 1955) Max Steiner
RCA LPM-1170

THE LAST HOLIDAY (Britain, 1950) Francis Chagrin
English Columbia 2702 (78)

THE LAST JUDGMENT (IL GIUDIZIO UNIVERSALE) (Italy, 1961) Alessandro Cicognini
RCA (S) 4

THE LAST OF THE MOHICANS (DER LETZTE MOKIKANER) (Germany, 1965) Peter Thomas
German Telefunken 14390

THE LAST OF THE SECRET AGENTS? (Paramount, 1966) Pete King
Dot 3714/25714

THE LAST REBEL (Columbia, 1971) Jon Lord/Tony Ashton
Capitol SW-827

LAST SUMMER (Allied Artists, 1969) John Simon
Mercury 61279
Warner Bros. 1791

THE LAST SUNSET (Universal, 1961) Ernest Gold
London 3320/320

THE LAST VALLEY (ABC, 1971) John Barry
Dunhill 50102

THE LAST WAGON (Fox, 1956) Lionel Newman
MGM 3480

LAST YEAR AT MARIENBAD (France, 1962) Francis Seyrig
Warner Bros. (S) 1548

LAURA (Fox, 1944) David Raksin
Camden 205 and 233
Cameo (S) 2003
Capitol (S) 1652
Columbia 744, 794, 1322/8124, 1627/8427 and 2034/8834
Decca 8629
Dot 3097/25097 and 3364/25364
Dunhill (S) 50008
Forum Circle (S) 9080
Harmony 7108
London 1700/124, 3322/322 and 3327/44031
Mercury 16399
RCA (S) 2380, (S) 2895, (S) 3887
Roulette 25023
Sunset 1106/5106
Ultra 7514/8514
Verve (6) 8694
Warner Bros. (S) 1368

THE LAW (WHERE THE HOT WIND BLOWS) (Italy, 1960) Roman Vlad
Everest 5076/1076
Mercury 20640/60640

LAWRENCE OF ARABIA (Columbia, 1962) Maurice Jarre
Ava (S) 23
Camden (S) 799
Capitol (S) 1877
Colgems (S). 5004
Colpix (S) 514, (S) 1000 and (S) 464
Liberty 3287/7287
London 3298/298 and 3516/516
Somerset 19300 and 20700
Stereo Fidelity 19300 and 20700
Time (5) 2078 and (5) 2112
United Artists 3303/6303

THE LEARNING TREE (Warners, 1969) Gordon Parks
Warner Bros. (S) 1812

THE LEFT HAND OF GOD (Fox, 1955) Victor Young
Decca 8285

THE LEGEND OF THE GLASS MOUNTAIN see THE GLASS MOUNTAIN

THE LEGION'S LAST PATROL see COMMANDO

LE MANS (Cinema Center, 1971) Michel Legrand
Columbia S-30891

THE LEOPARD (IL GATTAPARDO) (Fox, 1963) Nino Rota
Capitol (S) 9608
Fox (S) 5015
London 104

A LETTER TO THREE WIVES (Fox, 1948) Alfred Newman
Mercury 20037

LES LIASONS DANGEREUSES (DANGEROUS LOVE AFFAIRS) (France, 1961) Art Blakey
Epic 16022

LIBERTE I (France, 1963) J. Drejac
Philips 20071/60071

THE LIBERTINE (Audubon, 1969) Armando Trovajoli
United Artists UAS-6742

LIEUTENANT KIJE see THE CZAR WANTS TO SLEEP

THE LIFE AND DEATH OF COLONEL BLIMP (Britain, 1943) Allan Gray
English Decca 1724 (78)

LIFE BEGINS AT 8:30 (Fox, 1942) Alfred Newman
Decca 8123

THE LIFE OF ALBENIZ (Argentina, 1946) Isaac Albeniz
RCA 1092

THE LIFE OF EMILE ZOLA (Warners, 1937) Max Steiner
RCA LPM-1170

LIGHT FANTASTIC (Embassy, 1963) Joseph Liebman
Fox (S) 5016

A LIGHT IN THE PIAZZA (MGM, 1962) Mario Nascimbene
Command (S) 835

LILAC TIME (First National, 1928) Nathaniel Shilkret
RCA (S) 2560

LILI (MGM, 1953) Bronislau Kaper
Cameo (S) 4003
Capitol (S) 1599
Decca 8051
Dot 3097/25097 and 3364/25364
Harmony 7108
London 1700/124
MGM 187 and 3694
Mercury 20123
RCA (S) 2895 and (S) 3887
Richmond 20061/30061
Time (5) 2046 and (S) 304
Vox 25180
Warner Bros. 1242 and (S) 1368

LILIES OF THE FIELD (United Artists, 1963) Jerry Goldsmith
Capitol (S) 2063
Dunhill (S) 50015
Epic (S) 24094
United Artists 3376/6376

LILITH (Columbia, 1964) Kenyon Hopkins
Colpix (S) 520
Verve (6) 8694

LIMELIGHT (United Artists, 1952) Charles Chaplin
Camden 233
Columbia 503
Decca 8051
Dot 3276/25276
Epic 24014/26014

Fontana 67584
French Vogue SLD-837
Kapp (S) 3005
Liberty 13011/14011
London 1700/124, 1342, 3106/159, 3431/44066, and 44092
MGM 3480 and (S) 4064
Mercury 20123/60017
Paramount PAS-6062
RCA 1185
Richmond 20061/30061
Riviera 6580
Vox 25180
Warner Bros. (S) 1249

THE LIMPING MAN (STREET OF SHADOWS) (Britain, 1953) Eric Spear
English Parlophone 3645 (78)
RCA 20-5624 (45)

THE LION (THE RAGE OF THE LION) (Fox, 1963) Malcolm Arnold
London 76001

THE LION IN WINTER (Embassy, 1968) John Barry
Columbia (S) 3250 and (S) 9835
United Artists (S) 6669 and 6701

THE LIQUIDATOR (MGM, 1966) Lalo Schifrin
MGM (S) 4413

LISA (Fox, 1962) Malcolm Arnold
Columbia 1880/8680
Kapp (S) 1289
United Artists 3249/6249

LITTLE BIG HORN (Lippert, 1951) Paul Dunlap; song by Stanley Adams, Larry Stock, Maurice Sigler
RCA 47-4068 (45)

LITTLE BIG MAN (National General, 1970) John Hammond
Columbia 30545

LITTLE FAUSS AND BIG HALSY (Paramount, 1970) Johnny Cash, Carl Perkins
Columbia 30385

THE LITTLE FUGITIVE (Independent, 1953) Eddy Manson
Folkways 2070
Mercury 20123
MGM 3134

THE LITTLE SHEPHERD OF KINGDOM COME (Fox, 1961) Henry Vars
London 3247/237

LITTLE WOMEN (MGM, 1949) Adolph Deutsch, Max Steiner
MGM (S) 4144
RCA LPM-1170

LIVE FOR LIFE (France, 1967) Francis Lai
Camden (S) 2210
Mercury 21149/61149
Philips 200260/600260
Unart 20026/21026
United Artists 4165/5165 and 3633/6633

THE LIVING DESERT (Disney, 1953) Paul Smith
Vista 3326

LIVING FREE (Columbia, 1972) Sol Kaplan
RCA LSO-1172

THE LIVING IDOL (MGM, 1957) Edward Heyman, David Campbell
MGM 3480 and (S) 4064

LOLA MONTES (France, 1956) Georges Auric
Columbia 107
MGM 3480

LOLITA (MGM, 1962) Nelson Riddle; theme by Bob Harris
Epic 24014/26014
MGM (S) 4050, (S) 4064, (S) 4078 and (S) 4132

LOLLIPOP COVER (Independent, 1966) composer unlisted
Mainstream 56069/6069

THE LONELINESS OF THE LONG DISTANCE RUNNER (Britain, 1962) John Addison
Warner Bros. (S) 1548

LONG DAY'S JOURNEY INTO NIGHT (Embassy, 1962) Andre Previn
Columbia 1880/8680

THE LONG DUEL (Paramount, 1967) Patrick John Scott
Atco (S) 228

THE LONG HOT SUMMER (Fox, 1957) Alex North
Kapp (S) 3005
Roulette 25026
Wing 12136/12501

LONG JOHN SILVER (Australia, 1955) David Buttolph
RCA 3279

THE LONG SHIPS (Columbia, 1964) Dusan Radic
Colpix (S) 517
Dunhill (S) 50015

THE LONGEST DAY (Fox, 1962) Maurice Jarre; theme by Paul Anka
Fox (S) 5007
London 3313/44025 and 104
Time (5) 2078, (5) 2079, and (5) 2112

LORD JIM (Columbia, 1965) Bronislau Kaper
Colpix (S) 521

LORD LOVE A DUCK (United Artists, 1966) Neal Hefti
United Artists 3137/5137 and 3573/6573

LORD OF THE FLIES (Continental, 1962) Raymond Leppard
Ava (S) 30
London 3347/347
MGM (S) 4192

LOSS OF INNOCENCE (GREENGAGE SUMMER) (Britain, 1961)
Richard Addinsell
Colpix 508

THE LOST CONTINENT (Italy, 1957) Francesco Lavagnino
Columbia 107 and 2128 (45)
MGM 3635
Mercury 20188

LOST HORIZON (Columbia, 1937) Dimitri Tiomkin
Columbia 794
Coral 57006

THE LOST MAN (Universal, 1969) Quincy Jones
Uni 73060

THE LOST MOMENT (Universal, 1947) Daniele Amfitheatrof
Decca 8060

THE LOST WEEKEND (Paramount, 1945) Miklos Rozsa
RCA 1008 and 1245

LOUISIANA STORY (Independent, 1948) Virgil Thomson
Columbia 2087
Decca 3207
Epic 3809/1147

THE LOVE GODDESS (Continental, 1964) Percy Faith
Columbia 2209/9009

LOVE IN FOUR DIMENSIONS (Italy, 1965) Franco Mannino
Request 8090

LOVE IN THE AFTERNOON (FASCINATION) (Allied Artists, 1957)
Franz Waxman; "Fascination" theme by F. D. Marchetti
Camden (S) 373, and (S) 799, and (S) 2253
Decca 8629

London 571
Time (S) 304
United Artists 3315/6315

LOVE IN THE COUNTRY (n. d.) composer unlisted
Mercury 20887/60887

LOVE IS A BALL (United Artists, 1963) Michel Legrand
Philips 200082/600082

LOVE IS A FUNNY THING (France, 1970) Francis Lai
United Artists 5207

LOVE IS A MANY-SPLENDORED THING (Fox, 1955) Alfred Newman
Cameo (S) 4003
Capitol (S) 1652, (S) 1661
Columbia GP-10 1371/8172 and 2026/8826
Decca 8629
Dot 3097/25097, 3349/25349 and 3364/25364
Dunhill (S) 50008
Harmony 7108 and 7351/11151
Liberty 13011/14011
London 1700/124 and 3201
MGM 3220, 3397, (S) 4261, (S) 4132 and (S) 4213
Mercury 20123 and 20483/60162
Philips 200098/600098
RCA (S) 2380 and (S) 2897
Time (5) 2046 and (S) 304
Ultra 7514/8514
Warner Bros. (S) 1247

LOVE IS MY PROFESSION (France, 1959) Rene Cloerec
Everest 5076/1076

LOVE LETTERS (Paramount, 1945) Victor Young
Capitol (S) 1599, 753, 445, and 302
Columbia 612 and 1371/8172
Decca 8056 and 8285
Jubilee 1034
Liberty 3287/7287
MGM (S) 4432
Mercury 20369
Sunset 1106/5106
Warner Bros. (S) 1219

LOVE STORY (Paramount, 1970) Francis Lai
Paramount 6002
RCA LSC-3245

LOVE STORY see A LADY SURRENDERS

LOVE WITH THE PROPER STRANGER (Paramount, 1963) Elmer
Bernstein

Time (S) 2131

LOVERS AND LOLLIPOPS (Independent, 1956) Eddy Manson
Columbia 107

LOVERS AND OTHER STRANGERS (ABC, 1970) Fred Karlin
ABC 15

THE LOVERS OF TEREUL (France, 1963) Mikis Theodorakis
Philips 200071/600071

LOVES OF CARMEN (Fox, 1927) Manuel M. Ponce
RCA (S) 2560

THE LOVES OF ISADORA (Universal, 1968) Maurice Jarre
Kapp (S) 5511
Philips 600320

THE LOVES OF JOANNA GODDEN (Britain, 1947) Ralph Vaughan Williams
Entre 3029

THE LUCK OF GINGER COFFEY (Continental, 1965) Bernardo Segall
RCA (S) 3342

LUCKY KID see A KID FOR TWO FARTHINGS

LUCY GALLANT (Paramount, 1955) Van Cleave
Vik 1029

LUST FOR LIFE (MGM, 1956) Miklos Rozsa
Decca (7) 10015

LYDIA (United Artists, 1941) Miklos Rozsa
Camden 130 and 233
Colpix (S) 403

MACBETH (Columbia, 1972) Third Ear Band
English Harvest SHSP-4019

McCLINTOCK! (United Artists, 1963) Frank de Vol
Capitol (S) 2075
United Artists 4112/5112 and 3376/6376
Warner Bros. (S) 1535

THE McCONNELL STORY (Warner Bros. 1955) Max Steiner
RCA LPM-1170

MacKENNA'S GOLD (Columbia, 1969) Quincy Jones
RCA 4096
United Artists 6710

MADAME BOVARY (France, 1934) Darius Milhaud
Golden Crest (S) 4060

MADAME BOVARY (MGM, 1949) Miklos Rozsa
MGM 3507 and (S) 4112

MADAME X (Universal, 1966) Frank Skinner; theme by Charles Wildman
Decca (7) 9152, (7) 4743 and (7) 4754

MADAMIGELLA DI MAUPIN (Italy, 1966) Franco Mannino
Italian CAM 33-12

MADE FOR EACH OTHER (Fox, 1972) Trade Martin
Buddah BDS-5111

MADE IN PARIS (MGM, 1966) George Stoll
Command (S) 894

MADRON (MGM, 1970) Riz Ortolani
Quad 5001

THE MADWOMAN OF CHAILLOT (Warners, 1969) Michael Lewis
United Artists 6731
Warner Bros. 1805

THE MAGIC CHRISTIAN (Commonwealth United, 1970) Ken Thorne; theme by Paul McCartney
Apple 3364
Commonwealth United 6004

THE MAGIC GARDEN (PENNYWHISTLE BLUES) (South Africa, 1951) Willard Cele
London 1038 (78)

THE MAGIC WORLD (Britain, n.d.) William D. Van Ness
Design 21

THE MAGNIFICENT AMBERSONS (RKO, 1942) Bernard Herrmann
English Virtuoso 13010

MAGNIFICENT OBSESSION (Universal, 1954) Frank Skinner; based on themes by Chopin, Beethoven and Johann Strauss
Decca 8078 and 8085

THE MAGNIFICENT SEVEN (United Artists, 1960) Elmer Bernstein
DCP 3802/6802
London 3327/44031 and 3516/516
RCA (S) 4049
United Artists 3122/6122 and 3133/6133

MAJOR DUNDEE (Columbia, 1965) Daniele Amfitheatrof
Columbia 6380/2780

MAJORITY OF ONE (Warners, 1961) Philip W. Anderson, Max Steiner
Kapp (S) 1289

MALAMONDO (Magna, 1964) Ennio Morricone
Epic 24126/26126
RCA (S) 3342

MALEDETTO IMBROGLIO (Italy, 1959) Carlo Rustichelli
RCA (S) 4

MALTA, G. C. (Britain, 1943) Sir Arnold Bax
London 5054 (78)

A MAN, A HORSE AND A GUN see THE STRANGER RETURNS

A MAN ALONE (Republic, 1955) Victor Young
Camden (S) 927
MGM (S) 551

A MAN AND A WOMAN (France, 1966) Francis Lai
Camden (S) 2133
Columbia GP-10
Harmony 11315
London 571 and 44112
Mercury (S) 16348 and 21125/61125
Musicor 2133/3133
Philips 200231/600231
RCA (S) 3041
Solid 17013/18013
Unart 20019/21019 and 20015/21015
United Artists 4147/5147, 3570/6570, and 3625/6625

THE MAN BETWEEN (United Artists, 1953) John Addison
London 1389 and 1487

A MAN CALLED DAGGER (MGM, 1968) Steve Allen
MGM (S) 4516

A MAN CALLED HORSE (National General, 1970) Leonard Rosenman
Columbia 3530

A MAN CALLED PETER (Fox, 1955) Alfred Newman
Decca 8123

A MAN COULD GET KILLED (Universal, 1966) Bert Kaempfert
Decca (7) 4750
Epic 24224/26224
Harmony 7428/11228
Kapp 1501/3501
London 3474/474 and 44092
Mercury (S) 16348
Philips 200213/600213

Solid 17013/18013
United Artists 3526/6526

THE MAN FROM NOWHERE (Independent, 1969) composer unlisted
United Artists 6710

THE MAN IN THE GRAY FLANNEL SUIT (Fox, 1956) Bernard Herrmann
RCA 20-6528 (45)

MAN IN THE MIDDLE (Fox, 1963) Lional Bart
Fox (S) 4128

MAN OF A THOUSAND FACES (Universal, 1957) Frank Skinner
Decca 8623 and 8629

MAN OF THE WEST (United Artists, 1958) Leigh Harline
United Artists 40005

MAN ON FIRE (MGM, 1957) Sammy Fain
Coral 57125

THE MAN WHO KNEW TOO MUCH (Paramount, 1956) "Que Sera Sera" by Jay Livingston and Ray Evans
Coral 57125
London 3117/164
Richmond 20061/30061

THE MAN WHO UNDERSTOOD WOMEN (Fox, 1959) Robert Emmett Dolan
Fox 145 (45)

THE MAN WITH THE GOLDEN ARM (United Artists, 1955) Elmer Bernstein
Ava (S) 11 and (S) 49
Coral 57065
Decca (7) 4362, (7) 8257 and (7) 9079
Liberty 3353/7353
London 44078
Mercury 20702/60702
RCA (S) 3887
United Artists 30001

MARACAIBO (Paramount, 1958) Laurindo Almeida
Decca 8756

MARAT/SADE (United Artists, 1967) Richard Peaslee
United Artists 4153/5153

THE MARCH HARE (Britain, 1956) Philip Green
Capitol 40737 (45)

MARCHE OU MOURIR see COMMANDO

MARCIA O CREPA see COMMANDO

MARCO THE MAGNIFICENT (MGM, 1966) George Garvarentz
Columbia 6470/2870

LE MARIAGE PARFAIT see THE PERFECT MARRIAGE

MARJORIE MORNINGSTAR (Warners, 1958) Max Steiner
Capitol (S) 1599
Dunhill (S) 50015
Kapp (S) 3005
London 3149/193
Mercury 20371/60017
Philips 200620/600620
RCA 1044
Wing 12136/12501

MARNIE (Universal, 1964) Bernard Herrmann
Dance Along 1318
London 44126

MARRIAGE ITALIAN STYLE (Italy, 1965) Armando Trovajoli
Epic 24195/26195

MARRY ME! MARRY ME! (France, 1969) Emil Stern
RCA 1160

MARYJANE (American International, 1968) various composers
Sidewalk S-5911

M*A*S*H (Fox, 1970) Johnny Mandel
Columbia 3520

MASSACRE IN GRAND CANYON (Italy, 1965) Gianni Ferrio
Italian CAM 30-097

MASTER OF THE WORLD (American International, 1961) Les Baxter
Vee Jay (S) 4000

MASTERS OF THE CONGO JUNGLE (Fox, 1960) Richard Cornu
Fox (S) 4001

MATA-HARI (France, 1964) Georges Delerue
French Ducretet Thomson 460-V-665 (45)

THE MATING URGE (Independent, 1958) Stanley Wilson
International 7777

A MATTER OF INNOCENCE (Britain, 1968) Michel Legrand
Decca (7) 9160

MAYA (MGM, 1965) Riz Ortolani
MGM (S) 4376

MAYERLING (MGM, 1969) Francis Lai
English Philips 7876

ME AND THE COLONEL (Columbia, 1958) George Duning
RCA 1046

ME, NATALIE (National General, 1969) Henry Mancini
Columbia (S) 3350
United Artists 6731

MEDITERRANEAN HOLIDAY (Continental, 1964) Riz Ortolani
London 76003/82003

THE MEDIUM (Independent, 1951) Gian-Carlo Menotti
Mercury 7

MEDIUM COOL (Paramount, 1969) Mike Bloomfield
United Artists 6742

MEFIEZ-VOUS FILETTES see YOUNG GIRLS BEWARE

MELBA (United Artists, 1953) Mischa Spoliansky
Decca 8051
London 1094

MELODY (Britain, 1971) The Bee Gees
Atco 363

A MEMBER OF THE WEDDING (Columbia, 1952) Alex North
RCA (S) 1445

THE MEN (BATTLE STRIPE) (United Artists, 1950) Dimitri Tiomkin
Dot 3107
Hamilton 108/12108

MEN AGAINST (Italy, 1970) composer unlisted
RCA PSL-10473

MEN IN WAR (United Artists, 1957) Elmer Bernstein
Imperial 9032

MEN OF TWO WORLDS (Britain, 1946) Sir Arthur Bliss
English Decca 1174 (78)

LE MEPRIS see CONTEMPT

THE MERCENARY (Italy/Spain, 1970) Ennio Morricone
Italian United Artists 29-005

MERMOZ (France, 1944) Arthur Honegger
French Columbia 1059

METELLO (Italy, 1971) Ennio Morricone
RCA Italiana KOLS-1009

METTI, UNA SERA A CENA (Italy, 1972) Ennio Morricone
Italian Cinevox MDF-3316

MICHURIN (Russia, n.d.) Dmitri Shostakovich
Melodiya/Angel SR-40181

MICKEY ONE (MGM, 1965) Stan Getz
MGM (S) 4312

MIDNIGHT COWBOY (United Artists, 1969) John Barry
Mercury 61279
United Artists 5198 and 6731

MIDNIGHT LACE (Universal, 1961) Frank Skinner; theme by Joseph Lubin
London 3238/231
Mercury 20688/60688

A MILANESE STORY (Italy, 1962) John Lewis
Atlantic (S) 1388

MINNESOTA CLAY (Italy, 1966) Piero Piccioni
Italian CAM 30-114

THE MINX (Independent, 1969) Tom Dawes/Don Dannemann
Amsterdam 12007

THE MIRACLE WORKER (United Artists, 1962) Laurence Rosenthal
Columbia 1880/8680

MIRAGE (Universal, 1965) Quincy Jones
Mercury 21025/61025

THE MISFITS (United Artists, 1961) Alex North
Columbia 1627/8427
United Artists 3158/6158 and 4105/5105

MISS SADIE THOMPSON (Columbia, 1953) George Duning
Mercury 20123 and 25181

MISTER BUDDWING (MGM, 1966) Kenyon Hopkins
Verve (6) 8638

MR. HOBBS TAKES A VACATION (Fox, 1962) Henry Mancini
RCA (S) 2604

MR. HULOT'S HOLIDAY (France, 1954) Alain Romans
English Philips (S) 7858
French Victor 440.138 (45)

MISTER ROBERTS (Warners, 1955) Franz Waxman
RCA 1202

MR. ROBINSON CRUSOE (United Artists, 1932) Alfred Newman
Decca 8123 and 8312

MR. STEVE see THE STRANGE MR. STEVENS

MOBY DICK (Warners, 1956) Philip Sainton
RCA 1247

MODERN TIMES (United Artists, 1936) Charles Chaplin
Columbia 107 and 40692 (45)
Decca 8085
French Vogue SLD-837
Paramount PAS-6026
United Artists 4049, 30001 and UAS-5222

MODESTY BLAISE (Fox, 1966) John Dankworth
Fox (S) 4182 and (S) 3192

MOGAMBO (MGM, 1953) A. W. Watkins
Mercury 20156 and 20301

THE MOLE PEOPLE (Universal, 1956) Hans J. Salter
Coral 57240

THE MOLLY MAGUIRES (Paramount, 1970) Henry Mancini
Paramount 6000
RCA 4350

THE MOMENT OF TRUTH (Columbia, 1965) Piero Piccioni
Mainstream 56057/6057 and 56063/6063

MOMENT TO MOMENT (Universal, 1966) Henry Mancini
Command (S) 894
Dunhill (S) 50008
English RCA 1498 (45)
Kapp 1467/3467
RCA (S) 4140

UN MONDE NOUVEAU (France, 1966) Michel Colombier
French United Artists 36.072 (45)

MONDO CANE (Italy, 1963) Riz Ortolani, Nino Oliviero
Atco (S) 170
Camden (S) 799
Decca (7) 4669
Deram 12706
Kapp 1470/3470
Liberty 3491/7491
London 3347/347, 44078 and 44092
Mercury 20887/60887

Musicor 2049/3049
RCA (S) 3887
Somerset 20700
Stereo Fidelity 20700
United Artists 4105/5105, 3315, 6315, and 3360/6360

MONDO CANE #2 see MONDO PAZZO

MONDO HOLLYWOOD (Independent, 1967) various composers
Tower S-5083

MONDO PAZZO (Italy, 1964) Nino Oliviero
Command (S) 871
Fox 3147/4147

MONIKA (SUMMER WITH MONIKA) (Sweden, 1959) Les Baxter
Capitol 3259 (45)

LE MONOCLE RIT JAUNE (France, 1965) composer unlisted
French Ducretet Thomson 460-V-647 (45)

MONSIEUR VERDOUX (United Artists, 1947) Charles Chaplin
Paramount PAS-6026

LES MONTS D'OR (Russia, 1932) Dmitri Shostakovich
Columbia CB-15

THE MOONLIGHTER (Warners, 1953) Heinz Roemheld
Decca 8060

THE MOONSPINNERS (Disney, 1964) Ron Grainer
Vista 3323

MORE (Britain, 1969) The Pink Floyd
Tower 5169

MORE THAN A MIRACLE (MGM, 1967) Piero Piccioni
MGM (S) 4515, (S) 242
Mercury 21149/61149

MOULIN ROUGE (United Artists, 1952) Georges Auric
Camden 233
Capitol (S) 1599
Columbia 593, 6255 and 1322/8124
Decca 8051, 8312 and 8629
Fontana 67584
Forum Circle (S) 9080
Harmony 7351/11151
Kapp 1297/3297
London 979, 3298/298 and 44092
Mercury 20371/60017
Polydor 184023
RCA 1007, (S) 2895, (S) 2380, (S) 2381 and (S) 3887

Roulette 25023
Somerset 20700
Stereo Fidelity 20700
Time (5) 2046
United Artists 30001 and 3158/6158
Vox 25180
Warner Bros. (S) 1319

THE MOUNTAIN (Paramount, 1956) Daniele Amfitheatrof
Decca 8449

THE MOVING TARGET see HARPER

THE MUMMY (Universal, 1932) composer unlisted
Epic 24125/26125

MUNTELE RETRZAT (Rumania, 1967) Ion Dumitrescu
Electrola ECE-0210

MURDER AT THE GALLOP (MGM, 1963) Ron Goodwin
MGM (S) 4185

MURDER BY CONTRACT (Columbia, 1958) Perry Botkin
Decca 30912 (45) and 30936 (45)

MURDER, INC. (Fox, 1960) Frank de Vol
Canadian-American 1003
London 3238/231

MURDER WITHOUT CRIME (Britain, 1950) Philip Green
English Columbia 1702 (78)

MURDERER'S ROW (Columbia, 1966) Lalo Schifrin
Colgems (S) 5003

MURMUR OF THE HEART (France, 1971) Charlie Parker, Gaston Freche, Henri Renaud
Roulette SR-3006

THE MUSIC LOVERS (United Artists, 1970) Peter Illych Tchaikovsky
United Artists UAS-5217

MUTINY ON THE BOUNTY (MGM, 1962) Bronislau Kaper
Ava (S) 23
Capitol (S) 1877
Columbia 1880/8680
Command (S) 854
MGM (S) 4 and (S) 242
Mercury 20810/60810
RCA (S) 2604
Time (5) 2078, (5) 2112 and (S) 304
United Artists 3303/6303 and 3249/6249

Warner Bros. (S) 1476

MY FATHER'S HOUSE (Palestine, 1946) folk music
Disc 932 (78)

MY FOOLISH HEART (RKO, 1949) Victor Young
Columbia 794 and 1371/8172
Decca 8364
Dunhill (S) 50008
Jubilee 1034
London 1700/124
MGM (S) 4432
Mayfair 9642
Richmond 20006
RCA (S) 2895
Tops 1642

MY GEISHA (Paramount, 1962) Franz Waxman
Columbia 1880/8680
Epic 24014/26014
RCA (S) 1070

MY UNCLE (MON ONCLE) (France, 1958) Alain Romans, Frank Barcellini
Capitol (S) 8603
Columbia 1627/8427
English Philips (S) 7858
French Fontana 460.565 (45)
London 104

NAGIN (India, 1956) Herman Kumar
His Master's Voice 24

NAKED ANGELS (Favorite, 1969) various composers
Straight 1056

NAKED CITY (Universal, 1948) Miklos Rozsa
Decca (7) 10015

THE NAKED MAJA (United Artists, 1959) Francesco Lavagnino
United Artists 4031/5031

NAKED PREY (Paramount, 1966) native music
Folkways 3854

THE NAKED SEA (RKO, 1955) Laurindo Almeida, George Fields
Capitol 675 (45)
Liberty 3049

NAKED UNDER LEATHER see GIRL ON A MOTORCYCLE

NAPOLEON (France, 1954) Jean Francaix
Philips 432600

NED KELLY (Britain, 1970) Shel Silverstein
United Artists 5213

NEVADA SMITH (Paramount, 1966) Alfred Newman
Dot 3718/25718
Philips 200213/600213

NEVER LOVE A STRANGER (Allied Artists, 1958) Raymond Scott
Wing 12136/12501

NEVER ON SUNDAY (Greece, 1960) Manos Hadjidakis
Ascot 13501/16501
Atco (S) 170
Cameo (S) 4001 and (S) 4003
Capitol (S) 1661 and (S) 1986 and (S) 302
Carlton (S) 126
Columbia 1627/8427
Command (S) 835
DCP 3802/6802
Deram 12706
Dot 3349/25349 and 3616/35616
Kapp 1297/3297
Liberty 3306/7306
London 3247/237 and 3261/249
Mercury 20688/60688 and 20702/60702
RCA (S) 2897
Reprise (9) 6009
Richmond 20095/30095 and 20101/30101
Time (5) 2046
United Artists 3122/6122, 3158/6158, 3303/6303, 3575/6575 and 4070/5070

THE NEW INTERNS (Columbia, 1965) Earle Hagen
Colpix (S) 473

A NEW KIND OF LOVE (Paramount, 1963) Errol Garner, Leith Stevens
London 3347/347
Mercury 20859
Warner Bros. (S) 1535

NEW YORK CHIAMA SUPERDRAGO see SECRET AGENT SUPER DRAGON

NEW YORK EYE AND EAR CONTROL (Independent, 1964) composer unlisted
ESP-Disc 1016

NICHOLAS NICKLEBY (Universal, 1947) Lord Berners
Entre 3029

NIGHT AMBUSH (Britain, 1958) Mikis Theodrakis
English Columbia 3904 (45)

THE NIGHT HAS EYES (Britain, 1946) Charles Williams
English Saga 5018

NIGHTS OF CABIRIA (Italy, 1957) Nino Rota
Epic 3593
Italian Pathe 28 (45)

THE NIGHT OF THE HUNTER (United Artists, 1956) Walter Schumann
RCA 1136

THE NIGHT OF THE IGUANA (MGM, 1964) Benjamin Frankel
MGM (S) 4247

NIGHTFALL (Columbia, 1956) Peter DeRose
Coral 57065

NINE HOURS TO RAMA (Fox, 1963) Malcolm Arnold
London 76002

NO ORCHIDS FOR MISS BLANDISH (Britain, 1948) George Melachrino
His Master's Voice 3736 (78)

NO SUN IN VENICE (SAIT-ON JAMAIS) (France, 1958) John Lewis
Atlantic (S) 1284
Dot 3120
Philips 200225/600225

NO TIME FOR SERGEANTS (Warners, 1958) Ray Heindorf
MGM (S) 4064

NO TREES IN THE STREET (Britain, 1959) Laurie Johnson
English Nixa 24097 (45)

NO WAY TO TREAT A LADY (Paramount, 1968) Stanley Meyers
Dot 25846

NORTH BY NORTHWEST (MGM, 1959) Bernard Herrmann
Cub 9038 (45)
London 44126

NOT AS A STRANGER (United Artists, 1955) George Anthiel
RCA 1245
Vik 1029

NOT WITH MY WIFE, YOU DON'T! (Warners, 1966) Johnny Williams
Warner Bros. (S) 1668

NOTHING BUT A MAN (Independent, 1965) juke box music
Motown (S) 630

NOTHING BUT THE BEST (Britain, 1964) Ron Grainer
Colpix (S) 477

THE NOTORIOUS GENTLEMAN (THE RAKE'S PROGRESS) (Britain, 1945) William Alwyn
London 5054 (78)

LA NOTTE BIANCHE (THE SLEEPLESS NIGHT) (Italy, 1957) Nino Rota
Epic 3593

NOW VOYAGER (Warners, 1942) Max Steiner
Capitol 387
Columbia 794
Coral 57004

NUDE ODYSSEY (Italy, 1960) Francesco Lavagnino
RCA (S) 4

THE NUN'S STORY (Warners, 1959) Franz Waxman
Warner Bros. (S) 1306

NUTTY, NAUGHTY CHATEAU see CHATEAU EN SUEDE

O CANGACIERO (THE BANDIT) (Brazil, 1953) Gabriel Migliori
Columbia 1010
Riviera 6580

OBSESSION see THE HIDDEN ROOM

OCEANO (Italy, 1971) Ennio Morricone
RCA Italiana OLS-10

THE OCTOBER REVOLUTION (France, n.d.) Jean Wiener
English Philips (S) 7827

THE ODD COUPLE (Paramount, 1968) Neal Hefti
Dot 25862
United Artists 69

ODD MAN OUT (Britain, 1947) William Alwyn
Columbia 794

ODDS AGAINST TOMORROW (United Artists, 1959) John Lewis
Ascot 13500/16500
United Artists 4061/5061

ODETTE (Britain, 1950) Anthony Collins
English Columbia 1688

LES OEUFS DE L'AUTRUCHE see THE OSTRICH HAS TWO EGGS

OF HUMAN BONDAGE (Warners, 1946) Erich Wolfgang Korngold
RCA LSC-3330

OF HUMAN BONDAGE (MGM, 1964) Ron Goodwin
MGM (S) 4261
Time (5) 2169 and (S) 304
United Artists 3392/6392

OF LOVE AND DESIRE (Fox, 1963) Ronald Stein
Fox (S) 5014

OF MICE AND MEN (United Artists, 1939) Aaron Copland
MGM 3367 and 3334

OH, DAD, POOR DAD, MAMA'S HUNG YOU IN THE CLOSET AND I'M FEELIN' SO SAD (Paramount, 1967) Neal Hefti
RCA (S) 3750

THE OIL PRINCE (DER OLPRINZ) (Germany, 1965) Martin Boetticher
German Polydor 237494

OLD IRONSIDES (Paramount, 1926) Hugo Reisenfeld
RCA (S) 2560

THE OLD MAN AND THE SEA (Warners, 1958) Dimitri Tiomkin
Columbia 1183/8013
Kapp (S) 3005
Lion (S) 70136

OLD SUREHAND see FRONTIER HELLCAT

OLE GUAPA (n.d.) S. Malando
Vox 25180

OLIVER! (Columbia, 1968) Lional Bart
Command (S) 941
United Artists 6701

OLIVER TWIST (Britain, 1947) Sir Arnold Bax
Columbia 2092

OMAR KHAYYAM (Paramount, 1957) Victor Young
Decca 8449

ON ANY SUNDAY (Columbia, 1971) Dominic Frontiere
Bell 1206

ON HER BED OF ROSES (Independent, 1966) Joe Green
Mira (S) 3006

ON HER MAJESTY'S SECRET SERVICE (United Artists, 1969) John Barry
United Artists 5204

ON THE BEACH (United Artists, 1959) Ernest Gold
Decca (7) 4083

London 3247/237 and 3320/320
Roulette (S) 25098
Somerset 20700
Stereo Fidelity 20700
United Artists 3061/6061 and 3122/6122

ON THE DOUBLE (Paramount, 1961) Leith Stevens
Dot 16215 (45)

ON THE WATERFRONT (Columbia, 1954) Leonard Bernstein
Columbia 5651/6251
Decca 8396
Dot 3107 and 3364/25364
London 3327/44031

ONCE A THIEF (MGM, 1965) Lalo Schifrin
Verve (6) 8624

ONCE UPON A TIME IN THE WEST (Italy, 1969) Ennio Morricone
RCA Italiana OLS-3
United Artists 6710

ONE-EYED JACKS (Paramount, 1961) Hugo Friedhofer
Camden (S) 373
Liberty 16001/17001
Ultra 7514/8514
United Artists 3158/6158

100 RIFLES (Fox, 1969) Jerry Goldsmith
United Artists 6710

ONE MINUTE TO ZERO (RKO, 1952) Victor Young
Capitol 13708 (45)
Jubilee 1034
London 1667
RCA 1523

ONE NAKED NIGHT (Independent, 1964) Chet McIntyre
Vega 2002

ONE, TWO, THREE (United Artists, 1961) Andre Previn
United Artists 3197/6197

ONE WOMAN'S STORY see THE PASSIONATE FRIENDS

ONLY THE FRENCH CAN (FRENCH CAN-CAN) (France, 1956)
Georges van Parys
Columbia 880 and 107

OPEN CITY (Italy, 1946) composer unlisted
Epic 3593

ORPHEUS (France, 1950) George Auric
French Vega 30A98

THE OSCAR (Paramount, 1966) Percy Faith
Columbia 6550/2950
London 3474/474

THE OSTRICH HAS TWO EGGS (France, 1957) Henri Sauguet
Dot 3120

OTLEY (Columbia, 1969) Stanley Myers
Colgems (S) 112

D'OU VIENS-TU JOHNNY? (France, n.d.) J. J. Debout
French Philips 432.967 (45)

OUR MAN FLINT (Fox, 1966) Jerry Goldsmith
Capitol (S) 2455
Fox 3179/4179
Kapp 1467/3467
Metro (S) 565

OUR MOTHER'S HOUSE (Britain, 1967) Georges Delerue
MGM (S) 4495

OUR TOWN (United Artists, 1940) Aaron Copland
Concert Hall 2 and 51
Decca 7527
MGM 3334
Vanguard 1088/2115

OUR VERY OWN (RKO, 1950) Victor Young
Decca 27067 (45)

OUTLAW RIDERS (MGM, 1972) Simon Stokes
MGM S-26

OUTSIDE IN (Independent, 1972) Randy Edelman
MGM (S)37

THE OVERLANDERS (Britain, 1944) John Ireland
English Lyrita SRCS-45
Musical Heritage Society MHS-1481

PANIC BUTTON (Independent, 1964) Georges Garvarentz
Musicor 2026/3026

PAPA'S DELICATE CONDITION (Paramount, 1963) Joseph J. Lilley;
'Call Me Irresponsible'' by James van Heusen-Sammy Cahn
Capitol (S) 1877
Command (S) 871

PAR UN BEAU MATIN D'ETE (France, n.d.) composer unlisted
French Ducretet Thomson 460-V-671 (45)

THE PARADINE CASE (Selznick, 1948) Franz Waxman
Alco 10 (78)

LE PARADIS PERDU (France, n.d.) Hans May
French Victor 440. 138 (45)

THE PARENT TRAP (Disney, 1961) Paul Smith
Buena Vista (S) 3309 and (S) 3319
Camden (S) 373
London 3247/237
MGM (S) 4064
United Artists 3197/6197

PARIS BLUES (United Artists, 1961) Duke Ellington
Ascot 13502/16502
United Artists 4092/5092, 3158/6158 and 3197/6197

PARIS HOLIDAY (United Artists, 1959) Joseph J. Lilley
United Artists 40001

PARIS WHEN IT SIZZLES (Paramount, 1964) Nelson Riddle
Reprise (S) 6113

PARRISH (Warners, 1961) Max Steiner
Warner Bros. (S) 1413

THE PARTY (United Artists, 1968) Henry Mancini
RCA (S) 3997

PARTY GIRLS FOR THE CANDIDATE (Independent, 1965) Steve Karman
Jubilee 5029

PASSAGES FROM JAMES JOYCE'S "FINNEGANS WAKE" see FINNEGANS WAKE

PASSION (RKO, 1954) Louis Forbes
Decca 8085

THE PASSIONATE FRIENDS (ONE WOMAN'S STORY) (Britain, 1949) Richard Addinsell
Entre 3029

A PATCH OF BLUE (MGM, 1965) Jerry Goldsmith
Liberty 3498/7498
London 44092
Mainstream 56068/6068

PATHER PANCHALI (India, 1958) Ravi Shankar
World Pacific 1416

PATTON (Fox, 1970) Jerry Goldsmith
Fox S-4208
RCA 4350

LE PAVE DE PARIS (France, 1961) Joseph Kosma
French Philips 432.538 (45)

THE PAWNBROKER (Independent, 1965) Quincy Jones
Mercury 21011/61011

THE PEACH THIEF (Bulgaria, 1965) Simeon Pironkov
Roulette (S) 804

LE PEAU DE L'OURS (BEAR SKIN) (France, 1961) composer unlisted
Dot 3120

LA PEAU DOUCE see SOFT SKIN

THE PEKING MEDALLION see THE CORRUPT ONES

PENELOPE (MGM, 1966) Johnny Williams
MGM (S) 4426

PENNYWHISTLE BLUES see THE MAGIC GARDEN

THE PENTHOUSE (Britain, 1967) John Hawksworth
United Artists 4170/5170

THE PEOPLE NEXT DOOR (Embassy, 1970) Don Sebesky
Avco Embassy 11002

PEPE (Columbia, 1960) John Green; title song by Hans Wittstatt
Cameo (S) 2001
London 3238/231 and 3247/237
Richmond 20095/30095 and 20101/30101

THE PERFECT FURLOUGH (Universal, 1958) Frank Skinner
Imperial 5752 (45)
Medallion 605 (45)

THE PERFECT MARRIAGE (France, 1969) Peter Thomas
Polydor 242.217

A PERILOUS JOURNEY (Republic, 1953) Victor Young
Decca 8060

PERIOD OF ADJUSTMENT (MGM, 1962) Lyn Murray
Ava (S) 30

PERSONAL PROPERTY (MGM, 1937) Franz Waxman
World Artists (S) 3007

PETER THE GREAT (PETER THE FIRST, PART I) (Russia, 1937)
Vladimir Sherbachev
Russian Melodiya 11133

PETULIA (Warners, 1968) John Barry
Warner Bros. (S) 1755

PEYTON PLACE (Fox, 1957) Franz Waxman
RCA (S) 1042
Wing 12504

PHAEDRA (Greece, 1962) Mikis Theodorakis
Ascot 13505/16505
RCA (S) 2604
United Artists 4102/5102, 3303/6303 and 3249/6249

THE PHANTOM LOVERS (FANTASMI A ROMA) (Italy, 1960) Nino Rota
RCA (S) 4

THE PHANTOM OF THE OPERA (Universal, 1943) Edward Ward
London 6015 (45)

PICASSO (Italy, 1954) Roman Vlad
Folkways 3860

THE PICASSO SUMMER (Warners, 1970) Michel Legrand
Bell 6071
Warner Bros. 1925

PICCADILLY INCIDENT (Britain, 1946) Vivian Ellis
English Decca 1559 (78)

PICNIC (Columbia, 1955) George Duning
Colpix (S) 458 and (S) 464
Coral 57065 and 57125
Decca (7) 8320, 8407 and (7) 4362
Dunhill (S) 50015
London 3106/159 and 3421/44066
Mercury 20371/60017
RCA 2381
Time (5) 2046
Verve (6) 8694
Warner Bros. (S) 1247, (S) 1319 and (S) 1368

PIECES OF DREAMS (United Artists, 1970) Michel Legrand
Bell 6071

PIERROT LA TENDRESSE (France, n.d.) Guy Beart
French Philips 432.511 (45)

THE PILGRIM (First National, 1922) Charles Chaplin
Decca 4040

THE PINK PANTHER (United Artists, 1964) Henry Mancini
Command (S) 871
Metro (S) 551
RCA (S) 2795 and (S) 3491
Time (S) 2131
United Artists 3376/6736

PINKY (Fox, 1949) Alfred Newman
Capitol (S) 1652
Mercury 20037

PINOCCHIO (Disney, 1940) Leigh Harline
Vista (S) 3319

PIROGOV (Russia, n.d.) Dmitri Shostakovich
Melodiya/Angel SR-40160
Russian MK 01471

A PLACE IN THE SUN (Paramount, 1951) Franz Waxman
Decca 5414 and 8362
Dot 3097/25097
Hamilton 108/12108
MGM 3480
RCA LPM-1007

PLANET OF THE APES (Fox, 1968) Jerry Goldsmith
Project 3 (S) 5023

THE PLASTIC DOME OF NORMA JEAN (France, 1967) Michel Legrand
MGM (S) 4491

PLAY DIRTY (United Artists, 1969) Michel Legrand
United Artists 69

PLAY IT AGAIN, SAM (Paramount, 1972) Billy Goldenberg
Paramount PAS-1004

PLAYTIME (France, 1968) Jacques Tati
English Philips (S) 7858

PLEASE, NOT NOW (LE BRIDE SUR LE COU) (France, 1962) composer unlisted
French Barclay 72471 (45)

THE PLEASURE OF HIS COMPANY (Paramount, 1961) Alfred Newman
Camden (S) 373
Capitol (S) 1652

THE PLEASURE SEEKERS (Fox, 1964) Lionel Newman
RCA (S) 1101

PLEIN SOLEIL see PURPLE NOON

PLYMOUTH ADVENTURE (MGM, 1952) Miklos Rozsa
MGM 3507

A POCKETFUL OF MIRACLES (United Artists, 1961) Walter Scharf
United Artists 3197/6197

POLLYANNA (Disney, 1960) Paul Smith
Disneyland 1906

POPI (United Artists, 1969) Dominic Frontiere
United Artists 5194

POPSY POP (France, 1971) folk music
Arion 30-T-106

PORTE DE LILAS (France, 1957) George Brassens
Columbia 1178
Dot 3120

LES PORTES DE LA NUIT (France, 1947) Joseph Kosma
French Vega 30A98
London 3322/322

A PORTRAIT OF JENNIE (Selznick, 1948) Bernard Herrmann
Columbia 612
Decca 8237

LA POUPEE (THE DOLL) (French, n.d.) composer unlisted
French Philips 432.824 (45)

THE POWER AND THE PRIZE (MGM, 1956) Bronislau Kaper
MGM 3694

PREMIER RENDEZVOUS (France, n.d.) R. Sylviano
French Victor 440.138 (45)

THE PRESIDENT'S LADY (Fox, 1953) Alfred Newman
Capitol 2515
Decca 8123
Dot 15438
Heritage 0104
London 1428
MGM 3172

PRESSURE POINT (United Artists, 1962) Ernest Gold
London 3320/320

PRETTY BOY FLOYD (Continental, 1960) Del Serino, William Sanford
Audio Fidelity 5936

PRETTY POLLY see A MATTER OF INNOCENCE

THE PRIDE AND THE PASSION (United Artists, 1957) George Antheil
Capitol 873

THE PRIME OF MISS JEAN BRODIE (Fox, 1969) Rod McKuen
Fox (S) 4207
RCA 4350
Warner Bros. (S) 1787 and (S) 1853

THE PRINCE AND THE PAUPER (Warners, 1937) Erich Wolfgang Korngold
RCA 1782
Warner Bros. 1438

PRINCE BAYAYA (Czechoslovakia, 1954) Vaclav Trojan
Supraphon 168

PRISON TOWN see CITY OF WOMEN

LA PRISONIERE (France, 1969) music by Gustav Mahler, Luciano Berio, Anton Webern
Columbia 3320

PRIVATE HELL 36 (Filmakers, 1954) Leith Stevens
Coral 56122 and (7) 57283

THE PRIVATE LIVES OF ELIZABETH AND ESSEX (Warners, 1939) Erich Wolfgang Korngold
Decca 5413 and 8364
United Artists 3464/6464
Warner Bros. (S) 1438

THE PRIVATE WAR OF MAJOR BENSON (Universal, 1955) Joseph Gershenson
RCA 1245

THE PRIZE (MGM, 1964) Jerry Goldsmith
Capitol (S) 2063 and (S) 2075
Liberty 3498/7498
MGM (S) 4192
United Artists 3376/6376
Warner Bros. (S) 1535

THE PRODIGAL (MGM, 1955) Bronislau Kaper
London 3257/246
MGM 3172

THE PRODUCERS (Embassy, 1968) John Morris
RCA (S) 4008 and (S) 4049

THE PROFESSIONALS (Columbia, 1966) Maurice Jarre
Colgems (S) 5001

PROMISE AT DAWN (Embassy, 1970) Georges Delerue
Polydor 24-5502

PROMISE HER ANYTHING (Paramount, 1966) Lyn Murray
Command (S) 894
Kapp 1476/3476

THE PROPER TIME (Independent, 1961) Shelly Manne
Contemporary 3587/7587

THE PROUD AND THE BEAUTIFUL (LES ORGUEILLEUX) (France-Mexico, 1956) Paul Misraki
Columbia 1178

THE PROUD AND THE PROFANE (Paramount, 1956) Victor Young
Coral 57065

THE PROUD ONES (Fox, 1956) Lionel Newman
Coral 57065
MGM 3480

THE PROUD REBEL (Disney, 1958) Jerome Moross
Lion (S) 70136
MGM 12656 (45)

PRUDENCE AND THE PILL (Fox, 1968) Bernard Ebbinghouse
Fox (S) 4199

PSYCH-OUT (American International, 1968) various composers
Sidewalk (S) 5913

PSYCHE '59 (Royal, 1964) Kenneth V. Jones
Colpix (S) 464

PSYCHO (Paramount, 1960) Bernard Herrmann
London 44126

PUBLIC PIGEON NO. 1 (RKO, 1957) David Rose
MGM 3397

PURPLE NOON (France, 1961) Nino Rota
Polydor 184023

THE PYRAMID OF THE SUNGODS (Germany, 1965) Erwin Halletz
German Telfunken 14367

QUAI DES BRUMES (PORT OF SHADOWS) (France, 1938) Maurice Jaubert
French Vega 30A98

QUAI DES ORFEVRES (France, n.d.) Francis Lopez
French Victor 440.138 (45)

LE QUATORZE JUILLET (FOURTEENTH OF JULY) (France, 1932)
Maurice Jaubert
French Vega 30A98
French Victor 440.138 (45)
Disques Ades 15501

QUELLE JOIE DE VIVRE (CHE GIOIA VIVERE) (France, n.d.)
Francesco Lavagnino
French RCA 75.666 (45)

QUEMADA! see BURN!

QUICK BEFORE IT MELTS (MGM, 1964) David Rose
MGM (S) 4285

QUIET DAYS IN CLICHY (Independent, 1970) various artists
Vanguard 79303

THE QUIET MAN (Republic, 1952) Victor Young
Decca 8566

THE QUILLER MEMORANDUM (Fox, 1967) John Barry
Columbia 6660/3060 and 2708/9508

QUO VADIS? (MGM, 1951) Miklos Rozsa
Capitol 456, (S) 2627 and (S) 2837
Columbia 612
Liberty 6011/7711
MGM 3524 and (S) 4112
RCA 1007

RPM (Columbia, 1970) Perry Botkin, Jr. and Barry de Vorzon
Bell 1203

THE RACERS (Fox, 1955) Alex North
RCA (S) 1445

A RAGE TO LIVE (United Artists, 1965) Nelson Riddle
United Artists 3130/5130 and 3476/6476

THE RAIDER (WESTERN APPROACHES) (Britain, 1946) Clifton Parker
English Decca 1544 (78)

RAINIS (Russia, 1949) A. Skulte
Russian MK 019957

THE RAINMAKER (Paramount, 1957) Alex North
RCA 1434

THE RAINS OF RANCHIPUR (Fox, 1955) Hugo Friedhofer
Forum Circle (S) 9080
Roulette 25023

RAINTREE COUNTY (MGM, 1957) John Green
Dot 3097/25097
Hamilton 108/12108
MGM 3694 and (S) 4144
Mercury 20371/60017
RCA 6000 and (S) 1038
Wing 12136/12501

THE RAKE'S PROGRESS see THE NOTORIOUS GENTLEMAN

RAMONA (United Artists, 1928) L. Wolfe Gilbert
RCA (S) 2560

RAMPAGE AT APACHE WELLS see THE OIL PRINCE

THE RARE BREED (Universal, 1966) Johnny Williams
Decca (7) 4754

LE RAT D'AMERIQUE (France, 1964) Georges Garvarentz
French Barclay 80.198 and 70.534 (45)

THE RAT RACE (Paramount, 1960) Elmer Bernstein
Ava (S) 11
Dot 3306
English London 2288
Mercury 20702/60702

THE RAWHIDE YEARS (Universal, 1956) Arnold Hughes
Decca 29584 (45)

THE RAZOR'S EDGE (Fox, 1946) Alfred Newman
Mercury 20037

REACH FOR THE SKY (Britain, 1957) John Addison
His Master's Voice 8265 (45)
English Parlophone 4198 (45)

REAR WINDOW (Paramount, 1954) Franz Waxman
Decca 8085
MGM 3172
Mercury 20156

REBECCA (United Artists, 1940) Franz Waxman
Decca 30056 (45)

REBEL WITH A CAUSE see THE LONELINESS OF THE LONG DISTANCE RUNNER

REBEL WITHOUT A CAUSE (Warners, 1955) Leonard Rosenman
Columbia 940
Coral 57125 and 57009
Imperial 9021
RKO-Unique 109
Warner Bros. (S) 1478

THE RED HOUSE (United Artists, 1947) Miklos Rozsa
Capitol 456

RED LANTERNS (Greece, 1964) Starvros Xarchakos
Greek Odeon 37

THE RED MANTLE (HAGBARD AND SIGNE) (Iceland, 1968) Marc Fredericks
RCA LSP-4815

THE RED PONY (Republic, 1949) Aaron Copland
Decca 9616 and 3207

THE RED SHOES (Britain, 1948) Brian Easdale
Columbia 2083 and 5254/6028
Odyssey 32-16-0338

RED SKY AT MORNING (Universal, 1971) Billy Goldenberg
Decca 79180

THE RED TENT (Paramount, 1971) Ennio Morricone
Paramount PAS-6019

THE REIVERS (National General, 1969) John Williams
Columbia 3510

LES RENDEZ-VOUS DU DIABLE (France, 1959) Marius-Francois Gaillard
French Odeon 1221

REQUIEM FOR A HEAVYWEIGHT (Columbia, 1962) Laurence Rosenthal
Colpix (S) 458

RETOUR A L'AUBE (France, n.d.) Paul Misraki
French Victor 440.138 (45)

RETURN FROM THE ASHES (United Artists, 1965) John Dankworth
United Artists 3476/6476

RETURN OF THE 7 (United Artists, 1966) Elmer Bernstein
United Artists 69, 4146/5146 and 3570/6570

RETURN TO PARADISE (United Artists, 1953) Dimitri Tiomkin
Columbia 577, 6255 and 1371/8172
Coral 57006

Decca 4389
Liberty 3306/7306
MGM 3134
United Artists 30001

RETURN TO PEYTON PLACE (Fox, 1961) Franz Waxman
Imperial 5752 (45)
Kapp (S) 1289
London 3261/249
Medallion 605 (45)

REVENGE OF THE CREATURE (Universal, 1956) Herman Stein
Coral (7) 57240

RHODES OF AFRICA (Britain, 1936) Sir Hubert Bath
English Columbia 2830 (78)

RICHARD III (Britain, 1956) Sir William Walton
Angel (S) 36198
RCA 6126

RIDE THE HIGH COUNTRY (MGM, 1962) George Bassman
MGM (S) 4185
Warner Bros. (S) 1476

RIDER ON THE RAIN (France, 1970) Frances Lai
Capitol 584

RIFIFI (France, 1956) Georges Auric
Capitol (S) 8603
Deram 12706
Reprise (9) 6009

THE RISING OF THE MOON (Warners, 1957) Eamonn O. Gallagher
London (S) 44020

THE RIVER (Britain, 1951) Music of India
Polymusic 5003

THE RIVER OF NO RETURN (Fox, 1954) Lionel Newman
Columbia 1178

ROAD HOUSE (Fox, 1949) Alfred Newman
Decca 8109

ROAD TO HONG KONG (United Artists, 1962) Robert Farnon
Liberty 16002/17002

ROBBERY (Britain, 1967) Johnny Keating
London 76008/82008

THE ROBE (Fox, 1953) Alfred Newman
Capitol (S) 2627

Decca (7) 9012, 8060, 8312 and (7) 4362
Liberty 6011/7711
London 3257/246
MGM (S) 4033

ROCCO AND HIS BROTHERS (Italy, 1961) Nino Rota
Deram 12706
London 3261/249 and (S) 44020
Reprise (9) 6009
RCA (S) 2 and (S) 4

ROMANCE OF A HORSE THIEF (Allied Artists, 1971) Mort Schuman
Allied Artists 110-1010

ROMANOFF AND JULIET (Universal, 1961) Mario Nascimbene
Decca 31242 (45)
King 5509 (45)
United Artists 3464/6464

ROME ADVENTURE (Warners, 1960) Max Steiner
Dunhill (S) 50015
Kapp (S) 1289
Mercury 20810/60810
Warner Bros. (S) 1458

ROMEO AND JULIET (Britain, 1954) Roman Vlad
Epic 13104/15104

ROMEO AND JULIET (Paramount, 1968) Nino Rota
Camden 2340
Capitol 2993
Columbia 9823, 9906
Kapp 3610
RCA 4140
United Artists 6669, 6701

LA RONDE (France, 1950) Oscar Straus
Atco (S) 170
Capitol (S) 8603
Deram 13701
London 3298/298 and (S) 44020
Reprise (9) 6009

LA RONDE see also CIRCLE OF LOVE

ROOM AT THE TOP (Britain, 1959) Mario Nascimbene
Reprise (9) 6009
Warner Bros. (S) 1548

ROOM 43 (Britain, 1958) Kenneth V. Jones
Capitol (S) 1304 and 4275 (45)

THE ROOTS OF HEAVEN (Fox, 1958) Malcolm Arnold, Henri Patterson
Fox 3005

THE ROSE TATTOO (Paramount, 1955) Alex North
Columbia 727
Decca (7) 4083
MGM 3294
RCA (S) 1445

ROSEMARY (Germany, 1960) Norbert Schultze
Decca (7) 4083
Reprise (9) 6009

ROSEMARY'S BABY (Paramount, 1968) Krystof Komeda
Dot (S) 25875
Project 3 (S) 5027

ROTTEN TO THE CORE (Britain, 1954) Michael Dress, Robin Miller
English Parlophone 1262

ROYAL AFFAIRS IN VERSAILLES (France, 1957) Jean Francaix
French Pathe 1036

A ROYAL SCANDAL (Fox, 1945) Alfred Newman
Mercury 20036

RUBY GENTRY (Fox, 1952) Heinz Roemheld
Capitol 594 and (S) 1599
Columbia 593 and 612
Decca 8051 and 8312
Kapp (S) 3005
Liberty 3306/7306
MGM (S) 4033
Mercury 20123 and 16399
RCA (S) 2895

RUN, ANGEL, RUN (Fanfare, 1969) Stu Phillips
Epic 26474

RUN FOR YOUR WIFE (Italy, 1966) Nino Oliviero
RCA (S) 1129

RUN OF THE ARROW (RKO, 1957) Victor Young
Decca 8620
RKO-Unique 119

RUN WILD, RUN FREE (Columbia, 1969) David Whitaker
SGC 5003

THE RUSSIANS ARE COMING, THE RUSSIANS ARE COMING
(United Artists, 1966) Johnny Mandel

Camden 2106
United Artists 4142/5142 and 3570/6570

RYAN'S DAUGHTER (MGM, 1970) Maurice Jarre
MGM 27

S.W.A.L.K. see MELODY

SAADIA (MGM, 1953) Robert Inglez
English Parlophone 3876 (45)

SACCO AND VANZETTI (Italy, 1971) Ennio Morricone
RCA Italiana OLS-4

THE SACRED IDOL (n.d.) Les Baxter
Capitol 1293

SADDLE PALS (Republic, 1947) Ernest Gold
London 3320/320

SAINT JOAN (United Artists, 1957) Mischa Spoliansky
Capitol 865
Roulette 25023

SALADINO (Italy, 1966) Francesco Lavagnino
Italian CAM 100-007

SALLAH (Israel, 1964) Yohanan Zarai
Philips 200117/600117

SALOME (Columbia, 1953) George Duning, Daniele Amfitheatrof
Decca 6026

SALT AND PEPPER (United Artists, 1968) John Dankworth
United Artists (S) 5187

SALUTI E BACI (Italy, 1952) S. Barzizza
MGM 3485

SAMSON AND DELILAH (Paramount, 1950) Victor Young
Columbia 794
Decca 8566
Jubilee 1034
London 3257/246 and 3313/44025
Mercury 20369 and 16399
United Artists 3290/6290

THE SAND CASTLE (Independent, 1960) Alec Wilder
Columbia 1455/8249

THE SAND PEBBLES (Fox, 1966) Jerry Goldsmith
Camden (S) 2161
Command (S) 5005

Fox (S) 4189
Kapp 1512/3512
Mercury (S) 16348
Philips 200231/600231

THE SANDPIPER (MGM, 1965) Johnny Mandel
Camden (S) 926
Command (S) 887
Decca (7) 4647 and 75212
Dunhill (S) 50008
London 3474/474 and 44092
Mercury 21032/61032
Metro (S) 551
Solid 17013/18013
Time (5) 2189
United Artists 3526/6526

SANS FAMILE (THE ORPHAN) (France, 1958) Paul Misraki
Dot 3120

SAPPHIRE (Britain, 1959) Philip Green
Top Rank 112

SARATOGA TRUNK (Warners, 1944) Max Steiner
RCA LPM-1170

SATAN IN HIGH HEELS (Independent, 1962) Mundell Lowe
Charlie Parker (S) 406

SATAN NEVER SLEEPS (Fox, 1962) Richard Rodney Bennett
Command (S) 835

SATURDAY NIGHT AND SUNDAY MORNING (Britain, 1961) John Dankworth
London 3247/237 and (S) 44020
Warner Bros. (S) 1548

SAVAGE SEVEN (American International, 1968) various composers
Atco 245

SAYONARA (Warners, 1957) Franz Waxman; theme by Irving Berlin
Dot 3107, 3276/25276 and 33647/25364
Hamilton 108/12108
Kapp (S) 3005
Lion (S) 70136
MGM (S) 4064
RCA (S) 1041
Wing 12504

THE SCALPHUNTERS (United Artists, 1968) Elmer Bernstein
United Artists 69 and 4176/5176

SCANDALOUS JOHN (Disney, 1971) Rod McKuen
Vista 5004

THE SCAPEGOAT (MGM, 1959) Bronislau Kaper
Cub 9038 (45)

SCENT OF MYSTERY (Independent, 1960) Mario Nascimbene
Ramrod 6001

SCOTT OF THE ANTARCTIC (Britain, 1949) Ralph Vaughan Williams
London 977 and 9097

THE SEA HAWK (Warners, 1940) Erich Wolfgang Korngold
Warner Bros. (S) 1438

SÉANCE ON A WET AFTERNOON (Britain, 1964) John Barry
Columbia 2493/9293
Musicor 2133/3133

SEARCH FOR PARADISE (Cinerama, 1957) Dimitri Tiomkin
RCA 1034

THE SEARCHERS (Warners, 1956) Max Steiner
RCA 1287

SEARCHING WIND (Paramount, 1946) Victor Young
Decca 5370 and 27455 (45)

SEBASTIAN (Britain, 1968) Jerry Goldsmith
Dot (S) 25845

SECRET AGENT SUPER DRAGON (Italy, 1966) Benedetto Ghiglia
Italian CAM 33-16

THE SECRET OF SANTA VITTORIA (United Artists, 1969) Ernest Gold
United Artists 5200

SECRETS OF LIFE (Disney, 1956) Paul Smith
Disneyland 4006

SEPARATE TABLES (United Artists, 1958) David Raksin
Mercury 20483/60162

SERENADE (Warners, 1956) Nicholas Brodszky
MGM 3375 and 3397

SERENATA D'AMORE (Italy, n.d.) Heini Gaze
Decca (7) 4083
Dot 3120

SERGEANTS 3 (United Artists, 1962) Billy May
Reprise (9) 2013

SETTIMO PARALLELO (Italy, 1963) composer unlisted
Italian RCA 10327

THE SEVEN CAPITAL SINS (France, 1963) Michel Legrand
Atco (S) 170
Capitol (S) 8603
Philips 200071/600071

SEVEN GOLDEN MEN (Italy, 1965) Armando Trovajoli
French Philips 437.204 (45)
Italian CAM 33-1
United Artists 5193

THE SEVEN HILLS OF ROME (MGM, 1957) Victor Young, George Stoll
Mercury 20369
Epic 3593

SEVEN WONDERS OF THE WORLD (Cinerama, 1956) David Raksin, Jerome Moross
Coral 57065

THE SEVEN YEAR ITCH (Fox, 1955) Alfred Newman
Decca 8123 and 8312
Mercury 20154

THE 7TH DAWN (United Artists, 1964) Riz Ortolani
Command (S) 871
Musicor 2049/3049
United Artists 4115/5115 and 3376/6376

SEVENTH HEAVEN (Fox, 1927) Erno Rapee
RCA (S) 2560
Time (S) 304

THE SEVENTH VOYAGE OF SINBAD (Columbia, 1958) Bernard Herrmann
Colpix 504

SEX AND THE SINGLE GIRL (Warners, 1964) Neal Hefti
Warner Bros. (S) 1572

SHAFT (MGM, 1971) Isaac Hayes
MGM ENS-2-5002

SHAFT'S BIG SCORE (MGM, 1972) Gordon Parks; theme by Isaac Hayes
MGM 36

SHAKE HANDS WITH THE DEVIL (United Artists, 1959) William Alwyn
United Artists 4043/5043

SHAKESPEARE WALLAH (India, 1966) Satyajit Ray
Epic 13110/15110

SHALAKO (Cinerama, 1968) Robert Farnon
London 44112
Philips 600286

SHANE (Paramount, 1953) Victor Young
Columbia 593 and 659
Decca 8051
Mercury 20123
Philips 200213/600213
RCA 1007
Riviera 6580

SHENANDOAH (Universal, 1965) Frank Skinner
Decca (7) 9125

SHIP OF FOOLS (Columbia, 1965) Ernest Gold
Camden (S) 926
Command (S) 887
Decca (7) 4647
RCA (S) 2817 and (S) 3496
Mainstream 56063/6063

THE SHOES OF THE FISHERMAN (MGM, 1968) Alex North
Command (S) 941
MGM (S) 15
Philips 600301

THE SHOP ON MAIN STREET (Czechoslovakia, 1965) Zdenek Liska
Mainstream 56082/6082

THE SHOT FROM THE VIOLIN CASE (SCHUSSE AUS DEM GEIGEN-KASTEN) (Germany, 1965) Peter Thomas
German Polydor 237493

A SHOT IN THE DARK (United Artists, 1964) Henry Mancini
Dance Along 1318

SHOULDER ARMS (First National, 1918) Charles Chaplin
Decca 4040
French Vogue SLD-837

THE SHRIKE (Universal, 1955) Joseph Gershenson
Capitol 843
Columbia 777

THE SICILIAN CLAN (Fox, 1970) Ennio Morricone
Fox 4209

THE SIDEHACKERS (Independent, 1969) Mike Curb
Amaret 5004

SIGN OF THE GLADIATOR (American International, 1959) Dominic Frontiere
AIR 501

SIGNORE AND SIGNORI see THE BIRDS, THE BEES AND THE ITALIANS

THE SILENCERS (Columbia, 1966) Elmer Bernstein
RCA (S) 1120 and (S) 3496

SILENT MOVIE MUSIC (c1900-1928) themes and scores from early films
Asch 3856
Barbary 33030
Coral 57024
Decca 79079
Epic 3713
Golden Crest 4019
Liberty 3185
Major 1004
RCA 2560
Sutton 243

SILENT RUNNING (Universal, 1972) Peter Schickele
Decca 79188

THE SILK NOOSE (Britain, 1948) Charles Williams
English Columbia 1518 (78)

THE SILKEN AFFAIR (Britain, 1957) Peggy Stewart
RKO-Unique 414 (45)

SIMPLET (France, 1942) R. Dumas
French Decca 164.077

SINCE YOU WENT AWAY (United Artists, 1944) Max Steiner
Capitol 387
Columbia 612

THE SINGER NOT THE SONG (Britain, 1962) Philip Green
London 3238/231

SINGLE ROOM UNFURNISHED (Crown, 1967) James Sheldon
Sidewalk (S) 5917

SKI ON THE WILD SIDE (Independent, 1967) Billy Allen
MGM (S) 4493

SKIDOO (Paramount, 1968) Nilsson
RCA (S) 1152

THE SKYROCKET (Pathe, 1927) composer unlisted
RCA (S) 2560

SLAUGHTER ON TENTH AVE. (Universal, 1957) Richard Rodgers, adapted by Herschel Burke Gilbert
Decca (7) 8657

SLAUGHTERHOUSE-FIVE (Universal, 1971) Glenn Gould
Columbia S-31333

SLAVE TRADE IN THE WORLD TODAY (Continental, 1965) Teo Usuelli
London 76006

SLAVES (Continental, 1969) Bobby Scott
Skye 11

THE SLENDER THREAD (Paramount, 1966) Quincy Jones
Mercury 21070/61070

SMASHING TIME (Britain, 1968) John Addison
ABC (S) 6

THE SNOWS OF KILIMANJARO (Fox, 1952) Bernard Herrmann; theme by Alfred Newman
Columbia 8913
Decca 8123
London ST-44144
RCA LPM-1007
Somerset 19300
Stereo Fidelity 19300

SO BIG (Warners, 1953) Max Steiner
Decca 8060

SO LONG AT THE FAIR (Britain, 1950) Benjamin Frankel
English Columbia 1688 (78)

SODOM AND GOMORRAH (Fox, 1963) Miklos Rozsa
Capitol (S) 2627
MGM (S) 4112
RCA (S) 1076

SOFT SKIN (France, 1965) Georges Delerue
French Philips 77.233 and 434.887 (45)

SOL MADRID (MGM, 1968) Lalo Schifrin
MGM (S) 4541

SOLDIER IN THE RAIN (Allied Artists, 1963) Henry Mancini
English RCA 1498 (45)
Philips 600277
RCA (S) 3491

SOLDIER OF FORTUNE (Fox, 1955) Hugo Friedhofer
MGM 12023 (45)

SOLOMON AND SHEBA (United Artists, 1959) Mario Nascimbene
United Artists 4051/5051 and 3122/6122

SOME CAME RUNNING (MGM, 1959) Elmer Bernstein
Capitol 1109

SOME LIKE IT HOT (United Artists, 1959) Adolph Deutsch
Ascot 13500/16500
United Artists 3122/6122 and 3158/6158

SOMETHING MONEY CAN'T BUY (Universal, 1953) Nino Rota
Mercury 3081 (45) and 70196 (45)

SOMETHING TO LIVE FOR (Paramount, 1952) Victor Young
Decca 8051
Mercury 20369

SOMETHING WILD (United Artists, 1961) Aaron Copland
CBS 32-11-0001/32-11-0002

SON OF DRACULA (Universal, 1943) Hans J. Salter
Coral (7) 57240

SON OF FURY (Fox, 1942) Alfred Newman
Decca 18277 (45)

THE SONG OF BERNADETTE (Fox, 1943) Alfred Newman
Capitol 2627
Columbia 612
Decca 5358 and 8123
Liberty 6011/7711
Mercury 20037

SONG OF THE LAND (United Artists, 1953) M. Dupre
MGM 30838 (45)

SONG WITHOUT END (Columbia, 1960) George Duning
Colpix (S) 458, (S) 464 and (S) 506
Decca (7) 4083
Liberty 3306/7306

SONS AND LOVERS (Fox, 1960) Mario Nascimbene
Carlton (S) 126

THE SONS OF KATIE ELDER (Paramount, 1965) Elmer Bernstein
Columbia 6420/2820

THE SOUND AND THE FURY (Fox, 1959) Alex North
Decca 8885

SOUNDER (Fox, 1972) Taj Mahal
Columbia S-31944

SOUS LE TOITS DE PARIS see UNDER THE ROOFS OF PARIS

SOUTH SEAS ADVENTURE (Cinerama, 1958) Alex North
Audio Fidelity 1899/5899

THE SOUTHERN STAR (Columbia, 1969) George Garvarentz
Colgems 5009

SOUVENIR D'ITALIE see IT HAPPENED IN ROME

A SPANISH AFFAIR (Paramount, 1958) Daniele Amfitheatrof
Dot 3078

SPARA, GRINGO, SPARA (RAINBOW) (Italy, 1971) composer unlisted
Italian CAM SAG-9005

SPARTACUS (Universal, 1960) Alex North
Capitol (S) 2627
Decca (7) 9092 and (7) 4363
MGM (S) 3894
Mercury 20640/60640

SPELLBOUND (United Artists, 1946) Miklos Rozsa
Camden 181 and 233
Capitol 456, 453 and (S) 1599
Columbia 794
Decca 5413, 8127, 8364 and (7) 9079
Dot 3097/25097 and 3364/25364
Entre 3029
Forum Circle (S) 9080
Kapp (S) 3005
Liberty 13011/14011
London 44031
MGM 3172, (S) 3894, (S) 4007 and (S) 4112
Mercury 16399
Metro (S) 585
RCA 1008
Ron-lette 874/160
Roulette 25023
English Saga 5018
Warner Bros. (S) 1213

THE SPIDER'S WEB (Britain, 1965) Tony Crombie
English Ember 5030

SPIRIT OF ST. LOUIS (Warners, 1957) Franz Waxman
RCA 1472

SPITFIRE see THE FIRST OF THE FEW

SPLENDOR IN THE GRASS (Warners, 1961) David Amram
Columbia 1783/8583

THE SPORTING CLUB (Embassy, 1972) Michael Small
Buddah BDS-95002

THE SPY WHO CAME IN FROM THE COLD (Paramount, 1965)
Sol Kaplan
Capitol (S) 2455
Command (S) 894
Kapp 1467/3467
RCA (S) 1118 and (S) 3496

THE SPY WITH THE COLD NOSE (Britain, 1967) Riz Ortolani
Columbia 6670/3070

THE SQUARE ROOT OF ZERO (Independent, 1965) Elliot Kaplan
Mainstream 56070/6070

STAGECOACH (United Artists, 1939) Richard Hageman
London SP-44173

STAGECOACH (Fox, 1966) Jerry Goldsmith
Mainstream 56077/6077

LA STAGIONE DEI SENSI (Italy, 1971) composer unlisted
Ariete 2005

STAIRCASE (Fox, 1969) Dudley Moore
United Artists 6731

STAIRWAY TO HEAVEN (A MATTER OF LIFE AND DEATH)
(Britain, 1946) Allan Gray
Entre 3029

THE STALKING MOON (National General, 1969) Fred Karlin
United Artists 6710

STAR! (Fox, 1968) Various composers
Columbia (S) 9835

THE STAR (Fox, 1953) Victor Young
Decca 8051
Jubilee 1034
Mercury 20369

A STAR IS BORN (Selznick, 1937) Max Steiner
RCA LPM-1170

STARS AND STRIPES FOREVER (Fox, 1952) John Philip Sousa
MGM 3508

THE STERILE CUCKOO (Paramount, 1969) Fred Karlin
Mercury 61279
Paramount 5009

STILETTO (Embassy, (1969) Sid Ramin
Columbia (S) 3360

STOLEN HOURS (United Artists, 1963) Mort Lindsey
Capitol (S) 2063

A STOLEN LIFE (Warners, 1946) Max Steiner
RCA 1287

THE STONE (Greece, 1965) Stavros Xarchakos
Greek Odeon 30

THE STORY OF SHIRLEY YORK (Britain, 1950) George Melachrino
His Master's Voice 9678 (78)

A STORY OF THREE LOVES (MGM, 1953) Charles Williams
English Saga 5018

STOWAWAY IN THE SKY (France, 1960) Jean Prodromides
Capitol (S) 8603
Philips 200029/600029

LA STRADA (Italy, 1956) Nino Rota
Atco (S) 170
Cameo (S) 2001
Capitol (S) 8608
Columbia 2599, 1673/8473 and 107
Decca (7) 4233
Deram 12706
Epic 3593
Kapp (S) 3005 and 3610
Liberty 3491/7491
London 44020
MGM 3220 and 3397
Mercury 20648/60648
Musicor 2049/3049
Polydor 184023
Reprise (9) 6009
United Artists 3360/6360
Warner Bros. (S) 1548

STRANGE LADY IN TOWN (Warners, 1955) Dimitri Tiomkin
Coral 57006

THE STRANGE LOVE OF MARTHA IVERS (Paramount, 1946) Miklos Rozsa
Combo 113

THE STRANGE MR. STEVENS (L'ETRANGE MONSIEUR STEVE) (France, 1957) composer unlisted
Dot 3120

THE STRANGE ONE (Columbia, 1957) Kenyon Hopkins
Coral 57132

THE STRANGER RETURNS (A MAN, A HORSE AND A GUN) Italy, 1968) Stelvio Cipriani
RCA 4350
United Artists 6710

STRATEGIC AIR COMMAND (Paramount, 1955) Victor Young
Decca 8364
MGM 3172
Roulette 25023

STREET ANGEL (Fox, 1928) Erno Rapee
RCA (S) 2560

THE STREET OF DREAMS (Italy, n.d.) composer unlisted
Capitol (S) 8608

STREET OF SHADOWS see THE LIMPING MAN

STREET SCENE (United Artists, 1931) Alfred Newman
Capitol 406, 712
Decca 8123
Harmony 7108
MGM 3353, 3355
Warner Bros. (S) 1249

A STREETCAR NAMED DESIRE (Warners, 1951) Alex North
Capitol 387 and 8326
Columbia 2092 and 612
Dot 3107 and 3364/25364
Hamilton 108/12108
London 1513
RCA (S) 1445

STRIP-TEASE (France, n.d.) Serge Gainsbourg
French Philips 77.233 and 432.898 (45)

STROGOFF (Italy, 1971) Teo Usuelli
Italian Cinevox MDF 33-38

STRONGER THAN FIRE (STARKER ALS FLAMMEN) (Germany, 1963) Jewish folk music
Amadeo 9033

THE SUBTERRANEANS (MGM, 1960) Andre Previn
MGM (S) 3812

SUDDEN FEAR (RKO, 1952) Elmer Bernstein
Ava (S) 11

SUICIDE SQUADRON (Britain, 1942) Richard Addinsell, based on his "Warsaw Concerto"
Atco (S) 170
Camden (S) 637 and (S) 721
Capitol 406, (S) 8326, (S) 8496 and (S) 8593
Columbia 2092 and 5876/6476
Decca 5484 and (7) 9079
Harmony 7154 and 7258/11035
Kapp (S) 5003
Lion 70110
London 1513/112 and 3431/44066
MGM (S) 3868
Mayfair 9503
RCA 1879, (S) 2380 and (S) 1000
Rondo 528
Somerset 2100
Stereo Fidelity 8200
Telefunken 8037
Tops 1503
Vox 25180
Warner Bros. (S) 1249

THE SUITOR (LE SOUPIRANT) (France, 1963) Jean Paillaud
French Polydor 27.036 (45)

SUMMER AND SMOKE (Paramount, 1961) Elmer Bernstein
RCA (S) 1067

SUMMER MAGIC (Disney, 1963) Buddy Baker
Vista (S) 3319

SUMMER MANOUVERS (LES GRANDES MANOEUVRES) (France, 1955) George van Parys
English London 95012 (45)

SUMMER OF '42 (Warners, 1971) Michel Legrand
Bell 6071
Warner Bros. 1925

A SUMMER PLACE (Warners, 1959) Max Steiner
Camden (S) 926
Cameo (S) 4003
Columbia 1421/8218 and 1624/8427 and 9906
Decca (7) 8083
Dot 3276/25276
Dunhill (S) 50008
Kapp 1297/3297
Liberty 13011/14011
London 3231/224, 3247/237 and 3327/44031
Lion (S) 70136
MGM (S) 4132 and (S) 13
Philips 200213/600213
Richmond 20095/30095 and 20101/30101

Warner Bros. (S) 1413

SUMMERTIME (United Artists, 1955) I. Cini, Alessandro Cigognini
Capitol 10026
Decca (7) 4233
London 1700/124
MGM 3220 and 3397
Mercury 20188 and 20648/60648

THE SUN ALSO RISES (Fox, 1957) Hugo Friedhofer
Kapp 7001

SUNDAY, BLOODY SUNDAY (Britain, 1971) composer unlisted
RCA LSC-3245

SUNDAY IN NEW YORK (MGM, 1964) Peter Nero
RCA (S) 2827

SUNDAYS AND CYBELE (France, 1962) Maurice Jarre
Warner Bros. (S) 1548

THE SUNDOWNERS (Warners, 1960) Dimitri Tiomkin
Dot 3349/25349
London 3231/224, 3257/246 and 104
Mercury 20688/60688
Richmond 20095/30095

SUNFLOWER (Embassy, 1970) Henry Mancini
Avco Embassy 11001
Camden 2441

SUPERFLY (Warners, 1972) Curtis Mayfield
Curtom CRS-8014

THE SWAN (MGM, 1956) Bronislau Kaper
MGM 3397
Mercury 20156 and 20301

SWEDEN--HEAVEN AND HELL (Italy, 1969) Piero Umiliani
English Columbia 15000
Mercury 61279
United Artists 6742

SWEET BIRD OF YOUTH (MGM, 1962) Robert Armbruster
MGM (S) 4271

SWEET ECSTASY (France, 1963) Georges Garvarentz
Philips 200071/600071

SWEET LOVE, BITTER (Independent, 1967) Mal Waldron
Impulse (S) 9142

THE SWEET RIDE (Fox, 1968) Pete Rugolo
Fox (S) 4198

THE SWEET SMELL OF SUCCESS (United Artists, 1957) Elmer Bernstein
Ava (S) 11
Decca 8610 and 8614

SWEET SWEETBACK'S BAADASSSSS SONG (Cinemation, 1971) Melvin van Peeples
Stax 3001

THE SWIMMER (Columbia, 1968) Marvin Hamlisch
Columbia (S) 3210

SWISS FAMILY ROBINSON (Disney, 1960) William Alwyn
Vista (S) 3309 and (S) 3319

SYLVIA (Paramount, 1965) David Raksin
DCP 3806/6806
Mercury 21004/61004
RCA (S) 3342

SYMPHONY FOR TWO SPIES (Italy, 1966) Francesco de Masi
Italian CAM 33-5

SYNANON (Columbia, 1965) Neal Hefti
Liberty 3413/7413

TAKE A GIRL LIKE YOU (Britain, 1970) Stanley Myers
Pye NSPL-18353

TAKE THE HIGH GROUND (MGM, 1955) Dimitri Tiomkin
Capitol 594

TAKE THE MONEY AND RUN (Cinerama, 1969) Marvin Hamlisch
Command 941

TAKING OFF (Universal, 1971) various composers
Decca 79181

A TALE OF TWO CITIES (Britain, 1958) Richard Addinsell
English Saga 5018
Ron-lette 874/160

THE TALL HEADLINES (Britain, 1952) Hans May
Parlophone 3529 (78)

THE TALL MEN (Fox, 1955) Victor Young
Decca 8364

TAMMY AND THE BACHELOR (Universal, 1957) Frank Skinner; theme by Jay Livingston and Ray Evans
Ava (S) 23
Capitol (S) 1986
Columbia 1371/8172

Coral 57159
Decca 8629 and (7) 4362
Dot 3276/25276
MGM (S) 4064
Mercury 20371/60017
Richmond 20061/30061

TAMMY TELL ME TRUE (Universal, 1961) Percy Faith; theme by Dorothy Squires
Capitol (S) 1652
Columbia 1627/8427

TARANTULA (Universal, 1956) Henry Mancini
Coral (7) 57240

TARAS BULBA (United Artists, 1963) Franz Waxman
Ascot 13504/16504
Capitol (S) 1877 and (S) 2063
Decca (7) 4362
RCA (S) 2604
United Artists 3249/6249, 3303/6303 and 4100/5100

TARGET FOR TONIGHT (Britain, 1941) Leighton Lucas
His Master's Voice RAF-11 (78)

TARZAN THE APE MAN (MGM, 1959) Shorty Rogers
MGM 3798

A TASTE OF HONEY (Britain, 1962) John Addison
Kapp 1470/3470
London 3298/298, 3516/516
Mercury 20810/60810
United Artists 3249/6249 and 3315/6315

A TASTE OF VIOLENCE (France, 1963) Andre Hossein
Philips 200071/600071

A TAXI FOR TOBRUK (France, 1964) composer unlisted
Bel-Air 211035

THE TEAHOUSE OF THE AUGUST MOON (MGM, 1957) Saul Chaplin
Dot 3107 and 3364/25364

TELL ME LIES (Continental, 1968) Richard Peaslee
London 44112

TEMPI DURI PER I VAMPIRI see THE DEVIL'S COMMANDMENT

THE TEN COMMANDMENTS (Paramount, 1956) Elmer Bernstein
Capitol (S) 2627
Dot 3054/25054
Liberty 6011/7711
MGM (S) 4417

United Artists 69 and 3495/6495

TENDER IS THE NIGHT (Fox, 1962) Bernard Herrmann; title song by Sammy Fain
Command (S) 935
Fox (S) 3054
Mercury 20640/60640 and 20810/60810

THE TENTH VICTIM (Italy, 1965) Piero Piccioni
Mainstream 56071/6071

TEOREMA (Italy, 1968) various classical composers
Barclay 920.083
RCA LSC-3245

TERRAIN VAGUE (THE WASTELAND) (France, 1960) composer unlisted
Philips 432.523 (45)

THE TESTAMENT OF ORPHEUS (France, 1960) Jean Cocteau
French Columbia 1075

THAT DANGEROUS AGE (IF THIS BE SIN) (Britain, 1950) Mischa Spoliansky
Entre 3029

THAT DARN CAT (Disney, 1965) Bob Brunner; title song by Richard and Robert Sherman
Vista (S) 3334

THAT MAN IN INSTANBUL (Columbia, 1966) Georges Garvarentz
Mainstream 56072/6072

THAT NIGHT (RKO, 1957) Mario Nascimbene
Decca 8629 and 30385 (45)

THERESE DESQUEYROUX (France, 1962) Maurice Jarre
Ducretet Thomson 450-V-453 (45)

THESE WILDER YEARS (MGM, 1957) Jeff Alexander
MGM 3480

THEY CALL ME MISTER TIBBS! (United Artists, 1970) Quincy Jones
United Artists 5214

THEY CALL ME TRINITY (LO CHIAMAVANO TRINTA) (Italy, 1971) Franco Micalizzi
Ariete 2011

THEY SHOOT HORSES, DON'T THEY? (Cinerama, 1969) John Green
ABC 10

THE THING (RKO, 1951) Dimitri Tiomkin
Epic 24125/26125

THINGS TO COME (Britain, 1936) Sir Arthur Bliss
Ace of Diamonds SDD-255
London 15112
RCA 2257

THE THIRD DAY (Paramount, 1965) Percy Faith
Command (S) 887

THE THIRD MAN (Selznick, 1950) Anton Karas
Cameo (S) 4003
Capitol (S) 1877 and (S) 1986
Columbia 1271/8172 and 1178
Decca (7) 9079
Fontana 67584
Liberty 3353/7353
London 536, 158 and 3247/237
Mayfair 9642
RCA 2381
Reprise (9) 6009
Richmond 20060/30060
Time (5) 2046
Tops 1642
Vox 25180

30 IS A DANGEROUS AGE, CYNTHIA (Britain, 1968) Dudley Moore
London (S) 82010

36 HOURS (MGM, 1965) Dimitri Tiomkin
RCA (S) 3342
Vee Jay 1131

THIS COULD BE THE NIGHT (MGM, 1957) Nicholas Brodszky
Coral 57125

THIS EARTH IS MINE (Universal, 1959) Hugo Friedhofer
Decca (7) 8915

THIS ISLAND EARTH (Universal, 1956) Herman Stein
Coral (7) 57240

THIS MAN IS DANGEROUS (n.d.) composer unlisted
Riviera 6580

THIS MAN IS MINE (MILLIE, PHOEBE AND BILL) (Britain, 1945)
Allan Gray
Entre 3029

THIS PROPERTY IS CONDEMNED (Paramount, 1966) Kenyon Hopkins
Verve (6) 8664

THE THOMAS CROWN AFFAIR (United Artists, 1968) Michel Legrand
Bell 6071
Columbia 9823 and 9835
Project 3 (S) 5027
RCA (S) 4140
United Artists 69 and 5182

THOROUGHLY MODERN MILLIE (Universal, 1967) Elmer Bernstein and various composers
Camden (S) 2161
Mercury 21149/61149
Musicor 2133/3133
Somerset 27700
Stereo Fidelity 27700
United Artists 3633/6633

THOSE DARING YOUNG MEN IN THEIR JAUNTY JALOPIES (Paramount, 1969) Ron Goodwin
Paramount 5006

THOSE MAGNIFICENT MEN IN THEIR FLYING MACHINES (Fox, 1965) Ron Goodwin
Fox (S) 4174

THREE BITES OF THE APPLE (MGM, 1967) Eddy Manson with themes by David McCallum and Domenico Modugno
MGM (S) 4444

THREE COINS IN THE FOUNTAIN (Fox, 1954) Victor Young
Cameo (S) 4003
Capitol (S) 1986
Columbia 2026/8826
Harmony 7108 and 7351/11151
Liberty 13011/14011
London 1700/124 and 3201
MGM (S) 4132
Mercury 20371/60017
RCA 1291
Richmond 20060/30060
Time (S) 304 and (5) 2046
Warner Bros. (S) 1368

3 IN THE ATTIC (American International, 1969) Chad Stuart
Sidewalk (S) 5918

3 IN THE CELLAR (American International, n.d.) composer unlisted
AIR 1036

THUNDERBALL (United Artists, 1965) John Barry
Camden (S) 927
Capitol (S) 2455
Columbia 2493/9293 and 2708/9508

Command (S) 894
Kapp 1467/3467
London 44078 and 3514/514
Metro (S) 551
RCA (S) 3496
United Artists 4132/5132 and 3476/6476

THUNDERBIRDS (Republic, 1952) Victor Young
Decca 8051
Mercury 20369

TIARA TAHITI (Britain, 1963) Philip Green
London 3347/347

TICK ... TICK ... TICK (MGM, 1970) Tompall and the Glaser Brothers
MGM 4667

A TICKLISH AFFAIR (MGM, 1964) George Stoll, Robert Van Epps
Capitol (S) 2075

TIGER BAY (Britain, 1960) Laurie Johnson
Top Rank 112

THE TIGER TAMER (TIGER GIRL) (Russia, 1955) Moisei Vainberg
Monitor 530

TIGHT SPOT (Columbia, 1955) Morris Stoloff
MGM 3172
Vik 1029

TILL DEATH US DO PART (Britain, 1967) various composers
English Polydor (S) 583717

THE TIME MACHINE (MGM, 1960) Russell Garcia
Verve 10217 (45)

A TIME TO LOVE AND A TIME TO DIE (Universal, 1958) Miklos Rozsa
Decca 8778

TIME TO SING (MGM, 1968) various composers
MGM 4540

TO BED ... OR NOT TO BED (Italy, 1964) Piero Piccioni
Atco (S) 170
Camden 30-061 (45)
London 76005

TO CATCH A THIEF (Paramount, 1955) Lyn Murray
Coral 57125
Mercury 20156

TO DIE IN MADRID (France, 1966) Maurice Jarre
French Philips 77.233 and 432.881 (45)

TO EACH HIS OWN (Paramount, 1946) composer unlisted
Capitol (S) 1986

TO KILL A MOCKINGBIRD (Universal, 1962) Elmer Bernstein
Ava (S) 20 and (S) 23
MGM (S) 4192
RCA (S) 3491
Time (5) 2078

TO SIR, WITH LOVE (Columbia, 1967) Ron Grainer
Camden (S) 2210
Fontana 27569/67569
Mercury 21149/61149
United Artists 69 and 3633/6633

TOKYO OLYMPIAD (Japan, 1964) Toshiro Mayuzumi
Monument (1) 8046

TOM JONES (Britain, 1963) John Addison
Capitol (S) 2063
Command (S) 871 and (S) 899
Time (5) 2112 and (S) 2131
United Artists 3134/5134, 4113/5113, (S) 1535 and 3376/6376

TONITE LET'S ALL MAKE LOVE IN LONDON (Britain, 1967) documentary
English Instant 002

TOO LATE BLUES (Paramount, 1961) David Raksin
Columbia 1783/8583

TOO MUCH, TOO SOON (Warners, 1958) Ernest Gold
Lion (S) 70136
London 3320/320
Mercury 20318/60019
Wing 12136/12501

TOPKAPI (United Artists, 1964) Manos Hadjidakis
Musicor 2049/3049
Time (5) 2169
United Artists 4118/5118, 3392/6392 and 3608/6608

EL TOPO (Abkco, 1971) composer unlisted
Apple SWAO-3388

TORN CURTAIN (Universal, 1966) John Addison
Decca (7) 9155

A TOUCH OF EVIL (Universal, 1958) Henry Mancini
Challenge 602

RCA (S) 4049

THE TOUCHABLES (Britain, 1969) Ken Thorne
Fox 4206

TOUCHEZ PAS AU GRISBI (France, 1954) Jean Wiener
Angel 64014
Columbia 107
French Victor 440.138

THE TOWN WITHOUT A FACE (Czechoslovakia, 1963) Janos Cyulai-Gaal
Qualiton 7095 (45)

TOWN WITHOUT PITY (United Artists, 1961) Dimitri Tiomkin
DCP 3802/6802
London 104
United Artists 3197/6197

TOYS IN THE ATTIC (United Artists, 1963) George Duning
Capitol (S) 2063
London 3347/347
Warner Bros. (S) 1535

TRADE WINDS (United Artists, 1938) Alfred Newman
Capitol 804
Decca 5299 and 9048

THE TRAIN (United Artists, 1965) Maurice Jarre
United Artists 69, 4122/5122, 3476/6476 and 3608/6608

THE TRAP (Britain, 1967) Ron Goodwin
Atco (S) 204
English Polydor 582004 (45)

TRAPEZE (United Artists, 1956) Malcolm Arnold
Columbia 870

TREASURE OF SAN GENNARO (Paramount, 1968) Armando Trovajoli
Buddah (S) 5011

THE TREASURE OF SILVER LAKE (Germany, 1964) Martin Boetticher
German Polydor 46838

THE TREASURE OF THE AZTECS (Germany, 1965) Erwin Halletz
German Telefunken 14367

TRESPASS see FESTIVAL

THE TRIAL (LE PROCES) (France, 1963) Jean Ledrut
French Philips 432.844 (45)
Philips 200071/600071

THE TRIALS OF OSCAR WILDE (THE GREEN CARNATION) (Britain, 1960) Ron Goodwin
English RCA 4892 (45)

THE TRIP (American International, 1967) Mike Bloomfield
Sidewalk (S) 5908

TRIPLE CROSS (Warners, 1967) George Garvarentz
Unart 20015/21015
United Artists 3162/5162

TROUBLE MAN (Fox, 1972) Marvin Gaye
Tamla T-3221

THE TROUBLE WITH ANGELS (Columbia, 1966) Arthur Morton
Mainstream 56073/6073

THE TROUBLE WITH HARRY (Paramount, 1955) Bernard Herrmann
London 44126

THE TROUBLEMAKER (Independent, 1964) Cy Coleman
Ava (S) 49

TRUE FRIENDS (Russia, 1954) Mikhon Krennikov
Russian Melodiya 5520

TRUE GRIT (Paramount, 1969) Elmer Bernstein
Capitol 263
United Artists 6710

THE TRUTH (France, 1961) J. Tremble
French Victor 440.138 (45)

TUNES OF GLORY (Britain, 1961) Malcolm Arnold
London 3238/231, 3247/237 and 44020
Mercury 20688/60688
United Artists 4086/5086

TWELVE ANGRY MEN (United Artists, 1957) Kenyon Hopkins
Cadence 1322 (45)

THE 25TH HOUR (MGM, 1967) Georges Delerue
MGM (S) 4464

TWENTY-FOUR HOURS IN A WOMAN'S LIFE see AFFAIR IN MONTE CARLO

20,000 LEAGUES UNDER THE SEA (Disney, 1955) Paul Smith
Coral 57065

TWILIGHT OF HONOR (MGM, 1963) John Green
MGM (S) 4185 and (S) 4192

TWISTED NERVE (Britain, 1969) Bernard Herrmann
English Polydor 584728

"2" see I, A WOMAN--PART II

TWO FOR THE ROAD (Fox, 1967) Henry Mancini
Camden (S) 2161 and (S) 2162
MGM (S) 4491
RCA (S) 3802

TWO FOR THE SEESAW (United Artists, 1962) Andre Previn
Ascot 13505/16505
Columbia 2034/8834
United Artists 4103/5103 and 3249/6249

200 MOTELS (United Artists, 1971) Frank Zappa
United Artists UAS-9956

TWO LOVES (MGM, 1961) Bronislau Kaper
Command (S) 5005

TWO MULES FOR SISTER SARA (Universal, 1970) Ennio Morricone
Kapp 5512

2001: A SPACE ODYSSEY (MGM, 1968) various composers
Ampex 10129
Columbia (S) 7176
London SP-44173
MGM (S) 13

TWO-WAY STRETCH (Britain, 1960) Kenneth V. Jones
Mercury 20688/60688

ULYSSES (Continental, 1967) Stanley Myers
RCA (S) 1138

THE UMBRELLAS OF CHERBOURG (France, 1964) Michel Legrand
DCP 3806/6806
French Philips 77.233
Kapp 3610
London 44112
MGM (S) 4491
Philips 0054 (45)
RCA (S) 3491

UNCHAINED (Warners, 1955) Alex North
Camden (S) 795
Columbia 1371/8172
Dunhill (S) 50008
Harmony 7351/11151
London 1700/124
MGM 3127
RCA (S) 1445 and (S) 2895

Richmond 20060/30060

UNCLE TOM'S CABIN (ONKEL TOMS HUETTE) (Germany, 1965)
Peter Thomas
German Philips 843726
Philips 600272

UNDER PARIS SKIES (France, 1930) J. Drejac
Camden 233

UNDER THE ROOFS OF PARIS (France, 1930) Raoul Moretti
Capitol (S) 8603
Columbia 1178

UNDERCURRENT (MGM, 1946) Herbert Stothart
RCA 1008

UNE NUIT DE FOLIES (France, n.d.) Vincent Scotto
French Decca 164.077

THE UNFORGIVEN (United Artists, 1960) Dimitri Tiomkin
Ascot 13502/16502
Carlton (S) 126
Richmond 20095/30095
United Artists 4068/5068 and 3122/6122

THE UNINVITED (Paramount, 1944) Victor Young
Capitol (S) 1599, 570, 660, 689, and 690
Columbia GP-10 744, 811 and 1681/8481
Decca 8025 and 8056
MGM 3449 and (S) 4432
Norgran 134
RCA 1185 and 1333
Warner Bros. (S) 1291

L'UNIVERS D'UTRILLO (France, n.d.) Maurice Jarre
French Vega 30A98

UNTER GEIERN see FRONTIER HELLCAT

UOMO DI PAGLIA (Italy, 1957) Carlo Rustichelli
RCA (S) 4

UP THE DOWN STAIRCASE (Warners, 1967) Fred Karlin
United Artists 4169/5169

UP THE JUNCTION (Britain, 1968) Manfred Mann
Mercury (S) 61159

UP TIGHT (Paramount, 1969) Booker T. Jones
Stax (S) 2006

THE V.I.P.'S (MGM, 1963) Miklos Rozsa
Colpix (S) 464
Fox (S) 5105
London 3347/347
MGM (S) 4152, (S) 4192, and (S) 4144
Metro (S) 585
United Artists 3303/6303

VALLEY OF THE DOLLS (Fox, 1967) Johnny Williams; songs by Andre Previn
Alshire (S) 5097
Camden (S) 2210, (S) 2253
Decca (7) 4956
Fox (S) 4196
Mercury 21149/61149
RCA (S) 4022, (S) 3041
United Artists 69 and 3633, 6633

VANISHING POINT (Fox, 1971) various artists
Amos 8002

THE VANISHING PRAIRIE (Disney, 1954) Paul Smith
Columbia 6332
Vista 3326

VERA CRUZ (United Artists, 194) Hugo Friedhofer
Mercury 3135/7135

VERBOTEN (Columbia, 1959) Harry Sukman
Liberty 3135/7135

VERGOGNA SCHIFOSI (Italy, 1971) composer unlisted
Ariete 2003

LA VERITE see THE TRUTH

VERTIGO (Paramount, 1958) Bernard Herrmann
London 44126
Mercury 20384

A VERY PRIVATE AFFAIR (VIE PRIVEE) (France, 1963) Jean-Marie Riviere, Y. Spanos
French Victor 440.138
MGM 768 (45)

THE VICIOUS BREED (Britain, 1955) Charles Norman
Capitol 3728 (45)

THE VICTORS (Columbia, 1963) Sol Kaplan
Colpix (S) 516
Diplomat (S) 2305
London 3347/347
Time (5) 2112 and (S) 2131

Warner Bros. (S) 1535

VICTORY AT SEA (Independent, 1954) Richard Rodgers
Columbia 810
RCA (S) 2335, (S) 2226 and (S) 2523
Somerset 10900
Stereo Fidelity 10900

LA VIE CONJAGALE (France, 1965) Guy Beart
French Barclay 70.607 (45)

LA VIE DE CHATEAU (France, 1965) Michel Legrand
French Philips 437.146 (45)

LA VIE PRIVEE see A VERY PRIVATE AFFAIR

THE VIEW FROM POMPEY'S HEAD (Fox, 1955) Elmer Bernstein
Dot 3097/25097
Hamilton 108/12108

THE VIKINGS (United Artists, 1958) Mario Nascimbene
Ascot 13501/16501
United Artists 40003/5003 and 3122/6122

VILLA RIDES (Paramount, 1968) Maurice Jarre
Dot (S) 25870

VILLAGE HARVEST (Britain, 1945) Benjamin Britten
English Decca 874 (78)

VIOLATED (Independent, 1953) Tony Mottola
MGM 300

VIOLENT CITY see CITTA VIOLENTA

VIOLETTES IMPERIALES (France, 1955) Francis Lopez, Mireille Brocey
Columbia 551

THE VIRGIN AND THE GYPSY (Britain, 1970) Patrick Gowers
Steady S-122

LES VISITEURS DU SOIR (France, 1942) Maurice Thiriet
Columbia 1178
French Columbia 1059

VIVA MARIA (United Artists, 1965) Georges Delerue
Command (S) 894
United Artists 3135/5135, 3570/6570 and 3608/6608

VIVA MAX! (Commonwealth-United, 1969) Hugo Montenegro
RCA 4275

VIVA ZAPATA! (Fox, 1952) Manuel M. Ponce
Dot 3107
Hamilton 108/12108

VIVRE POUR VIVRE see LIVE FOR LIFE

VON RYAN'S EXPRESS (Fox, 1965) Jerry Goldsmith
Command (S) 887
Liberty 3498/7498

LE VOYAGE EN BALLON see STOWAWAY IN THE SKY

WAIT UNDER DARK (Warners, 1967) Henry Mancini
Decca (7) 4956
RCA 9340 (45)

WALK, DON'T RUN (Columbia, 1966) Quincy Jones
Mainstream 56080/6080

WALK ON THE WILD SIDE (Columbia, 1962) Elmer Bernstein
Ava (S) 23 and (S) 49
Liberty 3306/7306
MGM (S) 4078, (S) 13 and (S) 4271
Mainstream 56083/6083
Mercury 20810/60810
Somerset 19300
Stereo Fidelity 19300

A WALK THROUGH THE KURDISTAN WILDERNESS (Germany, 1965)
Raimund Rosenberger
German Telefunken 14390

WANTED FOR MURDER (Britain, 1946) Mischa Spoliansky
Entre 3029

WAR AND PEACE (Paramount, 1956) Nino Rota
Columbia 930
MGM 3480

WAR AND PEACE (Russia, 1964/1968) Vyacheslav Ovchinnikov
Melodiya/Capitol (S) 2918

THE WAR LORD (Universal, 1965) Jerome Moross
Decca (7) 9149

THE WAR LOVER (Columbia, 1962) Richard Addinsell
Colpix (S) 512 and (S) 458

THE WAR OF THE BUTTONS (France, 1963) Joseph Bergkmans
Philips 200071/600071

WARNING SHOT (Paramount, 1967) Jerry Goldsmith
Liberty 3498/7498

WATERHOLE #3 (Paramount, 1967) Roger Miller
Smash 27096/67096

WATERLOO (Columbia, 1971) Nino Rota
Paramount 6003

WATERMELON MAN (Columbia, 1970) Melvin van Peeples
Beverly Hills 26

WAY TO THE STARS (Britain, 1945) Nicholas Brodszky
English Columbia 2180 (78)

WAY ... WAY OUT (Fox, 1967) Lalo Schifrin
Fox (S) 3192

THE WAY WEST (United Artists, 1967) Bronislau Kaper
United Artists 69 and 3149/5149

WE HAVE MET BEFORE (Russia, n.d.) A. Lepin
Russian Melodiya 11797-98

WE STILL KILL THE OLD WAY (Italy, 1968) Luis Enrique Bacalov
United Artists 5183

WEST OF ZANZIBAR (Britain, 1954) George Sigara
London 1485

WESTERN APPROACHES see THE RAIDERS

WESTWARD HO, THE WAGONS (Disney, 1956) Paul Smith
Disneyland 4008

WHAT DID YOU DO IN THE WAR, DADDY? (United Artists, 1966)
Henry Mancini
Camden 2106
RCA (S) 3648

WHAT DO YOU SAY TO A NAKED LADY? (United Artists, 1970)
Steve Karmen
United Artists 5206 and 6742

WHAT PRICE GLORY? (Fox, 1926) Erno Rapee
Decca (7) 9079
MGM (S) 4033
RCA (S) 2604 and (S) 2560

WHAT RASCALS MEN ARE (GLI UOMINI CHE MASCALZONI) (Italy, n.d.) S. Bixio
Epic 3593

WHAT'S NEW, PUSSYCAT? (United Artists, 1965) Burt Bacharach
Camden (S) 926
Metro (S) 551

RCA (S) 3496
United Artists 4128/5128

WHAT'S UP, TIGER LILY? (Japan, 1966) John Sebastian
Kama Sutra (S) 8053

WHERE EAGLES DARE (MGM, 1969) Ron Goodwin
MGM (S) 16

WHERE THE BOYS ARE (MGM, 1961) George Stoll
MGM (S) 3988
Mercury 20688/60688

WHERE THE HOT WIND BLOWS see THE LAW

WHERE THE SPIES ARE (MGM, 1966) Brian Fahey
Metro (S) 565

WHERE'S JACK? (Paramount, 1969) Elmer Bernstein
Paramount 5005

WHERE'S POPPA? (United Artists, 1970) Jack Elliott
United Artists 5216

WHILE I LIVE (DREAM OF OLWEN) (Britain, 1947) Charles Williams
Columbia 744
Decca 8278
English Sage 5018
London 1513
MGM 3119 and 3354
Ron-lette 874/160
RCA 1002, 1020 and (S) 2380

WHILE THE CITY SLEEPS (RKO, 1956) Herschel Burke Gilbert
Coral 57065

THE WHISPERERS (Britain, 1967) John Barry
Columbia 2708/9508
Unart 20015/21015
United Artists 4161/5161

THE WHISPERING CITY (Canada, 1947) Andre Mathiew
English Decca 2526 (78)

THE WHITE-HAIRED GIRL (China, 1955) composer unlisted
English Topic 81 (78)

WHITE NIGHTS see NOTTE BIANCHI

THE WHITE ORCHID (United Artists, 1954) Chuy Hernandez
RCA 47-6032 (45)

WHITE ROSE OF ATHENS (Greece, n.d.) composer unlisted
Mercury 20688/60688

WHO IS HARRY KELLERMAN AND WHY IS HE SAYING THOSE TERRIBLE THINGS ABOUT ME? (National General, 1971) Shel Silverstein
Columbia 30791

WHO'S AFRAID OF VIRGINIA WOOLF? (Warners, 1966) Alex North
Command (S) 5005
Dunhill (S) 5001
Fox (S) 3192
London 44092
Warner Bros. (S) 1656

THE WILD AND THE WILLING (Britain, 1964) composer unlisted
English Columbia 8190 (45)

THE WILD ANGELS (American International, 1966) Mike Curb
Tower (S) 5043

THE WILD BUNCH (Warners, 1969) Jerry Fielding
Warner Bros. 1814

THE WILD EYE (Italy, 1968) Gianni Marchetti
RCA (S) 4003

WILD IN THE STREETS (American International, 1968) Barry Mann, Cynthia Weil
Tower 5099

WILD IS THE WIND (Paramount, 1957) Dimitri Tiomkin
Columbia 1090
Kapp (S) 3005
Lion (S) 70136
Mercury 20371/60017
Wing 12504

THE WILD ONE (CYCLIST RAIDERS) (Columbia, 1954) Leith Stevens
Decca 8349
Dot 3107
Liberty 3306/7306

WILD RACERS (American International, 1968) various composers
Sidewalk S-5914

THE WILD ROVERS (MGM, 1971) Jerry Goldsmith
MGM (S) 31

WILD WHEELS (Fanfare, 1969) Harley Hatcher
RCA 1156

WILL PENNY (Paramount, 1968) David Raksin
Dot 3844/25844

WINDJAMMER (Cinerama, 1958) Morton Gould
Columbia 1156/8651
Harmony 7131
Roulette 25023

THE WINGS OF EAGLES (MGM, 1957) Jeff Alexander
MGM 12430 (45) and 1467 (45)

WINNETOU I (APACHE GOLD) (Germany, 1964) Martin Boetticher
German Polydor 46838

WINNETOU II (Germany, 1965) Martin Boetticher
German Polydor 237422

WINNETOU III (Germany, 1965) Martin Boetticher
German Polydor 237494

WINNING (Universal, 1969) David Grusin
Decca (S) 79169

WIVES AND LOVERS (Paramount, 1963) Lyn Murray
Decca (7) 4669
Harmony 7428/11228
Solid 17013/18013
United Artists 3376/6376

A WOMAN IS A WOMAN (France, 1963) Michel Legrand
French Philips 432.595 (45)

WOMAN OF STRAW (United Artists, 1964) Muir Mathieson
United Artists 3392/6392

WOMAN OF THE RIVER (Columbia, 1957) Roman Vatro
MGM 3485

WOMAN TIMES SEVEN (Embassy, 1967) Riz Ortolani
Capitol (S) 2800

WOMAN TO WOMAN (Britain, 1947) George Melachrino
His Master's Voice 9535 (78)

THE WOMAN'S ANGLE (Britain, 1952) Kenneth Leslie Smith
English Columbia 1829 (78)

A WOMAN'S DEVOTION (Republic, 1956) Les Baxter
Capitol 3524 (45)

WOMEN IN LOVE (Britain, 1969) George Delerue
United Artists 6742

WOMEN OF THE WORLD (Italy, 1963) Riz Ortolani
Decca (7) 9112
United Artists 3360/6360 and 3376/6376

WONDERFUL COUNTRY (United Artists, 1959) Marlin Skiles
Ascot 13501/16501
United Artists 4050/5050 and 3122/6122

THE WONDERFUL WORLD OF THE BROTHERS GRIMM (MGM, 1962) Leigh Harline; songs by Bob Merrill
Capitol (S) 1986
Columbia 1880/8680
Kapp (S) 1289
MGM (S) 4077, (S) 4192 and (S) 4271
RCA (S) 604
United Artists 3249/6249

WONDERWALL (Britain, 1968) George Harrison
Apple (S) 3350

THE WORLD OF SUZIE WONG (Paramount, 1961) George Duning
London 3238/231
RCA (S) 1059
Mercury 20688/60688

WRITTEN ON THE WIND (Universal, 1957) Frank Skinner
Decca 8424 and 8629

THE WRONG BOX (Britain, 1966) John Barry
Columbia 2708/9508
Mainstream 56088/6088

WUTHERING HEIGHTS (United Artists, 1939) Alfred Newman
Columbia 794
Decca 5413, 8123 and 8364
Mercury 20037

WUTHERING HEIGHTS (American International, 1971) Michel Legrand
AIR 1039
Bell 6071

X-15 (United Artists, 1961) Nathan Scott
Reprise 20039 (45)

A YEAR IS WORTH A LIFETIME (Russia, n.d.) Dmitri Shostakovich
Melodiya/Angel SR-40181

YEARS OF LIGHTNING, DAYS OF DRUMS see JOHN F. KENNEDY: YEARS OF LIGHTNING, DAYS OF DRUMS

THE YELLOW CANARY (Fox, 1963) Kenyon Hopkins
Verve (6) 8548

THE YELLOW ROLLS-ROYCE (MGM, 1965) Riz Ortolani
Camden (S) 926
Command (S) 887
Decca (7) 4647
MGM 4292, (S) 242
Metro (S) 551
RCA (S) 3496
United Artists 3434/6434

THE YELLOW SUBMARINE (United Artists, 1968) The Beatles/ George Martin
Apple 153
Command (S) 941
United Artists 6701

YELLOWNECK (Republic, 1955) Lawrence Rosenthal
Decca 29356 (45)

YESTERDAY, TODAY AND TOMORROW (Italy, 1964) Armando Trovajoli
United Artists 3360/6360 and 3392/6392
Warner Bros. (S) 1552

LES YEUX CERNES (France, n.d.) composer unlisted
Ducretet Thomson 460-V-648 (45)

YOJIMBO (Japan, 1962) Masaru Sato
MGM (S) 4098

YOU ONLY LIVE ONCE (Sigma III, 1969) Jacques Loussier
London 561

YOU ONLY LIVE TWICE (United Artists, 1967) John Barry
Columbia 2708/9508
Deram 13701
London 3514/514 and 3516/516
Mercury 21149/61149
Project 3 5016
Unart 20015/21015
United Artists 4155/5155

YOUNG AND DANGEROUS (Fox, 1957) Paul Dunlap
Capitol 17764 (45)

YOUNG BILLY YOUNG (United Artists, 1969) Shelly Manne
United Artists 5199

YOUNG GIRLS BEWARE (MEFIEZ-VOUS FILLETTES) (France, 1957) Maurice Jarre
Dot 3120

THE YOUNG GIRLS OF ROCHEFORT (France, 1967) Michel Legrand
MGM (S) 4491
Mercury 61279

THE YOUNG LIONS (Fox, 1958) Hugo Friedhofer
Decca 8719

YOUNG MAN WITH A HORN (Warners, 1950) Ray Heindorf
Columbia 582

THE YOUNG ONES (LOS JOVENES) (Mexico, 1961) composer unlisted
Cameo 184 (45)

THE YOUNG PHILADELPHIANS (Warners, 1959) Ernest Gold
London 3320/320

THE YOUNG SAVAGES (United Artists, 1961) David Amram
Columbia 1672/8472

YOUNGBLOOD HAWKE (Warners, 1964) Max Steiner
RCA (S) 342

YOU'RE A BIG BOY NOW (MGM, 1967) John Sebastian
Kama Sutra (S) 8058

YOURS, MINE AND OURS (United Artists, 1968) Fred Karlin
United Artists 69 and 4181/5181

Z (Cinema V, 1969) Mikis Theodorakis
Columbia 3370
Mercury 61279
RCA 4350

ZABRISKIE POINT (MGM, 1970) various composers and artists
MGM 4668

ZACHARIAH (ABC, 1971) Jimmie Haskell
ABC 13

ZIGZAG (MGM, 1970) Oliver Nelson
MGM 21

ZITA (France, 1968) Francois de Roubaix
Philips (S) 600287

ZORBA THE GREEK (Fox, 1964) Mikis Theodorakis
Camden (S) 926
Columbia 9823
Command (S) 887 and (S) 899
Decca (7) 4647
Epic 24148/26148
Fox 3167/4167
Harmony 7428/11228
London 44078, 3516/516 and 44112
Mainstream 56063/6063

RCA (S) 3887
Time (5) 2189
United Artists 3476/6476

ZOYA (Russia, 1945) Dmitri Shostakovich
Melodiya/Angel SR-40160
Russian MK 01471

ZULU! (Embassy, 1964) John Barry
United Artists 4116/5116, 3392/6392 and 3424/6424

ZUMRAD (Russia, n.d.) S. Saifiddinov
Russian MK 20935/6

SHORTS

ACTUALITIES (France, n.d.) Darius Milhaud
Vega 30A98

THE AMERICAN ROAD (Ford, 1953) Alex North
RCA (S) 1445

ASSASSINATION OF THE DUC DE GUISE (France, 1908) Camille Saint-Saens
Golden Crest 4019

ASTROLOGIE (France, 1952) Pierre Henry
London Ducrete Thomson 93121

BAKERY BEAT (Cahill, 1966) Bob Porter
Charles Cahill and Associates 6227 (45)

BALLET MECHANIQUE (France, 1924) George Antheil
Columbia 4956
Urania (5) 134

BEAR COUNTRY (Disney, 1952) Paul Smith
Disneyland 4011

BEAVER VALLEY (Disney, 1950) Paul Smith
Disneyland 4011

BREAKTHROUGH (Independent, 1968) Paul Beaver, Bernard L. Krause
Limelight 86069

THE CIRCUS BABY (Weston Woods, 1958) Arthur Kleiner
Picture Book Parade 151

THE CITY (U.S. Government, 1939) Aaron Copland
MGM 3334 and 3367

THE COUNTRY FIDDLE (Independent, 1960) Pete Seeger
Folkways 3851

COURS DU SOIR (France, n.d.) Jacques Tati
English Philips (S) 7858

CURIOUS GEORGE RIDES A BIKE (Weston Woods, 1958) Arthur Kleiner
Picture Book Parade 152

THE DAYS OF WILFRED OWEN (Independent, 1966) Richard Lewine
Warner Bros. (S) 1635

DREAM OF A RAREBIT FIEND (Independent, 1903) composer unlisted
Folkways 3886-87

THE ENGLAND OF ELIZABETH (Britain, 1964) Ralph Vaughan Williams
RCA LSC-3280

ENTRE'ACTE (France, 1924) Erik Satie
Golden Crest 4019

FIVE CHINESE BROTHERS (Weston Woods, 1956) Arthur Kleiner
Picture Book Parade 151

GEORGIE (Weston Woods, 1957) Arthur Kleiner
Picture Book Parade 152

GOYA (Independent, 1952) Vicente Gomez
Decca 8236

GRANDMA MOSES (Radim, 1951) Hugh Martin
Columbia 2185

THE GREAT UNFENCED (Independent, 1964) Robert Muczynski
Music Library 7110

HERE AT THE WATER'S EDGE (Independent, 1964) traditional
Folkways 6161

IN PARIS PARKS (Independent, 1956) LaNoue Davenport
Classic Editions 1043

INDIAN SUMMER (Independent, 1960) Pete and Michael Seeger
Folkways 3851

INSTRUMENTS OF THE ORCHESTRA (Britain, 1947) Sir Benjamin Britten
Angel 35135
Capitol (S) 8373
Columbia 5183/6027 and 5768/6368

Deutsche Grammaphon 1 (3) 8654 and 1 (3) 8746
Mercury 50047, 50055 and 14033/18033
RCA 2596
Richmond 19040
Vox 9280

JAZZ DANCE (Independent, 1956) Roger Tilton
Jaguar 801

LABYRINTH (Canada, 1967) Eldon Rathburn
Labyrinth LAB-605S

LINES HORIZONTAL (Canada, 1960) Pete Seeger
Folkways 3851

THE LITTLE RED LIGHTHOUSE (Weston Woods, 1958) Arthur Kleiner
Picture Book Parade 151

LUCKY DUCK (Independent, 1928) H. Whitney
Golden Crest 4019

MAKE WAY FOR DUCKLINGS (Weston Woods, 1956) Arthur Kleiner
Picture Book Parade 152

THE MANY-COLORED PAPER (Independent, 1960) Pete Seeger
Folkways 3851

MARTIN AND GASTON (Britain, 1954) Temple Abady
MGM 3151

MIKE MULLIGAN AND HIS STEAM SHOVEL (Weston Woods, 1957) Arthur Kleiner
Picture Book Parade 151

MILLIONS OF CATS (Weston Woods, 1956) Arthur Kleiner
Picture Book Parade 151

NATURE'S HALF ACRE (Disney, 1951) Paul Smith
Disneyland 4011

THE OLD MILL (Disney, 1937) Leigh Harline
Disneyland 4021

THE OLYMPIC ELK (Disney, 1953) Paul Smith
Disneyland 4011

PACIFIC 231 (France, 1931) Arthur Honegger
Columbia 6059/6659
London 1156 and 9367/6367
MGM 3136
Vanguard (7) 1156
Westminster 18486/14486

PARBOLA (Independent, 1937) Darius Milhaud, based on his "Le-Creation du Monde"
Angel (S) 35932
Columbia 920
Everest 6017/3017
RCA (S) 2625
Vanguard 1090/2117

THE PHILANDERER (n.d.) B. Strawley
Golden Crest 4019

THE PLOW THAT BROKE THE PLAINS (U.S. Government, 1936)
Virgil Thomson
Decca 7527
RCA 1116 (78)
Vanguard 1071/2095

A PRINCE FOR CYNTHIA (Britain, 1954) Bruce Montgomery; 'Waltz'' by Norbert Glansberg
MGM 3151

PROWLERS OF THE EVERGLADES (Disney, 1954) Paul Smith
Disneyland 4011

PULL MY DAISY (Independent, 1958) David Amram
RCA VCS-7089

THE RED BALLOON (France, 1956) Maurice le Roux
Vega 30A98

THE REDWOODS (Sterling, 1967) Charles Ives' "The Unanswered Question" and Pete Seeger's 'Indian Summer"
Columbia MS-6483
RCA LSC-2893
Vanguard C-10013

RHAPSODY IN STEEL (Independent, 1958) Dimitri Tiomkin
U.S. Steel 502

THE RIVER (U.S. Government, 1936) Virgil Thomson
American Recording Society 8
Vanguard 1071/2095

SAMOA (Disney, 1956) Oliver Wallace
Disneyland 4003

SKATERDATER (Independent, 1965) Mike Curb
Mira 3004

SKELETON DANCE (Disney, 1929) standard
Disneyland 4021

STEAMBOAT WILLIE (Disney, 1928) standard
Disneyland 4021

STONE SOUP (Weston Woods, 1957) Arthur Kleiner
Picture Book Parade 152

THE STORY ABOUT PING (Weston Woods, 1956) Arthur Kleiner
Picture Book Parade 152

THE STORY OF MOBY DICK (Independent, 1957) Richard Mohaupt
Dot 3043

THE STRANGER LEFT NO CARD (Britain, 1954) Hugo Alfven
Cameo (S) 2001
London 979
MGM 3151
Warner Bros. (S) 1249

SWITZERLAND (Disney, 1956) Paul Smith
Disneyland 4003

THE TRUE STORY OF THE CIVIL WAR (Independent, 1957) Ernest Gold
Coral 59100

THE UNICORN IN THE GARDEN (Columbia, 1954) David Raksin
Classic Editions 1055

WELCOME TO THE QUEEN (Britain, 1954) Arthur Bliss
RCA (S) 2257

WHALER OUT OF NEW BEDFORD (Independent, 1962) Peggy Seeger, Ewan McColl
Folkways 3850

WINDSONG (Independent, 1958) Harry Partch
Composers Recordings 193

THE YANKEE PAINTER (Independent, 1964) Robert Muczynski
Music Library 7110

INDEX TO PART ONE